Human Sexuality in a Changing World

TENTH EDITION

Spencer A. Rathus
The College of New Jersey

Jeffrey S. Nevid
St. John's University

Lois Fichner-Rathus
The College of New Jersey

330 Hudson Street, NY NY 10013

VP, Editorial: Eric Stano
Marketing Manager: Christopher Brown
Program Manager: Erin Bosco
Managing Editor: Marita Bley
Project Coordination, Text Design,
 and Electronic Page Makeup: Integra Software Services, Inc.
Cover Designer: JayBird Design
Cover Art: Piotr Marcinski/Fotolia
Manufacturing Buyer: Carol Melville
Printer/Binder: LSC Communications Roanoke
Cover Printer: Lehigh Phoenix Color/Hagerstown

Acknowledgments of third-party content appear on pages 583–584, which constitute an extension of this copyright page.

PEARSON, ALWAYS LEARNING, and REVEL are exclusive trademarks in the United States and/or other countries owned by Pearson Education, Inc., or its affiliates.

Unless otherwise indicated herein, any third-party trademarks that may appear in this work are the property of their respective owners and any references to third-party trademarks, logos, or other trade dress are for demonstrative or descriptive purposes only. Such references are not intended to imply any sponsorship, endorsement, authorization, or promotion of Pearson's products by the owners of such marks, or any relationship between the owner and Pearson Education, Inc., or its affiliates, authors, licensees, or distributors.

Library of Congress Cataloging-in-Publication Data
Names: Rathus, Spencer A., author. | Nevid, Jeffrey S., author. |
 Fichner-Rathus, Lois, 1953- author.
Title: Human sexuality in a changing world/Spencer A. Rathus, Jeffrey S.
 Nevid, Lois Fichner-Rathus.
Description: Hoboken, NJ : Pearson Higher Education, [2018]
Identifiers: LCCN 2016041031 | ISBN 9780134525068 | ISBN 013452506X
Subjects: LCSH: Sex.
Classification: LCC HQ21 .R23 2018 | DDC 306.7—dc23 LC record
 available at https://lccn.loc.gov/2016041031

1 17

www.pearsonhighered.com

Student Edition
ISBN 10: 0-134-52507-8
ISBN 13: 978-0-134-52507-5

A la Carte
ISBN 10: 0-134-57009-X
ISBN 13: 978-0-134-57009-9

Dedicated to Our Children

Brief Contents

Contents

Feature Boxes

Preface

There are more things in heaven and earth, Horatio,

Than are dreamt of in your philosophy.

—Shakespeare, *Hamlet*

There are indeed more kinds of people in this world, and more ways in which people experience and express their sexuality, than most of us might imagine. Human sexuality may be intimately related to human biology, but it is also embedded within the fabric of human cultures and societies. The approach that has separated *Human Sexuality in a Changing World* from other human sexuality textbooks is its full embrace of the richness of human diversity. The new edition adds to the history of innovation by recognizing the key roles played by digital devices and the Internet in contemporary societies.

You may have noticed a change in title. Previous editions of the text were titled *Human Sexuality in a World of Diversity*, emphasizing the text's commitment to portraying the great diversity we find through the world, and in our own society, in attitudes and sexual behavior. The new title is *Human Sexuality in a Changing World*, signaling our continuing commitment to human diversity and adding a new commitment to portraying the ways in which the digital age in which we live has exploded the availability of sexual information and reshaped the ways in which many of us experience sexuality.

What's New in the Tenth Edition
New Chapter Structure

The new edition has 16 chapters as compared with the 19 chapters of previous editions. The reorganization will fit better with the semester calendar and is also more logical.

Following the introductory chapter and the chapters on sexual anatomy and physiology (Chapters 2 and 3), the text immediately delves into the basic matters of gender (Chapter 4) and sexual orientation (Chapter 5). The first group of chapters addresses the core of who a person is as a sexual being.

Having identified the sexual person, the new flow follows gender and sexual orientation with attraction and love (whom do we seek for sexual interaction?), patterns of sexual behavior, and the development of relationships. Development of relationships is followed logically by conception and pregnancy, contraception, and sexuality through the lifespan.

Finally, we explore the potpourri of crucial topics familiar to those who teach the course: sexual dysfunctions ("sexual problems and solutions"), sexually transmitted infections, atypical variations in sexual behavior (paraphilias), sexual coercion (rape and child abuse), and prostitution and pornography ("selling sex").

New Feature: Sex in the Digital Age

The tenth edition of the text proudly presents a new feature which testifies to the book's currency: Sex in the Digital Age. The typical American spends more than an hour online each day, and research suggests that much of this time is spent reading about and viewing sexual topics, including pornography. Sex in the Digital Age features include:

- Chapter 1   Thinking Critically about Sexual Advice on the Internet
- Chapter 2   Symptoms of Menopause? There's an App for That
- Chapter 3   SexInfo Online—Penis Enlargement
- Chapter 4   Gender-Hacking on OkCupid
- Chapter 5   Grindr
- Chapter 6   For Nice Jewish Boys, Swipe Right
- Chapter 7   Sex with *Her*
- Chapter 8   Swiping Right to Hook Up—Are We Heading Toward a Dating Apocalypse?
- Chapter 9   Fertility and Period Trackers
- Chapter 10   Using Apps to Predict Safe Periods for Sex
- Chapter 11   Sexting: Of Cell Phones, Sex, and Death

    What Happens When Your Extramarital Affair Becomes Exposed to 7 Billion People, Give or Take a Few?
- Chapter 12   Thinking Critically about Buying Viagra, Cialis, and Other Drugs Online
- Chapter 14   Total Web Cam Domination

    Cybersex Addiction: For Some, Sex Is Nothing but 'Net
- Chapter 15   Rape Prevention? There's an App for That (Actually There Are Several)

Heightened Use of Popular Culture to Stimulate Students and Illustrate Issues Involving Human Sexuality

Samples:

Chapter 4   Laverne Cox of *Orange Is the New Black* and Caitlyn Jenner to illustrate transgender issues among celebrities

Chapter 5   Miley Cyrus's statements suggestive of bisexuality in the chapter on sexual orientation

Chapter 8   Mila Kunis and Justin Timberlake in the film *Friends with Benefits* to illustrate contemporary wrinkles in sexual relationships

Chapter 14   Dakota Johnson in the film *Fifty Shades of Grey* as an illustration of sadomasochism

Chapter 15   Issues concerning Bill Cosby and alleged sexual assault in the chapter on sexual coercion

New References

The field of human sexuality may change more rapidly than any other, and the research in all these areas is thoroughly up to date. There are literally hundreds of new references that address updates in the area of sexual health and in the psychology of sex.

The Themes of Human Sexuality in a Changing World

The tenth edition of *Human Sexuality in a Changing World* builds on the strong themes for which it has come to be known:

1. The rich diversity found in gender roles, sexual attitudes, and sexual behaviors and customs
2. Critical thinking principles and skills
3. Making responsible sexual decisions
4. Sexual health
5. Recognition of popular media and helpful "apps"

THEME 1: HUMAN DIVERSITY   Colleges and universities are undertaking the mission of broadening students' perspectives so that they will appreciate and tolerate human diversity. The United States is a nation of hundreds of different ethnic and religious groups, many of which endorse culturally distinctive beliefs about appropriate gender roles for men and women, and distinctive sexual practices and customs. Diversity is even greater within the global village of the world's nearly 200 nations and the subcultures of those nations. *Human Sexuality in a Changing World* incorporates a multicultural, multiethnic perspective that reflects the diversity of sexual experience in our society and around the world. Our book thereby broadens students' understanding of the range of cultural differences in sexual attitudes and behavior worldwide and within our own society.

In addition, the "A World of Diversity" feature highlights the rich variety of human sexual customs and practices in our own society and in others around the world. Discussion of diversity encourages respect for people who hold diverse beliefs and attitudes. We also encourage students to question what is deemed appropriate for women and men in terms of social roles and sexual conduct in light of cultural traditions and standards.

THEME 2: CRITICAL THINKING   Colleges and universities in the new millennium are also encouraging students to become critical thinkers. Today's students are so inundated with information about gender and sexuality that it can be difficult to sort truth from fiction. Not only do politicians, theologians, and community leaders influence our gender- and sex-related attitudes and behaviors, but news outlets, TV programs, the Internet, and other media also brim with features about gender roles and issues concerning human sexuality.

Critical thinking means being skeptical of information that is presented in print or on the Internet, or uttered by authority figures or celebrities. Critical thinking requires thoughtful analysis and probing of the claims and arguments of others in light of evidence. Moreover, it requires a willingness to challenge conventional wisdom and common knowledge that many of us take for granted. It means scrutinizing definitions of terms, evaluating the premises or assumptions that underlie arguments, and examining the logic of arguments.

Throughout this book we raise issues that demand critical thinking. These issues are intended to stimulate student interest in analyzing and evaluating their beliefs and attitudes toward gender roles and sexuality in light of the accumulated scientific evidence. Moreover, this new edition fosters critical thinking through a section called "Thinking Critically about Human Sexuality" in Chapter 1, and by including "Critical Thinking" questions throughout each chapter.

THEME 3: RESPONSIBLE SEXUAL DECISION MAKING We also encourage students to make responsible sexual decisions. There are psychological and physical dangers in "going with the flow" or being passive about one's sexuality. Of course we do not encourage students to be sexually active (such a decision is personal). On the other hand, we do encourage students to make their own sexual decisions actively, on the basis of accurate information.

Decision making is deeply intertwined with individuals' sexual experiences. For example, each person needs to decide

- whom to date, and how and when to become sexually intimate
- whether to practice contraception and which methods to use
- how to protect himself or herself against HIV/AIDS and other STIs

Responsible sexual decision making is based not only on acquiring accurate information but also on carefully evaluating this information in the light of one's own moral values. We encourage students always to consider their own values, needs, and interests, rather than going along with the crowd or merely acceding to the wishes or demands of their partners. Throughout the text we provide students with the information they need to make responsible decisions about their physical health, the gender roles they will enact, sexual practices, birth control, and prevention of STIs.

THEME 4: SEXUAL HEALTH *Human Sexuality in a Changing World* places a strong emphasis on issues relating to sexual health, including extensive coverage of such topics as HIV/AIDS and other STIs, innovations in contraception and reproductive technologies, breast cancer, menstrual distress, sex and disabilities, and diseases that affect the reproductive tract. The text encourages students to take an active—in fact, a proactive—role in health promotion. For example, the book includes exercises and features that help students examine their bodies for abnormalities, reduce the risk of HIV infection, and cope with menstrual discomfort.

THEME 5: RECOGNITION OF POPULAR MEDIA AND HELPFUL "APPS" The tenth edition of *Human Sexuality in a Changing World* enriches coverage for students by referring to well-known people in the media and presenting websites and "apps" that will widen students' knowledge of issues relating to human sexuality and assist them in solving problems.

We cover the experiences of *Orange is the New Black* superstar Laverne Cox. We address Angelina Jolie's decision to have a preventive double mastectomy. We note the alleged sexual assaults of Bill Cosby.

We dwell in the digital age. Therefore, we also show students apps such as "Grindr," "Glow," and "Circle of Six," which, respectively, assist gay men in finding partners, help women calculate when they will ovulate, and prevent on-campus sexual violence.

Features of the Tenth Edition

Like previous editions, the tenth edition of *Human Sexuality in a Changing World* contains features that stimulate student interest and enhance understanding.

Learning Objectives

Featured at the beginning of each chapter, learning objectives help guide student reading by identifying main ideas and defining learning goals. These learning objectives appear again in the end of chapter summary, to help reinforce key information. They are also used to organize the Test Bank and Instructor Manual.

Real Students, Real Questions

What do students know about human sexuality? What are they too embarrassed to ask of professors, peers, or parents? This feature highlights questions, collected from college students from across the country, on any human sexuality topic concerning them—big or small. We then answer their questions. Sample questions include the following:

- One of my breasts is bigger than the other. Is this normal?
- How do you tell someone the relationship is over?
- How can I keep my partner interested in sex? We've been together for 5 years.

Sex in the Digital Age

These features in effect show what the electronic age—also known as the age of information—has brought to the world of human sexuality. Students locate their lovers with smartphones. They use apps such as Tinder and Grindr to search for new sex partners when they are on the street or at a bar or club. Most view pornography online, using their smartphones, tablet computers, laptops, or desktops rather than visit an adult bookstore or an adult theater. Women use apps such as Glow to track their periods and fertility. They also use rape preventions apps, which allow them to call in friends at a moment's notice. The applications of digital technology to human sexuality are virtually endless, and the text shows how people shape these apps and are shaped by them.

Sex in a World of Diversity

These features highlight the rich variety of human sexual customs and practices in our own society and in those throughout the world. Viewing human sexuality in a multicultural context helps students better understand how cultural beliefs, values, and attitudes can influence the expression of sexuality. Students may come to understand that their partners, who may not share the same ethnic or religious heritage as themselves, may feel different than they do about sexual intimacy. Students will learn about cultural differences related to gender roles, sexual orientation, sexual jealousy, and premarital and extramarital sexual patterns.

A Closer Look

The "A Closer Look" feature provides in-depth discussions of scientific techniques (for example, "Physiological Measures of Sexual Arousal") and skill-building exercises ("Breast Self-Examination," "Self-Examination of the Testes").

Self-Assessments

Self-scoring questionnaires stimulate students' interest and provide self-insight by helping them satisfy their curiosity about themselves. These questionnaires also enhance the relevance of the text to students' lives. Examples include "Would You Tell an Interviewer the Truth on a Survey about Your Sexual Behavior? The Social-Desirability Scale" and the "Triangular Love Scale" (which may help students decide whether they are "in love" and, if so, just what *type* of love they are in).

Truth-or-Fiction? Items

These unique chapter-opening devices motivate students by challenging common sense, stereotypes, and folklore. "Truth-or-Fiction Revisited" sections are interspersed throughout each chapter and provide feedback to students regarding the accuracy of their assumptions in light of the evidence presented in the chapter.

Running Glossary

Research shows that most students do not make use of glossaries at the end of books. Searching for the meanings of terms is a difficult task and distracts them from the subject matter. Therefore, *Human Sexuality in a Changing World* has a running glossary. Key terms are in bold type in the text and are defined in the margins near to where they appear. Students can readily find the meanings of key terms without breaking their concentration on the flow of the material.

A Comprehensive Media and Supplements Package

Human Sexuality in a Changing World presents instructors and students with a wide range of ancillaries and teaching aids.

Revel™

Educational technology designed for the way today's students read, think, and learn

When students are engaged deeply, they learn more effectively and perform better in their courses. This simple fact inspired the creation of Revel: an interactive learning environment designed for the way today's students read, think, and learn. Built in collaboration with educators and students nationwide, Revel replaces the textbook and gives students everything they need for the course.

Revel seamlessly blends authors' narrative, media, and assessment, enabling students to read, practice, and study in one continuous experience. This immersive educational technology is designed to measurably boost students' understanding, retention, and preparedness across an expanding range of discipline areas—for less than the cost of a traditional textbook.

Learn more about Revel at
http://www.pearsonhighered.com/revel/

Resources

INSTRUCTOR'S MANUAL   Updated for the tenth edition, this online instructor's manual is a wonderful tool for classroom preparation and management. Organized by the same learning objectives that appear throughout the text, each chapter begins with an "at a glance" grid, which makes it easy for instructors to survey the available teaching tools and find what they need. Each chapter contains a wealth of teaching tips, lecture launchers, discussion questions, activities, and references to online resources, and is hyperlinked to make navigation simple.

TEST BANK   A thoroughly revised and updated test bank helps instructors prepare for exams with challenging questions that target key concepts. Each chapter includes more than 100 questions, including multiple choice, true/false, short answer, and essay, each with a page reference, a difficulty rating, type designation, and reference to the textual learning objective it reinforces. This product is also available in MyTest and BlackBoard/WebCT cartridges for ease in creating exams.

POWERPOINT PRESENTATION   Highly visual, PowerPoint slides that support instructors in creating dynamic lectures. We also offer simple lecture PowerPoints that are easily modified to suit a variety of teaching styles.

Acknowledgments

We owe a great debt of gratitude to the many researchers and scholars whose contributions to the body of knowledge in the field of human sexuality are represented in these pages. Underscoring the interdisciplinary nature of the field, we have drawn on the work of scholars in such fields as psychology, sociology, medicine, anthropology, theology, and philosophy, to name a few. We are also indebted to the many researchers who have generously allowed us to quote from their work and reprint tabular material representing their findings. We also thank our professional colleagues who reviewed this text at various stages in its development:

Michael Bailey, Northwestern University; Keith E. Davis, University of South Carolina; Randy D. Fisher, University of Central Florida; Kam Majer, Glendale Community College; Patricia A. Tackett, San Diego State University; Michael L. Vinson, College of Charleston; and Mark A. Yarhouse, Regent University.

In addition, the following instructors provided invaluable feedback in their reviews. Several reviewers also supplied anonymous Real Students, Real Questions from their students, for which we are grateful:

Cindy Arem, Pima Community College; Rebecca L. Bosek, University of Alaska, Anchorage; Ted Coleman, California State University, San Bernadino; Ruth Conrad, Miami Dade College; Nancy P. Daley, The University of Texas at Austin; Darci Dance, Linn-Benton Community College; Dale Doty, Monroe Community College; Mary E. Doyle, Arizona State University; Laura Duvall, Heartland Community College; Steve Ellyson, Youngstown State University; Kathy Erickson, Pima Community College; Debra L. Golden, The Grossmont–Cuyamaca Community College; Jerry Green, Tarrant County College; Tawanda M. Greer, University of South Carolina; Chuck Hallock, University of Arizona; Mark L. Harmon, Reedley College– North Centers; Deborah Kindy, Sonoma State University; Amy Kolodji, Ithaca College; Gloria Lawrence, Wayne State College; Holly Lewis, University of Houston–Downtown; Sonya Lott-Harrison, Community College of Philadelphia; Ana Lucero-Liu, California State University, Northridge; Jason McCoy, Cape Fear Community College; Mary L. Meiners, San Diego Miramar College; Eva Mika, Loyola University Chicago; Ramona M. Noland, Sam Houston State University; Grace Pokorny, Long Beach City College; Jim Pond, Butler Community College; Marilyn Pugh, Texas Wesleyan University, North Texas; Rosalind Shorter, Jefferson Community College; Noam Shpancer, Otterbein University; Bette Speziale, Ohio State University; Virginia Sticinski, Delaware Technical Community College; Dana Stone, Virginia Tech; Virginia Totaro, Virginia Commonwealth University; Mixon Ware, Eastern Kentucky University; Mary Anne Watson, Metropolitan State College of Denver; O'Neal Weeks, Eastern Kentucky University; Steve Weinert, The Grossmont–Cuyamaca Community College; Lester Wright, Western Michigan University; and Brian Zamboni, Health University of Minnesota.

Last, we thank our long-time buddy David McPatchell, Associate Professor of Psychology, Compton Community College—and his students—for providing the heart of many of this edition's personal stories, including "Real Questions, Real Answers" features. It just would not have been the same without him—and them.

Spencer A. Rathus
Jeffrey S. Nevid
Lois Fichner-Rathus

Chapter 1
What Is Human Sexuality?

Learning Objectives

The Science of Human Sexuality

LO 1.1   Define the science of human sexuality.

Sexuality and Values

LO 1.2   Define the value systems people use in making sexual decisions.

Thinking Critically about Human Sexuality

LO 1.3   Explain how you can become a critical thinker.

Perspectives on Human Sexuality

LO 1.4   Discuss various ways of looking at human sexuality.

Research Methods in Human Sexuality

LO 1.5   Explain the steps in the scientific method.

LO 1.6   Explain what is meant by populations and samples.

LO 1.7   Describe methods of observation, including the case-study method, the survey, naturalistic observation, ethnographic observation, participant observation, and laboratory observation.

LO 1.8   Describe the correlational method.

LO 1.9   Explain how experiments seek to determine cause and effect.

Ethics in Research on Human Sexuality

LO 1.10 Describe the ethical concerns that govern the ways in which professionals interact with research participants and clients in treatment.

TRUTH OR FICTION?

Which of the following statements are the truth and which are fiction? Look for the Truth-or-Fiction items throughout this chapter to find the answers.

1   Scientific knowledge will enable you to make the right sexual decisions.   **T / F**?

2   You can trust the sexual advice that is posted on the Internet.   **T / F**?

3   In ancient Greece, a mature man would take a sexual interest in an adolescent boy, often with the blessing of the boy's parents.   **T / F**?

4   Throughout most of human history, and in many places around the world today, women are considered to be the property of their husbands.   **T / F**?

5   The production of sex manuals originated in modern times.   **T / F**?

6   The Graham cracker came into being as a means for helping young men control their sexual appetites.   **T / F**?

7   You could study the sexual behavior of millions of Americans and still not obtain an accurate picture of the sexual behavior of the U.S. population.   **T / F**?

8   Researchers created an artificial penis containing photographic equipment to study female sexual response.   **T / F**?

9   People who attend church regularly tend to be more satisfied with their relationships.   **T / F**?

Let's Google the islands off the coast of Europe and in the South Pacific—both in space and time. We go to Google Maps, find Inis Beag, click on the satellite image, further click on 1955 (no, you can't really do this—yet), and swoop in …

And suddenly we find ourselves visiting two islands that are a world apart—sexually as well as geographically. Our first stop is Inis Beag, which lies in the Atlantic, off the misty coast of Ireland. Our second stop will be Mangaia, which lifts languidly out of the blue waters of the Pacific.

The distant satellite image shows Inis Beag as a green jewel, fertile and inviting. The residents of this community do not believe that it is normal for women to experience orgasm. Anthropologists have reported that any woman who finds pleasure in sex—especially the intense waves of pleasure that can accompany orgasm—is viewed as deviant.

Premarital sex is all but unknown on Inis Beag. Before marriage, men and women socialize apart. Marriage comes late—usually in the middle 30s for men and the middle 20s for women. Mothers teach their daughters that they will have to submit to their husbands' animal cravings to obey God's injunction to "be fruitful and multiply."

But the women of Inis Beag need not be overly concerned about frequent sex because the men of the island believe, erroneously, that sexual activity will drain their strength. Consequently, men avoid sex on the eve of sporting activity or strenuous work. Because of taboos against nudity, married couples have sex with their undergarments on. Intercourse takes place in the dark—literally as well as figuratively.

During intercourse, the man lies on top. He is always the initiator. Foreplay is brief. The man ejaculates as fast as he can, in the belief that he is the only partner with sexual needs and to spare his wife as best he can. Then he turns over and falls asleep. Once more the couple have done their duty.

On to Mangaia, which is a pearl of an island. It lies on the other side of the world from Inis Beag—in more ways than one. From an early age, Mangaian boys and girls are encouraged to get in touch with their own sexuality through sexual play and masturbation. At about the age of 13, Mangaian boys are initiated into manhood by adults who instruct them in sexual techniques.

Boys practice their new techniques with girlfriends on secluded beaches or beneath the listing fronds of palms. They may visit girlfriends in huts where they sleep with their families. Parents often listen for their daughters to laugh and gasp so that they will know that they have reached orgasm with a visiting young "sleepcrawler." Parents often pretend to be asleep so as not to interfere with courtship and impede their daughters' chances of finding a mate. Daughters may receive a nightly succession of sleepcrawlers and have multiple orgasms with each one.

Mangaians look on virginity with disdain because virgins do not know how to provide sexual pleasure. Thus, the older male makes his contribution by initiating the girl.

Mangaians expressed concern when they learned that many Western women do not regularly experience orgasm. Orgasm is apparently universal among Mangaian women. Therefore, Mangaians could only assume that Western women suffered from some abnormality of the sex organs.

The residents of Inis Beag and Mangaia have similar anatomical features but vastly different attitudes toward sex. Their cultural settings influence their patterns of sexual behavior and the pleasure they gain—or fail to gain—from sex. Sex may be a natural function, but few natural functions have been influenced so strongly by religious and moral beliefs, cultural tradition, folklore, and superstition.

We are about to embark on the study of human sexuality. But why study human sexuality? Isn't sex something to do rather than to talk about? Isn't sex a natural function? Don't we learn what we need to know from personal experience or from our parents or from our friends?

Yes. And no. We can learn how our bodies respond to sexual stimulation through personal experience, but experience teaches us little about the biology of sexual response and orgasm. Nor does experience inform us about the variations in sexual behavior that exist around the world. Experience does not prepare us to recognize the signs of sexually transmitted infections (STIs) or to recognize the risks of pregnancy. What many of us learned about sex from our parents can probably be summarized in a single word: "Don't." The information we received from our friends was probably riddled with exaggeration, even lies. Many young people today receive accurate information through sex education courses in the schools, but they are usually taught about STIs and contraception, not about sexual techniques.

Real Students, Real Questions

Q *I am 17 years old, and in my family the topic of sex is nonexistent. How do I begin a conversation with my family?*

A Many people find it difficult to talk about sex. You'll find ideas for initiating conversations about sex with family members and other people throughout this text—conversations about contraception, STIs, and problems in relationships. In all cases, think about selecting a good time and place to talk. Consider asking permission to talk about a sensitive topic, as in "I know that talking about birth control is a no-no in this house, but I have some questions. Can we talk about them?" Or, "I could use some help. Can we talk about it?" People who care about you might just surprise you by accepting the challenge of trying to communicate about topics that have been off-limits. You can also check out the college counseling center; it is usually a safe place to explore ideas.

You may know more about human sexuality than your parents or grandparents did at your age, or do today. But how much do you really know? What causes an erection or vaginal lubrication? What factors determine sexual orientation? What are sexual dysfunctions and what causes them? How do our sexual responsiveness and interests change as we age? Can you contract an STI and not know it? If you have no symptoms, can you infect others?

These are just a few of the issues we will explore in this book. One feature of this text, "Real Students, Real Questions," illustrates some of the questions and erroneous ideas many of us have about sex.

The Science of Human Sexuality

LO 1.1 **Define the science of human sexuality.**

What is human sexuality? This is not a trick question. Consider the meaning, or rather meanings, of the word *sex*. One use of the term *sex* refers to our anatomic sex, female or male. The words *sex* or *sexual* are also used to refer to anatomic structures called *sex organs* or *sexual organs*, which play roles in reproduction and sexual pleasure. We may also speak of sex when referring to physical activities involving our sex organs for purposes of reproduction or pleasure, as in *having sex*. Sex also relates to erotic feelings, experiences, or desires, such as sexual fantasies and thoughts, sexual urges, or feelings of sexual attraction.

Many researchers reserve the word *sex* for reference to anatomic or biological categories but prefer the word **gender** when they are referring to social or cultural categories. For example, one might say that "reproductive anatomy appears to depend on the *sex* (not the *gender*) of the individual, but in so-called traditional societies, **gender roles** (not *sex roles*) are often seen as polar opposites." Although it is often preferred to speak of psychological and behavioral *gender differences* rather than *sex differences*, the use of "sex differences" is probably more correct when we are talking about differences between anatomic males and anatomic females.

The term **human sexuality** refers to the ways in which people experience and express themselves as sexual beings. Our awareness of ourselves as females or males is part of our sexuality, as is the capacity we have for erotic experiences and responses. Our knowledge of the gender roles in our culture also has a profound influence on us.

The Study of Human Sexuality

The study of human sexuality draws on the scientific expertise of anthropologists, biologists, medical researchers, sociologists, and psychologists, to name some of the professional groups involved in the field. These disciplines all make contributions because human sexuality reflects biological capabilities, psychological traits and experiences, and social and cultural influences. Biologists inform us about the physiological mechanisms of sexual arousal and response. Medical science teaches us about STIs and the biological bases of reproduction and sexual dysfunctions. Psychologists examine how our sexual behavior and attitudes are shaped by perception, learning, thought, motivation and emotion, and personality. Sociologists examine relationships between sexual behavior and religion, race, and social class. Anthropologists focus on cross-cultural similarities and differences in sexual behavior.

1 › T / F Truth or Fiction Revisited   Although science provides us with information, it cannot make sexual decisions for us. In making sexual decisions, we also turn to our **values**. The Declaration of Independence endorsed the fundamental values of "life, liberty, and the pursuit of happiness"—not a bad beginning. Religious traditions and other ethical systems also play a prominent role in shaping our values, as we see in the following section.

---

gender

The state of being male or being female, but usually used in reference to social and cultural differences rather than biological differences. When appropriate, we refer to the anatomic sex of an individual rather than her or his gender.

gender roles

Complex clusters of ways in which males and females are expected to behave within a given culture.

human sexuality

The ways in which people experience and express themselves as sexual beings.

values

The qualities in life that are deemed important or unimportant, right or wrong, desirable or undesirable.

Sexuality and Values

LO 1.2 Define the value systems people use in making sexual decisions.

Our society is pluralistic. It embraces a wide range of sexual attitudes and values. Some readers may be liberal in their sexual views and behavior. Others may be conservative. Some are "pro-choice" concerning abortion, others "pro-life." Some approve of premarital sex for couples who know each other casually. Others hold the line at emotional commitment. Still others believe in waiting until marriage. People's sexual attitudes, experiences, and behaviors are shaped to a large extent by cultural traditions and beliefs. They influence how, where, and with whom we become sexually involved.

As noted by feminists, some of the variability in sexual behavior between males and females reflects power rather than choice (Smith & Konik, 2011; Swirsky & Angelone, 2015). Throughout history and in many places, for example, women have been considered the property of men. Even today, women are often "given away" by their fathers to their husbands.

Let's consider the various value systems that people draw on in making sexual decisions.

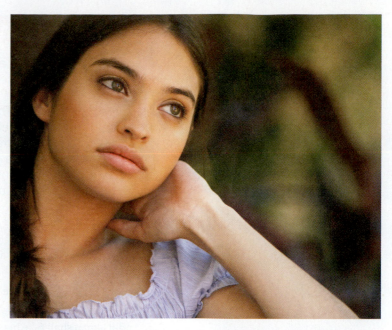

Sexuality and Values. How do you make sexual decisions? What value system or systems do you use?

Value Systems for Making Sexual Decisions

Although sex is a natural function, most of us who live in developed nations choose how, where, and with whom to become sexually involved. We face a wide array of decisions: Whom should I date? When should my partner and I become sexually intimate? Should I initiate sexual relations or wait for my partner to approach me? Should we use contraception? If so, which method? Should I use a condom to protect against STIs (or insist that my partner does so)? Should I be tested for HIV (the virus that causes AIDS)? Should I insist that my partner be tested for HIV before we have sex?

Value systems provide a framework for judging the morality of sexual options. Our value systems—our sexual standards—have many sources: parents, peers, religious training, ethnic subcultures, the larger culture, and our own appraisal of these influences. Value systems include legalism, situational ethics, ethical relativism, hedonism, asceticism, utilitarianism, and rationalism.

The legalistic approach formulates ethical behavior on the basis of a code of moral laws derived from an external source, such as a religion. The Hebrew and Christian Bibles contain many examples of the moral code of the Jewish and Christian religions. In the Book of Leviticus (20:10–17) in the Hebrew Bible we find many of the prohibitions against adultery, incest, same-sex sexual activity, and sex during menstruation that are followed by most people today:

10: And the man that committeth adultery with another man's wife, even he that committeth adultery with his neighbour's wife, the adulterer and the adulteress shall surely be put to death.

11: And the man that lieth with his father's wife hath uncovered his father's nakedness: both of them shall surely be put to death; their blood shall be upon them.

12: And if a man lie with his daughter-in-law, both of them shall surely be put to death: they have wrought confusion; their blood shall be upon them.

13: If a man also lie with mankind, as he lieth with a woman, both of them have committed an abomination: They shall surely be put to death; their blood shall be upon them.

Q *Is a person who takes a vow of chastity, such as a nun, no longer considered a sexual being?*

A A person who takes a vow of chastity only promises not to be a sexually active being. The reason usually involves dedication to values in which self-denial of sexual desires plays a key role, as in a religious tradition. But this doesn't mean that the person is no longer a sexual being. The person remains female or male, and continues to be subject to the sexual drives, sexual health issues, and cultural expectations that affect females and males.

14: And if a man take a wife and her mother, it is wickedness: they shall be burnt with fire, both he and they; that there be no wickedness among you.

15: And if a man lie with a beast, he shall surely be put to death: and ye shall slay the beast.

17: And if a man shall take his sister, his father's daughter, or his mother's daughter, and see her nakedness, and she see his nakedness; it is a wicked thing; and they shall be cut off in the sight of their people: he hath uncovered his sister's nakedness; he shall bear his iniquity.

18: And if a man shall lie with a woman having her sickness,[1] and shall uncover her nakedness; he hath discovered her fountain, and she hath uncovered the fountain of her blood: and both of them shall be cut off from among their people.

Many religious followers accept the moral codes of their religions as a matter of faith and commitment. Some people find it reassuring to be informed by religious authorities or scripture that a certain course of action is right or wrong. Others take a more liberal view. They say that the Bible reflects the social setting of the time in which it was written, not just divine inspiration. Now that population growth is exploding in many parts of the world, biblical injunctions to be fruitful and multiply may no longer be socially and environmentally sound. Prohibitions, such as that against sexual relations during menstruation, were likely based on prescientific perceptions of danger. Some people thus view religious teachings as a general guideline rather than a set of absolute rules.

Other value systems for making sexual decisions are shown in Table 1.1.

Many students will think critically about which values to apply to a given situation. They may also apply critical thinking to the claims and arguments about human sexuality they come across from authority figures, colleagues, friends, and advertisements. In the following section, we explore the nature of critical thinking.

Thinking Critically about Human Sexuality

LO 1.3 **Explain how you can become a critical thinker.**

We are flooded with so much information about sex that it is difficult to separate truth from fiction. Newspapers, TV shows, popular books and magazines, and the Internet contain one feature after another about sex. Many of them contradict one another, contain half-truths, or draw unsupported conclusions.

---

[1]That is, menstruation.

Table 1.1 Value Systems for Making Sexual Decisions

System	Core Belief	Example
Legalism	Ethical behavior is derived from an external source, such as a religion.	The Old Testament contains prohibitions against adultery, incest, sexual activity with people of one's own gender, and bestiality.
Situational Ethics	Ethical decision making should be guided by the situation and by genuine love for others.	A woman who has been taught that abortion is the taking of a human life may find herself with limited resources and decide in favor of an abortion.
Relativism	There is no objective way of justifying one set of moral values over another.	Cohabitation is tolerated in some cultures but considered immoral in others.
Hedonism	Pursuit of pleasure is the guide.	Hedonists might argue that, like hunger or thirst, sexual desires do not involve moral considerations.
Asceticism	One denies sexual desires to devote oneself to spiritual pursuits.	Many ascetics in Western and Eastern religions seek to transcend physical and worldly desires.
Utilitarianism	Moral conduct brings about the greatest good for the greatest number.	We should be honest simply because it serves the greater good for people to be true to their word and treat each other justly.
Rationalism	Sexual decisions should be based on intellect and reason, not blind obedience.	The rationalist might decide that the personal consequences of continuing an unhappy marriage outweigh the effects on the family or the community at large.

Most of us also tend to assume that authority figures such as doctors and government officials provide us with factual information and are qualified to make decisions that affect our lives. But when two doctors disagree on the need for breast surgery, or two officials disagree as to whether condoms should be distributed in public schools, how can both be correct? Critical thinkers never say that something is true because an authority figure says it is true. They demand *evidence*.

To help students evaluate claims, arguments, and widely held beliefs, most colleges encourage critical thinking. The core of critical thinking is skepticism—taking nothing for granted. Critical thinking means being skeptical of things that are presented in print, uttered by authority figures or celebrities, or passed along by friends. Another aspect of critical thinking is analysis and probing of claims and arguments. Critical thinking means scrutinizing definitions of terms and evaluating the premises of arguments and their logic. Critical thinkers maintain open minds. They suspend their beliefs until they have obtained and evaluated the evidence.

The "Sex in the Digital Age" feature examines application of critical thinking to the types of sexual information and advice we find on the Internet.

Critical Thinking
Are you a critical thinker? If not, why not? What kinds of intellectual and interpersonal conflicts are likely to be encountered by people who decide that they would like to become critical thinkers?

Perspectives on Human Sexuality

LO 1.4 **Discuss various ways of looking at human sexuality.**

Human sexuality is a complex topic. No single theory or perspective can capture all its nuances. In this book we explore human sexuality from many perspectives—historical, biological, evolutionary, cross-species, cross-cultural, sociological, psychological, and sociocultural.

The Historical Perspective

History places sexual attitudes and behavior in context. It informs us as to whether sexual behavior reflects trends that have been with us through the millennia or the customs of a particular culture and era. History shows little evidence of universal sexual trends. Attitudes and behaviors vary extensively from one time and place to another. Contemporary American society may be permissive when compared to the Victorian and post–World War II eras. Yet it looks staid when compared to the sexual

SEX IN THE DIGITAL AGE

THINKING CRITICALLY ABOUT SEXUAL ADVICE ON THE INTERNET

http://kinseyconfidential.org/
www.goaskalice.columbia.edu
www.cdc.gov
www.guttmacher.org/
www.aasect.org

"Kinsey Confidential?" "Go Ask Alice?" "CDC?" "Guttmacher Institute?" These are just a few of the Web sites offering sexual information and sexual advice that have flooded the Internet in recent years. On a recent day, "Kinsey Confidential" posted and answered questions including "My semen had a slight red color. What could cause that?" and "I want to give my girlfriend an 11-inch dildo. Is this safe?" The red color? Some blood in the semen is usually not a problem, but it is something to ask your doctor about if it's associated with discomfort between the legs or persists (see Chapter 3). The dildo? Think twice about it; maybe three times. "Go Ask Alice" posted and answered college students' questions including "What do I do about my man boobs?" and "Kissed by someone with HIV—Infected?" (The Web site also commented on corns between the toes.)

Kinsey Confidential is administered by the Kinsey Institute, which is associated with the Kinsey surveys of the 1940s and 1950s but which, since that time, has branched out in many different directions (Clay, 2015). (We rate it an A+.) "Go Ask Alice," it turns out, is administered by Columbia University, so its credibility is (likely) as strong as the credibility of the university. (A+) The CDC is the Centers for Disease Control and Prevention, which is a division of the U.S. Department of Health and Human Services. So, unless you mistrust the U.S. government, you can count on the CDC for factual information. The "Guttmacher Institute" is an admittedly liberal Web site—pro-family planning, pro-choice. On the other hand it accurately reports information obtained by surveys and other methods of research.

But these are just a few Web sites that offer sexual information and advice. How do we know whom to trust and whom not to trust? There are no easy answers. Many of us believe the things we see posted, and anecdotes about how Tyrone increased the size of his penis by 30% and how Maria learned to reach orgasm "every time" can have a powerful allure.

Be on guard. A price we pay for freedom of speech is that nearly anything can wind up posted on a Web site or in print. Authors can make extravagant claims with little fear of punishment. They can lie about the effectiveness of a new sexual cure-all as easily as they can lie about sightings of Elvis Presley or UFOs.

How can you protect yourself? Try some critical thinking:

1. **First, do "judge the book by its cover"**—at least in part. Does the Web site look well organized? Do the links within the Web pages work? A credible Web site will look professional and be well maintained.

2. **Ignore Web sites that make extravagant claims.** If it sounds too good to be true, it probably is. No method helps everyone who tries it. Few methods work overnight.

Really? How can you know what to believe on the Internet? How can you separate the electronic wheat from the electronic chaff?

3. **Check the credentials of the people who post the information.** Be suspicious if the author's title is "Dr." and is placed before the name. The degree could be a phony doctorate bought through the mail. It is better if the "doctor" has an Ph.D., Psy.D., Ed.D., M.D., or D.O. *after* her or his name.

4. **Check authors' affiliations.** Helping professionals who are affiliated with colleges, universities, clinics, and hospitals may have more to offer than those who are not.

5. **Check the *evidence* reported on the web site.** Unscientific Web sites (and books) usually make extensive use of *anecdotes*—unsupported stories or case studies about fantastic results with one or a few individuals. Responsible helping professionals test the effectiveness of techniques with large numbers of people. They carefully measure the outcomes. They use cautious language. For example, they say "It appears that . . ." or "It may be that . . . ."

6. **Check the reference citations for the evidence.** Legitimate research is reported in the journals, or on the Web sites you will find in the References section of this book. If there are no links to reference citations, or if the references look suspicious, you should be suspicious, too.

7. **Ask your instructor for advice.** Ask for advice on what to do, where to go (electronically, perhaps), whom to talk to, what to read.

8. **Talk to someone in your college or university health center.**

2 › T / F Truth or Fiction Revisited Actually, you cannot trust everything that is posted on the Internet. Much of the material may be written or posted by respected authorities, but always check out the authors' credentials. Be skeptical. Weigh the evidence. In general, there are few if any quick fixes to problems concerning sex and relationships. Do your homework.

excesses of some ancient societies, such as the ruling class of ancient Rome. History also shows how religion has been a major influence on sexual values and behavior. Let us trace some historical changes in attitudes toward sexuality. We begin by turning the clock back to the days before written records were kept—that is, to prehistory.

PREHISTORIC SEXUALITY: FROM FEMALE IDOLS TO PHALLIC WORSHIP

Information about life among our Stone Age ancestors is drawn largely from cave drawings, stone artifacts, and the customs of modern-day preliterate peoples whose existence has changed little over the millennia. From such sources, historians and anthropologists infer that there was a prehistoric gender-related division of labor. By and large, men hunted for game, and women tended to remain close to home. Women nurtured children and gathered edible plants and nuts, crabs, and other marine life that wandered along the shore or swam in shallow waters.

Art produced in the Stone Age suggests the worship of women's ability to bear children and perpetuate the species. Primitive statues and cave drawings portray women with large, pendulous breasts, rounded hips, and prominent sex organs. Most theorists regard the figurines as fertility symbols. Stone Age people may have been unaware of the male's contribution to reproduction.

As the glacial sheets of the last Ice Age retreated (about 11,000 BCE) and the climate warmed, human societies turned agrarian. Hunters and gatherers became farmers and herders. Villages sprang up around fields. Men tended livestock. Women farmed. As people grew aware of the male role in reproduction, **phallic worship** (worship of the penis) sprang into being. Knowledge of paternity is believed to have developed around 9000 BCE, resulting from observation of livestock. When people began to observe animals throughout the years, they also began to understand that a predictable period of time elapsed between copulation and the birth of offspring.

The penis became glorified in art as a plough, ax, or sword. **Phallic symbols** played roles in religious ceremonies in ancient Egypt. The ancient Greeks sometimes rendered phalluses as rings, sometimes as necklaces. In ancient Rome, a large phallus was carried like a float in a parade honoring Venus, the goddess of love.

The **incest taboo** may have been the first human taboo. All human societies apparently have some form of incest taboo, but societies have varied in terms of its strictness. Brother–sister marriages were permitted among the presumably divine rulers of ancient Egypt and among the royal families of the Incas, who inhabited what is now Peru, and of Hawaii, even though they were generally prohibited among commoners. Father–daughter marriages were permitted among the aristocracy and royalty of ancient Egypt. Incestuous relationships kept wealth and power, as well as "divinity," in the family.

THE ANCIENT HEBREWS

The ancient Hebrews viewed sex, at least in marriage, as a satisfying experience intended to fulfill the divine command to "be fruitful and multiply." The emphasis on the procreative function of sex led to some interesting social customs. For example, childlessness and the development of a repulsive abnormality, such as a boil, were grounds for divorce. Male–male and female–female sexual behavior were strongly condemned because they threatened the perpetuation of the family.

Although the ancient Hebrews believed that sex helped strengthen marital bonds and solidify the family, according to the Hebrew Bible, the prophet Abraham had several wives and concubines, and King Solomon had several hundred.

According to the Book of Proverbs, a good wife rises before dawn to tend to her family's needs, brings home food, instructs the servants, tends the vineyards, makes the clothes, keeps the ledger, helps the needy, and works well into the night. Even so, a wife was considered the property of her husband and could be divorced on a whim. A wife might have to share her husband with secondary wives and concubines, but she could be stoned to death for adultery—a fate still practiced in some Islamic cultures. Men who consorted with the wives of other men were considered to have violated the property rights of those men and might have to pay "damages."

The "Venus of Willendorf." This tiny buxom figurine may be a fertility symbol.

phallic worship
Worship of the penis as a symbol of generative power.

phallic symbol
An image of the penis.

incest taboo
The prohibition against intercourse and reproduction among close blood relatives.

Many Ancient Greek Ceramics Depict Male–Male Sexual Activity. The ancient Greeks believed that males were bisexual. A prominent mature Greek man might take an adolescent boy as a student and lover.

In case the notion that a woman is a man's property sounds ancient to you, we must note that in many cultures it remains current. For example, in Afghanistan some fathers have given other men their daughters as payment for gambling debts (Bearak, 2006).

THE ANCIENT GREEKS   The classical or golden age of Greece lasted from about 500 BCE to 300 BCE. Within this relatively short span lived the philosophers Socrates, Plato, and Aristotle; the playwrights Aristophanes, Aeschylus, and Sophocles; the natural scientist Archimedes; and the lawgiver Solon. Like the Hebrews, the Greeks valued family life, but Greek men also admired the well-developed male body and enjoyed nude wrestling in the arena. Erotic encounters and off-color jokes characterized the plays of Aristophanes and other playwrights. The Greeks viewed their gods as voracious seekers of sexual variety. Not only were they believed to have sexual adventures among themselves but they were also thought to have seduced mortals.

Three aspects of Greek sexuality are of particular interest to our study of sexual practices in the ancient world: male–male sexual behavior, pederasty, and prostitution. The Greeks viewed people as **bisexual**. Male–male sex was deemed normal and tolerated so long as it did not threaten the institution of the family. **Pederasty** means love of boys. Sex between men and prepubescent boys was illegal, but families were generally pleased if their adolescent sons attracted socially prominent mentors.

bisexual

Sexually responsive to either gender.

pederasty

Sexual love of boys.

3 › T / F   Truth or Fiction Revisited   It is true that men in ancient Greece might take on an adolescent male as a lover and pupil. Pederasty did not impede the boy's future male–female functioning, because the pederast himself was usually married, and Greeks believed people to be equally capable of male–female and male–male sexual activity. In Chapter 15 we will learn about priests who have abused boys and women teachers who have had relations with their male students. We learn about "boy play"—which is involuntary and clearly meets any definition of rape—in contemporary Afghanistan in the nearby "Sex in a World of Diversity" feature.

courtesan

A prostitute—especially the mistress of a noble or wealthy man.

concubine

A secondary wife, usually of inferior legal and social status.

Prostitution flourished at every level of society in ancient Greece. Prostitutes ranged from refined **courtesans** to **concubines**, who were usually slaves. Courtesans could play musical instruments, dance, engage in witty repartee, and discuss politics. They were also skilled in the arts of love. No social stigma was attached to visiting a courtesan. At the lower rungs of society were streetwalkers and brothel prostitutes. The latter were not hard to find: A wooden or painted penis invariably stood by the door.

The women of Athens were subject to the authority of their male next-of-kin before marriage and to their husbands afterward. They received no formal education and were consigned mostly to women's quarters in their homes. They were chaperoned when they ventured out of doors. A husband could divorce his wife without cause and was obligated to do so if she committed adultery.

4 › T / F   Truth or Fiction Revisited   Women in the ancient world were in fact largely treated as property. We still speak about fathers "giving away" their daughters to their husbands.

SEX IN A WORLD OF DIVERSITY

"BOY PLAY" IN AFGHANISTAN

By instructing American soldiers and Marines not to interfere, even if the incidents occurred on American bases, the Pentagon has chosen—reprehensibly—to sacrifice vulnerable children in order to maintain good relations with the Afghan police and militias it needs to fight the Taliban.

Editorial Board (2015), *New York Times*

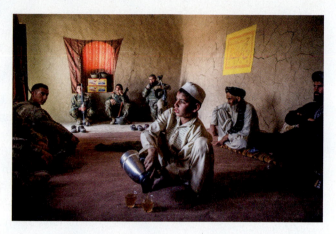

An Afghan "Tea Boy" with the Afghan army and U.S. soldiers.

The Afghan police commander, Sarwar Jan, had a toothache. Actually, having a "toothache problem" is what the local Afghans say to refer to people who engage in child sexual abuse. Despite his toothache, Jan was allied with the American soldiers and Marines at the base in Helmand Province, united by the common bond of fighting the Taliban—although Jan had earlier been arrested by Afghan authorities for supporting the Taliban. Jan arrived at the base with an entourage of "tea boys"—servants who often provide more than tea.

At about the time of Jan's arrival, Lance Corporal Gregory Buckley Jr. told his father that he repeatedly overheard Afghan police at the base sexually abusing boys they had abducted or bought from impoverished families. At night they heard the boys screaming. On one occasion another corporal walked in on several men lying on the floor beneath a sheet, with children between them.

The soldiers and Marines have informed their superiors about the abuse but been told to look the other way. Their mission is to fight the Taliban, not Afghan military commanders or police who engage in *bacha bazi*—the local term for "boy play." The abuse needed to be accepted because of the larger purpose and because "it's their culture." The culture Americans were fighting to preserve.

Buckley never brought his protest back to the United States. He and two other Marines were shot by one of Jan's tea boys. Two service members who were not shot have tried to compel their superiors to fight bacha bazi, and their careers are in jeopardy.

THE WORLD OF ANCIENT ROME   Much is made of the sexual excesses of the Roman emperors and ruling families. Julius Caesar is reputed to have been bisexual—"a man to every woman and a woman to every man." Other emperors, such as Caligula, sponsored orgies at which guests engaged in sexual practices including **bestiality** and **sadism**. Sexual excesses were found more often among the upper classes of palace society than among average Romans, however.

Romans disapproved of male–male sexual behavior as a threat to the integrity of the Roman family, which was viewed as the core of strength of the empire. Although Roman women were more likely than their Greek counterparts to share their husbands' social lives, they still were the property of their husbands.

Western society traces the roots of many of its sexual terms to Roman culture, as indicated by their Latin roots. **Fellatio**, for example, derives from the Latin *fellare*, meaning "to suck." **Cunnilingus** derives from *cunnus*, meaning "vulva," and *lingere*, "to lick." **Fornication** derives from *fornix*, an arch or vault. The term stems from Roman streetwalkers' practice of serving their customers in the shadows of archways near public buildings such as stadiums and theaters.

CHRISTIANITY   Christianity emerged within the Roman Empire during the centuries following the death of Jesus. Early Christian views on sexuality were largely shaped by Saint Paul and the church fathers in the first century and by Saint Augustine in the latter part of the fourth century. Adultery and fornication were rampant among the upper classes of Rome at the time, and early Christian leaders began to associate sexuality with sin.

bestiality
Sexual relations between a person and an animal.

sadism
The practice of achieving sexual gratification through hurting or humiliating others.

fellatio
A sexual activity involving oral contact with the penis.

cunnilingus
A sexual activity involving oral contact with the female genitals.

fornication
Sexual intercourse between people who are not married to one another.

In replacing the pagan values of Rome, the early Christians sought to restrict sex to marriage. They saw temptations of the flesh as distractions from spiritual devotion. Paul preached that celibacy was closer to the Christian ideal than marriage. He recognized that not everyone could achieve celibacy, however, so he said that it was "better to marry than to burn" (with passion, that is).

Christians, like the Hebrews before them, demanded virginity of brides. Prostitution was condemned. Christians taught that men should love their wives with restraint, not passion, because the goal was procreation and not pleasure—the spirit should rule the flesh. Divorce was outlawed. Unhappiness with one's spouse might reflect sinful restlessness. Dissolving a marriage might also jeopardize the social structure that supported the church. Masturbation, male–male sexual behavior, female–female sexual behavior, oral–genital contact, anal intercourse—all were viewed as abominations.

Saint Augustine (353–430 CE) associated sexual lust with the original sin of Adam and Eve in the Garden of Eden. Lust and shame were passed down through the generations. Lust made any sexual expression, even in marriage, inherently evil. Only through celibacy, according to Augustine, could men and women attain a state of grace.

There have been two conflicting concepts of woman in Christianity: One is of woman as Eve, the temptress; the other is of woman as Mary, Mother of God, virtuous and pure. Contemporary Western images of women still show the schism between the good girl and the bad girl—the Madonna and the whore.

During the Protestant Reformation, Martin Luther (1483–1546) and other Christian reformers such as John Calvin (1509–1564) split off from the Roman Catholic Church and formed their own sects, which led to the development of the modern Protestant denominations. Luther believed that priests should be allowed to marry and rear children. To Luther, marriage was as much a part of human nature as eating or drinking. Calvin rejected the Roman church's position that marital sex was permissible only for procreation. He believed that sex strengthened the marriage bond and helped relieve the stresses of everyday life.

Early European settlers brought to North America the religious teachings that had dominated Western thought and culture for centuries. Whatever their differences, each religion stressed the ideal of family life and viewed sex outside of marriage as immoral or sinful. A woman's place, by and large, was in the home and in the fields. Not until 1833, when Oberlin College opened its doors to women, were women permitted to attend college in the United States. (Not until 1920 did women gain the right to vote.)

ISLAM

> The Seraglio of the sultan of the Ottoman Empire housed about 1,600 virgins, each hoping to be chosen for one night of honor. The sultan makes [the Mormon] Brigham Young, who had only a few dozen wives, look like a piker. (Bentley, 2009)

Islam, the dominant religion in the Middle East, across North Africa and into parts of Southern Asia, was founded by the Prophet Muhammad. Muhammad was born in what is now Saudi Arabia, in about 570 CE. The Islamic tradition treasures marriage and sexual fulfillment in marriage. Premarital sex and adultery invite shame and social condemnation—and, as noted, in some fundamentalist Islamic states, the death penalty, by stoning.

Muhammad decreed that marriage represents the road to virtue. Islamic tradition permits a sexual double standard, however. Men under most circumstances may take up to four wives (we saw that the sultan of the Ottoman Empire had a few more), but women are permitted only one husband. Public social interactions between men and women are severely restricted in more conservative Islamic societies. Women are expected to keep their heads and faces veiled in public and to avoid all contact with men other than their husbands.

An Erotic Panel on the Kandariya Mahadev Temple, Khajuraho, India. This eleventh-century sculpture was carved on the side of a Hindu temple. Hindus today are more reserved in the expression of their sexuality.

INDIA   Perhaps no culture has cultivated sexual pleasure as a spiritual ideal to the extent of the ancient Hindus of India. From the fifth century CE onward, temples show sculptures of gods, nymphs, and ordinary people in erotic poses. Hindu sexual practices were codified in a sex manual, the *Kama Sutra,* which illustrates sexual positions, some of which would challenge a contortionist. It also holds recipes for alleged aphrodisiacs. This manual is believed to have been written sometime between the third and fifth centuries CE, when Christianity was ascending in the West.

In its graphic representations of sexual positions and practices, the *Kama Sutra* reflected the Hindu belief that sex was a religious duty, not a source of shame or guilt. Hindu deities were often portrayed as engaging in same-sex as well as male–female sexual activities. In the Hindu doctrine of karma (the passage of souls from one place to another), sexual fulfillment was regarded as one way to become reincarnated at a higher level of existence. Indian society grew more restrictive toward sexuality after about 1000 CE.

THE FAR EAST   In the cultures of the Far East, sexuality was akin to spirituality. To the Taoist masters of China, who influenced Chinese culture for millennia, sex was a sacred duty—a form of worship that led toward harmony with nature and immortality.

5 › T / F   Truth or Fiction Revisited   Consider this fact:

> Second century [Chinese] sex manuals … describe the beautiful bodies—"supple like grass"—of dancing girls, who "put forth all their charms so that one forgets life and death." (Bentley, 2009)

Therefore, it is not true that the production of sex manuals originated in modern times. The Chinese culture was the first to produce a detailed sex manual, which came into use about 200 years before the birth of Jesus.

In ancient China, the man was expected to extend intercourse as long as possible to absorb more of his wife's natural essence, or yin. Yin would enhance his own masculine essence, or yang. Moreover, he was to help bring his partner to orgasm so as to increase the flow of energy that he might absorb.

Taoists believed that it was wasteful for a man to "spill his seed." Masturbation, acceptable for women, was ruled out for men. Sexual practices such as anal intercourse and oral–genital contact (fellatio and cunnilingus) were permissible, so long as the man did not squander yang through wasteful ejaculation. Same-sex activity was not prohibited by Taoist holy writings, but some Taoists frowned on exclusive homosexuality. The good Chinese wife, like her Western counterparts, was limited to domestic roles.

THE VICTORIAN PERIOD   The middle and later parts of the nineteenth century in Western civilization are generally called the Victorian period, after Queen Victoria of England, who assumed the throne in 1837 and ruled until her death in 1901. Her name has become virtually synonymous with sexual repression. Victorian society in Europe and the United States, on the surface at least, was prim and proper. Even the legs of pianos were draped with cloth for the sake of modesty. Many women viewed sex as a marital duty to be performed for procreation or to satisfy their husbands' cravings. Consider the following quotation:

> I am happy now that Charles calls on my bed chamber less frequently than of old. As it is, I now endure but two calls a week and when I hear his steps outside my door I lie down on my bed, close my eyes, open my legs and think of England.
>
> —Alice, Lady Hillingdon

Women were assumed not to experience sexual desires or pleasures. "I would say," observed William Acton (1814–1875), an influential English physician, in 1857, "that the majority of women (happily for society) are not much troubled with sexual feeling of any kind."

6 › T / F Truth or Fiction Revisited   It was widely believed among medical authorities in England and the United States that sex drains the man of his vitality. Physicians thus recommended that intercourse be practiced infrequently. The Reverend Sylvester Graham (1794–1851) preached that ejaculation depleted men of "vital fluids" and preached against "wasting the seed" by masturbation or frequent marital intercourse (Haynes, 2012). (How frequent was "frequent"? In Graham's view, intercourse more than once a month could dangerously sap vital energies.) Graham therefore recommended that young men control their sexual appetites by a diet of simple foods based on whole-grain flours and invented what we now call the Graham cracker to serve this purpose.

Just How Repressed Was Sex during the Victorian Era? As this nineteenth-century nude study suggests, sexuality may not have been as repressed as advertised. The Greek statue in the background apparently attests that the photo is a work of art.

But the behavior of Victorians was not as repressed as advertised. Despite Acton's beliefs, Victorian women did experience sexual pleasure and orgasm. Consider some findings from an early sex survey conducted in 1892 by a female physician, Clelia Duel Mosher. Although her sample was small and nonrandom, 35 of the 44 women who responded admitted to desiring sexual intercourse. And 34 of them reported having orgasms. Women's diaries of the time also contain accounts of passionate love affairs.

Prostitution flourished during the Victorian era. Men apparently thought that they were doing their wives a favor by looking elsewhere. There may have been as many as 1 prostitute for every 12 men in London during the nineteenth century; in Vienna, perhaps 1 for every 7 men.

Same-sex sexual behavior was considered indecent in Victorian society. The celebrated, gay Anglo-Irish novelist and playwright Oscar Wilde—author of *The Picture of Dorian Gray, An Ideal Husband,* and *The Importance of Being Earnest*—was imprisoned after being convicted of "gross indecency."

BEGINNINGS OF THE SCIENTIFIC STUDY OF SEXUALITY   Against this backdrop of repression, scientists and scholars began to approach sexuality as an area of legitimate scientific study. The English physician Havelock Ellis (1859–1939) published a veritable encyclopedia of sexuality between 1897 and 1910, *Studies in the Psychology of Sex.* Ellis drew information from case histories, anthropological findings, and medical knowledge. He argued that sexual desires in women were natural and healthy. He wrote that many sexual problems had psychological rather than physical causes. Gay male and lesbian sexual orientations were natural variations in sexual orientation, not aberrations. Ellis saw gay male and lesbian sexual orientations as inborn dispositions, not as vices or character flaws.

The German psychiatrist Richard von Krafft-Ebing (1840–1902) described case histories of people with sexual deviations in his book, *Psychopathia Sexualis* (1886). Cases included sadomasochism (sexual gratification through inflicting or receiving pain), bestiality, and necrophilia (intercourse with dead people). Krafft-Ebing viewed deviations as mental diseases that could be studied and perhaps treated by medical science.

At about the same time, the Viennese physician Sigmund Freud (1856–1939) was developing his influential theory of personality. Freud believed that the sex drive was our principal motivating force.

Alfred Kinsey (1894–1956), an Indiana University zoologist, conducted the first large-scale studies of sexual behavior in the 1930s and 1940s. Kinsey conducted detailed interviews with nearly 12,000 people across the United States attempts to provide a comprehensive picture of American sexual behavior. The results of his surveys were published in two volumes, *Sexual Behavior in the Human Male* (Kinsey et al., 1948) and *Sexual Behavior in the Human Female* (Kinsey et al., 1953). The books made for dry reading. They were filled with statistical tables rather than racy pictures or vignettes. Nevertheless, they became best-sellers, exploding on a public that had not yet learned to discuss sex openly. Kinsey's work had some methodological flaws—especially in its selection of participants—but much of the criticism branded it as immoral and obscene. Many newspapers refused to report the results of his survey on female sexuality. A 1950s congressional committee claimed that Kinsey's work undermined the moral fiber of the nation, rendering it more vulnerable to a Communist takeover. Despite all the brouhaha, Kinsey and his colleagues made sex research a scientifically respectable field of study and helped lay the groundwork for discussing sexual behavior openly (DeLameter & Plante, 2015).

THE SEXUAL REVOLUTION   The period of the mid-1960s to the mid-1970s is often referred to as the *sexual revolution*. Dramatic changes occurred in American sexual attitudes and practices during the "Swinging Sixties." Our society was on the threshold of major social upheaval, not only in sexual behavior but also in science, politics, fashion, music, art, and cinema. The so-called Woodstock generation, disheartened by commercialism and the Vietnam War, tuned in (to rock music on the radio), turned on (to drugs), and dropped out (of mainstream society). The heat was on between the hippies and the hardhats. Long hair became the mane of men. Bell-bottomed jeans flared. Films became sexually explicit as censorship crumbled. Critics seriously contemplated whether the pornography "classic" *Deep Throat* had deep social implications. Hard rock music bellowed the message of rebellion and revolution.

The sexual revolution gained momentum from a timely interplay of scientific, social, political, and economic forces. The war (in Vietnam), the bomb (fear of the nuclear bomb), the pill (the introduction of the birth control pill), and the mass media (especially television) were four such forces. The pill lessened the risk of pregnancy, enabling young people to engage in recreational or casual sex. Pop psychology movements, such as the Human Potential Movement of the 1960s and 1970s (the "Me Decade"), spread the message that people should get in touch with and express their genuine feelings, including their sexual feelings. "Doing your own thing" became one catchphrase. "If it feels right, go with it" became another. The lamp was rubbed. Out popped the sexual genie.

The sexual revolution was tied to social permissiveness and political liberalism. The media dealt openly with sex. Popular books encouraged people to explore their

Critical Thinking
What, then, does history tell us about sex? Is there a universal standard for defining sexual values, or are there many standards?

sexuality. Film scenes of lovemaking became so commonplace that the movie rating system was introduced to alert parents.

During the sexual revolution, sexually explicit questionnaires proliferated in popular magazines, interviewers posed sexually explicit questions by telephone and in person, and some pioneers, including William H. Masters and Virginia Johnson, observed people engaging in sexual activity in the laboratory. In the 1960s, Masters and Johnson were condemned by many as destroying the moral fabric of the nation—a complaint similar to those leveled earlier against Kinsey. Today, research on sexual behavior continues, with more valid methods of sampling and a largely jaded citizenry. With the advent of the cable TV series *Masters of Sex*, Masters and Johnson became just another reality show.

RECENT TRENDS   More teenagers are sexually active today, and at younger ages, than they were a couple of generations ago. Two other features of the sexual revolution have become permanent parts of our social fabric: the liberation of female sexuality and widespread willingness to discuss sex openly. Countless pornography Web sites populate the Internet and can be accessed by children. As late as the 1950s and 1960s, men's magazines might reveal models' breasts, and nudist magazines might show some more. Today, however, with multiple Web sites offering the opportunity to download videos of celebrities such as Paris Hilton and Kim Kardashian engaging in sexual activity, pornography has nearly attained the status of wallpaper.

The Biological Perspective

The biological perspective focuses on the roles of hormones, the nervous system, the sex organs, genetics, and other biological factors in human sexuality. Sex, after all, serves the biological function of reproduction. We are biologically endowed with structures that make sexual behavior possible—and, for most people, pleasurable.

Study of the biology of sex informs us about the mechanisms of reproduction as well as of the mechanisms of sexual arousal and response. We learn that orgasm is a spinal reflex as well as a psychological event.

Genes lead to the timely development female and male sexual anatomy and physiology and, apparently, to stereotypical mating behavior in most species. In our discussion of the evolutionary perspective, we consider possible influences of genes on sexual and mating strategies in humans. Our physical traits, and perhaps our mating strategies, are determined or at least influenced by genes that we inherit from our parents. Genes are segments of **chromosomes**, which are composed of **DNA (deoxyribonucleic acid)**. Each human cell normally contains a complement of 46 chromosomes, which are arranged in 23 pairs. Each pair of chromosomes consists of 1,000 or so genes. A child normally inherits one member of each pair from each parent. Each child inherits half of his or her genes from each parent. The particular combinations of genes that one inherits account for whether one has blue eyes or brown eyes, light or dark hair, and a penis or a vagina.

The Evolutionary Perspective

Species vary not only in their physical characteristics but also in their social behavior, including their mating behavior. Scientists look to **evolution** to help explain such variability (Buss & Schmitt, 2011). The English naturalist Charles Darwin (1809–1882) showed that current species of animals and plants evolved from other life forms through **natural selection**, or "survival of the fittest." In each species, individuals vary, and some are better adapted to their environments than others. Better-adapted members are more likely to survive to reproduce and transmit their traits to succeeding generations. They are not necessarily the strongest or fleetest of foot, although these traits are adaptive for some species and enhance their reproductive success.

genes

The basic units of heredity, which consist of chromosomal segments of DNA.

chromosomes

The rodlike structures that reside in the nuclei of every living cell and carry the genetic code in the form of genes.

DNA

Deoxyribonucleic acid—the chemical substance whose molecules make up genes and chromosomes.

evolution

The development of a species to its present state, which is believed to involve adaptations to its environment.

natural selection

The evolutionary process by which adaptive traits enable members of a species to survive to reproductive age and transmit these traits to future generations.

New variations in species can also be introduced through random genetic changes called **mutations**. Although mutations occur randomly, they are subject to natural selection. Adaptive mutations enhance reproductive success. As more members of the species come to possess these traits, the species changes.

EVOLUTIONARY VIEWS OF MALE–FEMALE DIFFERENCES IN MATING STRATEGIES   With humans, natural selection may not only have led to the development of our sex organs, but also to sexual and mating strategies that promote the survival of our species. More specifically, researchers into evolutionary processes suggest that there may be a genetic basis to certain aspects of social behavior, including sexual behavior, among humans and some other animals (Buss & Schmitt, 2011; Kennair et al., 2015). If so, we may carry traits that helped our prehistoric ancestors survive and reproduce successfully. For example, some evolutionary psychologists argue that men are naturally more promiscuous than women because they are the genetic heirs of ancestors whose reproductive success was related to the number of women they could impregnate (Buss & Schmitt, 2011). Women, by contrast, can produce only a few offspring in their lifetimes. Thus, evolutionary theory suggests, woman may have to be more selective with respect to their mating partners. Women's reproductive success is enhanced by mating with the fittest males—not with any Tom, Dick, or Harry who happens by. Thus the male's "roving eye" and the female's selectivity may be embedded in their genes. Male–female differences in reasons for having sex may reflect evolutionary processes and are discussed further on the next page feature on the 13 basic reasons for having sex.

mutation
A random change in the molecular structure of DNA.

Critical Thinking
The biological, evolutionary, and cross-species perspectives may offer some insights into what kinds of sexual behavior are "natural." If a sexual behavior pattern is judged to be natural, does that mean that it is right or good? Explain your answer.

The Cross-Species Perspective

In an endeavor to discover what kinds of sexual behaviors are "natural," scientists have looked to the sexual behavior of other animal species. A surprising variety of sexual behaviors exist among nonhumans. There are animal examples, or analogues, of human male–male sexual behavior, female–female sexual behavior, oral–genital contact, and oral–oral behavior (i.e., kissing). Foreplay is also well known in the animal world. Turtles massage their mates' heads with their claws. Male mice nibble at their partner's necks. Most mammals use only a rear-entry position to mate, but some animals, such as apes, use a variety of positions.

Cross-species research reveals an interesting pattern. Sexual behavior among "higher" mammals, such as primates, is less directly controlled by instinct than it is among the "lower" species, such as birds, fish, or lower mammals. Experience and learning play more important roles in sexuality as we climb the evolutionary ladder.

Sociological Perspectives

Sociology tends to study the influences of groups of sexual behavior. Thus sociologists consider the behavior of humans by socioeconomic status level of education, sex (male or female), race and ethnicity, and age. They look at the roles of families, religion, urbanization, social movements, and nations. Sociological perspectives, like the historical perspective, provide insight into the ways in which cultural institutions and beliefs affect sexual behavior and people's sense of morality.

Societies differ, for example, in their attitudes toward childhood masturbation. Some societies, such as the Hopi Native Americans of the southwest United States, ignore it. Trobrianders encourage it. Other societies condemn it. Individuals in these societies tend to accept dominant beliefs or, if they challenge them, to be ostracized.

The members of all human societies share anatomic structures and physiological capacities for sexual pleasure, however. The same hormones flow through their arteries. Yet their sexual practices, and the pleasure they reap or fail to attain, may set them apart. If human sexuality were determined exclusively by biology, we might not find such diversity.

A CLOSER LOOK

THE 13 BASIC REASONS FOR HAVING SEX

In their seminal article "Why Humans Have Sex," Cindy Meston and David Buss (2007) note that the reasons might seem obvious. It feels good is one. It is the (most common) method of reproduction is another. It also relieves sexual tension.

But Meston and Buss point out that there are many other reasons. Let's think of some. Someone could say "He (or she) kept pushing me." Or "I wanted to feel closer to [fill in the name]." A sex worker might say, "I need to make a living." Or how about, "I wanted to stop him (or her) from having sex with someone else." Then again, one could think "I wanted to see if I would like it," or "I wanted to get back at my cheating boyfriend (or girlfriend)," even "I was bored."

How many reasons are there in all? Actually, we can't answer that question directly. But we can tell you what Meston and Buss did. They engaged in a pair of research studies. In the first, they asked study participants to "nominate" (or think up) reasons for having sex. They arrived at 237 answers (which we will not list here). Study 2 asked 1,549 participants to rate the degree to which each of the 237 answers had figured in to their own reasons for having sex. They then used a mathematical technique called factor analysis to see if the 237 reasons could be broken down into a manageable number of groups. They arrived at the four major factors shown in Table 1.2, and found, further, that each of the major factors could be broken down into two or more subfactors, totaling 13.

Many studies have further investigated the 13 basic reasons to see how, for example, they might fit people with a variety of personality traits, and to see whether they might dovetail

Fancy That! He has taken her out on an expensive dinner date. Will she feel that she should reciprocate by having sex with him? What are the 13 basic reasons that people have sex?

Table 1.2   The 13 Basic Reasons for Having Sex

Factor	Subfactor
Physical	• **Stress reduction** ("I thought it would relax me." "It could help me 'get sex out of my system' so I could focus on other things.") • **Pleasure** ("I wanted to feel the pure pleasure." "I was horny.") • **Physical desirability** ("The person had an attractive body [or face]." "The person was too sexy to resist.") • **Experience seeking** ("I wanted to experience what it would be like to have sex with another person." "I wanted adventure/excitement.")
Goal attainment	• **Resources** ("I wanted to make money." "I wanted to reproduce.") • **Social status** ("I wanted to brag to my friends about my conquest." "I was competing with someone else to 'get' the person.") • **Revenge** ("I wanted to even the score with a cheating partner." "I wanted to make someone else jealous.") • **Utilitarian** ("The person had taken me out on an expensive dinner." "I wanted to get out of doing something else.")
Emotional	• **Love and commitment** ("I wanted to express my love for the person." "It felt like a natural next step in my relationship.") • **Expression** ("I wanted to say 'Thank you'." "I wanted to celebrate a birthday/wedding anniversary/other special occasion.")
Insecurity	• **Self-esteem boost** ("I wanted to feel attractive." "I wanted my partner to notice me.") • **Duty/pressure** ("It was expected of me." "I didn't know how to say 'no'." "My partner kept insisting for a period of time.") • **Mate guarding** ("I wanted to prevent a breakup." "I wanted to decrease my partner's desire to have sex with someone else." "I was afraid my partner would have an affair if I didn't have sex with him/her.")

SOURCES: Kennair, L. E. O., et al. (2015). Sex and mating strategy impact the 13 basic reasons for having sex. *Evolutionary Psychological Science*, DOI: 10.1007/s40806-015-0024-6; Meston, C. M., & Buss, D. M. (2007). Why humans have sex. *Archives of Sexual Behavior, 36,* 477–507.

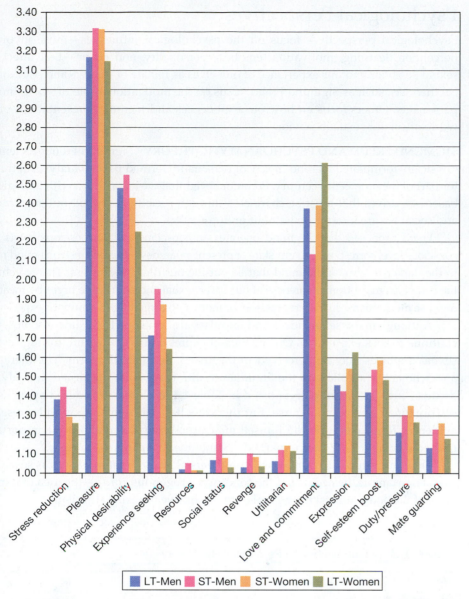

Figure 1.1 Relative Strength of Reasons for Having Sex Among Men Oriented Toward Long-Term Relationships (LT-Men), Men Oriented Toward Short-Term Relationships (ST-Men), Women Orientated Toward Short-Term Relationships (ST-Women), and Women Oriented Toward Long-Term Relationships (LT-Women).

Among all four groups, desire for pleasure was the strongest motive for having sex. The physical desirability of one's partner and feelings of love and commitment were tied overall. Men and women oriented toward short-term relationships were relatively more responsive to their partner's attractiveness than to feelings of love and commitment.

SOURCE: Kennair, L. E. O., et al. (2015). Sex and mating strategy impact the 13 basic reasons for having sex. *Evolutionary Psychological Science*, DOI: 10.1007/s40806-015-0024-6, Figure 1. With permission of Springer.

with evolutionary theory. Meston and Buss wrote that "Several evolution-based theories suggest that men will be more motivated by the desire for sexual variety, the chance for an opportunistic copulation, and the physical appearance of a potential partner, and that emotional factors, such as expressing love or intensifying psychological commitment, would figure more prominently in women's reasons for having sex" (2007, p. 478).

Figure 1.1 reported some of the findings of one such study, this one with 1,327 (473 male and 854 female) Norwegian university students who had engaged in sexual intercourse at least once. Participants were shown the 13 basic reasons and asked to indicate whether each explained their own reasons for sex, ranging from 1 for "none of my sexual experiences" to 5 for "all of my sexual experiences." Participants were also asked to indicate whether they were actively seeking short-term sexual

relationships or were in or were seeking long-term relationships. It comes as no surprise, perhaps that men and women actively seeking short-term sexual relationships were significantly more motivated by pleasure and the desire for experience than men and women who were oriented toward long-term relationships. Women oriented toward long-term relationships were most motivated to have sex by feelings of love and commitment. Men were more motivated than women by the physical desirability of their partners.

These differences aside, Figure 1.1 shows that all four groups were most strongly motivated by the desire for pleasure, with feelings of love and commitment and the physical desirability of one's partner sort of typing for second place. Few students overall were motivated to have sex for resources, revenge, social status, or utilitarian reasons.

Psychological Perspectives

Psychological perspectives focus on the psychological influences—those involving perception, learning, motivation, emotion, personality, and so on—that affect our sexual behavior and our experience of ourselves as female or male. Some psychological theorists, such as Sigmund Freud, focus on the motivational role of sex in human personality. Others focus on how our experiences and mental representations of the world affect our sexual behavior.

SIGMUND FREUD AND PSYCHOANALYTIC THEORY   Sigmund Freud, a Viennese physician, formulated a grand theory of personality termed **psychoanalysis** in the latter part of the nineteenth century. Freud believed that we are all born with biologically based sex drives that must be channeled through socially approved outlets if family and social life are to carry on without undue conflict.

Freud proposed that the mind operates on conscious and unconscious levels. The conscious level corresponds to our state of present awareness. The unconscious mind refers to the darker reaches of the mind that lie outside our direct awareness. The ego shields the conscious mind from awareness of our baser sexual and aggressive urges by means of **defense mechanisms** such as **repression**, or motivated forgetting of traumatic experiences.

Although many sexual ideas and impulses are banished to the unconscious, they continue to seek expression. One avenue of expression is the dream, through which sexual impulses may be perceived in disguised, or symbolic, form. The therapists and scholars who follow in the Freudian tradition are quite interested in analyzing dreams, and the dream objects listed in Table 1.3 are often considered symbols for sex organs or sexual intercourse. But this view has not been supported by research evidence. To his credit, Freud himself maintained skepticism about the importance of dream symbols. He once remarked, "Sometimes a cigar is just a cigar."

Freud introduced us to new and controversial ideas about ourselves as sexual beings. For example, he originated the concept of **erogenous zones**—the idea that many parts of the body, not just the genitals, are responsive to sexual stimulation.

psychoanalysis

The theory of personality originated by Sigmund Freud, which proposes that human behavior represents the outcome of clashing inner forces.

defense mechanisms

In psychoanalytic theory, automatic processes that protect the ego from anxiety by disguising or ejecting unacceptable ideas and urges.

repression

The automatic ejection of anxiety-evoking ideas from consciousness.

erogenous zones

Parts of the body, including but not limited to the sex organs, that are responsive to sexual stimulation.

Table 1.3 Dream Symbols in Psychoanalytic Theory

Symbols for the Male Sex Organs				
airplanes	fish	neckties	tools	weapons
bullets	hands	poles	trains	
feet	hoses	snakes	trees	
fire	knives	sticks	umbrellas	

Symbols for the Female Sex Organs				
bottles	caves	doors	ovens	ships
boxes	chests	hats	pockets	tunnels
cases	closets	jars	pots	

Symbols for Sexual Intercourse	
climbing a ladder	flying in an airplane
climbing a staircase	riding a horse
crossing a bridge	riding an elevator
driving an automobile	riding a roller coaster
entering a room	walking into a tunnel or down a hall

Symbols for the Breasts	
apples	peaches

Freud theorized that the content of dreams symbolized urges, wishes, and objects of fantasy that are censored in the waking state.

One of Freud's most controversial beliefs was that children normally harbor erotic interests. He believed that the suckling by the infant in the oral stage was an erotic act, and he believed the same about the anal bodily experimentation through which 2-year-olds find pleasure in the control of their sphincter muscles in the process of elimination. He theorized that it was normal for children to progress through stages of development in which the erotic interest shifts from one erogenous zone to another, as, for example, from the mouth or oral cavity to the anal cavity. According to his theory of **psychosexual development**, children undergo five stages of development: oral, anal, phallic, latency, and genital, which are named according to the main erogenous zones of each stage.

Freud believed that it was normal for children to develop erotic feelings toward the parent of the other sex during the phallic stage. These incestuous urges lead to conflict with the parent of the same sex. In later chapters we will see that these developments, which Freud termed the **Oedipus complex** when they involve a boy and his mother, have implications for the assumption of gender roles and sexual orientation.

LEARNING THEORIES To what extent does sexual behavior reflect experience? Would you hold the same sexual attitudes and do the same things if you had been reared in another culture? We think not. Even within the same society, family and personal experiences can shape unique sexual attitudes and behaviors.

Behaviorists such as John B. Watson (1878–1958) and B. F. Skinner (1904–1990) emphasized the importance of rewards and punishments in the learning process. Children left to explore their bodies without parental condemnation will learn what feels good and tend to repeat it. The Trobriand child who is rewarded for masturbation and premarital **coitus** through parental praise and encouragement will be more likely to repeat these behaviors than the child in a more sexually restrictive culture, who is punished for the same behavior. When sexual behavior (like masturbation) feels good, but parents connect it with feelings of guilt and shame, the child is placed in conflict and may vacillate between masturbating and swearing off of it. If, as young children, we are severely punished for sexual exploration, we may come to associate sexual stimulation in general with feelings of guilt or anxiety. Can such early learning experiences set the stage for sexual problems or dysfunctions in adulthood?

Observational learning refers to acquiring knowledge and skills by observing others. Observational learning includes seeing models in films and on television, hearing about them, and reading about them. According to **social–cognitive theory**, children acquire the gender roles deemed appropriate for people of their anatomic sex through reinforcement of what society considers to be gender-appropriate behavior and through observing the gender-role behavior of their parents, their peers, and other models.

COGNITIVE THEORIES Cognitive psychologists emphasize the importance of cognitive activity (problem solving, decision making, expectations, attitudes and beliefs, and so on). They recognize that the beliefs and attitudes taught to children can serve as *cognitive anchors* for a lifetime. If a person is reared as a Roman Catholic, he or she may subsequently judge people's behavior in terms of whether it is consistent with or deviates from Catholic doctrine. Even if the person leaves the church, he or she may still think of his or her place in the world in terms of distance from Catholicism. Catholic doctrine, for example, opposes use of artificial means of birth control. A Catholic may thus look on her or his use of birth control not simply as being what it is, but as being in keeping with or in conflict with that doctrine.

Feminist Theory

The Greek philosopher Aristotle is said to have described a female as a deformed male. We can only guess at the number of objectionable beliefs expressed in this

psychosexual development
In psychoanalytic theory, the process by which sexual feelings shift from one erogenous zone to another.

Oedipus complex
In psychoanalytic theory, a conflict of the phallic stage in which the boy wishes to possess his mother sexually and perceives his father as a rival in love.

behaviorists
Learning theorists who argue that a scientific approach to understanding behavior must refer only to observable and measurable behaviors.

coitus
Sexual intercourse.

social–cognitive theory
A cognitively oriented learning theory in which observational learning and values play key roles in determining behavior.

description, such as seeing the male as the ideal, focusing on the differences rather than the similarities between men and women, and the implicit right of men to hold power over women.

feminist theory

A theory that challenges acceptance of the male as the norm, traditional gender roles, and male oppression of females.

Feminism and **feminist theory** are born of protest against ideas such as those of Aristotle's—ideas that remain with us today in many if not most parts of the world (Petersen & Hyde, 2010). Definitions of *feminism* and of *feminist theory* are controversial, but it is clear enough that feminist theory focuses on the subordination of women to men; analyzing the relationships between sexism, heterosexism (prejudice or discrimination against homosexuals by heterosexuals), racism, and class oppression; and exploring means of resistance—on individual and societal levels (Petersen & Hyde, 2010).

Among other things, feminist theory challenges:

- Traditional views of men as breadwinners and women as homemakers
- Traditional views of men as political policymakers, especially because those policies affect women and children
- Traditional views of men as sexual "aggressors" and women as sexual "gatekeepers"
- Traditional gender roles that view men as objective and rational, and women as emotional and irrational

Some feminists challenge the concepts of femininity and masculinity because their existence tends to suggest that there is some sort of biological or "actual" basis to the distinction (Shields & Dicicco, 2011). They argue, instead, that femininity and masculinity might be purely social constructions that have the effect of giving women second-class citizenship—or, in many historic eras and parts of the world, no citizenship whatsoever.

In terms of topics most relevant to this book, we will find feminists asserting that men have no right to control women's bodies—for example, that abortion is the personal choice of a woman; that women have as much right as men to decide whether or not to engage in sexual activity, and with whom; that there are few if any female–male differences in mental abilities, such as those used in math and science; and that most medical research has been conducted by men for men, with men as subjects.

Although the extent and nature of male–female differences remain controversial, we can note that many traditions that subjugate women are falling by the wayside, at least in developed nations. Most Western women, for example, are now in the workforce. As a result, many men now share in child rearing and housekeeping with female partners. In the United States, as many women as men are pursuing careers in traditionally male domains, such as business, law, and medicine (Kimmel et al., 2012). Many women now feel free to initiate sex and relationships.

Queer Theory

The word *queer* was initially used as an insult to describe homosexuals. After approximately two centuries, the term became gradually replaced by the word *gay*. However, homosexuals have reappropriated the word *queer* as a sign of pride, as shown by the title of the former TV show, *Queer Eye for the Straight Guy*. As one result of this reappropriation, a widely cited theory of the psychology and sociology of gender roles and sexual orientation is termed **queer theory** (Allen & Rasmussen, 2015; Hegarty, 2011).

queer theory

A theory that challenges heteronormativity and heterosexism.

Queer theory challenges **heteronormativity**—the assumptions that heterosexuality is normal and superior to homosexuality (Herz & Johansson, 2015; Semp, 2011). Queer theory also challenges the assumption that people are naturally divided into heterosexuals and homosexuals (Downing, 2015; Downing & Gillett, 2011).

heteronormativity

The assumption that heterosexuality—being attracted to members of the other anatomic sex—is normal.

According to queer theory, the concepts of heterosexuality and homosexuality are social constructs that ignore commonly experienced mismatches among people's anatomic sex, society's gender roles, and individuals' sexual desires (Downing, 2015;

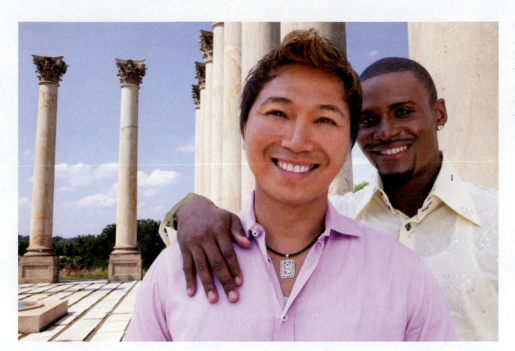

Queer Theory Queer theory asserts that heterosexuality and homosexuality are social constructs that ignore mismatches among people's anatomic sex, society's gender roles, and individual's sexual desires.

Downing & Gillett, 2011). Queer theory asserts that human sexuality has always been more varied than those in power—particularly male heterosexuals—are willing to admit. They point to historical examples such as ancient Greek bisexuality and to current **homophobia** as evidence. We will revisit concepts of queer theory in later chapters, particularly the chapters on gender and sexual orientation.

homophobia
Hatred of homosexuals.

Multiple Perspectives on Human Sexuality

Given the complexity and range of human sexual behavior, we need to consider multiple perspectives to understand sexuality. Each perspective—historical, biological, cross-species, sociological, psychological, feminist, and queer—has something

Real Students, Real Questions

Q *If there are so many ways of looking at sex, how can you tell what is the right way of thinking about things? It makes it hard to make decisions.*

A Yes, it can be hard to make sexual decisions, but it doesn't have to be! If the decisions are informed decisions, if they are consistent with your values, and—most important—if they are *your* decisions, you can be comfortable with them. Do not allow yourself to be pressured by someone else; if you're pressured and you go along with the pressure, it's not you making the decision. This textbook will suggest things to consider when making decisions about dozens of sexual topics. But in the end, the decisions have to be your decisions. What is right for someone else might not be right for you. One more thing: We don't know anyone who makes the right decision about every issue all the time. Be stubborn about matters of sexual health, but if you err in a judgment about another person, know that you're not alone. We've "been there."

to teach us. Let us venture a few conclusions based on our overview of these perspectives. First, human sexuality appears to reflect a combination of biological, psychological, and social factors that interact in complex ways. Second, there are few universal patterns of sexual behavior, and views on what is right and wrong show great diversity. Third, although our own cultural values and beliefs may be deeply meaningful to us, they may not indicate what is normal, natural, or moral in terms of sexual behavior. The complexity of human sexuality—a complexity that causes it to remain somewhat mysterious even to scientists—adds to the wonder and richness of our sexual experience.

Research Methods in Human Sexuality

Wardell B. Pomeroy, one of Alfred Kinsey's coresearchers in the 1940s, was interviewing a man about his first ejaculation. He asked, "When?" The man answered, "Fourteen." Pomeroy then asked, "How?" and was surprised to hear: "With a horse."

In his biography, *Sex the Measure of All Things: A Life of Alfred C. Kinsey,* Jonathan Gathorne-Hardy records what happened next. Pomeroy asked the man, "How often were you having intercourse with animals at 14?"

The man looked confused and said, "Well, yes, it is true I had intercourse with a pony at 14." Pomeroy, it turned out, had misheard the man's previous answer. It was "with whores," not "with a horse." So the man was stunned that Pomeroy had had the insight to ask him the horse question out of the blue (Drucker, 2012).

The question was asked during the Kinsey studies of sexual behavior in the United States—the best-known surveys in the history of studying sexual behavior. The survey method typically gathers information about sexual attitudes and behaviors through questionnaires or interviews.

In this section we see how scientists who study human sexuality carry out research. Many of them, such as Wardell Pomeroy and other members of the Kinsey team, interview respondents, but there are many other methods. But let us begin by exploring the scientific method. Science separates research findings from opinion, superstition, folklore, and error.

The Scientific Method

LO 1.5 **Explain the steps in the scientific method.**

empirical

Derived from or based on observation and experimentation.

Scientists who study sex take an **empirical** approach. They base their knowledge on research evidence, rather than on intuition, faith, or superstition. Critical thinking and the scientific approach share the hallmark of skepticism. Scientists question prevailing assumptions and theories about sexual behavior. They are willing to dispute the assertions of authority figures such as political and religious leaders—even other scientists. They also recognize that they cannot gain perfect knowledge. One era's "truths" may become another era's ancient myths and fallacies. Scientists are involved in the continuous quest for truth, but they do not see themselves as experiencing revelations or defining final truths.

The scientific method is a systematic way of gathering scientific evidence and testing assumptions (Williams, 2011). It has a number of elements:

1. **Formulating a research question.** An example of a possible research question is "Does alcohol inspire or impair sexual response?" Scientists formulate research questions on the basis of their observations of, or theories about, events or behavior. They then seek answers to such questions by conducting empirical research.

2. **Framing the research question in the form of a hypothesis.** Experiments are usually undertaken with a **hypothesis** in mind—a precise prediction that is tested through research. For instance, a scientist might theorize that alcohol enhances

hypothesis

A precise prediction about behavior that is tested through research.

sexual responsiveness either by directly stimulating sexual response or by reducing feelings of guilt associated with sex. He or she might then hypothesize that an intervention (called, in experimental terms, a *treatment*), such as drinking alcohol in a laboratory setting, will lead to heightened sexual arousal in the presence of sexually explicit films.

3. **Testing the hypothesis.** Scientists then test hypotheses through carefully controlled observation and experimentation. A specific hypothesis about alcohol and sexual arousal—that alcohol either increases or decreases sexual responsiveness—might be tested by administering a certain amount of alcohol to one group of people and then comparing their level of sexual arousal following specific types of sexual stimulation—such as exposure to sexually explicit films—to the level of sexual arousal of a group that was shown the films but not given any alcohol.

4. **Drawing conclusions.** Scientists then draw conclusions or inferences about the correctness of their hypotheses, based on their analyses of the results of their studies. If the results of well-designed research studies fail to bear out certain hypotheses, scientists can revise the theories that served as the frameworks for the hypotheses. Research findings often lead scientists to modify their theories, and in turn, generate new hypotheses.

GOALS OF THE SCIENCE OF HUMAN SEXUALITY The goals of the science of human sexuality are congruent with those of other sciences: to describe, explain, predict, and control the events (in this case, the sexual behaviors) that are of interest. Scientists attempt to be clear, unbiased, and precise in their descriptions of events and behavior.

Researchers attempt to relate their observations to other factors, or **variables**, that can help explain them. For example, researchers may attempt to explain variations in the frequency of sex by relating—or correlating—sexual frequency with **demographic** variables such as age, religious or social background, or cultural expectations. The variables that are commonly used to explain sexual behavior are biological (age, health), psychological (anxieties, skills), and sociological (educational level, socioeconomic status, ethnicity).

The concept of "controlling" human behavior does not mean coercing people to do the bidding of others. Rather, it means drawing from scientific knowledge to help people create their own goals and marshal their resources to meet them. Reputable scientists are held to ethical and professional standards that safeguard the rights of participants in research.

The science of human sexuality does not tell people how they ought to behave. Rather, it furnishes information that people may use to help themselves or others make decisions. For instance, the science of human sexuality provides information that increases the chances that a couple who is having difficulty becoming pregnant will be able to conceive. At the same time, it develops and evaluates means of birth control that can be used to help couples regulate their reproductive choices.

Let's now look at the ways in which sexologists study human sexuality. Researchers must first identify whom or what they will study, which brings us to the topic of sampling.

Populations and Samples: Representing the World of Diversity

LO 1.6 **Explain what is meant by populations and samples.**

Researchers seek to learn about **populations**—complete groups of people, animals, or events. Many researchers seek to learn about Americans, for example. Other researchers may identify American adults or American adolescents as their population. Still other researchers attempt to compare the sexual behavior of African Americans to that

variables

Quantities or qualities that vary or may vary.

demographic

Concerning the vital statistics (race, gender, age, religion, etc.) of human populations.

population

A complete group of organisms or events.

of Latin Americans and other Americans. These are termed the *populations of interest,* or *target populations.* These target populations are sizable; it would be expensive and difficult to try to study every individual in them.

Because of the difficulty in studying all members of a population, scientists select individuals from the population and study them. The individuals who participate in research are said to compose a **sample**. However, that sample must *represent* the target population. If we wished to study the sexual behavior of Asian Americans, for example, our population would consist of all Asian Americans. If we used only Asian American college students as our sample, we could not **generalize** our findings to all Asian Americans.

sample

Part of a population.

generalize

To go from the particular to the general.

SAMPLING METHODS: DOES SIZE MATTER?   Now and then, magazine editors boast that they have surveyed samples of 20,000 or 30,000 readers, but size alone does not mean that a sample is representative. *Psychology Today* and *Glamour* regularly poll readers, but their readers do not represent the general population. Readers of *Psychology Today* are "biased" in that they tend to be better educated and more liberal than the population at large (*Psychology Today,* 2006). Readers of *Glamour* are "biased" in that they are also better educated than the average American, and more likely to be concerned about their appearance and optimizing their sex lives.

7 › T / F   Truth or Fiction Revisited   It is true that you could study the sexual behavior of millions of Americans and still not obtain an accurate picture of the sexual behavior of the general American population. Researchers need to obtain samples that *represent* the target population. One way of acquiring a representative sample is by random sampling.

random sample

A sample in which every member of a population has an equal chance of participating.

stratified random sample

A random sample in which known subgroups in a population are represented in proportion to their numbers in the population.

Researchers use **random samples**, when possible, because every member of the target population has an equal chance of participating. In a **stratified random sample**, known subgroups of a population are represented in proportion to their numbers in the population. For instance, about 13% of the U.S. population is African American. Researchers could therefore decide that 13% of their sample must be African American if they are to represent the general U.S. population. The randomness of the sample would be preserved because the members of the subgroups would be selected randomly from their particular subgroups.

Random samples can be hard to come by, especially when it comes to asking people about their sexual attitudes or behavior. For instance, sexual research is almost invariably conducted with people who volunteer to participate. Volunteers tend to differ from people who refuse to participate, for example, by being more open about their sexuality (Quartaro & Spier, 2002; Zelenski et al., 2003).

One study attempted to assess the incidence of male–male sexual behavior that placed Hong Kong men at risk for contracting HIV/AIDS (for example, anal intercourse without use of condoms) by means of random telephone numbers generated by a computer (Lau et al., 2002). Eighty-five of 2,074 men contacted (4%) admitted to having sex with other men and described their sexual behavior. But how can we determine whether there were many others who had sex with men but denied doing so? How can we know whether the men who admitted to male–male sexual behavior accurately described their contacts?

The refusal of people who have been randomly selected to participate in a survey can ruin the representativeness of the sample, yet researchers cannot coerce people to participate in research. Therefore, researchers must use samples of volunteers, rather than true random samples. A low response rate to a voluntary survey is an indication that the responses do not represent the people for whom the survey was distributed.

Some samples, such as the Kinsey sample, are "samples of convenience." They consist of individuals who happen to be available to the researcher and do not represent the population at large. Convenience samples often consist of European

American, middle-class college students who volunteer for studies conducted at their schools. They may not even be representative of students in general.

Methods of Observation

LO 1.7 **Describe methods of observation, including the case-study method, the survey, naturalistic observation, ethnographic observation, participant observation, and laboratory observation.**

Once scientists have chosen those they will study, they observe them. In this section, we consider several methods of observation: the case study method, the survey method, naturalistic observation, ethnographic observation, participant observation, and laboratory observation.

THE CASE-STUDY METHOD A **case study** is a carefully drawn, in-depth biography of an individual or a small group. The focus is on understanding one or several individuals as fully as possible by unraveling the interplay of various factors in their backgrounds. In most case studies, the researcher comes to know the individual or group through interviews or other extended contacts. The interviewing pattern may build on itself with a good deal of freedom, as opposed to the printed set of questions used in survey questionnaires.

Researchers also conduct case studies by interviewing people who have known the individuals being studied, or by examining public records. Some case studies have been carried out on people who are dead. Sigmund Freud, for example, drew on historical records in his case study of the Renaissance inventor and painter Leonardo da Vinci. Freud concluded that Leonardo's artistic productions represented the sublimating, or channeling, of an attraction to other men.

Reports of innovative treatments for sexual dysfunctions often appear as detailed case studies. A clinician may report the background of the client in depth, describe the treatment and the apparent outcomes, and suggest factors that might have contributed to the treatment's success or failure. Case studies or multiple case studies (reports concerning a few people) that hold promise may be subjected to experimental studies involving treatment and control groups.

Despite the richness of material that may be derived from case studies, they are not as rigorous a research design as an experiment. People often have gaps in memory, especially concerning childhood events. There is also the potential of observer bias; that is, clinicians and interviewers may unintentionally guide people into saying what they expect to hear.

THE SURVEY METHOD Researchers may **survey** respondents by interviewing or administering questionnaires to thousands of people from particular population groups to learn about their sexual behavior and attitudes. Face-to-face interviews such as those used by Alfred Kinsey and his colleagues (1948, 1953) give the interviewer the opportunity to probe—to follow up on answers that seem to lead toward useful information. A skilled interviewer may be able to establish a sense of trust or rapport that encourages self-disclosure (Drucker, 2012).

Some of the major surveys described in this book were conducted by Kinsey and his colleagues (1948, 1953), by the Monitoring the Future research group at the University of Michigan (Herbenick et al., 2010a, 2010b, 2010c; Reece et al., 2010), and by the CDC's National Survey of Family Growth. These studies have reported the incidence and

case study

A carefully drawn, in-depth biography of an individual or a small group of individuals that may be obtained through interviews, questionnaires, and historical records.

survey

A detailed study of a sample obtained by means such as interviews and questionnaires.

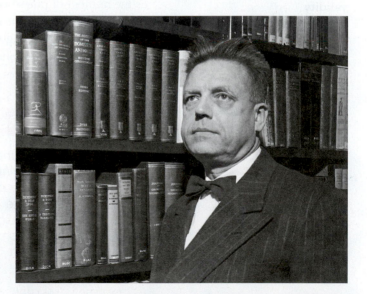

Alfred Kinsey. The "Kinsey Reports" shocked the United States of the 1950s. What kinds of surveys are there? How do researchers attempt to encourage people to participate? How do gaps in memory, volunteer bias, and social desirability distort the results of surveys?

frequency of sexual activities among men and women, married and single—solitary, male–female, male–male, and female–female. Many surveys have something to contribute to our understanding of human sexuality, but none perfectly represents the American population at large. People who agree to be polled on political matters may resist participation in surveys about their sexual behavior. Even the best surveys suffer from **volunteer bias**.

Let us review the methods of some surveys of human sexuality, beginning with those used by Kinsey and his colleagues.

volunteer bias

A slanting of research data that is caused by the characteristics of individuals who volunteer to participate, such as willingness to discuss intimate behavior.

The Kinsey Reports Alfred Kinsey and his colleagues (1948, 1953) interviewed 5,300 males and 5,940 females in the United States between 1938 and 1949. They posed questions about sexual experiences, including masturbation, oral sex, and intercourse before and in marriage. Kinsey did not try to obtain a random sample (Drucker, 2012). He believed that a high refusal rate would wreck his chances of representing the general population. Instead, he used group sampling. He recruited participants from the organizations and community groups to which they belonged, such as college fraternities and sororities. He contacted representatives of groups in diverse communities and tried to persuade them to secure the cooperation of fellow group members. If he showed these individuals that they would not be subjected to embarrassment or discomfort, Kinsey hoped that they would persuade other members to participate. In some cases he obtained the full participation of a group.

Yet, people of color, people in rural areas, older people, poor people, and Catholics and Jews were underrepresented in Kinsey's interviews (Drucker, 2012). It is thus unlikely that Kinsey's results accurately mirrored the U.S. population at the time. But some relationships Kinsey uncovered, such as the positive link between level of education and participation in oral sex, are probably generalizable.

confidentiality

Keeping records and the names of research participants or therapy clients private.

Kinsey took measures to urge honest answers. Participants were assured of **confidentiality**. Interviewers were trained to behave nonjudgmentally; they held a "calm and steady eye" and tone of voice. On the other hand, all of Kinsey's interviewers were men, and women respondents might have felt freer to open up to female interviewers.

reliability

The consistency or accuracy of a measure.

Kinsey checked the **reliability** of his data by reexamining hundreds of subjects after 18 months or more had passed. Their reports of the incidence of sexual activities (for example, whether or not they had ever engaged in premarital or extramarital coitus) were highly consistent, but reports of the frequency of sexual activities (such as the number of times one masturbates per week) were less consistent. People find it more difficult to estimate the frequencies of their activities than to answer whether or not they have ever engaged in them.

validity

With respect to interviews, questionnaires, and tests, the degree to which an item measures what it is supposed to measure.

Kinsey knew that consistency of responses across time did not guarantee **validity**. That is, repeat interviews did not show whether the reported behaviors actually took

Real Students, Real Questions

Q *I saw the movie* Kinsey; *is it really true that he had sex with people other than his wife for purposes of research?*

A We won't join the gossip about Kinsey, but we'll note that the history of legitimate sex research is tainted by occasional stories of problematic behavior. However, a checkered past doesn't mean we should toss the research enterprise into the wastebasket. It has saved lives and given countless people pleasure.

place as described. However, he found high consistency in the reports of 706 pairs of spouses, suggesting that their self-reports were reasonably accurate.

The National Survey of Adolescents and Young Adults   The Kaiser Family Foundation (2003) tried to obtain a nationally representative sample of 13- to 24-year-olds by selecting telephone numbers at random and conducting telephone interviews with 1,854 young people either in English or Spanish. They purposefully oversampled people in ethnic minority groups—African Americans, Latin Americans, and Asian Americans—because most studies do not generate enough information about them. Parents provided permission to interview minors (respondents younger than age 18). The response rate was 55%.

Note some of the study's major findings:

- About one adolescent in three reported being pressured into sex.

- Sixty percent of the sample agreed with the statement that "Waiting to have sex is a nice idea but nobody really does."

- One adolescent in three has engaged in oral sex, often to avoid intercourse.

- Seventy percent of sexually active young adults and 40% of sexually active adolescents reported that they or their partner had taken a pregnancy test.

- Four out of five adolescents reported that adolescents tend to drink or use drugs before sex.

- Although 90% of adolescents say that using condoms is a sign of respect and caring for one's partner, about half were reluctant to discuss condoms with their partners, fearing, for example, that raising the subject would be embarrassing or suggest that one is suspicious of one's partner.

The National Surveys of Family Growth (NSFG)   The National Surveys of Family Growth are conducted by the CDC as a means of assessing sexual behavior "relevant to demographic and public health concerns" (Mosher et al., 2005). One survey was run primarily in 2002, and results were published over the following years (Mosher et al., 2005). It involved face-to-face interviews in the homes of 12,571 people, including 4,928 men and 7,643 women aged 15 to 44. A more recent survey, published in 2011, reported the results of interviews with 22,682 face-to-face interviews of people aged 15 to 44, 12,279 with women and 10,403 with men over the years from 2006 to 2010 (Martinez et al., 2011). In the 2002 study, the interviewees responded to questions about their sexual behavior on laptop computers, to ensure their privacy and encourage honesty. The researchers who published in 2011 drew their sample from 110 locales across the United States and sampled randomly within those locales. All in all, the National Health and Social Life Survey (NHSLS) and NSFG may be the only surveys since Kinsey's day to offer a reasonably accurate—if not perfect—snapshot of the sexual behavior of the general population of the United States.

There have been some interesting findings about male–male and female–female sexual behavior. In the study published in 2005, 5.7% of the males had had oral sex with another male, and 3.7% had had anal sex with another male. In the study published in 2012, the figure was 5.5% for oral sex, and 5.7% reported oral or anal sex with another male—not exactly comparable. There was more comparability among females: in the 2005 study, 11% said yes when asked "Have you ever had any sexual experience of any kind with another female?" That figure rose to 17.4% in the study reported in 2012. Either female–female sexual activity has been increasing or there were differences in sampling or data collection and analysis between 2005 and 2012. In Chapter 5 we will see that smaller percentages of males and females identify themselves as homosexual or bisexual, adding more evidence that—as queer theorists suggest—there are discrepancies between sexual interests, sexual behavior, and self-identified sexual orientations. Ten percent of European American women reported having 15 or more sex partners, as compared with 9% of African American women and 5% of Latin American women.

Figure 1.2 Single (Never-Married) Females and Males, Aged 15–19, Who Report Ever Having Had Sexual Intercourse: United States, 1988–2010.

SOURCE: Martinez, G., Copen, C. E., & Abma, J. C. (2011). Teenagers in the United States: Sexual activity, contraceptive use, and childbearing, 2006–1010 National Survey of Family Growth. National Center for Health Statistics. *Vital Health Statistics, 23*(31), p. 6, Figure 1.

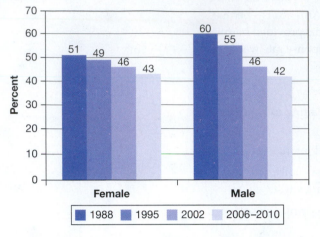

Figure 1.2 is from the study published in 2011. It compares the sexual experience of single females and males aged 15 to 19 over four time periods when the survey was conducted. The percentage of people in this age group, and their marital status, who have engaged in sexual intercourse has been dropping steadily. The researchers admit that no survey method can yield perfect results. Therefore, they include bands referred to as "confidence intervals" in the figure. The researchers use statistical methods to estimate that the "real" numbers are 95% likely to fall within these intervals. We place the word *real* in quotes to further suggest that the relationship between these survey results and reality is somewhat open to debate. Even so, the downward trend is striking.

Why is the **incidence** of sexual intercourse decreasing among young people? We will be thinking about answers throughout the text, but here let us note that one possibility is more awareness of the potential of unwanted pregnancies and STIs. There is certainly no reason to suggest that today's teens are less healthy than yesterday's. Nor is there reason to believe that the media are less sexually stimulating than they were. Today we have sex-laden reality TV shows that did not exist in 1988 and 1995. Pornography is readily available over the Internet for anyone who wants it.

incidence

A measure of the occurrence or the degree of occurrence of an event.

Magazine Surveys Readership surveys have also been conducted by popular magazines, such as *Psychology Today, Glamour, Ladies' Home Journal*, and *Cosmopolitan*. Although these surveys may obtain large numbers of respondents, their sampling techniques raise questions. Each sample represents, at best, the readers of the magazine in which the questionnaire appears. Moreover, we learn only about readers who volunteer to respond to these questionnaires, which is a small percentage of the overall readership. Finally, readers of these magazines are wealthier than the public at large, and readers of *Cosmopolitan, Psychology Today*, and *Glamour* tend to be more liberal (Cawley et al., 2011).

Limitations of the Survey Method One limitation of surveys involves the fact that they are self-reports of behavior and attitudes. Self-reports are subject to inaccuracies or biases because of factors such as faulty memory and tendencies to distort or conceal information resulting from embarrassment, shame, or guilt; or attempts to present a favorable image. People may not recall the age at which they first engaged in petting, or masturbated to orgasm. People may have difficulty recalling or calculating the **frequency** of certain behaviors, such as the weekly frequency of marital intercourse. Survey data may also be drawn from haphazard or nonrepresentative samples and not represent the target population.

frequency

The number of times an action is repeated within a given period.

Participants in surveys of sexual behavior may feel pressured to answer questions in the direction of **social desirability**. Some try to ingratiate themselves with their interviewers by offering what they believe to be socially desirable answers. Even though interviewers may insist that participants will remain anonymous, respondents may fear their identities could be exposed someday.

social desirability

A response bias to a questionnaire or interview in which the person provides a socially acceptable response.

One study asked 283 college students to record the incidence of their thoughts about sex, food, and sleep for a week. The men in the study reported significantly more thoughts about sex than the women did. However, the women also evidenced more interest in answering in a socially desirable direction (Fisher et al., 2012). So we can wonder whether women reported fewer thoughts about sex because frequent thoughts of sex are incompatible with the traditional feminine gender role (Fisher et al., 2012).

Some respondents choose to exaggerate. In our culture, men may tend to exaggerate their sexual exploits, and women may tend to downplay them (England & Bearak,

2014; Fisher et al., 2012). Some respondents exaggerate the bizarreness of their behavior or attitudes to draw attention to themselves or to foul up study results.

Because many people refuse to participate in surveys, samples are biased by large numbers of volunteers. Volunteers tend to be more sexually permissive and liberal-minded than nonvolunteers.

THE NATURALISTIC-OBSERVATION METHOD In **naturalistic observation**, also called the *field study*, scientists directly observe the behavior of animals and humans where it happens. For example, biologists might observe the behavior of animals in the wild, sociologists might observe the street life of prostitutes, and psychologists might observe patterns of body language in romantic couples.

Scientists try to observe their subjects *unobtrusively*; that is, they try not to influence the behavior of the individuals they study. Naturalistic observers sometimes find themselves in ethical dilemmas. They have allowed sick or injured animals to die, rather than intervene, when medical assistance could have saved them. They have allowed substance abuse and illicit sexual behavior to go unreported to authorities. The ethical trade-off is that unobtrusive observation may yield data that will benefit large numbers of people—the greatest good for the greatest number.

naturalistic observation
A method in which organisms are observed in their natural environments.

THE ETHNOGRAPHIC-OBSERVATION METHOD **Ethnographic observation** provides data concerning sexual behaviors and customs that occur among various ethnic groups—those that vary widely across cultures and those that are limited to one or few cultures. Anthropologists are the specialists who typically engage in ethnographic research. They have lived among societies of people in the four corners of the earth in order to observe and study human diversity. Margaret Mead (1935) reported on the social and sexual customs of various peoples of New Guinea. Bronislaw Malinowski (1929) studied the Trobriand Islanders, among others. Even so, ethnographic observation has its limits in the study of sexual behavior. Sexual activities are most commonly performed away from the watchful gaze of others, especially visitors from other cultures. Ethnographers may thus have to rely on methods such as interviewing.

ethnographic observation
A method of research that deals descriptively with specific cultures, especially preliterate societies.

The ethnographer who studies a particular culture or subgroup within a culture tries to do so unobtrusively, so as not to alter the behavior of the members of the group by focusing their attention on it. Falling prey to social desirability, some people may "straighten out their act" while the ethnographer is present. Other people may try to impress the ethnographer by acting in ways that are more aggressive or sexually provocative than usual. In either case, people supply distorted information.

participant observation
A method in which observers interact with the people they study as they collect data.

THE PARTICIPANT-OBSERVATION METHOD In **participant observation**, investigators learn about people's behavior by directly interacting with them (Boynton, 2008; Frank, 2007, 2015). Participant observation has been used in studies of male–male sexual behavior and mate-swapping. In effect, participation has been the "price of admission" for observation. In some cases, researchers have engaged in coitus with participants during "swinging parties," which raises questions as to what is permissible "for the sake of science."

We do not hear anymore about "scientific swinging" with the public, but there are more current uses of participant observation. One area of interest has been strip clubs. There are some 4,000 strip clubs in the United States, with an income of about $15 billion a year (Deveruex, 2011). As a graduate student in anthropology, Katherine Frank worked as a stripper in a southeastern city "both as a means of earning extra cash for graduate school and as part of a feminism theory project investigating female objectification and body image" (Sternberg, 2004). In reports of her experiences, Frank (2002, 2003) notes that many men told her they attend the clubs because they "just want to relax." She writes that male customers may encounter some stigma for visiting the clubs, but not as much as the strippers do. Some men, moreover, do business in strip clubs and charge the expenses to their corporate accounts.

Katherine Frank. Frank worked as a stripper in graduate school, both to augment her income and to learn about men who frequented strip clubs.

A Penile Strain Gauge. The gauge measures vasocongestion in the male genitals, providing an objective measure of sexual arousal.

laboratory observation

A method in which subjects are studied in a laboratory setting.

penile strain gauge

A device for measuring sexual arousal in men in terms of changes in the circumference of the penis.

vaginal plethysmograph

A tampon-like probe that is inserted in the vagina and suggests the level of vasocongestion by measuring the light reflected from the vaginal walls.

vasocongestion

Congestion from the flow of blood (from the Latin *vas*, meaning "vessel").

myotonia

Muscle tension.

THE LABORATORY-OBSERVATION METHOD Rather than study individuals in their natural settings, **laboratory observation** brings them into the laboratory, where their behavior can be more carefully monitored. In *Human Sexual Response* (1966), William Masters and Virginia Johnson were among the first to report direct laboratory observations of individuals and couples engaged in sex acts. In all, 694 people (312 men and 382 women) participated in the research. The women ranged from ages 18 to 78; the men were from 21 to 80 years old. There were 276 married couples, 106 single women, and 36 single men. The married couples engaged in intercourse and manual and oral stimulation of the genitals. The unmarried people participated in studies that did not require intercourse, such as measurement of female sexual arousal in response to insertion of a penis-shaped probe, and male ejaculation during masturbation.

Direct laboratory observation of biological processes was not invented by Masters and Johnson, but they were confronting a society that was still unprepared to speak openly of sex, let alone observe people having sex. Masters and Johnson were accused of immorality and voyeurism. Nevertheless, their methods offered the first reliable set of data on what happens to the body during sexual response. Their instruments—the **penile strain gauge** and the **vaginal plethysmograph**—permitted them to directly measure **vasocongestion** (blood flow to the genitals), **myotonia** (muscle tension), and other physiological responses.

8 › T / F Truth or Fiction Revisited Masters and Johnson did create an artificial penis containing photographic equipment to study female sexual response. The transparent device enabled them to observe changes in women's internal sexual organs as they became sexually aroused. From these studies, they observed that it is useful to divide sexual response into four stages (Masters and Johnson's "sexual response cycle"): excitement, plateau, orgasm, and resolution (see Chapter 7).

One confounding factor in Masters and Johnson's research is that people who participate in laboratory observation know that they are being observed and that their responses are being measured. The problem of volunteer bias, troublesome for sex surveys, is even thornier in laboratory observation. How many of us would assent to performing sexual activities in full view of researchers while we were connected to monitoring equipment? Some of the women observed by Masters and Johnson were patients of Dr. Masters who felt indebted to him and agreed to participate. Many were able to persuade their husbands to participate as well. Some were medical students and graduate students who may have been motivated to earn extra money (participants were paid for their time) as well as by scientific curiosity.

Researchers have since developed more sophisticated physiological methods of measuring sexual arousal and response. The laboratory method is now used, with some variations but with less controversy, in research centers across the country.

What Does a Woman Want? Using Objective and Subjective Measures to Find Out

> "The great question that has never been answered and which I have not yet been able to answer, despite my 30 years of research into the feminine soul, is, What does a woman want?"
>
> —*Sigmund Freud*

What sexually excites a man? What sexually excites a woman? Research using a variety of methods suggests that men's sexual responses are more predictable, and that what goes on in men's bodies is more likely to correlate with what they are thinking (Chivers et al., 2010; Huberman & Chivers, 2015). Consider some research by Meredith Chivers and her colleagues (Chivers & Bailey, 2007; Chivers et al., 2007). She showed erotic videos to men and women, both heterosexual and homosexual; the videos showed male–female sex, male–male sex, female–female sex, a man masturbating,

A CLOSER LOOK

ALTHOUGH VIAGRA WORKS FOR WOMEN, IT DOESN'T WORK FOR WOMEN

The use of Viagra, and the related drugs Cialis and Levitra, has revolutionized the treatment of erectile disorder in men. Erections are made possible by the flow of blood into the penis. Viagra and the other drugs are phosphodiesterase type 5 (PDE5) inhibitors, which is a complicated way of saying that they prevent blood from flowing out the penis prematurely; they help keep the penis sufficiently erect for sexual intercourse. We'll give you the full, unexpurgated explanation of how these drugs work in Chapter 12.

Sexual arousal in women, like sexual arousal in men, involves the flow of blood into the genital region, which has a number of effects, including stiffening the clitoris and helping with the production of vaginal lubrication. Yet women who try these drugs to help with sexual arousal typically find them to be of little if any use.

Enter sex researchers Meredith Chivers and Raymond Rosen (2010). They reviewed 16 studies that tested the effects of PDE5 inhibitors on women and determined that despite women's subjective reporting that the drugs were of little help, they increased genital vasocongestion as advertised.

How can we explain the disconnect between women's objective and subjective responses to PDE5 inhibitors? Chivers and Rosen suggest that the discrepancy is related to male–female differences in the connectedness of the biological (objective) and psychological (subjective) components of sexual response. Genital response in women is less likely to mean that they want to engage in sexual activity than it is in

A vaginal plethysmograph. The instrument provides an objective measure of sexual arousal.

men. For example, a woman who lacks sexual desire—or who lacks sexual desire with her usual partner—may see herself as having difficulty becoming sexually aroused, although sexual arousal itself is not necessarily the problem (Bloemers et al., 2013). Men would be unlikely to seek professional help when they lack desire, and women might not seek professional help when they have difficulty lubricating, because that particular difficulty can be aided with an artificial lubricant. On the other hand, the advent of the "little pink pill," Addyi, is intended to help women who wish to enhance their sexual desire.

---

a woman masturbating, a muscled man walking nude on a beach, and a well-toned nude woman doing calisthenics. The subjects watched on recliners while Chivers measured their arousal objectively and subjectively. The objective measures were made possible by plethysmographs connected to the viewers' genitals. Men wore an apparatus on the penis that gauged its swelling (that is, erection). Women inserted a tampon-shaped probe in the vagina that bounced light off the vaginal walls, providing a gauge of genital blood flow. In men, genital engorgement with blood produces erection. In women, it spurs lubrication—the seeping of moisture through the vaginal walls. The participants could rate their subjective feelings of arousal with a keypad.

Self-labeled heterosexual ("straight") men achieved erection while watching male–female or female–female sex, and while gazing at the masturbating and the exercising women. They were generally unresponsive when they watched a man masturbating or male–male sex. Gay males showed the opposite pattern of sexual arousal. For both straight and gay males, the subjective ratings matched the numbers provided by the plethysmograph. The men's subjective rating were congruent with their body's responses.

Not so with the women. Regardless of whether the women labeled themselves as heterosexual or lesbian, they responded with genital arousal when they viewed male–male sex, female–female sex, and male–female sex. Their genitals were more responsive to the exercising woman than the nude man. However, their self-reported arousal did not particularly match their body's responses. Heterosexual women reported less arousal when they watched female–female sex than their bodies indicated. They reported less arousal than their bodies showed when they watched male–male sex, but they reported *more* arousal than their bodies showed when they watched male–female sex. Lesbians showed objective and subjective arousal in response to female–female sex, but they reported less arousal than their bodies showed when they viewed male–male sex.

Chivers suggests that women are genitally aroused by a wider range of stimuli than men because these differences might reflect innate, evolutionary forces. Could female sexuality be divided into two systems: one physiological and the other subjective? According to this view, feminine lust would be a subjective phenomenon, and physiological genital arousal would not tell us much about desire—that is, what a woman cognitively "wants" might not always be the same as what her body responds to (Chivers et al., 2010). As another example, Chivers reports the results of a plethysmograph study showing surges of vaginal blood flow as women listened to descriptions of rape. Chivers uses an evolutionary hypothesis in a tentative explanation of female genital arousal in response to unwanted sex: Genital lubrication could be a reflexive response that reduces discomfort and the possibility of injury during intercourse. Ancestral females who did not lubricate in the presence of sexual cues might be more likely to sustain injuries that could lead to infertility and, possibly, death. They would thus be less likely to transmit this trait to their children. This is not to suggest that women want to be forced into sex—only that women, or some women, might have a built-in protective response in which they lubricate.

In the Chivers studies, both heterosexual and lesbian women showed greater sexual arousal in response to stimuli depicting female targets than to stimuli showing male targets. One possibility is that the women observers identify with the depicted female targets, imagining themselves in the place of the women receiving pleasure, whereas the men are more likely to attend to the physical attributes of the actors.

Sexologist Lisa Diamond suggests that the response of women to a wider range of sexual stimuli allows for quite a bit of plasticity in sexual response. She notes that "The actress Anne Heche began a widely publicized romantic relationship with the openly lesbian comedian Ellen DeGeneres after having had no prior same-sex attractions or relationships. The relationship with DeGeneres ended after two years, and Heche went on to marry a man" (Diamond, 2008). (One related study found that women who labeled themselves as bisexual showed greater genital response to narratives describing sexual interaction with female partners [Bouchard et al., 2015].) Diamond also related the history of Julie Cypher, who was in a heterosexual marriage but left it for the musician Melissa Etheridge. But the couple separated after 12 years and Cypher returned to heterosexual relationships. Diamond offers the possibility that many women's desires may be dictated more by intimacy or emotional connection than by the physical attractiveness—or even the anatomic sex—of one's partner.

Correlation

LO 1.8 Describe the correlational method.

What are the relationships between age and frequency of sex among married couples? What is the connection between socioeconomic status and teenage pregnancy? How about listening to sexually explicit rap music? And what about the age of sexual initiation? In each case, variables are being related to one another. The correlational method describes the relationship between variables in numerical terms, and as positive or negative.

A **correlation** is a statistical measure of the relationship between two variables. In correlational studies, two or more variables are related, or linked to, one another by statistical means. The strength and direction (positive or negative) of the relationship between any two variables is expressed with a statistic called a **correlation coefficient**.

Critical Thinking
Which strikes you as the truer measure of sexual arousal—the person's subjective reports of arousal or the levels shown on objective instruments such as the penile strain gauge or the vaginal photoplethysmograph? Support your answer. (*Hint:* Critical thinkers pay attention to definitions of terms. What does the word *truer* mean to you?)

Critical Thinking
Would you expect that there would be a positive or negative correlation between satisfaction in a relationship and communication? Explain.

correlation
A statistical measure of the relationship between two variables.

correlation coefficient
A statistic that expresses the strength and direction (positive or negative) of the relationship between two variables.

Research has shown relationships (correlations) between satisfaction with a relationship and a host of variables: communication skills, shared values, flexibility, frequency of social interactions with friends, and churchgoing, to name a few (see Figure 1.3). Although such research may give us an idea of the factors associated with satisfaction in a relationship, the researchers have not manipulated the variables of interest. For this reason we cannot say which, if any, of the factors is causally related to happiness in the relationship.

Research has also shown relationships between the use of sildenafil (Viagra) to enhance sexual response and risky sexual behavior among gay and bisexual men (Kim et al., 2002). Men who use Viagra also report a greater number of sex partners and higher levels of anal sex without using a condom. However, there is no evidence that Viagra *causes* risky sexual behavior. It is more likely that the effort to enhance sexual response explains both the use of Viagra and risky sex.

Correlations may be positive or negative. Two variables are positively correlated if one increases as the other increases. A Spanish study Figi of 412 university students correlated sociodemographic, psychological, and interpersonal variables with sexual behavior and feelings of intimacy (Yela, 2000). It was found that commitment, feelings of intimacy, and frequency of sexual relations correlated positively with feelings of love and sexual satisfaction for both men and women. However, the researcher did not manipulate the variables. Therefore, we cannot conclude that sexual satisfaction causes high coital frequency. It could also be that frequent sexual activity contributes to greater sexual satisfaction. It is also possible that there is no causal relationship between the variables. Perhaps both coital frequency and sexual satisfaction are affected by other factors, such as communication ability, marital satisfaction, general health, and so on (see Figure 1.3).

Figure 1.3 What Is the Relationship Between Frequency of Intercourse and Sexual Satisfaction?

Couples in relationships who engage in more frequent sexual relations report higher levels of sexual satisfaction, but why? Because researchers have not manipulated the variables, we cannot conclude that sexual satisfaction causes frequent sex. Nor can we say that frequent sex causes greater sexual satisfaction. Perhaps both variables are affected by other factors, such as communication ability, health, and general satisfaction with the relationship.

9 › T / F Truth or Fiction Revisited Evidence suggests that people who attend church regularly tend to be more satisfied with their relationships. Does satisfaction with a relationship motivate churchgoing? Does churchgoing enhance relationships? Or does a quest for stability contribute to both?

The Experimental Method

LO 1.9 Explain how experiments seek to determine cause and effect.

The best method for studying cause and effect is the **experiment**. Experiments permit scientists to draw conclusions about cause-and-effect relationships because the experimenter directly manipulates the variables of interest and observes their effects.

In an experiment on the effects of alcohol on sexual arousal, for example, a group of participants would receive an intervention, called a **treatment**, such as a dose of alcohol. (In other experiments, the intervention or treatment might involve the administration of a drug, exposure to violent pornography, a program of sex education, etc.). The participants would then be carefully observed to learn whether this treatment made a difference in their behavior—in this case, their sexual arousal.

In an experiment, the variables (treatments) that are hypothesized to have a causal effect are manipulated or controlled by the researcher. Consider an experiment designed to determine whether or not alcohol stimulates sexual arousal. The design might involve giving one group of participants a certain dosage of alcohol, and then

experiment

A scientific method that seeks to confirm cause-and-effect relationships by manipulating independent variables and observing their effects on dependent variables.

treatment

In experiments, an intervention that is administered to participants (e.g., a test, a drug, or sex-education program) so that its effects may be observed.

independent variable

A condition in a scientific study that is manipulated by the researchers so that its effects may be observed.

dependent variable

The measured result of an experiment that is believed to be a function of the independent variable.

Critical Thinking

Would it be possible to run an experiment to study the effects of rape on psychological health? Why or why not?

---

experimental group

A group of study participants who receive a treatment.

control group

A group of study participants who do not receive the experimental treatment. However, other conditions are held comparable to those of individuals in the experimental group.

selection factor

A bias that may operate in research when people are allowed to determine whether or not they will receive a treatment.

Critical Thinking

To run a true experiment on the effect of a new drug on people with HIV/AIDS, some people with HIV/AIDS would have to be assigned to a control group. To control for the effects of expectations, they might be told they are being given the real drug when they are really receiving "sugar pills" that look like the real thing. Can researchers justify withholding the real drug from people in the control group? What do you think?

---

measuring its effects. In such an experimental arrangement, the dosage of alcohol is considered an **independent variable**, whose presence and quantity is manipulated by the researchers. The measured results are called **dependent variables** because changes in their values are believed to depend on the independent variable or variables. In this experiment, measures of sexual arousal would be the dependent variables. Dependent variables are outcomes; they are observed and measured by the researchers, but not manipulated. Sexual arousal might be measured by means such as physiological measurement (gauging the degree of erection in the male, for example) or self-report (asking participants to rate their sexual arousal on a scale).

In a study of the effects of sex education on teenage pregnancy, sex education would be the independent variable. The incidence of teenage pregnancy would be the dependent variable. Researchers would administer the experimental treatment (sex education) and track the participants for a period of time to determine their pregnancy rates. Ideally, the incidence of pregnancy among these subjects would be compared to that among subjects who do not receive sex education but are similar to the subjects in all other respects.

EXPERIMENTAL AND CONTROL GROUPS   True experiments randomly assign subjects to experimental and control groups. Subjects in **experimental groups** receive the treatment. Subjects in **control groups** do not. All other conditions are held constant for both groups. By using random assignment and holding other conditions constant, researchers can be reasonably confident that the independent variable (treatment), and not extraneous factors (such as the temperature of the room in which the treatment was administered or differences between subjects in the experimental and control groups), brought about the results.

Why do experimenters assign subjects to experimental or control groups at random? Consider a study conducted to determine the effects of alcohol on sexual arousal in response to sexually explicit material, such as pornography. If we permitted participants to choose whether or not they would drink alcohol, we might not know if it was the alcohol itself that accounted for the results. Some other factor, called a **selection factor**, might discriminate between people who would or would not choose to drink alcohol. One difference might be that people who chose to drink might also have more permissive attitudes toward sexually explicit material than the others. Their permissiveness rather than the alcohol could affect their sexual responsiveness to these stimuli.

Although scientists agree that the experimental method provides the best evidence of cause and effect, experimenters cannot manipulate many variables directly. For example, we cannot conduct experiments to determine the effects of cohabitation on college students. We cannot assign an experimental group to cohabitation and a control group to separate living quarters. We can only compare groups who have chosen to cohabit to groups who have not. Our research may thus inform us that cohabitors who get married are more likely to eventually get divorced than married couples who have never cohabited, but it cannot show that these problems are *caused* by cohabiting (see Chapter 14). Cohabitors and noncohabitors may differ on other factors—such as nontraditional versus traditional attitudes—that give rise to different outcomes of marriage.

Similarly, we cannot conduct experiments to determine the effects of pornography on children and adolescents. Societal prohibitions and ethical standards preclude experimenters from exposing children or adolescents to erotic materials.

Ethics in Research on Human Sexuality

LO 1.10   **Describe the ethical concerns that govern the ways in which professionals interact with research participants and clients in treatment.**

Sex researchers are required to protect the people being studied. People cannot be subjected to physical or psychological harm and must participate of their own free will.

In colleges, universities, hospitals, and research institutions, ethics review committees help researchers weigh the potential harm of proposed studies in light of ethical guidelines. If the committee finds fault with a proposal, it may advise the researcher how to modify the research design to comply with ethical standards and withhold approval until the proposal has been modified. What kinds of ethical issues are raised concerning sex research? Let us consider a number of them.

- *Exposing participants to harm.* Individuals may be harmed if they are exposed to pain or placed in stressful situations. Nor would researchers expose children to erotic materials to determine their effects.

- *Confidentiality.* Sex researchers keep the identities and responses of participants confidential to protect them from possible harm or embarrassment.

- *Informed consent.* The principle of informed consent requires that people freely agree to participate after being given enough information about the procedures and purposes of the research, and its risks and benefits, to make an informed decision. Once the study has begun, participants must be free to withdraw at any time without penalty.

- *The use of deception.* Ethical conflicts may emerge when experiments require that participants not know all about the experiment's purposes and methods. For example, in experiments on the effects of violent pornography on aggression against women, participants may be misled into believing that they are administering electric shocks to women (who are actually confederates of the experimenter), even though no shocks are actually delivered. The experimenter seeks to determine participants' willingness to hurt women following exposure to aggressive erotic films. Such studies could not be carried out if participants knew that no shocks would actually be delivered.

Research is the backbone of human sexuality as a science. This textbook focuses on scientific findings that can illuminate our understanding of sexuality, help enhance sexual experience, prevent and treat sexually transmitted infections (STIs), and build more rewarding relationships.

Critical Thinking
What types of harm could occur if a researcher disclosed the identity of an individual participating in a sex survey and his or her sexual behavior?

Chapter Review

LO 1.1 Define the science of human sexuality.

Human sexuality concerns the ways in which we experience and express ourselves as sexual beings. The study of human sexuality draws on the expertise of psychologists, sociologists, anthropologists, biologists, medical researchers, and other scientists.

LO 1.2 Define the value systems people use in making sexual decisions.

Along with accurate knowledge about human sexuality, our values inform our sexual decisions. Value systems include legalism, situational ethics, ethical relativism, hedonism, asceticism, utilitarianism, and rationalism.

LO 1.3 Explain how you can become a critical thinker.

Critical thinking is a skeptical approach to evaluating arguments, widespread beliefs, and evidence. Critical thinkers examine definitions of terms and the premises of arguments.

LO 1.4 Describe various ways of looking at human sexuality.

The historical perspective suggests that there are few universal sexual trends. Ancient Hebrews, Greeks, and Romans dwelled in male-oriented societies that viewed women as property. Repressive Victorian sexual attitudes gave way to the sexual revolution of the 1960s and 1970s. The biological perspective focuses on biological sexual processes such as genetic, hormonal, and neural factors. Evolutionary theory has been active in studying the areas of mate selection and aggression—including sexual aggression. The evolutionary perspective suggests that social behaviors that enhance reproductive success may be subject to natural selection. Studying the behavior of other species may suggest that certain kinds of behaviors are "natural" in that other species do not plan and evaluate sexual behavior in the way that humans do. The sociological perspective studies the ways in which group membership influence human sexuality. Psychological perspectives focus on the processes of perception, learning, motivation, emotion, and personality that affect gender-related and sexual behavior. The theory of psychoanalysis proposes that biologically based sex drives come into conflict with social codes. Learning theories focus on factors such as rewards, punishments, and observational learning. Feminist theory challenges traditional views of men as breadwinners and women as homemakers; of men as political policymakers, especially because those policies affect women and children; of men as sexual "aggressors" and women as sexual "gatekeepers"; and traditional gender roles that view men as objective and rational, and women as emotional and irrational. Queer theory challenges heteronormativity—the viewpoint that heterosexuality is normal. According to queer theory, *heterosexuality* and *homosexuality* are social constructs that ignore commonly experienced mismatches among people's anatomic sex, society's gender roles, and individuals' sexual desires.

LO 1.5 Explain the steps in the scientific method.

The scientific method entails formulating a research question, framing a hypothesis, testing the hypothesis, and drawing conclusions about the hypothesis.

LO 1.6 Explain what is meant by populations and samples.

A population is a complete group of people or animals that researchers target for study. A sample is a subgroup of a population that researchers select to study the population. Researchers use random sampling when possible, to assure that every member of a population has an equal chance of being selected to represent the population. The results are subject to "volunteer bias" when people choose whether or not to participate in the study.

LO 1.7 Describe methods of observation, including the case-study method, the survey, naturalistic observation, ethnographic observation, participant observation, and laboratory observation.

Case studies are carefully drawn biographies of individuals or small groups. Surveys usually gather information about the behavior of large numbers of people through interviews or questionnaires. In naturalistic observation, scientists directly observe the behavior of animals and humans where it happens— "in the field." Ethnographic research provides us with data concerning sexual behaviors and customs that occur widely across cultures and those that are limited to one or few cultures. In participant-observation, investigators learn about people's behavior by personally interacting with them. In the laboratory-observation method, people engage in the behavior under study in the laboratory setting.

LO 1.8 Describe the correlational method.

Correlational research reveals the strength and direction of the relationships between variables, such as communication ability and satisfaction with a relationship. However, they do not show cause and effect.

LO 1.9 **Explain how experiments seek to determine cause and effect.**

Experiments allow scientists to draw conclusions about cause-and-effect relationships because they manipulate the variables of interest, control other variables, and observe their effects. Well-designed experiments randomly assign individuals to experimental and control groups to avoid the selection factor.

LO 1.10 **Describe the ethical concerns that govern the ways in which professionals interact with research participants and clients in treatment.**

Ethical standards require that potentially harmful research may be conducted only when the expected benefits clearly outweigh the risks to participants. Sex researchers keep the identities of participants confidential and obtain their informed consent, but they must now and then deceive people as to the purposes and methods of a study.

Test Your Learning

1. Critical thinking involves all of the following *except* _____
   (a) skepticism.
   (b) challenging tradition.
   (c) evaluating the premises of logic.
   (d) blindly following authority figures.

2. Stone Age art suggests that people worshiped _____
   (a) women's ability to bear children.
   (b) a scientific approach to human sexuality.
   (c) bisexuality in men.
   (d) men's ability to father children.

3. The ancient _____ were first to produce a sex manual.
   (a) Greeks
   (b) Romans
   (c) Chinese
   (d) Indians

4. Masters and Johnson are best known for using _____ in their research on human sexual response.
   (a) correlation coefficients
   (b) cross-cultural methods
   (c) the laboratory-observation method
   (d) the survey

5. Queer theory opposes _____
   (a) heteronormativity.
   (b) use of the word *queer*.
   (c) activism.
   (d) challenging prevailing views of gender and sexuality.

6. According to _____ theory, children acquire the gender roles deemed appropriate in a society through reinforcement and observation.
   (a) evolutionary
   (b) learning
   (c) feminist
   (d) psychoanalytic

7. In a(n) _____ sample, every member of the target population has an equal chance of participating.
   (a) distribution
   (b) digitized
   (c) egalitarian
   (d) random

8. The _____ reports interviewed 5,300 males and 5,940 females between 1938 and 1949.
   (a) Kaiser Family Foundation
   (b) Kinsey
   (c) Centers for Disease Control
   (d) Masters & Johnson

9. A scientific sample must be _____
   (a) large.
   (b) representative.
   (c) natural.
   (d) neutral.

10. Most researchers agree that the best means of learning about cause and effect is _____
    (a) the experiment.
    (b) the correlational method.
    (c) the survey.
    (d) the case study.
    (e) an online survey.

Chapter 2
Female Sexual Anatomy and Physiology

The French have a saying, *"Vive la différence!"* ("Long live the difference!"). The well-known saying is a celebration of the differences between men and women.

This chapter explores women's sexual anatomy and physiology. We will locate and study the female sex organs. Even generally sophisticated students may fill in some gaps in their knowledge. For example, most of you know what a vagina is, but how many of you realized that only the female has an organ that is exclusively dedicated to pleasure? Or that a woman's passing of urine does not involve the vagina?

Chapter 3 describes the sexual anatomy and physiology of men. Despite the obvious differences, we will see that there may be more similarities in the sex organs than you would imagine. As women readers encounter the features of their sexual anatomy in their reading, they may wish to examine their own genitals with a mirror. By following the text and the illustrations, students may discover some new anatomic features. They will see that their genitals can resemble those in the illustrations yet still be unique.

External Sex Organs

LO 2.1 **Describe the external female sex organs and their functions.**

Talking about one's sexual anatomy is often met with prejudice and misunderstanding. The derivation of the word *pudenda,* which refers to the external female genitals, speaks volumes about sexism in the ancient Mediterranean world.

Even today, this cultural heritage may lead women to develop negative attitudes toward their genitals. Girls and boys are both sometimes reared to regard their genitals with shame or disgust. Both may be reprimanded for expressing normal curiosity about them. They may be reared with a "hands-off" attitude, to keep their "private parts" private, even from themselves. This is unfortunate because knowledge of one's sexual anatomy contributes both to sexual health and pleasure.

Taken collectively, the external sexual structures of the female are termed the **pudendum**, or the vulva. **Vulva** is a Latin word that means "wrapper" or "covering." The vulva consists of the *mons veneris,* the *labia majora* and *minora* (major and minor lips),

pudenda
The external sexual structures of the female.

vulva
Another term for the external sexual structures of the female.

Figure 2.1   External Female Sex Organs.

This figure shows the vulva with the labia opened to reveal the urethral and vaginal openings.

mons veneris

A mound of fatty tissue that covers the joint of the pubic bones in front of the body, below the abdomen and above the clitoris.

labia majora

Large folds of skin that run downward from the mons along the sides of the vulva.

the *clitoris*, and the vaginal opening (see Figure 2.1). Figure 2.2 shows variations in the appearance of women's genitals.

The Mons Veneris

The **mons veneris** consists of fatty tissue that covers the joint of the pubic bones in front of the body, below the abdomen and above the clitoris. At puberty, the mons becomes covered with pubic hair that may be thick and curly but varies from person to person in waviness, texture, and color. The pubic hair captures the chemical secretions that exude from the vagina during sexual arousal. Their scent may allure lovers. The mons cushions a woman's body during sexual intercourse, protecting her and her partner from the pressure against the pubic bone that stems from thrusting. There is an ample supply of nerve endings in the mons, so that caresses can produce pleasurable sensations.

The Labia Majora

The **labia majora** are large folds of skin that run downward from the mons along the sides of the vulva. In some women, the labia majora are thick and bulging. In others, they are thinner, flatter, and less noticeable. When close together, they hide the labia minora and the urethral and vaginal openings. The outer surfaces of the labia majora, by the thighs, are covered with pubic hair and darker skin than that found on the thighs or labia minora. The inner surfaces of the labia majora

Figure 2.2   Normal Variations in the Vulva.

The features of the vulva show a great deal of variation. A woman's attitude toward her genitals is likely to reflect her general self-concept and early childhood messages rather than the appearance of her vulva per se.

are hairless and lighter in color. They are amply supplied with nerve endings that respond to stimulation and can produce sexual pleasure. The labia majora also shield the inner female genitals.

The Labia Minora

The **labia minora** are hairless, light-colored membranes, located between the major lips. They surround the urethral and vaginal openings. The outer surfaces of the labia minora merge with the major lips. At the top they join at the prepuce (hood) of the clitoris. The labia minora differ in appearance from woman to woman. The labia minora of some women form protruding flower shapes that are valued greatly in some cultures, such as that of the Khoikhoi people of Africa. (Khoikhoi women purposely elongate their labia minora by tugging at them.) Rich in blood vessels and nerve endings, the labia minora are highly sensitive to sexual stimulation. When stimulated, they darken and swell, engorging with blood.

labia minora

Hairless, light-colored membranes, located between the labia majora.

The Clitoris

Worldwide, the clitoris is known by many names, from *bijou* (French for "jewel") to *pokhotnik* (Russian for "lust"). The Tuamotuan people of Polynesia have ten words for it, emblematic of their interest in female sexuality.

The word **clitoris** derives from the Greek word *kleitoris,* meaning "hill" or "slope." It receives its name from the manner in which it slopes upward in the shaft and forms a mound of spongy tissue at the glans (see Figure 2.1). The body of the clitoris—the clitoral shaft—is about 1 inch long and ¼ inch wide. The shaft consists of erectile tissue that contains two spongy masses called **corpora cavernosa** ("cavernous bodies") that fill with blood (become engorged) and become erect in response to sexual stimulation. The stiffening of the clitoris is less apparent than the erection of the penis, because the clitoris does not swing free from the body. The **prepuce** (meaning "before a swelling"), or hood, covers the clitoral shaft. It is a sheath of skin formed by the upper part of the labia minora. The clitoral glans is a smooth, round knob or lump of tissue above the urethral opening. The glans is revealed by gently separating the labia minora and retracting the hood. It is highly sensitive to touch because of the rich supply of nerve endings.

The size of the clitoris varies from woman to woman. Because the clitoral glans is highly sensitive to touch, women usually prefer to be stroked or stimulated on the mons, or on the clitoral hood, rather than directly on the glans.

clitoris

A female sex organ consisting of a shaft and glans located above the urethral opening. It is extremely sensitive to sexual sensations.

corpora cavernosa

Masses of spongy tissue in the clitoral shaft that become engorged with blood and stiffen in response to sexual stimulation.

prepuce

The fold of skin covering the glans of the clitoris (or penis).

SEX IN A WORLD OF DIVERSITY

FEMALE GENITAL MUTILATION

Dateline, Kafr al Manshi Abou Hamar, Egypt—The men in this poor farming community were seething. A 13-year-old girl was brought to a doctor's office to have her clitoris removed, a surgery considered necessary here to preserve chastity and honor. The girl died, but that was not the source of the outrage. After her death, the government shut down the clinic, and that got everyone stirred up.

—Slackman (2007)

According to the World Health Organization, approximately 140 million Muslim women and girls have undergone genital mutilation (World Health Organization, 2015). And half a million women in the United States have been victimized by it, with many more in danger (Turkewitz, 2015). Despite the fact that people who practice it usually call it circumcision and compare it to male circumcision, social observers assert that female genital mutilation is an attempt by patriarchal societies to control the bodies and behavior of women (Amnesty International, 2012). In terms of their own perceptions, some groups in Egypt and in the Sudan simply perform clitoridectomies because it is a social custom that has been unchallenged in their own experience (Amnesty International, 2012). Because women tend to adopt the values of the larger cultures in which they dwell, nearly 80% of procedures are carried out by women who have undergone them themselves (World Health Organization, 2015).

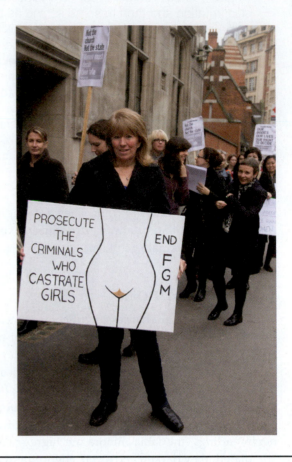

---

homologous

Similar in structure; developing from the same embryonic tissue.

analogous

Similar in function.

In some respects, the clitoris is the female counterpart of the penis. Both organs—clitoris and penis—develop from the same embryonic tissue, which makes them similar in structure, or **homologous** (see Chapter 3). They are not fully similar in function, or **analogous**, however. Both organs receive and transmit sexual sensations, but the penis is directly involved in reproduction and excretion by serving as a conduit for sperm and urine, respectively.

1 › T / F Truth or Fiction Revisited   The historic view of women as unresponsive to sexual stimulation is ironic because only women possess a sex organ—the clitoris—that is solely devoted to pleasurable sensations. The clitoris is the woman's most erotically charged organ; women most often masturbate through clitoral stimulation, not vaginal insertion.

clitoridectomy

Surgical removal of the clitoris.

Cutting out the clitoral hood—**clitoridectomy**—is common among Muslims in the Near East and Africa. As we see in the nearby Sex in a World of Diversity feature, it is a "rite of passage" to womanhood that leaves scars—physical and emotional.

vestibule

The area in the labia minora that contains the openings to the vagina and the urethra.

The Vestibule

The word **vestibule**, which means "entranceway," refers to the area within the labia minora that contains the openings to the vagina and the urethra. The vestibule is richly supplied with nerve endings and is very sensitive to tactile or other sexual stimulation.

urethral opening

The opening through which urine passes from the female's body.

Some perceive it as part of their submission to Islam. However, there is no support for it in the Koran—the Islamic bible (Nour, 2000). The typical young woman in this culture—like the typical woman in most patriarchal cultures—does not grasp that she is a victim (Amnesty International, 2012). She assumes that clitoridectomy is part of being female. As one young woman told gynecologist Nawal M. Nour (2000), the clitoridectomy hurt but was a good thing, because now she was a woman.

There are four major types of female genital mutilation (World Health Organization, 2015):

1. **Clitoridectomy:** partial or complete removal of the clitoris
2. **Excision:** partial or complete removal of the clitoris and the labia minora, with or without removal of the labia majora
3. **Infibulation:** narrowing of the vaginal opening by creating a seal formed by cutting and repositioning the inner, or outer, labia, with or without removal of the clitoris
4. **Other:** other procedures on the female genitalia that serve no medical purpose, such as pricking, piercing, scraping, and cauterizing (burning) the genital area

What effects does female genital mutilation have on women? A study of 250 female patients from the Maternal and Childhood Centers of Ismailia, Egypt, found that those who received the procedures were 80% more likely to complain of painful menstruation, 49% more likely to complain of vaginal dryness during intercourse, 45% more likely to lack sexual desire, 49% less likely to be pleased by sex, and 61% more likely to have difficulty reaching orgasm (El-Defrawi et al., 2001). Complications include severe bleeding, problems urinating, cysts, infections, infertility, complications in childbirth, greater risk of newborn deaths, and psychological and emotional stress (Womenshealth.gov, 2012; World Health Organization, 2015).

Do not confuse male circumcision with the maiming inflicted on girls in the name of circumcision. Nour (2000) depicts the male equivalent of female genital mutilation as cutting off the penis. The Pulitzer Prize–winning, African American novelist Alice Walker drew attention to the practice in her novel *Possessing the Secret of Joy* and called for its abolition in her book and film *Warrior Marks*.

The United States has outlawed ritual genital mutilation within its borders and directed American representatives to world financial institutions to deny aid to countries that have not established educational programs to bring an end to the practice. Yet, calls from Westerners to ban the practice have sparked arguments that people in one culture cannot dictate the cultural traditions of another. For Alice Walker, however, "Torture is not culture."

The World Health Organization (2015) summarizes its stand on the issue as follows:

> [Female genital mutilation] is recognized internationally as a violation of the human rights of girls and women. It reflects deep-rooted inequality between the sexes, and constitutes an extreme form of discrimination against women. It is nearly always carried out on minors and is a violation of the rights of children. The practice also violates a person's rights to health, security and physical integrity, the right to be free from torture and cruel, inhuman or degrading treatment, and the right to life when the procedure results in death.

The Urethral Opening

Urine passes from the female's body through the **urethral opening** (see Figure 2.1), which is connected by a short tube (the urethra) to the bladder (see Figure 2.3). The urethral opening lies below the clitoral glans and above the vaginal opening. The urethral opening, urethra, and bladder are unrelated to the reproductive system.

2 › T / F Truth or Fiction Revisited Many males (and even some females) believe erroneously that, for women, urination and coitus occur through the same bodily opening. The confusion may arise from the fact that urine and semen both pass through the penis of the male or because the urethral opening lies near the vaginal opening.

The proximity of the urethral opening to the external sex organs can pose hygienic problems for sexually active women (Belden, 2011). The urinary tract, which includes the urethra, bladder, and kidneys, may become infected by bacteria from the vagina or rectum. Disease organisms may pass from the partner's sex organs or hands to the

Figure 2.3 The Female Reproductive System.

This cross-section locates many of the internal sex organs that compose the female reproductive system. Note that the uterus is normally tipped forward.

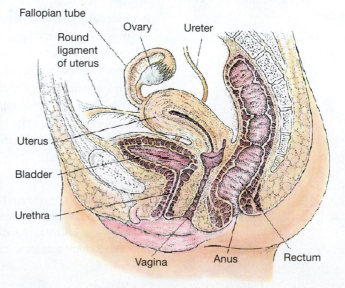

urethral opening during sexual activity. Anal intercourse followed by vaginal intercourse may transfer disease organisms from the rectum to the bladder. For similar reasons, women should first wipe the vulva, then the anus, when using the toilet.

cystitis

An inflammation of the urinary bladder.

Cystitis is a bladder inflammation that may stem from any of these sources. Its symptoms include burning and frequent urination (also called *urinary urgency*). Pus or a bloody discharge is common, and there may be discomfort above the pubic bone. These symptoms may disappear after several days, but consultation with a gynecologist is recommended because untreated cystitis can lead to kidney infections. "Honeymoon cystitis" is caused by the tugging on the bladder and urethral wall that occurs during vaginal intercourse. It may occur when beginning coital activity (although not necessarily on one's honeymoon) or when resuming coital activity after lengthy abstinence. Figure 2.3 shows the close proximity of the urethra and vagina.

A few precautions may help women prevent inflammation of the bladder:

- Drinking two quarts of water a day to flush the bladder.

- Drinking orange or cranberry juice to maintain an acid environment that discourages growth of infectious organisms.

- Decreasing use of alcohol and caffeine (from coffee, tea, or cola drinks) that may irritate the bladder.

- Washing the hands before masturbation or self-examination.

- Washing one's partner's and one's own genitals before and after intercourse.

- Preventing objects that have touched the anus (fingers, penis, toilet tissue) from subsequently coming into contact with the vulva.

- Urinating soon after intercourse to help wash away bacteria.

The Vaginal Opening

introitus

the vaginal opening

hymen

A fold of tissue across the vaginal opening that is usually present at birth and remains at least partly intact until a woman engages in coitus.

One does not see an entire vagina, but rather the vaginal opening, or **introitus**, when one parts the labia minora. The introitus lies below and is larger than the urethral opening. Its shape resembles that of the hymen.

The **hymen** is a fold of tissue across the vaginal opening that is usually present at birth and may remain at least partly intact until a woman engages in coitus. For this reason the hymen has been called the "maidenhead." Its presence has been taken as proof of virginity, and its absence as evidence of coitus. However, some women are born with incomplete hymens, and other women's hymens are torn accidentally, such as during horseback riding, strenuous exercise or gymnastics, or even when bicycling. A punctured hymen is therefore poor evidence of coital experience. A flexible hymen may also withstand many coital experiences, so its presence does not guarantee virginity. Nevertheless, many Muslim women in Europe are having *hymenoplasty* before marriage—an operation that restores the hymen to provide the illusion of virginity on their wedding night (Ostrzenski, 2011). One woman having the operation remarked, "In my culture, not to be a virgin is to be dirt. Right now, virginity is more important to me than life" (cited in Sciolino & Mekhennet, 2008).

3 › T / F Truth or Fiction Revisited Contrary to myth, it is not true that one may determine whether or not a woman is a virgin by examination of the hymen. Some people believe incorrectly that virgins cannot insert tampons or fingers into their vaginas, but most hymens will accommodate these intrusions.

Figure 2.4   Appearance of Various Types of Hymens and the Introitus (*at Right*) as It Appears Following Delivery of a Baby.

Annular hymen   Septate hymen   Cribriform hymen   Imperforate hymen   Parous introitus (after childbirth)

Figure 2.4 illustrates various vaginal openings. The first three show common shapes of hymens among women who have not had coitus. The fifth drawing shows a *parous* ("passed through") vaginal opening, typical of a woman who has delivered a baby. Now and then the hymen consists of tough fibrous tissue and is closed, or *imperforate,* as in the fourth drawing. An imperforate hymen may not be discovered until after puberty, when menstrual discharges begin to accumulate in the vagina. In these rare cases, a surgical incision will perforate the hymen. A woman may also have a physician surgically perforate her hymen if she would rather forgo the tearing and discomfort that may accompany her initial coital experiences. A woman may also stretch the vaginal opening over several days in preparation for intercourse by inserting a finger and gently pressing downward toward the anus. After several repetitions, she may insert two fingers and repeat the process, spreading the fingers slightly after insertion.

The hymen is found only in female horses and humans. It is not present in animal species closest to humans on the evolutionary scale, such as chimps and gorillas. The hymen remains something of a biological mystery because it serves no apparent biological function.

The Perineum

The **perineum** incorporates the skin and underlying tissue between the vaginal opening and the anus. The perineum is rich in nerve endings. Stimulation of the area may heighten sexual arousal. Many physicians make a routine perineal incision during labor, called an *episiotomy,* to facilitate childbirth.

perineum
The skin and underlying tissue that lies between the vaginal opening and the anus.

Structures That Underlie the External Sex Organs

Figure 2.5 shows what lies beneath the skin of the vulva. The *vestibular bulbs* and *Bartholin's glands* are active during sexual arousal and are found on both sides (shown on the right in Figure 2.5). Muscular rings (sphincters) that constrict bodily openings such as the vaginal and anal openings are also found on both sides.

The clitoral **crura** are wing-shaped, leglike structures that attach the clitoris to the pubic bone beneath. The crura contain corpora cavernosa, which engorge with blood and stiffen during sexual arousal.

crura
Anatomical structures resembling legs that attach the clitoris to the pubic bone.

Figure 2.5 Structures That Underlie the Female External Sex Organs.

If we could see beneath the vulva, we would find muscle fibers that constrict the various body openings, plus the crura ("legs") of the clitoris, the vestibular bulbs, and Bartholin's glands.

vestibular bulbs

Cavernous structures that extend downward along the sides of the introitus and swell during sexual arousal.

Bartholin's glands

Glands that lie just inside the minor lips and secrete fluid just before orgasm.

The **vestibular bulbs** are attached to the clitoris at the top and extend downward along the sides of the vaginal opening. Blood congests them during sexual arousal, swelling the vulva and lengthening the vagina. This swelling contributes to coital sensations for both partners.

Bartholin's glands lie just inside the minor lips on each side of the vaginal opening. They secrete a couple of drops of lubrication just before orgasm. This lubrication is not essential for coitus. In fact, the fluid produced by the Bartholin's glands has no known purpose. If the glands become infected and clogged, however, a woman may notice swelling and local irritation. It is wise to consult a gynecologist if these symptoms do not fade within a few days.

It was once believed that the source of the vaginal lubrication or "wetness" that women experience during sexual arousal was produced by the Bartholin's glands. It is now known that engorgement of vaginal tissues during sexual excitement causes moisture from the many small blood vessels that lie in the vaginal wall to be forced out and to pass through the vaginal lining, forming the basis of the lubrication. In less time than it takes to read this sentence (generally within 10 to 30 seconds), beads of vaginal lubrication or "sweat" appear along the interior lining of the vagina in response to sexual stimulation, in much the same way that rising temperatures cause water to pass through the skin as perspiration.

Pelvic floor muscles permit women to constrict the vaginal and anal openings. They contract automatically, or involuntarily, during orgasm, and their tone may contribute to coital sensations.

Internal Sex Organs

LO 2.2 Describe the internal female sex organs, their functions, and health problems that may affect them.

The internal sex organs of the female include the innermost parts of the vagina, the cervix, the uterus, and two ovaries, each connected to the uterus by a fallopian tube (see Figures 2.3 and 2.6). These structures comprise the female reproductive system.

The Vagina

vagina

The tubular female sex organ that contains the penis during sexual intercourse and through which a baby is born.

The **vagina** extends back and upward from the vaginal opening (see Figure 2.3). It is usually 3 to 5 inches long at rest. Menstrual flow and babies pass from the uterus to the outer world through the vagina. During coitus, the penis is contained within the vagina.

The vagina is commonly pictured as a canal or barrel; but, when at rest, it is collapsed, like the inner tube of a bicycle tire. The vagina expands in length and width during sexual arousal. The vagina can also expand to allow insertion of a tampon, as well as the passage of a baby's head and shoulders during childbirth.

The vaginal walls have three layers. The inner lining, or vaginal mucosa, is made visible by opening the labia minora. It is a mucous membrane similar to the skin that lines the inside of the mouth. It feels fleshy, soft, and corrugated. It may vary from very dry to very wet. The middle layer of the vaginal wall is muscular. The outer or deeper layer is a fibrous covering that connects the vagina to other pelvic structures.

The vaginal walls are rich with blood vessels but poorly supplied with nerve endings. Unlike the sensitive outer third of the vaginal barrel, the inner two-thirds are so insensitive to touch that minor surgery may sometimes be performed on those portions without anesthesia. The entire vaginal barrel is sensitive to pressure, however, which can be experienced as pleasurable.

Figure 2.6   Female Internal Reproductive Organs.

This drawing highlights the relationship of the uterus to the fallopian tubes and ovaries. Note the layers of the uterus, the ligaments that attach the ovaries to the uterus, and the relationship of the ovaries to the fimbriae of the fallopian tubes.

A CLOSER LOOK

THE G SPOT AND FEMALE EJACULATION: REALITIES OR MYTHS?

The Grafenberg spot, or G spot, is theorized to be a part of the vagina—a bean-shaped area in the anterior (front) wall that may have special erotic significance (Whipple, 2015). The G spot is believed to lie about 1 to 2 inches from the vaginal entrance and to consist of a soft mass of tissue that swells from the size of a dime to a half dollar when stimulated (see Figure 2.7). The name derives from the gynecologist Ernest Grafenberg, who first suggested the possible erotic import of the area. The spot can be directly stimulated by the woman's or her partner's fingers, or by penile thrusting in the rear entry or the female-superior positions. Some researchers suggest that stimulation of the spot produces intense erotic sensations and that, with prolonged stimulation, a distinct form of orgasm that is characterized by intense pleasure and, in some cases, a biological event formerly thought to be exclusively male: ejaculation. However, these claims are steeped in controversy (Leung, 2015; Ostrzenski, 2015).

In experiments dating to the 1980s, some researchers claim to have found evidence that many women produce an ejaculate as a result of sexual stimulation. Some researchers believe that this fluid is urine that some women release involuntarily during orgasm. Others believe that it differs from urine and represents a fluid that is released during sex by a system of ducts and glands called *Skene's glands*, in much the same way that semen is released by the prostate gland in men. Some women, on the other hand, may expel urine during sex, perhaps because of urinary stress incontinence.

Even supporters of the existence of the G spot admit that it is difficult to locate because it is not apparent to the eye or touch (Jannini et al., 2014). Most women who are knowledgeable about sexuality in general seem to believe that they have a G spot, even if they cannot locate it with any certainty. Because of difficulties such as these, some researchers wonder whether the notion of a G spot is something of a myth (Leung, 2015; Pan et al., 2015).

Figure 2.7   Stimulating the G Spot?

It is theorized that the G spot can be stimulated by fingers or by intercourse in the rear entry or the female-superior positions. Does stimulation of the G spot produce intense erotic sensations and a distinct form of orgasm?

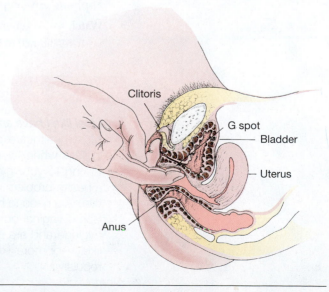

douche

Application of a jet of liquid to the vagina as a rinse.

vaginitis

Vaginal inflammation.

The vaginal walls secrete substances that help maintain the vagina's normal acidity (pH 4.0 to 5.0). Normally, they taste salty, but their odor and taste may vary during the menstrual cycle. The secretions may contain substances that act as sexual attractants. Women who frequently **douche** or use feminine deodorant sprays may remove or mask substances that arouse sex partners. Douching or spraying may also alter the natural chemical balance of the vagina, which can increase the risk of infections. Feminine deodorant sprays can also irritate the vagina and evoke allergic reactions. The normal, healthy vagina cleanses itself through regular chemical secretions that are evidenced by a mild white or yellowish discharge.

Vaginitis refers to any vaginal inflammation, whether it is caused by an infection, birth control pills, antibiotics that alter natural body chemistry, an allergic reaction, chemical irritation, or lowered resistance as may be caused by fatigue or poor diet. Changes in body chemistry or lowered resistance permit microscopic organisms normally found in the vagina to multiply to infectious levels. Vaginitis may be recognized by abnormal discharge, itching, burning of the vulva, and urinary urgency. Women with vaginitis are advised to seek medical attention, but let us note some suggestions that may help prevent vaginitis:

- Wash your vulva and anus regularly with mild soap. Pat dry (taking care not to touch the vulva after dabbing the anus).

- Wear cotton panties. Nylon underwear retains heat and moisture that cause harmful bacteria to flourish.

- Avoid pants that are tight in the crotch.

- Be certain that sex partners are well washed. Condoms may also reduce the spread of infections from one's sex partner.

- Use a sterile, water-soluble jelly such as K-Y jelly if artificial lubrication is needed for intercourse. Do not use Vaseline. Birth control jellies can also be used for lubrication.

- Avoid intercourse that is painful or abrasive to the vagina.

- Avoid diets high in sugar and refined carbohydrates; they alter the normal acidity of the vagina.

- Women who are prone to vaginal infections may find it helpful to douche occasionally with plain water, a solution of 1 or 2 tablespoons of vinegar in a quart of warm water, or a solution of baking soda and water. Douches consisting of unpasteurized, plain (unflavored) yogurt may help replenish the "good" bacteria that are normally found in the vagina and that may be destroyed by use of antibiotics. Be careful when douching, and do not douche when pregnant or when you suspect you may be pregnant. Consult your physician before deciding to douche or applying any preparations to the vagina.

- Watch your general health. Eating poorly or getting insufficient rest will reduce your resistance to infection.

Real Students, Real Questions

Q *I feel like I have an unpleasant odor from my vagina. Should I douche?*

A Most healthcare providers will recommend regular superficial washing, as when taking a shower, and then, if you remain concerned, talking to your gynecologist. An unpleasant odor can be a sign of a health problem. If you're 18 years old, or younger but sexually active, you need to have a gynecologist and to see her or him regularly. Some vaginal odor is normal. If you are attending to your personal hygiene and are not diagnosed with a health problem, a partner is as likely—or more likely—to find normal vaginal odors attractive rather than repulsive.

The Cervix

> When someone first said to me two years ago, "You can feel the end of your own cervix with your finger," I was interested but flustered. I had hardly ever put my finger in my vagina at all, and felt squeamish about touching myself there, in that place "reserved" for lovers and doctors. It took me two months to get up nerve to try it, and then one afternoon, pretty nervously, I squatted down in the bathroom and put my finger in deep, back into my vagina. There it was, feeling slippery and rounded, with an indentation at the center through which, I realized, my menstrual flow came. It was both very exciting and beautifully ordinary at the same time. Last week I bought a plastic speculum so I can look at my cervix. Will it take as long this time?

The **cervix** is the lower end of the uterus. Its walls, like those of the vagina, produce secretions that contribute to the chemical balance of the vagina (Belden, 2011). The opening in the middle of the cervix, or **os**, is normally about the width of a straw, although it expands to permit passage of a baby from the uterus to the vagina during childbirth. Sperm pass from the vagina to the uterus through the cervical canal.

cervix
The lower end of the uterus.

os
The opening in middle of the cervix.

CERVICAL CANCER   Cervical cancer is relatively uncommon in the United States, although there are about 13,000 new cases a year as well as 4,000 deaths (American Cancer Society, 2016a)[1]. The primary cause of cervical cancer is infection with the human papilloma virus (HPV; see Chapter 13). A vaccine has been developed that makes most women immune to the form of HPV connected with cancer. The woman is best vaccinated before she becomes sexually active and may be exposed to the virus (American Cancer Society, 2016a). Cervical cancer is more common among women who have had many sex partners, became sexually active at a relatively early age, have sex with partners who have had many sex partners, and have sex with uncircumcized males (American Cancer Society, 2016a). The mortality rate is higher for African American women than for European American women, at least in part because HPV tends to be diagnosed later in African Americans. However, the death rate has been declining, especially for African American women—down by more than 50% over the past 30 years (American Cancer Society, 2016a).

A **Pap test** examines a sample of cervical cells that are smeared on a slide to screen for cervical cancer and other abnormalities. The HPV test is also appropriate because it finds infections that can lead to cancer. We'll note here and elsewhere in the text that HPV infections are common, and most clear up by themselves. But there is also a vaccine for HPV, and we strongly advise readers to talk to their doctors about it.

Pap test
A test of a sample of cervical cells that screens for cervical cancer and other abnormalities.

According to the Centers for Disease Control and Prevention (2016), Cervical cancer is the easiest gynecologic cancer to prevent, with regular screening tests and follow-up. Two screening tests can help prevent cervical cancer or find it early—

- The Pap test (or Pap smear) looks for *precancers,* cell changes on the cervix that might become cervical cancer if they are not treated appropriately.

- The HPV test looks for the virus (human papilloma virus) that can cause these cell changes.

The Pap test is recommended for all women between the ages of 21 and 65 years old, and can be done in a doctor's office or clinic. During the Pap test, the doctor will use a plastic or metal instrument, called a *speculum,* to widen your vagina. This helps the doctor examine the vagina and the cervix, and collect a few cells and mucus from the cervix and the area around it. The cells are then placed on a slide or in a bottle of liquid and sent to a laboratory. The laboratory will check to be sure that the cells are normal.

---

[1]The numbers of affected individuals are rounded off from recent data. Go to the American Cancer Society's Web site for more precise numbers for any given year.

A Magnified Human Ovum (Egg Cell).
The ripe human ovum is almost large enough to be seen with the naked eye. The ovum of a chicken is a couple of inches across, of course.

radiotherapy

Treatment of a disease by X-rays or by emissions from a radioactive substance.

uterus

The hollow, muscular, pear-shaped organ in which a fertilized ovum implants and develops until birth.

fundus

The uppermost part of the uterus.

endometrium

The innermost layer of the uterus.

endometriosis

A condition caused by the growth of endometrial tissue in the abdominal cavity or elsewhere outside the uterus and characterized by menstrual pain.

myometrium

The middle, well-muscled layer of the uterus.

perimetrium

The outer layer of the uterus.

The only cancer for which the Pap test screens is cervical cancer. It does **not** screen for ovarian, uterine, vaginal, or vulvar cancers. So even if you have a Pap test regularly, if you notice any signs or symptoms that are unusual for you, see a doctor to find out why you're having them. If your Pap test results are normal, your doctor may tell you that you can wait three years until your next Pap test.

If you are 30 years old or older, you may choose to have an HPV test along with the Pap test. Both tests can be performed by your doctor at the same time. If your test results are normal, your chance of getting cervical cancer in the next few years is very low.

If you are 21 to 65 years old, it is important for you to continue getting a Pap test as directed by your doctor—even if you think you are too old to have a child or are not having sex anymore.

Most cases of cervical cancer can be successfully treated by surgery, **radiotherapy**, and chemotherapy if they are detected early. For women diagnosed with localized cancer, the survival rate is about 91% (American Cancer Society, 2016a). It is 57% for cancers that have not spread beyond the region and 16% for cancers that have metastasized (spread throughout the body).

The Uterus

The **uterus**, or womb (see Figures 2.3 and 2.6), is the organ in which a fertilized ovum implants and develops until birth. The uterus usually slants forward (*antroverted*), although about 10% of women have uteruses that tip backward (*retroverted*). In most instances a retroverted uterus causes no problems, but some women with one find certain positions of female–male coitus to be painful. A retroverted uterus normally tips forward during pregnancy. The uterus is suspended in the pelvis by flexible ligaments. In a woman who has not given birth, it is about 3 inches long, 3 inches wide, and 1 inch thick near the top. The uterus expands to house a fetus during pregnancy and shrinks after pregnancy, although not to its original size.

The uppermost part of the uterus is called the **fundus** (see Figure 2.6). The uterus is shaped like an inverted pear. If a ceramic model of a uterus were placed on a table, it would balance on the fundus. The central region of the uterus is called the *body*. The narrow lower region is the *cervix*, which leads downward to the vagina.

Like the vagina, the uterus has three layers (also shown in Figure 2.6). The innermost layer, or **endometrium**, is richly supplied with blood vessels and glands. Its structure varies according to a woman's age and phase of the menstrual cycle. Endometrial tissue is discharged through the cervix and vagina at menstruation. In some women, endometrial tissue may also grow in the abdominal cavity or elsewhere in the reproductive system. This condition is called **endometriosis**, and the most common symptom is menstrual pain. If untreated, it may lead to infertility.

The second layer of the uterus, the **myometrium**, is well muscled. It endows the uterus with flexibility and strength and creates the powerful contractions that propel a fetus outward during labor. The third or outermost layer, the **perimetrium**, provides an external cover.

ENDOMETRIAL CANCER   Cancer of the endometrial lining—the body of the uterus—is called *endometrial cancer*. There are about 55,000 new cases each year, and 10,000 deaths (American Cancer Society, 2016b). Endometrial cancer is rarer in women younger than 45. It is more common among European American women, but African American women are at greater risk of dying from it (American Cancer Society, 2016b). Risk factors are as follows:

- A shift in the balance between progesterone and estrogen toward higher estrogen levels

- Hormone replacement therapy

- Increased number of menstrual cycles during one's lifetime

- Obesity (fatty tissue can change other hormones into estrogen)
- Tamoxifen (a breast cancer–treatment drug, which acts like an antiestrogen medicine in breast tissue and like an estrogen in the uterus
- Ovarian tumors (which sometimes produce estrogen)
- Age
- A high-fat diet
- Diabetes
- Endometrial or colon cancer in the family
- A history of breast or ovarian cancer

The following factors help protect *against* endometrial cancer (American Cancer Society, 2016b):

- Use of birth control pills
- Pregnancy
- Use of an intrauterine device (IUD)
- Exercise

Endometrial cancer is symptomized by abnormal uterine staining or bleeding, especially after menopause. The most common treatment is surgery (American Cancer Society, 2016b), but women may also be treated with radiation therapy, hormonal therapy, and chemotherapy. The five-year survival rate for endometrial cancer is about 90% if it is discovered early and limited to the endometrium. (Endometrial cancer is usually diagnosed early because women tend to report postmenopausal bleeding to their doctors quickly.) The survival rate drops when the cancer invades surrounding tissues or metastasizes. (The survival rate drops to 15% when the cancer has metastasized.)

The Fallopian Tubes

The **fallopian tubes** are about 4 inches in length and extend from the upper end of the uterus toward the ovaries (see Figure 2.6). The part of each tube nearest the uterus is the *isthmus,* which broadens into the *ampulla* as it approaches the ovary. The outer part, or *infundibulum,* has fringelike projections called *fimbriae* that extend toward, but are not attached to, the ovary. Ova pass through the fallopian tubes on their way to the uterus. The fallopian tubes are not just passageways. They help nourish and conduct ova. The tubes are lined with tiny hairlike projections termed *cilia* ("lashes") that help propel ova through the tube at about 1 inch per day. Because ova must be fertilized within a day or two after they are released from the ovaries, fertilization usually occurs in the infundibulum within a couple of inches of the ovaries. The form of sterilization called *tubal ligation* ties off the fallopian tubes, so that ova cannot pass through them or become fertilized.

About 2% of pregnancies are **ectopic pregnancies**; that is, the fertilized ovum implants outside the uterus, most often in the fallopian tube where fertilization occurred. Ectopic pregnancies can eventually burst fallopian tubes, causing hemorrhaging and death, so such pregnancies are terminated before the tube ruptures. Ectopic pregnancies are not easily recognized, however, because their symptoms—missed menstrual period, abdominal pain, irregular bleeding—suggest many conditions. Any of these symptoms is an excellent reason to consult a gynecologist. Risk factors for ectopic pregnancy include a previous ectopic pregnancy, inflammation or infection of the fallopian tubes or uterus (as from the sexually transmitted infections gonorrhea or chlamydia), use of fertility drugs, or an unusually shaped fallopian tube (Mayo Clinic, 2012).

fallopian tubes

Tubes that extend from the upper uterus toward the ovaries and that conduct ova to the uterus.

ectopic pregnancy

A pregnancy in which the fertilized ovum implants outside the uterus, usually in the fallopian tube.

The Ovaries

ovaries

Almond-shaped organs that produce ova and the hormones estrogen and progesterone.

estrogen

A generic term for female sex hormones or synthetic compounds that promote the development of female sex characteristics and regulate the menstrual cycle.

progesterone

A steroid hormone secreted by the corpus luteum or prepared synthetically that stimulates proliferation of the endometrium and is involved in regulation of the menstrual cycle.

follicle

A capsule within an ovary that contains an ovum.

The two **ovaries** are almond-shaped organs that are each about 1½ inches long. They lie on either side of the uterus, to which they are attached by ovarian ligaments. The ovaries produce ova (egg cells) and the female sex hormones estrogen and progesterone. **Estrogen** is a generic term for several hormones (such as estradiol, estriol, and estrone) that promote the changes of puberty and regulate the menstrual cycle. Estrogen also helps older women maintain cognitive functioning and feelings of psychological well-being (Castanho et al., 2014). **Progesterone** is a hormone that also has multiple functions, including regulating the menstrual cycle and preparing the uterus for pregnancy by stimulating the development of the endometrium (uterine lining). Estrogen and progesterone levels vary with the phases of the menstrual cycle.

The human female is born with about 2 million ova, but they are immature in form. Of these, about 400,000 survive into puberty, each of which is contained in the ovary within a thin capsule, or **follicle**. During a woman's reproductive years, from puberty to menopause, only 400 or so ripened ova (typically 1 per month) will be released by their follicles for possible fertilization. How these ova are selected remains a mystery.

OVARIAN CANCER   Each year some 21,000 women in the United States are diagnosed with ovarian cancer, and about 14,000 die from it (American Cancer Society, 2016c). Ovarian cancer most often strikes women between the ages of 40 and 70 and ranks as the fifth-leading cancer killer of women, behind lung cancer, breast cancer, and colon cancer. It is more common in European American women that African American women.

Risk factors for ovarian cancer include (American Cancer Society, 2016c):

- Increased age (half of cases are found in women older than the age of 63)
- Obesity
- Use of the fertility drug clomiphene citrate
- Use of androgens
- Use of estrogen therapy (especially without progesterone)
- Family history of ovarian cancer, breast cancer, or colorectal cancer
- Personal history of breast cancer (especially if the woman is found to have an inherited mutation in the *BRCA1* or *BRCA2* genes)
- Use of talcum powder in the genital region

On the other hand, the following factors appear to lower the risk of ovarian cancer (American Cancer Society 2016c):

- Having had children
- Breast feeding
- Prolonged use of birth control pills
- Tubal ligation
- A low-fat diet
- Use of aspirin or acetaminophen

Early detection is the key to fighting ovarian cancer. When it is detected before spreading beyond the ovary, the five-year survival rate is 89% to 99%, depending on how aggressive the cancer is. When it has metastasized, the survival rate drops to as low as 17% (American Cancer Society, 2016c). Unfortunately, ovarian cancer is often "silent" in the early stages, showing no obvious signs or symptoms. And unfortunately again, early symptoms tend to overlap with symptoms caused by other thing, such as bloating—that is, enlargement of the abdomen, which is caused by the accumulation of fluid. Pelvic pressure or pain in the stomach, trouble eating of feeling full rapidly, and feeling the urge to urinate frequently are additional symptoms. The Pap test, which is useful in detecting cervical cancer, does not reveal ovarian cancer. Your gynecologist may detect the possibility of ovarian cancer during a regular pelvic examination. The most commonly used tests in screening for ovarian cancer are the transvaginal ultrasound (TVUS) and the CA-125 blood test. The TVUS inserts a wand into the vagina; the wand detects masses, but not whether they are cancerous. If ovarian cancer is suspected, the gynecologist usually does a biopsy—a minor surgical procedure in which the doctor obtains and then examines a sample or ovarian tissue.

Surgery, radiation therapy, and drug therapy are treatment options. One, two, or all of these methods may be recommended. Surgery usually includes the removal of one or both ovaries, the uterus, and the fallopian tubes.

HYSTERECTOMY   One in three women in the United States has a **hysterectomy** by the age of 60. Most women who obtain them do so between the ages of 35 and 45. The hysterectomy is the second-most commonly performed operation on women in the United States. (Cesarean sections are the most common.) A hysterectomy may be performed when a woman develops cancer of the uterus, ovaries, or cervix, or another disease that causes pain or excessive uterine bleeding. A **complete hysterectomy** is the surgical removal of the ovaries, fallopian tubes, cervix, and uterus. It is usually performed to reduce the risk of cancer spreading throughout the reproductive system. A **partial hysterectomy** is the removal of the uterus, but the ovaries and fallopian tubes are spared; thus, the woman continues to ovulate and produce adequate quantities of female sex hormones.

The hysterectomy can relieve symptoms associated with various gynecological disorders and improve the quality of life for many women. However, many gynecologists believe that hysterectomies are recommended too often, before proper diagnostic steps are taken or when less radical interventions might alleviate the problem (Corona et al., 2015). We strongly suggest that women whose physicians advise a hysterectomy seek a second opinion before proceeding.

hysterectomy
Surgical removal of the uterus.

complete hysterectomy
Surgical removal of the ovaries, fallopian tubes, cervix, and uterus.

partial hysterectomy
Surgical removal of the uterus but not the ovaries and fallopian tubes.

The Pelvic Examination

Women are advised to have an internal (pelvic) examination at least once a year by the time they reach their late teens (or earlier if they become sexually active) and twice yearly if they are older than age 35 or use birth control pills. The physician (usually a gynecologist) first examines the woman externally for irritations, swellings, abnormal vaginal discharges, and clitoral adhesions. The physician normally inserts a speculum to help inspect the cervix and vaginal walls for discharges (which can be signs of infection), discoloration, lesions, or growths. This examination is typically followed by a Pap test to detect cervical cancer. A sample of vaginal discharge may also be taken to test for the sexually transmitted infection (STI) gonorrhea (see Chapter 13).

To take a Pap test, or a Pap smear, the physician will hold open the vaginal walls with a plastic or (hopefully prewarmed!) metal speculum so that a sample of cells (a "smear") may be scraped from the cervix with a wooden spatula (see Figure 2.8). Women should not douche

Figure 2.8   Use of the Speculum and Spatula During a Pelvic Examination.

The speculum holds the vaginal walls apart while the spatula is used to gently scrape cells from the cervix. The Pap test screens for cervical cancer and other abnormalities.

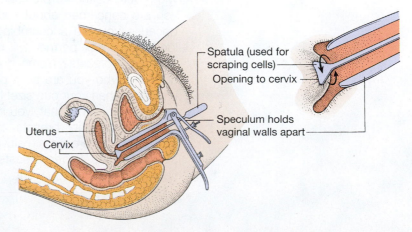

Spatula (used for scraping cells)
Opening to cervix
Speculum holds vaginal walls apart
Uterus
Cervix

before Pap tests or schedule them during menstruation because douches and blood confound analysis of the smear.

The speculum exam is normally followed by a bimanual vaginal exam in which the index and middle fingers of one hand are inserted into the vagina while the lower part of the abdomen is palpated (touched) by the other hand from the outside. The physician uses this technique to examine the location, shape, size, and movability of the internal sex organs, searching for abnormal growths and symptoms of other problems. Palpation may be somewhat uncomfortable, but severe pain is a sign that something is wrong. A woman need not hide such discomfort from the examiner. She may only be masking a symptom (that is, depriving the physician of useful information). Physical discomfort is usually mild, however, and psychological discomfort is sometimes lessened by discussing it.

Finally, the physician should do a recto-vaginal examination in which one finger is inserted into the rectum while the other is inserted into the vagina. This procedure provides additional information about the ligaments of the uterus, the ovaries, and the fallopian tubes. The procedure also helps the physician evaluate the health of the rectum.

Although it may be somewhat uncomfortable, the pelvic examination is not ordinarily painful. It is normal for a woman who has not had one, or who is visiting a new doctor, to be anxious about the examination. The doctor should be reassuring if the woman expresses concern. If the doctor is not, the woman should feel free to consult another doctor. She should not forgo the pelvic examination itself, however. It is essential for early detection of problems.

The Breasts

LO 2.3 Describe the composition and functions of the breasts.

In some cultures, the breasts are viewed merely as biological instruments for feeding infants. In American culture, however, breasts have such erotic significance that a woman's self-esteem may become linked to her bust line.

Real Students, Real Questions

Q *Is there any way to make my breasts larger without having plastic surgery?*

A You'll come across advertisements for dietary supplements that supposedly do the job, but we advise you not to take anything without discussing it with your healthcare provider. But think about why you are concerned about your breast size. Is it because you are succumbing to the popular idea that a sex partner will prefer a woman with large breasts? Some do, but many do not, and who you are as a person is more important than your cup size! If your partner doesn't agree with that, you need another partner, not larger breasts. In any case, small breasts are as sensitive to sexual stimulation as larger breasts, so show your partner what you want.

The breasts are **secondary sex characteristics**. Like the rounding of the hips, they distinguish females from males, but they are not directly involved in reproduction. Each breast contains 15 to 20 clusters of milk-producing **mammary glands** (see Figure 2.9). Each gland opens at the nipple through its own duct. The mammary glands are separated by soft, fatty tissue. It is the amount of this fatty tissue, not the amount of glandular tissue, that largely determines the size of the breasts.

4 › T / F Truth or Fiction Revisited
Breast size represents the amount of fatty tissue in the breast, but milk is produced by glandular tissue. Women vary less in their amount of glandular tissue than fatty tissue, so breast size does not determine the quantity of milk that can be produced.

The nipple, which lies in the center of the **areola**, contains smooth muscle fibers that erect the nipple when they contract. The areola, or area surrounding the nipple, darkens during pregnancy and remains darker after delivery. Oil-producing glands in the areola help lubricate the nipples during breast feeding. Milk ducts conduct milk from the mammary glands through the nipples. Nipples are richly endowed with nerve endings, so that stimulation of the nipples heightens sexual arousal for many women. Male nipples are similar in sensitivity.

Figure 2.10 shows some of the normal variations in the size and shape of the breasts of adult women. The sensitivity of the breasts to sexual stimulation is unrelated to their size. Small breasts may have as many nerve endings as large breasts, but they will be more densely packed.

Women can prompt their partners to provide breast stimulation by informing them that their breasts are sensitive to stimulation. They can also guide a partner's hands in ways that provide the type of stimulation they desire. The breasts vary in sensitivity with the phases of the menstrual cycle, and some women appear less responsive to breast

Figure 2.9   A Breast of an Adult Woman.
This drawing reveals the structures underlying the breast, including milk ducts and fat cells.

Nipple

Milk ducts

Areola

Fat cells

Pectoral muscle

Ribs

secondary sex characteristics
Traits that distinguish the sexes from one another but are not directly involved in reproduction.

mammary glands
Milk-secreting glands.

areola
The dark ring on the breast that encircles the nipple.

Figure 2.10   Normal Variations in the Size and Shape of the Breasts.
The size and shape of the breasts have little bearing on ability to produce milk or on sensitivity to sexual stimulation. Breasts have become highly eroticized in our culture.

stimulation than others. However, some less sensitive women may learn to enjoy breast stimulation by focusing on breast sensations during lovemaking in a relaxed atmosphere.

Breast Cancer

LO 2.4 Discuss risk factors for and detection and treatment of breast cancer.

mammography

A special type of X-ray test that detects cancerous lumps in the breast.

mastectomy

Surgical removal of the entire breast.

lumpectomy

Surgical removal of a lump from the breast.

Susan contracted breast cancer in her 30s. A lump "suddenly" appeared in her **mammography**. She and her family dwelled in fear over the next couple of weeks as tissue from the tumor was biopsied, found to be malignant, and arrangements were made to remove the breast. Given the "aggressiveness" of the tumor—the rapidity with which it had grown—every physician she consulted recommended **mastectomy** (surgically removing the breast) rather than **lumpectomy** (surgically removing a lump from the breast). The question arose as to whether Susan should remove the healthy breast as a precautionary measure. A blood test determined that she did not possess genetic mutations in the *BRCA1* or *BRCA2* genes that are connected with early-onset breast cancer, so the healthy breast was preserved. There was additional anxiety following the removal of the breast as tissues were examined to determine whether the cancer had spread within the breast or to lymph nodes. Fortunately, it had apparently remained within a duct despite the rapidity of its growth.

Susan then dealt with the psychological issues of feeling unwhole, which were to some degree mitigated by attending a support group of women undergoing similar experiences. Reconstruction of the breast was an unexpected and lengthy process during which the muscles that normally underlie breasts were gradually ballooned out to surround and support a silicone implant. A new cosmetic nipple was constructed from thigh tissue. It was decided that she did not need chemotherapy or radiation, but she did go on tamoxifen, a drug that decreases the body's supply of estrogen—a factor in the development of cancerous tissue in the breast. There was no evidence of remaining malignant tissue after Susan reached the "magical" five-year postsurgical survival date.

Breast cancer strikes more than 230,000 women in the United States each year and takes about 40,000 lives (American Cancer Society, 2016d). Men can also develop breast cancer, but the disease is 100 times more common in women (American Cancer Society, 2016d). People do not die from cancer in the breast per se, but rather from its spread to other body parts such as the brain, bones, lungs, or liver. Breast cancer is the second leading cancer killer of women, following lung cancer. Even so the incidence

Real Students, Real Questions

Q *One of my breasts is bigger than the other. Is this normal?*

A Sure. One hand is larger than the other, one foot, and for men, one testicle. Unless there's a huge difference, don't worry about it. It is mostly the amount of fatty tissue in the breasts that accounts for differences in the size of the breasts among women. Moreover, breasts expand with pregnancy, and smaller breasts tend to increase more dramatically in size than larger breasts. And because production of milk depends on the amount of glandular tissue in the breasts, not fatty tissue, the size of your breasts has nothing to do with the amount of milk you can produce if you have children. On the other hand, if you have noticed a change in the size of one breast relative to the other, or in the texture of your breast tissue or in the nipple or areola, bring it to the attention of your healthcare provider. It could mean nothing, but it's better to be sure.

of breast cancer has been on the decline, presumably related to decreased use of hormone replacement therapy following menopause.

In clinical breast examinations (CBEs), physicians feel the breasts for lumps that may be breast cancer during clinical examination. Women with breast cancer have lumps in the breast, but most lumps are *not* cancerous. Most are either **cysts** or **benign** tumors called **fibroadenomas**. Breast cancer involves lumps in the breast that are **malignant**. Women can also detect lumps in their own breasts by means of breast self-examination (BSE). But keep in mind that even though the American Cancer Society no longer recommends BSE, regular clinical visits are essential (American Cancer Society, 2016d).

More early cases of breast cancer are being detected because of an increased use of mammography, a kind of X-ray that detects cancerous lumps in the breast. Advances in early detection and treatment have led to increased rates of recovery among women from age 40 into their 70s (National Cancer Institute, 2015). On the other hand, health professionals admit that mammography has led to the detection and treatment of some localized cancers that might never have grown (National Cancer Institute, 2015). The American Cancer Society (2016d) counters that the majority of these small tumors would grow. In any event, the National Cancer Institute (2015) recommends that women aged 40 and older talk to their healthcare providers about the frequency of mammograms. The following factors increase the risk of breast cancer (American Cancer Society, 2016d):

- Gender—being female
- Family history of breast cancer, especially if a mother, sister, or daughter has been diagnosed with the disease
- Inherited mutation of *BRCA1* and *BRCA2* genes. In some families the lifetime risk of breast cancer from these mutations is 80% of *BRCA1* genes and 45% for *BRCA2* genes (American Cancer Society, 2016d). Ashkenazi Jewish women are at greater risk than the general population of BRCA mutations.
- Higher breast density
- First menstrual period before the age of 12, menopause after age 55, delayed childbearing, and never having children—all of which increase lifetime exposure to estrogen
- Long-term use of menopausal hormone therapy (especially women who have used a combination of estrogen and progestin for more than 5 years)
- Radiation therapy to the chest (as for Hodgkin lymphoma)
- Alcohol (the more you drink, the higher the risk)
- Use of DES
- Being overweight or obese (fatty tissue produces estrogen)
- Physical *in*activity (exercise may reduce the risk of breast cancer by decreasing the amount of fatty tissue in the body)

A number of women whose family histories and genetics seem to place them at extraordinarily high risk for breast cancer have chosen to have their breasts removed *prophylactically*—meaning to prevent disease, not to treat disease. In some cases women who developed cancer in one breast chose to have both removed at the same time. But in some case, women without any symptoms but just with the genetic risk have had them removed.

Film actress and United Nations special envoy Angelina Jolie lost her mother to breast cancer at the age of 56, and she, Angelina, shares, in her words, the "faulty" gene. Angelina's doctors estimated that she had an 87% chance of developing breast cancer herself, along with a 50% risk of developing ovarian cancer, which is genetically related. She writes, "I decided to be proactive and to minimize the risk as much I could. I made a decision to have a preventive double mastectomy.... I can tell my children that they don't need to fear they will lose me to breast cancer" (Jolie, 2013).

cysts
Sac-like structures filled with fluid or diseased material.

benign
Doing little or no harm.

fibroadenoma
A benign, fibrous tumor.

malignant
Lethal; causing or likely to cause death.

After learning that her genetic background put her risk of developing breast cancer at 87%, Angelina Jolie decided to have a preventive double mastectomy. She wrote, "I feel empowered that I made a strong choice that in no way diminishes my femininity."

A CLOSER LOOK

BREAST SELF-EXAMINATION

Regular visits to a physician and mammograms provide the best protection against breast cancer because they may lead to early detection and treatment. But many women find lumps themselves. It was once recommended that women conduct breast self-examinations (BSEs) at least once a month, but now the American Cancer Society considers BSEs to be optional. On the other hand, BSE may have psychological advantages for many women—empowering them to investigate their own bodies and to actively participate in their own disease prevention. Moreover, the American Cancer Society (2006) continues to recommend that women be *aware* of what is going on in their bodies. BSEs would appear to be one way to cultivate awareness.

The following instructions for BSE are based on American Cancer Society guidelines (see Figure 2.11). Additional material on BSE may be obtained from the American Cancer Society by calling 1-800-ACS-2345. However, women are advised to initiate BSEs with a health professional to determine their baseline "lumpiness" and to learn the proper technique.

1. **In the shower.** Examine your breasts during your bath or shower; hands glide more easily over wet skin. Keep your fingers flat and move gently over every part of each breast. Use the right hand to examine the left breast and the left hand for the right breast. Check for any lump, hard knot, or thickening.

2. **Before a mirror:** Inspect your breasts with your arms at your sides. Next, raise your arms high overhead. Look for any changes in the contour of each breast, a swelling, dimpling of skin, or changes in the nipple. Then rest your palms on your hips and press down firmly to flex your chest muscles. Your left and right breasts will not exactly match.

Few women's breasts are symmetrical. Regular inspection will allow you to determine what is normal for you and will give you confidence in your examination.

3. **Lying down.** To examine your right breast, put a pillow or folded towel under your right shoulder. Place your right arm behind your head. This position distributes breast tissue more evenly on the chest. With your left hand, fingers flat, press gently with the finger pads (the top thirds of the fingers) of the three middle fingers in small circular motions around an imaginary clock face. Begin at the outermost top of your right breast for 12 o'clock, then move to 1 o'clock, and so on around the circle back to 12 o'clock. A ridge of firm tissue in the lower curve of each breast is normal. Then move in 1 inch, toward the nipple. Keep circling to examine *every part of your breast,* including the nipple. This requires at least three more circles. Now slowly repeat the procedure on your left breast. Place the pillow beneath your left shoulder, place your left arm behind your head, and use the finger pads on your right hand.

After you examine your left breast fully, squeeze the nipple of each breast gently between your thumb and index finger. Any discharge, clear or bloody, should be reported to your doctor immediately.

5 › T / F Truth or Fiction Revisited The American Cancer Society has considered breast self-examination (BSE) to be optional since 2003. However, BSE does occasionally detect suspicious lumps that need to be followed up in the clinic.

Figure 2.11   A Woman Examines Her Breast for Lumps

In sum, the current recommendations for breast cancer screening of the American Cancer Society (2016d), are as follows:

Since 2003: BSE
- Age 20 and older, optional

Since 2003: Clinical breast exam (CBE),
- Ages 20–39, preferably every three years
- Ages 40 and older, preferably every year

Since 2015: Mammogram
- Ages 40–44, women should have the choice to request screening, and women with higher-risk profiles should be screened
- Ages 45–54, yearly
- Ages 55 and older, every two years, although women should have the choice to continue annual screening

In any event, the 5-year survival rate for women whose breast cancers have not spread beyond the breast is about 93%, up from nearly 80% in the 1950s (American Cancer Society, 2012d). The 5-year survival rate drops to about 80% if the cancer has spread to the surrounding region and to about 15% if it has spread to more distant sites.

Does abortion increase a woman's risk of breast cancer? Some writers have speculated that because pregnancy decreases the risk of breast cancer, having an abortion will indirectly increase the risk (Malec, 2003). But as we see in the following Truth-or-Fiction Revisited section:

6 › T / F Truth or Fiction Revisited An extensive review of carefully controlled studies does not find that abortion increases a woman's risk of breast cancer (Templeton & Grimes, 2011). Similarly, silicone breast implants have not been shown to increase the risk of breast cancer either, but they can lead to the development of scar tissue and obscure mammography readings (Lipworth et al., 2008).

TREATMENT Early detection of breast cancer offers many benefits. Smaller lumps are sometimes removed by lumpectomy, sparing the breast. More advanced cancers are likely to be treated by mastectomy.

Many drugs are also used to treat breast cancer, and others are in the research pipeline. For example, tamoxifen locks into the estrogen receptors of breast cancer cells, thereby blocking estrogen's stimulation of the cells to grow and proliferate. However, tamoxifen increases the risks of uterine cancer and of blood clots in the lungs, along with some other side effects. The risks of these side effects were lowest among women younger than the age of 50. The drug raloxifene has also been shown to reduce the risk of breast cancer (Wickerham D.L., et al., 2015). Moreover, raloxifene does not appear to have the side effects associated with tamoxifen. Other drugs are also being studied for use against breast cancer. Ask your gynecologist for the latest research results and which drugs, if any, are right for you.

Many women who have had mastectomies have had surgical breast implants to replace the tissue that has been removed. Other women have breast implants to augment their breast size. Research suggests that breast implants probably have no effect on the probability of developing breast cancer, rheumatoid arthritis, and a number of other health problems, casting doubts on previous studies that had implicated them in the development of these problems. Again, consult your gynecologist for the latest findings.

Critical Thinking
The American Cancer Society no longer recommends that women need to conduct BSEs as a means of detecting breast cancer early. Do you believe that it is a good idea for women to do BSEs anyhow? Why or why not?

SEX IN A WORLD OF DIVERSITY

AFRICAN AMERICAN WOMEN AND BREAST CANCER

Overall, African Americans are more likely than European Americans to develop cancer. The case is somewhat different with breast cancer. As a group, African American women are somewhat less likely than European American women to develop breast cancer. However, when they do, they frequently do so at an earlier age (Simon, 2011). Yet they tend to be diagnosed with the disease somewhat later, and they are also more likely to die from it (American Cancer Society, 2016d). Some aspects of the racial differences, such as the tendency to be diagnosed later, may reflect less access to health care.

On the other hand, genetic factors are also likely to be involved. It is usually estrogen that causes the proliferation of breast cancer cells, and thus some drugs, such as tamoxifen, treat breast cancer by suppressing the body's supply of estrogen. However, African American are more likely to develop tumors that are "estrogen-receptor negative." That is, they develop rapidly even in the absence of estrogen (Simon, 2011). These tumors are highly aggressive—that is, they grow very rapidly—and are a major factor in the higher mortality rate for African American women (Simon, 2011).

African American Women and Breast Cancer. African American women are less likely than European American women to develop breast cancer, but when they do, the cancer tends to be more "aggressive" and lethal. Most researchers attribute this racial difference to different varieties of breast cancer that tend to affect people from different races disproportionately.

The Menstrual Cycle

LO 2.5 **Describe the regulation and the phases of the menstrual cycle.**

menstruation

The cyclical bleeding that stems from the shedding of the uterine lining.

ovulation

The release of an ovum from an ovary.

Menstruation is the cyclical bleeding that stems from the shedding of the uterine lining (endometrium). Menstruation takes place when a reproductive cycle has not led to the fertilization of an ovum. The word *menstruation* derives from the Latin *mensis*, meaning "month." The menstrual cycle averages 28 days.

The cycle is regulated by the hormones estrogen and progesterone and can be divided into four phases. The first phase, the *proliferative phase*, follows menstruation. During this phase, estrogen levels increase, causing the ripening of perhaps 10 to 20 ova (egg cells) within their follicles and the proliferation of endometrial tissue in the uterus. During the second phase of the cycle, estrogen reaches peak blood levels, and **ovulation** occurs. Normally only one ovum reaches maturity and is released by an ovary during ovulation. Then the third phase (the *secretory*, or *luteal*, phase) of the cycle begins. The luteal phase begins right after ovulation and continues through the beginning of the next cycle.

The term *luteal phase* is derived from **corpus luteum**, the name given to the follicle that releases an ovum. The corpus luteum functions as an **endocrine gland** and produces large amounts of progesterone and estrogen. Progesterone causes the endometrium to thicken, so that it will be able to support an embryo if fertilization occurs. If the ovum goes unfertilized, however, estrogen and progesterone levels plummet. The drops trigger the fourth phase, the *menstrual phase*, which leads to the beginning of a new cycle.

Ovulation may not occur in every menstrual cycle. *Anovulatory* ("without ovulation") cycles are most common in the years just after **menarche** (the first menstrual period). They may become frequent again in the years before menopause, but they may also occur irregularly at any age.

Although the menstrual cycle averages 28 days, variations among women, and in the same woman from month to month, are common. Girls' cycles are often irregular for a few years after menarche but later assume regular patterns. Variations from cycle to cycle tend to occur during the proliferative phase that precedes ovulation. Menstruation tends to reliably follow ovulation by about 14 days.

Hormones regulate the menstrual cycle, but psychological factors can affect the secretion of hormones. Stress can delay or halt menstruation. For example, many women in otherwise good health stopped menstruating during imprisonment in Nazi concentration camps during World War II (Ofer & Weitzman, 1998).

corpus luteum
The follicle that releases an ovum and then produces copious amounts of progesterone and estrogen during the luteal phase of a woman's cycle.

endocrine gland
A ductless gland that releases its secretions directly into the bloodstream.

menarche
The first menstrual period.

SEX IN A WORLD OF DIVERSITY

HISTORICAL AND CROSS-CULTURAL PERSPECTIVES ON MENSTRUATION

In Peru, women speak of a "visit from Uncle Pepe," whereas in Samoa, menstruation is referred to as "the boogie man." One of the more common epithets for menstruation is "the curse." The Fulani of Upper Volta in Africa use a term that translates "to see dirt." Nationalism also rises to the call, with some nations blaming "the curse" on their historical enemies. The French once dubbed menstruation "the English" and its onset "the English are coming."

It is a common folk belief that menstruating women are contaminated. Men may thus avoid contact with menstruating women. To prevent their contaminating others, menstruating women in tribal societies have been dispatched to huts on the fringe of the village. In the traditional Navajo Native American culture, for instance, menstruating women would be consigned to huts that were set apart from other living quarters. In many Islamic societies, the menstrual flow is considered unclean, and menstruating women are not permitted to pray or enter a mosque.

Women in industrialized nations are not consigned to special huts, but throughout the history of Western culture, menstruation has been seen as unclean, contaminating, and sometimes even magical.

Ancient societies—and some contemporary ones—have limited understanding of bodily processes, or else they rely on

tradition more than science. Science teaches that there is no medical basis for isolating menstruating women or avoiding sex during menstruation.

We might laugh off these misconceptions as folly and ignorance, if it were not for their profound effect on women. Women who believe the myths about menstruation may see themselves as unclean and endure anxiety, depression, and lowered self-esteem. Negative cultural beliefs concerning menstruation may also exacerbate menstrual distress.

7 › T / F Truth or Fiction Revisited The ancient Romans did believe that menstrual blood soured wine and killed crops. In 77 CE, the Roman Pliny the Elder summed up Roman misbeliefs about menstrual blood in his *Natural History*:

Contact with it turns new wine sour, crops touched by it become barren, grafts die, seeds in gardens are dried up, the fruit of trees falls off.... [The] edge of steel and the gleam of ivory are dulled, hives of bees die, even bronze and iron are at once seized by rust, and a horrible smell fills the air; to taste it drives dogs mad and infects their bites with an incurable poison.

hypothalamus

A structure near the center of the brain that is involved in regulating body temperature, motivation, and emotion.

pituitary gland

The gland that secretes growth hormone, prolactin, oxytocin, and others.

hormone

A substance secreted by an endocrine gland that regulates various body functions.

testes

The male gonads, which produce the male sex hormone, testoterone.

testosterone

The male sex hormone that fosters the development of male sex characteristics and is connected with the sex drive.

Regulation of the Menstrual Cycle

The menstrual cycle involves finely tuned relationships between structures in the brain (the **hypothalamus** and the **pituitary gland**) and the ovaries and uterus. All these structures are parts of the endocrine system, which means that they secrete chemicals directly into the bloodstream (see Figure 2.12). The chemicals secreted by endocrine glands are called **hormones**. The ovaries and uterus are also reproductive organs.

The gonads—the ovaries in the female and the testes (or testicles) in the male—secrete sex hormones directly into the bloodstream. The female gonads, the ovaries, produce the sex hormones estrogen and progesterone. The male gonads, the **testes**, produce the male sex hormone **testosterone**. Males and females also produce relatively small amounts of the sex hormones of the opposite gender.

The hypothalamus is a pea-sized structure in the front part of the brain. It lies above the pituitary gland and below (hence the prefix *hypo-*, for "under") the thalamus. Despite its small size, it is involved in regulating many states of motivation, including hunger, thirst, aggression, and sex. For example, when the rear part of a male rat's hypothalamus is stimulated by an electric probe, the rat runs through its courting and mating sequence. It nibbles at a female's ears and at the back of her neck. When she responds, they copulate. Human sexuality is not so stereotyped or mechanical—although in the cases of people who have fallen into ruts, it may seem to be.

The pituitary gland, which is about the size of a pea, lies below the hypothalamus at the base of the brain. Because many pituitary secretions regulate other endocrine

Figure 2.12 Major Glands of the Endocrine System.

The endocrine system consists of glands that secrete chemicals called *hormones* directly into the bloodstream.

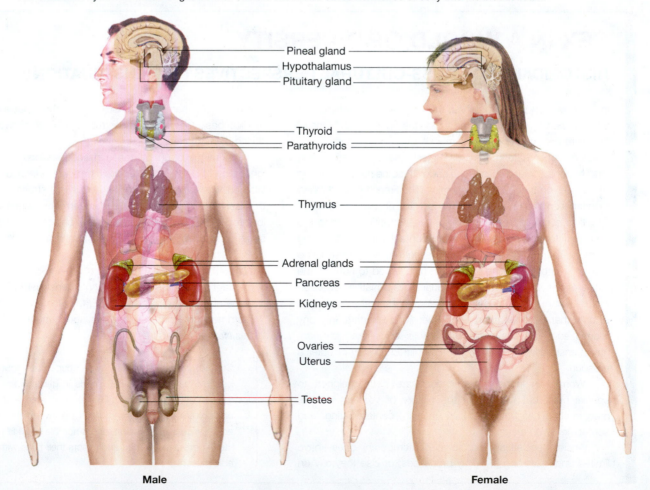

Pineal gland
Hypothalamus
Pituitary gland
Thyroid
Parathyroids
Thymus
Adrenal glands
Pancreas
Kidneys
Ovaries
Uterus
Testes

Male   **Female**

glands, the pituitary has also been called the *master gland*. Pituitary hormones regulate bone and muscle growth and urine production. Two pituitary hormones are active during pregnancy and motherhood: **prolactin**, which stimulates production of milk, and **oxytocin**, which stimulates uterine contractions in labor and the ejection of milk during nursing. The pituitary gland also produces **gonadotropins** (literally, "that which 'feeds' the gonads") that stimulate the ovaries: **follicle-stimulating hormone (FSH)** and **luteinizing hormone (LH)**. These hormones play key roles in regulating the menstrual cycle.

The hypothalamus receives information about bodily events through the nervous and circulatory systems. It monitors the blood levels of various hormones, including estrogen and progesterone, and releases a hormone called **gonadotropin-releasing hormone (Gn-RH)**, which stimulates the pituitary to release gonadotropins. Gonadotropins, in turn, regulate the activity of the gonads. It was once thought that the pituitary gland ran the show, but it is now known that the pituitary gland is regulated by the hypothalamus. Even the "master gland" must serve another.

Phases of the Menstrual Cycle

The menstrual cycle has four stages or phases: proliferative, ovulatory, secretory, and menstrual (see Figure 2.13). It might seem logical that a new cycle begins with the first day of the menstrual flow because this is the most clearly identifiable event of the cycle. Many women also count the days of the menstrual cycle beginning with the onset of menstruation. Biologically speaking, however, menstruation is really the culmination of the cycle. In fact, the cycle begins with the end of menstruation and the initiation of a series of biological events that lead to the maturation of an immature ovum in preparation for ovulation and possible fertilization.

THE PROLIFERATIVE PHASE The first phase, or **proliferative phase**, begins with the end of menstruation and lasts about 9 or 10 days in an average 28-day cycle (see Figures 2.13 and 2.14). During this phase the endometrium develops, or "proliferates." This phase is also known as the *preovulatory* or *follicular* phase because certain ovarian follicles mature and the ovaries prepare for ovulation.

Low levels of estrogen and progesterone are circulating in the blood as menstruation draws to an end. When the hypothalamus senses a low level of estrogen in the blood, it increases secretion of Gn-RH, which in turn triggers the pituitary gland to release a FSH. When FSH reaches the ovaries, it stimulates some follicles (perhaps

prolactin
A pituitary hormone that stimulates production of milk.

oxytocin
A pituitary hormone that stimulates uterine contractions in labor and the ejection of milk during nursing.

gonadotropins
Pituitary hormones that stimulate the gonads.

follicle-stimulating hormone (FSH)
A gonadotropin that stimulates development of follicles in the ovaries.

luteinizing hormone (LH)
A gonadotropin that helps regulate the menstrual cycle by triggering ovulation.

gonadotropin-releasing hormone (Gn-RH)
A hormone secreted by the hypothalamus that stimulates the pituitary to release gonadotropins.

proliferative phase
The first phase of the menstrual cycle, which begins with the end of menstruation and lasts about nine or ten days. During this phase, the endometrium proliferates.

Figure 2.13 The Phases of the Menstrual Cycle.

The menstrual cycle has proliferative, ovulatory, secretory (luteal), and menstrual phases.

Figure 2.14 Changes of the Menstrual Cycle.

This figure shows five categories of biological change: (a) changes in the development of the uterine lining (endometrium), (b) follicular changes, (c) changes in blood levels of ovarian hormones, (d) changes in blood levels of pituitary hormones, and (e) changes in basal temperature. Note the dip in temperature that is connected with ovulation.

10 to 20) to begin to mature. As the follicles ripen, they begin to produce estrogen. Normally, however, only one of them—called the *graafian follicle*—will reach full maturity in the days just preceding ovulation. As the graafian follicle matures, it moves toward the surface of the ovary, where it will eventually rupture and release a mature egg (see Figures 2.14 and 2.15).

Estrogen causes the endometrium in the uterus to thicken to about 1/8 inch. Glands develop that would eventually nourish an embryo. Estrogen also stimulates the appearance of a thin cervical mucus. This mucus is alkaline and provides a hospitable, nutritious medium for sperm. The chances are thus increased that sperm that enter the female reproductive system at the time of ovulation will survive.

THE OVULATORY PHASE During ovulation, or the **ovulatory phase**, the graafian follicle ruptures and releases a mature ovum *near* a fallopian tube—not *into* a fallopian tube (see Figure 2.15). The other ripening follicles degenerate and are reabsorbed by the body. If two ova mature and are released during ovulation and both are fertilized, fraternal (nonidentical) twins will develop. Identical twins occur when one fertilized ovum divides into two separate **zygotes**.

Ovulation is set into motion when estrogen production reaches a critical level. The hypothalamus detects the high level of estrogen and triggers the pituitary to release copious amounts of FSH and LH (see Figures 2.14 and 2.15). The surge of LH triggers ovulation, which usually begins 12 to 24 hours after the level of LH in the body has reached its peak. The synthetic hormone *clomiphene* is chemically similar to LH and has been used by women who ovulate irregularly to induce reliable ovulation and thus increase the chances of conceiving.

A woman's *basal body temperature*, taken by oral or rectal thermometer, dips slightly at ovulation (see Figure 2.14) and rises by about 1° F on the day following ovulation. Many women use this information to help them conceive or avoid conceiving.

Some women have discomfort or cramping during ovulation, termed **mittelschmerz**. This condition is sometimes confused with appendicitis. Mittelschmerz, however, may occur on either side of the abdomen, depending on which ovary is releasing an ovum. A ruptured appendix always causes pain on the right side.

THE SECRETORY PHASE The phase following ovulation is called the *postovulatory* or **secretory phase**. Some people refer to it as the *luteal phase*, which reflects the name given to the ruptured (graafian) follicle—the *corpus luteum*. Figures 2.14 and 2.15 show the transformation of the graafian follicle into the corpus luteum.

Under the influence of LH, the corpus luteum, which has remained in the ovary, begins to produce large amounts of progesterone and estrogen. Levels of these hormones peak at around the 20th or 21st day of an average cycle (see Figure 2.14). These hormones cause the glands in the endometrium to secrete nutrients to sustain a fertilized ovum that becomes implanted in the uterine wall.

If implantation does not occur, the hypothalamus responds to the peak levels of progesterone by signaling the pituitary to stop producing LH and FSH. This feedback process is similar to that of a thermostat in a house reacting to rising temperatures by shutting down the furnace. The levels of LH and FSH decline rapidly, leading the corpus luteum to decompose. After its decomposition, levels of estrogen and progesterone fall precipitously. The corpus luteum sows the seeds of its own destruction: Its hormones signal the brain to shut down secretion of substances that maintain it.

Figure 2.15 Maturation and Eventual Decomposition of an Ovarian Follicle.

Many follicles develop and produce estrogen during the proliferative phase of the menstrual cycle. Usually only one, the graafian follicle, ruptures and releases an ovum. The graafian follicle then develops into the corpus luteum, which produces copious quantities of estrogen and progesterone. Unless fertilization occurs, the corpus luteum decomposes.

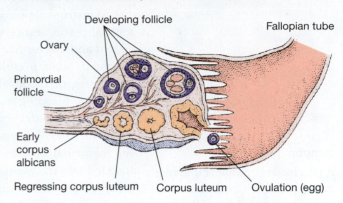

ovulatory phase

The second stage of the menstrual cycle, during which a follicle ruptures and releases a mature ovum.

zygote

A fertilized ovum (egg cell).

mittelschmerz

Pain that occurs during ovulation, midway between menstrual periods. (German for "middle pain.")

secretory phase

The third phase of the menstrual cycle, which follows ovulation. Also referred to as the *luteal phase*, after the *corpus luteum*, which begins to secrete large amounts of progesterone and estrogen following ovulation.

menstrual phase

The fourth phase of the menstrual cycle, during which the endometrium is sloughed off in the menstrual flow.

tampon

A plug made of cotton or a similar material that is inserted into the vagina to absorb the menstrual flow.

THE MENSTRUAL PHASE: AN END AND A BEGINNING The **menstrual phase** occurs when decreasing estrogen and progesterone levels can no longer sustain the uterine lining. The lining then disintegrates and is discharged from the body along with the menstrual flow.

The low estrogen levels of the menstrual phase signal the hypothalamus to release Gn-RH, which in turn stimulates the pituitary to secrete FSH. The FSH, in turn, prompts ovarian secretion of estrogen and the onset of another proliferative phase. Thus, a new cycle begins. The menstrual phase is a beginning as well as an end.

Menstrual flow contains blood from the endometrium (uterine lining), endometrial tissue, and cervical and vaginal mucus. Although the flow can appear persistent and last for five days or more, most women lose only a total of 2 or 3 ounces of blood (4 to 6 tablespoonfuls). A typical blood donor, by contrast, donates 16 ounces of blood at a sitting. Extremely heavy or prolonged (over a week) menstrual bleeding may reflect health problems and should be discussed with a healthcare provider.

Prior to 1933, women generally used external sanitary napkins or pads to absorb the menstrual flow. In that year, however, tampons were introduced. **Tampons** are inserted into the vagina and left in place to absorb menstrual fluid. Women who use tampons can swim without concern while menstruating, wear more revealing or comfortable apparel, and feel less burdened. Questions have arisen about whether or not tampons cause or exacerbate infections, such as *toxic shock syndrome (TSS)*, which is sometimes fatal. Signs of TSS include fever, headache, sore throat, vomiting, diarrhea, muscle aches, rash, and dizziness. Peeling skin, disorientation, and a plunge in blood pressure may follow. TSS is caused by the *Staphylococcus aureus* ("staph") bacterium, which is most likely to overbreed when highly absorbent tampons are left in place for many hours. As a result, many women now use regular rather than superabsorbent tampons. Others change their tampons three or four times a day, or alternate them with sanitary napkins. Women are encouraged to consult their healthcare providers about TSS.

Real Students, Real Questions

Q *As a guy, I don't really know what girls go through day to day when they have their period. I also don't have a sister. Do they use more than one tampon a day? Do they leave the tampon in? Do all girls use tampons? I want to understand what they actually have to go through.*

A In developed nations today, many women use tampons or feminine napkins and change them several times a day. So-called superabsorbent tampons, which could be left in for much or most of a day, have gone out of fashion because of the risk of toxic shock syndrome. In most cases, there is probably also less blood than you would imagine. However, many females experience premenstrual or menstrual pain (especially cramping) and some irritability. Both are uncomfortable, but absolutely normal. At the time of the sexual revolution, sexologists and social critics minimized premenstrual syndrome (PMS) and other menstrual problems as a way of minimizing gender differences in general. Today, however, menstrual problems are accepted as widely occurring and reflective of female sexual anatomy and physiology. Now the question is, how can we help women who encounter such difficulties? It's not how can we pretend they don't exist.

Sex During Menstruation

Many couples continue to have sex during menstruation; others abstain. Some people abstain because of religious prohibitions. Others express concern about the "fuss" or the "mess" of the menstrual flow.

> **8 › T / F Truth or Fiction Revisited** Despite traditional attitudes that associate menstruation with uncleanliness, there is no evidence that coitus during menstruation is physically harmful to either partner. Ironically, menstrual coitus may be helpful to the woman. The uterine contractions that occur during orgasm may help relieve cramping by dispelling blood congestion (Masters & Johnson, 1966). Orgasm from masturbation may have the same effect.

Women may be sexually aroused at any time during the menstrual cycle. The preponderance of the research evidence, however, points to a peak in sexual desire in women around the time of ovulation.

Human sexual patterns during the phases of the menstrual cycle reflect personal decisions and not just hormone fluctuations. Some couples may decide to increase their frequency of coitus at ovulation to optimize the chances of conceiving or to abstain during menstruation because of cultural or religious beliefs. Some may also increase their coital activity preceding menstruation to compensate for anticipated abstinence during menses or to increase coital activity afterward to make up for deprivation. In contrast, females of other species that are bound by the estrous cycle generally respond sexually only during **estrus**.

estrus
The period of time, as controlled by hormone levels, during which females in many species are most receptive to sexual activity.

Menopause, Perimenopause, and the Climacteric

LO 2.6 Define and discuss menopause, perimenopause, and the climacteric.

Two years after she had her breasts removed, Angela Jolie decided to remove her ovaries. In addition to having the *BRCA1* gene, three women in her family had died from cancer. As a result of the operation, she was placed in a "forced menopause"—meaning that female sex hormones from her ovaries would no longer be circulating in her bloodstream.

> I have a little clear patch that contains bio-identical estrogen. A progesterone IUD was inserted in my uterus. It will help me maintain a hormonal balance, but more important it will help prevent uterine cancer… I feel at ease with whatever will come, not because I am strong but because this is a part of life.
>
> —*Angelina Jolie (2013)*

Menopause, or the "change of life," is the cessation of menstruation. Menopause is a process that most commonly occurs between the ages of 46 and 50 and lasts for about two years. However, it may begin any time between the ages of 35 and 60.

Perimenopause refers to the beginning of menopause and is usually characterized by 3 to 11 months of amenorrhea (lack of menstruation) or irregular periods. Perimenopause ends with menopause. Menopause, in other words, is a specific event in a longer-term process known as the **climacteric** ("critical period"). The term *climacteric* specifically refers to the gradual decline in the reproductive capacity of the ovaries. The climacteric generally lasts about 15 years, from about ages 45 to 60. After age 35 or so, the menstrual cycles of many women shorten, from an average of 28 days to 25 days at age 40 and to 23 days by the mid-40s. By the end of her 40s, a woman's cycle may become erratic, with some periods close together and others missed.

In menopause, the pituitary gland continues to pour normal levels of FSH and LH into the bloodstream; but, for reasons that are not well understood, the ovaries gradually lose their capacity to respond. The ovaries no longer ripen egg cells or produce the sex hormones estrogen and progesterone.

menopause
The cessation of menstruation.

perimenopause
The beginning of menopause, as characterized by 3 to 11 months of amenorrhea or irregular periods.

climacteric
A long-term process, including menopause, that involves the gradual decline in the reproductive capacity of the ovaries.

Osteoporosis: Not for Women Only.
Men make up about one osteoporosis patient in five in the United States. Men are at lower risk for osteoporosis because they generally have larger, stronger bones than women do. Estrogen replacement lowers a woman's risk of osteoporosis, but there are risks to hormone replacement therapy (HRT).

The deficit in estrogen may lead to a number of unpleasant peri-menopausal sensations, such as night sweats and hot flashes (suddenly feeling hot) and hot flushes (suddenly looking reddened). Hot flashes and flushes may alternate with cold sweats, in which a woman feels suddenly cold and clammy. Anyone who has experienced "cold feet" or hands from anxiety or fear will understand how dramatic the shifting patterns of blood flow can be. Hot flashes and flushes stem largely from "waves" of dilation of blood vessels across the face and upper body. All of these sensations reflect *vasomotor instability*. That is, there are disruptions in the body mechanisms that dilate or constrict the blood vessels to maintain an even body temperature. Additional signs of estrogen deficiency include dizziness, headaches, pains in the joints, sensations of tingling in the hands or feet, burning or itchy skin, and heart palpitations. The skin usually becomes drier. Women may also encounter sleep problems, such as awakening more frequently at night and having difficulty falling back to sleep. Many perimenopausal women also experience migraine headaches.

There is some loss of breast tissue, vulvovaginal atrophy (loss of tissue in the genital region), and decreased vaginal lubrication during sexual arousal. Surveys by the North American Menopause Society (2013) asked women how vaginal discomfort affected them. This is what they reported:

- Eighty percent reported that vaginal discomfort negatively affected them, and 25% said it reduced their quality of life
- Thirty-six percent reported that it made them feel old, and 26% said it lowered their self-esteem
- three in four (75%) said that vaginal discomfort impaired their sex life, and one in three (33%) reported that it impacted their marriage or primary relationship
- Twenty-nine percent said that it had a negative effect on their sleep patterns

SEX IN THE DIGITAL AGE

EXPERIENCING THE SYMPTOMS OF MENOPAUSE? THERE'S AN APP FOR THAT

Many millions of American women have symptoms of menopause. In fact, the numbers increase by about 2 million per year, as women reach the latter years of middle adulthood. Yet there are few centralized sources of information about the symptoms and what to do about them. Treatment possibilities are also controversial because some of the most effective—hormone replacement therapies—are connected with risks of cardiovascular problems and cancer of the reproductive organs.

In an effort to help women, the North American Menopause Society (NAMS) created a free app, MenoPro, that works with smartphones and tablet

computers. A sister app is available to aid physicians in diagnostic work and in sifting through treatment options. Women answer series of questions to determine, first of all, whether their symptoms are connected with menopause and to help assess their severity. Based on their responses, they can receive information about nonprescription approaches such as changes in lifestyle and prescription medications, including hormone replacement therapies. By the way, women considering hormone therapy are encourage to try changes in their lifestyle for a few months before turning to medicine. Sometimes it's enough.

Long-term estrogen deficiency has also been linked to brittleness and porosity of the bones, known as **osteoporosis**. Bones break more readily, and some women develop "dowager's hump." Osteoporosis can be handicapping, even life-threatening. The increased brittleness of the bones increases the risk of serious fractures, especially of the hip, and many older women never recover from them. Estrogen deficiency can also impair cognitive functioning and feelings of psychological well-being.

osteoporosis

A condition caused by long-term estrogen deficiency that is characterized by a decline in bone density, such that bones become porous and brittle.

Hormone Replacement Therapy: Good Medicine or Menace?

Candace tried almost everything to manage her discomforts of perimenopause: a chiropractor, acupuncture, anti-anxiety pills, soy tablets, and herbal remedies. Finally, she relented and followed her doctor's recommendation that she use **hormone replacement therapy (HRT)**. The doctor's believed that for Candace, age 51, the immediate benefits, outweighed the risks (Rabin, 2006).

Some women with severe physical symptoms, like Candace, have been helped by HRT medication, which typically consists of synthetic estrogen and progesterone. The hormones are used to offset the losses of their naturally occurring counterparts. Hormone replacement therapy may help reduce the hot flushes and other symptoms brought about by hormonal deficiencies during menopause (Hunter, 2011). There is also evidence that estrogen replacement lowers women's risks of osteoporosis (Lindsay, 2011). The connection between estrogen and colon cancer is unclear (Clendenen et al., 2009). Use of vaginal estrogen has been shown to be helpful with vulvovaginal atrophy (North American Menopause Society, 2013). So do moisturizers.

Yet, HRT is controversial. Although it has been helpful to many women, the Women's Health Initiative study of some 16,600 postmenopausal women aged 50 to 79 found that exposure to a combination of estrogen and progestin appears to increase the risk of breast cancer, strokes, and blot clots, and did not have a protective effect on the heart (Chlebowski et al., 2003). (Progestin is used along with estrogen because estrogen alone exposes women to a greater risk of uterine cancer.) In addition to stimulating the growth of breast cancer, the combination of hormones also makes the tumors harder to detect, causing dangerous delays in diagnosis (American Cancer Society, 2016d). During the course of the Chlebowski study, of 8,506 women on HRT, 199 developed invasive breast cancers, as compared with 150 cases among the 8,102 women taking a placebo (Chlebowski et al., 2003). Also, despite having yearly mammograms, 25.4% of the women who developed cancer while using HRT had cancers that had begun to metastasize, as compared with 16% of those taking the placebo.

Although estrogen stimulates proliferation of breast cancer cells, research suggests that women who have had hysterectomies might actually have a lower risk of breast cancer (Anderson et al., 2012). The researchers point out the importance of distinguishing between hormone therapy that is estrogen-only versus estrogen plus progestin.

HRT also appears to increase the risk of lung cancer in postmenopausal women who smoke or smoked (Chlebowski et al., 2009). Rowan Chlebowski, the first author of the study that detected this association, writes, "The clear message is don't smoke and take hormones."

Levels of LDL ("bad cholesterol") rise among menopausal women, whereas levels of HDL ("good cholesterol") decrease (Altunkaynak et al., 2012). A number of studies suggest that HRT raises levels of HDL and lowers levels of LDL (Altunkaynak et al., 2012). Because high levels of LDL are connected with cardiovascular disease, it was believed that HRT would reduce the risk of heart disease in postmenopausal women. Although this view was supported in research following 120,000 nurses over the years, the women in the Hormone Replacement Therapy trial of the Women's Health Initiative apparently ran a slightly *greater* risk of heart attacks and strokes (Fletcher & Colditz, 2002).

hormone replacement therapy (HRT)

The administration of hormones such as estrogen and progestin to alleviate health problems associated with the loss of natural hormones.

Because of these concerns, the number of women using HRT has fallen. But more recent research from the Nurses Health Study (Grodstein et al., 2006) suggests that the women in the Women's Health Initiative trials might have been too old to profit from HRT—an average age of 64 when the average age of menopause is closer to 51. The arteries of women in their 50s are more elastic than those of women in their 60s, and estrogen might help them remain supple and reduce the buildup of plaque. But women in their 60s generally have less flexible arteries and some plaque. Because estrogen can increase the clotting of blood, it might pose a risk to the older women, even if it helps the younger women.

What can we conclude? Research results on the benefits and dangers of HRT are mixed, and women considering HRT are well advised to explore the latest findings with their healthcare providers. They might also consider alternatives. Selective serotonin reuptake inhibitors (SSRIs), such as Lexapro, Prozac, and Zocor are of help (Utian, 2012). Women using SSRIs to treat hot flashes usually take half the dose used to treat depression, which is their main usage, although they are also helpful with premenstrual syndrome (PMS), premenstrual dysphoric disorder (PMDD), eating disorders, and other problems.

Vaginal dryness can be treated with estrogens that are used locally—that is, placed in the vagina rather than the bloodstream, as hormones usually are. Creams (e.g., Estrace), suppositories (Vagifem), and a plastic ring (Estring) are available for this purpose.

Drinking milk, which is high in calcium, increases bone density among girls and is likely to help prevent against osteoporosis later in life. Calcium supplements and the bisphosphonates (Actonel or Fosamax) also help maintain bone strength.

Critical Thinking
Why might a woman be justified in complaining that she is confused about the evidence concerning the effects of HRT?

A CLOSER LOOK

MYTHS ABOUT MENOPAUSE

Menopause is certainly a major life change for most women. For many women, menopause symbolizes the many midlife issues they face, including changes in appearance, sexuality, and health. And yet, exactly what types of changes do we find? Many of us harbor misleading ideas about menopause—ideas that can be harmful to women. Consider the following myths and the realities. To which myths have you fallen prey?

- *Menopause is abnormal.* Of course not. Menopause is a normal development in women's lives.
- *The medical establishment considers menopause a disease.* No longer. Menopause is described as a "deficiency syndrome" today, referring to the decline in secretion of estrogen and progesterone. Unfortunately, the term *deficiency* also has negative meanings.
- *After menopause, women need complete replacement of estrogen.* Not necessarily. Some estrogen continues to be produced by the adrenal glands, fatty tissue, and the brain.
- *Menopause is accompanied by depression and anxiety.* Sometimes but not necessarily. A number of reviews of the literature have found no consistent relationship between menopause and these psychological symptoms. A Dutch study followed 2,103 females aged 46 to 54 for five years. During this time, the number of women who reached postmenopausal status doubled, and the

percentage of women reporting depression increased from 18.5 to 23.7% (Maartens et al., 2002). The increase is unlikely to be the result of chance, but more than three out of four women in the study did not report significant levels of depression or anxiety at any time during the experience of menopause.

- *A woman who has had a hysterectomy will not undergo menopause afterward.* Actually, it depends on whether the ovaries (the major producers of estrogen) were also removed. If they were not, menopause should proceed normally.
- *A woman's general level of activity is lower after menopause.* Many postmenopausal women become peppier and more assertive.
- *At menopause, women experience debilitating hot flashes.* Sometimes but not necessarily. Many women do not have hot flashes at menopause. Among those who do, the flashes are often mild. But let us recognize that some women do have disturbing hot flashes; we advise them to consult their gynecologists.
- *Menopause signals an end to a woman's sexual appetite.* It is not true that menopause signals an end to women's sexual appetite (Gass et al., 2011). In fact, some women feel newly sexually liberated because of the separation of sex from pregnancy.

Some women use HRT to help get through the years leading up to menopause and then stop it. At this time, it appears that the one thing we can predict is that different healthcare providers are likely to have different views on the matter.

Menstrual Problems

LO 2.7 **Define menstrual problems and discuss what can be done about them.**

Although menstruation is a natural biological process, the majority of women experience some discomfort prior to or during menstruation (Studd & Nappi, 2012). The problems we explore in this section include dysmenorrhea, mastalgia, menstrual migraine headaches, amenorrhea, PMS, and premenstrual dysphoric disorder (PMDD).

Dysmenorrhea

Pain or discomfort during menstruation—**dysmenorrhea**—is the most common menstrual problem. Most women at some time have at least mild menstrual pain or discomfort, so it is perfectly normal, even if annoying. Pelvic cramps are the most common manifestation of dysmenorrhea. They may be accompanied by headache, backache, nausea, or bloated feelings. Women who develop severe cases usually do so within a few years of menarche. **Primary dysmenorrhea** refers to menstrual pain or discomfort in the absence of known organic pathology. Women with **secondary dysmenorrhea** have identified organic problems that are believed to cause their menstrual problems. Their pain or discomfort is caused by, or secondary to, these problems. Endometriosis, pelvic inflammatory disease, and ovarian cysts are just a few of the organic disorders that can give rise to secondary dysmenorrhea.

Evidence is accumulating, however, that supposed primary dysmenorrhea is often secondary to hormonal changes, although the precise causes have not been delineated. For example, menstrual cramps sometimes decrease dramatically after childbirth, as a result of the massive hormonal changes that occur with pregnancy. Women who have been pregnant report a lower incidence of menstrual pain but a higher incidence of premenstrual symptoms and menstrual discomfort.

Menstrual cramps appear to result from uterine spasms that may be brought about by copious secretion of hormones called **prostaglandins**. Prostaglandins apparently cause muscle fibers in the uterine wall to contract, as during labor. Most contractions go unnoticed, but powerful, persistent contractions are discomfiting in themselves and may temporarily deprive the uterus of oxygen, another source of distress. Women with more intense menstrual discomfort apparently produce higher quantities of prostaglandins. Prostaglandin-inhibiting drugs, such as ibuprofen, indomethacin, and aspirin, are often helpful. Menstrual pain may also be secondary to endometriosis.

Pelvic pressure and bloating may be traced to pelvic *edema* (Greek for "swelling")—the congestion of fluid in the pelvic region. Fluid retention can lead to a gain of several pounds, sensations of heaviness, and **mastalgia**—a swelling of the breasts that sometimes causes premenstrual discomfort. Masters and Johnson (1966) noted that orgasm can help relieve menstrual discomfort by reducing the pelvic congestion that spawns bloating and pressure. Orgasm may also increase the menstrual flow and shorten this phase of the cycle.

Headaches frequently accompany menstrual discomfort. Most headaches (in both females and males) stem from simple muscle tension, notably in the shoulders, the back of the neck, and the scalp. Pelvic discomfort may cause muscle contractions, therefore contributing to the tension that produces headaches. Women who are tense about their menstrual flow are thus candidates for muscle tension headaches. Migraine headaches may arise from changes in the blood flow in the brain, however. Migraines are typically limited to one side of the head and are often accompanied by visual difficulties.

dysmenorrhea

Pain or discomfort during menstruation.

primary dysmenorrhea

Menstrual pain or discomfort that occurs in the absence of known organic problems.

secondary dysmenorrhea

Menstrual pain or discomfort that is caused by identified organic problems.

prostaglandins

Hormones that cause muscle fibers in the uterine wall to contract, as during labor.

mastalgia

A swelling of the breasts that sometimes causes premenstrual discomfort.

Amenorrhea

Amenorrhea is the absence of menstruation and is a primary sign of infertility. **Primary amenorrhea** describes the absence of menstruation in a woman who has not menstruated at all by about the age of 16 or 17. **Secondary amenorrhea** describes delayed or absent menstrual periods in women who have had regular periods in the past. Amenorrhea has various causes, including abnormalities in the structures of the reproductive system, hormonal abnormalities, growths such as cysts and tumors, and psychological problems, such as stress. Amenorrhea is normal during pregnancy and following menopause. Amenorrhea is also a symptom of **anorexia nervosa**, an eating disorder characterized by an intense fear of putting on weight and a refusal to eat enough to maintain a normal body weight, which often results in extreme (and sometimes life-threatening) weight loss. Hormonal changes that accompany emaciation are believed responsible for the cessation of menstruation. Amenorrhea may also occur in women who exercise strenuously, such as competitive long-distance runners (Berga & Naftolin, 2012). It is unclear whether the cessation of menstruation in female athletes is as a result of the effects of strenuous exercise itself, to related physical factors such as low body fat, to the stress of intensive training, or to a combination of factors.

Premenstrual Syndrome (PMS) and Premenstrual Dysphoric Disorder (PMDD)

The term **premenstrual syndrome (PMS)** describes the combination of physical and psychological symptoms that may affect women during the 4- to 6-day interval that precedes their menses each month. For many women, premenstrual symptoms persist during menstruation. **Premenstrual dysphoric disorder (PMDD)** is a more technical term used as a diagnostic category by the American Psychiatric Association (2013) in its *Diagnostic and Statistical Manual of the Mental Disorders* (the DSM–5). PMDD is more severe than PMS, and is characterized by the following symptoms:

- Depressed mood, as evidenced by crying and feelings of sadness, hopelessness, or worthlessness

- Withdrawal from activities that are usually sought out and enjoyed

- Difficulty concentrating and paying sustained attention to tasks

- Fatigue, lack of energy

- Feelings of tension and anxiety, being "on edge"

- Feelings of irritability or anger, possibly causing conflict with family members and others

- Feeling overwhelmed, that life is out of control

- Significant changes in appetite that can lead to binge eating or the craving of particular foods and often result in weight gain

- Problems in sleeping: sleeping too much (hypersomnia) or too little (insomnia)

- A variety of physical problems may also be present, such as swelling or tenderness of the breasts, pain in muscle, pain in joints, migraine headaches, and feeling bloated

Unlike PMS, PMDD is a persistent problem. The *DSM-V* does not apply the diagnosis unless the woman has experienced the problem during most menstrual cycles over a period of a year. Moreover, a number of the symptoms must be present. The *DSM-V* also requires that the symptoms impair the woman's life, perhaps her functioning at work or in an academic pursuit, perhaps in her social or family relationships.

The term *PMDD* is not always used precisely, and some make the mistake of confusing it with PMS. But the diagnosis of PMDD requires that five or more of the following symptoms be present most of the time during the week before the period and end within a few days after the period begins. At least one symptom must be one of the first four. In addition, to diagnose PMDD, the *DSM-V* requires that symptoms have been present for most menstrual cycles over the past year and that they notably impair functioning at work or school or in social activities and relationships.

Nearly three women in four experience some symptoms of PMS, and nearly half of women can be diagnosed with the problem (Direkvand-Moghadam et al., 2014). The most common symptoms are minor psychological discomfort, muscle tension, and aches or pains (Direkvand-Moghadam et al., 2014). The great majority of cases involve mild to moderate discomfort. Only a small minority of women report menstrual symptoms severe enough to impair their social, academic, or occupational functioning. The causes of PMS and PMDD are unclear, but researchers are looking to possible relationships between menstrual problems, including PMS and PMDD, and chemical imbalances in the body. Also, PMS and PMDD appear to be linked with imbalances in neurotransmitters such as serotonin (Direkvand-Moghadam et al., 2014). (Neurotransmitters are the chemical messengers in the nervous system.) Serotonin imbalances are also linked to changes in appetite. Women with PMS and PMDD show greater increases of appetite during the luteal phase than other women do. Another neurotransmitter, gamma-aminobutyric acid (GABA), also appears to be involved in premenstrual problems; medicines that affect the levels of GABA help many women with these problems (Bäckström et al., 2003). PMS and PMDD may well be caused by a complex interaction between ovarian hormones and neurotransmitters (Direkvand-Moghadam et al., 2014).

A couple of generations ago, premenstrual disorders were seen as "a woman's lot"—something women must put up with. No longer. Today there are many treatment options. These include exercise; dietary control (for example, eating several small meals a day rather than two or three large meals, limiting salt and sugar, supplementing diet with vitamins); hormone treatments (usually progestin); and medications that reduce anxiety or increase the amount of serotonin in the nervous system. If you have severe or disabling symptoms, you may be diagnosable with PMDD. What can women do about PMS or PMDD? Check with your gynecologist and consider the suggestions in the following section.

How to Handle Menstrual Discomfort

Most women experience some menstrual discomfort. Women with persistent menstrual distress may profit from the suggestions listed here. Researchers are exploring the effectiveness of these techniques in controlled studies. You might consider trying the suggestions that sound right for you—all of them, if you wish. Try them for a few months to see if you reap any benefits.

- Don't blame yourself! Menstrual problems were once erroneously attributed to women's "hysterical" nature. This is nonsense. Menstrual problems appear, in large part, to reflect hormonal variations or chemical fluctuations in the brain during the menstrual cycle. Researchers have not yet fully identified all the causal elements and patterns, but their lack of knowledge does not mean that women who have menstrual problems are hysterical.

- Keep a menstrual calendar so that you can track your menstrual symptoms systematically and identify patterns.

- Develop strategies for dealing with days that you experience the greatest distress—strategies that will help enhance your pleasure and minimize the stress affecting you on those days. Activities that distract you from your menstrual discomfort may be helpful. Go see a movie or get into that novel you've been meaning to read.

- Consider whether you harbor self-defeating attitudes toward menstruation that might compound distress. Do close relatives or friends see menstruation as an illness, a time of "pollution," a "dirty thing"? Have you adopted any of these attitudes—if not verbally, then in ways that affect your behavior, such as by restricting your social activities during your period?

- See a gynecologist about your concerns, especially if you have severe symptoms. Severe menstrual symptoms can be secondary to medical disorders such as endometriosis and pelvic inflammatory disease (PID). Check it out.

- Ask your gynecologist about oral contraceptives that reduce the number of menstrual periods to four per year (Seasonale or Seasonique) or one per year (Lybrel). Still others shorten periods.

- Develop nutritious eating habits—and continue them throughout the entire cycle (that means always). Consider limiting intake of alcohol, caffeine, fats, salt, and sweets, especially during the days preceding menstruation. A low-fat, vegetarian diet may reduce the duration and intensity of PMS.

- Eat several smaller meals (or nutritious snacks) throughout the day, rather than a few highly filling meals.

- Some women find that vigorous exercise—jogging, swimming, bicycling, fast walking, dancing, skating, even jumping rope—helps relieve premenstrual and menstrual discomfort. Evidence suggests that exercise helps to relieve and possibly prevent menstrual discomfort (Daley, 2009).

- Check with your doctor about vitamin and mineral supplements (such as calcium and magnesium).

- Ibuprofen (brand names Medipren, Advil, Motrin, etc.) and other medicines available over the counter may be helpful for cramping. Prescription drugs such as anti-anxiety drugs (e.g., alprazolam) and anti-depressant drugs (selective serotonin reuptake inhibitors or SSRIs) may also be of help. Anti-depressants affect levels of neurotransmitters in a way that can be helpful for women with PMS or PMDD. Their benefits do not mean that women with PMS or PMDD are depressed. Ask your doctor for a recommendation.

- Remind yourself that menstrual problems are time limited. Don't worry about getting through life or a career. Just get through the next couple of days.

In this chapter we have explored female sexual anatomy and physiology. In the following chapter, we turn our attention to the male.

Exercise as a Strategy for Coping with Menstrual Discomfort. Some women find that vigorous exercise helps relieve menstrual discomfort. There are many other strategies. Check with your doctor; in this "day and age," women should never suffer in silence.

Chapter Review

LO 2.1   Describe the external female sex organs and their functions.

The mons veneris is a mound of fatty tissue that covers the pubic area. The labia majora are large folds of skin that run downward from the mons along the sides of the vulva. The labia minora are hairless membranes that surround the urethral and vaginal openings. The clitoris is highly sensitive to sexual sensation but not directly involved in reproduction. The vestibule contains the openings to the vagina and the urethra. Urine passes from the female's body through the urethral opening. The vaginal opening, or introitus, lies below the urethral opening.

LO 2.2   Describe the internal female sex organs, their functions, and health problems that may affect them.

Menstrual flow and babies pass from the uterus to the outer world through the vagina. During coitus, the vagina contains the penis. The cervix contains an opening called the os. Cervical cancer is connected with HPV and detectable via a Pap test. The uterus is the pear-shaped organ in which a fertilized ovum implants and develops until birth. The uterine lining is called the endometrium. Ova pass through the fallopian tubes on their way to the uterus and are normally fertilized within these tubes. The ovaries produce ova and the sex hormones estrogen and progesterone.

LO 2.3   Describe the composition and functions of the breasts.

The breasts are secondary sex characteristics that contain mammary glands that make it possible for women to nurse children. Their size reflects the amount of fatty tissue present.

LO 2.4   Discuss risk factors for and detection and treatment of breast cancer.

Women with breast cancer have lumps in the breast, but most lumps are benign. Risk factors include family history, BRCA1 or BRCA2 mutations, exposure to estrogen, and alcohol.

LO 2.5   Describe the regulation and the phases of the menstrual cycle.

Menstruation is the cyclical bleeding that stems from the shedding of the endometrium when a reproductive cycle has not led to the fertilization of an ovum. The cycle has four phases: proliferative, ovulatory, secretory, and menstrual. During the first phase, ova ripen within their follicles and endometrial tissue proliferates. During the second phase, ovulation occurs. During the third phase, the corpus luteum produces copious amounts of progesterone and estrogen that cause the endometrium to thicken. If the ovum goes unfertilized, a plunge in estrogen and progesterone levels triggers the fourth, or menstrual, phase.

LO 2.6   Define and discuss menopause, perimenopause, and the climacteric.

Menopause is the cessation of menstruation. Perimenopause is the beginning of menopause and is characterized by irregular periods or amenorrhea. The climacteric is a multiyear process marked by declining levels of estrogen and ending in menopause. Hormone replacement therapy offsets losses of estrogen and progesterone and can help women with perimenopausal and postmenopausal symptoms, including night sweats, hot flashes, hot flushes, dry skin, loss of breast tissue, and decreased vaginal lubrication. But HRT has been linked to an increased risk of breast and endometrial cancers.

LO 2.7   Define menstrual problems and discuss what can be done about them.

Dysmenorrhea—painful menstruation—is the most common menstrual problem, and pelvic cramps are the most common symptom. Amenorrhea—the lack of menstruation—can be caused by abnormalities in the structures of the reproductive system, hormonal abnormalities, cysts, tumors, and stress. Premenstrual syndrome (PMS) can be characterized by depression and anxiety, irritability, difficulty concentrating, migraines, breast tenderness, and bloating. Premenstrual dysphoric disorder (PMDD) is like a severe case of PMS, said to occur when symptoms are extreme and impair functioning in school, at work, or in relationships.

Test Your Learning

1. HPV is connected with _____
   (a) cervical cancer.
   (b) endometrial cancer.
   (c) breast cancer.
   (d) ovarian cancer.

2. Urine passes through the _____
   (a) uterus.
   (b) urethra.
   (c) cervix.
   (d) introitus.

3. Menstrual cramps are thought to be caused by _____
   (a) estrogen.
   (b) progesterone.
   (c) prostaglandins.
   (d) testosterone.

4. Hot flashes and flushes stem largely from waves of dilation of _____
   (a) the cervix.
   (b) blood vessels.
   (c) ovarian follicles.
   (d) muscles.

5. The endometrium develops during the _____ phase of the menstrual cycle.
   (a) ovulatory
   (b) menstrual
   (c) secretory
   (d) proliferative

6. A surge of _____ triggers ovulation.
   (a) follicle stimulating hormone
   (b) luteinizing hormone
   (c) oxytocin
   (d) prolactin

7. The _____ is the only organ whose only known purpose is the experiencing of sexual pleasure.
   (a) cervix
   (b) vagina
   (c) breast
   (d) clitoris

8. For women who obtain HRT, combining estrogen with _____ lessens the risk of endometrial cancer.
   (a) progestin
   (b) prolactin
   (c) oxytocin
   (d) prostaglandins

9. Skeptics concerning the G spot are most likely to argue that _____
   (a) the anterior vaginal wall is not sensitive to erotic stimulation.
   (b) the G spot is not a discrete sex organ.
   (c) no research has been done into the existence of the G spot.
   (d) *G spot* is a silly name for a sex organ.

10. When the hypothalamus senses a low level of estrogen in the blood, it increases secretion of Gn-RH, which in turn triggers the pituitary gland to release _____
    (a) FSH.
    (b) LH.
    (c) the graafian follicle.
    (d) prolactin.

Answers: 1. a; 2. b; 3. c; 4. b; 5. d; 6. b; 7. d; 8. a; 9. b; 10. a

Chapter 3
Male Sexual Anatomy and Physiology

Learning Objectives

External Sex Organs

LO 3.1 Describe the external male sex organs and their functions.

LO 3.2 Discuss the pros and cons of circumcision.

Internal Sex Organs

LO 3.3 Describe the internal male sex organs and their functions.

Health Problems of the Urogenital System

LO 3.4 Discuss urethritis.

LO 3.5 Discuss testicular cancer.

LO 3.6 Discuss benign prostate hyperplasia.

LO 3.7 Discuss prostatitis.

LO 3.8 Discuss prostate cancer.

Male Sexual Functions

LO 3.9 Explain how erection occurs.

LO 3.10 Explain how ejaculation occurs.

TRUTH OR FICTION?

Which of the following statements are the truth, and which are fiction? Look for the Truth-or-Fiction items throughout this chapter to find the answers.

1 The penis contains bone and muscle. **T / F**?

2 The father determines the baby's sex. **T / F**?

3 *Semen* is a synonym for *sperm*. **T / F**?

4 Morning erections reflect the need to urinate. **T / F**?

5 Men can will themselves to have erections. **T / F**?

6 The penis has a mind of its own. **T / F**?

7 Many men who are paralyzed below the waist can attain erection, engage in sexual intercourse, and ejaculate. **T / F**?

In the predawn light of Western civilization, people engaged in phallic worship. Phallic symbols became glorified in art in the form of plows, axes, and swords. The ancient Greeks carried oversized images of fish as phallic symbols in their Dionysian processions, which celebrated the wilder and more frenzied aspects of human sexuality. The Greeks also adorned themselves with phallic rings and necklaces.

The ancient Romans honored Venus by outfitting a float in the shape of a large phallus and parading it through the streets. Men in Roman courts often swore to tell the truth with their hands on their genitals—as we swear to tell the truth by placing our hands on the Bible. The words *testes* and *testicles* derive from the same Latin word as "testify." The Latin *testis* means "witness."

Even today, men with large genitals are accorded respect from male peers and sometimes adoration from admirers (Crozier, 2012; Veale et al., 2015a). Given these cultural attitudes, it is not surprising that young men (and some not-so-young men) belittle themselves if they feel they do not measure up. Boys who mature late may be ridiculed by their peers. Adult men, too, may wonder whether their penises are large enough to satisfy lovers. Or they may fear that their partners' previous lovers had larger genitals.

In this chapter we examine male sexual anatomy and physiology, and we attempt to sort out truth from fiction. As in our exploration of female sexual physiology and anatomy, we begin with the external genitalia and then move inward. Once inside, we focus on the route of sperm through the male reproductive system.

Real Students, Real Questions

Q *Are men really that obsessed with their penises? Why?*

A Some are, and for them the obsession can be a serious psychological problem, although their concerns are often "exaggerated"—to choose an ironic term. A large penis is generally considered a plus in our culture. A large penis can earn the respect of peers in the locker room and, at least in the mind of the individual, a positive response from female partners. On the other hand, males with average or somewhat smaller-than-average penises tend to become less concerned with size so long as their sex partner or partners are adequately aroused by them.

External Sex Organs

LO 3.1 **Describe the external male sex organs and their functions.**

The external male sex organs include the penis and the scrotum (see Figures 3.1 and 3.2).

The Penis

The penis mightier than the sword.
    —*Mark Twain*

Is that a gun in your pocket, or are you just glad to see me?
    —*Mae West*

At first glance the penis may seem simple and obvious in its structures, particularly when compared to women's organs. Yet, as Figure 3.1 shows, the apparent simplicity of the penis is misleading. Much goes on below the surface.

The penis, like the vagina, is the sex organ used in sexual intercourse. But unlike the vagina, the penis serves as a conduit for urine. Both semen and urine pass through the urethral opening, or urethral *meatus* (pronounced me-ATE-us). The urethra is connected to the bladder, which is unrelated to reproduction, and to those parts of the reproductive system that transport semen.

1 › T / F **Truth or Fiction Revisited**   Fiction: there are no bones or muscles in the penis. Many mammals, including dogs, have penile bones that stiffen the penis to facilitate copulation. But despite the slang term *boner*, the human penis has no bones. Nor, despite another slang term, *muscle*, does the penis contain muscle tissue. However, muscles at the base of the penis, like the muscles surrounding the vaginal and urethral openings in women, are involved in urination and ejaculation.

Rather than bones or muscles, the penis contains three cylinders of spongy material that run its length and swell (become "engorged") with blood during sexual arousal, causing erection. The larger two, the **corpora cavernosa** (see Figures 3.1 and 3.2), lie side by side and function like the cavernous bodies in the clitoris. They fill with blood and stiffen when the male is aroused. In addition, a **corpus spongiosum** (spongy body) runs along the bottom, or ventral, surface of the penis. It contains the penile urethra that conducts urine to the urinary opening (urethral meatus) at the tip. Also at the tip, the spongy body enlarges into the glans, or head, of the penis.

The penile glans, like the clitoral glans, is highly sensitive to sexual stimulation, but direct, prolonged stimulation can become irritating. Most men prefer to masturbate by stroking the penile shaft rather than the glans. The **corona**, or coronal ridge, separates the glans from the body of the penis. It is also quite sensitive to sexual stimulation. The

corpora cavernosa
The larger two of the three cylinders of spongy tissue in the penis that become congested with blood and stiffen during sexual arousal.

corpus spongiosum
The spongy body that runs along the bottom of the penis, contains the penile urethra, and enlarges at the tip of the penis to form the glans.

corona
The ridge that separates the glans from the body of the penis.

Figure 3.1   The Penis.

During sexual arousal, the corpora cavernosa and corpus spongiosum become congested with blood, causing the penis to enlarge and stiffen.

Longitudinal Section

Cross Section

Figure 3.2 The Male Reproductive System.

The external male sex organs include the penis and the scrotum.

Urinary bladder
Vas deferens
Prostate gland
Corpus cavernosum
Penis
Urethra
Glans of penis
Prepuce (foreskin)

Seminal vesicle
Ejaculatory duct
Bulbourethral gland
Rectum
Corpus spongiosum
Epididymis
Testis
Scrotum

Seminiferous tubules

Real Students, Real Questions

Q *My penis curves to the right. Is this normal?*

A Sure. Penises do not tend to hang straight. As noted in the text, one testicle—usually the left testicle—tends to hang lower than the other because of the differential lengths of the spermatic cords. But you can consult your healthcare professional if you think the curvature is too great or find it in some way discomfiting.

---

frenulum

The sensitive strip of tissue that connects the underside of the penile glans to the shaft.

root

The base of the penis, which extends into the pelvis.

shaft

The body of the penis, which expands as a result of vasocongestion.

foreskin

The loose skin that covers the penile glans. Also referred to as the *prepuce.*

frenulum, a thin strip of tissue that connects the underside of the glans to the shaft, is also very sensitive. Most men find the top of the penis to be least sensitive.

The base of the penis, or **root**, extends into the pelvis. It is attached to the pelvic bone by leglike structures, called *crura,* similar to those that anchor the female's clitoris. The body of the penis is called the penile **shaft**. Unlike the clitoral shaft, it is free-swinging. Thus, the result of engorgement, erection, is obvious.

The skin of the penis is hairless and loose, allowing expansion during erection. It is fixed to the penile shaft just behind the glans. Some of it, however, like the labia minora in the female, folds over to partially cover the glans. This covering is the prepuce, or **foreskin**. It covers part or all of the penile glans just as the clitoral prepuce (hood) covers the clitoral shaft. The prepuce consists of loose skin that freely moves over the glans. However, *smegma*—a cheeselike, foul-smelling secretion—may accumulate below the foreskin, causing it to adhere to the glans.

CIRCUMCISION

LO 3.2 Discuss the pros and cons of circumcision.

Allison had her first son at the age of 37. Before the delivery, she focused on many issues. Was she going to use anesthesia during the delivery? (No.) Was she going to use disposable diapers or cloth diapers? (Cloth.) And was she going to breast-feed? (A resounding yes!) But she hadn't really thought about circumcision, so when her obstetrician recommended it, she just did it.

Figure 3.3   Normal Variations in the Male Genitals.

The penis and scrotum vary a good deal in appearance from one man to another. The penis in the photo to the right is uncircumcised.

Which is not to say the she regrets the decision, but just that not everyone in the United States does it. Male **circumcision** is surgical removal of the prepuce (see Figure 3.3). It has a long history as a religious rite. Jews traditionally carry out male circumcision shortly after a baby is born. Circumcision is performed as a sign of the covenant between God and the people of Abraham. Muslims also circumcise for religious reasons, although they tend do so some years later.

But the great majority of Americans are neither Jews nor Muslims, so circumcision has no religious meaning for them. For that reason, most American parents who decide to circumcise their sons do so for health reasons. And in recent years, opponents of circumcision have argued that it is a form of genital mutilation that is carried out without the consent of the person receiving it, who, in the United States, is usually a newborn baby. Moreover, circumcision is demonstrably painful, even if the boy does not remember the operation.

There is also some evidence that circumcision might reduce male sexual sensations because the foreskin is rich in nerve endings (Smith et al., 2010). Table 3.1 shows the findings of a British study of 6,293 men and 8,869 women (Homfray et al., 2015).

circumcision

Surgical removal of the foreskin of the penis.

Table 3.1 Variation in Prevalence of Sexual Function According to Circumcision Status Among Sexually Active Men, Aged 16–74

Experienced the following for 3 or more months over the last year	Circumcised men (%)	Uncircumcised men (%)
Lack of interest in sex	15.0	14.5
Lack of enjoyment in sex	4.8	4.8
Feeling anxious during sex	5.5	5.6
Feeling physical pain because of sex	1.8	1.9
Feeling no excitement or arousal during sex	3.2	3.5
Difficulty reaching orgasm	9.2	9.3
Reaching orgasm more quickly than you would like	14.0	15.3
Trouble getting or maintaining an erection	13.0	16.7*
Avoiding sex during due to sexual problems	10.9	10.2
Used sexual performance enhancing drugs (ever)	13.0	14.2

SOURCE: Adapted from Homfray et al., 2015. http://www.ncbi.nlm.nih.gov/pmc/articles/PMC4502984/table/T2/

*According to the authors, this difference was "close" to being large enough to be statistically significant; that is, not likely to be due to chance fluctuation.

Figure 3.4 Rates of Circumcision Performed on Male Newborn Infants Discharged From Short-Stay Hospitals, United States, 1979–2010.

SOURCE: Owings et al., 2013. http://www.cdc.gov/nchs/data/hestat/circumcision_2013/circumcision_2013.pdf

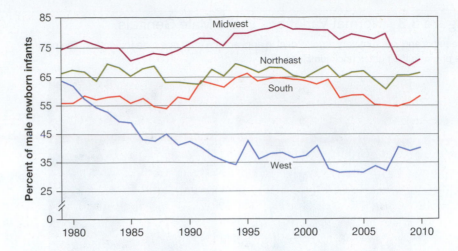

The participants were interviewed face-to-face online. Although it is difficult to estimate the extent to which findings might represent the British population at large, some interesting comparisons are possible. The findings suggest that circumcised men might be more subject to erectile problems than uncircumcised men, a difference that could represent less sensitivity to sexual stimulation. On the other hand, circumcised men were more likely to ejaculate more quickly than they would have liked, a finding that suggests that the *uncircumcised* men might have been more sensitive to sexual stimulation. Overall we would have to agree with the researchers that the study shows little if any difference in sexual pleasure, motivation, or response between the groups.

As shown in Figure 3.4, circumcision rates vary widely in the United States, from the majority of boys in the Midwest to about one in three in the West, where the number is depressed largely by the low rates of circumcision among Mexican immigrants and their descendants. Overall, about three boys in five in the United States are circumcised (Owings et al., 2013). Circumcision is uncommon in many other parts of the world, even in developed nations, and is rare in Latin America. Latin American immigration accounts for some of the disparity in circumcision rates across the United States (Morris et al., 2014). Figure 3.5 shows that the world's highest circumcision rates are found in countries where the population is largely or exclusively Muslim.

The American Academy of Pediatrics (AAP) issued statements that circumcision was unnecessary in 1999 and then again in 2005. For that reason, many health insurance companies stopped covering the cost of circumcision and many parents doubted its effectiveness. On the other hand, after much "obsessing" and a careful review of the research literature, the AAP reversed its position in 2012—sort of. The AAP

Figure 3.5 Prevalence of Circumcision around the Globe.

Circumcision is most prevalent in Islamic countries and in Israel. It is a religious rite in both places.

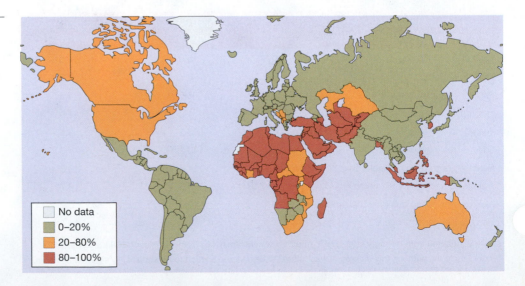

admitted that circumcision may protect heterosexual men, and their sex partners, against HIV (the virus that causes AIDS) and stated that the health benefits of circumcision were likely to outweigh any risks (American Academy of Pediatrics Task Force on Circumcision, 2012). But they still characterized circumcision as a family decision rather than wholeheartedly recommending it. But in 2014 the CDC strongly endorsed the health benefits of circumcision (Stobbe, 2014).

In fact, the evidence seems overwhelming that circumcision has many health benefits (Morris et al., 2014; Stobbe, 2014; Wright et al., 2012). Circumcision lessens the risk of infections of the urinary tract, including infections by the human papilloma virus (HPV) and by HIV (the virus that causes AIDS), and even the risk of prostate cancer, whose development appears to be facilitated by infections. Randomized trials in sub-Saharan Africa have shown that men who are circumcised are about 51% to 60% less likely to be infected with HIV via intercourse with prostitutes—a common sexual outlet in the region (Tobian & Gray, 2011). About 5 million African non-Muslim men have been circumcised to help prevent infection by HIV (Reed et al., 2015).

The protective effects of circumcision are likely to reflect a lower incidence of local inflammation and genital ulcers, both of which provide ports of entry for HIV, and the removal of cells in the foreskin—Langerhans cells—that are receptive to infection by HIV. Other studies have found that circumcised males are about 30% less likely to contract genital herpes (Morris et al., 2014; Tobian & Gray, 2011). In a study of 4,000 men, men who had been circumcised were 15% less likely to develop prostate cancer than those who had not (Wright et al., 2012).

Circumcision also has notable health benefits for *women*—that is, for the sex partners of circumcised men. Generally speaking, if a woman's male partner is less likely to have sexually transmitted infections, so is she. But more specifically, the female partners of circumcised men are 28% less likely to be infected with HPV (the virus that is connected with cervical cancer), 40% less likely to develop bacterial vaginosis, and 48% less likely to develop trichomoniasis (Tobian & Gray, 2011).

Physicians once agreed that circumcision is the treatment for **phimosis**, a condition in which is it difficult to retract the foreskin from the glans. But today, men with phimosis are less likely to be circumcised for that reason.

Here's what we need to know about male circumcision:

- Circumcision is recommended by the American Academy of Pediatrics and by the CDC.

- The majority of newborn boys in the United States are circumcised before the leaving the hospital in which they were born; many others are circumcised later on.

- There are cultural differences, with Jews and Muslims practicing universal male circumcision and Hispanic Americans least likely to be circumcised.

- Circumcision cuts down infection rates by many disease agents, including HIV, both for those who are circumcised and their sex partners.

- Circumcision can be painful, but health professionals can use local anesthetics to reduce the discomfort.

- There is no conclusive evidence that circumcision impairs sexual functioning or diminishes sexual pleasure.

phimosis
A condition in which the foreskin is so tight that it cannot be withdrawn from the glans.

Critical Thinking
What are the similarities and differences between male circumcision and female circumcision (clitoridectomy), as described in Chapter 2?

PENIS SIZE

IRAS: *Am I not an inch of fortune better than she?*

CHARMIAN: *Well, if you were but an inch of fortune better than I, where would you choose it?*

IRAS: *Not in my husband's nose.*

—William Shakespeare, *Antony and Cleopatra*

In our culture, the size of the penis is often seen as a measure of a man's masculinity and his ability to please his sex partner (Veale et al., 2015a). Shakespeare and other writers inform us that men have looked down at themselves for centuries, sometimes in delight but more often in chagrin. Some men are so distraught about the size of their penises that they become preoccupied with it and are at risk for developing what the American Psychiatric Association (2013) lists as a mental disorder: *body dysphoric disorder* (Veale et al., 2015a). Men who are heralded for their sexual or reproductive feats are presumed to have more prominent "testaments" to their manhood. Clinical experience with dysfunctional couples suggests that women are more likely to complain about their partner's communication ability or the feeling or tone of their relationship rather than the size of his penis (Zilbergeld, 1999). Many dissatisfied men are comparing their penis size with the size of penises they view in pornography (Cranney, 2015; Veale et al., 2015a).

One study presented women with three-dimensional models of penises and asked them to select the penis size they would prefer (Prause et al., 2015). The average model selected for a one-time encounter was 6.4 inches and for a long-term relationship, 6.3 inches. What is the reality? Consider a meta-analysis of 20 studies of penis size that yielded a total sample of 15,521 men (Veale et al., 2015b). People who had believed the commonly held notion that the average erect penis is 6 inches in length might be surprised to learn that the length of the average penis in the meta-analysis was 5.16 inches. (The average flaccid [soft] penis was 3.6 inches in length.) Now here is a disconnect: 85% of women say they are satisfied with the length of their partner's penis (Veale et al., 2015b). In other words, when women considered their relationships with their own partners, penis size was apparently one of a cluster of factors, and

SEX IN THE DIGITAL AGE

SEXINFO ONLINE—PENIS ENLARGEMENT?

Brought to you from the Sociology Department of the University of California at Santa Barbara: how to (maybe) and how *not* to increase the size of one's penis: http://www.soc.ucsb.edu/sexinfo/article/penis-enlargement

There are countless online ads that tout various ways of enlarging a man's penis. They pop up in your email almost daily, whether you are male or female, adult or child. Clicking on them usually brings a host of penis photos, along with whatever content there may be. The university Web page lists treatments that include surgery, diet supplements, drugs, pumps, and exercise. But no, the penis is not a muscle and exercise does not cause it to grow. On the other hand, exercise is good for the person's general health and improves the body's circulation. Because the circulatory system is involved in supplying the material (blood) for erection, perhaps exercise would be of some help in engorging the penis and making for a firmer erection. But it makes no sense to try any exercise that directly involves the penis (ouch). Try something aerobic, like fast walking or running or swimming.

The university also notes that some of the ads state that their methods are FDA approved (that is, approved by the Federal Drug and Alcohol Administration). However—a huge however—the products being hawked will have been approved for another purpose if they have been approved at all. For example, a number of pumps have been FDA approved as aids to gaining an erection, but not for enhancement of penis size.

Readers who are seriously concerned about their penis size might be well advised to discuss their concerns with their healthcare professional rather than seek solutions online. Sometimes awareness of the actual averages in penis size is of help. At other times, recognition that penis size is only one aspect of a meaningful sexual relationship brings some perspective.

perhaps a smaller-than-ideal penis was not a deal-breaker. This should not be surprising. Men who might stare at women with large breasts might also be content with their own partners' breast size.

Even when flaccid, the same penis can vary in size. Factors such as cold air or water or emotions of fear or anxiety can cause the penis (along with the scrotum and testicles) to draw closer to the body, reducing its size. These factors can trigger Koro syndrome in Chinese culture. The flaccid penis may expand in warm water or when the man is relaxed.

The Scrotum

The **scrotum** is a pouch of loose skin below the base of the penis that becomes covered lightly with hair at puberty. It has two compartments that hold the testes. Each testicle is held in place by a **spermatic cord**, a structure that contains the **vas deferens**, blood vessels and nerves, and the cremaster muscle. The **cremaster muscle** raises and lowers the testicle within the scrotum in response to temperature changes and sexual stimulation. (Sexual arousal draws the testes closer to the body.)

Sperm production is optimal at slightly below the 98.6° F that is normal for most of the body. Scrotal temperature tends to be from 5° to 6° F lower than body temperature. The scrotum is loose-hanging and flexible. It permits the testes and nearby structures to escape the higher body heat, especially in warm weather. In the middle layer of the scrotum is the **dartos muscle**, which, like the cremaster, contracts and relaxes reflexively in response to temperature changes. In cold weather, or when a man jumps into a body of cold water, the dartos muscle contracts and brings the testes closer to the body. In warm weather, it relaxes, allowing the testes to hang farther from the body. The dartos muscle also increases or decreases the surface area of the scrotum in response to temperature changes. Smoothing allows greater dissipation of heat in hot weather. Constricting the skin surface helps retain heat and wrinkles the scrotum in the cold.

The scrotum is developed from the same embryonic tissue that becomes the labia majora of the female. Thus, like the labia majora, it is quite sensitive to sexual stimulation.

Internal Sex Organs

LO 3.3 **Describe the internal male sex organs and their functions.**

The male internal sex organs include the testes, the organs that manufacture sperm and testosterone; the system of tubes and ducts that conduct sperm through the male reproductive system; and the organs that help nourish and activate sperm and neutralize some of the acidity that sperm encounter in the vagina (see Figure 3.2).

The Testes

The testes are the male gonads (*gonad* derives from the Greek *gone,* meaning "seed"). In slang, the testes are frequently referred to as "balls" or "nuts." These terms have been considered vulgar, but *balls* seems to be on the verge of being accepted in the mainstream media and is often used to signify courage or "guts," as in "He hasn't got the *balls* to challenge ..." You will also hear the Spanish word *cojones* (co-HO-nays) used by Anglo Americans, sometimes to avoid saying *balls*, sometimes because it seems a bit more ... macho.

The testes serve two functions analogous to those of the ovaries. They secrete sex hormones and produce mature **germ cells**. In the case of the testes, the germ cells are **sperm** and the sex hormones are **androgens**. The most important androgen is **testosterone**.

scrotum
The pouch of loose skin that contains the testes.

spermatic cord
The cord that suspends a testicle within the scrotum and contains a vas deferens, blood vessels, nerves, and the cremaster muscle.

vas deferens
A tube that conducts sperm from the testicle to the ejaculatory duct of the penis.

cremaster muscle
The muscle that raises and lowers the testicle in response to temperature changes and sexual stimulation.

dartos muscle
The muscle in the middle layer of the scrotum that contracts and relaxes in response to temperature changes.

germ cell
A cell from which a new organism develops.

sperm
The male germ cell.

androgens
Male sex hormones.

testosterone
A male steroid sex hormone.

Figure 3.6 Interstitial Cells.

Testosterone is produced by the interstitial cells, which lay between the seminiferous tubules in each testis. Sperm (see in the middle of the diagram) are produced within the seminiferous tubules.

Seminiferous   Interstitial
tubule   cells

interstitial cells

Cells that lie between the seminiferous tubules and secrete testosterone.

Leydig's cells

Another term for *interstitial cells.*

secondary sex characteristics

Traits that distinguish the genders but are not directly involved in reproduction.

seminiferous tubules

Tiny, winding, sperm-producing tubes within the lobes of the testes.

spermatogenesis

The process by which sperm cells are produced and developed.

TESTOSTERONE Testosterone is secreted by **interstitial cells**, which are also known as **Leydig's cells**. Interstitial cells lie between the seminiferous tubules and release testosterone into the bloodstream (see Figure 3.6). Testosterone stimulates prenatal differentiation of male sex organs, sperm production, and development of **secondary sex characteristics**, such as the beard, a deep voice, and muscle mass.

In men, several endocrine glands—a feedback loop among the hypothalamus, pituitary gland, and testes (see Figure 3.7)—keep blood testosterone levels at a more or less even level, although there are slight variations with stress, time of day or month, and other factors. This contrasts with the peaks and valleys in levels of female sex hormones during the phases of the menstrual cycle.

The pituitary hormones, follicle-stimulating hormone (FSH) and luteinizing hormone (LH), which regulate the activity of the ovaries, also regulate the activity of the testes. FSH regulates the production of sperm. LH stimulates secretion of testosterone by interstitial cells. Low testosterone levels signal the hypothalamus to secrete the hormone, LH-releasing hormone (LH–RH). Like dominoes falling in a line, LH–RH causes the pituitary gland to secrete LH, which in turn stimulates the testes to secrete testosterone. LH is also known as *interstitial-cell-stimulating-hormone* (ICSH).

When the level of testosterone in the blood system reaches a peak, the hypothalamus directs the pituitary gland *not* to secrete LH. This system for circling information around these three endocrine glands is called a *feedback loop.* This feedback loop is *negative.* That is, it increases in hormone levels in one part of the system trigger another part to shut down and vice versa.

The testes usually range between 1 and 1 ¾ inches in length. They are about half as wide and deep. The left testicle usually hangs lower because the left spermatic cord tends to be somewhat longer.

SPERM Each testicle is divided into many lobes, which are filled with winding **seminiferous tubules** (see Figure 3.2). Although packed into a tiny space, these tubules, placed end to end, would span the length of several football fields. Through **spermatogenesis**, these threadlike structures produce and store hundreds of billions of sperm over a lifetime.

Sperm cells develop through several stages. It takes about 72 days for the testes to manufacture a mature sperm cell. In an early stage, sperm cells are called

Figure 3.7 Hormonal Control of the Testes.

Several endocrine glands—the hypothalamus, the pituitary gland, and the testes—keep blood testosterone levels at a more or less constant level. Low testosterone levels signal the hypothalamus to secrete luteinizing hormone-releasing hormone (LH–RH). Like dominoes falling in line, LH–RH causes the pituitary gland to secrete LH, which in turn stimulates the testes to release testosterone. Follicle-stimulating hormone releasing hormone (FSH–RH) from the hypothalamus causes the pituitary to secrete FSH, which, in turn, causes the testes to produce sperm cells.

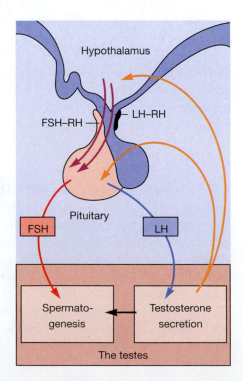

spermatocytes. Each one contains 46 chromosomes, including one X and one Y sex chromosome. Each spermatocyte divides into two **spermatids**, each of which has 23 chromosomes. Half the spermatids have X sex chromosomes, and the other half have Y sex chromosomes. Looking something like tadpoles when examined under a microscope, mature sperm cells, called **spermatozoa**, each have a head, a cone-shaped midpiece, and a tail. The head is about 5 microns (1/50,000 of an inch) long and contains the cell nucleus that houses the chromosomes. The midpiece contains structures that provide the energy that the tail needs to lash back and forth as it swims. Each sperm cell is about 50 microns (1/5,000 of an inch) long, one of the smallest cells in the body.

During fertilization, the 23 chromosomes from the father's sperm cell combine with the 23 chromosomes from the mother's ovum, furnishing the standard ensemble of 46 in the offspring. Among the 23 chromosomes borne by sperm cells is one sex chromosome—an X sex chromosome or a Y sex chromosome. Ova contain X sex chromosomes only. The union of an X sex chromosome and a Y sex chromosome leads to the development of male offspring. Two X sex chromosomes combine to yield female offspring.

2 › T / F Truth or Fiction Revisited It is true that the father determines the baby's anatomic sex—through the presence of an X (female) or Y (male) sex chromosome.

The testes churn out about 1,000 sperms per second or 30 *billion* per year. Mathematically speaking, 10 to 20 ejaculations hold enough sperm to populate the Earth. (Men are always so taken with themselves, notes the third author.)

Researchers have discovered that sperm cells possess receptors that detect attractants secreted by the ovum in humans and in some other animals (Alvarez et al., 2014; Yoshida, 2014). Sperm may in effect find their way to an egg cell by detecting its scent. In the future we may have contraceptives that prevent fertilization by blocking these receptors from sensing the odors of egg cells.

Sperm proceed from the seminiferous tubules through a maze of ducts that converge in a tube called the **epididymis**. The epididymis lies against the back wall of the testicle and stores sperm. It is some 2 inches in length and it consists of twisted passages that would extend 10 to 20 feet if straightened. Sperm are inactive when they enter the epididymis. They continue to mature as they make their way through the epididymis for another 2 to 4 weeks.

The Vas Deferens

Each epididymis empties into a vas deferens (also called *ductus deferens*). The vas is a thin, cylindrical tube about 16 inches long that serves as a conduit for mature sperm. In the scrotum, the vas deferens lies near the skin surface within the spermatic cord. Therefore, a **vasectomy**, an operation in which the right and left vas deferens are severed, is a convenient means of sterilization. The tube leaves the scrotum and follows a circuitous path up into the abdominal cavity. Then it loops back along the rear surface of the bladder (see Figure 3.8).

Human sperm cells magnified many times.

spermatocyte

An early stage in the development of sperm cells, in which each parent cell has 46 chromosomes, including one X and one Y sex chromosome.

spermatids

Cells formed by the division of spermatocytes. Each spermatid has 23 chromosomes.

spermatozoa

Mature sperm cells.

Figure 3.8 Passage of Spermatozoa.

Each testicle is divided into lobes that have threadlike seminiferous tubules. Through spermatogenesis, the tubules produce and store hundreds of billions of sperm over the course of a lifetime. During ejaculation, sperm cells travel through the vas deferens, up and over the bladder, into the ejaculatory duct, and then through the urethra. Secretions from the seminal vesicles and the bulbourethral glands join with sperm to compose semen.

Ureter
Bladder
Vas deferens
Seminal vesicle
Prostate gland
Urethra
Bulbourethral gland
Penis
Testis
Scrotum

Q *What does the ejaculate taste like, and is it harmful to ingest?*
A In a word, salty. Some people like the taste, others find it unpleasant, and still others are indifferent to it. Some find the taste to be sexually arousing. It is not clear as to how much of the response reflects natural individual differences and how much reflects what people expect as a result of cultural influences and tales from friends.

Ｔhe substances in the ejaculate are harmless. It is vaguely conceivable (no pun intended) that the fluid of the ejaculate could go down "the wrong pipe" and cause choking, but this possibility exists with the ingestion of any fluid, even water. By the way, the ejaculate is a low-calorie food—largely protein—when ingested.

The Seminal Vesicles

The two **seminal vesicles** are small glands, each about 2 inches long. They lie behind the bladder and open into the **ejaculatory ducts**, where the fluids they secrete combine with sperm (see Figure 3.7). The seminal vesicles were so named because they were mistakenly believed to be reservoirs for semen, rather than glands.

The fluid produced by the seminal vesicles is rich in fructose, a form of sugar, which nourishes sperm and helps them become active, or motile. Sperm motility is a major factor in male fertility. Before reaching the ejaculatory ducts, sperm are propelled along by contractions of the epididymis and vas deferens and by **cilia** that line the walls of the vas deferens. Once they become motile, they propel themselves by whipping their tails.

At the base of the bladder, each vas deferens joins a seminal vesicle to form a short ejaculatory duct that runs through the middle of the prostate gland (see Figure 3.8). In the prostate, the ejaculatory duct opens into the urethra, which carries sperm and urine out through the tip of the penis.

The Prostate Gland

The **prostate gland** lies beneath the bladder and approximates a chestnut in shape and size (about 3/4 inch in diameter). It contains muscle fibers and glandular tissue that secrete prostatic fluid. Prostatic fluid is milky and alkaline. It provides the characteristic texture and odor of the seminal fluid. The alkalinity neutralizes some of the acidity of the vaginal tract, prolonging the life span of sperm as seminal fluid spreads through the female reproductive system. The prostate is continually active in mature males, but sexual arousal further stimulates secretions. Secretions are conveyed into the urethra by a sieve-like duct system. There the secretions combine with sperm and fluid from the seminal vesicles.

Q *Is it possible to urinate with a full erection?*
A It's difficult, but possible. The ductwork of the male is constructed such that urination and ejaculation tend to be mutually exclusive. On the other hand, if a male with an erection makes an effort to relax his bladder fully (that is, to allow himself to urinate), he may well be able to do so, even if the flow of urine is delayed or slower than usual.

---

epididymis

A tube that lies against the back wall of each testicle and stores sperm.

vasectomy

Severing of the vas deferens, preventing sperm from reaching the ejaculatory duct.

seminal vesicles

Small glands that lie behind the bladder and secrete fluids that combine with sperm in the ejaculatory ducts.

ejaculatory duct

A duct formed by the convergence of a vas deferens with a seminal vesicle through which sperm pass through the prostate gland and into the urethra.

cilia

Hairlike projections from cells that beat rhythmically to produce locomotion or currents.

prostate gland

The gland that lies beneath the bladder and secretes prostatic fluid, which gives semen its characteristic odor and texture.

A CLOSER LOOK

LOW T, ANDROPAUSE, OR *MALE MENOPAUSE? AGE-RELATED MALE HYPOGONADISM* BY ANY OTHER NAME IS JUST AS UNSETTLING

Most of us are familiar enough with the slanderous phrase "raging hormones" when it comes to the alleged irritability shown by some women prior to menstruation and apparently related to the fluctuations of sex hormones. Yet men, too, can be said to be prey to "raging hormones." The male sex hormone testosterone is related to aggressiveness and tendencies to dominate other people. There is research evidence that aggressive boys, college students, and men have higher testosterone levels than their peers (Carre & Olmstead, 2015; Peterson & Harmon-Jones, 2011). High levels of testosterone also appear to reduce fear of the consequences of aggression (Crespi, 2015; King et al., 2005). For reasons such as these, social commentator Anna Quindlen wrote an article, "Is Testosterone Toxic?" We will see that the answer to Anna Quindlen's question might be yes—that is, testosterone might well be toxic—but not for reasons that she was writing about.

Historically speaking, more research has been done with men's health problems than women's. Yet the problems related to low levels of sex hormones in men do not yet even have an agreed-upon name. *Andropause* and *Low T* suggest a falloff in androgens (male sex hormones). *Viropause* suggests a decline in virility, which is not a scientific term and suggests a general loss of ability. *Manopause* and *male menopause* are unscientific knockoffs of the scientific term *menopause.* The more scientific term is *age-related male hypogonadism*.

For women, menopause is a time of relatively distinct age-related declines in sex hormones and fertility. In men, the decline in the production of male sex hormones and fertility is more gradual. It therefore is not surprising to find a man in his 70s or older fathering a child. However, many men in their 50s and 60s experience problems in achieving and maintaining erections, which may reflect circulatory problems, hormone deficiencies—or, commonly in developed nations, the use of medicines ("statins") to reduce levels of low-density lipoprotein ("bad cholesterol") in the blood. Blood pressure medications are also suspect.

Sexual performance is one part of the story. Between the ages of 40 and 70, the typical American male loses 12 to 20 pounds of muscle, about 2 inches in height, and 15% of his bone mass. (Men as well as women are at risk for osteoporosis.) The percentage of fat in the body nearly doubles. There is some loss in hearing and vision. There is loss of endurance as the cardiovascular system and lungs become less capable of adapting to exertion.

Some of these changes can be slowed or reversed. Exercise helps maintain muscle tone, keeps the growth of fatty tissue in check, and helps combat osteoporosis. A diet rich in calcium and vitamin D helps ward off bone loss. Hormone replacement therapy may help but is controversial. U.S. physicians write more than one million prescriptions for testosterone and related drugs for men each year, but it appears that long-term (12–36 months or longer) testosterone replacement therapy may heighten the risks of prostate cancer (Cui et al., 2015). Check with your physician.

Critical Thinking

Does the evidence suggest that men undergo an "andropause" that is similar to menopause? Explain.

A vasectomy prevents sperm from reaching the urethra but does not cut off fluids from the seminal vesicles or prostate gland. A man who has had a vasectomy thus emits an ejaculate that appears normal but contains no sperm.

Cowper's Glands

Cowper's glands

Structures that lie below the prostate and empty their secretions into the urethra during sexual arousal.

bulbourethral glands

Another term for *Cowper's glands*.

The two **Cowper's glands** are also known as the **bulbourethral glands**, in recognition of their shape and location. They lie below the prostate and empty their secretions into the urethra. During sexual arousal they secrete a drop or so of clear, slippery fluid that appears at the tip of the penis. The fluid may help buffer the acidity of the male's urethra and lubricate the urethral passageway, but not enough is produced to lubricate the vagina during intercourse.

Fluid from the Cowper's glands precedes the ejaculate and often contains sperm. Thus, male–female coitus may lead to pregnancy even if the penis is withdrawn before ejaculation. For this reason, people who practice the "withdrawal method" of birth control are often called "parents."

Semen

semen

The whitish fluid that constitutes the ejaculate, consisting of sperm and secretions from the seminal vesicles, prostate, and Cowper's glands.

The seminal vesicles secrete about 70% of the fluid that constitutes **semen**, the whitish, pasty fluid that is expelled through the tip of the penis during ejaculation. The remaining 30% of seminal fluid consists of sperm and fluids produced by the prostate gland and the Cowper's gland. Sperm themselves account for only about 1% of the volume of semen. This is why men with vasectomies ejaculate nearly as much semen as before the operation.

3 › T / F Truth or Fiction Revisited   Semen is *not* a synonym for sperm. Sperm and the fluids contributed by the seminal vesicles, the prostate gland, and the Cowper's glands make up semen, or seminal fluid.

Semen carries sperm through the male's reproductive system and the reproductive tract of the female. Semen contains water, mucus, sugar (fructose), acids, and bases. It activates and nourishes sperm, and the bases help shield sperm from vaginal acidity. The typical ejaculate contains between 200 and 400 million sperm and ranges between 3 and 5 milliliters in volume. (Five milliliters is equal to about one tablespoon.) The quantity of semen decreases with age and frequency of ejaculation.

Health Problems of the Urogenital System

Because the organs that comprise the urinary and reproductive systems are near each other and share some "piping," they are referred to as the *urinogenital* or *urogenital* system. A number of health problems affect the urogenital system. The type of physician who specializes in their diagnosis and treatment is a urologist.

Urethritis

LO 3.4 Discuss urethritis.

urethritis

An inflammation of the bladder or urethra.

Men, like women, are subject to bladder and urethral inflammations, which are generally referred to as **urethritis**. The symptoms include frequent urination (urinary frequency), a strong need to urinate (urinary urgency), burning during urination, and a penile discharge. People with symptoms of urinary frequency and urinary urgency feel the pressing need to urinate repeatedly, even though they may have just done so and may have but another drop or two to expel. The discharge may dry on the urethral opening, in which case it may have to be peeled off or wiped away before it is possible to urinate. The urethra also may become constricted when it is inflamed, slowing or even halting urination. (Sometimes it is sufficient to wipe a discharge off the tip of the penis. If that doesn't work, call your doctor or go to the emergency room.)

Preventive measures for urethritis parallel those suggested for cystitis (bladder infection):

- Drink more water.
- Drink cranberry juice (4 ounces, two or three times a day). Cranberry juice is highly acidic, and acid tends to eliminate many of the bacteria that can give rise to urethritis.
- Lower your intake of alcohol and caffeine.

Urethritis is usually treated with antibiotics.

Cancer of the Testes

LO 3.5 Discuss testicular cancer.

Cancer of the testicles remains a relatively rare form of cancer, accounting for about 8,400 new cases annually, and about 380 men will die from it every year (American Cancer Society, 2015e). Although testicular cancer is rare, it is the most common form of solid-tumor cancer to strike men between the ages of 20 and 34, accounting for nearly 10% of all deaths from cancer among men in that age group.

There is no evidence that testicular cancer results from sexual overactivity or masturbation. About 14% of men with testicular cancer had **cryptorchidism** as children, a condition in which one or both testicles fail to descend from the abdomen into the scrotum (American Cancer Society, 2015e). Family history also increases the risk. European Americans are 5 to 10 times more likely than African Americans to develop cancer of the testes, and more than twice as likely as Asian Americans (American Cancer Society, 2015e).

Although testicular cancer was generally fatal previously, the prognosis today is quite favorable, especially when the disease is detected early. Treatments include surgical removal of the diseased testis, radiation, and chemotherapy. The 5-year survival rate among cases that are detected before the cancer has spread beyond the testes is about 99% (American Cancer Society, 2015e). If it has spread to nearby lymph nodes, the 5-year survival rate is 96%. If it has spread beyond the lymph nodes, the 5-year survival rate drops to about 73%.

The surgical removal of a testicle may have profound psychological implications. Some men who have lost a testicle feel less "manly." Also, fears related to sexual performance can engender sexual dysfunctions. From a physiological standpoint, sexual functioning may remain unimpaired, as adequate testosterone may be produced by the remaining testis. There are a couple of caveats. One is that surgery to remove the lymph nodes behind the belly can accidentally damage nearby nerves that control ejaculation, causing sperm to be ejaculated into the urinary bladder. (Check on the success rate of potential surgeons!) This condition can render the man infertile. If both testes are removed, the man is infertile. However, with testosterone replacement therapy, he can usually obtain an erection and have sex. Because only a small amount of semen consists of sperm, sex can remain satisfying.

The early stages of testicular cancer usually produce no symptoms, other than the mass itself. Because early detection is crucial to survival, men are advised to examine themselves monthly following puberty and to have regular medical checkups. Self-examination may also reveal evidence of STIs and other problems.

cryptorchidism
A condition in which one or two testicles fails to descend from the abdomen into the scrotum.

Figure 3.9
Self-Examination of
the Testes

SELF-EXAMINATION OF THE TESTES   Self-examination (see Figure 3.9) is best performed shortly after a warm shower or bath, when the skin of the scrotum is most relaxed. The man should examine the scrotum for evidence of pea-sized lumps. Each testicle can be rolled gently between the thumb and the fingers. Lumps are generally found on the side or front of the testicle. The presence of a lump is not necessarily a sign of cancer, but it should be promptly reported to a physician for further evaluation. The American Cancer Society (2015e) lists these warning signals:

- A lump on a testicle
- Enlargement or swelling of a testicle
- Change in the consistency of a testicle
- Dull ache in the lower abdomen or groin (pain may be absent in cancer of the testes, however)
- Sensation of dragging and heaviness in a testicle

  Less common symptoms are:
- Growth of breast tissue; tender or swollen breasts
- Loss of sex drive
- Premature (prior to puberty) growth of hair on the face and body

Benign Prostatic Hyperplasia (BPH)

LO 3.6   **Discuss benign prostate hyperplasia.**

benign prostatic hyperplasia

Noncancerous enlargement of the prostate resulting from hormonal changes of aging and symptomized by urinary frequency, urinary urgency, and difficulty starting the flow of urine.

The prostate gland is tiny at birth and grows rapidly at puberty. It may shrink during adulthood, but usually becomes enlarged past the age of 50. The prostate gland becomes enlarged in about half the men past the age of 50 and 80% of men by age 80 (Lu & Chen, 2014). **Benign prostatic hyperplasia (BPH)** is noncancerous enlargement of the prostate gland as a result of hormonal changes associated with aging rather than other causes, such as inflammation from STIs. Because the prostate surrounds the upper part of the urethra (see Figure 3.2), enlargement constricts the urethra, causing urinary frequency (including increased frequency of nocturnal urination), urinary urgency, and difficulty starting the flow of urine. Several treatments are available to relieve the pressure on the urethra and increase the flow of urine. Two types of drugs help men with BPH. The first type, 5-ARIs (5-alpha reductase inhibitors), inhibits the production of the hormone DHT (a form of testosterone), which causes enlargement of the prostate. The 5-ARIs shrink the prostate, provide long-term improvement of symptoms, and reduce the risk of severe urinary retention and the need for surgery. The second type is alpha-blockers, which act by relaxing the muscles of the bladder to improve the flow of urine, providing symptom relief. Part of the prostate is also sometimes surgically removed.

Prostatitis

LO 3.7   **Discuss prostatitis.**

prostatitis

Inflammation of the prostate gland.

Prostatitis is inflammation of the prostate, which can be caused by various infectious agents. The chief symptoms are an ache or pain between the scrotum and anal opening and painful ejaculation. Men with prostatitis may also find visible blood in their urine or semen. Prostatitis is usually treated with antibiotics. Although aspirin, ibuprofen, and naproxen may relieve the pain and reduce inflammation, men with these symptoms should consult a physician. Painful ejaculation may discourage masturbation or coitus, which is ironic, because regular flushing of the prostate through ejaculation may be helpful in the treatment of the inflammation. Prostatitis is usually treated with antibiotics, most commonly ciproflaxin.

Cancer of the Prostate

LO 3.8 Discuss prostate cancer.

Prostate cancer is a serious and life-threatening problem. About one man in six in the United States will develop prostate cancer (American Cancer Society, 2015f). It is the second-most common form of cancer among men, after skin cancer, and the second-leading cause of cancer deaths in men, after lung cancer. There are about 220,000 new cases of prostate cancer in the United States each year, and about 27,500 deaths (American Cancer Society, 2015f). Prostate cancer involves the growth of malignant prostate tumors that can metastasize to bones and lymph nodes if not detected and treated early.

RISK FACTORS The American Cancer Society (2015f) lists the following risk factors:

- Age. Prostate cancer is rare before the age of 40. The risk rises rapidly after the age of 50, and most men with the disorder are 65 or older.

- Family history. The risk is more than twice as high for men who have a father or brother who has had the disease.

- Inherited mutations of the *BRCA1* or *BRCA2* genes. Mutations in these genes are why breast and ovarian cancers are significantly more common in some families. It is believed that mutations in these genes may also heighten the risk of prostate cancer in men.

- Race/ethnicity. Prostate cancer is more common among African American men than among European American or Latin American men. It is least prevalent among Asian Americans and Native Americans. African American men are 50% to 60% more likely than European American men to develop prostate cancer. In general, African American men have less access to health care than European American men do, so prostate cancer tends to be diagnosed later among them, and they are twice as likely to die from it (American Cancer Society, 2015f).

- Geography. Prostate cancer is most common in North America, northwestern Europe, Australia, and the Caribbean islands, but less common in Africa, Asia, and Central and South America. Also, men are less likely to contract and die from prostate cancer in countries with a higher prevalence of male circumcision (Wachtel et al., 2015).

The American Cancer Society (2015f) states that there is *no* clear connection between prostate cancer and the following:

- Diet. The American Cancer Society states that men who eat red meats or high-fat dairy foods may have a higher risk, but these men also tend to consume fewer fruits and vegetables. But there may be accumulating evidence that a high-fat Western-style diet increases the risk of prostate cancer (Yang et al., 2015).

- Obesity. However, may have less risk of developing a "less dangerous" form of cancer but a greater risk of developing a "more aggressive" form of cancer.

- Sexually transmitted infections.

- Vasectomy.

- Smoking. (But smoking is a major cause of the more deadly *lung cancer*.)

SYMPTOMS The early symptoms of cancer of the prostate may mimic those of benign prostate enlargement: trouble obtaining or maintaining an erection, urinary frequency and difficulty in urinating, blood in the urine, pain or burning

Critical Thinking

If a man has a strong family history of prostate cancer, is there any point to his making an effort to watch his diet? Explain.

Who Is at Higher Risk of Prostate Cancer? The African American man is, probably for genetic reasons. As we saw in the discussion of breast cancer in Chapter 2, cancer can affect people from different races and ethnic groups disproportionately. Health professionals recommend that African Americans begin screening for prostate cancer at 40, whereas European American men usually are not advised to begin screening until age 50.

Figure 3.10   Digital Rectal Examination (DRE) for Prostate Cancer

SOURCE: American Cancer Society, 2006.

when urinating, and pain in the lower back, pelvis, or upper thighs, weakness or numbness in the legs or feet, and loss of control of the bladder or bowels (American Cancer Society, 2015f). Most cases occur without noticeable symptoms in the early stages; therefore, screening for prostate cancer is an important topic of discussion for a man and his doctor.

DIAGNOSIS AND SCREENING   Health professionals detect and assess prostate cancer by a combination of tests. One of these is the digital rectal examination (DRE; see Figure 3.10). In this case, digital means "of the finger" and has nothing to do with computers or our "digital age." In the DRE, the physician inserts a finger into the rectum and feels for bumps or hard spots in the prostate gland. Unfortunately, many men are reluctant to have a rectal examination, even though it is only mildly uncomfortable and may save their lives. Some are embarrassed or reluctant to discuss urinary problems with their physicians. Some may resist the rectal examination because they associate rectal insertion with male–male sex. Some, of course, fear they may have cancer and choose to remain ignorant. But make no mistake: Failure to have regular examinationss is a major contributor to the death rate from prostate cancer.

These examinations include a PSA test, which is a blood test for *prostate-specific antigen*. PSA is a protein that helps transform a gel-like substance in the prostate gland to a liquid that transports sperm during ejaculation. In the diseased or enlarged prostate, PSA seeps into the blood at higher levels, yielding higher test scores. Results under 4 nanograms per milliliter (ng/mL) are considered normal (no disease). A result above 10 is considered high; results between 4 and 10 are "borderline."

The American Cancer Society recommends testing for prostate cancer as follows:

Testing should begin at the age of 50 for men who are considered to be at average risk for prostate cancer. This recommendation applies, for example, to European American men who do not have a close relative who has had prostate cancer.

Testing should start at the age of 45 for men who are considered to be at high risk for prostate cancer. These men include African Americans, especially African Americans with a "first-degree relative"—that is, a father, brother, or son—who has been diagnosed with prostate cancer, especially prostate cancers before the age of 65. African Americans at even higher risk have more than one-first-degree relative who has been diagnosed with the disease before the age of 65. These men are advised to begin testing at the age of 40.

These recommendations seem to be logical enough, but they are actually controversial. The issue, in a nutshell, is "overdiagnosis"—that is, physicians may find questionable or borderline readings and follow up on them with discomforting biopsies, and operating on small tumors when it might not have been necessary (Schröder et al., 2014).

A European study followed about 162,500 men for 13 years in The European Randomized study of Screening for Prostate Cancer (Schröder et al., 2014) and found that PSA screening does save lives. In the study, midlife PSA screening lowered the death rate from prostate cancer by 21%—a number not to be ignored. But look at it another way: a man's risk of dying from prostate cancer without screening is close to 3%, and PSA screening lowers it to 2.4%. The head of the study, Dr. Fritz H. Schröder of Erasmus University Medical Center in the Netherlands says that PSA screening detects a substantial number of cancerous growth, perhaps 30% to 50% of them, "that would never do any harm" (cited in Parker-Pope, 2014). "This overdiagnosis is unacceptable because it also leads to treatment," Dr. Schröder said.

Treatment can be painful and it frequently decreases a man's quality of life in terms of urination and sexual functioning.

A study in the United States—the Prostate Lung Colorectal and Ovarian (PLCO) cancer screening trial with some 77,000 men has also been underway for about 20 years. A recent analysis of study results concludes that PSA screening does in fact result in detecting more incidents of prostate cancer; however, in contrast to the European study, the PLCO study found no evidence that PSA screening actually reduced the number of deaths from prostate cancer (Shoag et al., 2015).

If cancer is suspected from PSA screening, DRE, or a combination of these tests, the doctor performs a biopsy. That is, the doctor uses a needle to take a sample of prostate tissue and sometimes of lymph nodes in the area. If a tumor is found, pathologists grade two samples of tissue and rate them from 1 to 5 on the so-called Gleason scale to provide a measure of the cancer's aggressiveness. The scores are added. Sums of 2 through 4 are considered low in aggressiveness (slow growing), 5 and 6 are intermediate, and 7 to 10 are high, with the worst prognoses. Doctors may do other tests such as bone scans, computed tomography (CT) scans, and magnetic resonance imaging (MRI) to see if the cancer has spread.

Early detection permits treatment before the cancer has metastasized. If it has, the survival rate drops dramatically. Still, the overall survival rate has improved from 50% in the 1960s to well above 80% (American Cancer Society, 2015f). A positive PSA result (one that is indicative of prostate cancer) exposes many men to "aggressive and unnecessary treatments" (Parker-Pope, 2009a) that can cause erectile dysfunction (difficulty achieving an erection) and incontinence. According to Otis Brawley (2009) of the American Cancer Society, the European results suggest that "the [PSA] test is about 50 times more likely to ruin your life than it is to save your life." Yet surgeon Gerald L. Andriole (2009) believes that middle-aged or older men whose life expectancy is 10 years or more "need to be informed about the potential pros and harms of screening. If they want to embark on it, that's fine. I'm still open to accepting that we learn a lot about a man's prostate and about the probability of him getting or having prostate cancer by measuring PSA."

Check with your physician (urologist) for the latest information.

TREATMENT The most widely used treatment for prostate cancer is surgical removal of the prostate gland. However, the surgery may damage surrounding nerves, leading to problems in urinary and sexual functions. Surgeons attempt to spare surrounding nerves, but cannot guarantee elimination of the risk of complications. Other treatments include radiation, hormone treatment, and anti-cancer drugs. Hormone treatment in the form of androgen (testosterone) suppression therapy and anti-cancer drugs may shrink the size of the tumor and relieve pain. Men who obtain surgery are more likely to have urinary incontinence (loss of control over urination) and sexual dysfunction (trouble attaining erection) than men who use radiation (American Cancer Society, 2015f). But many physicians argue that surgery remains the better choice in terms of survival rates. Among older men with slow-growing prostate cancer, physicians may prefer "watchful waiting" to surgery. The men may live long enough to die from causes other than cancer. Treatment choices are explored further in the "A Closer Look" feature about prostate cancer.

The 5-year survival rate for (local) prostate cancer (cancer that has remained within the prostate gland) is nearly 100%. If it is "regional"—that is, it has spread to nearby lymph nodes, the 5-year survival rate is also at nearly 100%. The significant problem rears its head when prostate cancer has spread to distant sites—that is, to distant lymph nodes, bone, or other organs. The 5-year survival rate then drops to 28% (American Cancer Society, 2015f). This is why it is so essential that men talk to their doctors about screening and make informed decisions.

A CLOSER LOOK

PROSTATE CANCER: TREAT IT OR WAIT IT OUT?

Each year more than 220,000 men are diagnosed with prostate cancer, but nobody can inform them what kind of treatment will most likely save their lives. Such are the findings of a report from the Agency for Healthcare Research and Quality (Wilt et al., 2008), which analyzed 592 published studies to try to advise men about the most successful treatments. The agency compared the successes and risks of eight treatments, from prostate removal to radioactive implants to rapid freezing and thawing to watchful waiting—that is, monitoring the disease (which is considered 100% curable as long as it doesn't metastasize) and doing nothing unless it progresses. The treatments also included minimally invasive surgery (laparoscopic or robotic-assisted prostatectomy); hormone therapy or testicle removal, both of which deprive the cancer of androgens; high-intensity ultrasound; and external-beam radiation therapy. None of the treatments emerged as more successful than watchful waiting.

The study, published in the *Annals of Internal Medicine,* affords men little guidance. Prostate cancer is usually slow growing, and many live with it for years and die from something else. But for some men, prostate cancer is more aggressive, and in 2015, about 27,500 men were expected to die from it.

Other findings are as follows:

- All treatments have side effects such as urinary incontinence, bowel problems, and erectile dysfunction. The chances of sexual dysfunction and bowel problems are similar for surgery and radiation, but urine leakage is six times more likely among surgery patients than patients treated with external-beam radiation therapy.
- External-beam radiation therapy and androgen deprivation each led to a higher frequency of bowel urgency (3%) than prostate removal (1%).

- Erectile dysfunction was more likely to be associated with androgen deprivation (86%) and radical prostatectomy (58%) than with watchful waiting (33%).
- One study concluded that men who were treated with surgery were less likely to have their cancer metastasize or to die than those who waited watchfully, but another study reported no difference in survival between the two.
- Hormone therapy before prostatectomy did not enhance survival rates or decrease recurrence rates.
- Combining radiation with hormone treatments may lower mortality, but when compared to radiation alone, the combination appears to increase the rates of impotence and abnormal breast development.

New treatments come along. One is a therapeutic prostate cancer vaccine, Provenge (American Cancer Society, 2015f). Therapeutic vaccines do not prevent a disease as childhood vaccines do. Instead, they are meant to trigger the body's immune system to attack a disease that is already in progress.

The American Cancer Society (2015f) advises that the treatment a man chooses should depend on the following:

- His age and how long he can expect to live
- Other health problems
- The stage and grade of his cancer (whether it has metastasized, and how aggressive it is)
- His feelings—and his doctor's—about whether the cancer needs to be treated
- The probability that a given treatment will cure the cancer
- His feelings about the treatment's side effects

Again, check with your doctor about the latest findings for the various treatments.

Male Sexual Functions

The male sexual functions of erection and ejaculation provide the means for sperm to travel from the male's reproductive tract to the female's. There the sperm cell and ovum unite to conceive a new human being. Of course, the natural endowment of reproduction with sensations of pleasure help ensure that reproduction will take place with or without knowledge of these biological facts.

Erection

LO 3.9   Explain how erection occurs.

erection

Enlargement and stiffening of the penis caused by engorgement with blood.

Erection is caused by the engorgement of the penis with blood, such that the penis expands and stiffens. The erect penis is an efficient funnel for depositing sperm deep within the vagina.

Erection is a hydraulic event. The spongy, cavernous masses of the penis fill with blood, causing the penis to enlarge, much like a sponge swells when it absorbs water. Erection involves both the vascular (circulatory) system and the nervous system.

In a few moments—10 or 15 seconds—the penis can double in length and firmness and will shift from a funnel for passing urine to one that expels semen. Muscles close off the bladder when the male becomes sexually aroused, preventing the mixture of semen and urine.

The corpora cavernosa are surrounded by a tough, fibrous covering. Just as the rubber of a balloon resists the pressure of pumped-in air, this covering resists expansion, stiffening the penis. The corpus spongiosum, which contains the urethra, also engorges with blood during erection. It does not become hard, however, because it lacks the fibrous casing. The penile glans, which is formed by the crowning of the spongiosum at the tip of the penis, turns a dark purplish hue as it becomes engorged, but it too does not stiffen.

Erection is reversed when more blood flows out of erectile tissue than flows in, restoring the prearousal circulatory balance and shrinking the spongy masses. Loss of erection occurs when sexual stimulation ceases, or when the body returns to a (sexual) resting state following orgasm. Loss of erection can also occur in response to anxiety or perceived threats (Cuzin et al., 2011). Such loss can be abrupt, as when a man in the "throes of passion" suddenly hears a noise suggestive of an intruder. A man who fears that he will be unable to perform successfully may experience **performance anxiety**, which can prevent him from obtaining or maintaining an erection.

Men have nocturnal erections every 90 minutes or so as they sleep. They generally occur during rapid eye movement (REM) sleep, which is associated with dreaming. It is so named because the sleeper's eyes dart about rapidly under the closed eyelids during this stage.

The mechanism of nocturnal erection is physiological. That is, dreams may not have erotic content. Morning erections are actually nocturnal erections. They occur when the man awakens during REM sleep.

performance anxiety
Feelings of dread and foreboding experienced in connection with sexual activity (or any other activity that might be judged by another person).

4 › T / F Truth or Fiction Revisited   Although men may need to urinate in the morning, morning erections do not reflect the need to urinate.

Spinal Reflexes and Sexual Response

Men may become sexually aroused by a range of stimuli, including tactile stimulation provided by their partners, visual stimulation (as from scanning photos of nudes on the Internet), or sexual fantasies. Regardless of the source of stimulation, the man's sexual responses, erection, and ejaculation occur by reflex.

Sexual reflexes are automatic, unlearned responses to sexual stimulation. Examples in women include vaginal lubrication and orgasm. We need not try to become aroused. We need only expose ourselves to sexual stimulation and allow reflexes to do the job for us.

5 › T / F Truth or Fiction Revisited   Men cannot will themselves to have erections. People do not control sexual reflexes voluntarily, as they might lift an arm, but they can set the stage for them to occur by seeking sexual stimulation. Efforts to control sexual responses consciously by "force of will" can backfire and make it more difficult to become aroused (for example, to attain erection or vaginal lubrication).

The reflexes governing erection and ejaculation are controlled in the spinal cord. They are thus called *spinal reflexes*. Erectile responses to direct stimulation such as

Figure 3.11   Erection Is a Reflex.

Reflexes need not involve the brain, although messages to the brain may make us aware when reflexes are occurring. Reflexes are the product of "local government" in the spine.

1. A man's penis is stimulated

2. The nerve impulse travels from site of touch to lower part (sacral area) of spinal cord

Sacral area

Sensory neuron — Gray matter

White matter

4. Erection occurs

3. Nerve impulse travels back to penis

Effector neuron — Spinal cord

sacrum

The thick, triangular bone located near the bottom of the spinal column.

Critical Thinking

Because erection and ejaculation are reflexes, how is it that people can purposefully cause them to happen?

---

touching or licking involve a simple spinal reflex that does not require the direct participation of the brain (see Figure 3.11). Erections can also be initiated by the brain, such as when a man has sexual fantasies or catches a glimpse of an attractive person. In such cases, stimulation from the brain travels to the spinal cord, where the erectile reflex is triggered.

Tactile stimulation (touching) of the penis or nearby areas (lower abdomen, scrotum, inner thighs) causes sensory neurons to transmit nerve messages (signals) to an erection center in the lower back, in an area of the spinal cord called the **sacrum**. The sacral erection center controls reflexive erections—that is, erections occurring in response to direct stimulation of the penis and nearby areas. When direct penile stimulation occurs, messages in the form of nerve impulses are received by this erection center, which in turn sends impulses to the genitalia via nerves that serve the penis. These impulses cause arteries carrying blood to the corpora cavernosa and corpus spongiosum to dilate, so that more blood flows into them, causing erection.

The sacral erection center makes it possible for men whose spinal cords have been injured or severed above the center to achieve erections (and ejaculate) in response to direct tactile stimulation of the penis. Erection occurs even though their injuries prevent nerve signals from reaching their brains. Because of the lack of communication between the genital organs and the brain, there are no sensations, but many spinal-injured men report that sex remains psychologically pleasurable because they can observe the responses of their partners.

THE ROLE OF THE BRAIN   If direct penile stimulation triggers erection at the spinal level, what is the role of the brain? Although it may seem that the penis sometimes has "a mind of its own," the brain plays an important role in regulating sexual responses.

Tactile (touch) stimulation of the penis may trigger erection through the spinal cord, but sexual sensations are then normally relayed to the brain, which generally results in pleasure and perhaps in a decision to focus on erotic stimulation. The sight of one's partner, erotic fantasies, memories, and so forth can result in messages being sent by the brain through the spinal cord to the arteries servicing the penis, maintaining or strengthening the erection.

When the brain originates messages that trigger the erectile reflex, it transmits nerve impulses to a second and higher erection center located in the upper back in the lumbar region of the spinal cord. This higher spinal erection center serves as a "switch board" between the brain and the penis, allowing perceptual, cognitive, and emotional responses to make their contributions. When the nerve pathways between the brain and the upper spinal cord are blocked or severed, men cannot achieve erections in response to mental stimulation alone.

The brain can also stifle sexual response. A man who is highly anxious about his sexual abilities may be unable to achieve an erection even with intense penile stimulation. Or a man who believes that sexual pleasure is sinful or dirty may be filled with anxiety and guilt and be unable to achieve erection with a partner.

In some males, especially adolescents, the erectile reflex is so easily tripped that incidental rubbing of the genitals against his own undergarments, the sight of an attractive passer-by, or a fleeting sexual fantasy produces erection. Spontaneous erections may occur under embarrassing circumstances, such as before classes change in middle or high school, or on a beach. In an effort to distract himself from erotic fantasies and to allow an erection to subside, many a male adolescent desperately renews his interest in his algebra or language textbook in class before the bell rings. (A well-placed towel may serve in a pinch on the beach.)

As men mature, they need more penile stimulation to achieve full erection. Partners of men in their 30s and 40s should not feel that their attractiveness has waned if their lovers no longer have instant "no-hands" erections when they disrobe. It takes men longer to obtain erection as they age, and direct stimulation becomes more important.

THE ROLE OF THE AUTONOMIC NERVOUS SYSTEM (ANS) Stimulation that brings about an erection can originate in the brain, but erection is not a voluntary response, like raising your arm. Whatever the original or dominant source of stimulation—direct penile stimulation or sexual fantasy—erection remains an unlearned, automatic reflex.

Automatic responses, such as erection, involve the division of the nervous system called the **autonomic nervous system (ANS)**. *Autonomic* means "automatic." The ANS controls automatic bodily processes such as heartbeat, pupil dilation, respiration, and digestion. In contrast, voluntary movement (like raising an arm) is under the control of the *somatic* division of the nervous system.

The ANS has two branches: the sympathetic and the parasympathetic. These branches have largely opposing effects; when they are activated at the same time, their effects become balanced out to some degree. In general, the **sympathetic** branch is in command during processes that involve a release of bodily energy from stored reserves, such as during running, performing some other athletic task, or being gripped by fear or anxiety. The sympathetic branch also governs the general mobilization of the body, such as by increasing the heart rate and respiration rate in response to a threat.

The **parasympathetic** branch is most active during processes that restore reserves of energy, such as digestion. When we experience fear or anxiety, the sympathetic branch of the ANS quickens the heart rate. When we relax, the parasympathetic branch curbs the heart rate. It also activates digestive processes, but inhibits digestive activity. Because the sympathetic branch is in command when we feel fear or anxiety, such stimuli can inhibit the activity of the parasympathetic system, possibly causing indigestion.

The divisions of the ANS play different roles in sexual arousal and response. The nerves that cause penile arteries to dilate during erection belong to the parasympathetic branch of the ANS. The parasympathetic system largely governs erection. The nerves governing ejaculation belong to the sympathetic branch, however. One implication of this division of neural responsibility is that intense fear or anxiety, which involves sympathetic nervous system activity, may inhibit erection by counteracting the activity of the parasympathetic nervous system. Because sympathetic arousal helps trigger

autonomic nervous system (ANS)
The division of the nervous system that regulates automatic bodily processes, such as heartbeat, pupil dilation, respiration, and digestion.

sympathetic
The branch of the ANS most active during emotional responses that spend energy, such as fear and anxiety. The sympathetic ANS largely controls ejaculation.

parasympathetic
The branch of the ANS most active during processes that restore energy, like digestion. The parasympathetic ANS largely controls erection.

ejaculation, anxiety or fear may also accelerate ejaculation, causing *premature ejaculation* (Graziottin & Althof, 2011; see Chapter 12).

The connection between emotions, sympathetic activity, and ejaculation can set up a vicious cycle. Anxiety in a sexual encounter may trigger premature ejaculation. During a subsequent sexual encounter, the man might fear recurrence of premature ejaculation. The fear may bring on the reality. He may face further sexual encounters with yet greater fear, perhaps further hastening ejaculation—but possibly inhibiting erection. Methods for helping men with erectile dysfunction and premature ejaculation aim at reducing their levels of anxiety and thereby lessening sympathetic activity.

6 › T / F Truth or Fiction Revisited   Because erections seem spontaneous at times and often occur when the man would rather not have them, it may seem to men that the penis has a mind of its own. But despite this common folk belief, the penis possesses no guiding intelligence. It consists of spongy masses of erectile tissue, not the lovely dense gray matter that renders your thought processes so incisive.

ERECTILE ABNORMALITIES   Some men find that their erect penises are slightly curved or bent. Some degree of curvature is normal, but men with **Peyronie's disease** have excessive curvature that can make erections painful. The condition is caused by buildup of fibrous tissue in the penile shaft. Although some cases of Peyronie's disease appear to clear up on their own, most require medical attention.

Some men experience erections that persist for hours or days. This condition is called *priapism,* after Priapus of Greek myth, the son of Dionysus and Aphrodite who personified male procreative power. Priapism is often caused by leukemia, sickle cell anemia, or diseases of the spinal cord, although in some cases the cause remains unknown. Priapism occurs when the mechanisms that drain the blood that erects the penis are damaged and cannot readily return the blood to the circulatory system. Priapism may become a medical emergency because erection prolonged beyond 6 hours can starve penile tissues of oxygen, leading to tissue deterioration. Medical intervention in the form of drugs or surgery may be required to reverse the condition.

Ejaculation

LO 3.10 Explain how ejaculation occurs.

Ejaculation, like erection, is a spinal reflex. It is triggered when sexual stimulation reaches a critical point or threshold. Ejaculation generally occurs together with **orgasm**, the sudden muscle contractions that occur at the peak of sexual excitement and result in the abrupt release of sexual tension that had built up during sexual arousal. Orgasm is generally pleasurable. *Ejaculation,* however, refers only to the expulsion of semen from the tip of the penis. Orgasm and ejaculation are *not* synonymous, however. For example, **paraplegics** can ejaculate if the area of the lower spinal cord that controls ejaculation is intact. They do not experience the subjective aspects of orgasm, however, because the sensations of orgasm do not reach the brain.

7 › T / F Truth or Fiction Revisited   Many men who are paralyzed below the waist can attain erection, engage in sexual intercourse, and ejaculate, as long as the spinal centers controlling erection and ejaculation remain intact.

Prepubertal boys may experience orgasms even though they emit no ejaculate (these are so-called *dry orgasms*). Boys do not begin to produce seminal fluid (and sperm) until puberty. Mature men can also experience dry orgasms. These may take the form of "little orgasms" preceding a larger orgasm, or they can follow "wet orgasms" when sexual stimulation is continued but seminal fluids have not been replenished. Also, older men may not produce enough ejaculate to have a (noticeably) wet orgasm.

Peyronie's disease

Excessive curvature of the penis that can make erections painful.

orgasm

The climax of sexual excitement.

paraplegic

A person with sensory and motor paralysis of the lower half of the body.

Ejaculation occurs in two stages. The first phase, often called the **emission stage**, involves contractions of the prostate, seminal vesicles, and the upper part of the vas deferens (the **ampulla**). The force of these contractions propels seminal fluid into the prostatic part of the urethral tract—a small tube called the **urethral bulb**—which balloons as muscles close at either end, trapping the semen. It is at this point that the man perceives orgasm as inevitable. The man feels that nothing can prevent ejaculation.

In the second or **expulsion stage**, seminal fluid is propelled through the urethra and out of the urethral opening at the tip of the penis. In this stage, muscles at the base of the penis and elsewhere contract rhythmically, expelling semen. The second stage is generally accompanied by the sensations of orgasm.

In ejaculation, seminal fluid is released from the urethral bulb and expelled by contractions of the pelvic muscles that surround the urethral channel and the crura of the penis. The first few contractions are most intense and occur at 0.8-second intervals. Subsequent contractions weaken. The interval between them increases. Seminal fluid is expelled in spurts during the first few contractions. In young men, seminal fluid may be propelled 12 to 24 inches. But in some men, semen travels but a few inches, or oozes from the penile opening. The force of the expulsion varies with the condition of the man's prostate, his general health, and his age. More intense orgasms tend to accompany more forceful ejaculations.

Like erection, ejaculation is regulated by two centers in the spinal cord, one in the sacral region and one in the higher lumbar region. When sexual arousal reaches the point of ejaculatory inevitability, the lumbar ejaculatory center triggers the first stage of ejaculation, seminal emission. The lower, or sacral, ejaculatory center triggers the second stage of orgasm.

Although ejaculation occurs by reflex, a man can delay ejaculation by maintaining the level of sexual stimulation below the critical threshold, or "the point of no return." Men who ejaculate prematurely have been successfully treated in programs that train them to learn to recognize their point of no return and maintain sexual stimulation below it. (Issues concerning the definition and treatment of premature ejaculation are explored in Chapter 12, which discusses sexual dysfunctions.) Recognizing the point of no return and keeping stimulation beneath the critical level can also prolong coitus and enhance sexual pleasure for couples even when the man does not experience premature ejaculation.

RETROGRADE EJACULATION In **retrograde ejaculation**, the ejaculate empties into the bladder rather than being expelled from the body. During normal ejaculation, an external sphincter opens, allowing seminal fluid to pass out of the body. Another sphincter, this one internal, closes off the opening to the bladder, preventing the seminal fluid from backing up into the bladder. In retrograde ejaculation, the actions of these sphincters are reversed. The external sphincter remains closed, preventing the expulsion of the seminal fluid, whereas the internal sphincter opens, allowing the ejaculate to empty into the bladder. The result is an apparently dry orgasm. Retrograde ejaculation may be caused by prostate surgery (less so now than in former years), drugs such as tranquilizers, certain illnesses, and accidents. Retrograde ejaculation is usually harmless in itself because the seminal fluid is later discharged with urine. But infertility can result, and there may be changes in the sensations associated with orgasm. Persistent dry orgasms should be medically evaluated.

Male sexual functions, like female sexual functions, are complex. They involve the cooperation of the nervous system, the endocrine system, the cardiovascular system, and the musculoskeletal system. In Chapter 4 we examine the similarities and differences between females and males with respect to sexual differentiation, behavior, and personality. In Chapter 7 we learn more about how the female and male sex organs respond to sexual stimulation.

emission stage
The first phase of ejaculation, which involves contractions of the prostate gland, seminal vesicles, and the upper part of the vas deferens.

ampulla
A sac or dilated part of a tube or canal.

urethral bulb
The small tube that makes up the prostatic part of the urethral tract and balloons out as muscles close at either end, trapping semen prior to ejaculation.

expulsion stage
The second stage of ejaculation, during which muscles at the base of the penis and elsewhere contract rhythmically, forcefully expelling semen and providing pleasurable sensations.

retrograde ejaculation
Ejaculation in which the ejaculate empties into the bladder.

Chapter Review

LO 3.1 Describe the external male sex organs and their functions.

The external male sex organs include the penis and the scrotum, both of which are sensitive to sexual stimulation. Semen and urine pass out of the penis through the urethral opening. The scrotum is the pouch that contains the testes.

LO 3.2 Discuss the pros and cons of circumcision.

Circumcision has been carried out for religious and hygienic reasons. Research shows that circumcision makes a male less vulnerable to certain health problems but decreases sexual sensations.

LO 3.3 Describe the internal male sex organs and their functions.

The internal male sex organs consist of the testes, tubes and ducts that conduct sperm, and organs that nourish and activate sperm. Testes secrete male sex hormones and produce sperm. The hypothalamus, pituitary gland, and testes keep blood testosterone levels at more or less even levels through a negative feedback loop. Each epididymis empties into a vas deferens that conducts sperm over the bladder. The seminal vesicles open into the ejaculatory ducts where their fluids nourish sperm. Semen is made up of sperm and fluids contributed by the seminal vesicles, prostate gland, and Cowper's glands.

LO 3.4 Discuss urethritis.

Men, like women, are subject to bladder and urethral inflammations, which are generally referred to as urethritis.

LO 3.5 Discuss testicular cancer.

Cancer of the testes is the most common form of solid-tumor cancer to strike young men between the ages of 20 and 34. Treatment is typically removal of the cancerous testis.

LO 3.6 Discuss benign prostate hyperplasia.

Benign prostate hyperplasia (BPH) is noncancerous enlargement of the prostate, which is caused by testosterone and connected with aging.

LO 3.7 Discuss prostatitis.

Prostatitis is an inflammation of the prostate gland that is typically symptomized by discomfort between the legs, behind the testes, and, sometimes, by visible blood in the urine. It is treated with antibiotics.

LO 3.8 Discuss prostate cancer.

Risk factors for prostate cancer include genetics, aging, and race (African American men are at higher risk). Treatments include surgery, chemotherapy, radiation, and watchful waiting.

LO 3.9 Explain how erection occurs.

The penis erects when caverns within it become engorged with blood, expanding and stiffening it. Erection occurs in response to sexual stimulation but is also common during REM sleep. There are two erection centers in the spinal cord. Although erection is a reflex, penile sensations are relayed to the brain, where they generally result in pleasure.

LO 3.10 Explain how ejaculation occurs.

The parasympathetic branch of the autonomic nervous system largely governs erection, whereas the sympathetic branch largely controls ejaculation. Ejaculation, like erection, is a reflex. It is triggered when sexual stimulation reaches a threshold. The emission phase of ejaculation involves contractions of the prostate, seminal vesicles, and the upper part of the vas deferens. In the expulsion stage, muscles propel semen out of the penis.

Test Your Learning

1. _____ is characterized by prolonged erection.
   (a) Phimosis
   (b) Peyronie's disease
   (c) Ejaculation
   (d) Priapism

2. During the emission stage of ejaculation, semen is propelled into the _____
   (a) urethral bulb.
   (b) prostate gland.
   (c) sacrum.
   (d) bladder.

3. Both males and females have _____
   (a) sperm.
   (b) semen.
   (c) vas deferens.
   (d) corpora cavernosa.

4. Male circumcision removes the _____
   (a) frenulum.
   (b) prepuce.
   (c) glans.
   (d) corona.

5. Scrotal temperature tends to be _____ body temperature.
   (a) 5° to 6° F higher than
   (b) 5° to 6° F lower than
   (c) the same as
   (d) an unpredictable

6. _____ stimulates secretion of testosterone by interstitial cells.
   (a) Progestin
   (b) Prolactin
   (c) Luteinizing hormone
   (d) Follicle-stimulating hormone

7. _____ nanograms of prostate specific antigen per milliliter of blood are considered normal.
   (a) Fewer than 4
   (b) 4–10
   (c) 10–20
   (d) More than 20

8. Both semen and urine pass through the _____
   (a) vas deferens.
   (b) bladder.
   (c) urethral meatus.
   (d) intestines.

9. Men have erections every _____ minutes or so while they sleep.
   (a) 30
   (b) 60
   (c) 90
   (d) 120

10. The human penis contains _____
    (a) corpora cavernosa.
    (b) bone.
    (c) muscle.
    (d) interstitial tissue.

Answers: 1. d; 2. a; 3. d; 4. b; 5. b; 6. c; 7. a; 8. c; 9. c; 10. a

Chapter 4
Gender: Identity, Roles, Differences

Learning Objectives

TRUTH OR FICTION?

Which of the following statements are the truth, and which are fiction? Look for the Truth-or-Fiction items throughout this chapter to find the answers.

1 If male sex hormones were not present during critical stages of prenatal development, we would all develop external female sexual organs. **T / F**?

2 A woman with Turner syndrome cannot become pregnant, but she can carry and deliver a baby. **T / F**?

3 Seventeen of 18 boys who appeared to have female external sex organs suddenly developed male sex organs at puberty, when male sex hormones went to work. **T / F**?

4 The sex of a baby crocodile is determined by the temperature at which the egg develops. **T / F**?

5 Thousands of people have changed their anatomic sexes through gender-reassignment surgery. **T / F**?

6 Men act more aggressively than women do. **T / F**?

7 A 2½-year-old child may know that he is a boy but might think that he can grow up to be a mommy. **T / F**?

gender

The psychological state of being female or being male, as influenced by cultural concepts of stereotypical gender-appropriate traits and behavior. Compare and contrast the concept of gender with that of *anatomic sex*, which is based on the physical differences between females and males.

sexual differentiation

The process by which males and females develop distinct reproductive anatomy.

Laverne Cox and Caitlyn Jenner are two of the transgender superstars. Laverne Cox captivated viewers of the Netflix series *Orange Is the New Black* with her portrayal of the character Sophia Burset. Laverne was the first openly "trans" actress to be nominated for a Primetime Emmy Award. Caitlyn Jenner, of course, had been the 1970s Olympian decathalon winner Bruce Jenner for six decades and then the father figure in the reality show, *Keeping Up with the Kardahians*. Considered the world's greatest athlete after the Olympics, one-time *Playgirl* cover, and father of six children, Jenner came out as trans in 2015, at the age of 66. The change, which electrified the nation, led to a new reality series for Jenner, a series that sought to educate the public about trans people as well as to entertain.

This chapter addresses the biological, psychological, and sociological aspects of gender. First we define **gender** as the psychological sense of being female or being male and the roles society ascribes to gender. Anatomic sex is based on, well, anatomy. But gender is a complex concept that is based partly on anatomy, partly on the psychology of the individual, and partly on culture and tradition.

First we focus on **sexual differentiation**—the process by which males and females develop distinct reproductive anatomy. We then turn to gender roles—the clusters of behavior that are deemed "masculine" or "feminine" in a particular culture. The chapter examines research findings on gender differences. We then consider gender typing—the processes by which boys come to behave in line with what is expected of men (most of the time) and girls behave in accordance with what is expected of women (most of the time). We will also explore the concept of psychological androgyny, which applies to people who display characteristics associated with both gender roles in our culture.

Viewing the July 2015 Cover of *Vanity Fair*, featuring Caitlyn Jenner.

Prenatal Sexual Differentiation

LO 4.1 Describe the processes of prenatal sexual differentiation.

Over the years, less-than-scientific ideas have been proposed to account for sexual differentiation. Aristotle believed that the anatomic difference between males and

Figure 4.1   Development of the Internal Sex Organs From an Undifferentiated Stage at About 5 or 6 Weeks After Conception.

females was as a result of the heat of semen during sexual relations. Hot semen generated males, whereas cold semen made females. Aristotle may have given in to stereotyping—the stereotypes of "hot-blooded male" and the "frigid female." Others believed that sperm from the right testicle made females, and sperm from the left testicle made males.

chromosome

A rodlike structure found in the nuclei of cells that carries the genetic code in the form of genes.

When a sperm cell fertilizes an ovum, 23 **chromosomes** from the male parent normally combine with 23 chromosomes from the female parent. The resulting *zygote*, the beginning of a new human being, is only 1/175 of an inch long. Yet, on this tiny stage, one's stamp as a unique individual has already been ensured—whether one will have black or blond hair, grow bald or develop a widow's peak, or become female or male.

The chromosomes from each parent combine to form 23 pairs. The 23rd pair makes up the sex chromosomes. An ovum carries an X sex chromosome, but a sperm cell can carry either an X or a Y sex chromosome. The denotation of *X* and *Y* refers to the shapes of the chromosomes. If a sperm cell with an X sex chromosome fertilizes the ovum, the newly conceived individual will have an XX sex chromosomal structure and normally develop as a female. If the sperm cell carries a Y sex chromosome, the child will normally develop as a male (XY).

After fertilization, the zygote divides repeatedly. After a few short weeks, one cell has become billions of cells. At about three weeks a primitive heart begins to drive blood through the embryonic bloodstream. At about five to six weeks, when the

embryo

The stage of prenatal development that begins with implantation of a fertilized ovum in the uterus and concludes with development of the major organ systems at about two months after conception.

embryo is only 1/4- to 1/2-inch long, primitive gonads, ducts, and external genitals whose anatomic sex cannot be distinguished visually have formed (see Figures 4.1 and 4.2). Each embryo possesses primitive external genitals, a pair of sexually undifferentiated gonads, and two sets of primitive duct structures, the Müllerian (female) ducts and the Wolffian (male) ducts.

During the first six weeks or so of prenatal development, embryonic structures of females and males develop along similar lines and resemble primitive female structures. At about the seventh week after conception, the genetic code (XX or XY) begins to assert itself, causing changes in the gonads, genital ducts, and external genitals. Genetic activity on the Y sex chromosome causes the testes to begin to differentiate (National Center for Biotechnology Information, 2006). Ovaries begin to differentiate if the Y chromosome is absent. The reproductive organs of some rare individuals who have only one X sex chromosome instead of the typical XY or XX arrangement also become female in appearance because they too lack the Y sex

Figure 4.2 Development of the External Sex Organs From an Undifferentiated Stage at about 5 or 6 Weeks After Conception.

Undifferentiated

Glans area
Urethral fold
Urethral groove
Lateral buttress
Anal pit
Anal tubercle

Genital tubercle

45–50 mm

Male   **Female**

Glans
Site of future origin of prepuce
Urethral fold
Urogenital groove
Lateral buttress (corpus or shaft)
Labioscrotal swelling
Urethral folds partly fused (perineal raph)
Anal tubercle
Anus

Fully Developed

Male   **Female**

Urethral meatus   Clitoral shaft
Glans penis   Prepuce
Prepuce   Clitoral glans
Shaft or body of penis (corpus)   Urethral meatus
Penoscrotal raph   Labia minora
                                         Labia majora
Scrotum   Vagina

Perineal raph

Perineal tissues including external sphincter

chromosome. (One could thus say that the basic blueprint of the human embryo is female). The genetic instructions in the Y sex chromosome cause the embryo to deviate from the female developmental course.

By about the seventh week of prenatal development, strands of tissue begin to organize into seminiferous tubules. Female gonads begin to develop somewhat later than male gonads. The forerunners of follicles that will bear ova are not found until the fetal stage of development, about 10 weeks after conception. Ovaries begin to form at 11 or 12 weeks.

Genetic Factors in Sexual Differentiation

LO 4.2 **Discuss sex chromosomal abnormalities that may affect sexual differentiation.**

What roles do genes play in sexual differentiation? Some of the answers to this question are fascinating. Animal studies suggest a role for genes in the determination of mating and other behavior patterns in humans. For example, the interaction of a number of genes has led to the development of three different types of males in a crustacean as well as to a quite complex mating strategy (Benvenuto et al., 2015). One anatomic-sex-determining gene called *transformer (tra)* is needed in the development of female fruit flies. Chromosomal (XX) females with inactive tra attempt to mate with other females, but they are attractive to males because they still emit female phero-mones (Griffith, 2014). Researchers conclude that among fruit flies, sexual differentia-tion, sexual orientation, and sexual behavior are all determined by the interactions of genes (Griffith, 2014).

The SRY gene—which stands for *sex-determining region Y* gene—is also connected with sexual differentiation. In an article that could have been titled "The Mouse That Roared," researcher Stephen Maxson (1998) reported that a number of genes that are involved in determining maleness in mice, including SRY, are connected with aggressiveness. SRY is also involved in anatomic sex determination in humans (Savic et al., 2010), leading to formation of the testes. Another gene involved in anatomic sex determination has also been researched in mice: *Sox 9*. Sox 9 appears to regulate the expression of SRY (Czech et al., 2012). Females with XX sex chromosomal structure normally suppress the action of their own Sox 9, which in turn prevents the expres-sion of SRY. However, when these XX mice are chemically prevented from turning off Sox 9, they develop as males—albeit sterile males.

The Role of Sex Hormones in Sexual Differentiation

Once genes have done their work and testes develop in the embryo, they begin to produce male sex hormones, or androgens. Without androgens, we would all develop female external reproductive organs. The most important androgen, testosterone, spurs differentiation of the male (Wolffian) duct system (see Figure 4.1). Each Wolffian duct develops into an epididymis, vas deferens, and seminal vesicle. The external genitals, including the penis, begin to take shape at about the eighth week of development under the influence of another androgen, dihydrotestosterone (DHT).

1 › T / F   Truth or Fiction Revisited   It is true that without male sex hormones, or androgens, we would all develop female external reproductive organs. However, *Müllerian inhibiting substance (MIS)*, a testicular hormone that is secreted during the fetal stage, prevents the Müllerian ducts from developing into the female duct system. Moreover, those of us with apparent female external sex organs but with XY sex chromosomal structure would be infertile.

Small amounts of androgens are produced in female fetuses, but they are not normally sufficient to cause male sexual differentiation. In female fetuses, the relative absence of androgens causes degeneration of the Wolffian ducts and prompts devel-opment of female sexual organs. The Müllerian ducts evolve into fallopian tubes, the uterus, and the upper two-thirds of the vagina. Although female sex hormones are crucial in puberty, they are not involved in fetal sexual differentiation. If a fetus with an XY sex chromosomal structure failed to produce testosterone, it would develop external female sexual organs, but be infertile.

Descent of the Testes and the Ovaries

The testes and ovaries develop from slender structures high in the abdominal cavity. By about 10 weeks after conception, they have descended so that they are almost even with the upper edge of the pelvis. The ovaries remain there for the rest of the prena-tal period. Later they rotate and descend farther to their adult position in the pelvis. About 4 months after conception, the testes normally descend into the scrotal sac via the **inguinal canal**. Then the passageway closes.

Critical Thinking
Critical thinkers do not oversimplify or overgeneralize. Consider this statement: *In the absence of prenatal male sex hormones we would all develop as females.* Question: In what way would we all develop as females?

inguinal canal
A fetal canal that connects the scrotum and the testes, allowing their descent.

In a small percentage of males, one or both testes do not descend and remain in the abdomen at birth. The condition is termed **cryptorchidism**. In most cases of cryptorchidism, the testes migrate to the scrotum during infancy. In still other cases, the testes descend by puberty. Men with undescended testes are usually treated through surgery or hormonal therapy because they are at higher risk for cancer of the testes. Sperm production is also impaired because the undescended testes are subjected to a higher-than-optimal body temperature, causing sterility.

cryptorchidism
The condition defined by undescended testes.

Sex Chromosomal Abnormalities

Abnormalities of the sex chromosomes can have profound effects on sexual characteristics, physical health, and psychological development. **Klinefelter syndrome**, a condition that affects about 1 in 500 males, is caused by an extra X sex chromosome, so the man has an XXY rather than an XY pattern. Men with this pattern fail to develop appropriate secondary sex characteristics. They have enlarged breasts, poor muscular development, and because they fail to produce sperm, they are infertile. They may be mildly retarded.

Klinefelter syndrome
A sex-chromosomal disorder caused by an extra X sex chromosome.

Turner syndrome occurs in about 1 of every 2,500 females and is a consequence of having one rather than two X sex chromosomes. Individuals with this abnormality are at risk of developing heart disease, short arms and legs, kidney problems, hypothyroidism (producing too little thyroid hormone), and diabetes. Turner syndrome does not cause general cognitive impairment, but women may have specific problems in spatial relationships and math. Females with the syndrome may not naturally undergo puberty, so hormone treatments are usually begun when pubertal changes would start to spur growth of secondary sex characteristics. Nevertheless, nearly all women with the syndrome are infertile.

Turner syndrome
A genetically determined condition associated with the presence of only one complete X chromosome and with characteristics including usually infertile ovaries, absence of menstruation, and short stature.

2 › T / F Truth or Fiction Revisited   Interestingly, however, if another woman donates an ovum (egg cell), and it is fertilized in a laboratory dish, it can usually be implanted in a woman with Turner syndrome and the embryo can develop normally to term.

The brain, like the genital organs, undergoes prenatal sexual differentiation (Reddy et al., 2015). Testosterone causes cells in the hypothalamus of male fetuses to become insensitive to the female sex hormone estrogen. In female fetuses the hypothalamus develops sensitivity to estrogen.

Sensitivity to estrogen is important in the regulation of the menstrual cycle after puberty. The hypothalamus detects low levels of estrogen in the blood at the end of each cycle and initiates a new cycle by stimulating the pituitary gland to secrete follicle-stimulating hormone (FSH). FSH, in turn, stimulates estrogen production by the ovaries and the ripening of an immature follicle in an ovary.

Gender Identity

LO 4.3 Define gender identity and the roles of nature and nurture in gender identity.

Our **gender identity** is our psychological awareness or sense of being male or being female. It is one of the most obvious and important aspects of our self-concepts (Meyer-Bahlburg, 2015). **Sex assignment** (also called *gender assignment*) reflects the child's anatomic sex, and around the world it usually occurs at birth, although with the use of imaging techniques such as ultrasound in developed, it can also occur during prenatal development, once the male genitals become visible. But as we will see in Chapter 10, ultrasound is used commonly to determine the sex of the fetus in countries such as India and China where strong preference for sons prevails, and if the fetus is discovered to be female, it may be aborted.

gender identity
One's sense of being male or female.

sex assignment
The labeling of a newborn as male or female. Also termed *gender assignment*.

Most children first become aware of their anatomic sex by about the age of 18 months. By 36 months, most children have acquired a firm sense of gender identity (Fausto-Sterling, 2012).

Nature and Nurture in Gender Identity

Is gender identity fully a product of an announcement made by parents or other adults? Is that all it takes? Or are there also built-in biological determinants of gender identity? Could it be that our brains are biologically programmed along stereotypical masculine or feminine lines by prenatal sex hormones? Or do environmental influences, in the form of postnatal learning experiences, shape our self-concepts as being males or females? Or does gender identity reflect an intermingling of biological and environmental influences?

Gender identity, like prenatal sex differentiation, is almost always consistent with chromosomal sex, but such consistency does not certify that gender identity is biologically determined. Caregivers also rear us as males or females, according to our anatomic sex. How, then, might we sort out the roles of nature and nurture, of biology and the environment?

Some clues are found in the experiences of rare individuals known as **intersexual** people, or reproductive anatomy that is not consistent with usual concepts of female and male. Some intersexual people have external sex organs that are ambiguous. Others have the external organs of one sex but the internal organs of the other.

Researchers have wondered whether the gender identity of intersexual children reflects their chromosomal and gonadal sex or the gender to which they were assigned at birth, and according to which they were reared. Before going further, let us distinguish between true hermaphrodites and intersexuals.

Individuals born with both ovarian and testicular tissue are called **hermaphrodites**, after the Greek myth of the son of Hermes and Aphrodite, whose body became united with that of a nymph while he was bathing. True hermaphrodites may have one gonad of each anatomic sex (a testicle and an ovary), or gonads that combine testicular and ovarian tissue.

Regardless of their genetic sex, hermaphrodites often assume the gender identity and gender role of the gender assigned at birth. Figure 4.3 shows a genetic female (XX) with a right testicle and left ovary. This person married and became a stepfather with a firm male identity, despite his XX chromosomal structure. The roles of biology and environment remain tangled, however, because true hermaphrodites have gonadal tissue of females and males.

INTERSEXUALISM   True hermaphroditism is quite rare. The most common form of female intersexualism is **congenital adrenal hyperplasia (CAH)**, in which a genetic (XX) female has female internal sexual structures (ovaries), but masculinized external genitals (www.congenitaladrenalhyperplasia.org; see Figure 4.4). The clitoris is enlarged and may resemble a small penis. Congenital adrenal hyperplasia is caused by high levels of androgens, which are usually produced by the fetus's own adrenal glands. In other cases, mothers may have received synthetic androgens during their pregnancies. In the 1950s and 1960s, before these side effects were known, synthetic androgens were sometimes prescribed to help prevent miscarriages in women with histories of miscarriage.

Swedish investigator Anna Servin and her colleagues (2003) studied gender-typed behaviors and interests in 26 girls aged 2 to 10 with CAH and in 26 girls without CAH who were matched for age. Girls with CAH showed more interest in masculine-typed toys, such as transportation toys, and less interest in feminine-typed toys, such as dolls. The girls with CAH were also more likely to have boys as playmates and to desire masculine-typed careers. Parents rated the behavior of daughters with CAH as being more "boy-like" in choice of toys and

intersexual

A person who possesses the gonads of one anatomic sex but external genitalia that are ambiguous or typical of the other anatomic sex. Also termed *pseudohermaphrodite*.

hermaphrodite

A person who possesses both ovarian and testicular tissue.

congenital adrenal hyperplasia (CAH)

A form of intersexualism in which a genetic female has internal female sexual structures but masculinized external genitals.

Figure 4.3
A Hermaphrodite.

This genetic (XX) female has one testicle and one ovary and the gender identity of a male.

aggressiveness. Servin, her colleagues, and other investigators interpret the results as supporting a hormonal contribution to styles of play between girls with and without CAH, although other researchers also find a role for socialization (Fine, 2014; Wong et al., 2012).

There are several varieties of **androgen-insensitivity syndrome**, which is another type of intersexualism. One involves genetic (XY) males who, as a result of a mutated gene, have lower-than-normal prenatal sensitivity to androgens. As a result, their genitals do not become normally masculinized. At birth their external genitals are feminized, including a small vagina, and their testes are undescended. Because of insensitivity to androgens, the male duct system (epididymis, vas deferens, seminal vesicles, and ejaculatory ducts) fails to develop. Nevertheless, the fetal testes produce Müllerian inhibiting substance (MIS), preventing the development of a uterus or fallopian tubes. Genetic males with androgen-insensitivity syndrome usually have no or sparse pubic and axillary (underarm) hair because the development of hair in these locations is dependent on androgens.

Girls with *partial androgen-insensitivity syndrome (PAIS)* or *complete androgen-insensitivity syndrome (CAIS)* are also intersexuals. PAIS and CAIS occur in 1 in 2,000 to 5,000 girls with a single X sex chromosome and in girls with XX chromosomal structure who lose some X sex chromosomal material. Girls with CAIS develop typical external genital organs, but their internal reproductive organs do not develop or function normally. By contrast, girls with PAIS develop masculinized external genitals and are sometimes raised as boys, sometimes as girls. A study by Melissa Hines and her colleagues (2003, 2015) compared 22 women with CAIS and single X sex chromosomal structure with 22 women who had the normal XX sex chromosomal structure. They found no differences between the women with CAIS and controls in self-esteem, general psychological well-being, gender identity, sexual orientation, gender-typed behavior patterns, marital status, personality traits, or hand preferences. The researchers conclude that two X sex chromosomes and ovaries are not essential to the development of feminine-typed behavior patterns in humans.

Dominican Republic syndrome is a form of intersexualism that was first documented in a group of 18 boys in two villages in the Dominican Republic (Lang & Kuhnle, 2008; Newman, 2012). Dominican Republic syndrome is a genetic enzyme disorder that prevents testosterone from masculinizing the external genitalia. The boys were born with normal testes and internal male reproductive organs, but their external genitals were malformed. Their penises were stunted and resembled clitorises. Their scrotums were incompletely formed and resembled female labia. They also had partially formed vaginas. Because the boys resembled girls at birth, they were reared as females. At puberty, however, their testes swung into normal testosterone production, causing startling changes: Their testes descended, their voices deepened, their musculature filled out, and their "clitorises" expanded into penises.

3 › T / F Truth or Fiction Revisited Of the 18 Dominican Republic boys who were reared as girls, 17 shifted to a male gender identity. Sixteen of the 18 assumed a stereotypical masculine gender role. Of the remaining 2, 1 identified himself as a male but continued to maintain a feminine gender role, including wearing dresses. The 18th continued to see herself/himself as female and later sought gender-reassignment surgery to counter the pubertal masculinization. Despite being reared as girls, 16 of the 18 made the transition to the male role without conflict, suggesting the importance of biology in gender identity (Bailey, 2003b).

Many scientists conclude that gender identity is influenced by complex interactions of biological, psychological, and social factors. But could the "complex-interaction" approach be a way of avoiding the hot-potato issue as to whether nature (biological factors) or nurture (psychosocial factors) is more important? To place the

Figure 4.4 An intersexual person.

In congenital adrenal hyperplasia, a genetic (XX) female has female internal sexual structures (ovaries) but masculinized external genitals.

androgen-insensitivity syndrome

A form of intersexualism in which a genetic male is prenatally insensitive to androgens such that his genitals are not normally masculinized.

Dominican Republic syndrome

A form of intersexualism in which a genetic enzyme disorder prevents testosterone from masculinizing the external genitalia.

Critical Thinking
How do intersexual people provide researchers with a special opportunity to explore the origins of gender identity?

A CLOSER LOOK

XY BOYS WHO ARE REARED AS GIRLS

Are children "psychosexually neutral" at birth? Can you surgically reassign a boy as a female, rear him as a girl, and have him feel that he truly is a girl as the years go on? Will cosmetic surgery, female sex hormone treatments, and laces and ribbons do it? Or will he be maladjusted and his male gender identity sort of "break through"? Naturally, we cannot seek to answer these questions by randomly selecting male babies and reassigning their genders. Evidence on the matter derives from studies of children who have lost their penises or failed to develop them through accidents or unusual medical conditions.

David Reimer

Getting Down to Cases

For example, one of a pair of male twins, David Reimer, lost much of his penis as a result of a circumcision accident. As this case study is related by Colapinto (2000), the parents wondered what to do. Johns Hopkins sexologist John Money advised gender reassignment as a girl, believing that gender identity was sufficiently malleable that the boy could undergo sex-reassignment surgery (have his testes removed and an artificial vagina constructed) along with female hormone treatments, and then be successfully reared as a girl.

For a number of years, David, the gender-reassigned twin, unlike his brother, seemed to develop like a "real girl," albeit with a number of "tomboyish" traits. But at the age of 14,

when "she" was informed about the circumcision accident and the sex reassignment, David immediately decided to pursue life as a male. As an adult, he recalled that he had never felt quite comfortable as a girl—a view confirmed by the recollections of his mother. At the age of 25, he married a woman and adopted her children. This outcome would appear to support the view that gender identity may be determined to a considerable extent in the uterus, as the fetal brain is being exposed to androgens (Friedman, 2015a; Kranz et al., 2014).

Is It a Boy or a Girl? We don't have the answer, but the anatomic sex of this hatchling will depend on the temperature at which the egg was incubated. Clue: Some like it hot.

emphasis on nature is to lessen the role of personal choice and thus has major political consequences. Although some place relatively greater emphasis on psychosocial factors (Bradley et al., 1998; Money, 1994), others emphasize the role of biological factors (Diamond, 2011; Kovic et al., 2015). However, as noted in the nearby "A Closer Look" titled "XY Boys Who Are Reared as Girls," the theory that newborns are psychosexually neutral and that gender identity depends mainly on environmental factors has had rough sledding in recent years.

In case you have had enough discussion of the complex issues surrounding the origins of anatomic sex and gender identity in humans, consider the crocodile. Crocodile eggs do not carry sex chromosomes. Their anatomic sex is determined by the ambient temperature. Do male crocodiles have a right to be concerned about global warming?

4 › T / F   Truth or Fiction Revisited   The crocodile offspring's anatomic sex is determined by the temperature at which the eggs develop (Ackerman, 1991). Some (males) like it hot (at least in the mid-90s° F), and some (females) like it cooler, under the mid-80s° F.

Reimer committed suicide with a sawed-off shotgun in 2004, at the age of 38. When Colapinto received the news from David's father, he wrote, "I was shocked, but I cannot say I was surprised. Anyone familiar with David's life—as a baby, after a botched circumcision, [after] an operation to change him from boy to girl—would have understood that the real mystery was how he managed to stay alive for 38 years, given the physical and mental torments he suffered in childhood and that haunted him the rest of his life" (2004).

Another Case Study

Susan Bradley and her colleagues (1998) report on the development of another boy who suffered a circumcision accident in infancy. Again, John Money recommended sex reassignment, and the surgery was carried out at the age of 21 months. In this case, as Money found out in a follow-up at the age of 9, the individual was also tomboyish in behavior and personality traits but considered herself to be a girl.

She was interviewed subsequently at the ages of 16 and 26, and her situation had grown more complex. She considered herself to be bisexual and had sexual relationships with both men and women. However, when last interviewed, she had begun living with a woman.

A Larger Study

Researchers also recount the development of 27 children who had been born without penises due to a rare condition called *cloacal exstrophy* (Reiner, 2000). However, the children had normal testicles, male sex chromosomal structure, and male sex hormones. Nevertheless, the sex of 25 of the 27 children was reassigned shortly after birth. They were surgically castrated and reared as girls by their parents. As the years went on, all 25—5 to 16 years old at the time of the report—showed rough-and-tumble play considered stereotypical of males. Of the 25, 14 declared themselves to be males. Reiner (2000) suggests that "with time and age, children may well know what their gender is, regardless of any and all information and child-rearing to the contrary," he said. "They seem to be quite capable of telling us who they are." Reiner also noted that the 2 of the 27 children who were not sex-reassigned fit in with male peers and appeared to be better adjusted than the children who were reassigned.

Swedish neuroscientists Ivanka Savic and her colleagues (2010) report evidence that gender identity and sexual orientation (heterosexual or homosexual) can develop during the intrauterine period. However, sexual differentiation of the sex organs occurs during the first 2 months of pregnancy, whereas sexual differentiation of the brain begins later, during the second half of pregnancy. Sexual differentiation of the genitals and the brain both depend on surges of testosterone, but because they happen at different times, they occur independently. Therefore, it is possible that an individual's sex organs can develop in one direction while his or her brain develops in the other direction.

As Marianne J. Legato (2000), a professor of medicine at Columbia University, describes it, "When the brain has been masculinized by exposure to testosterone, it is kind of useless to say to this individual, 'You're a girl.' It is this impact of testosterone that gives males the feelings that they are men." The view that newborns are psychosexually neutral and that gender identity depends mainly on nurture has become increasingly criticized in recent years.

Being Transgender

LO 4.4 Discuss being transgender.

Yes, my teenage son is transgender. No, you may not ask about his genitals.

I am the mother of a 16-year-old transgender boy. For years, our child, whom we had thought was our daughter, suffered from depression, anxiety, an eating disorder, self-cutting, and suicidal thoughts before he came to us with his big secret. He was, in fact, male and he had hidden this through episodes of bullying and transfers to five different schools in three years. His life had been painful and he had wanted to end it at times. Finally, with the help of a kind and understanding therapist, he'd decided at the age of 15 to share with us who he truly was inside. We immediately showered him with love and support and watched with amazement as his anxiety and depression all but disappeared. Living as his true self was the blessing he'd been looking for, and our family was so much better off with a happy and more adjusted son.

—Sharon Dunski (2015)

Why would Sharon Dunski be referring to the issue as to the nature of her son's genitals? The answer is that many transgendered ("trans") individuals undergo cosmetic surgery to provide the appearance of the genitals of the gender with which they identify. But many others do not. And as actress Laverne Cox told Katie Couric:

Laverne Cox Trans star of *Orange Is the New Black* at the Emmy Awards.

transgender

Describing people who feel as though they possess the body of the wrong (anatomic) sex and desire to live as a member of the other anatomic sex. Some but not all trans people seek gender-reassignment surgery. (Also termed *trans*)

trans

a more current popular term for *transgender*.

autogynephilic

Descriptive of trans men who are sexually stimulated by fantasies that their own bodies are female.

The preoccupation with transition and surgery objectifies trans people. And then we don't get to really deal with the real lived experiences. The reality of trans people's lives is that so often we are targets of violence. We experience discrimination disproportionately to the rest of the community.

—Laverne Cox (2014)

Transgender (or **trans**) individuals wishes to possess the anatomic features of people of the other sex and to live as a person of the other anatomic sex. The term *transsexual* was previously used for transgender. Note that we are not using the term transgender*ism* because it sounds like a psychiatric or medical condition or disorder. We will use *transgender* and, where appropriate, the derivative term *trans*, which is coming into more common usage.

What motivates trans people to wish to live as people of the other anatomic sex? It appears that they experience incongruity between their genital anatomy and their gender identity. Although they have the anatomic sex of a male or a female, they *feel* that they are members of the other anatomic sex. The discrepancy motivates them to wish to be rid of their own primary sex characteristics (their external genitals and internal sex organs) and to live as members of the other anatomic sex. A male-to-female trans perceives himself to be a female who, through some quirk of fate, was born with the wrong genital equipment. A female-to-male trans perceives herself to be a man trapped in a woman's body.

But some researchers contend that many men who seek to become women tend to fall into other categories: either men who are extremely feminine, or men who are sexually aroused by the idea of becoming a woman. The first category includes gay trans men—men who are extremely feminine gays and not fully satisfied by sexual activity with other males (Blanchard, 1989; Cantor, 2011). The second category refers to males who are **autogynephilic**, or sexually stimulated by fantasies of their own bodies as being female (Moser, 2010; Nuttbrock et al., 2011).

We must inform you that the American Psychiatric Association (2013) includes the category of *gender dysphoria* in the fifth edition of its *Diagnostic and Statistical Manual of the Mental Disorders* (the *DSM–V*). The Association writes that "Gender dysphoria as a general descriptive term refers to an individual's [emotional]/cognitive discontent with the assigned gender but is more specifically defined when used as a diagnostic category." As a diagnostic category, it "refers to the distress that may accompany the incongruence between one's experienced or expressed gender and one's assigned gender" (p. 451). Therefore, if there is no distress, or if the distress does not reach the level of being "clinically significant," trans people are not considered to have a mental disorder (Zucker, 2015). In previous editions, trans people in general were considered to have a gender identity disorder (GID). Perhaps in the next edition, the American Psychiatric Association will do away with any reference to trans people.

Identifying as being transgender is far from rare. A study based on state and federal data estimates that there are about 1.4 million trans individuals in the United States (Flores et al., 2016). Trans people are more likely to be from ethnic and racial minority groups, especially Latin Americans. Young adults aged 18–24 were more likely than older groups to report that they were transgender. If we assume that younger adults, especially given the recent presence of trans individuals in the media, are more likely than older adults to be open about their gender identity, there might be more trans people among older age groups than older people will recognize or report. Note, too, that the estimate of 1.4 million does not include children; therefore, there could be 2 million or more trans people in the United States overall.

Real Students, Real Questions

Q *Can a man who has sex reassignment surgery get pregnant, or is that option futuristic?*

A No, he can't. Getting pregnant in the future is also unlikely. However—there's often a however in these matters—she could provide sperm prior to the change, use it to fertilize an egg from a donor, and the donor or another woman might carry the embryo to term.

Gay trans males usually show cross-gender preferences in play and dress in early childhood. Some report that they felt they belonged to the other anatomic sex as long as they can remember (Zucker, 2005a, 2005b). Some male-to-female trans men recall that, as children, they preferred playing with dolls, enjoyed wearing frilly dresses, and disliked rough-and-tumble play. They were often perceived by their peers as "sissy boys." Some female-to-male trans people report that as children they disliked dresses and acted like "tomboys." They preferred playing "boys' games" and playing them with boys. Female-to-male trans individuals appear to have an easier time adjusting than male-to-female trans individuals. Even in adulthood, it may be easier for a female trans to don men's clothes and pass as a slightly built man than it is for a brawny man to pass for a tall woman.

Many trans individuals undergo hormone treatments and surgery to create the appearance of the external genitals typical of the other anatomic sex. This can be done more precisely with male-to-female than female-to-male trans individuals. After surgery, people can participate in sexual activity and even attain orgasm, assuming that the muscles that surrounded the base of the penis—and now the constructed vaginal barrel—remain untouched. One survey found that 85% of trans women attained orgasm during sexual activity (Lawrence, 2005). They cannot, however, conceive or bear children.

5 › T / F Truth or Fiction Revisited   Gender-reassignment surgery cannot implant the internal reproductive organs of the other anatomic sex. Therefore, it is not accurate to say that people have actually changed their sexes—again, referring to anatomic sex—through gender-reassignment surgery. Instead, surgery creates the appearance of the external genitals typical of the other anatomic sex.

Gender Reassignment

Some trans people seek gender reassignment, and surgery is one of the options. The surgery has had at least four names over the years, and we list them here just so that you will recognize what is meant if you come across one of them:

- Sex reassignment surgery
- Gender reassignment surgery
- Gender reconstructive surgery
- Gender confirmation surgery

Because the surgery is irreversible, health professionals conduct careful evaluations to determine that people seeking reassignment are competent to make such decisions and that they have thought through the consequences. They usually require that the trans individual live openly as a member of the other anatomic sex for an extended trial period before surgery.

After the decision is reached, a lifetime of hormone treatments is begun. Male-to-female trans receive estrogen, which fosters the development of female secondary sex characteristics. It causes fatty deposits to develop in the breasts and hips, softens the skin, and inhibits growth of the beard (Fisher et al., 2015). Female-to-male trans receive androgens, which promote the development of male secondary sex characteristics. The voice deepens, hair becomes distributed according to the male pattern, muscles enlarge, and the fatty deposits in the breasts and hips are lost. The clitoris may also grow more prominent. In the case of male-to-female trans, "phonosurgery" can raise the pitch of the voice (Cavalot & Cossu, 2015). Practitioners note that the process is facilitated if it is begun prior to puberty because the biological changes of puberty can then be chemically suppressed, enabling male-to-female trans to avoid developing male secondary sex characteristics and a masculine body shape (Steensma & Cohen-Kettenis, 2015). It goes without saying that practitioners must be very certain that youth—who are legally minors—with gender dysphoria will retain their feelings (Pomara et al., 2015).

Despite its complexity and intimacy, sex-reassignment surgery is largely cosmetic. Medical science cannot construct internal genital organs or gonads. Male-to-female surgery is generally more successful. The penis and testicles are first removed. Tissue from the penis is placed in an artificial vagina so that sensitive nerve endings will provide sexual sensations (Perovic, 2015). A penis-shaped form of plastic or balsa wood is used to keep the vagina distended during healing.

In female-to-male trans, the internal sex organs (ovaries, fallopian tubes, uterus) are removed, along with the fatty tissue in the breasts. Some female-to-male trans engage in a series of operations, termed **phalloplasty**, to construct an artificial penis, but the penises don't work very well, and the procedures are costly (Arnez et al., 2015). Therefore, many female-to-male trans are content to have hysterectomies, mastectomies, and testosterone treatments.

phalloplasty

The surgical creation of an artificial penis.

Some trans people hesitate to undertake surgery because they are repulsed by the prospect of extreme medical intervention. Others forgo surgery so as not to jeopardize high-status careers or family relationships. Such people continue to think of themselves as members of the other anatomic sex, even without surgery.

OUTCOMES OF GENDER REASSIGNMENT SURGERY   Most reports of the postoperative adjustment of trans individuals are positive (Murad et al., 2010; Rolle et al., 2015). A Canadian follow-up study of 116 trans at least one year after surgery found that most were content with the results and were reasonably well adjusted (Blanchard et al., 1985). Positive results for surgery have also been reported in studies involving hundreds of Dutch trans (Cohen-Kettenis & Klink, 2015).

A study of 326 Dutch candidates for reassignment surgery found that about two-thirds (222) began hormone treatment, whereas 103 did not (Smith et al., 2005). Of the 222, about 15% dropped out before surgery. Generally speaking, after surgery the group was no longer gender dysphoric and most individuals functioned well sexually, psychologically, and socially. Only two male-to-female trans regretted their decision. Male-to-female trans outnumbered female-to-males, but postoperative adjustment was more favorable for female-to-males. One reason may be that society is more accepting of women who desire to become men (Smith et al., 2005). Female-to-male trans tend to be better adjusted socially before surgery as well so their superior postoperative adjustment may simply represent a selection factor.

Murad and his colleagues (2010) analyzed 28 studies with 1833 individuals (1093 male-to-female and 801 female-to-male) who underwent gender reassignment.

SEX IN THE DIGITAL AGE

GENDER-HACKING ON OKCUPID

I had just graduated from college … and was trying to navigate dating in the real world. So, like everyone else in my age bracket, I went on OkCupid.

Here's the thing about OkCupid—before you even fill out a profile, you're asked for your gender and what gender you're interested in. Which, yeah, makes total sense for a dating website, sure. But at the time, this wasn't simple for me—I wasn't really sure *what* gender I fit into. In college I had always identified as a butch lesbian, but I had recently started coming to terms with the fact that I might be a dude in a woman's body.

I didn't want to let this confusion limit my dating opportunities. So I came up with the following solution: I set up two essentially identical profiles—one as a woman looking for women, one as a man looking for men. I had always identified myself as queer, so it seemed logical to stick with what I knew. Both profiles included the same picture and the same answers to all the questions (more or less). Neither mentioned anything about my gender; I let people figure that one out on their own, just as I was trying to figure it out on *my* own.

Looking back now, this was the first time I had ever confidently presented myself to the world as male without apologizing or explaining or worrying what people would think. So when I went to check the activity on OkCupid, I was delighted to see I had roughly the same number of messages in the inboxes of both accounts. And not a single one of them said anything about my gender; they just accepted me for whatever I'd said I was. Man, it felt *great*.

—Tucker

Following the procedures 80% of the participants reported significantly less gender dysphoria and a more positive quality of life. Nearly three-quarters (72%) reported improvement in their sex lives.

Having noted these generally positive results for gender reassignment, we should note that practitioners in the field urge caution. Not all children and adolescents with gender dysphoria develop into adults who desire gender reassignment (Cohen-Kettenis & Klink, 2015). Some decide to retain the gender identity consistent with their anatomic sex and recognize themselves as being gay males or lesbians (Steensma & Cohen-Kettenis, 2015). On the other hand, it seems that when gender dysphoria is genuine and persistent, it may be cruel to withhold gender reassignment (Dunski, 2015; Steensma & Cohen-Kettenis, 2015).

Gender Roles and Stereotypes

LO 4.5   **Discuss gender roles and stereotypes.**

"Why can't a woman be more like a man?" This is the title of a song in the musical *My Fair Lady*. In the song, Professor Henry Higgins laments that women are emotional and fickle, whereas men are logical and dependable. The "emotional woman" is a stereotype. The "logical man" is also a stereotype—albeit more generous. Even emotions are stereotyped. People assume that women are more likely to experience feelings of

Table 4.1 Stereotypical Gender-Role Traits as Found in 26 Nations.

Stereotypes of Males		Stereotypes of Females	
Active	Opinionated	Affectionate	Nervous
Adventurous	Pleasure seeking	Appreciative	Patient
Aggressive	Precise	Cautious	Pleasant
Arrogant	Quick	Changeable	Prudish
Autocratic	Rational	Charming	Self-pitying
Capable	Realistic	Complaining	Sensitive
Coarse	Reckless	Complicated	Sentimental
Conceited	Resourceful	Confused	Sexy
Confident	Rigid	Dependent	Shy
Courageous	Robust	Dreamy	Softhearted
Cruel	Sharp witted	Emotional	Sophisticated
Determined	Show-off	Excitable	Submissive
Disorderly	Steady	Fault finding	Suggestible
Enterprising	Stern	Fearful	Superstitious
Hardheaded	Stingy	Fickle	Talkative
Individualistic	Stolid	Foolish	Timid
Inventive	Tough	Forgiving	Touchy
Loud	Unscrupulous	Frivolous	Unambitious
Obnoxious		Fussy	Understanding
		Gentle	Unstable
		Imaginative	Warm
		Kind	Weak
		Mild	Worrying
		Modest	

Note: Psychologists John Williams and Deborah Best (1994) found that people in 30 countries largely agreed on what constituted masculine and feminine gender-role stereotypes.
SOURCE: Data from Williams and Best (1994, p. 193, Table 1).

Critical Thinking
Why would a researcher bother to study whether traditional gender-role stereotypes are found around the world?

stereotype
A fixed, conventional and often distorted idea about a group of people.

gender roles
Complex clusters of behavioral expectations for males and females.

sexism
The prejudgment that, because of her or his sex, a person will possess negative traits.

fear, sadness, and sympathy, whereas men are more likely to experience anger and pride (Leaper & Farkas, 2015). A **stereotype** is a fixed, conventional—and often distorted—idea about a group of people. Sex assignment—our identification of ourselves as female or male—does not determine the roles or behaviors that are deemed masculine or feminine in our culture. Cultures have broad expectations for the personalities and behaviors of men and women, and these are termed **gender roles**. A survey of gender-role stereotypes across 26 nations confirmed that they are widespread (Cuddy et al., 2015; Williams & Best, 1994; see Table 4.1).

One of the effects of stereotyping is sexism, as we see in the following section.

Sexism

Where are we with **sexism** today? Haven't we come a long way since the "discovery" of rampant sexism 50 years ago—at least in developed nations? Even in an age where many consciously strive to avoid standard types of sexism, two types of sexism remain prevalent (Becker & Swim, 2012; Denmark & Williams, 2014). First is "benevolent sexism," the tendency to help women as—what we used to call—the "weaker sex." The other is "modern sexism"—the proclamation that sexism as we knew it is dead; we live in a "post-sexist" society in which both women and men are judged only on their merit when it comes to hiring them or guiding them into various lines of academic and vocational work.

Would that it were so. The reality seems to be that we have all encountered the prejudgment that because of her or his anatomic sex, a person will possess certain negative traits. These negative traits are assumed to disqualify the person for certain vocations or prevent him or her from performing adequately in these jobs or in some social situations.

In personal and social relationships, we still interpret the same behavior in prejudicial ways when performed by women or by men. A "sensitive" woman is simply sensitive, but a sensitive man may be seen as a "sissy." We may see a man as "self-assertive," but a woman who behaves in the same way is often seen as "pushy."

Children develop stereotypes about what is "man's work" and "woman's work" (Rathus, 2017). Women have been historically excluded from "male occupations," and stereotypical expectations concerning "men's work" and "women's work" filter down to the primary grades. For example, according to traditional stereotypes, women are not expected to excel in math. Exposure to such negative expectations may discourage women from careers in science and technology (Master et al., 2014). Even when they choose a career in science or technology, women are often subject to discrimination in hiring, promotions, allocation of facilities for research, and funds to conduct research (Denmark & Williams, 2014; Rennie, 2014). Similarly, only recently have men begun to enter occupational domains previously restricted largely to women, such as secretarial work, nursing, and teaching in the primary grades.

Sexism is psychologically damaging. One experiment found that women who were led to believe that sexism was pervasive reported lower self-esteem than women who were led to think that sexism was rare (Schmitt et al., 2003). In another experiment, men and women were led to believe that they were rejected from taking a course either as a result of sexism or personal reasons (Major et al., 2003). Attributing the rejection to prejudice rather than to personal deservingness had the effect of protecting their self-esteem ("It's not me; it's society").

Fortunately, it appears that education can modify sexist attitudes. One study reported on the degree to which women's studies courses can help individuals become more aware of sexism and develop more egalitarian attitudes (Stake & Hoffman, 2001). In the study, 548 women's studies students completed questionnaires prior to and following the courses in areas such as openness to women's studies, egalitarian attitudes toward females and gender issues, and awareness of sexism and discrimination against females. As compared with students who did not take women's studies, the students in the courses reported increased awareness of sexism and other kinds of prejudice, more egalitarian attitudes toward women and other stigmatized groups, and more interest in engaging in activism for social causes.

Gender Roles and Sexual Behavior

LO 4.6 **Explain the relationship between gender roles and sexual behavior.**

Gender roles affect relationships and sexual behavior. Children learn at an early age that men usually approach women and initiate sexual interactions, whereas women usually serve as the gatekeepers in romantic relationships. As gatekeepers, women are expected to wait to be approached and to screen suitors. Men are expected to make the first (sexual) move, and women are to determine how far they will go.

The cultural expectation that men are initiators and women are gatekeepers is embedded within the larger stereotype that men are sexually aggressive and women are sexually passive. Men are expected to have a higher number of sexual partners than women do, and do so (Fisher et al., 2012; Liu et al., 2015; Schmitt et al., 2012). Men not only initiate sexual encounters; they are also expected to dictate all the "moves" thereafter, just as they are expected to take the lead on the dance floor. People who adhere to the masculine gender-role stereotype, whether male or female, are more likely to engage in risky (unprotected) sexual behavior (Fields et al., 2015; Parent et al., 2012). According to the stereotype,

A Nurse and a Patient. If you think there might be something wrong with this picture, could it be because you have fallen prey to traditional gender-role stereotypes? Tradition has prevented many women from seeking jobs in "male" preserves such as construction work and the military. Tradition has also prevented many men from obtaining work in "female" domains such as secretarial work, nursing, and teaching at the primary school level.

SEX IN A WORLD OF DIVERSITY

THIRD GENDER/THIRD SEX

The terms *third gender* and *third sex* have been used to describe people who are considered to be neither women nor men, along with the social category in societies that recognize three or more sexes. Being neither male nor female has ramifications not only in terms of the person's anatomic sex but also in terms of the person's gender role, gender identity, and sexual orientation. In some cultures or to some individuals, a third sex or gender may represent an intermediate state between men and women, or it may represent a state of being both, as in the case of "the spirit of a man in the body of a woman." It may also represent the state of being neither (neuter), the ability to cross or swap sexes and gender roles, or another category that is independent of being male or being female. This last definition is favored by those who argue for a strict interpretation of the "third gender" concept.

The term *third gender* has been used to describe the Hijras of India and Pakistan, the Fa'afafine of Polynesia, and the Sworn virgins of the Balkans. In the Western world, lesbian, gay, transgender, and intersex people have also been described as belonging to a third sex or gender, although many object to being so categorized.

A small number of individuals within a population do not differentiate sexually into typical male or female bodies (Das, 2013; Hollimon, 2015). Some of them are intersexual. But we may also distinguish between anatomic (and XX or XY) sex and gender, which refers not only to biological sex but also to the psychological and sociological constructs of sex or gender. Many gender theorists find that a two-gender system is apparently neither inborn nor universal. A sex/gender system that recognizes only the following two social norms has been labeled "heteronormativity," but feminists and queer theorists consider it to be too limited to describe the variety of sexual interests and behaviors we find in the real world.

Let's have a look at some *non*-heteronormative patterns around the world.

Ladyboys Standing Outside a Nightclub in Thailand. Many ladyboys are exploited as prostitutes; "sex tourists" from distant countries travel to see them.

South-Central Asia

The Hijra of India, Pakistan, and Bangladesh are probably the most well-known and populous third sex type in the

women are supposed to let male partners determine the choice, timing, and sequence of sexual positions and techniques. Unfortunately, the stereotype favors men's sexual preferences, denying women the opportunity to give and receive their preferred kinds of stimulation.

According to another stereotype, men become sexually aroused at puberty and remain at the ready throughout adulthood. Women, however, do not share men's natural interests in sex, and a woman discovers her own sexuality only when a man ignites her sexual flame. Despite the stereotype, it is not clear that women are biologically less arousable than men; however, they are more likely to desire to limit sexual activity to intimate, committed relationships (Schmitt et al., 2012). On the other hand, researchers (Fisher et al., 2012; Hakim, 2015) find consistent empirical support for the view that men generally have more sexual desire than women.

Questions remain as to the extent to which the gender differences associated with gender-role stereotypes reflect nature or the influences of culture and modern world (Das, 2013). The Mumbai-based community health organization called The Humsafar Trust estimates there are between 5 and 6 million hijras in India. In different areas they are known as Aravani/Aruvani or Jogappa. British photographer Dayanita Singh writes about her friendship with a Hijra, Mona Ahmed, and their two different society's beliefs about gender: "When I once asked her if she would like to go to Singapore for a sex change operation, she told me, 'You really do not understand. I am the third sex, not a man trying to be a woman. It is your society's problem that you only recognize two sexes'" (Singh et al., 1999). Hijra social movements have campaigned for recognition as a third sex, and in 2005, Indian passport application forms were updated with three gender options: M, F, and E.

The "Ladyboys" of Thailand

Also commonly referred to as a third sex are the *kathoeys* (or *"ladyboys"*) of Thailand. Many see kathoeys as belonging to a third gender, including many kathoeys themselves, but for others, gender identity is not so clear. Sam Winter (2003) writes:

> We asked ... 190 [kathoeys] to say whether they thought of themselves as men, women, *sao praphet song* ["a second kind of woman"] or *kathoey*. None thought of themselves as male, and only 11% saw themselves as kathoey (i.e., "non-male"). By contrast 45% thought of themselves as women, with another 36% as *sao praphet song*.... Unfortunately we did not include the category *phet tee sam* (third sex/gender); conceivably if we had done so there may have been many respondents who would have chosen that term.... Around 50% [of non-transgender Thais] see them as males with the mistaken minds, but the other half see them as either women born into the wrong body (around 15%) or as a third sex/gender (35%).

There is "ladyboy tourism" in Thailand, with many locals and Westerners seeking out ladyboy prostitutes (Enteen, 2014). There are special beauty contests for ladyboys. There are many who exploit the Hijra of the Asian subcontinent and the ladyboys of Thailand.

The Western World

A historic note about terminology in the West: Some writers have suggested that a "third sex" emerged around 1700 in England. They described a subculture of gay effeminate males and meeting places ("molly houses"), as well as a marked increase among the general population in hostility toward effeminate or gay males. Writers such as Karl Heinrich Ulrichs, Magnus Hirschfeld, John Addington Symonds, Edward Carpenter, Aimée Duc described themselves and those like them as being of an "inverted" or "intermediate" sex. They also argued for social acceptance of such sexual intermediates. In retrospect we would likely say these men were gay—not "inverted" or "intermediate"—and that they were experimenting with a way of trying to come out and gain social acceptance. But you may come across this usage of the term third sex.

Indigenous Cultures of North America: "Two Spirits"

Native American cultures are also very much associated with multiple genders. They often contain social gender categories that are collectively known as "berdache" or Two-Spirit. Individual examples include the Winkte of Lakota culture, the ninauposkitzipxpe ("manly-hearted woman") of the North Piegan (Blackfoot) community, and the Zapotec Muxe. Various scholars have debated the nature of such categories, as well as the definition of the term *third gender* (Hollimon, 2015; Mirande, 2015). Different researchers may characterize the berdache as a gender-crosser, a mixed gender, an intermediate gender, or distinct third and fourth genders that are not dependent on male and female as primary categories.

tradition. Gender differences are also vastly more pervasive than those involving sexual behavior, as we see next.

Gender Differences

If females and males were not anatomically different, this book would not have been written. But how do females and males differ in cognitive abilities, personality, and social behavior, if at all?

Differences in Cognitive Abilities

LO 4.7 Discuss gender differences in cognitive abilities.

Although females and males do not differ noticeably in overall intelligence in our culture, gender differences appear in certain cognitive abilities beginning in childhood

Critical Thinking
Do you believe it would be "politically correct" to endorse or deny gender differences in cognitive abilities? Explain your answer.

(Halpern, 2012). Females are somewhat superior to males in verbal ability. Males, on the other hand, seem to be somewhat superior in visual–spatial skills. The picture for mathematics ability is more complex, with females excelling in some areas and males excelling in others. Let's take a closer look at these gender differences.

VERBAL ABILITY Verbal abilities include reading, spelling, grammar, oral comprehension, and word fluency. In the United States and Canada, females, as a group, surpass males in verbal ability throughout their lives (Halpern, 2012). Girls seem to acquire language faster than boys, utter their first word sooner, and develop larger vocabularies. Boys in the United States are more likely than girls to have reading problems, ranging from reading below grade level to learning disorders (Halpern, 2012).

Why do females excel in verbal abilities? For one thing, parents talk more to their infant daughters than to their infant sons. Encouragement of verbal interaction may be connected with girls' relative verbal precocity. Because of this early language advantage, girls may rely more on verbal skills to interact with people, thus furthering their abilities in this area (Halpern, 2012).

When we reflect on gender differences in reading, remember that in many repressive societies, girls are prevented from learning how to read—or even allowed to attend school. Biological factors such as the organization of the brain may also play a role in reading ability. In cultures in which boys and girls are both encouraged to learn to read, we may still consider whether the culture stamps reading as a gender-neutral, masculine, or feminine activity (Helgeson, 2015). In nations in which reading is looked on as a masculine activity boys do better than in societies is which reading is stereotyped as feminine. People tend to apply themselves more diligently to pursuits that they believe are "meant" for them—whether it is the life of the nomad, ballet, ice hockey, or reading.

VISUAL–SPATIAL ABILITIES *Visual–spatial abilities* refer to the abilities to visualize objects or shapes, to mentally manipulate and rotate them, and to find one's way by navigating the outer world. As you can imagine, these abilities are important in such fields as art, architecture, and engineering. Boys begin to outperform girls on many types of visual–spatial tasks starting at age 8 or 9, and the difference persists into adulthood (Halpern, 2012; Sneider et al., 2015; Yazzie, 2010). The gender difference is particularly notable on mental rotation tasks (see Figure 4.5), which require imagining how objects will look if they are rotated in space.

What is the basis for the gender difference in visual–spatial skills? A number of biological and environmental explanations have been offered. One biological theory

---

Figure 4.5 Rotating Geometric Figures in Space.

Visual–spatial skills—for example, the ability to rotate geometric figures in space—are considered part of the male gender-role stereotype. But such gender differences are small and can be modified by training.

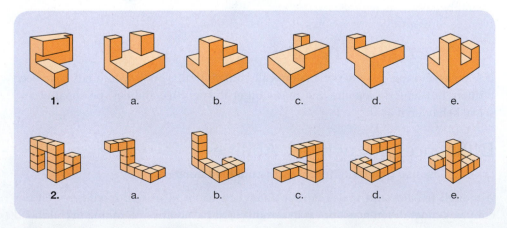

that has received some attention is that visual–spatial ability is influenced by sex-linked recessive genes on the X sex chromosome. But this theory has not been supported by research (Halpern, 2012).

Some researchers link visual–spatial performance to evolutionary theory and sex hormones. It may be related to a genetic tendency to create and defend a territory (Halpern, 2012; Stanyon & Bigoni, 2014). One environmental theory is that gender stereotypes influence the spatial experiences of children. For example, gender-stereotyped "boys' toys," such as blocks, Legos, and Erector sets, provide more practice with spatial skills than gender-stereotyped "girls' toys," such as baby dolls, Barbies, and play kitchens. Boys are also more likely to engage in sports, which involve moving balls and other objects through space (Ryan et al., 2015). Boys are allowed to travel farther from home than girls are, which gives them greater opportunities for exploration—and a larger "home range" (Halpern, 2012). It is no secret that participation in spatially related activities is associated with better performance on visual–spatial tasks.

MATHEMATICAL ABILITY The possibility—or presence—of gender differences in ability in math is a highly controversial topic in the social sciences because of its ramification for the future of females in the sciences, technology, and math. For half a century or more, it has been believed that male adolescents generally outperform females in mathematics, and research has tended to support that belief (Else-Quest et al., 2013; Miller & Halpern, 2014). However, research on the issue has been mixed, and gender differences are either non-existent or not as large as has been believed.

A study by Janet Shibley Hyde and her colleagues (Hyde, 2014; Hyde et al., 2008) of some 7 million 2nd- through 11th-graders found no gender differences for performance in mathematics on standardized tests. The complexity of the test items apparently made no difference. Nevertheless, most Americans continue to have different expectations for boys and girls, and these expectations may still dissuade girls from pursuing careers in science and math (Else-Quest et al., 2013).

But girls appear to be more vulnerable than boys to losing their self-confidence when faced with difficult math problems (Galdi et al., 2014). Mathematically gifted sixth-grade girls fare poorly when they are overly perfectionistic or anxious about taking tests, especially tests that are timed. Many female adolescents, especially when they are under pressure, are apparently vulnerable to feeling threatened by the stereotype that males are better than females at math. The threat is experienced as anxiety that distracts them from the tasks at hand and impairs their performance (Hyde, 2014; Passolunghi et al., 2014). On the other hand, when female adolescents' mothers strongly reject gender stereotypes concerning ability in math and science, their daughters are less likely to show stereotype vulnerability in tackling math problems (Tomasetto et al., 2011).

What, then, shall we conclude about gender differences in cognitive abilities? First, it may be that girls show greater verbal ability than boys but that boys have somewhat better visual–spatial skills (Miller & Halpern, 2014; Voyer & Voyer, 2014). However, gender differences in cognitive skills are group differences, not individual differences. That is, the difference in, say, reading skills between a male who reads well and a male who is dyslexic is greater than the average group gender difference

Are There Gender Differences in Cognitive Abilities? The physical differences between females and males are well established—and well celebrated! But are there cognitive differences between females and males? If so, what are they? How large are they? Are they the result of nature (heredity) or nurture (environmental influences such as educational experiences and cultural expectations)? Or do they reflect the interaction of nature and nurture as the person develops?

SEX IN A WORLD OF DIVERSITY

WOMEN IN STEM FIELDS

Despite research suggesting that there is no overall gender difference in performance on standardized mathematics achievement tests, most Americans continue to have different expectations for boys and girls, and these expectations may still dissuade some math-proficient girls from entering so-called STEM (science, technology, engineering, and mathematics) fields (Leaper et al., 2012). In the case of computer science, the media representation of the stereotypical computer genius is of a somewhat socially withdrawn, nerdish male (Cheryan et al., 2013, 2015; Master et al., 2014, 2015). Girls may not feel that they will belong.

Thus, there is reason to believe that women have the capacity to be entering STEM fields in greater numbers. So why, in the 21st century in the United States, do women remain underrepresented in STEM fields? There are a number of possibilities (Else-Quest et al., 2013; Hyde et al., 2014):

- Women who are proficient in math are more likely than math-proficient men to prefer careers that do not require skills in math.
- More males than females obtain extremely high scores on the SAT mathematics test and the quantitative reasoning sections of the Graduate Record Exam.
- Women who are proficient in math are more likely than men with this proficiency to have high verbal competence as well, which encourages many such women to choose careers other than those in STEM fields.
- In some STEM fields, women with children find themselves penalized in terms of promotions.

Women's preferences may well be a key reason why there are more men entering and remaining in STEM fields today. However, we need to note two caveats. One caveat, as shown by Table 4.2, is that women are tossing these stereotypes out the

Table 4.2 Bachelor's Degrees Conferred by Degree-Granting U.S. Institutions, by Gender of Student.

Discipline	Males	Females
Architecture	3,540	2,500
Biology	25,382	39,229
Business management	189,486	176,004
Chemistry	6,673	6,268
Computer and information science	9,143	1,636
Education	21,757	84,028
Engineering	65,829	15,553
Mathematics	10,723	8,119
Physics	4,263	1,002
Psychology	24,073	78,683

SOURCE: National Center for Education Statistics (2013).

window by entering STEM fields, and other fields still dominated by men, in increasing numbers. For example, women are currently receiving more bachelor's degrees than men in biology and nearly as many in chemistry (Table 4.2). The number of women receiving degrees in business management—the most popular undergraduate degree—is approximately the same as the number of men doing so. Men remain far ahead in the numbers of degrees received in computer and information science, engineering, and physics. Women, on the other hand, obtain many times the numbers of degrees obtained by men in education and psychology. The second caveat is that women's preferences cannot be fully divorced from society's expectations. As long as gender stereotypes and media representations about who belongs in STEM fields remain, at least some women will be discouraged from entering them.

in reading ability. Moreover, despite group differences, millions of females exceed the average American male in visual–spatial skills. Similarly, despite group differences, millions of males exceed the average American female in writing, spelling, and articulation. Hundreds of thousands of American women perform well in domains that once were considered masculine, such as medicine and law (Whitmarsh & Wentworth, 2012). Moreover, in most cases, differences in cognitive skills are small in societies in which women are empowered, including most parts of the United States, Canada, Europe, Japan, and South Korea (Else-Quest et al., 2010; Else-Quest & Grabe, 2012).

Differences in Personality

LO 4.8 **Discuss gender differences in personality.**

There are also many gender differences in personality. According to a meta-analysis of the research literature, females exceed males in extraversion, anxiety, trust, and nurturance (Feingold, 1994). Overall, however, differences in personality tend to be small (Bailey, 2003b). Males do tend to exceed females in assertiveness, tough-mindedness, and self-esteem. One study using the "Big Five Inventory" investigated gender differences in personality in 55 nations, with a sample size of 17,637 (Schmitt et al., 2008). Responses revealed that women reported higher levels of anxiety, extraversion (outgoingness), agreeableness, and conscientiousness than men did in most nations.

Two factors may largely account for the relatively lower self-esteem of females:

- Parents, on average, prefer to have boys.
- Society has created an unlevel playing field in which females have to perform better than males to be seen as doing equally well.

Differences in Social Behavior

LO 4.9 Discuss gender differences in social behavior.

There are important gender differences in social behavior, particularly in matters concerning sex and aggression. Consider communication styles. Research shows that males tend to dominate classroom discussions unless teachers take steps to encourage gender equity in the classroom (McHugh & Hambaugh, 2010). As girls mature, it appears that they often learn to "take a backseat" to boys and let the boys do most of the talking when they are in mixed-gender groups, especially if they are reared in "traditional" communities or regions of the nation. Women are more willing than men to disclose their feelings and personal experiences, however (Valkenburg et al., 2011). The stereotype of the "strong and silent" male may not discourage men from hogging the conversation, but it may inhibit them from expressing their personal feelings.

DIFFERENCES IN SEXUALITY According to almost any measure that is used, men show more interest in sex than women do, although the gender difference may not be as large as is generally believed and may also be influenced by sex-role expectations (Fisher, Moore, et al., 2012). Women are more likely to want to combine sex with a romantic relationship (Thompson & O'Sullivan, 2011). Men also report being more interested than women in casual sex and in multiple sex partners (Schmitt et al., 2012).

DIFFERENCES IN AGGRESSIVENESS Males tend to behave more aggressively than females, whether we are talking about rough-and-tumble play in childhood, going hunting, fighting in the military, body contact sports, or the incidence of violent crime (Hay et al., 2011). The key question is: Why?

DIFFERENCES IN WILLINGNESS TO SEEK HEALTH CARE Men's life expectancies are seven years shorter, on average, than women's. Female and male anatomy and physiology predispose them to different health issues, but part of the difference, according to surveys of physicians and of the general population, is women's greater willingness to seek health care (Glaesmer et al., 2012). Men often let symptoms go until a problem that could have been prevented or readily treated becomes serious or life-threatening. Women, for example, are much more likely to check themselves for breast cancer than men are to even recognize the symptoms of prostate cancer. Many men have a "bullet-proof mentality." They are too strong to see the doctor in their 20s, too busy in their 30s, and too frightened later on.

Gender Typing: Origins of Gender Differences

LO 4.10 Discuss biological and psychological perspectives on gender typing.

We have described biological sexual differentiation, and we have explored gender differences in cognitive abilities, personality, and social behavior. Now let us consider gender typing, the process by which males and females come to develop personality traits and behavior patterns that society considers to be consistent with their gender, male or female—at least most of the time.

Biological Perspectives: It's Only Natural

Biological views on gender typing tend to focus on the roles of hormones, genetics, and brain structures in predisposing men and women to gender-linked behavior patterns. It is largely assumed that a major mechanism by which heredity expresses itself in this realm is through prenatal sex hormones.

SEX HORMONES Researchers suggest that the development of gender differences in personality, along with the development of anatomic gender differences, may be related to prenatal levels of sex hormones. Although results of many studies attempting to correlate prenatal sex hormone levels with subsequent gender-typed play have been mixed, a study of 212 pregnant women conducted by Bonnie Auyeung and her colleagues (2009) found that fetal testosterone was related to masculine or feminine-typed play at the age of 8½ years. Other studies show that children display gender-typed preferences—with boys preferring transportation toys and girls preferring dolls—as early as the age of 13 months (Knickmeyer et al., 2005).

Also consider some cross-species research. The gender differences in activity preferences of children are also found in rhesus monkeys. For example, male rhesus juveniles and boys are more likely than female rhesus juveniles and girls to engage in-rough-and-tumble play (Wallen & Hassett, 2009). Researchers also introduced wheeled toys and plush toys into a 135-member rhesus monkey troop and found that male monkeys, like boys, showed consistent, strong preferences for the wheeled toys, whereas female monkeys, like girls, showed greater flexibility in preferences, sometimes playing with the plush toy and sometimes playing with the wheeled toy (Hassett et al., 2008). Do these cross-species findings suggest that such preferences in humans can develop without human gender-typed-socialization experiences?

THE EVOLUTIONARY PERSPECTIVE From the evolutionary perspective, the story of the survival of our ancient ancestors is etched in our genes. Genes that bestow attributes that increase an organism's chances of surviving to produce viable offspring are most likely to be transmitted to future generations. We thus possess the genetic remnants of traits that helped our ancestors survive and reproduce (Bugental et al., 2015; Buss, 2009b). This heritage influences our social and sexual behavior as well as our anatomic features.

According to the evolutionary perspective, men's traditional roles as hunters and warriors and women's roles as caregivers and gatherers of fruits and vegetables are bequeathed to us in our genes. Men are better suited to war and the hunt because of physical attributes passed along since ancestral times. Upper-body strength, for example, would have enabled them to throw spears and overpower adversaries. Men also possess perceptual–cognitive advantages, such as superior visual–motor skills that favor aggression. Visual–motor skills would have enabled men to aim spears or bows and arrows.

Women, it is argued, are genetically predisposed to be empathic and nurturing because these traits enabled ancestral women to respond to children's needs and to enhance the likelihood that their children would flourish and eventually reproduce, thereby transmitting their own genetic legacy to future generations. Prehistoric women thus tended to stay close to home, care for the children, and gather edible plants, whereas men ventured from home to hunt and raid their neighbors' storehouses.

The evolutionary perspective is steeped in controversy. Although scientists do not dispute the importance of evolution in determining physical attributes, many are reluctant to attribute complex social behaviors, such as aggression and gender roles, to heredity. The evolutionary perspective implies that stereotypical gender roles—men as breadwinners and women as homemakers, for example—reflect the natural order of things. Critics contend that, among humans, biology is not destiny, and behavior is not dictated by genes.

PRENATAL BRAIN ORGANIZATION   The organization of the brain is largely genetically determined, and prenatal exposure to sex hormones is a way in which the genetic code expresses itself (Avinum & Knafo-Noam, 2015). Is it possible that the cornerstone of gender-typed behavior is laid in the brain before the first breath is taken?

The hemispheres of the brain are specialized to carry out certain functions (Shaywitz et al., 1995). In most people, the right hemisphere ("right brain") appears to be specialized to perform visual–spatial tasks. The "left brain" appears to be more essential to verbal functions, such as speech, in most people.

We know that sex hormones are responsible for prenatal sexual differentiation of the genitals and for the gender-related structural differences in the hypothalamus of the developing prenatal brain. Sexual differentiation of the brain may also partly explain men's superiority at spatial-relations tasks, such as interpreting road maps and visualizing objects in space. Matthias Riepe and his colleagues (Grön et al., 2000) have studied the ways in which humans and rats use the hippocampus when they are navigating mazes. Males use the hippocampus in both hemispheres when they are navigating (Grön et al., 2000). Females, however, rely on the hippocampus in the right hemisphere in concert with the right prefrontal cortex—an area of the brain that evaluates information and makes plans. Researchers have also found that females, as a group, rely more than men do on landmarks when they are finding their way ("Go a block past Ollie's Noodle Shop, turn left, and go to the corner past Café Lalo") (Andersen et al., 2012). Men tend to rely more on geometry, as in finding one's position in terms of coordinates or on a map ("You're on the corner of Eleventh Avenue and 57th Street, and you want to get to Seventh Avenue and 55th Street, so . . .") (Andersen et al., 2012).

Testosterone in the brains of male fetuses spurs greater growth of the right hemisphere and slows the rate of growth of the left hemisphere (Cohen-Bendahan et al., 2005; Siegel-Hinson & McKeever, 2002). This difference may be connected with the ability to accomplish spatial-relations tasks, and with preferences for childhood toys.

Might boys' inclinations toward aggression and rough-and-tumble play also be prenatally imprinted in the brain? Some theorists argue that prenatal sex hormones may masculinize or feminize the brain by creating predispositions that are consistent with gender-role stereotypes, such as rough-and-tumble play and aggressive behavior in males (Cohen-Bendahan et al., 2005).

The gender differences in activity preferences of children are also found in rhesus monkeys. For example, male rhesus juveniles and boys are more likely than female rhesus juveniles and girls to engage in rough-and-tumble play (Wallen & Hassett, 2009). Researchers also introduced wheeled toys and plush toys into a 135-member rhesus monkey troop and found that male monkeys, like boys, showed consistent, strong preferences for the wheeled toys, whereas female monkeys, like girls, showed greater flexibility in preferences, sometimes playing with the plush toys and sometimes playing with the wheeled toys (Hassett et al., 2008). Do these cross-species findings suggest that such preferences in humans can develop without human gender-typed socialization experiences?

Another study investigated the gender-typed visual preferences of human infants at the early ages of 3 to 8 months (Alexander et al., 2009). The researchers hypothesized that preferences for gender-typed toys might be at least in part inborn and would therefore emerge in children before they were self-aware of their gender identity. The researchers assessed interest in a toy truck and doll in 30 infants by using eye-tracking technology to indicate the direction of visual attention. They did find the hypothesized gender differences in visual interest: Girls showed a visual preference for the doll over the truck, and boys showed a higher number of visual fixations on the truck than on the doll. As noted, these gender differences emerge much earlier than self-awareness of one's sex, and there has been relatively little time for social influences to take effect.

Critical Thinking
Why do you think some feminists and queer theorists argue that evolutionary theory is little more than a sophisticated excuse for maintaining the status quo in the centers of power in society?

SEX IN A WORLD OF DIVERSITY

THE EYE THAT ROVES AROUND THE WORLD?

One of the more controversial gender differences is the suggestion that males are naturally polygamous and females are naturally monogamous (Schmitt, 2008; Schmitt & Jonason, 2014). If this were so, it would place a greater burden on societies in which men are expected to remain loyal to their mates. If the man strayed, after all, he could have the attitude, "Don't blame me. It's in my genes." Women, moreover, might wonder how realistic it is to expect that their partners will remain faithful.

Evolutionary psychologists have hypothesized *sexual strategies theory*, which holds that men and women differ in their long-term and short-term mating strategies, with men more interested in sexual variety in the short term (Kennair et al., 2015). In the long term, both males and females may seek a heavy investment in a relationship, and feelings of love, companionship, and a sharing of resources. Even so, men are hypothesized to place more value on signals of fertility and reproductive value, as found in a woman's youth and physical appearance. But women are hypothesized to place relatively more value on a man's social status, maturity, and resources—cues that are relevant to his ability to provide over the long term. The qualities that men and women seek are believed to help solve adaptive problems that humans have faced over their evolutionary history.

Do Men Around the World Have Roving Eyes? A study of 10 different areas of the world found that in every culture surveyed, men were more likely than women to desire multiple sex partners. According to the sexual strategies theory, this gender difference reflects human adaptation to environmental forces. Here's a question for critical thinking: Does this research finding mean that it is "unnatural" to expect men to remain faithful to their partners?

Table 4.3 Gender Differences in the Percentage of Men and Women Who Desire More Than One Sex Partner "in the Next Month" across 10 World Regions.

	Percentage of Men Wanting More Than One Sex Partner	Percentage of Women Wanting More Than One Sex Partner
North America	23.1	2.9
South America	35.0	6.1
Western Europe	22.6	5.5
Eastern Europe	31.7	7.1
Southern Europe	31.0	6.0
The Middle East	33.1	5.9
Africa	18.2	4.2
Oceania	25.3	5.8
South/Southeast Asia	32.4	6.4
East Asia	17.9	2.6

Note: The chances that any gender differences within a given region are the result of chance is less than 1 in 1,000 (p < 0.001).

SOURCE: David P. Schmitt (2003). Universal sex differences in the desire for sexual variety: Tests from 52 nations, 6 continents, and 13 islands. *Journal of Personality and Social Psychology, 85*(1), 85–104, Table 5. Copyright © 2003 by the American Psychological Association. Reprinted with permission.

Psychological Perspectives

Developmentally speaking, children acquire awareness of gender-role stereotypes by the tender ages of 2½ to 3½ (Rathus, 2017). When asked to describe gender differences, boys and girls generally agree that boys build things, play with transportation toys such as cars and fire trucks, enjoy helping their fathers, and hit other children.

Figure 4.6   Mean Number of Sexual Partners Desired by Men and Women in the Next 30 Years, Across 10 World Regions.

SOURCE: David P. Schmitt (2003). Universal sex differences in the desire for sexual variety: Tests from 52 nations, 6 continents, and 13 islands. *Journal of Personality and Social Psychology,* 85(1), 85–104. Copyright © 2003 by the American Psychological Association. Reprinted with permission.

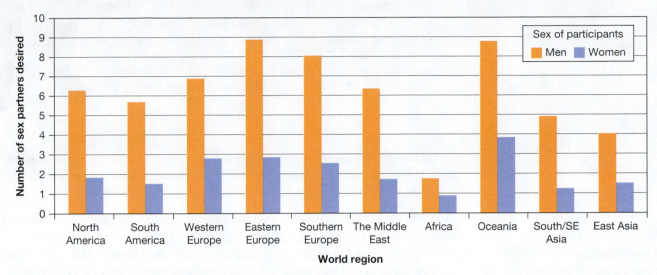

But in the short term, men are more interested in one-night stands and relatively brief affairs. Women, evolutionarily speaking, would have little to gain from such encounters. Impregnation requires a long-term commitment to childrearing, and evolutionary forces would favor the survival of the children of women who created a long-term nurturing environment. But men would have a greater chance of contributing their genes to future generations by impregnating as many women as possible.

Because a "universal" form of behavior is more likely to be embedded in people's genes, the evolutionary theory of different sexual strategies would find support if males and females from various cultures showed similar gender differences in short-term mating strategies. In seeking just such evidence, David Schmitt (2003) supervised a survey of 16,288 people across 10 major regions of the world, including North America, South America, Western Europe, Eastern Europe, Southern Europe, The Middle East, Africa, Oceania, South/Southeast Asia, and East Asia. He found that, indeed, gender differences in the desire for sexual variety are apparently universal.

Table 4.3 and Figure 4.6 reveal Schmitt's findings concerning desire for variety in short- and long-term relationships. When asked whether they would like to have more than one sex partner in the next month, men from all 10 areas of the world were significantly more likely than women to say that they would. For example, 23.1% of North American men would like more than one partner, as compared with just 2.9% of North American

women (see Table 4.3). When asked about the mean (average) number of sex partners they would like to have over the next 30 years, men from every area said they would like to have significantly more sex partners than did the women (see Figure 4.6).

We cannot conclude that these research findings, intriguing as they are, "prove" the validity of the evolutionary approach to understanding gender differences in "sexual strategies." For example, we could point to details in Figure 4.6, such as the fact that Oceanic women reported that they wanted more sex partners in the long term than did African men. We can also accept the universality of the finding but consider rival explanations for the data. For example, in a world with common global communication, it might not be surprising that there is worldwide overlap in gender roles. This overlap might affect the ways in which parents and cultural institutions influence children around the world.

Critical Thinking
According to evolutionary theory, men have inherited a tendency to be interested in having multiple sex partners. Does this mean that it is "unnatural" or counterproductive for societies to promote monogamous relationships for men?

Both boys and girls also agree that girls enjoy playing with dolls, help their mothers cook and clean, and are talkative, dependent on others for help, and nonviolent. They perceive the label "cruel" to be a masculine trait, whereas "cries a lot" is perceived as feminine. By the time they are age 3, most children have become aware of the stereotypical ways in which men and women dress and the types of occupations that are considered appropriate for each (Rathus, 2017).

Q *Aren't there cultures in which women do the hunting and gathering and men take care of the children?*

A There certainly have been some. In her 1935 book *Sex and Temperament in Three Primitive Societies*, anthropologist Margaret Mead described the Tchambuli of New Guinea as follows: "The men 'primped' and spent their time decorating themselves while the women worked and were the practical ones—the opposite of how it seemed in early 20th century America." But, frankly, what makes this finding notable is its rarity.

Many psychologists have attempted to explain how children acquire such knowledge and adopt stereotypical behavior patterns in terms of psychoanalytic, social–cognitive, or cognitive–developmental theories.

PSYCHOANALYTIC THEORY Sigmund Freud explained gender typing in terms of identification. Appropriate gender typing, in Freud's view, requires that boys come to identify with their fathers and girls with their mothers. **Identification** is completed, in Freud's view, as children resolve the **Oedipus complex** (sometimes called the *Electra complex* in girls).

According to Freud, the Oedipus complex occurs during the phallic period of psychosexual development, from the ages of 3 to 5. During this period the child develops incestuous wishes for the parent of the other anatomic sex and comes to perceive the parent of the same sex as a rival. The complex is resolved by the child's forsaking incestuous wishes for the parent of the other anatomic sex and identifying with the parent of the same anatomic sex. Through identification with the same-sex parent, the child comes to develop preferences and behavior patterns that are typically associated with that sex. But children display stereotypical gender-typed behaviors earlier than Freud would have predicted. Babies show visual preferences for sex-typed toys at 3 to 8 months (Alexander et al., 2009). During the first year, boys are more independent than girls. Girls are more quiet and restrained. Because of their lack of empirical support, many researchers believe that Freud's views are now of historic interest only.

SOCIAL–COGNITIVE THEORY Social–cognitive theorists explain the development of gender-typed behavior in terms of processes such as observational learning, identification, and socialization (Golombok et al., 2008; Zosuls et al., 2009). In social–cognitive theory, identification is seen as a continuous learning process in which rewards and punishments influence children to imitate adult models of the same sex. In identification, the child not only imitates the behavior of the model but tries to become broadly like the model.

Socialization also plays a role in gender typing. Parents, teachers, other adults—even other children—provide children with information about the gender-typed behaviors they are expected to display (Leaper, 2013). Almost from the moment a baby comes into the world, she or he is treated in ways that are consistent with gender stereotypes. Parents tend to talk more to baby girls, and fathers especially engage in more roughhousing with boys. When children are old enough to speak, caregivers and even other children begin to tell them how they are expected to behave. Parents may reward children for behavior they consider gender appropriate and punish (or fail to reinforce) them for behavior they consider inappropriate for their gender. Girls are encouraged to practice caregiving behaviors, which

---

identification

In psychoanalytic theory, the process of incorporating within ourselves our perceptions of the behaviors, thoughts, and feelings of others.

Oedipus complex

According to psychoanalytic theory, a conflict of the phallic stage in which the boy wishes to possess his mother sexually and perceives his father as a rival in love. (Sometimes called the Electra complex in girls.)

socialization

The process of guiding people into socially acceptable behavior patterns by means of information, rewards, and punishments.

are intended to prepare them for traditional feminine adult roles. Boys are handed Legos or doctor sets to help prepare them for traditional masculine adult roles.

Fathers generally encourage their sons to develop assertive, instrumental behavior (that is, behavior that gets things done or accomplishes something) and their daughters to develop nurturing, cooperative behavior. Fathers are likely to cuddle their daughters gently. They are likely to carry their sons like footballs or toss them into the air. Fathers also tend to use heartier and harsher language with their sons, such as "How're yuh doin', Tiger?" and "Hey you, get your keester over here." Being a nontraditionalist, your first author made sure to toss his young daughters into the air, which raised immediate objections from the relatives, who chastised him for being too rough. This, of course, led him to modify his behavior. He learned to toss his daughters into the air when the relatives were not around.

In traditional households, boys are more likely to receive toy cars and guns and athletic equipment and to be encouraged to compete aggressively from an early age. Girls are spoken to more often, whereas boys are handled more frequently and more roughly.

Maternal employment is associated with somewhat less polarized gender-role concepts for girls and boys (Goldberg et al., 2012; Greene et al., 2013). The daughters of employed women also have higher educational and career aspirations than the daughters of unemployed women, and they are more likely to choose careers that are nontraditional for women (Greene et al., 2013).

Social–cognitive theorists believe that aggression is largely influenced by learning. Boys are permitted, even encouraged, to engage in more aggressive behavior than girls.

Cognitive theorists address ways in which children integrate gender-role expectations within their self-concepts. Let us consider two cognitive approaches to gender typing: cognitive–developmental theory and gender schema theory.

COGNITIVE–DEVELOPMENTAL THEORY Psychologist Lawrence Kohlberg (1966) proposed a cognitive–developmental view of gender typing. Children form concepts, or **schemas**, about gender and then conform their behavior to their gender concepts. These developments occur in stages and are entwined with general cognitive development.

According to Kohlberg, gender typing entails the emergence of three concepts: *gender identity*, *gender stability*, and *gender constancy*. Gender identity is usually acquired by the age of 3. By the age of 4 or 5, most children develop a concept of **gender stability**—the recognition that people retain their genders for a lifetime.

7 › T / F Truth or Fiction Revisited   Prior to the age of 4 or 5 or so, children may have not developed the concept of gender stability. As a result, boys may think that they will become mommies when they grow up, and girls may believe that they can become daddies.

The more sophisticated concept of **gender constancy** develops in most children by the age of 7 or 8. They recognize that gender does not change, even if people alter their dress or behavior. So gender remains constant even when appearances change. A woman who wears her hair short (or shaves it off) remains a woman. A man who dons an apron and cooks dinner remains a man.

Gender Typing Through Observational Learning. According to social–cognitive theory, people learn about the gender roles that are available to them—and expected of them—at an early age. Gender schema theory adds that once children have learned the expected gender roles in their culture, they blend these roles with their self-concepts. Their self-esteem comes to be dependent on their adherence to the expected gender roles, often creating psychological issues for those whose interests and desires are inconsistent with stereotypical gender roles.

schema

Concept; way of interpreting experience or processing information.

gender stability

The concept that people retain their genders for a lifetime.

gender constancy

The concept that people's genders do not change, even if they alter their dress or behavior.

According to cognitive–developmental theory, children are motivated to behave in ways that society considers to be consistent with their gender once they have established the concepts of gender stability and gender constancy (Halim et al., 2014; Liben et al., 2014).

Boys and girls who come to recognize that their genders will remain a fixed part of their identity will show preferences for "masculine" and "feminine" activities, respectively. Researchers find, for instance, that boys who had achieved gender constancy played with an uninteresting gender-typed toy for a longer period of time than did boys who hadn't yet achieved gender constancy (Frey & Ruble, 1992). Both groups of boys played with an interesting gender-typed toy for about an equal length of time.

Cross-cultural studies of the United States, Samoa, Nepal, Belize, and Kenya find that the concepts of gender identity, gender stability, and gender constancy emerge in the order predicted by Kohlberg. However, gender-typed play often emerges at an earlier age than would be predicted by the cognitive–developmental theory. Many infants show visual preferences for gender-typed toys by 3 to 8 months (Alexander et al., 2009).

gender schema

A cluster of mental representations about male and female physical qualities, behaviors, and personality traits.

GENDER SCHEMA THEORY   Gender schema theory proposes that children develop a **gender schema** as a means of organizing their perceptions of the world (Bem, 1993). A gender schema is a cluster of mental representations about masculine and feminine physical qualities, behaviors, and personality traits. Gender gains prominence as a schema for organizing experience because of society's emphasis on it.

Children's gender schemas determine how important gender-typed traits are to them. Consider the dimension of *strength–weakness*. Children may learn that strength is connected with maleness and weakness with femaleness. (Other dimensions, such as *light–dark*, are not gender-typed and thus may fall outside children's gender schemas.) Children also gather that some dimensions, such as *strong–weak*, are more relevant to children of one anatomic sex (in this case, the male) than the other.

Once children acquire a gender schema, they begin to judge themselves according to traits considered appropriate to their anatomic sex (Fagot et al., 2000; Grace et al., 2008). In doing so, they blend their developing self-concepts with the prominent gender schema of their culture. Children with self-concepts that are consistent with the prominent gender schema of their culture are likely to develop higher self-esteem than children whose self-concepts are inconsistent. Jack learns that muscle strength is a characteristic associated with "manliness." He is likely to think more highly of himself if he perceives himself as embodying this attribute than if he does not. Jill is likely to discover that the dimension of kindness–cruelty is more crucial than strength–weakness to the way in which women are perceived in society.

According to gender schema theory, gender identity itself is sufficient to inspire gender-appropriate behavior. Once children develop a concept of gender identity, they begin to seek information concerning gender-typed traits and try to live up to them (Halim et al., 2014; Wong & Hines, 2015). Jack will retaliate when provoked because boys are expected to do so. Jill will be "sugary and sweet" if such is expected of little girls. Thus, gender-typed behavior would emerge earlier than would be proposed by cognitive–developmental theory. But even gender-schema theory cannot explain why boys and girls tend to show visual preferences for gender-typed toys before they are 1-year old.

In the following section, we see that some people have traits that are stereotypical of both males and females and that they promote psychological adjustment in a complex society.

Psychological Androgyny and the Reconstruction of Masculinity–Femininity: The More Traits, the Merrier?

LO 4.11   **Define psychological androgyny and discuss its possible advantages.**

Most people think of masculinity and femininity as opposite ends of one continuum. For them, it's a zero-sum game: The more masculine a person is, the less feminine he or she must be, and vice versa. So a man who exhibits stereotypical feminine traits of nurturance, tenderness, and emotionality is often considered less masculine than other men. Women who compete with men in business are perceived not only as more masculine but also as less feminine than other women.

Other investigators, such as Sandra Bem, argue that masculinity and femininity comprise separate personality dimensions (DiDonato & Berenbaum, 2011). A person who is highly masculine, whether male or female, may also possess feminine traits—and vice versa. People who exhibit "masculine" assertiveness and instrumental skills (skills in the sciences and business, for example) along with "feminine" nurturance and cooperation fit both the masculine and feminine gender-role stereotypes. They are said to show **psychological androgyny**. Assertiveness and instrumental skills are consistent with the masculine stereotype. Nurturance and cooperation are consistent with the feminine stereotype. People low in the stereotypical masculine and feminine traits are "undifferentiated," according to gender-role stereotypes.

People who are psychologically androgynous may be capable of summoning a wider range of masculine and feminine traits to meet the demands of various situations and to express their desires and talents (Cooper et al., 2011; Prakash et al., 2010). Researchers, for example, have found psychologically androgynous persons of both genders to show "masculine" independence under group pressures to conform and "feminine" nurturance in interactions with children (DiDonato & Berenbaum, 2011). Psychologically androgynous adolescents are less likely to stereotype occupations as masculine or feminine (Kulik, 2000).

Many people who oppose the constraints of traditional gender roles may perceive psychological androgyny as a desirable goal. Some feminist writers, however, have criticized psychological androgyny on grounds that the concept is defined in terms of, and thereby perpetuates, belief in the existence of masculine and feminine gender roles (Denmark et al., 2008).

Other critics suggest that some benefits of psychological androgyny are actually confounded with masculinity. For example, psychologically androgynous people tend to have higher self-esteem and to be generally better adjusted psychologically than people who are feminine or undifferentiated (DiDonato & Berenbaum, 2011; Parent et al., 2011). Does this mean that masculine traits such as assertiveness and independence may be related to psychological well-being, whether or not they are combined with feminine traits such as warmth, nurturance, and cooperation?

psychological androgyny
A state characterized by possession of both stereotypical masculine traits and stereotypical feminine traits.

Critical Thinking
Explain why feminists have criticized the concept of psychological androgyny.

"Rosie the Riveter"—She is a fictional woman who represented women aiding the war effort during World War II—wears overalls and a bandanna. Her arm is muscular and her gaze is pointed, but she also has long eyelashes and a sensuous mouth. She perhaps illustrates the concept of psychological androgyny.

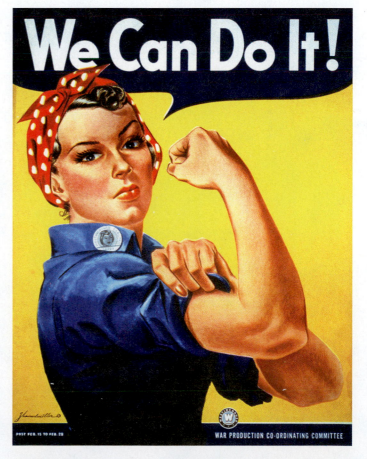

Q *Are there more similarities or differences between men and women?*

A Here's a shocking answer: It depends on how you look at it. We are used to focusing on the differences, but we'll take a flyer and say there are more similarities. For example, men and women share well more than 99% of their genetic material. They both walk upright, use language, think, perform in the sciences and the arts, play tennis and golf, have iPods and smartphones attached to their ears, and on and on. And, sadly, they both pay taxes and carry mortgages.

In any event, not all males are extremely "masculine," and not all females are overwhelmingly "feminine." Perhaps it is fortunate that few of us are completely masculine or feminine, despite our anatomic sex.

In this chapter we have explored what it means to be female, male, or another sex within a cultural setting such as ours. In the following chapter we consider how feelings of attraction and love develop in females, males, and others.

Chapter Review

LO 4.1 Describe the processes of prenatal sexual differentiation.

During the first 6 weeks or so of prenatal development, embryonic structures of both sexes resemble female structures. At about the seventh week, the genetic code (XX or XY) begins to cause changes in the gonads, genital ducts, and external genitals. Testosterone spurs differentiation of the male (Wolffian) duct system. In the absence of testosterone, the Wolffian ducts degenerate, and female sex organs develop. The testes and ovaries develop in the abdominal cavity. A few months after conception, the ovaries descend to the pelvic region, and the testes descend into the scrotal sac.

LO 4.2 Discuss sex chromosomal abnormalities that may affect sexual differentiation.

These abnormalities include Klinefelter syndrome (in which a male has an XXY sex chromosomal structure) and Turner syndrome (in which a woman has just one X sex chromosome.

LO 4.3 Define gender identity and the roles of nature and nurture in gender identity.

Gender identity is almost always consistent with anatomic sex. However, research with intersexual people suggests that prenatal exposure to androgens may masculinize the brain as well as the sex organs.

LO 4.4 Discuss being transgender.

Transgender, or *trans*, individuals desire to have the genital organs of, and to live as, a member of the other anatomic sex. Gender reassignment involves use of sex hormones and may include genital surgery.

LO 4.5 Discuss gender roles and stereotypes.

Cultures have broad expectations of men and women that are termed *gender roles.* In our culture the stereotypical female is seen as nurturing, gentle, dependent, kind, helpful, patient, and submissive. The stereotypical male is self-assertive, tough, competitive, gentlemanly, and protective. Sexism is the prejudgment that because of gender, a person will possess negative traits.

LO 4.6 Explain the relationship between gender roles and sexual behavior.

Gender roles encourage many males to take the initiative in matters of sex.

LO 4.7 Discuss gender differences in cognitive abilities.

Females excel somewhat in verbal skills, and males exceed females somewhat in spatial-relations skills. Recent research challenges the view that males perform better in math, showing no overall differences on math achievement tests.

LO 4.8 Discuss gender differences in personality.

Females are usually more extraverted and nurturing. Males are usually more aggressive and tough minded.

LO 4.9 Discuss gender differences in social behavior.

Males often dominate classroom discussions, and females are usually more likely to share their feelings. Men are relatively more interested in sex with multiple partners, and women are usually more interested in combining sex with romance.

LO 4.10 Discuss biological and psychological perspectives on gender typing.

Evolutionary theory explains gender differences in terms of adaptation to environmental forces. Testosterone in the brains of male fetuses spurs greater growth of the right hemisphere, which may be connected with spatial-relations tasks. Freud explained gender typing in terms of identification with the parent of the same anatomic sex. Social–cognitive theorists explain the development of gender-typed behavior in terms of processes such as observational learning, identification, and socialization. According to Kohlberg, gender typing entails the emergence of gender identity, gender stability, and gender constancy. Gender schema theory proposes that children blend their developing self-concepts with the prominent gender schema of their culture.

LO 4.11 Define psychological androgyny and discuss its possible advantages.

There is a question as to whether masculinity and femininity comprise two independent personality dimensions or a single bipolar dimension. People who combine stereotypical masculine and feminine behavior patterns are termed *psychologically androgynous.*

Test Your Learning

1. Müllerian inhibiting substance prevents the Müllerian ducts from developing into _____
   - (a) the female duct system.
   - (b) the male duct system.
   - (c) interstitial cells.
   - (d) external genital organs.

2. Congenital adrenal hyperplasia is caused by excessive levels of _____
   - (a) androgens.
   - (b) estradiol.
   - (c) pheromones.
   - (d) Müllerian inhibiting substance.

3. Transgendered people are most likely to have _____
   - (a) an extra X chromosome.
   - (b) androgen insensitivity syndrome.
   - (c) aggressive tendencies.
   - (d) gender dysphoria.

4. The masculine gender-role stereotype is seen as all of the following *except* _____
   - (a) sensitive.
   - (b) tough.
   - (c) protective.
   - (d) gentlemanly.

5. Which gender difference is supported by evidence?
   - (a) Males are better writers.
   - (b) Females are better in math and science.
   - (c) Females are more aggressive.
   - (d) Males have more reading problems.

6. According to sexual strategies theory, _____
   - (a) women choose the best-looking men.
   - (b) only humans have long-term mates.
   - (c) men are more interested in short-term sexual variety.
   - (d) women seek sex without commitment.

7. According to Kohlberg, gender _____ develops last.
   - (a) stability
   - (b) identity
   - (c) exclusivity
   - (d) constancy

8. The concept of the third gender challenges _____
   - (a) feminist theory.
   - (b) queer theory.
   - (c) heteronormativity.
   - (d) transgender activism.

9. Research shows that following gender reassignment surgery, most male-to-female trans _____
   - (a) are orgasmic during sexual intercourse.
   - (b) regret their decision to have the operation.
   - (c) develop psychological disorders they did not show evidence of previously.
   - (d) eventually discontinue hormone treatments.

10. The most common form of female intersexualism is _____
    - (a) Dominican Republic syndrome.
    - (b) congenital adrenal hyperplasia.
    - (c) being transgender.
    - (d) gender instability.

Answers: 1. a; 2. a; 3. d; 4. a; 5. d; 6. c; 7. d; 8. c; 9. a; 10. b

Chapter 5
Sexual Orientation

Learning Objectives

Getting Oriented Toward Sexual Orientation

LO 5.1 Describe the various sexual orientations and discuss controversies in defining them.

Perspectives on Sexual Orientation

LO 5.2 Explain how sexual orientation has been viewed historically and scientifically.

Sexual Orientation in Contemporary Society

LO 5.3 Discuss contemporary U.S. attitudes toward homosexuality.

Adjustment of Lesbians and Gay Males

LO 5.4 Discuss the psychological adjustment of lesbians and gay males.

LO 5.5 Describe concerns about and processes of "coming out."

Same-Sex Marriage

LO 5.6 Discuss the status of same-sex marriage in the United States, including changing attitudes toward same-sex marriage.

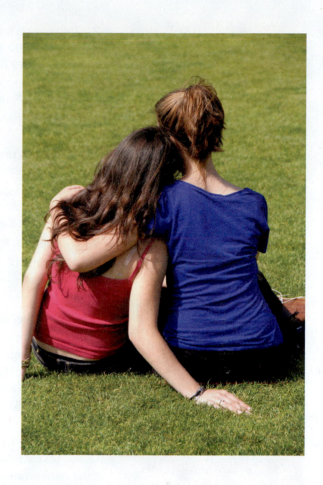

Singer Miley Cyrus at the 2015 MTV Video Music Awards. In the same year, Miley told *Paper magazine*, "Yo, I'm down with any adult—anyone over the age of 18 who is down to love me. I don't relate to being boy or girl, and I don't have to have my partner relate to boy or girl."

Miley Cyrus became well known to the public through her role as Hannah Montana, a Disney Channel series that ran from 2006 to 2011. She played Miley Stewart, who was your average American schoolgirl during the day but led a double life as teen idol recording artist Hannah Montana at night. When the series ended, Miley could be said to have embarked on another double life: she shot dramatically from wholesome teenager to a flesh-baring, twerking, on-stage pop star under her own name.

It could be stretching the point to suggest that sexually speaking, Miley could be considered to be leading yet a third double life. She is an LGBT activist who reports having sexual relationships with both men and women. She reports romantic relationships with women that were as serious as the relationships with men such as Liam Hemsworth and Nick Jonas. "I'm very open about it," she told a British magazine. "I'm pansexual.... I'm going on dates, but I change my style every two weeks, let alone who I'm with" (Elle UK, 2015). She elaborated her feelings in an interview with *Paper* magazine:

> I am literally open to every single thing that is consenting and doesn't involve an animal and everyone is of age. Everything that's legal, I'm down with. Yo, I'm down with any adult—anyone over the age of 18 who is down to love me. I don't relate to being boy or girl, and I don't have to have my partner relate to boy or girl. I've had [relationships with women] but people never really looked at it, and I never brought it into the spotlight (Petrusich, 2015).

Getting Oriented toward Sexual Orientation

LO 5.1 Describe the various sexual orientations and discuss controversies in defining them.

This chapter is about sexual orientation. **Sexual orientation** concerns the *direction* of one's romantic interests and erotic attractions—toward members of one's own anatomic sex, the other anatomic sex, or both. People who are exclusively erotically

sexual orientation

The direction of one's sexual and romantic interests—toward members of the same gender, the other gender, or both.

attracted to people of their own anatomic sex are labeled **homosexual** (from the Greek *homos*, meaning "same"). People who are **heterosexual** (from the Greek *heteros*, meaning "other") are exclusively erotically attracted to people of the other anatomic sex. It's not just about sexual activity, however. Homosexuals and heterosexuals also prefer to develop romantic relationships with, respectively, people of their own anatomic sex or people of the other anatomic sex.

Miley Cyrus referred to herself as *pansexual*. *Pan-* derives from Greek terms and is a prefix meaning "all." The term in use by researchers is *bisexual*, not pansexual, with *bi-* meaning "two" (as a *bicycle* has two wheels). The direction of one's erotic and romantic attractions is referred to as one's sexual orientation. We will see that homosexual people, like heterosexual people, incorporate their sexual orientation within their personal sexual identity, to find lovers, and to establish satisfying lifestyles. For some homosexuals, recognition and incorporation of their sexual orientation into their identity is a struggle because homosexuals in our culture have faced and—in many locations and with many people—continue to face a backdrop of social intolerance, even if they commit themselves to long-term relationships and marriage with same-sex partners.

One's **sexual identity** refers to one's sense of who one is in terms of one's sexual anatomy; cultural stereotypes of masculinity and femininity; one's place in a given cultural setting as a man, woman, or somewhere in between; and the anatomic sex of those to whom one is sexually attracted. The term *sexual orientation,* then, is more narrow than sexual identity in that it refers only to one's erotic attractions toward, and interests in developing romantic relationships with, members of one's own anatomic sex or the other sex. Many homosexual people refer to heterosexual people as being *straight,* or as *straights.*

The term *homosexual* denotes sexual interest in members of one's own *anatomic sex* and applies to both men and women. Homosexual men are often referred to as **gay males**. Homosexual women are often called **lesbians**. Gay males and lesbians are also sometimes referred to collectively as "gays" or "gay people." We commonly hear the term *gay marriage* used as being synonymous with *same-sex marriage,* and in this case "gay" refers to lesbians as well as to gay males.

Coming to Terms with Terms

Now that we have defined homosexuality, let us note that the term has been controversial over the years. Some homosexuals and other people object to the term *homosexuality* because they feel that it appears to focus on sexual behavior. The term *homosexual* actually refers to feelings of attraction and desires for romantic relationships, and not directly to behavior. The direction of one's feelings of attraction and desires for romantic relationships may *lead* to sexual behavior, but it is not the same thing. Moreover, the term bears a social stigma and has been historically associated with concepts of deviance and mental illness. In this book, your authors speak of male–female sexual behavior (not *heterosexual* behavior), male–male sexual behavior, and female–female sexual behavior to help distinguish sexual behavior from sexual orientation.

Nor are the collective terms *gays* and *gay people* without controversy. Because the term *gay* is commonly used to refer to men only, critics argue that the term renders lesbians "invisible." Thus, many people would prefer terms such as a *gay male sexual orientation* or a *lesbian sexual orientation.*

Sexual Orientation, Sexual Identity, and Heteronormativity

Again, one's sexual orientation is just one part of one's sexual identity. Because gay males and lesbians are attracted to members of their own anatomic sex, some people assume that they would prefer to be members of the other sex. This is not so.

homosexual orientation
Erotic attraction to, preference for, and developing romantic relationships with members of the same gender. (From the Greek *homos,* meaning "same," not the Latin *homo,* which means "man").

heterosexual orientation
Exclusive erotic attraction to, preference for, and developing romantic relationships with members of the other gender.

sexual identity
one's sense of who one is in terms of one's sexual anatomy; cultural stereotypes of masculinity and femininity; one's place in a given cultural setting as a man, woman, or somewhere in between; and the anatomic sex of those to whom one is sexually attracted.

gay males
Males who are sexually attracted to and desire to form romantic relationships with other males.

lesbians
Females who are sexually attracted to and interested in forming relationships with other females. (After *Lesbos,* the Greek island on which, legend has it, female–female sexual activity was idealized.)

Critical Thinking
Critical thinkers pay close attention to the meanings—and implications—of terms. Why do your authors prefer to use the terms *male–male sexual behavior* or *female–female sexual behavior* rather than *homosexual behavior*?

heteronormativity
The assumption that heterosexuality—being attracted to members of the other anatomic sex—is normal.

1 ⟩ T / F   Truth or Fiction Revisited   The category of homosexuality refers to individuals who are satisfied with their own anatomic sex. The aspect of their sexual identity that refers to their knowledge of their own anatomic sex is consistent with their anatomic sex. That is, a gay male is satisfied with having a penis. A lesbian is satisfied with having a vagina and breasts. Feeling dissatisfied with one's own anatomic sex is characteristic of transgenderism, or being "trans," as we saw in Chapter 4. Being trans is distinct from the definition of homosexuality and from the experiences of homosexuals.

Does this mean that the sexual identity of homosexuals is "split" or in "conflict" because homosexuals are satisfied with their own genitals but are erotically attracted to people of the other anatomic sex? The question itself is **heteronormative**. By that we mean that the question assumes that it is normal for men—or for people with male genitals—to be erotically attracted to women. Likewise, it assumes that it is normal for women—that is, for people with female genitals—to be sexually attracted to men. Homosexuals generally argue that heteronormativity is one aspect of millennia of prejudice against homosexuals. Yes, reproduction requires the union of sperm and ova, but, again, there is a distinction between one's sexual orientation and one's behavior. Many homosexuals have sexual relations with people of the other anatomic sex to reproduce. Others, including one gay couple we know, mixed their sperm in a "cocktail" and used it to impregnate a surrogate mother to have a child. And many homosexuals, like many heterosexuals, do not reproduce.

When heterosexuals think about homosexuals, they tend to focus almost exclusively on sexual aspects of male–male and female–female relationships. But, as noted, the relationships of homosexuals, like those of heterosexuals, involve more than sexual behavior. Homosexuals, like heterosexuals, spend only a small amount of time engaged in sexual activity. More basic to a gay male or lesbian sexual orientation is the interest in forming romantic attachments with members of one's own anatomic sex. These attachments, like male–female attachments, provide a framework for love and intimacy. Sexual orientations, again, are not defined by sexual activity per se, but rather by the *direction* of one's romantic interests and erotic attractions (Savin-Williams, 2014).

Classification of Sexual Orientation: Is Yes or No Enough?

Determining a person's sexual orientation might seem to be a clear-cut task. Some people are exclusively homosexual and limit their sexual activities to partners of their own anatomic sex. Others are strictly heterosexual and limit their sexual activities to partners of the other anatomic sex. Some people fall in between.

Many heterosexual people have had sexual experiences with people of their own anatomic sex (Savin-Williams et al., 2012). Historically speaking, we have noted that in the absence of heterosexual outlets, adolescents and isolated populations such as prison inmates may have sexual experiences with people of their own anatomic sex while they maintain their heterosexual identities and a preference for sexual activities with people of the other anatomic sex.

Gay males and lesbians, too, may engage in male–female sexual activity while maintaining a homosexual orientation. Some gay males and lesbians marry members of the other anatomic sex but harbor unfulfilled desires for members of their own anatomic sex. Some of them are not completely aware that they would prefer sexual and romantic relationships with members of their own anatomic sex. Others are aware of their feelings but believe they will be better adjusted if they behave as if they had a heterosexual orientation. Then, too, some people are bisexual but may not act on their attraction to members of their own anatomic sex (Rosenthal et al., 2012).

Real Students, Real Questions

Q *Are some people so unsuccessful with the opposite sex that they become gay?*

A No. It seems that sexual orientation has nothing to do with success or failure with members of one anatomic sex or the other. Many individuals recognize that they are heterosexual or homosexual before they have any sexual experiences with other people.

On the other hand, many people see themselves as gay or heterosexual long before they ever have sex with members of their own sex (Thompson & Morgan, 2008; Savin-Williams & Diamond, 2000). Some people, homosexual and heterosexual alike, adopt a celibate lifestyle for religious or ascetic reasons.

People's erotic interests and fantasies may also shift over time. Men who consider themselves to be "100% heterosexual" are least likely to change their sexual orientation (Savin-Williams et al., 2012). Gay males and lesbians may experience sporadic **heteroerotic** interests. Heterosexual people may have occasional **homoerotic** interests. To some extent, women's sexual orientations are more flexible or plastic than men's, with women being somewhat more dependent on social experience (Savin-Williams et al., 2012). Lisa M. Diamond (2003b) conducted a survey of lesbian and bisexual women that involved three interviews over a 5-year period. She found that more than 25% of the women relinquished their lesbian or bisexual orientation as time went on. Half of these relabeled themselves as heterosexual, and the other half renounced any effort at self-labeling. Some heterosexual people report fantasies about sexual activity with people of their own anatomic sex.

Attraction to people of the other anatomic sex and people of one's own anatomic sex may therefore not always be mutually exclusive. People may have various degrees of sexual interest in, and sexual experience with, people of either anatomic sex (Vrangalova & Savin-Williams, 2012). For this reason, some investigators have proposed additional sexual orientations, one of them being "mostly heterosexual" (Savin-Williams & Vrangalova, 2013).

heteroerotic

Of an erotic nature and involving members of the other gender.

homoerotic

Of an erotic nature and involving members of one's own gender.

2 › T / F Truth or Fiction Revisited   There is a body of research evidence that suggests that people can indeed be bisexual. Many of them are "mostly heterosexual," but they still are attracted to people of their own anatomic sex.

Kinsey and his colleagues recognized early on that the boundaries between gay male and lesbian sexual orientations, on the one hand, and a heterosexual orientation, on the other, are sometimes blurry. As Kinsey and his colleagues noted,

> The world is not to be divided into sheep and goats.… Only the human mind invents categories and tries to force facts into separated pigeonholes. The living world is a continuum in each and every one of its aspects. (1948, p. 639)

Kinsey and his colleagues (1948, 1953) found evidence of a continuum of sexual orientation among the people they surveyed, with bisexuality representing a midpoint between exclusively heterosexual and exclusively homosexual sexual orientations (see Figure 5.1). People are located on the continuum according to their patterns of sexual attraction and behavior. People in category 0 are considered exclusively heterosexual. People in category 6 are considered exclusively gay.

Figure 5.1   The Kinsey Continuum.

Kinsey and his colleagues conceived of a 7-point heterosexual—homosexual continuum that classifies people according to their homosexual behavior and the magnitude of their attraction to members of their own gender. People in category 0, who accounted for most of Kinsey's study participants, were considered exclusively heterosexual. People in category 6 were considered exclusively homosexual.

How Many People, Then, Are Heterosexual, Homosexual, and Bisexual?

Kinsey and his colleagues (1948, 1953) reported that about 4% of men and 1% to 3% of women in their samples were exclusively gay (category 6 on their scale). A larger percentage of people were considered predominantly gay (4 or 5 on their scale) or predominantly heterosexual (1 or 2 on their scale). All in all, Kinsey's data suggested that close to 10% of the U.S. population was gay or predominantly gay, a number that exceeds most current estimates. Some were classified as equally gay and heterosexual in orientation and could be labeled bisexual (scale point 3). Most people were classified as exclusively heterosexual (scale point 0).

But statistics concerning *past* sexual activity with a member of one's own anatomic sex can be misleading. They may represent a single episode or a brief period of adolescent experimentation. Half of the men who reported male–male sexual activity in Kinsey's sample limited it to the ages of 12 to 14. Another third had male–male sexual experience by the age of 18, but not again.

Kinsey's research, consistent with more recent research, also showed that sexual behavior patterns can change, sometimes dramatically so. Sexual experiences or feelings involving people of one's own anatomic sex are common, especially in adolescence, and do not necessarily mean that one will engage in sexual activity exclusively with people of one's own anatomic sex in adulthood (Savin-Williams et al., 2012). On the other hand, it seems insulting to homosexuals to suggest that many people "outgrow" having youthful sexual activity with members of their own anatomic sex when they "grow up." It seems less biased and more realistic to simple not that many youth have limited opportunities for sexual expression and that there is a tendency to experiment with a variety of sexual outlets. Once people become clear about what they want and the objects of their desire are available, they tend to head toward those objects.

The controversy over how many people belong to sexual minorities continues. According to a number of investigators (Herbenick et al., 2010a, 2010b, 2010c; Reece et al., 2010a), about 7% of American women and men define themselves as being "other than heterosexual," but the behavior of the other 93% doesn't exactly match up with the way in which people label themselves. For example, nearly twice as many people—about 14%—say they have had oral sex with a person of the same anatomic sex.

THE GALLUP TRACKING SURVEY A recent and carefully conducted survey of sexual orientation in the United States was conducted by the Gallup organization as part of the Gallup Daily tracking survey leading up to the 2012 presidential election (Gates & Newport, 2012). The Gallup organization used random telephone dialing and asked about sexual orientation as one among many questions having to do with political preferences. The findings were compiled and organized by the Gallup organization along with the Williams Institute at the law school of the University of California at Los Angeles, and the main findings are shown in Table 5.1.

It is clear that emerging and younger adults—the 18- to 29-year-olds in the study—were most likely to identify themselves as lesbian, gay, bisexual, or transgender. Note the systematic falloff for females in every racial/ethnic group in the survey. There is also a falloff for males, but a "rebound" among African American and Asian American males aged 65 and older. Why do we see these dropoffs? If one assumes that biological factors are the major contributor to sexual orientation, one has to ask how biology would have changed over the years in these various age cohorts, or else why older cohorts, beginning in their 30s, are less likely to identify themselves as LGBT. Perhaps, in our more liberated times, young adults are more likely to feel free to identify themselves as LGBT, or more likely to be in touch with their sexual orientations? These inferences are speculative.

Table 5.1 People in the United States Who Identify Themselves as Lesbian, Gay, Bisexual, or Transgender (LGBT), in Percentages.

	African American	Asian American	European American	Latin American
Ages 18–29				
Female	9.6	8.0	8.6	6.6
Male	6.1	4.8	3.9	5.8
Ages 30–49				
Female	3.4	2.7	3.3	3.4
Male	3.6	4.1	3.1	3.6
Ages 50–64				
Female	2.6	1.2	2.3	2.0
Male	2.3	1.7	3.0	3.3
Ages 65+				
Female	2.0	0.4	1.5	1.5
Male	4.1	5.2	2.4	1.4

SOURCE OF DATA: Based on Gallup organization and the Williams Institute at the law school of UCLA, October 18, 2012. Based on telephone interviews June 1–September 30, 2012 of 121,290 Americans.

Gates, G. J., & Newport, F. (2012, October). Gallup special report: The LGBT vote in the 2012 presidential election. The Williams Institute. http://williamsinstitute.law.ucla.edu/research/census-lgbt-demographics-studies/gallup-special-report-lgbt-vote-18oct-2012/ (accessed October 20, 2012).

Why do we see the "rebound" among older African American and Asian American males, when the same age cohort, for women, shows relatively rare self-identification as LGBT? It is tempting to think that males of the age cohort are possibly more outspoken and of an age at which they might be thinking, "Why does it matter anymore to admit to the truth?" But perhaps women from that cohort (across all racial/ethnic groups) are less likely to have examined their sexual orientations across the years? We must admit that we don't have the answers and are not comfortable with our speculations.

In the youngest age cohort, we must also note that females are significantly more likely than males to identify themselves as being LGBT. Is the gender difference the result of more common presence of biological factors that influence a lesbian, bisexual, or transgender orientation in females? Does the difference reflect greater erotic plasticity in females? Or more willingness to admit to a lesbian, bisexual, or transgender orientation? (Females, presumably, more so than males, would *not* be influenced by a desire to be masculine or "tough.")

Interestingly, 18- to 29-year-old African Americans are most likely to label themselves as LGBT. Among African Americans, males in the 50- to 64-year-old age cohort are least likely to label themselves as gay, bisexual, or transgender. Might one reason be that this was the group most likely to be devastated by the HIV/AIDS epidemic?

NATIONAL HEALTH STATISTICS REPORTS   The U.S. Department of Health and Human Services conducts annual national surveys about health-related behavior and behavior. A recent report (Ward et al., 2014) is based on face-to-face interviews with 34,557 adults aged 18 and older. Beginning in 2013, the survey has asked male respondents whether they are gay, straight, bisexual, or something else and given them the opportunity to day "I don't know the answer." Females have been asked whether they are "lesbian or gay," straight, bisexual, or something else, and as with the males, they could report "I don't know the answer."

The results show strikingly fewer respondents reporting themselves to be gay, lesbian, bisexual, or transgender. Among all respondents, male and female included, 96.6% said they were straight; only 1.6% said they were gay or lesbian, and 0.7%

Table 5.2 Health-Related Behaviors of Gay Men and Women Who Are Homosexual, Straight, or Bisexual.

	Men			Women		
	Gay	Straight	Bisexual	Lesbian	Straight	Bisexual
Cigarette smoker	26%	20%	29%	26%	15%	29%
Had 5 or more drinks in one day in past year	39%	31%	52%	26%	14%	34%
Met federal guidelines for aerobic physical activity	64%	56%	55%	51%	48%	56%

SOURCE: Ward, B. W., Dahlhamer, J. M,Galinsky, A.M., Joestl, S.S. Sexual orientation and health among U.S. adults: National Health Interview Survey, 2013. National health statistics reports; no 77. Hyattsville, MD: National Center for Health Statistics. 2014.

reported that they were bisexual. Only 1.1% said they were "something else"; very few reported that they did not know. As with the Gallup survey, younger respondents (the group aged 18–44) were more likely than older groups to report a lesbian, gay, or bisexual orientation. Table 5.2 shows that gay males, lesbians, and bisexuals were more likely to smoke and binge drink than straight males and females, but their exercise regimens were at least equal to those of straight individuals.

THE YOUGOV SURVEY A survey by YouGov (2015) shows much more interesting results than the Gallup or National Health Interview surveys. The question is how accurate those results are. Yougov is a private organization that takes nearly instant polls on questions that clients want answered. That is not the problem; Gallup is also private. The question comes about because YouGov bases its results on the responses of 1,000 individuals drawn from a much larger sample base that stands ready to provide such answers. It is not clear how well that sample represents the population at large. Nevertheless, the YouGov survey clearly merits a mention, and its age-related findings are generally consistent with those of other surveys.

YouGov used the 0–6-point Kinsey scale as its jumping-off point. The organization asked respondents to indicate whether they were "completely" heterosexual, completely homosexual, or somewhere in between. As you can see in Figure 5.2, the great majority of YouGov respondents, as those in the other surveys, reported that they were (completely) heterosexual. And, as in the other surveys, emerging and young adults (in this case, as in the Gallup survey, the 18- to 29-year-olds) were more likely than older age groups to report they were somewhere in between being completely heterosexual and completely homosexual (see Figures 5.2 and 5.3).

The three surveys reported here provide interesting information about the sexual orientations of U.S. adults today. They agree that most Americans are completely heterosexual. They also agree that, by and large, older Americans are more likely than younger Americans to say that they are exclusively or

Figure 5.2 Self-Placement of YouGov Poll Respondents Along the Kinsey Continuum.

SOURCE: YouGov. (2015). A third of young Americans say they aren't 100% heterosexual. https://today.yougov.com/news/2015/08/20/third-young-americans-exclusively-heterosexual/

1 in 3 young Americans not 100% heterosexual

U.S. adults were asked to place themselves on the Kinsey scale, ranging from 0 (completely heterosexual) to 6 (completely homosexual)

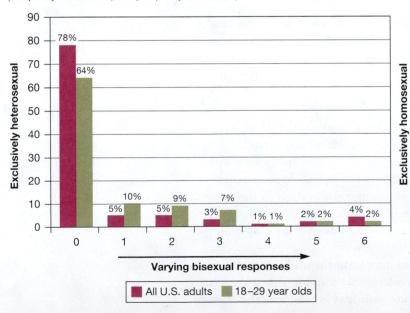

Varying bisexual responses

■ All U.S. adults   ■ 18–29 year olds

completely heterosexual. Having said that, they disagree on how many Americans can be said to be somewhere in between exclusive heterosexuality and exclusive homosexuality.

A Challenge to the Kinsey Continuum: How Many Dimensions of Sexual Orientation Are There?

Alfred Kinsey believed that exclusive heterosexual and gay sexual orientations lay at opposite poles of one continuum. Therefore, the more heterosexual a person is, the less homosexual that person is, and vice versa. Viewing homosexual and heterosexual orientations as opposite poles of one continuum is akin to the traditional view of masculinity and femininity as opposite poles of one continuum, such that the more masculine one is, the less feminine, and vice versa. But in Chapter 4 we saw that we may also regard masculinity and femininity as independent personality dimensions.

Similarly, it may be that these sexual orientations—heterosexuality and homosexuality—are separate dimensions rather than polar opposites (Vrangalova & Savin-Williams, 2012). There are apparently separate dimensions of responsiveness to male–female sexual stimulation (heteroeroticism) and sexual stimulation that involves someone of the same anatomic sex (homoeroticism), as shown in Figure 5.4. According to this model, bisexuals are high in both dimensions, whereas people who are low in both are essentially asexual (Bogaert, 2006). According to Kinsey, bisexual individuals would be *less* responsive to stimulation by people of the other anatomic sex than heterosexual people are, but *more* responsive to stimulation by people of their own anatomic sex. However, the two-dimensional model allows for people to be as responsive to stimulation by people of the other anatomic sex as heterosexual people are, and as responsive to stimulation by people of their own anatomic sex as gay males and lesbians are.

Concerning the possibility of there being two dimensions of sexual orientation, one research group (Vrangalova & Savin-Williams, 2012) studied the responses of 1,784 individuals to an online survey advertised on Facebook. The respondents provided information about three aspects of their sex lives: their self-reported sexual orientation, the people to whom they were sexually attracted, and their actual sexual experiences. The findings were consistent with a five-point continuum of sexual orientation: heterosexual, "mostly" heterosexual, bisexual, "mostly" gay/lesbian, and gay/lesbian. The "mostly" participants, whether mostly heterosexual or mostly gay/lesbian, generally reported patterns of sexual attraction and sex partners at odds with their self-reported sexual orientation. But in contrast to the Kinsey view, their findings also supported the two-dimensional view of same- and other-sex sexuality shown in Figure 5.4. That is, having more sexual attraction to members of the other anatomic sex did not necessarily imply less sexual attraction to people of the same anatomic sex, and vice versa.

AND HOW ABOUT EROTIC PLASTICITY? Another challenge to the Kinsey continuum involves the concept of erotic plasticity, and the possibility the females have more erotic plasticity than males. In one experiment concerning the issue, Chivers and Bailey (2005) exposed men and women to visual male and female sexual stimuli.

Figure 5.3 Varying Degrees of Bisexuality Reported by YouGov Respondents, by Age.

SOURCE: YouGov. (2015). A third of young Americans say they aren't 100% heterosexual. https://today.yougov.com/news/2015/08/20/third-young-americans-exclusively-heterosexual/

Bisexuality by age
American adults were asked to place their sexuality on a scale of 0 to 6, where 0 is completely heterosexual and 6 is completely homosexual %

■ Completely heterosexual or homosexual (0 or 6 on Kinsey scale)
■ Varying degrees of bisexuality (1–5 on Kinsey scale)

Figure 5.4   Heterosexuality and Homosexuality as Separate Dimensions.

According to this model, homosexuality and heterosexuality are independent dimensions. One can thus be high or low on both dimensions at the same time. Most people are high on one dimension. Bisexuals are high on both dimensions. People who are extremely low on both may be considered to be *asexual*.

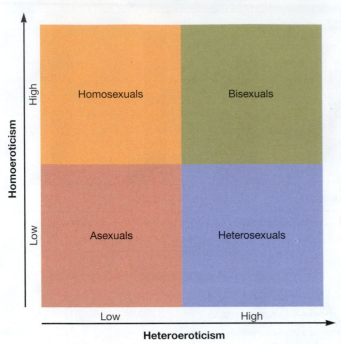

They measured the subjects' genital responses as well as their self-reports of sexual arousal. Male heterosexuals responded genitally only to the female stimuli, and gay males showed the reverse pattern. Their genital responses bore out their verbal reports. But the women, both heterosexual and lesbian, were more likely to be aroused by both male and female sexual stimuli.

Chivers and Bailey's findings are consistent with research showing that women's sexual orientations are more flexible than men's and apparently more intertwined with their social experience (Diamond, 2000, 2003a, 2012; Mock & Elbach, 2012). When we discuss **homophobia**, or hatred of homosexuals, we will see that men tend to be more homophobic than women. Homophobia is connected with traditional "tough" masculine attitudes (Davies, 2004). However, it may also be that part of the reason for this gender difference in homophobia is that heterosexual men have a more difficult time than heterosexual women understanding how any man could be attracted to a person of the same anatomic sex.

Bisexuality

Bisexuality refers to people who are sexually attracted to both males and females. They are sometimes said to "swing both ways," or to be "A/C–D/C" (as in "alternating current" and "direct current"). Yet, many have a somewhat stronger attraction to people of one gender than the other. In fact, Weinrich and Klein (2002) speak of bisexuals as being "bi-gay," "bi-straight," or "bi-bi," meaning that some have a stronger leaning toward people of their own anatomic sexgender (bi-gays), some toward people of the other anatomic sex (bi-straights), and still others appears to be equally attracted to people of their own sex and the other sex (bi-bi's). We have seen that studies vary widely in their estimates of how many people are bisexual, with the National Health Interview Survey (Ward et al., 2014) reporting only about 1% of the population to be bisexual and the YouGov (2015) survey reporting that as many as 29% of 18- to 29-year-olds and 7% of people aged 65 and older show varying degrees of bisexuality. This is what can only be called a huge discrepancy, and it is possible that the truth lies somewhere in between.

homophobia

A cluster of negative attitudes and feelings toward gay people, including intolerance, hatred, and fear.

bisexuality

Erotic attraction to and interest in developing romantic relationships with males and females.

Some gay people (and some heterosexual people) believe that claims to bisexuality are a "cop-out" that people use to deny being gay. Perhaps people who say they are bisexual fear leaving their spouses or "coming out" (declaring their gay male or lesbian sexual orientation publicly). Others view bisexuality as a form of sexual experimentation with people of one's own anatomic sex by people who are mostly heterosexual. But many avowed bisexuals and researchers assert that bisexuals can maintain erotic interests in, and romantic relationships with, members of both anatomic sexes. They insist that bisexuality is an authentic sexual orientation with its own developmental patterns, and not just a "cover" for a gay male or lesbian sexual orientation (Savin-Williams et al., 2012).

Some bisexual people follow lifestyles that permit them to satisfy their dual inclinations. Others feel pressured by heterosexual and homosexual people alike to commit themselves one way or the other (Savin-Williams et al., 2012). Some gay people also mask their sexual orientation by adopting a bisexual lifestyle. That is, they get married to someone of the other anatomic sex or form enduring male–female partnerships, but also enter into clandestine sexual liaisons with members of their own anatomic sex.

Still, it appears that many bisexual men remain reasonably comfortable in committed heterosexual relationships, such as marriages. An in-depth study of 20 married men who scored as bisexual on the Kinsey Scale found that they encountered some anxiety, some feelings of guilt, and some sense of loss, but not to the point where they experienced high levels of stress (Edser & Shea, 2002). By and large, the men were psychologically, stable and most of their marriages were in what the authors call "relatively good condition." The authors conclude that long-term committed relationships with women are a "viable option" for bisexual men. The authors were not moralistic; that is, they were not suggesting that bisexual men *should* seek committed relationships with women. They merely pointed out that such relationships can work.

Perspectives on Sexual Orientation

LO 5.2 **Explain how sexual orientation has been viewed historically and scientifically.**

Gay male and lesbian sexual orientations have existed throughout history. Attitudes toward them have varied widely. They have been tolerated in some societies, openly encouraged in others, but condemned in most. In this section we review historical and other perspectives on gay male and lesbian sexual orientations.

Historical Perspectives

In Western culture, few sexual practices have met with such widespread censure as sexual activities with members of one's own anatomic sex. But it was not always that way. In ancient Greece, for example, established men frequently formed sexual relationships with adolescent males at about the age of first growing a beard. The main sexual activity depicted on Greek vases is of the older male inserting his penis between the boy's thighs (not in the anus) and thrusting until he ejaculates.

A few centuries later, the Romans described highly feminine gay men who dressed flamboyantly, had showy hair styles and mannerisms, and cruised certain neighborhoods, searching for partners. The Apostle Paul commented on this behavior as the key sign of the decadence of Rome, and the Christian Church assumed a strongly negative attitude toward homosexuality.

In the fifteenth century, Florence, a Christian city, was reputed to house numerous "sodomites." (Jews and Christians have traditionally referred to male–male sexual activity as the sin of Sodom—hence the origins of the term *sodomy*, which generally alludes to anal intercourse, and sometimes to oral–genital contact. According to the book of Genesis, the city of Sodom was destroyed by God. Yet it is unclear what behavior incurred God's wrath. Pope Gregory III was not ambiguous, however, in his eighth-century account of the city's obliteration as a punishment for sexual activity with members of the same anatomic sex.) Sodomy was so common in Florence, and (theoretically) so disturbing to the city's governors, that they created the "Office of the Night" in 1432, which enabled the populace to anonymously accuse individuals of sodomy. During the 70 years that the office was in operation, some 17,000 men were investigated as possible sodomites, nearly half of the male population of Florence throughout that period! Fewer than 3,000 were actually convicted, however, and those who were convicted were required to pay a fine rather than tossed into prison (Grey 2014).

The book of Leviticus was also clear in its condemnation:

> If a man lies with a man as with a woman, both of them have committed an abomination; they shall be put to death, their blood is upon them. (Leviticus 20:13)

Sexual activity with members of one's own anatomic sex was not the only sexual act considered sinful by the early Christians. Any nonprocreative sexual act was considered sinful, even within marriage. With the fall of the Roman Empire, the influence of Christianity spread across Western Europe. Christian beliefs were eventually encoded into secular law. By the late Middle Ages, most civil statutes throughout Western Europe contained penalties for nonprocreative sexual acts involving the discharge of semen, including oral or anal sex, masturbation, male–male sexual behavior, and bestiality. Male–male and female–female sexual practices continue to be condemned by most Christian and Jewish denominations, and by Islam.

The legal system in some states, grounded in this religious tradition, maintains criminal penalties for sexual practices commonly associated with male–male and female–female sex, such as anal and oral sex. But much of the criminalization of male–male and female–female sex has been directed against men. In any event, court decisions, including the 2015 U.S. Supreme Court decision legalizing same-sex marriage throughout the country, has led to the extremely rare enforcement of any such laws that remain on the books.

Cross-Cultural Perspectives

Male–male sexual behavior has been practiced in many preliterate societies. In their review of the literature on 76 preliterate societies, Ford and Beach (1951) found that in 49 societies (64%), male–male sexual interactions were viewed as normal and deemed socially acceptable for some members of the group. The other 27 societies (36%) had sanctions against male–male sexual behavior. Nevertheless, male–male sexual activity persisted. In another cross-cultural analysis, Broude and Greene (1976) found that male–male sexual behavior was present but uncommon in 41% of a sample of 70 of the world's non-European societies. It was rare or absent in 59% of these societies. Broude and Greene also found evidence of societal disapproval and punishment of male–male sexual activity in 41% of a sample of 42 societies for which information was available.

Sexual activities between males are sometimes limited to rites that mark the young male's initiation into manhood. In some preliterate societies, semen is believed to boost strength and virility. Older males thus transmit semen to younger males through oral or anal sexual activities. Among the Sambian people of New Guinea, a tribe of warlike headhunters, 7- to 10-year-old males leave their parents' households and live in a "clubhouse" with other prepubertal and adolescent males. There they undergo sexual rites of passage. To acquire the fierce manhood of the headhunter, they fellate older males and drink semen (Bailey, 2003b). They are encouraged to take in as much semen as they can, as if it were mother's milk. Ingestion of semen is believed to give rise to puberty. Following puberty, adolescents are fellated by younger males. In their late teens or early twenties, however, young men are expected to take brides and enter into exclusively male–female sexual relationships.

These practices of Sambian culture might seem to suggest that the sexual orientations of males are fluid and malleable. But the practices involve *behavior* and not *sexual orientation*. Male–male sexual behavior among Sambians takes place within a cultural context that bears little resemblance to consensual male–male sexual activity in Western society. The prepubertal Sambian male does not *seek* sexual liaisons with other males. He is removed from his home and thrust into male–male sexual encounters by older males.

Cross-Species Perspectives

Biologists have observed male–male and female–female sexual behavior in at least 450 different animal species in every part of the world (Hird, 2006; Vasey et al., 2014). Rare it's not.

SEX IN A WORLD OF DIVERSITY

ETHNICITY AND SEXUAL ORIENTATION: A MATTER OF BELONGING

Lesbians and gay males frequently suffer the slings and arrows of an outraged society. Because of societal prejudices, it is difficult for many young people to come to terms with an emerging lesbian or gay male sexual orientation. You might assume that people who have been subjected to prejudice and discrimination—members of ethnic minority groups in the United States—would be more tolerant of a lesbian or gay male sexual orientation.

3 › T / F Truth or Fiction Revisited However, members of ethnic minority groups in the United States tend to be less tolerant of homosexuals than European Americans are (Guittar & Pals, 2014, McGee, 2016.).

Within traditional Latin American culture, the family is the primary social unit. Men are expected to support and defend the family, and women are expected to be submissive, respectable, and deferential to men. Because women are expected to remain virgins until marriage, men sometimes engage in male–male sexual behavior without considering themselves gay (Barrett et al., 2005). Latin American culture frequently denies the sexuality of women. Thus, women who label themselves lesbians are doubly condemned because they are lesbians and because they are confronting others with their sexuality. Because lesbians are independent of men, most Latin American heterosexual people view Latina lesbians as threats to the tradition of male dominance (Harris et al., 2015).

Asian American cultures emphasize respect for elders, obedience to parents, and sharp distinctions in gender roles (Harris et al., 2015; Kumashiro, 2004). The topic of sex is generally taboo within the family. Asian Americans, like Latin Americans, tend to assume that sex is unimportant to women. Women are also generally considered less important than men. Open admission of a lesbian or gay male sexual orientation is seen as rejection of traditional cultural roles and a threat to the continuity of the family line (Collins, 2004).

Because many African American men have had difficulty finding jobs, gender roles among African Americans have been more flexible than those found among European Americans and most other ethnic minority groups (Chisholm & Greene, 2008). Nevertheless, the African American community appears to strongly reject gay men and lesbians, pressuring them to remain secretive about their sexual orientations. Greene (2000, 2012) hypothesizes a number of factors that influence African Americans to be hostile toward lesbians and gay men. One is allegiance to Christianity and Biblical scripture. Another is internalization of the dominant culture's stereotyping of African Americans as highly sexual beings. That is, many African Americans may wish to assert their sexual "normalcy."

Prior to European colonization, sex may not have been discussed openly by Native Americans, but sex was generally seen as a natural part of life. Individuals who incorporated both traditional feminine and masculine styles were generally accepted and even admired. The influence of the religions of colonists led to greater rejection of lesbians and gay men, and pressure to move off the reservation to the big city (Adams & Phillips, 2006; Balsam et al., 2004). Native American lesbians and gay men, like Asian American lesbians and gay men, thus often feel doubly removed from their families.

If any generalization is possible, it may be that lesbians and gay men find more of a sense of belonging in the gay community than in their ethnic communities.

Ethnicity and Sexual Orientation. The experiences of lesbians and gay men can differ according to their ethnicity. For example, traditional Latin American culture supports strong differences in gender roles. Men are expected to support and defend the family. Women are expected to be submissive, respectful of traditional gender roles, and deferential to men.

On the other hand, what you see isn't always what you get (Vasey et al., 2014). A male baboon may present his rear and allow himself to be mounted by another male. This behavior may resemble anal intercourse among gay men. Is the behavior sexually motivated, however? Mounting behavior among male baboons may represent a type of dominance ritual in which lower-ranking males adopt a submissive (feminine) posture to ward off attack from dominant males. (Some male–male acts among people also involve themes of dominance, as in the case of a dominant male prisoner forcing a less dominant one to submit to anal intercourse.) In other cases, male baboons may be seeking favors or protection from more dominant males. Among juvenile animals, male–male behaviors may also be a form of play. Females may also attempt to mount other females, but here too, the motives may not be the same as those of humans.

Sexual motivation appears to play a role in some, but not all, male–male and female–female sexual interactions among animals. Fellatio and anal intercourse to ejaculation among juvenile male orangutans may be a case in point, as may be thrusting by one adult female gorilla against another.

> **4 › T / F Truth or Fiction Revisited** Actually, same-sex sexual activity has been found among hundreds of species. The motivations for male–male and female–female sexual activity among other-than-human species is not always clear, however.

Biological Perspectives

Biological perspectives focus on the possible roles of evolution, genetics, and hormonal influences in shaping sexual orientation.

THE EVOLUTIONARY PERSPECTIVE It might seem odd that evolutionary theorists have endeavored to explain gay male and lesbian sexual orientations. After all, gay males and lesbians are not motivated to engage in sexual activity with members of the other anatomic sex. How, then, can gay male and lesbian sexual orientations confer any evolutionary advantage?

To answer the question, we must look to the group or the species rather than the individual. Some investigators suggest that male–male and female–female sexual behavior derive from individual selection for reciprocal *altruism* (Kirkpatrick, 2000; Rind, 2015). That is, strong male–male and female–female alliances have advantages for group survival in that they bind group members together emotionally. This hypothesis remains quite speculative.

However, researchers have also compared the family trees of homosexuals with those of heterosexuals and found that there is a significant increase in fecundity in the women related to the homosexuals in the maternal line but not in women in the paternal line (Ciani et al., 2012). These findings suggest the possibility that genetic factors that are linked to the X sex chromosome and might influence homosexual orientation in males are not eliminated by natural selection because they also increase fecundity in women carriers. That is, the women related to gay males apparently bear more children, compensating for the lesser likelihood that homosexuals will reproduce.

GENETICS, THE BRAIN, AND SEXUAL ORIENTATION Considerable evidence exists that gay male and lesbian sexual orientations run in families (Jannini et al., 2010a). Twin studies shed light on the possible role of heredity (Bailey, 2003b). **Monozygotic (MZ) twins**, or identical twins, develop from a single fertilized ovum and share 100% of their heredity. **Dizygotic (DZ) twins**, or fraternal twins, develop from two fertilized ova. Like other brothers and sisters, DZ twins share only 50% of their heredity. Thus, if a gay male or lesbian sexual orientation were transmitted genetically, it should be found about twice as often among identical twins of gay males and lesbians as among fraternal twins. Because MZ and DZ twins who are reared together share similar environmental influences, differences in the degree of

monozygotic (MZ) twins

Twins who develop from the same fertilized ovum; identical twins.

dizygotic (DZ) twins

Twins who develop from different fertilized ova; fraternal twins.

concordance (agreement) for a given trait between the types of twin pairs are further indicative of genetic origins. Several studies have identified gay men who had either identical (MZ) or fraternal (DZ) twin brothers to examine the prevalence of a gay male sexual orientation in their twins. In one of the most carefully conducted twin studies, about 52% of identical (MZ) twin pairs were found to be "concordant" for a gay male sexual orientation, as compared with 22% of fraternal (DZ) twins and only 11% of adoptive brothers (Bailey, 2003a; Bailey & Pillard, 1991). Bear in mind that MZ twins are more likely to be dressed alike and treated alike than DZ twins. Thus, their greater concordance for a gay sexual orientation may at least in part reflect environmental factors (Hines, 2011b; Jannini et al., 2010b).

Researchers have found evidence linking a region on the X sex chromosome to a gay male sexual orientation (Bailey et al., 1999). One group of researchers (Hamer et al., 1993) found that gay males in a sample of 114 gay men were more likely to have gay male relatives on their mothers' side of the family than would be expected, based on the prevalence of a gay male sexual orientation in the general population. However, they did not have a greater than expected number of gay male relatives on the paternal side of the family. This pattern of inheritance is consistent with genetic traits, such as hemophilia, that are linked to the X sex chromosome, which men receive from their mothers.

The researchers then examined the X sex chromosome in 40 pairs of gay male, nontwin brothers. In 33 of the pairs, the brothers had identical DNA markers on the end tip of the X chromosome. For brothers overall in the general population, about half would be expected to have inherited this chromosomal structure. It is suspected, therefore, that this chromosomal region may hold genetic material that predisposes men to a gay male sexual orientation.

The researchers cautioned that they had not found a particular gene linked to sexual orientation, just a general location of where the gene may be found. Nor do scientists know how such a gene, or combination of genes, might account for sexual orientation. Perhaps a particular gene or gene combination governs the development of proteins that sculpt parts of the brain in ways that favor the development of a gay male sexual orientation. On the other hand, a number of the gay brothers, 7 of the 40 pairs, did *not* share the chromosomal marker.

In a search for possible differences in the brain among heterosexuals, gay men, and lesbians, Swedish researchers (Savic & Lindström, 2008) conducted MRI scans of the brains of 90 subjects—25 heterosexual men (HeM) and women (HeW), and 20 gay men (HoM) and lesbians (HoW). They found that the brains of the heterosexual men and the lesbians were slightly asymmetrical; the right hemisphere was slightly larger than the left hemisphere. This difference was not found among the brains of gay men and heterosexual women. The researchers also measured the blood flow to the amygdala, an area of the brain involved in the emotional response to threats, and they found that it was wired similarly in gay men and heterosexual women and also in lesbians and heterosexual men (see Figure 5.5). The researchers admitted that their methodology cannot show whether the differences in brain shape and interconnectivity are inherited or as a result of environmental factors such as exposure to testosterone in the womb. Nor can they conclude that the differences in the brain are responsible for sexual orientation. But even at this stage in the research, it would appear that the brains of heterosexuals and homosexuals *might* be different in ways that are consistent with their sexual orientations.

concordance

Agreement.

Figure 5.5   PET Scans of the Amygdalas of Heterosexuals and Homosexuals.

The amygdalas of gay men (HoM) and heterosexual women (HeW) appear to have similar patterns of blood flow, as shown by PET scanning. Moreover, the patterns of blood flow of the amygdalas of lesbians (HoW) and heterosexual men (HeM) also appear to be similar.

SOURCE: I. Savic, and P. Lindström. (2008). PET and MRI show differences in cerebral asymmetry and functional connectivity between homo- and heterosexual subjects. Published online on June 16, 2008. *Proceedings of the National Academy of Sciences.* USA, 10.1073/pnas.0801566105.

HORMONAL INFLUENCES ON SEXUAL ORIENTATION Sex hormones strongly influence the mating behavior of other species (Hines et al., 2015; Pradhan et al., 2015). Researchers have thus looked into possible hormonal factors in determining sexual orientation in humans.

Testosterone is essential to male sexual differentiation. Thus, levels of testosterone and its by-products in the blood and urine have been studied as possible influences on sexual orientation. Research has failed to connect sexual orientation in people of either anatomic sex with differences in the levels of either male or female sex hormones *in adulthood* (Hines, 2011b). In adulthood, testosterone appears to have **activating effects**. That is, it affects the intensity of sexual desire, but not the preference for partners of the same or the other anatomic sex.

But can sex hormones influence the developing human embryo and fetus (Garcia-Falgueras & Swaab, 2010)? Swedish neuroscientists Ivanka Savic and her colleagues (2010) report evidence that one's gender identity as being male or being female and one's sexual orientation (heterosexual, homosexual, or bisexual) can develop during the intrauterine period. They point out that sexual differentiation of the sex organs occurs during the first two months of pregnancy, whereas sexual differentiation of the brain begins later, during the second half of pregnancy. Sexual differentiation of the genitals and the brain both depend on surges of testosterone, but because they happen at different times, they can occur independently. Therefore, it is possible that an individual's sex organs can develop in one direction, whereas the biological factors that may underlie one's sexual orientation develop in another direction.

When drugs such as letrozole are given during critical prenatal periods in which the brains of the fetuses of rats are becoming sexually differentiated, a majority of the male offspring show erections in the presence of male rats. Yet about half of them also engage in sexual activity with sexually receptive females. Their blood levels of testosterone and other sex hormones are in the normal range as adults. It seems clear that modification of hormone levels in utero during critical periods of sexual development can affect sexual orientation in mammals and that blood tests for sex hormones during adulthood are unlikely to be related to sexual orientation (Olivera-Hernandez et al., 2016).

Melissa Hines and her colleagues (2015) also note that female embryos and fetuses who are exposed prenatally to higher-than-typical concentrations of male sex hormones because, for example, of genetic conditions or the mother's use of hormones during pregnancy show:

- increased male-stereotyped play during childhood
- increased likelihood of developing a lesbian sexual orientation
- possible changes in gender identity (a greater chance of viewing the self as being male), and
- heightened tendencies to display physically aggressive behavior.

THE STRUCTURE OF THE BRAIN Evidence suggests that there may be structural differences between the brains of heterosexual and gay men. In 1991, Simon LeVay, a neurobiologist at the Salk Institute in La Jolla, California, carried out autopsies on the brains of 35 AIDS victims—19 gay men and 16 (presumably) heterosexual men. He found that a segment of the hypothalamus (specifically, the *third interstitial nucleus of the anterior hypothalamus*) in the brains of the gay men was less than half the size of the same segment in the heterosexual men. Other investigators bear out this finding (Hines, 2011a; Roselli et al., 2011). The same brain segment was larger in the brain tissues of heterosexual men than in brain tissues obtained from a comparison group of six presumably heterosexual women. No significant differences in size were found between the brain tissues of the gay men and the women, however.

Findings about differences in brain structure among heterosexual and homosexual males are intriguing but preliminary. There are also other questions. For example,

---

activating effects

Those effects of sex hormones that influence the level of the sex drive but not sexual orientation.

Critical Thinking
Some people believe that sexual orientation is inborn; others believe that it represents the choice of the individual. Why are people who believe that sexual orientation is inborn more tolerant of homosexuals?

A CLOSER LOOK

PHEROMONES AND SEXUAL ORIENTATION

In the film *Scent of a Woman,* Al Pacino played a blind man who was drawn to women by their odor. Are there odors that are characteristic of the other gender? If so, does one's response to these odors play a role in one's sexual orientation?

Some answers are suggested by a study by Swedish researchers (Savic et al., 2005) who used PET scans to show that gay and heterosexual men respond differently to smelling chemicals that may affect sexual arousal, and that the gay men respond similarly to heterosexual women (see Figure 5.6). The Swedish study investigated the effects of two chemicals: a testosterone derivative produced in men's sweat and an estrogen-like compound found in women's urine. Most odors activate neurons in specific regions of the brain, increasing the blood flow to these regions and causing them to "light up" when imaged by the PET scan. The estrogen-like compound activated the usual smell-related areas in women, but it lit up the hypothalamus—a structure involved in sexual behavior—in heterosexual men. The chemical extracted from male sweat, in contrast, did the opposite; it activated the

hypothalamus in women and the usual smell-related areas in men. Each chemical seemed to be just another odor with one gender but a pheromone with the other. However, gay men in the study responded to the chemicals as women did. That is, their hypothalamus was lit up by the chemical drawn from male sweat.

It must be noted that the Swedish study does not reveal cause and effect. A "snapshot" was taken of brain functioning at a point in time. The snapshot did not show how the brain's responses develop. Were the activity patterns in heterosexual and gay men a cause of their sexual orientation or an effect of their sexual orientation? If sexual orientation has a genetic basis or is influenced by hormones in the womb or at puberty, it might be that the neurons in the hypothalamus become hardwired in a way that shapes sexual orientation. Conversely, the findings could mean that experience leads straight and gay men to respond in different ways. In any event, the study does suggest a role for pheromones in human sexual response and lays the groundwork for further research.

Figure 5.6   Who Lights Up Your Hypothalamus?

Certain areas of the hypothalamus "light up" when heterosexual males smell an estrogen-like compound ("estratetraenol") found in women's urine, when heterosexual women smell an androgen-like compound ("androstadienone"), and when gay males smell the androstadienone. The hypothalamus of gay males responds similarly to that of heterosexual women when the person is presented with the odor of androstadienone.

SOURCE: Adapted with permission from I. Savic, H. Berglund, and P. Lindström (2005). Brain response to putative pheromones in homosexual men. *Proceedings of the National Academy of Sciences,* Vol. 102, pp. 7356–7361, 7539. Copyright © 2005 National Academy of Sciences, U.S.A.

are these differences found in all gay males? (Apparently not.) Are these differences causal in sexual orientation, or are they merely markers of sexual orientation?

Consider another structural difference between males and females, and between "straight" men and gay men. A number of studies suggest that the ratio of the length of the second finger (index finger) and the fourth finger (ring finger) is related to prenatal levels of male and female sex hormones and also to sexual orientation among males (e.g., Xu & Zheng, 2015). However, nobody would suggest that a person's finger ratio is a causal factor in sexual orientation. On the other hand, findings of digit ratio studies and findings of structural differences in the brain all suggest the plausibility of a role for sex hormones in the development of sexual orientation.

Psychological Perspectives

Psychoanalytic theory and learning theory provide two of the major psychological approaches to understanding the origins of sexual orientation.

PSYCHOANALYTIC VIEWS   We are going to make you aware of the psychoanalytic approach to the origins of homosexuality, but let us also make it clear at the outset that there is no adequate scientific evidence to support this view. Why, then, you may ask, do we bother discussing it at all? The answer is that many people still believe in it (it is "out there" in the culture), so it is useful to know "where they are coming from"—especially if you are a gay male or a lesbian.

In any event, Sigmund Freud, the originator of psychoanalytic theory, believed that children are naturally open to all forms of sexual stimulation. In Freud's view, a gay male or lesbian sexual orientation results from failure to successfully resolve the Oedipus complex by identifying with the parent of the same gender. In men, faulty resolution of the Oedipus complex is most likely to result from the so-called classic pattern of an emotionally "close-binding" mother and a "detached–hostile" father. A boy reared in such a family may come to identify with his mother and even to "transform himself into her" (Freud, 1922/1959, p. 40). He may thus become effeminate and develop sexual interests in men.

castration anxiety

In psychoanalytic theory, a man's fear that his genitals will be removed. Castration anxiety is an element of the Oedipus complex and is implicated in the directionality of erotic interests.

Freud believed that unresolved **castration anxiety** plays a role in a gay male sexual orientation. By the time the Oedipus complex takes effect, the boy will have learned from self-stimulation that he can obtain sexual pleasure from his penis. In his youthful fantasies, he associates this pleasure with mental images of his mother. Similarly, he is likely to have learned that females do not possess a penis. Somewhere along the line, the psychoanalyst theorizes that the boy may also have been warned that his penis will be removed if he plays with himself. From all this, the boy may surmise that females—including his mother—once had penises, but that they were removed.

During the throes of the Oedipus complex, the boy unconsciously comes to fear that his father, his rival in love for the mother, will retaliate by removing the organ that the boy has come to associate with sexual pleasure. His fear causes him to repress his sexual desire for his mother and to identify with the potential aggressor—his father. The boy thus overcomes his castration anxiety and is headed along the path of adult heterosexuality.

If the Oedipus complex is not successfully resolved, castration anxiety may persist. When sexually mature, the man will not be able to tolerate sex with women. His lack of a penis will arouse unconscious castration anxiety within himself.

The Electra complex in little girls follows a somewhat different course. Freud believed that little girls become envious of boys' penises because they lack their own. Jealousy leads little girls to resent their mothers, whom they blame for their anatomic "deficiency," and to turn from their mothers to their fathers as sexual objects. They now desire to possess the father because the father's penis provides what they lack. But incestuous desires bring the girl into competition with her mother. Motivated by fear that her mother will withdraw her love if the desires persist, the girl normally represses them and identifies with her mother. She supplants her childhood desire for a penis with a desire to marry a man and bear children. The baby, emitted from between her legs, serves as the ultimate penis substitute.

A nagging problem for Freudian theory is that many of its concepts, such as castration anxiety and penis envy, are believed to operate at an unconscious level. As such, they lie beyond the scope of scientific observation and measurement (Hergenhahn & Henley, 2014).

> **5 › T / F Truth or Fiction Revisited**   The Freudian belief that "castration anxiety" in gay males is aroused by knowledge of male–female intercourse has not been scientifically demonstrated. Moreover, gender nonconformity and gender preferences in gay males all occur earlier than Freud's psychoanalytic theory would suggest.

LEARNING THEORIES   Heather Hoffmann (2012) of Knox College notes that "the effects of learning on sexual orientation are rarely addressed in the literature." The scientific literature has come to focus on "orientation dispositions," such as the influence of sex hormones during prenatal development. The scientific thrust agrees with the political view that sexual orientation is inborn or innate; it is not a choice. The belief that sexual orientation is a choice brings the issue of "character" into the explanation of homosexuality. Even the suggestion that early experiences determine sexual orientation is a huge political problem because it suggests that homosexual adults can prey on children and, in doing so, convert the children from heterosexual to homosexual. Therefore, let us make it clear that there is no evidence that sexual orientation is either a choice or pressed on children by early sexual interactions with older people of the same anatomic sex.

Let us also recall that some youth have same-sex experiences because of the lack of opportunities with people of the other anatomic sex. Prison inmates may also have same-sex experiences because of lack of opportunity. So, as we saw, do Sambian youth have same-sex experiences with adult males. Yet the Sambian male youth take female brides upon maturity and subsequently engage in male–female sexual behavior. Moreover, the overwhelming majority of gay males and lesbians were aware of sexual interest in people of their own anatomic sex *before* they had sexual encounters with them, pleasurable or otherwise (Savin-Williams & Diamond, 2000).

Gender Nonconformity

Gender nonconformity means not behaving in a way that is consistent with the gender-role stereotype associated with one's anatomic sex in a given culture. On average, gay males tend to be somewhat feminine and lesbians to be somewhat masculine, but there is a good deal of variation within each group (Burri & Rahman, 2015; Rieger & Savin-Williams, 2012). Gender nonconformity begins in childhood. Gay males and lesbians are more likely than heterosexuals to report childhood behavior stereotypical of people of the other anatomic sex (Green, 2008; Lippa, 2008). Many gay males and lesbians recall acting and feeling "different" from their childhood peers. Many gay males from a variety of groups, such as college students, prisoners, psychiatric patients, and activists, report that they avoided participating in competitive sports as children, were more fearful of physical injury, and were more likely to avoid getting into fights than heterosexual males (Dawood et al., 2009; Rieger & Savin-Williams, 2012). Some gay males recall feeling different as early as the age 3 or 4, a feeling that was related to behavior that is stereotypical of the other gender.

Gay males are also more likely to recall feeling more sensitive than their heterosexual peers during childhood (Green, 2008; Lippa, 2008). They cried more easily. Their feelings were more readily hurt. They had more artistic interests. They had fewer male buddies and more female playmates (Bos et al., 2008). Gay males were more likely than their heterosexual counterparts to have preferred "girls' toys." They preferred playing with girls to playing with trucks or guns or engaging in rough-and-tumble play (Dawood et al., 2009). Their preferences often led to their being called "sissies." Gay men also recall more cross-dressing during childhood. They preferred the company of older women to older men and engaged in childhood sex play with other boys rather than with girls.

GENDER NONCONFORMITY AND THE BUTCH–FEMME DIMENSION There is also evidence of masculine-typed behavior among lesbians as children (Rieger & Savin-Williams, 2012). Lesbians as a group were more likely than heterosexual women to perceive themselves as having been "tomboys." They were more likely to prefer rough-and-tumble games to playing with dolls, and they enjoyed wearing boys' clothing rather than "cutesy" dresses.

A study by Devendra Singh and colleagues (1999) relates gender nonconformity in lesbians to the butch–femme dimension and biological factors. The investigators compared self-identified **butch** and **femme** lesbians on various personality, behavioral, and biological measures. They found that butch lesbians were significantly more likely than femme lesbians to recall gender-atypical behavioral preferences in childhood. Butch lesbians also had higher waist-to-hip ratios and higher testosterone levels in their saliva, both of which are more typical of males. The Singh group suggests that their findings support the validity of the butch–femme distinction, and that the distinction may be related to differences in exposure to prenatal androgens (male sex hormones).

All in all, the origins of sexual orientation remain complex and somewhat mysterious. The literature strongly suggests that heredity and prenatal sex hormones play causative roles. The structure of the brain is at least a marker for many if not all homosexuals, and digit ratio would appear to be another marker. Early experiences may play some role, but the beliefs that sexual orientation is a choice or a result of early experiences with older gay or lesbian people are not supported by the evidence.

Sexual Orientation in Contemporary Society

LO 5.3 **Discuss contemporary U.S. attitudes toward homosexuality.**

Same-sex sexual activity has been outlawed or frowned upon in nearly every society for thousands of years. In some societies even today, recognition that one is lesbian or gay can lead to a death sentence. Yet after decades of debate and majority negative public opinion the United States has undergone a profound sudden shift in attitudes toward homosexuals and transgendered individuals (Leubsdorf & Nelson, 2015). The shift preceded the Supreme Court ruling of 2015 that people of the same sex have a constitutional right to get married. Why the change? Many reasons. More and more states were recognizing same-sex marriage. LGBT characters were populating TV shows and movies. Much survey data suggest that greater acceptance has also come from more people knowing someone who is gay. As more LGBT people come out, the people around them realize that they are friends,

butch

A lesbian who assumes a traditional masculine gender role.

femme

A lesbian who assumes a traditional feminine gender role.

family, co-workers, and public role models. It is inconsistent to enjoy personalities such as Ellen DeGeneres, Anderson Cooper, Elton John, Neil Patrick Harris, and Ellen Page and to condemn their sexual orientations.

Sexual Orientation and the Law

During the past generation, gay people have organized effective political groups to fight discrimination and to overturn the sodomy laws that have traditionally targeted them. Despite their success, sodomy laws are still on the books in many states. Sodomy laws prohibit "unnatural" sexual acts, even between consenting adults. Certain sexual acts that many gay people (and heterosexual people) practice, such as anal intercourse and oral–genital contact, fall under the legal definition of sodomy in many states. Although sodomy laws are usually written to apply equally to all adults, the vast majority of prosecutions have been directed against gay people.

A 1986 Supreme Court decision (*Hardwick v. Bowers*) let stand a Georgia sodomy law that makes oral–genital or anal–genital sexual contact crimes punishable by up to 20 years in prison, even when engaged in by consenting adults. The decision was a blow to gay rights organizations, which had looked to the Supreme Court to overturn state sodomy laws.

However, in 2003, by a vote of 6 to 3, the Supreme Court reversed that decision by striking down a Texas law against "deviant sexual intercourse with another individual of the same sex." The Texas law "demeans the lives of homosexual persons," wrote Justice Anthony M. Kennedy, explaining the majority vote. Over the years, the Constitution's right to privacy has been in conflict with laws against same-gender sexual behavior. Gay males and lesbians "are entitled to respect for their private lives," Kennedy wrote further. In an interview, he added that "the state cannot demean their existence or control their destiny by making their private sexual conduct a crime."

In 2015, of course, the Supreme Court ruled that the rights of gay males and lesbians to marry could not be denied by the states, turning the legal environment for homosexuals topsy-turvy, as we see later in the chapter.

Activism

Gay activism is the term in general use, but we would have preferred *same-sex activism*, or *LGBT activism*, because "gay" activism could be said to render lesbians invisible. But just as one cannot ignore minority group members such as lesbians, one cannot ignore the terms in common use—those that instantly convey the meaning on wishes to communicate.

But let us focus on former *New York Times* columnist Frank Rich for a moment. Like many other young people in the 1960s, Rich was involved in the civil rights movement. He was shocked by the violent confrontation between protesters and police in Selma, Alabama, in 1965 and in Chicago in 1968. But he had never heard about the days of rioting that rocked Greenwich Village when the police raided

Gay Liberation This sculpture by George Segal commemorates the Stonewall riots in New York's Greenwich Village, in which members of the gay community engaged in violent protests against a raid on the Stonewall Inn by Manhattan police. The spontaneous events are seen as a catalyst in the fight for lesbian, gay, bisexual, and transgender (LGBT) rights. In 2016, two weeks after 49 people were killed in a "gay bar" in Orlando, President Obama named the Inn a national monument. A couple of days later, Pope Francis told reporters that Christians and the Roman Catholic church should ask forgiveness of gay people for its treatment of them over the, well, millennia (Reuters, 2016).

George Segal, Gay Liberation (inaugurated in Greenwich Village in 1992). Bronze, covered in white lacquer; life-sized. Christopher Park, Greenwich Village, New York.

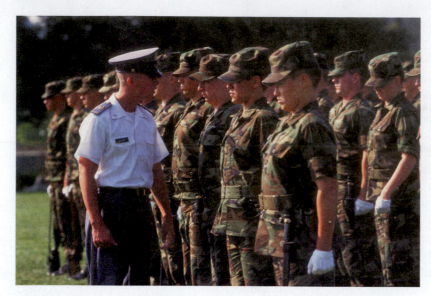

What Is the Sexual Orientation of These Soldiers? During Bill Clinton's presidency, a "Don't Ask–Don't Tell" policy was adopted toward gay people in the military. If they divulged their sexual orientation, they could be removed from the military, but superiors were not allowed to ask them about it. In 2011 President Barack Obama directed that gay males and lesbians could their country.

the Stonewall Inn, a "gay bar," in the wee hours of the morning. Looking back, Rich (2009) realizes that in the 1960s he did not know one gay or lesbian friend, student, or teacher throughout his high school and college career. The *New York Times*, the paper for which he now writes, did not allow journalists to use the word *gay* until 1987. Nobody he knew had come out as gay or lesbian, and, as he put it, the "issue of gay civil rights wasn't on our radar screen."

After the Stonewall incident, all of that changed. "Gay activism" made strides forward in the 1990s in obtaining medical resources for gay males struck by HIV/AIDS. It remains front and center in the nation's civil rights movement. Nowhere in the United States have gay males and lesbians been more politically effective than in San Francisco. They are well represented on the city police force and in other public agencies. The coming out of many gay males and lesbians, and their flocking to more tolerant urban centers, has rendered them formidable political forces in these locales and throughout the nation.

In 2016, 49 patrons of the Pulse Club in Orlando, Florida—a "gay" night club—were gunned down by a terrorist who spouted radical Islamic propaganda but was also seen on Grindr and at the club itself. The killer's motives are not fully understood, but what is clear is that President Obama declared the Stonewall Inn to be a national monument a couple of weeks later. Moreover, 49 marchers at the June 2016 New York Gay Pride parade wore hoods, suggestive that the slain were among them.

Gay activism has focused on ending discrimination against gay males and lesbians on all fronts. Notable among these are obtaining partner job benefits (health plan, retirement, and so on), serving openly in the military, and having governments permit gays to get married. Two of the largest issues gay males and lesbians faced were the repeal of the Defense of Marriage Act (DOMA) and the legalization of same-sex marriage. DOMA, signed into law by president Bill Clinton in 1996, defines marriage as occurring only between a man and a woman, therefore denying equal protection and due process to gay males and lesbians. DOMA was found unconstitutional by the Supreme Court in 2013. The Supreme Court then legalized same-sex marriage nationwide in 2015. In the previous edition of this book, replacement of the Don't Ask–Don't Tell order in the military—instituted by President Bill Clinton in 1993 and considered a "cop-out" by most gays—with the right to serve openly was a key concern. However, in 2011, President Barack Obama gave gay males and lesbians the right to openly serve their country.

"Gay activism"—or same-sex activism, or LGBT activism—has successfully moved its agenda in the twenty-first century. The times they are a-changing, and more swiftly than most people had expected. Later we discuss same-sex marriage.

Stereotypes and Sexual Behavior

Among heterosexuals, sexual aggressiveness is linked to the masculine gender role. Sexual passivity is linked to the feminine role. Some heterosexual people assume (often erroneously) that in gay male and lesbian relationships, one partner consistently assumes the masculine role in sexual relations, and the other assumes the feminine.

Many gay and lesbian couples vary the active and passive roles, however. Among gay male couples, for example, roles in anal intercourse (*inserter* versus *insertee*) and in fellatio are often reversed. Contrary to popular assumptions, sexual behavior between

SEX IN THE DIGITAL AGE

GRINDR

Grindr is the most popular dating App for gay men. It is a location-based App in which men can exchange photos and messages and arrange to hook up. The key appeal of Grindr is its ease of use. Users can check out thumbnails of other users, mark the ones they like as favorites and transmit messages to them. And the people who come up in the App are nearest to the user. There is no question as to whether the people users see are gay—or at least interested in a hookup with a man. There's no guessing (Woo, 2013).

But is that it? Are users of Grindr only seeking to hook up for casual sex?—no. A Grindr user survey found that 67% of users were also looking for new friends, 62% wanted to chat, and 38% wanted dates (Woo, 2013). Some were just passing time. Keep in mind, though, that some respondents might have said they were seeking friends because it is more socially acceptable than saying they just wanted sex. (Many men used to say that they bought *Playboy* magazine to read the stories.) Seventy percent of users are young adults, 40% in their 20s and 30% in their 30s. The highest number of users per 1,000 residents is found in the city of San Francisco (Figure 5.7).

Gay Dating Apps Scruff, Hornet, and Grindr. For gay men flocking to smartphone dating applications, making a connection increasingly comes with messages about HIV status, testing, and drug regimens. Some Apps let users declare their HIV status, remind them to get tested, and locate the nearest clinics.

Figure 5.7 Grindr Users per 1,000 Residents, Selected Cities, United States.

More than five million people use the Grindr app, and they spend an average of 90 minutes each day using the app.

SOURCE OF DATA: *Wired magazine* (2015, March). Hookup City.

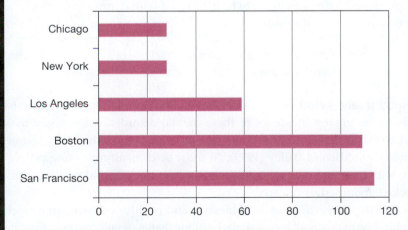

Because Grindr is frequently used for spontaneous hookups, you might assume that users are more willing than less- "laid back" gay males to engage in high-risk sexual behavior, such as anal sex without the use of condoms. A study of 375 young men who had sex with men reported in the *Journal of Urban Health* (Landovitz et al., 2013) supported this view. Seventy percent of them reported engaging in unprotected anal intercourse (UAI) with other men and they had an unrealistically low estimate of the risk of becoming infected with HIV from UAI. Five of six had been tested for HIV within the past year, and 4.5% were infected. The infected men had more frequent anal sex with other men.

Another study found different results concerning UAI (Rice et al., 2012). Sixty percent of the sample of 195 participants used condoms with partners met on Grindr, as opposed to with 42% of partners met in other ways. Only one in seven had UAI with his last Grindr partner.

lesbians seldom reflects distinct butch (active, assertive)–femme (passive, submissive) gender roles. Most lesbians report providing and receiving oral–genital stimulation, alternating roles or acting simultaneously. Many gay males and lesbians claim that the labels of *masculine* and *feminine* only represent the "straight community's" efforts to pigeonhole them in terms "straights" can understand. Many theorists do not accept the idea that stereotypical masculine and feminine gender roles are natural and precisely clustered with specific traits.

Adjustment of Lesbians and Gay Males

LO 5.4 Discuss the psychological adjustment of lesbians and gay males.

We cannot paint a picture of the psychological adjustment of lesbians and gay males with a broad brush, except to say that it depends on the social context in which they find themselves. As we see in the section on homophobia, there are nations in which recognition of a lesbian or gay male sexual orientation is tantamount to a death sentence. In the United States we can speak of some trends. One is that social acceptance of lesbians and gay males is rising throughout the country, and self-acceptance tends to mirror social acceptance. Yet there are places—most of them socially conservative—in which the majority of people still do not understand and ostracize homosexuals. In these places, some homosexuals are still driven from their families of origin, either because of violence or severe disapproval. In other parts of the country, such as the large cities, there are lesbian and gay communities that familiarize the population at large with who they are, and there are families that are as welcoming of homosexual children as of heterosexual children. We know of several families who have in one way or another communicated the message to their teenagers that it is all right if they are homosexuals.

But there is also the history of misunderstanding and ostracism by many mental health professionals. Until 1973, the American Psychiatric Association listed homosexuality as a mental disorder in its prestigious *Diagnostic and Statistical Manual (DSM) of the Mental Disorders*. That is, the *DSM* once considered the fact of homosexuality itself, not the psychological problems displayed by homosexuals, to be a disorder. Given this backdrop of heteronormativity, it is useful to consider the findings of a study by Michael King and his colleagues (2008). The researchers identified 13,706 research articles on the mental health of gay males, lesbians, and bisexuals. Of these, 476 were selected for analysis. The researchers ultimately compared the mental health of 214,344 heterosexuals and 11,971 nonheterosexuals. A sophisticated statistical averaging technique called *meta-analysis* found that lesbian, gay, and bisexual people were more than twice as likely as heterosexuals to attempt suicide. Lesbian, gay, and bisexual people were 1.5 times as likely to be diagnosed with depression, anxiety, and dependence on alcohol and other substances.

6 › T / F Truth or Fiction Revisited Actually, the *DSM* of the American Psychiatric Association has not considered homosexuality to be a mental disorder since 1973.

In retrospect it seems clear enough that societal and familial oppression contributed strongly to the greater incidence of these mental disorders among gay males, lesbians, and bisexuals (Health risks among sexual minority youth, 2015). "Surely," wrote psychologist J. Michael Bailey (1999), "it must be difficult for young people to come to grips with their homosexuality in a world where homosexual people are often scorned, mocked, mourned, and feared."

There is also the connection between lifestyle and health—physical and psychological—among gay males and lesbians, and among heterosexual people. Gay men and lesbians occupy all socioeconomic and vocational levels and follow a variety of lifestyles. It is worth mentioning the classic research of Alan P. Bell and Martin S. Weinberg (1978), who found variations in adjustment in the LGBT community that seem to mirror the variations in the heterosexual community. Gay people who lived with partners in stable, intimate relationships—so-called *close couples*—were about as well adjusted as married heterosexual couples. Older gay people who lived alone and had few sexual contacts were more poorly adjusted. So, too, are many heterosexual people who have similar lifestyles. All in all, Bell and Weinberg found that differences in adjustment were more likely to reflect the lifestyle of the individual than his or her sexual orientation.

A CLOSER LOOK

LESBIAN AND GAY MALE PARENTS AND THEIR FAMILIES

Real Students, Real Questions

Q *Are there studies that show the effects of being raised by homosexual parents?*

A There are loads of them. Let's have a look…

Research shows that the children of gay male and lesbian couples adjust as well as other children as long as the social climate of their environment is supportive of LGBT families. Nor are the children of gay male or lesbian couples more likely to be gay male or lesbian themselves.

"Where did you get that beautiful necklace?" I asked the little girl in the pediatrician's office. "From my Moms," she answered. It turned out that her family consisted of two women, each of whom had a biological child, one girl and one boy. About 23% of lesbians in the United States are parents, as compared with about 68% of heterosexual women, and most lesbians become parents through prior relationships with men (Brewster et al., 2014). Yet some lesbians become pregnant via donor insemination (Bos, 2013) and others adopt (Farr & Patterson, 2013). Gay fathers, similarly, are most likely to have fathered children in prior relationships with women (Tornello & Patterson, 2015). However, some gay couples use surrogate mothers (Berkowitz, 2013), and as with lesbian mothers, some adopt children (Farr & Patterson, 2013).

Research on parenting by lesbians and gay males has fallen into two general categories: the general adjustment of the children and whether the children are more likely than other children to be lesbian or gay themselves. Research by Charlotte Patterson (2006; Patterson & Farr, 2011) has generally found that the psychological adjustment of children of lesbian and gay parents—whether conceived by intercourse or donor insemination, or adopted—is comparable to that of children of heterosexual parents. Despite continuing barbs thrown about the legitimacy of same-sex relationships and same-sex marriage, lesbians and gay men frequently create and sustain positive family relationships (Lick et al., 2011; Tasker & Granville, 2011). It almost goes without saying that the psychological adjustment of lesbian and gay couples and their children is superior in communities in which there is social support for lesbian and gay families (Lick et al., 2012; Oswald et al., 2013). Locales in which there is greater density of lesbian and gay populations generally offer more support.

Now let's consider the sexual orientation of the children of lesbian and gay parents. In doing so, we begin more than a generation back with the research of psychiatrist Richard Green. In a classic study, Green (1978) observed 37 children and young adults, 3–20 years old, who were being reared—or had been reared—by lesbians or transgendered people. All but one of the children reported or recalled preferences for toys, clothing, and friends (male or female) that were typical (stereotypical) for their gender and age. All of the 13 older children who reported sexual fantasies or sexual behavior were heterosexually oriented. In a subsequent study, Green and his colleagues (1986) compared the children of European American mothers who were currently single, 50 of whom were lesbians and 40 heterosexual. Boys from the two groups showed no significant differences in intelligence test scores, sexual orientation, gender-role preferences, relationships with family and peer groups, or adjustment to life with a single parent. Girls showed slight differences, including somewhat more flexibility in gender roles. Green concluded that the mother's sexual orientation had no connection with the sexual orientation of their children and general parental fitness. A study by Charlotte Patterson and her colleagues (Farr et al., 2010) suggested that many adoption agencies now agree with Green's conclusions.

Another review by Patterson and her colleague Rachel Farr (Farr & Patterson, 2013) addressed the personal and social development of children who have lesbian or gay parents. Patterson found that the sexual orientation of the children was generally heterosexual, as among the general population. When parents had gotten divorced and created families with same-gender partners because of their sexual orientations, their children experienced a period of adjustment that entailed some difficulties—as do children when heterosexual parents get divorced. Children who are adopted by lesbian or gay parents tend to be well adjusted. Wanting the child is more important to the child's adjustment than the sexual orientation of the parents.

Most gay males and lesbians who share close relationships with their partners are satisfied with the overall quality of their relationships. Researchers find that heterosexual and gay couples report similar levels of satisfaction with their relationships (Henderson et al., 2009; Kurdek, 2005). Moreover, gay males and lesbians in enduring relationships generally report high levels of love, attachment, closeness, caring, and intimacy. Like heterosexual people, gay men and lesbians are happier in relationships in which they share power and make joint decisions (Henderson et al., 2009).

Homophobia

Iranian president Mahmoud Ahmadinejad was already known to be a denier—a Holocaust denier—but when he was asked at Columbia University about the execution of two gay men, he said, "In Iran we don't have homosexuals like in your country" (Daily Mail, 2007).

Homophobia is also rampant in the Western world and accounts for the greatest challenge to the adjustment of gay males and lesbians. It takes many forms, including the following:

- Using derogatory names (such as *queer, faggot,* and *dyke*)
- Telling disparaging "queer jokes"
- Barring gay people from housing, employment, or social opportunities
- Taunting (verbal abuse)
- **Gay bashing** (physical, sometimes lethal, abuse)

gay bashing

Violence against homosexuals.

According to the FBI, about one in every five hate crimes in the United States is directed against gay males or lesbians (FBI, 2014; see Fig. 5.8). *Homophobia* derives from root words meaning "fear of homosexuals." Although some psychologists link homophobia to fears of a gay male or lesbian sexual orientation within oneself, homophobic attitudes may also be embedded within a cluster of stereotypical gender-role attitudes toward family life (Rosky, 2009; Lewis & White, 2009). These attitudes support male dominance and the belief that it is natural and appropriate for women to sacrifice for their husbands and children. People who have a strong stake in maintaining stereotypical gender roles may feel more readily threatened by homosexuals because gay people appear to confuse or reverse these roles. Men have more at stake in maintaining the tradition of male dominance, so perhaps it is not surprising that college men are more intolerant of gay males than college women (Rosky, 2009; Lewis & White, 2009).

Homophobic attitudes are more common among males who identify with a traditional tough male gender role, a conservative political orientation (Rosky, 2009; Lewis & White, 2009), those who hold a fundamentalist religious orientation (Davies, 2004), and those who identify with Nazi beliefs and regalia (Zezima, 2006). But those who actually engage in violence against gay males and lesbians, and especially those who kill, tend to be criminal psychopaths (Parrot et al., 2006). That is, they are in frequent conflict with the law and do not feel guilt or shame when they inflict pain (Parrott et al., 2006).

Although strides toward social acceptance of gay people have been made since Kinsey's day, the advent of HIV/AIDS has added fuel to the fires of homophobia (Herek et al., 2005). When HIV/AIDS first appeared, it primarily struck the gay male community. Some homophobes in the larger society preached that the epidemic was a God-sent plague intended to punish homosexuals people for sinful behavior. Perhaps the epidemic serves as a pretext for some people to attack gay males, whom they blame for spreading the disease.

Figure 5.8 According to the FBI, More Than One Hate Crime in Five in the United States Is Directed Against Gay Males and Lesbians.

SOURCE: FBI, 2014. https://www.fbi.gov/news/stories/2014/december/latest-hate-crime-statistics-report-released

Bias Breakdown
Breakdown of the 5,922 single-bias hate crime incidents reported in 2013:

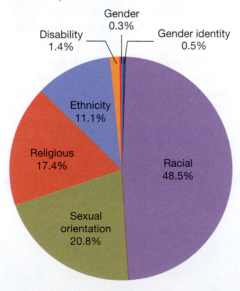

"Treatment" of Gay Male and Lesbian Sexual Orientations

Because the great majority of individuals are heterosexual, let us assume that most readers of this book will also be heterosexual. We have a question for you: Would you be interested in changing your sexual orientation? Does the idea of obtaining some sort of treatment that would cause you to prefer having romantic and sexual relationships with people of your own anatomic sex appeal to you? The answer is likely to be no, and the great (great!) majority of gay males and lesbians would also not be interested in changing their sexual orientations.

Yet some gay males and lesbians do express an interest in converting from homosexual to heterosexual, for such reasons as religious beliefs or the desire to create a typical family life. But more and more helping professionals have come to believe that gay males and lesbians would not wish to change their sexual orientation if it were not for social pressure and prejudice. Let us note that the American Psychological Association has taken the position that it is unethical to attempt conversion therapy. The association argues that gay males and lesbians would not seek to change their sexual orientation if homophobia did not exist in society. Therefore, the real issue is to change social and cultural prejudices against individuals with minority sexual orientations.

Nonetheless, you need to know that a few therapists have reported changing the sexual orientations of some individuals. Among the best known of these are the famous sex researchers William Masters and Virginia Johnson (1979), who employed methods that mirrored those used to treat sexual dysfunctions (see Chapter 12) to "reverse" clients' gay male or lesbian sexual orientations. For example, they involved gay males in a graded series of pleasurable activities with women, such as massage and genital stimulation. Masters and Johnson reported a failure rate of 20% for the gay men and 23% for the lesbians they treated in their therapy program. However, these patients do not represent the general gay population:

- Most of the patients were bisexuals. Only about one in five engaged exclusively in male–male or female–female sexual activities.
- More than half were married.
- All were highly motivated to switch their sexual orientations.

7 › T / F Truth or Fiction Revisited   It has *never* been shown that conversion therapy has successfully changed an individual's sexual orientation. We must distinguish between sexual orientation and sexual activity. Conversion therapy did change some people's sexual behavior, at least temporarily. We have no long-term follow-ups to see where the Masters and Johnson subjects are today.

Also remember that sexual behavior is *not* the equivalent of sexual orientation. There is no evidence that Masters and Johnson changed anyone's sexual *orientation*.

In any event, the state of California outlawed conversion therapy for minors in 2012. New Jersey followed suit in 2013. The American Psychological Association now holds that conversion therapy can cause "depression, anxiety and self-destructive behavior" (Zernike, 2013). Interestingly, Exodus International, a Christian group that had pushed for conversion therapy for 37 years, apologized to gay males and lesbians for the damage it had caused, and disbanded.

Coming Out

LO 5.5 Describe concerns about and processes of "coming out."

Because of the backdrop of social condemnation and discrimination, gay males and lesbians in our culture often struggle to come to terms with their sexual orientation (Legate et al., 2012). Homosexuals usually speak of the process of accepting their sexual

Critical Thinking
We live in a society in which many people are prejudiced against homosexuals. Under these circumstances, is it possible to know whether a homosexual who seeks to change his or her sexual orientation is acting of his or her own free will?

orientation as "coming out" or as "coming out of the closet." Coming out is a two-pronged process: coming out to oneself (recognizing one's sexual orientation) and coming out to others (declaring one's orientation to the world). Coming out can create a sense of pride in one's sexual orientation and foster the ability to form emotionally and sexually satisfying relationships with gay male or lesbian partners (Legate et al., 2012).

COMING OUT TO ONESELF Coming out to oneself means recognizing that one is a gay male or a lesbian, or bisexual. According to Ritch Savin-Williams and Lisa Diamond (2000), coming out to oneself is a process that involves four steps or features:

- Attraction to members of the same anatomic sex
- Self-labeling as gay or lesbian
- Sexual contact with members of the same anatomic sex
- Disclosure of one's sexual orientation to other people

The researchers by and large found a 10-year gap between initial attraction to members of one's own gender, which tended to occur at about the age of 8 or 9, and disclosure of one's orientation to other people, which usually occurred at about age 18. In keeping with gender differences noted in Chapter 4, females were more likely to focus on the emotional or romantic aspects of their budding feelings. Males were more likely to focus on the sexual aspects. Males—who are generally more open than females to sexual experimentation—were likely to become involved in sexual activity with other males before they labeled themselves as being gay. Females, on the other hand, were more likely to see themselves as being lesbians before pursuing relationships with other females. Males also tend to form their sense of whom they are attracted to and come out about two years earlier than females (Grov et al., 2006).

We noted that one's geographic location affects his or her adjustment. It also turns out that younger cohorts—people aged 18 to 24—in New York and Los Angeles also came out earlier than older cohorts (Grov et al., 2006). For some people, coming to recognize and accept a gay male or lesbian sexual orientation involves gradually stripping away layers of denial. For others, it may be a sudden awakening.

COMING OUT TO OTHERS There are different patterns of coming out to others. Coming out occasionally means an open declaration to the world. More often, a person may inform only one or a few select people. For example, the person might tell friends but not family members.

Despite changing times, many gay men and lesbians remain reluctant to declare their sexual orientation, even to friends and family. Disclosure is fraught with the risk of loss of jobs, friendships, familial disapproval, and social standing (Legate et al., 2012; Rosario et al., 2009). On the other hand, if the organization at which the individual works is generally supportive of gays, coming out can be related to greater job satisfaction and less anxiety (Legate et al., 2012). Also, "butch" lesbians are more comfortable with coming out to others than "femme" lesbians (Rosario et al., 2009). According to Wandrey and her colleagues (2015), bisexual women face particular issues and quandaries, including both homophobia and **biphobia**, along with the ability to "pass" as being heterosexual or lesbian, as best fits the situation.

Christian Grov and his colleagues (2006) found no racial differences in the ages at which European Americans and African Americans came out to themselves and others. However, African Americans were less likely than European Americans to come out to their parents, which is consistent with findings that African American families tend to have more conservative views than European American families.

Critical Thinking
How do you account for the differences in the processes of coming out in males and females?

---

biphobia
Negative attitudes and feelings toward bisexual people, including intolerance, hatred, and fear.

Coming Out. Coming out to one's parents can be a scary thing, and many lesbians and gay males avoid it for years, or even for a lifetime. On the other hand, some parents have suspected or known about their children's sexual orientation for quite some time, and even though they may have initially had deep concerns, they may be more accepting than the "children" (who may already be in their 30s or 40s) expect.

Real Students, Real Questions

Q *I don't understand why people can be supportive of gays/lesbians, but not supportive of marriage for gays/lesbians. Can you explain?*

A *Marriage* seems to be the trip word. Many people who are otherwise tolerant of gay males and lesbians see marriage as something defined by scripture to apply only to a man and a woman. Of course, one could ask whether one can be truly tolerant of gays and lesbians if one restricts marriage to males and females. On the other hand, let's not minimize the struggle that many well-meaning people experience when they attempt to reconcile social trends and their own feelings with religious dogma. The Book of Leviticus and other parts of the Old Testament, and the writings of early Christian theologians such as St. Augustine proscribe many sexual acts other than male–male and female–female acts, for example, masturbation and sex without being married. Gay marriage is just one of the sources of internal conflict for many people. On the other hand, polls show that Americans are in fact becoming more tolerant of gay marriage.

Same-Sex Marriage

LO 5.6 **Discuss the status of same-sex marriage in the United States, including changing attitudes toward same-sex marriage.**

> No union is more profound than marriage, for it embodies the highest ideals of love, fidelity, devotion, sacrifice, and family. In forming a marital union, two people become something greater than once they were. As some of the petitioners in these cases demonstrate, marriage embodies a love that may endure even past death. It would misunderstand these men and women to say they disrespect the idea of marriage. Their plea is that they do respect it, respect it so deeply that they seek to find its fulfillment for themselves. Their hope is not to be condemned to live in loneliness, excluded from one of civilization's oldest institutions. They ask for equal dignity in the eyes of the law. The Constitution grants them that right....
>
> [T]he right to marry is a fundamental right inherent in the liberty of the person, and under the Due Process and Equal Protection Clauses of the Fourteenth Amendment couples of the same-sex may not be deprived of that right and that liberty. The Court now holds that same-sex couples may exercise the fundamental right to marry. No longer may this liberty be denied to them.
>
> —Supreme Court Justice Anthony Kennedy, 2015, p. 33

With a single swipe in 2015, the U.S. Supreme Court cut through thousands of years of history, decades of debate, and piecemeal state-by-state advances toward the legalization of same-sex marriage in the United States. At the time, some 30 of the 50 states had already recognized gay marriage, either by legislative action or by court decisions based on the concept of equal protection for all under the law. Same-sex marriage was also recognized in countries including our next-door neighbors Canada and Mexico, the Netherlands, Sweden, and Norway in Europe, and Israel and South Africa.

Although the Supreme Court decision was handed down overnight, the struggle to obtain the right to marry people of one's own anatomic sex was fought for decades. In 1996 the government had enacted DOMA, which in retrospect seems to be little more than an effort to forestall what many saw even then as the inevitable. Even so, DOMA was passed by both the Senate and the House with veto-proof majorities, and President Bill Clinton signed it into law. DOMA did not prevent the states from legalizing same-sex marriage, but it denied federal marriage benefits to same-sex couples. But in 2013—as prelude to the ruling of 2015—the Supreme Court struck down DOMA as being unconstitutional.

The Fifth Amendment of the U.S. Constitution requires that the federal government not deprive people of life, liberty, or property without "due process of the law" and guarantees that all individuals will receive "equal protection" under the law. Section 1 of the Fourteenth Amendment further prohibits states from depriving individuals of rights, again on the basis of due process and equal protection.

Think once more of Leviticus in the Bible: "If a man lies with a man as with a woman, both of them have committed an abomination; they shall be put to death, their blood is upon them" (Leviticus 20:13). The U.S. Supreme Court in effect upheld the separation of church and state; the Court agreed that the United States is a nation of laws and not a theocracy, as are a number of nations around the world. Justice Kennedy recognized, as we see in his following statement, that people may disagree with the Court ruling on religious grounds, but, he asserts, states may not "bar same-sex couples from marriage":

[It] must be emphasized that religions, and those who adhere to religious doctrines, may continue to advocate with utmost, sincere conviction that, by divine precepts, same-sex marriage should not be condoned. The First Amendment ensures that religious organizations and persons are given proper protection as they seek to teach the principles that are so fulfilling and so central to their lives and faiths, and to their own deep aspirations to continue the family structure they have long revered. The same is true of those who oppose same-sex marriage for other reasons. In turn, those who believe allowing same-sex marriage is proper or indeed essential, whether as a matter of religious conviction or secular belief, may engage those who disagree with their view in an open and searching debate. The Constitution, however, does not permit the State to bar same-sex couples from marriage on the same terms as accorded to couples of the opposite sex.

—Supreme Court Justice Anthony Kennedy, 2015, p. 32

Following the Supreme Court Decision …

As Justice Kennedy anticipated, some conservative, religious individuals defied the Supreme Court order, citing the religious freedom guaranteed in the First Amendment of the Constitution. In one county in Kentucky, a public official, Kim Davis, refused to grant same-sex couples marriage licenses, despite the court decision and a specific order from federal judge David Bunning to do so. Some Republican candidates for the presidency (prior to the presidential election of 2016) went so far as to declare, that Bunning's order was part of a "War on Christianity." Bunning noted that Davis held a government position, and that the government could not discriminate against same-sex couples. Davis was also the chief clerk in her office and had instructed deputy clerks also not to issue marriage licenses. Davis was jailed for contempt of court and released when she agreed to allow her deputies to issue the licenses.

It is of interest that the American public at large, including 80% of Democrats and 66% of Republicans said that treating people equally was more important than

U.S. Supreme Court Justice Anthony Kennedy. Kennedy wrote the Supreme Court decision that legalized same-sex marriage throughout the United States.

Two women exchange rings during a mass gay wedding ceremony that took place on June 28, 2016 in Atlanta.

a person's religious views (Craighill & Somashektar, 2015). But as we will see, many fewer Republicans are in favor of same-sex marriage itself.

Changing Attitudes toward Same-Sex Marriage

A generation ago, the great majority of Americans were opposed to sexual relations between people of the same sex and also to same-sex marriage (Leubsdorf & Nelson, 2015). As recently as 2001, only one American in three (35%) favored same-sex marriage, whereas in 2015 the majority (60%) favored same-sex marriage (McCarthy, 2015).

8 › T / F Truth or Fiction Revisited   Yes, a majority of Americans in 2015 and 2016 reported that they favor same-sex marriage. The number of people supporting same-sex marriage has risen throughout the century, and younger people are more likely than older people to favor same-sex marriage. Thus, the numbers supporting same-sex marriage are likely to continue to increase.

Younger Americans have been more accepting of same-sex marriage than older Americans, including 39% of those born between 1928–1945 and 70% of those born in or since 1981 (Pew Research Center, 2015). Same-sex marriage remains one of the key social issues that divide Americans. Back in 2001, when a minority of Americans favored same-sex marriage, even the majority of Democrats did not break that mold; only 43% of Democrats supported same-sex marriage. In 2015, there was a vast change. In that year two-thirds of Democrats (66%) and three out of five Independents (61%) supported same-sex marriage, as compared with only a third (32%) of Republicans (Pew Research Center, 2015). There are two key details: First, each of the three groups has increased support for same-sex marriage over time (even Republicans increased their support from 21% to 32%). But, vitally important, the divide between Democrats and Republicans on the issue is greater now than it was in 2001. Back then the difference in opinion was 22% (43% minus 21%). In 2015 the difference had risen to 34% (66% minus 32%). This issue along with other social issues, such as abortion, is likely to divide Democrats and Republicans for some time to come. On the other hand, the rights of gay males and lesbians to get married has been affirmed by the U.S. Supreme Court. That affirmation is unlikely to change.

Chapter Review

LO 5.1 **Describe the various sexual orientations and discuss controversies in defining them.**

Heterosexuals are attracted to members of the other anatomic sex. Homosexuals are attracted to members of the same anatomic sex. Bisexuals are attracted to both males and females. Most homosexuals are content with their anatomic sex. The term *heteronormative* applies to the view that heterosexuality is the norm. Research into bisexuality raises the question as to whether heterosexuality and homosexuality are polar opposites on a single dimension, or whether they make up independent dimensions. Evidence suggests that fewer than 5% of the population is exclusively gay male or lesbian. The best evidence we have suggests that about 3% of American males are exclusively gay, and about 2% of American women are exclusively lesbian. According to the 2015 YouGov poll, which is an outlier, only two-thirds of 18- to 29-year-olds are exclusively heterosexual.

LO 5.2 **Explain how sexual orientation has been viewed historically and scientifically.**

The Judeo-Christian and Islamic traditions frown on homosexuality and other forms of nonprocreative sex. Ancient Greek men often had sexual relationships with adolescent males. Research with MZ and DZ twins suggests a role for genetic factors in the development of sexual orientation. Prenatal sex hormones are also believed to play a role; female embryos exposed to androgens tend to develop more masculine behavior patterns and are also more likely to be lesbians. Early experience with parents and early sexual experience do not appear to sway sexual orientation. Many homosexuals showed gender nonconformity in childhood.

LO 5.3 **Discuss contemporary U.S. attitudes toward homosexuality.**

Most Americans are growing more tolerant of homosexuals. A majority would now support either gay marriage or civil unions. Most would grant gay people equal rights to jobs and housing. Men—especially men who are heavily invested in traditional gender roles—are more likely than women to be homophobic. In some parts of the world, homosexuals face the threat of death.

LO 5.4 **Discuss the psychological adjustment of lesbians and gay males.**

Homosexuals are more likely than heterosexuals to encounter anxiety and depression and to have suicidal thoughts, apparently because of social prejudice. Most professionals agree that homosexuals who seek to change their sexual orientation are influenced by social prejudice, and so-called conversion therapy has been outlawed for minors in many jurisdictions.

LO 5.5 **Describe concerns about, and processes of, coming out.**

Coming out to oneself is a gradual process in which the individual eventually comes to accept his or her homosexual orientation. Coming out to others is for many an anxiety-evoking process characterized by fear of social disapproval, loss of a job, and the like. Savin-Williams and Diamond describe coming out as involving four steps or features: experiencing attractions to people of the same anatomic sex, self-labeling as gay or lesbian, sexual contact with peoples of the same sex, and disclosure of one's sexual orientation to others.

LO 5.6 **Discuss the status of same-sex marriage in the United States, including changing attitudes toward same-sex marriage.**

In 2013, the U.S. Supreme Court found the Defense of Marriage Act, which defined marriage as between a man and a woman, to be unconstitutional because it denied equal protection to gay males and lesbians. In 2015, the Court further found states' prohibitions against same-sex marriage to be unconstitutional on the same grounds. Support for same-sex marriage has been growing over the years, and today a majority of Americans support it. Support is highest among young people, women, Democrats, liberals, Hispanics, and professional people.

Test Your Learning

1. In ancient _____, men often had sexual relationships with adolescent males.
   - (a) Egypt
   - (b) Greece
   - (c) Rome
   - (d) Macedonia

2. _____ are most likely to share a homosexual orientation.
   - (a) Monozygotic twins
   - (b) Dizygotic twins
   - (c) Parents and their biological children
   - (d) Adoptive parents and their adopted children

3. Psychoanalytic theory ties male homosexuality to faulty resolution of the _____ complex.
   - (a) inferiority
   - (b) Electra
   - (c) whore–Madonna
   - (d) Oedipus

4. The hypothalamus of gay males responds similarly to that of _____ when gay males are presented with the odor of a testosterone derivative.
   - (a) heterosexual men
   - (b) heterosexual women
   - (c) lesbians
   - (d) bisexuals

5. Homosexuals differ from transgendered people in that homosexuals _____
   - (a) are satisfied with their anatomic sex.
   - (b) are dissatisfied with their anatomic sex.
   - (c) are confused about their gender identity.
   - (d) seek therapy to change their sexual orientation.

6. Ivanka Savic and her colleagues suggest that sexual differentiation and sexual orientation may reflect the timing of prenatal surges of _____
   - (a) dopamine.
   - (b) serotonin.
   - (c) estrogen.
   - (d) testosterone.

7. According to Savin-Williams and Diamond, the first step in the development of sexual orientation in homosexuals is _____
   - (a) sexual activity with members of the same anatomic sex.
   - (b) attraction to members of the same gender.
   - (c) acceptance of one's sexual orientation.
   - (d) self-labeling as gay or lesbian.

8. _____ tried to develop methods to "reverse" a homosexual orientation.
   - (a) Masters and Johnson
   - (b) Laumann
   - (c) Freud
   - (d) Kinsey

9. In contrast to Kinsey and his colleagues, Vrangalova and Savin-Williams (2012) see sexual attraction to people of one's own anatomic sex or the other anatomic sex as _____
   - (a) one-dimensional.
   - (b) two-dimensional.
   - (c) three-dimensional.
   - (d) four-dimensional.

10. Which of the following groups is most likely to favor same-sex marriage?
    - (a) very religious, small-town individuals.
    - (b) people aged 65 and older.
    - (c) Republicans.
    - (d) Democrats.

Answers: 1. b; 2. a; 3. d; 4. b; 5. a; 6. d; 7. b; 8. a; 9. b; 10. d

Chapter 6
Attraction and Love

 Learning Objectives

Physical Attractiveness: Flooding the Senses with Attraction

LO 6.1 Describe cultural standards for physical attractiveness.

LO 6.2 Describe nonphysical traits that affect perceptions of physical attractiveness.

The Attraction–Similarity Hypothesis: Who is "Right" for You?

LO 6.3 Explain the role of similarity in the formation of romantic relationships.

Love: "The Morning and the Evening Star"?

LO 6.4 Discuss the meaning of love.

LO 6.5 Discuss the meaning of romantic love.

Contemporary Models of Love: Dare Science Intrude?

LO 6.6 Discuss theories of love.

LO 6.7 Explain how people's preferences for partners differ for short- and long-term relationships.

TRUTH OR FICTION?

Which of the following statements are the truth, and which are fiction? Look for the Truth-or-Fiction items throughout this chapter to find the answers.

1 Beauty is in the eye of the beholder.   **T / F**?

2 Women find men with deeper voices to be more attractive.   **T / F**?

3 People are regarded as more attractive when they are smiling.   **T / F**?

4 Women who are randomly assigned names like Kathy and Jennifer are rated as more attractive than women assigned names like Harriet and Gertrude.   **T / F**?

5 "Opposites attract." That is, we are more apt to be attracted to people who disagree with our views and tastes than to people who share them.   **T / F**?

6 It is possible to be in love with someone who is not also a friend.   **T / F**?

7 Committed couples can remain in love even after passion fades.   **T / F**?

Sexual attraction is an elixir of life, from love at first sight to the spark of romance that enlivens a relationship for years. It imbues the great love affairs of literature and film, whether the star-crossed lovers of Shakespeare's *Romeo and Juliet* or James Cameron's *Titanic* of the long-smoldering attraction between Humphrey Bogart's and Ingrid Bergman's characters in *Casablanca*. . . .

Sexual attraction is not simply a topic of titillation. It permeates our conversations—from gossip columns highlighting celebrity fashion missteps to Web sites devoted to ranking who is hot and who is not, advertisers exploit it to sell everything from cars to iPods. Lack of sexual attraction is often a deal breaker in romances, killing possible partnerships before they even get off the ground. And when sexual attraction fades with time, it can propel a partner into the arms of another.

—*Meston & Buss, 2009 [p. 1]*

Attraction and one of its possible consequences, love, are the subjects of this chapter. Investigators define feelings of attraction as psychological forces that draw people together. We will see that many factors enter into personal attraction. The first of these is physical appearance.

Physical Attractiveness: Flooding the Senses with Attraction

LO 6.1 Describe cultural standards for physical attractiveness.

We might like to think of ourselves as so sophisticated that physical attractiveness does not move us. We might like to claim that sensitivity, warmth, and intelligence are more important to us. However, we may never learn about other people's personalities if they do not meet our minimal standards for physical attractiveness. Research for many decades has shown—and keeps on showing—that physical attractiveness is a major determinant of interpersonal and sexual attraction (Lippa, 2012; Meltzer et al., 2014). The power of Tinder—in which people express interest in others on the basis of their photo alone—also testifies to the importance of physical appearance in consideration of partners for dates, sex, and long-term relationships.

Men appear to be more responsive to visual stimuli than women, although women are also clearly attuned to appealing eyefuls—and what they mean to them

(Chivers, 2010; Thompson, 2011). Evolutionary psychologists note that it would make sense for males and females to be more attracted to one another when the woman is ovulating: that is, capable of conceiving a child. It would be likely that women might act somewhat differently or that men would pick up on certain cues—perhaps unconsciously—that would communicate a woman's phase of the menstrual cycle (Haselton & Gildersleeve, 2011, 2015). Interestingly, women tend to dress and ornament themselves in more appealing ways when they are in the fertile phase of their ovulatory cycle (Haselton et al., 2007; Starratt & Alesia, 2014). Forty-two judges selected photos of women as "trying to look more attractive" in their fertile (59.5 percent) phase as compared with their luteal phase (40.5 percent). Other research shows that men's "mate-retention efforts" increase as their partners are approaching ovulation, and perhaps the men perceive subtle changes in their partners' appearance that make them more attractive (Haselton & Gildersleeve, 2011, 2015).

Although physical appeal is important in sexual attraction, other factors matter and may even challenge the equation that good looks equals sexual attractiveness. First of all, people differ to some degree in terms of the features, for example eye color, and general appearance of people they find most attractive. And how often do we hear "How did he/she wind up with her/him?" Common experience also tells us that we often nominate different people as being the most attractive celebrities, and then someone else says "I can't see it at all." Second, there is the issue of whether or not it seems that an individual would be able to provide a high-quality relationship (Eastwick & Hunt, 2014). Again, we're talking common sense: what good does it do one to enter a relationship with an attractive person if that person will make you miserable? And because men are somewhat more attuned to the visual than women, we would expect women to be somewhat more flexible in mate choice in that they may be more willing to trade (some) good looks for a good relationship. Remember that evolutionary theory proposes that women on some level recognize that they are more likely than men to be reproductively successful if they can rear their children in high-quality relationships.

Is Beauty in the Eye of the Beholder?

Are our standards for beauty subjective, or is there broad agreement on what is attractive? Cross-cultural studies of preliterate societies have found that people universally want physically appealing partners (Ford & Beach, 1951). However, is that which appeals in one culture unimportant or even repulsive in others?

In certain African tribes, as among the Khoikhoi, long necks and round, disk-like lips are signs of feminine beauty. Women thus stretch their necks and lips to make themselves more appealing. Women of the Nama tribe persistently tug at their labia majora to make them "beautiful"—that is, prominent and elongated (Ford & Beach, 1951).

1 › T / F Truth or Fiction Revisited Beauty may not be completely in the eye of the beholder. As noted in the nearby "Sex in a World of Diversity" feature, "Wide-Eyed with . . . Beauty?" some aspects of beauty seem to be largely cross-cultural.

Generally speaking, taller men are considered to be more attractive by women (Furnham, 2009; Meston & Buss, 2009; Sohn, 2015). Height plays a key role in choice of a mate because it suggests social dominance, status, access to resources, protection, and a positive heritable trait (Meston & Buss, 2009). Undergraduate women prefer their dates to be about 6 inches taller than they are. Undergraduate men, on the average, prefer women who are about 4 to 5 inches shorter (Furnham, 2009). Consistent with stereotypical gender roles, tall women are not viewed as positively as tall men are. In a survey of 2,000 personal ads and about 400 undergraduates, only 23 percent of men and 4 percent of women indicated that they would accept a date in which the

SEX IN A WORLD OF DIVERSITY

WIDE-EYED WITH … BEAUTY?

Research suggests that European Americans, African Americans, Asian Americans, and Latin Americans tend to agree on the facial features that they find to be attractive (Cunningham et al., 1995). They all prefer female faces with large eyes; greater distance between the eyes; small noses; narrower faces with smaller chins; high, expressive eyebrows; larger lower lips; and a well-groomed, full head of hair.

Consider the methodology of a study that compared the facial preferences of people in Japan and England. Perrett (cited in Brody, 1994) created computer composites of the faces of 60 women. Part A is a composite of the 15 women who were rated the most attractive. He then used computer enhancement to exaggerate the differences between the composite of the 60—that is, the average face—and the composite of the 15 most attractive women. Perret found that both Japanese and British men deemed women with large eyes, high cheekbones, and narrow jaws to be the most attractive. Computer enhancement resulted in the image shown in Part B. The enhanced composite has still higher cheekbones and a narrower jaw than Part A. Part B was then rated as the most attractive image. Similar results were found for the image of a Japanese woman.

Cunningham and his colleagues (1995) reported historical anecdotes that suggest that the facial preferences of people as diverse as Europeans, Black Africans, Native Americans, Indians necessary? and Chinese are quite consistent. They quoted from Charles Darwin's 1871 treatise, *The Descent of Man, and Selection in Relation to Sex:*

> Mr. Winwood Reade … who has had ample opportunities for observation [with Black Africans] who have never associated with Europeans is convinced that their ideas of beauty are, on the whole, the same as ours; and Dr. Rohlfs writes to me the same effect with respect to Borneo and the countries inhabited by the Pullo tribes…. Capt. Burton believes that a woman whom we consider beautiful is admired throughout the world.

Darwin believed that our physical preferences were largely inborn and related to the survival of our species. What do you think? Do you believe that "their ideas of beauty are, on the whole, the same as ours"? Or do you think that research hasn't yet ferreted out significant cultural or ethnic differences that might exist? If there is ethnic consistency in these preferences, how would you explain them? For example, do you believe

- that they are coincidental?
- that there has been more exchange of ideas among cultures than believed?
- that there is something instinctive about them?

A   **B**

(Perrit, 1994)

In both England and Japan, large eyes, high cheekbones, and narrow jaws contribute to perceptions of the attractiveness of women. Part A shows a composite of the faces of 15 women rated as the most attractive of a group of 60. Part B is a composite in which the features of these 15 women are exaggerated—that is, developed further in the direction that separates them from the average of the 60. Raters tend to find face B to be yet more attractive than face A.

woman was taller. But short men and tall women were more flexible; otherwise their potential dating pool would be much smaller.

Because their height discourages shorter men from asking them out, some tall women walk with a hunch, as if to minimize their height. A neighbor of the first and third authors of this text refers to herself—humorously, of course—as 5 feet 13 inches tall.

anorexia nervosa

A potentially life-threatening eating disorder characterized by refusal to maintain a healthy body weight, intense fear of becoming overweight, a distorted body image, and, in females, lack of menstruation (amenorrhea).

"Thin is in" in the dominant European American culture of the United States. Some young women are so affected by the cultural ideal that they suffer from the eating disorder called **anorexia nervosa**, in which they literally starve themselves. Both females and males find slenderness (though not anorexic thinness) attractive. In a survey of 22,815 U.S. adults, it was found that men and women both said that it is desirable or essential for potential partners to be good looking (92 percent of men and 84 percent of women) and slender (80 percent of men and 58 percent of women) (Fales et al., 2016). Older men and women were relatively less demanding. On the other hand, women were more likely to express a desire for men who had a steady income (74 percent versus 97 percent) and made a lot of money (47 percent versus 69 percent). These findings are all consistent with evolutionary theory: Men are relatively more concerned with the (apparent) fertility of their partners, and women are relatively more concerned with a partner's ability to help provide an environment conducive to successful child-rearing.

European American males are more likely than African American and Latino males to want to date slender and buffed women. African American and Latino men are significantly more likely to be interested in women with large or thick bodies.

A CLOSER LOOK

THE ALLURE OF THE COLOR RED

When you go to buy a box of Valentine's Day candy, what color will the box be? Green? Blue? The answer, of course, is red. What is the most popular color of women's lipstick? Yellow? Brown? Again, the answer is red (Elliot, 2015). Red has been the most popular lipstick color since the hot days that saw the construction of the pyramids in ancient Egypt (Elliot & Niesta, 2008). Red is similarly the most popular color for women's lingerie.

At a traffic light, the color red means stop. But when it comes to sexual attraction, the color red is more likely to mean go.

But why is the color red associated with feelings of attraction? Could the answer be cultural conditioning? Anthropologists have found evidence that females used red ochre as a face and body paint in rituals carried out before the dawn of history (Y. Lee, 2006). We find red used in ancient myths and folklore as a symbol of passion and fertility (Elliot & Pazda, 2012; Elliot et al., 2013). Red has been associated with lust in literature, most notably in Nathaniel Hawthorne's novel of illicit romance and consequences—*The Scarlet Letter*. Red has been used as a symbol of prostitution for centuries, as in the term *red-light district* (Moore, 2010).

The link between red and physical attraction may also be rooted in our biological heritage. Many nonhuman female primates; including baboons, chimpanzees, gorillas, and rhesus monkeys, show reddened genital regions and sometimes reddened chests and faces when they are nearing ovulation—the time of the month when they are fertile (Barelli et al., 2008; Engelhardt et al., 2012). Reddening of the skin is caused by elevated estrogen levels (relative to progesterone), which increase the flow of blood under the surface of the skin. It is widely believed that reddish skin tones are a sexual signal that

Why Did They Deck Her out in Red? The answers may lie in our cultural conditioning and in our genetic heritage. Red is suggestive of a healthy circulatory system and of sexual arousal.

attracts mates (Huchard et al., 2009). Research has found that male primates are in fact especially attracted to females when they display red, as shown by attempts at sexual relations (Meier et al., 2012).

Although being a heavy woman is connected with a negative body image in the dominant culture, African American and Latina women are significantly more likely than European American women with similar body shapes to be satisfied with their bodies (La Rocque & Cloe, 2011). Moreover, women who are displeased with their bodies are more likely to avoid sexual activity, although women with a history of sexual satisfaction and with strong sexual desire are more likely to engage in sexual activity despite their body images (La Rocque & Cloe, 2011; Milhausen et al., 2015).

The dominant culture also prefers the hourglass figure. Studies find that women of average weight with a waist-to-hip ratio of 0.7 to 0.8 are rated as most attractive and desirable for relationships (Dural et al., 2015). Neither gaunt nor obese women are found to be as attractive.

Cohen and Tannenbaum (2001) conducted an Internet study in which they posted various women's body shapes and asked lesbian and bisexual women to indicate which were most sexually attractive to them. Respondents included 209 women self-identified as lesbian and 141 women self-identified as bisexual. The women, like heterosexual men, found women with a 0.7 waist-to-hip body ratio to be the most sexually attractive.

As in the case of other female primates, women's estrogen levels relative to progesterone are elevated near ovulation, enhancing the flow of blood beneath the surface of the skin (Lynn et al., 2007). At this time of the month, women also tend to choose clothing that leaves more skin visible (Durante et al., 2008), use sexier gaits and walk more slowly ahead of men (Gueguen, 2012), and are more readily sexually aroused (Rupp et al., 2009). For men, then, as with other male primates, the reddening of a woman's skin at the time of ovulation may be a sexual signal.

Andrew Elliot and Daniela Niesta (2008) ran a series of experiments in which men did, indeed, rate the same woman as more attractive when her photograph was shown against a red background compared with a variety of other background colors. One experiment revealed that the red-related difference in attractiveness was found in male raters but not in female raters. As you can see in Figure 6.1, male raters found women more attractive when they were shown with red backgrounds as opposed to white, but female raters did not show the same preference.

Andrew Elliot and his colleagues (2010) also ran experiments with women and found that they rated photos of men as being more attractive when the photos were bordered in red or the men were wearing red clothing. Women are more interested in the status of potential partners than men are, and it seems that they connect the color red with status in males. Cross-cultural research links the color red in males with power and social dominance, and the Elliot group found that women rated males in red as having more status than males in white, blue, or green. The color red had no effect on women's ratings of males as being likeable, agreeable, or outgoing—status was the lone association. But, as with men viewing women, red is "sexy."

A biological possibility as to why women are more attracted to males who are associated with the color red is that testosterone is involved in oxygenating blood and increasing its flow to the skin (giving off a reddish hue) and to the genitals, leading to sexual excitement. Red coloration can also be an indicator of health, because highly oxygenated blood levels can be maintained only by organisms in good health (Elliot et al., 2010).

Reddening of the skin, then, is a cue that is connected with attraction. Body odor—or scent—is another cue. Female strippers and lap dancers earn higher tips when they are ovulating (Haselton & Gildersleeve, 2011). We may wonder if the "mechanism" connected with attraction was indeed body odor, however. A critical thinker might ask whether ovulation might have in some way prompted the women to behave in a manner that was more appealing to men.

Figure 6.1 Rated Attractiveness as a Woman Shown in a Photograph, as Related to the Color of the Background and the Gender of the Rater.
SOURCE: Elliot, A. J., & Niesta, D. (2008). Romantic red: Red enhances men's attraction to women. *Journal of Personality and Social Psychology, 95*(5), 1150–1164.

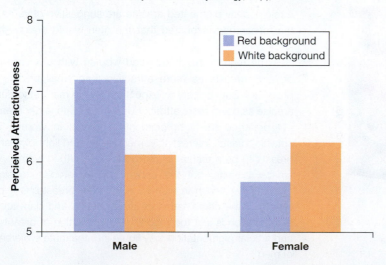

Critical Thinking
Do you think the study that concluded that heterosexual women find men with deeper voices to be more attractive during the late follicular phase of the menstrual cycle is consistent with evolutionary theory? Explain.

However, they differed from the men in that their first choice was for heavy women with a 0.7 waist-to-hip body ratio and large breasts. Their second choice was for heavy women with the same waist-to-hip body ratio but with small breasts. The authors of the study suggest that lesbians rejected societal emphasis on excessive slenderness.

It will come as little surprise that people who are attractive know it. In one study, men and women rated each other for attractiveness and also rated themselves (Marcus & Miller, 2003). By and large, the individuals' self-ratings meshed with those by others, both female and male. Women's judgments were most closely related to how men perceived them, suggesting that they were reflecting men's opinions of them more so than women's.

The voice is another physical feature in attraction. An experiment manipulated men's voices and asked women to rate them for attractiveness. Heterosexual women at the fertile (late-follicular) phase of the menstrual cycle found men with more "masculine"—that is, deeper—voices to be more attractive (Feinberg et al., 2006). The study did not assess possible differences between heterosexual and lesbian women.

2 ❭ T / F   Truth or Fiction Revisited   It is only partly true that women preferred men with deeper voices. First of all, the finding was true for heterosexual women only. Second it was true for heterosexual women only during the time of the month when they were fertile.

A CLOSER LOOK

THIN MAY BE IN, BUT NOT WITH BUST SIZE

It is generally believed that men prefer women with large breasts. For this reason, as well as dissatisfaction with their own body image, many women with small breasts decide to obtain breast implants (Moser & Alken, 2011). *Do men prefer women with large breasts?*

Studies have assessed men's interest in women of various breast sizes by tracking their eye movements when they were viewing images of women with different sized breasts (Dixson et al, 2011; 2015). The researchers predicted that the men would have a greater number of visual fixations on larger breasts and also rate them as more attractive. They predicted that the coloration of the areolae would also play

Critical Thinking
Critical thinkers look for rival explanations for research findings. For example, could it be that in our visual culture, with its ubiquitous sexual and anatomic images, that the men were just scanning the breasts and the areolae for differences, but they had no particular arousing quality? Can you think of other rival explanations for the results?

a role. Lightly pigmented areolae are suggestive of youth, so the researchers expected that the men would prefer lighter areolae.

The men in the study rated women with medium-sized or large breasts as more attractive than small breasts, as predicted. But contrary to expectations, the men rated darker areolae as being more attractive in women with larger breasts, but preferred the light pigmented areolae in women with smaller breasts. Interestingly, men associated light pigmented breasts to be a marker of reproductive health in women with smaller breasts, but the darker colored areolae to signify reproductive health in women with larger breasts. Is it possible that the combination of large breasts and dark areolar pigmentation is just too much? This interaction of breast size and areolar pigmentation may figure into the mate preferences of men.

shutterstock.com 213084793

What size breasts do men prefer? What about the pigmentation of the areolae?

Smell: Does the Nose Know Best?

Although the sense of smell plays a lesser role in governing sexual arousal in humans than in lower mammals, research shows that humans can detect literally millions of different odors (Hoover, 2010). Odors can be powerful sexual turn-ons or turn-offs. Perfume companies, for example, bottle fragrances purported to be sexually arousing.

Most Westerners prefer their lovers to be clean and fresh smelling (Boston Women's Health Book Collective, 2005). People in the United States have learned to remove or mask odors by the use of soaps, deodorants, and perfumes or colognes. The ancient Egyptians invented scented bathing to rid themselves of offensive odors (Illes, 2000).

ATTRACTION TO—OR DISLIKE OF—BODY ODORS OF HETEROSEXUAL MALES AND FEMALES VERSUS GAY MALES AND LESBIANS There is reason to believe that body odors play a role in the selection of sex partners (Meston & Buss, 2007; Moshkin et al., 2011). Yolanda Martins and her colleagues (2005) hypothesized that preferences for axillary (underarm) odors would be related to people's sexual orientation: heterosexual male or female, and gay male or lesbian. They collected samples of axillary odors from 24 volunteers—6 exclusively male heterosexual, 6 exclusively female heterosexual, 6 exclusively gay male, and 6 exclusively lesbian, according to the Kinsey heterosexuality–homosexuality scale described in Figure 10.1.

A study of 46 male and 19 female college students compared the pleasantness or unpleasantness of male and female armpit odors as related to the phases of women's menstrual cycles (Moshkin et al., 2011). Men rated women's armpit odors as more pleasant when women were in the ovulatory phases of their cycles. The women were less likely to rate intense male body odor as unpleasant when they were in the ovulatory phase.

The researchers had a number of interesting findings. For example:

- Heterosexual males and females and lesbians preferred axillary odors taken from heterosexual males over those taken from gay males.

- Gay males preferred axillary odors taken from other gay males.

- Heterosexual males and females and lesbians aged 25 and older preferred axillary odors taken from lesbians to those from gay males.

- When axillary odors of heterosexual females were compared to those of lesbians, all groups except for heterosexual males preferred the odors from heterosexual females.

- Heterosexual males preferred the odor from lesbians over the odor taken from gay male donors.

The researchers suggest that the data show that gay males and lesbians may produce axillary odors that can be distinguished from those of heterosexuals. It would also appear that gay males may perceive these typical odorants differently from the way in which heterosexual males do. We can note, at least in the few studies that have investigated the relationships between body odor and sexual orientation, that gay males are most likely to be attracted to the body odors of other gay males, and that heterosexual males are least likely to prefer the body odors of gay males.

PHEROMONES

> Pheromones have been found across the animal kingdom, sending messages between courting lobsters, alarmed aphids, suckling rabbit pups, mound-building termites and trail-following ants.
>
> —*T. D. Wyatt (2009)*

For centuries, people have searched for a love potion—a magical formula that could make other people fall in love with you or be strongly attracted to you. But some scientists suggest that such potions may already exist in the form of chemical secretions

A CLOSER LOOK

STRIPPERS: A TREAT FOR THE EYES OR THE NOSE?

Many patrons of bars and strip clubs say they go "just to see what's going on" (or off?). But it could also be that many of them go to titillate their senses of smell, especially during lap dances. A study published in *Evolution and Human Behavior* (Miller et al., 2007) found that women strippers' tips were related to their "time of month."

When strippers were ovulating, they made twice as much money in tips as when they were menstruating—and one and one-half the amount of money they made when they were neither ovulating nor menstruating. When women are ovulating, they are usually somewhat more interested in sex, and it is possible that they subtly communicated their interest through their movements. However, it is also possible that they emitted olfactory cues that were more arousing to their patrons, who, in turn, showed their enhanced appreciation via their wallets (Haselton & Gildersleeve, 2011). It could also be that subliminal menstrual odors—which, in biological terms, are a sign of an infertile period of time—communicated unavailability at some fundamental sexual level.

This stripper will probably earn higher tips when she is ovulating. Why? Will she behave differently? Will customers perceive something to be different?

known as pheromones. Pheromones may enhance people's moods, have effects on fertility, and provide a basis for sexual communication below the level of conscious awareness (T. D. Wyatt, 2014).

Pheromones are odorless chemicals that in many animals are detected through a "sixth sense"—the *vomeronasal organ (VNO)*. People possess VNOs in the mucous lining of the nose (Touhara & Vosshall, 2009; T. D. Wyatt, 2014). During prenatal development, the VNO shuttles sex hormones into the brain, aiding in the sexual differentiation of the embryo (Rodriguez et al., 2000). But before birth, the human VNO shrinks, and some researchers suggest that it stops working (Kouros-Mehr et al., 2001). But if it does continue to work, it might detect pheromones and direct information about them to the hypothalamus, where they might affect sexual response (T. D. Wyatt, 2014). Infants may use pheromones to recognize their mothers, and adults might respond to them in seeking a mate (Meston & Buss, 2009). Male rodents such as mice are extremely sensitive to several kinds of pheromones (Stowers & Kuo, 2015). Male rodents show less sexual arousal when their sense of smell is blocked, but the role of pheromones in sexual behavior becomes less vital as one moves upward through the ranks of the animal kingdom.

Only a few years ago, most researchers did not believe that pheromones played a role in human behavior, but today the issue has attracted new interest. In a typical study, Winnifred Cutler and her colleagues (1998) had heterosexual men wear a suspected male pheromone, whereas a control group wore a placebo. The men using the pheromone increased their frequency of sexual intercourse with their female partners but did not increase the frequency of masturbation. The researchers conclude that the substance increased the sexual attractiveness of the men to their partners, although they do not claim that it directly stimulated sexual behavior.

Real Students, Real Questions

Q *I keep attracting the same kind of guy—one that is not good for me. Why do I do this?*

A We don't know you well enough to give you a precise answer, but your complaint sounds familiar enough. Try listing the traits you want in a guy. Seriously—write them down. Then write down how you go about meeting guys and how you decide to get intimate with them, or whether you just let it happen.

    Should you meet guys in other places, in other ways? Should you get to know them better before getting intimate? Should you end things early on if things aren't going the way you want them to? Just be honest with yourself and figure it out. It's more likely because of poor choices, lack of self-confidence, low self-esteem (if you think you're not worth very much, maybe you allow people to treat you as if you aren't), or—gulp—laziness, rather than something like a deep unconscious desire to punish yourself.

Experiments that expose men and women to suspected pheromones (*androstadienone* produced by males and *estratetraenol* produced by females) find that they enhance the moods of women but not of men; the substances also apparently reduce feelings of nervousness and tension in women, but again, not in men (Krajnik et al., 2014; Jacob & McClintock, 2000). The findings about estratetraenol are not surprising. This substance is related to estrogen, and women tend to function best during the time of the month when estrogen levels are highest (Ross et al., 2000). The fact that the women responded positively to the androstadienone is of greater interest. Women may thus generally feel somewhat better when they are around men, even if male chemicals have not been shown to have direct sexual effects. Of course, being in a good mood can indirectly contribute to a woman's interest in sex.

Male perspiration primes women's emotional responses (Hummer & McClintock, 2009; Preti et al., 2003). It induces feelings of relaxation and helps lessen stress (Preti et al., 2003). It even affects the menstrual cycle. Researchers extracted samples from the underarms of men who avoided using deodorant for a month. The samples were blended and applied to the upper lips of 18 women, aged 25 to 45. The women did not know the source or makeup of the chemicals on the swabs. The women then rated their moods over a six-hour period and reported feeling more relaxed and in better moods. Analysis of their blood revealed a rise in levels of luteinizing hormone (LH), which surges before ovulation. There was no indication that the women were sexually aroused, but it might be that men's perspiration provides "chemical communication" when they meet women, allowing them to coordinate reproductive efforts below the level of awareness. These substances do not directly stimulate behavior, as pheromones do with lower animals.

In a double-blind experiment, 36 university women were randomly assigned to wear a perfume laced with a suspected pheromone extracted from their underarm secretions or a placebo (McCoy & Pitino, 2002). The women recorded their sexual behaviors over three menstrual cycles (12 weeks). Three-quarters (74 previously) of the women who used the suspected pheromone showed significant increases in their frequency of sexual intercourse, sleeping next to a partner, formal dates, and kissing, petting, and other displays of affection, as compared with one-quarter (23 previously) of the users of the placebo. Perhaps the suspected pheromone increased the women's attractiveness to men.

Nonphysical Traits Affect Feelings of Attraction

LO 6.2 Describe nonphysical traits that affect perceptions of physical attractiveness.

Although there are physical standards for beauty in our culture, nonphysical traits also affect our perceptions of beauty. For example, the perceived beauty of a partner is likely to be enhanced by nonphysical traits such as familiarity, liking, respect, and sharing of values and goals (Morry et al., 2011; Reis et al., 2011; Sprecher & Fehr, 2011).

3 › T / F   Truth or Fiction Revisited   People rate the attractiveness of faces higher when they are smiling than when they are not smiling (O'Doherty et al., 2003a). So there is reason to "put on a happy face" when you meet people.

HOW BEHAVIOR AND NAMES AFFECT PERCEPTIONS OF PHYSICAL ATTRACTIVENESS: ON THE IMPORTANCE OF NOT BEING EARNEST   Gender-role expectations may affect perceptions of attractiveness. For example, women are more likely to be attracted to socially dominant men than men are to be attracted to socially dominant women (Graziano & Bruce, 2008). Women who viewed videos of prospective dates found men who acted outgoing and self-expressive more appealing than men who were passive (Riggio & Woll, 1984; Riggio et al., 2015). Another study found that highly feminine women are more likely to be attracted to dominant "macho" men than less feminine women are (Maybach & Gold, 1994). And yet, men who viewed videos in the Riggio and Woll (1984) study were put off by outgoing, self-expressive behavior in women. In still another study, women rated videos of dominant college men (defined in this study as social control over a troublesome interaction with an instructor) as more appealing than submissive men. Again, male viewers were put off by similarly dominant women (Sadalla et al., 1987). Men are more likely to be jealous of socially dominant men, whereas women are more likely to be jealous of physically attractive women (Dijkstra & Buunk, 2002).

4 › T / F   Truth or Fiction Revisited   It is true that names can also affect perceptions of attractiveness. In one study, women who were randomly assigned names like Kathy, Jennifer, and Christine were rated more attractive than women assigned the names Harriet, Gertrude, and Ethel (Garwood et al., 1980). Seems silly, does it not? After all, our parents name us, and there need be no relationship between our names and our physical appeal. On the other hand, we may choose to keep our names or to use nicknames. So if you are unhappy with your name, why not assume a more popular nickname? Beginning college or a new job is an ideal time for doing so. Men, too, can doff their Sylvesters and Ernests, if they prefer. If you have an unusual name and are content with it, be yourself, however.

SOME THOUGHTS ON THE EVOLUTIONARY VIEW OF SEXUAL ATTRACTIVENESS   On the surface, gender differences in perceptions of attractiveness seem unbearably sexist—and perhaps they are. But some evolutionary psychologists believe that evolutionary forces favor the continuation of gender differences in preferences for mates because certain preferred traits provide reproductive advantages (Conroy-Beam et al., 2015; Fales et al., 2016; Schmitt et al., 2012). Some physical features, such as cleanliness, good complexion, clear eyes, good teeth, good hair, firm muscle tone, and a steady gait, are universally appealing to both females and males. Perhaps they are markers of reproductive potential (Buss, 2005). Age and health may be relatively more important to a woman's appeal, because these characteristics tend to be associated with her reproductive capacity (the "biological clock" limits her reproductive potential). Physical characteristics associated with a woman's youthfulness, such as smooth skin, firm muscle tone, and lustrous hair, may thus have become more closely linked to a woman's appeal (Buss, 2005). A man's reproductive value, however, may depend more on how well he can provide for his family than on his age

Q *What do you do if you're attracted to your best friend's boyfriend (or girlfriend)?*

A Generally speaking, flirting with or "messing around with" your friend's boyfriend or girlfriend is a no-no. You may win the boyfriend or girlfriend, but you'll probably lose the friend, and possibly, the respect of people who know both of you. Having said that, the reality of the situation must also accept the fact that what you are essentially doing is making a decision regarding who is more important to you—your friend or his or her partner. You probably can't have both. This also goes for "exes." Even if the relationship between your friend and his or her partner comes to an end, seeing the ex-partner may still be a sore point, so you may still be unable to have both.

or physical appeal. The value of men as reproducers, therefore, is more intertwined with factors that contribute to a stable environment for childrearing—such as economic status and reliability (Fales et al., 2016). Evolutionary psychologists argue that these gender differences in mate preferences may have been passed down through the generations as part of our genetic heritage (Buss, 2009b).

The Attraction–Similarity Hypothesis: Who is "Right" for You?

LO 6.3 **Explain the role of similarity in the formation of romantic relationships.**

Do not despair if you are less than exquisite in appearance, along with most of us mere mortals. You may be saved from permanently blending in with the wallpaper by the effects of the attraction–similarity hypothesis.

The **attraction–similarity hypothesis** holds that people tend to develop romantic relationships with people who are similar to themselves in physical attractiveness and other traits (Morry et al., 2011; Sprecher & Fehr, 2011). There are some gender differences: Research shows that men are more likely than women to communicate positive feelings and present themselves in a positive light when they are conversing with a woman who is similar in physical attractiveness (van Straaten et al., 2009). Women did not show the same selectivity in talking with men. These findings are consistent with research showing that physical attractiveness is a more important criterion for men than women in mate selection. Yet, as we will see in the following chapter, women can be as direct as men in signaling interest when they begin conversations.

People who are involved in committed relationships are most likely to be similar to their partners in their attitudes and cultural attributes (Morry et al., 2011). People are more often than not similar to their mates in height, weight, personality traits, intelligence, educational level, religion, and even in use of alcohol and tobacco (DeCuyper et al., 2012; Sprecher et al., 2015). Nearly 95 percent of marriages and 80 to 90 percent of cohabiting unions were between partners of the same race at the time of the 2010 U.S. census (U.S. Census Bureau, 2011). The concept of "like marrying like" is termed **homogamy**. Research shows that marriages between people from similar backgrounds tend to be more stable (DeCuyper et al., 2012), perhaps because partners are more likely to share values and attitudes (Willetts, 2006).

Most people also tend to follow *age homogamy*—to select a partner who falls in their own age range, with husbands 2 to 5 years older than wives (Skopek et al., 2011; Zhang et al., 2011). But age homogamy reflects the tendency to marry in early

attraction–similarity hypothesis

The view that people tend to develop romantic relationships with people who are similar to themselves in factors such as physical attractiveness, cultural background, personality traits, and interests.

homogamy

Like marrying like.

Who Is Right for You? Research shows that people tend to pair off with others who are similar in physical characteristics and personality traits.

adulthood. Persons who marry late or who remarry tend not to select partners so close in age because they are "out in the world"—rather than in school or fresh out of school—and tend to work with or otherwise meet people from different age groups.

Attitudes: Do "Opposites Attract" or Do "Birds of a Feather Flock Together"?

propinquity

Nearness.

Why do the great majority of us have partners from our own backgrounds? One reason is **propinquity**; that is, relationships are made in the neighborhood and not in heaven. Although mobility has increased in Western societies in recent decades, we tend to live among people who are reasonably similar to us in background and thus come into contact with them. Another is that we are drawn to people who are similar in their attitudes. People similar in background are more likely to be similar in their attitudes. Similarity in attitudes and tastes is a key contributor to attraction, friendships, and love relationships (Brown et al., 2003; Morry & Gaines, 2005).

Let us also note a gender difference. Evidence shows that women place greater emphasis on attitude similarity as a determinant of attraction to a stranger of the other gender than do men, whereas men place more value on physical attractiveness (Furnham, 2009). We also tend to assume that people we find attractive share our attitudes (Montoya et al., 2008). A powerful physical attraction can motivate them to pretend that their preferences, tastes, and opinions coincide. When sexual attraction is strong, perhaps we want to think that we can iron out all the kinks in the relationship. Although similarity may be important in determining initial attraction, compatibility appears to be a stronger predictor of maintaining an intimate relationship (Amodio & Showers, 2005).

Real Students, Real Questions

Q *Is it okay to be attracted to your stepbrother (or stepsister)?*
A It is not unusual to be attracted to one's stepbrother or stepsister. Stepbrothers and stepsisters are not blood relations, and many excellent partnerships have developed between them. However, if they are raised together, a change from a fraternal to a romantic relationship may raise conflicting feelings or issues that you will need to sort through.

5 › T / F   Truth or Fiction Revisited   It is usually not true that "opposites attract." We are talking about similarity in attitudes, level of education, and preferences in taste, as well as physical features. We are less likely to be attracted to people who disagree with our views and tastes than to people who share them.

RECIPROCITY: IF YOU LIKE ME, YOU MUST HAVE EXCELLENT JUDGMENT   Has anyone told you that you are good looking, brilliant, and emotionally mature to boot? That your taste is elegant? Ah, what superb judgment!

SEX IN THE DIGITAL AGE

FOR NICE JEWISH BOYS, SWIPE RIGHT[1]

Not long ago, Jordan Rodman, a 23-year-old publicity assistant, was paying her respects at a *shiva* on the Upper West Side when her online dating life became a topic of conversation.

"Someone came up to me and was like, 'Oh, Jordan, I know this guy and he saw you on JSwipe and I think you *x*-ed him but he thought you were really beautiful,'" she said. Ms. Rodman shrugged. She had plenty of other takers on her favorite new app, JSwipe, which blends the Jewish exclusivity of JDate with the romance-by-swiping proficiency of Tinder. The app is a faddish take on the age-old desire to marry within the tribe. Instead of attributes like favorite movies, users indicate their degree of Jewishness (among them: Just Jewish, Orthodox and Willing to Convert).

Swipe right and a Star of David with a happy face appears; swipe left and it wears a frown. When a couple match, animated figures appear doing the hora.

The similarities to Tinder are not by coincidence. "As soon as I touched Tinder, I was like, 'Oh my God, this is the next step that needs to exist in the Jewish community,'" said David Yarus, a 28-year-old entrepreneur who said he made the app "kind of as a joke." But he is taking it seriously now.

"I've unlocked this alignment of truth in my life where my passion and my profession and my expertise is all the same thing right now," he said. Mr. Yarus describes typical JSwipe users as "millennial Jews around the world whose grandparents and mothers are saying, 'When are you going to marry someone Jewish?'"

He counts himself among the target audience. Though Mr. Yarus grew up in an observant Jewish household in Miami Beach and attends a synagogue in the tradition of the Carlebach spiritual movement in Crown Heights, Brooklyn, he calls himself "post-affiliation." ("I don't do labels," he says.)

The app, Mr. Yarus said, currently has 250,000 users in 70 countries, with the bulk of users in New York, Los Angeles, and Tel Aviv. He hopes to reach a half million by Passover next year. (Tinder, by comparison, reportedly has about 50 million users.)

"We're like, young punks working out of a factory that are trying to make love free for the Jewish community," Mr. Yarus said.

Much of the growth has been through word of mouth.

"I'm going to Florida in like two weeks to visit my *bubbe*" — Yiddish for grandmother — "in Boca, and obviously she's going to love it," said Ms. Rodman, who uses the app a few times a week. "It'll be a really good bonding activity."

She is also curious to see what kind of men will appear, as the app makes suggestions based on location. For example, on the Upper West Side, where she lives, "You'll get the Shulis, the Yonis, all the guys dressed in their I.D.F. uniforms," she said, referring to the Israel Defense Forces. "As you head more downtown, you get the Alexes, the Joshes, and the Bens, and they have all their Birthright pictures in the desert."

One guy she won't meet is Michael Brand, a 39-year-old risk vice president at J.P. Morgan, who visited Boca Raton, Florida, last summer and downloaded JSwipe there for the first time. "To be perfectly frank, I really didn't take the app too seriously," he said. But soon, he matched with Samantha Rudnick, 26, a marketing strategist in Florida, though they didn't talk until her 3-year-old niece commandeered her phone and sent him a string of garbled messages.

"I think he texted back asking if I was all right," Ms. Rudnick said.

The toddler's opening line worked. Mr. Brand proposed in January at Disney World, in front of Cinderella's Castle. The couple will wed this month. "It was love at first swipe," he said.

In Jewish tradition, the number 18 has special meaning. It is associated with the letters in the Hebrew word *Chai*, which means "life" in English.

reciprocity

Mutual exchange.

When we feel admired and complimented, we tend to return these feelings and behaviors. This is called **reciprocity**. Reciprocity is a potent determinant of attraction (Levine, 2000; Sprecher, 1998). We tend to be much more warm, helpful, and candid when we are with strangers who we believe like us (Sprecher, 1998). We even tend to welcome positive comments from others when we know them to be inaccurate (Levine, 2000).

Perhaps the power of reciprocity has enabled many couples to become happy with one another and reasonably well adjusted. By reciprocating positive words and actions, a person can perhaps stoke neutral or mild feelings into robust, affirmative feelings of attraction.

Attraction can lead to feelings of love. Let us now turn to that most fascinating topic.

Love: "The Morning and the Evening Star"?

LO 6.4 Discuss the meaning of love.

For thousands of years, poets have sought to capture love in words. A seventeenth-century poet wrote that his love was like "a red, red rose." The novelist Sinclair Lewis wrote of love as "the morning and the evening star." Love is beautiful and elusive. It shines, brilliant and heavenly. Passion and romantic love are also earthy and sexy, brimming with sexual desire.

Our culture idealizes the concept of romantic love. Thus, we readily identify with the plight of the "star-crossed" lovers in *Romeo and Juliet* and *West Side Story*, who sacrificed their lives for love. We learn that "love makes the world go round" and that "love is everything." Like other aspects of sexual and social behavior among humans, the concept of love must be understood within a cultural context.

We can trace the concept of love at least as far back as the classical age of Greece. The Greeks distinguished four concepts related to the modern meanings of love:

storge

Loving attachment and nonsexual affection; the type of emotion that binds parents to children.

agape

Selfless love; a kind of loving that is similar to generosity and charity.

philia

Friendship love, which is based on liking and respect rather than sexual desire.

eros

The kind of love that is closest in meaning to the modern-day concept of passion.

- Storge: loving attachment, deep friendship, or nonsexual affection
- Agape: selfless giving
- Philia: friendship
- Eros: passion

Storge is the emotion that binds friends and parents and children. Some scholars believe that even romantic love is a form of attachment that is similar to the type of attachments infants have to their mothers (Hazan & Selcuk, 2015).

Agape is similar to compassion (Fehr et al., 2014). It implies the wish to share one's bounty and is epitomized by anonymous donations of money. Agape, according to F. R. Lee's (2006) research, is the kind of love least frequently found between adults in committed relationships.

Philia is based on liking and respect, rather than sexual desire. It involves the desire to do and enjoy things with the other person and to see him or her when one is lonely or bored.

Eros was a character in Greek mythology (transformed by the Romans into Cupid) who would shoot the unsuspecting with love arrows, causing them to fall madly in love with whomever was nearby at the time. Erotic love embraces sudden passionate desire: "love at first sight" and "falling head over heels in love." Younger college students are more likely to believe in love at first

Storge. Friends share the type of "love" referred to as storge, meaning a nonsexual affection.

sight and that "love conquers all" than older (and wiser?) college students (Knox et al., 1999). Passion can be so gripping that one is convinced that life has been changed forever (Aron et al., 2008). This feeling of sudden transformation was captured by the Italian poet Dante Alighieri (1265–1321), who exclaimed upon first beholding his beloved Beatrice, "*Incipit vita nuova*," which can be translated as "My life begins anew." Unlike the ancient Greeks, we tend to use the word "love" to describe everything from feelings of affection toward another to romantic ardor to sexual intercourse ("making love"). Still, different types or styles of love are recognized in our own culture, as we will see.

Romantic Love

LO 6.5   Discuss the meaning of romantic love.

The experience of romantic love, as opposed to loving attachment or sexual arousal per se, occurs within a cultural context in which the concept is idealized (Aron et al., 2008). Western culture has a long tradition of idealizing the concept of romantic love, as represented, for instance, by romantic fairy tales that have been passed down through the generations. In fact, our exposure to the concept of romantic love may begin with hearing the fairy tales of Sleeping Beauty, Cinderella, and Snow White—along with their princes charming. Later, perhaps, the concept of romantic love blossoms with exposure to romantic novels, television and film scripts, and the heady tales of friends and relatives.

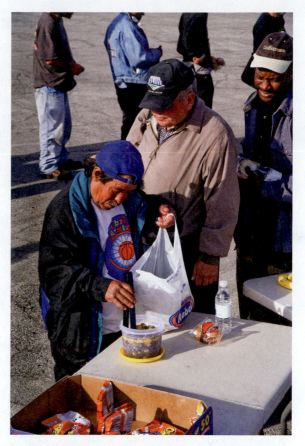

Agape. The type of love called agape is epitomized by charitable donations, especially anonymous donations.

During adolescence, strong sexual arousal along with an idealized image of the object of our desires leads us to label our feelings as love. We may learn to speak of "love" rather than "lust," because sexual desire in the absence of a committed relationship might be viewed as primitive or animalistic. Being "in love" ennobles attraction and sexual arousal, not only to society but also to oneself. Unlike lust, love can be discussed even at the dinner table. If others think we are too young to experience "the real thing"—which presumably includes knowledge of and respect for the other person's personality traits—our feelings may be called "puppy love" or a "crush."

Western society maintains much of the double standard toward sexuality. Thus, women are more often expected to justify sexual experiences as involving someone they love. Young men usually need not attribute sexual urges to love. So men are more apt to deem love a "mushy" concept. The vast majority of people in the United States nonetheless believe romantic love is a prerequisite for marriage or another kind of long-term or permanent relationship. Romantic love is rated by young people as the single-most important reason for marriage (Hatfield et al., 2012; Reis & Aron, 2008). You can explore your self-perceptions of being a romantic or a realist when it comes to love by completing the Triangular Love Scale later in this chapter.

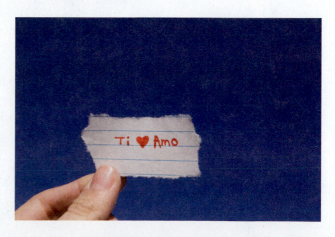

When reciprocated, romantic love is usually a source of deep fulfillment and ecstasy (Hatfield et al., 2012). How wonderful when love meets its match! When love is unrequited, however, it can lead to emptiness, anxiety, or despair. Romantic love can thus teeter between states of ecstasy and misery. Perhaps no other feature of our lives can lift us up as high or plunge us as low as romantic love.

Infatuation versus "True Love": Will Time Tell?

Perhaps you first noticed each other when your eyes met across a classroom. Or perhaps you met when you were both assigned to the same Bunsen burner in chemistry lab—less romantic but closer to the flame. However it happened, the meeting triggered such an electric charge through your body that you could not get him (or her) out of your mind. But were you truly in love, or was it merely a passing fancy? Was it infatuation or the "real thing"—a "true," lasting, and mutual love? How do you tell them apart?

infatuation

A state of intense absorption in or focus on another person, which is usually accompanied by sexual desire, elation, and general physiological arousal or excitement; passion.

Perhaps you don't, at least not at first. **Infatuation** is a state of intense absorption in or focusing on another person (Aloni & Bernieri, 2004). It is usually accompanied by sexual desire, elation, and general physiological arousal or excitement. Some refer to passion as infatuation. Others dub it a "crush." Both monikers suggest that it is a passing fancy. In infatuation, your heart may pound whenever the other person draws near or enters your fantasies.

For the first month or two, infatuation and the more enduring forms of romantic love are hard to differentiate. At first, both may be characterized by intense focusing or absorption. Infatuated people may become so absorbed that they cannot sleep, work, or carry out routine chores. Logic and reason are swept aside (Aron et al., 2008; Hatfield et al., 2012). Infatuated people hold idealized images of their love objects and overlook the faults of their loved one. Caution may be cast to the winds. In some cases, couples in the throes of infatuation rush to the altar, only to find a few weeks or months later that they are not well suited.

As time goes on, signs that distinguish infatuation from a lasting romantic love begin to emerge. The partners begin to view each other more realistically and determine whether or not the relationship should continue. Although the tendency to idealize one's lover is strongest at the outset of a relationship, we should note that a so-called positive illusion tends to persist in relationships (Aron et al., 2008). That is, people maintain some tendency to differentiate their partners from the average and also to differentiate the value of their relationships from the average.

Infatuation is based on feelings of passion but not on the deeper feelings of attachment and caring that typify a more lasting mutual love (Hatfield et al., 2012). Although infatuation may be a passing fancy, it can be supplanted by the deeper feelings of attachment and caring that characterize enduring love relationships.

Contemporary Models of Love: Dare Science Intrude?

LO 6.6 Discuss theories of love.

Despite the importance of love, scientists have historically paid little attention to it (Reis et al., 2013). Some people believe that love cannot be analyzed scientifically. Love, they maintain, should be left to the poets, philosophers, and theologians. Others think that love is sort of a silly topic for the purview of science.

Yet, researchers today are applying the scientific method to the study of love. They recognize that love is a complex concept, involving many areas of experience—biological, emotional, cognitive, and motivational (Berscheid, 2010; Hatfield et al., 2012). Let us begin with some biological comments and then move on to some psychological approaches.

Biological Mechanisms

Some investigators focus on the bodily changes that occur when we experience feelings of romantic love. There are many. Some of the research focuses on the search for distinct neural pathways (roadmaps in the brain) that define feelings of love (Ackerman, 2012). Others involve chemistry, with special focus on

- monoamines and neuropeptides—including dopamine and naturally produced opium look-alikes we call *endorphins*—that are involved in the brain's pleasure system.

- the hormones oxytocin and vasopressin, which we come across repeatedly in this book.

There are always interesting new studies arriving on our desks. For example, we tend to have heightened levels of nerve growth factor (Ackerman, 2012), which partly explains—at least on a biological level—why new lovers are so acutely aware of everything going on around them and why everything seems so bathed in a luxurious light. (How's that for a sad attempt at poetry in a textbook?)

fMRI research (research using functional magnetic resonance imaging) shows heightened activity in a part of the brain called the *caudate nucleus* (see Figure 6.2). What is perhaps of interest here is that the caudate nucleus is part of the brain's "limbic system," which is intimately connected with emotional arousal.

Let us now consider several psychologically oriented views of love. They may touch indirectly on things that happen in the body, but as we will see, they do so almost apologetically.

Figure 6.2 The Caudate Nucleus.

A part of the brain that is particularly active when we are in the throes of a new romantic love.

The Basal Nuclei

Lateral ventricle

Caudate nucleus

Putamen

Globus pallidus

Third ventricle   Thalamus

Love as Appraisal of Arousal

Social psychologists Ellen Berscheid and Elaine Hatfield (Berscheid, 2010; Hatfield et al., 2011) defined romantic love in terms of a state of intense physiological arousal, and the cognitive appraisal of that arousal as love. The physiological arousal may be experienced as a pounding heart, sweaty palms, and butterflies in the stomach when one is in the presence of or thinking about one's love interest (Diamond, 2014). Cognitive appraisal of the arousal means attributing it to some cause, such as fear or love. The perception that one has fallen in love is thus derived from several simultaneous events: (1) a state of intense physiological arousal that is connected with an appropriate love object (that is, a person, not an event like a rock concert), (2) a cultural setting that idealizes romantic love, and (3) the attribution of the arousal to feelings of love toward the person.

Styles of Love

Some researchers speak in terms of styles of love. Susan and Clyde Hendrick and their colleagues speak of love as a positive emotion that contributes to happiness, feelings of psychological well-being, and optimism about the future (Hatfield et al., 2012). The Hendricks developed a Love Attitude Scale that suggests the existence of six styles of love. The following is a list of the styles. Each one is exemplified by statements similar to those on the original scale. As you can see, the styles owe a debt to the Greeks:

Critical Thinking
The student of psychology or sociology might wonder what all of this biological research *means*. Does it mean, for example, that students of human sexuality must memorize every corner of the brain and every neurological activity? Or does it call, rather, for a more general appreciation that thoughts and emotions are based in the body—and particularly in the brain—and that these scientific facts are not to be ignored when we discuss the nature of human beings? How can you best make use of this information?

- *Romantic love (eros):* "My lover fits my ideal." "My lover and I were attracted to one another immediately."

- *Game-playing love (ludus):* "I keep my lover up in the air about my commitment." "I get over love affairs pretty easily."

- *Friendship (storge, philia):* "The best love grows out of an enduring friendship."

- *Logical love (pragma):* "I consider a lover's potential in life before committing myself." "I consider whether my lover will be a good parent."

- *Possessive, excited love (mania):* "I get so excited about my love that I cannot sleep." "When my lover ignores me, I get sick inside."

- *Selfless love (agape):* "I would do anything I can to help my lover." "My lover's needs and wishes are more important than my own."

Most people who are "in love" experience a number of these styles, but the Hendricks found some interesting gender differences in styles of love. College men are significantly more likely than college women to develop game-playing and romantic love styles. College women are more apt than college men to develop friendly, logical, and possessive love styles. (There were no gender differences in selfless love.) The Hendricks have also found that romantically involved couples tend to experience the same kinds of love styles. They also found evidence that couples with romantic and selfless styles of love are more likely to remain together. A game-playing love style leads to unhappiness, however, and is one reason that relationships come to an end.

Sternberg's Triangular Theory of Love

LO 6.7 **Explain how people's preferences for partners differ for short- and long-term relationships.**

Robert Sternberg (1988) offers a "triangular theory" of love that organizes the relationships among kinds of love discussed by many theorists, including passionate love, romantic love, and companionate love (Hatfield et al., 2012). The three building blocks, or components, of loving experiences are as follows:

1. **Intimacy:** The experience of warmth toward another person that arises from feelings of closeness and connectedness to the other. Intimacy also involves the desire to give and receive emotional support and to share one's innermost thoughts with the other.

2. **Passion:** An intense romantic or sexual desire for another person, which is accompanied by physiological arousal.

3. **Commitment:** A component of love that involves commitment to maintain the relationship through good times and bad.

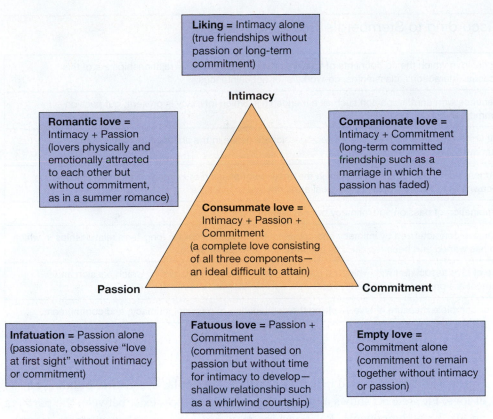

Liking = Intimacy alone (true friendships without passion or long-term commitment)

Romantic love = Intimacy + Passion (lovers physically and emotionally attracted to each other but without commitment, as in a summer romance)

Companionate love = Intimacy + Commitment (long-term committed friendship such as a marriage in which the passion has faded)

Consummate love = Intimacy + Passion + Commitment (a complete love consisting of all three components— an ideal difficult to attain)

Infatuation = Passion alone (passionate, obsessive "love at first sight" without intimacy or commitment)

Fatuous love = Passion + Commitment (commitment based on passion but without time for intimacy to develop— shallow relationship such as a whirlwind courtship)

Empty love = Commitment alone (commitment to remain together without intimacy or passion)

Figure 6.3 The Triangular Model of Love.

According to psychologist Robert Sternberg, love consists of three components, as shown by the vertices of this triangle. Various kinds of love consist of different combinations of these components. Romantic love, for example, consists of passion and intimacy. Consummate love—the cultural ideal—consists of all three.

SOURCE: Sternberg, 1988. The triangle of love: Intimacy, passion, commitment. By permission of Robert Sternberg.

Sternberg's model is triangular in that various kinds of love can be conceptualized in terms of a triangle in which each vertex (corner?) represents one of the building blocks (see Figure 6.3). The strength of each component can be represented by the shape of the triangle. For example, a love in which all three components were equally balanced—as in consummate love—would be represented by an equilateral triangle, as in Figure 6.4.

The Hendricks noted that couples who are romantically involved tend to share similar love styles. In terms of Sternberg's model, couples are well matched if they possess corresponding levels of passion, intimacy, and commitment. Compatibility can be represented visually in terms of the congruence (fit) of the love triangles (see Figure 6.5). Figure 6.5A shows a perfect match, in which the triangles are congruent.

Figure 6.4 Compatibility and Incompatibility, According to the Triangular Model of Love.

Compatibility in terms of Sternberg's types of love can be represented as triangles. View A shows a perfect match in which triangles are congruent. View B depicts a good match; the partners are similar according to the three dimensions. View C shows a mismatch; major differences exist between the partners on all three components.

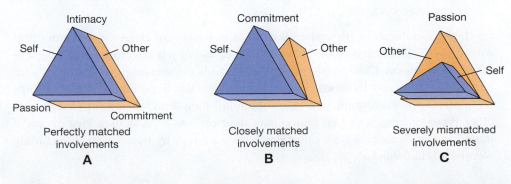

Perfectly matched involvements
A

Closely matched involvements
B

Severely mismatched involvements
C

Figure 6.5 Types of Love, According to Sternberg's Triangular Model.

1. Nonlove	A relationship in which the components of love are absent. Most personal relationships are of this type—casual interactions, classmates, co-workers, or acquaintances.
2. Liking	An experience with another person such as a friendship in which intimacy is present, but passion and commitment are lacking.
3. Infatuation	"Love at first sight," in which one experiences passionate desire in the absence of intimacy and commitment.
4. Empty love	Commitment (to maintain the relationship) in the absence of passion or intimacy. Stagnant relationships with decaying emotional intimacy or physical attraction are of this type.
5. Romantic love	The combination of passion and intimacy but not commitment.
6. Companionate love	A kind of love characterized by intimacy and commitment. It often occurs in long-term relationships in which passion has waned and been replaced by a kind of committed friendship.
7. Fatuous love	The type of love associated with whirlwind romances and "quickie marriages" in which passion and commitment are present, but intimacy is not.
8. Consummate love	The full or complete measure of love involving the combination of passion, intimacy, and commitment.

SOURCE: Adapted from Sternberg (1988).

Figure 6.5B depicts a good match; the partners are similar in the three building blocks of love. Figure 6.5C shows a mismatch; major differences exist between the partners on all three components. Relationships may run aground when partners are mismatched. A relationship may fizzle, rather than sizzle, when one partner experiences more passion than the other, or when one wants a long-term commitment when the other's idea of commitment is to stay the night.

Various combinations of the three elements of love characterize different types of love relationships (see Figures 6.3 and 6.5). For example, infatuation (passionate love) is typified by strong sexual desire but not by intimacy and commitment. The partners may each feel passionate love for the other, or, as in the case of Tom, such feelings may go unrequited:

> Tom sat behind Lisa in physics class. Tom hated physics, but he could not say the same for Lisa. One look at her was enough to change his life. He had fallen madly in love with her. Instead of listening to the teacher or looking at the blackboard, he would gaze at Lisa throughout the class. Lisa was aware of this and was not happy about it. She did not much care for Tom, and when he tried to start a conversation with her, she moved on as quickly as possible. Tom's staring and his awkwardness in talking to her made her feel uncomfortable. Tom, on the other hand, could think of little else besides Lisa, and his grades began to suffer as he spent the time he should have been devoting to his homework thinking about her. He was a man obsessed. The obsession might have gone on for quite some time had not both Tom and Lisa graduated that June and gone to different colleges. Tom never saw Lisa again, and after several unanswered love letters, he finally gave up on her. (Sternberg, 1988, p. 123)

Liking is a basis for friendship. It consists of feelings of closeness and emotional warmth without passion or commitment. Liking is not felt toward passing acquaintances. It is reserved for people to whom one feels close enough to share one's innermost feelings and thoughts. We sometimes develop these intimate relationships without making the commitment to maintaining a long-term relationship that typifies other types of love, however. Liking may develop into a passionate love or into a more committed form of love called companionate love by many writers, including Sternberg (Hatfield et al., 2012).

6 › T / F Truth or Fiction Revisited   It is possible to be in love with someone who is not also a friend. Being in love can refer to states of passion or infatuation, whereas friendship is usually based on shared interests, liking, and respect. Friendship and passionate love do not necessarily overlap. There is nothing that prevents people in love from becoming good friends, however—perhaps even the best of friends. Sternberg's model recognizes that the intimacy we find in true friendships and the passion we find in love are blended in two forms of love—romantic love and consummate love. These love types differ along the dimension of commitment, however.

Romantic love has both passion and intimacy but lacks commitment. Romantic love may burn brightly and then flicker out. Or it may develop into a more complete love (consummate love) in which all three components flower. Desire is accompanied by a deeper intimacy and commitment. The flames of passion can be stoked across the years, even if they do not burn quite as brightly as they once did. Consummate love is most special and certainly an ideal toward which many Westerners strive.

In empty love, by contrast, there is little else than commitment. Neither the warm emotional embrace of intimacy nor the flame of passion exists. With empty love, one's lover is a person whom one tolerates and remains with because of a sense of duty. Remaining in an empty-love relationship is often based either on the belief that one should persist in a relationship or that one's community or family members believe that it is right to persist in a relationship.

Sometimes a love relationship has both passion and commitment but lacks intimacy. Sternberg calls this *fatuous (foolish) love*. Fatuous love is associated with whirlwind courtships that burn brightly but briefly as the partners come to the realization that they are not well matched. Intimacy can develop in such relationships, but couples who rush into promises of marriage often find that the realities of their relationships give the lie to their expectations.

7 › T / F   Truth or Fiction Revisited   It is true that couples can remain "in love" after passion fades; for example, they can experience companionate love. Companionate love need not be lacking in romance, however. Although passion may have ebbed, sexual pleasure can help strengthen bonds.

In companionate love, intimacy and commitment are strong, but passion is lacking. This form of love typifies long-term (so-called *platonic*) relationships and marriages in which passion has ebbed but a deep and abiding friendship remains for those with whom our lives are entwined (Hatfield et al., 2012; Hendrick & Hendrick, 2003).

The balance among Sternberg's three aspects of love is likely to shift through the course of a relationship (Hatfield et al., 2012). A strong dose of all three components—found in consummate love—typifies, for many of us, an ideal relationship. At the outset of a relationship, passions may be strong but intimacy weak. Couples may only first be getting to know each other's innermost thoughts and feelings. Time alone does not cause intimacy and commitment to grow, however. Some couples are able to peer into each other's deeper selves and form meaningful commitments at relatively early stages in their relationships. Yet some couples who have been together for many years may remain distant or waver in their commitment. Some couples experience only a faint flickering of passion early in the relationship. Then it becomes quickly extinguished. For some, the flames of passion burn ever brightly. Many couples, though, find that passion tends to fade while intimacy and commitment grow stronger.

Knowledge of the components of love can help couples avoid pitfalls. Couples who recognize that passion exerts a strong pull early in a relationship may be

Critical Thinking
Why do you think that most people in the United States believe that people should get married only when they experience romantic love?

Sternberg's Triangular Love Scale

Which are the strongest components of your love relationship? Intimacy? Passion? Commitment? All three components? Two of them?

To complete the following scale, fill in the blank spaces with the name of one person you love or care about deeply. Then rate your agreement with each of the items by using a 9-point scale in which 1 = "not at all," 5 = "moderately," and 9 = "extremely." Use points in between to indicate intermediate levels of agreement between these values. Then consult the scoring key in the Appendix.

Intimacy Component

____ 1. I am actively supportive of _____'s well-being.

____ 2. I have a warm relationship with _____.

____ 3. I am able to count on _____ in times of need.

____ 4. _____ is able to count on me in times of need.

____ 5. I am willing to share myself and my possessions with _____.

____ 6. I receive considerable emotional support from _____.

____ 7. I give considerable emotional support to _____.

____ 8. I communicate well with _____.

____ 9. I value _____ greatly in my life.

____ 10. I feel close to _____.

____ 11. I have a comfortable relationship with _____.

____ 12. I feel that I really understand _____.

____ 13. I feel that _____ really understands me.

____ 14. I feel that I can really trust _____.

____ 15. I share deeply personal information about myself with _____.

Passion Component

____ 16. Just seeing _____ excites me.

____ 17. I find myself thinking about _____ frequently during the day.

____ 18. My relationship with _____ is very romantic.

____ 19. I find _____ to be very personally attractive.

____ 20. I idealize _____.

____ 21. I cannot imagine another person making me as happy as _____ does.

____ 22. I would rather be with _____ than anyone else.

____ 23. There is nothing more important to me than my relationship with _____.

____ 24. I especially like physical contact with _____.

____ 25. There is something almost "magical" about my relationship with _____.

____ 26. I adore _____.

____ 27. I cannot imagine life without _____.

____ 28. My relationship with _____ is passionate.

____ 29. When I see romantic movies and read romantic books, I think of _____.

____ 30. I fantasize about _____.

Commitment Component

____ 31. I know that I care about _____.

____ 32. I am committed to maintaining my relationship with _____.

____ 33. Because of my commitment to _____, I would not let other people come between us.

____ 34. I have confidence in the stability of my relationship with _____.

____ 35. I could not let anything get in the way of my commitment to _____.

____ 36. I expect my love for _____ to last for the rest of my life.

____ 37. I will always feel a strong responsibility for _____.

____ 38. I view my commitment to _____ as a solid one.

____ 39. I cannot imagine ending my relationship with _____.

____ 40. I am certain of my love for _____.

____ 41. I view my relationship with _____ as permanent.

____ 42. I view my relationship with _____ as a good decision.

____ 43. I feel a sense of responsibility toward _____.

____ 44. I plan to continue my relationship with _____.

____ 45. Even when _____ is hard to deal with, I remain committed to our relationship.

SOURCE: Sternberg, 1988. The triangle of love: Intimacy, passion, commitment. By permission of Robert Sternberg.

less likely to let passion rush them into a premature long-term legal commitment. Couples who recognize that it is normal for passion to fade may avoid assuming that their love is at an end when it may, in fact, be changing into a deeper, more intimate and committed form of love. This knowledge may also encourage couples to focus on finding ways of rekindling the embers of romance, rather than looking to escape at the first signs that the fires may be cooling.

Real Students, Real Questions

Q *What is the secret to a loving relationship?*

A There are a few secrets: First is honesty—that is, being honest about your likes and dislikes, your feelings, and your values. Another is sharing interests and values with your partner. You can't expect a relationship to endure if you're only pretending to agree with your partner about your likes and dislikes. A third is respect. You probably cannot truly love your partner if you do not respect him or her as a person.

Chapter Review

LO 6.1 Describe cultural standards for physical attractiveness.

Physical appearance is a key determinant of sexual attraction. In our culture, slenderness is in style. Men prefer medium to large breasts. Women prefer taller men.

LO 6.2 Describe nonphysical traits that affect perceptions of physical attractiveness.

Females and males both consider smiling faces more attractive. Socially dominant men, but not women, are usually found attractive. Women place relatively greater emphasis on traits like vocational status and earning potential, whereas men give relatively more consideration to physical attractiveness. Some evolutionary psychologists believe that evolutionary forces favor such gender differences in preferred traits because these traits provide reproductive advantages.

LO 6.3 Explain the role of similarity in the formation of romantic relationships.

Despite the adage "opposites attract," research tends to support the attraction–similarity hypothesis, which holds that people tend to develop romantic relationships with people who are similar to themselves in attractiveness, cultural background, and interests. Our feelings are warmer toward people who appear to like us. Through reciprocation of positive words and actions, neutral or mild feelings may be stoked into strong feelings of attraction.

LO 6.4 Discuss the meaning of love.

The ancient Greeks had four concepts related to the modern meanings of love: storge (loving attachment, as between parents and children), agape (generosity and charity), philia (friendship, liking, respect), and eros (passion).

LO 6.5 Discuss the meaning of romantic love.

Western culture has a tradition of idealizing the concept of romantic love. Most people in the United States see romantic love as a prerequisite to marriage. At first, infatuation and more enduring forms of romantic love may be indistinguishable.

LO 6.6 Discuss theories of love.

Berscheid and Hatfield define romantic love in terms of intense physiological arousal and cognitive appraisal of that arousal as love. Cultural belief in romantic love contributes to that labeling of arousal. Hendrick and Hendrick suggest that there are six styles of love among college students: romantic love, game-playing love, friendship, logical love, possessive love, and selfless love. Sternberg suggests that there are three distinct components of love: intimacy, passion, and commitment. Romantic love is characterized by the combination of passion and intimacy. Consummate love—the cultural ideal—is described by all three components.

LO 6.7 Explain how people's preferences differ for short-term and long-term relationships.

People may pay more attention to superficial characteristics such as physical attractiveness when they are selecting partners for short-term relationships.

Test Your Learning

1. _____ is found to be universally attractive in women.
   - **(a)** A good complexion
   - **(b)** Slenderness
   - **(c)** Plumpness
   - **(d)** Socially dominant behavior

2. According to evolutionary theory, women would be most attracted to someone who is _____
   - **(a)** younger than they are.
   - **(b)** not good looking.
   - **(c)** less well educated than they are.
   - **(d)** likely to hold a steady job.

3. Loving attachment, deep friendship, or nonsexual affection describe the ancient Greek concept of _____
   - **(a)** agape.
   - **(b)** storge.
   - **(c)** eros.
   - **(d)** philia.

4. People who say "I keep my lover up in the air about my commitment," or "I get over love affairs pretty easily" appear to be in the _____ style of love.
   - **(a)** logical
   - **(b)** romantic
   - **(c)** game-playing
   - **(d)** possessive

5. According to Sternberg, romantic love involves _____
   - **(a)** passion and intimacy.
   - **(b)** passion and commitment.
   - **(c)** intimacy and commitment.
   - **(d)** passion alone.

6. It would appear that the single most important element in attraction is _____
   - **(a)** the way someone smells,
   - **(b)** physical attractiveness,
   - **(c)** relationship value,
   - **(d)** slenderness.

7. People are generally viewed as being more attractive when they are presented against a background color of _____
   - **(a)** blue.
   - **(b)** green.
   - **(c)** white.
   - **(d)** red.

8. Helen Fisher and her colleagues found that the _____ is highly active when we experience a new romantic love.
   - **(a)** reticular activating system
   - **(b)** prefrontal cortex
   - **(c)** metatarsal-phalangeal joint
   - **(d)** caudate nucleus

9. In animals, the the *vomeronasal organ* detects _____
   - **(a)** intelligence.
   - **(b)** hormones.
   - **(c)** pheromones.
   - **(d)** color.

10. The Hendricks found that college men were significantly more likely than college women to develop a _____ love style.
   - **(a)** friendly
   - **(b)** logical
   - **(c)** romantic
   - **(d)** possessive

Answers: 1. a; 2. d; 3. d; 4. c; 5. a; 6. b; 7. d; 8. d; 9. d; 10. c

Chapter 7
Sexual Response and Sexual Behavior

⌄ Learning Objectives

Sexual Response

LO 7.1 Describe the sexual response cycle, according to Masters and Johnson.

LO 7.2 Discuss other views of sexual response.

LO 7.3 Discuss controversies about orgasm.

LO 7.4 Discuss the effects of drugs on sexual response.

LO 7.5 Describe the role of the brain in sexual response.

LO 7.6 Discuss the organizing and activating influences of sex hormones.

Sex without a Partner

LO 7.7 Discuss attitudes toward masturbation.

LO 7.8 Describe ways in which people masturbate.

Sex with a Partner

LO 7.9 Discuss purposes and methods of precoital partnered sex.

Sexual Intercourse: Positions and Techniques

LO 7.10 Describe methods of sexual intercourse.

Sexual Fantasies

LO 7.11 Discuss kinds and uses of sexual fantasies.

TRUTH OR FICTION?

Which of the following statements are the truth, and which are fiction? Look for the Truth-or-Fiction items throughout this chapter to find the answers.

1 Orgasms attained through sexual intercourse are more intense than those attained through masturbation.   **T / F**?

2 "Spanish fly" will not turn your date on, but it may cure his or her warts.   **T / F**?

3 Alcohol enhances sexual response.   **T / F**?

4 Electrical stimulation of certain areas in the human brain can yield sensations similar to those of sexual pleasure and gratification.   **T / F**?

5 Married people rarely if ever masturbate.   **T / F**?

6 Statistically speaking, oral sex is the norm for today's young couples.   **T / F**?

7 Sexual fantasies are abnormal.   **T / F**?

8 When lovers fantasize about other people, the relationship is in trouble.   **T / F**?

What turns you on? What springs your heart into your mouth, tightens your throat, and opens the floodgates into your genitals? The sight of your lover undressing, a photo of a celebrity, a sniff of musky perfume, a sip of wine?

Many factors contribute to sexual arousal. Some people are aroused by magazines with photographs of nude or seminude models that have been airbrushed to perfection. Some need only to imagine Hollywood's latest sex symbol. Some become aroused by remembrances of past lovers. Some are stimulated by sexual fantasies of flings with strangers.

People vary greatly in the cues that excite them sexually and in the frequency with which they experience sexual thoughts and feelings. Some young people seem perpetually aroused or arousable. Some people rarely or never entertain sexual thoughts or fantasies.

In this chapter we look at factors that contribute to sexual arousal and the processes that relate to sexual response. Because our experience of the world is initiated by our senses, we begin the chapter by asking: What are the roles of the senses in sexual arousal? In our discussion, we will explore the possible role of pheromones.

Sexual Response

Although we may be culturally attuned to focus on sex differences rather than similarities, Masters and Johnson (1966) found that the physiological responses of men and women to sexual stimulation (whether from coitus, masturbation, or other sources) are quite alike. The sequence of changes in the body that takes place as men and women become progressively more aroused is referred to as the *sexual response cycle*.

The Four-Phase Masters and Johnson Sexual Response Cycle

LO 7.1 **Describe the sexual response cycle, according to Masters and Johnson.**

Masters and Johnson divided the **sexual response cycle** into four phases: excitement, plateau, orgasm, and resolution. Figure 7.1 suggests the levels of sexual arousal associated with each phase. Both males and females experience vasocongestion and myotonia early in the response cycle. **Vasocongestion** is the swelling of the genital tissues with blood, which causes erection of the penis and engorgement of the area

sexual response cycle
Masters and Johnson's model of sexual response, which consists of four phases.

vasocongestion
The swelling of the genital tissues with blood, which causes erection of the penis and engorgement of the area surrounding the vaginal opening.

Figure 7.1   Levels of Sexual Arousal during the Phases of the Sexual Response Cycle.

Masters and Johnson (1966) divide the sexual response cycle into four phases: excitement, plateau, orgasm, and resolution. During the resolution phase, the level of sexual arousal returns to the prearoused state. For men, there is a refractory period after orgasm. As shown by the broken line, however, men can become rearoused to orgasm after the refractory period has passed and their level of sexual arousal returns to preplateau levels. Pattern A for women shows a typical response cycle, with the broken line suggesting multiple orgasms. Pattern B shows the cycle of a woman who reaches the plateau phase, but for whom arousal is "resolved" without reaching the orgasmic phase. Pattern C shows the possibility of orgasm in a highly aroused woman who passes quickly through the plateau phase.

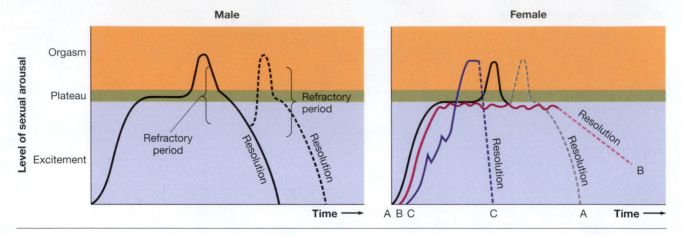

myotonia

Muscle tension.

excitement phase

The first phase of the sexual response cycle, which is characterized by erection in the male, vaginal lubrication in the female, and muscle tension and increases in heart rate in both males and females.

sex flush

A reddish rash that appears on the chest or breasts late in the excitement phase of the sexual response cycle.

plateau phase

The second phase of the sexual response cycle, which is characterized by increases in vasocongestion, muscle tension, heart rate, and blood pressure in preparation for orgasm.

surrounding the vaginal opening. The testes, nipples, and even earlobes become engorged as blood vessels in these areas dilate.

Myotonia refers to muscle tension. Myotonia causes voluntary and involuntary muscle contractions, which produce facial grimaces, spasms in the hands and feet, and eventually, the spasms of orgasm. Let us follow these and the other bodily changes that constitute the sexual response cycle.

EXCITEMENT PHASE   In younger men, vasocongestion during the **excitement phase** produces penile erection as early as 3 to 8 seconds after stimulation begins. Erection may occur more slowly in older men, but the responses are essentially the same. Erection may subside and return as stimulation varies. The scrotal skin thickens, losing its baggy appearance. The testes increase in size. The testes and scrotum become elevated.

In the female, vaginal lubrication may start 10 to 30 seconds after stimulation begins. Vasocongestion swells the clitoris, flattens the labia majora and spreads them apart, and increases the size of the labia minora. The inner two-thirds of the vagina expand. The vaginal walls thicken and, because of the inflow of blood, turn from their normal pink to a deeper hue. The uterus becomes engorged and elevated. The breasts enlarge, and blood vessels near the surface become more prominent.

The skin may take on a rosy **sex flush** late in this phase. It varies with intensity of arousal and is more pronounced in women. The nipples may become erect in both sexes, especially in response to direct stimulation. Men and women show some increase in myotonia, heart rate, and blood pressure.

PLATEAU PHASE   A plateau is a level region, and the level of arousal remains somewhat constant during the plateau phase of sexual response. Nevertheless, the **plateau phase** is an advanced state of arousal that precedes orgasm. Men in this phase show a slight increase in the circumference of the coronal ridge of the penis. The penile glans turns a purplish hue, a sign of vasocongestion. The testes are elevated further into position for ejaculation and may reach one and one-half times their unaroused size. The Cowper's glands secrete a few droplets of fluid that are found at the tip of the penis (see Figure 7.2).

Figure 7.2   The Male Genitals During the Phases of the Sexual Response Cycle.

1. Excitement Phase

Vasocongestion of penis results in erection

Meatus dilates

Testes begin elevation
Scrotal skin tenses, thickens

2. Plateau Phase

The coronal ridge of the glans increases in diameter and turns a deeper reddish purple

The Cowper's glands may release fluid

The testes become completely elevated and engorged when orgasm is imminent

Cowper's gland

3. Orgasmic Phase

Contractions of vas deferens and seminal vesicles expel sperm and semen into urethra
Prostate expels fluid into the urethra

Sperm and semen expelled by rhythmic contractions of urethra

Rectal sphincter contracts

4. Resolution Phase

Erection subsides

Testes descend

Scrotum thins, folds return

In women, vasocongestion swells the tissues of the outer third of the vagina, contracting the vaginal opening (thus preparing it to "grasp" the penis) and building the orgasmic platform (see Figure 7.3). The inner part of the vagina expands fully. The uterus becomes fully elevated. The clitoris withdraws beneath the clitoral hood and shortens. Thus, a woman (or her partner) may feel that the clitoris has become lost. This may be mistaken as a sign that the woman's sexual arousal is waning, although it is actually increasing.

Coloration of the labia minora appears, which is referred to as the **sex skin**. The labia minora become a deep wine color in women who have borne children and bright red in women who have not. Further engorgement of the areolas of the breasts may make it seem that the nipples have lost part of their erection (see Figure 7.4). The Bartholin's glands secrete a fluid that resembles mucus.

sex skin

Reddening of the labia minora that occurs during the plateau phase.

Real Students, Real Questions

Q *Sometimes I don't get lubricated, and intercourse is painful. Why don't I get lubricated?*

A There are many possibilities. Sometimes a woman needs more time or a more comfortable setting. If you suspect a health problem, check with your gynecologist. You can also try an artificial lubricant, like K-Y jelly. But by and large, simply ask yourself two questions: Do you know what turns you on? Are you making sure you get it? Maybe this means getting a new partner!

Figure 7.3   The Female Genitals During the Phases of the Sexual Response Cycle.

1. Excitement Phase

The clitoral glans and the labia swell resulting from vasocongestion

Vagina begins to lubricate

Clitoris

Labia majora

Labia minora

2. Plateau Phase

Clitoris retracts under hood

Bartholin's glands secrete fluid

Labia minora increase in size and turn reddish purple

Uterus elevates and increases in size

Inner two-thirds of vagina expands and lengthens

Outer third of vagina forms orgasmic platform

3. Orgasmic Phase

Uterus contracts

Orgasmic platform contracts

Rectal sphincter contracts

4. Resolution Phase

Clitoris descends to unaroused position

The labia return to their unaroused state

Uterus shrinks, returns to its normal position

Cervix drops to its unaroused position

Vagina returns to its unaroused position

Figure 7.4   The Breasts During the Phases of the Sexual Response Cycle.

1. Excitement Phase

Breast increases in size

Nipple becomes erect

Veins become more visible

2. Plateau and Orgasmic Phases

Vasocongestion of areola makes nipple seem less erect

Breast increases still more in size

Rashlike sex flush may appear

3. Resolution Phase

Reduction of areola causes increased prominence of nipple

Breast size is reduced to normal in 5–10 minutes

Sex flush disappears rapidly

About one man in four and about three women in four show a sex flush, which often does not appear until the plateau phase. Myotonia may cause spasmodic contractions in the hands and feet and facial grimaces. Breathing becomes rapid, like panting, and the heart rate may increase to 100 to 160 beats per minute. Blood pressure continues to rise. The increase in heart rate is usually less dramatic with masturbation than during coitus.

ORGASMIC PHASE

Aching of the vaginal regions and trembling in the thighs. Every muscle in the body tightens and then a huge amount of energy is released. It feels like it comes from between my legs and ascends up my spine, absolutely zapping my brain. Oftentimes I hold my breath, my eyes shut tight, and colors appear behind my eyelids. Immediately afterward I'm very photosensitive, giddily happy, tingly, relieved, and energized.

—A 24-year-old woman, Meston & Buss, 2009 (p. 38)

The **orgasmic phase** in the male consists of two stages of muscular contractions. In the first stage, contractions of the vas deferens, the seminal vesicles, the ejaculatory duct, and the prostate gland cause seminal fluid to collect in the urethral bulb at the base of the penis (see Figure 7.2). The bulb expands to accommodate the fluid. The internal sphincter of the urinary bladder contracts, preventing seminal fluid from entering the bladder in a backward, retrograde ejaculation. The normal closing off of the bladder also serves to prevent urine from mixing with semen. The collection of semen in the urethral bulb produces feelings of ejaculatory inevitability—the sensation that nothing will stop the ejaculate from "coming." This sensation lasts for about 2 to 3 seconds.

In the second stage, the external sphincter of the bladder relaxes, allowing the passage of semen. Contractions of muscles surrounding the urethra and urethral bulb and the base of the penis propel the ejaculate through the urethra and out of the body. Sensations of pleasure tend to be related to the strength of the contractions and the amount of seminal fluid. The first three or four contractions are generally most intense and occur at 0.8-second intervals (five contractions every 4 seconds). Another two to four contractions occur at a somewhat slower pace. Rates and patterns vary somewhat from man to man.

Orgasm in the female is manifested by 3 to 15 contractions of the pelvic muscles that surround the vaginal barrel. The contractions first occur at 0.8-second intervals, producing, as in the male, a release of sexual tension. Another three to six weaker and slower contractions follow. The spacing of these contractions is generally more variable in women than in men. The uterus and the anal sphincter also contract rhythmically. Uterine contractions occur in waves from the top to the cervix. In both sexes, muscles go into spasm throughout the body. Blood pressure and heart rate reach a peak, with the heart beating up to 180 times per minute. Respiration may increase to 40 breaths per minute.

orgasmic phase

The phase of the sexual response cycle that is characterized by a rapid succession of muscular contractions in the genital regions of both males and females, and also by ejaculation by the male.

resolution phase

The fourth phase of the sexual response cycle, during which the body gradually returns to its prearoused state.

RESOLUTION PHASE   The period following orgasm, in which the body returns to its prearoused state, is called the **resolution phase**. Following ejaculation, the man loses his erection in two stages. The first occurs in about a minute. Half the volume of the erection is lost as blood from the corpora cavernosa empties into the other parts of the body. The second stage occurs over a period of several minutes: The remaining tumescence subsides as the corpus spongiosum empties. The testes and scrotum return to normal size, and the scrotum regains its wrinkled appearance.

In women, orgasm also triggers release of blood from engorged areas. In the absence of continued stimulation, swelling of the areolas decreases; then the nipples return to normal size. The sex flush lightens rapidly. In about 5 to 10 seconds the clitoris descends to its normal position. The clitoris, vaginal barrel, uterus, and labia gradually shrink to their prearoused sizes. The labia minora turn lighter (the "sex skin" disappears) in about 10 to 15 seconds.

Most muscle tension (myotonia) tends to dissipate within 5 minutes after orgasm in both men and women. Blood pressure, heart rate, and respiration may also return to their prearousal levels within a few minutes. About 30% to 40% of men and women find their palms, the soles of their feet, or their entire bodies covered with a sheen of perspiration. Both men and women may feel relaxed and satiated. However, …

Although the processes by which the body returns to its prearousal state are similar in men and women, there is an important sex difference during the resolution phase. Unlike women, men enter a **refractory period** during which they are physiologically incapable of experiencing another orgasm or ejaculation. The refractory period of adolescent males may last only minutes, whereas that of men age 50 and older may last from several minutes (yes, it could happen) to a day. Women do not undergo a refractory period and so can become quickly rearoused to the point of repeated (multiple) orgasms if they desire and receive continued sexual stimulation (see Figure 7.1).

refractory period

A period of time following a response (e.g., orgasm) during which an individual is no longer responsive to stimulation (e.g., sexual stimulation).

Myotonia and vasocongestion may take an hour or more to dissipate in people who are aroused but who do not reach orgasm. Persistent pelvic vasocongestion may cause "blue balls" in males—the slang term for a throbbing ache. Some men insist that their dates should consent to coitus because it is unfair to stimulate them to the point where they have this condition. This condition can be relieved through masturbation as well as coitus, however—or allowed to dissipate naturally. Although it may be uncomfortable, it is not dangerous and should not be an excuse to pressure or coerce another person into any sexual activity. "Blue" sensations are not limited to men. Women, too, may experience unpleasant pelvic throbbing if they have become highly aroused and do not find release. Women, too, can relieve the throbbing through masturbation.

> **1 › T /F   Truth or Fiction Revisited**   Masters and Johnson (1966) actually found that orgasms experienced during masturbation were generally more physiologically intense than those experienced during intercourse. Perhaps masturbation allows one to focus only on one's own pleasure and ensure that one receives effective stimulation to climax. This does not mean that orgasms during masturbation are more enjoyable or gratifying than those experienced through partnered sex. Given the sexual arousal we experience from sensing a partner, we are unlikely to break off relationships in favor of masturbation. "Physiological intensity," in sum, does not directly translate into subjective pleasure or fulfillment.

Kaplan's Three Stages of Sexual Response: An Alternative Model

LO 7.2   Discuss other views of sexual response.

Perhaps the only alternative view of the sexual response cycle that has received continued attention is the one proposed by Helen Singer Kaplan. Kaplan was a prominent sex therapist and author of several professional books (1974, 1987) on sex therapy. Whereas Masters and Johnson had proposed a four-stage model of sexual response, Kaplan developed a three-stage model consisting of (1) desire, (2) excitement, and (3) orgasm. Kaplan's model is an outgrowth of her clinical experience in working with people with sexual dysfunctions. She believes that their problems can best be classified according to these three phases. Kaplan's model recognizes sexual dysfunctions involving desire (low or absent desire), excitement (such as problems with erection in the male or lubrication in the female), and orgasm (such as premature ejaculation in the male or orgasmic dysfunction in the female).

Masters and Johnson view sexual response as composed of successive stages; the order is crucial and invariant. Kaplan treats her phases as relatively independent components of sexual response whose sequence is somewhat variable. For example, a person may experience sexual excitement and even orgasm, even though sexual desire remains low.

Kaplan's model is noteworthy for designating desire as a separate phase of sexual response. Problems in lack of sexual interest or desire are among the most common brought to the attention of sex therapists.

Controversies about Orgasm

LO 7.3   Discuss controversies about orgasm.

Few other topics in human sexuality have aroused more controversies over the years than orgasm. We do not have all the answers, but some intriguing research findings have shed light on some lingering controversies. For example, are women capable of having multiple orgasms? Are men?

MULTIPLE ORGASMS   Kinsey and colleagues (1953) reported that 14% of their female respondents regularly had **multiple orgasms**, surprising fellow scientists as well as the community at large. Many people were aghast that women could have more than one orgasm at a time. There were comments (mostly by men, of course!) that the women in the Kinsey surveys must be "nymphomaniacs" who were incapable of being satisfied with the "normal" complement of one orgasm per occasion. However, only 13 years later, Masters and Johnson (1966) reported that most if not all women are capable of multiple orgasms. Although all women may have a biological capability for multiple orgasms, not all women report them. A survey of 720 nurses showed that 43% reported experiencing multiple orgasms (Darling et al., 1991). Nearly half of them

multiple orgasms

One or more additional orgasms following the first, which occur within a short period of time and before the body has returned to a preplateau level of arousal.

experienced multiple orgasms when they used a vibrator. They generally applied the vibrator to the clitoris and reported that orgasms experienced with the vibrator were more intense than other kinds. Two-thirds of the women, by the way, used the vibrators in conjunction with sexual activity with their husbands.

By Masters and Johnson's definition, men are not capable of achieving multiple orgasms because they enter a refractory period following ejaculation. Men who want more than one orgasm during one session may have to pause for a while. Women, however, can maintain a high level of arousal between multiple orgasms and have them in rapid succession because women do not have a refractory period. Women can continue to have orgasms if they continue to receive effective stimulation (and, of course, are interested in continuing). Some men thus refrain from reaching orgasm until their partners have had the desired number. The differential capacity for multiple orgasms is one of the major sex differences in sexual response.

Some men have two or more orgasms without ejaculation ("dry orgasms") preceding a final ejaculatory orgasm. These men may not enter a refractory period following their initial dry orgasms and may therefore be able to maintain their level of stimulation at near-peak levels.

Masters and Johnson (1966) found that some women experienced 20 or more orgasms by masturbating. Still, few women have multiple orgasms during most sexual encounters, and many are satisfied with just one per occasion. Some women who have read or heard about female orgasmic capacity wonder what is "wrong" with them if they are content with just one. Nothing is wrong with them, of course: A biological capacity does not create a behavioral requirement.

DO ORGASMS INCREASE THE LIKELIHOOD OF CONCEPTION?   The evolutionary perspective has some interesting suggestions about women's orgasm—or at least the circumstances under which she is likely to have an orgasm. Notes William McKibbin of the University of Michigan:

> It's almost like an arms race, with women maybe evolving the orgasm to select high-quality sperm, men counter-evolving an interest in orgasms to help ensure paternity, and women perhaps evolving the tendency to fake, obscuring paternity (in Dingfelder, 2011, p. 44).

The point is that orgasms apparently increase the probability that a sexual act will lead to conception by holding the sperm within their bodies, increasing the likelihood that one of them will fertilize an ovum (Puts et al., 2012; Welling, 2014). It has even been speculated that a woman can choose or choose not to have an orgasm as a "subconscious last-minute call" as to whether they wish their partner to fertilize them (Dingfelder, 2011). The operative word is "speculate."

HOW MANY KINDS OF ORGASMS DO WOMEN HAVE? ONE, TWO, OR THREE? Until Masters and Johnson published their laboratory findings, many people believed that there were two types of female orgasm, as proposed by the psychoanalyst Sigmund Freud: the clitoral orgasm and the vaginal orgasm. *Clitoral orgasms* were achieved through direct clitoral stimulation, such as by masturbation. Clitoral orgasms were seen by psychoanalysts (mostly male psychoanalysts, naturally) as emblematic of a childhood fixation—a throwback to an erogenous pattern acquired during childhood masturbation.

The term *vaginal orgasm* referred to an orgasm achieved through sexual intercourse, and it was theorized to be a sign of mature sexuality. Freud argued that women achieve sexual maturity when they forsake clitoral stimulation for vaginal stimulation. This view would be little more than an academic footnote but for the fact that some adult women who continue to require direct clitoral stimulation to reach orgasm, even during coitus, have been led by traditional (generally male) psychoanalysts to believe that they are sexually "fixated" at an immature stage or are sexually inadequate.

Despite Freudian theory, Masters and Johnson (1966) were able to find only one kind of orgasm, physiologically speaking, regardless of the source of stimulation (manual–clitoral or penile–vaginal). By monitoring physiological responses to sexual stimulation, they found that the female orgasm involves the same biological events whether it is reached through masturbation, petting, coitus, or even stimulation of the breasts. In men, also, it does not matter how orgasm is achieved—through masturbation, petting, oral sex, coitus, or by fantasizing about a fellow student in chem lab. Orgasm still involves the same physiological processes: Involuntary contractions of the pelvic muscles at the base of the penis expel semen and release sexual tension. A woman or a man might prefer one source of orgasm to another—with a lover rather than by masturbation, or with one person rather than another, but the biological events that define orgasm remain the same.

The purported distinction between clitoral and vaginal orgasms also rests on an assumption that the clitoris is not stimulated during coitus. Masters and Johnson showed this assumption to be false. Penile coital thrusting draws the clitoral hood back and forth against the clitoris. Vaginal pressure also heightens blood flow in the clitoris, helping set the stage for orgasm (Pauls, 2015). Medical researcher Rachel N. Pauls (Pauls, 2015; Oakley et al., 2013) argues that whatever sexual stimulation is provided to reach orgasm, the clitoris is the center for orgasmic response.

Another issue concerning orgasm is women is whether it is a "by-product" of sexual activity or whether it has evolved as an adaptation that promotes reproductive success (Welling, 2014). Theorists who see the female orgasm as a by-product note that female orgasm is not required for reproductive purposes. Evolutionary psychologist Lisa Welling (2014) argues that the female orgasm is an adaptation that does promote reproductive success because it rewards sexual activity, strengthens pair bonds, and actually—through the pelvic contractions—heightens the probability of conception.

Effects of Drugs on Sexual Arousal

LO 7.4 Discuss the effects of drugs on sexual response.

We all know that alcohol stimulates sexual response, do we not? Actually, it may and it may not. Let's review what we know about the effect of various substances and sexual response.

APHRODISIACS: OF SPANISH FLIES AND RHINO HORNS

> The only known aphrodisiac is variety.
>
> —Marc Connolly

An **aphrodisiac** arouses or increases one's capacity for sexual pleasure or response. You may have heard of "spanish fly," an alleged aphrodisiac once extracted from a spanish beetle. (The beetle from which it was taken, *lytta vesicatoria,* is near extinction.) A few drops in a date's drink were believed to make you irresistible. Spanish fly is but one of many purported aphrodisiacs. It is toxic, however, not sexually arousing. Spanish fly is now synthesized—but not as an aphrodisiac.

aphrodisiacs
Drugs or other agents that are sexually arousing or that increase sexual desire.

2 › T /F Truth or Fiction Revisited Despite the widespread belief that Spanish fly is an aphrodisiac, it is true that it will *not* turn your date on, but it might cure his or her warts. Spanish fly contains *cantharidin,* a skin irritant that is used medically to burn off warts. If it can burn off warts, consider the damage it can do when taken internally. It irritates the urinary tract and can damage tissue or cause death (Bengoa Vallejo et al., 2008). It inflames the urethra, producing a burning sensation in the penis that is sometimes misinterpreted as sexual feelings.

A Plate of Oysters. Various substances, including certain foods, have been touted as aphrodisiacs. We have two words of advice: "Buyer beware."

Foods that in some way resemble male genitals have now and then been considered aphrodisiacs. They include oysters, clams, bull's testicles ("prairie oysters"), tomatoes, and "phallic" items such as celery stalks, bananas, and even ground-up rhinoceros, reindeer, and elephant horns (which is one derivation of the slang term *horny*). Even potatoes—both white and sweet—have been held to be aphrodisiacs. None of these foods or substances has been shown to be sexually stimulating, however. Sadly, myths about the sexually arousing properties of substances drawn from rhinoceroses or elephants may be contributing to the rapidly diminishing numbers of these animals (Ascher, 2006).

Other drugs and psychoactive substances may have certain effects on sexual arousal and response. The drug arginine, an amino acid extracted from the African yohimbe tree, does stimulate blood flow to the genitals. However, its effects are limited and unreliable (West & Krychman, 2015).

"POPPERS"   Amyl nitrate (in the form of "snappers" or "poppers") has been used mostly by gay men (and by some heterosexuals) in the belief that it heightens sensations of arousal and orgasm. Poppers dilate blood vessels in the brain and genitals, producing sensations of warmth in the pelvis and possibly facilitating erection and prolonging orgasm. Amyl nitrate does have some legitimate medical uses, such as helping reduce heart pain (angina) among cardiac patients. It is inhaled from ampules that "pop" open for rapid use when heart pain occurs. Poppers can cause dizziness, fainting, and migraine-type headaches, however. They should be taken only under a doctor's care for a legitimate medical need, not to intensify sexual sensations.

VIAGRA, CIALIS, AND LEVITRA   The drug Viagra was originally developed as a treatment for angina (heart pain) because it increases the blood flow to the heart—modestly. However, it also dilates blood vessels in the genital organs, thereby facilitating vasocongestion and erection—and, according to some reports, sexual response in women as well. Viagra and similar drugs—Levitra and Cialis—are treatments for erectile dysfunction (once termed *impotence*). Is Viagra also an aphrodisiac? No. Although Viagra and its cousins facilitate erection, erection still requires a sexual turn-on.

ADDYI   The drug Addyi (flibanserin) has been dubbed the "female Viagra"—but it isn't. It doesn't directly facilitate sexual arousal in women but appears to work on the appetitive phase of arousal—that is, sexual desire. In one clinical trial, women using the drug reported 4.4 "satisfying sexual experiences" a month, as compared with 3.7 satisfying experiences for women given a placebo ("sugar pill") (Editorial Board, 2015a). The difference is "statistically significant"—that is, unlikely to be as a result of chance alone. But Addyi is controversial because it appears to operate on the premise that low ("hypoactive") sexual desire is a "mental disorder" in women. If a woman has less frequent or generally lower sexual desire than her partner, should she be "treated" for that? More on this in Chapter 12.

WELLBUTRIN   Other drugs also appear to have aphrodisiac effects, apparently because they act on the brain mechanisms controlling the sex drive. For example, drugs that affect brain receptors for the neurotransmitter dopamine, such as the anti-depressant drug bupropion (trade name Wellbutrin) and the drug L-dopa used in the treatment of Parkinson's disease, can increase the sex drive (Saks, 2008).

anaphrodisiacs

Drugs or other agents whose effects are antagonistic to sexual arousal or sexual desire.

ANAPHRODISIACS   Aphrodisiacs are thought to stimulate a sexual response. **Anaphrodisiacs** would have the opposite effect. These include substances such as potassium nitrate (salt-peter), which have been considered inhibitors of sexual response, or anaphrodisiacs. Saltpeter, however, only indirectly dampens sexual arousal. As a diuretic that can increase the need for urination, it may make the thought of sex unappealing, but it does not directly dampen sexual response.

Other chemicals do dampen sexual arousal and response. Tranquilizers and central nervous system depressants, such as barbiturates, can lessen sexual desire and impair sexual performance. These drugs may paradoxically enhance sexual arousal in some people, however, by lessening sexual inhibitions or the fear of possible repercussions from sexual activity. Anti-hypertensive drugs, which are used in the treatment of high blood pressure, may produce erectile and ejaculatory difficulties in men and reduction of sexual desire in men and women. Certain anti-depressant drugs, such as fluoxetine (brand name Prozac), amitriptyline (brand name Elavil), and imipramine (brand name Tofranil), appear to dampen the sex drive (Kennedy & Rizvi, 2009). Anti-depressants may also impair erectile response and delay ejaculation in men and orgasmic responsiveness in women (Kennedy & Rizvi, 2009). (Because they delay ejaculation, some of these drugs are used to treat premature ejaculation.)

Nicotine, the stimulant in tobacco smoke, constricts the blood vessels. Thus, it can impede sexual arousal by reducing the capacity of the genitals to become engorged with blood. Chronic smoking can also reduce the blood levels of testosterone in men, which, in turn, can lessen sex drive or motivation.

PSYCHOACTIVE DRUGS   Psychoactive drugs, such as alcohol and cocaine, are widely believed to have aphrodisiac effects. Do any psychoactive drugs stimulate a sexual response? Perhaps some do, but their effects may also reflect our expectations of them, or their effects on sexual inhibitions, rather than direct stimulation of sexual response.

ALCOHOL   Small amounts of alcohol are stimulating, at least in part because alcohol stimulates release of the neurotransmitter dopamine, which in turn stimulates the reward system in the brain (Ding et al., 2016; Topper et al., 2014). However, large amounts of alcohol curb sexual response. This fact should not be surprising because alcohol is a depressant; it reduces central nervous system activity. Large amounts of alcohol can severely impair sexual performance in both men and women.

> **3 › T /F   Truth or Fiction Revisited**   This item is both true and false. How? Alcohol stimulates sexual response in the short run, so it may enhance sexual response. But too much alcohol depresses the nervous system, and sexual response along with it.

People who drink moderate amounts of alcohol may also feel more sexually aroused because of their expectations about alcohol, not because of its chemical properties (Davis, 2010; Gil-Rivas, 2012). That is, people who expect alcohol to enhance sexual responsiveness may play the role. Expectations that alcohol serves as an aphrodisiac may lead men with problems achieving erection to turn to alcohol as a cure. The fact is that alcohol is a depressant, and a few drinks can reduce sexual response rather than enhance it (Cooper et al., 2015).

Alcohol may also lower sexual inhibitions, because it allows us to ascribe our behavior to the effects of the alcohol rather than to our own decision-making processes. Alcohol is connected with a liberated social role and thus provides an excuse for dubious behavior. "It was the alcohol," people can say, "not me." People may express their sexual desires and do things when drinking that they would not do when sober. For example, a person who feels guilty about sex may become sexually active when drinking because he or she can later blame the alcohol.

Binge drinking—having five or more drinks in a row for a male, or four or more for a female—is connected with high-risk sexual behavior, sexual promiscuity, and sexual assault (Bird et al., 2016; Ragsdale et al., 2012). Nevertheless, more than two out of five college students binge at least twice a month, and half this number binge three or more times every two weeks (Patrick & Schulenberg, 2011; Squeglia et al., 2012).

What Are the Effects of Alcohol on Sex Behavior? Small doses of alcohol can be stimulating, induce feelings of euphoria, and lower inhibitions, all of which could be connected with sexual interest and could facilitate social and sexual behavior. Alcohol also reduces fear of consequences of engaging in risky behavior—sexual and otherwise, and it provides an excuse for otherwise unacceptable behavior, such as sexual intercourse on the first date (or upon a casual meeting). That is, drinkers can say, "It was the alcohol, not me." Alcohol is also expected to be sexually liberating, and people often live up to social and cultural expectations. Yet, as a depressant drug, large amounts of alcohol will biochemically dampen sexual response.

Alcohol can also induce feelings of euphoria. Euphoric feelings may enhance sexual arousal and also wash away qualms about expressing sexual desires. Alcohol also appears to impair the ability to weigh information ("information processing") that might otherwise inhibit sexual impulses (Orchowski et al., 2012; Purdie et al., 2011). When people drink, they may be less able to foresee the consequences of misconduct and less likely to ponder their standards of conduct.

HALLUCINOGENICS There is no evidence that marijuana and other hallucinogenic drugs directly stimulate sexual response, yet marijuana use is connected with increased sexual activity and engaging in unprotected sex (Anderson & Stein, 2011). However, fairly to strongly intoxicated marijuana users claim to have more empathy with others, to be more aware of bodily sensations, and to experience time as passing more slowly. These sensations can heighten subjective feelings of sexual response and apparently contribute to women's sexual enjoyment and physical responsiveness, but marijuana use, especially at high doses, may decrease testosterone levels in males and have an inhibitory effect on erection (Gorzalka et al., 2010).

Other hallucinogenics, such as LSD and mescaline, have also been reported by some users to enhance sexual response. Again, these effects may reflect dosage level, as well as expectations, user experiences, attitudes toward the drugs, and altered perceptions.

STIMULANTS Stimulants such as amphetamines ("speed," "uppers," "bennies," "dexies") and methamphetamine ("meth") are reputed to heighten arousal and sensations of orgasm (Frohmader et al., 2010). The drugs can also elevate the mood, and sexual pleasure may be in part heightened by general elation. But overdoses of these drugs can give rise to irritability, restlessness, hallucinations, paranoid delusions, insomnia, loss of appetite—and, at their worst, cardiac problems. Moreover, methamphetamine is highly addictive.

Cocaine is a natural stimulant that is extracted from the leaves of the coca plant—the plant from which the soft drink Coca-Cola obtained its name. In fact, Coke—Coca-Cola, that is—contained cocaine as part of its original formula. Cocaine was removed from the secret formula in 1906 and replaced with extra caffeine. The drug is ingested in various forms, snorted as a powder, smoked in hardened rock form ("crack" cocaine) or in a freebase form, or injected directly into the bloodstream in liquid form. Cocaine produces a euphoric rush, which tends to ebb quickly. Physically, cocaine constricts blood vessels (reducing the oxygen supply to the heart), elevates blood pressure, and boosts heart rate. There is also evidence that cocaine has complicated effects on hormone levels in mammals, which may induce feelings of anxiety and inhibit sexual response (Kohtz et al., 2010; Matsui et al., 2015).

Despite any effects on sexual arousal, high doses of stimulants can cause irritability, restlessness, hallucinations, paranoid delusions, insomnia, loss of appetite—and in high doses, cardiac arrest. Use of crack cocaine is connected with a higher number of sex partners (Maranda et al., 2004).

Erogenous Zones and the Brain

LO 7.5 **Describe the role of the brain in sexual response.**

Erogenous zones are parts of the body that are especially sensitive to tactile sexual stimulation—to strokes and other caresses. Primary erogenous zones are erotically sensitive because they are richly endowed with nerve endings. Secondary erogenous zones become erotically sensitized through experience.

Primary erogenous zones include the genitals; the inner thighs, perineum, buttocks, and anus; the breasts (especially the nipples); the ears (particularly the earlobes); the mouth, lips, and tongue; the neck; the navel; and, yes, the armpits. Preferences vary somewhat from person to person, reflecting possible biological, attitudinal, and experiential differences. Areas that are exquisitely sensitive for some people may produce virtually no reaction, or discomfort, in others. Many women, for example, report little sensation when their breasts are stroked or kissed. Many men are uncomfortable when their nipples are caressed. On the other hand (or foot), many people find the areas between their toes sensitive to erotic stimulation and enjoy keeping a toehold on their partners during coitus.

Secondary erogenous zones become eroticized through association with sexual stimulation. For example, a woman might become sexually aroused when her lover gently caresses her shoulders because such caresses have been incorporated into the couple's lovemaking. A few of the women observed by Masters and Johnson (1966) reached orgasm when the smalls of their backs were rubbed.

People are also highly responsive to images and fantasies. This is why the brain is sometimes referred to as the primary sexual organ or an erogenous zone. Some women reported reaching orgasm through fantasy alone to interviewers in the Kinsey studies (Kinsey et al., 1953). Men regularly experience erection and nocturnal emissions ("wet dreams") without direct stimulation of the genitals.

The brain plays a central role in sexual functioning (Fisher, 2000). Direct genital stimulation may trigger spinal reflexes that produce erection in the male and vaginal lubrication in the female without the direct involvement of the brain. The same reflexes, however, may also be triggered by sexual stimulation that originates in the brain in the form of erotic memories, fantasies, visual images, and thoughts. The brain may also inhibit sexual responsiveness, as when we experience guilt or anxiety in a sexual situation, or when we suddenly realize in the midst of a sexual encounter that we have left the car lights turned on. Let us explore the brain mechanisms involved in sexual functioning.

Parts of the brain, in particular the cerebral cortex and the limbic system, play key roles in sexual functioning (see Figure 7.5). Cells in the cerebral cortex fire (transmit messages) when we experience sexual thoughts, images, wishes, fantasies, and the like. Cells in the cerebral cortex interpret sensory information as sexual turn-ons or turn-offs. The sight of your lover disrobing, the anticipation of a romantic kiss, a passing sexual fantasy, or an erotic photo can trigger the firing of cortical cells. These cells, in turn, transmit messages through the spinal cord that send blood rushing to the genitals, causing erection or vaginal lubrication. The cortex also provides the conscious sense of self.

Critical Thinking

Critical thinkers are cautious in their interpretation of research findings. There is evidence that use of crack cocaine is connected with having more sex partners. Does this connection mean that cocaine causes people to have more sex partners? Can you think of other possible explanations of the relationship?

Figure 7.5 Parts of the Brain Involved in Sexual Functioning.

A view of the brain, split from top to bottom. Cells in the cerebral cortex transmit messages when we experience sexual thoughts and mental images. Cells in the cortex interpret sensory information as sexual turn-ons or turn-offs. The cerebral cortex may then transmit messages through the spinal cord that send blood coursing to the sex organs, leading to erection or vaginal lubrication. The limbic system lies along the inner edge of the cerebrum. When part of a male rat's hypothalamus is electrically stimulated, the rat engages in its courting and mounting routine. Klüver and Bucy (1939) found that destruction of areas of the limbic system triggered continuous sexual behavior in monkeys. Electrical stimulation of the hippocampus and septal nuclei produces erections in monkeys.

Cerebral cortex

Corpus callosum

Septal nuclei

Hypothalamus

Cingulate gyrus of cerebral cortex

Fornix

Hippocampus

Amygdala

The cortex judges sexual behavior to be proper or improper, moral or immoral, relaxing or anxiety- or guilt-provoking.

Areas of the brain below the cortex, especially the limbic system, also play roles in sexual processes (Kimble, 1992). For example, when the rear part of a male rat's hypothalamus is stimulated by an electrical probe, the animal mechanically runs through its courting and mounting routine. It nibbles at the ears and the back of the neck of a female rat and mounts her when she responds. People, of course, are influenced by learning, fantasy, and values as well as simple brain (or spinal) stimulation.

The importance of the limbic system in the sexual behavior in animals was demonstrated in experiments by Heinrich Klüver and Paul Bucy of the University of Chicago in 1939. Klüver and Bucy reported that destruction of areas of the limbic system triggered persistent sexual behaviors that included masturbation and male–female and male–male mounting attempts. The monkeys even tried to mount the experimenters. For obvious ethical reasons, researchers have not injured or destroyed parts of people's brains to observe the effects on humans.

Electrical stimulation of the hippocampus and septum of the limbic system can produce erections in laboratory monkeys (Ferris et al., 2004). Electrical stimulation of a pathway in the thalamus, moreover, can produce a seminal discharge in these monkeys—without erection. Stimulation of certain areas in the thalamus and hypothalamus may induce ejaculation. It remains to be seen how these findings will be useful with humans.

Critical Thinking
If you electrically stimulate part of a rat's brain, it mechanically runs through a mating routine. Does it seem useful or wise to attempt to apply this research finding to humans?

ON PUSHING THE RIGHT BUTTONS: ARE THERE PLEASURE CENTERS IN THE BRAIN? Research with electrical probes suggests that "pleasure centers" may exist in and near the hypothalamus in other animals and perhaps even in people. Classic research found that when electrodes are implanted in certain parts of the limbic system, investigators find that laboratory animals such as rats (Olds, 1956; Olds & Milner, 1954) will repeatedly press controls to receive bursts of electricity. Of course we cannot know what the rats experience, but people report that stimulation of these so-called pleasure centers leads to feelings of sexual arousal and gratification.

Heath (1972) found that electrical stimulation of the septal region of the limbic system resulted in orgasm-like sensations in two people. Delgado (1969) reported that two female epileptic patients who received limbic stimulation as part of a diagnostic evaluation became sexually aroused by the stimulation:

> [One] reported a pleasant tingling sensation in the left side of her body "from my face down to the bottom of my legs." She started giggling and [stated] that she enjoyed the sensation "very much." Repetition of these stimulations made the patient more communicative and flirtatious, and she ended by openly expressing her desire to marry the therapist. [The other patient reported] a pleasant sensation of relaxation and considerably increased her verbal output, which took on a more intimate character. [She] expressed her fondness for the therapist [whom she had just met], kissed his hands, and talked about her immense gratitude. (p. 145)

4 › T /F Truth or Fiction Revisited It is apparently true that electrical stimulation of certain areas in the human brain can yield sensations similar to those of sexual pleasure and gratification. We might wonder whether we would bother to develop sexual relationships if such centers could be stimulated directly. But before you run to the store for electrodes, consider that few researchers suggest that we will someday replace lovers with electronic kits.

Sex Hormones and Sexual Response

LO 7.6 Discuss the organizing and activating influences of sex hormones.

In a TV situation comedy, a male adolescent was described as a "hormone with feet." Ask parents why teenagers act the way they do, and you are likely to hear a one-word answer: hormones!

Hormones are chemicals that are secreted by the ductless glands of the endocrine system directly into the bloodstream. The word *hormone* derives from the Greek *horman*, meaning "to stimulate" or "to goad." We could say that hormones very much goad us into sexual activity. Hormones also regulate various bodily functions, including growth and resistance to stress, as well as sexual functions.

The hypothalamus and pituitary gland regulate gonadal secretion of sex hormones, specifically testosterone in males and estrogen and progesterone in females. At puberty, a surge of sex hormones causes the blossoming of reproductive maturation: the sperm-producing ability of the testes in males and the maturation of ova and ovulation in females. Sex hormones released at puberty also cause the flowering of secondary sex characteristics. In males, the vocal cords lengthen (and the voice consequently lowers), and facial and pubic hair grow. In females, the breasts and hips become rounded with fatty tissue, and pubic hair grows.

ORGANIZING AND ACTIVATING INFLUENCES Sex hormones have organizing and activating effects on behavior. That is, they exert an influence on the type of behavior that is expressed (an organizing effect) and the frequency or intensity of the drive that motivates the behavior and the ability to perform the behavior (activating effects). For example, sex hormones predispose lower animals and possibly people toward stereotypical masculine or feminine mating behaviors (an organizing effect). They also facilitate sexual response and influence sexual desire (activating effects).

Although sex hormones clearly determine the sex of the sex partners that many lower animals will seek, their roles in human sexual behavior may be relatively more subtle and are not as well understood. Much of our knowledge of the organizing and activating effects of sex hormones comes from research with other species in which hormone levels were manipulated by castration or injection. Ethical standards prohibit such research with human infants, for obvious reasons.

The activating effects of testosterone can be clearly observed among male rats. For example, males who are castrated in adulthood and thus deprived of testosterone discontinue sexual behavior. If they are given injections of testosterone, however, they resume stereotypical male sexual behaviors, such as mounting females.

In rats, testosterone apparently organizes or differentiates the brain in the masculine direction such that adult male rats display stereotypical masculine behaviors—including sniffing (especially sniffing of females), and mounting females—upon activation by testosterone. Male fetuses and newborns normally have sufficient amounts of testosterone in their blood systems to organize their brains in the masculine direction. Female fetuses and newborns normally have lesser amounts of testosterone. Their brains thus become organized in a feminine direction. When female rodents are prenatally exposed to large doses of testosterone, their sexual organs become somewhat masculinized, and they are predisposed toward masculine mating behaviors in adulthood (Banszegi et al., 2010).

Are Adolescents "Hormones with Feet"? Research shows that levels of androgens are connected with sexual interest in both male and female adolescents. Hormone levels are more likely to predict sex behavior in adolescent males, however, perhaps because society places greater restraints on female sexuality.

hormone
A chemical that is secreted directly into the bloodstream by a ductless gland, and that influences the functions of the body and/or behavior.

In rats and other rodents, sexual differentiation of the brain is not complete at birth. Female rodents and monkeys who are given testosterone injections shortly before or shortly following birth (depending on the species) show typical masculine sexual patterns in adulthood, mounting other females and resisting mounting by males (Phoenix, 2009).

Questions remain about the organizing effects of sex hormones on human sexual behavior. Prenatal sex hormones play a role in the sexual differentiation of the genitalia and of the brain structures, such as the hypothalamus. Their role in patterning sexual behavior in adulthood remains unclear, however. It has been speculated that prenatal sexual differentiation of the brain may also be connected with sexual orientation.

What of the activating effects of sex hormones on human sex drive and behavior? Although the countless attempts to extract or synthesize aphrodisiacs have failed to produce the real thing, men and women normally produce a genuine aphrodisiac— testosterone. Testosterone activates the sex drives of both men and women (Nappi & Albani, 2016).

SEX HORMONES AND MALE SEXUAL BEHAVIOR   Male sex hormones are known to influence the sex drive and sexual response in nonhuman animals and men (Nieschlag et al., 2012). Evidence of the role for hormones in the sex drive is found among men who have declines in testosterone levels as the result of aging or chemical or surgical castration. Surgical castration (removal of the testes) is sometimes performed as a medical treatment for cancer of the prostate or other diseases of the male reproductive tract, such as genital tuberculosis. But some convicted sex offenders have voluntarily undergone castration as a condition of release.

Men who are surgically or chemically castrated usually exhibit a gradual decrease in the incidence of sexual fantasies and loss of sexual desire (Barbaree & Blanchard, 2008). They also gradually tend to lose the capacities to attain erection and to ejaculate—an indication that testosterone is important in maintaining sexual functioning as well as drive, at least in males. Castrated men show great variation in their sexual interest and functioning, however. Some continue to experience sexual desires and are able to function sexually for years, even decades. Learning appears to play a large role in determining continued sexual response following castration. Males who were sexually experienced before castration show a more gradual decline in sexual activity. Those who were sexually inexperienced at the time show relatively little or no interest in sex. Male sexual motivation and functioning thus involve interplay of hormonal influences and experience.

Further evidence of the relationship between hormonal levels and male sexuality is found in studies of men with hypogonadism, a condition marked by abnormally low levels of testosterone production. Hypogonadal men generally suffer loss of sexual desire and a decline in sexual activity (Nieschlag et al., 2012). Here again, hormones do not tell the whole story. Hypogonadal men are capable of erection, at least for a while, even though their sex drives may wane. The role of testosterone as an activator of sex drives in men is further supported by evidence of the effects of testosterone replacement in hypogonadal men. When such men receive testosterone injections, their sex drives, fantasies, and activity are often restored to former levels (Nieschlag et al., 2012).

Although minimal levels of androgens are critical to male sexuality, there is no one-to-one correspondence between hormone levels and the sex drive or sexual performance in adults. In men who have ample supplies of testosterone, sexual interest and functioning depend more on learning, fantasies, attitudes, memories, and other psychosocial factors than on hormone levels. At puberty, however, hormonal variations may play a more direct role in stimulating sexual interest and activity in males. Udry (2001) found, for example, that testosterone levels predicted sexual interest, masturbation rates, and the likelihood of engaging in sexual intercourse among teenage boys. A positive relationship also has been found between testosterone levels in adult men and frequency of sexual intercourse (Nieschlag et al., 2012). Moreover, drugs that reduce the levels of androgen in the blood system, called **antiandrogens**, lead to reductions in the sex drive and in sexual fantasies (Nieschlag et al., 2012).

Men and women produce small amounts of the sex hormones of the other sex. Testosterone, the major form of androgen, or male sex hormone, is secreted in small amounts by the adrenal glands (located above the kidneys) in both sexes, but in much larger amounts by the testes. The ovaries produce small amounts of androgens but much larger amounts of the female sex hormones, estrogen and progesterone. The testes similarly produce small amounts of estrogen and progesterone.

SEX HORMONES AND FEMALE SEXUAL BEHAVIOR   The female sex hormones estrogen and progesterone play prominent roles in promoting the changes that occur during puberty and in regulating the menstrual cycle. Female sex hormones do not appear to play a direct role in determining sexual motivation or response in human females, however.

In most mammals, females are sexually receptive only during **estrus**. Estrus is a brief period of fertility that corresponds to time of ovulation; during estrus, females are said to be "in heat." Estrus occurs once a year in some species; in others, it occurs periodically during the year in mating seasons. Estrogen peaks at time of ovulation, so there is a close relationship between fertility and sexual receptivity in most female mammals. Human females' sexuality is not clearly linked to hormonal fluctuations, however. Unlike females of most other species of mammals, the human female is sexually responsive during all phases of the reproductive (menstrual) cycle—even during menstruation, when ovarian hormone levels are low—and after menopause.

There is evidence, however, that sexual responsiveness in women is influenced by the presence of circulating androgens, or male sex hormones, in their bodies. The adrenal glands of women produce small amounts of androgens, just as they do in males (Davis & Braunstein, 2012). The fact that women normally produce smaller amounts of androgens than men does not mean that they necessarily have weaker sex drives. Rather, women appear to be more sensitive to smaller amounts of androgens. Even so, women's sexual activity increases at points in the menstrual cycle when levels of androgens in the bloodstream are high.

Women who have **ovariectomies**, which are sometimes carried out when a hysterectomy is performed, no longer produce female sex hormones. Nevertheless, they may continue to experience sex drives and interest as before. Loss of the ovarian hormone estradiol may cause vaginal dryness and make coitus painful, but it does not necessarily reduce sexual desire. (The dryness can be alleviated by a lubricating jelly or by estrogen-replacement therapy.) However, women whose adrenal glands and ovaries have been removed, so that they no longer produce androgens, gradually lose sexual desire (Davis & Braunstein, 2012). An active and enjoyable sexual history seems to ward off this loss, however, suggestive of the impact of cognitive and experiential factors on human sexual response.

Research provides further evidence on the links between testosterone levels and women's sex drives. Androgen levels predict sexual interest among teenage girls. In contrast to boys, however, girls' androgen levels were unrelated to the likelihood of coital experience. Androgens apparently affect sexual desire in both sexes, but sexual interest may be more likely to be directly translated into sexual activity in men than in women (Carvalho & Nobre, 2010a; Petersen & Hyde, 2011). This sex difference may be explained by society's placement of greater restraints on female sexuality.

Androgens thus play a prominent role in activating and maintaining women's sex drives. As with men, however, women's sexuality is too complex to be explained fully by hormone levels. For example, an active and enjoyable sexual history seems to ward off the loss of sexual interest that generally follows the surgical removal of the adrenal glands and ovaries.

antiandrogen
A substance that decreases the levels of androgens in the bloodstream.

estrus
A brief period of fertility that corresponds to time of ovulation.

ovariectomy
Surgical removal of the ovaries.

Sex without a Partner

The human body is sensitive to many forms of sexual stimulation. Biology is not destiny, however: A biological capacity does not impose a behavioral requirement. Cultural expectations, personal values, and individual experience—not only our biological capacities—determine our sexual behavior. What is right for you is right for you—and not necessarily for your neighbor.

We begin by reviewing the techniques that people practice on their own to derive sexual pleasure. We then consider techniques that involve a partner.

Various forms of sexual expression do not require a partner or are not generally practiced in the presence of a partner. Masturbation is one of the principal forms of one-person sexual expression. Masturbation involves direct stimulation of the genitals. Other forms of individual sexual experience, such as sexual fantasy, may or may not be accompanied by genital stimulation.

The word *masturbation* is not simply a descriptive term. It derives from the Latin *masturbari*, from the roots for "hand" and "to defile." The derivation provides clues to historical cultural attitudes toward the practice (Polansky, 2006). **Masturbation** may be practiced by manual stimulation of the genitals, perhaps with the aid of artificial stimulation, such as a vibrator. It may employ an object, such as a pillow or a **dildo** that touches the genitals. Even before we conceive of sexual experiences with others, we may learn early in childhood that touching our genitals can produce pleasure.

Pleasure is not the only reason that people masturbate. Table 7.1 lists reasons reported for masturbation, according to the findings of the NHSLS.

Within the Judeo-Christian tradition, masturbation has been condemned as sinful (Kaestle & Allen, 2011). Early Judeo-Christian attitudes toward masturbation reflected the censure that was applied toward nonprocreative sex. Masturbation has also been referred to as "onanism" or "onania," names derived from the biblical story of Onan (Obald, 2012). According to the book of Genesis (38:9–11), Onan was the second-born son of Judah. Judah's first son, Er, died without an heir. Biblical law required that if a man died without a male heir, his brother must take the widow as a wife and rear their first son as his brother's heir. Judah thus directed Onan to "Go in unto thy brother's wife, and perform the duty of a husband's brother unto her, and raise up seed to thy brother." But Onan "spilled [his seed] upon the ground" during relations with his deceased brother's wife and was struck down by God for his deed.

Although "onanism" has come to be associated with masturbation, scholars have noted that Onan's act was **coitus interruptus**, not masturbation. Both acts,

masturbation

Sexual self-stimulation.

dildo

A penis-shaped object used in sexual activity.

coitus interruptus

The practice of withdrawing the penis prior to ejaculation during sexual intercourse. Also called *withdrawal method*.

Table 7.1 Reasons for Masturbation (Percentage of Respondents Who Report Reason), According to the NHSLS

Reasons for Masturbation	Men	Women
To relax	26	32
To relieve sexual tension	73	63
Partners are unavailable	32	32
Partner does not want to engage in sexual activity	16	6
Boredom	11	5
To obtain physical pleasure	40	42
To help get to sleep	16	12
Fear of HIV/AIDS and other STIs	7	5
Other reasons	5	5

SOURCE: Adapted with permission from E. O. Laumann, J. H. Gagnon, R. T. Michael, & S. Michaels (1994). *The social organization of sexuality: Sexual practices in the United States.* Chicago: University of Chicago Press, Table 3.3, p. 86.

however, involve nonprocreative sex—"spilling the seed." Whatever its biblical origins, masturbation is prohibited under Jewish law. St. Augustine was influenced by ancient Persian beliefs, which condemned all nonprocreative sex as sinful (van Oort, 2012). Historians suspect that people in ancient times condemned sex that did not lead to pregnancy because of the need for an increase in their numbers. The need for progeny is also linked to the widespread view that marital intercourse is the only morally acceptable avenue of sexual expression.

Historical Medical Views of Masturbation

LO 7.7   Discuss attitudes toward masturbation.

> In solitude he pollutes himself, and with his own hand blights all his prospects for both this world and the next. Even after being solemnly warned, he will often continue this worse than beastly practice, deliberately forfeiting his right to health and happiness for a moment's mad sensuality.
>
> —J. H. Kellogg, M.D., *Plain Facts for Old and Young*, 1888

In the eighteenth century, the medical profession "translated" sin into disease (van Oort, 2012). Thus, until recent times, masturbation was thought to be physically and mentally harmful, as well as degrading. The eighteenth-century physician Benjamin Rush, a signer of the Declaration of Independence, believed that masturbation caused tuberculosis, "nervous diseases," poor eyesight, memory loss, and epilepsy.

Many clergy and medical authorities of the nineteenth century were persuaded that certain foods had a stimulating effect on the sex organs. They therefore advised parents to modify their children's diets to eliminate foods that were believed to excite the sexual organs—notably meat, coffee, tea, and chocolate. Rather, parents should substitute "unstimulating" foods, primarily grain products. In the 1830s, the Reverend Sylvester Graham developed a cracker, since called the graham cracker, to help people control their sexual impulses (Ley, 2012).

Another household name belongs to a man who made his mark by introducing a bland diet that was also intended to help people, especially youngsters, control sexual impulses. One of the more influential medical writers of the nineteenth century was the superintendent of the Battle Creek Sanatorium in Michigan, Dr. J. H. Kellogg (1852–1943), better known now as the creator of the modern breakfast cereal. Kellogg identified 39 "signs of masturbation," including acne, paleness, heart palpitations, rounded shoulders, weak backs, and convulsions. Kellogg, like Graham, believed that sexual desires could be controlled by a diet of simple foods, especially grains, including the corn flakes that have since borne his name (Ley, 2012).

Many nineteenth-century physicians also advised parents to take measures to prevent their children from masturbating. Kellogg suggested that parents bandage or cage their children's genitals, or tie their hands. Some contraptions devised to prevent masturbation were barbarous (see Figure 7.6).

Several nineteenth-century scholars of sexuality joined the crusade against masturbation. Richard von Krafft-Ebing (in *Psychopathia Sexualis*, 1886) and Havelock Ellis (in *Studies in the Psychology of Sex*, 1900) condemned masturbation as psychologically dangerous. Male masturbation—or so it was mistakenly believed—arrested the development of normal erotic instincts and led to erectile dysfunction with women. Thus, it encouraged male–male sexual activity.

Despite this history, there is no scientific evidence that masturbation is harmful. It doesn't cause insanity, grow hair on the hands, or cause warts or any of the other ills once ascribed to it, except for rare

Figure 7.6   Devices Designed to Curb Masturbation.

Because of widespread beliefs that masturbation was harmful, various contraptions were introduced during the nineteenth century to prevent the practice in children. Some of the devices were barbarous.

A CLOSER LOOK

GOOD VIBES

The use of vibrators during sexual activity is one of the more apparent examples of the old General Electric slogan, "Better living through electricity." Surveys with nationally representative samples reveal that half of U.S. residents use vibrators, slightly less than half of men (Reece et al., 2009) and more than half of women (Herbenick et al., 2009). Vibrators are incorporated into both solo and partnered sexual activities (Herbenick et al., 2011). These include—but are not limited to!—clitoral stimulation, (attempted) stimulation of the G-spot (we say "attempted" because, as noted in Chapter 2, the existence of a G-spot remains controversial), securing of the base of a condom (to prevent leakage), anal stimulation (eternal and internal), the simulation of cunnilingus, and couples sex play (Herbenick et al., 2011).

Given these varied usages, and the penetration (excuse the pun) of the vibrator into sexual activity in the United States, we must consider the vibrator to be a normal (at least statistically normal) aid in the achievement of sexual pleasure. Looking at vibrator use a bit more deeply, the survey of 1,047 men aged 18–60 found that 45% had incorporated a vibrator into their sexual activities over the course of their lifetime, and 10% had done so in the past month (Reece et al., 2009). Responses of 2,056 women aged 18–60 to a survey found that 52.5% had incorporated vibrators into their sexual activities over their lifetime (Herbenick et al., 2009).

What do we know about the men and women who used vibrators? Responses to other survey questions showed that men who used vibrators were more likely to pay attention to their sexual health, such as being more likely to engage in testicular self-examinations. Men who had used vibrators also reported more positively on their erectile functioning, their satisfaction with intercourse, their ability to reach orgasm, and their sexual desire. As with the men, use of a vibrator among women was connected with more healthful behaviors such as obtaining gynecological examinations and doing self-genital examinations. And as with the men, vibrator use was positively correlated with sexual desire and arousal and orgasm, and negatively correlated with sexual pain. More than 70% of the women reported that they had never had negative side effects from vibrator use.

We also have a study of beliefs about the use of vibrators by women (Herbenick et al., 2011; Table 7.2). Participants included a nationally representative sample of both women and men. The only way to sum up the results is to say that the great majority of both genders agreed with the positive statements about women's usage of vibrators, and that the great majority *disagreed* with the *negative* statements. It would appear that today, the general public favors, or is not concerned about, women's use of vibrators.

Let us dispel a couple of myths about semen. For one thing, it is impossible to become pregnant by swallowing semen. For another, semen is not fattening. The average ejaculate contains about five calories. On the other hand, it is not our intention to encourage swallowing of semen. The aesthetics of swallowing semen have little or nothing to do with concerns about pregnancy or weight. They involve the preferences of the individual.

Table 7.2 Women's and Men's Beliefs about Women's Use of Vibrators.

Belief items	Female respondents		Male respondents	
	Disagree or strongly disagree	Agree or strongly agree	Disagree or strongly disagree	Agree or strongly agree
POSITIVE BELIEFS				
Makes it easier for a woman to have an orgasm	27%	73%	18.7%	81.3%
Can enhance a woman's sexual relationship with her partner	25.6%	74.4%	18.1%	81.9%
Helps women to become more sexually independent	33.5%	66.4%	39.2%	60.8%
Can take the pressure off a woman's partner to give her an orgasm	32.2%	67.8%	32.4%	67.5%
Is a healthy part of many women's sex lives	23.4%	76.6%	19.8%	80.2%
Can make sex with a partner more exciting	24.8%	75.2%	19.6%	80.4%
NEGATIVE BELIEFS				
Makes women too dependent on them for pleasure	66.3%	33.7%	65%	35%
Is embarrassing for women	71.7%	28.3%	76.6%	23.4%
Is something that only women who are lonely do	84.7%	15.3%	85.4%	14.6%
Is intimidating to women's partners	63.3%	36.7%	70.4%	29.6%

SOURCE: Adapted from Debra Herbenick, Michael Reece, Vanessa Schick, Kristen N. Jozkowski, Susan E. Middelstadt, Stephanie A. Sanders, Brian S. Dodge, Annahita Ghassemi & J. Dennis Fortenberry (2011): Beliefs About Women's Vibrator Use: Results From a Nationally Representative Probability Survey in the United States, *Journal of Sex & Marital Therapy*, 37(5), 329–345, p. 339, Table 4. *Journal of sex & marital therapy* by ROUTLEDGE. Reproduced with permission of ROUTLEDGE in the format republish in a book/textbook via Copyright Clearance Center.

injuries to the genitals resulting from rough stimulation. Nor is masturbation in itself psychologically harmful, although it may suggest an adjustment problem if people use masturbation as an exclusive sexual outlet when they have opportunities for sexual relationships. Sex therapists have used masturbation as a treatment for individuals with low sexual desire and for women who have difficulty reaching orgasm (Kaestle & Allen, 2011; ter Kuile et al., 2012; see Chapter 12).

Of course, people who consider masturbation wrong, harmful, or sinful may experience anxiety or guilt about it (Zuckerman, 2012). But these negative reactions are linked to their beliefs about masturbation, not masturbation per se. Nevertheless, feelings of guilt can lower the incidence and frequency of masturbation (Ortega et al., 2005).

Surveys indicate that most people in our society masturbate at some time (see Table 7.3). But individuals are now masturbating at earlier ages than in Kinsey's day (Dekker & Schmidt, 2002). The incidence of masturbation is generally greater among men than women.

> **5 › T /F   Truth or Fiction Revisited**   Masturbation is not rare among married people. The NHSLS reported that only 43% of the married men and 63% of the married women sampled in the NHSLS study said that they did not masturbate at all during the past year. When you broaden the view to include all people living with a sex partner, the NHSLS reported that 85% of the men and 45% of the women had masturbated during the past year.

Females and males with more education reported more frequent masturbation in the NHSLS. Perhaps people with more schooling are more likely to learn that masturbation itself is harmless or are less likely to follow traditional social restrictions. Traditional religious beliefs appear to restrain masturbation. Conservative Protestants are less likely to masturbate than liberal and moderate Protestants.

Women who have masturbated during adolescence are more likely to find gratification in sex with others in adulthood than women who had not (Hogarth & Ingham, 2009). This correlational evidence cannot be used to conclude that adolescents should be encouraged to masturbate to foster sexual fulfillment in adulthood. A selection factor may explain the link (see Figure 7.7). That is, people who masturbate early may

---

Figure 7.7   What Are the Connections Between Masturbation During Adolescence and Sexual Satisfaction Later on?

There is a positive correlation between masturbation during adolescence and sexual satisfaction during adult relationships. What hypotheses can we make about the causal connections? Does experience with masturbation teach people about their sexual needs so that they are more likely to obtain adequate sexual stimulation later on in life? Are people who masturbate early generally more open to exploring their sexuality and learning about the types of stimulation that arouse them? Such attitudes might also increase the likelihood that people would seek the coital stimulation they need to achieve sexual gratification in adult relationships.

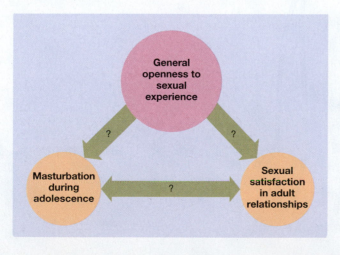

be more open to exploring their sexuality. These attitudes would carry over into adulthood and increase the likelihood that women would seek the stimulation they need to obtain sexual gratification. Adolescent masturbation may also set the stage for sexual satisfaction in adulthood by providing information about the types of stimulation that lead to sexual gratification.

Researchers also find that women achieve orgasm more reliably through masturbation than through sexual intercourse (Hogarth & Ingham, 2009; ter Kuile et al., 2012). This finding does not necessarily mean that women prefer masturbation. It does suggest, though, that women know what stimulation they need to reach orgasm better than their partners do and, through masturbation, can focus on providing themselves with that stimulation.

In our efforts to correct misinformation about masturbation, let us not suggest that there is anything wrong with choosing *not* to masturbate. Readers are encouraged to make their own choices on the basis of their own values.

Masturbation Techniques

LO 7.8 **Describe ways in which people masturbate.**

> *Sex is like bridge—if you don't have a good partner, you'd better have a good hand.*
>
> —Bathroom graffiti

The comment observed once upon a time on bathroom walls may be humorous, but in terms of masturbation techniques, it is only part of the story.

TECHNIQUES USED BY MALES Although masturbation techniques vary widely, most men do report that they masturbate by manual manipulation of the penis (see Figure 7.8). Kinsey and his colleagues (1948) reported that they typically take one or two minutes to reach orgasm. Men tend to grip the penile shaft with one hand, jerking it up and down in a milking motion. Some men move the whole hand up and down the penis, whereas others use two fingers, generally the thumb and index finger. Men usually shift from a gentler rubbing action during the flaccid or semi-erect state of arousal to a more vigorous milking motion once

Figure 7.8   Male Masturbation.

Masturbation techniques vary widely, but most men report that they masturbate by manual manipulation of the penis. They tend to grip the penile shaft with one hand and jerk it up and down in a milking motion.

full erection takes place. Men are also likely to stroke the glans and frenulum lightly at the outset, but their grip tightens and their motions speed up as orgasm nears. At orgasm, the penile shaft may be gripped tightly, but the glans has become sensitive, and contact with it is usually avoided. (Likewise, women usually avoid stimulating the clitoris directly during orgasm because of increased sensitivity.)

Some men use soapsuds (which may become irritating) as a lubricant for masturbation during baths or showers. Other lubricants, such as petroleum jelly or K-Y jelly, are less irritating and also more effective at reducing friction and simulating the moist conditions of coitus.

A few men prefer to masturbate by rubbing the penis and testicles against clothing or bedding. A few men rub their genitals against inflatable sex dolls sold in sex shops. These dolls may come with artificial mouths or vaginas that can be filled with liquid to mimic the sensations of coitus. Artificial vaginas are also for sale.

Sex dolls are becoming more realistic, and more expensive (Yeoman & Mars, 2012; Cott, 2015). As we see in the Sex in the Digital Age feature, some have realistic skin and are being fitting with artificial intelligence that will enable them to move their eyes, mouths, and limbs and have "conversations" with their purchasers. Sex within a "relationship" (Knafo, 2015)? Japan and South Korea are apparently taking the lead in fashioning the dolls, although there is activity in the United States as well.

Some men strap vibrators to the backs of their hands. Electrical vibrators save labor but do not simulate the type of up-and-down motions of the penis that men favor. Hence, they are not used very often. Most men use fantasy, photos, videos, or the Internet. With the exception of a real-life partner—a notable exception, indeed—the Internet offers one-stop sex shopping for millions.

Techniques Used by Females

Techniques of female masturbation also vary widely, but some general trends have been noted. Most women masturbate by massaging the mons, labia minora, and

---

SEX IN THE DIGITAL AGE

SEX WITH *HER*

The digital age is in the cloud all around us. It's in our smartphones, desktops, and cars. It's also in our beds.

Matt McMullen, creator of the sex doll he calls the RealDoll may be about to swerve his business off the road into the "uncanny valley" (Cott, 2015). Users of sex dolls for sham oral, vaginal, and anal sex are very aware that their sex dolls are just that—dolls. But McMullen is developing artificial intelligence to integrate speech and companionship into his dolls.

In the movie *Her*, Scarlett Johansson portrayed Samantha—the disembodied, sultry voice of a digital operating system that made herself/itself "available" to the actor Joaquin Phoenix, initially through his smartphone. She offered companionship and even sex, by conniving to connect electronically through the nervous system

of a human volunteer that Phoenix rejected, possibly because the volunteer made the operating system all too real, or even creepy, or challenged his fantasies about "her." In any event, the operating system reaches into other people's appliances as well, and Phoenix soon learns that she is "cheating" on him with countless thousands of other people.

Back to McMullen's RealDoll about to be fitted with the artificial intelligence. Add in realistic soft skin and body types and you suddenly have a "sex partner" that's approximating the human. That's the uncanny valley: the idea that the closer robots become to real humans, the more we are likely to be repulsed by them.

And can "real men" who actually talk to their lovers be far behind?

Apparently we will be finding out.

Figure 7.9 Female Masturbation.

Techniques of female masturbation vary so widely that Masters and Johnson reported never observing two women masturbating in precisely the same way. Most women masturbate by massaging the mons, labia minora, and clitoral region, however, either with circular or back-and-forth motions.

clitoral region with circular or back-and-forth motions. They may also straddle the clitoris with their fingers, stroking the shaft rather than the glans (see Figure 7.9). The glans may be lightly touched early during arousal, but because of its exquisite sensitivity, it is rarely stroked for any length of time during masturbation. Women typically achieve clitoral stimulation by rubbing or stroking the clitoral shaft or pulling or tugging on the vaginal lips. Some women also massage other sensitive areas, such as their breasts or nipples, with the free hand. Many women, like men, fantasize during masturbation.

In contrast to the male myth that women usually masturbate by simulating penile thrusting through the insertion of fingers or phallic objects into their vaginas, relatively few women actually do. Kinsey and his colleagues (1953) reported that only one in five women inserted objects into the vagina during masturbation. Some women experimented with vaginal insertion but gave it up as they became more familiar with their sexual anatomy and capabilities. Others practiced the technique because their male partners found it sexually stimulating to watch them. Still, some women reported erotic pleasure from deep vaginal penetration.

Even when women use insertion, they usually precede or combine it with clitoral stimulation. Sex shops sell dildos, which women can use to rub their vulvas or to insert. Penis-shaped vibrators may be used in the same way. Many women masturbate during baths; some spray their genitals with jets of water.

Handheld electrical vibrators (see Figure 7.10) massage the genitals in a way that can be erotic (Herbenick et al., 2009; Shick et al., 2011). But some women find this type of stimulation too intense and

Figure 7.10 Electric Vibrators and Other Sex Toys.

Both females and males use devices like these in the place of real penises, to try to increase the volume of the penis, or for other sexual ends. If they are to be used at all, they should be used with extreme caution.

favor vibrators that strap to the back of the hand, helping the fingers to vibrate during manual stimulation of the genitals. But this type of vibration may numb the hand attached to the vibrator. Women experiment with different vibrators to find one with the shape and intensity of vibration that suits them.

Women may stimulate their nipples during masturbation or seek nipple stimulation from their partners during partnered sex. Functional magnetic resonance imaging (fMRI) research has shown the stimulation of the nipples not only activates the parts of the brain that represent the chest, but also those parts of the brain that indicate arousal in the genital reason (Komisaruk et al., 2011). Thus, there is a clear neurological basis for women's reporting that stimulation of the nipples is sexually arousing. We suspect that stimulation of men's nipples is also connected to the genitals in the male brain, but we have yet to see evidence supporting this suspicion.

Real Students, Real Questions

Q *Are vibrators bad for your health in any way?*

A Could be. Use some common sense. As a rule of thumb, vibrators that penetrate the body are more potentially harmful than vibrators that strap onto the back of the hand (or foot, or whatever). And vibrators that have sharp or pointed edges, even if they're called something apparently harmless, like "ticklers," are more potentially dangerous than those that have smooth edges or those that don't directly touch the body at all. If you're going to use a vibrator, start by seeing how it affects a nongenital area of the body. When you move it to the genital region, apply it gently at first. You may also have a partner use a vibrator to provide you with sexual stimulation, but be very specific and cautious in showing him or her what to do. When in doubt, stop, or at least slow down.

Sex with a Partner

Partners' feelings for one another, and the quality of their relationships, may be stronger determinants of their sexual arousal and response than the techniques they employ (Chivers & Timmers, 2012; Stephenson et al., 2012). Partners are most likely to experience mutually enjoyable sexual interactions when they are sensitive to each other's sexual needs and incorporate techniques with which they are both comfortable. As with other aspects of sharing relationships, communication is the most important "sexual" technique. Let us begin our discussion of sex with others as many sexual episodes begin—with a discussion of foreplay.

Precoital and Noncoital Partnered Sex

LO 7.9 **Discuss purposes and methods of precoital partnered sex.**

Precoital partnered sex is also known as "foreplay." The term *foreplay* sounds a bit old-fashioned. It implies that the kinds of methods that partners use to sexually arouse one another—and themselves, of course—are intended to culminate in intercourse. Not necessarily. Most of the methods we will discuss can lead to orgasm, or in the case of mouth-to-mouth kissing, they can set the stage for orgasm when another technique is applied. In fact, many people prefer one or more of these methods to intercourse, at least some of the time. Females having sex with females, of course, will not be having penile–vaginal intercourse, although they may choose to simulate intercourse manually or with the use of a sex toy.

foreplay

Physical interactions that are sexually stimulating and set the stage for intercourse.

But various forms of noncoital sex, such as cuddling, kissing, petting, and oral–genital contact, are in fact used as **foreplay**. The pattern and duration of foreplay vary widely within and across cultures.

There is a general assumption in the United States and Canada that women in heterosexual relationships want more foreplay than men do, which may be more or less the case. But a side effect of this stereotype is that men often wind up receiving less foreplay than they would actually like (Miller & Byers, 2004). Because women usually require a longer period of stimulation during sex with a partner to reach orgasm, increasing the duration of foreplay may increase female coital responsiveness. On the other hand, men have become more aware of this since Kinsey's day, and women sometimes want men to "get on with it" (Miller & Byers, 2004).

A telephone survey with more than 1,000 French subjects in heterosexual relationships found that simultaneous orgasms and feelings of closeness were highly important for about 36% of the respondents (Colson et al., 2006). Foreplay, by contrast, was mentioned as being crucial by only about 13%, which, of course, begs the question as to whether the couple would reach simultaneous orgasm and closeness without some form of foreplay.

Although, as noted, kissing, genital touching, and oral–genital contact may all be experienced as ends in themselves and not as preludes to coitus, some people object to petting for petting's sake, equating it with masturbation or at least as a form of sexual activity without a "product" or "result." Many people behave as though all sexual contact must lead to coitus, perhaps because of the importance that our culture places on it and because of some people's traditional idea that purely recreational (nonprocreative) sex is of questionable moral value.

Kissing. Romantic kissing is common in the United States, Europe, the Middle East, and Asia. But it is not a universal part of lovemaking.

Kissing

Mid-twentieth century anthropological research found that romantic kissing was unknown in some cultures, such as among the Thonga of Africa and the Siriono of Bolivia. Variations in styles of kissing also exist across cultures (Ford & Beach, 1951). Instead of kissing, the Balinese of Indonesia brought their faces close enough to each other to smell each other's perfume and feel the warmth of each other's skin. This practice has been dubbed "rubbing noses" by Europeans. Researchers have also not found romantic kissing in Central America or New Guinea, or among the native peoples who dwell along the Amazon River. Why, some of these peoples ask, would people want to "share their dinner"?

Anthropologists Willaim Jankowiak and Shelly Volsche (2015) of the University of Nevada did an up-to-date review of cultural practices and found that romantic kissing prevailed in about half the world's cultures. A nation, by the way, can have more than

Real Students, Real Questions

Q *What is tantric sex?*

A Tantric sex is something like foreplay taken to the outer limits, which could lead some to have a tantrum. (Bad pun.) Practitioners of tantric sex point to Eastern philosophies as their points of inspiration. They speak of releasing body energies and auras and herbs and ritual cleansing baths and massages and aromatics and healing and ... did we mention herbs? It's yoga, it's *Kama Sutra*. We'll summarize it like this: We don't know of any scientific or government accrediting agency that trains and supervises tantric sex practitioners. Having said that, it's probably as much fun as an erotic massage in a bubble bath—depending on who's doing what to whom. Light the candles.

one culture. As you can see in Table 7.4, there are some surprises. Romantic kissing was present in all of the 10 cultures studied in the Middle East. Romantic kissing is clearly popular—although by no means universal—in North America, Europe, and Asia, but not so in black African cultures, and Central and South America. Findings are mixed among Pacific Islanders.

Couples may kiss for their own enjoyment or as a prelude to intercourse, in which case it is a part of foreplay. In *simple kissing*, the partners keep their mouths closed. Simple kissing may develop into caresses of the lips with the tongue, or into nibbling of the lower lip. In what Kinsey called *deep kissing*, which is also called *French* or *soul kissing*, the partners part their lips and insert their tongues into each other's mouths. Some prefer the lips parted slightly. Others open their mouths widely.

Kissing may also be an affectionate gesture without erotic significance, as in kissing someone good night. Some people kiss relatives and close friends affectionately on the lips. Others limit kissing relatives to the cheek. Sustained kissing on the lips and deep kissing are almost always erotic gestures.

Kissing is not limited to the partner's mouth. Kinsey found that more than nine husbands in ten kissed their wives' breasts. Women may prefer several minutes of body contact and gentle caresses before desiring to have their partner kiss their breasts, or lick or suck their nipples. Women also usually do not prefer sucking until they are highly aroused. Many women are reluctant to tell their partners that sucking hurts because they do not want to interfere with their partner's pleasure.

Touching

Hugging or holding another person can feel good. Touching or caressing erogenous zones with the hands or other parts of the body can be highly arousing. Even simple handholding can be sexually stimulating for couples who are sexually attracted to one another. The hands are rich in nerve endings.

Touching is a common form of foreplay. Both men and women generally prefer manual or oral stimulation of the genitals as a prelude to intercourse. Women generally prefer that direct caressing of the genitals be focused around the clitoris but not directly on the extremely sensitive clitoral glans. Men sometimes assume (often mistakenly) that their partners want them to insert their finger or fingers into the vagina as a form of foreplay. But not all women enjoy this form of stimulation. Some women go along with it because it's what their partners want or something they think their partners want.

Masters and Johnson (1979) noted sex differences with respect to preferences in foreplay. Men typically prefer direct stroking of their genitals by their partner early in lovemaking. Women, however, tend to prefer that their partners caress their genitals after a period of general body contact that includes holding, hugging, and nongenital massage. This is not a hard and fast (or slow) rule, but it concurs with other observations that men tend to be more genitally oriented than women. Women are more likely to view sex within a broader framework of affection and love.

TECHNIQUES OF MANUAL STIMULATION OF THE GENITALS   Here again, variability in technique is the rule, so partners need to communicate their preferences. The man's partner may use two hands to stimulate his genitals. One may be used to fondle the scrotum, by gently squeezing the skin between the fingers (taking care not to apply pressure to the testes themselves). The other hand may

How Touching? Touching is a common form of foreplay. Most people like manual or oral stimulation of the genital organs as a prelude to sexual intercourse.

circle the coronal ridge and engage in gentle stroking of the penis, followed by more vigorous up and down movements as the man becomes more aroused.

The penis may also be gently rolled back and forth between the palms as if one were making a ball of clay into a sausage—increasing pressure as arousal progresses. Note that men who are highly aroused or who have just had an orgasm may find direct stimulation of the penile glans uncomfortable.

The woman may prefer that her partner approach genital stimulation gradually, following stimulation of other body parts. Genital stimulation may begin with light, stroking motions of the inner thighs and move on to the vaginal lips (labia) and the clitoral area. Women may enjoy pressure against the mons pubis from the heel of the hand, or tactile stimulation of the labia, which are sensitive to stroking motions. Clitoral stimulation can focus on the clitoral shaft or the region surrounding the shaft, rather than the clitoris itself, because of the extreme sensitivity of the clitoral glans to touch.

Moreover, the clitoris should not be stroked if it is dry, lest it become irritated. Because it produces no lubrication of its own, a finger may enter the outer portion of the vagina to apply some vaginal lubrication to the clitoral region.

Some, but not all, women enjoy having a finger inserted into the vagina, which can stroke the vaginal walls or simulate thrusting of the penis. Vaginal insertion is usually not preferred, if at all, until the woman has become highly aroused. Many women desire that their partners discontinue stroking motions while they are experiencing orgasm, but others wish stimulation to continue. Men and women may physically guide their partners' hands or otherwise express their preferences as to the types of strokes they find most pleasurable.

If a finger is to be inserted into the vagina, it should be clean. Fingernails should be well trimmed. Inserting fingers that have been in the anus into the vagina is dangerous. The fingers may transfer microbes from the woman's digestive tract, where they do no harm, to the woman's reproductive tract, where they can cause serious infections.

FISTING Some individuals engage in "fisting," which is the insertion of the fist or hand into the rectum, usually after the bowels have been evacuated with an enema. Fisting is more common among male–male than male–female couples, and it carries the risk of infection or injury to the rectum or anus. A survey of 75 gay men in Australia found that fisting was usually done with gloves, although fingering was not (Richters et al., 2003).

Stimulation of the Breasts

Men are more likely to stimulate women's breasts than to have their own breasts fondled, even though the breasts (and especially the nipples) are erotically sensitive in both females and males. Most, but not all, women enjoy stimulation of the breasts (see Figure 7.11). Masters and Johnson (1966) report that some women are capable of achieving orgasm from stimulation of the breasts alone.

The hands and the mouth can be used to stimulate the breasts and the nipples. Because the desired type and intensity of stimulation of the breasts varies from person to person, partners need to communicate their preferences.

Oral–Genital Stimulation

Oral stimulation of the male genitals is called **fellatio**. Fellatio is referred to by slang terms such as "a blow job," "sucking," "sucking off," and "giving head." Oral stimulation of the female genitals is called **cunnilingus**, which is referred to by slang expressions such as "eating" (a woman) and "going down" on her.

The popularity of oral–genital stimulation has increased dramatically since Kinsey's day, especially among young married couples. Kinsey and his colleagues (1948, 1953) found that at least 60% of married, *college-educated* couples had experienced oral–genital contact. Such experiences were reported by only about 20% of couples who had only a

fellatio

Oral stimulation of the male genitals.

cunnilingus

Oral stimulation of the female genitals.

Figure 7.11 Erotic Touch.
Erotic touch is a pleasurable, intimate behavior by itself and need not necessarily lead to other sexual activities.

high school education and 10% who had only a grade-school education. The more recent National Survey of Sexual Health and Behavior, from the Center for Sexual Health Promotion (2011) founded by Kinsey, shows that within any given recent year, upward of 70% of men and women will have given and received oral sex. The numbers are especially high in the 20s and the 30s, when the sex drive is high and people are sexually experienced.

Among married couples, 80% of the men and 71% of the women have performed oral sex. Similarly, 80% of the men and 74% of the women have received oral sex (Laumann et al., 1994). A more recent study from the Kinsey Institute also speaks to the widespread use of oral sexual stimulation (Table 7.3).

> **6 › T /F Truth or Fiction Revisited** Oral sex is in fact the norm for today's young couples, statistically speaking. A great majority of young couples report participating in this form of sexual expression.

Research suggests that women frequently engage in fellatio as part of what evolutionary psychologists refer to as "mate retention" behaviors (Sela et al., 2015). That is, apart from whatever pleasure women may derive themselves from fellatio, they often perform it to please their partners. It is not surprising, then, that women who are agreeable and conscientious are more likely than other women to engage in the practice (Sela et al., 2015).

As with touching, oral–genital stimulation can be used as a prelude to intercourse or as a sexual end in itself. If orgasm is reached through oral–genital stimulation, a partner may be concerned about tasting or swallowing the ejaculate. There is no evidence that swallowing semen is harmful to one's health unless the man has an infection that

Table 7.3 Percentage of Americans Performing Certain Sexual Behaviors in the Past Year (N = 5865).

Age Groups		Masturbated Alone	Masturbated with Partner	Received Oral from Women	Received Oral from Men	Gave Oral to Women	Gave Oral to Men	Vaginal intercourse	Received Penis in Anus	Inserted Penis into Anus
14–15	Men	62%	5%	12%	1%	8%	1%	9%	1%	3%
	Women	40%	8%	1%	10%	2%	12%	11%	4%	
16–17	Men	75%	16%	31%	3%	18%	2%	30%	1%	6%
	Women	45%	19%	5%	24%	7%	22%	30%	5%	
18–19	Men	81%	42%	54%	6%	51%	4%	53%	4%	6%
	Women	60%	36%	4%	58%	2%	59%	62%	18%	
20–24	Men	83%	44%	63%	6%	55%	7%	63%	5%	11%
	Women	64%	36%	9%	70%	9%	74%	80%	23%	
25–29	Men	84%	49%	77%	5%	74%	5%	86%	4%	27%
	Women	72%	48%	3%	72%	3%	76%	87%	21%	
30–39	Men	80%	45%	78%	6%	69%	5%	85%	3%	24%
	Women	63%	43%	5%	59%	4%	59%	74%	22%	
40–49	Men	76%	38%	62%	6%	57%	7%	74%	4%	21%
	Women	65%	35%	2%	52%	3%	53%	70%	12%	
50–59	Men	72%	28%	49%	8%	44%	8%	58%	5%	11%
	Women	54%	18%	1%	34%	1%	36%	51%	6%	
60–69	Men	61%	17%	38%	3%	34%	3%	54%	6%	6%
	Women	47%	13%	1%	25%	1%	23%	42%	4%	
70+	Men	46%	13%	19%	2%	24%	3%	43%	2%	2%
	Women	33%	5%	2%	8%	2%	7%	22%	1%	

SOURCE: Center for Sexual Health Promotion. (2011). *National Survey of Sexual Health and Behavior (NSSHB)*. Indiana University, Bloomington: School of Health, Physical Education, and Recreation. http://www.nationalsexstudy.indiana.edu/graph.html (Accessed February 22, 2012). Used with permission.

Figure 7.12 Fellatio.

Fellatio involves stimulation of the male penis and surrounding genital area with the mouth, lips, and tongue.

can be transmitted through oral contact with semen. Oral contact with the genitals of an infected partner, even without semen, may transmit harmful organisms. Couples are therefore advised to practice "safer sex" techniques (see Chapter 13) unless they know that they and their partners are free of sexually transmitted infections.

TECHNIQUES OF FELLATIO Although the word *fellatio* is derived from a Latin root meaning "to suck," sucking is generally not highly arousing. The up-and-down movements of the penis in the partner's mouth, or the licking of the penis, are generally the most stimulating (see Figure 7.12). Gentle licking of the scrotum may also be highly arousing.

The mouth stimulates the penis because it contains warm, moist mucous membranes, as does the vagina. Muscles of the mouth and jaw can vary pressure and movements. Erection may be stimulated by gently pulling the penis with the mouth (being careful not to touch the penis with the teeth) and simultaneously providing manual stimulation.

Higher levels of sexual arousal or orgasm can be promoted by thrusting the penis in and out of the mouth. The speed of the motions can be varied, and manual stimulation near the base of the penis (firmly encircling the lower portion of the penis or providing pressure behind the scrotum) can also be stimulating.

TECHNIQUES OF CUNNILINGUS Women can be highly aroused by their partner's tongue because it is soft, warm, and well lubricated (see Figure 7.13). In contrast to a finger, the tongue can almost never be used too harshly. A woman may thus be more receptive to direct clitoral contact by a tongue. Cunnilingus provides such intense stimulation that many women find it to be the best means for achieving orgasm.

In performing cunnilingus, the partner may begin by kissing and licking the woman's abdomen and inner thighs, gradually nearing the vulva. Gentle tugging at or sucking of the labia minora can be stimulating, but the partner should take care not to bite. Many women enjoy licking of the clitoral region, and others desire sucking of the clitoris itself. The tongue may also be inserted into the vagina where it may imitate thrusting.

We should note here that there has been a recent rise in oropharyngeal cancer (cancer of the throat) among men who have engaged in cunnilingus with women who are infected with the human papilloma virus (HPV) (Chaturvedi et al., 2011). In Chapter 2 we noted that HPV is also connected with cancer of the cervix. Researchers also point out, however, that despite the incidence of throat cancer, there are fewer

Figure 7.13 Cunnilingus.

Cunnilingus is the stimulation of the vulva with the mouth, lips, and tongue.

than 10,000 cases per year, and that most people infected with HPV do not develop cancer (Gillison, 2011). Even so, health professionals are wondering whether it would be worthwhile to vaccinate boys with Gardasil or Cervarix, one of the vaccinations used with girls to help prevent development of cervical cancer (Cullen, 2011).

"69" The term *sixty-nine* describes simultaneous oral–genital stimulation. The numerals *6* and *9* are used because they resemble two partners who are upside-down and facing each other.

The "69" position has the psychologically positive feature of allowing couples to experience simultaneous stimulation, but it can be awkward if two people are not similar in size. Some couples avoid "69" because it deprives each partner of the opportunity to focus fully on receiving or providing sexual pleasure.

The "69" technique may be practiced side by side or with one partner on top of the other. There are no strict rules, and couples often alternate positions.

ABSTAINING FROM ORAL SEX Despite the popularity of oral sex among couples today, many people choose to abstain. Some people object on grounds of cleanliness. They view the genitals as "dirty" because of their proximity to the urinary and anal openings. Concerns about offensive odors or cleanliness may be relieved by thoroughly washing the genitals beforehand. Some abstain because they are concerned or embarrassed about providing (or receiving) a direct view of parts of the body we have been reared to keep private.

Some prefer not to taste or swallow semen because they find it to be dirty, sinful, or repulsive. Others are put off by the taste or texture. Semen has a salty taste and a texture similar to the white of an egg. If couples are to engage in unprotected oral sex, open discussion of feelings can enhance pleasure and diminish anxiety. For example, a man can be encouraged to warn his partner or remove his penis from her or his mouth when he is nearing ejaculation.

Sexual Intercourse: Positions and Techniques

LO 7.10 **Describe methods of sexual intercourse.**

Sexual intercourse, or *coitus* (from the Latin *coire*, meaning "to go together"), is sexual activity in which the penis is inserted into the vagina. Each position of sexual intercourse must allow the genitals to be aligned so that the penis is contained by

Table 7.4 Monthly Coital Frequency between Men and Women Aged 25–45 Years

Characteristic		Men	Women
Age	25–29	6.81	6.92
	30–34	6.30	6.17
	35–39	5.11	6.22
	40–45	4.83	6.22
Married	No	5.31	5.46
	Yes	5.81	6.27
Race	European American	5.23	6.39
	African American	5.70	5.74
	Latin American	7.40	7.27
	Asian American	4.05	5.12
Education	Less than high school	6.91	6.72
	High School	5.70	6.70
	More than high school	5.13	5.42
Body Mass Index (BMI)	18 or less	7.00	5.00
	19–24	6.12	6.54
	25–29[1]	5.35	6.59
	30 or above[2]	5.68	6.16
Currently pregnant	No	6.17	6.43
	Yes	4.11	5.05

[1]Overweight

[2]Obese

SOURCE: Adapted from Eisenberg, M., Shindel, A. W., Smith, J. F., Breyer, B. N., and Lipshultz, L. I. (2010). Socioeconomic, anthropomorphic, and demographic predictors of adult sexual activity in the United States: Data from the national survey of family growth. *Journal of Sexual Medicine 7*, 50–58, Tables 1 and 3.

the vagina. In addition to varying positions, couples also vary the depth and rate of thrusting (in-and-out motions) and additional sexual stimulation.

Table 7.4 shows the monthly frequency of sexual intercourse reported by heterosexual men and women aged 25 to 45 (Eisenberg et al., 2010). Overall, younger people within the age group were more likely than older people to engage in sexual intercourse. Married people had a higher monthly frequency than unmarried people. Latin Americans were most likely to report having sex and Asian Americans least likely. People with less education had a higher frequency of coitus (but don't drop out of college!). There was also a relationship between frequency of coitus and body mass index (BMI). People with a BMI above 25 are considered overweight, and those with a BMI over 30 are labeled obese. Men of normal weight were more sexually active than overweight people, but, strangely, obese people had a higher frequency of sexual activity than people in the overweight category. The thinnest women reported the lowest frequency of sexual activity, suggesting, perhaps, that women's efforts to meet the very thin cultural ideal are having a negative effect on their health. Pregnant women had less frequent sex than women who were not pregnant, but notice that pregnant women still had sex on about a weekly basis.

Although the number of possible coital positions is virtually endless, we will focus on four of the most commonly used positions: the male-superior (man-on-top) position, the female-superior (woman-on-top) position, the lateral-entry (side-entry) position, and the rear-entry position. We discuss anal intercourse as well, a sexual technique used by both male–female and male–male couples.

The Male-Superior (Man-on-Top) Position

The male-superior position ("superiority" is used purely in relation to body position, but has sometimes been taken as a symbol of male domination) has also been called the **missionary position**. In this position, the partners face one another. The man lies above the woman, perhaps supporting himself on his hands and knees rather than applying his full weight against his partner (see Figure 7.14). Still, movement is easier for the man than for the woman, which suggests that he is responsible for directing their activity.

Many students of human sexuality suggest that it is preferable for the woman to guide the penis into the vagina, rather than having the man do so. The idea is that the woman can feel the location of the vaginal opening and determine the proper angle of entry. It is easier to accomplish this if the woman feels comfortable "taking charge" of lovemaking. With the breaking down of the traditional stereotype of the female as passive, women are feeling more comfortable assuming this role. On the other hand, if the couple prefers that the man guide his penis into his partner's vagina, the slight loss of efficiency need not trouble them, as long as he moves prudently to avoid hurting his partner.

The male-superior position has the advantage of permitting the couple to face one another so that kissing is easier. The woman may run her hands along her partner's body, stroking his buttocks and perhaps cupping a hand beneath his scrotum to increase his stimulation.

But the male-superior position makes it difficult for the man to caress his partner while simultaneously supporting himself with his hands. So the position may not be favored by women who enjoy having their partners provide manual clitoral stimulation during coitus. This position can be highly stimulating to the man, which can make it difficult for him to delay ejaculation. The position also limits the opportunity for the woman to control the angle, rate, and depth of penetration. It may thus be more difficult for her to attain the type of stimulation she may need to achieve orgasm, especially if she favors combining penile thrusting with manual clitoral stimulation. Finally, this position is not advisable during the late stages of pregnancy. At that time the woman's distended abdomen would force the man to arch severely above her, lest he place undue pressure on her abdomen.

The Female-Superior (Woman-on-Top) Position

In the female-superior position, the couple face one another with the woman on top. The woman straddles the male from above, controlling the angle of penile entry and the depth of thrusting (see Figure 7.15). Some women maintain a sitting position; others lie on top of their partners. Many women vary their position.

In the female-superior position the woman is psychologically, and to some degree physically, in charge. She can move as rapidly or as slowly as she wishes with little effort, adjusting her body so as to vary the angle and depth of penetration. She can reach behind her to stroke her partner's scrotum, or lean down to kiss him.

Figure 7.14   The Male-Superior (Man-on-Top) Coital Position.
The man-on-top position requires somewhat more physical effort on the part of the male; it is the most common position for coitus in Western cultures.

missionary position

The coital position in which the man is on top. Also termed the *male-superior position.*

Figure 7.15 The Female-Superior (Woman-on-Top) Coital Position.

The female-superior position allows the woman more control over angle and depth of penetration and the greater control over the orgasm.

As in the male-superior position, kissing is relatively easy. This position has additional advantages. The man may readily reach the woman's buttocks or clitoris to provide manual stimulation. Assuming that the woman is shorter than he is, it is rather easy for him to stimulate her breasts orally (a pillow tucked behind his head may help). The woman can, in effect, guarantee that she receives adequate clitoral stimulation, either by the penis or manually by his hand or her own. This position thus facilitates orgasm in the woman. Because it tends to be less stimulating for the male, it may help him to control ejaculation. For these reasons, this position is commonly used by couples who are learning to overcome sexual difficulties.

The Lateral-Entry (Side-Entry) Position

In the lateral-entry position, the man and woman lie side by side, facing one another (see Figure 7.16). This position has the advantages of allowing each partner relatively free movement and easy access to the other. The man and woman may kiss freely, and they can stroke each other's bodies with a free arm. The position is not physically taxing, because both partners are resting easily on the bedding. Thus, it is an excellent position for prolonged coitus or for coitus when couples are somewhat fatigued.

Let us note some disadvantages to this position. First, inserting the penis into the vagina while lying side by side may be awkward. Many couples thus begin coitus in another position and then change into the lateral-entry position—often because they wish to prolong coitus. Second, one or both partners may have an arm lying beneath the other that will "fall asleep" or become numb because of the constricted blood supply. Third, women may not receive adequate clitoral stimulation from the penis in this position. Of course, such stimulation may be provided manually (by hand) or by switching to another position after a while. Fourth, it may be difficult to achieve deeper

Figure 7.16 The Lateral-Entry (Side-by-Side) Coital Position.

The side-by-side position requires less physical effort for both partners and allows more freedom of movement for mutual caressing during intercourse.

penetration of the penis. The lateral position is useful during pregnancy (at least until the final stages, when the distension of the woman's abdomen may make lateral entry difficult).

The Rear-Entry Position

In the rear-entry position, the man faces the woman's rear. In one variation (Figure 7.17), the woman supports herself on her hands and knees while the man supports himself on his knees, entering her from behind. In another, the couple lie alongside one another and the woman lifts one leg, draping it backward over her partner's thigh. The latter position is particularly useful during the later stages of pregnancy.

The rear-entry position may be highly stimulating for both partners. The man may enjoy viewing and pressing his abdomen against his partner's buttocks. He man can reach around or underneath to provide additional stimulation of the clitoris or breasts, and she may reach behind (if she is on her hands and knees) to stroke or grasp her partner's testicles.

Potential disadvantages to this position include the following: First, this position is the mating position used by most other mammals, which is why it is sometimes referred to as *doggy style*. Some couples may feel uncomfortable about using the position because of its association with animal mating patterns. The position is also impersonal in the sense that the partners do not face one another, which may create a sense of emotional distance. Because the man is at the woman's back, the couple may feel that he is very much in charge; he can see her, but she cannot readily see him. Physically, the penis does not provide adequate stimulation to the clitoris. The penis also tends to pop out of the vagina from time to time. Finally, air tends to enter the vagina during rear-entry coitus. When it is expelled, it can sound as though the woman has passed air through the anus—a possibly embarrassing though harmless occurrence.

Anal Intercourse

Anal intercourse is insertion of the penis into the rectum. It is practiced by male–female couples and male–male couples. The rectum is richly endowed with nerve endings and highly sensitive to sexual stimulation. Both partners may reach orgasm through anal sex. Anal intercourse is also referred to as "Greek culture," or lovemaking in the "Greek style" because of male bisexuality in ancient Greece. It is also the major act that comes under the legal definition of sodomy.

In anal intercourse, the penetrator can situate himself behind his partner, or lie above or below his partner face to face. The receiving partner can supplement anal stimulation with manual stimulation of the clitoral region or penis to reach orgasm. Because the rectum produces no natural lubrication, couples are advised to use an artificial lubricant, such as K-Y jelly.

People often want their partner's fingers in the anus at the height of passion or at the moment of orgasm. A finger in the rectum can heighten sexual sensation because the anal sphincters contract during orgasm.

Many couples are repulsed by the idea of anal intercourse. They view it as unnatural, immoral, or risky. Others find anal sex to be an enjoyable sexual variation, though perhaps not a regular feature of their sexual diet.

One research team (Reynolds et al., 2015) recruited four female focus groups to investigate why women engaged in anal intercourse and how they responded to it. The study was "qualitative" rather than "quantitative," so we don't have percentages. Some engaged in anal sex because they wanted it, others to please male partners, and

Figure 7.17   Rear-Entry Coital Position.

Some people enjoy the sensations provided by the rear-entry position; it may also be more comfortable for pregnant women.

Critical Thinking
What are the relationships between level of education and sexual practices such as oral sex and anal sex? How do you account for the relationships?

still others in exchange for something else, such as a romantic dinner or cunnilingus. Some women enjoyed anal sex because it felt good or brought the sexual relationship to a special level of intimacy. But other women disliked the experience and found it painful. Some reported rectal bleeding. Still others felt shame and disgust, or were offended by male attempts to find lubrication, such as applying spit to their penises. But even those women who enjoyed anal sex said they preferred vaginal sex.

Now let's consider some numbers. The NHSLS found that one man in four (26%) and one woman in five (20%) reported having engaged in anal sex at some time (Laumann et al., 1994). The more recent National Survey of Sexual Health and Behavior (Center for Sexual Health Promotion, 2011; see Table 7.4) found that some 21% to 27% of people in their 20s and 30s had engaged in anal intercourse in the past year—something of a jump upward. Other surveys report numbers in the same ballpark (e.g., Ompad et al., 2006). As with oral sex, there is a higher incidence of anal sex among more highly educated people. Education appears to be a liberating influence on sexual experimentation.

Religion appears to be a restraint on anal sex. About 34% of the men and 36% of the women in the NHSLS who said they had no religion reported engaging in anal sex at some time. Figures for male Christians ranged from the lower to upper 20s, and for female Christians, from the midteens to the lower 20s (Laumann et al., 1994, p. 99).

Many couples kiss or lick the anus in their foreplay. This practice is called **anilingus**. Oral–anal sex carries a health risk because microorganisms causing intestinal diseases and many sexually transmitted infections (STIs) can be spread through oral–anal contact.

Many couples avoid anal intercourse because of the fear of HIV/AIDS and other STIs. HIV and microorganisms causing STIs such as gonorrhea, syphilis, and hepatitis can be spread by anal intercourse. Cells in the rectum are especially susceptible to infection by some organisms, and small tears in the rectal tissues may allow other microbes to enter the recipient's blood system (see Chapter 13). However, if both partners are infection free, they are at no risk of contracting STIs.

Not all gay males enjoy or practice anal intercourse. Of those who do, most alternate between being the inserter and the insertee. The incidence of anal intercourse—especially without using condoms—among gay males declined as gays became aware of the connection between anal sex and transmission of HIV. However, now that highly active antiretroviral therapy (HAART) is prolonging the lives of many people with HIV/AIDS, some gay males are again forgoing use of condoms in anal intercourse (Pines et al., 2015; Rich et al., 2015). Men report that they prefer to forgo condoms because condoms reduce sexual sensations and emotional connectedness with a partner (Bancroft et al., 2005a; Crosby et al., 2005). Moreover, gays—like heterosexuals—are more likely to forgo condoms with strangers when they are under the influence of alcohol and drugs (Irwin et al., 2006; Rich et al., 2015).

anilingus

Oral stimulation of the anus. Slang: *rimming, rim job.*

Sexual Fantasies

LO 7.11 Discuss kinds and uses of sexual fantasies.

People may use sexual fantasies either when they are alone or to heighten sexual excitement with a partner. Some couples find it sexually arousing to share fantasies or to enact them. Sexual fantasies may also be experienced without sexual behavior, as in erotic dreams or daydreams. Masturbators often require some form of cognitive stimulation, such as fantasy or viewing erotica, to reach orgasm.

There are many theories about sexual fantasies. One view that apparently has little, if any, research evidence behind it is that people who fantasize about sex are less likely to have enjoyable sex lives. That is, the fantasy takes the place of life. But fantasies can also enhance sexual arousal, providing greater pleasure.

Real Students, Real Questions

Q *If you have anal sex, is there any way that the sperm can get to the egg once they are inside?*

A No and yes. When the penis is withdrawn from the anus, there will be some sperm at the tip. Or there will be sperm all along the shaft if thrusting continues after ejaculation. Some of the sperm may find their way along the outside of the woman's body to the vaginal opening, and from there, into the vagina. So the "no" refers to the fact that there's no direct internal passage between the rectum and the vagina. The "yes" refers to the off chance that fertilization could occur through a much more indirect route. Highly improbable, but not impossible.

7 › T /F Truth or Fiction Revisited   Research suggests that sexual fantasies are normal. Most people have them—even during sex with another person. Fantasies heighten their sexual arousal during activity with their partners (Dawson et al., 2012). Males seem to engage in sexual fantasies more often than females, but most females do so also—at least within our American culture.

A survey of 349 university students and employees, aged 18 to 70, who were involved in heterosexual relationships found that the great majority—98% of the men and 80% of the women—reported sexual fantasies about someone *other* than their sex partner (Hicks & Leitenberg, 2001). These fantasies were more common among people who had been in their relationships longer, perhaps providing sexual novelty. Women were more likely than men to fantasize about *prior* sex partners, suggesting, perhaps, that they had less need to mentally stray from familiar relationships. According to a *New York Times* poll, men are somewhat more likely than women—52% versus 40%—to think it is acceptable to fantasize about sex with someone other than their partner (Eggers, 2000).

Evolutionary theorists conjecture that women are relatively more likely to fantasize about the images of familiar lovers because female reproductive success in ancestral times was more likely to depend on a protective relationship with a reliable partner (Buss, 2009b; Schmitt, 2014). Women can bear and rear relatively few offspring. Thus, they would have a relatively greater genetic investment in each reproductive opportunity.

In keeping with gender-role stereotypes, studies also find that males are more likely to fantasize about forcing women into sexual activity. Women are more likely to fantasize about being victimized (Critelli & Bivona, 2008; Dawson et al., 2012). Women are also more likely than men to fantasize that they are sexually desirable in their partner's eyes (Bogaert et al., 2015)

Research also shows that women are more likely to report that they have more frequent and arousing sexual fantasies at time of ovulation (Dawson et al., 2012). In this study, heterosexual women kept diaries in which they recorded their fantasies, and ovulation was assessed by means of self-administered urine tests. The number of males in their fantasies increases during ovulation, but not the number of females. Fantasies

It is normal to use sexual fantasies while masturbating or even while having sex with a partner.

during ovulation are also more likely to emphasize sex within a relationship rather than explicit sexual content.

Researchers, by the way, use the frequency and variety of sexual fantasies as one measure of the sex drive (T. D. Fisher et al., 2012). The sex drive—and the frequency of sexual fantasizing—is related to testosterone levels in both males and females. One study surveyed the frequency of sexual activity and sexual fantasies among women who had had their ovaries and uteruses surgically removed (Shifren et al., 2000). The women were then administered various doses of testosterone or a placebo via skin patches. Women given higher doses of testosterone doubled or tripled their reported incidence of sexual fantasies, masturbation, and sexual intercourse.

There are also "deviant" sexual fantasies, such as sadistic rape fantasies. Research evidence with personality tests suggests that men with frequent deviant sexual fantasies are more likely to be socially isolated and emotionally unstable (Bartels & Gannon, 2011; Maniglio, 2011). Yet, the extent to which deviant sexual fantasies contribute to crimes involving sex and aggression remained clouded. Nevertheless, many helping professionals work with men who have deviant sexual fantasies in the hope that by changing their fantasies the men will be less likely to commit crimes of violence (Schmidt et al., 2012). And when it comes to fantasies about being victimized, Nancy Friday (2008) reports the following from a woman she interviewed:

> My fantasies are so personal, and the pleasure I get from them derives so much, I think, from the fact that they are private and locked away in my imagination, that I wouldn't dream of trying to make them come true.... But act my fantasies out? Make them come true? No, absolutely not. My real life's not what they're about; I don't want those things to really happen to me, I simply want to imagine what it would be like. So that's where they'll stay.

As with masturbation, mental excursions into fantasy during coitus may be used to enhance sexual arousal and response (Murray & Milhausen, 2012). Fantasies enable couples to inject sexual variety into their sexual activity without being unfaithful. Researchers find that most married people have coital fantasies (Bader, 2003; Murray & Milhausen, 2012). A survey of a sample of 178 students, faculty, and staff members at a college in Vermont found that 84% reported fantasizing at least occasionally during intercourse (Cado & Leitenberg, 1990).

8 › T /F Truth or Fiction Revisited There does not appear to be any connection between sexual dissatisfaction with one's relationship and the use of sexual fantasies during sexual activity with a partner (Davidson & Hoffman, 1986). Thus, coital fantasies are not a form of compensation for an unrewarding sexual relationship.

Coital fantasies, like masturbation fantasies, run a gamut of themes. They include making love to another partner, group sex, orgies, images of past lovers or special erotic experiences, and making love in fantastic and wonderful places, among others. Heterosexual men are likely to fantasize about women, and gay men are more likely to fantasize about men (Chivers et al., 2004). Heterosexual women and lesbians are more flexible in their selection of the gender of the objects of their fantasies (Chivers et al., 2004; Chivers & Timmers, 2012).

Partners may be reluctant to share their fantasies, or even to admit to them, especially when the fantasy includes people other than the partner. The fantasizer might fear being accused of disloyalty or that the partner will interpret fantasies as a sign of rejection: "What's the matter? Don't I turn you on anymore?"

Chapter Review

LO 7.1 Describe the sexual response cycle, according to Masters and Johnson.

Masters and Johnson found that the physiological responses of men and women to sexual stimulation are similar, including vasocongestion and myotonia. Sexual excitement is characterized by erection in the male and vaginal lubrication in the female. The plateau phase is an advanced state of arousal that precedes orgasm. The third phase of the sexual response cycle is characterized by orgasmic contractions of the pelvic musculature. During the resolution phase, the body returns to its prearoused state.

LO 7.2 Discuss other views of sexual response.

Kaplan developed a three-stage model of sexual response consisting of desire, excitement, and orgasm.

LO 7.3 Discuss controversies about orgasm.

Multiple orgasm is the occurrence of one or more additional orgasms following the first, within a short period of time and before the body has returned to a preplateau level of arousal. Freud theorized two types of female orgasm: clitoral and vaginal. Masters and Johnson found only one kind of orgasm among women. Anatomical research appears to confirm the central role of the clitoris in female orgasm.

LO 7.4 Discuss the effects of drugs on sexual response.

Alleged aphrodisiacs such as Spanish fly and foods that resemble the genitals have not been shown to contribute to sexual arousal. Viagra, Cialis, and Levitra facilitate erection in the male but do not directly influence sexual arousal. Addyi (flibanserin) appears to enhance sexual desire in women, but the premise that hypoactive sexual desire is a "mental disorder" is controversial, to say the least. The male sex hormone testosterone heightens the sex drive in both males and females. Anaphrodisiacs include amyl nitrate. Alcohol may stimulate and then depress sexual response. Some effects of alcohol and cocaine may reflect our expectations or their effects on sexual inhibitions, rather than direct stimulation of sexual response. Some people report initial increased sexual pleasure with cocaine use, but frequent use can lead to sexual dysfunctions.

LO 7.5 Describe the role of the brain in sexual response.

The cerebral cortex interprets sensory information as sexual turn-ons or turn-offs. It transmits messages through the spinal cord that cause vasocongestion. Stimulation of parts of the limbic system causes sexual arousal and sensations similar to those of orgasm.

LO 7.6 Discuss the organizing and activating influences of sex hormones.

Sex hormones have organizing and activating effects. Men and women normally produce one genuine aphrodisiac: testosterone.

LO 7.7 Discuss attitudes toward masturbation.

Masturbation is self-stimulation of the genitals for purposes such as relieving sexual tension and obtaining sexual pleasure. Within the Judeo-Christian tradition, masturbation has been condemned as sinful, as have been many other nonprocreative sexual acts. Masturbation itself is rarely if ever physically harmful, although people whose values oppose masturbation may experience guilt and anxiety if they masturbate. Surveys indicate that most people have masturbated. Males are more likely than females to masturbate.

LO 7.8 Describe ways in which people masturbate.

Males tend to masturbate by using a manual milking motion. Females tend to stroke the mons and the area around the clitoral shaft. Males and females may both use vibrators or other sex toys. Females do not necessarily insert vibrators or other sex toys into the vagina.

LO 7.9 Discuss purposes and methods of precoital and noncoital partnered sex.

Precoital and noncoital sexual activities include romantic kissing, touching, and other activities that heighten sexual arousal and either result in orgasm or set the stage for intercourse. Women have traditionally desired longer periods of foreplay than men do. Most, but not all, women enjoy stimulation of the breasts by the hands and mouth. The majority of young couples use oral–genital stimulation. Kissing, licking, or sucking the male genitals is called fellatio. Kissing or licking or sucking the female genitals is called cunnilingus.

LO 7.10 Describe various methods of sexual intercourse.

Four of the most commonly used coital positions are the male-superior position, the female-superior position, the lateral-entry position, and the rear-entry position. The female-superior position allows the female to better obtain the stimulation needed to reach orgasm. Anal intercourse may be carried out in male–female and male–male sex. Artificial lubrication facilitates anal intercourse.

LO 7.11　Discuss kinds and uses of sexual fantasies.

Sexual fantasies are often incorporated with masturbation or with partnered sex to heighten sexual response. Sexual fantasies range from the realistic to flights of fancy. Many people fantasize about sexual activities that they would not actually engage in. Sexual fantasies can also heighten sexual excitement during coitus. Sexual fantasies are normal in that most people have them and that they are not signs of psychological disorders or troubled relationships.

Test Your Learning

1. Alcohol is known to have _____
   (a) depressing effects only.
   (b) stimulating effects only.
   (c) both stimulating and depressing effects.
   (d) neither stimulating nor depressing effects.

2. When the rear part of a male rat's _____ is stimulated by electricity, the animal runs through its sexual routine mechanically.
   (a) thalamus
   (b) hypothalamus
   (c) occipital lobe
   (d) larynx

3. According to Masters and Johnson, sexual arousal is characterized by vasocongestion and _____
   (a) myotonia.
   (b) blurry vision.
   (c) cramping.
   (d) constriction of blood vessels.

4. The hormone _____ activates the sex drives of both men and women.
   (a) prolactin
   (b) oxytocin
   (c) progesterone
   (d) testosterone

5. Foods such as oysters and bananas have been considered aphrodisiacs because they _____
   (a) are chemically similar to compounds secreted by the male genitals.
   (b) are enjoyed by women.
   (c) are popular among the upper classes.
   (d) resemble the male genitals.

6. Which of the following is connected with cancer of the throat?
   (a) Human papilloma virus
   (b) Bacterial vaginosis
   (c) Hepatitis
   (d) Herpes

7. According to the NHSLS, the most common reason for masturbating is to _____
   (a) relax.
   (b) get to sleep.
   (c) relieve sexual tension.
   (d) obtain physical pleasure.

8. A woman is most likely to reach orgasm in the _____ coital position.
   (a) male-superior
   (b) female-superior
   (c) lateral-entry
   (d) rear-entry

9. Couples are least likely to report engaging in _____
   (a) fellatio.
   (b) cunnilingus.
   (c) penile–vaginal intercourse.
   (d) anal intercourse.

10. According to Kinsey, women who masturbated during adolescence _____
   (a) grew hair in the palms of their hands.
   (b) had difficulty forming social relationships in adulthood.
   (c) were more likely to find sexual gratification with others in adulthood.
   (d) were less likely to find sexual gratification with others in adulthood.

Answers: 1. c; 2. b; 3. a; 4. d; 5. d; 6. a; 7. d; 8. b; 9. d; 10. c.

Chapter 8
Relationships and Communication

 ## Learning Objectives

Beginning Relationships

LO 8.1 Explain ways in which couples meet, including the role of dating apps.

LO 8.2 Describe "hookup culture," its pleasures, and pitfalls.

Jealousy: Is the World a Real-Life *Temptation Island*?

LO 8.3 Discuss the effects of jealousy on a relationship.

Loneliness

LO 8.4 Discuss the causes and effects of loneliness.

Sexual Communication

LO 8.5 Describe methods of sexual communication.

TRUTH OR FICTION?

Which of the following statements are the truth, and which are fiction? Look for the Truth-or Fiction items throughout this chapter to find the answers.

1 Couples who meet in the "real" world are more likely to report being satisfied with one another and less likely to break up than couples who meet online. **T / F**?

2 People can have intimate relationships without being sexually intimate. **T / F**?

3 Many people remain lonely because they fear being rejected by others. **T / F**?

4 Conflict is destructive to a relationship. **T / F**?

5 "Love is all you need." That is, when partners truly love one another, they instinctively know how to satisfy each other sexually. **T / F**?

6 Retaliation is the best course of action when you are criticized. **T / F**?

7 Relationships come to an end when the partners cannot resolve their differences. **T / F**?

In the film *Friends with Benefits*, Jamie (played by Mila Kunis) and Dylan (played by Justin Timberlake) develop a friendship after Jamie recruits Dylan for a job in New York City. They are attracted to one another but neither one desires to develop a serious romantic relationship. One evening they are watching television and start to talk about sex and relationships. One thing leads to another, as the saying goes, and they decide to have sex—a physical connection—but without deep feelings or commitment.

The movie is a romantic comedy, so it runs through the requisite complications. Jamie and Dylan undergo changes. Jamie decides she is no longer interested in sex without anything deeper, so she breaks things off. She enters into a relationship with a new man, Parker (played by Bryan Greenberg), looking for romance, but Parker ends that relationship, informing her that he isn't seeking anything deeper. Because this is a romantic comedy, it is almost mandatory that it have a happy ending. In this case, Jamie and Dylan go on their first "real date"—heading apparently toward love and marriage, which, according to the song, "go together like the horse and carriage."

Friends with benefits has entered the contemporary social and sexual lexicon as one of the kinds of relationships (or non-relationships) that people in our society are

friends with benefits

A noncommitted, "casual" sexual relationship in which a couple also does nonsexual things together

Mila Kunis and Justin Timberlake in the film *Friends with Benefits*.
"Friends with benefits" have an ongoing sexual relationship and also "hang out" together, but it is understood that the relationship is not headed toward a long-term commitment.

having today. In this kind of relationship, a couple has an ongoing sexual relationship but also does nonsexual things together (Jonason et al., 2015). It is understood that if either wishes to begin a serious romantic relationship with someone else, this relationship will come to an end. Peter Jonason and his colleagues (2015) refer to friends with benefits as one kind of casual sexual relationship. They discuss two others: one-night stands and booty-call relationships. One-night stands refer to situations in which people meet and have sex one time. A one-night stand may also be referred to as a **hookup**. In the Jonason group's parlance, a **booty-call relationship** is physical only. It differs from hookup in that the couple may have sex repeatedly. It is less than a friends-with-benefits relationship in that all they do is have sex. In contrast to the casual sexual relationship is the **serious romantic relationship**, in which people have sex in the context of monogamy, high levels of commitment, and the possibility of marriage.

Men are more eager than women to engage in the three kinds of casual sexual relationships (Jonason et al., 2015), and we will ponder the reasons for this difference later in the chapter. In the film *Friends with Benefits*, Jamie was interested in a serious romantic relationship with Parker, but Parker was thinking more along with lines of friends with benefits. Jamie's relationship with Dylan began as a friends-with-benefits relationship but was "morphing" into a serious romantic relationship as the film drew to a close.

In a booty-call relationship, one person calls the other when he or she is in the mood for sex. The image aroused is of the call taking place in the night. The term is of interest. Booty Call was the name of a 1997 comedy, and the term *booty* may be used more widely in Hip-Hop culture. The word *booty* literally refers to a haul or to loot gotten illicitly, yet it also refers to the back storage area of a car, or trunk, and hence the buttocks, especially a woman's posterior. The booty call has been seen as a compromise between male and female ideal mating strategies. For men, it makes sex available without a significant investment. It may afford women the opportunity to test a variety of mates (Jonason et al., 2009a). But as a casual sexual relationship, the booty call is more desirable to men.

In this chapter we see how individuals meet and have casual sexual encounters or form serious romantic relationships. We find that Internet apps have their pluses and minuses and are playing larger roles than ever. We define intimacy and see that not all relationships—not even all long-term, committed relationships—achieve this level of interrelatedness. Moreover, some of us remain alone, and, perhaps, lonely. Finally, we see how couples can use communication to enhance their sexual relationships.

Beginning Relationships

LO 8.1 Explain ways in which couples meet, including the role of dating apps.

Many couples meet each other by being in the same place at the same time—at school, at work, at church, in the neighborhood. Many meet by chance. Others are brought together by third parties, such as family or friends. There were times and places, of course, when marriages were arranged by families.

In the United States, in the remote year of 1940, 24% of heterosexual romantic couples in the united states met through family, 21% through friends, 21% through school, 13% through neighbors, 13% through church, 12% at a bar or restaurant, and 10% through co-workers (Ansari & Klinenberg, 2015). (The number exceeds 100% because some categories overlapped.)

By the early 2000s, 22% of straight couples were meeting online. However, nearly 70% of same-sex couples were meeting online (Rosenfeld & Thomas, 2012). Why? Are gay males and lesbians more likely to have computers and smartphones? Any discrepancy in the availability of electronic equipment cannot explain this vast discrepancy. One reason might be that there are fewer gays and lesbians than straight people, so there is relatively less opportunity to meet them in one's usual daily activities. Another reason could be the large number of online services that exist to connect gays and lesbians. Can you think of other reasons?

hookup

A brief, possibly spontaneous casual sexual encounter

booty-call relationship

A relationship characterized by repeated sexual episodes without commitment of deep emotional feeling

serious romantic relationship

A relationship characterized by high commitment, sexual exclusivity, and the possibility of marriage

Figure 8.1 Snapshot, USA: Where Married Couples Met.

SOURCE: Cacioppo, J. T., et al. (2013). Marital satisfaction and break-ups differ across on-line and off-line meeting venues. *Proceedings of the National Academy of Sciences, 110*(25), 10135–10140, p. 10136.

Meeting Venue

A

Offline Meeting Site

B

Social psychologist John Cacioppo and his colleagues (2013) recently surveyed a nationally representative sample of more than 19,000 Americans to learn how they met their spouses and how the method of meeting might have affected their marital satisfaction. Part A of Figure 8.1 shows that more than one in three couples (35%) met online and the remaining couples (65%) met offline—that is, in the "real" world. Part B reveals that the greatest number of those who met offline met at work (22%) or through a friend (19%). Meeting at school played less of a role (11%), in part because people are settling down later than they did in the last century, and also because of greater mobility—that is, people are less likely to remain in the neighborhood of their secondary schools or institutions of higher education. But of course meeting online takes a large chunk out of it as well!

Of couples who met online, nearly half (45%) used a dating Web site. The two most popular Web sites were eHarmony and Match.com, each accounting for about one-quarter of marriages. Do the math and you will see that about 4% of recently married couples met on eHarmony and another 4% met on Match.com!

And here is what may be a surprising finding by the Cacioppo group: Couples who met online were slightly *more* likely to report satisfaction with their partners and slightly *less* likely to undergo separations or divorce. Why? One possibility is that the matching algorithms used by dating Web sites may actually be at least somewhat effective in helping individuals find compatible partners. But another possibility is what social scientists refer to as the selection factor. That is, people who use dating Web sites are not the same as people who do not. For one thing, they are actively looking for a partner; finding a partner may therefore be more important to them, relatively speaking, than if they had bumped into someone in their building's elevator. At least they may be putting more thought into it. In the case of finally meeting someone with whom a person has shared a great deal of e-mail, the couple already know quite a bit about one another—things that run more deeply than superficial attraction, such as likes and dislikes, histories, even the way in which they each phrase sentences to express ideas.

1 › T / F Truth or Fiction Revisited Actually, couples who meet online are somewhat more likely to be satisfied with their partners and less likely to undergo separations or divorce than couples who meet in the "real world"—for example, at work, through a friend, or at school. Could this be because they have been working harder at trying to meet someone? Or perhaps because people who can use Web sites are somewhat more sophisticated than those who cannot? What do you think?

Northwestern University researcher Eli Finkel and his colleagues (2012) note that online dating sites offer users three things:

1. They provide access to other people who are also seeking potential dating partners—people they would be unlikely to meet in their everyday lives.
2. They facilitate communication between potential partners, enabling them to explore each other online before they have a face-to-face meeting.
3. They make some attempt to match potential partners according to demographic variables such as (desired) race, religion, and age; and according to personality traits. Potential partners thereby obtain a great deal of factual information about potential partners before meeting them

Yet the investigators note certain pitfalls related to these services. First, three-dimensional flesh-and-blood people tend to be reduced to a photograph and a pack of statistics, eliminating the subtle factors of interaction that often allow people to judge whether those they meet could be potential partners (Ankee & Yazdanifard, 2015). Moreover, the sheer number of people displayed to the user of the service makes it necessary to eliminate people who might have worked out just fine if they had met offline. Online meetings provide opportunities for extended communication before offline meetings. While such communication allows people to probe beneath the surface, it may also display too much too soon. Overly rapid self-disclosure can "turn other people off" (Park et al., 2011).

There is also reason to believe that when sites do not have enough respondents, they "stretch" the limits of the variables that are supposed to match. That is, if you're looking for someone who is at least 6'2" tall, but the Web site has hardly anyone who reaches even 6', you may wind up with "matches" who are 5'7" tall (Finkel et al, 2012).

Online dating has revolutionized the ways in which couples seek partners and start relationships. Using the power of the Internet has enabled many people who lack other significant means for finding potential partners to explore the universe of possibly compatible individuals who are also seeking partners. It even offers shy people a safer way to initiate a relationship; people who might be somewhat tongue-tied in person may find it easier to type messages at a keyboard. Knowing in advance that there are certain common backgrounds and common interests can give an individual a running start in developing a relationship if and when a couple does choose to meet in person. On the other hand, online dating sites remove the advantage of being able to "play it cool" because registering on the site means that one is looking for a partner. That disadvantage might be a small price to pay for those who desire relatively safe awareness of and access to the "universe" of potential partners.

> ### Critical Thinking
> Thirty-five percent of people who get married in the United States are now meeting online. Nearly 60% of the U.S. population now sees nothing wrong with premarital sex among adults. In Chapter 11 you will see that about 8 million U.S. couples are living together (cohabiting) without being married. Do all these changes in courtship and "dating" challenge your own beliefs? If so, how? Do you see the rapidly changing lifestyles of Americans as something good or something bad? (Or as in between?) Explain your answers.

Hooking Up

LO 8.2 Describe "hookup culture," its pleasures, and pitfalls.

Justin Garcia of the Kinsey Institute and his colleagues (2012, 2015) note that people in the United States are living in unprecedented times. Americans are delaying marriage to attend school, establish careers, and often, to experiment in the search for Ms. or Mr. Right. On the other hand, puberty is coming earlier. There is therefore a prolonged period of time during which individuals are sexually motivated—or ready to be sexually motivated—but there is no traditional sexual outlet. Nor are enduring romantic relationships always available, or desirable. As a result, more and more people, especially late adolescents, emerging adults, and young adults are turning to casual sex or hooking up. That is, they have brief sexual encounters with no particular emotional attachment, no sense that they are initiating a relationship, and no commitment.

Garcia and his colleagues (2012, 2015) trace hooking up culture to the 1920s, when couples began going out in cars and to movie theaters. Other might point to the 1960s, when the sexual revolution swept the land. The sexual revolution was part of a broader rebelliousness that also involved protests against the Vietnam War and the Civil Rights and feminist movements, and coed college dormitories. The "pill" divorced sex from the repercussions of unwanted pregnancy, if not from the perils of sexually transmitted infections. In the 2000s, premarital sex and hooking up among

Figure 8.2 Percentage of the U.S. Population Agreeing That Premarital Sex Among Adults Is "Not Wrong at All."

SOURCE OF DATA: Twenge, J. M., Sherman, R. A., & Wells, B. E. (2015). Changes in American adults' sexual behavior and attitudes, 1972–2012. *Archives of Sexual Behavior*, DOI: 10.1007/s10508-015-0540-2.

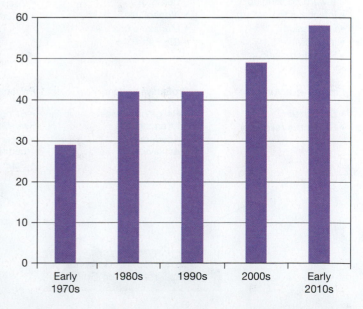

gay males and lesbians became staples in the media, as in the TV series *Queer as Folk, The L-Word, Sex and the City,* and *Girls* depicted the "demure" sex as being as capable of initiating sexual activity as the male (Taylor, 2013).

The cultural shift is reflected in public attitudes toward hooking up. As shown in Figure 8.2, back in the 1970s, in the early days of the sexual revolution, 29% of a sample of the U.S. population said that premarital sex among adults was "not wrong at all" (Twenge et al., 2015). Over the years, the percentage of the population who say that premarital sex among adults is not wrong has grown. The most recent General Social Survey, which questions a nationally representative sample of 33,380 U.S. adults, found that 58% now agree that premarital sex among adults is "not wrong at all." The number of sex partners has also increased throughout the years.

FACTORS IN HOOKING UP The incidence of hooking up has increased, and the public is generally more tolerant of it. But that doesn't mean that everyone hooks up, and among those who do, the frequency of hooking up also differs (Lyons et al., 2015). A research team at Syracuse University (Fielder et al, 2013) studied the literature on sexual hookups among first-year female college students and found a number of factors that contributed to the probability that a college woman would engage in a sexual hookup on a given occasion. As shown in Figure 8.3, they were able to group the contributors into three main factors: the women's personalities ("Personality System"), their patterns of behavior ("Behavior System"), and the situational variables in play ("Perceived Environment System"). Each of these systems contained a number of *Risk factors*—that is, factors that increased the probability of a hookup—and a number of *protective factors*—or factors that decreased the likelihood of a hookup.

Studies generally support the accuracy of the listed factors. Of these factors, the use of alcohol on the occasion sharply increases the likelihood of hooking up, partly because alcohol clouds perceptions and decreases the accessibility of one's values (Claxton et al., 2015). We may also note that drinking alcohol gives one a social role to play—aggressiveness in males and sexual availability in females. In Chapter 15 we will see that drinking also plays an important role in rape.

Viewing pornography also plays a role (Braithewaite et al., 2015a). Use of the Internet has exploded the availability and viewing of pornography. Pornography appears to enhance the likelihood of hooking up in many ways. Viewing pornography can be sexually arousing both for males and females, although females show less interest in it. Pornography also suggests various things that people engaged in sexual acts can do. Beyond these types of things, pornography usually shows uncommitted sex among youngish strangers, or at least among people whose relationships—if there are any—are unclear.

Figure 8.3 Prediction of Sexual Hookups by First-Year College Women: Risk Factors and Protective Factors.

Why do you think the authors label certain factors as "risk factors" and others as "protective factors"? Do you agree with the labeling?

SOURCE: Fielder, R. L., Walsh, J. L., Carey, K. B., & Carey, M. P. (2013). Predictors of sexual hookups: A theory-based, prospective study of first-year college women. *Archives of Sexual Behavior, 42,* 1425–1441, p. 1427; permission conveyed through Copyright Clearance Center, Inc.

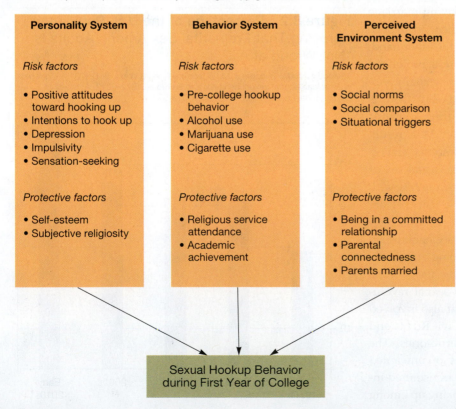

Personality System	**Behavior System**	**Perceived Environment System**
Risk factors	*Risk factors*	*Risk factors*
• Positive attitudes toward hooking up • Intentions to hook up • Depression • Impulsivity • Sensation-seeking	• Pre-college hookup behavior • Alcohol use • Marijuana use • Cigarette use	• Social norms • Social comparison • Situational triggers
Protective factors	*Protective factors*	*Protective factors*
• Self-esteem • Subjective religiosity	• Religious service attendance • Academic achievement	• Being in a committed relationship • Parental connectedness • Parents married

Sexual Hookup Behavior during First Year of College

(Portraying middle-aged or older married couples engaged in loving sex is, to say the least, a niche market.) Therefore, pornography that depicts consenting sex tends to embrace the message that sex is there to be enjoyed, so why not participate?

We spoke of risk factors and protective factors regarding the likelihood of hooking up. Why "risk factors" as opposed to something like "pro-hooking-up factors"? After all, there can be benefits to hooking up, such as sexual enjoyment, feeling attractive and empowered, and feeling close to another person, even if briefly (Fielder et al., 2013; Snapp et al., 2015). In fact, one recent study of 879 U.S. college students who had engaged in hooking up found that the reactions of 62% of the sample were positive, as compared with 38% who reported negative reactions (Strokoff et al., 2015). Those with a positive reaction reported hope that the hookup might lead to a deeper relationship or that their expectations (that it was just a brief sexual encounter) had been realistic. Those who had a negative reaction were likely to report that they felt used, confused, and disappointed. But even in this study showing that a majority of students who had hooked up had positive feeligs about the experience also revealed that about one-third of participants did not.

Many people who engage in casual sex or hookups have regrets or problems of one kind or another. Given the ways in which their evolutionary histories have led to (somewhat) different mating strategies for males and females, it is not surprising that women, overall, are more likely than men to have regrets (Galperin et al., 2013; Townsend et al., 2015). Studies of college students find that for many students casual sex is related to psychological distress, such as feelings of depression (Bersamin et al., 2014). A study of 483 first-year college women found that half reported hookup sex during the year and 62% reported romantic sexual relationships (Fielder et al., 2014). Hookup sex increased the likelihood that the women would encounter feelings of depression and sexually transmitted infections. One reason for the infections is that the partners are less likely to use condoms during impulsive hookups than within romantic relationships. But these results were not universal.

intimacy
Feelings of closeness and connectedness that are marked by sharing of innermost thoughts and feelings.

Developing Intimacy: Sharing Innermost Thoughts and Feelings

Intimacy consists of feelings of emotional connectedness with another person and the desire to share innermost thoughts and feelings (Burke & Young, 2012). Partners in the throes of romantic love usually want to disclose everything to, and know everything about, one another (Kito, 2005; Vaculík & Hudecek, 2005). Along with sex, intimacy is one of the key ingredients in passionate relationships (Burke & Young, 2012). Feelings of intimacy and affection tend to grow as romantic relationships develop (Perlman & Sprecher, 2012; Rubin & Campbell, 2012). Relationships also develop from being more casual and superficial to being relatively committed. As couples age, intimacy becomes one of the most valued—if not the most valued—components of the relationship (Villar et al., 2005). Intimate relationships are also characterized by trust, caring, and acceptance.

Sternberg's (2007) triangular theory of love regards intimacy as a basic component of romantic love, but people can be intimate and not in love, at least not in romantic love. Close friends and family members become emotionally intimate when they care deeply for each other and share their feelings and experiences.

Intimate relationships are characterized by trust, caring, and acceptance.

2 › T / F Truth or Fiction Revisited   It is true that people need not be *sexually* intimate to be emotionally intimate. Nor does sexual intimacy automatically create emotional intimacy. Often, people who are sexually involved may not achieve emotional closeness. They can be more emotionally intimate with friends than with lovers.

SEX IN THE DIGITAL AGE

SWIPING RIGHT TO HOOK UP: ARE WE HEADING TOWARD A DATING APOCALYPSE?

CNN commentator Mel Robbins (2015) asks the question, "Has Tinder replaced dating with hookup culture?" She is referring to an article in *Vanity Fair,* which referred to a "dating apocalypse," in which in an evening at a Manhattan sports bar, all the twenty somethings are drinking, focusing on their screens, and swiping left or right, looking for people with whom they might hook up later on. Nascent investments bankers from the Ivy League are making dates, sometimes two or three, because, you never know, something better might come along from the endless supply of what the guys call "Tinderellas."

"Guys view everything as a competition," one of them named Alex says. "Who's slept with the best, hottest girls?" With dating apps, "you're always sort of prowling. You could talk to two or three girls at a bar and pick the best one, or you can swipe a couple hundred people a day—the sample size is so much larger. It's setting up two or three Tinder dates a week and, chances are, sleeping with all of them, so you could rack up 100 girls you've slept with in a year" (Sales, 2015). Alex is a Tinder King, meaning that he can lure a woman into bed with him on the basis of a few texts, even though he alerts them that he is not seeking a relationship.

All the literature shows, of course, that women, relatively speaking, are more interested in having sex within relationships than men are (Gorelik & Shackelford, 2014; Kennair et al., 2015). As reported by Leif Kennair and his colleagues (2015), based on research with 1,372 college students, men are relatively more interested than women in short-term goals for having sex, such as experiencing pleasure, enjoying the physical desirability of their partners, reducing stress, and boosting their self-esteem and social status. Women are relatively more interested than men in the long-term strategies of finding love and commitment, and of expressing their feelings through sex.

If Tinder-type dating "sucks for women," as Robbins puts it, it's because they allow themselves to enter the world of hooking up online. Of course some women enjoy multiple hookups, but by and large it's a man's pursuit. The mating strategies of men and women do not necessarily coincide. As theorized by evolutionary psychologists, many men try to rack up as many conquests as they can—attempting, subconsciously perhaps, to sire as many offspring as possible. Women, of course, can carry only a relative few children to term, and their mating strategies, therefore, entice many or most women to try to hold on to

at least some of them men with whom they have sex. Put it this way, many men who use Tinder are just prowling and looking for a good time. Women are usually fooling themselves if they think that they are auditioning for long-term relationships.

Groucho Marx once quipped that he wouldn't want to belong to a club that would take members like him. Men who meet women via apps like Tinder often seem to function as if they're thinking, "Why would I want to have a relationship with someone who would hook up with me so readily?"

Having noted these issues with Tinder and like-minded apps, Finkel (2015) rises to the defense of Tinder. He acknowledges that the "old" or standard way to find an enduring relationship online is to use an app like Match.com or eHarmony, which use elaborate algorithms to examine your profile and the profiles of potential partners and to enable communication between you and your possible match. Critics, as we have seen, argue that Tinder and similar apps such as Zoosk and Hinge are useful for one-night (or one-hour) stands, but not for initiating long-term, meaningful relationships. Not necessarily, argues Finkel. Finkel believes that the kinds of information required to determine whether someone is a good match for you only comes to light after you have actually met—despite the hollering of a mathematical algorithm that you were made for each other. The Tinder advantage is the way it expands the dating pool. How you use Tinder is then up to you. Its payoff need not involve playing musical beds if users have other possibilities in mind as well.

Because intimacy involves the sharing of innermost thoughts and feelings, honesty is a core feature of intimacy. A person need not be an "open book" to develop and maintain intimacy, however. Some aspects of experience are better kept even from one's most intimate partners, especially when they are embarrassing or threatening (Anderson et al., 2011). We would not expect partners to disclose every passing sexual fantasy. Nor should we expect intimate partners to divulge the details of past sexual experiences. Honesty means *saying what one means,* not providing hurtful details.

Intimacy is important not only to interpersonal relationships but also to one's health. Researchers have found that intimacy fosters well-being and that its absence can be psychologically and physically harmful (Rubin & Campbell, 2012; Perlman & Sprecher, 2012).

INTIMACY AND SELF-ESTEEM   Some social scientists suggest that getting to know and like yourself is an initial step toward intimacy with others. By coming to know and value yourself, you identify your own feelings and needs and develop the security to share them. Research suggests that partners with low self-esteem are more likely to harbor self-doubts that can interfere with the development and maintenance of romantic relationships (Leary & Tangney, 2012). For example, experiments show that when their partner is in a "bad mood," people with low self-esteem tend to feel more responsible for that mood, to feel more rejected, and, consequently, to behave in a more hostile manner (Bellavia & Murray, 2003). Yet, people with high self-esteem seem to be more likely to use their partners' acceptance and approval as a way of maintaining their self-esteem when self-doubts arise (Murray et al., 2001). That is, even when we feel rather good about ourselves, we can come to rely on our partners' impressions of us.

Too much self-esteem can also be detrimental to a relationship if it takes the form of narcissism, or being wrapped up in oneself. Research shows that narcissists tend to play love games with their partners; they show less commitment and are more likely to have alternatives handy if relationships do not work out (Campbell et al., 2002). The same researchers found that self-esteem, as opposed to narcissism, was positively linked to romantic love.

Two other ingredients of an intimate relationship are trust and caring. *Trust* enables partners to feel confident that disclosing intimate feelings will not lead to ridicule or rejection. Trust usually builds gradually, as partners learn whether it is safe to share confidences.

A German study of 72 adolescents who were followed from the ages of 14 through 20 found that the quality of their relationships with their parents contributed to their ability to trust romantic partners (Seiffge-Krenke & Kuehnemund, 2001). Research also shows that people come to trust their partners when they see that their partners have made sincere investments in the relationship, as evidenced, for example, by making sacrifices to be with them, such as incurring the disapproval of their family (Van Lange & Rusbult, 2012). Commitment and trust in a relationship can be seen as developing according to a model of **mutual cyclical growth:**

- Feelings that one needs one's partner to promote commitment to and dependence on the relationship.
- Commitment to the relationship encourages the partners to do things that are good for the relationship (that is, to perform "pro-relationship acts").
- One's partner perceives the pro-relationship acts.
- Perception of the pro-relationship acts enhances the partner's trust in the other partner and in the relationship.
- Feelings of trust increase the partners' willingness to depend on the relationship.

Caring is an emotional bond that allows intimacy to develop. Caring means that partners try to satisfy each other's needs, gratify each other's interests, and make sacrifices, if necessary. Research shows that willingness to sacrifice is connected with commitment to the relationship, level of satisfaction in the

Critical Thinking
Critical thinkers pay attention to the definitions of terms. Which do you think more truly defines an "intimate relationship"? A sexual relationship or one built on sharing of inmost thoughts and feelings? Can one engage in sexual relationships without developing caring for another person and a desire to share thoughts and feelings? Without developing feelings of jealousy when the other person has sexual relations with other people? What do you think?

mutual cyclical growth
The view that the need for one's partner promotes commitment; commitment promotes acts that enhance the relationship; and these acts build trust, increasing one's partner's commitment to the relationship.

relationship, and interestingly, poor alternatives to the relationship (Rusbult et al., 2012; Van Lange & Rusbult, 2012). In other words, it may not be easy to find partners if one does not sacrifice for relationships (Katz & Tirone, 2009). Is self-sacrifice thus self-serving?

MAKING A COMMITMENT   People may open up to strangers on airplanes or trains or to healthcare providers and still find it hard to talk openly with people to whom they are closest. This phenomenon is true even though we know that we will not see the strangers again, or that the health professionals are required to keep our personal matters confidential. Truly intimate relationships are marked by commitment to maintain the relationship through thick and thin (Sternberg, 2004).

Numerous studies find that men tend to be more reluctant than women to make commitments. David Popenoe, co-director of the National Marriage Project at Rutgers University in New Jersey, conducted a study with 60 unmarried heterosexual men and found that the commonness of cohabitation is one reason why they are reluctant to make a commitment. In cohabitation, sex—traditionally a key reason for men to marry—is readily available. Popenoe notes, "In a sense, with cohabitation he gets a quasi-wife without having to commit" (Hussain, 2002).

In committed relationships, a delicate balance exists between individuality and mutuality. In healthy unions, a strong sense of togetherness does not eradicate individuality. Partners in such relationships remain free to be themselves. Neither seeks to dominate or submerge himself or herself into the personality of the other. Each partner maintains individual interests, likes and dislikes, and needs and goals.

Factors that can throw continuing relationships into a downward spiral include boredom, as in falling into a rut in leisure activities or sexual practices. Yet, boredom does not always end relationships. Consider a study of 12 men who admitted to experiencing sexual boredom in long-term heterosexual relationships (Tunariu & Reavey, 2003). The men were not happy with sexual boredom, particularly in a culture in which men are viewed as highly sexual, and romantic love is supposed to remain passionate. On the other hand, they viewed their boredom as a normal trade-off for so-called true love and long-term companionship.

Other factors that contribute to the discontinuation of a relationship include evidence of negative evaluation (such as bickering, and forgetting anniversaries and other important dates or pretending that they do not exist), lack of fairness in the relationship (such as one partner's always deciding how the couple will spend their free time), jealousy, and general dissatisfaction. Which leads us to the question: How does jealousy affect relationships?

Jealousy: Is the World a Real-Life *Temptation Island*?

LO 8.3 Discuss the effects of jealousy on a relationship.

O! beware, my lord, of jealousy;
It is the green-ey'd monster …

—William Shakespeare, *Othello*

Thus was Othello, the Moor of Venice, warned of jealousy in the Shakespearean play that bears his name. Othello could not control his feelings, however, and killed his beloved wife, Desdemona. The English poet John Dryden labeled jealousy a "tyrant of the mind." Anthropologists find evidence of jealousy in all cultures, although it may vary in amount and intensity across and within cultures. It appears to be more common and intense among cultures with a stronger machismo tradition, in which men are expected to display their virility. It is also powerful in cultures in which men view a woman's infidelity as a threat to their honor. But jealousy is found among gay males and lesbians as well as among heterosexuals (Peluso, 2008).

The emotion of jealousy accounted in part for the popularity of the reality TV show *Temptation Island.* On this show, people in committed relationships were exposed to attractive others, and the audience was apparently intrigued by the question of how much temptation the contestant on the show could withstand. No doubt, members of the audience also speculated on how much temptation they themselves could withstand.

Sexual jealousy is aroused when we suspect that an intimate relationship is threatened by a rival. Lovers can become jealous when others show sexual interest in their partners or when their partners show an interest (even a casual or nonsexual interest) in another. Jealousy can lead to loss of feelings of affection, feelings of insecurity and rejection, anxiety and loss of self-esteem, and feelings of mistrust of one's partner and potential rivals (Guerrero et al., 2011). It is one of the commonly mentioned reasons why relationships fail. Feelings of possessiveness, related to jealousy, also place stress on a relationship. In extreme cases, jealousy can cause depression or give rise to spouse abuse, suicide, or, as with Othello, murder (Harmon-Jones et al., 2009). But milder forms of jealousy are not necessarily destructive to a relationship. They may even serve the positive function of revealing how much one cares for one's partner. For this reason, we can distinguish between *normal jealousy*, which reflects occasional self-doubts and the belief that one's partner is attractive, and *obsessional jealousy*, in which the individual, like Othello, is consumed by his or her fears of interference in the relationship.

What causes jealousy? Experience and personality variables play roles. People may become mistrustful of their partners because former partners have cheated. People with low self-esteem may experience sexual jealousy because they become overly dependent on their partners. They may fear that they will not be able to find another partner if their present partner leaves.

Jealousy and Evolutionary Theory

Researchers (e.g., Sagarin et al., 2012; Shackelford et al., 2005; Zandbergen & Brown, 2015) find that sex differences in jealousy appear to support evolutionary theory. Males seem to be more upset by sexual infidelity, females by emotional infidelity (Sagarin et al., 2012; Zandbergen & Brown, 2015). That is, males are made more insecure

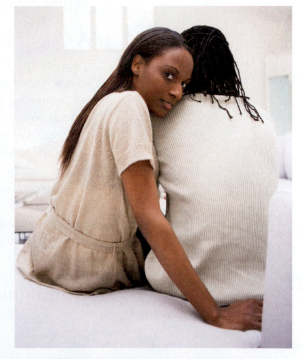

Jealousy. How do we explain feelings of jealousy? What does jealousy do to an intimate relationship?

Real Students, Real Questions

Q *My boyfriend wants me to move in with him, but I am not sure if I am ready. How can I decide? Also, how do you know when you are ready to marry someone?*

A If you're not sure you're ready, don't do it. If he cares about you, he'll wait until you're ready. If he won't wait, it could be that you haven't lost anything you need to worry about. (We can talk tough when we have to.) How do you know when you are ready to marry someone? One thing we're rather sure of is that you'll know when it's time. You'll probably know who you are, where you're going, who he is, where he's going, and whether you want to go there together.

and angry when their partners have sexual relations with someone else. Females are made more insecure and angry when their partners become emotionally attached to someone else. Why? Evolutionary theory hypothesizes that sexual jealousy was shaped by natural selection as a method of ensuring males that their female partner's offspring are their own, and of ensuring females that their male partners will continue to provide resources to facilitate childrearing (Bendixen et al., 2015; Buss, 2009a).

Lack of Sex Differences in Responses to Affairs Among Gay Males and Lesbians

Interestingly, the hypothesized gender difference in reactions to infidelity disappear when one's partner has an affair with someone of his or her own gender (Sagarin et al., 2003). Is it because the affair carries no threat of impregnation (a view that would be consistent with evolutionary theory)? Or is it because the victim consoles himself or herself by thinking that he or she really isn't competing in the same arena with the intruder? Are both explanations and other explanations possible?

A Cognitive Perspective on Jealousy

In recent years, cognitive theory has gained importance in many areas of the behavioral sciences, and sexual jealousy is no exception. In two studies, Stacie Bauerle and her colleagues (2002) presented 156 college undergraduates and 128 members of the general population with various scenarios in which their partners were unfaithful. By and large, jealousy increased when the individuals attributed their partner's infidelity to internal causes, such as clear personal choice. When they attributed the infidelity to external causes, such as alcohol or social pressure, the individuals in the study reported feeling significantly less jealous. ("Don't blame me; it was the alcohol.")

Many lovers—including many college students—play jealousy games. They let their partners know that they are attracted to other people. They flirt openly or manufacture tales to make their partners pay more attention to them, to test the relationship, to inflict pain, or to take revenge for a partner's disloyalty.

Communicative Responses to Jealousy

Researchers have found four types of communicative responses to situations that create feelings of jealousy (Guerrero et al., 2014):

1. Destructive communication. Such communications include insults, threats, and in the worst case, violence. They also tend to bring relationships to an end.

2. Constructive communication. Such communication involves discussing the context of feelings of jealousy and exploring ways to restore and strengthen the relationship. Constructive communication tends to increase satisfaction with the relationship.

3. Avoidance. Avoidance means remaining silent and acting as if the events that led to feelings of jealousy had not happened.

4. Rival-focused communication. Such communications involve claims that one possesses one's partner, following or stalking one's partner, derogating one's rival, and, sometimes, directly contacting and confronting one's rival. Rival-focused communication, like destructive communication, is extremely harmful to the relationship.

loneliness
Painful isolation.

solitude
Characterized by self-discovery, inner peace, reflection, and spirituality.

Loneliness

LO 8.4 **Discuss the causes and effects of loneliness.**

Many people start relationships because of loneliness. Loneliness and solitude (being alone) are not synonymous. **Loneliness** is a state of painful isolation, of feeling cut off from others. **Solitude**, however, can be quite positive. Inner-directed solitude can be characterized by self-discovery and inner peace. Outer-directed solitude can refer to spirituality or allow us to reflect on the world around us. Solitude is usually a matter of choice; loneliness is not.

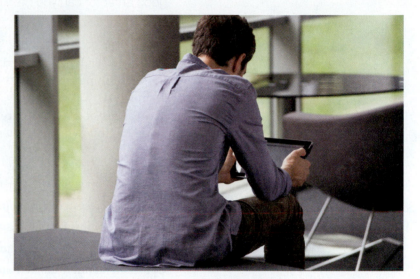

Lonely people tend to spend a lot of time by themselves, eat dinner alone, spend weekends alone, and participate in few social activities. They are unlikely to date. Some lonely people report having many friends, but a closer look suggests that these "friendships" are shallow. Lonely people are unlikely to share confidences. Loneliness tends to peak during adolescence, when peer relationships begin to supplant family ties.

Loneliness or Solitude? Solitude can be a positive experience, allowing us to think or read or write. But loneliness is painful social isolation that can be detrimental to both our psychological and our physical health.

Effects of Loneliness

Loneliness is associated with a host of problems in psychological adjustment. A study of 90 adolescents aged 16 to 18 found that feelings of loneliness were connected with low self-confidence, introversion, unhappiness, and emotional instability (Cheng & Furnham, 2002). Loneliness is also often connected with feelings of depression. A study of 101 dating couples with a mean age of 21 found that poor relationships contributed to feelings of loneliness and to depression—even though the individuals had partners (Segrin et al., 2003).

Loneliness is connected with physical health problems as well as with psychological problems such as depression. Studies find that lonely people have higher blood pressure than people who were not lonely (Hawkley et al., 2003; Shankar et al., 2011). Lonely people also found stressful experiences to be more discomfiting, an observation that suggests the value of social support when we are undergoing stress (Hawkley et al., 2003). Social isolation has also been shown to predict cancer, cardiovascular disease, various other diseases, eating disorders such as anorexia nervosa and bulimia nervosa, and a higher mortality rate (Hawkley & Cacioppo, 2003; Holt-Lunstad et al., 2015; Levine, 2012). It appears that one causal

Critical Thinking
What is the difference between loneliness and solitude? Do you know people who get by just fine by themselves and others who cannot get through one day without social interactions? How would you explain the difference between them? How would you characterize yourself when it comes to your ability to "swim alone"?

pathway between loneliness and illness involves stress. Stress impairs the functioning of the immune system, and lonely people perceive stress to be more aversive (Cacioppo et al., 2003).

The causes of loneliness are many and complex. Lonely people tend to have several of the following characteristics:

- Lack of social skills. Lonely people often lack the interpersonal skills to make friends or cope with disagreements.

- Lack of interest in other people.

- Lack of empathy. Empathy is a key aspect of satisfaction in romantic relationships.

- Failure to disclose personal information to potential friends.

- Cynicism about human nature (for example, seeing people as only out for themselves).

- Demanding too much too soon. The lonely perceive other people as cold and unfriendly in the early stages of a relationship.

- General pessimism. When we expect the worst, we often get … you guessed it.

- An external locus of control. That is, lonely people do not see themselves as capable of taking their lives into their own hands and achieving their goals.

3 › T / F Truth or Fiction Revisited   It is true that many people remain lonely because of fear of rejection. This fear is often connected with self-criticism of social skills and expectations of failure in relating to others (Gable, 2012).

Sexual Communication

LO 8.5   **Describe methods of sexual communication.**

Some relationships work out. Others don't. In Western culture, where people tend to form relationships with more than one partner as they develop, perhaps the majority of relationships draw to an end. Termination of a relationship is not always a bad thing. As people spend time together, they learn more about whether they are well matched or poorly matched. Most also learn how to compromise to help build relationships and how to approach resolving conflicts in a constructive way (Rosenblatt & Rieks, 2009).

Conflict Resolution

Some researchers, such as John M. Gottman (Cleary Bradley et al., 2011; Madhyastha et al., 2011), have focused on the ways in which couples resolve conflicts. Gottman has videotaped couples as they do so and also monitored their physiological responses, including their heart rates, sweating, and large motor movement. He found that deterioration of satisfaction in the relationship could be predicted by physiological measures, particularly on the part of the male. The calmer the couple's bodily responses, the more their relationship improved as time went on. On the other hand, couples whose heart rates were more rapid, who sweated more, and who moved about agitatedly had relationships that deteriorated over the next 3 years.

4 › T / F   Truth or Fiction Revisited   Gottman and Gottman also found that conflict itself is not necessarily destructive to a relationship (Gottman & Gottman, 2008; Gottman & Silver, 2015). The important thing is the way in which the couple attempts to resolve it. Couples who were open and calm during the conflict tended to improve their satisfaction. Couples who were defensive experienced deterioration in the relationship.

A notable trait that contributed to deterioration of the relationship was stonewalling by the male. *Stonewalling* means that there is little movement of the head, few if any nods, and few of the verbal acknowledgments made by listeners who are participating in a discussion. Deterioration of the relationship was also predicted by excessively agreeable, compliant behavior on the part of the female or by her verbalizing feelings of contempt. Facial expressions predicted deterioration, especially facial expressions that suggested disgust on the part of the female, fear on the face of the male, and then miserable smiles by both parties. These nonverbal behaviors were accompanied by more defensiveness, excuses, and denial of responsibility.

Stonewallers suffer not only in terms of their relationships. Stonewalling predicted loneliness after the relationship ended, and loneliness, in turn, was connected with deteriorating health.

Good outcomes for relationships could also be predicted by positive attributes during conflict, such as displays of humor, empathy, and affection; by mutual effort to solve problems; and by determination to listen to one's partner nondefensively. These positive elements kept physiological responses in check as well.

Other researchers have generally found evidence in support of Gottman's conclusions about couples in conflict (Caughlin et al., 2012; Noller, 2012). For example, the ways in which couples communicate to resolve conflicts are the key to the survival or termination of a relationship. Couples who validated each other's feelings in a respectful and helpful manner were most satisfied with their relationships. Couples who were hostile or explosive, or who attempted to avoid conflict, were less satisfied with their relationships.

5 › T / F   Truth or Fiction Revisited   Despite the Beatles' song lyrics, love is not all you need. You also need communication. Couples learn about each other's desires and needs through communication. Otherwise, this knowledge remains a mystery.

Communication Skills for Enhancing Relationships: How to Do It

Couples therapists and sex therapists might find less work if more couples communicated effectively about their sexual feelings. Unfortunately, when it comes to sex, *talk* may be the most overlooked four-letter word.

Many couples suffer for years because one or both partners are unwilling to speak up. Or problems arise when one partner misinterprets the other. Clear communication

SEX IN A WORLD OF DIVERSITY

RELATIONSHIP SATISFACTION AMONG LGBT COUPLES

Numerous researchers have studied the factors that predict satisfaction in a relationship or the deterioration and ending of a relationship. Much of this research has sought to determine whether there are differences in the factors that satisfy heterosexual and same-sex couples, and the interesting finding is that we are hard-pressed to find differences (Holmstrom, 2009). One difference that stands out favors the gay and lesbian couples: They tend to distribute household chores evenly and not in terms of gender-role stereotypes (Kurdek, 2005, 2006; Wong, 2012). Now for the similarities: Sexual satisfaction is tied to satisfaction with the relationship in both heterosexual and lesbian women (Wong, 2012). Male–female and same-sex couples are all more satisfied when they receive social support from their partners, there is sharing of power in the relationship, they fight fair, and they perceive their partners to be committed to the relationship. But there are a couple of differences that favor stability in the relationships of the male–female couples: They are more likely to have the support of their families and less likely to be stigmatized by society at large.

Couples therapists who work with LGBT individuals and couples will find problems akin to those in male–female couples, such as infidelity, and many that need special sensitivity to these commonly stigmatized subpopulations (Schwartz & Young, 2009):

- Lesbian and gay identity development and how it affects the functioning of the couple
- Parenting and its impact on the couple
- Lesbians and gay males as members of families
- The kinds of stressors that impact individuals who are underrepresented in the LGBT literature, including older LGBT people, LGBT individuals who are members of ethnic minority groups, and LGBT individuals who are members of religious groups
- Legal issues and their impact on the couple
- Workplace issues and their impact on the couple

can take the guesswork out of relationships, avert misunderstandings, relieve resentments and frustrations, and increase sexual and general satisfaction with the relationship (Gottman & Gottman, 2008).

OBSTACLES TO SEXUAL COMMUNICATION   Why is it so difficult for couples to communicate about sex? There are several reasons.

Some couples believe that talking about sex is vulgar. But vulgarity, like beauty, is to some degree in the eye of the beholder. One couple's vulgarity may be another couple's love talk. Some people may maintain a Victorian belief that any talk about sex is not fit for mixed company, even between intimate partners. Sex is something you may do, but not something to be talked about. Other couples may be willing in principle to talk about sex but may find it difficult to actually do so because they lack an agreeable, common language.

How, for example, are they to refer to their genitals or to sexual activities? One partner may prefer to use coarse four-letter (or five-letter) words to refer to them. The other might prefer more clinical terms. A partner who prefers slang for the sexual organs might be regarded by the other as vulgar or demeaning. One who uses clinical terms, such as *fellatio* or *coitus*, might be regarded as, well, clinical. Some couples try to find a common verbal ground that is not vulgar at one extreme or clinical at the other. They might speak, for example, of "doing it" or "having sex" rather than "engaging in sexual intercourse." (The title of the Eddie Cantor musical of the 1930s suggests that some people once spoke of "making whoopie.") Or they might speak of "kissing me down there" rather than of practicing fellatio or cunnilingus.

Many couples also harbor irrational beliefs about relationships and sex, such as the notion that people should somehow know what their partners want, without having to ask. The common misconception that people should know what pleases their partners undercuts communication. Men, in particular, seem burdened with the stereotype that they should have a natural expertise at sex. Women may feel it is "unladylike" to talk openly about their sexual needs and feelings. Both partners may hold the idealized romantic notion that "love is all you need" to achieve sexual happiness.

A related irrational belief is that if our partners truly loved us, they would somehow "read our minds" and know what types of sexual stimulation we desire. Unfortunately, or fortunately, others cannot read our minds. We must assume the responsibility for communicating our preferences.

Some people communicate more effectively than others, perhaps because they are more sensitive to others' needs or because their parents served as good models as communicators. But communication skills can be acquired at any time. Learning takes time and work, but the following guidelines should prove helpful if you want to enhance your communication skills. These skills can also improve communication in areas of intimacy other than the sexual.

GETTING STARTED   How do you broach tough topics? Here are some ideas. You can start by talking about talking. You can inform your partner that it is difficult for you to talk about problems and conflicts: "You know, I've always found it awkward to find a way of bringing things up" or "You know, I think other people have an easier time than I do when it comes to talking about some things." You can allude to troublesome things that happened in the past when you attempted to resolve conflicts. This approach encourages your partner to invite you to proceed.

Broaching the topic of sex can be difficult. Couples who gab endlessly about finances, children, and work might clam up about sex. So it may be helpful to agree first to talk about talking about sex. You can admit that it is difficult to talk about sex. You can say that your sexual relationship is important to you and that you want to do everything you can to enhance it. Gently probe your partner's willingness to set aside time to talk about sex, preferably when you can dim the lights and avoid interruptions.

The "right time" may be when you are both relaxed, rested, and unpressed for time. The "right place" can be any place where you can enjoy privacy and speak undisturbed. Sex talk need not be limited to the bedroom. Couples may feel more comfortable talking about sex over dinner, when cuddling on the sofa, or when just relaxing together.

Another possibility is to request permission to raise an issue. You can say something like this: "There's something on my mind. Do you have a few minutes? Is now a good time to tell you about it?" Or you can say, "There's something that we need to talk about, but I'm not sure how to bring it up. Can you help me with it?"

You can also tell your partner that it is okay to point out ways in which you can become a more effective lover. For example, you can say, "I know that you don't want to hurt my feelings, but I wonder if I'm doing anything that you'd rather I didn't do?"

LISTENING   Effective listening involves such skills as active listening, paraphrasing, the use of reinforcement, and valuing your partner even when the two of you disagree. To listen actively rather than passively, first adopt the attitude that you may actually learn something—or perceive things from another vantage point—by listening.

Even when you disagree with what your partner is saying, you can maintain good relations and keep channels of communication open by saying something like "I really appreciate your taking the time to try to work this out with me" or "I hope you'll think it's okay if I don't see things entirely in the same way, but I'm glad that we had a chance to talk about it."

When you disagree with your partner, do so in a way that shows that you still value your partner as a person. In other words, say something like "I love you very much, but it annoys me when you …" rather than "You're really contemptible for doing …." In this manner, you encourage your partner to disclose sensitive material without risk of attack or of losing your love or support.

Critical Thinking
Have you had difficulty getting started in discussing a "tough topic" with a family member or friend? (Not necessarily a sexual problem—could be that a roommate doesn't shower or that a family member disapproves of your style of life.) What did you do about it? Some people avoid bringing up problems indefinitely. Others seem to enjoy confronting others. And then there are those who have some trepidation but manage to get things out into the open eventually? Where are you along this continuum? Are you comfortable with there you are? If not, what can you do to change things?

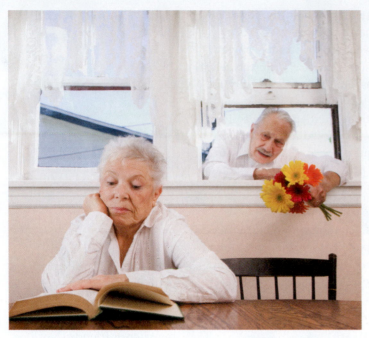

Forget the Flowers. Try Communicating. Would it have been easier for him if he had just listened to her? Listening can take some skills, especially when a couple are in conflict.

LEARNING ABOUT YOUR PARTNER'S NEEDS

Listening is basic to learning about another person's needs, but sometimes it helps to go a few steps further. You can ask open-ended questions that allow for a broader exploration of issues, such as:

"What do you like best about the way we make love?"

"Do you think that I do things to bug you?"

"Does it bother you that I go to bed later than you do?"

"Does anything disappoint you about our relationship?"

"Do you think that I do things that are inconsiderate when you're studying for a test?"

Closed-ended questions that call for a limited range of responses are most useful when you're looking for a simple yes-or-no type of response: "Would you rather make love with the stereo off?"

Self-disclosure is essential to developing intimacy (Derlega et al., 2008). You can also use self-disclosure to learn more about your partner's needs because communicating your own feelings and ideas invites reciprocation. For example, you might say, "There are times when I feel that I disappoint you when we make love. Should I be doing something differently?"

You can ask your partner to level with you about an irksome issue. You can say that you recognize that it might be awkward to discuss it but that you will try your best to listen conscientiously and not get too disturbed. You can also limit yourselves to one such difficult issue per conversation. If the entire emotional dam were to burst, the job of mopping up could be overwhelming.

PROVIDING INFORMATION There are skillful ways of communicating information, including "accentuating the positive" and using verbal and nonverbal cues. It is irrational to expect that your partner can read your mind. He or she can tell when you're wearing a grumpy face, but your expression does not provide much information about your specific feelings. When your partner asks, "What would you like me to do?" don't say, "Well, I think you can figure out what I want" or "Just do whatever you think is best." Only you know what pleases you.

Let your partner know when he or she is doing something right! Speak up or find another way to express your appreciation. Accentuating the positive is rewarding and also informs your partner about what pleases you. In other words, don't just wait around until your partner does something wrong and then seize the opportunity to complain!

Sexual activity provides an excellent opportunity for direct communication. You can say something like "Oh, that's great" or "Don't stop." Or you can ask for feedback, as in "How does that feel ...?"

Feedback provides direct guidance about what is pleasing. Partners can also make specific requests and suggestions.

Sexual communication also occurs without words. Facial expressions and body language communicate likes and dislikes. Our partners may lean toward us or away from us when we touch them, or they may relax or tense up. In any case, they speak volumes in silence. The following exercises may help couples use nonverbal cues to communicate their sexual likes and dislikes.

- *Take turns petting.* Taking turns petting can help partners learn what turns one another on. Each partner takes turns caressing the other, stopping frequently enough to receive feedback by asking questions like "How does that feel?" The recipient is to provide feedback, which can be expressed verbally ("Yes, that's it—yes, just like that" or "No, a little lighter than that") or nonverbally, as in making appreciative or disapproving sounds. The knowledge gained through this exercise can be incorporated into the couple's regular pattern of lovemaking.

- *Direct your partner's hand.* Gently guiding your partner's hand—to show your partner where and how you like to be touched—is a most direct way of communicating sexual likes. Women might show partners how to caress the breasts or clitoral shaft in this manner. Men might cup their partners' hands to show them how to stroke the penile shaft or caress the testes.

- *Signal your partner.* Couples can use agreed-upon nonverbal cues to signal sexual pleasure. For example, one partner may rub the other in a certain way, or tap the other, to signal that something is being done right. The recipient of the signal takes mental notes and incorporates the pleasurable stimulation into the couple's lovemaking. This is a sort of "hit or miss" technique, but even near misses can be rewarding.

MAKING REQUESTS   A basic part of improving relationships or lovemaking is asking partners to change their behavior—to do something differently or to stop doing something that hurts or is ungratifying. The skill of making requests now comes to the fore.

Be specific in requesting changes. Telling your partner something like "I'd like you to be nicer to me" may accomplish little. Your partner may not know that his or her behavior is not nice and may not understand how to be "nicer." It is better to say something like "I would appreciate it if you would get coffee for yourself, or at least ask me in a more pleasant way." Or, "I really have a hard time with the way you talk to me in front of your friends. It's as if you're trying to show them that you have control over me or something." Similarly, it may be less effective to say, "I'd like you to be more loving" than to say, "When we make love, I'd like you to kiss me more and tell me how you care about me."

Of course, you can precede your specific requests with openers such as "There's something on my mind. Is this a good time for me to bring it up with you?"

You are more likely to achieve desired results by framing requests in I-talk than by heaping criticisms on your partner. For example, "I would like it if we spent some time cuddling after sex" is superior to "You don't seem to care enough about me to want to hold me after we make love." Saying "I find it very painful when you use a harsh voice with me" is probably more effective than "Sometimes people's feelings get hurt when their boyfriends [girlfriends] speak to them harshly in front of their friends or families."

You can try out I-talk in front of a mirror or with a confidante before using it with your partner. In this way, you can see whether your facial expression and tone of voice are consistent with what you are saying. Friends may provide constructive feedback.

DELIVERING CRITICISM   Delivering criticism effectively is a skill. It requires focusing partners' attention on the problem without inducing resentment or reducing them to trembling masses of guilt or fear.

First, weigh your goals forthrightly. Is your primary intention to punish your partner, or are you more interested in gaining cooperation? If your goal is punishment, you may as well be coarse and disparaging, but understand that you are inviting reprisals. If your goal is to improve the relationship, however, a tactful approach may be in order.

Deliver criticism privately—not in front of friends or family. Your partner has a right to be upset when you make criticism public. Making private matters public prompts indignation and cuts off communication.

Criticism. Criticism can be hard to take. How can you deliver criticism to a partner in such a way as to enhance the relationship? How can you receive criticism in a helpful way?"

Be specific about the behavior that disturbs you so that you bypass the trap of disparaging your partner's personality or motives. For example, you may be more effective by saying, "I could lose this job because you didn't write down the message" than by saying, "You're completely irresponsible" or "You're a flake." Similarly, you may achieve better results by saying, "The bathroom looks and smells dirty when you throw your underwear on the floor" rather than "You're a filthy pig." Complain about specific, modifiable behavior rather than trying to overhaul another individual's whole personality.

Your partner will feel less threatened if you express displeasure in terms of your own feelings rather than by directly attacking his or her personality. Attacks often arouse defensive behavior, and sometimes retaliation. When confronting your partner for failing to be sensitive to your sexual needs when making love, it will likely be more effective to say, "You know, it really upsets me that you don't seem to care about my feelings when we make love" than to say, "You're so wrapped up in yourself that you never think about anyone else."

Keep criticism and complaints to the present. Think how many times have you been in an argument and heard things like "You never appreciated me!" or "Last summer you did the same thing!" Bringing up the past muddles current issues and heightens resentments. When your partner forgets to jot down a telephone message, it is more useful to state, "This was a vital phone call" than "Three weeks ago you didn't tell me about the phone call from Chris, and as a result I missed out on seeing *Terminator 17*." It's better to leave who did what to whom last year (or even last week) alone.

Avoid blunt criticisms or personal attacks and suggest constructive alternatives. Avoid saying, "You're really a lousy lover." Say instead, "Can I take your hand and show you what I'd like?"

Whenever possible, express criticism positively and combine it with a concrete request. When commenting on your partner's failure to display affection during love-making, say, "I love it when you kiss me. Please kiss me more" rather than "You never kiss me when we're in bed and I'm sick of it."

RECEIVING CRITICISM

Honest criticism is hard to take, particularly from a relative, a friend, an acquaintance, or a stranger.

—Franklin P. Jones

Delivering criticism can be tricky, especially when you want to inspire cooperation. Receiving criticism can be even trickier. Nevertheless, the following suggestions offer some help.

When you hear "It's time you did something about ...," it is understandable if the hair on the backs of your arms does a headstand. After all, it's a blunt challenge. When we are confronted harshly, we are likely to become defensive and think of retaliating. But if your objective is to enhance the relationship, take a few moments to stop and think. To resolve conflicts, we need to learn about the other person's concerns, keep lines of communication open, and find ways of changing problem behavior.

So when your partner says, "It's about time you did something about the bathroom," stop and think before you summon up your most menacing voice and say, "Just what the hell is that supposed to mean?" Ask yourself what you want to find out.

Just as it's important to be specific when delivering criticism, it helps if you encourage the other person to be specific when you are on the receiving end of criticism. In the example of the complaint about the bathroom, you can help your partner be specific and perhaps avert the worst by asking a clarifying question, such as "Can you tell me exactly what you mean?" or "The bathroom?"

Consider a situation in which a lover says something like "You're one of the most irritating people I know." Rather than retaliating and further harming the relationship, you might say something like "How about forgoing the character assassination and telling me what I did that's bothering you?" This response requests an end to insults and asks your partner to be specific.

Even when you disagree with a criticism, you can keep lines of communication open and show respect for your partner's feelings by acknowledging and paraphrasing the criticism.

On the other hand, if you are at fault, you can admit it. For example, you can say, "You're right. It was my day to clean the bathroom and it totally slipped my mind" or "I was so busy, I just couldn't get to it." Now the two of you should look for a way to work out the problem. When you acknowledge criticism, you cue your partner to back off and look for ways to improve the situation. What if your partner then becomes abusive and says something like "So you admit you blew it?" You might then try a little education in conflict resolution. You could say, "I admitted that I was at fault. If you're willing to work with me to find a way to handle it, great; but I'm not going to let you pound me into the ground over it."

Now, if you think that you were not at fault, express your feelings. Use I-talk and be specific. Don't seize the opportunity to angrily point out your partner's shortcomings. By doing so, you may shut down lines of communication.

6 › T / F   Truth or Fiction Revisited   Retaliation is not the best course of action when you are criticized. We suggest that you do not seize the opportunity to strike back by saying, "Who're you to complain about the bathroom? What about your breath and that pigsty you call your closet?" Retaliation is tempting and may make you feel good at the moment, but it can do a relationship more harm than good in the long run.

NEGOTIATING DIFFERENCES   Negotiate your differences if you feel that there is merit on both sides of the argument. You may want to say something like "Would it help if I …?" And if there's something about your obligation to clean the bathroom that seems totally out of place, perhaps you and your partner can work out an exchange—that is, you get relieved of cleaning the bathroom in exchange for tackling a chore that your partner finds equally odious.

If none of these approaches helps resolve the conflict, perhaps your partner is using the comment about the bathroom to express anger over other issues. You may find out by saying something like "I've been trying to find a way to resolve this thing, but nothing I say seems to be helping. Is this really about the bathroom, or are there other things on your mind?"

WHEN COMMUNICATION IS NOT ENOUGH: HANDLING IMPASSES Communication helps build and maintain relationships, but sometimes partners have profound, substantial disagreements. In fact, it is normal to have disagreements from time to time. Even when their communication skills are superbly tuned, partners now and then reach an impasse. Couples who reach an impasse may find these suggestions helpful.

Research shows that taking your partner's perspective (that is, looking at things from your partner's point of view) during a dispute results in more positive feelings about the relationship and greater effort to respond in a constructive manner (Arriaga & Rusbult, 1998; Driver et al., 2003). Thus, if there is an impasse, ill feeling may be resolved by (honestly) saying something like "I still disagree with you, but

I can understand why you take your position." But if you do not follow your partner's logic, you can say something like "Please believe me: I'm trying very hard to look at this from your point of view, but I can't follow your reasoning. Would you try to help me understand your point of view?"

Sometimes when you reach a stalemate, it helps to allow the problem to "incubate" for a while. If you and your partner put the issue aside for a time, perhaps a resolution will dawn on one of you later.

Although we tend to form relationships with people who share similar attitudes, there is never a perfect overlap. A partner who pretends to be your clone will most likely become a bore. Assuming that your relationship is generally rewarding and pleasurable, you may find it possible to tolerate some differences. Part of respecting other people is allowing them to be who they are. When we have a solid sense of who we are as individuals and what we stand for, we are more apt to tolerate differentness in our partners.

7 › T / F Truth or Fiction Revisited It is not necessarily true that relationships come to an end when the partners cannot resolve their differences. You and your partner can agree to disagree on various issues (Rosenblatt & Rieks, 2009). Remember that disagreement itself is not necessarily destructive to a relationship—unless you are convinced that it must be. Two people cannot see everything in the same way. Failure to disagree ever will leave at least one partner feeling frustrated now and then. Conflict is nearly inevitable in a relationship. The key to satisfaction with the relationship is how the couple go about trying to resolve the conflict.

Chapter Review

LO 8.1 **Explain ways in which couples meet, including the role of dating apps.**

Recent research shows that more than a third of married couples have met online. The most common places that married couples have met in the "real world" are at work, through friends, at school, and at social get-togethers. In earlier years, couples were relatively more likely to meet in their neighborhoods, through family, friends, and in school, and in some cases to marry "high-school sweethearts." But marriages are occurring at later ages today, and people are moving around more to attend school and establish careers.

LO 8.2 **Describe "hookup culture," its pleasures, and pitfalls.**

Because of delaying marriage or the establishment of long-term partnerships, many people in the United States today are "hooking up" for brief or one-time sexual encounters. One reason is that fewer people today believe that premarital sex is wrong. Some other factors involved in hooking up include impulsivity, use of alcohol and other drugs, social comparison ("everyone's doing it"), and situational triggers. Many people—especially women—have regrets about hooking up, including disappointment that hooking up is unlikely to lead to a long-term romantic relationship.

LO 8.3 **Discuss the effects of jealousy on a relationship.**

Jealousy can harm or end relationships, especially when there is destructive or rival-directed communication.

According to evolutionary theory, males are more jealous when their partners have sexual relations with an outsider, whereas females are more concerned when their partners develop emotional closeness with an outsider.

LO 8.4 **Discuss the causes and effects of loneliness.**

Loneliness is a state of painful isolation, of feeling cut off from others. Causes of loneliness include lack of social skills, lack of interest in other people, lack of empathy, fear of rejection, lack of self-disclosure, cynicism about people, demanding too much too soon, pessimism, and an external locus of control. People can overcome loneliness by challenging self-defeating attitudes, developing social skills, and placing themselves among others.

LO 8.5 **Describe methods of sexual communication.**

Developing communication skills is an important way of leading to the resolution of conflicts in a relationship, but many people find it difficult to talk openly about sex. Listening and learning about one's partner's needs is essential. People also need to be able to communicate what they want, including making requests. Exercises such as taking turns petting and directing one's partner's hand are highly useful. Delivering criticism requires thought and tact, and receiving criticism is usually not easy. Communication also enables couples to negotiate differences and handle impasses.

Test Your Learning

1. Sexual satisfaction for lesbians is connected with _____
   - (a) their sexual orientation.
   - (b) their relationship.
   - (c) social stigmatization.
   - (d) issues in the workplace.

2. Evolutionary theory predicts that _____ will be most jealous about their partners' sexual infidelity.
   - (a) heterosexual males
   - (b) heterosexual females
   - (c) gay males
   - (d) lesbians

3. About _____% of couples today meet their partners through online dating services.
   - (a) 10
   - (b) 20
   - (c) 35
   - (d) 50

4. Which of the following is not part of an intimate relationship?
   - (a) selfishness
   - (b) trust
   - (c) caring
   - (d) honesty

5. Hooking up _____
   - (a) is a healthful way to avoid deep relationships.
   - (b) causes severe feelings of depression.
   - (c) exposes about 80% of participants to HIV.
   - (d) has become more common over the past decades.

6. It is not true that _____
   - (a) strong emotional feelings automatically lead to good relationships.
   - (b) jealousy harms a relationship.
   - (c) intimacy is an important part of a romantic relationship.
   - (d) communication skills are important to relationships.

7. Which statement is accurate?
   - (a) People need to be sexually intimate to have an emotionally intimate relationship.
   - (b) People need not be sexually intimate to have an emotionally intimate relationship.
   - (c) Love is necessary for intimacy.
   - (d) Intimacy requires total honesty.

8. Men are generally more interested than women in _____
   - (a) multiple sex partners.
   - (b) love.
   - (c) enduring relationships.
   - (d) feelings of commitment.

9. Kurdek finds that LGB couples tend to differ from heterosexual couples in that they _____
   - (a) distribute household chores more evenly.
   - (b) avoid conflict at all costs.
   - (c) do not consider sexual activity per se to be an important aspect of their relationship.
   - (d) believe that love conquers all and that it is not necessary to work on relationships.

10. Perhaps the most difficult aspect of sexual communication is _____
    - (a) taking turns petting.
    - (b) making requests.
    - (c) listening.
    - (d) receiving criticism.

Chapter 9
Conception, Pregnancy, and Childbirth

Learning Objectives

Conception: Against All Odds

LO 9.1   Describe the process of conception.

Infertility and Assisted Reproductive Technology

LO 9.2   Discuss fertility problems and ways in which people with such problems can become parents.

Pregnancy

LO 9.3   Discuss signs of pregnancy and sexual activity during pregnancy.

Prenatal Development

LO 9.4   Discuss the key events of the stages of prenatal development.

LO 9.5   Discuss the effects of environmental hazards on the child.

LO 9.6   Discuss the effects of genetic abnormalities on the child.

Childbirth

LO 9.7   Discuss the stages of childbirth.

LO 9.8   Describe various methods of childbirth.

LO 9.9   Discuss various birth problems.

The Postpartum Period

LO 9.10 Discuss events of the postpartum period, including mood changes and breast-feeding versus bottle-feeding.

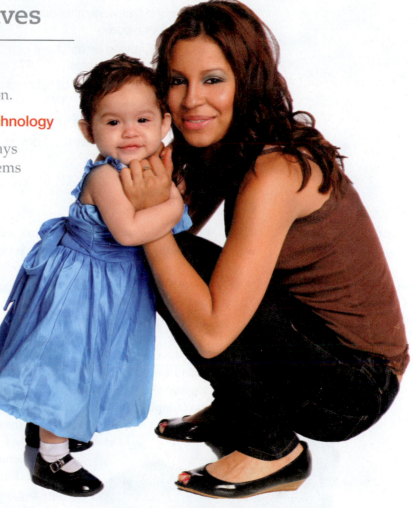

zygote

A fertilized ovum.

Down syndrome

A chromosomal abnormality that leads to mental retardation, caused by an extra chromosome on the twenty-first pair.

On a balmy day in October, Marta and her partner Jorge rush to catch the train to their jobs in the city. Marta's workday is outwardly the same as any other. Within her body, however, a remarkable drama is unfolding. Yesterday, hormones had caused an ovarian follicle to rupture, releasing its egg cell, or ovum. How this particular follicle was selected to ripen and release its ovum this month remains a mystery. But for the next day or so, Marta will be capable of conceiving.

The previous morning Marta had used her ovulation-timing kit, which showed that she was about to ovulate. That night, Marta and Jorge had made love, hoping that Marta would conceive. Jorge ejaculated hundreds of millions of sperm within Marta's vagina. Only a few thousand survived the journey through the cervix and uterus to the fallopian tube that contained the ovum, released just hours earlier. Of these, a few hundred remained to bombard the ovum. One succeeded in penetrating the ovum's covering, thereby fertilizing it and resulting in conception. From a single cell formed by the union of sperm and ovum, a new life begins to form. The **zygote** is but 1/175 of an inch across—a tiny beginning for the drama about to occur.

Marta is age 37, which raises some concern about the possibility of Down syndrome and other chromosomal abnormalities, which become more common as the age of the parents increases. However, blood work and ultrasound "pictures" taken toward the end of the first three months suggest that the chromosomal structure of her fetus is normal and the shape of the head and body of the fetus also do not suggest problems. The tests also reveal the anatomic sex of the fetus. Many parents prefer to know the sex of their baby before it is born. "Why," some say, "should the doctor know and we not know?" But Marta and Jorge ask their doctor not to inform them. "Why ruin the surprise?" Jorge tells his friends.

Conception: Against All Odds

LO 9.1 **Describe the process of conception.**

Conception is the union of a sperm cell and an ovum. On the one hand, conception is the beginning of a new human life. It is also the end of a fantastic voyage, however, in which a viable ovum, one of only several hundred that will mature and ripen during a woman's lifetime, unites with one of several hundred *million* sperm produced by the man in the average ejaculate.

Ova carry X sex chromosomes. Sperm carry either X or Y sex chromosomes. Girls are conceived from the union of an ovum and an X-bearing sperm, boys from the union of an ovum and a Y-bearing sperm. Sperm that bear Y sex chromosomes appear to be faster swimmers than those bearing X sex chromosomes. This is one of the reasons that between 120 and 150 boys are conceived for every 100 girls. What seem to be natural balancing factors favor the survival of female fetuses, however. Male fetuses are more likely to be lost in a **spontaneous abortion**, which often occurs during the first month of pregnancy. In many cases of early sponta- neous abortion, the woman never realizes that she had been pregnant. Despite spontaneous abortions, boys still outnumber girls at birth. Boys suffer from a higher incidence of infant mortality, however. Thus, the numbers of boys and girls in the population are further equalized by the time they mature to the point of pairing off.

The 200 to 400 million sperm in an average ejaculate may seem excessive because only 1 can fertilize an egg. But here's a fun question: How many sperm does it take to make a chicken? Answer: Chickens are usually inseminated with millions of sperm, which, for some unknown reason seems to be necessary for the proper development of the embryo! (Hemmings & Birkhead, 2015).

Back to humans: Only 1 sperm in 1,000 arrives in the vicinity of an ovum. Millions deposited in the vagina flow out of the woman's body because of gravity, unless she remains prone for quite some time. Normal vaginal acidity kills many more. Many surviving sperm swim against the current of fluid coming from the cervix, through the os and into the uterus. Surviving sperm may reach the fallopian tubes 60 to 90 minutes after ejaculation. About half the sperm end up in the wrong tube—that is, the one not containing the egg. Perhaps some 2,000 sperm find their way into the right tube. Fewer still manage to swim the final two inches against the currents generated by the cilia that line the tube.

The journey of sperm may be blind but it is not random. Sperm cells are appar- ently attracted by the odor of a chemical secreted by ova. They seem to be guided by a change in calcium ions that occurs when an ovum is released (Cerezales et al., 2015; G. D. Smith et al., 2014).

> **1 › T / F** **Truth or Fiction Revisited** It is *not* true that sperm travel about at random inside the woman's reproductive tract, so that reaching the ovum is a matter of luck. Sperm cells are apparently attracted by the odor of a chemical secreted by ova. They seem to be "egged on" (pardon the pun) by a change in calcium ions that occurs when an ovum is released.

Fertilization normally occurs in a fallopian tube. Ova contain chromosomes, pro- teins, fats, and nutritious fluid and are surrounded by a gelatinous layer called the **zona pellucida**. This layer must be penetrated if fertilization is to occur. Sperm that have completed their journey secrete the enzyme **hyaluronidase**, which briefly thins the zona pellucida, enabling one sperm to penetrate. Once a sperm has entered, the zona pellucida thickens, locking other sperm out. The corresponding chromosomes in the sperm and ovum line up opposite each other. Conception occurs as the chromo- somes from the sperm and ovum combine to form 23 new pairs, which carry a unique set of genetic instructions.

conception

The union of the sperm cell and an ovum (egg cell).

spontaneous abortion

The sudden, involuntary expul- sion of the embryo or fetus from the uterus before it is capable of independent life. Also termed *miscarriage*.

zona pellucida

A gelatinous layer that surrounds an ovum.

hyaluronidase

An enzyme that briefly thins the zona pellucida, enabling one sperm to penetrate.

Figure 9.1 Human Sperm Swarming Around an Ovum in a Fallopian Tube.

Fertilization normally occurs in a fallopian tube, not in the uterus. Sperm secrete the enzyme *hyaluronidase*, which thins the layer surrounding the ovum, allowing one sperm cell to penetrate.

Figure 9.2 A Basal Body Temperature (BBT) Chart.

Because most women have somewhat irregular menstrual cycles, they may not be able to predict ovulation perfectly. The BBT chart helps them to do so. Body temperature is fairly even before ovulation but dips slightly just before ovulation. On the day after ovulation, a woman's body temperature increases about 0.4° to 0.8° F above the level before ovulation.

Optimizing the Chances of Conception

Couples may wish to optimize their chances of conceiving during a particular month so that birth occurs at a certain time. Others may have trouble conceiving and want to maximize their chances for a few months before seeing a fertility specialist. Fairly simple procedures can increase the chances of conceiving for couples without serious fertility problems.

The ovum can be fertilized for about 4 to 20 hours after ovulation. Sperm are most active within 48 hours after ejaculation. So one way to optimize the chances of conception is to engage in coitus within a few hours of ovulation. There are several ways to predict ovulation.

USING THE BASAL BODY TEMPERATURE CHART Few women have perfectly regular cycles, so they can only guess when they are ovulating. A basal body temperature (BBT) chart (see Figure 9.2) can provide a more reliable estimate.

Body temperature is fairly even before ovulation. Early-morning temperature is usually below 98.6° F. But just before ovulation, basal temperature dips slightly. Then, on the day after ovulation, temperature tends to rise by about 0.4° F to 0.8° F and to remain higher until menstruation. A woman can detect these changes by tracking her temperature after awakening in the morning but before rising from bed. Thermometers that provide finely graded readings, such as electronic digital thermometers, best detect the minor changes. The couple records the woman's temperature and the day of the cycle (as well as the day of the month) and indicates whether they have engaged in coitus. With regular charting for 6 months, the woman may learn to predict the day of ovulation more accurately—assuming that her cycles are fairly regular.

Opinion is divided as to whether it is better for couples to have coitus every 24 hours or every 36 to 48 hours for the several-day period during which ovulation is expected. More frequent coitus around the time of ovulation may increase the chances of conception. Relatively less frequent (that is, every 36 to 48 hours) coitus leads to a higher sperm count during each ejaculation. Most fertility specialists recommend that couples seeking to conceive a baby have intercourse once every day or two during the week in which the woman expects to ovulate. Men with lower than normal sperm counts may be advised to wait 48 hours between ejaculations.

ANALYZING URINE OR SALIVA FOR LUTEINIZING HORMONE Over-the-counter kits are more accurate than the basal body temperature method and predict ovulation by analyzing the woman's urine or saliva for the surge in **luteinizing hormone (LH)** that precedes ovulation by about 12 to 24 hours.

TRACKING VAGINAL MUCUS Women can track the thickness of their vaginal mucus during the menstrual cycle by rolling it between their fingers and noting changes in texture. The mucus is thick, white, and cloudy during most phases of the cycle but turns thin, slippery, and clear for a few days before ovulation. A day or so after ovulation the mucus again thickens and becomes opaque.

ADDITIONAL CONSIDERATIONS Having sex in the male-superior position allows sperm to be deposited deeper in the vagina and minimizes leakage of sperm out of the vagina as a result of gravity. Women may improve their chances of conceiving by lying on their backs and drawing their knees close to their breasts after ejaculation. This position, perhaps aided by use of a pillow to support the buttocks, may prevent sperm from dripping out and will elevate the pool of semen in relation to the cervix. Gravity will therefore work for, rather than against, conception. Women may lie still for about 30 to 60 minutes after ejaculation.

luteinizing hormone (LH)

A hormone secreted by the pituitary gland that stimulates ovulation in women (and the synthesis of male sex hormones in males).

SEX IN THE DIGITAL AGE

FERTILITY AND PERIOD TRACKERS

Been obsessed with work, running to the gym, Food Network, and more? Maybe you got confused about your window for getting pregnant this month, or, on the other hand, maybe an app blinked at you, buzzed at you, or just calmly informed you by text that your window of opportunity to conceive is about to open.

Rather than filling in printed charts, many women are using apps that help them predict when they will be ovulating and when they will have their periods. Depending on whether or not they desire to conceive a child, they either have sex just before or during ovulation to conceive, or avoid sex then, as a contraceptive measure. Women who are trying to get pregnant are more likely to have sex on days 12–14 of their cycles.

Apps like Fertility Tracker Mobile, Virtual Nurse—Birth Control, and Glow are examples of such calculators and trackers. Glow, which wins the best-name contest, works well with your smartphone or with your Apple Watch. Based on your entries, it will inform you when your next window of opportunity is due, giving you a day-by-day countdown, if you want that. It also collects data about a users' sex lives—if users decide to upload the data.

Most Glow users who report the data (54%) usually have sex in the missionary position, 20% in the woman-on-top position, and 17% with the woman in front of the man (doggy style). Users report they're a bit more likely to have an orgasm on top (60%) than on the bottom (53%). (Big surprise?)

Women with severely retroverted or "tipped" uteruses may profit from supporting themselves on their elbows and knees and having their partners enter them from behind. Again, this position helps prevent semen from dripping out.

The man should penetrate as deeply as possible just before ejaculation, hold still during ejaculation, then withdraw slowly in a straight line to avoid dispersing the pool of semen.

Selecting the Sex of Your Child

Parents have wished that they could select the sex of their children for thousands of years. In many cultures, one sex—usually male—has been preferred over the other. In other cases, parents who already have girls (or boys) would like to be able to "balance" their family by having a boy (or girl). Then, too, there are sex-linked diseases that show up only in sons. In such cases, parents would feel safer if they could have only daughters.

Folklore is replete with methods. Some cultures advised sex under the full moon to conceive boys. The Greek philosopher Aristotle suggested that making love during a north wind will beget sons. A south wind would produce daughters. Sour foods were once suggested for parents desirous of having boys. Those who wanted girls were advised to consume sweets. Husbands who yearned to have boys might be advised to wear their boots to bed. It goes without saying that none of these methods worked (but we will say it anyhow).

These methods, or nonmethods, would supposedly lead to the conception of children of the desired sex. However, methods after conception have also been used, such as the abortion of fetuses because of their sex. There are also many cultures in which infanticide has been used. Because boys have usually been considered more desirable than girls, female infanticide has been more common than male infanticide.

Today, there is a reliable method for selecting the sex of your child prior to implantation: preimplantation genetic diagnosis (PGD). PGD was developed to detect genetic disorders, but it also allows health professionals to learn of the sex of the embryo (Fovargue & Bennett, 2016). In PGD, ova are fertilized in vitro, leading to conception of perhaps six to eight embryos. After a few days of cell division, a cell is extracted from each. The sex chromosomal structure of the cell is examined microscopically to determine whether the embryo is female or male. Embryos of the desired sex are implanted in the woman's uterus, where one or more can grow to term. PGD is a foolproof sex-selection method, but it is medically invasive and expensive, and implantation cannot be guaranteed. Yet, when implantation does occur, the sex of the embryo is known.

Infertility and Assisted Reproductive Technology

LO 9.2 **Discuss fertility problems and ways in which people with such problems can become parents.**

infertility

Inability to conceive a child.

For couples who want children, few problems are more frustrating than the inability to conceive. Physicians often recommend that heterosexual couples try to conceive on their own for 6 months before seeking medical assistance. The term **infertility** is usually not applied until the couple has tried to get pregnant for more than a year, but women older than the age of 35 are advised to seek help within 6 months of attempts (Path2Parenthood, 2016).

Because the incidence of infertility increases with age, it is partially the result of a rise in couples who postpone childbearing until their 30s and 40s. About one American couple in six or seven has fertility problems (Path2Parenthood, 2016). However, about half of them eventually succeed in conceiving a child. Many treatment options are available, as we will see.

motility

Self-propulsion. A measure of the viability of sperm cells.

Male Fertility Problems

The fertility lies with the man in about 40% of cases. In about 20% of cases, problems are found in both partners.

The following fertility problems are found in men (Path2Parenthood, 2016):

autoimmune response

The production of antibodies that attack naturally occurring substances that are (incorrectly) recognized as being foreign or harmful.

- Low sperm count
- Deformed sperm
- Low sperm **motility**
- Chronic diseases such as diabetes, as well as infectious diseases such as sexually transmitted infections
- Injury to the testes
- An **autoimmune response**, in which antibodies produced by the man deactivate his own sperm
- A pituitary imbalance or thyroid disease

Critical Thinking

Sex selection raises many moral and ethical questions. Many people wonder whether people have the "right" to select the sex of their children, especially when the selection is based on nonmedical reasons. What do you think? Why?

Problems in producing normal, abundant sperm may be caused by genetic factors, advanced age, hormonal problems, diabetes, injuries to the testes, varicose veins in the scrotum, drugs (alcohol, narcotics, marijuana, tobacco), blood pressure medications, environmental toxins, excess heat, and stress. Sperm production gradually declines with age, but normal aging does not necessarily produce infertility. Men in late adulthood have fathered children (although, as noted at the beginning of the chapter, their children are at greater risk of having abnormalities).

Low sperm count (or no sperm) is the most common problem. Sperm counts of 40 million to 150 million sperm per milliliter of semen are considered normal. A count of fewer than 20 million is regarded as low. Sperm production may be low among men with undescended testes that were not surgically corrected before puberty. Also, frequent ejaculation can reduce sperm counts. Sperm production may be impaired in men whose testicles are consistently one or two degrees above the typical scrotal temperature of 94° to 95°F. Frequent hot baths and tight-fitting underwear may also be responsible for low sperm production, at least temporarily.

2 › T / F Truth or Fiction Revisited   Some men may encounter fertility problems from prolonged athletic activity, use of electric blankets, or even long, hot baths. In such cases the problem can be readily corrected. Male runners with fertility problems are often advised to take time off to increase sperm counts. Pressure, which can be caused by certain bicycle seats, may also impair fertility; have your doctor recommend a comfortable, safe seat. Aging and certain prescription and illicit drugs are other causes (Path2Parenthood, 2016).

Sometimes the sperm count is adequate, but prostate, hormonal, or other factors deprive sperm of motility or deform them. Motility can also be hampered by scar tissue from infections. Scarring may prevent sperm from passing through parts of the male reproductive system, such as the vas deferens. To be considered normal, sperm must be able to swim for at least 2 hours after coitus and most (60% or more) must be normal in shape.

Sperm counts have been increased by surgical repair of the varicose veins in the scrotum. Microsurgery can also open blocked passageways that prevent the outflow of sperm. Researchers are also investigating the effects on sperm production of special cooling undergarments. Most men whose infertility is the result of higher-than-normal scrotal temperatures show increased sperm count and quality when they wear such undergarments.

ARTIFICIAL INSEMINATION   The sperm of men with low sperm counts can be collected and frozen. The sperm from multiple ejaculations can then be injected into a woman's uterus at the time of ovulation. This is one kind of **artificial insemination**. Also, the sperm of men with low sperm motility can be injected into their partners' uteruses, so that the sperm begin their journey closer to the fallopian tubes. Sperm from a donor can be used to artificially inseminate a woman whose male partner is infertile. The child then bears the genes of one of the parents (the mother). A donor can be chosen who resembles the partner in physical traits and ethnic background.

artificial insemination
The introduction of sperm in the reproductive tract through means other than sexual intercourse.

A variation of artificial insemination has been used with some men with very low (or zero!) sperm counts in the semen, immature sperm, or immotile sperm. Immature sperm can be removed from a testicle by a thin needle and then directly injected into an egg in a laboratory dish. The method has even been successful with a few men who only have tailless spermatids in the testes.

Women also use artificial insemination to become pregnant when they do not have or wish to use a male partner. They may purchase sperm from a sperm bank, which preserves sperm in frozen "sperm straws."

Frozen "Sperm Straws" at a Sperm Bank. Sperm are preserved at sperm banks for use in artificial insemination.

Female Fertility Problems

Women encounter the following major fertility problems (Path2Parenthood, 2016):

- Irregular ovulation, including failure to ovulate
- Obstructions or malfunctions of the reproductive tract, which are often caused by infections or diseases involving the reproductive tract
- Endometriosis (inflammation of tissue sloughed off during menstruation)
- Declining hormone levels of estrogen and progesterone that occur with aging and may prevent the ovum from becoming fertilized or remaining implanted in the uterus

The most common problem in women is irregular ovulation or lack of ovulation. Many factors can play a role in failure to ovulate, including hormonal irregularities, malnutrition, genetic factors, stress, and chronic disease. Failure to ovulate may occur in response to low levels of body fat, as in the cases of women athletes and women who have eating disorders (Eguiguren & Ackerman, 2016; Gordon & LeBoff, 2014).

Ovulation may often be induced by the use of fertility drugs such as *clomiphene* (Clomid). Clomiphene stimulates the pituitary gland to secrete follicle-stimulating hormone (FSH) and luteinizing hormone (LH), which in turn stimulate the maturation of ova. Clomiphene leads to conception in most cases of infertility that are due *solely* to irregular or absent ovulation. But because infertility can have multiple causes, only about half of the women who use clomiphene become pregnant. Another infertility drug, Pergonal, contains a high concentration of FSH, which directly stimulates maturation of ovarian follicles. Like clomiphene, Pergonal has high success rates with women whose infertility is the result of lack of ovulation. These drugs may cause multiple births by stimulating more than one ovum to ripen during a month (Chehab et al., 2015).

Local infections that scar the fallopian tubes and other organs impede the passage of sperm or ova. Such infections include pelvic inflammatory disease, which is an inflammation of the woman's internal reproductive tract that can be caused by various infectious agents, such as the bacteria responsible for gonorrhea and chlamydia (see Chapter 13).

In **endometriosis**, cells break away from the uterine lining (the endometrium) and become implanted and grow elsewhere. When they develop on the surface of the ovaries or fallopian tubes, they may block the passage of ova or impair conception. About one case in six of female sterility is believed to be the result of endometriosis. Hormone treatments and surgery sometimes reduce the blockage to the point that women can conceive. A physician may suspect endometriosis during a pelvic exam, but it is diagnosed with certainty by **laparoscopy**. A long, narrow tube is inserted through an incision in the navel, permitting the physician to inspect the organs in the pelvic cavity visually. (The incision is all but undetectable.)

Suspected blockage of the fallopian tubes may also be checked by a **Rubin test** or a **hysterosalpingogram** (or "hysterogram"). In a Rubin test, carbon dioxide gas is blown through the cervix. Its pressure is then monitored to determine whether it flows freely through the fallopian tubes into the abdomen or is trapped in the uterus. In the common hysterosalpingogram, the movement of an injected dye is monitored by X-rays. This procedure may be uncomfortable. Several methods help many couples with problems such as blocked fallopian tubes bear children.

IN VITRO FERTILIZATION   When Louise Brown was born in England after being conceived by the method of **in vitro fertilization (IVF)**, the event made headlines around the world. Louise was dubbed the world's first "test-tube baby," but Louise did *not* develop in a test tube.

---

endometriosis

An abnormal condition in which endometrial tissue is sloughed off into the abdominal cavity rather than out of the body during menstruation. The condition is characterized by abdominal pain and may cause infertility.

laparoscopy

A medical procedure in which a long, narrow tube (laparoscope) is inserted through an incision in the navel, permitting the visual inspection of organs in the pelvic cavity.

Rubin test

A test in which carbon dioxide gas is blown through the cervix and its progress through the reproductive tract is tracked to determine whether or not the fallopian tubes are blocked.

hysterosalpingogram

A test in which a dye is injected into the reproductive tract and its progress is tracked by X-rays to determine whether or not the fallopian tubes are blocked.

in vitro fertilization (IVF)

A method of conception in which mature ova are surgically removed from an ovary and placed in a laboratory dish along with sperm.

3 › T / F   Truth or Fiction Revisited   With a so-called test-tube baby, conception actually takes place in a laboratory dish (not a test tube), and the embryo is then implanted in the mother's uterus, where it develops to term. Before in vitro fertilization, fertility drugs stimulate ripening of ova. Ripe ova are then surgically removed from an ovary and placed in a laboratory dish along with the father's sperm. Fertilized ova are then injected into the mother's uterus to become implanted in the uterine wall.

Several attempts may be needed to achieve a pregnancy because only a minority of attempts leads to births. Yet several embryos may be injected into the uterus at once, heightening the odds. IVF remains costly but is otherwise routine—if not guaranteed.

Laura Schieve and her colleagues (1999) studied nearly 10,000 births from IVF and found that the greatest success rates were achieved when professionals attempted to implant two embryos: 43% success among 20- to 29-year-olds and 36% success among 30- to 34-year-olds. For each age group, multiple births (of dizygotic twins) occurred in about half of the cases. IVF is associated with some greater risks for mother and child, such as high blood pressure in the mother and spontaneous abortion. Discuss the risks and rewards with your gynecologist.

SEX IN A WORLD OF DIVERSITY

LGBT FAMILY BUILDING

Not only heterosexual couples want children. So do single people. And so too do singles and couples who belong to the gay, lesbian, bisexual, or trans community.

Some gay and lesbian couples, of course, bring children from previous marriages or other kinds of relationships. But if they want children, they have to make decisions as to who the children will be and how to make it happen. Trans individuals who have had genital surgery are also sterile, so they cannot father or bear offspring.

Lesbians, of course, can conceive through sexual intercourse with a friend or confidant, but many prefer not to do so. They can also conceive through assisted productive technologies such as at-home insemination, intrauterine insemination (IUI), in vitro

fertilization (IVF), and reciprocal in vitro fertilization (RIVF). All of these methods require donor sperm, from either a known or anonymous source. IUI, known better perhaps as artificial insemination, is a low-tech method in which sperm are inserted directly into the uterus. If IUI does not work, a woman may consider IVF. When both members of a lesbian couple are fertile, they sometimes choose to harvest the eggs from one partner, have them fertilized with donor sperm, and then insert the resulting embryos in the other partner, who may become pregnant through this process. The other partner may do the same. That's why this method is called *reciprocal* IVF. It permits both partners to play a role in bearing the child.

Gay males will need a surrogate mother to become impregnated by their sperm and carry the embryo and fetus to term. Sometimes the sperm of the two potential fathers' is mixed so that the couple do not know who the biological father is. (But in cases known to the authors, father–child resemblances are clear enough.) DNA testing can also make the determination if the men want to know. But both men played a role in the process and as long as their relationship remains stable, they usually make no effort to precisely determine paternity.

Path2Parenthood (www.path2parenthood.org) invites people with questions or issues relating to fertility to be in touch with them.

gamete intrafallopian transfer (GIFT)

A method of conception in which sperm and ova are inserted into a fallopian tube to encourage conception.

zygote intrafallopian transfer (ZIFT)

A method of conception in which an ovum is fertilized in a laboratory dish and then placed in a fallopian tube.

donor IVF

A variation of in vitro fertilization in which the ovum is taken from one woman, fertilized, and then injected into the uterus or fallopian tube of another woman.

embryonic transfer

A method of conception in which a woman volunteer is artificially inseminated by the male partner of the intended mother, after which the embryo is removed from the volunteer and inserted within the uterus of the intended mother.

intracytoplasmic Sperm Injection (ICSI)

ICSI is sometimes used when the man has too few sperm for IVF, or when IVF fails. A thin (very thin!) needle injects a single sperm directly into an ovum.

surrogate mother

A woman who is impregnated, through artificial insemination, with the sperm of a prospective father, carries the embryo and fetus to term, and then gives the child to the prospective parents.

GIFT In **gamete intrafallopian transfer (GIFT)**, sperm and ova are inserted together into a fallopian tube for fertilization. Unlike IVF, conception occurs in a fallopian tube rather than a laboratory dish.

ZIFT **Zygote intrafallopian transfer (ZIFT)** is a combination of IVF and GIFT. Sperm and ova are combined in a laboratory dish. After fertilization, the zygote is placed in the mother's fallopian tube to begin its journey to the uterus for implantation. ZIFT has an advantage over GIFT in that the fertility specialists can ascertain that fertilization has occurred before insertion is performed.

DONOR IVF Donor IVF is a variation of IVF. It is used when a woman does not produce ova of her own but when her uterus is apparently capable of providing an adequate environment to bring a baby to term. An ovum is harvested from another woman—the donor. It is fertilized in vitro, often by sperm from the partner of the recipient. Then, as in other cases of IVF, the fertilized ovum is placed directly into the uterus of the recipient. The embryo becomes implanted and undergoes the remainder of prenatal development in the recipient's uterus. This procedure is known as an *embryonic transplant*.

EMBRYONIC TRANSFER Embryonic transfer can be used with women who do not produce ova of their own. A woman volunteer is artificially inseminated by the male partner of the infertile woman, or by donor sperm. Five days later the embryo is removed from the volunteer and inserted within the uterus of the mother-to-be, where it is hoped that it will become implanted.

INTRACYTOPLASMIC SPERM INJECTION Intracytoplasmic sperm injection (ICSI) can be used when a man has too few sperm for IVF, or when IVF fails. ICSI injects a sperm cell directly into an ovum. However, these methods may be associated with an increase in birth defects, such as heart, stomach, kidney, and bladder problems; cleft palate; hernia; and, in boys, malformation of the penis.

SURROGATE MOTHERHOOD Surrogate mothers bring babies to term for other women who are infertile. (The word *surrogate* means "substitute.") Surrogate mothers may be artificially inseminated by the partners of infertile women, in which case the baby thus carries the genes of the father. But sometimes—as with 53-year-old singer-songwriter James Taylor and his 47-year-old wife—ova are surgically extracted from the biological mother, fertilized in vitro by the biological father, and then implanted in another woman's uterus, where the baby is brought to term. Surrogate mothers are usually paid fees and sign agreements to surrender the baby. (These contracts have been annulled in some states, however, so surrogate mothers cannot be forced to hand over their babies.) In the case of Taylor and his wife, the surrogate mother was a friend of the family, and she delivered twins.

Biologically, surrogate motherhood might seem the mirror image of the more common artificial insemination technique in which a fertile woman is artificially inseminated with sperm from a donor. But the methods are psychologically very different. For example, sperm donors usually do not know the identity of the women who have received their sperm, nor do they follow the child's prenatal development. Surrogate mothers, however, are involved throughout the course of prenatal development.

Ethical and legal dilemmas revolve around the fact that artificially inseminated surrogate mothers have a genetic link to their babies (Lewin, 2014). If they change their minds and do not want to hand the babies over to the contractual parents, there can be legal struggles.

ADOPTION Adoption is another way for people to obtain children. Despite occasional conflicts that pit adoptive parents against biological parents who change their minds about giving up their children, most adoptions result in the formation of loving new families.

Many Americans find it easier to adopt infants from other countries or infants/children with special needs. Until the past generation, most adopted children were

European American babies adopted within a few days of birth. But the more widespread use of contraception and the decisions by many unwed mothers to keep their babies has contributed to a scarcity of European American babies. Today, however, greater numbers of adopted children are older, have spent some time in foster care, are of other races, have special needs, or were born in other countries (Priest et al., 2014). Similarly, a generation or so ago, most adoptive parents were infertile married European American couples of secure socioeconomic status. However, today many adoption agencies allow more diversity in their pool of adopting people: single people, older people, and gay males and lesbians.

Most adopted children and adoptive parents fare well, but everything is relative. Adopted children are apparently at higher risk for being insecure with their caregivers than biological children are (Gilmore, 2008; Pace et al., 2014). Everything else being equal, the younger the child at the time of adoption, the more smoothly the adoption seems to go (Klahr et al., 2011). Although adoptive parents of children from other races and ethnic backgrounds may make strong efforts to "expose" their adoptive children to their cultures of origin, children adopted at younger ages acquire the language and customs of their adoptive parents more readily (Gauthier et al., 2011). Insecurities and anxiety are most likely to emerge in middle childhood, when they do at all, because of increased understanding of what adoption means. One aspect of coping with adoption is that it often seems to be an inexplicable rejection by the birth mother, which has detrimental effects on the development of the child's self-esteem (Gilmore, 2008; MacCallum & Keeley, 2008). Institutionalization prior to adoption, which can be a form of social deprivation, can heighten problems. Postinstitutionalized children are at still greater risk of being insecure with the adoptive parents, and the insecurity can be found early (Pace et al., 2015). One study found such children to show higher cortisol (a stress hormone) levels than noninstitutionalized children in the presence of their mothers (Wismer Fries et al., 2008).

An aspect of adoption that is often not considered is its effects on the relinquishing mother (Aloi, 2009). These mothers often encounter senses of loss and guilt, along with wondering how their child is developing and adjusting.

Pregnancy

LO 9.3 **Discuss signs of pregnancy and sexual activity during pregnancy.**

Women react to pregnancy in different ways. For those who are psychologically and economically prepared, pregnancy may be greeted with joyous celebration. But an unwanted pregnancy may evoke feelings of fear and hopelessness.

In this section we examine biological and psychological aspects of pregnancy: signs of pregnancy, prenatal development, complications, effects of drugs and sex, and the psychological experiences of pregnant women and fathers.

Early Signs of Pregnancy

For many women the first sign of pregnancy is missing a period. But some women have irregular menstrual cycles or miss a period because of stress. Missing a period, then, is not a fully reliable indicator. Some women experience cyclic bleeding or spotting during pregnancy, although the blood flow is usually lighter than normal. If a woman's BBT remains high for about 3 weeks after ovulation, there is reason to suspect pregnancy even if she spots 2 weeks after ovulation.

Pregnancy Tests

Women can confirm pregnancy in a minute or two by using over-the-counter test kits that detect HCG in the urine as early as 10 days after conception. A blood test—the *beta subunit HCG radioimmunoassay (RIA)*—can detect **human chorionic gonadotropin (HCG)**

Critical Thinking
Do some or all methods of overcoming infertility strike you as being "unnatural"? Explain. Would your judgment as to whether or not these methods are natural affect your willingness to try one or more of them? Explain.

human chorionic gonadotropin (HCG)

A hormone produced by women shortly after conception, which stimulates the corpus luteum to continue to produce progesterone. The presence of HCG in a woman's urine indicates that she is pregnant.

in the woman's blood as early as the eighth day of pregnancy, about 5 days preceding her expected period.

Laboratory-based tests are considered 98% to 99% accurate. Home-based tests performed by laypeople are also considered to be quite accurate. Women are advised to consult their physicians if they suspect that they are pregnant or wish to confirm a home pregnancy test result.

Early Effects of Pregnancy

Just a few days after conception, a woman may note tenderness of the breasts. Hormonal stimulation of the mammary glands may make the breasts more sensitive and cause sensations of tingling and fullness.

morning sickness

Symptoms of pregnancy, including nausea, aversions to specific foods, and vomiting.

Morning sickness, which can actually occur throughout the day, refers to the nausea, food aversions, and vomiting that many women experience during pregnancy. Women carrying more than one child usually experience more nausea. Although called morning sickness, it is not a "sickness" at all, but rather a perfectly normal part of pregnancy. The nausea and vomiting experienced by pregnant women apparently reflects bodily changes that promote the development of the placenta (Bustos et al., 2016; Cardwell, 2012). Although it may have provided an evolutionary advantage, the usefulness of morning sickness has waned over the millennia, especially with the advent of refrigeration to help safely store foods.

miscarriage

The spontaneous or accidental expulsion of an embryo or fetus from the uterus, sometimes referred to as *spontaneous abortion*.

4 › T / F Truth or Fiction Revisited Biologists Samuel Flaxman and Paul Sherman (2000) reviewed records of some 20,000 pregnancies and found that morning sickness was associated with a healthy outcome, including lower incidences of miscarriage and stillbirth. The researchers suggest that the food aversions protect the mother and fetus from likely sources of toxins and disease-causing agents, which are most commonly found in spoiled meat.

All this may be of little consolation to pregnant women. In some cases, morning sickness is so severe that the woman cannot eat regularly and must be hospitalized to ensure that she and the fetus receive adequate nutrition. In milder cases, having small amounts of food throughout the day is of help. Many women find that eating a few crackers at bedtime and before getting out of bed in the morning are of help. Other women profit from medication. Women are advised to discuss the situation with their obstetricians rather than assume that they have to tough it out. Morning sickness usually—but not always—subsides by about the twelfth week of pregnancy. In the case of carrying twins, morning sickness may be more severe and last longer.

Pregnant women may experience greater-than-normal fatigue during the early weeks, so that they sleep longer and fall asleep more readily than usual. Frequent urination, which may also be experienced, is caused by pressure from the swelling uterus on the bladder.

Morning Sickness Does Not Spare Royalty. On the other hand, few can afford to treat morning sickness with a hospital stay. So-called morning sickness can last all day long and may be an evolutionary adaptation that prevents pregnant women from eating harmful foods. Morning sickness, despite its discomforting nature, is usually also a signal that the pregnancy is progressing in a healthful manner.

Miscarriage

Miscarriages have many causes, including chromosomal defects in the fetus and abnormalities of the placenta and uterus. Miscarriage is more common among older mothers (Klemetti et al., 2014; Mills & Lavender, 2014). About three in four miscarriages occur in the first 16 weeks of pregnancy, and most of these occur in the first 7 weeks. Some miscarriages occur so early that the woman does not know she was pregnant.

After a miscarriage, the mother or couple may feel a deep sense of loss and undergo a period of mourning. Emotional support from friends and family often helps the mother or couple cope with the loss. In most cases women who miscarry can carry subsequent pregnancies to term.

Sex During Pregnancy

Most health professionals agree that coitus is safe for pregnant women until labor begins, provided that the pregnancy is proceeding normally and the woman has no history of miscarriages. Women who experience bleeding or cramps during pregnancy may be advised by their obstetricians not to engage in coitus.

A study of 188 women showed a decline in sexual activity as pregnancy progresses (Pauleta et al., 2010). The frequency of intercourse was greatest during the first trimester, followed by the second and then the third. Nearly one in four of the women (23.4%) reported having fear of sexual intercourse during the pregnancy. About 10% said they feared intercourse could harm the baby. A few were concerned that sex would be painful.

About one in four (24.5%) said they experienced loss of sexual desire on the part of their partners. Two of five (41.5%) of the women said that they themselves felt less sensual or attractive. Nearly all (98%) of the women reported having vaginal intercourse during pregnancy. Nearly two in five (38%) reported having oral sex. Smaller numbers masturbated (20%) or had anal sex (7%).

In another study, three women in five (61%) reported having intercourse at least once a month during the third trimester (Fox et al., 2008); 24% reported intercourse at least once a week. During the two weeks prior to delivery, 40% reported having intercourse, and almost one woman in five (17%) reported having intercourse during the two days prior to delivery.

As the woman's abdominal region swells, the male-superior position becomes unwieldy. For heterosexual couples, the female-superior, lateral-entry, and rear-entry positions are common alternatives. Manual and oral sex can continue as usual. Some women are concerned that the uterine contractions of orgasm may dislodge an embryo, but such concerns are usually unfounded. Still, women and their partners are advised to ask their obstetricians about sex during pregnancy.

Psychological Changes During Pregnancy

A woman's psychological response to pregnancy reflects her desire to be pregnant, her physical changes, and her attitudes toward these changes. Women who choose to become pregnant and who have the financial, social, and psychological resources to meet the needs of pregnancy and childrearing will welcome pregnancy. Some describe it as the most wondrous experience of their lives. Other women may get pregnant accidentally, or may question their ability to handle pregnancy and childbirth. Or they may fear that pregnancy will impair their careers or their partner's feelings about them.

The first trimester may be difficult for women who are ambivalent or unhappy about the pregnancy. At that stage symptoms such as morning sickness are most pronounced, and women must come to terms with being pregnant. The second trimester is generally smoother. Morning sickness and other symptoms largely vanish. It is not yet difficult to move about, and childbirth remains a while off. Women first note fetal movement during the second trimester, and for many the experience is stirring:

> I was lying on my stomach and felt— something, like someone lightly touching my deep insides. Then I just sat very still and … felt the hugeness of having something living growing in me. Then I said, No, it's not possible, it's too early yet, and then I started to cry…. That one moment was my first body awareness of another living thing inside me. (Boston Women's Health Book Collective, 2005)

Critical Thinking
How would you explain the relationship between a woman's experience of the physical aspects of pregnancy and her desire to have a child? Why might some women consider "morning sickness" to be a blessing and other women consider it a curse?

During the third trimester it is normal, especially for first-time mothers, to worry about the mechanics of delivery and whether the child will be normal. The woman becomes increasingly heavy and literally "bent out of shape." It may become difficult to get up from a chair or out of bed. She must sit farther from the steering wheel when driving. Muscle tension from supporting the extra weight in her abdomen may cause backaches. She may feel impatient in the days and weeks just before delivery.

The mother's partner, like the mother, responds to pregnancy according to the degree to which he or she wants the child. Many partners look forward to the child with great anticipation. In such cases, pregnancy may bring partners closer together. But partners who are financially or emotionally unprepared may consider the pregnancy a "trap." And some mothers, of course, do not have partners. For single moms in the making, pregnancy is often much more frightening.

Real Students, Real Questions

Q *How often do pregnant women have to go to the doctor during the pregnancy, assuming everything is going okay, and what kinds of things happen during the visits?*

A If you think you're pregnant, arrange for prenatal care as soon as possible. If you're not sure how to do that, check in with your college health center or an organization such as Planned Parenthood. If you're young, 18 to 35 years old, you'll probably have a low-risk pregnancy and will be asked to see the doctor once a month for the first seven months, then every two to three weeks from the 28th through the 36th weeks, and then every week from the 35th week until delivery. If you're older or at high risk, your doctor will arrange to see you more often. The first visit is usually longest. You'll provide a full medical history and have a thorough physical examination, including measurements of height and weight, respiration rate (breathing), blood pressure, and pulse rate. You'll have a breast examination, Pap test, and tests for chlamydia and gonorrhea. Your state might require testing for HIV/AIDS. You may have blood, skin, and urine tests to check for anemia, blood type, cystic fibrosis, Gaucher's disease, hepatitis, rubella, sickle-cell anemia, Tay–Sachs disease, thalassemias, tuberculosis, diabetes, and Down syndrome.

At follow-ups the doctor will check your urine, blood pressure, fluid retention (swollen hands, face, feet), as well as check the growth of your uterus, examine your abdomen for the position of the fetus, and listen for the fetal heartbeat. Ultrasound will be used to show the size and position of the fetus, check the placenta, confirm the due date, detect multiple pregnancies and certain abnormalities, and of course, check out the anatomic sex of the fetus. Invasive tests such as amniocentesis and chorionic villus sampling are unusual if not quite rare today, and only recommended when blood tests and ultrasounds show ambiguous results.

During the third trimester the doctor will usually perform a biophysical profile, which combines ultrasound with a fetal monitor to check out the fetal heartbeat and movement more closely.

Prenatal Development

We can date pregnancy from the onset of the last menstrual cycle before conception, which makes the normal gestation period 280 days. We can also date pregnancy from the date at which fertilization was assumed to have taken place, which normally corresponds to 2 weeks after the beginning of the woman's last menstrual cycle. In this case, the normal gestation period is 266 days.

Once pregnancy has been confirmed, the delivery date may be calculated by *Nagele's rule:*

- Jot down the date of the first day of the last menstrual period.
- Add 7 days.
- Subtract 3 months.
- Add 1 year.

For example, if the last period began on November 12, 2019, adding 7 days yields November 19, 2019. Then subtracting 3 months yields August 19, 2019. Adding one year gives a "due date" of August 19, 2020. Few babies are born exactly when they are due,* but the great majority are delivered during a 10-day period that spans the date.

Stages of Prenatal Development

LO 9.4 Discuss the key events of the stages of prenatal development.

Shortly after conception, the single cell that results from the union of sperm and egg begins to multiply—becoming two cells, then four, then eight, and so on. During the weeks and months that follow, tissues, structures, and organs begin to form, and the fetus gradually takes on the shape of a human being. By the time the fetus is born, it consists of hundreds of billions of cells—more cells than there are stars in the Milky Way galaxy. Prenatal development can be divided into three periods: the *germinal stage,* which corresponds to about the first 2 weeks; the *embryonic stage,* which coincides with the first 2 months; and the *fetal stage.* We also commonly speak of prenatal development in terms of three trimesters of 3 months each.

THE GERMINAL STAGE Within 36 hours after conception, the zygote divides into 2 cells. It then divides repeatedly, becoming 32 cells within another 36 hours as it continues its journey to the uterus.

> **5 › T / F Truth or Fiction Revisited** For the first week after conception, a fertilized egg cell is not attached to its mother's body. It takes the zygote perhaps 3 or 4 days to reach the uterus. This mass of dividing cells then wanders about the uterus for perhaps another 3 or 4 days before it begins to become implanted in the uterine wall. Implantation takes about another week. This period from conception to implantation is termed the **germinal stage**, or the **period of the ovum** (see Figure 9.3). And during this stage, there is no external source of nutrition.

Several days into the germinal stage, the cell mass takes the form of a fluid-filled ball of cells, which is called a **blastocyst**. Already some cell differentiation has begun. Cells begin to separate into groups that will eventually become different structures. Within a thickened mass of cells that is called the **embryonic disk**, two distinct inner layers of cells are beginning to form. These cells will become the embryo and eventually the fetus. The outer part of the blastocyst, called the **trophoblast**, consists of several membranes from which the amniotic sac, placenta, and umbilical cord eventually develop.

germinal stage
The period of prenatal development before implantation in the uterus.

period of the ovum
Germinal stage.

blastocyst
A stage within the germinal stage of prenatal development, at which the embryo is a sphere of cells surrounding a cavity of fluid.

embryonic disk
The platelike inner part of the blastocyst, which differentiates into the ectoderm, mesoderm, and endoderm of the embryo.

trophoblast
The outer part of the blastocyst, from which the amniotic sac, placenta, and umbilical cord develop.

---

*The Rathi wish to boast, however, that their daughters Allyn and Jordan were born precisely on their due dates. At least one of them has been just as compulsive ever since. Nevid adds that he and his wife Judy had their son Michael within 1 day of the due date. (Close—but no cigar.)

Figure 9.3 The Ovarian Cycle, Conception, and the Early Days of the Germinal Stage.

The zygote first divides about 36 hours after conception. Continuing division creates the hollow sphere of cells termed the *blastocyst*. It is the blastocyst that becomes implanted in the wall of the uterus.

embryonic stage

The stage of prenatal development that lasts from implantation through the eighth week and is characterized by the differentiation of the major organ systems.

cephalocaudal

From the head downward.

proximodistal

From the central axis of the body outward.

ectoderm

The outermost cell layer of the newly formed embryo, from which the skin and nervous system develop.

neural tube

A hollow area in the blastocyst from which the nervous system will develop.

endoderm

The inner layer of the newly formed embryo, from which the lungs and digestive system develop.

mesoderm

The central layer of the embryo, from which the bones and muscles develop.

Implantation may be accompanied by some bleeding, which results from the usual rupturing of some small blood vessels that line the uterus. Bleeding can also be a sign of a miscarriage—although most women who experience implantation bleeding do not miscarry but go on to have normal pregnancies and deliver healthy babies.

THE EMBRYONIC STAGE The period from implantation to about the eighth week of development is called the **embryonic stage**. The major organ systems of the body begin to differentiate during this stage.

Development of the embryo follows two trends: **cephalocaudal** and **proximodistal** (see Figure 9.4). Growth of the head (the cephalic region) takes precedence over the growth of the lower parts of the body. You can also think of the body as containing a central axis that coincides with the spinal cord. The growth of the organ systems that lie close to this axis (that is, *proximal* to the axis) takes precedence over the growth of those that lie farther away toward the extremities (that is, *distal* to the axis). Relatively early maturation of the brain and organ systems that lie near the central axis allows these organs to facilitate further development of the embryo and fetus.

As the embryonic stage unfolds, the nervous system, sensory organs, hair, nails, teeth, and the outer layer of skin begin to develop from the outer layer of cells, or **ectoderm**, of the embryonic disk. By about 3 weeks after conception, two ridges appear in the embryo. The ridges fold together to form the **neural tube**. This tube develops into the nervous system. The inner layer of the embryonic disk is called the **endoderm**. From this layer develop the respiratory and digestive systems, and organs such as the liver and the pancreas. A short time later in the embryonic stage, the middle layer of cells, or **mesoderm**, differentiates and develops into the reproductive, excretory, and circulatory systems, as well as the skeleton, muscles, and the inner layer of the skin.

Figure 9.4   Human Embryos and Fetuses.

Development is cephalocaudal and proximodistal. Growth of the head takes precedence over the growth of the lower parts of the body.

A	B	C	D	E	F	G
14 days	18 days	24 days	4 weeks	6–6 1/2 weeks	7–7 1/2 weeks	9 weeks

H
11 weeks

I
15 weeks

During the third week of development, the head and blood vessels begin to form. By the fourth week, a primitive heart begins to beat and pump blood in an embryo that measures but a fifth of an inch in length. The heart will normally continue to beat without rest for every minute of every day for the better part of a century. By the end of the first month of development we can see the beginnings of the arms and legs— "arm buds" and "leg buds." The mouth, eyes, ears, and nose begin to take shape. The brain and other parts of the nervous system begin to develop.

The arms and legs develop in accordance with the proximodistal principle. First the upper arms and legs develop. Then the forearms and lower legs appear. Next the hands and feet form, followed by webbed fingers and toes by about 6 weeks to 8 weeks into development. The webbing is gone by the end of the second month. By this time the head has become rounded, and the limbs have elongated and separated. Facial features are visible. All this has occurred in an embryo that is about 1 inch long and weighs 1/30th of an ounce. During the second month, nervous impulses also begin to travel through the developing nervous system.

amniotic sac

The protective sac containing the fetus.

amniotic fluid

Fluid within the amniotic sac that suspends and protects the fetus.

placenta

An organ connected to the fetus by the umbilical cord. The placenta serves as a relay station between mother and fetus, allowing the exchange of nutrients and wastes.

umbilical cord

A tube that connects the fetus to the placenta.

The embryo—and later, the fetus—develop within a protective environment in the mother's uterus called the **amniotic sac**, which is surrounded by a clear membrane. The embryo and fetus are suspended within the sac in **amniotic fluid**. The amniotic fluid acts like a shock absorber. It cushions the embryo from damage that might result from the mother's movements. The fluid also helps maintain a steady temperature.

Nutrients and waste products are exchanged between mother and embryo (or fetus) through a mass of tissue called the **placenta**. The placenta is unique in origin. It develops from material supplied by both mother and embryo. Toward the end of the first trimester, it becomes a flattish, round organ about seven inches in diameter and one inch thick—larger than the fetus itself. The fetus is connected to the placenta by the **umbilical cord**. The mother is connected to the placenta by the system of blood vessels in the uterine wall. The umbilical cord develops about 5 weeks after conception and reaches 20 inches in length. It contains two arteries through which maternal nutrients reach the embryo. A vein transports waste products back to the mother.

The circulatory systems of mother and embryo do not mix. A membrane in the placenta permits only certain substances to pass through, such as oxygen (from the mother to the fetus); carbon dioxide and other wastes (from the embryo or fetus to the mother, to be eliminated by the mother's lungs and kidneys); nutrients; some microscopic disease-causing organisms; and some drugs, including aspirin, narcotics, alcohol, and tranquilizers.

The placenta is also an endocrine gland. It secretes hormones that preserve the pregnancy, stimulates the uterine contractions that induce childbirth, and helps prepare the breasts for breastfeeding. Some of these hormones may also cause the signs of pregnancy. HCG stimulates the corpus luteum to continue to produce progesterone. The placenta itself secretes increasing amounts of estrogen and progesterone. Ultimately, the placenta passes from the woman's body after delivery. For this reason, it is also called the "afterbirth."

THE FETAL STAGE   The fetal stage begins by the ninth week and continues until birth. By about the ninth or tenth week the fetus begins to respond to the outside world by turning in the direction of external stimulation. By the end of the first trimester the major organ systems, the fingers and toes, and the external genitals have been formed. The sex of the fetus can be determined visually. The eyes are clearly distinguishable.

During the second trimester the fetus increases dramatically in size, and its organ systems continue to mature. The brain now contributes to the regulation of basic body functions. The fetus increases in weight from 1 *ounce* to 2 *pounds* and grows from about 4 to 14 inches in length. Soft, downy hair grows above the eyes and on the scalp. The skin turns ruddy because of blood vessels that show through the surface. (During the third trimester layers of fat beneath the skin will give the red a pinkish hue.)

Usually by the middle of the fourth month the mother can feel the first fetal movements. By the end of the second trimester the fetus moves its limbs so vigorously that the mother may complain of being kicked—often at 4:00 a.m. It opens and shuts its eyes, sucks its thumb, alternates between periods of wakefulness and sleep, and perceives lights and sounds. The fetus also does somersaults, which the mother will definitely feel. Fortunately, the umbilical cord will not break or strangle the fetus, no matter what acrobatic feats the fetus performs.

An illustration of a Fetus at 9 Weeks. Developmental changes are most rapid and dramatic during prenatal development. Within a few months, the human embryo, then the fetus, advances from weighing a fraction of an ounce to several pounds, and from one cell to billions of cells. Development is cephalocaudal and proximodistal. Growth of the head takes precedence over the growth of the lower parts of the body.

Near the end of the second trimester the fetus approaches the **age of viability**. Still, only a minority of babies born at the end of the second trimester who weigh under two pounds will survive—even with intense medical efforts.

During the third trimester, the organ systems continue to mature and enlarge. The heart and lungs become increasingly capable of maintaining independent life. Typically, during the seventh month the fetus turns upside down in the uterus so that it will be head first, or in a **cephalic presentation**, for delivery. But some fetuses do not turn during this month. If such a fetus is born prematurely it can have either a **breech presentation** (bottom first) or a shoulder-first presentation, which can complicate problems of prematurity. The closer to term (the full 9 months) the baby is born, the more likely it is that the presentation will be cephalic. If birth occurs at the end of the eighth month, the odds are overwhelmingly in favor of survival.

During the final months of pregnancy, the mother may become concerned that the fetus seems to be less active than before. Generally, the change in activity level is normal. The fetus has grown so large that it is cramped, and its movements are restricted.

age of viability

The age at which a fetus can sustain independent life.

cephalic presentation

Emergence of the baby head first from the womb.

breech presentation

Emergence of the baby bottom or feet first from the womb.

Environmental Influences on Prenatal Development

LO 9.5 **Discuss the effects of environmental hazards on the child.**

Advances in scientific knowledge have made us more aware of the changes that take place during prenatal development. They have also heightened our awareness of the problems that can occur and what might be done to prevent them. These include the mother's diet, maternal diseases and disorders, and the mother's use of drugs.

THE MOTHER'S DIET It is a common misconception that the fetus will take what it needs from its mother. If this were true, pregnant women would not have to be highly concerned about their diets. But malnutrition in the mother, especially during the last trimester when the fetus should be making rapid gains in weight, has been linked to low birth weight, prematurity, stunted growth, retardation of brain development, cognitive deficiencies, behavioral problems, and even cardiovascular disease (Monk et al., 2013; de Souza et al., 2011).

Generally speaking, the slimmer a woman is prior to pregnancy, the more weight she is advised to gain during pregnancy. For example, a woman with a body mass index (BMI)* of less than 18.5 is advised to gain 28 to 40 pounds (Rasmussen et al., 2009; see Table 9.1). Normal-weight women, those with a BMI of 24.9 or less, are advised to gain 25 to 35 pounds. However, 55% of pregnant women in the United States are overweight or obese (Parker-Pope, 2009b). Women who are overweight, with a BMI of 25 to 29.9 are advised to gain 15 to 25 pounds. And obese women, those with a BMI over 30, are advised to limit their weight gain to 11 to 20 pounds. Regular weight gains are most desirable.

Table 9.1 Body Mass Index (BMI) and Weight Status

BMI	Weight Status
Below 18.5	Underweight
18.5–24.9	Normal
25.0–29.9	Overweight
30.0 and Above	Obese

MATERNAL DISEASES AND DISORDERS Environmental influences or agents that can harm the embryo or fetus are called **teratogens**. These include drugs taken by the mother, such as alcohol and even aspirin, as well as substances produced by the mother's body, such as Rh-positive antibodies. Other teratogens include the metals lead and mercury, radiation, and disease-causing organisms such as viruses and bacteria. Although many disease-causing organisms cannot pass through the placenta to infect the embryo or fetus, some extremely small organisms, such as those

teratogens

Environmental influences or agents that can harm an embryo or fetus.

---

*The formula for calculating your BMI is: weight (lb)/[height (in)]^2 × 703. That is, divide your weight in pounds (lbs) by your height in inches (in.) squared, and multiply by a conversion factor of 703. For example:

Weight = 150 lbs, Height = 5'5" (65')

Calculation: [150 ÷ (65)^2] × 703 = 24.96.

Figure 9.5 Critical Periods in Prenatal Development.

The developing embryo is most vulnerable to teratogens when the organ systems are taking shape. The periods of greatest vulnerability of organ systems are shown in gray. Periods of lesser vulnerability are shown in yellow.

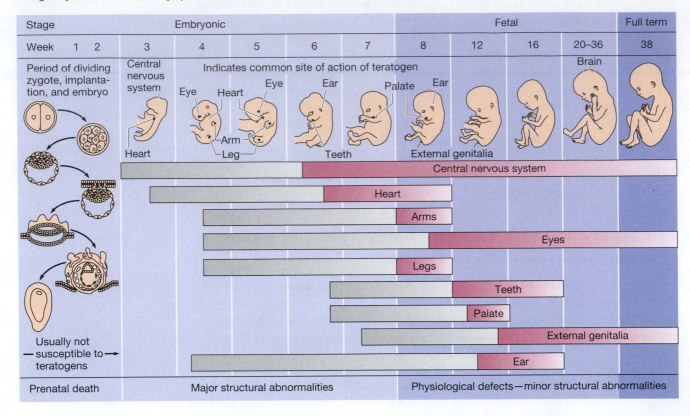

causing syphilis, measles, mumps, and chicken pox, can. Some disorders such as toxemia are not transmitted to the embryo or fetus but can adversely affect the environment in which it develops.

critical period of vulnerability

A period of time during which an embryo or fetus is vulnerable to the effects of a teratogen.

CRITICAL PERIODS OF VULNERABILITY The times at which exposure to particular teratogens can cause the greatest harm are termed **critical periods of vulnerability**. Critical periods correspond to the times at which the structures most affected by the teratogens are developing (see Figure 9.5). The heart, for example, develops rapidly from the third to the fifth week after conception. It may be most vulnerable to certain teratogens at this time. The arms and legs, which develop later, are most vulnerable from the fourth through the eighth week of development. Because the major organ systems differentiate during the embryonic stage, the embryo is most vulnerable to the effects of teratogens. Let us now consider some of the most damaging effects of specific maternal diseases and disorders.

Rubella

A viral infection that can cause mental retardation and heart disease in an embryo. Also called *German measles*.

RUBELLA (GERMAN MEASLES) **Rubella** is a viral infection. Women who contract rubella during the first month or two of pregnancy, when rapid differentiation of major organ systems is taking place, may bear children who are deaf or who develop mental retardation, heart disease, or cataracts. Risk of these defects declines as pregnancy progresses. Yet because of a successful vaccination program, the Centers for Disease Control and Prevention (CDC) has declared that rubella has been eliminated in the United States (Mayo Clinic, 2016).

syphilis

A sexually transmitted bacterial infection.

stillbirth

The birth of a dead fetus.

SYPHILIS Maternal **syphilis** may cause miscarriage or **stillbirth**, or be passed along to the child in the form of congenital syphilis. Congenital syphilis can impair the vision and hearing, damage the liver, or deform the bones and teeth.

Routine blood tests early in pregnancy can diagnose syphilis and other problems. Because the bacteria that cause syphilis do not readily cross the placental membrane during the first months of pregnancy, the fetus will probably not contract syphilis if an infected mother is treated successfully with antibiotics before the fourth month of pregnancy. However, an infected and untreated woman has about a 40% chance of having a child who is stillborn or dies shortly after birth (Centers for Disease Control and Prevention, 2013a). The baby has a 40% to 70% chance of being infected in utero and of developing congenital syphilis, and about 12% of those infected die.

HIV/AIDS   Acquired immunodeficiency syndrome (AIDS) is caused by the *human immunodeficiency virus (HIV)*. HIV is blood-borne and is sometimes transmitted through the placenta to infect the fetus. The rupturing of blood vessels in mother and baby during childbirth provides another opportunity for transmission of HIV. *However, the majority of babies born to mothers who are infected with HIV do not become infected themselves.* Using antiviral medication can also minimize the probability of transmission. It also appears that women can decrease the risk of becoming infected with HIV by regular use of antiviral drugs such as Truvada (Callahan et al., 2015; Conniff & Evensen, 2016). HIV can also be transmitted to children by breastfeeding. Newborns can be infected while in the uterus and during childbirth (Mofenson, 2000; Wood et al., 2000).

> **acquired immunodeficiency syndrome (AIDS)** A condition caused by HIV that destroys white blood cells in the immune system, leaving the body vulnerable to various "opportunistic" diseases.

Children from ethnic and racial minority groups are at greater risk of being infected with HIV. African Americans account for approximately half of the pediatric cases of HIV/AIDS, and Latin Americans (especially those of Puerto Rican origin) account for almost one-fourth of them (Bangs & Davis, 2015; Office of Minority Health & Health Disparities [OMHD], 2010). As we will see in Chapter 13, inner-city neighborhoods, where there is widespread intravenous drug use, are especially hard hit (OMHD, 2010).

PREECLAMPSIA   Preeclampsia, also known as *toxemia*, is a life-threatening condition characterized by high blood pressure. It may afflict women late in the second or early in the third trimester of pregnancy. The first stage is termed *preeclampsia*. It is diagnosed by protein in the urine, swelling from fluid retention, and high blood pressure. It may be mild at first, but as preeclampsia worsens, the mother may have headaches and visual problems from high blood pressure, along with abdominal pain. If left untreated, the disease may progress to the final stage, *eclampsia*. Eclampsia can lead to maternal or fetal death. Babies born to women with toxemia are often undersized or premature.

> **preeclampsia** A life-threatening condition that is characterized by high blood pressure; also known as *toxemia*.

The disorder appears to be linked to malnutrition. Ironically, undernourished women may gain weight rapidly through fluid retention, but their swollen appearance

---

A CLOSER LOOK

PREVENTING YOUR BABY FROM BEING INFECTED WITH HIV

Pregnant women who are infected with HIV or other STIs should discuss these conditions with their physicians. Measures can be taken that will help prevent their babies from being infected. The current recommendations concerning transmission of HIV from mother to baby include ART, Cesarean section (C-section), and formula feeding. ART stands for antiretroviral therapy—the use of a combination of drugs that reduce the amount of HIV in the bloodstream. C-sections help to prevent transmission of HIV to the baby because the baby is not exposed to the mother's blood to the extent that it is during vaginal delivery, when blood vessels rupture. HIV is also found in breast milk; hence the recommendation for formula feeding. All in all, the combination of ART and C-section has reduced the risk that the mother will transmit HIV to her baby to about 1 in 400 (Townsend et al., 2014). Using formula feeding cuts the risk further (Rutstein et al., 2015; Unger et al., 2014).

For up-to-date information on HIV/AIDS, call the National AIDS Hotline at 1-800-342-AIDS. If you want to receive information in Spanish, call 1-800-344-SIDA.

may discourage them from eating. Pregnant women who gain weight rapidly but have not increased their food intake should consult their obstetricians.

ectopic pregnancy

A pregnancy in which the fertilized ovum becomes implanted someplace other than the uterus.

ECTOPIC PREGNANCY   In an **ectopic pregnancy**, the fertilized ovum implants itself someplace other than the uterus. Most ectopic pregnancies occur in a fallopian tube ("tubal pregnancies") when the ovum is prevented from moving into the uterus because of obstructions caused by infections. Ectopic pregnancies are more common among older women. If ectopic pregnancies do not abort spontaneously, they must be removed by surgery or aborted by use of drugs such as methotrexate because the fetus cannot develop to term. Delay in removal may cause hemorrhaging and the death of the mother. A woman with a tubal pregnancy will not menstruate but may notice spotty bleeding and abdominal pain.

Rh incompatibility

A condition in which antibodies produced by a pregnant woman are transmitted to the fetus and may cause brain damage or death.

RH INCOMPATIBILITY   In **Rh incompatibility**, antibodies produced by the mother are transmitted to the fetus or newborn infant. *Rh* is a blood protein found in some people's red blood cells. Rh incompatibility occurs when a woman who does not have this blood factor, and is thus *Rh-negative,* is carrying an *Rh-positive* fetus, which can happen if the father is Rh-positive. The negative–positive combination is found in about 10% of U.S. couples. However, it becomes a problem only in a minority of resulting pregnancies. In such cases the mother's antibodies attack the red blood cells of the fetus, which can cause brain damage or death. Rh incompatibility does not usually adversely affect a first child because women will usually not yet have formed antibodies to the Rh factor.

Because mother and fetus have separate circulatory systems, it is unlikely that Rh-positive fetal red blood cells will enter the Rh-negative mother's body. The probability of an exchange of blood increases during childbirth, however, especially when the placenta becomes detached from the uterine wall. If an exchange of blood occurs, the mother will then produce antibodies to the baby's Rh-positive blood. The mother's antibodies may enter the fetal bloodstream and cause a condition called *fetal erythroblastosis*, which can result in anemia, mental deficiency, or even the death of the fetus or newborn infant.

Fortunately, blood-typing of pregnant women significantly decreases the threat of uncontrolled erythroblastosis. If an Rh-negative mother is inoculated with Rhogan within 72 hours after delivery of an Rh-positive baby, she will not develop the dangerous antibodies and will not pass them on to the fetus in a subsequent pregnancy. A fetus or newborn child at risk for erythroblastosis may also receive a preventive blood transfusion, to remove the mother's Rh-positive antibodies from its blood.

DRUGS TAKEN BY THE MOTHER (OR HER PARTNER)   Some widely used drugs, including nonprescription drugs, are linked with birth abnormalities. In the 1960s, the drug thalidomide was marketed to pregnant women as a presumably safe treatment for nausea and insomnia. However, the drug caused birth deformities, including stunted or missing limbs. Maternal use of illegal drugs such as cocaine and marijuana may also place the fetus at risk.

Paternal use of certain drugs also may endanger the fetus. One question is whether drugs alter the genetic material in the father's sperm. The use of certain substances by those who come into contact with a pregnant woman can harm the fetus. For example, the mother's inhalation of secondhand tobacco or marijuana smoke can hurt the fetus.

Several antibiotics may harm a fetus, especially if they are taken during certain periods of fetal development. Tetracycline may yellow the teeth and deform the bones (Vennila et al., 2014). Other antibiotics have been implicated in deafness and jaundice. Acne drugs such as Accutane can cause physical and mental handicaps in the children of women who use them during pregnancy. Antihistamines, used commonly for allergies, may deform the fetus.

If you are pregnant, or suspect that you are, it is advisable to consult your obstetrician before taking any and all drugs, not just prescription drugs. Your obstetrician can usually direct you to a safe and effective substitute for a drug that could harm a fetus.

HORMONES   The hormones progestin and DES have sometimes been used to help women at risk of miscarriage maintain their pregnancies. When taken at about the time that sex organs differentiate, progestin (which is similar in composition to male sex hormones) can masculinize the external sex organs of embryos with female (XX) sex chromosomal structures. Progestin taken during the first trimester has also been linked to increased levels of aggressive behavior during childhood.

DES (**diethylstilbestrol**), a powerful estrogen, was given to many women at risk for miscarriage from the 1940s through the 1960s to help maintain their pregnancies. DES is suspected of causing cervical and testicular cancer in some of the children whose mothers used it when pregnant (Centers for Disease Control and Prevention, 2005b). Other problems have been reported as well. Daughters whose mothers used DES during their pregnancies have a higher-than-expected rate of miscarriages and premature deliveries. It was once suspected that men who were exposed prenatally to DES had higher than expected rates of infertility. However, research reveals no connection between in utero exposure to DES and male infertility. DES users themselves appear to be at high risk of some serious medical problems, such as breast cancer (Centers for Disease Control and Prevention, 2005b).

DES
(Diethylstilbestrol) An estrogen that was once given to women at risk for miscarriage to help maintain pregnancy.

VITAMINS   Many pregnant women are prescribed daily doses of multivitamins to maintain their own health and to promote the development of a healthy pregnancy. "Too much of a good thing" may be hazardous, however. High doses of vitamins such as A, B6, D, and K have been linked to birth defects. Vitamin A excesses have been linked with cleft palate and eye damage, whereas excesses of vitamin D are linked to mental retardation.

NARCOTICS   Narcotics such as heroin and methadone can readily pass from mother to fetus through the placental membrane. Narcotics are addictive. Fetuses of mothers who use them regularly during pregnancy can become addicted in utero. At birth, such babies may undergo withdrawal and show muscle tension and agitation. Women who use narcotics are advised to notify their obstetricians so that measures can be taken to aid the infants before and after delivery.

TRANQUILIZERS AND SEDATIVES   Tranquilizers (benzodiazepines) cross the placental membrane and affect the fetus, but there is relatively little information on possible harm. One current article suggests that low doses of lorazepam may be safe but that diazepam is to be avoided (Kim & Hebert, 2015). Ask your obstetrician. Sedatives and anticonvulsants, such as the barbiturate *phenobarbital*, are suspected of adversely affecting the developing nervous system of the fetus (Eadie & Vajda, 2016). Again: Use no drugs during pregnancy without the knowledge and approval of your obstetrician.

MARIJUANA   The active ingredient in marijuana, THC, readily crosses the placenta. Now that recreational use of marijuana has been legalized in many states, it is more crucial than ever to consider the effects of using marijuana during pregnancy. Research into the cognitive effects of maternal prenatal use of marijuana has yielded mixed results. Some studies suggest that there may be no impairment, but others suggest that cognitive skills, including learning and memory, may be impaired (Giussani, 2011; Huizink, 2013). Fetal exposure to marijuana may also impair systems in the brain that regulate emotional behavior (Dvorak & Day, 2014; Wang et al., 2004).

Researchers have also found evidence that suggests that maternal use of marijuana during pregnancy predisposes offspring to dependence on opiates (narcotics derived from the opium poppy). The fetal brain, like the adult brain, has cannabinoid receptors—called CB-1-receptors—and other structures that are altered by exposure to marijuana. The alterations make the individual more sensitive to the reinforcing properties of opiates, even in adulthood (Hurd et al., 2014).

ALCOHOL   Mothers who drink heavily during pregnancy expose the fetus to greater risk of birth defects, infant mortality, sensory and motor problems, and mental retardation (Paintner et al., 2012). Nearly 40% of children whose mothers drank heavily during pregnancy develop **fetal alcohol syndrome (FAS)**. FAS is a cluster of symptoms typified by developmental lags and characteristic facial features, such as an underdeveloped upper jaw, flattened nose, and widely spaced eyes. Infants with FAS are often smaller than average and have smaller than average brains. They may be mentally retarded, lack coordination, and have deformed limbs and heart problems. They are more susceptible to developing conduct disorders in middle childhood (Disney et al., 2008).

fetal alcohol syndrome (FAS)
A cluster of symptoms caused by maternal drinking, in which the child shows developmental lags and characteristic facial features such as an underdeveloped upper jaw, flattened nose, and widely spaced eyes.

6 › T / F   Truth or Fiction Revisited   It has *not* been shown that pregnant women can have one or two alcoholic beverages a day without harming their babies. Although research suggests that light drinking is unlikely to harm the fetus in most cases, FAS has been found even among the children of mothers who drank only two ounces of alcohol a day during the first trimester (Astley & Clarren, 2001). Moreover, individual sensitivities to alcohol may vary widely. The critical period for the development of the facial features associated with FAS seems to be the first 2 months of prenatal development, when the head is taking shape. Here is the key takeaway: *There is no guaranteed safe minimum amount of drinking during pregnancy* (Charness et al., 2016; Kelly et al., 2013).

CIGARETTE SMOKING   Cigarette smoke contains many ingredients, including the stimulant nicotine, the gas carbon monoxide, and hydrocarbons ("tars"), which are carcinogens. Fortunately, only the first two of these, nicotine and carbon monoxide, pass through the placenta and reach the fetus. That's the end of the fortunate news. Cigarette smoke also lessens the amount of oxygen received by the fetus. Maternal smoking increases the risk of spontaneous abortion and complications during pregnancy such as premature rupturing of the amniotic sac, stillbirth, premature birth, low birth weight, and early infant mortality (Beyerlein et al., 2011). Maternal smoking may also lead to attention deficit hyperactivity disorder and impair the child's intellectual development (Kuja-Halkola et al., 2014; Thapar et al., 2012). In one study, women who smoked during pregnancy were 50% more likely than women who did not smoke to have children whose intelligence test scores placed them in the mentally retarded range (that is, beneath an IQ score of 70) when the children were 10 years old (Drews et al., 1996).

Low birth weight is a common risk factor for infant disease, mortality, and problems in learning in school (Kuja-Halkola et al., 2014). The combination of smoking and drinking alcohol places the child at greater risk of low birth weight than either practice alone (Bottorff et al., 2014; Spencer, 2006). Maternal smoking affects the fetal heart rate and increases the risk of sudden infant death syndrome (SIDS) (Gordon et al., 2002; Smylie et al., 2014). Maternal smoking has also been linked to reduced lung function in newborns (Sasaki et al., 2008) and asthma in childhood (Goodwin et al., 2009). Evidence also points to reduced attention spans, hyperactivity, and lower IQ and achievement test scores in children exposed to maternal smoking during and after pregnancy.

Smoking by other household members may endanger a fetus because secondary smoke (smoke exhaled by the smoker or emitted from the tip of a lit cigarette) may be absorbed by the mother and passed along to the fetus (Evlampidou et al., 2015; Niu et al., 2015). Passive exposure to secondhand smoke during infancy is also linked to increased risk of SIDS (Gordon et al., 2002).

Tempting?—Don't Do It! Cigarettes diminish the baby's oxygen supply and increase the risk of miscarriage. Alcohol? There is no safe limit for drinking while pregnant. Some women exercise control over cigarettes by thinking, "It's only for a few months." (Then, however, some quitters stay quit.)

Our clinical experience suggests that it may be easier for pregnant women to quit smoking if they consider quitting as limited to the term of their pregnancy rather than as permanent. Then, of course, if they should remain abstinent after delivery, perhaps they will not be disappointed.

METHAMPHETAMINE   Prenatal exposure to methamphetamine is associated with increased emotional reactivity, anxiety, and hyperactivity by the age of 5 (LaGasse et al., 2012).

OTHER AGENTS   X-rays increase the risk of malformed organs in the fetus, especially within a month and a half after conception. (Ultrasound has *not* been shown to harm the embryo or fetus.)

Chromosomal and Genetic Abnormalities

LO 9.6   **Discuss the effects of genetic abnormalities on the child.**

Not all of us have the normal complement of chromosomes. Some of us have genes that threaten our health or our existence (see Table 9.2).

DOWN SYNDROME   Children with Down syndrome have characteristic round faces; wide, flat noses; protruding tongues; and a downward sloping crease of skin in the inner corners of the eyes. They often suffer from respiratory problems and heart malformations; these problems tend to claim their lives by middle age—the "prime of life" for most people. The individuals with Down syndrome are also moderately mentally retarded, but they usually can learn to read and write. With a little help from family and social agencies, they may hold jobs and lead largely independent lives.

The risk of giving birth to a child with Down syndrome increases with the mother's age (see Table 9.3). Down syndrome is usually caused by an extra chromosome on the twenty-first pair ("Trisomy 21"). In most cases, Down syndrome is transmitted by the mother. About 5,300 children with Down Syndrome are born each year in the United States, and there are about 3,100 Down Syndrome-related elective pregnancy terminations each year (de Graaf et al., 2015).

Table 9.2 Some Chromosomal and Genetic Abnormalities

Health Problem	Comments
Cystic fibrosis	A genetic disease in which the pancreas and lungs become clogged with mucus, which impairs the processes of respiration and digestion.
Down syndrome	A condition characterized by a third chromosome on the twenty-first pair. The child with Down syndrome is mentally retarded and has a characteristic fold of skin over each eye and mental retardation. The risk of having a child with the syndrome increases as parents increase in age.
Hemophilia	A sex-linked disorder in which blood does not clot properly.
Huntington disease	A fatal neurological disorder with an onset that occurs in middle adulthood.
Neural tube defects	Disorders of the brain or spine, such as *anencephaly*, in which part of the brain is missing, and *spina bifida*, in which part of the spine is exposed or missing. Anencephaly is fatal shortly after birth, but some spina bifida victims survive for a number of years, albeit with severe handicaps.
Phenylketonuria	A disorder in which children cannot metabolize phenylalanine, which builds up in the form of phenylpyruvic acid and causes mental retardation. The disorder can be diagnosed at birth and controlled by diet.
Retinal blastoma	A form of blindness caused by a dominant gene.
Sickle-cell disease	A blood disorder that mostly afflicts African Americans, in which deformed blood cells obstruct small blood vessels, decreasing their capacity to carry oxygen and heightening the risk of occasionally fatal infections
Tay-Sachs disease	A fatal neurological disorder that primarily afflicts Jews of European origin.

Table 9.3 Likelihood of Giving Birth to an Infant With Down Syndrome, According to Maternal Age

SOURCE: National Down Syndrome Society. (2012). What is the Likelihood of Having a Child with Down Syndrome? http://www.ndss.org/Down-Syndrome/What-Is-Down-Syndrome/

Maternal Age	Incidence of Down syndrome
20	1 in 2,000
25	1 in 1,200
30	1 in 900
35	1 in 350
40	1 in 100
45	1 in 30
49	1 in 10

recessive trait

A trait that is not expressed when the gene or genes involved have been paired with dominant genes. Recessive traits are transmitted to future generations, however, and are expressed if they are paired with other recessive genes.

amniocentesis

A procedure for drawing off and examining fetal cells in the amniotic fluid to determine the presence of various disorders in the fetus.

It's a Girl! (Or a Boy!) Ultrasound is used to help test for many kinds of birth defects. After a few months ultrasound also reveals the anatomic sex of the fetus.

SICKLE-CELL DISEASE AND TAY-SACHS DISEASE Sickle-cell disease and Tay-Sachs disease are genetic disorders that are most likely to afflict certain racial and ethnic groups. Sickle-cell disease is most prevalent in the United States among African Americans, affecting 90,000–100,000 people (Sickle-Cell Disease, 2015). In sickle-cell disease, the red blood cells assume a sickle shape—hence the name—and they form clumps that obstruct narrow blood vessels and diminish the supply of oxygen. As a result, victims can suffer problems ranging from swollen, painful joints to potentially lethal problems such as pneumonia and heart and kidney failure. Infections are a leading cause of death among those with the disease. However, mortality rates have fallen as a result of a pneumonia vaccine, early diagnosis, and early treatment (Sickle-Cell Disease, 2015).

Tay-Sachs disease is a fatal neurological disease of young children. Only 1 in 100,000 people in the United States is affected, but among Jews of Eastern European background the figure rises steeply to 1 in 3,600 (Bodurtha & Strauss, 2012). The disease is characterized by degeneration of the central nervous system and gives rise to retardation, loss of muscle control, paralysis, blindness, and deafness. Victims seldom live beyond the age of 5.

SEX-LINKED GENETIC ABNORMALITIES Some genetic defects, such as hemophilia, are sex linked, in that they are carried only on the X sex chromosome. They are transmitted from generation to generation as **recessive traits**. Females, each of whom has two X sex chromosomes, are less likely than males to be afflicted by sex-linked disorders because the genes that carry the disorder would have to be present on both of their sex chromosomes for the disorder to be expressed. Sex-linked disorders are more likely to afflict sons of female carriers because they have only one X sex chromosome, which they inherit from their mothers. England's Queen Victoria was a hemophilia carrier and transmitted the condition to many of her children, who in turn carried it into several ruling families of Europe. For this reason, hemophilia has been dubbed the "royal disease."

AVERTING CHROMOSOMAL AND GENETIC ABNORMALITIES Health professionals gather information about a couple's medical background and family history of genetic defects to help them appraise the risks of passing along genetic defects to their children. Some couples facing a high risk of passing along genetic defects to their children decide to adopt. Other couples decide to terminate the pregnancy if the fetus is discovered to have certain abnormalities. Although we will discuss **amniocentesis** and chorionic villus sampling (CVS), it should be noted that their use is declining because blood tests and ultrasound are becoming more sophisticated and used more frequently to assess the presence of Down syndrome and other disorders (Brody, 2013). By the time an amniocentesis would be scheduled, a woman may have had several blood tests and ultrasounds, which provide evidence of chromosomal as well as genetic abnormalities, and also provide reasonably clear pictures of the embryo and fetus.

Amniocentesis and CVS are invasive techniques that may still be recommended to confirm ambiguous findings from blood tests and ultrasounds. Amniocentesis is usually performed about 4 months into pregnancy but is sometimes done earlier. Fluid is drawn from the amniotic sac (or "bag of waters") with a syringe. Fetal cells in the fluid are grown in a culture and examined under a microscope for the presence of biochemical and chromosomal abnormalities. CVS is performed at about 10 weeks. A narrow tube is used to snip off material from the chorion, which is a membrane that contains the amniotic sac and fetus. The material is analyzed. Amniocentesis and CVS both carry some risk of miscarriage and may be unnecessary—ask for a second opinion if the recommendation is made and you are concerned about it (Akolekar et al., 2014). We're not saying that you should refuse the tests, only that you may wish to seek the opinion of other health professionals if they are recommended.

A CLOSER LOOK

THE EFFECTS OF PARENTS' AGE ON CHILDREN: DO MEN REALLY HAVE ALL THE TIME IN THE WORLD?

What if 30-year-old women started looking at 50-year-old men as damaged goods, what with their washed-up sperm, meaning those 50-year-olds might actually have to date (gasp!) women their own age? What if men, as the years passed, began to look with new eyes at Ms. Almost Right?

—Lisa Belkin

The artist Pablo Picasso fathered children in his 70s. Former Senator Strom Thurmond fathered a child in his 90s. It has been widely known that women's chances of conceiving children decline as they age. The traditional message has been "Women: You'd better hurry up. Men: You have all the time in the world" (Belkin, 2009).

Not so, apparently. True: From a biological vantage point, the 20s may be the ideal age for women to bear children. Teenage mothers have a higher incidence of infant mortality and children with low birth weight (Martin et al., 2008; Save the Children, 2014). Early teens who become pregnant may place a burden on bodies that may not have adequately matured to facilitate pregnancy and childbirth. Teenage mothers also are less educated and less likely to obtain prenatal care.

What about women older than 30 years old? Women's fertility declines gradually until the mid-30s, after which it declines more rapidly. Women beyond their middle-30s may have passed the point at which their reproductive systems function most efficiently. Women possess their ova in immature form at birth. Over 30 years, these cells are exposed to the slings and arrows of an outrageous environment of toxic wastes, chemical pollutants, and radiation, thus increasing the risk of chromosomal abnormalities such as Down syndrome. Women who wait until their 30s or 40s to have children also increase the likelihood of having stillborn or preterm babies, or children with autism (Martin et al., 2008; Sandin et al., 2012). But with adequate prenatal care, the risk of bearing a premature or unhealthy baby still is relatively small, even for older first-time mothers (Martin et al., 2008). This news should be encouraging for women who have delayed, or plan to delay, bearing children until their 30s or 40s.

Older fathers are more likely to produce abnormal sperm, leading to fertility problems (Parner et al., 2012). But that's only the tip of the iceberg. University of Queensland researchers analyzed data from some 33,000 U.S. children and found that the older the father is at conception, the lower a child's score may be on tests of reading skills, reasoning, memory, and concentration. The ages of 29 and 30 are something of a turning point for men, because children conceived past these ages are at greater risk for the psychological disorders of schizophrenia and bipolar disorder (Perrin et al., 2007). Children born to men past the age of 40 also have a greater risk of autism and **schizophrenia** (Callaway, 2012; Reichenberg et al., 2006; see Figure 9.6).

These findings do not mean that the majority of children born to men past their reproductive "prime" will develop these problems, but it does mean that men's age, as women's, is related to risks for their children. As noted by one of the researchers in schizophrenia, "It turns out the optimal age for being a mother is the same as the optimal age for being a father" (Malaspina, 2009).

Figure 9.6 Risky Business?

Chance of autism spectrum disorder among 132,271 subjects by paternal age.

SOURCE: *Archives of General Psychiatry*, September 2006.

Chance of autism spectrum disorder among 132,271 subjects, by paternal age:

6 in 10,000

15- to 29-year-old fathers

9 in 10,000

30- to 39-year-old fathers

32 in 10,000

40- to 49-year-old fathers

52 in 10,000

50-year-old fathers and older

Childbirth

Early in the ninth month of pregnancy, the fetus's head settles in the pelvis. This shift is called *dropping* or *lightening*. The woman may actually feel lighter because of lessened pressure on the diaphragm. About a day or so before the beginning of labor, the woman may notice blood in her vaginal secretions because fetal pressure on the pelvis may rupture superficial blood vessels in the birth canal. Tissue that had plugged the cervix, possibly preventing entry of infectious agents from the vagina, becomes dislodged. There is a resultant discharge of bloody mucus. At

schizophrenia

A severe psychological disorder characterized by problems in thought, language, and perception.

Real Students, Real Questions

Q *What triggers childbirth?*

A It is speculated that hormones secreted by the fetus may stimulate the placenta and the mother's uterus to secrete prostaglandins that, in turn, cause uterine muscles to contract. These contractions might feel similar to premenstrual cramping. Thus, it could be that the fetus has a mechanism for signaling the mother that it is ready to sustain independent life. Other possible triggers include the possible "urge" of the uterus to empty itself when it reaches a certain fullness or aging of the placenta. Later, during labor, the mother's pituitary gland releases oxytocin, the hormone that stimulates contractions strong enough to expel the baby. Some common causes of prematurity include infection, inflammation, and maternal smoking.

about this time 1 woman in 10 also has a rush of warm "water" from the vagina. The "water" is amniotic fluid, and it means that the amniotic sac has burst. Labor usually begins within a day after rupture of the amniotic sac. For most women the amniotic sac does not burst until the end of the first stage of childbirth. Other signs of impending labor include indigestion, diarrhea, abdominal cramps, and an ache in the small of the back. Labor begins with the onset of regular uterine contractions.

The first uterine contractions are relatively painless and are called **Braxton-Hicks contractions**, or *false labor contractions*. They are false because they do not widen the cervix or advance the baby through the birth canal. They tend to increase in frequency but are less regular than labor contractions. Real labor contractions, by contrast, become more intense when the woman moves around or walks.

The initiation of labor may involve the secretion of hormones by the fetal adrenal and pituitary glands that stimulate the placenta and mother's uterus to secrete **prostaglandins**. Prostaglandins stimulate the uterine musculature to contract. It would make sense for the fetus to have a mechanism for signaling the mother that it is mature enough to sustain independent life. The mechanisms that initiate and maintain labor are not fully understood, however. Later in labor the pituitary gland releases **oxytocin**, a hormone that stimulates contractions strong enough to expel the baby.

Stages of Childbirth

LO 9.7 Discuss the stages of childbirth.

Childbirth begins with the onset of labor and has three stages. In the first stage uterine contractions **efface** and **dilate** the cervix to about 4 inches (10 cm) in diameter, so that the baby may pass. Stretching of the cervix causes most of the pain of childbirth. A woman may experience little or no pain if her cervix dilates easily and quickly. The first stage may last from a couple of hours to more than a day. About 12 to 24 hours of labor is considered average for a first pregnancy. In later pregnancies labor takes about half this time.

The initial contractions are usually mild and spaced widely, at intervals of 10 to 20 minutes. They may last 20 to 40 seconds. As time passes, contractions become more frequent, long, strong, and regular.

Transition is the process that occurs when the cervix becomes nearly fully dilated and the baby's head begins to move into the vagina, or birth canal. Contractions

---

Braxton-Hicks contractions
So-called false labor contractions that are relatively painless.

prostaglandins
Uterine hormones that stimulate uterine contractions.

oxytocin
A pituitary hormone that stimulates uterine contractions.

efface
To become thin.

dilate
To open or widen.

transition
The process during which the cervix becomes nearly fully dilated and the head of the fetus begins to move into the birth canal.

Figure 9.7 The Stages of Childbirth.

During the first stage, uterine contractions efface and dilate the cervix to about 4 inches so that the baby may pass through. The second stage begins with movement of the baby into the birth canal and ends with the birth of the baby. During the third stage, the placenta separates from the uterine wall and is expelled through the birth canal.

1. The second stage of labor begins

2. Further descent and rotation

3. The crowning of the head

4. Anterior shoulder delivered

5. Posterior shoulder delivered

6. The third stage of labor begins with separation of the placenta from the uterine wall

usually come quickly during transition. Transition usually lasts about 30 minutes or less and is often accompanied by feelings of nausea, chills, and intense pain.

The second stage of childbirth follows transition and begins when the cervix has become fully dilated and the baby begins to move into the vagina and first appears at the opening of the birth canal (see Figure 9.7). The woman may be taken to a delivery room for the second stage of childbirth. The second stage is shorter than the first stage. It lasts from a few minutes to a few hours and ends with the birth of the baby.

Each contraction of the second stage propels the baby farther along the birth canal (vagina). When the baby's head becomes visible at the vaginal opening, it is said to have *crowned*. The baby typically emerges fully a few minutes after crowning.

An **episiotomy** may be performed on the mother when the baby's head has crowned. The purpose is to prevent random tearing of the **perineum** that can occur if

episiotomy

A surgical incision in the perineum that widens the birth canal, preventing random tearing during childbirth.

perineum

The area between the vulva and the anus.

it becomes extremely effaced. Episiotomies are controversial, however. The incision can cause infection and pain, and create discomfort and itching as it heals. In some cases, the discomfort interferes with coitus for months. Although a European study did find a significant reduction in the incidence of anal tears with episiotomy (Frethelm et al., 2013), the overall episiotomy rate has been declining.

With or without an episiotomy, the baby's passageway to the external world is a tight fit. As a result, the baby's facial features and the shape of its head may be temporarily distended. The baby may look as if it has been through a prizefight. Its head may be elongated, its nose flattened, and its ears bent. Although parents may be concerned about whether the baby's features will assume a more typical shape, they almost always do.

The third, or placental, stage of childbirth may last from a few minutes to an hour or more. During this stage, the placenta is expelled. Detachment of the placenta from the uterine wall may cause some bleeding. The uterus begins the process of contracting to a smaller size. The attending physician sews up the episiotomy or any tears in the perineum.

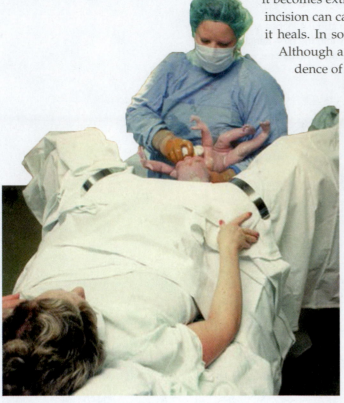

Coming Into the World. Childbirth progresses through three stages. During the first stage, uterine contractions efface and dilate the cervix so that the baby may pass. The second stage is the birth of the baby and lasts from a few minutes to a few hours. During the third stage, the placenta is expelled.

IN THE NEW WORLD   As the baby's head emerges, mucus is cleared from its mouth by means of suction aspiration to prevent the breathing passageway from being obstructed. Aspiration is often repeated once the baby is fully delivered. (Newly delivered babies are no longer routinely held upside down to help expel mucus. Nor is the baby slapped on the buttocks to stimulate breathing, as in old films.)

Once the baby is breathing adequately, the umbilical cord is clamped and severed about 3 inches from the baby's body. (After the birth of your first and third authors' third child, your first author was invited by the obstetrician to cut the umbilical cord—but the third author seized the scissors and cut the umbilical cord herself, squirting blood on the obstetrician's glasses. "Who gave the obstetrician the right to determine who would cut the umbilical cord!" she wanted to know.) The stump of the umbilical cord dries and falls off in its own time, usually in 7 to 10 days.

7 › T / F   Truth or Fiction Revisited   It is *not* true that the cutting of the umbilical cord determines whether the baby will have an "inny" or an "outy." The cord dries and falls off on its own.

While the mother is in the third stage of labor, a nurse may perform procedures on the baby, such as placing drops of silver nitrate or an antibiotic ointment into the eyes. This procedure is required by most states to prevent bacterial infections in the newborn's eyes. Typically, the baby is also footprinted and (if the birth has taken place in a hospital) given an identification bracelet. Because neonates do not manufacture vitamin K on their own, the baby may also receive an injection of the vitamin to ensure that her or his blood will clot normally in case of bleeding.

Methods of Childbirth

LO 9.8   Describe various methods of childbirth.

Until the twentieth century, childbirth usually occurred at home and involved the mother, a midwife, family, and friends. These days, women in the United States and Canada typically give birth in hospitals attended by obstetricians who use surgical instruments and anesthetics to protect mothers and children from infection, complications, and severe pain. Medical procedures save lives but also make childbearing more impersonal. Social critics argue that these procedures have medicalized a natural process: They have usurped control over women's bodies and, through the use of drugs, denied many women the experience of giving birth.

ANESTHETIZED CHILDBIRTH   During the past two centuries, science and medicine have led to the expectation that women should experience minimal discomfort during childbirth. Today only a minority of American women use no anesthesia.

General anesthesia first became popular when Queen Victoria of England delivered her eighth child under chloroform in 1853. General anesthesia, like the chloroform of old, induces unconsciousness. The drug sodium pentothal, a barbiturate, induces general anesthesia when it is injected into a vein. Barbiturates may also be taken orally to reduce anxiety while the woman remains awake. Women may also receive tranquilizers such as Valium or narcotics such as Demerol to help them relax and to blunt pain without inducing sleep.

Anesthetic drugs, as well as tranquilizers and narcotics, decrease the strength of uterine contractions during delivery. They may therefore delay the process of cervical dilation and prolong labor. They also weaken the woman's ability to push the baby through the birth canal. Because these drugs cross the placental membrane, they also lower the newborn's overall responsiveness.

Regional or **local anesthetics** block pain in parts of the body without generally depressing the mother's alertness or putting her to sleep. In a *pudendal block*, the external genitals are numbed by local injection. In an *epidural block* and a *spinal block*, an anesthetic is injected into the spinal canal, which temporarily numbs the mother's body below the waist. To prevent injury, the needles used for these injections do not come into contact with the spinal cord itself. Although local anesthesia decreases the responsiveness of the newborn baby, there is little evidence that medicated childbirth has serious, long-term consequences on children.

PREPARED CHILDBIRTH: THE LAMAZE METHOD   The French obstetrician Fernand Lamaze visited the Soviet Union in 1951 and found that many Russian women bore babies without anesthetics and without reporting a great deal of pain. Lamaze returned to Western Europe with some of the techniques the women used; they are now termed the **Lamaze method**, or *prepared childbirth*. Lamaze (1981) argued that women can learn to conserve energy during childbirth and reduce the pain of uterine contractions by associating the contractions with other responses, such as thinking of pleasant mental images such as beach scenes or engaging in breathing and relaxation exercises.

A pregnant woman typically attends Lamaze classes with a "coach"—usually the father or partner—who will aid her in the delivery room by timing contractions, offering emotional support, and coaching her in the breathing and relaxation exercises. The woman and her partner also receive general information about childbirth. The partner is integrated into the process, and many couples report that their relationships are strengthened as a result.

The Lamaze method is flexible about the use of anesthetics. Many women report some pain during delivery and obtain anesthetics. However, the Lamaze method appears to help women to gain a greater sense of control over the delivery process.

CESAREAN SECTION (C-SECTION)   In a **cesarean section**, the baby is delivered through surgery rather than through the vagina. The term *section* is derived from the Latin for "to cut." Julius Caesar is said to have been delivered in this way, but health professionals believe that this is unlikely. In a cesarean section ("C-section" for short) the woman is anesthetized, and incisions are made in the abdomen and uterus so that the surgeon can remove the baby. The incisions are then sewn up and the mother can begin walking, usually on the same day, although with some discomfort for a while.

---

general anesthesia
The use of drugs to put people to sleep and eliminate pain, as during childbirth.

local anesthesia
A type of anesthesia that eliminates pain in a specific area of the body, as during childbirth.

Lamaze method
A childbirth method in which women learn about childbirth, learn to relax and to breathe in patterns that conserve energy and lessen pain, and have a coach (usually the father) present at childbirth. Also termed *prepared childbirth*.

Cesarean section
A method of childbirth in which the fetus is delivered through a surgical incision in the abdomen.

Figure 9.8 The Increase in C-Sections.

Since 1996, the percentage of American women undergoing C-sections has mushroomed from about one in five (21%) to nearly one in three (32.2%). But the use of C-sections appears to have leveled off and undergone a slight decline since 2011.

SOURCES: U.S. National Center for Health Statistics (2012); Hamilton, B. E., Martin, J. A., Osterman, M. J. K., & Curtin, S. C. (2015). Births: Preliminary data for 2014. *National Vital Statistics Reports, 64*(6). Hyattsville, MD: National Center for Health Statistics.

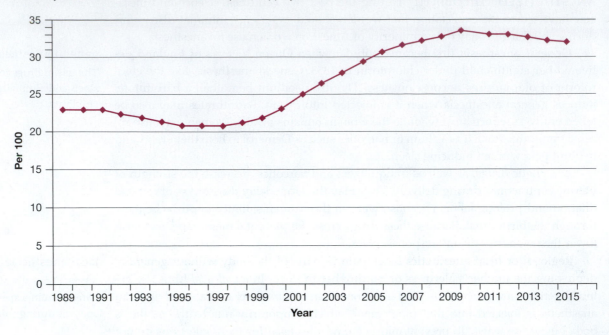

Although most C-sections are without complications, some cause urinary tract infections, inflammation of the wall of the uterus, blood clots, or hemorrhaging.

C-sections are most likely to be advised when normal delivery is difficult or threatening to the health of the mother or child. Vaginal deliveries can become difficult if the baby is large, the mother's pelvis is small or misshapen, the mother is tired or weakened, or the mother is aging. Herpes and HIV infections in the birth canal can be bypassed by C-section. C-sections are also likely to be performed if the baby presents for delivery in the breech position (feet downward) or the **transverse position** (lying crosswise), or if the baby is in distress. Yet some women request C-sections to avoid the discomforts of vaginal delivery or to control the timing of the delivery. Women are also having children at more advanced ages, when there is more risk to the urogenital system from vaginal delivery.

transverse position

A crosswise birth position.

8 › T / F Truth or Fiction Revisited   Use of the C-section has mushroomed over the past several decades, but now it seems to have leveled off or be in slight decline (Hamilton et al., 2016). Even so, nearly one birth in three (32.2% in 2014 and 32% in 2015) was by C-section (Hamilton et al., 2015; National Vital Statistics Report, 2016; see Figure 9.8). Compare this figure to about 1 in 20 births in 1965. Much of the increase in the rate of C-sections reflects advances in medical technology, such as use of fetal monitors that allow doctors to detect fetal distress, concern about malpractice suits, concern about maternal–newborn transmission of infections, and simply, current medical practice patterns.

Medical opinion once held that once a woman had a C-section, subsequent deliveries also had to be by C-section. Otherwise, uterine scars might rupture during labor (Begum et al., 2014). Research has shown that the rate of uterine rupture during a vaginal delivery following a C-section is about 5% (Peaceman et al, 2009), which is about twice the risk of uterine rupture among women delivering vaginally who have not had a previous C-section. However, maternal deaths as a result of uterine rupture during delivery are rare. In any event, only a small minority of women who have previously had a C-section deliver subsequent babies vaginally.

Consumer advocates advise pregnant women who would like to deliver vaginally, if possible, to ask about the rates of C-sections when they are choosing a physician and a hospital. Women can try to choose obstetricians who have lower rates or who are open to a second opinion for elective surgery. But it should not be forgotten that there are excellent reasons for having C-sections. It makes no sense to avoid a C-section if vaginal delivery might put the mother or the baby at risk.

Birth Problems

LO 9.9 Discuss various birth problems.

Most deliveries are uncomplicated, or "unremarkable," in the medical sense—although childbirth is the most remarkable experience of many parents' lives. Problems can and do occur, however. Some of the most common birth problems are anoxia and the birth of preterm and low–birth weight babies.

ANOXIA   Prenatal **anoxia** can cause various problems in the neonate and affect later development. It leads to complications such as brain damage and mental retardation. Prolonged anoxia during delivery can also result in cerebral palsy and possibly death.

The baby is supplied with oxygen through the umbilical cord. Passage through the birth canal squeezes the umbilical cord. Temporary squeezing, like holding one's breath for a moment, is unlikely to cause problems. (In fact, slight oxygen deprivation at birth is not unusual because the transition from receiving oxygen through the umbilical cord to breathing on its own may not happen immediately after the baby emerges.) Anoxia can result if constriction of the cord is prolonged, however. Prolonged constriction is more likely to occur with a breech presentation, because the baby's head presses the umbilical cord against the birth canal during delivery. Fetal monitoring can help detect anoxia early, however, before damage occurs. A C-section can be performed if the fetus appears to be in distress. Children who were deprived of oxygen at birth often show problems in learning and memory, motor development, and spatial relations (Thaler et al., 2013).

PRETERM AND LOW BIRTH-WEIGHT CHILDREN   A neonate is considered to be premature, or **preterm**, if it is born before 37 weeks of gestation. The normal period of gestation is 40 weeks. Prematurity is generally linked with low birth-weight because the fetus normally makes dramatic gains in weight during the last weeks of pregnancy.

Regardless of the length of its gestation period, a newborn baby is considered to have a low birth-weight if it weighs less than 5 pounds (about 2,500 grams). Preterm and low birth-weight babies face a heightened risk of infant mortality from causes ranging from asphyxia and infections to sudden infant death syndrome (SIDS) (Save the Children, 2013). Neurological and developmental problems are also common among preterm infants, especially those born at or prior to 25 weeks of gestation (Clark et al., 2013).

Twins and other multiple birth groupings are more likely to be of low birth-weight than individual births (Shiozaki et al., 2014). There is also a relationship between prematurity and the spacing of babies. Women who have babies less than 18 months or more than 59 months apart have the highest risk of giving birth to premature infants (Fuentes-Afflick & Hessol, 2000). On the other hand, it is common for women carrying more than one child to deliver prematurely, apparently because the babies are running out of space.

Critical Thinking
Critical thinkers tackle controversial issues. What are the pros and cons of the following aspects of childbirth: Episiotomy? Use of anesthesia? C-section?

anoxia
Oxygen deprivation.

preterm
Born before 37 weeks of gestation.

Too Early. A baby is considered premature if it is born before 37 weeks of gestation. Premature babies are vulnerable to various developmental problems.

SEX IN A WORLD OF DIVERSITY

MATERNAL AND INFANT MORTALITY AROUND THE WORLD

Modern medicine has made vast strides in decreasing the rates of maternal and infant mortality, but the advances are not equally spread throughout the world. Save the Children, a nonprofit relief and development organization, tracks the likelihood that a woman will die in childbirth and that an infant will die during its first year. The likelihood of maternal and infant mortality is connected with what Save the Children (2014) terms the "mother's index," which includes factors such as the lifetime risk of maternal death during pregnancy and delivery, the younger-than-age-5 mortality rate for children, the years of formal schooling of mothers, economic status (as measured by national income per person), and participation of women in national government—a measure of the extent to which a society empowers women. Figure 9.9 shows the various reasons why children die, according to a recent edition of *State of the World's Mothers* (Save the Children, 2014).

Number 1 on the mother's index in 2014 was Finland, where the chances of the woman dying are about 1 in 12,200, and where only 3 infants in 1,000 die during the first 5 years (see Table 9.4). Women receive an average of 17 years of formal schooling (the same as in the United States), per capita income is $46,490 (about the same as the United States), and 42 to 43% of national government seats are held by women (as compared to only about 19% in the United States). In the United States, 1 in 2,400 women stands a lifetime risk of dying during pregnancy or childbirth (forty-sixth in the world), and a child has a 7.1 in 1,000 chance of dying under the age of 5 (forty-first in the world). Half the countries in the world have a higher percentage of females in national government than the United States. The performance of the United States in the rankings is related to the large number of "nations within the nation." For example, there is great disparity in wealth,

Figure 9.9   Global Causes of Infant Mortality.

SOURCE: Data from Save the Children, 2014.

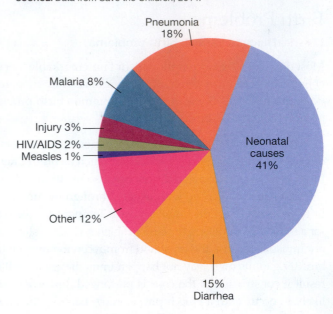

and richer Americans fare better in the rankings than poorer Americans. High-quality medical intervention is more available in some parts of the country than others. Many mobile Americans base their residence, in part, on the availability of good medicine.

Readers may wonder why the United States is not at the top of the list. One answer is that states with above-average

surfactant

Substances that prevent the walls of the airways from sticking together.

respiratory distress syndrome

A cluster of breathing problems, including weak and irregular breathing, to which preterm babies are especially vulnerable.

Preterm babies are relatively thin because they have not yet formed the layer of fat that accounts for the round, robust appearance of most full-term babies. Their muscles are immature, weakening their sucking and breathing reflexes. Also, in the last weeks of pregnancy fetuses secrete **surfactant**, which prevents the walls of their airways from sticking together. Muscle weakness and incomplete lining of the airways with surfactant can cause a cluster of problems known as **respiratory distress syndrome**, which is responsible for many neonatal deaths. Preterm babies may also suffer from underdeveloped immune systems, which leave them more vulnerable to infections.

Preterm infants usually remain in the hospital for a time. There, they can be monitored and placed in incubators that provide a temperature-controlled environment and offer some protection from disease. If necessary, they may also receive oxygen. Although remarkable advances are being made in the medical field's ability to help preterm babies survive, the likelihood of developmental disabilities continues to increase dramatically for babies who are born at 25 weeks of gestation or earlier (Cole, 2000).

Table 9.4 Maternal and Child Mortality in Selected Countries as Related to Income Level and Empowerment of Women

Country	Lifetime Risk of Maternal Mortality (1 in number shown)	Younger-than-age-5 mortality rate (per 1,000 live births)	Average years of formal schooling for women	National income per person (in U.S. dollars)	Participation of women in national government (percentage of seats held by women)
Finland	12,200	2.9	16.9	$46,490	42.5
Ireland	8,100	4.0	18.7	$39,930	19.0
Italy	20,300	3.7	16.1	$35,290	20.6
France	6,200	4.1	16.3	$42,420	25.1
Germany	10,600	4.0	16.4	$44,270	32.4
Poland	14,400	5.8	15.4	$12,480	21.8
Japan	13,100	3.4	15.3	$44,900	11.3
Mexico	790	15.7	13.7	$9,420	11
Sweden	14,100	2.8	16.0	$53,150	44.7
Canada	5,200	5.6	15.1	$45,560	28.0
United Kingdom	4,600	5.1	16.7	$37,840	22.6
United States	2,400	7.1	16.8	$48,620	18.9
Russia	2,000	11.9	14.3	$10,730	12.1
China	1,700	14.6	11.9	$4,940	21.3
Cuba	1,000	5.8	15.4	$5,460	45.2
Israel	5,100	4.3	15.7	$28,930	21.7
Nigeria	29	124.1	9.0	$1,280	6.6
India	170	61.3	10.7	$1,410	10.9
Afghanistan	32	101.1	8.8	$470	27.6

SOURCES: Save the Children (2013, 2014).

poverty rates, large rural populations, and less-than-average levels of education have the highest maternal and infant mortality rates. According to a report by the Centers for Disease Control and Prevention's National Center for Health Statistics (http://www.cdc.gov/nchs/linked.htm), African American women have the highest infant mortality rate at 13.60 per 1,000 live births, as compared to 4.55 per 1,000 births for the group with the lowest mortality rate: Cuban Americans. European American women had 5.66 infant deaths per 1,000 births, as compared with 8.45 for Native Americans, 7.82 for Puerto Ricans, 5.47 for Mexican Americans, 4.67 for Asian Americans, and 4.65 for Central and South Americans. How do you explain these ethnic differences?

STILLBIRTH Stillbirth means that the baby is born dead. Stillbirth is no surprise. The baby is "silent" prior to birth—no heartbeat is heard and no movement is felt (Trulsson & Rådestad, 2004). Stillbirth is connected with fetal abnormalities, infection, medical conditions of the mother, and pregnancy complications such as preeclampsia and problems with the placenta (Pasupathy & Smith, 2005). However, the majority of cases have no clear cause and are considered unexplained. Even so, many "unexplained" deaths are connected with restriction of growth of the fetus. Growth restriction, in turn, may be associated with the mother's age and smoking (Cnattingius, 2004). The risk of stillbirth is also connected with the functioning of the placenta early in the pregnancy. Pregnancies at risk must be carefully monitored. Sometimes corrective actions can be taken to improve placental circulation.

Subsequent pregnancies are likely to be experienced with extreme anxiety by parents (Brisch et al., 2005; Turton et al., 2006). In the case of a miscarriage, parents may feel that they have to get safely through the first trimester for the subsequent pregnancy to be valid. In the case of a stillbirth, they are likely to have misgivings for the entire gestation period, and through labor. This is a painful process, but it is to be expected.

The Postpartum Period

LO 9.10 Discuss events of the postpartum period, including mood changes and breast-feeding versus bottle-feeding.

postpartum

Following birth.

The weeks after delivery are called the **postpartum** period. The first few days of postpartum are frequently happy ones. The long wait is over, as are the discomforts of childbirth. However, the majority of new mothers also have periods of tearfulness, sadness, and irritability. In most cases these are normal.

Psychological Issues Women Encounter During the Postpartum Period

Following delivery, many women experience psychological problems described by the American Psychiatric Association (2013) as baby blues, postpartum anxiety, and more serious mood disorders, which occasionally include "psychotic features." These problems are far-flung; researchers find them in China, Turkey, Guyana, Australia, and South Africa—occurring with similar frequency (American Psychiatric Association, 2014; O'Hara & McCabe, 2013).

Baby blues affect the majority of women in the weeks after delivery. Researchers believe they are common because they are caused by the hormonal changes that accompany and follow delivery (American Psychiatric Association, 2014). They last for about 10 days and are not severe enough to impair the mother's functioning. Don't misunderstand: The baby blues are seriously discomforting and not to be ignored. (Don't say, "Oh, you're just experiencing what most women experience.") The point is that most women tolerate the baby blues, even though with great difficulty at times, partly because they know that the mood problems are transient.

A minority of women, but perhaps as many as one in seven, encounter the more serious mood disorder referred to technically as major depression "with perinatal onset"—but more commonly known as **postpartum depression, or PPD**. *Perinatal onset* refers to the period just before or after birth. The disorder most often begins about a month after delivery and may linger for weeks, even months. It is characterized by serious sadness, feelings of hopelessness and helplessness, feelings of worthlessness, difficulty concentrating, and major changes in appetite (usually loss of appetite) and sleep patterns (frequently insomnia). There can also be severe fluctuations in mood, with women sometimes feeling elated. Some women show obsessive concern with the well-being of their babies at this time. PPD can also interfere with the mother–baby relationship in the short term.

postpartum depression (PPD)

Persistent and severe mood changes during the postpartum period, involving feelings of despair and apathy and characterized by changes in appetite and sleep, low self-esteem, and difficulty concentrating.

Many researchers suggest that PPD is caused by the interaction of psychological factors and physiological (mainly hormonal) factors, including the sudden drop in estrogen that is characteristic of the period following delivery (O'Hara & McCabe, 2013). Feelings of depression before getting pregnant are a risk factor for the postpartum problem, as are concerns about all the life changes that motherhood creates, relationship problems, and having a sick or unwanted baby. There are major changes in body chemistry during and after pregnancy, and as noted, women around the world seem to experience similar disturbances in mood, even when their life experiences and support systems are radically different (O'Hara & McCabe, 2013). But it is clear that stress can heighten the risk of PPD (Hillerer et al., 2014).

According to the American Psychiatric Association (2013), postpartum mood episodes are accompanied by "psychotic features" in about 1 woman in 1,000. A psychotic feature may mean a break with reality. Mothers with these features may have delusional thoughts about the infant that place the infant at risk of injury or death. Some women experience delusions that the infant is possessed by the devil, and some have "command hallucinations" to kill the infant; they experience a command to kill the infant as though it is coming from outside themselves—perhaps from a commanding person or some kind of divine or evil spirit—even though the idea originates within. But they may not be able to tell the difference, and the infant may be in serious jeopardy. Women with postpartum psychosis frequently have a history of psychological disorders, substance abuse, or problems such as negligence or abuse in their families of origin (Comtois et al., 2008; Kimmel et al., 2015). Remember, too, that psychotic features are rare, and when they occur, they do not always place the baby at risk.

Women who experience milder mood disorders in the periods before and after birth usually profit from social support and a history of high self-esteem. They may benefit from counseling, even if counseling does little more than explain that many women encounter baby blues and get over it. Drugs that increase estrogen levels or act as antidepressants may help, but most women get over the problem on their own. At the very least, women should know that the problem does not necessarily mean that there is something wrong with them or that they are failing to live up to their obligations.

Critical Thinking
How have women you know reacted emotionally in the hours, days, and weeks following childbirth?

Breastfeeding Versus Bottle-Feeding

In many developing nations, women have no choice: If their infants are going to be nourished, they will have to breastfeed. Yet even in developed nations, where formula is readily available, breast milk today is considered by most health professionals to be the "medical gold standard," and by many (perhaps most) mothers to be the "moral gold standard" (Walker, 2010). Largely for this reason, the majority of mothers in the United States and Canada today breastfeed their children (see Figure 9.10). The American Academy of Pediatrics (2012) recommends that women exclusively breastfeed infants for the first 6 months, gradually introduce complementary foods over the next 6 months, and continue breastfeeding as long as the mother and infant wish to do so.

Breastfeeding is, of course, the "natural" way to nourish a baby. Infant formulas were developed in the 1930s. Over the next several decades, the incidence of breastfeeding declined because women were entering the workforce, bottle feeding was seen as "scientific," and the women's movement encouraged women to become liberated from traditional roles (Weaver, 2012). Thus, breastfeeding has political and social aspects as well as nutritional aspects (Bakalar, 2014). Much of the decision whether to breastfeed involves domestic and occupational arrangements, day care, social support, reactions to public breastfeeding, and beliefs about mother–infant bonding.

African American women are less likely than Asian American, European American, and Latin American women to breastfeed (see Figure 9.10), which may be connected with higher rates of infant mortality, asthma, diabetes, and obesity among black children (Black Breast-Feeding, 2015). In fact, breastfeeding appears to be associated with lower rates of obesity when the children reach 35 years of age (Fergusson et al., 2014). A survey of 35 African American and Latin American mothers or pregnant adolescents (ages 12 to 19) found that those who recognized the benefits of breastfeeding were more likely to do it (Hannon et al., 2000). They reported benefits such as promoting mother–infant bonding and the infant's health. A survey of 349 Latin American mothers found that younger mothers and mothers born in the United States were more likely to breastfeed (Newton, 2009). Barriers to breastfeeding include fear of pain, embarrassment by public exposure, and unease with the act itself. However, an influential person—such as the woman's partner or mother—often encourages the mother to breastfeed (Hunter & Cattelona, 2014). Community support through volunteer workers ("Birth Sisters"), visiting nurses, and community clinics also encourages women to breastfeed (Frick et al., 2012; Wambach et al., 2011). Better-educated women are more likely to breastfeed, even among low-income women (Wambach et al., 2011).

Breastfeeding Is Considered to Be the "Gold Standard" for Mothers in the United States and Canada Today. What are the advantages of breastfeeding? Under what circumstances should women not breastfeed their children?

Figure 9.10 Who Breastfeeds?

Although the majority of mothers breastfeed, many are unsure of its benefits over baby formula.

SOURCE: CDC, *Healthy Styles Survey*, 2010.

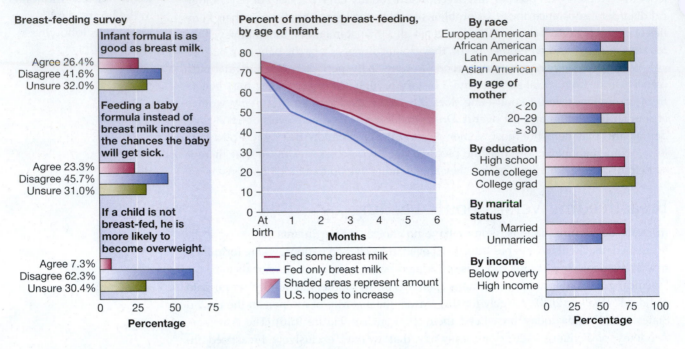

In any event, breastfeeding has become more popular during the past generation, largely because of increased knowledge of its health benefits, even among women at the lower end of the socioeconomic spectrum (Weaver, 2012). Most American mothers—more than 70%—breastfeed their children, at least for a while.

Breastfeeding reduces the risk of infectious diseases to the baby by transmitting the mother's antibodies to the baby (see Table 9.5). Breastfeeding also reduces the incidence of allergies in babies, sudden infant death syndrome, diabetes, and many other health problems, both in developed and developing countries (American Academy of Pediatrics, 2015). Uterine contractions that occur during breastfeeding help return the uterus to its typical size. Breastfeeding similarly promotes a return to prepregnancy body weight (American Academy of Pediatrics, 2015). In addition, breastfeeding delays resumption of normal menstrual cycles but is not a perfectly reliable birth-control method.

Table 9.5 Advantages of Breast Milk Over Formula

There are numerous advantages to breast milk (American Academy of Pediatrics, 2015; Breastfeeding, 2010):

- Breast milk conforms to human digestion processes (i.e., it is unlikely to upset the infant's stomach).
- Breast milk alone is adequate for the first 6 months after birth. Other foods can merely supplement breast milk through the first year.
- As the infant matures, the composition of breast milk changes to help meet the infant's changing needs.
- Breast milk contains the mother's antibodies and helps the infant ward off health problems ranging from ear infections, pneumonia, wheezing, bronchiolitis, and tetanus to chicken pox, bacterial meningitis, and typhoid fever.
- Breast milk helps protect against the form of cancer known as childhood lymphoma (a cancer of the lymph glands).
- Breast milk decreases the likelihood of developing serious cases of diarrhea.
- Infants who are nourished by breast milk are less likely to develop allergic responses and constipation.
- Breastfed infants are less likely to develop obesity later in life.
- Breastfeeding is associated with better neural and behavioral organization in the infant.

There are also some downsides to breastfeeding. For example, breast milk is one of the bodily fluids that transmit HIV (the virus that causes AIDS). Researchers estimate that as many as one-third of the world's infants who have HIV/AIDS were infected in this manner (UNICEF, 2012; Rose et al., 2014). Alcohol, many drugs taken by the mother, and environmental hazards such as polychlorinated biphenyls (PCBs) can also be transmitted to infants through breast milk. Therefore, breast milk is not always as pure as it would seem to be. Moreover, for breast milk to contain the necessary nutrients, the mother must be adequately nourished herself. In many cases, mothers in developing countries do not eat sufficiently well to pass along proper nutrition to their infants.

Other negatives to breastfeeding include the mother's assumptions of the sole responsibility for nighttime feedings. She also encounters the physical demands of producing and expelling milk, a tendency for soreness in the breasts, and the inconvenience of being continually available to meet the infant's feeding needs.

The hormones prolactin and oxytocin are involved in breastfeeding. **Prolactin** stimulates production of milk, or **lactation**, 2 to 3 days after delivery. Oxytocin causes the breasts to eject milk and is secreted in response to suckling. When an infant is weaned, secretion of prolactin and oxytocin is discontinued, and lactation comes to an end.

prolactin
A pituitary hormone that stimulates production of milk.

lactation
Production of milk by the mammary glands.

Resumption of Ovulation and Menstruation

For close to a month after delivery, women experience a reddish vaginal discharge called **lochia**. A nonnursing mother does not resume actual menstrual periods until 2 to 3 months postpartum. The first few cycles are likely to be irregular. Many women incorrectly assume that they will resume menstruating following childbirth by having a menstrual period and ovulating 2 weeks later. In most cases the opposite is true. Ovulation precedes the first menstrual period after childbirth. Thus, a woman may become pregnant before the menstrual phase of her first postpartum cycle. Some women who suffered premenstrual syndrome before their pregnancies find that their periods give them less discomfort after the birth of their children.

lochia
A reddish vaginal discharge that may persist for a month after delivery.

Critical Thinking
What are the "political" issues involved in breastfeeding versus bottle-feeding?

Resumption of Sexual Activity

The resumption of coitus depends on a couple's level of sexual interest, the healing of episiotomies or other injuries, fatigue, the recommendations of obstetricians, and of course, tradition. Obstetricians usually advise a 6-week waiting period for safety and comfort. One study of 570 women found that they actually resumed sexual intercourse at an average of 7 weeks after childbirth (Byrd et al., 1998).

9 › T / F Truth or Fiction Revisited   It is true that couples should abstain from coitus for at least 6 weeks following childbirth. However, many other kinds of sexual activities are safe and do not cause discomfort. (Check with your obstetrician.)

Women will typically prefer to delay coitus until it becomes physically comfortable, generally when the episiotomy or other lacerations have healed and the lochia has ended. This may take several weeks. Women who breastfeed may also find they have less vaginal lubrication, and the dryness can cause discomfort during coitus. K-Y jelly or other lubricants may help in such cases.

The return of sexual interest and resumption of sexual activity may take longer for some couples than for others. Sexual interest depends more on psychological than on physical factors. Many couples encounter declining sexual interest and activity in the first year following childbirth, generally because child care can sap energy and limit free time. Not surprisingly, couples whose sexual relationships were satisfying before the baby arrived tend to show greater sexual interest and to resume sexual activity earlier than those who had less satisfying relationships beforehand.

Chapter Review

LO 9.1 Describe the process of conception.

Conception is the union of a sperm cell and an ovum, which normally occurs in a fallopian tube. Male fetuses have a higher rate of miscarriage. Chromosomes from the sperm cells combine to form 23 new pairs.

LO 9.2 Discuss fertility problems and ways in which people with such problems can become parents.

Male fertility problems mainly involve low sperm count and motility. Female fertility problems include failure to ovulate, infections, endometriosis, and obstructions in the reproductive tract. Fertility drugs stimulate ovulation. Artificial insemination may use sperm from a donor. In vitro fertilization (IVF) may be used when the fallopian tubes are blocked. Some couples adopt.

LO 9.3 Discuss signs of pregnancy and sexual activity during pregnancy.

Early signs of pregnancy include a missed period and the presence of human chorionic gonadotropin (HCG) in the blood or urine. "Morning sickness" is believed to be linked with a healthy pregnancy. Miscarriages have many causes, including chromosomal defects in the fetus. Most health professionals agree that under normal circumstances, sexual intercourse is safe until the start of labor.

LO 9.4 Discuss the key events of the stages of prenatal development.

During the germinal stage, the dividing mass of cells receives no external nourishment and travels to the uterus, where it becomes implanted. The embryo and fetus exchange nutrients and wastes with the mother through the placenta and umbilical cord. Major organ systems develop during the embryonic period, when the embryo is most vulnerable to teratogens. The fetal stage is mainly characterized by maturation of organs and gains in size.

LO 9.5 Discuss the effects of environmental hazards on the child.

Maternal malnutrition is linked with low birth weight, prematurity, and cognitive problems. Maternal diseases and disorders can harm the embryo and are called *teratogens*. Syphilis can cause miscarriage or stillbirth. Babies born to HIV-infected mothers may become infected by childbirth unless the mother uses antiretroviral drugs; C-sections also help prevent transmission. In Rh incompatibility, antibodies produced by the mother can kill the fetus or cause brain damage. Maternal use of alcohol is linked to fetal alcohol syndrome (FAS). Maternal cigarette smoking deprives the fetus of oxygen and is linked with low birth weight, stillbirth, and academic problems later on.

LO 9.6 Discuss the effects of genetic abnormalities on the child.

Chromosomal abnormalities such as Down syndrome become more likely as parents age. Parental blood tests can reveal genes and markers for many disorders. Amniocentesis and CVS may be used to confirm findings of blood tests.

LO 9.7 Discuss the stages of childbirth.

Before labor begins, blood typically appears in the birth canal. Some women have a rush of amniotic fluid. Oxytocin stimulates contractions strong enough to expel the baby. Childbirth begins with the onset of regular contractions of the uterus, which efface and dilate the cervix, causing most of the discomfort of childbirth. The second stage begins when the baby appears and ends with birth. The third stage expels the placenta.

LO 9.8 Describe various methods of childbirth.

General anesthesia puts the woman to sleep. Local anesthetics deaden pain without putting the mother to sleep. A C-section delivers a baby surgically by cutting through the abdomen and the uterus.

LO 9.9 Discuss various birth problems.

Prenatal oxygen deprivation can damage the nervous system and kill the baby. Preterm and low birth-weight babies face a heightened risk of infant mortality from causes ranging from asphyxia and infections to SIDS. Preterm babies are also subject to respiratory distress syndrome.

LO 9.10 Discuss events of the postpartum period, including breastfeeding versus bottle-feeding.

Women may encounter baby blues and more severe postpartum depression, problems that apparently reflect hormonal changes following birth. Breastfeeding is connected with fewer infections and allergic reactions in the baby. Obstetricians usually advise waiting 6 weeks following childbirth before resuming sexual intercourse.

Test Your Learning

1. The enzyme hyaluronidase _____
   (a) stimulates production of milk.
   (b) passes through the placenta.
   (c) stimulates contractions of labor.
   (d) thins the zona pellucida.

2. The most common cause of male infertility is _____
   (a) low sperm motility.
   (b) low sperm count.
   (c) injury to the testes.
   (d) higher-than-normal scrotal temperature.

3. The presence of human chorionic gonadotropin is assessed to determine _____
   (a) blocked fallopian tubes.
   (b) sickle-cell anemia.
   (c) pregnancy.
   (d) Down syndrome.

4. If we date pregnancy from the onset of the last menstrual cycle before conception, the normal gestation period is _____ days.
   (a) 266
   (b) 272
   (c) 280
   (d) 288

5. A breech presentation is _____
   (a) bottom or feet first.
   (b) head first.
   (c) sideways.
   (d) shoulder first.

6. The critical period for the development of the facial features associated with FAS seems to be the first _____ of prenatal development.
   (a) week
   (b) 2 weeks
   (c) month
   (d) 2 months

7. The pudendal block is an example of _____
   (a) general anesthesia.
   (b) local anesthesia.
   (c) a birth problem.
   (d) anoxia.

8. Which of the following is most likely to afflict African Americans?
   (a) Tay-Sachs disease
   (b) Hemophilia
   (c) Sickle-cell disease
   (d) Retinal blatoma

9. An underdeveloped upper jaw is characteristic of _____
   (a) children whose mothers smoked during pregnancy.
   (b) fetal alcohol syndrome.
   (c) prenatal exposure to PCBs.
   (d) prenatal exposure to stress.

10. Mothers in _____ are most likely to die in childbirth.
    (a) Mexico
    (b) Cuba
    (c) Finland
    (d) Afghanistan

Chapter 10
Contraception and Abortion

Learning Objectives

Contraception

LO 10.1 Discuss historic issues concerning the legalization of contraception in the United States.

Hormonal Methods of Contraception

LO 10.2 Explain how hormonal methods of contraception work, and discuss their advantages and disadvantages.

Barrier Methods of Contraception

LO 10.3 Explain how barrier methods of contraception work, and discuss their advantages and disadvantages.

Fertility Awareness Methods of Contraception

LO 10.4 Explain how fertility awareness methods of contraception work, and discuss their advantages and disadvantages.

Sterilization

LO 10.5 Describe methods of sterilization, and discuss the prospects of reversibility.

Non-Methods of Contraception

LO 10.6 Identify "non-methods" of contraception, and explain why they are not dependable.

Abortion

LO 10.7 Discuss the history of abortion in the United States and controversies concerning abortion.

Methods of Abortion

LO 10.8 Discuss methods of abortion.

Which of the following statements are the truth, and which are fiction? Look for the Truth-or-Fiction items throughout this chapter to find the answers.

1 Ancient Egyptians used crocodile dung as a contraceptive. **T / F**?

2 There is an oral contraceptive that can be taken the morning after unprotected intercourse. **T / F**?

3 Sterilization operations can be surgically reversed. **T / F**?

4 Contraceptives not only prevent conception, they also provide protection against sexually transmitted infections. **T / F**?

5 Douching quickly after unprotected intercourse is a reasonably good contraceptive method. **T / F**?

6 Abortions were legal in the newly founded United States. **T / F**?

7 The D&C is the most widely used abortion method in the United States. **T / F**?

It was a stifling day in July 1912. Margaret Sanger (1883–1966), a nurse practitioner, was summoned to the house of a woman near death from a botched self-induced abortion. Her husband had called a doctor, and the doctor sent for Sanger. Together, doctor and nurse worked feverishly through the days and nights that followed to stem an infection that had taken hold in the woman. Sanger later commented,

> Never had I worked so fast, never so concentratedly. The sultry days and nights were melted into a torpid inferno. It did not seem possible there could be such heat, and every bit of food, ice, and drugs had to be carried up three flights of stairs…. (Sanger, 1938, page 90)

After 2 interminable weeks, the woman began to recover. Her neighbors, who had feared the worst, came to express their joy. But the woman, who smiled wanly at those who came to see her, appeared more depressed and anxious than would be expected of someone who was recovering from a grave illness. By the end of the third week, when Sanger prepared to leave her patient, the woman, Mrs. Sachs, voiced the fear that was haunting her. Her face registered deep despair as she explained to Sanger that she dreaded becoming pregnant again and facing a choice between attempting another abortion, which she feared might kill her, and bearing a baby whose care it was beyond her means to support. She pleaded for information about contraception but Sanger could offer none. In 1912, it was a crime even for health professionals like Sanger to dispense information about contraceptives. Abortions, too, were illegal. Sanger tried to comfort her and promised to return to talk again.

Three months later Sanger received another urgent call. It was Mr. Sachs. His wife was sick again—from the same cause. Sanger recalled,

> For a wild moment I thought of sending someone else, but actually, of course, I hurried into my uniform, caught up my bag, and started out. All the way I longed for a subway wreck, an explosion, anything to keep me from having to enter that home again. But nothing happened, even to delay me. I turned into the dingy doorway and climbed the familiar stairs once more. The children were there, young little things.
>
> Mrs. Sachs was in a coma and died within ten minutes. I folded her still hands across her breast, remembering how they had pleaded with me, begging so humbly for the knowledge which was her right. I drew a sheet over her

Margaret Sanger Testifying Before a Senate Committee

pallid face. Jake was sobbing, running his hands through his hair and pulling it out like an insane person. Over and over again he wailed, "My God! My God! My God!" (Sanger, 1938, pages 91–92.)

Today, partly because of the work of Margaret Sanger, who went on to become a key advocate for birth control, information about contraceptives is disseminated freely throughout the United States (Engelman, 2011; Stearns et al., 2015).

Methods of birth control include contraception and abortion. The term *contraception* refers to techniques that prevent conception. The term *abortion* refers to the termination of a pregnancy before the embryo or fetus is capable of surviving outside the womb, as we see later in the chapter.

Contraception

LO 10.1 Discuss historic issues concerning the legalization of contraception in the United States.

People have been devising means of contraception since they became aware of the relationship between coitus and conception. Ironically, the safest and most effective method of contraception is also the least popular: abstinence. The bible contains many references to contraceptive techniques, including vaginal sponges and contraceptive concoctions. It also refers to **coitus interruptus**, or withdrawal. The story of onan, for example, implies knowledge of the withdrawal method.

coitus interruptus

A method of contraception in which the penis is withdrawn from the vagina before ejaculation. Also known as the *withdrawal method*.

Ancient Egyptian methods of birth control included douching with wine and garlic after coitus, and soaking crocodile dung in sour milk and stuffing the mixture deep within the vagina. The dung blocked the passage of many—if not all—sperm through the cervix and also soaked up sperm. The dung may also have done its job through a social mechanism. It may have discouraged all but the most ardent suitors.

> **1 › T / F Truth or Fiction Revisited** It is true that ancient Egyptians used crocodile dung as a contraceptive. (No comment.)

Ancient Greek and Roman women placed absorbent materials within the vagina to absorb semen. The use of sheaths or coverings for the penis has a long history. Sheaths worn over the penis as decorative covers can be traced to ancient Egypt (1350 BCE). Sheaths of linen were first described in European writings in 1564 by the Italian anatomist Fallopius (from whom the name of the fallopian tube is derived). Linen sheaths were used, without success, as a barrier against syphilis. The term **condom** was not used to describe penile sheaths until the eighteenth century. At that time, sheaths made of animal intestines became popular as a means of preventing sexually transmitted infections and unwanted pregnancies. Among the early advocates of condoms as a method of contraception was the Italian adventurer and writer Giovanni Casanova (1725–1798). We now associate his name with men who are known for their amorous adventures. James Boswell (1740–1795), the biographer of Samuel Johnson, described his use of "armor," or condoms, in his graphic *London Journal.* On one occasion, however, he was so enamored with a street prostitute that he neglected to use his armor and contracted gonorrhea. Condoms made of rubber (hence the slang "rubbers") were introduced shortly after Charles Goodyear invented vulcanization of rubber in 1843. Many other forms of contraception were also used widely in the nineteenth century, including withdrawal, vaginal sponges, and douching.

condom

A sheath made of animal membrane or latex that covers the penis and serves as a barrier to sperm.

Critical Thinking
Critical thinkers pay attention to definitions of terms. The Roman Catholic Church opposes the use of artificial contraception. What is meant by *artificial* contraception?

Contraception in the United States: The Political Battle

As methods of contraception grew more popular in the nineteenth century, opponents waged a battle to make contraception illegal. One powerful opponent of contraception was Anthony Comstock, who served for a time as the secretary of the New York society for the suppression of vice. Comstock lobbied successfully for passage of a federal law in 1873—the Comstock law—that prohibited the dissemination of birth-control information through the mail on the grounds that it was "obscene and indecent." Many states passed even more restrictive laws. They outlawed passage of information from one person to another, even from physician to patient.

Consider the resistance that Margaret Sanger met when she challenged the laws restricting information about contraception (Engelman, 2011). In 1914, she established the National Birth Control League, which published the magazine *The Woman Rebel. Rebel* did not publish birth-control information but challenged the view that it was obscene. Nevertheless, charges were brought against Sanger, and she fled to Europe before her trial. During her self-imposed exile, she visited birth-control clinics in the Netherlands. When the charges against her in the United States were dropped in 1916, Sanger returned and established a birth-control clinic in Brooklyn, New York. The clinic was closed by the police, and Sanger was arrested. Released on bail, she reopened the clinic and was thereupon sentenced to 30 days in jail. She successfully appealed the sentence. In 1918, the courts ruled that physicians must be allowed to disseminate information that might aid in the cure and prevention of disease. Dismantling of the Comstock law had begun. With the financial support of a wealthy friend, Katherine Dexter McCormack, Sanger spurred research into the use of hormones as one approach to contraception. In 1960, only 6 years before Sanger's death, oral contraception—"the pill"—was finally marketed in the United States. In 1965, the Supreme Court struck down the last impediment to free use of contraception: a law preventing the sale of contraceptives in Connecticut (*Griswold v. Connecticut,* 1965). In 1973, abortion was, in effect, legalized by the Supreme Court in the case of *Roe v. Wade,* permitting women to terminate unwanted pregnancies.

Today, contraceptives are advertised in popular magazines and sold through vending machines in college dormitories. U.S. history is not a one-way road to unrestricted use of birth control, however. Recent Supreme Court decisions have set aside bits and pieces of *Roe v. Wade,* giving the states more discretion over the regulation of abortion and restricting access to abortions for minors. On the other hand, in 2016 the Supreme Court struck down a Texas law which requiring that physicians who perform abortions have admitting privileges at nearby hospitals and that the clinics meet standards for performing more complex surgical procedures. Texas claimed that its law was an attempt to protect the health of women. The Supreme Court's decision said that the claim of interest in women's health was a thinly veiled effort to prevent abortions and placed an undue burden on women, given that few abortion clinics in Texas could meet the requirements of the state law. The battles go on.

Methods of Contraception

There are many methods of contraception, including hormonal methods (the pill, the contraceptive patch, and injectable contraceptives), intrauterine contraceptive devices, diaphragms, cervical caps, spermicides, condoms, douching, withdrawal (coitus interruptus), and timing of ovulation (rhythm methods).

Hormonal Methods of Contraception

LO 10.2 Explain how hormonal methods of contraception work, and discuss their advantages and disadvantages.

Hormonal birth-control methods include "the pill," the contraceptive patch, injectable contraceptives, some intrauterine contraceptive devices, and the under-the-skin implant.

Oral Contraceptives ("The Pill")

oral contraceptive

A contraceptive consisting of sex hormones and taken by mouth.

An **oral contraceptive** is commonly referred to as a birth-control pill, or simply "the pill." However, there are many kinds of birth-control pills that vary in the type and dosages of hormones they contain. Birth-control pills fall into two major categories: combination pills and mini-pills. Available only by prescription, birth-control pills are the most popular form of contraception among single women of reproductive age (Zieman et al., 2015–2016). According to National Health Statistics Reports (Daniels et al., 2013), about 82% of adult women aged 15–44 have used the pill at one time or another.

combination pill

A birth-control pill that contains estrogen and progesterone.

Combination pills (such as Ortho-Novum, Ovcon, and Loestrin) contain a combination of synthetic forms of the hormones estrogen and progesterone (progestin). Most combination pills provide a steady dose of synthetic estrogen and progesterone. Other combination pills, called *multiphasic* pills, vary the dosage of these hormones across the menstrual cycle to reduce the overall dosages to which the woman is exposed as well as reduce possible side effects. The **mini-pill** contains synthetic progesterone (progestin) only.

mini-pill

A birth-control pill that contains progesterone only.

HOW THEY WORK Women cannot conceive when they are already pregnant because their bodies suppress maturation of egg follicles and ovulation. The combination pill fools the brain into acting as though the woman is already pregnant, so that no additional ova mature or are released. If ovulation does not take place, a woman cannot become pregnant.

In a normal menstrual cycle, low levels of estrogen during and just after the menstrual phase stimulate the pituitary gland to secrete follicle-stimulating hormone (FSH), which in turn stimulates the maturation of ovarian follicles. The estrogen in the combination pill inhibits FSH production, so that follicles do not mature. The progesterone (progestin) inhibits the pituitary's secretion of luteinizing hormone (LH), which would otherwise lead to ovulation. The woman continues to have menstrual periods, but there is no unfertilized ovum to be sloughed off in the menstrual flow.

The combination pill is taken for 21 days of the typical 28-day cycle. Then, for 7 days, the woman either takes no pill at all or an inert placebo pill to maintain the habit of taking a pill a day. The sudden drop in hormone levels causes the endometrium to disintegrate and menstruation to follow 3 or 4 days after the last pill has been taken. Then the cycle is repeated.

The progestin in the combination pill also increases the thickness and acidity of the cervical mucus. The mucus thus becomes a more resistant barrier to sperm and inhibits development of the endometrium. Therefore, even if an egg were somehow to mature and become fertilized in a fallopian tube, sperm would not be likely to survive the passage through the cervix. Even if sperm were somehow to succeed in fertilizing an egg, the failure of the endometrium to develop would mean that the fertilized ovum could not become implanted in the uterus. Progestin may also impede the progress of ova through the fallopian tubes and make it more difficult for sperm to penetrate ova.

The mini-pill contains progestin but no estrogen. Mini-pills are taken daily through the menstrual cycle, even during menstruation. They act in two ways. They thicken the cervical mucus to impede the passage of sperm through the cervix, and they render the inner lining of the uterus less receptive to a fertilized egg. Thus, even if the woman does conceive, the fertilized egg will pass from the body rather than becoming implanted in the uterine wall.

In Chapter 2 we noted that hormonal preparations such as Seasonique and Lybrel provide birth control as well as decrease the woman's number of periods.

EFFECTIVENESS The failure rate of the birth-control pill associated with perfect use is very low—0.5% or less depending on the type of pill. The failure rate increases to 9% in typical use (see Figure 10.1). Failures can occur when women forget to take the pill for 2 days or more, when they do not use backup methods when they first go on the pill, and when they switch from one brand to another. But forgetting to take the pill for a day or two might allow ovulation—and fertilization.

REVERSIBILITY Oral contraceptives may temporarily reduce fertility after they are stopped but they are not associated with permanent infertility. Nearly all women begin ovulating regularly within 3 months of suspending use (Hatcher et al., 2011). When a woman appears not to be ovulating after going off the pill, a drug such as clomiphene is often used to induce ovulation.

ADVANTAGES AND DISADVANTAGES The great advantage of oral contraception is that when used properly it is nearly 100% effective. Unlike many other forms of contraception, such as the condom or diaphragm, its use does not interfere with sexual spontaneity or diminish sexual sensations. The sex act need not be interrupted, as it would be by use of a condom.

Birth-control pills may also have some *healthful* side effects. They appear to reduce the risk of pelvic inflammatory disease (PID), benign ovarian cysts, and fibrocystic (benign) breast growths. The pill regularizes menstrual cycles and reduces menstrual cramping and premenstrual discomfort. The pill may also be helpful in the treatment of iron-deficiency anemia and facial acne. The combination pill reduces the risks of ovarian and endometrial cancer, even for a number of years after the woman has stopped taking it (Melo & Creinin, 2016).

Taking the Pill. What are the advantages and disadvantages of the birth control pill? Will there ever be a birth control pill for men?

The pill does have some disadvantages. It provides no protection against sexually transmitted infections (STIs). Moreover, it may reduce the effectiveness of antibiotics used to treat STIs. Going on the pill requires medical consultation, so a woman must plan to begin using the pill at least several weeks before becoming sexually active or before discontinuing the use of other contraceptives, and she must incur the expense of medical visits. Marchbanks and her colleagues (2002) compared 4,575 women with breast cancer with 4,682 controls and found no increased risk for breast cancer among women who were using or had used oral contraceptives. Moreover, the pill did not increase the risk of breast cancer in women with a family history of the disorder.

The main drawbacks of birth-control pills are potential side effects and possible health risks. Although a good deal of research suggests that the pill is safe for healthy women, many researchers (e.g., Melo & Creinin, 2016) suggest caution among women with medical conditions such as hypertension, diabetes, migraine headaches, fibrocystic breast tissue, uterine fibroids, or elevated cholesterol.

The estrogen in combination pills may produce side effects such as nausea and vomiting, fluid retention (feeling bloated), weight gain, increased vaginal discharge, headaches, tenderness in the breasts, and dizziness. Many of these are temporary. When they persist, women may be switched from one pill to another, perhaps to one with lower doses of hormones. Pregnant women produce high estrogen levels in the corpus luteum and placenta. The combination pill artificially raises levels of estrogen, so it is not surprising that some women who use it have side effects that mimic the early signs of pregnancy, such as weight gain or nausea ("morning sickness"). Weight gain can result from estrogen (through fluid retention) or progestin (through increased appetite and development of muscle). Oral contraceptives may also increase blood pressure in some women, but clinically significant elevations are rare in women using the low-dose pills that are available today (Zieman et al., 2015–2016). Still, it is wise for women who use the pill to have their blood pressure checked regularly. Women who encounter problems with high blood pressure from taking the pill are usually advised to switch to another form of contraception.

Hormone withdrawal symptoms are experienced by many women when they discontinue the pill (Spencer & Bonnema, 2011). These include headaches, pelvic pain, bloating, and breast tenderness.

Many women have avoided using the pill because of the risk of blood clots. The lower dosages of estrogen found in most types of birth-control pills today are associated with much lower risk of blood clots than was the case in the 1960s and 1970s when higher dosages were used (Melo & Creinin, 2016; Zieman et al., 2015–2016). Still, women who are at increased risk for blood clotting, such as women with a history of circulatory problems or stroke, are typically advised not to use the pill.

Women who are considering using the pill need to weigh the benefits and risks with their healthcare providers. For the great majority of young, healthy women in their 20s and early 30s, the pill is unlikely to cause blood clots or other cardiovascular problems (Zieman et al., 2015–2016). Although research has found the pill to be safe for most women who do not smoke and are younger than age 35, pill users may have a slightly higher chance than nonusers of developing blood clots in the veins and lungs, stroke, and heart attack.

Some women should not be on the pill at all: women who have had circulatory problems or blood clots; women who have suffered a heart attack or stroke; or women who have a history of coronary disease, breast, or uterine cancer, genital bleeding, liver tumors, or sickle cell anemia (because of associated blood-clotting problems). Because of their increased risk of cardiovascular problems, caution should be exercised when the combination pill is used with women older than 35 years of age who smoke (Zieman et al., 2015–2016). Nursing mothers should also avoid using the pill because the hormones may be passed to the baby in the mother's milk.

Since the risks of cardiovascular complications generally increase with age, many women older than the age of 35 have been encouraged by their gynecologists to use other forms of birth control. However, the American College of Obstetricians and Gynecologists believes that healthy nonsmokers can use the pill safely at least until the age of 45. This number keeps expanding, with many women now being advised to continue using pills to regulate their periods into their 50s.

The pill may also have psychological effects. Some users report depression or irritability. Switching brands or altering doses may help. Evidence is lacking concerning the effects of lower-estrogen pills on sexual desire.

Progestin fosters male secondary sex characteristics, so women who take the mini-pill may develop acne, facial hair, thinning of scalp hair, reduction in breast size, vaginal dryness, and missed or shorter periods. Irregular bleeding, or so-called breakthrough bleeding, between menstrual periods is a common side effect of the mini-pill. Irregular bleeding should be brought to the attention of a health professional. Because they can produce vaginal dryness, mini-pills can hinder vaginal lubrication during intercourse, decreasing sexual sensations and rendering sex painful.

Researchers have also examined suspected links between the use of the pill and certain forms of cancer, especially breast cancer. Results from several large-scale studies show no overall increase in the rates of breast cancer among pill users, but it remains possible that some subgroups of women who use the pill may be at increased risk. The evidence linking use of the pill with cervical cancer is mixed, with some studies showing a link and others showing none (Zieman et al., 2015–2016).

Women considering the pill are advised to have a thorough medical evaluation to rule out conditions that might make usage unsafe. The evaluation should include a detailed medical and family history, and a physical examination including a Pap smear, assessment of blood pressure, screening for STIs, urinalysis, breast and pelvic examination, and possibly an electrocardiogram (ECG). Women who begin to use the pill, regardless of their age or risk status, should pay attention to changes in their physical condition, have regular checkups, and promptly report any physical complaints or unusual symptoms to their physicians.

The "Morning-After" Pill: The "Emergency Contraceptive"

About 11% of U.S. women aged 15–44 have used the so-called morning-after pill, or postcoital contraceptive (Daniels et al., 2013). The morning after pill actually refers to several types of pills that have high doses of hormones. Because they are not taken regularly, they do not prevent ovulation. Instead, they prevent fertilization or prevent the fertilized egg from implanting in the uterus. The morning-after pill, sold as Plan B One-Step, Next Choice, and Next Choice One Dose, contains the hormone levonogestrel, a form of progesterone. It is available to women aged 17 and older without prescription.

Morning-after pills are best taken within 24 hours after sex, but are effective up to 5 days (120 hours) afterward. Women who wait to see whether they have missed a period are no longer candidates for the morning-after pill.

Another morning-after pill (brand name Ella) is available by prescription only. It contains ulipristal acetate. It is about twice as effective as Plan B and Next Choice.

Morning-after pills have a higher hormone content than most birth-control pills. For this reason, nausea is a common side effect. Nausea is usually mild and passes within a day or two after treatment, but it can be treated with antinausea medication.

Because morning-after pills often prevent fertilized ova from implanting in the uterus, they may be looked upon as an early method of abortion. Be aware that our description here is fraught with political baggage because supporters of the morning-after pill are concerned that pro-life advocates could turn a great deal of attention to the morning-after pill, and some have done so (Dye, 2013). But it is our function as textbook authors to provide information, not judgments.

We should also note that some women swallow several regular birth-control pills to ward off pregnancy after unprotected sex. Sometimes they actually work, but women are strongly advised to call their doctors about it. But for women who do not have access to doctors, or do not want to involve them, Plan B and Next Choice are available.

Critical Thinking
Is the use of the mini-pill or of the intrauterine contraceptive device a method of contraception or of abortion? Does it matter? Explain your views.

Plan B. Plan B—one of the "morning-after" pills—is available without prescription for women age 17 and older.

2 › T / F Truth or Fiction Revisited Yes, there is a morning-after pill, but it is certainly not recommended as a regular form of birth control. They are *one-time* forms of emergency protection, which may be most appropriate to use following rape or when regular contraceptive devices fail (for example, if a condom breaks or a diaphragm becomes dislodged). The morning-after pill generally prevents implantation, but if it fails, the fetus may be damaged by exposure to the hormones.

The Contraceptive Patch

The contraceptive patch is another method of delivering estrogen and progestin to prevent ovulation and implantation. The patch is thin and measures about 2 inches by 2 inches. It is worn on the abdomen, buttocks, upper arm, or upper torso. The patch contains a week's worth of hormones and releases them gradually into the bloodstream. It has been used by 10%–11% of U.S. women aged 15–44 (Daniels et al., 2013).

Like the birth-control pill, when used correctly, the patch is more than 99% effective, but in typical use 9% of women who use it become pregnant within a year (Figure 10.1). Women who use the patch need not think about contraception daily. Also, like the pill, the patch doesn't interrupt sex. Its side effects and potential hazards are similar to those of the pill.

Injectable Contraceptives

One U.S. woman in four aged 15–44 has used an injectable hormone preparation such as Lunelle and Depo-Provera, which are available by prescription (Daniels et al., 2013). Lunelle is similar to the combination pill in that it contains estrogen and progestin. It is injected monthly. Like the mini-pill, Depo-Provera contains progestin only. It prevents pregnancy for 3 months. Injectables are the second-most popular hormonal contraceptive method after the pill (Daniels et al., 2013).

Lunelle prevents ovulation; thickens cervical mucus, which prevents the sperm from reaching the egg; and changes the lining of the uterus to prevent implantation. Depo-Provera prevents ovulation. Lunelle, like oral contraceptives, has a failure rate of less than 1% when used properly.

Injectable contraceptives have the advantages of being highly effective, permitting spontaneous sex, and of remaining effective without being taken every day. They have side effects similar to those of other types of hormonal contraceptives, including oral contraceptives. These include vaginal bleeding, headaches, tenderness in the breasts, irregular menstrual cycles, weight gain, bloating, nausea, and vomiting. Injectable contraceptives are usually not recommended for women who smoke, have elevated blood pressure, have breast or uterine cancer, have a history of blood clots, have a history of heart attack or stroke, have diabetes, have liver disease, or are allergic to hormones.

The effects of Lunelle and Depo-Provera are reversible, but ovulation may take 10 months or so to return (Allen et al., 2016). Neither contraceptive affords protection against STIs.

Intrauterine Contraception (IUC) Devices

intrauterine contraceptive (IUC) device

An object inserted into the uterus and left in place to prevent conception.

Camel drivers setting out on long desert journeys once placed round stones in the uteruses of female camels to prevent them from becoming pregnant and lost to service. The stones may have acted as primitive **intrauterine contraception (IUC) devices**—also known as IUDs. IUC devices are small objects of various shapes that are inserted into the uterus. They have been used by humans since ancient Greek times. Today, they are inserted into the uterus by a physician or nurse practitioner and usually left in place for a year or more. Fine plastic threads or strings hang down from the IUC device into the vagina, so that the woman can check to see that it remains in place.

IUC devices are used by more than 180 million women around the world (Ohly & Westhof, 2016). Most of them live in China, where nearly one in three married women uses an IUC device during her childbearing years. By contrast, IUC devices are used by only about 7.7% of women aged 15–44 in the United States (Daniels et al., 2013).

IUC devices achieved their greatest popularity in the United States in the 1960s and 1970s. They were used by 18%–19% of U.S. women aged 15–44 in the year 1982. Then there was a sharp drop off in their use during the 1980s after use of a popular model, the Dalkon Shield, was linked to a high incidence of pelvic infections and tubal infertility.

Women may choose from a number of IUC devices: the TCu380A copper T intrauterine device, the LNG-20 intrauterine system which has 52 mg of levonorgestrel, and the LNG-14 which contains 13.5 mg of levonorgestrel (Ohly & Westhof, 2016). The copper device contains no hormones but is toxic to sperm. Levonorgestrel is a form of progesterone which thickens cervical mucus, blocking the movement of sperm, and also suppressing development of the uterine lining, which may reduce menstrual cramping and heavy bleeding. Ask your doctor which IUC device is preferable for you.

After the fears that attended use of IUC devices were shown to be exaggerated or baseless, IUC devices began to make a comeback in popularity in the United States (Brody, 2012). Many now see the UIC device as safe, convenient, and effective, and the number of women using the IUC device has tripled over the past 10 years, such that they now account for 10% of prescribed contraceptives. (Keep in mind that many contraceptives, such as condoms and the sponge, do not require a prescription.) The IUC device is 99% effective in preventing pregnancy, and if inserted soon following coitus without a condom, it may be as useful in preventing implantation as the morning-after pill, acting by preventing the uterine lining changes that permit implantation. IUC devices may help protect against cervical cancer.

EFFECTIVENESS   The failure rate associated with use of the IUC device is less than 1%. Most failures occur within 3 months of insertion, often because the device shifts position or is expelled.

The IUC device may irritate the muscular layer of the uterine wall, causing contractions that expel it through the vagina. The device is most likely to be expelled during menstruation, so users are advised to check their sanitary napkins or tampons before discarding them. Women who use IUC devices are advised to check the string several times a month to ensure that it is in place.

REVERSIBILITY   IUC devices may be removed readily by professionals. Nine out of 10 former IUC device users who try to become pregnant do so within a year (Zieman et al., 2015–2016).

ADVANTAGES AND DISADVANTAGES   The IUC device's advantages are it is highly effective, it does not diminish sexual spontaneity or sexual sensations, and once in place, the woman need not do anything more to prevent pregnancy. The IUC device also does not interfere with the woman's normal hormonal production. Users continue to produce pituitary hormones that stimulate ovarian follicles to mature and rupture, thereby releasing mature ova and producing female sex hormones.

A disadvantage is that insertion can be discomforting. Another disadvantage is side effects. The most common side effects are excessive menstrual cramping, irregular bleeding (spotting) between periods, and heavier than usual menstrual bleeding (Ohly & Westhof, 2016). These usually occur shortly following insertion and are among the primary reasons women ask to have the device removed. A more serious concern is the possible risk of PID, a serious disease that can become life threatening if left untreated. Women who use the IUC device may have an increased risk of PID. The risk of infection is associated more with the insertion of the device (bacteria may enter the woman's reproductive tract during insertion) than with use of the device itself. Risk factors for PID include a recent episode of gonorrhea or chlamydia, recurrent episodes of these STIs, sexual contact with multiple partners, or sexual contact with a partner who has had multiple partners.

Another risk is that the IUC device may perforate (tear) the uterine or cervical walls, which can cause bleeding, pain, and adhesions. Perforations are not common but can be serious when they occur (Zieman et al., 2015–2016). IUC-device users are also at greater risk for ectopic pregnancies, both during and after usage, and for miscarriage.

Another drawback to the IUC device is its cost. The typical cost of insertion in a family-planning clinic is a few hundred dollars. But users can think of the cost as being averaged out over the years that the device is in use. Moreover, the IUC device, like the pill, offers no protection against STIs. Finally, like the pill, IUC device places the burden of contraception entirely on the woman.

Under-the-Skin Implants

Another long-acting reversible contraceptive is implanted beneath the skin of the upper arm and gradually releases the hormone etonogestrel. The implant is a small matchstick-like plastic rod and it remains effective for 3 years. Like the IUC device, the implant is nearly 100% effective. Even so, only about 2% of U.S. women aged 15–44 use implants (Daniels et al., 2013).

Etonogestrel is a form of progesterone. It prevents ovulation and thickens cervical mucus, which make it more difficult for sperm to travel in the woman's reproductive tract—if an ovum were present, it would be harder to reach and fertilize it.

ADVANTAGES AND DISADVANTAGES   Once the implant is in place, its effectiveness is unrelated to the couple's reliability and motivation. It is close to perfectly effective. There is no need to shop and spend for additional birth-control supplies during the implant's period of effectiveness; although there is an up-front cost, there are no monthly costs. Fertility returns rapidly when the implant is removed. It can also be used by women who are breast-feeding.

Possible disadvantages include changes to the woman's menstrual cycle. Menstrual flow typically diminishes, and after a year or so, some women stop having periods. But other women report heavier, longer periods along with increased spotting between menstrual periods. These changes do not signify problems regaining fertility when the implant stops working or is removed. The implant offers zero protection against STIs.

Barrier Methods of Contraception

LO 10.3   **Explain how barrier methods of contraception work, and discuss their advantages and disadvantages.**

Barrier methods such as the diaphragm prevent sperm from reaching ova. However, as we'll see, many of them are best used with chemicals that kill sperm (spermicides).

The Diaphragm

Diaphragms were once used by about one-third of American couples who practiced birth control. When invented in 1882, they were a breakthrough. Their popularity declined only in the 1960s with the advent of the pill and the IUC device. They were still used by 17% of U.S. women aged 15–44 in 1982, but are used by only about 3% of women today (Daniels et al., 2013).

---

diaphragm

A rubber cup or dome, fitted to the contour of a woman's vagina, coated with a spermicide and inserted before coitus to prevent conception.

Figure 10.1   A Diaphragm.

The diaphragm is a shallow cup or dome made of latex. Diaphragms must be fitted to the contour of the vagina by a health professional. The diaphragm forms a barrier to sperm but should be used in conjunction with a spermicidal cream or jelly.

Rubber dome

Coil spring

Spermicide

Diaphragm

The diaphragm is a shallow cup or dome made of thin latex rubber (see Figure 10.1). The rim is a flexible metal ring covered with rubber. Diaphragms come in different sizes to allow a precise fit.

Diaphragms are available by prescription and must be fitted to the contour of the vagina by a health professional. Several sizes and types of diaphragms may be tried during a fitting. Women practice insertion in a health professional's office so they can be guided as needed.

HOW IT WORKS   The diaphragm is inserted and removed by the woman, much like a tampon. It is akin to a condom in that it forms a barrier against sperm when placed snugly over the cervical opening. Yet it is unreliable as a barrier alone. Thus, the diaphragm should be used in conjunction with a spermicidal cream or jelly. One might even say that the diaphragm's main function is to keep the spermicide in place.

HOW IT IS USED   The diaphragm should be inserted no more than 2 hours before coitus because the spermicides that are used may begin to lose effectiveness beyond this time. Some health professionals, however, suggest that the diaphragm may be inserted up to 6 hours preceding intercourse. (It seems reasonable to err on the side of caution and assume that there is a 2-hour time limit.) The woman or her partner places a tablespoonful of spermicidal cream or jelly on the inside of the cup and spreads it inside the rim. (Cream spread outside the rim might cause the diaphragm to slip.) The woman opens the inner lips of the vagina with one hand and folds the diaphragm with the other by squeezing the ring. She inserts the diaphragm against the cervix, with the inner side facing upward (see Figure 10.2). Her partner can help insert the diaphragm, but the woman is advised to check its placement. Some women prefer a plastic insertion device, but most find it easier to insert the diaphragm without it. The diaphragm should be left in place *at least 6 hours* to allow the spermicide to kill sperm remaining in the vagina (Zieman et al., 2015–2016). It should not be left in place for longer than 24 hours, to guard against toxic shock syndrome (TSS).

After use, the diaphragm should be washed with mild soap and warm water and stored in a dry, cool place. When cared for properly, a diaphragm can last about 2 years. Women may need to be refitted after pregnancy or a change in weight of about 10 pounds or more.

EFFECTIVENESS   If used consistently and correctly, the failure rate of the diaphragm is estimated at 6% during a year of use. In typical use, however, the failure rate is believed to be twice as high—12% (see Figure 10.1). Some women become pregnant because they do not use the diaphragm during every coital experience. Others may insert it too early or not leave it in long enough. The diaphragm may not fit well, or it may slip—especially if the couple is acrobatic. A diaphragm may develop tiny holes or cracks. Women are advised to inspect the diaphragm for signs of wear and consult their health professionals when in doubt (Nelson & Russo, 2016). Effectiveness also is seriously compromised when the diaphragm is not used along with a correctly applied spermicide.

REVERSIBILITY   The effects of the diaphragm are fully reversible. To become pregnant, the woman simply stops using it. The diaphragm has not been shown to influence subsequent fertility.

Figure 10.2   Insertion and Checking of the Diaphragm.

Women are instructed in insertion of the diaphragm by a health professional. In practice, a woman and her partner may find joint insertion an erotic experience.

Uterus

Cervix

Vagina

Diaphragm

ADVANTAGES AND DISADVANTAGES When used correctly, the diaphragm is a safe and reasonably effective means of birth control and does not alter the woman's hormone production or reproductive cycle. The diaphragm can be used as needed, whereas the pill must be used daily and the IUC device remains in place whether or not the woman has sex. Another advantage is the virtual absence of side effects. The few women who are allergic to the rubber in the diaphragm can switch to a plastic model.

The major disadvantage is the high failure rate of typical users. Nearly one in eight typical users, who also uses a spermicide, becomes pregnant during a year of use (Figure 10.1). Another disadvantage is the need to insert the diaphragm before intercourse, which the couple may find disruptive. The woman's partner may find the taste of the spermicide unpleasant during oral sex. The pressure exerted by the diaphragm against the vaginal and cervical walls may also irritate the urinary tract and cause urinary or vaginal infections. Switching to a different size diaphragm or one with a different type of rim may alleviate this problem. About 1 woman or man in 20 may develop allergies to the particular spermicide that is used, which can lead to irritation of the genitals. This problem may be alleviated by switching to another brand.

Spermicides

Spermicides are agents that kill sperm. They coat the cervical opening, blocking the passage of sperm and killing sperm by chemical action. They come as jellies and creams, suppositories, aerosol foam, and a contraceptive film. Spermicides should be left in place in the vagina (no douching) for several hours after having sex (Zieman et al., 2015–2016). Only about 7% of U.S. women aged 15–44 use spermicidal foam alone, and about 4% use spermicidal jellies or creams (Daniels et al., 2013).

Spermicidal jellies and creams come in tubes with plastic applicators that introduce the spermicide into the vagina (see Figure 10.3). Spermicidal foam is a fluffy white cream with the consistency of shaving cream. It is contained in a pressurized can and is introduced with a plastic applicator in much the same way as spermicidal jellies and creams.

Vaginal suppositories are inserted into the upper vagina, near the cervix, where they release spermicide as they dissolve. Unlike spermicidal jellies, creams, and foam, which become effective immediately when applied, suppositories must be inserted no less than 10 to 15 minutes before coitus so that they have sufficient time to dissolve.

Spermicidal film consists of thin, 2-inch-square sheets that are saturated with spermicide. When placed in the vagina, they dissolve into a gel and release the

---

Figure 10.3 The Application of Spermicidal Foam.

Spermicidal jellies and creams come in tubes with plastic applicators. Spermicidal foam comes in a pressurized can and is applied with a plastic applicator in much the same way as spermicidal jellies and creams.

Uterus

Cervix

Foam applicator

Foam

Vagina

spermicide. The spermicidal film should be inserted at least 5 minutes before intercourse to allow it time to melt and for the spermicide to be dispersed. It remains effective for upwards of 1 hour. One disadvantage of the film that some users have noted is a tendency for it to adhere to the fingertips, which makes it difficult to insert correctly.

In typical use, the yearly failure rate of spermicides used alone is a whopping 28% (Figure 10.1). When used correctly and consistently, the failure rate is estimated to drop to about 6%. Spermicides are more effective when combined with other forms of contraception, such as the condom or diaphragm.

The major advantages of spermicides are that they do not alter the woman's natural biological processes and are applied only as needed. Spermicides have not been linked with any changes in reproductive potential. So couples who wish to become pregnant simply stop using them. They do not require a doctor's prescription or a fitting, and can be bought in virtually any drugstore.

The major disadvantage is the high failure rate among typical users. Foam often fails when the can is not shaken enough, when too little is used, when it is not applied deeply enough within the vagina near the cervix, or when it is used after coitus has begun.

Spermicides are generally free of side effects but occasionally can irritate the vagina or penis. Irritation is sometimes alleviated by changing brands. Partners may find the taste of spermicides unpleasant.

It was once thought that spermicides that contain nonoxynol-9 might afford protection against STIs such as HIV/AIDS, genital herpes, trichomoniasis ("trich"), syphilis, and chlamydia. Yet researchers have found that nonoxynol-9 provides no protection against STIs (Zalenskaya et al., 2011). In a study of the effectiveness of the spermicide as a means of preventing HIV infection among African and Thai prostitutes, the group using nonoxynol-9 actually had a significantly higher rate of HIV infection (15%) than the group using the placebo (10%) (Stephenson, 2000). Commentators suggest that local irritation caused by nonoxynol-9 might have made the vaginal tract an easier port of entry for HIV (Weiss et al., 2008, Gordon et al., 2016).

The Contraceptive Sponge

The contraceptive sponge is a soft, disposable device. Unlike the diaphragm, the sponge does not need to be fitted. Like the diaphragm, it provides a barrier that holds a spermicide, but the spermicide is built in. The sponge can also be inserted into the vagina several hours before coitus and has the additional advantage of absorbing sperm. It is odorless and tasteless, and users found it less drippy than the diaphragm. On the negative side, the failure rate for typical use is 12% for women who have not had children, and 24% for women who have. About 1 user in 20 (male and female) is mildly irritated by the spermicide. There is also a remote chance of TSS: one case arose for every 4 *million* days of use. Only about 4.3% of U.S. women aged 15–44 have ever used the sponge.

The Cervical Cap

The cervical cap, like the diaphragm, is a dome-shaped cup. It comes in different sizes and must be fitted by a health professional. It is smaller than the diaphragm—about the size of a thimble—and is meant to fit snugly over the cervical opening.

Like the diaphragm, the cap is intended to be used with a spermicide applied inside it. When inserting it, the woman (or her partner) fills the cap about a third full of spermicide. Then, squeezing the edges together, she inserts the cap high in the vagina, so that it presses firmly against the cervix. The woman can test the fit by running a finger around the cap to ensure that the cervical opening is covered. It should be left in place for at least 8 hours after intercourse. The cap provides continuous protection for about 48 hours without the need for additional spermicide. To reduce the risk of TSS, the cap should not be left in place longer than 48 hours. Like the diaphragm, the cervical cap forms a barrier and also holds spermicide in place. It prevents sperm from passing into the uterus and fallopian tubes and kills sperm by chemical action. The cap should be cleaned after use and checked for wear and tear. When cared for properly, it can last upward of 3 years.

The failure rate in typical use is high, ranging from 18% in women who have not borne children to 36% in women who have (Zieman et al., 2015–2016). Failures may be attributed, at least in part, to the cap becoming dislodged and to changes in the cervix during the menstrual cycle, which can cause the cap to cover the cervix less snugly.

Similar to the diaphragm, the cap is a mechanical device that does not affect the woman's hormonal production or reproductive cycle. The cap may be especially suited to women who cannot support a diaphragm because of lack of vaginal muscle tone. Because of concern that the cap may irritate cervical tissue, however, users are advised to have regular Pap tests.

Some women find the cervical cap uncomfortable. It can also become dislodged during sex or lose its fit as the cervix changes over the menstrual cycle. Side effects include urinary tract infections and sensitivities to the rubber or spermicide. Other disadvantages include the expense and inconvenience of being fitted by a health professional. Moreover, some women are shaped so that the cap does not remain in place. For these reasons, and because they may be difficult to obtain, cervical caps are not very popular in the United States.

The Condom

prophylactic

An agent that protects against disease.

Condoms are also called "rubbers," "safes," **prophylactics** (because latex condoms protect against STIs), and "skins" (referring to those that are made from lamb intestines). Condoms lost popularity with the advent of the pill and the IUC device. They are less effective than either of them, may disrupt sexual spontaneity, and can lessen sexual sensations because they prevent contact between the penis and the vaginal wall.

Condoms have regained popularity, however, because latex condoms can help prevent the spread of HIV/AIDS and other STIs and, to a lesser extent, because of concerns about side effects of the pill and the IUC device. Let's provide some numbers: In 1982 about 52% of U.S. women aged 15–44 had ever had sex with a male partner wearing a condom; that percentage expanded to 93%–94% today (Daniels et al., 2013).

The current popularity of condoms has been spurred by the increased assertiveness of women. By using a condom, the man assumes much of the responsibility for contraception. Condoms are the only contraceptive device worn by men, and the only readily reversible method of contraception that is available to men. Condoms are inexpensive and can be obtained without prescription from pharmacies, family-planning clinics, and vending machines.

Some condoms are made of latex rubber. Thinner, more expensive condoms ("skins") are made from the intestinal membranes of lambs. The latter allow greater sexual sensation, but only latex condoms are effective against HIV. Condoms made of animal intestines have pores large enough to permit HIV and other viruses, such as the one that causes hepatitis B, to slip through (Zieman et al., 2015–2016). A few condoms are made from other materials, such as plastic (polyurethane). Questions remain about the effectiveness of polyurethane condoms. Some condoms have plain ends. Others have nipples or reservoirs (see Figure 10.5) that catch semen and may help prevent the condom from bursting during ejaculation.

HOW THEY WORK   A condom serves as a barrier, preventing the passage of sperm and disease-carrying microorganisms.

A CLOSER LOOK

ERRORS IN USING CONDOMS

All right, you're going to be using condoms because they have no side effects (other than some decrease in sexual sensations) and are the one method that places the responsibility squarely on the shoulders of the man. Condoms are highly effective—when used properly. However, the authors of a review of the literature (Sanders et al., 2012) found that many couples experience problems such as the following in using condoms:

- Breakage: From 1% to 41% of condom users report discovering that the condom they were using was broken. In fact, 2% to 11% of users say they have used sharp objects to open the condom package, clearly exposing the condom to cutting.
- Slippage: From 13% to 19% of users reported that a condom had slipped, allowing semen to leak.
- Leakage: Condoms can also leak when they do not slip, with 8% of men and 13% of women reporting at least one such experience.
- Late application: In perhaps the most common error, 17% to 51% of users report putting on the condom after they have begun sexual intercourse. Better late than never? Perhaps, but …
- Early removal: At least as problematic as late application is removing a condom before the couple has finished having sexual intercourse—an error that is nevertheless reported by 14% to 45% of users.
- Unrolling a condom before putting it on: Manufacturers intend for condoms to be unrolled onto the penis, yet 2% to 25% of users unroll them first and then struggle to put them on—increasing the chances of breakage and leakage.
- No space at the tip: Space should be left at the tip of the condom to collect semen without placing undue pressure on the condom, yet from 24% to 46% of users fail to leave such a reservoir for semen.
- Failing to remove air: Users should squeeze out air from the tip of the condom to help make room for semen, but 48% of women and 42% of men admit to failing to do so.
- Inside-out condoms: No, condoms are not manufactured inside out, but 4% to 30% of users report rolling condoms on inside out, and then removing them and applying them the correct way, but exposing the woman to semen during the process.
- Failing to unroll all the way: Condoms should be completely unrolled, but 11% of women and 28% of men have begun intercourse before the condom was completely unrolled.
- Assuming the condom is not damaged: 83% of women and 75% of men admit to having sex without checking whether or not the condom is damaged.
- Lack of lubrication: From 16% to 26% of users use condoms with no lubrication, increasing friction and the risk of breakage. Meanwhile, from 3% to 5% of users use the wrong lubrication with latex condoms, such as an oil-based lubrication that can degrade the rubber, increasing the risk of breakage.
- Incorrect withdrawal: Then there are users—perhaps as many as half!—who do not withdraw the penis promptly and carefully after ejaculating, increasing the possibility of leakage.
- Condom reuse: Condoms are meant to be used once, but a few people admit to reusing the same condom during a given sexual encounter—increasing the probabilities of leakage and breakage.
- Incorrect storage: Finally, from 3% to 19% of users store condoms in ways that will promote degradation, such as exposing them to high temperatures, bending, and so on.

The Condom. Some single women carry condoms in case their partner is not prepared.

HOW THEY ARE USED   The condom is rolled onto the penis once erection is achieved and before contact between the penis and the vagina (see Figure 10.4). If the condom is *not* used until moments before the point of ejaculation, sperm-carrying fluid from the Cowper's glands or from preorgasmic spasms may already have passed into the vagina. Nor does the condom afford protection against STIs if it is fitted after penetration.

Figure 10.4 Applying a Condom.

First the rolled-up condom is placed on the head of the penis, and then it is rolled down the shaft of the penis. If a condom without a reservoir tip is used, a one-half-inch space should be left at the tip for the ejaculate to accumulate.

Some condoms break or fall off during intercourse or when withdrawing the penis afterward. Condoms may also slip down the shaft of the penis without falling off. To use a condom most effectively and to help prevent it from either breaking or falling off, a couple should observe the following guidelines (which are adapted from the Centers for Disease Control pamphlet, *Condoms and Sexually Transmitted Diseases … Especially AIDS* [Food and Drug Administration, 2015] as well as other sources):

- Use a condom each and every time you have intercourse.
- Handle the condom carefully, making sure not to damage it with your fingernail, teeth, or sharp objects.
- Place the condom on the erect penis before it touches the vulva.
- Uncircumcised men should pull back the foreskin before putting on the condom.
- If you use a spermicide, place some inside the tip of the condom before placing the condom on the penis. (The couple may apply additional spermicide inside the vagina to provide extra protection.)
- Do not pull the condom tightly against the tip of the penis.
- For a condom without a reservoir tip, leave a small empty space—about a half-inch—at the tip for semen, but do not allow air to get trapped at the tip.
- Unroll the condom all the way to the bottom of the penis.
- Ensure that adequate vaginal lubrication during intercourse is present, using lubricants if necessary. But use only water-based lubricants such as contraceptive jelly or K-Y jelly. Never use oil-based lubricants, which can weaken the latex material, such as petroleum jelly (Vaseline), cold cream, baby oil or lotion, mineral oil, massage oil, vegetable oil, Crisco, hand or body lotions, and most skin creams.
- If the condom breaks during intercourse, withdraw the penis immediately and use a spermicide.
- After ejaculation, carefully withdraw the penis while it remains erect.
- Hold the rim of the condom against the base of the penis as the condom is withdrawn to prevent slippage.
- Check the removed condom for tears or cracks. If any are found, use a spermicide.

Because condoms can be eroded by exposure to body heat or other sources of heat, they should not be kept for any length of time in a pocket or the glove compartment of a car. The "Closer Look" feature describes condom use errors that will compromise their effectiveness.

EFFECTIVENESS   In typical use, the failure rate of the male condom is estimated at 18% (see Figure 10.1). In other words, 18 women out of 100 whose partners rely on condoms alone can expect to become pregnant during a year of use. The rate drops if the condom is used with a spermicide. The effectiveness of a condom and spermicide combined rivals that of the pill when used correctly.

REVERSIBILITY   The condom is simply a mechanical barrier to sperm and does not compromise fertility. Therefore, a couple who wish to conceive a child simply discontinue its use.

ADVANTAGES AND DISADVANTAGES   Condoms have the advantage of being readily available. They can be purchased without prescription. They require no fitting and can remain in sealed packages until needed. They are readily discarded after use. The combination of condoms and spermicides increases effectiveness. Some condoms contain a spermicide as a lubricant. When in doubt, ask a pharmacist.

Condoms do not affect production of hormones, ova, or sperm. Women whose partners use condoms ovulate normally. Men who use them produce sperm and ejaculate normally. With all these advantages, why are condoms not more popular?

A CLOSER LOOK

DON'T LIKE YOUR CONDOM? TRY THE "CONDOM BUFFET"

Why does the burden of birth control so often fall on the woman? One reason is that men frequently do not want to use condoms. Why are men reluctant? For numerous reasons, such as interference with sexual spontaneity, lessening of sexual sensations, and condom-related problems in achieving and maintaining of an erection (Graham et al., 2014; Hill et al., 2014). But some women are also put off by condoms because condoms sometimes cause them pain (Mullinax et al., 2016). A study with young heterosexual men by Stephanie Sanders and her colleagues (Sanders et al., 2014) of the Kinsey Institute found that erection problems with condoms could become chronic and that in many cases they were the result of poorly fitting condoms.

What, then, to do? Sanders (2015) suggests presenting men with a condom "buffet." That is, men alone—without the added pressure of having a partner present—can try out various condoms for fit and comfort, along with lubricants (Dodge et al., 2014; Reese et al., 2014). Sanders (2015) says "If you want to be good at sports or music, you have to practice and use the right equipment, and the same is true of condom use. You don't have to use the standard condom your grandfather used." And people wear different-sized sneakers, she adds.

Condoms of course are the contraceptive that also prevents STIs. Therefore, the condom is also recommended for men who have sex with men. The condom buffet appears to be

of help with this population as well. Sanders and her colleagues (Emetu et al., 2014) ran a pilot study with college men who have sex with men, and spending time trying one a variety of condoms reduced their incidence of unprotected sex.

One reason is that it may render sex less spontaneous. The couple must interrupt lovemaking to apply the condom. Condoms also lessen sexual sensations, especially for the man. Latex condoms do so more than animal membrane sheaths. Condoms also sometimes slip or tear, allowing sperm to leak through.

On the other hand, condoms are almost entirely free of side effects. They offer protection against STIs that is unparalleled among contraceptive devices. They can be used without prior medical consultation. Both partners can share putting on the condom, which makes it an erotic part of their lovemaking. The use of textured or ultra-thin condoms may increase sensitivity, especially for the male. Sex in the age of HIV/AIDS has given condoms a new respectability, even a certain trendiness. Advertisers now also target women in their ads, suggesting that women, like men, can come prepared with condoms.

It is tempting to claim that the condom never has side effects. Let us settle for "close to never." Some people have allergic reactions to the spermicides with which some lubricated condoms are coated or that the woman may apply. Some people are allergic to latex.

Women have a right to insist that their male sex partners wear latex condoms if their partners are not latex-sensitive. STIs such as gonorrhea and chlamydia (see Chapter 13) do more damage to a woman's reproductive tract than to a man's. Condoms can help protect women from vaginitis, PID, infections that can harm a fetus or cause infertility, and HIV.

Fertility Awareness Methods of Contraception

LO 10.4 Explain how fertility awareness methods of contraception work, and discuss their advantages and disadvantages.

There are several fertility awareness methods, which are also referred to as *rhythm methods*. They all rely on awareness of the occurrence of the fertile segments of the woman's menstrual cycle. You will also hear them referred to as *natural birth control* or *natural family planning*. Each of them aims to avoid coitus on days when conception is likely. Fertility awareness methods are used by a small minority of women, more so by women in committed relationships. Because the rhythm method does not employ artificial devices, it is acceptable to the Roman Catholic Church.

A number of rhythm methods are used to predict the likelihood of conception. They are the mirror images of the methods that couples use to increase their chances of conceiving (see Chapter 9). Methods for enhancing the chances of conception seek to predict time of ovulation so the couple can arrange to have sperm present in the woman's reproductive tract at about that time. As methods of *birth control,* rhythm methods predict ovulation so that the couple can *abstain* from intercourse when the woman is fertile. About 18% of U.S. women aged 15–44 have used the calendar method of birth control; about 4% have used the basal body temperature method or tracked their cervical mucus (Daniels et al., 2013).

The Calendar Method

calendar method

A fertility awareness (rhythm) method of contraception that relies on prediction of ovulation by tracking menstrual cycles, typically for a 10- to 12-month period, and assuming that ovulation occurs 14 days before menstruation.

The **calendar method** assumes that ovulation occurs 14 days before menstruation. The couple abstains from intercourse during the period that begins 4 days prior to day 13 (because sperm are unlikely to survive for more than 72 hours in the female reproductive tract) and ends 3 days after day 15 (because an unfertilized ovum is unlikely to remain receptive to fertilization for longer than 48 hours). The period of abstention thus covers days 10 to 17 of the woman's cycle.

When a woman has regular 28-day cycles, predicting the period of abstention is relatively straightforward. Women with irregular cycles are generally advised to chart their cycles for 10 to 12 months to determine their shortest and longest cycles. The first day of menstruation counts as day 1 of the cycle. The last day of the cycle is the day preceding the onset of menstruation.

Consider a woman whose cycles vary from 23 to 33 days. In theory she will ovulate 14 days before menstruation begins. (To be safe she should assume that ovulation will take place anywhere from 13 to 15 days before her period.) Applying the rule of "3 days before" and "2 days after," she should avoid coitus from day 5 of her cycle, which corresponds to 3 days before her earliest expected ovulation (computed by subtracting 15 days from the 23 days of her shortest cycle and then subtracting 3 days), through day 22, which corresponds to 2 days after her latest expected ovulation (computed by subtracting 13 days from the 33 days of her longest cycle and then adding 2 days). Another way of determining this period of abstention would be to subtract 18 days from the woman's shortest cycle to determine the start of the "unsafe" period and 11 days from her longest cycle to determine the last "unsafe" day. The woman in the example has irregular cycles. She thus faces an 18-day abstention period each month—quite a burden for a sexually active couple.

Most women who follow the calendar method need to abstain from coitus for at least 10 days during the middle of each cycle. Moreover, the calendar method cannot ensure that the woman's longest or shortest menstrual cycles will occur during the

10- to 12-month period of baseline tracking. Some women, too, have such irregular cycles that the range of "unsafe" days cannot be predicted reliably even if baseline tracking is extended.

The Basal Body Temperature (BBT) Method

In the **basal body temperature (BBT) method**, the woman tracks her body temperature upon awakening each morning to detect the small changes that occur directly before and after ovulation. A woman's basal body temperature sometimes dips slightly just before ovulation and then tends to rise between 0.4° and 0.8° Fahrenheit just before, during, and after ovulation. It remains elevated until the onset of menstruation. (The rise in temperature is caused by the increased production of progesterone by the corpus luteum during the luteal phase of the cycle.) Thermometers that provide finely graded readings, such as electronic thermometers, are best suited for determining minor changes. A major problem with the BBT method is that it does not indicate the several *unsafe* preovulatory days during which sperm deposited in the vagina may remain viable. Rather, the BBT method indicates when a woman *has* ovulated. Thus, many women use the calendar method to predict the number of "safe" days before ovulation and use the BBT method to determine the number of "unsafe" days after. A woman would avoid coitus during the "unsafe" preovulatory period (as determined by the calendar method) and then for 3 days when her temperature rises and remains elevated. A drawback of the BBT method is that changes in body temperature may also result from factors unrelated to ovulation, such as infections, sleeplessness, or stress. So, some women triple-check themselves by also tracking their cervical mucus.

The Cervical Mucus (Ovulation) Method

The **ovulation method** tracks changes in the **viscosity** of the cervical mucus. Following menstruation, the vagina feels rather dry. There is also little or no discharge from the cervix. These dry days are relatively safe. Then a mucous discharge appears in the vagina that is first thick and sticky, and white or cloudy in color. Coitus (or unprotected coitus) should be avoided at the first sign of any mucous. As the cycle progresses, the mucus discharge thins and clears, becoming slippery or stringy, like raw egg white. These are the **peak days**. This mucus discharge, called the *ovulatory mucus*, may be accompanied by a feeling of vaginal lubrication or wetness. Ovulation takes place about a day after the last peak day (about 4 days after this ovulatory mucus first appears). Then the mucus becomes cloudy and tacky once more. Intercourse may resume 4 days following the last peak day. However, many women have difficulty detecting changes in the mucus discharge. Such changes may also result from infections, certain medications, or contraceptive creams, jellies, or foam. Sexual arousal may also induce changes in viscosity.

OVULATION-PREDICTION KITS   Predicting ovulation is more accurate with an ovulation-prediction kit. Kits allow women to test their urine regularly for the presence of LH. LH levels surge about 12 to 24 hours before ovulation. Kits can be used to help couples conceive or avoid pregnancy. Ovulation kits can be costly, however.

EFFECTIVENESS   The estimated first-year failure rate of rhythm methods is 24%, which reminds us of the joke: "What do you call people who use the rhythm method? Parents!" *But*—and this is a big "but"—fewer failures occur when these methods are applied conscientiously, when a combination of rhythm methods is used, and when the woman's cycles are regular.

ADVANTAGES AND DISADVANTAGES   Because they are a natural form of birth control, rhythm methods appeal to many people who, for religious or other reasons,

Recording Basal-Body Temperature. Now there's an app for that.

basal body temperature (BBT) method

A fertility awareness method of contraception that relies on prediction of ovulation by tracking the woman's temperature over the menstrual cycle.

ovulation method

A fertility awareness method of contraception that relies on prediction of ovulation by tracking the viscosity of cervical mucus.

viscosity

Stickiness, consistency.

peak days

The days during the menstrual cycle during which a woman is most likely to be fertile.

SEX IN THE DIGITAL AGE

USING APPS TO PREDICT SAFE PERIODS FOR SEX

There are many ways to predict ovulation. Women who wish to become pregnant, as noted in Chapter 9, will time sex for a couple of days before ovulation and during ovulation. Women who wish to avoid pregnancy will limit sex to days more distant from ovulation. A number of apps can help women limit sexual activity to "safe" periods by counting days, tracking body temperature and the like. The apps are "friendlier" and probably more accurate than jotting things down on a paper calendar or in a notebook. They include:

- Clue (relies on the calendar method)
- Kindara (tracks basal body temperature)
- Ovia (tracks cervical mucus)

- Glow (uses the symptothermal method—combines the calendar method, the temperature method, and the cervical mucus method)

The following figure is from the Kindara.com Web site. It's what you'll be looking at on your mobile phone it you use the app. Go to https://www.kindara.com/avoid-pregnancy

It's a good idea to use a back-up birth control method, such as condoms, while you're testing out a birth-control app. You can also check out how well you are using your app by buying an ovulation test kit or a fertility monitor and using it for a while along with the app.

prefer not to use artificial means. Because no devices or chemicals are used, there are no side effects. Nor do they cause loss of sensation, as condoms do. Nor is there disruption of sex, as with condoms, diaphragms, or foam—although sex could be said to be quite "disrupted" during the period of abstention. Rhythm methods are inexpensive, except for ovulation-prediction kits. Both partners may share the responsibility for rhythm methods. The man, for example, can take his partner's temperature or assist with charting. All rhythm methods are fully reversible.

Rhythm methods may be unsuitable for women with irregular cycles. Moreover, the rhythm method requires abstaining for many days, perhaps weeks, each month. Rhythm methods also require that records of the menstrual cycle be kept for many months before implementation. Rhythm methods cannot be used spontaneously. Nor do rhythm methods afford protection against STIs.

Sterilization

LO 10.5 **Describe methods of sterilization, and discuss the prospects of reversibility.**

Sterilization permanently makes the individual incapable of fertilizing a partner or of conceiving. Many people decide to be sterilized when they plan to have no children or no more children. With the exception of abstinence, sterilization is the most effective form of contraception. Yet the prospect of sterilization arouses strong feelings because a person is transformed all at once, and presumably permanently, from someone who might be capable of bearing children to someone who cannot. This transformation involves a change in self-concept, which may disturb people who link fertility to their self-identity. Still, sterilization is the most widely used form of birth control among couples in committed relationships aged 30 and older.

sterilization

Surgical procedures that render people incapable of reproduction without affecting sexual activity.

Male Sterilization

The male sterilization procedure used today is the **vasectomy**. About one man in seven or eight in the United States has had a vasectomy (Franzese & Panaggio, 2016).

A vasectomy is usually carried out in a doctor's office, under local anesthesia, in 15 to 20 minutes. Small incisions are made in the scrotum. Each vas deferens is cut, a small segment is removed, and then the ends are tied off or cauterized to prevent them from growing back together (see Figure 10.5). Sperm no longer reach the urethra and are reabsorbed harmlessly by the body.

vasectomy

The surgical method of male sterilization in which sperm are prevented from reaching the urethra by cutting each vas deferens and tying it back or cauterizing it.

Figure 10.5 Vasectomy.

The male sterilization procedure is usually carried out in a doctor's office, using local anesthesia. Small incisions are made in the scrotum. Each vas deferens is cut, and the ends are tied off or cauterized to prevent sperm from reaching the urethra. Sperm are harmlessly reabsorbed by the body after the operation.

1. Location of vas deferens

2. Injection of local anesthetic

3. Incision over vas deferens

4. Isolation of vas deferens from surrounding tissue

5. Removal of segment of vas deferens; tying of ends

6. Return of vas deferens to position; incision is closed and process is repeated on the other side

The man can usually resume sexual relations within a few days. However, healthcare providers recommend follow-ups to check for the presence of sperm in the ejaculate because sperm can be found for many weeks and sometimes months even when operations have been successful. And rarely—in about 1 case in 500—the vas "recanalizes," meaning that the severed ends rejoin spontaneously (Jayaraman & Mann, 2012).

Vasectomy does not diminish sex drive or result in any change in sexual arousal, erectile or ejaculatory ability, or sensations of ejaculation. Male sex hormones and sperm are still produced by the testes. Without a passageway to the urethra, however, sperm are no longer expelled with the ejaculate. Because sperm account for only about 1% of the ejaculate, the volume of the ejaculate is not noticeably different.

Over the years there has been some concern as to whether or not vasectomy raises the risk of prostate cancer. A New Zealand study comparing the incidence of vasectomy among 923 men who had had prostate cancer and a matched group of 1,224 who had not (Cox et al., 2006) found no connection between the two. Individuals considering vasectomy should discuss the most recent available findings with their physicians.

Reversibility is simple in concept but not in practice. Thus, vasectomies should be considered permanent. In an operation to reverse a vasectomy, called a **vasovasotomy**, the ends of the vas deferens are sewn together, and in a few days they grow together. Estimates of success at reversal, as measured by subsequent pregnancies, are quite variable and have been reported to range from 16 to 79% (Brechin & Bigrigg, 2006; Zieman et al., 2015–2016). Even so, the man still produces viable sperm and they can be harvested, if with some difficulty, and used to fertilize ova via methods such as intracytoplasmic sperm injection (Karpman et al., 2006).

Few serious complications from vasectomies have been reported, but minor complications are not uncommon. They typically involve temporary local inflammation or swelling after the operation. Ice packs and anti-inflammatory drugs, such as aspirin, may help reduce swelling and discomfort.

Female Sterilization

About 20% of American women between the ages of 15 and 44 have been surgically sterilized (Daniels et al., 2013). The percentages are higher among older women in committed relationships. **Tubal sterilization**, also called *tubal ligation*, is the most common method of female sterilization. Tubal sterilization prevents ova and sperm from passing through the fallopian tubes.

The surgical procedures for tubal sterilization occlude fallopian tubes. The two main methods of doing so are *mini-laparotomy* and *laparoscopy*. In a **mini-laparotomy**, a small incision is made in the abdomen, just above the pubic hairline, to provide access to the fallopian tubes. Each tube is cut and tied back or clamped. In sterilization, or tubal ligation, by **laparoscopy** (see Figure 10.6), sometimes called "belly button surgery," the fallopian tubes are approached through a small incision in the abdomen just below the navel. The surgeon uses a narrow, lighted instrument called a *laparoscope* to view the tubes. A small section of each of the tubes is cauterized, cut, or clamped. The woman usually returns to her daily routine in a few days and can resume sex when it becomes comfortable. In an alternative sterilization procedure, a **culpotomy**, the fallopian tubes are approached through an incision in the back wall of the vagina.

None of these methods disrupts the sex drive or sexual response. Surgical sterilization does not induce premature menopause or alter the woman's production of sex hormones. The menstrual cycle is undisturbed. The unfertilized egg is reabsorbed by the body rather than sloughed off in the menstrual flow.

A **hysterectomy** also sterilizes a woman, but a hysterectomy is a major operation that is commonly performed because of cancer or other diseases of the reproductive tract; it is inappropriate as a method of sterilization.

---

vasovasotomy

The surgical reversal of vasectomy in which the cut or cauterized ends of the vas deferens are sewn together.

tubal sterilization

The method of female sterilization in which the fallopian tubes are surgically blocked; also called *tubal ligation*.

mini-laparotomy

A kind of tubal sterilization in which an incision is made in the abdomen to access the fallopian tubes.

laparoscopy

Tubal sterilization by means of a *laparoscope*, which is inserted through a small incision just below the navel and used to cauterize, cut, or clamp the fallopian tubes.

culpotomy

A kind of tubal sterilization in which the fallopian tubes are approached through an incision in the back wall of the vagina.

hysterectomy

Surgical removal of the uterus.

Figure 10.6   Tubal Ligation by Laparoscopy.

During this method of female sterilization, the surgeon approaches the fallopian tubes through a small incision in the abdomen just below the navel. A narrow instrument called a *laparoscope* is inserted through the incision, and a small section of each fallopian tube is cauterized, cut, or clamped to prevent ova from joining with sperm.

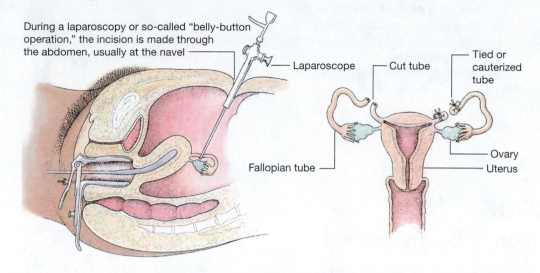

During a laparoscopy or so-called "belly-button operation," the incision is made through the abdomen, usually at the navel

Laparoscope

Cut tube

Tied or cauterized tube

Fallopian tube

Ovary

Uterus

Overall, about 1 woman in 200 (0.4%) is likely to become pregnant in the first year following a tubal sterilization (Zieman et al., 2015–2016), most likely the result of a failed surgical procedure or an undetected pregnancy at the time of the procedure. Like vasectomy, tubal ligation should be considered irreversible. Reversals are successful, as measured by subsequent pregnancies, in 43% to 88% of cases (Zieman et al., 2015–2016). Reversal is difficult and costly, however. But if you think you might ever change your mind about pregnancy later on, you may mention that to the surgeon before sterilization and ask for an opinion.

3 › T / F   Truth or Fiction Revisited   Not all sterilization operations can be surgically reversed. Therefore, sterilization is not advised for individuals who believe they might change their minds. Nevertheless, the woman continues to ovulate, and even if the tubes cannot be rejoined, it may be possible to harvest her ova, fertilize them in vitro, and insert them into the uterus for implantation.

Some women have medical complications, such as abdominal infections, excessive bleeding, punctures of nearby organs, and scarring. The use of general anesthesia (typical in laparoscopies and in some mini-laparotomies) poses additional risks, as in any major operation. (Most of the deaths that are attributed to tubal sterilization actually result from the anesthesia. But there are only 2 to 5 deaths per 100,000 operations.)

Advantages and Disadvantages of Sterilization

The major advantages of sterilization are effectiveness and permanence. Sterilization is nearly 100% effective. The permanence is also its major drawback, however. People sometimes change their minds about wanting to have children.

Sterilization procedures create varying risks of complications following surgery, with women generally incurring greater risks than men. Sterilization affords no protection against STIs.

A CLOSER LOOK

SELECTING A METHOD OF CONTRACEPTION

If you believe that you and your partner should use contraception, how will you determine which method is right for you? There is no simple answer. What is right for your peers may be wrong for you. You and your partner will make your own selections, but there are some issues you may want to consider:

1. *Convenience.* Is the method convenient? Does it require a device that must be purchased in advance? If so, is a prescription required? Will the method work at a moment's notice, or, as with the birth-control pill, will it require time to reach maximum effectiveness?

2. *Moral acceptability.* A method that is morally acceptable to one person may be objectionable to another. For example, those who strictly follow the teachings of the Roman Catholic Church may find any artificial means of contraception to be objectionable.

Selecting a Method of Contraception. Should you and your partner use contraception? If so, how can you determine which method is right for you? Issues you may want to consider include convenience, effectiveness, moral acceptability, safety, reversibility, and cost. Other issues include whether the method allows you and your partner to share the responsibility and whether it also affords protection from sexually transmitted infections.

3. *Cost.* Methods vary in cost. Some more costly methods involve devices (such as the diaphragm, the cervical cap, and the IUC device or hormones that require medical visits in addition to the cost of the devices themselves.

4. *Sharing responsibility.* Most forms of birth control place the burden of responsibility largely, if not entirely, on the woman. The woman must consult with her doctor to obtain birth-control pills or other prescription devices such as diaphragms, cervical caps, and IUC devices. The woman must take birth-control pills reliably or check to see that her IUC device remains in place.

   Some couples prefer methods that allow for greater sharing of responsibility, such as alternating use of the condom and diaphragm. A man can also share the responsibility for the birth-control pill by accompanying his partner on her medical visits and sharing the expense.

5. *Safety.* How safe is the method? What are the side effects?

6. *Reversibility.* In most cases the effects of birth-control methods can be fully reversed by discontinuing their use. In other cases, reversibility may not occur immediately, as with oral contraceptives. It's most cautious to consider sterilization irreversible.

7. *Protection against sexually transmitted infections (STIs).*

4 ❯ T / F Truth or Fiction Revisited   The truth is that only some contraceptives, such as the condom, have any efficacy as preventing STIs as well as conception. Other barrier methods may offer *some* protection, but don't assume that they will!

8. *Effectiveness.* Techniques and devices vary widely in their effectiveness in actual use. The failure rate for a particular method refers to the percentage of women who become pregnant when using the method for a given period of time, such as during the first year of use. Most contraceptive

"Non-Methods" of Contraception

LO 10.6 Identify "non-methods" of contraception, and explain why they are not dependable.

Non-methods may sound like an ironic lead-in to this topic, but we use the term because many people think that the following methods work. If they do, they work occasionally, and frankly, sometimes because of luck. "Luck" isn't all that dependable if you're trying to prevent a pregnancy.

Douching

Many couples believe that if a woman **douches** shortly after coitus, she will not become pregnant. Women who douche for contraceptive purposes often use syringes to flush the vagina with water or a spermicidal agent.

douche

To rinse or wash the vaginal canal by inserting a liquid and allowing it to drain out.

methods are not used correctly much or even all of the time. Failure rates among typical users are often considerably higher because of incorrect, unreliable, or inconsistent use. Table 10.1 shows the failure rates, reversibility, and degree of protection against STIs associated with various contraceptive methods.

Table 10.1 Failure Rates, Reversibility, and Protection Provided against Sexually Transmitted Infections by Various Methods of Birth Control (in Percent of Women Who Become Pregnant within the First Year of Use)

| Method | Percent (%) of Women Who Have an Unplanned Pregnancy within the First Year of Use | | Is It Reversible? | Does It Protect Against Sexually Transmitted Infections (STIs)? |
	Typical Use[1]	Consistent, Correct Use		
None	85	85	yes	no
Spermicides	29	18	yes	no
Rhythm Methods	20		yes	no
Calendar		9		
Ovulation Method		3		
Basal Body Temperature		2		
Post-Ovulation		3		
Withdrawal	27	4	yes	no
Cervical Cap[2]	20–40	10–30	yes	some
Diaphragm[2]	16	6	yes	some
Condom alone				
Female condom	21	5	yes	(scarce information)
Male condom	15	2	yes	yes
The Pill	8	0.3	yes	no, but may *reduce* the risk of pelvic inflammatory disease
Progestin Only		0.5		
Combined		0.1		
IUD	0.2–0.8	0.2–0.6	yes, except if fertility is impaired	no
Depo-Provera	3	0.3	yes	no
Injectable Contraceptives	0.5	0.5	yes	no
Female Sterilization	0.5	0.5	questionable	no
Male Sterilization	0.15	0.10	questionable	no

[1] Accidental pregnancies among typical couples.
[2] With spermicide.
SOURCES: American Academy of Family Physicians (2012), Cleland et al., 2012; Hatcher et al. (2011).

5 › T / F Truth or Fiction Revisited Douching is ineffective, however, because large numbers of sperm move beyond the range of the douche seconds after ejaculation. In addition, squirting a liquid into the vagina may even propel sperm *toward* the uterus. Regular douching may also alter the natural chemistry of the vagina, increasing the risk of vaginal infection. In short, douching is a non-method of contraception.

The Withdrawal Method

Withdrawal means that the man removes his penis from the vagina before ejaculating. Withdrawal—also referred to as *coitus interruptus*—has a first-year failure rate among typical users of about 22% (Figure 10.1). There are several reasons for these failures. The man may not withdraw in time. Even if the penis is withdrawn just before ejaculation, some ejaculate may still fall on the vaginal lips, and sperm may find their way to the fallopian tubes. Sperm may also be present in the *pre*ejaculatory secretions of fluid from the Cowper's glands. Because of its unreliability and high failure rate, withdrawal is *not* a viable method of contraception. Even so, about three U.S. women in five, aged 15–44, have used the withdrawal method at least once (Daniels et al., 2013).

induced abortion

The purposeful termination of a pregnancy before the embryo or fetus is capable of sustaining independent life.

Figure 10.7 When Women Have Abortions (in Weeks).

Eighty-eight percent of abortions occur during the first 12 weeks of pregnancy.

SOURCE: www.guttmacher.org

When women have abortions*
One-third of abortions occur at six weeks of pregnancy or earlier; 89% occur in the first twelve weeks, 2010

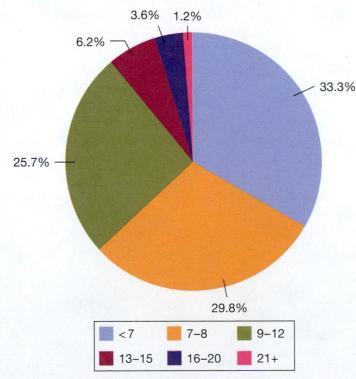

<7	7–8	9–12
13–15	16–20	21+

* In weeks from the last menstrual period.

Abortion

LO 10.7 Discuss the history of abortion in the United States and controversies concerning abortion.

In common usage, the term *abortion* usually refers to an **induced abortion** (in contrast to a spontaneous abortion, or miscarriage)—that is, the purposeful termination of a pregnancy. Perhaps more than any other contemporary social issue, induced abortion (hereafter referred to simply as *abortion*) has divided neighbors and family members into opposing camps.

In the United States, the abortion rate increased steadily from the early 1970s through 1980, leveled off somewhat in the 1980s, reached a peak in about 1990, when there were about 1.4 million abortions, and has declined to about 1.06 million abortions per year (Jones & Jerman, 2014). The great majority of abortions in the United States occur during the first trimester (see Figure 10.7). This is when they are safest to the woman and least costly.

About 30% of U.S. women will have an abortion by the time they reach 45 (Jones & Jerman, 2014). According to the Guttmacher Institute (2014), of women who have abortions:

• Eighteen percent are teenagers

• Thirty-three percent are aged 20–24, and 24% are aged 25–29

- Thirty-six percent are European American, 30% are African American, and 25% are Latina American
- Forty-five percent are single
- Forty-two percent live below the federal poverty level
- Twenty-eight percent are Roman Catholic; 37% are Protestant
- Seventy-five percent say they cannot afford a child, or that having a child would interfere with their school work, or ability to care for existing family members

Abortion is practiced widely in Canada, Japan, Russia, and many European nations. It is less common in developing nations, in part because of sparse medical facilities. Abortion is rarely used as a primary means of birth control. It usually comes into play when other methods have failed.

There are many reasons why women have abortions, including psychological factors as well as external circumstances. Abortion is often motivated by a desire to reduce the risk of physical, economic, psychological, and social disadvantages that the woman perceives for herself and her present and future children should she carry the pregnancy to term.

The national debate over abortion has been played out in recent years against a backdrop of demonstrations, marches, and occasional acts of violence, such as firebombing of abortion clinics, even murder. Most who label themselves pro-life believe that human life begins at conception and view abortion as the killing of an unborn child. Some pro-life people brook no exception to their opposition to abortion, but most would permit abortion to save the mother's life or when a pregnancy results from rape or incest.

Critical Thinking
Why do you think people refer to themselves as "pro-choice" or "pro-life" as opposed to "pro-abortion" or "anti-abortion"?

Perspectives on Abortion

Attitudes toward abortion have varied across cultures and eras. Abortion was permitted in ancient Greece and Rome, but women in ancient Assyria were impaled on stakes for attempting abortion. The Bible does not specifically prohibit abortion (Sagan & Dryan, 1990). For much of its history, the Roman Catholic Church held to Thomas Aquinas's belief that ensoulment of the fetus did not occur until 40 days after conception for boys and 90 days for girls. In 1869, Pope Pius IX declared that human life begins at conception. Thus, an abortion at any stage of pregnancy became murder in the eyes of the church and grounds for excommunication.

6 ❯ T / F   Truth or Fiction Revisited   It is true that abortions were legal in the United States before the Civil War. In fact, abortion was legal in the United States from 1607 to 1828 (Hitt, 1998; Rosen & Imperato, 2015). Women were permitted to terminate a pregnancy until "quickening" occurred (the point at which the woman was first able to feel the fetus stirring within her).

Restrictive abortion laws emerged because of a national desire to increase the population and because of concerns voiced by physicians about protecting women from botched abortions. By 1900, virtually all states in the union had enacted legislation banning abortion *at any point* during pregnancy, except when necessary to save the woman's life (Rosen & Imperato, 2015).

Abortion laws remained essentially unchanged until the late 1960s, when some states liberalized their abortion laws under mounting public pressure. Then, in 1973, the U.S. Supreme Court, in effect, legalized abortion nationwide in the landmark *Roe v. Wade* decision. *Roe v. Wade* held that a woman's right to an abortion was protected under the right to privacy guaranteed by the Constitution. The decision legalized abortions for any reason during the first trimester. In its ruling, the Court also noted

Pro-Choice or Pro-Life? Where Do You Stand?

What does it mean to be "pro-life" on the abortion issue? What does it mean to be "pro-choice"? Which position is closer to your own views on abortion?

The following self- assessment will afford you insight into whether you are more in agreement with pro-life or pro-choice lines of reasoning about abortion. To find out which position is closer to your own, indicate your level of agreement or disagreement with each of the following items by circling the answer that most closely represents your feelings.

Use the code below to circle the answer that fits your belief. Then refer to the key in the Appendix to interpret your score.

Strongly agree = +2

Agree = +1

Not sure = 0

Disagree = –1

Strongly disagree = –2

1. Abortion is never justified.	–2 –1 0 +1 +2
2. Abortion pills are a benefit to women and society.	–2 –1 0 +1 +2
3. One's religion should determine whether one has an abortion.	–2 –1 0 +1 +2
4. There is no logical answer to the question as to when human life begins.	–2 –1 0 +1 +2
5. No decent person can condone abortion.	–2 –1 0 +1 +2
6. Abortion should be allowed to save the mother's life.	–2 –1 0 +1 +2
7. Health professionals who conduct abortions are committing murder.	–2 –1 0 +1 +2
8. Nobody has the right to tell a woman what she can do with her body.	–2 –1 0 +1 +2
9. Roe v. Wade is a Supreme Court decision that should be overturned.	–2 –1 0 +1 +2
10. Only judges who support the Roe. V. Wade decision should be appointed to the Supreme Court.	–2 –1 0 +1 +2
11. A human embryo is a human life.	–2 –1 0 +1 +2
12. The right to have an abortion fills a societal need.	–2 –1 0 +1 +2
13. Victims of rape and incest have the right to have an abortion.	–2 –1 0 +1 +2
14. A society that allows abortion cannot be considered a humane or just society.	–2 –1 0 +1 +2
15. It is all right for pregnant women who fear that they cannot adequately raise a child to consider an abortion.	–2 –1 0 +1 +2
16. Abortion leaves a permanent stain on the soul of a woman.	–2 –1 0 +1 +2
17. Demonstrators against abortion should be kept away from abortion clinics.	–2 –1 0 +1 +2
18. Only abortion clinics that can provide hospital-type services should be able to operate.	–2 –1 0 +1 +2
19. A woman's body is her own.	–2 –1 0 +1 +2
20. Abortion is murder.	–2 –1 0 +1 +2

© Spencer A. Rathus

that a fetus is not considered a person and is thus not entitled to constitutional protection. The Court ruled that states may regulate a woman's right to have an abortion during the second trimester to protect her health, as in requiring her to obtain an abortion in a hospital rather than a doctor's office. The Supreme Court also held that when a fetus becomes viable, its rights override the mother's right to privacy. Because the fetus may become viable early in the third trimester, states may prohibit third-trimester abortions, except when an abortion is medically necessary to protect a woman's health.

Since *Roe v. Wade*, most states have also enacted laws requiring parental consent or notification before a minor may have an abortion. According to a CBS News Poll taken in 2005, 80% of adults in the United States say that at least one parent should be notified before minor girls can have abortions. Yet, with or without such rules, most girls seeking abortion do consult their parents. On the other hand, a survey reported in the *Journal of the American Medical Association* found that 48% of a sample of 950 girls visiting Planned Parenthood said that they would stop using all of the organization's services if their parents were notified of the visits (Reddy et al., 2002).

Let's look at why the controversy over abortion has existed. Many opponents of abortion argue that abortion is the taking of a human life—tantamount to murder. Therefore, it is useful to discuss the issue as to when human life begins.

When Does Human Life Begin?

The issue as to when human life begins is at the heart of the abortion controversy. It is a question that you will have to answer for yourself. We can only note that moral concerns about abortion often turn on the question of when human life begins. For some Christians, the matter revolves around when they believe the fetus obtains a soul. Scientists, too, have attempted to define when human life can be said to begin. Astronomer Carl Sagan, for example, wrote that fetal brain activity can be considered a scientific marker of human life (Sagan & Druyan, 1990). Brain activity is needed for thought, the quality that is considered most "human" by many. Brain-wave patterns typical of children do not begin until about the thirtieth week of pregnancy. But opponents argue that a newly fertilized ovum carries the *potential* for human thought in the same way that the embryonic or fetal brain does. It could even be argued that sperm cells and ova are living things in that they carry out the biological processes characteristic of cellular life. All in all, the question of when *human* life begins is apparently not going to be resolved by science.

Attitudes Toward Legalized Abortion: A Nation Divided

National public opinion polls taken since *Roe v. Wade*, including the Gallup Poll taken in 2015, have consistently shown that a majority of people in the United States support a woman's right to have an abortion *under at least some circumstances* (see Figures 10.8 and 10.9). Reduced support for legal abortion is associated with religious commitment, conservative attitudes on premarital sex, and belief in having large families. Democrats are significantly more likely than Republicans to label themselves as pro-choice and favor abortion either under all or some circumstances (Saad, 2012).

Critical Thinking
One of the issues concerning abortion is whether it is the taking of a human life. How do *you* define *human life*? When do *you* believe human life begins? At conception? When the embryo becomes implanted in the uterus? When the fetus begins to assume a human shape or develops human facial features? When the fetus is capable of sustaining independent life? Do your beliefs have anything to do with the concept of ensoulment? Explain.

Figure 10.8   Response to the Question, "With Respect to the Abortion Issue, Would You Consider Yourself to Be Pro-Choice or Pro-Life?", 1996–2015.

Figure 10.9 Responses to the Question, "Do You Think Abortions Should Be Legal Under Any Circumstances, Legal Only Under Certain Circumstances, or Illegal in All Circumstances?".

The majority of American still prefer that abortion be legal under some (or all) circumstances.

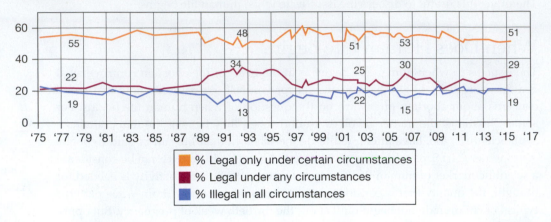

- % Legal only under certain circumstances
- % Legal under any circumstances
- % Illegal in all circumstances

Many people in the pro-choice movement argue that if abortions were to be made illegal again, thousands of women, especially poor women, would die or suffer serious physical consequences from botched or nonsterile abortions. People in the pro-life movement counter that alternatives to abortion, such as adoption, are available. Pro-choice advocates argue that the debate about abortion should be framed not only by notions of the mother's right to privacy but also by the issue of the quality of life of an unwanted child. They argue that minority and physically or mentally disabled children are often hard to place for adoption. These children often spend their childhoods being shuffled from one foster home to another. Pro-life advocates counter that killing a fetus eliminates any potential that it might have, despite hardships, of living a fruitful and meaningful life. Many pro-life individuals also argue that all human life is precious in the eyes of God.

Figure 10.9 shows the breakdown of Americans who have considered themselves to be pro-life and pro-choice according to national surveys done from 1996 to 2015 (Gallup Poll, 2015). You can see that the percentages of people who label themselves pro-life or pro-choice have been close over the years, although in 2015 the number who consider themselves pro-choice is greater than those who label themselves pro-life. In 2012, 72% of Republicans self-identified as pro-life compared to 22% who labeled themselves pro-choice. Among Democrats, the picture was quite different: 58% self-identified as pro-choice and 34% as pro-life. On the other hand, looking at all American adults, including Independents, only a minority of respondents—19% in the 2015 poll—would restrict abortion under all circumstances (see Figure 10.10). But there is yet another caveat: Of those who would permit abortion under certain circumstances, the majority would permit it in only a few circumstances. Such few circumstances might include rape, incest, health or life of the mother, and deformity in the fetus.

Despite polls such as these, *Roe v. Wade* is not in the personal memories of most women who choose to have abortions in the United States today. Many of them have a hard time recognizing that abortion was ever illegal and cannot imagine what it would mean if abortion were to be made illegal again.

So, are we a nation divided? Do people divide themselves into two camps, pro-life and pro-choice? Yes, but most people would allow abortion at certain times during pregnancy or under certain circumstances. It would be pushing the point to suggest that there is a broad consensus in the center, but only a minority of people are at the extremes—either favoring or restricting abortion under all circumstances.

Methods of Abortion

LO 10.8 Discuss methods of abortion.

Regardless of the moral, legal, and political issues that surround abortion, there are many abortion methods. Let us explain what they are, and why a woman might choose one rather than another.

The sooner a woman has an abortion, the less invasive the procedure. Figure 10.10 shows that the great majority of abortions—nearly 90%—are conducted during the first trimester. Note that the figure dates pregnancy from the last menstrual period. Assume that the woman became pregnant about 2 weeks later. Therefore, fully one-third take place within the first 5 weeks of pregnancy.

Vacuum Aspiration

In **vacuum aspiration**, the cervix is usually dilated first by insertion of progressively larger curved metal rods, or "dilators," or by insertion, hours earlier, of a stick of seaweed called *Laminaria digitata*. *Laminaria* expands as it absorbs cervical moisture, providing a gentler means of opening the os. Then a tube connected to an aspirator (suction machine) is inserted into the uterus. The uterine contents are evacuated (emptied) by suction (see Figure 10.11). Possible complications include perforation of the uterus, infection, cervical lacerations, and hemorrhaging, but these are not common.

vacuum aspiration

Removal of the uterine contents by suction; an abortion method used early in pregnancy.

Dilation And Curettage (D&C)

The **D&C** was once the customary method of performing abortions. It now accounts for only a small number of abortions in the United States. It is usually performed 8 to 20 weeks following the last menstrual period (LMP). Once the cervix has been dilated, the uterine contents are scraped from the uterine lining with a blunt scraping tool.

D&C

Abbreviation for *dilation and curettage*, an operation in which the cervix is dilated and uterine contents are then gently scraped away.

1. Vacurette is inserted through cervical canal

2. Suction is turned on; material flows through tubing

Collection hose
Vacuum tube to bottles
Collection bottles

3. Empty uterus collapses

Pump compartment

Figure 10.10   Vacuum Aspiration.

This is the safest and most common method of abortion, but it can be performed only during the first trimester. An angled tube is inserted through the cervix into the uterus, and the uterine contents are then evacuated (emptied) by suction.

D&Cs are carried out in a hospital, usually under general anesthesia. The scraping increases the chances of hemorrhaging, infection, and perforation. Because of these risks, D&Cs have largely been replaced by the vacuum aspiration method. D&Cs are still used to treat various gynecological problems, however, such as abnormally heavy menstrual bleeding.

> **7 › T / F Truth or Fiction Revisited** It is not true that the D&C is the most widely used type of abortion method; vacuum aspiration—also called *suction curettage*—accounts for more than 90% of abortions in the United States. It is relatively painless and inexpensive. It can be done with little or no anesthesia in a medical office or clinic, but only during the first trimester. Later, thinning of the uterine walls increases the risks of perforation and bleeding.

Dilation And Evacuation (D&E)

D&E
Abbreviation for *dilation and evacuation*, an abortion method in which the cervix is dilated before vacuum aspiration.

The **D&E** is used most commonly during the second trimester, when vacuum aspiration alone would be too risky. The D&E combines suction and the D&C. First, the cervix is dilated. The cervix must also be dilated more fully than with vacuum aspiration to allow for passage of the larger fetus. Second, a suction tube is inserted to remove some of the contents of the uterus. But suction alone cannot safely remove all uterine contents. So the remaining contents are removed with forceps. A blunt scraper may also be used to scrape the uterine wall to make sure that the lining has been removed fully. Like the D&C, the D&E is usually performed in the hospital under general anesthesia. Most women recover quickly and relatively painlessly. In rare instances, however, complications such as excessive bleeding, infection, and perforation of the uterine lining arise.

Inducing Labor by Intra-Amniotic Infusion

intra-amniotic infusion
An abortion method in which a substance is injected into the amniotic sac to induce premature labor; also called *instillation*.

Second-trimester abortions are sometimes performed by chemically inducing premature labor and delivery. The procedure, which must be performed in a hospital, is called *instillation*, or **intra-amniotic infusion**. It is usually performed when fetal development has progressed beyond the point at which other methods are deemed safe. A saline (salt) solution or a solution of prostaglandins (hormones that stimulate uterine contractions during labor) is injected into the amniotic sac. Prostaglandins may also be administered by vaginal suppository. Uterine contractions (labor) begin within a few hours after infusion. The fetus and placenta are expelled from the uterus within the next 24 or 48 hours.

Intra-amniotic infusion accounts for only a small number of abortions. Medical complications, risks, and costs are greater with this procedure than with other methods of abortion. Overly rapid labor can tear the cervix, but previous dilation of the cervix with *Laminaria* lessens the risk. Perforation, infection, and hemorrhaging are rare if

Real Students, Real Questions

Q *Will having an abortion make it difficult for me to get pregnant again?*

A There is usually no connection between having an abortion and getting pregnant again, as long as the abortion is carried out *competently* by a licensed physician. If you are contemplating having an abortion, ask the doctor where she or he studied medicine, where he or she is licensed to practice, and inquire about her or his experience. The diploma and license should be displayed on the wall of her or his office.

A CLOSER LOOK

THE POLITICAL BATTLE OVER PARTIAL-BIRTH ABORTION

Most Americans believe that early abortions should be permitted, but there is great concern over the late-term surgical abortion method generally known as *partial-birth abortion* and referred to, medically, as an *intact dilation and extraction,* or *intact D and X.* In this method, the cervix is dilated and a fetus that may be 10 inches long is extracted through the birth canal. Brain tissue is destroyed to rapidly terminate any life functions in the fetus.

Support of abortion rights drops off rapidly as the stages of pregnancy progress. Most people who support early first-trimester abortions oppose partial-birth abortion because of its timing. Others oppose it because of the nature of the disposal of the fetus. However, many pro-choice people argue in favor of partial-birth abortions for at least two reasons. One is that they are relatively rare and usually performed when the health of the mother is at stake. Another is the "slippery-slope" argument, or fear that surrendering a woman's right to have a partial-birth abortion could eventually lead to surrendering other rights to her own body.

The general attitudes of the medical profession toward the partial-birth abortion may be expressed in the fact that the procedure is rarely found in medical books. Many states have passed bills to outlaw partial-birth abortion, and a number of them have been struck down by the courts on the grounds that the bans do not provide for a health exception—that is, an exception in the case where the mother's life is at stake. The battle will likely continue.

In the year 2000, the U.S. Supreme Court struck down a Nebraska statute *(Stenberg v. Carhart)* that banned partial-birth abortion on two grounds. One was that the definition of partial-birth abortion was too vague. The second was that the law did not make an exception for the case in which the procedure was necessary to protect the mother's health. But in 2003 Congress passed the Partial-Birth Abortion Ban Act, calling for the fining or imprisonment of a physician who performs such an abortion. In 2007 the Supreme Court held that the law does not violate the Constitution of the United States. The decision allows no exception for the health of the mother.

As of this writing, 32 states have also enacted bans on partial-birth abortion. All of the states have a health exception; 29 of these only allow the procedure when the life of the mother is at stake (Guttmacher Institute, 2015).

Critical Thinking

What are the political consequences of labeling this abortion method "partial-birth abortion" as opposed to "intact D&X"?

---

prostaglandins are used, but about half the recipients experience nausea and vomiting, diarrhea, or headaches. Saline infusion can cause shock and even death if the solution is carelessly introduced into the bloodstream.

Hysterotomy

The **hysterotomy** is, in effect, a cesarean section. Incisions are made in the abdomen and uterus, and the fetus and uterine contents are removed. Hysterotomy may be performed during the late second trimester, between the sixteenth and twenty-fourth weeks following the last menstrual period. It is performed rarely, usually only when intra-amniotic infusion is not advised. A hysterotomy is major surgery that must be carried out under general anesthesia in a hospital. Hysterotomy involves risks of complications from the anesthesia and the surgery itself.

hysterotomy
Abortion of the fetus by Cesarean section.

Abortion Drugs

Between 200,000 and 250,000 U.S. women use drugs to terminate pregnancies each year (Jones & Jerman, 2014). We provide a large range for this number because the use of abortion drugs is such a private matter.

The drug mifepristone induces early abortion by blocking the effects of progesterone. Progesterone is the hormone that stimulates proliferation of the endometrium, allowing implantation and development of the placenta. The typical course is for the woman to take three mifepristone pills. Twenty-four to 72 hours after taking mifepristone, the woman takes a second oral drug, misoprostol, which causes uterine contractions to expel the embryo.

As the abortion debate continues, so does research into the use of other drugs. A combination of the cancer drug methotrexate and misoprostol can also be used to terminate early pregnancy. Methotrexate is toxic to the trophoblastic tissue of the embryo, and—as in combination with mifepristone—misoprostol causes the uterus to expel the embryo.

Real Students, Real Questions

Q *I had an abortion. Should I tell the father—even if we are not seeing each other?*

A Complicated question. What would be your motive? To show him what he lost? To punish him? We are doubtful that he would fully understand the extent of *your* loss. So if your motive is to make him understand, you might be headed down a blind alley. Looking at it from another point of view, we can't think of any reason you would be *obligated* to tell him. After all, it was, and is, your body. Have an honest talk with yourself about your motives, and maybe your answer will develop from that.

Chapter Review

LO 10.1 Discuss historic issues concerning the legalization of contraception in the United States.

Contraception is a technique that prevents a sperm cell and ovum from uniting or prevents a newly formed embryo from implanting in the uterus. Anthony Comstock lobbied for passage of a federal law in 1873 that prohibited the dissemination of birth-control information through the mail on the grounds that it was obscene and indecent. In 1918, the courts ruled that physicians must be allowed to disseminate information that might aid in the cure and prevention of diseases. Dismantling of the Comstock law had begun.

LO 10.2 Explain how hormonal methods of contraception work, and discuss their advantages and disadvantages.

Hormone methods supply estrogen and progestin, or just the latter. Birth-control pills include combination pills (estrogen and progestin) and mini-pills (progestin). Combination pills fool the brain into acting as though the woman is already pregnant, so no additional ova are released. Mini-pills contain progestin, thicken the cervical mucus to impede the passage of sperm through the cervix, and render the inner lining of the uterus less receptive to a fertilized egg. Other methods of supplying these hormones include skin patches and injections. "Morning-after" pills have high hormone content that prevents fertilization or implantation of a fertilized ovum. Most intrauterine contraceptive (IUC) devices thicken cervical mucus and apparently irritate the uterine lining, causing inflammation and the production of antibodies that may prevent ova from becoming implanted. (The copper device is toxic to sperm.) As with "the pill," the woman need do nothing after the IUC device is inserted.

LO 10.3 Explain how barrier methods of contraception work, and discuss their advantages and disadvantages.

Barrier methods such as the diaphragm prevent sperm from reaching ova. However, as we'll see, many of them are best used with chemicals that kill sperm (spermicides).

The diaphragm covers the cervix and should be used with a spermicide. The contraceptive sponge absorbs sperm and also contains a spermicide. The cervical cap covers the cervix. Latex condoms afford protection against sexually transmitted infections as well as conception. The major disadvantage concerns failure rates.

LO 10.4 Explain how fertility awareness methods of contraception work, and discuss their advantages and disadvantages.

Rhythm methods of contraception rely on awareness of the occurrence of fertile segments of the menstrual cycle. The calendar method informs women with regular cycles when they are likely to ovulate. Women may also track their basal body temperature and the thickness of their cervical mucus. Ovulation detection kits and online applications (apps) provide more accurate data. In effect, the apps do the calculating for the woman.

LO 10.5 Describe methods of sterilization, and discuss the prospects of reversibility.

Sterilization is considered permanent, although it may be reversed in many cases. The male vasectomy consists of cutting the vas deferens. Female sterilization methods prevent ova and sperm from passing through the fallopian tubes.

LO 10.6 Identify "non-methods" of contraception, and explain why they are not dependable.

Douching is ineffective because sperm may pass beyond the range of the douche within seconds after ejaculation. Withdrawal has a high failure rate.

LO 10.7 Discuss the history of abortion in the United States and controversies concerning abortion.

Induced abortion is the intentional termination of a pregnancy. In the 1973 *Roe v. Wade* decision, the U.S. Supreme Court, in effect, legalized abortion nationwide. Opinions regarding the law vary across cultures and eras. Some pro-life activists have been challenging the extent of the *Roe v. Wade* decision; some would like it completely overturned. Others are strong supporters of the law. The abortion controversy is largely about when human life begins. Some argue that it begins at conception; others say it begins when the fetus becomes viable; and still others are somewhere in between, as, for example, when they maintain that life begins when neural activity begins in the fetal brain.

LO 10.8 Discuss methods of abortion.

Abortion methods in use today include vacuum aspiration, D&C, D&E, induction of labor by intra-amniotic infusion, hysterotomy, and drugs such as mifepristone. Partial-birth abortion (intact D&X) is the most controversial method because it occurs closest to the age of viability, and sometimes when the fetus might be viable with contemporary medical procedures.

Test Your Learning

1. Which of the following is termed a *non-method* of birth control in the text?

    (a) Sterilization
    (b) The condom
    (c) Withdrawal
    (d) Fertility awareness techniques

2. Which of the following is the most effective method of birth control?

    (a) The female condom
    (b) Oral contraceptives
    (c) The contraceptive sponge
    (d) Douching

3. Which of the following methods of birth control has the most side effects?

    (a) The IUC device
    (b) The male condom
    (c) The diaphragm
    (d) Tracking basal body temperature

4. Which is true of attitudes toward abortion in the United States?

    (a) Most people would allow abortion under some circumstances.
    (b) Most people would allow abortion for women who cannot afford to raise children.
    (c) All Roman Catholics oppose abortion.
    (d) Few parents want to be notified if an underage daughter is seeking an abortion.

5. The most common method of abortion practiced in the United States today is _____

    (a) the D&C.
    (b) the D&E.
    (c) vacuum aspiration.
    (d) ectopic pregnancy.

6. Of the following, _____ is(are) the most widely used contraceptive.

    (a) Injectable contraceptives
    (b) The contraceptive sponge
    (c) The diaphragm
    (d) The pill

7. The most controversial abortion method is the _____

    (a) mini-pill.
    (b) D&C.
    (c) hysterotomy.
    (d) intact D&X.

8. Rhythm methods rely on _____

    (a) fertility awareness.
    (b) hormonal preparations.
    (c) barriers.
    (d) spermicides.

9. Research with African and Thai prostitutes shows that nonoxynol-9 _____ the chances of being infected with HIV.

    (a) decreases
    (b) increases
    (c) has no measurable effect on
    (d) has mixed effects on

10. The Supreme Court struck down a Nebraska statute (*Stenberg v. Carhart*) that banned partial-birth abortion because _____

    (a) partial-birth abortion was politically popular.
    (b) partial-birth abortion was a medical issue and not a legal issue.
    (c) the Court was conservative.
    (d) the law did not make an exception when the procedure was necessary to protect the mother's health.

Answers: 1. c; 2. b; 3. a; 4. a; 5. a; 6. d; 7. d; 8. a; 9. b; 10. d

Chapter 11
Sexuality Through the Lifespan

Learning Objectives

Childhood

LO 11.1 Describe sexually related behaviors in infancy and early childhood.

Preadolescence (9 to 13 years)

LO 11.2 Describe sexual behaviors in preadolescence.

LO 11.3 Discuss the purposes and outcomes of sex education.

Adolescence

LO 11.4 Describe the milestones of puberty.

LO 11.5 Describe sexuality in adolescence, including teenage pregnancy.

Adulthood

LO 11.6 Describe what being single means today.

LO 11.7 Discuss cohabitation, including the relationship between cohabitation and marriage.

LO 11.8 Discuss marriage, including sex in marriage and marital satisfaction.

LO 11.9 Discuss infidelity.

LO 11.10 Discuss the incidence of divorce and issues connected with divorce.

Sex in the later years

LO 11.11 Describe physical changes in the later years and how they affect sexual behavior.

Sex and disability

LO 11.12 Discuss the relationships between disabilities and sexual behavior.

TRUTH OR FICTION?

Which of the following statements are the truth, and which are fiction? Look for the Truth-or-Fiction items on the pages that follow to find the answers.

1 Many boys are born with erections.   **T /F**?

2 Infants often engage in pelvic thrusting at 8 to 10 months of age.   **T /F**?

3 Most children do not talk with their parents about sex.   **T /F**?

4 Sex education encourages sexual activity among children and adolescents.   **T /F**?

5 Nocturnal emissions in boys accompany erotic dreams.   **T /F**?

6 Petting is practically universal among adolescents in the United States.   **T /F**?

7 Being single has become a more common U.S. lifestyle over the past few decades.   **T /F**?

8 Cohabitation has become a normal stage in courtship.   **T /F**?

9 Most of today's sophisticated young people see nothing wrong with an occasional extramarital fling.   **T /F**?

10 Few senior women can reach orgasm.   **T /F**?

11 People who are paralyzed because of spinal cord injuries cannot become sexually aroused or engage in sexual intercourse.   **T /F**?

Children tend to play at sex for many years before they are ready for "real" sex. Our sexuality is—or can be—an integral part of our lives for our lifetimes.

We begin long before we are capable of understanding anything about sex, but reliable information about children's sexuality is hard to come by. Few empirical studies on the sexual behavior of children are available (Kenny & Wurtele, 2012; Thigpen, 2009). Few studies ask children about their sexual behavior. We tend to rely on retrospective reports by adults or on observations by caregivers (Frank, 2015; Kenny & Wurtele, 2012).

Childhood

LO 11.1 **Describe sexually related behaviors in infancy and early childhood.**

Our sexuality includes our relationships, and infants begin to learn about love and trusting others through being touched, held, and cared for. But infants—even fetuses—engage in a variety of sexual behaviors, although the "meaning" of these behaviors, if there is one, is a matter of speculation. Imaging techniques such as ultrasound have shown, for example, that male fetuses have erections. Male and female fetuses suck their fingers. The sucking reflex allows babies to obtain nourishment, but infants also appear to reap pleasure from sucking fingers, pacifiers, nipples, or whatever else fits into the mouth. None of this is surprising, given the sensitivity of the mouth's mucous lining.

Stimulation of the genitals in infancy can also produce pleasure. Parents who touch their infants' genitals while changing or washing them may discover the infants smiling or becoming excited. Infants discover the pleasure of self-stimulation ("masturbation") for themselves when they gain the ability to manipulate their genitals with their hands.

Infants' Sexual Response

Boys have erections in utero. Erection is a reflex that begins to operate early in life. Signs of sexual arousal in infant girls, such as vaginal lubrication, are less readily detected. However, evidence of lubrication and genital swelling has been reported (Mazur, 2006).

But do not interpret children's reflexes according to adult concepts of sexuality. The reflexes of lubrication and erection do not necessarily signify "interest" in sex. We cannot say what, if anything, infants' sexual reflexes "mean" to them.

1 › T /F   Truth or Fiction Revisited   Many boys are in fact born with erections. Most boys continue to have erections during the first few weeks of life.

Pelvic thrusting is observed in infant monkeys, apes, and humans. These observations led ethologist John Bowlby (1969) to suggest that infantile sexual behavior may be the rule in mammals, not the exception—although the "meaning" of pelvic thrusting in human infants clealrly does not involve sexual "intent."

2 › T /F   Truth or Fiction Revisited   Pelvic thrusting has been observed in humans at 8 to 10 months of age and may be an expression of excitement, affection, or both. Typically, the infant clings to the parent, nuzzles, and thrusts and rotates the pelvis for several seconds.

At least some infants seem capable of involuntary muscular contractions that resemble orgasm. Kinsey and his colleagues (1953) noted that baby boys show behaviors that resemble orgasm as early as 5 months, and baby girls as early as 4 months. Orgasms in boys are similar to those in men in terms of involuntary contraction of muscles, but ejaculation occurs only after puberty.

Masturbation is typical for infants and young children and may start as early as 5 months of age (Narchi, 2003; Zhu et al., 2011). Infants may masturbate by rubbing their genitals against a soft object, such as a towel, bedding, or a doll. As they mature and develop sensorimotor coordination, infants may engage in manual stimulation of the genitals.

Masturbation to orgasm is rare until the second year (Reinisch, 1990). Some children begin masturbating to orgasm later. Some never do. All in all, however, orgasm from masturbation is found frequently among children, as among adults (Reinisch, 1990).

Children may develop curiosity about sex as early as 12 to 15 months of age. Later on they play "doctor" and show their curiosity about the sexual anatomy of other people in other ways, such as wanting to watch a parent take a shower or bath (De Graaf & Rademakers, 2011).

Children in the United States typically do not engage in genital play with others until about the age of 2. Then, perhaps as an expression of curiosity, they may investigate other children's genitals or may hug, cuddle, kiss, or climb on top of them. Rough-and-tumble play, including touching the genitals, is common among children.

Co-Sleeping

An issue that concerns many parents is whether it is "safe" for infants to share their beds. Parents have several motives for co-sleeping, for example, infants are more likely to get back to sleep in their parents' beds when they awaken in the night. Co-sleeping also simplifies breastfeeding at odd hours. But the American Academy of Pediatrics does not recommend co-sleeping (Ratnayake, 2011) for fear that parents may accidentally suffocate children. Nevertheless, the majority of U.S. mothers have slept at least occasionally with their infants, and perhaps one in five mothers receives information about co-sleeping from their physicians (Krouse et al., 2012).

Critical Thinking
What are the scientific problems in attempting to explain or interpret the meaning of pelvic thrusting in infants? Is it possible that pelvic thrusting in infants has nothing to do with sexuality per se?

Research does not reveal harmful effects for co-sleeping. For example, an Austrian study found no significant connections between children's sleeping arrangements and their social development (Rothrauff et al., 2004). Another research group followed the development of children in 205 families from infancy to 18 years of age (Okami et al., 2002). They found that the children who shared beds with their parents during infancy showed superior intellectual development at the age of 6, as compared with children who did not co-sleep. No sexual problems were connected with co-sleeping, at any age.

Early Childhood (3 to 8 Years)

Recollections from early childhood illustrate children's interest in sexual anatomy and behavior. Children in early childhood often show each other their bodies (Pike, 2005). The unwritten rule seems to be "I'll show you mine if you'll show me yours."

MASTURBATION   Because of the difficulties in conducting research into childhood sexuality, statistics on masturbation and other sexual activities are largely speculative (de Graaf & Rademakers, 2011). Parents may not wish to answer questions about their children's sexual behavior. Or they may want to present their children as little "gentlemen" and "ladies" by underreporting their sexual activity. Many parents will not even allow their adolescents, let alone their younger children, to be interviewed about sex. And when we try to look back as adults, our memories may be cloudy.

A study by William Friedrich and colleagues (1998) of the Mayo Institute relied on interviews with the mothers of more than 1,100 children. The goal of the study was to establish what kinds of sexual behaviors can normally be expected in childhood. The study did not provide data about masturbation per se, but, as shown in Table 11.1, it offered some insight into how many children touch their "private parts." Friedrich suggests that behavior that occurs in at least 20% of children is normal from a statistical point of view.

MALE–FEMALE SEXUAL BEHAVIOR   It is quite common for 3- and 4-year-olds to express affection through kissing. Curiosity about the genitals increases in this stage. Sex games like "show" and "playing doctor" may begin earlier, but they become common between the ages of 3 and 7 (de Graaf & Rademakers, 2011). Much of this sexual activity takes place in same-sex groups, although mixed-sex sex games are not uncommon. Children may show their genitals to each other, touch each other's genitals, or masturbate together.

Critical Thinking
Why is it difficult to obtain accurate information about sexual behavior in children?

Table 11.1 Some Common Sexual Behaviors During Childhood

	Boys	Girls
Ages 2–5		
Touches or tries to touch mother's or other women's breasts	42.4%	43.7%
Touches private parts when at home	60.2%	43.8%
Tries to look at people when they are nude or undressing	26.8%	26.9%
Ages 6–9		
Touches private parts when at home	39.8%	20.7%
Tries to look at people when they are nude or undressing	20.2%	20.5%

SOURCE: Data from W. M. Friedrich, J. Fisher, D. Broughton, M. Houston, and C. R. Shafran (1998). Normative sexual behavior in children: A contemporary sample. *Pediatrics, 101*(4) e9.

A CLOSER LOOK

HOW SHOULD PARENTS REACT WHEN CHILDREN MASTURBATE?

Few parents in developed nations still believe that childhood masturbation sets the stage for physical and mental maladies. Yet some parents react to childhood masturbation with concern, revulsion, or shock. Parents who are unaware that masturbation is commonplace among children may erroneously think that children who masturbate are oversexed or abnormal. They may pull a child's hands away and scold her or him. Some may slap the child's hand. Once the child is capable of understanding speech, the parent may say things like, "Don't touch down there! That's a bad thing to do. Stop doing that." Or parents may not respond verbally but move the child's hands away from the genitals or pick up the child when he or she is found masturbating.

Sex educators argue that punishment may cause children to become secretive and guilty about masturbation (University of Michigan, 2009). Sex guilt tends to persist and may impede sexual pleasure in marriage. But most sex educators agree that children need to learn that public masturbation is not acceptable in our culture. The child who masturbates publicly can be told something like this by the age of 4: "It's okay in your room but not in the grocery store."

Not all authorities, and certainly not all parents, endorse tolerance. Some object to masturbation on religious or moral grounds. We must also recognize that some religious leaders believe that it does a child—and a parent—little good to be relaxed about bodily pleasures if the payoff is going to hell. Parents must examine their own values and decide for themselves how to react when they discover their children masturbating.

Real Students, Real Questions

Q *Will masturbating earlier make you develop sooner?*

A Physically? No. Emotionally or mentally? Let's simply say that masturbation will help one get in touch with one's sexuality—with what feels good and what happens when it feels good—at whatever age one masturbates. One may also need to deal with parental response to masturbation, but that's a separate (and often difficult) matter.

MALE–MALE AND FEMALE–FEMALE SEXUAL BEHAVIOR Same-sex sexual play in childhood does not foreshadow adult sexual orientation (Reinisch, 1990). It may, in fact, be more common than heterosexual play. It typically involves handling the other child's genitals, although it may include oral or anal contact. It may also include an outdoor variation of the game of "show" in which boys urinate together and see who can reach farthest or highest.

Preadolescence (9 to 13 Years)

LO 11.2 **Describe sexual behaviors in preadolescence.**

Some preadolescent behaviors are sexually related rather than sexual per se. For example, preadolescents typically form relationships with a "best friend" of the same sex that enables them to share secrets and confidences. Preadolescents also tend to socialize with larger networks of friends in sex-segregated groups. Preadolescents grow increasingly preoccupied with, and self-conscious about,

Real Students, Real Questions

Q *How can you tell the difference between normal childhood sex play or exploration and signs of sexual abuse?*

A It's not always easy. Children often know or suspect when something is wrong. Abuse most often comes from someone older and close to the child—not a stranger—so parents need to be open to listening to the child, even when he or she implicates a family member or close friend. Children who are abused often act depressed—withdrawn, listless—or, at the other extreme, aggressive. They may not have the concept of abuse or the words to talk about it. Or they may fear *they* have done something wrong. Children need to be taught the difference between "good touching" and "bad touching." They need to know they can tell you what's on their mind without being judged or scolded. By and large, a good deal of abuse can be avoided simply by having children play with children who are pretty much their own age. They may play "doctor" or "show," but such games are usually not abusive.

their bodies. Peers pressure preadolescents to conform to dress codes, the "proper" slang, and group norms concerning sex and drugs. Peer disapproval can be an intense punishment.

Sexual urges are experienced by many preadolescents but may not emerge until adolescence. Sigmund Freud had theorized that sexual impulses are hidden (latent) during preadolescence, but many preadolescents are quite active sexually.

Masturbation

Kinsey and his colleagues (1948, 1953) reported that masturbation is the primary means of achieving orgasm during preadolescence for both boys and girls. They found that 45% of males and 15% of females masturbated by age 13. Although the frequencies of masturbation reported by Kinsey and his colleagues are suspect, other studies agree that adolescent males are more likely than females to masturbate (Petersen & Hyde, 2011; Robbins et al., 2011).

Male–Female Sexual Behavior

Preadolescent sex play often involves mutual display of the genitals, with or without touching. Such sexual experiences are quite common and do not appear to affect future sexual adjustment (Martinez et al., 2011). Although preadolescents tend to socialize in same-sex groups, interest in the other sex among heterosexuals tends to gradually increase as they approach puberty. Group activities and mixed-sex parties often provide preadolescents with their first exposure to heterosexual activities (Connolly et al., 2004). But couples may not begin to pair off until middle adolescence.

Male–Male and Female–Female Sexual Behavior

Some preadolescent sexual behavior between members of the same sex is exploration. Some reflects a gay male or lesbian sexual orientation. Some incidents reflect lack of availability of partners of the other sex. As with younger children, preadolescent

Sex Education. Despite the availability of sex education in most schools, many young people still learn about sex from their peers. Survey data show that most parents want sex education to cover abstinence, avoiding pregnancy, sexually transmitted infections, abortion, and sexual orientation. However, we may do a poorer job of teaching our children about sex than most developed nations do.

experiences with children of the same sex may be more common than heterosexual experiences (Martinez et al., 2011). These activities are usually limited to touching each other's genitals or mutually masturbating. Because preadolescents generally socialize with peers of their own sex, their sexual explorations are also often with peers of their own sex. Most same-sex sexual experiences involve single episodes or short-lived relationships.

Sex Education

LO 11.3 **Discuss the purposes and outcomes of sex education.**

Sixty or 70 years ago in the United States, people did not generally talk openly about sex. Sure, there were dirty jokes. Friends confided in one another, or asked for opinions. Mothers may have "warned" their daughters about the onset of menstruation or about the aggressive "advances" of boys, but there was little if any formal discussion about human anatomy, sexually transmitted infections (STIs), and methods of preventing unwanted pregnancies. In fact, many young people weren't sure exactly how females got pregnant, and there were myths such as the (erroneous!) belief that a female cannot get pregnant the first time she has sex. The message from mother and church was simple: "Don't." And hundreds of thousands of teenage girls became pregnant each year, and many youngsters would up infected with the STIs of the day, such as gonorrhea and syphilis.

Since that time, the numbers of teenagers getting pregnant showed some increase and the threat of HIV/AIDS emerged. Even so, many parents felt that sex education should not be taught outside the home or the church, and some still felt that sex should not be discussed at all.

It is interesting, then, that some kind of formal sex education for children or adolescents is now nearly universal in the United States. There is more than discussion; adolescents often practice unrolling condoms on bananas and the like. Figure 11.1 shows the results of a survey run by the government National Survey of Family Growth (Martinez et al., 2010) that recruited some 7,000 females and

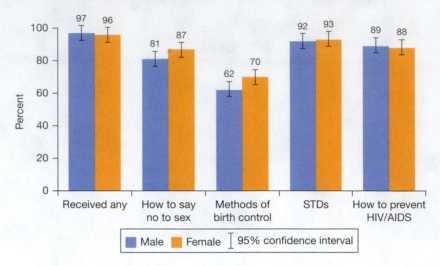

Figure 11.1 Teenagers Aged 15–19 Who Reported Receiving Formal Sex Education Before the Age of 18.

SOURCE: Martinez, G., Abma, J., & Copen, C. (2010). Educating teenagers about sex in the United States. NCHS data brief, no. 44. Hyattsville, MD: National Center for Health Statistics, Figure 1.

6,000 males. Ninety-seven percent of males and 96% of females had received at least some formal sex education. That information was most likely to be about the nature and prevention of HIV/AIDS. A strong runner-up was learning "how to say no to sex." The teenagers were less likely to be taught about methods of birth control, but even so, 70% of females and 62% of males received that information.

3 › T /F Truth or Fiction Revisited Figure 11.2 shows that the majority of teenagers aged 15 to 19 actually have talked with a parent about sex. Females are more likely to do so than males, and nearly four out of five (79%) reported doing so.

Parents are most likely to talk to their children and adolescents about abstinence—how to say no to sex—although females (63%) were much more likely than males (42%) to discuss that issue (Martinez et al., 2010). About half of the children and adolescents (55% of females and 50% of males) reported discussing STIs with their parents. More than half of females (51%) were told about birth control, as compared with fewer than one-third (31%) of males; and nearly twice as many females (38%) as males (20%) were told where to get birth control. In other words, many youngsters were told "Don't get pregnant" and "Don't get sick," but not all of them were given the specifics as to how to avoid these problems.

Some people argue that sex education ought to be left to parents and religious authorities. But the data suggest that adolescents will all too often learn about sex from peers and the Internet.

4 › T /F Truth or Fiction Revisited Many parents worry that teaching about sexual techniques and contraception encourages sexual activity, but research does not support this concern (Kirby, 2011; Kraft et al., 2012).

Adolescence

Adolescence is bounded by the onset of puberty at the lower end and the assumption of adult responsibilities at the upper end. (Yes, by this definition, some people remain adolescents forever.) In our society adolescents are "neither fish nor fowl," as

Figure 11.2 Teenagers 15–19 Who Talked With a Parent About Sex.

SOURCE: Martinez, G., Abma, J., & Copen, C. (2010). Educating teenagers about sex in the United States. NCHS data brief, no. 44. Hyattsville, MD: National Center for Health Statistics, from Figure 3.

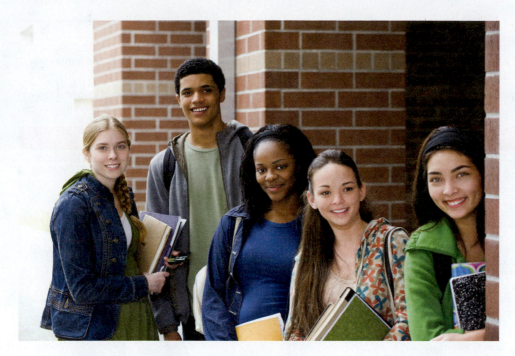

Adolescence. Adolescence begins with puberty. Many adults see adolescents as impulsive and as needing to be controlled for "their own good." However, adolescents have a sex drive that is heightened by surges of sex hormones, and they are flooded with sexual themes in the media. Therefore, it is not surprising that many of them are in conflict with their families about issues of autonomy and sexual behavior.

the saying goes—neither children nor adults. Adolescents may be able to reproduce and be taller than their parents, but they may not be allowed to get driver's licenses or attend R-rated films. They are prevented from working long hours and must usually stay in school until age 16. They cannot marry until they reach the "age of consent." The message is clear: Adults see adolescents as impulsive and as needing to be restricted for "their own good." Given these restrictions, a sex drive that is heightened by surges of sex hormones, and media inundation with sexual themes, it is not surprising that many adolescents are in conflict with their families about going around with certain friends, sex, and using the family car.

Puberty

LO 11.4 Describe the milestones of puberty.

Puberty begins with the appearance of **secondary sex characteristics** and ends when the long bones make no further gains in length. The appearance of pubic hair is often the first visible sign of puberty. Puberty also involves changes in **primary sex characteristics**. Most major changes occur within 3 years in girls and within 4 years in boys.

Reproduction becomes possible toward the end of puberty. The two principal markers of reproductive potential are menarche in the girl and the first ejaculation in the boy. But these events may not signify immediate fertility.

PUBERTAL CHANGES IN FEMALES In girls, the pituitary gland signals the ovaries to increase estrogen production at puberty. Estrogen may stimulate the growth of breast tissue ("breast buds") as early as the age of 8 or 9, but the breasts usually begin to enlarge during the tenth year. The development of fatty tissue and ducts elevates the areas of the breasts surrounding the nipples and causes the nipples to protrude. The breasts typically reach full size in about 3 years, but the mammary glands do not mature fully until a woman has a baby. Events of puberty for girls are shown in Table 11.2.

Estrogen also promotes the growth of the fatty and supporting tissue in the hips and buttocks, which, along with the widening of the pelvis, causes the hips to become rounded. Growth of fatty deposits and connective tissue varies considerably. For this reason, development of breasts and hips differs.

puberty

The biological stage of development during which reproduction first becomes possible. Puberty begins with the appearance of secondary sex characteristics and ends when the long bones make no further gains in length.

secondary sex characteristics

Physical characteristics that differentiate males and females and that usually appear at puberty but are not directly involved in reproduction, such as the bodily distribution of hair and fat, development of the muscle mass, and deepening of the voice.

primary sex characteristics

Physical characteristics that differentiate males and females and are directly involved in reproduction, such as the sex organs.

Table 11.2   Five Stages of Pubertal Development for Females

Girls usually start to show the physical changes of puberty between the ages of 9 and 13, which is slightly sooner than boys. The female sex hormone estrogen and other hormones cause the physical changes.

Many girls are fully developed by the age of 16. Some girls will continue to develop through age 18. Here are the five stages of pubertal development and what happens:

Stage	Characteristics
Stage 1: Between ages 8 and 12	• No visible signs of physical development, but the ovaries are enlarging and hormone production is beginning.
Stage 2: May begin anywhere from ages 8 to 14.	• Height and weight increase rapidly. • Fine hair growth begins close to the pubic area and underarms. • Breast buds appear; nipples become raised and this area may be tender. • Sweat and oil glands become more active, which can result in acne.
Stage 3: May begin anywhere from ages 9 to 15.	• Breasts become rounder and fuller. • Hips may start to widen in relation to waist. • Vagina begins secreting a clear or whitish fluid. • Pubic hair becomes darker, thicker, and curlier. • Height and weight continue to increase. • For some girls, ovulation and menstruation (periods) begin but may be irregular.
Stage 4: May begin anywhere from ages 10 to 16.	• Underarm hair becomes darker. • Pubic hair starts to form a triangular patch in front and around sides of genital area. • The nipple and the dark area around the breast (areola) may stick out from the rest of the breast. • For many girls, ovulation and menstruation (periods) begin, but may be irregular.
Stage 5: May begin anywhere from ages 12 to 19.	• Adult height is probably reached. • Breast development is complete. • Pubic hair forms a thick, curly, triangular patch. • Ovulation and menstruation (periods) usually occur regularly. • Overall look is that of a young adult woman.

SOURCE: U.S. Department of Health and Human Services. *Sexual development of girls.* http://www.4parents.gov/sexdevt/girlswomen/girls_sexdevt/index.html (Accessed July 3, 2016).

Beginning at about the age of 11, girls' adrenal glands produce small amounts of androgens, which, along with estrogen, stimulate the growth of pubic and underarm hair. Excessive androgen production can darken or increase the amount of facial hair. Androgens and estrogen have other functions as well.

Estrogen causes the labia, vagina, and uterus to develop during puberty, and androgens cause the clitoris to develop. The vaginal lining varies in thickness according to the amount of estrogen in the bloodstream.

Estrogen typically brakes the female growth spurt some years before testosterone brakes that of males. Girls deficient in estrogen during their late teens may grow quite tall, but most girls reach their heights because of normal, genetically determined variations.

menarche

The onset of menstruation; first menstruation.

Menarche (first menstruation) commonly occurs between the ages of 11 and 14. But it is normal for menarche to occur as early as 9 or as late as 16 (Natsuaki et al., 2011). In the middle 1800s, European girls first menstruated at about 16, as shown in Figure 11.4. During the past century and a half, however, the processes of puberty have occurred at progressively earlier ages in Western nations, an example of the secular trend in development. By the 1960s, the average age of menarche in the United States had plummeted to its current figure of 12½.

No single theory of the onset of puberty has found wide acceptance. In any event, the average age of the advent of puberty for girls and boys appears to have leveled off in recent years. The dramatic drop suggested in Figure 11.3 has come to an end.

What accounts for the earlier age of puberty? One hypothesis is that increases in body weight trigger menarche (Terasawa et al., 2012; Wagner et al., 2015). Rapid weight increases even in infancy are associated with earlier menarche (Salgin et al., 2015). Body fat could trigger the changes because fat cells secrete the protein leptin. Leptin would then signal the brain to secrete a cascade of hormones that raise estrogen levels in the body. Menarche comes later to girls who have a lower percentage of body fat, such as athletes or those with eating disorders (Javed et al., 2015).

The average body weight for triggering menarche depends on the girl's height (Novotny et al., 2011). In developed nations, girls today are larger than those of the early twentieth century, probably because of improved nutrition and health care. It seems that the age threshold for reaching menarche may have been attained because the average age has leveled off in recent years.

The age at menarche has been shown to be related to adverse health outcomes later in life. For example, earlier menarche has been associated with higher risk of breast cancer and possibly a higher risk of endometrial cancer, adult obesity, and menstrual problems (Bandera et al., 2015).

Estrogen production becomes cyclical in puberty and regulates the menstrual cycle. A girl's initial menstrual cycles are typically **anovulatory**. Girls cannot become pregnant until ovulation occurs, which may lag menarche by a year or two.

PUBERTAL CHANGES IN MALES At puberty the hypothalamus signals the pituitary to increase production of follicle-stimulating hormone (FSH) and luteinizing hormone (LH). These hormones stimulate the testes to increase their output of testosterone. Testosterone prompts growth of the male genitals: the testes, scrotum,

Figure 11.3   Age at Menarche.

The age at menarche has been declining since the mid-1800s among girls in Western nations, apparently because of improved nutrition and health care. Menarche may be triggered by the accumulation of a critical percentage of body fat.

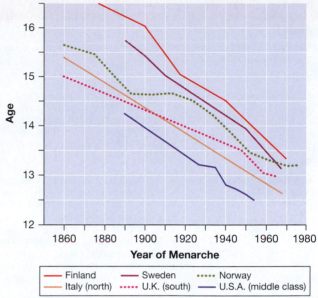

anovulatory

Without ovulation.

SEX IN A WORLD OF DIVERSITY

THE MANY MEANINGS OF MENARCHE

In different times, in different places, menarche has had different meanings. The Manus of New Guinea greet menarche with elaborate ceremony (Lohmann, 2004). The other girls of the village sleep in the menstruating girl's hut. They feast and party. In the West, menstruation has historically received a mixed response. The menstrual flow itself has generally been seen, erroneously, as polluting, and the frequent discomforts of menstruation have led menstruating women to be stereotyped as irrational (Hubbard, 2009). Menarche itself has generally been perceived as the event in which a girl suddenly develops into a woman, but because of taboos and prejudice against menstruating women, girls historically matured in ignorance of menarche.

Most American girls receive advance information about menstruation, not only from family and girlfriends but also from school health classes (Allison & Hyde, 2011). The old horror stories are pretty much gone, at least in societies in developed countries. However, most girls experience at least some menstrual discomfort and need to discreetly dispose of the menstrual flow. Most girls can separate pride in "becoming women" from the realities of some discomfort and the fact that menarche usually means that the girl will not be growing much taller because of the braking effects of estrogen.

Table 11.3 Five Stages of Pubertal Development for Males

Boys usually start to show the physical change of puberty between the ages of 11 and 14, which is slightly older than when girls start puberty. The male sex hormone testosterone and other hormones cause the physical changes.

Here are the five stages and what happens:

Stage	Characteristics
Stage 1: May begin as early as age 9 and continue until 14.	• No sign of physical development, but hormone production is beginning.
Stage 2: May begin anywhere from ages 11 to 13.	• Height and weight increase rapidly. • Testicles become larger and scrotum hangs lower. • Scrotum becomes darker in color. • Fine hair growth begins at the base of the penis. • Hair growth may begin on the legs and underarms.
Stage 3: May begin anywhere from ages 12 to 14.	• The penis, scrotum, and testicles grow. • Pubic hair becomes darker, thicker, and curlier. • Muscles become larger and shoulders become broader. • Sweat and oil glands become more active, which can result in acne. • Sperm production may begin. • Temporary swelling and tenderness may occur around nipples. • Height and weight continue to increase. • Hair growth on the legs and underarms continues.
Stage 4: May begin anywhere from ages 13 to 16.	• Sperm production has usually begun. • The larynx (Adam's apple) increases in size. Vocal chords become longer and thicker, and the voice begins to break or crack, then becomes low. • Height and weight continue to increase. • Penis and testicles continue to grow. • Pubic hair increases in amount and becomes darker, coarser, and curly.
Stage 5: May begin anywhere from ages 14 to 18.	• Growth of facial hair begins. • Chest hair growth may begin (not all males get much chest hair). • Adult height is reached. • Penis and testicles have reached full adult size. • Pubic, underarm, and leg hair are adult color, texture, and distribution. • Overall look is that of a young adult man.

SOURCE: U.S. Department of Health and Human Services. *Sexual development of boys.* http://www.4parents.gov/sexdevt/boysmen/boys_sexdevt/index.html (Accessed July 3, 2016)

nocturnal emission

Involuntary ejaculation of seminal fluid while asleep. Also referred to as a *wet dream*, although the individual need not be dreaming about sex, or dreaming at all, at the time.

and penis (see Table 11.3). It fosters differentiation of male secondary sex characteristics: the growth of facial, body, and pubic hair; and the deepening of the voice. Testicle growth, in turn, accelerates testosterone production and pubertal changes. The testes continue to grow, and the scrotal sac becomes larger and hangs loosely from the body. The penis widens and lengthens, and pubic hair appears.

By age 13 or 14, erections become common. Many middle school boys dread that they may be caught between classes with erections, or asked to stand before the class. Testosterone causes the prostate and seminal vesicles—the organs that produce semen—to grow and produce semen. Boys typically experience their first ejaculation by age 13 or 14, often through masturbation. But there is much variation. Mature sperm are not usually found in the ejaculate until about a year after the first ejaculation, at age 14 on average. But sperm may be present in the first ejaculate, so pubertal boys should not assume that they have an infertile "grace period" following first ejaculation. About a year after first ejaculation, boys may also begin to experience **nocturnal emissions**, which are also called "wet dreams" because of the belief that nocturnal emissions accompany erotic dreams—which need not be so.

SEX IN THE DIGITAL AGE

SEXTING: OF CELL PHONES, SEX, AND DEATH

Jessica Logan was 18 years old when she committed suicide. She had used her cell phone to snap and send nude photos of herself to her boyfriend. After they broke up, he forwarded the photos to other girls at their high school. The girls taunted Jessica mercilessly, calling her a whore and a slut. Jessica told her depressing tale in a local TV interview, and 2 months later—finding no peace—she hanged herself in her bedroom.

Jessica's sending of her photos to her boyfriend is an example of "sexting"—short for *sex texting.* It refers to sending or receiving text messages with sexual content. Sexting can be used to titillate the recipient, to highlight the intimacy of one's relationship, to humiliate someone—or to ask or arrange for a sexual encounter (Walrave et al., 2015).

In other "case studies," a 15-year-old Pennsylvania girl has been charged with producing and sending child pornography after sending nude photos of herself to other adolescents. A 19-year-old Florida college student was expelled and ordered to register as a sex offender for 25 years because he shared nude photos of his girlfriend with other people. The same sexting that is a crime for teenagers is legal for adults. Teenagers don't see their sexting as child pornography, although in many locales the law does (Najdowski et al., 2015).

A survey of high school students in Texas found that 28% said they had transmitted a nude photo of themselves in a text message or an email (Temple et al., 2012). Three in 10 (31%) had requested a "sext" message, and more than half (57%) had asked someone else to send them a sexual text or e-mail. Girls who had engaged in sexting were significantly more like than those who had not to begin dating early and to engage in risky sexual behavior.

Consider the Following Before Pressing "Send":

- **Don't believe that anything you sext will remain private.** Many teens say they have received a sext that was meant to be private; some say they forwarded a sext to someone other than the intended recipient.

- **Whatever you sext may never go away.** Potential employers, college recruiters, teachers and coaches, parents, love interests, friends, enemies, and total strangers may be able to access your posts, even after (long after!) you have deleted them.
- **Don't give in to peer pressure to sext.** Many adolescent girls say that "pressure from guys" is a reason they sext. Boys may also sext because of peer pressure.
- **Consider the recipient's reaction before you press send.** You may intend for a message to be fun but the recipient may not perceive it that way; for example, girl may send sexually suggestive content as a "joke," but guys may think that such a girl will hook up in real life.
- **Nothing you post or send will necessarily remain anonymous.** Some teens sext to people they have "met" only online. Those people can often track you down on the basis of your screen name and other information you have provided.

5 › T /F Truth or Fiction Revisited Despite the term *wet dreams*, nocturnal emissions need not accompany boys' erotic dreams.

Underarm hair appears at about age 15. Facial hair is at first a fuzz on the upper lip. A beard does not appear for another 2 or 3 years. Only half of U.S. boys shave (of necessity) by age 17. The beard and chest hair continue to develop past the age of 20. At age 14 or 15 the voice deepens because of the growth of the voice box and the lengthening of the vocal cords. Development is gradual, and the voices of adolescent boys sometimes crack embarrassingly.

Boys and girls undergo general growth spurts during puberty. Girls usually shoot up before boys. Individuals differ, however, and some boys spurt sooner than some girls.

Increases in muscle mass increase body weight. The shoulders and the circumference of the chest widen. At the age of 18 or so, men stop growing taller because estrogen prevents the long bones from making further gains in length. (Males normally produce some estrogen in the adrenal glands and testes.) Nearly one in two boys experiences temporary enlargement of the breasts, or **gynecomastia**, during puberty, which is also caused by estrogen.

In both females and males, sex hormones course through the bloodstream in copious amounts, stoking a relatively strong sex drive. Thus, many adolescents seek sexual outlets, such as masturbation.

gynecomastia

Overdevelopment of a male's breasts.

Types of Sexual Behaviors in Adolescence

LO 11.5   Describe sexuality in adolescence, including teenage pregnancy.

Adolescents are generally pressed by high levels of sex hormones and interested in seeking sex outlets. These outlets include masturbation and sex with others, including members of the other sex and the same sex.

MASTURBATION   Masturbation is the most common sexual outlet in adolescence. Most adolescents masturbate at some time. The well-known Kinsey studies, published in the mid-twentieth century (Kinsey et al., 1948, 1953), suggested that masturbation was nearly universal among male adolescents but less common among adolescent females. This sex difference is confirmed in nearly every survey (Hakim, 2015; Schmitt et al., 2012). Boys who masturbate may do so several times a week, on average, much more frequently than most girls who masturbate. It is unclear whether this sex difference reflects a stronger sex drive in boys, greater social constraints on girls, or both. The erroneous belief that masturbation is harmful and guilt about masturbation lessen the incidence of masturbation.

MALE–FEMALE SEXUAL BEHAVIOR   Adolescents today start dating and going out earlier than in past generations. Teens who date earlier are more likely to engage in sexual activity during high school (Temple et al., 2012; Waylen et al., 2010). Teens who initiate sexual activity earlier are also less likely to use contraception and more likely to become pregnant (Temple et al., 2012).

6 › T /F Truth or Fiction Revisited   It is true that petting is practically universal among American adolescents and has been for many generations. Adolescents use petting to express affection, satisfy their curiosities, heighten their sexual arousal, and reach orgasm while avoiding pregnancy and maintaining virginity. Girls are more likely than boys to be coerced into petting and to feel guilty about it (Gavin et al., 2009).

Figure 11.4   Percentage of Never-Married Teenagers, Aged 15-19, Who Have Had Sexual Intercourse.

SOURCE: Martinez, G., & Abma, J. C. (2015). Sexual activity, contraceptive use, and childbearing of teenagers aged 15–19 in the United States. U.S. Department of Health and Human Services, National Center for Health Statistics. NCHS Data Brief, No. 209, Figure 1.

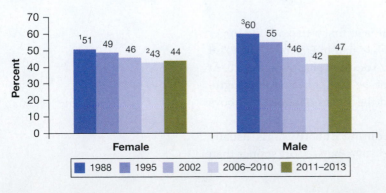

Since the early 1990s, the percentage of high school students who have engaged in sexual intercourse has been gradually declining. The incidences of kissing, "making out," oral sex, and sexual intercourse all increase with age. Figure 11.4 summarizes some findings about teenage male–female sexual behavior with results from the National Survey of Family Growth (Martinez & Abma, 2015). There was a gradual decline in the incidence of sexual intercourse between 1988 and the first decade of the twenty-first century, but the percentage of never-married teenagers between the ages of 15 and 19 who have had sex has leveled off in the mid-40s. It should not be surprising that the probability of having had sex rises dramatically

Figure 11.5 Methods of Contraception Ever Used Among Females Aged 15–19 Who Ever Had Sexual Intercourse: United States, 2002, 2006–2010, and 2011–2013.

SOURCE: Martinez, G., & Abma, J. C. (2015). Sexual activity, contraceptive use, and childbearing of teenagers aged 15–19 in the United States. U.S. Department of Health and Human Services, National Center for Health Statistics. NCHS Data Brief, No. 209, Figure 4.

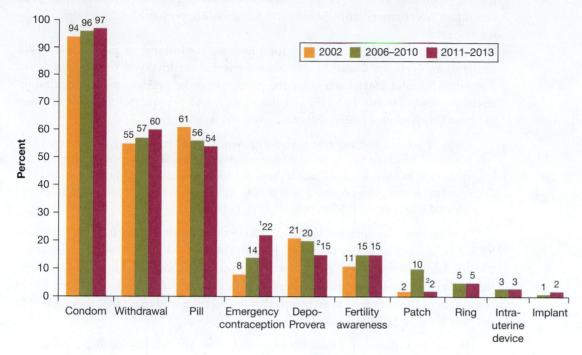

between the ages of 15 and 19. Figure 11.5 shows that more than 90% of the girls aged 15–19 who have had sex have used a condom at one time or another, and majorities have used withdrawal (a "non-method" of birth control) or the pill.

Some teenagers do not plan their first sexual experience. Rather, they perceive it as simply happening to them (Martinez et al., 2011). Females are more likely than males to say they didn't want it to happen (see Table 11.4). The largest number of females had mixed feelings about it, but most males reported that they wanted it (Martinez et al., 2011).

The main reason that females give for abstaining from sex is that it is against their religious beliefs or moral values. For males, religious or moral beliefs and not having found the right person are somewhat of a tie.

The incidences of kissing, petting, oral sex, and sexual intercourse all increase with age (McLeod & Knight 2010). For example, according to a Centers for Disease Control and Prevention (CDC) survey, 42% of girls aged 15 to 17 reported engaging in oral sex as compared to 72% of girls aged 18 to 19 (Mosher et al., 2005). Among adolescents who have not engaged in sexual intercourse, the lowest rates of oral sex—about 19%—were for adolescents who cited moral or religious reasons for abstaining from sexual intercourse. Some adolescent couples use oral sex as a means of maintaining virginity and preventing pregnancy.

Table 11.4 Attitudes of Teenagers Ages 15–19 Toward Their First Sexual Intercourse

	Didn't Want It to Happen	Had Mixed Feelings	Really Wanted It to Happen
Females	10.8%	48%	41.2%
Males	5%	32.5%	62.5%

SOURCE: Martinez, G., Copen, C. E., & Abma, J. C. (2011). Teenagers in the United States: Sexual activity, contraceptive use, and childbearing, 2006–2010. National Survey of Family Growth. National Center for Health Statistics. *Vital Health Statistics, 23*(31).

MOTIVES FOR INTERCOURSE Premarital intercourse is motivated by a number of factors. The pubertal surge of sex hormones directly activates sexual arousal, at least among boys (Petersen & Hyde, 2011). But about half of the men (51%) and one-quarter of the women (24%) in the National Health and Social Life Survey (NHSLS) reported that the main reason for their first experience was curiosity, or "readiness for sex" (Michael et al., 1994, p. 93). Hormonal changes stoke the development of secondary sex characteristics. Some early maturers are pressured into dating or sex—ready or not.

Motives including love, desire for pleasure, conformity to peer norms, peer recognition, even the desire to dominate someone are involved in sexual activity. The NHSLS found that affection for the partner was the primary reason for first intercourse among nearly half (48%) of the women and one-quarter (25%) of the men sampled (Michael et al., 1994). Betsy believed she was in love:

> I was 17 when I had my first sexual experience. I had been going out with my boyfriend for about five months, during which time he had been continually pressuring me to have sex. He made it seem as though I had to comply or he would end the relationship. Because I was deeply in love with him (or so I thought), I allowed it to happen. (McIntyre et al., 1991, p. 64)*

Adolescents may consider intercourse a sign of maturity, a way for girls to reward a loyal boyfriend, or a way to punish parents (McBride et al., 2003; O'Donnell et al., 2003b). Adolescents whose friends have had sex are more likely to have sex themselves (Fava & Bay-Cheng, 2012). Sometimes the pressure comes from partners. About one-quarter (24%) of the women sampled in the NHSLS study said that they agreed to sex only for their partner's sake (Michael et al., 1994):

> *Megan* (18, California): I have felt pressure before. My first boyfriend pressured me because he knew I loved him and that he could take advantage of my feelings. I was blinded by my feelings and I had sex with him. I hated it.

> *Amy* (18, Washington, D.C.): I was sexually pressured by my second boyfriend. He didn't love me, but he did want to have sex. I helped him sneak into my room in the middle of the night. Just before we were about to have sex, I realized that it wasn't something I wanted to do. I wanted my first time to be with someone I loved and who loved me. I stopped him, although he tried everything to get me to say yes. The next day we broke up, and I couldn't have been happier. (McIntyre et al., 1991, pp. 4–6)*

About 8% of the men in the NHSLS study say they went along with intercourse for the sake of their partners (Michael et al., 1994). As one young man describes it:

> *Matt* (18, New York): My girlfriend pressured me and I didn't handle it very well. I submitted so she wouldn't be mad or disappointed. (McIntyre et al., 1991, p. 65)**

The relationship between teens and their parents is a factor (Belgrave et al., 2000; Langille & Curtis, 2002). Adolescents with permissive parents are more likely to have premarital intercourse (Mundy, 2000). Parents who show interest in their children's behavior and communicate their expectations with understanding and respect often influence their children to show sexual restraint (National Campaign to Prevent Teen and Unplanned Pregnancy, 2012).

MALE–MALE AND FEMALE–FEMALE SEXUAL BEHAVIOR About 4.5% of the male adolescents and 10.6% of the female adolescents in the National Survey of Family

---

*Copyright 1991 by McIntyre, Formichella, Osterhout, and Green by arrangement with AVON BOOKS.

**Ibid

Growth (Mosher et al., 2005) report ever having "same-sex sexual contact." Among all respondents aged 15 to 44, the percentages grow to 6% for males and 11.2% for females. But the percentages drop to 2.9% for males and 4.4% for females when asked about the incidence of same-sex sexual activity in the past year. Same-sex sexual activity in adolescence can reflect limited availability of partners as well as one's sexual orientation. Despite sensationalist news stories, seduction of adolescents by gay male and lesbian adults is relatively rare.

Many gay males and lesbians develop a firm sense of their sexual orientation in adolescence. Other adolescents can be particularly cruel in their stigmatization, referring to gay and lesbian peers as "homos," "queers," "dykes," and other derogatory names. Although the nation is growing more accepting of LGBT individuals, many adolescent gay males and lesbians continue to feel isolated and cloak their sexual orientation.

Teenage Pregnancy

Believe it or not, the title of this section is "loaded": It suggests that there is a problem with teenage pregnancy. So let's toss in a couple of caveats at the beginning. First, throughout most of history, even most of the history of the United States, girls first became pregnant in their teens. Second, throughout most cultures in the world today, girls are first becoming pregnant in their teens (Save the Children, 2015). But in the United States today, the great majority of teenagers who become pregnant do so accidentally and without committed partners (Guttmacher Institute, 2012). Most young adults in developed nations defer pregnancy until after they have completed some or all of their education. Many defer pregnancy until they are well into their careers—in their late 20s, their 30s, occasionally their 40s. So it is in our place and time that we have a topic called "Teenage Pregnancy," implying that there might be a problem with it.

So in our culture, today, why do teenage girls become pregnant? For one thing, adolescent girls typically get little advice in school or at home about how to deal with boys' sexual advances. Another reason is failure to use contraception. Some initiate sex at very early ages, when they are least likely to use contraception (Martin et al., 2015; Martinez & Abma, 2015). Only about three-quarters (77%) of adolescent girls, especially those age 17 and under, used contraception the first time they had sex (Martinez & Alba, 2015). Moreover, about three teenage girls in five have used the withdrawal method of birth control at one time or another (Martinez & Abma, 2015).

Some teenage girls purposefully get pregnant to try to force their partners to make a commitment to them. Some are rebelling against their parents or the moral standards of their communities. But most girls are impregnated because they and their partners do not know as much about reproduction and contraception as they think they do or because they miscalculate the odds of getting pregnant. Even those who have been to all the sex education classes and who have access to family-planning clinics slip up now and then, especially if their partners push them or do not want to use condoms.

Figure 11.6 strongly suggests the decline in teenage birth rates in the United States over the past 55–60 years.

Figure 11.6 Percentage of Birth Rates for Teenagers Aged 15–19, by Age Group, United States, 1960–2013.

SOURCE: Martin, J. A., Hamilton, B. E., Osterman, M. J. K., Curtin, S. C., & Mathews, T. J. (2015). Births: Final Data for 2013. U.S. Department of Health and Human Services, National Center for Health Statistics, Figure 3.

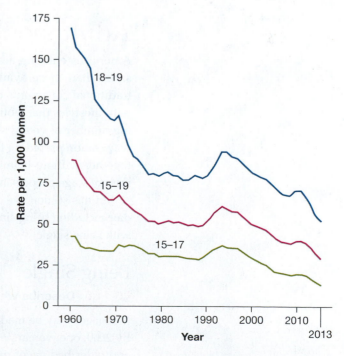

Critical Thinking
Where do you stand on the issue of whether school districts should make contraceptive devices available to students? On what do you base your views? As an intellectual exercise, can you argue a point of view opposed to your own?

The decline is most dramatic for teens aged 18 and 19. We may assume that this age group has greater control of their sexuality (and their boyfriends) than younger teenage girls do. But the 18–19-year-olds are having more sex than their younger counterparts, so, overall, they are more likely to get pregnant. The current numbers are all record lows. The rates have fallen by 57% just from 1991. Furthermore, the decline from 2012 to 2013 has been comparable for all races and ethnic groups: down 9% for European Americans, 10% for Latin Americans, and 11% for African Americans.

Why has the decline occurred? A number of factors appear to have contributed. One is a federal government-funded increase in access to family planning, which includes contraceptive services and counseling. There are success stories on the state level as well, as with the making of contraceptive implants available to teens in Colorado. The Colorado Department of Public Health and Environment has been offering free intrauterine devices (IUDs) and implants, and the number of teenage births dropped 40% between 2009 and 2013 (Tavernise, 2015). The teenage rate of abortions also fell, by 42%. Let us also suggest that sex education programs have played a role, as did the poor economy over those years. When income is in doubt, even young people are less likely to get pregnant. And, unfortunately, most pregnant teenagers will become single mothers.

And what about abstinence-only programs? Abstinence is certainly a way to prevent pregnancy and HIV/AIDS, but does sex education that advises "abstinence only" work? It turns out that states most likely to teach "abstinence only" are also those with the highest rates of teenage pregnancy. However, one study with 662 African American children (mean age = 12.2 years) reduced the incidence of sexual intercourse over the next 2 years through an 8-hour program that discussed the practical problems rather than the moral issues associated with teenage pregnancy (Jemmott et al., 2010). About one-third of youngsters in the program reported engaging in intercourse over the next 2 years, as opposed to nearly half of those who were in a control group in which there was a general discussion of health. "Moralistic" programs that promote abstinence until marriage are less effective (Kohler et al., 2008). In any event, three out of four large school districts in the United States also provide instruction about methods of contraception and prevention of STIs.

Adulthood

Americans entering adulthood today face a wider range of sexual choices and lifestyles than those available to earlier generations. The sexual revolution loosened traditional constraints on sexual choices, especially for women. Couples experiment with lifestyles that would have been unthinkable in previous generations. An increasing number of young people choose to remain single as a way of life, not merely as a way station preceding the arrival of Mr. or Ms. Right. Fifty years ago, a couple's living together without being married was dubbed "living in sin"; today it has become a normal stage of courtship.

In this section, we discuss diverse forms of adult sexuality in the United States today, including being single, cohabitation, and marriage. Let us begin as people begin—with being single.

Being Single

LO 11.6 Describe what being single means today.

Marriages may be made in heaven, but many Americans are saying heaven can wait. By 2000, one woman in four and three men in ten in the United States 15 years of age and older had never married. Half a century earlier, in 1950, one woman in five and

Singles. There is no single "singles scene." Although some singles meet in singles' bars, many meet in more casual settings, such as the neighborhood laundromat. Many singles who are seeking partners advertise online; some do so in newspapers or magazines, although newspapers and magazines are so … 2000.

about one man in four aged 15 and older had never been married. The rate of marriages had also fallen off. More than four men in five (84%) in the 20 to 24 age range were unmarried, up from 55% in 1970. By 2000, the number of single women in this age group had doubled to 73% from 36% in 1970 (U.S. Bureau of the Census, 2006). But—and this is a big but—many singles are among the formerly married, divorced or widowed (Larson, 2015).

7 › T /F Truth or Fiction Revisited Recent years have seen a sharp increase in the numbers of single young people in our society. Being single, not married, is now the most common lifestyle among people in their early 20s. In the year 2014, single adults made up more than half the adult population in 27 of the 50 states (H. Schwartz, 2014).

Several factors contribute to the increased proportion of singles. For one thing, more people are postponing marriage to pursue educational and career goals. Many young people are deciding to "live together" (cohabit), at least for a while, rather than get married. Also, as you can see in Figure 11.7, people are getting married later. The typical man in the United States gets married at age 29–30 today, compared with age 23 to 24 just 60 years ago, according to the U.S. Bureau of the Census. The typical woman gets married today at about 27; 60 years earlier, the typical woman married at age 20. But divorce and widowhood also contribute to the numbers of singles.

One-parent family groups have doubled to more than one-quarter of all families as compared with three decades ago (U.S. Bureau of the Census, 2015). Five times as many of these households are headed by women as men. Some of these individuals started their families as single mothers, but the increased prevalence of divorce also swells the ranks. Thirty-five percent of these families live below the poverty level.

Many single people do not choose to be single. Some remain single because they have not yet found Mr. or Ms. Right. Yet, many young people see being single as an alternative, open-ended way of life—not a temporary stage that precedes marriage. As career options for women have expanded, women are not as financially dependent on men as their mothers and

Figure 11.7 Median Age at First Marriage: 1950 to Present.

SOURCE: U.S. Census Bureau, Current Population Survey, Annual Social and Economic Supplements, 1947 to 2014. https://www.census.gov/hhes/families/files/graphics/MS-2.pdf

grandmothers were. A number of career women, like career-oriented men, choose to remain single (at least for a time) to focus on their careers. So do older singles. Many of them are lonely, but others—single by choice—build communities and connections that are as rewarding as marriage, and they value their independence (Larson, 2015).

Being single is not without its problems. As noted, many single people are lonely. Some singles express concerns about a lack of a steady, meaningful social relationship. Others, usually women, worry about their physical safety. Some people living alone find it difficult to satisfy their needs for intimacy, companionship, sex, and emotional support. Despite these concerns, most singles are well adjusted and content. Singles who have a greater number of friends and a supportive social network tend to be more satisfied with their lifestyles.

There is no typical "singles scene." Single people differ in their sexual interests and lifestyles. Many achieve emotional and psychological security through a network of intimate relationships with friends. Most are sexually active and practice **serial monogamy** (Nield et al., 2015). Other singles have a primary sexual relationship with one steady partner but occasional flings. A few—more commonly men than women—pursue casual sexual encounters, or "one-night stands."

Some singles remain celibate, either by choice or because of lack of opportunity. People choose **celibacy** for a number of reasons. Nuns, priests, and monks do so for religious reasons. Others believe that celibacy allows them to focus their energies and attention on work or to commit themselves to an important cause. They see celibacy as a temporary accommodation to other pursuits. Others remain celibate because they view sex outside of marriage as immoral. Still others are celibate because they find the prospects of sexual activity aversive or unalluring, or because of fears of STIs.

Cohabitation: Living Together

LO 11.7 **Discuss cohabitation, including the relationship between cohabitation and marriage.**

The majority of Americans in their 20s and 30s cohabit at some point (Jayson, 2013; see Table 11.5). **Cohabitation** has become part of the social mainstream. We no longer hear it referred to as "living in sin" or "shacking up" as we did in previously generations. People today refer to cohabitation with value-free expressions such as "living together." Does the current tolerance reflect society's adjustment to the numbers of cohabiting couples? Have numbers of cohabiting couples increased as a consequence of tolerance? Yes, and yes.

The numbers of households consisting of an unmarried adult male and female couple living together in the United States has increased more than 10-fold since 1960, from fewer than half a million couples to nearly 8 million couples today (see Figure 11.8). Another half million households consist of same-sex partners.

Critical Thinking

People face a variety of sources of pressure to get married. Which arguments for getting married or remaining single make sense to you? Why?

serial monogamy

A pattern of involvement in one exclusive relationship after another, as opposed to engaging in multiple sexual relationships at the same time.

celibacy

Complete sexual abstinence. (Sometimes used to describe the state of being unmarried, especially in the case of people who take vows to remain celibate.)

cohabitation

Living together as though married but without legal sanction.

Table 11.5 Percentage of Men and Women Ages 15–44 Who Have Even Cohabited With a Person of the Opposite Sex

	1995	2002	2006–2010	2011–2013
Percent of men 15-44 years of age who have ever cohabited with a female partner	n.a.	48.8%	49%	52.9%
Percent of women 15-44 years of age who have ever cohabited with a male partner	41.2%	50.0%	52%	57.3%

SOURCE: Key statistics from the National Survey of Family Growth. (2015). CDC/National Center for Health Statistics. http://www.cdc.gov/nchs/nsfg/key_statistics.htm Accessed October 3, 2015.

Today a woman's first union is more likely to be by cohabitation than marriage (Fig. 11.9). Cohabitation is a stage of courtship for many couples. People cohabit for many reasons. Cohabitation, like marriage, is an alternative to living alone. Partners may have deep feelings for each other but not be ready to get married. For many of these people, cohabitation represents a trial marriage. Some couples prefer cohabitation because it provides an abiding relationship without the legal entanglements of marriage. And in some subcultures, cohabitation is the norm.

8 › T /F   Truth or Fiction Revisited Cohabitation has, in fact, become a normal stage in courtship for many couples. Some see it as a chance to get to know the other person better before making a permanent commitment.

Willingness to cohabit was once related to more liberal attitudes toward sexual behavior, less traditional views of marriage, and less traditional views of gender roles (Hsueh et al., 2009; Rhoades et al., 2009). But cohabitation has cast such a wide net that it has drawn in more and more people with moderate and, now and then, conservative backgrounds.

Many cohabitants are less committed to their relationships than married people are (Rhoades et al., 2009; Wilcox, 2015). It is more often the man who is unwilling to make a marital commitment (Peplau, 2003). Mark, a 44-year-old computer consultant, lives with Nancy and their 7-year-old daughter, Janet. Mark says, "We feel we are not primarily a couple but rather primarily individuals who happen to be a couple. It allows me to be a little more at arm's length. Men don't like committing, so maybe this is just some sort of excuse." David Popenoe of Rutgers University notes that many men cohabit because they get a "quasi-wife" without having to make a commitment (Hussain, 2002).

Economic factors also come into play. Partners may decide to cohabit because of the economic advantages of sharing household expenses. Cohabiting individuals who receive public assistance risk losing support if they get married. Some older couples cohabit rather than marry because of resistance from adult children. Some children fear that a parent will be victimized by a needy senior citizen. Others may not want their inheritances to come into question or may not want to decide where to bury the remaining parent. Younger couples may cohabit secretly to maintain parental support that they might lose if they were to get married or reveal their living arrangements.

COHABITATION AND LATER MARRIAGE: BENEFIT OR RISK? The longer a couple continue to cohabit, the more likely it is that they will get married (see Table 11.6). Cohabiting couples

Figure 11.8 Number of Cohabiting, Unmarried Adult Couples of the Opposite Sex, by Year, United States.

SOURCE: U.S. Census Bureau.

Figure 11.9 Type of First Unions among Women Aged 15–44, United States.

In 1995 a woman's first union was more likely to be marriage, by 39% to 34%. But by 2006–2010, her first union was twice as likely to be cohabitation, by 48% to 23%.

SOURCE: Copen, C. E., Daniels, K., & Mosher, W. D. (2013, April 4). First premarital cohabitation in the United States: 2006–2010 National Survey of Family Growth. National Health Statistics reports; no. 64. Hyattsville, MD: National Center for Health Statistics.

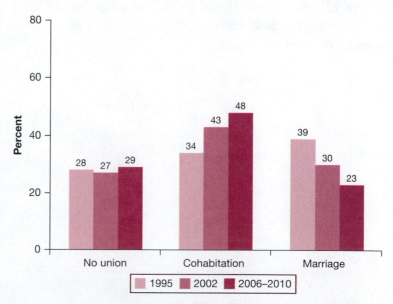

Table 11.6 Outcome of First Premarital Cohabitation

Probability that the first premarital cohabitation will remain intact, transition to marriage, or disrupt (break up) by duration of cohabitation among women 15–44 years of age, 2006–2010.

	After 1 year	After 3 years
Remain intact	67.0%	32.2%
Transition to marriage	19.4%	40.3%
Disrupt (break up)	13.6%	27.4%

SOURCE: Key statistics from the National Survey of Family Growth. (2012). CDC/National Center for Health Statistics. http://www.cdc.gov/nchs/nsfg/key_statistics.htm (accessed October 3, 2015).

may believe that cohabitation will strengthen eventual marriage by helping them iron out the kinks in their relationship. However, cohabitors who later marry also run a serious risk of getting divorced. According to Pamela Smock's (2000) survey at the Institute for Social Research at the University of Michigan, 40% of couples who cohabited before tying the knot got divorced later on. Cohabitors who marry may run a greater—not lesser—risk of divorce than noncohabitors. Some studies suggest that the likelihood of divorce within 10 years of marriage is nearly twice as great among married couples who cohabited before marriage (Smock, 2000).

Marriage: Tying the Knot

LO 11.8 **Discuss marriage, including sex in marriage and marital satisfaction.**

Throughout history marriage has allowed for the orderly transition of wealth from one generation to another, the establishment and maintenance of a home life, an institution for rearing children, and sexual exclusivity. In some cases, of course, marriages have included more than two partners, and in many, only the women have been required to limit their sex lives to their husbands. The Bible, for example, speaks of all those cases in which men of means had concubines as well as wives. Today, in developed nations, premarital sexual relations have become the norm, at least statistically speaking, but in these same nations, sexual exclusiveness is considered necessary or desirable once couples make the decision to exchange vows of faithfulness.

Figure 11.10 shows the marital status of 35- to 44-year-olds each decade from 1960, as compiled by the U.S. Bureau of the Census (Wilcox & Marquardt, 2011). This is the group of Americans who are mature enough to have completed graduate school or to have established themselves in careers. This is also a group that is young enough not to have generally suffered being widowed.

Before the number of single adults (just!) passed the number of married adults, the overall percentage of American males aged 15 and older who are married declined from 69.3% in 1960 to 52.8% in 2010. For females the decline is from 65.9% in 1960 to 49.9% in 2010.* On the other hand, we can say that nearly two-thirds of American men and women ages 35 to 44 are married.

Marriage has a varied history. The ancient Hebrews, Greeks, and Romans lived in patriarchies in which the wife was the husband's property—a chattel whose responsibilities consisted of childrearing and homemaking. Marriages were usually arranged by men, sometimes for financial or political gain. In classical Greece, men turned to prostitutes for sensual sex and sophisticated conversation. In the Christian tradition, male dominance was legitimized by biblical scripture, as in this passage from the New Testament: "Wives, submit to your own husbands, as unto the Lord. For the husband is the head of the wife, as Christ is the head of the church" (Ephesians 5:23–24).

In developed nations women have come to be viewed as loving companions rather than chattels. But the notion that a married woman

Figure 11.10 Percentages of Persons Age 35–44 Who Are Married, by Sex, 1960–2010, United States

SOURCE: U.S. Census Bureau.

might seek fulfillment through a career unrelated to her husband's needs is less than a century old—a recent development. The idea that women have a right to sexual fulfillment is also "new." Male–female American couples today are more likely to share or even reverse marital roles than in the past.

Today's same-sex marriages do not follow any of the old traditions, of course. If one partner dominates, it is not because of his or her sex. Again, if one is the breadwinner, it is not because of her or his sex. Yet same-sex marriages, as male–female marriages, value sharing lives and remaining faithful (Macedo, 2015).

WHY DO PEOPLE GET MARRIED?   Even in this era of serial monogamy and cohabitation, people still get married. Why? Marriage meets a number of personal and cultural needs. For traditionalists, it legitimizes sexual relations. Marriage still provides a traditional institution in which children can be supported and socialized. Marriage (theoretically) restricts sexual relations so that a man can be assured—or at least assume—that his wife's children are his. Unless one has signed a prenuptial agreement to the contrary, marriage permits the orderly transmission of wealth from one family to another and from one generation to another. Notions such as romantic love, equality, and the radical concept that men as well as women would do well to aspire to the ideal of faithfulness are recent additions to the structure of marriage in Western society. Not until the nineteenth century did the notion of love as a basis for marriage become widespread in Western culture.

Today, because more people believe that premarital sex is acceptable between two people who feel affectionate toward each other, the desire for sex is less likely to motivate marriage. But marriage provides a sense of security and opportunities to share feelings, experiences, and ideas with someone with whom one forms a special attachment. Even younger people still buy into the notion that marriage is important for people who plan to spend the rest of their lives together (Wilcox, 2015).

Broadly speaking, many people in the United States today want to get married because they believe that they will be happier.

TYPES OF MARRIAGE   There are several types of marriage. Among male and female couples, we have two types: monogamy and polygamy. In **monogamy**, a husband and wife are wed only to each other. But let us not confuse monogamy, which is a form of matrimony, with sexual exclusivity. People who are monogamously wed often do have extramarital affairs, as we shall see, but they are married to one person at a time. In polygamy, a person has more than one spouse (of the other sex) and is permitted sexual access to each of them. In same-sex marriage (also referred to as gay marriage), an individual is married to someone of the same sex.

monogamy
Marriage to one person.

---

*U.S. Census Bureau, *Current Population Reports*, "America's Families and Living Arrangements" for 2010 (Table UC3), available online at www.census.gov/population/www/socdemo/hh-fam/cps2010.html.

polygyny

A form of marriage in which a man is married to more than one woman at the same time.

polyandry

A form of marriage in which a woman is married to more than one man at the same time.

Polygyny has been the most prevalent form of polygamy among the world's preliterate societies (Ford & Beach, 1951; Frayser, 1985). **Polyandry** is relatively rare. In polygynous societies, including many Islamic societies, men are permitted to have multiple wives. Practically speaking, in many cases, only wealthy men can afford to support multiple wives and the children of these unions. But few societies have enough women to allow most men to have multiple wives.

ARRANGED MARRIAGE   Traditional societies such as those of modern-day India and Pakistan and in olden Europe frequently use arranged marriages, in which the families of the bride and groom more or less arrange for the union (Harris, 2015; Stopes-Roe & Cochrane, 2011). Arranged marriage by traditional Jewish families was one of the main themes of the musical *Fiddler on the Roof*.

As in *Fiddler*, one of the purposes of arranged marriage is to make certain that the bride and groom come from similar backgrounds so that they will carry on their families' religious and cultural traditions. Supporters of arranged marriage argue that it is wiser to follow family wisdom than one's own heart, especially because the attraction couples feel is often infatuation and not a deep, abiding love. Couples also begin arranged marriages with low expectations and are then pleasantly surprised when things go reasonably well. Proponents also claim a lower divorce rate for arranged marriages than for "self-arranged marriages," but it must be noted that couples who enter arranged marriages are also more traditional.

OTHER WRINKLES IN MARRIAGE   Marriages are generally based on the expectation of sexual exclusivity. Alternative or nontraditional lifestyles, however, such as open marriages and group marriages, permit intimate relationships with people outside the marriage. Such alternative lifestyles attracted a flurry of attention during the heyday of the sexual revolution in the 1960s and 1970s, but even then were more often talked about than practiced (Davis, 2010). Today, they find still fewer adherents.

Then of course there is same-sex marriage, which we discussed in detail in Chapter 5.

WHOM DO WE MARRY: ARE MARRIAGES MADE IN HEAVEN OR IN THE NEIGHBORHOOD?   In contemporary Western culture, mate selection is presumably free. Parents seldom arrange marriages, although they may still encourage their child to date that wonderful son or daughter of the solid churchgoing couple who lives down the street. Nevertheless, factors such as race, social class, religion, and level of education often—but clearly not always—determine the categories of people within which we seek mates. People in our culture tend to marry others from the same geographical area, social class, and religion (Braithwaite et al., 2015b; Schramm et al., 2012; Schwartz & Mare, 2012). Because neighborhoods are often made up of people from a similar social class, storybook marriages like Cinderella's are the exception to the rule.

We tend to choose mates who are similar to us in physical attractiveness and attitudes. As relationships progress through stages such as meeting, dating, perhaps cohabiting, and marriage, we tend to become more selective—that is, to narrow our choices to people yet more similar to us in background, attitudes, and interests (Schramm et al., 2012; Schwartz & Mare, 2012). We are more often than not similar to our mates in height, weight, personality traits, intelligence, engagement in exercise, even on use of alcohol and tobacco (Ask et al., 2012; Vinkhuyzen et al., 2012). We also tend to think about whether potential mates are likely to meet our material, sexual, and psychological needs.

Singing the song "Tradition." In the musical *Fiddler on the Roof*, the tradition of arranged marriage comes into conflict with the preferences of the younger generation.

A Case of Attraction–Similarity?
Although there are many—many!—exceptions, we tend to marry people who are similar to us in physical appeal and attitudes. We also tend to be similar in height and weight, intelligence, and even use of alcohol and other drugs.

The concept of "like marrying like" is termed **homogamy**. Most of the time, we also marry people of the same racial and ethnic background, educational level, and religion. Even so, more and more Americans are intermarrying because of love.

We also tend to follow *age homogamy*—to select a partner who falls in one's own age range (Gustafson & Fransson, 2015; Michael et al., 1994). Age homogamy may reflect the tendency to marry early in adulthood. Persons who marry late or who remarry tend not to select partners so close in age. Bridegrooms tend to be 2 to 5 years older than their wives, on average, in European, North American, and South American countries (Buss, 1994).

Some marriages also show a mating gradient. The stereotype has been that an economically established older man would take an attractive, younger woman as his wife. But by and large, we are attracted to and marry the boy or girl (almost) next door or at the office. Most marriages seem to be made not in heaven, but in the neighborhood.

All in all, keep in mind that we become attracted to people we meet and spend time with. You are a college student. If you are young and single—not a returning student, and not an online student—you may be meeting people who are more diverse in background and ethnicity than those who are nearby "at home." Therefore, you might find yourself becoming attracted to individuals who are in many ways more different from you than you would have anticipated in, say, high school. On the other hand, some students go to colleges that will have students who are yet more like them than were those at home, as in the case of students who enroll at Catholic colleges or Protestant evangelical colleges. They are seeking people who are yet more like them than they found at home, and they may set firm limits on whom they will consider as potential partners. Of course, if those relationships do not work out, and they are in a different city 10 years later, …

MARITAL SEX Patterns of marital sexuality vary across cultures, yet anthropologists note common threads. Privacy for sexual relations is valued in almost all cultures. Most cultures also place restrictions on sex during menstruation, during some stages of pregnancy, and for a while after childbirth.

Until the sexual revolution of the 1960s and 1970s, Western culture could have been characterized as restrictive, even toward marital sex. We usually think of

homogamy

The practice of marrying people who are similar in social background and standing. (From the Greek roots *homos*, meaning "same," and *gamos*, meaning "marriage.")

the sexual revolution in terms of the changes in sexual behaviors and attitudes that occurred among young, unmarried people. But the revolution also ushered in profound changes in marital sexuality. Compared to Kinsey's "pre-revolution" samples from the late 1930s and 1940s, married couples today experiment more with sex, and do so for longer periods of time. They report greater sexual satisfaction. The sexual revolution helped dislodge the view that sexual pleasure is meant for men and that it is the duty of women to satisfy their husbands' sexual needs. Scientific findings were also liberalizing influences. Kinsey's and Masters and Johnson's findings that normal women were capable not only of orgasm but also of multiple orgasms punctured traditional beliefs that sexual gratification was the birthright of men. TV shows, films, and radio talk shows began to portray women as sexual initiators who enjoy sex. The affluence of the post-World War II years also encouraged more young people to pursue a college education and live away from home. College liberates not only through exposure to great books and scientific knowledge but also through interaction with students from different backgrounds.

The development of effective contraceptives separated sex from reproduction. Motives for sexual pleasure became more open. All these liberalizing forces have led to changes in the frequency of marital sex and in techniques of foreplay and coitus since Kinsey's day (Eisenberg et al., 2010).

Married women in Kinsey's sample reported an average (median) length of foreplay of about 12 minutes. Kinsey found that men at lower educational levels engaged in briefer foreplay, generally lasting but a minute or two before penetration. The length of foreplay rose to 5 to 15 minutes among college-educated men. Marital foreplay has gained in duration and variety since Kinsey's day. Couples in more recent surveys report using a wider variety of foreplay techniques, including oral stimulation of the breasts and oral–genital contact (Laumann et al., 1994).

How often do married couples engage in coitus? Table 11.7 summarizes results from the Kinsey surveys. The frequency of coitus was negatively related to age. That is, older couples engaged in coitus less frequently.

Married men and women in the National Survey of Family Growth reported engaging in sexual relations 5 to 6 times a month (Eisenberg et al., 2010). These figures are not all that different from Kinsey's.

The frequency of sexual relations declines with age, however (Eisenberg et al., 2010; Schroder & Schmiedeberg, 2015). At the ages of 50 to 59, for example, people reported an average of sexual relations 4 to 5 times per month. Regardless of a couple's age, sexual frequency also appears to decline with the duration of the relationship (Schroder & Schmiedeberg, 2015). Novelty apparently heightens interest in sex.

METHODS OF COITUS   In coitus, as in foreplay, the marital bed since Kinsey's day has become a stage on which the players act more varied roles. Today's couples use greater variety in positions.

As many as 70% of Kinsey's males used the male-superior position only (Kinsey et al., 1948). Perhaps 3 couples in 10 used the female-superior position frequently. Approximately 1 in 4 or 5 couples used the lateral-entry position frequently, and about 1 in 10 couples used the rear-entry position. Younger and more highly educated men showed greater variety, however. An important difference between Kinsey's and the NHSLS samples involves the length of intercourse. In Kinsey's time it was widely believed that the "virile" man ejaculated rapidly during intercourse. Kinsey estimated that most men reached orgasm within 2 minutes after penetration, many within 10 or 20 seconds. Yet some clinicians at the time were already asserting that a man's ejaculation was "premature" unless he delayed it until his partner was ready to reach orgasm. Men now spend more time on their partner's needs: The "duration of the last sexual event" of three out of four married couples was 15 minutes to an hour (Michael et al., 1994).

Table 11.7 Median Weekly Frequency of Marital Sexual Relations, Male and Female Estimates Combined, According to the Kinsey Surveys

Age	Frequency
16–25	2.45
26–35	1.95
36–45	1.40
46–55	0.85
55–60	0.50

SOURCES: A. C. Kinsey, W. B. Pomeroy, and C. E. Martin, (1948). *Sexual behavior in the human male.* Philadelphia: W. B. Saunders; A. C. Kinsey, W. B. Pomeroy, C. E. Martin, and P. H. Gebhard. (1953). *Sexual behavior in the human female.* Philadelphia: W. B. Saunders.

MARITAL SATISFACTION   Marital satisfaction is a complex phenomenon that includes the following (Wilcox & Marquardt, 2011):

- Commitment
- Adequate income (yes, money matters)
- Sharing housework
- Generosity toward one's spouse (Dew & Wilcox, 2011)
- The support of one's family and friends (yes, in-laws can make a difference one way or the other)
- Agreement on attitudes toward having and raising children
- Sexual satisfaction, and
- For many couples, belief in the religious or spiritual value of marriage (George et al., 2015)

There are many ways to view the link between sexual satisfaction and marital satisfaction. Does marital satisfaction lead to feelings of attraction and sexual desire for one's spouse? Does "good sex" contribute to happiness with a marriage? The answer to both questions is likely yes.

Now consider the spiritual value of marriage. There's little doubt about it: The data obtained by the National Marriage Project (Wilcox & Marquardt, 2011) do show that people who believe that their marriage fulfills a religious need or value and who attend church (or the synagogue or the mosque) regularly tend to be happier with their marriages and less prone to getting divorced. Does this finding mean that you should look for or develop a spiritual value or role for your marriage even if you don't believe in it? It's not something you can fake. You can also be completely committed to your marriage—or not—regardless of your religious beliefs.

Now let's talk a bit more about sexual satisfaction. One index of sexual satisfaction is orgasmic consistency. For women, sexual satisfaction is positively correlated with orgasmic consistency and the frequency with which partners stimulate their genitals, and negatively correlated with masturbation (Klapilová et al., 2015). For men, sexual satisfaction is positively correlated with the frequency of penile–vaginal intercourse and their partner's orgasm. A higher frequency of intercourse and female orgasmic consistency predicts sexual satisfaction in both sexes. We can infer that it is usually easier for the man to reach orgasm, so the woman's reaching orgasm is a sign of the success of their sexual partnership.

The National Health and Social Life Survey (NHSLS) found that more than 90% of the men and about 70% of women reported reaching orgasm "always" or "usually" with their primary partner during the 12 months before the survey (Carpenter et al., 2009). Seventy-five percent of men and almost 29% of women reported reaching orgasm every time. Only 2% of the married women reported never reaching orgasm with their husbands during the past year.

Women in their 40s were somewhat more likely to reach orgasm than younger and older women. Women in their 40s have presumably have had more opportunity to learn about their sexuality and are more secure in their relationships than younger women are. Married women were most likely to reach orgasm consistently, followed by cohabiting women, then single women. Security apparently promotes orgasmic consistency.

More recent analysis of the NHSLS data by Laura Carpenter and her colleagues (2009) found that among 1,053 heterosexual women and men aged 40 to 59, women were less likely to be sexually satisfied than men were. Interestingly, there was an apparent reversal of gender-role stereotypes among these people in midlife: Women's emotional satisfaction was closely related to their "bodily sexual practices"—that is, to what sources of sexual stimulation they received—whereas the men's physical satisfaction was relatively more strongly related to factors in the relationship.

Critical Thinking
Agree or disagree with the following statement, and support your answer: Marriage is an old-fashioned, outdated lifestyle that has become irrelevant for today's sophisticated young people.

Q *How can I keep my partner interested in sex? We have been together for 5 years.*

A Do you have any "barriers" to sex? Kids running into the room? Incredibly stressful jobs? Impossibly long commutes? Fatigue? (Too much) alcohol? If so, you may want to consider reengineering your life in general. But if you've just got a little sexual boredom going, you may want to remember that the greatest aphrodisiac is variety. How about a new perfume or cologne? How about a change in hairstyle? Nightclothes or lingerie? How about a weekend away? How about trying something new? A 75-year-old endocrinologist said he and his wife watched pornography while they were having sex. He said it was pretty much a yawner for her, but she appreciated what it did for him. In sum: Remove barriers. Create novelty. And if you happen to be a 75-year-old endocrinologist . . .

Infidelity

LO 11.9 **Discuss infidelity.**

President Bill Clinton. Senator John Ensign. Senator John Edwards. Representative Newt Gingrich. Governor Elliot Spitzer. Senator David Vitter. Governor Mark Sanford. Governor David Paterson. What do these left-wing, right-wing, and "moderate" politicians have in common? They have all admittedly engaged in marital infidelity. They are not alone.

Some people engage in extramarital sex for variety (Balon, 2015). Some have affairs to break the routine of a confining marriage (Balon, 2015; Friedman, 2015). Others enter affairs for reasons similar to the nonsexual reasons adolescents often have for sex: as a way of expressing hostility toward a spouse or retaliating for injustice. Husbands and wives who engage in affairs often report that they are not satisfied with or fulfilled by their marital relationships. Curiosity and desire for personal growth are often more prominent motives than marital dissatisfaction. Middle-aged people may have affairs to boost their self-esteem or to prove that they are still attractive.

Many times the sexual motive is less pressing than the desire for emotional closeness. Some women say they are seeking someone whom they can talk to or communicate with (Lamanna & Riedmann, 2005). There is a sex difference here (Friedman, 2015b; Petersen & Hyde, 2011). According to Janis Abrahms Spring, author of *After the Affair*, women are usually seeking "soul mates," whereas men are seeking "playmates." Women tend to justify affairs when they are for love, but men do so when the affair is *not* for love.

Women are less accepting of sex without emotional involvement (Petersen & Hyde, 2011). Men are more likely than women to distinguish between sex and love, whereas women see love and sex as going together so that falling in love justifies sex (Petersen & Hyde, 2011). But these are *group* differences. Many individual men are interested primarily in the extramarital relationship rather than the sex per se. Similarly, some women are out for the sex and not the relationship.

From an evolutionary perspective, infidelity can be seen as a short-term mating strategy—one that is more adaptive for men than women. Infidelity increases the opportunity for men to spread their "seed," but women, who can bear and rear only relatively few offspring, are more likely to achieve reproductive success within the environment of a protective pair-bond. Genetic factors associated with the action of the hormones vasopressin and oxytocin—which are involved in pair bonding—may play a role in infidelity (Balon, 2015; Zietsch et al., 2015). Australian psychologist Brendan Zietsch and his colleagues (2015) found that a large number of women who engage in extramarital affairs show variation in receptors for vasopressin, suggesting that they may be less likely to form monogamous pair bonds. Swedish researcher Hasse Walum and his colleagues (2012) found that men and women with variants in the receptor genes for both oxytocin and vasopressin were less likely to form strong pair-bonds and experience marital satisfaction. Blocking the reception of oxytocin in the brains of species of monogamous mice apparently impairs their pair-bonding; that is, they stray (Walum et al., 2015). Conversely, enhancing the availability of oxytocin in the brains of species of mice that do not normally form pair-bonds apparently makes them faithful to the next mouse with whom they couple (Walum et al., 2015).

"So," asks psychiatrist Richard Friedman (2015b), "do we get a moral pass if we happen to carry ... 'infidelity' genes? Hardly. We don't choose our genes and can't control them (yet), but we can usually decide what we do with the emotions and impulses they help create." Also keep in mind that not all humans who stray have variants of vasopressin and oxytocin receptor genes. But these genes may play a role.

PATTERNS OF INFIDELITY   Let us begin with a few definitions. **Extramarital sex** is usually conducted without the spouse's knowledge or approval. Secret affairs are referred to as **conventional adultery**, infidelity, or simply "cheating." Conventional adultery runs the gamut from the "one-night stand" to the affair that persists for years. In **consensual adultery**, extramarital relationships are conducted openly—that is, with the knowledge and consent of the partner. In what is called **swinging**, or *mate-swapping* the partner participates.

How many people "cheat" on their spouses? Viewers of TV talk shows may get the impression that everyone cheats, but reliable surveys paint a different picture. More than 90% of the married women and 75% of the married men in the NHSLS reported remaining loyal to their spouses (Laumann et al., 1994). The vast majority of people who were cohabiting also reported that they were sexually faithful to their partners. But results from the Laumann group reported more recently find that the lifetime rate of infidelity for men aged 60 and older increased to 28% in 2006, up from 20% in 1991 (Parker-Pope, 2008a). For older women, the lifetime incidence rose to 15%, up from 5% in 1991. The researchers also found changes in newer marriages. About 20% of the men and 15% of the women younger than age 35 say they were unfaithful at some time, up from about 15% for men and 12% for women in 1991. A *USA Today*/Gallup Poll found that 54% of respondents said they personally knew someone who had been unfaithful (Blow, 2009).

Having presented the percentages of reported extramarital sex, we point out that these reports cannot be verified. People may be reluctant to reveal they have "cheated" even when they are assured of anonymity (Parker-Pope, 2008a). One study surveyed 4,884 married women, using both face-to-face interviews and anonymous computer questionnaires (Whisman & Snyder, 2007). Only 1% of women said they had been unfaithful during the previous year in the face-to-face interviews. However, 6% of the same sample admitted to infidelity on the computer questionnaire.

ATTITUDES TOWARD INFIDELITY   Although Americans, especially younger Americans, may not see marriage as "very important" anymore, they still seem to value keeping one's promises. About 9 out of 10 Americans say that affairs are "always wrong" or "almost always wrong" (Friedman, 2015b). Most married couples embrace monogamy as the cornerstone of their relationship.

extramarital sex
Sexual relations between a married person and someone other than his or her spouse.

conventional adultery
Extramarital sex that is kept hidden from one's spouse.

consensual adultery
Extramarital sex that is engaged in openly with the knowledge and consent of one's spouse.

swinging
A form of consensual adultery in which both spouses share extramarital sexual experiences. Also referred to as *mate-swapping*.

SEX IN THE DIGITAL AGE

WHAT HAPPENS WHEN YOUR EXTRAMARITAL AFFAIR BECOMES EXPOSED TO 7 BILLION PEOPLE, GIVE OR TAKE A FEW?

Ashley Madison, as most of the developed world knows by now, is the name of one of the most popular dating Web sites. It differs a bit from match.com and eHarmony.com because people sign up to engage in extramarital affairs. When you check out the splash page, it says that the dating service is intended for "discreet" affairs. It boasts a "Trusted Security Award" and claims to be a "Secure Site." Users can begin their online adventures with a pseudonym and list their sexual preferences and turn-ons. Users start to pay for the service once they begin chatting and exchanging photos with other members (Grandoni, 2015).

Despite the promise of security, the Web site was hacked in 2015. In one of the clearest displays of the value of the maxim, "Buyer Beware," information about members' communications was released to anyone who cared to search for it. The Web site had long guaranteed that they could scrub their profiles and activities from the site for a fee of $19. But computer experts say this information is never completely wiped clean; rather, the normally used access information is deleted. Therefore, there are workarounds, some of which are relatively simple searches. One experts says, "Once something is published on the Internet, it's there forever" (Grandoli, 2015).

In case you think that cheating on spouses is rare, Ashley Madison held personal

www.ashleymadison.com uses an advertising photo similar to this one to suggest that its information about which married person is hooking up with whom is kept under the rug. Ashley Madison billboards advertise "Life is short, have an affair." Although the "shhh" appears to promise confidentiality, the site was recently hacked and the identities of millions of subscribers were exposed, leading to divorces and some suicides.

information on about 37 million members (gasp), 10,000 of whom were U.S. government officials (double gasp), and even a few celebrities (yawn) (Grandoni, 2015; Perlroth, 2015). Thinking about the government officials for a moment, they are required to live spotless lives so that they do not become subject to blackmail. On the other hand, now that their information has been released, there may be little left to blackmail them about.

For many site users, the results have been devastating. "Kimberly" confronted her husband when she found he was using the Web site. She told him to pack up and leave, even though she isn't completely certain whether he actually had affairs. "I'm done," she says. "Even if it's just him on there looking. I don't trust him" (cited in Pagliery, 2015). "Stacy" says that her soon-to-be-divorced husband's Ashley Madison membership "proves his adulterous behavior. It [will] give me more ability to negotiate what I'm requesting in the settlement" (Pagliery, 2015). "Ana" is finalizing a divorce and generally unconcerned about her sexual exploits becoming known to her husband, but she does fear that her behavior might look suspect at he financial firm where she works, possibly causing her to be fired (Pagliery, 2015). Canadian police reported at least two suicides related to exposure of extramarital behavior (Perlroth, 2015).

9 › T /F   Truth or Fiction Revisited   It is *not* true that most of today's sophisticated young people see nothing wrong with an occasional extramarital fling. The sexual revolution never extended itself to infidelity—at least among most married people. The difference apparently has to do with the fact that married people have made a commitment to one another to remain faithful.

EFFECTS OF INFIDELITY   The discovery of infidelity can evoke a range of emotional responses. The spouse may be filled with anger, jealousy, and even shame. Feelings of inadequacy and doubts about one's attractiveness and desirability may surface. Infidelity may be seen by the betrayed spouse as a serious breach of trust and intimacy. Marriages that are not terminated in the wake of the disclosure may survive in a damaged condition.

Women more often than men intertwine sex with relationships, and men might not view their own infidelity as a reason to leave a primary relationship. Women are more concerned about remaining monogamous. Therefore, if a woman is sleeping with another man, she may already have a foot out the door. A wife's affair may be an unforgivable blow to the husband's ego or pride (Rasmussen & Kilborne, 2008). A woman may be more likely to see the transgression as a threat to the structure of her life.

Divorce: Breaking Bonds

LO 11.10 Discuss the incidence of divorce and issues connected with divorce.

> My wife and I were considering a divorce, but after pricing lawyers we decided to buy a new car instead.
>
> —*Henny Youngman*

> Whenever I date a guy, I think, is this the man I want my children to spend their weekends with?
>
> —*Rita Rudner*

Some 40 to 50% of the Marriages in the United States end in divorce (Wilcox & Marquardt, 2010, 2011). The divorce rate in the United States rose steadily from 1960 to 1980, then declined gradually before leveling off in the 2000s (see Figure 11.19). Divorced women outnumber divorced men, in part because men are more likely to remarry.

Why did the incidence of divorce rise in the 1960s? Until the mid-1960s, adultery was the only legal grounds for divorce in most states. But no-fault divorce laws have been enacted in nearly every state, allowing a divorce to be granted without a finding of marital misconduct. The increased economic independence of women has also contributed to the divorce rate. More women today have the economic means of breaking away from a troubled marriage, and, in male–female marriages, about two divorces in three are initiated by women (Doherty 2014). Today, more people consider marriage an alterable condition than in prior generations.

People today also hold higher expectations of marriage than did their parents or grandparents. They expect marriage to be personally fulfilling as well as an institution for family life and rearing children. Most people want to be happy in marriage. Today, the most common reasons given by women for divorce are problems in communication and a lack of understanding. Key predictors of divorce today include husband's criticism, defensiveness, contempt, and stonewalling—not lack of financial support (Horan et al., 2015; Mahoney & Knudson-Martin, 2009).

On the other hand, the following factors decrease the chances of getting divorced (Wilcox & Marquardt, 2011):

- Having a high annual income
- Having a baby 7 months or more after getting married, as opposed to having a baby before getting married
- Getting married when you're older than 25 years of age, as opposed to being a teenager
- Having an intact family of origin, rather than parents who are separated or divorced
- Having a religious affiliation
- Having a college education

But as is the case with martial satisfaction, starting to go to church or to try to believe in God (if you don't already) isn't going to save a troubled marriage. Nor has anyone ever shown that getting a college education in order to save a marriage works! These are all "selection factors"—meaning, in a nutshell, that if you belong to one of these groups, your marriage has a better chance of surviving. But trying to join one of these groups to save a marriage makes no sense. Work on the marriage instead.

THE COST OF DIVORCE   Divorce is usually connected with financial and emotional problems. When a household splits, the resources often cannot maintain the previous standard of living for each partner. Divorce hits women in the pocketbook harder than men. According to a Population Reference Bureau report, a woman's household income drops by about 24% (Bianchi & Spain, 1997). A man's income declines by about 6%. Women who have not pursued a career may have to struggle to compete with younger, more experienced workers. Divorced mothers often face the combined stress of having the sole responsibility for childrearing and the need to increase their incomes. Divorced fathers may find it difficult to pay alimony and child support while establishing a new lifestyle.

Divorce can also prompt feelings of failure as a spouse and parent, loneliness and uncertainty about the future, and depression. Married people appear to be better able to cope with the stresses and strains of life, perhaps because they can lend each other emotional support. Divorced and separated people have the highest rates of physical and mental illness (Levite & Cohen, 2012; Meadows, 2009). They also have high rates of suicide (Donald et al., 2006; Milner et al., 2012). On the other hand, divorce may permit personal growth and renewal—an opportunity to take stock of oneself and establish a new, more rewarding life.

Children are often the biggest losers when parents get a divorce, yet chronic marital conflict is also connected with psychological distress in children (Robbers et al., 2011). Boys have greater problems adjusting to conflict or divorce, such as having conduct problems at school and increased anxiety and dependence. The children of divorce are more likely to have psychological problems and conduct disorders, have lower self-esteem, abuse drugs and alcohol, and do more poorly in school (Amato, 2006; Fletcher & Sindelar, 2012). There are individual differences in all of this, and boys tend to fare worse than girls (Kim, 2011). But, by and large, the fallout for children is at its worst during the first year after the breakup. Children tend to rebound in a year or two.

Researchers attribute children's problems following divorce not only to the divorce itself but also to a consequent decline in the quality of parenting. Children's adjustment is enhanced when both parents maintain parenting responsibilities and set aside their differences long enough to agree on childrearing practices (Hetherington, 2006). Children of divorce also benefit when their parents avoid saying negative things about each other in the children's presence (Hetherington, 2006; Kim, 2011).

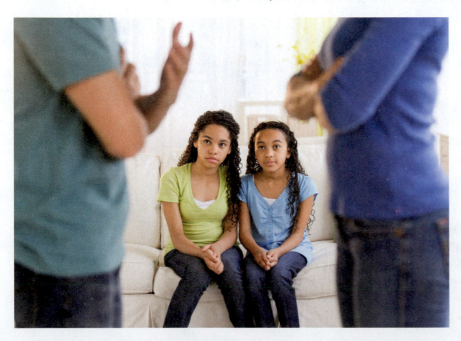

Despite the difficulties in adjustment, most divorced people eventually bounce back. Most remarry. Among older people, divorced men are more likely than divorced women to remarry—in part because men usually die earlier than women (and so fewer prospective husbands are available), and in part because older men tend to remarry younger women (Wilcox & Marquardt, 2011).

LIFE IN BLENDED FAMILIES: HIS, HERS, THEIRS, AND ... Because of the high incidence of divorce and remarriage, the stepfamily is becoming a more common family unit in the United States. Although many stepfamilies disband, often because of conflict over stepchildren (such as parental favoritism for their own [Golish, 2003; Hofferth & Anderson, 2003]), levels of happiness in others can be as high as they were in original marriages (Braithwaite et al., 2001). In any event, one child in eight is living in a stepfamily (National Stepfamily Resource Center, 2015).

The rule of thumb about the effects of living in stepfamilies is that there is no rule of thumb. Living in a stepfamily may have no measurable psychological effects (Coleman et al., 2000). Stepparents may claim stepchildren as their own (Marsiglio, 2004). One study of the effects of stepparenting on middle schoolers found that good stepmother–stepchild relationships were linked with less aggressive behavior in both boys and girls and with higher self-esteem among stepdaughters (Anderson et al., 1999). But not everything comes up roses in stepfamilies. There are some risks. Infanticide (killing infants) is a rarity in the United States, but the crime occurs much more often in stepfamilies than in families with biological kinship (Daly & Wilson, 2003, 2005). There is also a significantly higher incidence of sexual abuse by stepparents than by natural parents.

Why do we find these risks in stepfamilies? According to evolutionary psychologists, people often behave as if they want their genes to flourish in the next generation. Thus, it could be that stepparents are less devoted to rearing the children of other people than their own. They may even see "foreign" children as competitors for resources with their own children. Or a stepfather may see a woman's possession of children by another man as lessening her capacity to bear and rear his children (Daly & Wilson, 2003, 2005).

Sex in the Later Years

LO 11.11 **Describe physical changes in the later years and how they affect sexual behavior.**

What is the fastest growing segment of the U.S. population? People age 65 and older. The "graying" of the United States may have a profound effect on our views of the sexuality of older people. Many people think of sex as appropriate only for the young. This belief falls within a constellation of unfounded cultural myths about older people, which includes the notions that older people are sexless, older people with sexual urges are abnormal, and older men with sexual interests are "dirty old men."

Researchers find that sexual daydreaming, sex drive, and sexual activity may decline with age, whereas negative sexual attitudes may increase (Loe, 2012). However, research does not support the belief that people lose their sexuality as they age (Connaughton & McCabe, 2015; Laumann et al., 2006). Most older people report that they like sex, and a majority report that orgasm is important to their sexual fulfillment. Sexual activity among older people, as among other groups, is influenced not only by physical structures and changes but also by psychological well-being, feelings of intimacy, and cultural expectations (Loe, 2012).

Physical Changes

Although many older people retain the capacity to respond sexually, physical changes do occur as the years pass (see Table 11.8). If we are aware of them, we will not view them

Sex in the Later Years? The stereotype suggests that the sex lives of older people are behind them. As goes the song from *Porgy and Bess*, "It ain't necessarily so."

Table 11.8 Changes in Sexual Response Connected With Aging

Changes in the Female	Changes in the Male
Reduced muscle tension (myotonia)	Longer time to achieve erection and orgasm
Reduced lubrication	Need for more direct stimulation to achieve erection and orgasm
Reduced elasticity in the vaginal walls	Less semen emitted during ejaculation
Smaller increases in breast size during sexual arousal	Softer erections
Reduced intensity of spasms of orgasm	Testicles may not elevate as high before ejaculation
	Reduced intensity of spasms of orgasm
	Less felt need to ejaculate
	Longer refractory period

SOURCE: Based on *The Kinsey Institute New Report on Sex*, 1990, p. 227. Reprinted by permission of The Kinsey Institute for Research in Sex, Gender, and Reproduction, Inc.

as abnormal or find ourselves unprepared to cope with them. Many potential problems can be averted by changing our expectations or making behavioral changes to accommodate aging.

Let's not start this section with a deeply biological focus on changes in cells, hormones, and the like. Let's talk first about what happens when we look in the mirror. Many of us are dismayed by visible changes that occur as we age. We develop wrinkles. Our hair turns gray. Our muscle tone decreases. We tend to put on weight, especially if we do not exercise regularly. All in all, we are likely to feel less attractive than we did. And the fact is that our partners may find us to be less attractive. Nevertheless, in enduring intimate relationships, feelings of love, intimacy, and sharing life can outweigh those changes and feelings. But if we are single in our later years, perhaps because of divorce or becoming widowed, the future, including the sexual future, may look more bleak.

Yet, older people can also lead sexually fulfilling lives. If they fine-tune their expectations, they may find themselves leading some of the most sexually fulfilling years of their lives (McCarthy & Pierpaoli, 2015; Menard et al., 2015).

CHANGES IN THE FEMALE Many of the physical changes in older women stem from decline in the production of estrogen. The vaginal walls lose much elasticity and the thick, corrugated texture of the childbearing years. The vaginal walls grow paler and thinner, perhaps making coitus irritating to the walls. Also, the thinning of the walls may place greater pressure against the bladder and urethra during sex, leading now and then to urinary urgency and burning urination. The condition may persist for days.

The vagina also shrinks. The labia majora lose much of their fatty deposits and thin. The introitus constricts, and penile entry may become difficult. On the other hand, increased friction between the penis and vaginal walls may heighten sexual sensations. Following menopause, there is atrophy (loss of tissue) in the genital region. Women also produce less vaginal lubrication, and lubrication may take minutes, not seconds, to appear. Lack of adequate lubrication is a key reason for painful coitus. As noted in Chapter 2, these vaginal changes can lead to loss of intimacy with women's partners and decreases in enjoyment of sex (North American Menopause Society, 2013). It can generally reduce women's quality of life. Although many men who are partnered with women see the effects of menopause as a shared process, they are generally not sure what to do about it, how to help. On the other hand, they also realized that menopause "liberated" the partnership from contraceptive constraints (Liao et al., 2015).

Many of these changes may be slowed or reversed through estrogen-replacement therapy, although estrogen replacement has its hazards (see Chapter 2). Natural lubrication may be increased through more elaborate foreplay. Older men too will likely need more time to become aroused. An artificial lubricant can also ease problems in penile entry and thrusting.

Women's breasts show smaller increases in size with sexual arousal as they age, but the nipples still become erect. Because the muscle tone of the urethra and anal sphincters decreases, the spasms of orgasm become less powerful and fewer in number. Thus, orgasms may feel less intense, but the subjective experience of orgasm may remain satisfying.

10 › T /F Truth or Fiction Revisited Despite loss of muscle tone and decreases in lubrication, most women actually retain their ability to reach orgasm well into their advanced years. Nevertheless, the uterine contractions that occur during orgasm may become discouragingly painful for some older women.

CHANGES IN THE MALE Age-related changes tend to occur more gradually in men than women and are not clearly connected with any one biological event (Loe, 2012). Male adolescents may achieve erection in seconds through sexual fantasy alone. After about age 50, men take progressively longer to achieve erection. Erections become less firm, perhaps because of lowered testosterone levels (Laumann et al., 2006). Older men may require prolonged direct stimulation of the penis to obtain an erection. Couples can adjust to these changes by extending the length and variety of foreplay.

Erectile dysfunction is not inevitable with aging, but it becomes increasingly common. If we look at population growth in late adulthood, and consider the findings of the Massachusetts Male Aging Study, which predicted more than 600,000 new cases annually in the year 2000, we can now expect approximately 1 million new cases of erectile dysfunction in the United States each year. Erectile dysfunction is associated with aging, cardiovascular problems (and the statins used to reduce cholesterol!), diabetes, a sedentary life style, overweight, and even glaucoma (Besiroglu et al., 2015).

Men generally require more time to reach orgasm as they age, which may reflect lowered testosterone levels. Testosterone production usually declines gradually from about age 40 to age 60 and can also lead to erectile dysfunction (Luo et al., 2015). However, the declines in testosterone levels and sexual functioning are not inevitable and may be related to the man's general health. Sperm production tends to decline as the seminiferous tubules degenerate, but viable sperm may be produced by men in their 70s, 80s, and 90s. But aging increases the chances of having children with genetic and chromosomal disorders, as in women.

Nocturnal erections tend to diminish in intensity, duration, and frequency as men age, but they do not normally disappear in healthy men (Loe, 2012). The refractory period tends to lengthen with age. An adolescent may require but a few minutes to regain erection and ejaculate again after a first orgasm, whereas a man in his 30s may require half an hour. Past age 50, the refractory period may increase to hours.

Older men produce less ejaculate, and it may seep out rather than shoot out. The contractions of orgasm become weaker and fewer. Still, an older male may enjoy orgasm as thoroughly as he did at a younger age. Following orgasm, erection subsides more rapidly than in a younger man.

Q *I caught my grandparents having sex. Now they will not talk to me, and they act differently toward me. What can I do?*

A Lesson for everyone: You gotta knock. Or you have to say "Anyone home?" or whatever, when entering someone's home. Your grandparents aren't talking to you? They're embarrassed, and for a number of reasons. One is that they were likely brought up in more traditional times. There is also the stereotype that sex is for young people. Why not drop them a handwritten note (without a return address so that they'll open it). Say you're sorry you didn't knock or whatever. Ask them to forgive you. And say something humorous like you wish your love life was as good as theirs. If you do that and they don't get over it, you tried. End of story.

Patterns of Sexual Activity

Despite the decline in physical functions, older people can continue to lead a fulfilling sex life. Years of sexual experience may more than compensate for any diminution of physical response (McCarthy & Pierpaoli, 2015; Menard et al., 2015). Coital frequency tends to decline with age. Several factors play a role in declining activity, including physical problems, boredom, and cultural attitudes. Despite general trends, sexuality among older people is variable (Menard et al., 2015). Many older people engage in intercourse, oral sex, and masturbation as often (or more) as when they were younger; some become disgusted by sex; others simply lose interest.

Couples may accommodate the physical changes of aging by broadening their sexual repertoire to include more diverse forms of stimulation. Many older people report using petting, oral–genital stimulation, sexual fantasy, pornography, anal stimulation, vibrators, and other techniques to offset problems in achieving lubrication or erection. Sexual satisfaction may be derived from manual or oral stimulation, cuddling, caressing, petting, and tenderness—all of which have been summarized as "good enough sex, or GES" (McCarthy & Pierpaoli, 2015)—as well as intercourse to orgasm. The availability of a sexually interested and supportive partner may be the most important determinant of continued sexual activity (McCarthy et al., 2013; Menard et al., 2015).

Sex and Disability

LO 11. 12 Discuss the relationships between disabilities and sexual behavior.

Like older people, people with disabilities (especially those whose physical disabilities render them dependent on others) are often stereotyped as sexless and childlike. Such views are based on misconceptions about the sexual functioning of people with disabilities. Some of these myths and stereotypes may be eroding, however, in part because of the success of the civil and social rights movements, and in part because of the attention focused on the sexuality of people with disabilities in films such as *Born on the Fourth of July* and *My Left Foot*.

A person may have been born with or acquire a bodily impairment or may suffer a loss of function or a disfiguring change in appearance. Although the disability may require the person to make adjustments to perform sexually, most people with disabilities have the same sexual needs, feelings, and desires as people without disabilities. Their ability to express their sexual feelings and needs depends on the physical limitations imposed by their disabilities, their adjustment to their disabilities, and the availability of partners. The establishment of mature sexual relationships generally demands some distance from one's parents. Therefore, people with disabilities who are physically dependent on their parents may find it especially difficult to develop sexual relationships. Parents who acknowledge their children's sexual development can be helpful by facilitating dating. Far too often, parents become overprotective.

Physical Disabilities

According to researchers in the field of sexuality and physical disability (Eisenberg et al., 2015; Nosek, 2011), sexual wellness, among the disabled, as among the population at large, involves:

- Positive sexual self-concept; seeing oneself as valuable sexually and as a person
- Knowledge about sexuality
- Positive, productive relationships
- Coping with barriers to sexuality (social, environmental, physical, and emotional)
- Maintaining the best possible general and sexual health, given one's limitations

This model applies to all of us, of course. Let us now consider aspects of specific physical disabilities and human sexuality.

MULTIPLE SCLEROSIS Multiple sclerosis (MS) is a chronic, unpredictable disease that affects the nervous system. The tissue called *myelin*, which surrounds and protects nerve cells, disintegrates and leaves scar tissue in its place. MS impairs sexual functioning, and people with MS report more sexual problems than people without the disorder (Vitkova et al., 2014). However, there is a good deal of individual difference, and the progression of the disorder, and its effects, do not follow a straight line. Many people with MS in good relationships enjoy fine sex lives for many years.

CEREBRAL PALSY Cerebral palsy and related disorders of the nervous system do not necessarily impair sexual interest, capacity for orgasm, or fertility. Depending on the nature and degree of muscle spasticity or lack of voluntary muscle control, however, afflicted people may be limited to certain types of sexual activities and coital positions (M. A. Schwartz, 2015).

People with disabilities such as cerebral palsy often suffer social rejection during adolescence and perceive themselves as unfit for or unworthy of intimate sexual relationships, especially with people who are not disabled. They are often socialized into an asexual role. Counseling can help them understand and accept their sexuality, promote a more positive body image, and provide the social skills to establish intimate relationships.

SPINAL CORD INJURIES People who suffer physical disabilities as the result of traumatic injuries or physical illness must not only learn to cope with their physical limitations but also to adjust to a world designed for nondisabled people. The majority of persons who suffer disabling spinal cord injuries are young, active males. Automobile or pedestrian accidents account for about half of these cases. Other common causes include stabbing or bullet wounds, sports injuries, and falls. Depending on the location of the injury to the spinal cord, a loss of voluntary control (paralysis) can occur in either the legs (*paraplegia*) or all four limbs (*quadriplegia*). A loss of sensation may also occur in parts of the body that lie beneath the site of injury.

11 › T /F Truth or Fiction Revisited Actually, many people who are paralyzed as a result of spinal cord injuries usually can become sexually aroused and engage in coitus. The effect of spinal cord injuries on sexual response depends on the site and severity of the injury.

Men have two erection centers in the spinal cord: a higher center in the lumbar region that controls psychogenic erections and a lower one in the sacral region that controls reflexive erections. When damage occurs at or above the level of the lumbar center, men lose the capacity for psychogenic erections—the kinds of erections that occur in response to mental stimulation alone, such as when viewing erotic films or fantasizing. They may still be able to achieve reflexive erections from direct stimulation of the penis because these erections are controlled by the sacral erection center located in a lower portion of the spinal cord. However, they cannot feel any genital sensations because the nerve connections to the brain are severed. Men with damage to the sacral erection center lose the capacity for reflexive erections but can still achieve psychogenic erections so long as their upper spinal cord remains intact. Overall, researchers find that about 3 of 4 men with spinal cord injuries are able to achieve erections but only about 1 in 10 men continues to ejaculate naturally. Others can ejaculate with a vibrator. Their brains may help to fill in some of the missing sensations associated with coitus and even orgasm.

Although the frequency of sexual activity among spinal cord–injured men tends to decline following the injury, about one-third continue to engage in sexual intercourse (Hess & Hough, 2012). Such men typically report increased interest in alternative sexual activities, especially those involving areas above the level of the spinal injury, such as the mouth, lips, neck, and ears.

Retention of sexual response in women depends on the site and severity of the spinal cord injury. Women may lose the ability to experience genital sensations or to lubricate normally during sexual stimulation (Hess & Hough, 2012). However, sensations in the breasts may not be affected, making the breasts more erotogenic. Most women with spinal cord injuries can engage in coitus, become impregnated, and deliver vaginally. A survey of 68 spinal cord–injured women showed that about half were able to achieve orgasm as a result of audiovisual erotic material combined with manual genital stimulation (Sipski et al., 2001). Spinal cord–injured women can heighten their sexual pleasure by using sexual imagery and manual stimulation (Sipski et al., 2001).

Couples facing the challenge of spinal cord injury may expand their sexual repertoire to focus less on genital stimulation (except to attain the reflexes of erection and lubrication) and more on the parts of the body that retain sensation. Stimulation of some areas of the body, such as the ears, the neck, and the breasts (in both men and women), can yield pleasurable erotic sensations.

One of the greatest impediments to sexual fulfillment among people with disabilities is difficulty in finding a loving and supportive partner. Some people engage in sexual relations with people with disabilities out of sympathy. By and large, however, the partners are other people with disabilities or nondisabled people who have overcome stereotypes that portray disabled people as undesirable. Many partners have had a prior positive relationship with a person with a disability, usually during childhood. Experience facilitates acceptance of the idea that a disabled person can be desirable. Depending on the nature of the disability, the nondisabled partner may need to be open to assuming a more active sexual role to compensate for the limitations of the partner with the disability. Two partners with disabilities need to be sensitive to each other's needs and physical limitations. People with disabilities and their partners may also expand their sexual repertoires to incorporate ways of pleasuring each other that are not fixated on genital stimulation. As with older people, GES can make a significant contribution to the quality of life of disabled individuals.

Chapter Review

LO 11.1 Describe sexually related behaviors in infancy and early childhood.

Male fetuses have erections; male and female fetuses suck their fingers. Pelvic thrusting has been observed as early as 8 months of age. Masturbation may begin at 6 to 12 months. Co-sleeping has not been shown to affect sexual development. Statistics concerning the incidence of masturbation at ages 3 to 8 is speculative. In early childhood, children show curiosity about the genitals and may play "doctor."

LO 11.2 Describe sexual behaviors in preadolescence.

Preadolescents tend to socialize with same-sex peers and to become self-conscious about their bodies. Masturbation is the primary means of obtaining orgasm in preadolescence. Preadolescent sex play often involves mutual display of the genitals, with or without touching. Much preadolescent same-sex sexual behavior involves exploration and is short-lived.

LO 11.3 Discuss the purposes and outcomes of sex education.

Sex education is intended to prevent unwanted pregnancy, unwanted sex, and sexually transmitted infections. Adolescents talk to their parents about sex more frequently than commonly believed. Sex education has not been shown to increase sexual activity among adolescents.

LO 11.4 Describe the milestones of puberty.

Puberty is ushered in by sex hormones. Puberty begins with the appearance of secondary sex characteristics and ends when the long bones make no further gains in length. During puberty the individual's body matures, setting the stage for reproduction. Most major changes in primary sex characteristics occur within 3 years in girls and within 4 years in boys.

LO 11.5 Describe sexuality in adolescence, including teenage pregnancy.

Masturbation is a major sexual outlet during adolescence. Many adolescents use petting as a way of achieving sexual gratification without becoming pregnant or losing their virginity. The incidence of premarital sex, especially for females, has increased dramatically since Kinsey's day. Some adolescents report same-sex experience, mostly with age-mates. Adolescence is often more tumultuous for gay males and lesbians, largely because of social stigmatization. Factors in teenage pregnancy include lack of closeness with parents, low interest and achievement in academics, and inconsistent use of contraceptives.

LO 11.6 Describe what being single means today.

Recent years have seen an increase in the numbers of single young people in our society. Reasons include increased permissiveness toward premarital sex and, particularly for women, and the desire to become established in a career. Some people remain single or celibate for religious reasons. Divorced people are also numbered among singles.

LO 11.7 Discuss cohabitation, including the relationships between cohabitation and marriage.

Since the 1960s, the numbers of inhabiting couples have mushroomed from about half a million to nearly 8 million, with another half million cohabiting same-sex couples. Cohabitation is more prevalent among less well educated and less affluent people. Some couples prefer cohabitation because it provides a consistent intimate relationship without the legal and economic entanglements of marriage. Cohabitors who later marry may run a greater risk of divorce than noncohabitors, perhaps because cohabitors have tended to be more liberal than people who do not live together before getting married.

LO 11.8 Discuss marriage, including sex in marriage and marital satisfaction.

Fewer people in the United States are married than in the past; the number has decreased from about two-thirds to one-half over the past 50 years. (At the same time, more people are cohabiting than ever before.) The major male–female marriages consist of two types: monogamy and polygamy. Same-sex marriage is recognized in the United States and many other nations. Americans tend to practice *homogamy*—that is, to marry partners similar to themselves in ethnic and religious background, attitudes and interests. Married couples today experiment more with sex than in Kinsey's day. Wives take more active sexual roles. Marital satisfaction involves factors such as commitment, adequate income, generosity, sharing of key attitudes, sexual satisfaction—and for those who are religious, belief in the spiritual value of marriage.

LO 11.9 Discuss infidelity.

People may have affairs for sexual variety, to punish their spouses, to achieve emotional closeness with someone, or to prove that they are attractive. In swinging, or mate-swapping, the partner participates. Extramarital sex continues to be viewed negatively by most people in our society.

LO 11.10 **Discuss the incidence of divorce and issues connected with divorce.**

Forty to 50% of the marriages in the United States end in divorce. Reasons for divorce include relaxed restrictions on divorce, greater financial independence among women, and the idea that marriages should be happy. Divorce often leads to financial and emotional problems.

LO 11.11 **Describe physical changes in the later years and how they affect sexual behavior.**

Partners may become less attractive to one another. It becomes more difficult for males to attain and maintain erections, and for females to lubricate. Many potential sexual problems can be averted by flexibility and "good enough sex."

LO 11.12 **Discuss the relationships between physical disabilities and sexual behavior.**

Cerebral palsy does not usually impair sexual interest, capacity for orgasm, or fertility, but afflicted people may be limited to certain types of sexual activities and coital positions. People with spinal cord injuries may be paralyzed and lose sensation below the waist but still respond reflexively to direct genital stimulation.

Test Your Learning

1. According to Kinsey, children first engage in behaviors that resemble orgasm _____
   (a) in infancy.
   (b) between the ages of 5 and 6.
   (c) between the ages of 6 and 11.
   (d) between the ages of 12 and adulthood.

2. It is *not* true that _____
   (a) teenage girls become pregnant despite using the withdrawal method of contraception.
   (b) pregnant teenagers obtain a good deal of support from their partner.
   (c) most teenage pregnancies are by choice.
   (d) the rate of teenage pregnancies has been declining.

3. Puberty ends _____
   (a) with the appearance of primary sex characteristics.
   (b) with the appearance of secondary sex characteristics.
   (c) when people assume adult responsibilities.
   (d) when the long bones make no further gains in length.

4. Estrogen does *not* cause _____
   (a) growth of the uterus.
   (b) growth of fatty and supporting tissue in the breasts and buttocks.
   (c) growth of underarm and pubic hair.
   (d) thickening of the vaginal lining.

5. Sex games like "show" and "playing doctor" become common between the ages of _____
   (a) 1 and 2.
   (b) 3 and 7.
   (c) 8 and 10.
   (d) 11 and 15.

6. All of the following are connected with getting married at later ages today *except* _____
   (a) living together first to test compatibility.
   (b) women's desire to focus on careers.
   (c) social pressure to remain single.
   (d) advanced education.

7. Which is true about cohabitation?
   (a) The numbers of couples who are cohabiting has been decreasing.
   (b) Religious organizations view cohabitation as being as virtuous as marriage.
   (c) Cohabitation is seen by many as a normal stage in courtship.
   (d) The great majority of cohabiting couples have children.

8. Which of the following is not true of late adulthood?
   (a) The testes increase in size.
   (b) Some men develop erectile dysfunction.
   (c) Most older men still like sex.
   (d) Testosterone production increases.

9. Polyandry is a form of marriage in which _____
   (a) one wife has more than one husband.
   (b) one husband has more than one wife.
   (c) there are multiple wives and husbands.
   (d) there is rapid divorce and remarriage.

10. The term *homogamy* refers to _____
    (a) like marrying like.
    (b) same-sex marriage.
    (c) polygyny.
    (d) polyandry.

Answers: 1. a; 2. b; 3. d; 4. c; 5. b; 6. c; 7. c; 8. d; 9. a; 10. a

Chapter 12
Sexual Problems and Solutions

TRUTH OR FICTION?

Which of the following statements are the truth, and which are fiction? Look for the Truth-or-Fiction items throughout the chapter to find the answers.

1   Sexual dysfunctions are rare.   **T / F**?

2   The most common cause of painful intercourse in women is vaginal infection.   **T / F**?

3   Sex therapy teaches a man with erectile disorder how to "will" an erection.   **T / F**?

4   A doctor made a somewhat unusual presentation to a medical convention by dropping his pants to reveal an erection.   **T / F**?

5   Many sex therapists recommend masturbation as the treatment for women who have never been able to reach orgasm.   **T / F**?

6   A man can prevent ejaculation by squeezing his penis when he feels that he is about to ejaculate.   **T / F**?

Derek, 59, and his wife Pam, 47, had not attempted sexual intercourse for 5 years. Sexual relations had been limited to fondling, caressing, and occasional oral–genital contact. They had given up attempting intercourse because of Derek's difficulty in attaining and sustaining erections. But recently they had begun trying again. Some nights Derek would have an erection enabling him to penetrate, only to find that he quickly lost the erection. Many nights he was unable to perform at all. Each failure was another blow to his self-esteem. Pam accused him of not being able to perform because he was no longer attracted to her. She asked him if he had other women or was spending his time alone by masturbating to online pornography. By the time the couple came for treatment, the marriage was in jeopardy and they could barely manage to talk about the problem.

Terry, 24, has decided she is built different from friends and women she reads about. They all reach orgasm, it seems, at the drop of a hat. But she has never managed "one of those things." Her partner David, also 24, is considerate, but Terry knows that he, too, is frustrated and feels guilty with every ejaculation. Why, she imagines he thinks, should he enjoy sex if Terry cannot? Terry and David anticipate sex with anxiety rather than pleasure, and David has begun having difficulty attaining erection. Terry wonders whether she should try to fake orgasm to hold on to him. But she fears she would not know how.

—The Authors' Files

Derek and Terry have sexual problems. The American Psychiatric Association refers to them as **sexual dysfunctions**—persistent or recurrent problems in becoming sexually aroused or reaching orgasm. Many of us have sexual problems from time to time. Men occasionally have difficulty obtaining an erection or ejaculate sooner than they or their partners would like. Women occasionally have difficulty lubricating or reaching orgasm. But sexual dysfunctions, as they are defined by the association, are persistent and cause significant distress.

People with serious sexual problems, or sexual dysfunctions, may avoid sexual opportunities for fear of failure. They may anticipate that sex will result in frustration or pain rather than pleasure and gratification. Because our culture emphasizes sexual competence, people with sexual problems may feel inadequate or incompetent—and these feelings diminish their self-esteem (Brassard et al., 2015; Vlachopoulos, 2015). They may also experience guilt, shame, frustration, depression, and anxiety.

Many people with sexual problems find it difficult to talk about them, even with long-term partners or helping professionals. A woman who cannot reach orgasm with her partner may not want to "make a fuss." A man may find it difficult to admit to having erectile problems to his physician during a physical examination. Many physicians are also uncomfortable talking about sex and may never ask about sexual matters.

We do not have precise figures on the occurrence of sexual problems or dysfunctions. Table 12.1 summarizes epidemiological data from surveys around the world. Although there is wide variation in the figures gleaned from the surveys, we can make some generalizations:

- Women are more likely than men to report having sexual problems.

- The occurrence of nearly every kind of sexual problem increases with age, with premature (early) ejaculation being the notable exception.

- The most common sexual problems in women are lack of interest in sex and difficulty reaching orgasm.

- The least common sexual problem is sexual pain.

- Despite the stereotype that men are "always ready" for sex, many men actually report having little interest in sex.

1 › T / F Truth or Fiction Revisited   It is *not* true that sexual dysfunctions are rare. Nearly half of women and at least one-third of men will report having a sexual problem as one time or another.

sexual dysfunctions
Persistent or recurrent difficulties in becoming sexually aroused or reaching orgasm.

Critical Thinking
When does a sexual problem become a sexual dysfunction? Where do you draw the line? How can *concern* about a sexual problem develop into a *problem*?

Table 12.1 Prevalence of Sexual Problems Based on Epidemiological Studies From Around the World

	Women	Men
At least one current sexual problem	40%–45%	20%–30%
Low sexual interest or desire	17%–55%	8%–25%
Arousal and lubrication problems in woman; erectile disorder (ED) in males	8%–28%	1%–40%*
Difficulty reaching orgasm**	16%–25%***	12%–19%
Premature (Early) ejaculation		8%–30%
Sexual Pain	1%–27%	1%–6%

SOURCES: American Psychiatric Association (2013); Harlow et al., 2014; Lewis, et al. (2010).

* The prevalence may double from the 40s to the 60s and again from the 60s to the 70s and older, with some studied showing rates much higher than those shown in the table.

** Difficulty reaching orgasm in women; "delayed ejaculation" in men.

*** Outliers put the percentage as high as 80% for older women.

Types of Sexual Problems

LO 12.1   **Identify and define the kinds of sexual problems that come to the attention of helping professionals.**

We may think of sexual problems as fitting into categories based on what we know about sexual desire and response:

- First are problems relating to sexual interest or desire
- Second are problems relating to becoming sexually aroused
- Third are problems relating to orgasm
- But then there are also problems involving sexual pain

As we discuss these problems, we will make you aware of how they are viewed by the American Psychiatric Association in its *Diagnostic and Statistical Manual of Mental Disorders (DSM-V)*, which is currently in its fifth edition (2013). The *DSM-V* refers to these problems as "dysfunctions." Why do we refer to the *DSM-V*? One reason is that it contains a good deal of useful information. Another reason is that if you go to a health professional for help with a sexual problem, the professional may well be thinking of the problem as it is described in the *DSM-V*. You should know that.

It is also useful to know that the association classifies sexual dysfunctions as being lifelong or acquired. Acquired dysfunctions follow a period of normal functioning. The association also classifies sexual problems as being generalized or situational. *Generalized* sexual problems occur in all situations. A man with generalized erectile disorder has trouble obtaining an erection in all situations. *Situational* sexual problems affect sexual functioning only in some situations, as, for example, during intercourse but not masturbation, or with one partner but not with another. If a man has never been able to obtain an erection during sexual relations with a partner but can do so when he is masturbating, his sexual problem is lifelong and situational.

Sexual Problems Relating to Lack of Interest or Desire

Many women have little or no interest in sex, or they used to have an interest but now they do not. They may no longer have erotic thoughts or fantasies. Nor do they initiate sexual activity, and they may be unreceptive to a partner's advances.

Some women who lack desire may harbor deep-seated anger and resentment toward their partners for reasons having nothing to do with sex (McCabe et al., 2010). However, they find it difficult to turn off these feelings when they go to bed. In such

---

Real Students, Real Questions

Q *What does prude mean? Is this considered a sexual dysfunction?*

A The word *prude* has the same origin as the word *proud*, and it refers to being highly or evenly excessively proper or modest in one's own speech, behavior, and dress. In other words, prudes prefer not to curse, kiss in public, or dress seductively. They also typically disapprove of such displays by others. What they do privately in a committed relationship might be quite different. In fact, they might enjoy sex a great deal, so there is no necessary connection between public prudery and sexual functioning or dysfunctioning. The origins of prudery are uncertain. Being reared strictly may have something to do with it, although many young people rebel, especially in open societies. And there might just be a genetic component.

cases, lack of desire may be situational—related to sex with her partner. In other cases, sexual trauma is implicated. Survivors of sexual abuse may urn off their thinking when it comes around to sex. Childhood sexual abuse is often found in cases of lack of desire (Colangelo & Keefe-Cooperman, 2012). Feelings of helplessness, anger, or guilt, or even flashbacks to incidents of abuse, may surface when the woman thinks about sex. Other psychosocial causes include anxiety or guilt about sex (McCabe et al., 2010).

The Association Psychiatric Association's name for this problem is a mouthful: **female sexual interest/arousal disorder**. The current diagnostic category combines what were previously termed "hypoactive sexual desire disorder" (lack of interest in sex) and "female sexual arousal disorder" (trouble getting aroused). The association decided to combine the two because "difficulties in desire and arousal often simultaneously characterize the complaints of women with this disorder" (2013, p. 434).

Men, like women, can lose interest in sex or, rarely, never have had interest in sex. The American Psychiatric Association (2013) gives this problem in men its own diagnosis: **male hypoactive desire disorder**. It isn't—as with women—lumped in, say, with erectile disorder. But in another mirror image with women, men with this issue may not consider it much of a problem unless a partner complains.

In any event, the problem is characterized by few if any erotic thoughts or fantasies, and little if any desire for sexual activity. The problem may be lifelong, but usually follows periods of more normal sexual desire and activity. It may be generalized—that is, apply to all situations and sexual opportunities—or it may be situational, as when occurring with a long-term partner. As with lack of sexual interest in women, the diagnosis is made only when the lack of desire is connected with "clinically significant distress."

Sexual Problems Relating to Becoming Aroused

Women with this problem encounter persistent difficulties becoming sexually excited or sufficiently lubricated in response to sexual stimulation. In some cases, these difficulties are lifelong. In others, they develop after a period of normal functioning. In some cases, difficulties are generalized; they occur during both masturbation and sex with a partner. More often they occur in certain situations. For example, they occur with some partners and not with others, or during intercourse but not during oral sex or masturbation.

Despite problems in becoming sexually aroused, women with sexual arousal disorders can often engage in sexual intercourse, even if lower-than-optimal levels of lubrication produce discomfort.

A woman who does have interest in sex may have difficulty becoming aroused for physical reasons. A thorough evaluation by a medical specialist is recommended. Any neurological, vascular, or hormonal problem that interferes with the lubrication or swelling response of the vagina to sexual stimulation may contribute to problems in women's sexual arousal. For example, diabetes mellitus may damage the nerves and blood vessels servicing the clitoral region. Reduced estrogen production can result in vaginal dryness.

But difficulty becoming sexually aroused, like lack of sexual interest or desire, more commonly has situational or psychological causes. If a woman's partner has erectile disorder, she will obviously not be able to reach orgasm through intercourse. As with lack of interest, the problem may lie in the relationship—or lack of relationship—with a partner (McCabe et al., 2010). A history of sexual trauma may also be implicated.

Difficulty becoming sexually aroused in men—that is, difficulty attaining and maintaining an erection—is termed **erectile disorder**. With all the TV commercials for Viagra and Cialis, and all the online offers to buy these drugs without prescription, erectile disorder (or ED) is among the most familiar of sexual problems. When

female sexual interest/ arousal disorder

An American Psychiatric Association diagnosis that combines problems in sexual desire and becoming sexually aroused in women. These problems cause clinically significant distress.

male hypoactive desire disorder

An American Psychiatric Association diagnosis referring to persistent or recurrent problems in lack of sexual desire that cause significant distress.

Critical Thinking
There is no consensus among clinicians and researchers concerning the definition of low sexual desire. How much sexual interest or desire would seem to be normal to you? Is there a sex difference? Explain your answer.

erectile disorder

Persistent difficulty achieving or maintaining an erection sufficient to allow the man to engage in or complete sexual intercourse. Also termed *erectile dysfunction*.

The Emotional Toll of Erectile Disorder. Erectile disorder is characterized by persistent difficulty in achieving or maintaining an erection sufficient to allow the completion of sexual activity. Tens of millions of men in the United States experience some degree of erectile dysfunction, and the incidence increases with age. Occasional erectile problems are common and may be caused by fatigue, alcohol, or anxiety about a new partner. However, fear of recurrence can create a vicious cycle, in which anxiety leads to failure, and failure heightens anxiety.

vasocongestion

Engorgement of blood vessels with blood, which swells the genitals and breasts during sexual arousal.

we are sexually stimulated, our bodies normally respond with **vasocongestion**, which produces erection in the male. But men with ED do not achieve or sustain an erection sufficient to enable sexual activity. ED was once labeled *impotence*, but that term has what we may call "excess meanings" and is no longer widely used.

In many cases ED is limited to sexual activity with one's partner, or with some partners and not others. It can therefore be classified as *situational.* In some cases, the problem occurs during any sexual activity, including masturbation. In these instances, it is considered *generalized.* Some men with ED are unable to attain an erection with their long-term partners. Others can achieve erection but not sustain it (or recover it) long enough for penetration and ejaculation.

ED usually develops after a period of normal functioning. Many men engage in years of successful sexual activity before the problem begins. Occasional problems in achieving or maintaining erection are quite common at any age and may have a variety of causes, such as fatigue or a couple of drinks too many. As we will see, erectile problems grow more common with age, especially in men who are taking prescribed medications for high blood pressure and high cholesterol.

Sexual Problems Relating to Orgasm

female orgasmic disorder

An American Psychiatric Association diagnosis describing persistent or recurrent problems in women's reaching orgasm even when they obtain sexual stimulation that brings most women to orgasm.

Women with this problem—listed as **female orgasmic disorder** by the American Psychiatric Association—are unable to reach orgasm or have difficulty reaching orgasm following what would usually be an adequate amount of sexual stimulation. Women who have never had an orgasm by any means are sometimes labeled **anorgasmic** or *pre*orgasmic.

anorgasmic

Never having had an orgasm.

A woman who reaches orgasm through masturbation or oral sex may not necessarily reach orgasm during sexual intercourse. Penile thrusting during intercourse may not provide sufficient clitoral stimulation. Sometimes reaching orgasm is impaired by factors such as sexual guilt or performance anxiety. Women who try to force an orgasm may find themselves unable to do so. They may assume what sex pioneers William Masters and Virginia Johnson labeled a **spectator role** and observe rather than fully participate in their sexual encounters. "Spectatoring" may further decrease the likelihood of orgasm.

spectator role

A role, usually taken on because of performance anxiety, in which people observe rather than fully participate in their sexual encounters.

There are two problems relating to orgasm in men, one of which is rare (delayed orgasm) and one of which is very common (premature ejaculation).

Real Students, Real Questions

Q *I was molested as a child, and the thought of sex does not interest me. What can I do about this?*

A We will offer you some generalizations, but we will also admit, right at the beginning, that we do not know enough about your particular situation to be more specific. We also suggest that you might want to talk the situation over with a helping professional who has expertise in the area. Having said that, you might begin by allowing a good relationship to develop with a decent, caring person. If you are comfortable in the relationship and are engaging in some cuddling and so on, you might find some interest in sex developing. If such a relationship does not stir sexual feelings, it still would not hurt to discuss the situation with a professional. Also consider the possibility that your history of being abused may not be the cause of your current lack of interest in sex. For the third time: Have a talk with a helping professional.

Delayed ejaculation disorder has also been referred to as *male orgasmic disorder, retarded ejaculation,* and *ejaculatory incompetence.* The problem may be lifelong or acquired, generalized or situational. There are very few cases of men who have never ejaculated. In most cases the disorder is limited to sexual intercourse. The man may find it relatively easy to ejaculate during masturbation or oral sex, but find it difficult, if not impossible—despite high levels of sexual excitement—to ejaculate during intercourse. One might think that female partners could possibly enjoy such a problem because it would enable a man to last longer. But the experience can be frustrating for both partners (Althof, 2012). Delayed ejaculation is relatively infrequent in the general population and in clinical practice, where it is among the least frequently diagnosed disorders.

Delayed ejaculation may be caused by physical problems such as multiple sclerosis or neurological damage that interferes with neural control of ejaculation. It may also be a side effect of certain drugs. Various psychological factors may also play a role, including performance anxiety, sexual guilt, and hostility toward the partner. Emotional factors such as fears of pregnancy and anger toward one's partner can also play a role.

Men with delayed ejaculation and their partners may "try harder" to have him come. But trying harder may worsen rather than help sexual problems. Trying harder can transform sexual relations into a job to get done, a chore rather than an opportunity for pleasure and gratification.

Premature (early) ejaculation—"coming" too soon—is the most common male sexual problem among younger men (see table 12.1). Because men lose their erections when they ejaculate, premature ejaculation usually prevents their female partners (or the men themselves) to fully enjoy sexual relations (American Psychiatric Association, 2013). In the case of male–male sexual activity, it may deprive the receiving partner from enjoying anal intercourse.

The degree of prematurity or rapidity varies. Some men ejaculate during foreplay, or even at the sight of their partner disrobing. But most ejaculate either just before or immediately upon penetration, or following a few coital thrusts. The point is that the man's partner—and he—would rather wait a while. In determining what is too rapid, some clinicians argue that the focus should be on whether the couple is satisfied with the duration of sexual intercourse rather than on a specific time period. According to Ronald Lewis and his colleagues (2010), premature ejaculation "always or nearly always occurs prior to or within about 1 minute of vaginal penetration, and

delayed ejaculation
A sexual problem in which a male persistently and recurrently has difficulty reaching orgasm, causing clinically significant distress.

premature (early) ejaculation
A sexual dysfunction in which ejaculation occurs with minimal sexual stimulation and before the partners desire it.

the inability to delay ejaculation on all or nearly all vaginal penetrations, and negative personal consequences such as distress, bother, frustration, and/or the avoidance of sexual intimacy" (p. 1600).

Some suggest that the label of early or premature ejaculation should be applied when men persistently or recurrently lack voluntary control over their ejaculations. This may sound like a contradiction in terms because ejaculation is a reflex, and reflexes need not involve thought or conscious control. However, a man may control ejaculation by regulating the amount of sexual stimulation he experiences so that it remains low enough not to trigger the ejaculation reflex until the partners are ready.

Sexual Pain

For most of us, sexual intercourse is a source of pleasure. For some of us, however, it gives rise to pain and discomfort. Still others may experience pleasure, but pain is the price they pay for it. The American Psychiatric Association (2013) lumps all sexual pain problems together in the category of **genito-pelvic pain/penetration disorder**. The diagnosis can apply to both women and men. The problem has been broadly referred to as **dyspareunia**, which simply translates into painful sex.

Painful intercourse is less common in men and is generally associated with genital infections that cause burning or painful ejaculation. Smegma under the penile foreskin of uncircumcised men may also irritate the penile glans during sexual contact.

Two sexual pain problems apply to women only: **vulvodyinia**, and **vaginismus** (Simonelli et al., 2014). These terms were previously used by the American Psychiatric Association and are still used by many helping professionals. However, they are absent in the current edition of *DSM-V*. This technical change is not likely to affect your sex life, but we thought we should make you aware of it in case you come across these terms in magazines, the doctor's office, and the like.

Painful sexual activity is particularly common among women, although—sadly!—about half of women with the problem do not seek professional help for it (Harlow et al., 2014). Pain is usually a sign that something is physically wrong, and painful sex may result from physical causes, emotional factors, or an interaction of the two. On the other hand, lack of adequate lubrication is the most common cause of sexual pain during intercourse, or attempted intercourse.

2 › T / F Truth or Fiction Revisited   Actually, the most common cause of painful intercourse in women is not vaginal infection. It is lack of adequate lubrication.

If a woman finds intercourse painful because of lack of lubrication, she may seek additional foreplay or artificial lubrication. And sometimes she—and maybe we're being a bit nosy here—may really want to ask herself if she wants to be where

genito-pelvic pain/penetration disorder

A catchall American Psychiatric Association diagnosis referring to a number of sexual pain problems in women and men.

dyspareunia

A sexual dysfunction characterized by persistent or recurrent pain during sexual intercourse.

vulvodyinia

A problem characterized by symptoms such as severe vulval pain, burning, and itching.

vaginismus

A sexual dysfunction characterized by involuntary contraction of the muscles surrounding the vaginal barrel, preventing penile penetration or rendering penetration painful.

she is with her partner, or with *this* partner. The normal changes of aging also commonly play a role in painful sex among perimenopausal and postmenopausal women (Ussher et al., 2015). Vaginal infections or sexually transmitted infections (STIs) may produce painful sex. Allergic reactions to spermicides, even the latex material in condoms, can give rise to painful sex. Pain during deep thrusting may indicate endometriosis, pelvic inflammatory disease (PID), or structural disorders of the reproductive system. Check with your gynecologist.

A severe kind of sexual pain experienced by women (formerly called *vulvodynia* by the association and still referred to as vulvodyinia by many other professionals) is characterized by intense vulval pain, particularly chronic burning sensations, irritation, and soreness. There is commonly no identifiable cause—which can be highly frustrating—although a history of local infections, damage to local nerves, and allergies are among the suspects (Mayo Clinic, 2014). Cold compresses, local anesthetics, and topical creams with estrogen or cortisone may provide relief (Mayo Clinic, 2014). The Mayo Clinic also recommends considering tricyclic antidepressants (you would be taking them "off label"—meaning for sexual pain and not for depression), anticonvulsants, antihistamines (to reduce itching), biofeedback therapy (to learn to relax muscles in the pelvic floor), and in the most severe cases, nerve blocks or surgery. Consult your gynecologist; you need not ignore this problem or try to go it alone. It is unfortunate that the American Psychiatric Association lumps this problem in with general sexual pain disorders because this one—vulvodyinia—is so clearly medical in origin.

Psychological factors such as unresolved guilt or anxiety about sex or the lingering effects of sexual trauma may also be involved in many cases of sexual pain. These factors may inhibit lubrication and may cause involuntary contractions of the vaginal musculature (*vaginismus*), making penetration painful or uncomfortable. Powerful muscle contractions may make entry by the penis painful or impossible. Some women with such muscle contractions are unable to tolerate penetration by any object, including a finger, tampon, or a physician's speculum.

Involuntary contraction of vaginal muscles is usually considered to be caused by psychological fear of penetration rather than physical injury or defect (Simonelli et al., 2014). Some think of vaginismus as a conditioned response to a painful experience. Women with the problem often have histories of sexual trauma, rape, even botched abortions that resulted in vaginal injuries. Still, they may want sex and they may be capable of sexual response and orgasm. However, fear of penetration triggers the involuntary spasm of the vaginal musculature at the point of penile insertion. In general, women who experience painful sex may develop a fear of penetration, which then leads to involuntary vaginal contractions.

Real Students, Real Questions

Q *Do women find a man ejaculating disgusting? Is that a dysfunction?*

A Some women find ejaculation disgusting. Others are turned on by it. Still others have no particular feelings about it. The reasons for these variations are unclear. Finding ejaculating disgusting is not in itself a sexual dysfunction. If it gives rise to loss of sexual desire or difficulty becoming sexually aroused, it might contribute to one.

Origins of Sexual Problems

We human beings are complex, with complex bodies as well as complex mental processes. We are also reared in families within cultural settings. For these reasons, we need to consider possible biological, psychological, and social factors in sexual problems. For example, biological and psychosocial factors—hormonal deficiencies, depression, dissatisfaction with one's relationship, and so on—can contribute to lack of sexual desire. Moreover, these factors can interact in a number of ways.

Biological Factors

LO 12.2 Discuss biological factors in the development of sexual problems.

Researchers find that health problems—especially cardiovascular disorders, hypertension, and obesity—can contribute to several kinds of sexual problems in men (Tan et al., 2012), but mostly to sexual pain in women (van Lankveld et al., 2010). Even when biological factors are involved in sexual problems, psychological factors such as anger, anxiety, and depression can prolong or worsen them (Tan et al., 2012).

Among the medical conditions that diminish sexual desire are testosterone deficiencies, thyroid overactivity or underactivity, and temporal lobe epilepsy (Ramasamy et al., 2014). Sexual desire is stoked by testosterone, which is produced by men in the testes and both men and women in the adrenal glands. Women may experience less sexual desire when their adrenal glands are surgically removed (Cappelletti & Wallen, 2015). Low sexual interest, along with erectile problems, is also common among men with **hypogonadism**, which is treated with testosterone (Ramasamy et al., 2014).

hypogonadism

An endocrine disorder that reduces the output of testosterone.

The reduction in testosterone levels that occurs in middle and later life may in part explain a gradual decline in sexual desire among men (Ramasamy et al., 2014). But women's sexual desire may also decline with age, because of physical and psychological changes, as we will see. Some medications, especially those used to control anxiety or hypertension, may also reduce desire. Changing medications or doses may reinstate the person's previous level of desire. We will editorialize by arguing that physicians need to do a better job of explaining the possible sexual side effects of the medications they prescribe so that patients can make more informed decisions.

Fatigue may lead to erectile problems and delayed ejaculation in men, and to inadequate lubrication and difficulty reaching orgasm in women. But these will be isolated incidents unless the person attaches too much meaning to them and becomes concerned about future performances. Painful sex—when not simply a result of inadequate lubrication—often reflects underlying infections. Medical conditions that affect sexual response include heart disease, diabetes mellitus, multiple sclerosis, spinal cord injuries, complications from surgery (such as removal of the prostate in men), hormonal problems, and the use of some medicines, such as those used to treat hypertension and psychiatric disorders (Dan et al., 2014; Martin et al., 2014; Shafer, 2016).

Fatigue and Sexual Dysfunction.
They were tired and it didn't happen. Should they keep trying or wait until they've had a good night's sleep?

HIV/AIDS AND SEXUAL PROBLEMS There is little doubt that HIV/AIDS is associated with sexual problems in both men and women. Men with HIV/AIDS are also more likely to have hypogonadism and ED, which apparently can be worsened by antiretroviral therapy (Santi et al., 2014; Zona et al., 2012). Antiretroviral therapy is known to increase levels of estrogen in men. A study of 78 seropositive gay males found a host of sexual dysfunctions ranging from loss of interest in sex to delayed ejaculation and ED (Cove & Petrak, 2004). Because the men were more capable of obtaining and maintaining erections without condoms than with condoms, many of them used condoms inconsistently.

HIV-seropositive women, too, encounter various sexual problems, from lack of interest to difficulty becoming sexually aroused and reaching orgasm (Florence et al., 2004). Researchers attribute the problems to psychological factors—anxiety, irritability, and depression—as well as to the physical effects of HIV/AIDS.

ERECTILE PROBLEMS   Biological causes of ED affect the flow of blood to and through the penis—a problem that becomes more common as men age. They may also damage the nerves involved in erection (Shafer, 2016). Erectile problems can arise when clogged or narrow arteries leading to the penis deprive the penis of oxygen. For example, men with diabetes mellitus, a disease that can damage blood vessels and nerves, have more trouble attaining and maintaining erections. Eric Rimm (2000) of the Harvard School of Public Health studied 2,000 men and found that ED was connected with a large waist, physical inactivity, and drinking too much alcohol (or not having any alcohol!). The common condition among these men may have been **atherosclerosis**, or hardening of the arteries, which is related to high levels of "bad cholesterol" (LDL, or low-density lipoprotein). Atherosclerosis can impede the flow of blood to the penis just as it impedes the flow of blood to the heart. Exercise, weight loss, eating fewer animal fats, and use of medicines called statins (such as Zocor and Lipitor) help to lower cholesterol levels. However, statins may also contribute to erectile problems (Katsiki et al., 2015). Ask your doctor if there is anything you can do to significantly lower your LDL other than take statins. If your doctor says no, you may wind up having to choose between your sex life and your health. This is tough language, but the choices are difficult.

Middle-aged and older men might try weight control and regular exercise. The findings of the Massachusetts Male Aging Study suggest that men who exercise regularly seem to do a better job of warding off erectile problems (Derby, 2000). Men who burn 200 calories or more a day in physical activity, an amount that be achieved by briskly walking for 2 miles, cut their risk of ED by about half. Exercise seems to prevent atherosclerosis, thus keeping the arteries clearer for the flow of blood into the penis.

But men (and women!) need to think about one particular form of exercise—bicycling. Bicycling, done properly, is not a problem. However, the use of standard narrow bicycle seats is a problem. Use of these seats exerts continual pressure in the perineal area (which lies between the penis or vulva and the anus), causing vascular (blood-flow) problems and possible nerve damage (Sommer et al., 2010). Frank Sommer and his colleagues (2010) recommend use of a "properly fitted" bicycle, meaning a bicycle with a wide enough seat and a seat position which does not place pressure on the perineal area. Such seats are widely available for men, and women are advised to consider them as well.

Nerve damage resulting from prostate surgery may impair erectile response (Koehler et al., 2012; Martin et al., 2014). ED may also result from multiple sclerosis (MS), a disease in which nerve cells lose the protective coatings that facilitate transmission of neural messages (Keller et al., 2012). MS has also been implicated in delayed ejaculation.

The bacteria that cause syphilis, an STI, can invade the spinal cord and affect the cells that control erections, resulting in ED. Chronic kidney disease, hypertension, cancer, emphysema, and

atherosclerosis
Hardening and narrowing of the arteries; a condition caused by the buildup of a hard substance known as *plaque* on the inside walls of arteries.

They're Having a Great Time, But Are They Risking Their Sex Life? Bicycles can provide exercise, but male riders with narrow seats can place pressure against the perineal area, leading to vascular (blood flow) problems and nerve damage in the region—also impairing sexual response.

tumescence

Swelling; erection.

heart disease can all impair erectile response because can endocrine disorders that interfere with the production of testosterone (Shafer, 2016).

People with sexual problems are generally advised to undergo a physical examination to determine whether their problems might be biologically based. Men with ED may be evaluated in a sleep center to determine whether they attain erections while asleep. The technique is termed nocturnal penile **tumescence** (NPT). Healthy men usually have erections during rapid-eye-movement (REM) sleep, which occurs every 90 to 100 minutes. Men with biologically based ED often do not have nocturnal erections.

Prescription drugs and illicit drugs account for many cases of ED. Antidepressant medication and antipsychotic drugs may impair erectile functioning and cause delayed ejaculation (Montejo et al., 2015). Tranquilizers such as Valium and Xanax may prevent both men and women from reaching orgasm. Some drugs used to treat high cholesterol and high blood pressure can impair erectile response. Switching to other blood pressure drugs or adjusting doses may help. Other drugs that can lead to ED include adrenergic blockers, diuretics, anti-convulsants, anti-Parkinson drugs, and dyspepsia and ulcer-healing drugs (Shafer, 2016).

People and physicians need to be very, very aware of the sexual side effects of some drugs used to treat depression. So-called selective serotonin reuptake inhibitors—SSRIs for short—are widely prescribed not only for depression but also for panic disorder, obsessive-compulsive disorder, anorexia nervosa, and other health issues. Most physicians are aware that these drugs have "some" effect on sexual arousal in "some" patients. However, the fact of the matter is that they almost completely impair sexual arousal in many patients, especially older patients (Montejo et al., 2015). Moreover, even when the patients lower the dosage or discontinue the drugs, sexual functioning does *not* necessarily bounce back.

Some drugs that are helpful with depression may not impair sexual functioning—at least in the short run. Bupropion, at least when used temporarily, *sometimes* improves sexual functioning and may be prescribed along with an SSRI to help prevent sexual side effects. Ask your physician.

Speaking of "pills," it should be noted that regular use of over-the-counter painkillers such as aspirin, acetaminophen (e.g., Tylenol), ibuprofen (e.g., Advil and Motrin), and naproxen (e.g., Aleve) may also be connected with erectile problems (Gleason et al., 2011). These drugs are also called NSAIDs—an abbreviation for nonsteroidal anti-inflammatory drugs. They have important uses and should not necessarily be completely avoided. For example, 81 mg of aspirin a day, which is a small dose, has been shown to help avert heart attacks. The thing to keep in mind is that even though you can buy these drugs without a prescription, they are serious medicines. As always, we advise checking with your doctor when there is a question about the use of medicines.

Central nervous system depressants such as alcohol, heroin, and methadone can reduce sexual desire and impair sexual arousal (del Rio et al., 2015; Shafer, 2016). Narcotics also depress testosterone production, thereby reducing sexual desire and leading to erectile failure. Marijuana use has been associated with reduced sexual desire and performance (del Rio et al., 2015; Shafer, 2016).

Regular use of stimulants such as cocaine can cause ED or delay ejaculation and reduce sexual desire in both women and men (Ciccarone, 2011; Hart et al., 2012). Some people report increased sexual pleasure from initial use of cocaine, but repeated use can lead to dependency on the drug for sexual arousal. Long-term use may compromise the ability to experience sexual pleasure.

Finally, there is the question as to whether taking various kinds of pills together, whether they are prescription drugs or nonprescription drugs, is related to erectile problems. To make a long story short, it is (Londoño et al., 2012). As men age, they tend to be prescribed more drugs, especially cholesterol-fighting drugs (statins, as discussed previously), and drugs that fight high blood pressure (hypertension). Both kinds of drugs are implicated in erectile problems. A study of several thousand male patients at the Kaiser-Permanente clinics in California calculated the relationships between self-reported erectile problems of patients, their age, and the kinds and numbers of drugs used (Londoño et al., 2012). As expected, erectile problems were associated with aging: Older men were more likely to report having ED. Older men also use more drugs. However, older men who used, say, three or more different types of drugs were more likely to report erectile problems than men of the same age who used zero to two types of drugs. The problems were also "dose-related"; that is, men who used higher doses of the same drugs reported erectile problems more frequently than men who used lower doses. It really didn't matter what the drugs were in this particular study. Again, check with your doctor about using drugs. Ask about their interactions with one another, their doses, and whether you have to stay on them indefinitely.

How do people get "trapped" into heavy drug use (and we're talking about pre-scribed drugs and over-the-counter drugs such as aspirin here)? One "problem" is that the drugs "work"—that is, the blood pressure medicines actually lower blood pressure, and statins actually lower blood levels of harmful cholesterol. Therefore, doctors are understandably reluctant to discontinue them. Patients can ask doctors about substitutes, but doctors often respond—accurately—that there are no substitutes. Another problem is that patients may have more than one doctor, perhaps a family doctor and one or two specialists, and they may all be prescribing something. A third problem is that patients may be mixing these drugs with NSAIDs, antihistamines (for allergies), and alcohol (which is a drug). It can be quite a brew. It can be wonderful and it can save lives. But there can also be problems. Patients need to inform their doctors about *everything* they are taking, and they need to be open about sexual concerns.

SEXUAL AROUSAL IN WOMEN   Aging can also affect the sexual response of women. Perimenopausal and postmenopausal women usually produce less vaginal lubrication than younger women and the vaginal walls become thinner—changes that can render sex painful (van Lankveld et al., 2010). These physical changes, along with negative stereotypes of older women and men, can create performance anxiety and fumbling performances, and discourage both partners from attempting sexual activity

Medications and Sexual Problems.
Use of the right drugs can be healthful and even life-saving. However, research shows that taking many different drugs, including over-the-counter drugs, can inhibit sexual response. Tell your physician about *all* the drugs you are taking and their doses.

(Brotto et al., 2010; McCabe & Connaughton, 2014). In such cases, artificial lubrication can help supplement the woman's own production, and estrogen replacement may halt or reverse some of the sexual changes of aging (Wierman et al., 2010). But partners also need to have realistic expectations and consider enjoyable sexual activities they can engage in without discomfort or high demands (Althof, 2010). As we saw in the chapter on sex through the lifespan, many older people are quite content with what we can call "good enough sex."

Women also develop vascular or nervous disorders that impair genital blood flow, reducing lubrication and sexual excitement, rendering intercourse painful, and reducing their ability to reach orgasm. As with men, these problems become more likely as women age.

Psychosocial Factors

Abrupt changes in sexual desire are more often explained by psychological and interpersonal factors such as depression, stress, and problems in the relationship than by biological causes (McCabe & Connaughton, 2014; Stephenson & Meston, 2015; Stephenson et al., 2013). Anxiety is the most commonly reported factor. Anxiety may dampen sexual ardor. Performance anxiety (anxiety over being evaluated negatively), anxiety involving fears of pleasure or loss of control, and deeper sources of anxiety relating to fears of injury can all contribute to making sex a feared obligation rather than a source of excitement and pleasure. Depression is also a common cause of lack of desire. As noted previously, childhood sexual abuse or sexual assault has also been linked to low sexual desire (Colangelo & Keefe-Cooperman, 2012).

Psychosocial factors connected with sexual dysfunctions include cultural influences, economic problems, psychosexual trauma, dissatisfaction with one's relationship, lack of sexual skills, irrational beliefs, and performance anxiety (McCabe & Connaughton, 2014).

CULTURAL INFLUENCES   Children reared in sexually repressive cultural or home environments may learn to respond to sex with feelings of anxiety and shame, rather than anticipation and pleasure (Woo et al., 2011). People whose parents instilled in them a sense of guilt over touching their genitals may find it difficult to accept their sex organs as sources of pleasure (McCarthy et al., 2006).

In most cultures, sexual pleasure has traditionally been a male preserve. Young women may be reared to believe that sex is a duty to be performed for their husbands, not a source of personal pleasure. Although the traditional double standard has diminished in developed countries, some girls are still exposed to repressive attitudes (Allen, 2015; Rani & Sharma, 2015; Simmons, 2015). Women are more likely than men to be taught to suppress sexual desires. Self-control and vigilance—not sexual awareness and acceptance—become identified as feminine virtues. Women reared with such attitudes may not learn about their sexual potentials or express their erotic desires to their partners.

Many women who are exposed to negative attitudes about sex during childhood and adolescence find it difficult to suddenly view sex as a source of pleasure and satisfaction as adults. A lifetime of learning to turn themselves off sexually may impair sexual arousal and enjoyment when an acceptable opportunity arises (Woo et al., 2011).

PSYCHOSEXUAL TRAUMA

LO 12.3   Discuss psychosocial factors in the development of sexual problems.

Women and men who were sexually victimized in childhood are more likely to experience lack of sexual desire and difficulty in becoming sexually aroused (Colangelo & Keefe-Cooperman, 2012; McCabe & Connaughton, 2014; Yehuda et al., 2015). Some learning theorists speak of conditioned anxiety in explaining these sexual problems. Sexual stimuli come to elicit anxiety when they have been paired with traumatic

Critical Thinking
Are there any sexual attitudes common to people of your demographic background that can give rise to sexual problems or dysfunctions? What are these attitudes? Do you share them? Explain.

experiences, such as rape, incest, or sexual molestation. Unresolved anger, misplaced guilt, and feelings of disgust also make it difficult for victims of sexual trauma to respond sexually, even years later and with loving partners.

SEXUAL ORIENTATION   Some gay males and lesbians test their sexual orientation by developing heterosexual relationships, even by entering heterosexual marriages and rearing children with their spouses. Others may wish to maintain the appearance of heterosexuality to avoid the social stigma attached to a gay male or lesbian sexual orientation. In such cases, problems with heterosexual partners can signify lack of heteroerotic interest (McCarthy et al., 2006).

INEFFECTIVE SEXUAL TECHNIQUES   In some relationships, couples fall into a narrow sexual routine because one partner controls the timing and sequence of sexual techniques. A woman who remains unknowledgeable about the erotic importance of her clitoris may be unlikely to seek direct clitoral stimulation. A man who responds to one erectile failure by trying to force an erection may be unintentionally setting himself up for repeated failure. Couples in which the partners fail to communicate their sexual preferences or to experiment with new techniques may find themselves losing interest. Brevity of foreplay and coitus may contribute to female orgasmic disorder.

EMOTIONAL FACTORS   Orgasm involves a sudden loss of voluntary control. Fear of losing control or "letting go" may block sexual arousal. Other emotional factors, especially depression, are often implicated in sexual problems (Carvalho & Nobre, 2010b). Depression can contribute to lack of sexual desire. Stress can also interfere with sexual interest and response.

PROBLEMS IN THE RELATIONSHIP   Problems in the relationship are not easily left at the bedroom door (Brotto et al., 2010; Carvalho & Nobre, 2010a). Heterosexual and homosexual couples alike usually find that sex is no better than other facets of

> **Critical Thinking**
> Given our cultural values, why might it lead to a problem in a relationship if a woman were to exhibit sexual competence?

A Vicious Cycle? Conflict in the Relationship and Lack of Sexual Desire. Conflicts in a relationship may dampen sexual interest. Lack of sexual interest may then further strain the relationship.

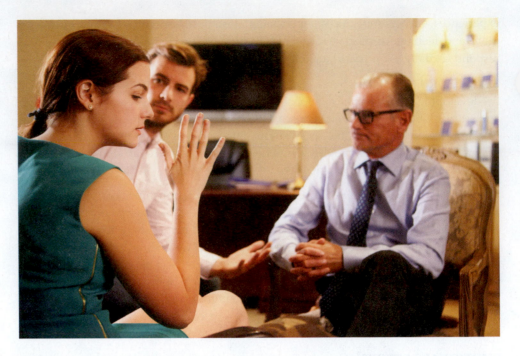

Irrational Beliefs and Sexual Problems. She tells the psychologist, "He seems to think that if I truly loved him, I'd know what he wants. I've tried, but I can't read his mind." The psychologist then helps the couple communicate better.

their relationship (IsHak et al., 2010). Partners who have general trouble communicating may also be unable to communicate their sexual desires. Couples who harbor resentments may make sex their combat arena. They may fail to become aroused by their partners or "withhold" orgasm to make their partners feel guilty or inadequate (McCabe & Connaughton, 2014).

LACK OF SEXUAL SKILLS   Sexual competency involves sexual knowledge and skills that are acquired through learning. We generally learn what makes us and others feel good through trial and error and by talking and reading about sex. Some people may not develop sexual competency because of a lack of opportunity to acquire knowledge and experience—even within a committed relationship. People with sexual problems may have been reared in families in which discussions of sexuality were off limits and early sexual experimentation was harshly punished.

IRRATIONAL BELIEFS   Irrational beliefs and attitudes may contribute to sexual problems. We cannot expect our partners to read our minds. We cannot assume that if they truly cared for us, they would know what we need, or want. Communication is one of the keys to sexual satisfaction.

performance anxiety

Anxiety concerning one's ability to perform behaviors, especially behaviors that may be evaluated by other people.

PERFORMANCE ANXIETY Anxiety—especially **performance anxiety**—plays an important role in sexual problems (Althof & Needle, 2011; Althof et al., 2014). Performance anxiety occurs when a person becomes overly concerned with how well he or she performs a certain act or task. Performance anxiety may place a dysfunctional individual in a spectator rather than a performer role. Rather than focusing on erotic sensations and allowing reflexes like erection, lubrication, and orgasm to occur naturally, he or she focuses on self-doubts and thinks, "Will I be able to do it this time? Will this be another failure?"

In men, performance anxiety can inhibit erection while also triggering early ejaculation (Althof et al., 2014). Erection, mediated by the parasympathetic nervous system, can be blocked by activation of the sympathetic nervous system in the form of anxiety. Because ejaculation, like anxiety, is mediated by the sympathetic nervous system, arousal of this system in the form of anxiety can increase the level of stimulation and thereby heighten the potential for early ejaculation.

In women, performance anxiety can reduce vaginal lubrication and contribute to orgasmic disorder (Goldstein et al., 2006). Women with performance anxieties may try to force an orgasm, only to find that the harder they try, the more elusive it becomes.

Solutions

When Kinsey conducted his surveys in the 1930s and 1940s, there was no effective treatment for sexual problems. At the time, the predominant model of therapy for sexual problems was long-term psychoanalysis. Psychoanalysts believed that the sexual problem would abate only if the presumed unconscious conflicts that lay at the root of the problem were resolved through long-term therapy. Evidence of the effectiveness of psychoanalysis in treating sexual problems remains lacking, however.

Since that time cognitive and behavioral models of short-term treatment, collectively called **sex therapy**, have emerged. Sex therapy aims to modify problematic cognitions (beliefs and attitudes) and sexual behavior as directly as possible. Sex therapists also recognize the roles of childhood conflicts and the quality of the partners' relationship. Therefore, they draw from various forms of therapy, as needed (Althof, 2010; Althof et al., 2014; Frühauf et al., 2013).

Although the particular approaches vary, sex therapists aim to:

1. Change self-defeating beliefs and attitudes.
2. Enhance sexual knowledge.
3. Teach sexual skills.
4. Improve sexual communication.
5. Reduce performance anxiety.

sex therapy

A collective term for short-term behavioral models for treatment of sexual dysfunctions.

Recent research shows that sex therapy is effective for treatment of lack of sexual interest or desire in women, and also in female orgasmic disorder (Frühauf et al., 2013). Sex therapy may involve partners, although individual therapy is preferred in some cases. Therapists find that granting people "permission" to sexually experiment or discuss negative attitudes about sex helps many people overcome sexual problems without the need for more intensive therapy.

Today, biological treatments have also been emerging for various sexual problems. Most public attention has been focused on Viagra and Cialis, drugs that are helpful in most cases of ED. But Addyi, a drug meant to boost women's sexual desire, has joined the arsenal. (Note, however, that sex therapy is effective in the treatment of lack of desire.) Biological treatments for other sexual problems are also emerging. Moreover, there are research findings to the effect that psychotherapy combined with drugs such as Viagra and Cialis can be more effective than the medicine alone (Schmidt et al., 2014).

In this section we explore psychological and behavioral approaches to the treatment of sexual problems. Let us begin with the pioneering work of Masters and Johnson.

The Masters and Johnson Approach

LO 12.4 **Discuss the historic Masters and Johnson approach to sex therapy.**

Masters and Johnson (1970) pioneered the use of direct cognitive-behavioral approaches to treating sexual problems. They treated couples in a 2-week residential program. Then the couples were female–male, and they used a female–male therapy team. Masters and Johnson considered the couple, not the individual, to be dysfunctional. A couple may describe the husband's ED as the problem, but this problem is likely to have led to further problems in the relationship by the time they seek therapy. Similarly, a man whose wife has a problem reaching orgasm is likely to be anxious about his ability to provide effective sexual stimulation.

sensate focus exercises

Exercises in which sex partners take turns giving and receiving pleasurable stimulation in nongenital areas of the body.

The dual-therapist team permits each partner to discuss problems with someone of his or her own gender. Anxieties and resentments are aired, but the focus of treatment is on behavioral change. Couples perform daily sexual homework assignments, such as **sensate focus exercises**, in the privacy of their rooms.

Sensate focus sessions are carried out in the nude. Partners take turns giving and receiving stimulation in nongenital areas of the body. Without touching the breasts or genitals, the giver massages or fondles the receiving partner to provide pleasure under relaxing and nondemanding conditions. Because genital activity is restricted, there is no pressure to "perform." The giving partner is freed to engage in trial-and-error learning about the receiving partner's preferences. The receiving partner is also freed to enjoy the experience without feeling rushed to reciprocate or obliged to perform by becoming sexually aroused. The receiving partner's only responsibility is to direct the giving partner as needed. In addition to these general sensate focus exercises, Masters and Johnson used specific assignments designed to help couples overcome particular sexual problems.

Although Masters and Johnson were pioneers in sex therapy, many sex therapists have departed from their format. For example, many do not require residential programs. Many question the necessity of female–male therapist teams. Nor does it seem to matter whether sessions are conducted within a short period of time, as with Masters and Johnson, or spaced over time.

Integration of Sex Therapy and Psychotherapy

LO 12.5 **Discuss the integration of sex therapy and psychotherapy.**

Sex therapy, as noted, has cognitive components—for example, addressing self-defeating attitudes and expectations, and sex education. Few therapists use strict Masters and Johnson guidelines anymore, but many of their innovations are incorporated into their methods (Althof, 2010). Moreover, because sexual activity is so often embedded in relationships, many therapists (Althof, 2010) use psychotherapy and couple therapy to help couples learn how to share the power in relationships, how to improve sexual communication, and how to negotiate differences. The combination of sex therapy and couple therapy appears to be a powerful tool for enhancing relationships as well as sex lives.

The Treatment of Specific Sexual Problems

LO 12.6 **Discuss the treatment of specific sexual dysfunctions.**

Let us now consider some of the specific techniques that sex therapists have introduced in treating several sexual problems.

LACK OF SEXUAL DESIRE Some therapists help kindle the sexual appetites of people with little or no sexual desire by prescribing self-stimulation exercises combined with erotic fantasies (Knudson & Kingsberg, 2010). Sex therapists may also assist dysfunctional couples by prescribing sensate focus exercises, enhancing communication, and expanding the couple's repertoire of sexual skills. Sex therapists recognize that lack of desire is often a complex problem, and they may employ counseling or psychotherapy to uncover and resolve psychological conflicts (Carvalho & Nobre, 2010b).

Some men lack sexual because of hormonal deficiencies, especially deficiencies in testosterone. Testosterone replacement therapy restores desire in some men who had low testosterone levels (Brock et al., 2015). Among women, as among men, lack of sexual desire is sometimes connected with low levels of androgens. One study of postmenopausal women found that after using testosterone patches of various doses for 24 weeks, women taking 150-µg testosterone had a mean increase of 1.2 satisfying sexual episodes per 4-week period, whereas women taking 300 µg testosterone had

A CLOSER LOOK

THE "LITTLE PINK PILL" FOR WOMEN

In its traditional gender-stereotyped color, the "little pink pill" for women arrived in 2015. It was the female counterpart to the traditional, gender-stereotyped blue pill—Viagra.

Except it wasn't, and it isn't.

Viagra and its sister (should we instead write "brother") drugs Cialis and Levitra enhance (most) men's abilities to obtain and maintain and erection by capturing men's blood flow into the penis. That is, Viagra, in its complicated biochemical way, contributes to a man's sexual arousal, making sexual intercourse possible for many men with ED.

Viagra, it turns out, works in pretty much the same way in women. That is, it helps women engorge the clitoral region with blood, an action that is the equivalent of promoting erection in men. As part of its biochemical actions, it similarly enhances vaginal lubrication, facilitating intercourse.

The most common sexual problem reported by women is lack of sexual desire, or lack of interest in sex. Many women with

low sexual desire don't believe they have a problem, but others would like to have more of a sex life, either for their own sake, for their partner's, or both.

Unlike Viagra and other drugs that help men "rise" to the occasion as needed, flibanserin (brand name, Addyi), which must be taken daily, seems to have moderate effects at best. In one trial, for example, women who took the drug reported having 4.4 "satisfying sexual experiences a month" as compared with 3.7 satisfying experiences for women who took a placebo (Editorial Board, 2015a; Thorp et al., 2014).

Then there are the side effects, including low blood pressure and loss of consciousness. Drinking alcohol increases the risks and, remember, the drug is to be taken daily, not upon demand. Doctors and pharmacists cannot prescribe or dispense the drug without taking an online tutorial and demonstrating that they understand the risks. Moreover, it is known that the drug boosts the action of the neurotransmitter serotonin in the brain (Stahl, 2015), but many drugs do that and their exact actions on sexual desire remain somewhat unclear.

So, if the drug is risky and its effects are "underwhelming," why was it approved and why is it being prescribed? Part of the answer is political. The Food and Drug Administration (FDA) rejected applications to market the drug in 2010 and 2013, but women's advocates argued that the FDA was showing a gender bias in denying women the drug. Several drugs to help men had been approved, but none for women. On the physical risk-reward side, the drug had shown some positive effects and was not thought to be deadly. Yes, there were side effects, but they didn't affect every user equally. Men's drugs also had side effect and men's drugs also had some mixed results in the arena of effectiveness.

Now that the drug is out there, facts about its track record will accumulate quickly. Users will tell one another it's worth it or it isn't. We can't say the jury is out; the drug was approved. We can say that we'll see what happens over the next few years. Other women's drugs will also likely be coming on the market, and we'll see how people respond to them as well.

---

an increase of 2.1 episodes over the same period (Davis et al., 2008). Those using the patch also reported heightened sexual desire.

SEX THERAPY FOR ERECTILE DISORDER   Men with ED may ask their therapists to "teach" them or "show" them how to obtain an erection. Some of our clients have asked us to tell them what fantasies they should entertain to obtain an erection, or how they should touch their partners or be touched. Erection is a reflex, however, not a skill. A man need not learn how to have an erection any more than he need learn how to breathe.

3 › T / F   Truth or Fiction Revisited   It is *not* true that sex therapy teaches a man with erectile disorder how to "will" an erection. Men with ED are actually taught that it is not possible to "will" an erection. One can only set the stage for erection (or vaginal lubrication) to occur and then allow it to happen reflexively.

Figure 12.1   Behavioral Approach to Treatment of Erectile Disorder.

In one part of a sex therapy program designed to overcome erectile disorder, a man's partner repeatedly "teases" him to erection and allows the erection to subside. Thus, the partner avoids creating performance anxiety that could lead to loss of erection. Through repeated regaining of erection, the man loses the fear that loss of erection means it will not return.

People who have difficulty becoming sexually aroused frequently develop performance anxiety. When therapists work with a couple, they may recommend that the couple engage initially in nondemanding sexual contacts—contacts that do not demand lubrication or erection. They may start with nongenital sensate focus exercises in the style of Masters and Johnson. After a couple of sessions, sensate focus extends to the genitals. The position shown in Figure 12.1 allows a woman easy access to a male partner's genitals. She repeatedly "teases" him to erection and allows the erection to subside. Thus, she avoids creating performance anxiety that could lead to loss of erection. By repeatedly regaining his erection, the man loses the fear that loss of erection means it will not return. He learns also to focus on erotic sensations for their own sake. He experiences no demand to perform, as the couple is asked to refrain from coitus.

When the dysfunctional partner can reliably achieve sexual excitement (denoted by erection in the male and lubrication in the female), the couple does not immediately attempt coitus because this might rekindle performance anxiety. Rather, the couple engages in a series of nondemanding, pleasurable sexual activities, eventually culminating in coitus.

In the Masters and Johnson approach, the couple begin coitus after about 10 days of treatment. The woman teases the man to erection while she is sitting above him, straddling his thighs. When he is erect, she inserts the penis—to avoid fumbling attempts at entry—and moves slowly back and forth in a *nondemanding way*. Neither attempts to reach orgasm. If erection is lost, teasing and coitus are repeated. Once the couple become confident that erection can be retained—or reinstated if lost—they may increase coital thrusting gradually to reach orgasm.

But note that ED is frequently, and perhaps most often, biologically related. Put it this way: a sex therapist is unlikely to try the Masters and Johnson approach to treating ED with a 60-year-old man who is taking medicines for high blood pressure and high cholesterol. Let's consider biological treatment of erectile disorder.

BIOLOGICAL APPROACHES TO ERECTILE DISORDER   You have likely heard the sales pitch "What happens in Las Vegas stays in Las Vegas." However, one event at the 1983 Las Vegas convention of the American Urological Association spread quickly beyond the borders of "sin city" into the consciousness of sexologists everywhere.

4 › T / F   Truth or Fiction Revisited   What happened is that the British scientist Giles Brindley, who had been invited by the association to discuss the confusing issues surrounding male sexual response, dropped his pants to reveal a rather sizeable erection. He was demonstrating the effects of a chemical compound called *alprostadil*. The erection was not the result of sexual stimulation or sexual fantasies, but of an injection of alprostadil directly into his penis. Alprostadil is a vasodilator; it relaxes the muscles surrounding the arteries in the penis, allowing more blood to flow in, increasing vasocongestion and causing erection. Brindley was giving a "live" demonstration of a biological method of treating erectile disorder.

According to an observer (Lamar, 2012): "With his pants at his knees, [Brindley] waddled down the stairs, approaching (to their horror) the urologists and their partners in the front row. As he approached them, erection waggling before him, four or five of the women in the front rows threw their arms up in the air, seemingly in unison, and screamed loudly."

Table 12.2 Biological Treatments of Erectile Problems

Medication	
Oral medication	Oral forms of several compounds—sildenafil (Viagra), vardenafil (Levitra), and tadalafil (Cialis)—relax the muscles that surround the small blood vessels in the penis, allowing them to dilate so that blood can flow into them more freely. Apomorphine increases brain levels of the neurotransmitter dopamine. Called "Uprima," the drug is in clinical trials. Bremelanotide apparently acts directly on the central nervous system and, as the book goes to press, is also in clinical trials.
Hormone therapy	Helps men (and women) with abnormally low levels of male sex hormones.
Injections	Muscle relaxants such as *alprostadil* and *phentolamine* are injected into the corpus cavernosum of the penis, relaxing the muscles that surround the arteries in the penis, allowing the vessels to dilate and blood to flow more freely.
Suppository	Alprostadil is inserted into the tip of the penis in gel form.
Vacuum Pump	
Vacuum pump	A *vacuum constriction device* creates a vacuum when it is held over the penis. The vacuum induces erection by increasing the flow of blood into the penis. Rubber bands around the base of the penis maintain the erection.
Surgery	
Vascular surgery	Helps when blood vessels that supply the penis are blocked.
Penile implants	May be used when other treatments fail because of biological problems.

Biological and biomedical approaches are helpful in treating ED, especially when organic factors are involved. Many of these involve changes in lifestyle that have the "side effect" of improving the man's general health. Other treatments include surgery, medication, and vacuum pumps (see Table 12.2).

When we consider the factors associated with ED, we find that many men can modify their lives to remove or reduce their impact. Because ED is connected with obesity, men can lose weight by dieting and exercising in the effort to restore erectile functioning (Segraves, 2015). Even if there is not complete reversal of the problem, there may be improvement. Men can also consider their use of drugs ranging from prescription drugs to alcohol to over-the-counter drugs such as pain killers, anti-inflammatory drugs, and anti-allergy drugs. It may be possible to avoid some of these drugs or to lower the dose (Londoño, et al., 2012). Men should *not* lower the doses of prescription drugs without medical advice, but they can inform their doctors that they would like to do so if it is safe, and they can lower their use of alcohol and other drugs. It may be that a drink a day is good for your heart, but two drinks a day is unnecessary for that purpose and may have overall depressive effects. Consider little things, such as getting a more sensible bicycle seat, that can have big effects (Sommer et al., 2010).

Two types of surgery may be used with ED: vascular surgery and the installation of penile implants. *Vascular surgery* can help in cases in which the blood vessels that supply the penis are blocked, or in which structural defects in the penis restrict blood flow. Arterial bypass surgery reroutes vessels around the blockage. A *penile implant* may be used when other treatments fail. Implants are either malleable (semi-rigid) or inflatable (see Figure 12.2). The semi-rigid implant is made of rods that remain in a *permanent* semi-rigid position. It is rigid enough for intercourse but permits the penis to hang reasonably close to the body at other times. The inflatable type requires that cylinders be implanted in the penis. A fluid reservoir is placed near the bladder, and a tiny pump is inserted in the scrotum. To attain erection, the man squeezes the pump, releasing fluid into the cylinders. Some adverse side effects of penile implants have been reported, including destruction of erectile tissue, impairing the man's ability to have normal erections. Penile implants do not affect sex drive, sexual sensations, or ejaculation.

Implant surgery is irreversible. Therefore, the National Institutes of Health recommend that penile implants be used only when less invasive techniques, such as sex therapy and medication, are unsuccessful.

Figure 12.2   A Penile Implant.

Penile implants provide erection when the man's cardiovascular system does not do the job. This implant consists of cylinders that are implanted in the penis. A fluid reservoir (*top left*) is placed near the bladder. A pump (*lower middle*) is typically inserted in the scrotum. Squeezing the pump forces fluid into the cylinders, inflating the penis. A release valve returns the fluid to the reservoir, deflating the penis.

Medication is also used to help men with erectile problems. For example, hormone (testosterone) treatments help restore the sex drive and erectile ability in many men with abnormally low levels of testosterone (Brock et al., 2015). Hormone therapy does not appear to help men with normal hormone levels.

The muscle relaxants *alprostadil* (brand names Caverject and Edex) and *phentolamine* (Invicorp) can be injected into the corpus cavernosum of the penis. These chemicals relax the muscles that surround the small blood vessels in the penis. The vessels dilate and allow blood to flow in more freely. Alprostadil erections last for an hour or more and occur whether or not there is sexual stimulation. A physician teaches the man how to inject himself. If phentolamine is used along with the protein VIP, erection occurs only when sexual stimulation is applied.

Penile injections may have side effects, including pain from the injection itself and prolonged, painful erections (*priapism*) (Ralph & McNicholas, 2000). Many men find the idea of penile injections distasteful (the "wince factor") and refuse them.

Alprostadil is also available as a suppository in gel form (brand name MUSE). It is then inserted into the tip of the penis by an applicator. The suppository helps men get around the "wince factor" that many experience with injections. "Putting a needle in your penis is not everybody's idea of foreplay," notes Dr. John Seely (in Kolata, 2000b).

Other medications are taken orally. For example, the oral form of sildenafil is sold as Viagra, and the oral form of vardenafil is sold as Levitra. The oral form of tadalafil (Cialis) lasts up to 36 hours. Users in France dub it "the weekend pill."

Real Students, Real Questions

Q *I know that Viagra helps put more blood into the penis; but how does it do that? How does it actually work?*

A The answer is chemical and it applies to Levitra and Cialis as well as Viagra. The end point is to allow the arteries in the penis to dilate and fill up with blood to produce an erection. Chemically, what has to happen for arteries to dilate is that the brain sends a signal along a nerve fiber ending in a nonadrenergic–noncholinergic (NANC) cell in an artery; the NANC cell produces nitric oxide and injects it into the bloodstream and nearby cells. The nitric oxide causes a chemical called cyclic guanosine monophosphate (cGMP) to be produced, which relaxes the muscles that line an artery, increasing the flow of blood. However, a chemical called phosphodiesterase (PDE) deactivates cGMP. The specific type of PDE found in the penis is called PDE5.

Viagra, Levitra, and Cialis are all PDE5 inhibitors. That is, they work by deactivating PDE5. Step by step:

1. A man takes Viagra, Levitra, or Cialis.

2. The chemical in the pill circulates throughout his bloodstream.

3. The chemical attaches to PDE5 in his penis and deactivates most of it.

4. When he is sexually aroused, his brain sends the usual message to the cells in his penis, resulting in the output of nitric oxide.

5. In turn, the nitric oxide produces cGMP.

6. Because most PDE5 has been deactivated, cGMP builds up, allowing the arteries in the penis to dilate and produce a fuller erection.

NOTE: Although Viagra and its chemical cousins are marketed as PDE5 inhibitors, their effects are somewhat broader, which is why they sometimes produce migraines.

The drug apomorphine (Uprima) heightens brain levels of dopamine, a neurotransmitter that is involved in erection. Uprima is available in the United Kingdom and without prescription online, but it is advisable to consult your physician before using it. Researchers became aware of the potential benefits of dopamine-enhancing drugs through research with Parkinson's disease. Parkinson's is apparently caused by the loss of dopamine-producing cells, and is connected with loss of motor coordination and ED. L-dopa and other drugs that are used to treat Parkinson's raise dopamine levels and frequently have the "side effect" of erection (Senbel, 2011).

SEX IN THE DIGITAL AGE

THINKING CRITICALLY ABOUT BUYING VIAGRA, CIALIS, AND OTHER DRUGS ONLINE

Viagra, Levitra, and Cialis are prescription drugs. Many men who might otherwise use them are reluctant to discuss ED with their physicians. The anonymity of doing things on the Internet is a lure; you don't have to admit your personal worries to your doctor face to face. Some men, unfortunately, do not even have a regular physician. What to do?

Many have discovered that by searching "Viagra" on the Net, they can find many Web sites where they can "consult" with online physicians, obtain a prescription, and order the drug for home delivery. Easy! A few questions and a fee—and they've got it. But is it wise? Perhaps, perhaps not.

Prescriptions are needed for various drugs because physicians are better equipped than most lay people to diagnose an individual's health problems, understand the chemical nature and side effects of the drugs that are available for treatment, and predict how the drugs will affect the individual patient. The physicians are also usually prepared to deal with the unexpected effects of the drugs, and there can be many.

So ask yourself what kind of physician will prescribe drugs online, without personally knowing the patient. Is it possible that some of them would have difficulty establishing private practices or getting jobs in hospitals? If you have a question about the drug once you use it, will you be able to get back to the prescriber easily for an answer, or will you wind up with an embarrassing call to your own physician or a trip to the emergency department?

You will find that many of the sites are online pharmacies that also advertise Propecia for treatment of hair loss, drugs that reverse the loss of pubic hair (yes, pubic hair), weight-control drugs that prevent the absorption of some of the fat in food (e.g., Xenical), herbal supplements, and so on. What you will tend to hit in your search are chemical armories of weapons that sound as if they can stop you from aging, or even reverse the aging process. It may sound as if they will help you remain (or return you to status as) a stud-muffin. But the fact is that medical science isn't there yet.

While surfing the Net, you will also come across sites that claim to have "natural" preparations, including a variety of herbs that are as effective as Viagra, but without the side effects, and without the need to get a prescription. Use some critical thinking: Are you convinced of the effectiveness and safety of these preparations? Because they are foods (sort of) rather than drugs, they escape the scrutiny of the FDA; the government is not watching over them. Be warned.

In sum, even if it is convenient to buy a drug online, you are well advised to get your prescription face to face—from a doctor you know and trust.

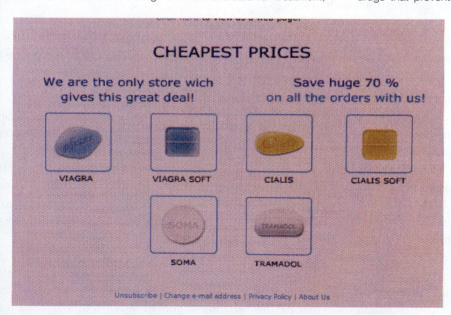

CHEAPEST PRICES

We are the only store wich gives this great deal!

Save huge 70 % on all the orders with us!

VIAGRA   VIAGRA SOFT   CIALIS   CIALIS SOFT

SOMA   TRAMADOL

Unsubscribe | Change e-mail address | Privacy Policy | About Us

Should You Buy Viagra or Cialis Online? Many Web sites enable men to consult with physicians and order Viagra or Cialis online. Is it wise to purchase prescription drugs without personally seeing the doctor? Prescriptions are needed for drugs when the person's diagnosis is in question and when the drugs have side effects. Physicians are better equipped than most laypeople to diagnose health problems, understand the chemical composition and effects of drugs, and predict how drugs will affect the individual.

Sounding like something from the "What will they think of next?" category, a vacuum pump helps men achieve erections through vacuum pressure. The device (brand name ErecAid) consists of a cylinder that is connected to a hand-operated vacuum pump. It creates a vacuum when it is held over the limp penis. The vacuum induces erection by increasing the flow of blood into the penis. Rubber bands around the base of the penis can maintain the erection for as long as 30 minutes.

The device has been used successfully by men with both organically and psychologically based erectile failure. However, side effects such as pain and black-and-blue marks are common. The rubber bands prevent normal ejaculation, so semen remains trapped in the urethra until the bands are released. The quality of the erections produced by the device is also considered inferior to spontaneous erections.

WOMEN WHO EXPERIENCE DIFFICULTY IN BECOMING SEXUALLY AROUSED
Psychological treatments for women who find it difficulty to become sexually aroused parallel those for orgasmic disorder and are discussed later in this chapter. They involve sex education (labeling the parts, discussing their functions, and explaining how to arouse them), searching out and coping with possible cognitive interference (such as negative sexual attitudes), creating nondemand situations in which sexual arousal may occur, and—when appropriate—working on problems in the relationship.

Yet many cases of female sexual arousal disorder reflect impaired blood flow to the genitals, just as in ED. Female sexual arousal involves vaginal lubrication, which permits sexual intercourse without a great deal of pain-causing friction. Lubrication is made possible by vasocongestion—the flow of blood into the genitals. Lack of lubrication can reflect the physical effects of aging, menopause, and surgically induced menopause, as through surgery.

Sometimes all that is necessary to deal with lack of lubrication is an artificial lubricant such as K-Y Jelly. But lessened blood flow to the genitals can also sap sexual pleasure and, as a consequence, lessen a woman's desire for sex.

The development of treatments for women has lagged behind the development of treatments for men. Ironically, the treatments that are emerging are highly similar to those that help men with ED.

For example, many trials have been undertaken with Viagra for women (Nurnberg et al., 2008). Researchers are also developing alprostadil (the vasodilator) for use with women, largely in the form of creams that are inserted into the vagina to enhance the flow of blood and hence lubrication.

orgasmic disorder

An American Psychiatric Association diagnosis characterizing women who persistently or recurrently have difficulty reaching orgasm despite attaining a level of sexual stimulation of sufficient intensity to usually result in orgasm.

ORGASMIC DISORDERS Because few men have difficulty reaching orgasm, our discussion will focus mainly on women. Women who have never experienced orgasm often harbor negative sexual attitudes that cause anxiety and inhibit sexual response. Treatment in such cases may first address these attitudes.

Masters and Johnson used a male–female couple-oriented approach in treating anorgasmic women, beginning sensate focus exercises. Then, during genital massage and later, during coitus, the woman guides her partner in the caresses and movements that she finds sexually exciting. They reported that taking charge helps free the woman from the traditional role of the passive, subordinate female.

Masters and Johnson recommend the position shown in Figure 12.3 to give the woman's partner access to her breasts and genitals. The gender of the partner clearly does not matter, although Masters and Johnson spoke of female–male couples. The woman guides her partner's hands to show the types of stimulation she enjoys. Genital play is *nondemanding.* The goals are to learn to provide and enjoy effective sexual stimulation, not to reach orgasm. The clitoris is not stimulated early because doing so may produce a high level of stimulation, or even hurt, before the woman is prepared.

After a number of occasions of genital play, a male–female couple undertake coitus in the female-superior position (see Figure 12.4). This position allows the woman

Figure 12.3   A Position for Nondemanding Stimulation of the Female Genitals.
This position gives the woman's partner access to her breasts and genitals. The woman can guide her partner's hands to demonstrate the types of stimulation she enjoys.

freedom of movement and control over her genital sensations. The couple engages in several sessions of deliberately slow thrusting to sensitize the woman to sensations produced by the penis and to break the common counterproductive pattern of desperate, rapid thrusting.

Orgasm cannot be willed or forced. When a woman receives effective stimulation, feels free to focus on erotic sensations, and feels that nothing is being demanded of her, she will generally reach orgasm. Once the woman is able to attain orgasm in the female-superior position, the couple may extend their sexual repertoire to other positions.

Masters and Johnson prefer working with the couple in cases of anorgasmia, but other sex therapists prefer to work with the woman individually through masturbation.

5 › T / F Truth or Fiction Revisited   Many sex therapists do recommend masturbation as a treatment for women who have never been able to reach orgasm (Cohen & Goldstein, 2016). Masturbation allows people to get in touch with their sexual responses at their own pace. The sexual pleasure they experience helps counter lingering sexual anxieties.

Figure 12.4   The Female-Superior Position.
In treatment of female orgasmic disorder, the couple is usually advised to undertake coitus in the female-superior position after a number of occasions of genital play. This position allows the woman freedom of movement and control over her genital sensations. She is told to regard the penis as her "toy." The couple engages in several sessions of deliberately slow thrusting to sensitize the woman to sensations produced by the penis and to break the common counterproductive pattern of desperate, rapid thrusting.

Although there is some variation among therapists, the following elements are commonly found in directed masturbation programs:

1. *Education.* The woman and her partner (if she has one) are educated about female sexuality.
2. *Self-exploration.* Self-exploration is encouraged as a way of increasing the woman's sense of body awareness. She may hold a mirror between her legs to locate her sexual anatomic features.
3. *Self-massage.* The woman creates a private, relaxing setting for self-massage. She begins to explore the sensitivity of her body to touch, discovering and repeating the caresses she finds pleasurable. Nonalcohol-based oils and lotions may be used to enhance the sensuous quality of the massage and to provide lubrication for the external genitalia. To prevent performance anxiety, the woman does not attempt to reach orgasm during the first few occasions.
4. *Giving oneself permission.* The woman may be advised to challenge lingering guilt and anxiety about sex. For example, she might repeat to herself, "This is my body. I have a right to learn about my body and receive pleasure from it."
5. *Use of fantasy.* Arousal is heightened through the use of sexual images, fantasies, and fantasy aids, such as erotic written or visual materials.
6. *Use of a vibrator.* A vibrator may provide more intense stimulation.
7. *Involvement of the partner.* Once the woman is capable of regularly achieving orgasm through masturbation, the focus may shift to her sexual relationship with her partner. Nondemanding sensate focus exercises may be followed by nondemanding coitus. The female-superior position is often used so that the woman can control the depth, angle, and rate of thrusting. She thus ensures that she receives the kinds of stimulation she needs to reach orgasm.

Our focus has been on sexual techniques, but it is worth noting that a combination of approaches that focus on sexual techniques and underlying interpersonal problems may be more effective than focusing on sexual techniques alone—at least for couples whose relationships are troubled (Firestone et al., 2006).

DELAYED EJACULATION Treatment of male orgasmic disorder generally focuses on increasing sexual stimulation and reducing performance anxiety (Althof, 2012). Masters and Johnson treated the problem within the context of the couple and prescribed sensate focus exercises for several days, during which the man made no attempt to ejaculate. The couple then brought the man to orgasm in any way it could, usually manually. Masters and Johnson dealt only with male–female couples, but we can assume that therapy with a male–male couple would in many cases stop here, with orgasm by manual or oral means. In the context of the male–female relationship, once the man could ejaculate in his partner's presence, she would bring him to the point at which he was about to ejaculate. Then, in the female-superior position, she inserted the penis and thrusted vigorously to bring him to orgasm. A male–male couple might experiment with anal intercourse at this point.

PREMATURE (EARLY) EJACULATION In the Masters and Johnson approach, sensate focus exercises are followed by practice in the training position shown in Figure 12.1. The woman teases her partner to erection and uses the **squeeze technique** when he indicates that he is about to ejaculate. She squeezes the tip of the penis, which temporarily prevents ejaculation. This process is repeated three or four times in a 15- to 20-minute session before the man purposely ejaculates.

Critical Thinking

Are there any sex therapy methods that seem "over the top" to you? Explain.

---

squeeze technique

A method for treating early ejaculation whereby the tip of the penis is squeezed temporarily to prevent ejaculation.

6 › T / F   Truth or Fiction Revisited   It is true that a man can be prevented from ejaculating by squeezing his penis when he feels that he is about to ejaculate. In using the squeeze technique, the partner holds the penis between the thumb and first two fingers of the same hand. The thumb presses against the frenulum. The fingers straddle the coronal ridge on the other side of the penis. Squeezing the thumb and forefingers together fairly hard for about 20 seconds (or until the man's urge to ejaculate passes) prevents ejaculation. The erect penis can withstand fairly strong pressure without discomfort, but erection may be partially lost.

After 2 or 3 days of these sessions, Masters and Johnson have a male–female couple begin coitus in the female-superior position because it creates less pressure to ejaculate. The woman inserts the penis. At first she contains it without thrusting, allowing the man to get used to intravaginal sensations. If he signals that he is about to ejaculate, she lifts off and squeezes the penis. After some repetitions, she begins slowly to move backward and forward, lifting off and squeezing as needed. The man learns gradually to tolerate higher levels of sexual stimulation without ejaculating.

The "stop–start" method for treating early ejaculation was introduced formally by urologist James Semans (1956). However, many men with early ejaculation have thought to use stopping and starting on their own (Porst et al., 2007). Semans's approach can be applied to manual stimulation, oral sex, or coitus. For example, the man's partner can manually stimulate him until he is about to ejaculate. He then signals his partner to suspend sexual stimulation and allows his arousal to subside before stimulation is resumed. This process enables the man to recognize the cues that precede his point of ejaculatory inevitability, or "point of no return," and to tolerate longer periods of sexual stimulation.

A CLOSER LOOK

IS VIAGRA FOR WOMEN?

As women age, they, like men, experience a reduced flow of blood to the genital region (Brotto et al., 2010). The clitoris becomes less engorged during sexual arousal and may be connected with feelings of lessened sexual arousal overall. Postmenopausal women experience vaginal dryness because of drop-off in estrogen (Wierman et al., 2010). Many older women say that they have lost interest in sex or have difficulty becoming aroused.

Researchers have suspected that PDE5 inhibitors such as Viagra would increase vasocongestion in the genital region of women as it does with men. Shouldn't these drugs, then, enhance the sexual experiences of women as well as men? Meredith Chivers and Raymond Rosen (2010) report that the use of PDE5 does in fact increase women's vasocongestion. However, the women do not reliably report "feeling" more sexually aroused or enjoying sex more. Why? There is apparently a gender difference in the connection between vasocongestion and the subjective sense of being sexually aroused. In men, the connection seems to be reliable, but in women, there is often either a minor connection or no connection between subjective feelings and physiological events in the genital region.

Put it another way. Use of a PDE5 inhibitor will usually increase vaginal lubrication in women, but that fact will not necessarily affect their sexual desire. Why? Part of the problem may be in the relationship. Part of the problem might lie in a deteriorating body image. The "medicalization" of sex therapy is unlikely to enhance the quality of a relationship or change one's body image. Counseling or psychotherapy may be better advised.

Some drugs that are usually used to treat psychological problems have been helpful in treating premature ejaculation (McMahon, 2011). Clomipramine, which is used to treat people with obsessive-compulsive disorder or schizophrenia, can impair erectile response at high doses. But in a study with 15 couples, low doses helped men engage in coitus five times longer than usual without ejaculating (Althof, 1994). Anti-depressant drugs are associated with ED, buy in younger men who do not have erectile problems, they have been shown to be helpful in treatment of premature ejaculation (Waldinger, 2011).

Why do drugs used to treat psychological problems help with early ejaculation? The psychological problems are frequently connected with imbalances in body chemistry, such as neurotransmitters—the chemical messengers of the brain. Neurotransmitters are also involved in other bodily functions, including ejaculation. "Anti-depressant" drugs all work by increasing the action of the neurotransmitter serotonin. Serotonin, in turn, may inhibit the ejaculatory reflex (Waldinger, 2011). But note the cautions about using SSRIs expressed previously in the chapter! It remains to be seen whether medications continue to show positive effects and compare their effectiveness with psychological sex therapy techniques.

Sexual Pain

Again, many cases of sexual pain stem from lack of adequate lubrication, which may in turn reflect insufficient foreplay or problems in the relationship. But if the problem is not successfully managed by increasing lubrication, painful sex may call for medical intervention to ascertain whether there are any underlying medical problems and treat them (van Lankveld et al., 2010).

When sexual pain is caused by vaginismus, treatment of vaginismus through a cognitive-behavioral approach may reduce pain. Many sex therapists treat vaginismus by "exposure"—that is, by insertion of fingers or vaginal dilators of increasing size under circumstances in which the woman remains relaxed (Macey et al., 2015; Pacik, 2015). In one study, women with vaginismus performed vaginal penetration exercises in the company of a female therapist (ter Kuile et al., 2009). When the woman is able to tolerate dilators (or fingers) equivalent in thickness to the penis, the couple may try coitus, but the woman should control insertion. Circumstances should remain relaxed and nondemanding. The idea is to avoid resensitizing her to fears of penetration. Because vaginismus often occurs among women with a history of sexual trauma, such as rape or incest, treatment for the psychological effects of these experiences may also be in order.

Critical Thinking

If you had a sexual dysfunction, do you think that you would be willing to participate in sex therapy? Explain. (And do you think women or men are likely to be more willing to engage in sex therapy? Why?)

Chapter Review

LO 12.1 Identify and define the kinds of sexual problems that come to the attention of helping professionals.

Sexual problems that persist and cause significant distress are labeled sexual dysfunctions by the American Psychiatric Association. Men are more likely to reach orgasm too quickly (premature ejaculation), and women are more likely to have lack of desire, difficulty reaching orgasm, and painful sex. Men also encounter lack of desire and often develop erectile disorder, especially as they age and begin taking medicines to control their blood pressure and cholesterol. Sexual pain disorders include dyspareunia, or painful sex, which may be experienced by both women and men, and the women's problems of vulvodyinia, in which the vulval region is intensely painful with burning and itching, and vaginismus, in which involuntary contraction of vaginal muscles make penetration painful.

LO 12.2 Discuss biological factors in the development of sexual problems.

Fatigue may lead to erectile disorder in men and to orgasmic disorder and dyspareunia in women. Dyspareunia may reflect inadequate lubrication, vaginal infections, and sexually transmitted infections. Biological factors are likely involved in most cases of erectile disorder. Medications for various health problems may impair sexual functioning. Aging can also impair sexual functioning.

LO 12.3 Discuss psychosocial factors in the development of sexual problems.

Psychosocial factors connected with sexual problems include cultural influences (e.g., sexually repressive environments), psychosexual trauma, problems in the relationship, lack of sexual skills, irrational beliefs, and performance anxiety. Some people lack the opportunity to acquire sexual knowledge and experience. An excessive need for approval and perfectionism can contribute to sexual problems.

Performance anxiety may place people with sexual problems in a spectator role rather than performer role.

LO 12.4 Discuss the historic Masters and Johnson approach to sex therapy.

Sex therapy modifies dysfunctional behavior by changing self-defeating beliefs and attitudes, fostering sexual skills and knowledge, enhancing sexual communication, and using exercises that enhance sexual stimulation while reducing performance anxiety. Masters and Johnson employed an in-residence program that focused on the couple as the unit of treatment. Sensate focus exercises were used to enable the partners to give each other pleasure in a nondemanding situation.

LO 12.5 Discuss the integration of sex therapy and psychotherapy.

Many therapists combine sex therapy with couple therapy or other forms of therapy to deal with related psychological problems and problems in relationships.

LO 12.6 Discuss the treatment of specific sexual dysfunctions.

Androgens heighten the sex drive in people with androgen deficiencies. Noninvasive biological treatments facilitate blood flow to the genitals or affect levels of neurotransmitters. Viagra, Cialis, and Levitra may help men with erectile disorder, and Addyi may help women who are concerned about lack of sexual desire. Masters and Johnson used a couples approach in treating anorgasmic women. Other therapists prefer directed masturbation to enable women to learn about their own bodies at their own pace and free them of the need to rely on partners. Dyspareunia may be treated by tackling health problems, ensuring that the woman is adequately lubricated, or, among older women, considering use of estrogen replacement. Vaginismus is generally treated with a series of dilators.

Test Your Learning

1. According to epidemiological studies, _____ is the most frequently reported sexual problem by women.
   - **(a)** vaginismus
   - **(b)** lack of sexual desire
   - **(c)** difficulty reaching orgasm
   - **(d)** problems in a relationship

2. Which of the following is most likely to have biological causes?
   - **(a)** Vulvodyinia
   - **(b)** Vaginismus
   - **(c)** Female orgasmic disorder
   - **(d)** Performance anxiety

3. According to epidemiological studies, men are least likely to experience _____
   - **(a)** erectile disorder.
   - **(b)** sexual pain.
   - **(c)** premature ejaculation.
   - **(d)** delayed ejaculation.

4. According to the text, _____ is most likely to be connected with a history of sexual trauma.
   - **(a)** erectile disorder
   - **(b)** premature ejaculation
   - **(c)** performance anxiety
   - **(d)** vaginismus

5. Alprostadil has been used in the treatment of _____
   - **(a)** premature ejaculation.
   - **(b)** erectile disorder.
   - **(c)** female orgasmic disorder.
   - **(d)** lack of sexual desire.

6. According to the text, a low level of _____ can lessen sexual desire in both men and women.
   - **(a)** male sex hormones
   - **(b)** sildenafil
   - **(c)** Depo-Provera
   - **(d)** alprostadil

7. All of the following are sex therapy methods, with the exception of _____
   - **(a)** penile implants.
   - **(b)** improving sexual communication.
   - **(c)** reducing performance anxiety.
   - **(d)** sensate focus exercises.

8. _____ is sometimes treated with a series of rings of plastic dilators.
   - **(a)** Dyspareunia
   - **(b)** Female sexual arousal disorder
   - **(c)** Vaginismus
   - **(d)** Erectile disorder

9. Addyi is used to treat _____
   - **(a)** lack of sexual desire in women.
   - **(b)** lack of sexual desire in men.
   - **(c)** dyspareunia.
   - **(d)** premature ejaculation.

10. Sex therapists are most likely to recommend masturbation as a treatment for _____
    - **(a)** premature ejaculation.
    - **(b)** female orgasmic disorder.
    - **(c)** vaginismus.
    - **(d)** delayed ejaculation.

Answers: 1. b; **2.** a; **3.** b; **4.** d; **5.** b; **6.** a; **7.** a; **8.** c; **9.** a; **10.** b

Chapter 13
Sexually Transmitted Infections

Learning Objectives

LO 13.1 Describe features of the epidemic of sexually transmitted infections.

Bacterial Infections

LO 13.2 Discuss the transmission, effects, and treatment of gonorrhea.

LO 13.3 Discuss the transmission, effects, and treatment of syphilis.

LO 13.4 Discuss the transmission, effects, and treatment of chlamydia.

LO 13.5 Discuss the transmission, effects, and treatment of other bacterial sexually transmitted infections.

Vaginal Infections

LO 13.6 Discuss the transmission, effects, and treatment of various vaginal infections.

Viral Infections

LO 13.7 Discuss the transmission, effects, and treatment of HIV/AIDS.

LO 13.8 Discuss the transmission, effects, and treatment of genital herpes.

LO 13.9 Discuss the transmission, effects, and treatment of human papilloma virus.

LO 13.10 Discuss the transmission, effects, and treatment of the Zika virus and other viral sexually transmitted infections.

Ectoparasitic Infestations

LO 13.11 Discuss the transmission, effects, and treatment of ectoparasitic infestations.

Preventing STIs: It's More Than Safer Sex

LO 13.12 Explain ways of preventing sexually transmitted infections.

TRUTH OR FICTION?

Which of the following statements are the truth, and which are fiction? Look for the Truth-or-Fiction items throughout this chapter to find the answers.

1   Most women who contract gonorrhea do not develop symptoms.   **T / F**?

2   Christopher Columbus brought more than beads, blankets, and tobacco back to Europe from the New World: He also brought syphilis.   **T / F**?

3   Gonorrhea and syphilis can be contracted from toilet seats in public restrooms.   **T / F**?

4   If a syphilitic sore goes away by itself, the infection does not require medical treatment.   **T / F**?

5   Men can develop vaginal infections.   **T / F**?

6   As you are reading this, you are engaged in search-and-destroy missions against foreign agents within your body.   **T / F**?

7   Most people who are infected by HIV remain symptom free and seem to be healthy for years.   **T / F**?

8   Genital herpes can be transmitted only during flare-ups of the infection.   **T / F**?

9   Pubic lice are of the same family of animals as crabs.   **T / F**?

Harold and Carin, both 20, have been seeing each other for months. They both want to have sex but have hesitated because of fears about of HIV/AIDS and other sexually transmitted infections (STIs). Harold wants them both to be tested for HIV, the virus that causes AIDS. Carin resists because she feels insulted. Harold doesn't know what to make of her refusal, and they drift apart.

Baron, 18, got drunk at a party 3 days ago and had unprotected anal intercourse in the bathroom with another guy. He can't recall the other man's name, or whether he ever knew it. He confides to his roommate about it, and his roommate says he should see a doctor right away. Why bother, Baron wonders, trembling; either he was infected with HIV or he wasn't, right? (Wrong, actually, as we will see.) The next day his roommate tells him he nothing against gays, but the situation is weird and he's moving out. Baron says he isn't gay, but he wonders about that too. And should he get himself to a doctor?

Keisha, a 24-year-old law student, was diagnosed, she has had no recurrences since the initial outbreak 2 years earlier. But she knows that herpes is a lifelong infection and may recur from time to time. She also knows that she may inadvertently transmit the herpes virus to sex partners. She has begun thinking seriously about Steve, a keeper. She would like to tell him that she has herpes before they have sex, but she fears that it might scare him off.

Melanie and Craig have a 12-year-old daughter Lin. Melanie's doctor said it was time for Lin to be vaccinated against HPV. Why, Melanie wondered, should a 12-year-old be vaccinated against an STI? She brought it up with Craig, and he couldn't think of a reason either. Melanie called her older sister and she advised against doing it; it would only encourage Lin to have sex. Melanie planned to think about it later, but instead she pushed the matter out of her mind.

José, 21, a computer whiz, is planning some day to run AI for a large corporation. He lives off-campus with several of his buddies in a run-down house they've dubbed "The Nuclear Dumpsite." He has been seeing Maria, a theater major, for several months. They have been practicing "safer sex"— at least most of the time. During the past week he noticed a burning sensation while urinating. It passes so he figures that it was probably nothing to worry about. But he's not sure and wonders whether he should see a doctor—or tell Maria about it.

LO 13.1 Describe features of the epidemic of sexually transmitted infections.

Harold, Carin, Baron, Keisha, Melanie, and José express some of the fears and concerns of a generation of young people who are becoming sexually active at a time when the threats of HIV/AIDS and other **sexually transmitted infections (STIs)** hang over every sexual opportunity and decision.

STIs are rampant. HIV/AIDS is indeed a scary thing—a very scary thing. But HIV/AIDS is only one of many STIs, and other STIs actually pose wider threats (American Sexual Health Association, 2015; HIV in the United States, 2015; Reported STDs in the United States, 2014):

- More than half the people in the United States will be infected with an STI at some point during their lifetime.

- The incidence of chlamydia has increased to about 3 million cases per years, and it remains largely undiagnosed.

- There are some 820,000 new cases of gonorrhea each year, and drug-resistant strains of gonorrhea are evolving.

- Most chlamydia and gonorrhea infections occur among 15- to 24-year-olds.

- About one in six Americans is infected with *Herpes simplex* virus (HSV)-2.

- Despite widespread knowledge of how HIV is transmitted, the number of new cases of HIV infection has remained stubbornly stable at about 40,000 to 50,000 in the United States each year.[1]

College students have become reasonably well versed about HIV/AIDS. However, many are unaware that chlamydia can go undetected for years. Moreover, if it is left untreated, it can cause pelvic inflammation and infertility. Many college students appear to be ignorant about human papillomavirus (HPV) and its links to genital warts, cervical cancer, even cancer of the throat (Chaturvedi et al., 2011). But the Centers for Disease Control and Prevention (CDC) estimates that as many as 6 million new cases of HPV infection occur each year in the United States—more than syphilis, genital herpes, and HIV/AIDS combined. Whereas about 1.2 million Americans are living with HIV/AIDS, another 50 to 60 million are infected with other STI-causing viruses, such as those causing herpes, hepatitis, and cervical cancer.

Sexually transmitted infections are transmitted through sexual means, such as vaginal or anal intercourse or oral sex. Some writers call them sexually transmitted *diseases (STDs)* rather than *infections*. They were previously called *venereal diseases (VDs)*—after Venus, the Roman goddess of love. We refer to them as STIs because a person can be infected before developing a disease. HPV, for example, is an organism that infects people; genital warts and cancers are the kinds of diseases that can develop from infection.

sexually transmitted infections (STIs)

Infections that can be communicated through sexual contact.

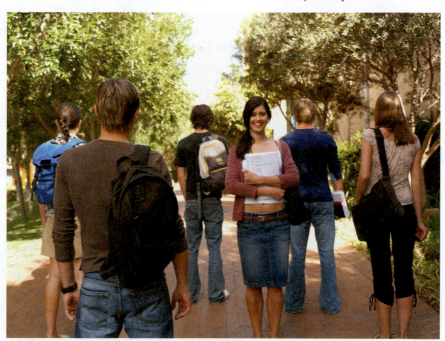

Who Is at Risk? Anyone can contract sexually transmitted infections (STIs). In fact, the majority of people will contract an STI at some time in their lives. What will you do to learn about them and protect yourself?

---

[1]According to the Centers for Disease Control's *HIV Surveillance Report* (Vol. 26, November 2015), the estimated number of new HIV diagnoses in 2014 was 44,073, including 174 diagnoses among children below the age of 13.

Some STIs are spread through nonsexual contact as well. For example, HIV and viral hepatitis may be spread by sharing contaminated hypodermic syringes such as those used by people "shooting up" drugs. And a few STIs (such as the parasitic infection we sometimes refer to as "crabs") may be picked up from bedding or other objects, such as moist towels. Zika is transmitted by mosquitoes as well as sexual contact.

The United States is believed to have the highest rate of infection by STIs in the industrialized world. In a recent year, for example, more than 100 cases of gonorrhea were reported per 100,000 people in the United States (Reported STDs in the United States, 2014) as compared with 18.6 per 100,000 in Canada and 3 per 100,000 in Sweden.

Do not read the remainder of this paragraph unless you are ready for the truth: Some of you readers have STIs and do not know it. But ignorance is not bliss. Some STIs do not produce noticeable symptoms but can be harmful if left untreated. STIs can also be painful and—in the cases of HIV/AIDS, advanced syphilis, and the cervical cancer that can follow infection with HPV—lethal. Hundreds of thousands of women become infertile each year because of STIs that are spreading through their reproductive system (STDs and Infertility, 2015). Overall, STIs are believed to account for 15% to 30% of cases of infertility among women. In addition to their biological effects, STIs exact an emotional toll and can strain relationships to the breaking point.

Why the surge in the incidence of STIs? One factor is the number of young people who have sex. Many of them fail to use latex condoms consistently, if at all. Some people do not use condoms because the woman is on the pill or using another form of hormonal birth control (Morrison & Nanda, 2012). Hormonal methods of birth control may prevent conception, but they do not prevent STIs. Another reason is that people with some infections, such as chlamydia, are symptom-free. Therefore, they may unwittingly transmit them to others. Other risk factors include early sexual involvement and sex with multiple partners (Sex and Infertility, 2015). Drug use is also associated with an increased risk of STIs (George et al., 2014; Yu et al., 2015). People who abuse drugs are more likely than others to engage in risky sexual practices. Moreover, certain forms of drug use, such as needle sharing, can directly transmit infectious organisms such as HIV. Another risk factor, ironically, is the apparent success of antiretroviral therapy in treating HIV/AIDS. As a result, many individuals who had become more cautious in their sexual behavior have once again thrown caution to the wind (Grady, 2012; McNeil, 2012).

Bacterial Infections

Bacteria are one-celled microorganisms, some are essential to human life and some are harmful. Bacteria play vital roles in our bodies' digestive systems. Bacteria are essential to fermentation. Without bacteria, there would be no wine. Unfortunately, bacteria also cause many diseases such as pneumonia, tuberculosis, and meningitis—along with the common STIs gonorrhea, syphilis, and chlamydia.

Gonorrhea

LO 13.2 **Discuss the transmission, effects, and treatment of gonorrhea.**

Gonorrhea—also known as "the clap" or "the drip"—was once the most widespread bacterial STI in the United States, but it has been replaced by chlamydia. The rate of infection declined 74% between 1975 and 1997, and 22% between 2000 and 2010, possibly because of safer sex practices and use of antibiotics (Sexually transmitted disease surveillance, 2015; see Figure 13.1). It is estimated that there are about 820,000 new cases of gonorrhea a year in the United States. People aged 20–24 are in the age group most likely to contract gonorrhea.

Gonorrhea is caused by the gonococcus bacterium (see Table 13.1). A penile discharge that was probably gonorrhea is described in ancient Egyptian and Chinese

---

Critical Thinking
Why do you think the United States has the largest incidence of STIs in the industrialized world? Can you think of social and cultural forces that may be at work?

bacteria
One-celled microorganisms that have no chlorophyll and can give rise to many illnesses.

gonorrhea
An STI caused by the *Neisseria gonorrhoeae* bacterium and characterized by a discharge and burning urination.

writings and is mentioned in the Hebrew Bible (Leviticus 15). Ancient Jews and Greeks assumed that the discharge was an involuntary loss of seminal fluid. In about 400 BCE the Greek physician Hippocrates suggested that the loss stemmed from excessive sex or "worship" of Aphrodite (whom the Romans would later rename *Venus*). The term *gonorrhea* is credited to the Greek physician Galen, who lived in the second century ce. Albert L. S. Neisser identified the gonococcus bacterium that bears his name in 1879: *Neisseria gonorrhoeae*.

TRANSMISSION   Gonococcal bacteria require a warm, moist environment, like that found along the mucous membranes of the urinary tract in both genders or the cervix in women. Outside the body, they die in about a minute. There is no evidence that gonorrhea can be picked up from public toilet seats or by touching dry objects. In rare cases, gonorrhea is contracted by contact with a moist, warm towel or sheet used immediately beforehand by an infected person. Gonorrhea is almost always transmitted by unprotected vaginal, oral, or anal sex, or from mother to newborn during delivery.

A person who performs fellatio on an infected man may develop **pharyngeal gonorrhea**, which produces a throat infection. Mouth-to-mouth kissing and cunnilingus are less likely to spread gonorrhea. The eyes provide a good environment for the bacterium. Thus, a person whose hands come into contact with infected genitals and who inadvertently touches his or her eyes afterward may infect them. Babies have contracted gonorrhea of the eyes (**ophthalmia neonatorum**) when passing through the birth canals of infected mothers. This disorder may cause blindness but has become rare because the eyes of newborns are treated routinely with silver nitrate or penicillin ointment, which kill gonococcal bacteria.

A gonorrheal infection may be spread from the penis to the partner's rectum during anal intercourse. A cervical gonorrheal infection can be spread to the rectum if an infected woman and her partner follow vaginal intercourse with anal intercourse. Gonorrhea is less likely to be spread by vaginal discharge than by penile discharge.

Gonorrhea is highly contagious. Women stand nearly a 50% chance of contracting gonorrhea after one exposure. Men have a 25% risk of infection (Zieman et al., 2015–2016). The risks to women are apparently greater because women retain infected semen in the vagina. The risk of infection increases with repeated exposure.

SYMPTOMS   Most men experience symptoms 2 to 5 days after infection. Symptoms include a penile discharge that is clear at first (see Figure 13.1). Within a day it turns yellow to yellow-green, thickens, and becomes puslike. The urethra becomes inflamed, and urination is accompanied by a burning sensation. From 30% to 40% of males have swelling and tenderness in the lymph glands of the groin. Inflammation and other symptoms may become chronic if left untreated.

The initial symptoms of gonorrhea usually abate within a few weeks without treatment, leading people to think of gonorrhea as being no worse than a bad cold. However, the gonococcus bacterium will usually continue to damage the body internally.

The primary site of infection in women is the cervix, where it causes cervicitis. **Cervicitis** may cause a yellowish to yellow-green puslike discharge that irritates the vulva. If the infection spreads to the urethra, women may also note burning urination.

1 › T / F   Truth or Fiction Revisited   Despite the facts that many women who contract gonorrhea have a discharge and some local irritation, it is true that most women who contract gonorrhea do not have noticeable symptoms. *About 80% of the women who contract gonorrhea have no symptoms during the early stages of the infection.* Because many infected women do not seek treatment until symptoms develop, they may innocently infect another sex partner.

When gonorrhea is not treated early, it may spread through the urogenital systems in both genders and strike the internal reproductive organs. In men, it can lead to

pharyngeal gonorrhea
A gonorrheal infection that is characterized by a sore throat.

ophthalmia neonatorum
A gonorrheal infection of the eyes of newborn children who contract the disease by passing through an infected birth canal.

cervicitis
Inflammation of the cervix.

Figure 13.1   Gonorrheal Discharge.

Gonorrhea in the male often causes a thick, yellowish, puslike discharge from the penis.

Table 13.1 Causes, Modes of Transmission, Symptoms, Diagnosis, and Treatment of Major STIs

STI and Pathogen	Transmission	Symptoms	Diagnosis	Treatment
Bacterial Infections				
Gonorrhea ("the clap," "the drip"): Gonococcus bacterium (*Neisseria gonorrhoeae*)	Vaginal, oral, or anal sex; from mother to newborn during delivery	In men, yellowish, thick penile discharge, burning urination; in women, increased vaginal discharge, burning urination, irregular menstrual bleeding (most women are symptom-free early on)	Clinical inspection, culture of sample discharge	Antibiotics
Syphilis: *Treponema pallidum*	Vaginal, oral, or anal sex; touching an infectious chancre; congenitally	Primary stage: hard, round painless chancre or sore at site of infection within 2 to 4 weeks; may progress if untreated	Primary-stage: clinical examination and by examination of fluid from a chancre; secondary-stage: blood test (the VDRL)	Antibiotics
Chlamydia and nongonococcal urethritis (NGU): *Chlamydia trachomatous* bacterium	Vaginal, oral, or anal sex; touching eyes after touching genitals of an infected partner; to newborns via childbirth	Often symptom free, but women and men may have frequent and painful urination, lower abdominal discomfort, and discharge; sore throat from oral sex	Abbott Test-pack analyzes cervical smear; in men, penile fluid is analyzed	Antibiotics
Vaginal Infections				
Bacterial vaginosis: *Gardnerella vaginalis* bacterium and others	Overgrowth of organisms in vagina; allergic reactions; sexual contact	May be symptom free; irritation and inflammation in genitals, discharge, painful urination	Culture and examination of bacterium	Metronidazole, clindamycin
Candidiasis (moniliasis, thrush, "yeast infection"): *Candida albicans*—a yeastlike fungus	Overgrowth of fungus in vagina; sexual contact; sharing washcloth with infected person	In women, vulval itching and soreness; white, cheesy, foul-smelling discharge; in men, itching and reddening of penis, burning urination	Clinical examination	Single-dose oral fluconazole, or suppositories of miconazole, clotrimazole, or butaconazole
Trichomoniasis ("trich"): *Trichomonas vaginalis*—a protozoan (one-celled animal)	Almost always transmitted sexually	In women, foamy, yellowish, odorous discharge; vulval itching or burning; may be symptom free; men usually symptom free, possible mild urethritis	Microscopic examination of a smear of vaginal secretions or culture of sample	Metronidazole
Viral Infections				
Oral herpes: *Herpes simplex virus type 1 (or HSV-1)*	Contact with sores or blisters; sharing cups, towels, toilet seats	Cold sores or fever blisters on the lips, mouth, or throat; herpetic sores on genitals	Clinical examination	Lip balms, cold sore medications

epididymitis

Inflammation of the epididymis.

pelvic inflammatory disease (PID)

Inflammation of the pelvic region; symptoms are abdominal pain, tenderness, nausea, fever, and irregular menstrual cycles; PID may lead to infertility.

epididymitis, which can cause fertility problems. Swelling and feelings of tenderness or pain in the scrotum are the principal symptoms of epididymitis. Fever may also be present. Occasionally the kidneys are affected.

In women, the bacterium can spread through the cervix to the uterus, fallopian tubes, ovaries, and other parts of the abdominal cavity, causing **pelvic inflammatory disease (PID)**. Symptoms of PID include cramps, abdominal pain and tenderness, cervical tenderness and discharge, irregular menstrual cycles, coital pain, fever, nausea, and vomiting. PID may also be present in the absence of symptoms. PID can cause scarring that blocks the fallopian tubes, leading to infertility. PID is a serious illness that requires aggressive treatment with antibiotics. Surgery may be needed to remove infected tissue. Unfortunately, many women become aware of a gonococcal infection only when they develop PID. These consequences are all the more unfortunate because gonorrhea, when diagnosed and treated early, clears up rapidly in more than 90% of cases.

DIAGNOSIS AND TREATMENT Diagnosis of gonorrhea involves clinical inspection of the genitals by a physician (e.g., a family practitioner, urologist, or gynecologist) and the culturing and examination of a sample of genital discharge.

Table 13.1 (continued)

STI and Pathogen	Transmission	Symptoms	Diagnosis	Treatment
Genital herpes: *Herpes simplex virus type 2 (or HSV-2)*	Vaginal, oral, or anal sex; most contagious during flare-ups	Painful, reddish bumps that turn into pus-filled blisters around genitals, thigh, or buttocks, or in vagina or on cervix; possible burning urination, fever, aches and pains, swollen glands; vaginal discharge	Clinical examination; culture of fluid from sore	No cure, but antiviral drugs may provide relief and promote healing
Viral hepatitis: hepatitis A, B, C, and D type viruses	Sexual contact, especially involving the anus; transfusion of contaminated blood	Varies; symptom free to mild flulike symptoms to fever, abdominal pain, vomiting, and "jaundiced" (yellowish) skin and eyes	Blood tests; liver biopsy	Bed rest, fluids, and, sometimes, antibiotics to ward off opportunistic infections; alpha interferon
HIV/AIDS	Sexual contact, contaminated hypodermic syringes, transfusions of infected blood, and from mother to infant during childbirth or breastfeeding	May be symptom free for years or have mild flulike symptoms; eventual "full-blown" AIDS is symptomized by fever, weight loss, fatigue, diarrhea, and lethal opportunistic infections	Blood, saliva, or urine tests detect HIV antibodies; other tests confirm the presence of the virus itself	A "cocktail" of antiretroviral drugs (ART) appears to stem the progress of HIV/AIDS
Human Papillomavirus (HPV)	Sexual and other forms of contact, as with infected towels or clothing	May be symptom free or have painless warts on genital organs; may lead to cervical and other cancers, such as throat cancer in men who perform cunnilingus on infected women.	Clinical inspection, Pap test, DNA test	Warts can be removed by freezing, burning, surgery, and medications; a vaccine can protect most people from infection
Zika	Sexual contact and bites by mosquitoes carrying the virus	Embryos and fetuses developing within infected mothers may develop microcephaly; fever, rash, joint pain, red eyes	Blood test	Body usually clears itself of the virus; no vaccine is available as this book goes to press
Ectoparasitic Infestations				
Pediculosis ("crabs"): *Pthirus pubis (public lice)*	Sexual contact or by contact with an infested towel, sheet, or toilet seat	Intense itching in pubic area and other hairy regions to which lice can attach	Clinical examination	Prescription lindane and non-prescription medications (brand names Nix, RID, Triple X)
Scabies: *Sarcoptes scabiei*	Sexual contact or contact with infested clothing or bed linen, towels, and other fabrics	Intense itching; reddish lines on skin where mites have burrowed in; welts and pus-filled blisters	Clinical inspection	Lindane

Antibiotics are the standard treatment for gonorrhea. Penicillin was once the favored antibiotic, but the rise of penicillin-resistant strains of the bacterium has required use of alternative antibiotics (Gonococcal Infections, 2015). A combination of certriazone and azithromycin is generally recommended in the United States. Other antibiotics that are used to treat gonorrhea include ciprofloxacin and ofloxacin. Because gonorrhea and chlamydia often occur together, people who are infected with gonorrhea may also be treated for chlamydia with another antibiotic. Sex partners of people with gonorrhea should also be examined.

Key facts about sexually transmitted infections discussed in the chapter are summarized in Table 13.1.

Syphilis

LO 13.3   Discuss the transmission, effects, and treatment of syphilis.

Nobody wanted to be associated with **syphilis**. In Naples they called it "the French disease." In France it was "the Neapolitan disease." Many Italians called it "the Spanish disease," but in Spain they called it "the disease of Española" (modern Haiti).

Critical Thinking
How do penicillin-resistant strains of a bacterial agent evolve?

syphilis
An STI that is caused by the *Treponema pallidum* bacterium, which may progress through several stages of development from a chancre to a rash to damage to vital body systems.

Figure 13.2   Treponema pallidum.

Treponema pallidum is the bacterium that causes syphilis. Because of the spiral shape, *T. pallidum* is also called a spirochete.

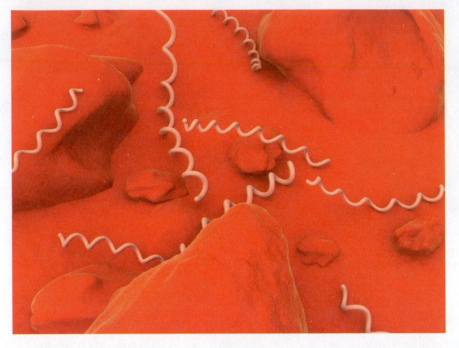

In 1530, the Italian physician Girolamo Fracastoro wrote a poem about a shepherd boy named Syphilus, who was afflicted with the disease as retribution for insulting the sun god Apollo.

Syphilis is caused by a bacterium isolated in 1905 by the German scientist Fritz Schaudinn: *Treponema pallidum* (*T. pallidum*, for short) (see Figure 13.2). The name contains roots meaning a "faintly colored (pallid) turning thread," describing the corkscrew-like shape of the microscopic organism. Because of the spiral shape, *T. pallidum* is also called a '*spirochete,* from Greek roots meaning "spiral" and "hair."

The incidence of syphilis decreased in the United States with the introduction of penicillin (see Figure 13.3). Figure 13.4 shows that the rates of infection are highest in the southern United States, Washington, DC, California, and New York. But despite the availability of penicillin, there has been a recent resurgence in rates of syphilis to more than 11,000 cases per year, in part because the advent of effective drugs for HIV/AIDS has contributed to a new wave of risky sexual behavior among many individuals (Sexually transmitted disease surveillance, 2015). About six of seven new cases are found among men who have sex with men (Syphilis Statistics, 2015). Even so, the rates among women and infants (resulting from **congenital syphilis**) have also risen.

Depending on when syphilis is diagnosed and treated, its effects can range from negligible to harmful to lethal. They include heart disease, blindness, confusion, and death. Syphilis killed the painter Paul Gauguin.

congenital syphilis

A syphilis infection that is present at birth.

Figure 13.3   Reported Cases of Syphilis, According to Year and Stage of Infection, 1941–2014.

Because of frequent testing for syphilis, treatment with antibiotics, and preventive measures, the number of newly reported cases of syphilis has declined since the 1940s, but there have been recent upsurges.

SOURCE: Centers for Disease Control and Prevention. *Sexually Transmitted Disease Surveillance 2014.* Atlanta: U.S. Department of Health and Human Services; 2015. Figure 31.

Figure 13.4   Rates of Primary and Secondary Syphilis—Reported Cases by State, United States and Outlying Areas, 2014.

Rates of syphilis are highest in the southern United States, the District of Columbia, California, and New York State.

SOURCE: Centers for Disease Control and Prevention. *Sexually Transmitted Disease Surveillance 2014.* Atlanta: U.S. Department of Health and Human Services; 2015. Figure 35.

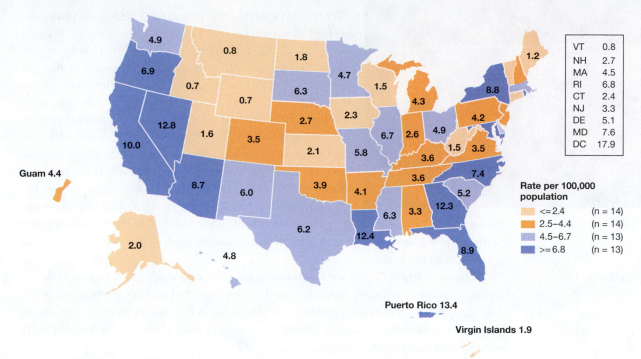

VT	0.8
NH	2.7
MA	4.5
RI	6.8
CT	2.4
NJ	3.3
DE	5.1
MD	7.6
DC	17.9

Guam 4.4

Rate per 100,000 population

	<=2.4	(n = 14)
	2.5–4.4	(n = 14)
	4.5–6.7	(n = 13)
	>=6.8	(n = 13)

Puerto Rico 13.4

Virgin Islands 1.9

NOTE: The total rate of primary and secondary syphilis for the United States and outlying areas (Guam, Puerto Rico, and Virgin Islands) was 6.4 per 100,000 population.

THE ORIGINS OF SYPHILIS The origins of syphilis are controversial. The Columbian theory holds that Christopher Columbus returned to Spain from his first voyage to the West Indies (1492–1493) with more than beads, blankets, and tobacco. Then, from Spain, Spanish mercenaries may have carried the disease to Naples when they were hired to protect that city from French invaders. Then the French army may have contracted syphilis from prostitutes, who also practiced their profession with the Spaniards and Neapolitans. Sailors may have eventually spread syphilis to the East.

2 › T / F   Truth or Fiction Revisited   It is generally accepted that Columbus exhibited symptoms of advanced syphilis when he died in 1506. However, it is unclear whether or not Columbus brought syphilis back to Europe from the New World.

TRANSMISSION   Syphilis, like gonorrhea, is most often transmitted by vaginal or anal intercourse, or oral–genital or oral–anal sex with an infected person. The spirochete is usually transmitted when open lesions on an infected person come into contact with the mucous membranes or skin abrasions of the partner's body during sexual activity. Syphilis may also be contracted by touching an infectious **chancre**, but not from using the same toilet seat as an infected person.

chancre

A sore or ulcer.

3 › T / F   Truth or Fiction Revisited   It is not true that gonorrhea and syphilis can be contracted from toilet seats in public rest rooms.

Pregnant women may transmit syphilis to their fetuses because the spirochete can cross the placental membrane. Miscarriage, stillbirth, or congenital syphilis may result. Congenital syphilis may impair vision and hearing or deform bones and teeth.

Figure 13.5 Syphilis Chancre.

The first stage, or primary stage, of a syphilis infection is marked by the appearance of a painless sore or chancre at the site of the infection.

Blood tests are administered routinely during pregnancy to diagnose syphilis in the mother so that congenital problems in the baby may be averted. The fetus will probably not be harmed if an infected mother is treated before the fourth month of pregnancy.

SYMPTOMS AND COURSE OF ILLNESS Syphilis develops through several stages. In the first or *primary stage* of syphilis, a painless chancre (a hard, round, ulcer-like lesion with raised edges) appears at the site of infection 2 to 4 weeks after contact. When women are infected, the chancre usually forms on the vaginal walls or the cervix. It may also form on the external genitalia, most often on the labia. When men are infected, the chancre usually forms on the penile glans. It may also form on the scrotum or penile shaft. If the mode of transmission is oral sex, the chancre may appear on the lips or tongue (see Figure 13.5). If the infection is spread by anal sex, the rectum may serve as the site of the chancre. The chancre disappears within a few weeks, but if the infection remains untreated, syphilis will continue to work within the body.

The *secondary stage* begins a few weeks to a few months later. A skin rash develops, consisting of painless, reddish, raised bumps that darken after a while and burst, oozing a discharge. Other symptoms include sores in the mouth, painful swelling of joints, a sore throat, headaches, and fever. A person with syphilis may thus wrongly assume that he or she has the flu.

These symptoms also disappear. Syphilis then enters the *latent stage* and may lie dormant for 1 to 40 years. But spirochetes continue to multiply and burrow into the circulatory system, central nervous system (brain and spinal cord), and bones. The person may no longer be contagious to sex partners after several years in the latent stage, but a pregnant woman may pass along the infection to her newborn at any time.

In many cases the disease eventually progresses to the late or *tertiary stage*. A large ulcer may form on the skin, muscle tissue, digestive organs, lungs, liver, or other organs. This destructive ulcer can often be successfully treated, but still more serious damage can occur as the infection attacks the central nervous system or the cardiovascular system (the heart and the major blood vessels). Either outcome can be fatal. **Neurosyphilis** can cause brain damage, resulting in paralysis or the mental illness called **general paresis**.

neurosyphilis

Syphilitic infection of the central nervous system, which can cause brain damage and death.

general paresis

A progressive form of mental illness caused by neurosyphilis and characterized by gross confusion.

VDRL

Named after the Venereal Disease Research Laboratory, a test for the presence of antibodies to *Treponema pallidum* in the blood.

antibodies

Specialized proteins that are produced by the white blood cells of the immune system in response to disease organisms and other toxic substances, and that recognize and attack the invading organisms or substances.

4 ▶ T / F Truth or Fiction Revisited The primary and secondary symptoms of syphilis inevitably disappear, but it is *not* true that the infection does not require medical treatment if a syphilitic chancre (sore) goes away by itself. The belief that medical treatment is unnecessary if the symptoms of an STI disappear by themselves is unfounded. Gonorrhea and syphilis, for example, both can damage the body even when their early symptoms have abated.

DIAGNOSIS AND TREATMENT Primary-stage syphilis is diagnosed by clinical examination. If a chancre is found, fluid drawn from it can be examined under a microscope. The spirochetes are usually quite visible. Blood tests are not definitive until the secondary stage begins. The most frequently used blood test is the **VDRL**, which tests for the presence of **antibodies** to *Treponema pallidum* in the blood.

Penicillin is the treatment of choice for syphilis, usually a single injection of long-acting Benzathine penicillin. Options for non-pregnant individuals who are allergic to penicillin include doxycycline, tetracycline, and ceftriaxone (Syphilis Treatment and Care, 2015). Sex partners of persons infected with syphilis should also be evaluated by a physician.

Chlamydia

LO 13.4   **Discuss the transmission, effects, and treatment of chlamydia.**

Chlamydia, another bacterial STI, is more common than gonorrhea and syphilis in the United States (STI surveillance, 2015). Chlamydia infections are caused by the *Chlamydia trachomatis* bacterium, a parasitic organism that can survive only within cells. The bacterium can cause several different types of infection, including *nongonococcal urethritis (NGU)* in men and women, *epididymitis* (infection of the epididymis) in men, and *cervicitis* (infection of the cervix), *endometritis* (infection of the endometrium), and PID in women.

The CDC estimates that there are about 3 million new chlamydia infections each year. The incidence of chlamydia infections is especially high among female teenagers and college students. The rate of infection is highest among young people aged 20–24 and 15–19 (Figure 13.6). Women are more likely to be infected than men. The highest infection rates are found in the south and southwest, and also in Washington, DC and Illinois (see Figure 13.7).

TRANSMISSION   *Chlamydia trachomatis* is usually transmitted through vaginal or anal sexual intercourse (Chlamydia—CDC fact sheet, 2014). *Chlamydia trachomatis* may also cause an eye infection if a person touches his or her eyes after handling the genitals of an infected partner. Oral sex with an infected partner can infect the throat. Newborns can acquire potentially serious chlamydia eye infections as they pass through the cervix of an infected mother during birth. Even newborns delivered by Cesarean section may be infected if the amniotic sac breaks before delivery.

Figure 13.6   New Cases of Chlamydia by Age and Sex, United States, 2014.

People in the United States are most likely to contract chlamydia in their early 20s, although the ages of 15–19 are not far behind. The incidence of new infections then tapers off as people become more likely to enter long-term relationships and have fewer sex partners. They also might grow more wise and careful.

SOURCE: Centers for Disease Control and Prevention. *Sexually Transmitted Disease Surveillance 2014.* Atlanta: U.S. Department of Health and Human Services; 2015. Figure 5.

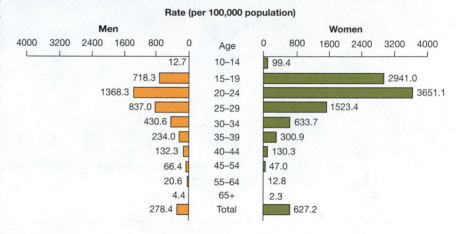

SYMPTOMS   Chlamydia infections usually produce symptoms that are similar to, but milder than, those of gonorrhea. In men, *Chlamydia trachomatis* can lead to nongonococcal urethritis (NGU). *Urethritis* is an inflammation of the urethra. NGU refers to forms of urethritis that are not caused by the gonococcal bacterium. (NGU is generally diagnosed only in men. In women, an inflammation of the urethra caused by *Chlamydia trachomatis* is called a chlamydia infection or simply chlamydia.) NGU was formerly called nonspecific urethritis or NSU. Many organisms can cause NGU. *Chlamydia trachomatis* accounts for about half of the cases among men.

Nongonococcal urethritis in men may produce a thin, whitish discharge from the penis and some burning or other pain during urination. These contrast with the yellow-green discharge and more intense pain produced by gonorrhea. There may be soreness in the scrotum and feelings of heaviness in the testes. NGU is more prevalent among men in the United States than gonorrhea (Hatcher et al., 2011). Young male adults are at the highest risk of contracting gonorrhea and NGU, presumably because of their high levels of sexual activity.

In women, chlamydial infections usually give rise to infections of the urethra or cervix (Chlamydia—CDC fact sheet, 2014). Women, like men, may experience burning when they urinate, genital irritation, and a mild (vaginal) discharge. Women are also likely to encounter pelvic pain and irregular menstrual cycles. The cervix may look swollen and inflamed. However, as many as 25% of men and 70% of women

Figure 13.7 Chlamydia—Rates of Reported Cases by State, United States and Outlying Areas, 2014.

SOURCE: Centers for Disease Control and Prevention. *Sexually Transmitted Disease Surveillance 2014.* Atlanta: U.S. Department of Health and Human Services; 2015. Figure 3.

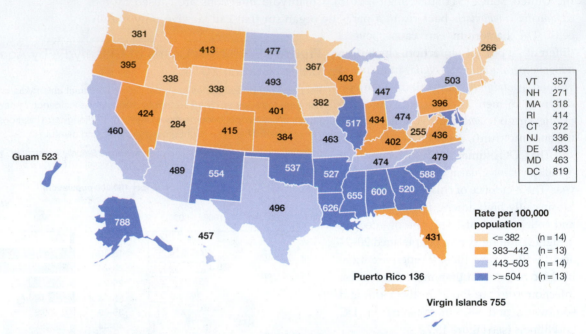

VT	357
NH	271
MA	318
RI	414
CT	372
NJ	336
DE	483
MD	463
DC	819

Rate per 100,000 population

- <= 382 (n = 14)
- 383–442 (n = 13)
- 443–503 (n = 14)
- >= 504 (n = 13)

NOTE: The total rate of reported cases of chlamydia for the United States and outlying areas (Guam, Puerto Rico, and Virgin Islands) was 452.6 per 100,000 population.

infected with chlamydia have no noticeable symptoms (Chlamydia—CDC fact sheet, 2014). For this reason, chlamydia has been dubbed the "silent disease." Symptom-free people may go untreated and unknowingly pass their infections to new partners. In women, an untreated chlamydial infection can spread throughout the reproductive system, leading to PID and scarring the fallopian tubes, resulting in infertility. About half of the more than 1 million annual cases of PID are attributed to chlamydia. Women exposed to *Chlamydia trachomatis* also stand a greater chance of incurring an ectopic (tubal) pregnancy.

Untreated chlamydial infections can also damage the internal reproductive organs of men. About 50% of cases of epididymitis are caused by chlamydial infections (Chlamydia—CDC fact sheet, 2016). Yet, only about 1% or 2% of men with untreated NGU caused by *Chlamydia trachomatis* go on to develop epididymitis. The long-term effects of untreated chlamydial infections in men remain undetermined.

DIAGNOSIS AND TREATMENT Various tests are used in the laboratory or the physician's office to verify a diagnosis of chlamydia in women. The tests analyze a cervical smear and are highly reliable. In men, a swab may be inserted through the penile opening to extract fluid that is analyzed for the presence of *Chlamydia trachomatis.*

Antibiotics other than penicillin are highly effective in eradicating chlamydia infections. These include azithromycin, doxycycline, ofloxacin, and amoxicillin (Chlamydia—CDC fact sheet, 2016). Sex partners are treated when possible to prevent the infection from bouncing back and forth. Both partners may be unaware that they are infected and oblivious to the internal damage the infection is causing. Because of the risks posed by untreated chlamydial infections, especially to women, and the high rate of symptom-free infections, many physicians screen young women for chlamydia during regular checkups.

A CLOSER LOOK

SEX AND THE SINGLE (INFECTED) SENIOR

"What is happening in retirement communities, assisted living facilities and nursing homes?," asks Ezekial Emanuel (2014), vice provost at the University of Pennsylvania. "You might imagine quiet reading, crossword puzzles, bingo, maybe some shuffleboard. Think again. Think about sex—unsafe sex."

The USDHHS reported in 2013 that more than 2 million Medicare beneficiaries obtained free screenings for STIs. Between 60,000 and 70,000 obtained free tests for HIV. About as many Medicare recipients obtained STI screenings as obtained colonoscopies.

As shown in Figure 13.8 the number of seniors with chlamydia increased 31% between 2007 and 2011. The seniors

showed a stunning increase of 52% in those with syphilis. The rise is almost as great as that among 20- to 24-year-olds, who showed an increase of 35% in cases of chlamydia during the same period, and 64% (!) in cases of syphilis. Four key factors appear to be contributing to the incidence of STIs among seniors:

First, retirement communities and assisted living facilities pack people in as in crowded college dorms. Then stuff happens. A woman described what happened after her father moved into an assisted-living facility: three women stopped by to meet him within a half an hour. Emanuel suggests that they didn't introduce themselves "to compare Medicare pharmacy plans and premiums."

Second, older people today are more robust than they were in earlier generations, and they are living longer. Therefore they can remain sexually active much longer (DeLamater & Koepsel, 2015). Surveys such as the National Survey of Sexual Health and Behavior find that more than half of senior men and about 40% of senior women remain sexually active.

Even when they are highly sexually active, seniors do not seem to have gotten "the safe sex memo." Or, if they did, many of them ignored it, assuming it was unlikely to apply to them. Pregnancy was no longer an issue, and most of them grew up before the Age of AIDS. So why would they use condoms? The 2010 National Survey of Sexual Health and Behavior found that college-age Americans use condoms in nearly half of their sexual encounters. Compare that to only 6% of the time among people aged 61 and older. According to a study in the *Annals of Internal Medicine*, older men who use Viagra and other drugs to enhance sexual functioning are much less likely to use condoms than men in their 20s.

It seems that public health campaigns on safe sex need to be aimed at single seniors as well as college students. Actually, quips Emanuel, "there is an untapped market: over 40 million Americans who are unfamiliar with latex protection. Maybe Durex and Trojan can mail free condoms to every Social Security recipient?"

Figure 13.8 Increased Incidence from 2007 to 2011 of Chlamydia and Syphilis Among People Aged 65 and Older, as Compared to Increased Incidence of These STIs among 20- to 24-Year-Olds.

SOURCE: Emanuel, 2014.

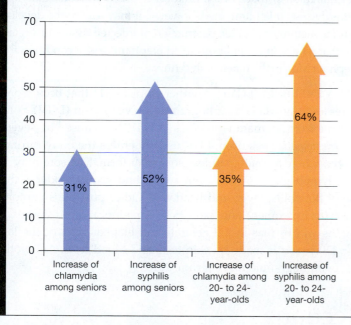

Other Bacterial Diseases

LO 13.5 **Discuss the transmission, effects, and treatment of other bacterial sexually transmitted infections.**

Several other bacterial STIs occur in the United States and Canada, but less frequently. These include chancroid, shigellosis, granuloma inguinale, and lymphogranuloma venereum.

CHANCROID Chancroid, or "soft chancre," is caused by the bacterium *Hemophilus ducreyi*. It is more commonly found in the tropics and Eastern nations than in Western countries. The chancroid sore consists of a cluster of small bumps or pimples on the

chancroid
An STI caused by the *Hemophilus ducreyi* bacterium. Also called *soft chancre*.

genitals, perineum (the area of skin that lies between the genitals and the anus), or the anus itself. These lesions usually appear within 7 days of infection. Within a few days the lesion ruptures, producing an open sore or ulcer. Several ulcers may merge with other ulcers, forming giant ulcers. There is usually an accompanying swelling of a nearby lymph node. In contrast to the syphilis chancre, the chancroid ulcer has a soft rim (hence the name) and is painful in men. Women frequently do not experience any pain and may be unaware of being infected. The bacterium is typically transmitted through sexual or bodily contact with the lesion or its discharge. Diagnosis is usually confirmed by culturing the bacterium, which is found in pus from the sore, and examining it under a microscope. Antibiotics are usually effective in treating the disease.

shigellosis

An STI caused by the *Shigella* bacterium.

SHIGELLOSIS   **Shigellosis** is caused by the *Shigella* bacterium and is characterized by fever and severe abdominal symptoms, including diarrhea and inflammation of the large intestine. About 25,000 cases of shigellosis are reported each year in the United States. Shigellosis can result from food poisoning, but it is also often contracted by oral contact with infected fecal material, which may stem from oral–anal sex. Shigellosis often resolves itself, but people with the disease may become severely dehydrated from the diarrhea. Severe cases are usually treated with antibiotics.

granuloma inguinale

A tropical STI caused by the *Calymmatobacterium granulomatous* bacterium.

GRANULOMA INGUINALE   Rare in the United States, **granuloma inguinale**, like chancroid, is more common in tropical regions. It is caused by the bacterium *Calymmatobacterium granulomatous* and is not as contagious as many other STIs. Primary symptoms are painless red bumps or sores in the groin area that ulcerate and spread. Like chancroid, it is usually spread by intimate bodily or sexual contact with a lesion or its discharge. Diagnosis is confirmed by microscopic examination of tissue of the rim of the sore. Numerous antibiotics are effective in treating this disease. If left untreated, however, it may lead to the development of fistulas (holes) in the rectum or bladder, destruction of infected tissues or organs, or scarring of skin tissue that results in a condition called **elephantiasis**, a condition that afflicted the so-called Elephant Man in the nineteenth century.

elephantiasis

A disease characterized by enlargement of parts of the body, especially the legs and genitals, and by hardening and ulceration of the surrounding skin.

lymphogranuloma venereum (LGV)

A tropical STI caused by the *Chlamydia trachomatis* bacterium.

LYMPHOGRANULOMA VENEREUM (LGV)   Another tropical STI that occurs only rarely in the United States and Canada is **lymphogranuloma venereum (LGV)**. Some U.S. soldiers returned home from Vietnam with cases of LGV. It is caused by several strains of the *Chlamydia trachomatis* bacterium. LGV usually enters the body through the penis, vulva, or cervix, where a small, painless sore may form. The sore may go unnoticed, but a nearby lymph gland in the groin swells and grows tender. Other symptoms mimic those of flu: chills, fever, and headache. Other possible symptoms include backache (especially in women) and arthritic complaints (painful joints). If LGV is untreated, growths and fistulas in the genitals and elephantiasis of the legs and genitals may occur. Diagnosis is made by skin tests and blood tests. Antibiotics are the usual treatment (Lymphogranuloma venerum, 2015).

Vaginal Infections

LO 13.6 **Discuss the transmission, effects, and treatment of various vaginal infections.**

A vaginal infection or inflammation is technically termed **vaginitis**. Vaginitis is typically symptomized by genital irritation or itching and burning during urination, but the most common symptom is an odious discharge.

vaginitis

Any type of vaginal infection or inflammation.

Most cases of vaginitis are caused by organisms that reside in the vagina or by sexually transmitted organisms. Organisms that reside in the vagina may overgrow when the environmental balance of the vagina is upset by factors such as birth-control pills, antibiotics, dietary changes, excessive douching, or nylon underwear or pantyhose. (See Chapter 2 for ways to reduce the risk of vaginitis.) Still other cases are caused by sensitivities or allergic reactions to various chemicals.

The great majority of vaginal infections involve bacterial vaginosis (BV), candidiasis (commonly called a "yeast" infection), or trichomoniasis ("trich"). Bacterial vaginosis is the most common form of vaginitis, followed by candidiasis, then by trichomoniasis, but some cases involve combinations of the three.

The microbes causing vaginal infections in women can also infect the man's urethral tract. A "vaginal infection" can be passed back and forth between sex partners.

5 › T / F   Truth or Fiction Revisited   Men can not literally develop vaginal infections. Only women have vaginas. However, the pathogens that cause vaginal infections in women may also cause problems for men.

Bacterial Vaginosis

Formerly called *nonspecific vaginitis*, **bacterial vaginosis (BV)** is most often caused by overgrowth of the bacterium *Gardnerella vaginalis*. The bacterium is mainly transmitted sexually. The most characteristic symptom in women is a thin, foul-smelling vaginal discharge, but infected women often have no symptoms. Diagnosis requires culturing the bacterium in the laboratory. Besides causing troublesome symptoms in some cases, BV may increase the risk of various gynecological problems, including infections of the reproductive tract (Bacterial Vaginosis, 2015). Oral treatment with metronidazole (brand name Flagyl) is recommended and is effective in most cases. Topical treatments with metronidazole or clindamycin are also effective. But recurrences are common.

Questions remain about whether a male partner should also be treated. The bacterium can usually be found in the urethra of a symptom-free male. Being symptom free, the male may unknowingly transmit the bacterium others.

Candidiasis

Candidiasis is caused by a yeastlike fungus, *Candida albicans*. It is also known as *moniliasis, thrush,* or, more simply, a yeast infection. **Candidiasis** commonly produces soreness, inflammation, and intense (sometimes maddening!) itching around the vulva that is accompanied by a white, thick, curdlike vaginal discharge (see Figure 13.9). Yeast generally produces no symptoms when the vaginal environment is normal. Yeast infections can also occur in the mouth in both men and women and in the penis in men.

Infections most often arise from changes in the vaginal environment that allow the fungus to overgrow. Factors such as the use of antibiotics, birth-control pills, intrauterine devices (IUDs), pregnancy, and diabetes may alter the vaginal balance, allowing the fungus that causes yeast infections to grow to infectious levels. Wearing nylon underwear and tight, restrictive, poorly ventilated clothing may also set the stage for a yeast infection.

Diet may play a role in recurrent yeast infections. Reducing intake of substances that produce excessive excretion of urinary sugars (such as dairy products, sugar, and artificial sweeteners) apparently reduces the frequency of recurrent yeast infections. Eating a pint of yogurt containing active bacterial (*Lactobacillus acidophilus*) cultures daily may reduce the rate of recurrent infections.

Candidiasis can be passed back and forth between sex partners through vaginal intercourse. It may also be passed back and forth between the mouth and the genitals through oral–genital contact and infect the anus through anal intercourse. However, most infections in women are believed to be caused by an overgrowth of "yeast" normally found in the vagina, not by sexual transmission. Still, it is advisable to evaluate partners simultaneously. Whereas most men with *Candida* have no symptoms, some may develop NGU or a genital thrush that is accompanied by itching and burning during urination or by reddening of the penis. Candidiasis may also be transmitted nonsexually, as between women who share a washcloth.

bacterial vaginosis
A form of vaginitis usually caused by the *Gardnerella vaginalis* bacterium.

Critical Thinking
Critical thinkers pay attention to definitions of terms. What does it mean to say that men have a vaginal infection?

candidiasis
A form of vaginitis caused by a yeastlike fungus, *Candida albicans*.

Figure 13.9   Candidiasis.

A "yeast infection" is caused by the Candida albicans fungus and causes soreness, inflammation, and itching around the vulva, accompanied by a thick, white vaginal discharge.

Nearly 75% of adult women will experience at least one episode of candidiasis, and 40% to 45% will have recurrent infections (Vulvovaginal Candidiasis, 2015). Short-term regimens of "azole" drugs are effective in treating candidiasis. A single dose of oral fluconazole, or vaginal suppositories or creams containing miconazole, clotrimazole, butaconazole, or terconazole are recommended. These treatments are sold over the counter, but it is wise to ask the pharmacist which preparations contain these medicines (or read the labels). We advise women with vaginal complaints to consult their physicians before using any of these medications to ensure that they receive the proper diagnosis and treatment.

Trichomoniasis

trichomoniasis

A form of vaginitis caused by the protozoan *Trichomonas vaginalis*.

Trichomoniasis ("trich") is the most common STI. It is caused by *Trichomonas vaginalis*, a one-celled parasite. There are about 7.4 million new cases a year among women (and men) in the United States (Trichomoniasis—CDC fact sheet, 2016). Symptoms include burning or itching in the vulva, mild pain during urination or coitus, and an odorous, foamy whitish to yellowish green discharge. Lower abdominal pain is reported by some infected women. Many women notice symptoms appearing or worsening during, or just following, their menstrual periods. Trichomoniasis facilitates the transmission of HIV and is linked to the development of tubal adhesions that can result in infertility. As with many other STIs, many infected women have no symptoms.

Candidiasis often reflects the overgrowth of organisms normally found in the vagina, but trich is almost always sexually transmitted. Because the parasite can survive for several hours on moist surfaces outside the body, trich can be communicated from contact with infected semen or vaginal discharges on towels, washcloths, and bedclothes. This parasite is one of the few disease agents that can be picked up from a toilet seat, but it would have to come into contact with the penis or vulva.

Trichomonas vaginalis can cause NGU in the male, which can be symptom free or cause a slight penile discharge that is usually noticeable before first urination in the morning. There may be tingling, itching, and other irritating sensations in the urethral tract. But most infected men are symptom free and can unwittingly transfer the organism to other sex partners. Diagnosis is frequently made by microscopic examination of a smear of a woman's vaginal fluids.

Except during the first three months of pregnancy, trichomoniasis is usually treated in both women and men with metronidazole (brand name Flagyl). If both partners are treated, the success rate approaches 100% (Trichomoniasis, 2016).

Viral Infections

Viruses are tiny particles of dna coated with a protein. They cannot reproduce on their own. When they invade a body cell, however, they can direct the cell's own reproductive machinery to spin off new viral particles that spread to other cells, causing infection. Our immune systems defeat many viruses, and many others are not lethal. In this section we discuss viral STIs, some of which are indeed deadly: HIV/AIDS, Herpes simplex virus, viral hepatitis, HPV, and molluscum contagiosum.

HIV/AIDS

human immunodeficiency virus (HIV)

A sexually transmitted virus that destroys white blood cells in the immune system, leaving the body vulnerable to life-threatening diseases.

acquired immunodeficiency syndrome (AIDS)

A condition caused by the human immunodeficiency virus (HIV) and characterized by destruction of the immune system so that the body is stripped of its ability to fend off life-threatening diseases.

LO 13.7 **Discuss the transmission, effects, and treatment of HIV/AIDS.**

The **human immunodeficiency virus (HIV)** is the virus that causes AIDS, which stands for **acquired immunodeficiency syndrome (AIDS)**. HIV attacks and disables the immune system, the body's natural line of defense, stripping it of its ability to fend off disease-causing organisms. AIDS is considered fatal, although many people are currently living with HIV/AIDS indefinitely due to the development of powerful antiretroviral medications. (HIV is a *retrovirus*—that is, a virus that reproduces by inserting copies of its DNA into the cells of its hosts.) For people in industrialized

Table 13.2 Estimated Numbers of People in the United States Living With HIV/AIDS by Race/Ethnicity, 2014

Race/Ethnicity	Number of Cases	Total Number of People in United States Living with HIV/AIDS (%)	Racial/Ethnic Group of Population of United States (%)
African American	504,833	40.5	13.2
Asian American	9,873	>1.0	5.4
European American	439,575	35.3	62.1
Latin American	255,036	20.5	17.4
Native American	3,524	>1.0	1.2
Multiple races	(33,274)	N/A	2.5

SOURCES: Centers for Disease Control and Prevention. HIV Surveillance Report, 2014; vol. 26. http://www.cdc.gov/hiv/library/reports/surveillance/. Published November 2015. (Accessed January 1, 2016); United States Census Bureau, 2015. QuickFacts, United States. 2014 estimates. Published December 2, 2015. http://quickfacts.census.gov/qfd/states/00000.html (Accessed July 8, 2016).

nations such as the United States and Canada, European nations, and Asian nations such as Japan and South Korea, HIV/AIDS may become a chronic but manageable condition for most people—like diabetes. But for many millions in developing nations, where medications are too expensive or difficult to deliver, a diagnosis of HIV/AIDS remains a death sentence. And in the United States, about 13,000 people continue to die of HIV/AIDS each year.

PREVALENCE OF HIV/AIDS The World Health Organization (2015a) estimates that 36.9 million people around the world are living with HIV/AIDS. The organization further estimates that in 2014, 2 million people were infected with HIV and 1.2 million died from causes related to HIV/AIDS.

Approximately 1.2 million Americans are living with HIV/AIDS (HIV in the United States, 2015). More than half a million Americans have died from it. The incidence of HIV/AIDS is highest among men who have sex with men, people of color (see Table 13.2 and Figure 13.10), people who share needles when they inject drugs, and people who engage in unprotected, male–female sex.

Figure 13.10 Estimates of the Annual Prevalence of New HIV Infections in the United States for the Most Affected Subpopulations

SOURCE: HIV among Gay and Bisexual Men, 2015. Centers for Disease Control and Prevention. http://www.cdc.gov/hiv/group/msm/index.html Accessed January 1, 2016.

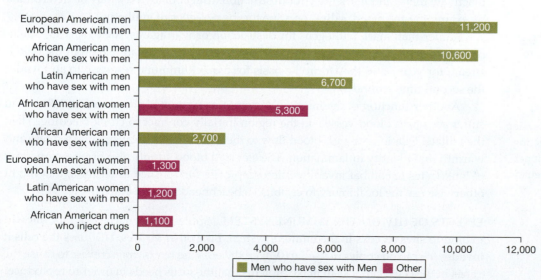

Table 13.3 Cumulative Estimated Number of AIDS Diagnoses Among Adolescents and Adults in the United States, 2014

Transmission Category	Males	Females	Total
Men who have sex with men	592,621	–	592,621
Injection drug use	201,009	93,515	294,524
Men who have sex with men and inject drugs	87,850	–	87,850
Male–female sex	88,352	155,667	244,019
Other*	11,828	6,125	17,953
TOTAL			1,236,967

*Includes hemophilia, blood transfusion, perinatal exposure, and risk not reported or not identified.

SOURCE: Centers for Disease Control and Prevention. HIV Surveillance Report, 2014; vol. 26. http://www.cdc.gov/hiv/library/reports/surveillance/. Published November 2015. Accessed July 8, 2016.

About half of the people infected with HIV around the world are female, but in the United States, HIV/AIDS is predominantly found among men who have sex with men or who share needles when injecting drugs (HIV in the United States, 2015; see Table 13.3). But male–female sex is the fasting-growing exposure category in the United States. Among women, male–female sexual contact accounts for more than half of the cases (see Table 13.3).

THE IMMUNE SYSTEM AND HIV/AIDS   AIDS is caused by a virus that attacks the body's **immune system**—the body's natural line of defense against disease-causing organisms. The immune system combats disease in several ways. It produces white blood cells that envelop and kill **pathogens** such as bacteria, viruses, and funguses; worn-out body cells; and cancer cells. White blood cells are called **leukocytes**. Leukocytes engage in microscopic search-and-destroy missions. They identify and eradicate foreign agents and debilitated cells.

6 › T / F Truth or Fiction Revisited   It is true that as you read this, you are engaged in search-and-destroy missions against foreign agents within your body. The white cells in your immune system continuously seek and destroy foreign pathogens within your body.

Leukocytes recognize foreign agents by their surface fragments. The surface fragments are termed **antigens** because the body reacts to their presence by developing specialized proteins, or antibodies. Antibodies attach themselves to the foreign bodies, inactivate them, and mark them for destruction. (Infection by HIV may be determined by examining the blood, saliva, or urine for the presence of antibodies.)

Rather than mark pathogens for destruction or war against them, special "memory lymphocytes" are held in reserve. Memory lymphocytes can remain in the bloodstream for years, and they form the basis for a quick immune response to an invader the second time around.

Another function of the immune system is to promote **inflammation**. When you suffer an injury, blood vessels in the region initially contract to check bleeding. Then they dilate. Dilation expands blood flow to the injured region, causing the redness and warmth that identify inflammation. The elevated blood supply also brings in an army of leukocytes to combat invading microscopic life forms, such as bacteria, that might otherwise use the local injury to establish a beachhead into the body.

EFFECTS OF HIV ON THE IMMUNE SYSTEM   Spikes on the surface of HIV allow it to bind to sites on cells in the immune system. Like other viruses, HIV uses the cells it invades to spin off copies of itself. HIV uses the enzyme *reverse transcriptase* to cause the genes in the cells it attacks to make proteins that the virus needs in order to reproduce.

immune system

A term for the body's complex of mechanisms for protecting itself from disease-causing agents such as pathogens.

pathogen

An agent, especially a microorganism, that can cause a disease.

leukocytes

White blood cells that are essential to the body's defenses against infection.

antigen

A protein, toxin, or other substance to which the body reacts by producing antibodies.

inflammation

Redness and warmth that develop at the site of an injury, reflecting dilation of blood vessels that permits the expanded flow of leukocytes to the region.

HIV attacks the immune system by destroying a type of lymphocyte called the *CD4 cell* (see Figure 13.11). The CD4 cell, also known as *T-cell* or *helper T-cell*, is the "quarterback" of the immune system. CD4 cells "recognize" invading pathogens and signal B-lymphocytes or B-cells—another kind of white blood cell—to produce antibodies that inactivate pathogens and mark them for annihilation. CD4 cells also signal another class of T-cells, called *killer T-cells*, to destroy infected cells. By attacking and destroying helper T-cells, HIV disables the cells on which the body relies to fend off diseases. As HIV cripples the body's defenses, the individual develops infections that would not otherwise take hold. Cancer cells might also proliferate. Although the CD4 cells appear to be its main target, HIV also attacks other types of white blood cells.

The blood normally contains about 1,000 CD4 cells per cubic millimeter. The numbers of CD4 cells may remain at about this level for years following HIV infection. Many people show no symptoms and appear healthy while CD4 cells remain at this level. Then, for reasons that are not clearly understood, the levels of CD4 cells begin to drop off, although symptoms may not appear for a decade or more. As the numbers of CD4 cells decline, symptoms generally increase, and people fall prey to diseases that their weakened immune systems are unable to fight off. People become most vulnerable to opportunistic infections when the level of CD4 cells falls below 200 per cubic millimeter.

PROGRESSION OF HIV/AIDS   HIV follows a complex course once it enters the body. A recently infected individual may experience mild flulike symptoms—fatigue, fever, headaches, muscle pain, lack of appetite, nausea, swollen glands, and possibly a rash. Such symptoms usually disappear within a few weeks, and people may dismiss them as a case of the flu. People who enter this symptom-free or carrier state generally look and act well and do not realize that they are infectious. Thus, they can unwittingly pass the virus on to others.

7 › T / F **Truth or Fiction Revisited**   Most people who are infected with HIV remain symptom free for years. Others enter a symptomatic state that is typically denoted by symptoms such as chronically swollen lymph nodes and intermittent weight loss, fever, fatigue, and diarrhea. This symptomatic state does not constitute full-blown AIDS, but shows that HIV is undermining the integrity of the immune system.

Even during the years when HIV appears to be dormant, billions of viral particles are being spun off. In a seesaw battle, the great majority of them are wiped out by the immune system. Eventually, in almost all cases, the balance tips in favor of HIV. Then the virus's numbers swell. Perhaps a decade or more after the person is infected with HIV, the virus begins to overtake the immune system. It obliterates the cells that house it and spreads to other immune-system cells. About half of the people with HIV develop AIDS within 10 years of initial infection. For this reason, people who know that they are infected with HIV may feel that they are carrying time bombs within them.

AIDS is called a *syndrome* because it is characterized by a variety of different symptoms. The beginnings of full-blown cases of AIDS are often marked by such symptoms as swollen lymph nodes, fatigue, fever, night sweats, diarrhea, and weight loss (a "wasting syndrome") that cannot be attributed to dieting or exercise. AIDS is connected with the appearance of diseases such as tuberculosis, pneumocystis carinii pneumonia (PCP); Kaposi's sarcoma (a form of cancer); toxoplasmosis of the brain (an infection of parasites); or *Herpes simplex* with chronic ulcers. These are termed **opportunistic diseases** because they are not likely to emerge unless a weakened immune system grants the opportunity.

About 10% of people with AIDS have the wasting syndrome—the unintentional loss of more than 10% of a person's body weight that is connected with HIV/AIDS,

Figure 13.11   HIV (the AIDS Virus) Attacks a White Blood Cell.

HIV progressively weakens the immune system, leaving the body vulnerable to infections and diseases that would otherwise be fended off.

opportunistic diseases

Diseases that take hold only when the immune system is weakened and unable to fend them off.

some other infections, and cancer. As HIV/AIDS progresses, the individual becomes thinner and more fatigued. He or she becomes unable to perform ordinary life functions and falls prey to opportunistic infections. If left untreated, AIDS almost always results in death within a few years.

TRANSMISSION   HIV can be transmitted by certain contaminated bodily fluids—blood, semen, vaginal secretions, or breast milk. The first three of these may enter the body through vaginal, anal, or oral–genital intercourse with an infected partner. An African study that followed **seropositive** mothers and their babies for 2 years found that the probability of transmission of HIV via breast milk was about 16.2% (1 in 6) (Nduati et al., 2000). Today antiretroviral therapy can significantly reduces the risk of mother–infant transmission of HIV by breast milk, but the medicines are often unavailable and the HIV infections both in mother and child often go undiagnosed in time to obtain help (Becquet & Dabis, 2013).

Other avenues of infection include sharing a hypodermic needle with an infected person (as do many people who inject drugs), transfusion with contaminated blood, transplants of organs and tissues that have been infected with HIV, artificial insemination with infected semen, or being stuck by a needle used previously on an infected person. HIV may enter the body through tiny cuts or sores in the mucous lining of the vagina, the rectum, and even the mouth. These cuts or sores can be so tiny that you are not aware of them.

Transmission of HIV through kissing, even prolonged "French" kissing, is considered unlikely. When a person injects drugs, a small amount of his or her blood remains inside the needle and syringe. If the person is infected with HIV, the virus may be found in the blood remaining in the needle or syringe. Others who use the needle inject the infected blood into their bloodstream. HIV can also be spread by sharing needles used for other purposes, such as injecting steroids, ear piercing, or tattooing.

HIV can also be transmitted from mother to fetus during pregnancy or from mother to child through childbirth or breastfeeding. Transmission is most likely during childbirth.

Male-to-female transmission through vaginal intercourse is more than twice as likely as female-to-male transmission (see Table 13.3), partly because more of the virus is found in the ejaculate than in vaginal secretions. A man's ejaculate may also remain for many days in the vagina, providing greater opportunity for infection to occur. Male–female or male–male anal intercourse is especially risky because it often tears or abrades rectal tissue, facilitating entry of the virus into the bloodstream (Chandra et al., 2012; Duby et al., 2015).

Male–female transmission via sexual intercourse is the primary route of HIV infection in Africa, Latin America, and Asia. Worldwide, male–female sexual intercourse accounts for the majority of cases of HIV/AIDS (World Health Organization, 2015a). In the United States, many cases of male–female transmission occur among people who inject drugs and their sex partners.

HIV may also be spread by donor semen, such as that used in artificial insemination. Cases have also been reported of women who have become infected with hepatitis B, gonorrhea, trichomoniasis, and chlamydia by donor semen.

FACTORS AFFECTING THE RISK OF SEXUAL TRANSMISSION OF HIV   Some people seem more likely to communicate HIV, and others seem to be especially vulnerable to infection. Several factors appear to affect the risk of HIV infection and development of AIDS:

- The probability of transmission rises with the number of sexual contacts with an infected partner.

- The probability of transmission is affected by the type of sexual activity. Anal intercourse provides a convenient port of entry for HIV because it abrades the rectal lining and rectal cells are particularly vulnerable.

---

seropositive

Having a pathogen (such as HIV) or antibodies to that pathogen in the bloodstream.

- STIs such as genital warts, gonorrhea, trichomoniasis, and chlamydia inflame the genital region, which heightens the risk of sexual transmission of other STIs. STIs that produce genital ulcers, such as syphilis and genital herpes, heighten vulnerability to HIV infection.

- Circumcision is associated with a lower risk of HIV infection in men who have sex with women (Gray & Wawer, 2012; Hoffman et al., 2015). Analysis of data from the African country of Uganda also found that circumcision lowered the risk of infection from HPV by 35%, and the risk from HSV-2, the virus that causes herpes, by 28% (Tobian et al., 2009).

- Genetic factors may also be at work. About 1% of people of Western European descent have inherited a gene from both parents that prevents HIV from entering cells in the immune system and are therefore apparently immune to HIV infection. Perhaps 20% of individuals of Western European descent have inherited the gene from one parent; HIV disease appears to progress more slowly in them. Some prostitutes in Thailand and Africa, where HIV infection has run rampant, also appear to be immune to HIV infection (Shacklett & Ferre, 2011).

HOW HIV IS *NOT* TRANSMITTED   There is much misinformation about the transmission of HIV. Let us consider some of the ways in which HIV is not transmitted:

- HIV is not transmitted by donating blood. AIDS cannot be contracted by donating blood because needles are discarded after a single use.

- HIV is not transmitted through casual, everyday contact. There is no evidence of transmission of HIV through hugging; shaking hands; sharing crowded public transportation; handling money, doorknobs, or other objects that have been touched by infected people; sharing drinking fountains, public telephones, public toilets, or swimming pools; or wearing clothing that has been worn by an infected person.

- HIV is not transmitted by insect bites or bites from other animals.

- HIV is not transmitted by airborne germs or contact with contaminated food.

- HIV is not transmitted through sharing work or home environments. No cases of HIV transmission have been documented based on nonsexual contact in schools or in the workplace.

- HIV is apparently not transmitted by kissing, but check out the nearby "A Closer Look" feature.

DIAGNOSIS OF HIV INFECTION AND AIDS   There are three kinds of tests for diagnosing infection by HIV: antibody tests, antigen/antibody tests, and nucleic acid (RNA) tests. Antibody tests search for proteins that are made by your immune system to fight HIV, not HIV itself. Antigen and RNA tests detect HIV itself.

The Home Access HIV-1 Test System and OraQuick are available over the counter (Home Tests, 2015). With the Home Access HIV-1 test system, you prick your finger to collect a sample of blood and send it off to a lab, which may provide results the next business day. With OraQuick, you use a mouth swab to check for antibodies in your saliva. A saliva test is not quite as accurate as a blood test, in part because the level of antibodies is higher in blood than in saliva, but it is reasonably accurate, provides results in about 20 minutes, and might encourage people who avoid blood tests to be tested. Although HIV antibodies can be detected in saliva, HIV itself is not found in saliva in measurable quantities. This is why kissing is not considered an avenue of transmission of HIV.

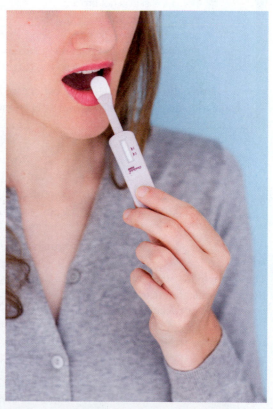

OraQuick. The over-the-counter OraQuick test informs people as to whether they have HIV antibodies in their saliva within a few minutes. What are the barriers to testing oneself?

A CLOSER LOOK

IS KISSING SAFE?

In a presentation on the safety of kissing that leaves us less than happy, the Centers for Disease Control and Prevention looks as though it comes close to speaking out of two sides of its mouth. But actually it doesn't. The following information was downloaded from the federal Centers for Disease Control and Prevention (http://www.cdc.gov/hiv/basics/transmission.html), as updated on December 14, 2015:

> Only certain body fluids—blood, semen (*cum*), pre-seminal fluid (*pre-cum*), rectal fluids, vaginal fluids, and breast milk—from a person who has HIV can transmit HIV. These fluids must come in contact with a mucous membrane or damaged tissue or be directly injected into the bloodstream (from a needle or syringe) for transmission to occur. Mucous membranes are found inside the rectum, vagina, penis, and mouth. . . .
>
> In extremely rare cases, HIV has been transmitted by:
>
> - Eating food that has been pre-chewed by an HIV-infected person. The contamination occurs when infected blood from a caregiver's mouth mixes with food while chewing. The only known cases are among infants.
> - Being bitten by a person with HIV. Each of the very small number of documented cases has involved severe trauma with extensive tissue damage and the presence of blood. There is no risk of transmission if the skin is not broken. . . .
> - Deep, open-mouth kissing if both partners have sores or bleeding gums and blood from the HIV-positive partner gets into the bloodstream of the HIV-negative partner. HIV is not spread through saliva.

Here's the takeaway. HIV is all but absent in saliva. If you engage in deep kissing—also known as open-mouthed kissing,

Tongue Play. Is kissing safe? Yes, as long as only saliva is being exchanged. However, the transfer of blood, as from a love bite, has apparently led to some cases of infection by HIV.

tongue kissing, or French kissing—with a person who is infected with HIV, there is no evidence that you will catch HIV from that person's *saliva*.

However, there is a remote chance you could be infected by sharing blood. How might that happen? One possibility is that the two of you might have brushed your teeth recently, creating tiny abrasions or cuts in your gums. Some blood from your kissing partner might make its way into your mouth and into one of those temporary ports of entry. It's an extremely slight risk, but it does exist.

Here's our recommendation: If you really don't know your partner, don't engage in deep kissing. (Why would you deep kiss a stranger anyway?) If you have gotten to know your partner for a while and you have no reason to be suspicious that his or her sexual or injecting drug history places him or her at risk of being infected with HIV, kiss away. (That does *not* mean you can also risk unprotected sex!)

If an initial test result is positive (meaning that the test detects the presence of the antibodies), follow-up testing to detect HIV itself—and not antibodies—is recommended. If the first test was a laboratory blood test, the follow-up testing may use the same sample.

The follow-up tests in use include antibody *differentiation tests*, which distinguishes the virus from the antibodies; *HIV-1 nucleic acid tests*, which detect the virus RNA itself; and the *Western blot* and indirect *immunofluorescence* assay, which also detect antibodies, but are more precise than the initial tests.

TREATMENT OF HIV/AIDS   A combination, or "cocktail," of antiviral drugs has become the standard treatment for HIV/AIDS. This combination—referred to as ART[2] (for "antiretroviral therapy")—decreases the likelihood that HIV will develop resistance to treatment. It has created hope that AIDS will become increasingly

ART
The acronym for "antiretroviral therapy," which refers to the combination or cocktail of drugs used to treat HIV/AIDS. (Previously termed highly active antiretroviral therapy, or *HAART*.)

---

[2]Previously termed HAART, the acronym for "highly active antiretroviral therapy."

manageable, a chronic health problem as opposed to a terminal illness. However, ART is expensive, and many people who could benefit from it cannot afford it. The side effects of these medicines can be unpleasant, including nausea and, in the case of protease inhibitors, unusual accumulations of fat, such as "buffalo humps" in the neck. Moreover, there are some treatment failures.

It is possible to obtain the benefits of ART by taking a three-in-one pill, Atripla, whose sandwiched ingredients are released at different rates. Another combination pill, Quad, contains four antiviral drugs and appears to be somewhat more effective than Atripla, with a different constellation of side effects (DeJesus et al., 2012). Quad contains tenofovir and emtricitabine (the two ingredients in Truvada), elvitegravir, and cobicistat. After a year, 88% of the study participants taking Quad had no detectable virus in their bloodstreams, as compared with 84% of participants taking Atripla. However, having no detectable level of the virus in one's bloodstream does not mean that the individual is "cured." Decades of research experience have shown that without continued use of antiviral drugs, blood levels of the virus will eventually rebound. Yet, 88% and 84% are both impressive numbers, especially when a person might continue to survive with a low detectable level of the virus. Physicians will therefore be comparing side effects, including ability to tolerate the drugs, and costs.

ART has cut the U.S. death rate from HIV/AIDS-related causes by about 75% since the mid- to late-1990s (HIV in the United States, 2015). Yet, ART-resistant strains of HIV may evolve. For this and other reasons, many HIV-infected people go on drug "vacations" after using ART for a number of months or years. Promising results are also reported in treating the opportunistic infections such as PCP and fungal infections that take hold in people with weakened immune systems.

One "downside" of ART is that its existence has lured many people into believing that they can engage in unprotected sex with impunity and decreased use of condoms

A CLOSER LOOK

PREVENTING HIV INFECTION WITH TRUVADA

Recent research has looked into medicines that lower the risk of being infected with HIV. The method is called *pre-exposure prophylaxis*, or PrEP. Studies reported in 2015 suggest that it may be possible to ward off HIV infections by taking the two-antiretroviral-drug cocktail called Truvada—a combination of tenofovir and emtricitabine. Jonathan Volk and his colleagues (2015) at Kaiser Permanente's San Francisco Medical Center followed 657 men who had sex with men for more than 2 years. The men took Truvada as prescribed but made no effort to limit their numbers of sexual contacts. Moreover, the researchers found that taking Truvada decreased the likelihood that the men would use condoms.

Lower condom use was connected with a higher incidence of contracting sexually transmitted infections in general, but not HIV. Not one of the men in the study became infected with HIV during the course of the study.

All the men in the study received Truvada; none received a placebo. Therefore, the study does not qualify as a carefully run experiment. However, an English study of the benefits of Truvada did randomly assign some participants to a placebo, and some of those who took the placebo did become infected with HIV (McCormack & Dunn, 2015). After a while that study

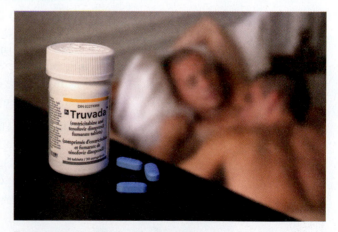

Truvada. Viagra isn't the only blue pill on the block. When used as a prophylactic agent, Truvada, consisting of the antiretroviral drugs tenofovir and emtricitabine, has been shown to lower the risk of being infected with HIV.

was stopped early, because it became clear that Truvada was effective and that the men taking the placebo were being exposed to risk for no good scientific reason.

(Paz-Bailey et al., 2013). However, despite the advent of ART, more than 13,000 people in the United States still die of HIV/AIDS each year (HIV in the United States, 2015). The CDC attributes these deaths to lack of early testing and treatment for some people, failure of some people with HIV/AIDS to follow ART treatment regimens, and, in some cases, treatment failure. People who assume that HIV/AIDS is no longer a deadly syndrome therefore need to recognize that ART does not help everyone with HIV/AIDS.

Unfortunately, the advances in treatment in the United States do not extend to everyone in the world, not even to everyone in the United States. Among women in the United States today, the risks of HIV/AIDS fall most heavily on poor women, mostly African American or Latina American, who live in urban areas. African American and Latin American women account for nearly three-quarters of women with HIV/AIDS in the United States, although they make up only about 30% of the female population.

Genital Herpes

LO 13.8 **Discuss the transmission, effects, and treatment of genital herpes.**

genital herpes

An STI caused by the *Herpes simplex* virus type 2 and characterized by painful shallow sores and blisters on the genitals.

Genital herpes is an STI caused by a variant of the *Herpes simplex* virus. The hysteria that surrounded the rapid spread of genital herpes in the 1970s and 1980s died down because of the advent of AIDS. In fact, the prevalence of people infected with HSV-2, which causes genital herpes, has been decreasing from about 19.5% of the U.S. population aged 14–49 in the 1990s to about 15% of that age group in more recent years (Herpes simplex virus, 2015). The great majority of individuals infected with HSV-2 are not aware that they have it. HSV-1, however, which causes those common fever blisters in the mouth and on the lips, may also affect the genital region via oral sex—and its prevalence has been on the increase among college students.

Although most people infected with HSV-2 are not aware of it, at some point it may develop into recurrent painful blisters and sores in the genital or anal region. After an initial attack, it continues to remain an unwelcome guest in the body. Recurrent outbreaks often happen at the worst times, such as around final exams. This is because stress can depress the functioning of the immune system and heighten the likelihood of outbreaks.

Infected people may also continue to pass the infection along to sex partners, even when they do not have an outbreak. Flare-ups may continue to recur, sometimes with annoying frequency, but some people have no recurrences. Still other people have mild, brief recurrences that become less frequent over time.

TRANSMISSION   Herpes can be transmitted through oral, anal, or vaginal sex with an infected person. The herpes viruses can also survive for several hours on toilet seats or other objects, where they can be picked up by direct contact. Oral herpes is easily contracted by drinking from the same cup as an infected person, by kissing, even by sharing towels. But genital herpes is generally spread by vaginal, oral, or anal sex.

8 › T / F Truth or Fiction Revisited   It is not true that genital herpes can be transmitted only during flare-ups of the infection. Although people are most contagious during flare-ups, genital herpes can also be transmitted between outbreaks.

ocular herpes

A herpes infection of the eye, usually caused by touching an infected area of the body and then touching the eye.

Herpes can also be spread from one part of the body to another by touching the infected area and then touching another body part. One potentially serious result is a herpes infection of the eye: **ocular herpes**. Thorough washing with soap and water after touching an infected area may reduce the risk of spreading the infection to other parts of the body. Still, it is best to avoid touching the infected area altogether, especially if there are sores or blisters.

Women with genital herpes are more likely than the general population to have miscarriages. Passage through the birth canal of an infected mother can infect babies with genital herpes, damaging or killing them. Obstetricians therefore often perform cesarean sections if the mother has active lesions or **prodromal symptoms** at the time of delivery. Herpes can also place women at greater risk of genital cancers, such as cervical cancer. (All women, not just women with herpes, are advised to have regular pelvic examinations, including Pap tests for early detection of cervical cancer.)

SYMPTOMS Genital lesions or sores appear about 6 to 8 days after infection with genital herpes. At first they appear as reddish, painful bumps, or papules, along the penis or the vulva (see Figure 13.12). They may also appear on the thighs or buttocks, in the vagina, or on the cervix. These papules turn into groups of small blisters that are filled with fluid containing infectious viral particles. The blisters are attacked by the body's immune system (white blood cells). They fill with pus, burst, and become extremely painful, shallow sores or ulcers that are surrounded by a red ring. People are especially infectious during such outbreaks, as the ulcers shed millions of viral particles. Other symptoms may include headaches and muscle aches, swollen lymph glands, fever, burning urination, and a vaginal discharge. The blisters crust over and heal in one to three weeks. Internal sores in the vagina or on the cervix may take 10 days longer than external (labial) sores to heal. Physicians thus advise infected women to avoid unprotected intercourse for at least 10 days following the healing of external sores.

When symptoms disappear, the virus remains in the body, burrowing into nerve cells in the base of the spine, where it may lie dormant for years or a lifetime. The infected person is least contagious during this dormant stage.

Recurrences may be related to factors such as infections (as in a cold), stress—as noted previously, fatigue, depression, exposure to the sun, and hormonal changes, such as those that occur during pregnancy or menstruation. Recurrences tend to occur within 3 to 12 months of the initial episode and to affect the same part of the body.

Symptoms of oral herpes include sores or blisters on the lips, the inside of the mouth, the tongue, or the throat. Fever and feelings of sickness may occur. The gums may swell and redden. The sores heal over in about 2 weeks, and the virus retreats into nerve cells at the base of the neck, where it lies dormant between flare-ups. Most people with oral herpes experience recurrences.

DIAGNOSIS AND TREATMENT Genital herpes is first diagnosed by clinical inspection of herpetic sores or ulcers in the mouth or on the genitals. A sample of fluid may be taken from the base of a genital sore and cultured in the laboratory to detect the growth of the virus.

Clinical trials of experimental vaccines for genital herpes are underway, but none has been approved by the Federal Drug Administration (American Osteopathic College of Dermatology, 2015). Antiviral drugs such as acyclovir (brand name Zovirax), famciclovir (Famvir), and valacyclovir (Valtrex) can relieve pain, speed healing, and reduce the duration of viral shedding. Acyclovir can be applied directly to the sores in ointment form, but must be taken orally, in pill form, to help combat internal lesions in the vagina or on the cervix. Oral administration of antiviral drugs may reduce the severity of the initial episode and, if taken regularly, the frequency and duration of recurrent outbreaks. On the other hand, users may develop tolerance for these drugs, meaning that larger doses must be used to maintain effectiveness.

Warm baths, loose fitting clothing, aspirin, and cold, wet compresses may relieve pain during flare-ups. People with herpes are advised to maintain regular sleeping habits and to learn to manage stress.

Figure 13.12 Herpes Lesions on the Male Genitals.

Herpes lesions or sores can appear on the genitals in both men and women. In contrast to the syphilis chancre, they can be quite painful. Herpes is most likely to be transmitted during outbreaks of the disease (when the sores are present, that is), but it can be transmitted at other times as well. Stress increases the likelihood of outbreaks. Antiviral drugs tend to decrease the frequency, duration, and discomfort of outbreaks.

prodromal symptoms
Warning symptoms that signal the onset of a disease.

COPING WITH GENITAL HERPES The psychological problems connected with herpes can be more distressing than the physical effects of the illness. The prospects of a lifetime of recurrences and concerns about infecting one's sex partners exacerbate the emotional impact of herpes. People with herpes often feel angry, especially toward those who transmitted the disease to them. They may feel anxious about making a long-term commitment or bearing children.

Yet most people with herpes learn to cope. Some are helped by support groups that share ways of living with the disease. A caring and trusting partner is important. Joanne, a 26-year-old securities analyst, kept her herpes a secret from Jonathan during the first month they were dating. But when they approached the point of becoming sexually intimate, she felt obligated to tell him that she carried the virus:

> "I feared that telling him would scare him off. After all, who wants to have a relationship with someone who can give them herpes? After the first few dates I felt that this was the person I could spend the rest of my life with. I knew he also felt the same way. I had to tell him before things became too intense between us. Believe me, it wasn't easy blurting it out. He wasn't shocked or anything, although he did ask me all kinds of questions about it. I remember telling him that I got recurrences about once a year or so for about a week at a time. I told him that there was always the potential that I could infect him but that we would play it safe and avoid having sex whenever I had an outbreak. I also told him that even at other times I couldn't guarantee that it would be perfectly safe. He said at first that he needed some time to think about it. But later, that very night in fact, he called to tell me that he didn't want this to come between us and that we should try to make our relationship work."
>
> Joanne and Jonathan were married about 6 months later. A year after that their daughter Andrea was born. Jonathan remains uninfected. Joanne's occasional outbreaks are treated with acyclovir ointment and pass within a week or so.
>
> —*The Authors' Files*

The attitudes of people with herpes also play a role in adjusting. People who view herpes as a manageable illness or problem, and not as a medical disaster or character deficit, seem to find it easier to cope.

Human Papillomavirus

LO 13.9 Discuss the transmission, effects, and treatment of human papillomavirus.

human papillomavirus (HPV)
The world's most common STI, which is linked to genital warts, cervical cancer in women, and throat cancer in men.

Critical Thinking
What role is played by STIs in considering whether or not to have a male baby circumcised?

---

genital warts
An STI that is caused by the human papilloma virus and takes the form of warts that appear around the genitals and anus.

Human papillomavirus (HPV) is the world's most common STI, with signs of infection found in nearly half of the adult women in some countries. According to the Centers for Disease Control and Prevention, "HPV is so common that nearly all sexually active men and women get the virus at some point in their lives" (Genital HPV infection—Fact sheet, 2016). Fortunately, HPV infections clear up by themselves within 2 years in about 90% of cases. Women are more susceptible than men to HPV infection because cells in the cervix divide swiftly, facilitating the multiplication of HPV. Women who initiate coitus before the age of 18 and who have many sex partners are particularly susceptible to infection. It is estimated that nearly half of the sexually active teenage women and college women are currently infected with HPV (Genital HPV infection, 2012).

One study looked at 308 male–female college couples, all in newly formed relationships (Burchell et al., 2011). The researchers identified 179 pairs who were "discordant" for HPV infection; that is, one member of the couple was infected, and other one was not. However, 6 months later, HPV had been transmitted to 73 of the uninfected partners (41% of them).

Genital warts are one of the symptoms of infection by HPV, although many infected people either do not have the warts, or do not find them. Genital warts are similar to common plantar warts—itchy bumps that vary in size and shape. Genital warts are hard and yellow-gray when they form on dry skin. They take on pink, soft, cauliflower shapes in moist areas such as the lower vagina (see Figure 13.13). In men they appear on the penis, foreskin, and scrotum, and in the urethra. They appear on the vulva, along the vaginal wall, and on the cervix in women. They can also occur outside the genital area—for example, in the mouth; on the lips, eyelids, or nipples; around the anus; or in the rectum.

Genital warts may not cause any symptoms, but those that form on the urethra can cause bleeding or painful discharges. Genital warts are annoying but not deadly. However, HPV has been connected with cancers of the genital organs, particularly cervical cancer and penile cancer (The Link Between HPV and Cancer, 2015). In sum, HPV has been linked to:

- Nearly all cases of cervical cancer
- Sixty-nine percent of cases of vulvar cancer
- Seventy-five percent of cases of vaginal cancer
- Sixty-three percent of cases of penile cancer
- Ninety-one percent of cases of anal cancer
- Seventy-two percent of cases of cancer at the back of the throat.

HPV has been connected with throat cancer in people, mostly men, who perform cunnilingus on HPV-infected women (The Link Between HPV and Cancer, 2015). Men who have been circumcised are significantly less likely to carry HPV than men who have not been circumcised. All in all, it would seem wise for women to safeguard themselves from HPV-related cervical cancer by limiting their number of sex partners (to reduce their risk of exposure to HPV), thinking about the extracurricular sexual activities of their partners, and having regular Pap smears.

All sexually active individuals, female and male, should be regularly checked for the types of health problems that can develop from infection by HPV. On the other hand, as noted, the majority of cases of HPV infection do clear up "on their own." That is, the immune system eradicates HPV in most cases. But if you have been infected, or suspect that you have been infected, it would be wise to be followed by a physician.

HPV can be transmitted sexually through skin-to-skin contact during vaginal, anal, or oral sex. It can also be transmitted by other forms of contact, such as touching infected towels or clothing. The incubation period may vary from a few weeks to a couple of years.

Freezing a genital wart (*cryotherapy*) with liquid nitrogen is a preferred treatment for that particular problem. One alternative treatment involves painting or coating the warts over several days with podofilox solution or gel, imiquimod cream, trichloroacetic acid (TCA), or bichloroacetic acid (BCA). An alcohol-based podophyllin solution causes the warts to dry up and fall off. Although the warts may be removed, treatment does not rid the body of the virus. There may be recurrences. Podophyllin is not recommended for use with pregnant women or for treatment of warts that form on the cervix. The warts can also be treated by a doctor with electrodes (burning) or surgery (by laser or surgical removal).

HPV VACCINES Vaccines are available for prevention of HPV infections. Cervarix and Gardasil protect girls and women against the types of HPV responsible for most cancers of the cervix (Jena et al., 2015). Gardasil also protects against genital warts, anal, vaginal, and vulvar cancers. Either vaccine is recommended for 11- and 12-year-old girls, although girls may receive them as early as age 9 and women may obtain them up to the age of 26 (Cifu & Davis, 2014). In our experience, these types of age

Figure 13.13 Genital Warts.

Genital warts are caused by HPV and may have a cauliflower-like appearance. Many—perhaps most—cases occur where they can go visually undetected. HPV is implicated in cervical cancer, and women should be checked regularly for genital warts and other possibly "silent" STIs.

frames can change rapidly; check with your physician. Gardasil also protects males against genital warts and anal cancer that is caused by HPV (Genital HPV Infection, 2012). The vaccine is also apparently beneficial for men who have anal sex with other men (Palefsky et al., 2011). Ask your physician whether one of these vaccines would be helpful for you. Some critics have expressed fear that the availability of the HPV vaccine would encourage sexual activity among teens, and this concern has depressed the vaccination rate (Rubin, 2015). However, there is no evidence that use of the vaccine has increased sexual activity among teenage girls (Jena et al., 2015).

Viral Hepatitis

LO 13.10 **Discuss the transmission, effects, and treatment of other viral sexually transmitted infections.**

hepatitis

An inflammation of the liver.

Viral hepatitis refers to various types of liver infections (**hepatitis** is an inflammation of the liver) that are caused by viruses. The major types are *hepatitis A* (formerly called infectious hepatitis), *hepatitis B* (formerly called serum hepatitis), *hepatitis C* (formerly called hepatitis non-A, non-B), and *hepatitis D*.

Most people with hepatitis have no symptoms. When symptoms do appear, they often include **jaundice**, feelings of weakness and nausea, loss of appetite, abdominal discomfort, whitish bowel movements, and brownish or tea-colored urine. The symptoms of hepatitis B tend to be more severe and long-lasting than those of hepatitis A or C. In about 10% of cases, hepatitis B can lead to chronic liver disease. Hepatitis C tends to have milder symptoms but often leads to chronic liver disease such as cirrhosis or cancer of the liver. Hepatitis D—also called *delta hepatitis* or *type D hepatitis*—occurs only in the presence of hepatitis B. Hepatitis D, which has symptoms similar to those of hepatitis B, can produce severe liver damage and often leads to death.

jaundice

A yellowish discoloration of the skin and the whites of the eyes.

The hepatitis A virus is transmitted through contact with infected fecal matter found in contaminated food or water, and by oral contact with fecal matter, as through oral–anal sexual activity (licking or mouthing the partner's anus). (It is largely because of the risk of hepatitis A that restaurant employees are required to wash their hands after using the toilet.) Eating raw infested shellfish is also a common means of transmitting hepatitis A.

Hepatitis B can be transmitted sexually through anal, vaginal, or oral intercourse with an infected partner; through transfusion with contaminated blood supplies; by sharing contaminated needles or syringes; and by contact with contaminated saliva, menstrual blood, nasal mucus, or semen. Sharing razors, toothbrushes, or other personal articles with an infected person can also transmit hepatitis B. Hepatitis C and hepatitis D can also be transmitted sexually or through contact with contaminated blood. A person can transmit the viruses that cause hepatitis even if he or she is unaware of having any symptoms of the disease.

Hepatitis is usually diagnosed by testing blood samples for the presence of hepatitis antigens and antibodies. There is no cure for viral hepatitis. Bed rest and fluids are usually recommended until the acute stage of the infection subsides, generally in a few weeks. Full recovery may take months. A vaccine provides protection against hepatitis B and also against hepatitis D, since hepatitis D can occur only if hepatitis B is present.

Zika

Although the Zika virus is spread primarily by mosquitoes, it can also be spread through sexual contact, even before symptoms develop. An infected pregnant woman can also transmit the virus to her embryo or fetus, and it is a cause of **microcephaly** and other serious brain defects (Zika Virus, 2016). (It is not known to be transmitted from mother to child by breast feeding.) The virus can also be spread by blood transfusion.

As this book goes to press, cases of Zika infection in the mainland United States are the result of travel by people who have been in places, such as Brazil, where the spread of the disease has been rampant. Zika has also been found in Puerto Rico and the U.S. Virgin Islands. Many infected people do not develop symptoms, and in many others the symptoms are mild. Symptoms include fever, joint pain, rash and red eyes (conjunctivitis). Many infected people never know they had the disease. The virus tends to be cleared from the blood in about a week, although it lasts longer in some people.

Infection appears to protect people from future infection, a fact that presents hope that a vaccine will be developed. The best prevention is to avoid mosquito bites and also to avoid sexual contact with people traveling in from areas known to have cases of infection until the virus would have been cleared from the body (at least a week). As always: ask your doctor.

Microcephaly

abnormal smallness of the head resulting from incomplete development of the brain.

Molluscum Contagiosum

Molluscum contagiosum is an STI that is characterized by painless raised lesions that appear on the genitals, buttocks, thighs, or lower abdomen and caused by a pox virus. Pinkish in appearance with a waxy or pearly top, the lesions usually appear within 2 to 3 months of infection. Most infected people have between 10 and 20 lesions, although the number of lesions can range from 1 to 100 or more. The lesions are generally not associated with serious complications and often disappear on their own within 6 months. Or they can be treated by squeezing them (like "popping" a blackhead) to exude the whitish center plug. Solutions of podophyllin, trichloroacetic acid (TCA), or silver nitrate are also used. Freezing with liquid nitrogen (*cryotherapy*) can also be used to remove the lesions. However, do not try to treat any lesions on your own. See your doctor.

molluscum contagiosum

An STI that is caused by a pox virus that causes painless raised lesions to appear on the genitals, buttocks, thighs, or lower abdomen.

Ectoparasitic Infestations

LO 13.11   **Discuss the transmission, effects, and treatment of ectoparasitic infestations.**

Ectoparasites, as opposed to endoparasites, live on the outer surfaces of animals (*ecto* means "outer"). *Trichomonas vaginalis* is an endoparasite (*endo* means "inner"). Ectoparasites are larger than the agents that cause other STIs. In this section we consider two types of STIs caused by ectoparasites: pediculosis and scabies.

ectoparasites

Parasites that live on the outside of the host's body.

pediculosis

A parasitic infestation by pubic lice (*Pthirus pubis*) that causes itching.

Pediculosis

Pediculosis is the name given to an infestation of a parasite whose proper Latin name, *Pthirus pubis* (pubic lice), sounds rather too dignified for these bothersome (dare we say ugly?) creatures that are better known as "crabs" (Fig. 13.14).

Figure 13.14   Pubic Lice.

Pediculosis is an infestation by pubic lice (*Phthirus pubis*). Pubic lice are commonly called "crabs" because of their appearance under a microscope.

9 › T / F   Truth or Fiction Revisited   It is *not* true that pubic lice are of the same family of animals as crabs, but when viewed under a microscope, they look similar to crabs. They belong to a family of insects called *biting lice*. Another member of the family, the human head louse, is an annoying insect that clings to hair on the scalp and often spreads among schoolchildren.

In the adult stage, pubic lice are large enough to be seen with the naked eye. They are spread sexually but can also be transmitted by contact with an infested towel, sheet, or—yes—toilet seat. They can survive for only about 24 hours without a human host, but they may deposit eggs that can take up to 7 days to hatch in bedding or towels. Therefore, all bedding, towels, and clothes that have been used by an infested person must be washed in hot water and dried on the hot cycle, or dry-cleaned to ensure that they are safe. Fingers may also transmit the lice from the genitals to other hair-covered parts of the body, including the scalp and armpits. Sexual contact should be avoided until the infestation is eradicated.

Itching, ranging from the mildly irritating to the intolerable, is the most prominent symptom of a pubic lice infestation. The itching is caused by the "crabs" attaching themselves to the pubic hair and piercing the skin to feast on the blood of their hosts. (Yecch!) The life span of these insects is only about 1 month, but they are prolific egg-layers and may spawn several generations before they die. An infestation can be treated effectively with a prescription medication, a 1% solution of lindane (brand name Kwell), which is available as a cream, lotion, or shampoo. Nonprescription medications containing pyrethrins or piperonyl butoxide (brand names RID, Triple X, and others) will also do the job. Kwell is not recommended for use by pregnant or lactating women. A careful reexamination of the body is necessary after several days of treatment to ensure that all lice and eggs were killed.

Scabies

Scabies (short for *Sarcoptes scabiei*) is a parasitic infestation caused by a tiny mite that may be transmitted through sexual contact or contact with infested clothing, bed linen, towels, and other fabrics. The mites attach themselves to the base of pubic hair and burrow into the skin, where they lay eggs and subsist for the duration of their 30-day life span. Like pubic lice, scabies are often found in the genital region and cause itching and discomfort. They are also responsible for reddish lines (created by burrowing) and sores, welts, or blisters on the skin. Unlike lice, they are too tiny to be seen by the naked eye. Diagnosis is made by detecting the mite or its by-products on microscopic examination of scrapings from suspicious-looking areas of skin. Scabies are most often found on the hands and wrists, but they may also appear on the genitals, buttocks, armpits, and feet. They do not appear above the neck—thankfully!

Scabies, like pubic lice, may be treated effectively with 1% lindane (brand name Kwell). The entire body from the neck down must be coated with a thin layer of the medication, which should not be washed off for 8 hours. But lindane should not be used by women who are pregnant or lactating. To avoid reinfection, sex partners and others in close bodily contact with infected individuals should also be treated. Clothing and bed linen that the infected person has used must be washed and dried on the hot cycle or dry-cleaned. As with "crabs," sexual contact should be avoided until the infestation is eliminated.

Critical Thinking
If pubic lice can be transmitted by contact with an infested toilet seat, why is it referred to as a sexually transmitted infection?

---

scabies

A parasitic infestation caused by a tiny mite (*Sarcoptes scabiei*) that causes itching.

Preventing STIs: It's More Than Safer Sex

LO 13.12 **Explain ways of preventing sexually transmitted infections.**

Prevention is the best way to control the spread of STIs, especially those for which there is no cure or vaccine. Prevention of even one case of an STI can prevent its spread to others—perhaps eventually to you.

There are many things that you can do to lower the risk of contracting STIs. "Safer sex" is only one aspect of prevention.

Abstinence or Monogamy

The only fully effective strategies to prevent the sexual transmission of STIs are abstinence or maintaining a monogamous sexual relationship with an uninfected partner. If you are celibate, or if you and your sex partner are not infected and neither of you engages in sexual activity with anyone else, you have little to be concerned about. But most people are sexually active and may not have not committed themselves to a monogamous relationship. Even for those who seek monogamous relationships, there must always be that first time.

Know About the Risks

Be aware of the risks of STIs. Many of us try to put the dangers of STIs out of our minds—especially in moments of passion. Make a pact with yourself to refuse to play the dangerous game of pretending that the dangers of STIs do not exist or that you are somehow immune.

If virtually all young people in the United States are aware of the sexual transmission of HIV, why do so many continue to engage in risky sex? For one thing, teens do not perceive risky behavior to be as dangerous as adults do. This generalization extends to drinking, smoking, failure to use seat belts, and drag racing, as well as sex. Young people also profit from being taught specific skills to protect themselves from engaging in risky sex, such as communication skills for discussing safer sex options with their partners, assertiveness skills for ensuring that their needs are respected by their partners, social skills to resist peer pressures, and correct use of condoms.

Researchers have identified several factors that underlie risky sexual behavior among young people:

1. *Perceived low risk of infection.* Given the current low rate of known infections among heterosexuals who do not inject drugs, many heterosexuals may dismiss HIV/AIDS as a problem that affects other types of people. Even gay men may operate under the "I'm not the type" fallacy and underestimate their personal risk.

2. *Negative attitudes toward condom use.* For some, the risk of being infected with HIV seems to fly out of the minds when the opportunity for sex arises. Some claim that a condom dampens romantic ardor in moments of passion and decreases sexual sensations. Some people consider them too much of a fuss.

3. *Myth of personal invulnerability.* Some people subscribe to a myth of personal invulnerability and believe that they are somehow immune to HIV/AIDS and other STIs. One junior at the University of Miami (Ohio) explained to an interviewer why she did not insist that her partners use a condom: "I

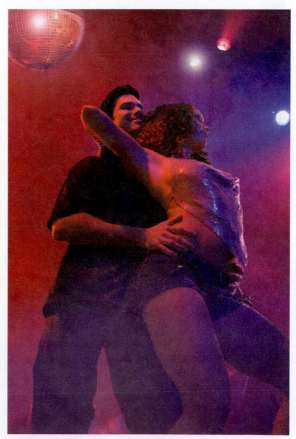

Stay Sober! Is any additional commentary necessary?

have an attitude—it may be wrong—that any guy I would sleep with would not have AIDS." The adventurous spirit that we often associate with youth may confer a dangerous sense of immortality and a greater willingness to take risks.

4. *Impulsivity.* Young men who are impulsive and quick to become sexually aroused are more likely to engage in risky sex (Derefinko et al., 2014).

Stay Sober

Alcohol—especially binge drinking—and other drugs increase the likelihood of engaging in risky sex.

Inspect Yourself and Your Partner

Inspect yourself for a discharge, bumps, rashes, warts, blisters, chancres, sores, lice, or foul odors. Do not expect to find tell-tale signs of an HIV infection, but infected people often have other STIs. Check out any unusual feature with a physician before you engage in sexual activity.

You may be able to work an inspection of your partner into foreplay—a reason for having sex the first time with the lights on. In particular, a woman may hold her partner's penis firmly, pulling the loose skin up and down, as if milking it. Then she can check for a discharge at the penile opening. The man may use his fingers to detect any sign of a vaginal discharge. Other visible features of STIs include herpes blisters, genital warts, syphilitic chancres or rashes, and pubic lice.

If you find anything that doesn't look, feel, or smell right, bring it to your partner's attention. Treat any unpleasant odor as a warning sign. If you notice any suspicious signs, refrain from further sexual contact until your partner has the chance to seek a medical evaluation. It is advisable to be informed about the common signs and symptoms of STIs, but you need not become a medical expert.

Condoms are one of the simplest and best forms of protection against AIDS. But they're only effective if they are used properly every time you have sex. Why risk not using them? For more information about condoms, AIDS and AIDS prevention, call 1-800-342-AIDS.

AMERICA RESPONDS TO AIDS

Of course, your partner may become defensive or hostile if you express a concern that he or she may be carrying an STI. Try to be empathetic. The social stigma attached to people with STIs makes it difficult to accept the possibility of infection. It may be appropriate to point out that STIs are quite common (among college students, bankers, military personnel, or … fill in the blanks) and that many people are unaware that they carry them.

But if you are not sure that sex is safe, stop. Think carefully about the risks, and seek expert advice.

Use Latex Condoms

Latex condoms are effective in blocking nearly all sexually transmissible organisms. Improper use or inconsistent use is a common reason for failures in using condoms to prevent STI transmission. Yet even when used properly, condoms may be of limited or no value against disease-causing organisms that are transmitted externally, such as those causing herpes, genital warts, and ectoparasitic infestations.

Condoms made from animal membranes ("skins") are less effective barriers against STIs because they contain pores that allow tiny microbes, including HIV, to penetrate. Even latex condoms are not always 100% effective in preventing the transmission of HIV and other STIs. Condoms (and the people who use them) are fallible. Condoms can break or slip off.

Use Barrier Devices During Oral Sex

Use a condom before practicing fellatio and a dental dam (a square piece of latex rubber used by dentists during oral surgery) to cover the vagina before engaging in cunnilingus.

Avoid Risky Sex

Avoid unprotected vaginal intercourse (intercourse without the use of a latex condom). Unprotected anal intercourse is one of riskiest practices. Other high-risk behaviors include unprotected oral sex, oral–anal sex, insertion of a hand or fist ("fisting") into someone's rectum or vagina, or any activity in which you or your partner would come into contact with the other's blood, semen, or vaginal secretions. If you do engage in anal sex and are uncertain as to whether you or your partner is infected, use a latex condom. Oral–anal sex, or anilingus (sometimes called *rimming* or a *rim job*), should be avoided because of the potential of transmitting microbes between the mouth and the anus.

Also avoid sexual contact with people with STIs, people who practice high-risk sexual behaviors, people who inject drugs, and prostitutes or people who frequent prostitutes.

Wash the Genitals Before and After Sex

Washing the genitals before and after sex removes a quantity of potentially harmful agents. Washing together can be erotic foreplay. Right after sex, washing with soap and water may help reduce the risk of infection. Do not, however, deceive yourself into believing that washing your genitals is an effective substitute for safe sex. Most STIs are transmitted internally. Washing is useless against them.

Douching right after sex might have some limited benefits for women. But frequent douching should be avoided because it may change the vaginal flora and encourage the growth of infectious organisms.

Have Regular Medical Checkups

A sexually active person should have regular health checkups, at least once a year. Many community clinics and family-planning centers scale their charges to ability to pay. Checkups are a small investment to make in one's own health. Many people are symptomless carriers of STIs, especially of chlamydial infections. Medical checkups enable them to learn about and receive treatment for disorders that might otherwise go unnoticed. Many physicians advise routine testing of asymptomatic young women for chlamydial infections to prevent the hidden damage that can occur if the infection goes untreated.

Discuss Whether You and Your Partner Should Be Tested Before Having Sex

Some couples reach a mutual agreement to be tested for HIV and other STIs before they begin having sex. (Some people simply insist that their prospective partners be tested.) But many people resist testing or feel insulted when partners raise the issue. People usually assume that they are free of STIs if they are symptom free and have been reasonably selective in their choice of partners. But STIs can infect anyone and the absence of symptoms is no guarantee of freedom from infection. Unless you have been celibate or involved in a monogamous relationship with an uninfected partner, you should consider yourself at risk of carrying or contracting an infectious STI.

Engage in Forms of Sex Other than Intercourse and Oral–Genital Contact

Other forms of sex, such as hugging, massage, caressing, mutual masturbation, or rubbing bodies together without vaginal, anal, or oral contact, are low-risk ways of finding sexual pleasure, so long as semen or vaginal fluids do not come into contact with mucous membranes or breaks in the skin. Sharing sexual fantasies can be titillating, as can taking a bath or shower together. Vibrators, dildos, and other sex toys may also be erotically stimulating and carry a low risk of infection, if they are washed thoroughly with soap and water before and between use. (Be sure to remove *all* the soap, which can otherwise be irritating.

Talk to a Doctor If You Suspect That You Have Been Exposed to an STI

Many STIs are detectable in the early stages of development and are best treated early. If you have engaged in risky sex or have developed symptoms, see a doctor as soon as possible.

HIV/AIDS: EXPOSURE VERSUS INFECTION! Now for some words about HIV/AIDS. We begin with a fact: There is a difference between being *exposed* to HIV and being *infected* with HIV. If you have been *exposed* to HIV, the virus may be traveling though your bloodstream. If you have been *infected*, the HIV has entered cells in your body. Exposure precedes infection, and you may have a window of opportunity to prevent exposure from transforming into infection. If you think that you have done something that may have exposed you to HIV, see a doctor as soon as possible. Post-exposure prophylaxis nPEP with antiretroviral medicines may prevent HIV in your bloodstream from infecting cells. nPEP should be begun as soon as possible after exposure. If you want details, you can go to http://www.cdc.gov/hiv/guidelines/preventing.html. Then click on non-occupational post-exposure prophylaxis or occupational post-exposure prophylaxis. But it is more important that you get yourself to a doctor.

Get to Know Your Partner Before Having Sex

Be selective in your choice of sex partners. Having sex with multiple partners—especially one-night stands—increases your risk of sexual contact with an infected person. It also lessens the opportunity to get to know your partner well enough to know whether he or she has had risky sex.

Avoid Other High-Risk Behaviors

Avoid contact with bodily substances (blood, semen, vaginal secretions, fecal matter) from other people. Do not share hypodermic needles, razors, cuticle scissors, or other implements that could contain another person's blood. Be careful when handling wet towels, bed linen, or other material that might contain bodily substances.

Chapter Review

LO 13.1 Describe features of the epidemic of sexually transmitted infections.

More than 19 million people in the United States contract an STI each year. Although public attention has been riveted on HIV/AIDS, other STIs such as chlamydia and HPV pose wider threats.

LO 13.2 Discuss the transmission, effects, and treatment of gonorrhea.

Gonorrhea is caused by the *gonococcus* bacterium. Men's symptoms include a penile discharge and burning urination. Most women are asymptomatic, but if untreated, gonorrhea can develop into pelvic inflammatory disease (PID).

LO 13.3 Discuss the transmission, effects, and treatment of syphilis.

Syphilis is caused by the *Treponema pallidum* bacterium. Syphilis undergoes several stages of development, beginning with a chancre. It can lie dormant for many years but eventually be lethal.

LO 13.4 Discuss the transmission, effects, and treatment of chlamydia.

Chlamydial infections are caused by *Chlamydia trachomatous.* Symptoms resemble those of gonorrhea but tend to be milder.

LO 13.5 Discuss the transmission, effects, and treatment of other bacterial sexually transmitted infections.

Other bacterial infections include chancroid, shigellosis, granuloma inguinale, and lymphogranuloma venereum. Bacterial infections are treated with antibiotics.

LO 13.6 Discuss the transmission, effects, and treatment of various vaginal infections.

Vaginitis is usually known by a foul-smelling discharge, genital irritation, and burning during urination. Most cases of vaginitis involve bacterial vaginosis, candidiasis (caused by a fungus), or trichomoniasis (caused by a protozoan). These microbes are normally found in the body but can "overgrow."

LO 13.7 Discuss the transmission, effects, and treatment of HIV/AIDS.

HIV causes AIDS by attacking the body's immune system, making the person vulnerable to opportunistic diseases—such as serious infections and cancers—that are normally held in check. HIV is found in blood, semen, vaginal secretions, and breast milk. Common avenues of transmission include vaginal and anal sex, sharing hypodermic needles, childbirth, and breast-feeding. HIV infection can be diagnosed through tests of blood, saliva, or urine. The only effective treatment of HIV/AIDS is ART, which uses a "cocktail" of antiretroviral agents.

LO 13.8 Discuss the transmission, effects, and treatment of genital herpes.

Genital herpes is caused by HSV-2, which produces painful shallow sores and blisters on the genitals. Antiviral drugs can relieve pain and speed healing during flare-ups.

LO 13.9 Discuss the transmission, effects, and treatment of human papillomavirus.

HPV causes genital warts and has been linked to cervical cancer in women and throat cancer in sex partners of infected women who engage in cunnilingus. Most cases of HPV infection clear by themselves, but those that do not can cause serious health problems.

LO 13.10 Discuss the transmission, effects, and treatment of the Zika virus and other viral sexually transmitted infections.

The several types of hepatitis are caused by different viruses. Most cases are transmitted sexually or by contact with contaminated blood or fecal matter.

LO 13.11 Discuss the transmission, effects, and treatment of ectoparasitic infestations.

Pediculosis ("crabs") is caused by pubic lice (*Pthirus pubis*). Pubic lice attach themselves to pubic hair and feed on the blood of their hosts, which often causes itching. Infestations can be treated with lindane. Scabies (*Sarcoptes scabiei*) is caused by a tiny mite that causes itching and can be treated with lindane.

LO 13.12 Explain ways of preventing sexually transmitted infections.

Ways of preventing STIs include abstinence, monogamy with an uninfected partner, knowing one's partner, remaining sober (enough) at get-togethers, and using latex condoms.

Test Your Learning

1. Which of the following is the most widespread STI?

   (a) Scabies
   (b) HIV/AIDS
   (c) Genital herpes
   (d) HPV

2. Treponema pallidum is the organism that causes _____

   (a) gonorrhea.
   (b) syphilis.
   (c) chlamydia.
   (d) genital herpes.

3. The Abbott Testpack is used to diagnose _____

   (a) trichomoniasis.
   (b) HIV infection.
   (c) chlamydia.
   (d) candidiasis.

4. Miconazole is used to treat _____

   (a) candidiasis.
   (b) hepatitis.
   (c) pediculosis.
   (d) syphilis.

5. ART is used to treat _____

   (a) *Herpes simplex* virus, type 1.
   (b) HPV.
   (c) pthirus pubis.
   (d) HIV/AIDS

6. General paresis may develop during the _____ stage of syphilis.

   (a) primary
   (b) secondary
   (c) tertiary
   (d) All of the above

7. As many as half of some populations of college women are infected with _____

   (a) gonorrhea.
   (b) genital herpes.
   (c) HPV.
   (d) HIV/AIDS

8. HIV is *not* found in infectious amounts in _____

   (a) breast milk.
   (b) saliva.
   (c) blood.
   (d) semen.

9. _____ often reflects the overgrowth of organisms normally found in the vagina.

   (a) Gonorrhea
   (b) Candidiasis
   (c) Molluscum contagiosum
   (d) Chlamydia

10. Women infected with _____ are likely to encounter pelvic pain and irregular menstrual cycles.

    (a) hemophilus ducreyi
    (b) *Herpes simplex* virus, type 2
    (c) human papilloma virus
    (d) chlamydia trachomatis

Answers: 1. d; 2. b; 3. c; 4. a; 5. d; 6. c; 7. c; 8. b; 9. b; 10. d

Chapter 14
Atypical Sexual Variations

Learning Objectives

Normal Versus Deviant Sexual Behavior

LO 14.1 Explain the distinction between normal and deviant sexual behavior.

Paraphilic Disorders

LO 14.2 Enumerate and define paraphilic disorders.

Theoretical Perspectives

LO 14.3 Discuss biological perspectives on paraphilic disorders.

LO 14.4 Discuss psychoanalytic perspectives on paraphilic disorders.

LO 14.5 Discuss cognitive-behavioral perspectives on paraphilic disorders.

LO 14.6 Discuss sociological perspectives on paraphilic disorders.

LO 14.7 Discuss the "Lovemap."

Treatment Of Paraphilic Disorders

LO 14.8 Discuss the psychoanalytic treatment of paraphilic disorders.

LO 14.9 Discuss the cognitive-behavioral treatment of paraphilic disorders.

LO 14.10 Discuss medical treatment of paraphilic disorders.

Which of the following statements are the truth, and which are fiction? Look for the Truth-or-Fiction items throughout this chapter to find the answers.

1 Strippers are exhibitionists.   **T / F**?

2 People who enjoy watching their mates undress are voyeurs.   **T / F**?

3 Exhibitionists and voyeurs are never violent.   **T / F**?

4 Some people cannot become sexually aroused unless they are bound, flogged, or humiliated by their sex partners.   **T / F**?

5 It is normal to enjoy some mild forms of pain during sexual activity.   **T / F**?

6 There is a subculture in the United States in which sexual sadists and sexual masochists form liaisons to inflict and receive pain and humiliation during sexual activity.   **T / F**?

7 Painful stimuli may activate the reward regions of the brain.   **T / F**?

His sister once called Archie a "dredge to society."

By the time he came to the clinic, the now 55-year-old plumber had been cross-dressing for decades. There was a time when he would go out in public as a woman, but as his prominence in the community grew, he and his wife Myrna, who knew of his "peccadillo," decided he must limit his cross-dressing to home. Myrna had learned of his behavior because he borrowed many of her clothes. In order to keep Archie at home, Myrna offered to help him with his "weirdness."

But eventually Myrna had had it, in part because a teenage daughter nearly walked into their bedroom while they were acting out Archie's fantasies. Archie accompanied Myrna to the clinic, under threat of divorce. Myrna described how Archie had imposed his will on her for 20 years. Archie would wear her undergarments and masturbate while she watched and told him how disgusting he was. (The couple also regularly had what Myrna called "normal" sex, and Myrna enjoyed it.)

With Myrna out of the consulting room, Archie confided that he grew up in a family with several older sisters. He described how underwear had been perpetually hanging out to dry in the house's single bathroom. As an adolescent, Archie experimented with rubbing against articles of underwear, then with trying them on. On one occasion a sister walked in while he was modeling panties before the mirror. She told him he was a "dredge to society," and he straightaway experienced unparalleled sexual excitement. He masturbated immediately when she left the room, and his orgasm was the most intense of his young life.

Archie did not think that there was anything wrong with wearing women's undergarments and masturbating. He found the prospect of giving it up extraordinarily painful. But Myrna at this point felt that she must separate from Archie's "sickness." She didn't care what he did anymore, so long as he did it by himself. "Enough is enough," she said.

Actually, these feelings embodied the compromise that the couple worked out. Archie would engage in his fantasies by himself. He would do so when Myrna was not at home, and she would not hear of his activities. He would also be very, very careful to choose times when the children would not be around.

Six months later the couple were together and content. Archie had replaced Myrna's input into his fantasies with transvestic-sadomasochistic magazines. Myrna said, "I see no evil, hear no evil, smell no evil." They continued to have sex. After a while, Myrna forgot to check to see which underwear had been used.

—*The Authors' Files*

Archie is a transvestite. He seeks sexual satisfaction by dressing in women's clothing. Some transvestites can be sexually aroused only by cross-dressing. Others, like Archie, are in long-term, committed, male–female relationships and also have sex with their regular partners. Yet they seek additional sexual gratification through dressing as women. Women, of course, commonly wear pants and other clothes that have been traditionally deemed male attire, yet their doing so is not transvestic because wearing "men's clothing" is a common style and is not sexually arousing to them.

The American Psychiatric Association (2013) lists Archie's kind of behavior in its *Diagnostic and Statistical Manual of the Mental Disorders*. Over the years "mental disorder" and many other terms have been used to describe Archie's behavior, including mental illness, abnormal behavior, deviant behavior, character disorder, and perversion. These labels have also been applied to exhibitionism, voyeurism, sadism, masochism, and numerous other sexual behaviors in which sexual excitement is triggered by stimuli that most people find to be non-arousing.

Normal Versus Deviant Sexual Behavior

LO 14.1 **Explain the distinction between normal and deviant sexual behavior.**

One common approach to defining normal versus deviant traits or behavior is statistical. We can readily agree that the great majority of human adults range in height from, say, 4' 10" to 6' 6". People who are shorter or taller are clearly statistically abnormal, but that is not necessarily a bad thing unless it is connected with biological health problems. From this perspective, rare or unusual sexual behaviors are atypical and might also be labeled abnormal or deviant. The statistical approach may seem value-free because the yardstick of normality or typicality is based on the frequency of behavior, not on judgment of its social acceptability. But having sex while standing, or more than seven times a week, might be considered abnormal or deviant by this yardstick.

Another approach is to consider sexual behaviors abnormal or deviant when they run counter to one's religious values, or when they make most of us wince (as in sadism or masochism), or when they seem inexplicable (as in being turned on more by a woman's shoe than by the woman herself) (O'Donohue, 2014; Balon, 2015b). Behaviors that counter someone's religious values—such as premarital sex—may be common enough, but that individual might label them deviant because they deviate from what the person has been led to believe is normal, right, or proper. There will clearly be great disagreement among the general population as to what is normal and what is abnormal when we base our judgments on religious values.

What is considered normal and is typical in one culture or at a particular time may also be considered abnormal in other cultures and at other times. What is "normal" behavior for the female adolescent Trobriand Islander (see Chapter 1) might be considered deviant—nymphomaniacal, in fact—by most other cultural standards.

In our own culture, sexual practices such as oral sex and masturbation were once considered to be deviant or abnormal. Today, however, they are practiced by such wide majorities that few people would label them as abnormal or deviant. Concepts of "normalcy" and "deviance," then, also reflect the mores and customs of a particular culture at a given time.

But the basis used for determining the patterns of sexual behavior discussed in this chapter is that they involve the persistent preference for nongenital sexual outlets (O'Donohue, 2013; Balon, 2015b). If a man prefers fondling a woman's panties to having sex with her, or prefers to masturbate against her foot rather than have sex, his behavior is likely to be labeled deviant. Such behaviors have a bizarre or "kinky" quality (A. D. Fisher et al., 2011). The behaviors may also cause significant distress to the individual engaging in the behavior or to others.

The American Psychiatric Association (2013) refers to these behaviors as representing *paraphilic disorders*, from the roots *para-*, meaning "unusual" or "alongside of," and *philia*, meaning "love." As noted previously, the American Psychiatric Association

Critical Thinking
Why is statistical rarity an inadequate standard for considering a sexual practice to be normal or abnormal?

lists these behaviors as mental disorders. But milder forms of these behaviors may be practiced by many people and may be considered to fall within the more typical spectrum of human sexuality.

Paraphilic Disorders

LO 14.2   Enumerate and define the paraphilic disorders.

paraphilic disorder

An atypical pattern of sexual arousal or behavior that becomes problematic in the eyes of the individual or society, such as fetishistic disorder or exhibitionistic disorder. The urges are recurrent and are either acted on or are distressing to the individual. (From Greek roots meaning "to the side of" [*para-*] and "loving" [*philos*].)

Paraphilic disorders involve sexual arousal in response to unusual stimuli such as children or other nonconsenting people (such as unsuspecting people whom one watches or to whom one exposes one's genitals), nonhuman objects (such as shoes, leather, rubber, or undergarments), or pain or humiliation (Balon, 2015b). The psychiatric diagnosis of paraphilic disorder requires that the person has acted on the urges, is distinctly distressed by them, or that they impair the functioning of the individual, as in impairing social relationships, work life, and so on.

People with paraphilic disorders usually feel that their urges are obsessional—insistent, demanding, or compulsory. They may describe themselves as overcome by them. People with paraphilic disorders tend to experience their urges as beyond their control, as drug addicts or compulsive gamblers do. For these reasons theorists have speculated that paraphilic disorders may represent a type of sexual compulsion or an addiction.

Paraphilic disorders vary in severity. In some cases, the person can function sexually in the absence of the unusual stimuli and seldom, if ever, acts on his or her deviant urges. In other cases, the person resorts to paraphilic behavior only in times of stress. In more extreme forms the person repeatedly engages in paraphilic behavior and may become preoccupied with thoughts and fantasies about these experiences. In such cases the person may not be able to become sexually aroused without either fantasizing about the paraphilic stimulus or having it present. For some people, paraphilic behavior is the only means of attaining sexual gratification.

The person with a paraphilic disorder typically replays the paraphilic act in sexual fantasies to stimulate arousal during masturbation or sexual relations. It is as if he or she is mentally replaying a videotape of the paraphilic scene. But the scene grows stale after a while, and the individual feels the urge to perform another paraphilic act to make a new "video."

Some paraphilic disorders are mostly harmless and victimless, such as *fetishistic disorder* and cross-dressing to achieve sexual arousal, as in the case of Archie (*transvestic fetishistic disorder*). Even being humiliated by one's partner may be relatively harmless if the partner consents. Other paraphilic behaviors, such as exposing oneself in public or enticing children into sexual relations, do have victims and may cause harm, sometimes severe physical or psychological harm. They are also against the law (Balon, 2015b). Sexual sadism, in which sexual arousal is connected to hurting or humiliating another person, can be a most harmful paraphilic disorder when it is forced on a nonconsenting person. Some brutal rapes involve sexual sadism.

Real Students, Real Questions

Q   *Is having sex underwater considered atypical? Can it cause infection?*

A   It's not a paraphilic disorder, and we hate to burst your bubble (pardon the pun), but it's not really all that unusual. You're unlikely to get anyone infected with salt water, although there can be some irritation. The same goes for the chlorine in a pool, but irritation is no fun, and the water is no lubricant. Remember to hold your breath or get scuba gear.☺

Except in the case of sexual masochism, paraphilic disorders are believed to occur almost exclusively among men (American Psychiatric Association, 2013). The prevalence of paraphilic disorders in the general population remains unknown because people are generally unwilling to talk about them. Much of what we have learned about paraphilic disorders derives from the reported experiences of people who have been apprehended for performing illegal acts (such as exposing themselves in public) and the few who have voluntarily sought help. The characteristics of people who have not been identified or studied remain virtually unknown.

We discuss the major types of paraphilic disorders in this chapter, beginning with fetishistic disorder. The one exception is *pedophilia.* In pedophilistic disorder, children become the objects of sexual arousal. Pedophilistic disorder often takes the form of sexual coercion of children, as in incest or sexual molestation (Lalumière, et al., 2005a; Seto, 2008). It is discussed in the following chapter as a form of sexual coercion.

Fetishistic Disorder

The roots of the word *fetish* come from the French *fétiche,* which is thought to derive from the Portuguese *feitico,* meaning "magic charm." The "magic" in this case lies in an object's ability to arouse a person sexually. In **fetishistic disorder**, an inanimate object elicits sexual arousal. Articles of clothing (for example, women's panties, bras, lingerie, stockings, gloves, shoes, or boots) and materials made of rubber, leather, silk, or fur are among the more common fetishistic objects (Kafka, 2010). Leather boots and high-heeled shoes are popular. There are also baby diaper fetishists and a community referred to as Adult Baby/Diaper Lovers (Hawkinson & Zamboni, 2014).

The fetishist may act on the urges to engage in fetishistic behavior, such as by masturbating by stroking an object or while fantasizing about it, or he may be distressed about such urges or fantasies and not act on them (Kafka, 2010). In a related paraphilic disorder, **partialism**, people are excessively aroused by a particular body part, such as the feet, breasts, or buttocks.

fetishistic disorder

A paraphilic disorder in which an inanimate object such as an article of clothing or items made of rubber, leather, or silk elicit sexual arousal.

partialism

A paraphilic disorder related to fetishistic disorder in which sexual arousal is exaggeratedly associated with a particular body part, such as feet, breasts, or buttocks.

Fetishism. In fetishistic disorder, inanimate objects such as leather shoes or boots, or parts of the body such as feet, elicit sexual arousal. Many fetishists cannot achieve sexual arousal without contact with the desired objects or without fantasizing about them. Women's undergarments and objects made of rubber, leather, silk, or fur are common fetishistic objects. Why is it that some men seek "footjobs" by women, in which women rub their genitals with their feet until they ejaculate?

Most fetishes and partialisms are harmless. Fetishistic practices are almost always private and involve masturbation or are incorporated into sex with a willing partner (Darcangelo, 2008). Only rarely have fetishists coerced others into paraphilic activities. However, some partialists have touched parts of women's bodies in public. And some fetishists commit burglaries to acquire the fetishistic objects. Now and then we hear of someone who has stolen hundreds of pairs of women's shoes, for example.

TRANSVESTIC FETISHISTIC DISORDER Fetishistic disorder appears to include **transvestism**. Whereas other fetishists become sexually aroused by handling the fetishistic object while they masturbate, transvestites become excited by wearing articles of clothing—the fetishistic objects—of the other gender (Blanchard, 2010). A fetishist may find the object or gender involving the object to be erotically stimulating. For the transvestite, the object is sexually alluring only when it is worn. Transvestites are mostly males. Many, like Archie, whom we met at the beginning of the chapter, are in committed male–female relationships and otherwise stereotypically masculine in behavior.

Like fetishistic disorder in general, the origins of transvestism remain obscure. Evidence of biological hormonal and neurological abnormalities in transvestism is mixed (Bailey, 2003b). Långström and Zucker (2005) surveyed 2,450 Swedes and found transvestism in about 2.8% of men and 0.4% of women. A history of transvestism was associated with separation from parents, same-sex sexual experiences, use of pornography, high rates of masturbation, and other paraphilic disorders—namely, sexual masochism, exhibitionistic disorder, and voyeuristic disorder.

Some men cross-dress for reasons other than sexual arousal and so are not "true transvestites." Some men make a living by impersonating women like Marilyn Monroe and Madonna on stage and are not motivated by sexual arousal. Among some segments of the gay male community, it is fashionable to masquerade as women. Gay men do not usually cross-dress to become sexually stimulated, however.

Transvestic behaviors may range from wearing a single female garment when alone to sporting dresses, wigs, makeup, and feminine mannerisms at a transvestite club. Some transvestites become sexually aroused by masquerading as women and attracting the interest of unsuspecting males. They sometimes entice these men or string them along until they find some excuse to back out before their anatomic sex is revealed. The great majority of transvestites do not engage in anti-social or illegal behavior. Most practice their sexual predilection in private and would be horrified or embarrassed to be discovered by associates while dressed in female attire.

transvestism

A paraphilic disorder in which a person repeatedly cross-dresses to achieve sexual arousal or gratification, or is troubled by persistent, recurring urges to cross-dress.

Transvestism. This man, like Archie, is wearing women's underwear in his own home. Some transvestites cross-dress in public. Transvestites are sexually aroused by dressing in women's clothing, and some cannot be sexually aroused by other stimuli, such as women themselves.

A study of male heterosexual cross-dressers in New England found that most of their wives were tolerant, but many who found out about their husbands' cross-dressing years into the marriage felt betrayed and angry (Reynolds & Caron, 2000). A common concern of the wives was that outsiders would learn about their husbands' behavior.

Exhibitionistic Disorder

If fetishistic disorder is often victimless, the same cannot be said for exhibitionistic disorder. **Exhibitionistic disorder** ("flashing") involves persistent, powerful urges and sexual fantasies involving exposing one's genitals to unsuspecting strangers for the purpose of achieving sexual arousal or gratification (Langstrom, 2010). The urges are either acted on or are disturbing to the individual. Exhibitionists are almost always males, but there are some cases of female exhibitionists (Hugh-Jones et al., 2005). Males who expose themselves to females usually seek sexual release by masturbating to memories of the incidents afterward. After a while the novelty of incidents tends to wear off and exhibitionists seek new victims to create new memories.

What we know of exhibitionists, as with most other people with paraphilic disorders, is almost entirely derived from studies of men who have been apprehended or treated by mental-health professionals (Langevin et al., 2004). Such knowledge may yield a biased picture because relatively few incidents result in apprehension and conviction. The characteristics of most perpetrators may thus differ from those of people who have been made available for study.

About 4% of the males in a national probability sample reported exposing their genitals to obtain sexual pleasure; the prevalence dropped to about 2% for women (Murphy & Page, 2008). A survey of college women at U.S. universities found exposure to exhibitionistic disorder to be widespread. About 32% to 39% report running into a "flasher" (Murphy & Page, 2008). A majority of the women had been approached for the first time (some had been approached more than once) by 16 years of age. Only a few had reported these incidents to the police. The clinical definition of exhibitionistic disorder involves exposure to a stranger, but about one-third (36%) of the incidents among the college women were committed by acquaintances, relatives, or "good friends."

The typical exhibitionist is young, either lonely or in an unhappy male–female relationship, and sexually repressed. An exhibitionist may claim that sex with his regular partner is reasonably satisfactory, but that he also experiences the compulsion to expose himself to strangers. Many exhibitionists are single, however. They typically have difficulties relating to women and have been unable to establish meaningful heterosexual relationships (Leue et al., 2004; Murphy & Page, 2008).

Exhibitionistic disorder usually begins before age 18 (American Psychiatric Association, 2013). The urge to exhibit oneself, if not the actual act, usually begins in early adolescence, generally between the ages of 13 and 16. The frequency of exhibitionistic disorder declines markedly after the age of 40 (American Psychiatric Association, 2013). The typical exhibitionist does not attempt further sexual contact with the victim. Thus, he does not usually pose a physical threat (American Psychiatric Association, 2013). We say *usually*, but if the victim confronts the exhibitionist and insults or attacks him, the situation may escalate into a violent one (McNally & Fremouw, 2014).

exhibitionistic disorder

A paraphilic disorder characterized by persistent, powerful urges and sexual fantasies involving exposing one's genitals to unsuspecting strangers for the purpose of achieving sexual arousal or gratification.

Critical Thinking
Critical thinkers pay close attention to definitions. Why are (most) stripteasers and nude sunbathers *not* exhibitionists?

An Exhibitionist at a Cricket Match. Whatever else his motives might have been, this streaker was trying to shock the crowd by exposing himself.

The police sometimes trivialize exhibitionistic disorder as a "nuisance crime," but the psychological consequences among victims, especially young children, indicate that exhibitionistic disorder is not victimless. For example, victims may feel violated and be bothered by recurrent images or nightmares; harbor misplaced guilt that they had unwittingly enticed the exhibitionist; blame themselves for reacting excessively or for failing to apprehend the perpetrator; and develop fears of venturing out on their own. Moreover, exhibitionists are highly likely to repeat their crimes, even if they spend time in prison for them (Kaser-Boyd, 2015; Langevin et al., 2004).

Some theorists see exhibitionistic disorder as a means of expressing hostility toward women (Murphy & Page, 2008). Exposure may be an attempt to strike back at women because of a belief that women have wronged him or damaged his self-esteem by failing to notice him or take him seriously. The direct expression of anger may be perceived as too risky, so the exhibitionist vents his rage by humiliating a defenseless stranger. The urge to expose oneself often occurs when the exhibitionist feels that his masculinity has been insulted. Are exhibitionists attempting to assert their masculinity by evoking a response from victims?

Other studies show exhibitionists to be shy, dependent, passive, lacking in sexual and social skills, even inhibited (Leue et al., 2004). They tend to have doubts about their masculinity, and to suffer from feelings of inadequacy and inferiority. Exhibitionists who are socially shy or inadequate may be using self-exposure as a substitute for intimate relationships.

The preferred victims are typically girls or young women. The typical exhibitionist drives up to, or walks in front of, a stranger and exposes his penis. After his victim has registered fear, disgust, confusion, or surprise, an exhibitionist will typically cover himself and flee. He usually masturbates, either while exposing himself or shortly afterward while thinking about the act and the victim's response (American Psychiatric Association, 2013). Some exhibitionists ejaculate during the act.

Exhibitionists and some other people with paraphilic disorders may find the risk of being caught to heighten their erotic response because it causes a rush of stress hormones that are chemically similar to testosterone (Haake et al., 2003). The exhibitionist may even purposefully increase the risk by exposing himself in the same location in his own easily identifiable car.

Courts tend to be hard on exhibitionists, partly because of evidence that shows that some exhibitionists progress to more serious crimes of sexual aggression (McLawsen et al., 2012). Still, most exhibitionists do not appear to become rapists or child molesters.

Definitions of exhibitionistic disorder also bring into focus the boundaries between normal and abnormal behavior (Hugh-Jones et al., 2005; O'Donohue, 2014). For example, people in intimate relationships may enjoy showing their bodies to their partners to sexually arouse them. That is normal. And we might ask, are exotic dancers (stripteasers) exhibitionists? No—or at least, being an exhibitionist is not part of the job description.

1 › T / F Truth or Fiction Revisited It is *not* true that strippers are exhibitionists. They are more successful at their work if they sexually excite their audiences, but their audiences are not unsuspecting victims. They pay for the privilege of watching them. Strippers' main motive is (usually) to earn a living (Philaretou, 2006).

It is also normal to become sexually excited while stripping before one's sex partner. Such stripping is done to sexually excite a willing partner, not to surprise or shock a stranger.

OBSCENE TELEPHONE CALLING, SEXTING, AND CHAT-SCATOPHILIA Like exhibitionists, obscene phone callers (almost all of whom are male) seek to become sexually aroused by shocking their victims (Balon, 2015b). Whereas an exhibitionist exposes his genitals to produce the desired response, the obscene phone caller "exposes" himself verbally by uttering obscenities and sexual provocations to a nonconsenting person. The *DSM* (American Psychiatric Association, 2013) labels this type of paraphilic disorder **telephone scatologia**. People practicing "chat-scatophilia" are sexually aroused by sending obscene e-mails, instant messages, and chat-room messages (Balon, 2015b). Sexting, of course, is also often associated with exhibitionism. As noted by Leah Kaylor and he colleagues, technology has devised new ways to express deviance (Kaylor et al., 2016). (Sexting is discussed in the "Sex in the Digital Age" feature on page 355 of Chapter 11.)

Relatively few obscene callers are women (Quayle, 2008). Women who are charged with such offenses are generally motivated by rage for some actual or fantasized rejection rather than the desire for sexual arousal. They use the phone to hurl sexual invectives against men whom they feel have wronged them. By contrast, male obscene phone callers are generally motivated by a desire for sexual excitement and usually choose their victims randomly from the phone book or by chance dialing. They typically masturbate during the phone call or shortly afterward. Most obscene telephone callers also engage in other paraphilic acts, especially voyeuristic disorder and exhibitionistic disorder (Heil & Simons, 2008).

There are many patterns of obscene phone calling. Some callers limit themselves to obscenities. Others make sexual overtures. Some just breathe heavily into the receiver. Others describe their masturbatory activity to their victims. Some profess to have previously met the victim at a social gathering or through a mutual acquaintance. Some even present themselves as "taking a sex survey" and ask a series of personally revealing questions.

The typical obscene phone caller is a socially inadequate heterosexual male who has had difficulty forming intimate relationships with women (Leue et al., 2004). The relative safety and anonymity of the telephone may shield him from the risk of rejection (Leue et al., 2004). A reaction of shock or fright from his victims may fill him with feelings of power and control that are lacking in his life, especially in his relationships with women. The obscenities may vent rage that he holds against women who have rejected him.

Obscene phone calls are illegal, but it has been difficult for authorities to track down perpetrators. Call tracing can help police track obscene or offending phone callers. Call tracing works in different ways in different locales. Caller ID shows the caller's telephone number on a display panel on the receiving party's telephone. In some locales, people can program their telephone service so that a caller who calls from a private number or one without caller ID received a message stating that the recipient accepts only calls from people who identify their phone numbers or names. These services may deter some obscene callers, but others may use public phones instead of their home phones. Check with your local telephone company if you are interested in these services.

What should a woman do if she receives an obscene phone call? Above all, women are advised to remain calm and not reveal shock or fright because such reactions tend to reinforce the caller and increase the probability of repeat calls. Women may be best advised to say nothing at all and gently hang up the receiver. A woman might alternatively offer a brief response that alludes to the caller's problems before hanging up. She might say in a calm but strong voice, "It's unfortunate you have this problem. I think you should seek professional help." If she should receive repeated calls, the woman might request an unlisted number or contact the police. Many women list themselves only by their initials in the phone directory so as to disguise their gender. But because this practice is so widespread, obscene callers may assume that people listed by initials are women living alone.

Sexting. Former Congressman Anthony Weiner and Huma Abedin, assistant to Hillary Clinton, at the Metropolitan Museum of Art in June 2016. Two months later, Abedin separated from Weiner because of his continual sexting with other women.

telephone scatologia

A paraphilic disorder characterized by the making of obscene telephone calls.

Voyeurism. Voyeurs are turned on by watching unsuspecting strangers undressing or engaging in sexual behavior. They may show endless patience, waiting hours for a glimpse.

voyeuristic disorder

A paraphilic disorder characterized by strong, repetitive urges and related sexual fantasies of observing unsuspecting strangers who are naked, disrobing, or engaged in sexual relations.

Voyeuristic Disorder

Voyeuristic disorder could be considered the flip side of the coin of exhibitionistic disorder. It involves strong, repetitive urges to observe unsuspecting strangers who are nude, undressing, or involved in sexual relations (Voyeuristic disorder, 2012). The voyeur becomes sexually aroused by watching and typically does not seek sexual relations with the "victim." Like fetishistic disorder and exhibitionistic disorder, voyeuristic disorder is found almost exclusively among males (Langstrom, 2010). It usually begins before age 15.

The voyeur may masturbate while peeping or afterward while replaying the incident in his mind. He may fantasize about sex with the observed person but have no intention of actually seeking sexual relations with her (Lavin, 2008).

Are people voyeurs who become sexually aroused by the sight of their lovers undressing? What about people who enjoy watching pornographic films or stripteasers? No, no, and no. The people being observed are not unsuspecting strangers. The lover knows that his or her partner is watching. Porn actors and strippers know that others will be viewing them. They would not be performing if they did not expect or have an audience.

2 › T / F Truth or Fiction Revisited It is *not* true that people who enjoy watching their mates undress are voyeurs. In such cases the person who is disrobing is knowingly and willingly observed, and the observer's enjoyment is normal (Montemurro et al., 2003). True voyeurs want to peep on *unsuspecting* strangers. Women who attend male strip clubs also enjoy "bonding" with their friends and other women at the clubs (Montemurro et al., 2003).

Voyeurs are also known as *peepers* and *peeping Toms.* Why "peeping Toms"? According to an old English legend, Lady Godiva asked the townspeople not to look at her while she rode horseback in the nude to protest the oppressive tax that her husband, a landowner, had imposed on them. A tailor named Tom of Coventry was the only townsperson not to grant her request.

Voyeurs often put themselves in risky situations in which they face the prospect of being caught. They may risk injury by perching themselves in trees or otherwise assuming precarious positions to catch a preferred view of their target. They will occupy rooftops and fire escapes in brutal winter weather. Peepers can be exceedingly patient. They may wait hour after hour, night after night, for a furtive glimpse of the target. One 25-year-old recently married man secreted himself in his mother-in-law's closet, waiting for her to disrobe. Part of the sexual excitement seems to stem from the risks voyeurs run. The need for risk may explain why voyeurs are not known to frequent nude beaches or nudist camps where it is acceptable to look (though not to stare) at nude people.

3 › T / F Truth or Fiction Revisited We cannot say that exhibitionists and voyeurs are *never* violent. Exhibitionistic disorder and voyeuristic disorder per se are not violent in themselves, but some exhibitionists and voyeurs have been known to be violent; moreover, if provoked or angered, they may react violently (Kaser-Boyd, 2015; McNally & Fremouw, 2014). Voyeurs who break into and enter homes or buildings, or who tap at windows to gain the attention of victims, are among the more dangerous.

Compared to other types of sex offenders, voyeurs tend to be less sexually experienced and are less likely to be married (Lavin, 2008). Like many exhibitionists, voyeurs tend to harbor feelings of inadequacy and to lack social and sexual skills (Leue et al., 2004). They may thus have difficulty forming romantic relationships with women. For this shy and socially inadequate type of voyeur, "peeping" affords sexual gratification without the risk of rejection. But not all voyeurs are socially awkward and inept with women.

Sexual Masochism Disorder

People who *prefer* or *require* having pain or humiliation inflicted on them by their sex partners are referred to as having **sexual masochism disorder**. A sexual masochist either acts on or is distressed by persistent urges and sexual fantasies involving pain or humiliation to achieve sexual excitement. Sexual masochists may derive pleasure from various types of punishing experiences, including being restrained (a practice known as **bondage**), blindfolded (sensory bondage), spanked, whipped, or made to perform humiliating acts, such as walking around on all fours and licking the boots or shoes of the partner, or being subjected to vulgar insults. Some masochists have their partners urinate or defecate on them. Some masochists prefer a particular source of pain. Others seek an assortment. But we should not think that sexual masochists enjoy types of pain that do not involve sex. Sexual masochists are no more likely than anyone else to derive pleasure from the pain they experience when they stub their toe or touch a hot stove. Pain must often be part of an elaborate sexual ritual to provide erotic gratification (Hucker, 2008).

4 › T / F   Truth or Fiction Revisited   It is true that in some cases, a sexual masochist cannot become sexually aroused unless he or she is bound, flogged, or humiliated by his or her sex partner. Sexual masochism is the only paraphilic disorder that is found among women with some frequency (Logan, 2008).

The word *masochism* derives from the name of the Austrian storyteller Leopold von Sacher-Masoch (1835–1895). He wrote tales of men who derived sexual satisfaction from having a female partner inflict pain on them, typically by flagellation (beating or whipping). Sexual masochists and **sexual sadists** often form sexual relationships or join "kink" communities to meet each other's needs (Yates et al., 2008). Some sexual masochists enlist the services of prostitutes or obtain the cooperation of their regular sexual partners to enact their masochistic fantasies. Archie wanted to be insulted by his wife when he cross-dressed and masturbated in front of her, adding a touch of sexual masochism to his transvestism.

5 › T / F   Truth or Fiction Revisited   It is considered normal—or typical—to enjoy some mild forms of pain during sexual activity. Love bites, hair pulls, and minor pinches or scratches are examples of sources of pain that are considered to fall within normal limits (O'Donohue, 2014). But if pain becomes a requirement for sexual gratification, or if the painful experiences endanger the health of the recipient, its purposes and uses need to be reconsidered.

sexual masochism

A paraphilic disorder characterized by the desire or need for pain or humiliation to enhance sexual arousal so that gratification may be attained.

bondage

Ritual restraint, as by shackles, as practiced by many sexual masochists.

sexual sadists

People who become sexually aroused by inflicting pain or humiliation on others.

Real Students, Real Questions

Q   *Do people get genital piercings for sexual pleasure?*

A   Some do, but the results are iffy at best, and body piercings can carry dangers. Please check with your doctor before having any piercings. You will be surprised to hear that some are probably fine, but others are not fine. In any event, the kinds of piercings usually recommended for women who are looking to enhance their sexual pleasure are clitoral hood piercings, clitoral piercings, and labial piercings. Of these, clitoral piercings are the most dangerous because they pass through the most nerves and blood vessels. Piercings of nipples, male sex organs, and navels are usually more for aesthetic purposes and have a subcultural message or appeal rather than for an aphrodisiacal effect. The really frightening thing here is how some people will allow anyone with a storefront to pierce their bodies—anywhere. Don't be one of them. If you decide to go in this direction, use a reputable piercing studio that employs only trained and licensed employees.

SEX IN THE DIGITAL AGE

TOTAL WEB CAM DOMINATION

"I worked in a house of domination in 2008. Men (and a few women) who had seen my videos (I've been working in porn since 2000) would call the house to make an appointment, booking hour-long sessions for just under $200 a pop.

"My clients came from every socioeconomic class and had a wide variety of desires. In the dungeon, I made my money like a diner waitress (which I'd also been)—get them in, get them out. Some got straight to the point, like the construction worker who showed up once a week on his lunch break to touch my bare feet and jerk off.

"But most of my clients wanted more—they wanted to understand. A regular once asked me, 'How do you know if love is real?' I thought, 'Lord, where do I begin?'

"Once, a man booked a session with me and then claimed he was a Broadway producer—he said he'd flown into town because he was a longtime fan and wanted to meet me. I said, 'Sure you are, now get on your knees.' For the entire hour he insisted, saying, 'Look me up. I've got a Tony.' Usually when a client left I'd close the front door quickly, but this time I watched him walk to the curb, where a uniformed driver ushered him into a limousine. Later I found his face in *The New York Times*.

"That was when I started to realize I was not maximizing my earning potential. In the seven years since, the Internet has revolutionized virtual one-on-one encounters. For a number of reasons—faster home Internet connections and a rise in video content piracy, to name two—webcam shows have skyrocketed. In 2013 my coworker Maitresse Madeline combined the webcam with the Internet auction. She invited me to auction off a single hour-long webcam session. I was excited by the prospect of reach—the winner of the auction could be anyone, anywhere.

Of Sex and Dungeons. This woman dominates masochistic men in a sort of medieval setting.

"The week of the auction, we posted a video of me challenging my fans to make a bid. We watched the numbers rise to $2,000, then $5,000, then $10,000. I didn't dare believe it was for real. Every good sex worker knows: Don't count the money until it's in your bra (or G-string or boot).

"The final bid came from an Australian man. A few weeks later, he sent the payment $42,000. He had paid the same amount for an hour with Madeline months before. (He still has not booked the shows.) To celebrate, Madeline and I scheduled a photo shoot, throwing all $84,000 in cash on the studio floor, dressing up in latex, and rolling in it."

—Lorelei Lee

It may seem contradictory for pain to become connected with sexual pleasure. The association of sexual arousal with mildly painful stimuli is actually quite common, however. Kinsey and his colleagues (1953) reported that perhaps as many as one person in four has experienced erotic sensations from being bitten during lovemaking. The eroticization of mild forms of pain (love bites, hair pulls, minor scratches) may fall within the normal range of sexual variation. Pain from these sources increases overall bodily arousal, which may enhance sexual excitement. Some of us become sexually excited when our partners "talk dirty" to us or call us vulgar names. When the urge for pain for purposes of sexual arousal becomes so persistent or strong that it overshadows other sources of sexual stimulation, or when the masochistic experience causes physical or psychological harm, we may say that the boundary between normality and abnormality has been breached.

Some theorists suggest that independent and responsible selfhood becomes burdensome or stressful at times (Knoll & Hazelwood, 2009). Sexual masochism can be conceptualized as sometimes providing a temporary reprieve from the responsibilities of independent selfhood. It is a blunting of one's ordinary level of self-awareness by focusing on immediate painful and pleasant sensations, and on the experience of being a sexual object.

Sexual masochism can range from relatively benign to potentially lethal practices, like **hypoxyphilia**. Hypoxyphiliacs put plastic bags over their heads, nooses around their necks, or pressure on their chests to temporarily deprive themselves of oxygen and enhance their sexual arousal. They usually fantasize that they are being strangled by a lover. They try to discontinue oxygen deprivation before they lose consciousness, but some miscalculations result in death by suffocation or strangulation (Behrendt et al., 2002; Santtila et al., 2002).

hypoxyphilistic disorder

A practice in which a person seeks to enhance sexual arousal, usually during masturbation, by becoming deprived of oxygen.

Sexual Sadism Disorder

Sexual sadism disorder is sort of the opposite of sexual masochism disorder. Sexual sadism disorder is named after the infamous Marquis de Sade (1774–1814), a Frenchman who wrote tales of becoming sexually aroused by inflicting pain or humiliation on others. The virtuous Justine, the heroine of his best-known novel of the same name, endures terrible suffering at the hands of fiendish men. She is at one time bound and spread-eagled so that bloodhounds can savage her. She then seeks refuge with a surgeon who tries to dismember her. Later she falls into the clutches of a saber-wielding mass murderer, but Nature saves her with a timely thunderbolt.

sexual sadism

A paraphilic disorder characterized by the desire or need to inflict pain or humiliation on others to enhance sexual arousal so that gratification is attained.

Sexual sadism disorder is characterized by persistent, powerful urges and sexual fantasies involving the inflicting of pain and suffering on others to achieve sexual excitement or gratification (Balon, 2015b). The urges are acted on or are disturbing enough to cause personal distress. Some sexual sadists cannot become sexually aroused unless they make their sex partners suffer. Others can become sexually excited without such acts.

Some sexual sadists hurt or humiliate willing partners, such as prostitutes or masochists. Others—a small minority—stalk and attack nonconsenting victims (Yates et al., 2008).

SEXUAL SADOMASOCHISM Sexual **sadomasochism (S&M)** involves *mutually gratifying sexual interactions* between *consenting partners*. Occasional S&M is quite common among the general population. Couples may incorporate mild or light forms of S&M in their lovemaking now and then, such as mild dominance and submission games or gentle physical restraint. It is also not uncommon for lovers to scratch or bite

sadomasochism (S&M)

A mutually gratifying sexual interaction between consenting sex partners in which sexual arousal is associated with the infliction and receipt of pain or humiliation.

BDSM. This man could never save money or concentrate sufficiently to climb the ladder of success because of his investment of money and time in dominatrix prostitutes.

their partners to heighten their mutual arousal during coitus. They generally do not inflict severe pain or damage, however.

Twenty-two percent of the men and 12% of the women surveyed by Kinsey and his colleagues (1953) reported at least some sexual response to sexual sadomasochistic stories. Although mild sexual sadomasochism may fall within the boundaries of normal sexual variation, sexual sadomasochism becomes pathological when such fantasies are acted on in ways that become destructive, dangerous, or distressing to oneself or others.

6 › T / F Truth or Fiction Revisited   There is a subculture—the S&M subculture—in the United States in which sexual sadists and sexual masochists form liaisons to inflict and receive pain and humiliation during sexual activity (Heil & Simons, 2008). It is catered to by sex shops that sell S&M paraphernalia and magazines. Paraphernalia includes leather restraints and leather face masks that resemble the ancient masks of executioners. People in the subculture seek one another out through mutual contacts, S&M social organizations, or personal ads in S&M magazines.

Participants in sexual sadomasochistic behavior often engage in highly elaborate rituals involving dominance and submission. Rituals are staged, as if they were scenes in a play (Gross, 2006). In the "master and slave" game, the sadist leads the masochist around by a leash. The masochist performs degrading or menial acts. In bondage and discipline (B&D), the dominant partner restrains the submissive partner and flagellates (spanks or whips) or sexually stimulates her or him. The erotic appeal of bondage is connected with controlling or being controlled.

Various sources of pain may be used during S&M encounters, but pain is not always employed. When it is, it is usually mild or moderate. Psychological pain, or humiliation, may be as common. Pain may also be symbolic, as in the case of a sadist who uses a harmless, soft rubber paddle to spank the masochist. Thus, the erotic appeal of pain for some S&M participants may derive from the ritual of control rather than pain itself. Extreme forms of pain, such as torture or severe beatings, are rarely reported by sexual sadomasochists. Masochists may seek pain, but they usually avoid serious injury and dangerous partners (Gross, 2006).

S&M participants may be heterosexual, gay, lesbian, or bisexual (Heil & Simons, 2008). They may assume either the masochistic or the sadistic role, or may alternate roles. People who seek sexual excitement by enacting both sadistic and masochistic roles are known as *sexual sadomasochists*. In heterosexual relationships the partners may reverse traditional gender roles. The man may assume the submissive or masochistic role, and the woman may take the dominant or sadistic role (Gross,

Dakota Johnson as Anastasia Steele in the 2015 film *Fifty Shades of Grey*, which is based on the best-selling novel of the same name. The movie depicts tycoon Christian Grey's (played by Jamie Dornan) seduction of Anastasia into a sex life of bondage and discipline, dominance and submission.

2006). The majority of S&M participants are male, but a sizable minority are female (American Psychiatric Association, 2013). Most are in committed relationships.

The causes of sexual masochism disorder and sexual sadism disorder, as of other paraphilic disorders, are unclear, but pain has some biological links to pleasure (Berridge & Kringelbach, 2015; Ellingsen et al., 2013). Natural chemicals called *endorphins*, similar to opiates, are released in the brain in response to pain and produce feelings of euphoria and well-being. The neurotransmitter dopamine activates the reward regions of the brain and can also be released in response to painful stimuli (Budygin et al., 2012). Perhaps, then, pleasure is derived from pain because of the release or augmentation of endorphins and dopamine. But these findings fall short of explaining the erotic appeal of sexual sadomasochistic encounters that involve minimal or symbolic pain. Nor do they explain the erotic appeal to the sadist of inflicting pain.

7 › T / F Truth or Fiction Revisited   It is true that painful stimuli may activate the reward regions of the brain. This research finding may, in part, explain the development of sexual masochism.

Whatever their causes, the roots of sexual masochism disorder and sexual sadism disorder apparently date to childhood (Barbaree & Blanchard, 2008). Sexual sadomasochistic behavior commonly begins in early adulthood, but sexual sadomasochistic fantasies are often present in childhood (American Psychiatric Association, 2013).

Frotteuristic Disorder

Vivian used to take the F train home to Queens. She shivered at the memory. "Men used to touch women on the train and stand close to them and ruin their clothes."

Stephanie said she had dealt many times with men rubbing up against her or trying to touch her on crowded No. 4 or 5 trains in the morning when she takes her daughter to school. "It's worse in the summer months when everyone is wearing less clothing," she said. (Hartocollis, 2006)

A CLOSER LOOK

WOMEN FROM THE "KINK" COMMUNITY

When you come across sexual sadomasochistic magazines or Web sites, photos may seem to be as likely to show women as men cracking whips, tied up, blindfolded, wearing leather, and the like. Although the great majority of people diagnosed with paraphilic disorders are male, an exception is made in the case of sexual masochism, in which women may be as likely as men to participate.

A recent study of women in the so-called *kink community* recruited 1,580 women via online kink forums and kink community events (Rehor, 2015). The study defined *kink* behavior as including BDSM kinds of behavior (bondage, discipline, dominance, submission, sadistic and masochistic behavior), exhibitionism, voyeurism, fetishism, and some others.

A majority of the women enjoyed activities such as caressing and cuddling, kissing, sucking (all more than 99%), applying body paint or oil or food, playing with wax candles, and using feathers or fur. Many did *not* require pain to become sexually aroused. However, more than half had engaged in sadomasochistic activities such as spanking (96%), slapping breasts or buttocks, applying clothespins to the breasts or genitals, pinching, whipping, and caning. Yet they generally avoided practicing these activities in ways that were dangerous or likely to lead to medical problems. Bondage was highly preferred, with 85% of participants reporting use of bondage toys and being immobilized. Most of the women (83%) created or watched kink-related pornography, live performances, and the like. The most popular role-play scenario involved master and slave fantasies (84%). Also popular were playing out danger, job (boss/underling), animal, and medical examination fantasies.

The study did not attempt to address the prevalence of kinky behavior in the general population. Nor did it try to investigate the causes of the women's sexual desires. It did describe the behavior of many women involved in these activities.

frotteurism

A paraphilic disorder characterized by recurrent, powerful sexual urges and related fantasies involving rubbing against or touching a nonconsenting person.

toucherism

A practice related to frotteurism and characterized by the persistent urge to fondle nonconsenting strangers.

zoophilistic disorder

A paraphilic disorder involving persistent or repeated sexual urges and related fantasies involving sexual contact with animals.

Some people who use the subway run into pickpockets; some women who use the subway find themselves victimized by frotteurs. **Frotteurism** (also known as *mashing* or *groping*) is rubbing against or touching a nonconsenting person (Langstrom, 2010). As with other paraphilic disorders, a diagnosis of frotteurism requires either acting on these urges or being distressed by them. Mashing has been reported exclusively among males (American Psychiatric Association, 2013).

Most mashing takes place in crowded places, such as buses, subway cars, or elevators. The man finds the rubbing or the touching, not the coercive nature of the act, to be sexually stimulating. While rubbing against a woman, he may fantasize a consensual, affectionate sexual relationship with her. Typically, the man incorporates images of his mashing within his masturbation fantasies (Lussier & Piché, 2008). Mashing also incorporates a related practice, **toucherism**, which is fondling nonconsenting strangers.

Mashing may be so fleeting and furtive that the woman may not realize what has happened. Mashers therefore stand little chance of being caught.

Although this masher was married, many mashers have difficulties forming relationships with women and are handicapped by fears of rejection. Mashing provides sexual contact in a relatively nonthreatening context.

Other Paraphilic Disorders

The paraphilic disorders we have been discussing, fetishistic disorder through frotteuristic disorder, are the most common. But there are others, such as zoophilistic disorder.

ZOOPHILISTIC DISORDER   **Zoophilistic disorder** is one of the rarest paraphilic disorder. A person with the disorder experiences repeated, intense urges and related fantasies involving sexual contact with animals. As with other paraphilic disorders, the urges may be acted on or cause personal distress. A child or adolescent who shows some sexual response to an occasional episode of rough-and-tumble play with the family pet is not displaying zoophilistic disorder.

The term *bestiality* applies to actual sexual contact with an animal. Human sexual contact with animals, mythical and real, has a long history. Michelangelo's painting *Leda and the Swan* depicts the Greek god Zeus taking the form of a swan to mate with a woman, Leda. Zeus was also portrayed as taking the form of a bull or serpent to mate with humans. In the Old Testament, God is said to have put to death people who had sexual relations with animals. The Greek historian Herodotus notes that goats at the Egyptian temple at Mendes were trained to copulate with people.

Although the prevalence of zoophilistic disorder in the general population is unknown, Kinsey and his colleagues (1948, 1953) found that about 8% of the men and 3% to 4% of the women interviewed admitted to sexual contacts with animals. Men more often had sexual contact with farm animals, such as calves and sheep. Women more often reported sexual contacts with household pets. Men were more likely to masturbate or copulate with the animals. Women more often reported general body contact. Urban–rural differences emerged. Rates of bestiality were higher among boys reared on farms. Compared with only a few city boys, 17% of farm boys had reached orgasm at some time through sexual contact with dogs, cows, and goats. These contacts were generally restricted to adolescence, when human outlets were unavailable. Still, adults sometimes engage in sexual contacts with animals, generally

Q *Are there cultures that allow sex with animals/pets?*

A No modern cultures do, but ancient cave paintings and other artifacts suggest that sex with animals might have been allowed and sometimes incorporated into magical rituals before the advent of the so-called Abrahamic religions of Judaism, Christianity, and Islam. Many Egyptian gods were depicted as part animal, suggesting that sex with animals might have been included in some rituals. Goats and baboons might have been occasional sex partners in ancient Egypt.

because of curiosity or novelty or for a sexual release when human partners are unavailable. Zoophilistic disorder is often associated with problems such as alcoholism and intellectual deficiency (Lesjak et al. 2004).

NECROPHILISTIC DISORDER In **necrophilistic disorder**, a rare paraphilic disorder, a person desires sex with corpses. Three types of necrophilistic disorder have been identified (Holmes & Holmes, 2002). In *regular necrophilistic disorder*, the person has sex with a deceased person. In *necrophilic homicide*, the person commits murder to obtain a corpse for sexual purposes. In *necrophilic fantasy^the person fantasizes about sex with a corpse but does not actually carry out necrophilic acts. Necrophiles often obtain jobs that provide them with access to corpses, such as working in cemeteries, morgues, or funeral homes. The primary motivation for necrophilistic disorder appears to be the desire to sexually possess a completely unresisting and nonrejecting partner (Holmes & Holmes, 2002). Many necrophiles have serious psychological disorders.

necrophilistic disorder

A paraphilic disorder characterized by desire for sexual activity with corpses.

LESS COMMON PARAPHILIC DISORDERS In **klismaphilistic disorder**, sexual arousal is derived from use of enemas. Klismaphiles generally prefer the receiving role to the giving role. Klismaphiles may have derived sexual pleasure in childhood from the anal stimulation provided by parents giving them enemas.

In **coprophilistic disorder**, sexual arousal is connected with feces. The person may desire to be defecated on or to defecate on a sex partner. The association of feces with sexual arousal may also be a throwback to childhood. Many children appear to obtain anal sexual pleasure by holding in and then purposefully expelling feces. It may also be that the incidental connection between erections or sexual arousal and soiled diapers during infancy eroticizes feces.

In **urophilistic disorder**, sexual arousal is associated with urine. As with coprophilistic disorder, the person may desire to be urinated on or to urinate on a sexual partner. Also like coprophilistic disorder, urophilistic disorder may have childhood origins. Stimulation of the urethral canal during urination may become associated with sexual pleasure. Or urine may have become eroticized by experiences in which erections occurred while the infant was clothed in a wet diaper.

klismaphilistic disorder

A paraphilic disorder in which sexual arousal is derived from use of enemas.

coprophilistic disorder

A paraphilic disorder in which sexual arousal is attained in connection with feces.

urophilistic disorder

A paraphilic disorder in which sexual arousal is associated with urine.

Theoretical Perspectives

The paraphilic disorders are fascinating and perplexing variations in sexual behavior. We may find it difficult to understand how people can become sexually excited by fondling an article of clothing or by cross-dressing. It may also be difficult to

SEX IN THE DIGITAL AGE

CYBERSEX ADDICTION: FOR SOME, SEX IS NOTHING BUT 'NET

"How can I compete with hundreds of anonymous others who are now in our bed, in his head? Our bed is crowded with countless faceless strangers, where once we were intimate."

—A 34-year-old woman, married 14 year to a minister

"Porn sites get more visitors each month than Netflix, Amazon and Twitter combined."

— The Huffington Post

"Sex on the 'Net is like heroin. It grabs [people] and takes over their lives. And it's very difficult to treat because the people affected don't want to give it up."

—Mark Schwartz, Masters and Johnson Institute

It appears that about one-third of Internet visits are directed to sexually oriented Web sites, with ample opportunity to contact potential sex partners—paid and amateur (*The Huffington Post*, 2013). Of 9- to 17-year-olds who go online at least once a week, more than half have encountered online pornography, usually accidentally, and 38% have had pornographic advertisements pop up when they were doing something completely unrelated (Tsaliki, 2011). The availability of Internet pornography has all but killed pornographic magazines and any attendance at movie houses showing pornographic films (Dhuffar & Griffiths, 2015). For most people these cybersex experiences are harmless enough, but the accessibility and anonymity of sex on the Internet are fueling what many health professionals have labeled a new

form of addiction—*cybersex addiction*—that is spreading rapidly and bringing turmoil into the lives of those afflicted with it (Green et al., 2012). The American Psychiatric Association added the broader category of *Internet addiction* to its list of disorders in 2013.

Is cybersex addiction a paraphilic disorder? It shares certain characteristics: It tends to be repetitive and individuals with the problem have difficulty controlling it. Moreover, many cybersex users come to prefer their online images to the real people in their lives such that they sometimes develop problems in becoming sexually aroused by their flesh-and-blood partners (Griffiths, 2012). We might also ask whether cybersex addiction is truly an addiction. It depends on how one defines *addiction*. Addiction to a substance such as alcohol or nicotine usually means that usage of the substance has changed the

identify with people who feel compelled to exhibit their genitals or to rub their genitals against unsuspecting victims in crowded places. Perhaps we can recognize some voyeuristic tendencies in ourselves, but we cannot imagine peeping through binoculars while perched in a nearby tree or, for that matter, risking the social and legal consequences of being discovered in the act. Nor might we understand how people can become sexually turned on by inflicting or receiving pain. Let us consider explanations that have been advanced from various theoretical perspectives.

Biological Perspectives

LO 14.3   Discuss biological perspectives on the paraphilic disorders.

Researchers are investigating whether there are biological factors in paraphilic behavior. The biological perspective looks into factors such as the endocrine system (hormones) and the nervous system in paraphilic behavior. The tendency of paraphilic disorders to cluster within some families also raises the question as to whether genetic factors may be involved (Labelle et al., 2012).

body so that having the substance in the body is the "new normal." But we speak more generally of being psychologically dependent on or addicted to something when it seems to be irresistible and interferes with vocational, academic, or social functioning.

Surveys show that many people, mostly men, now spend dozens of hours each week surfing pornographic and other sex-related Web sites (Cooper et al., 2004a, 2004b; Daneback et al., 2006). Yet there are also female addicts. Interestingly, a recent study of women cybersex users found no connection between their use of Internet pornography and their being in a relationship or finding sexual gratification with their flesh-and-blood sexual contacts (Laier et al., 2014).

Like drug addicts, cybersex addicts typically deny that they have a problem and refuse help unless their real relationships or jobs are in jeopardy. Those in relationships typically deny that cybersex excursions are cheating or infidelity (Jones & Hertlein, 2012; Schneider et al., 2012). Those most strongly hooked on online sex may spend hours a day masturbating to pornographic images or—less commonly—having "online sex" with someone who "popped up" online when visiting a pornographic website (Daneback et al., 2006).

Based on a survey of 9,265 men and women who admitted surfing the 'Net for sex, Cooper and his colleagues (2000) concluded that the 'Net is "the crack cocaine of sexual compulsivity," with at least 1% of respondents deeply addicted to online sex.

Cybersex compulsives are like drug addicts (Ayres & Haddock, 2009). They "use the Internet as an important part of their sexual acting out, much like a drug addict who has a drug of choice. [Especially vulnerable are those] whose sexuality may have been suppressed and limited all their lives [who] suddenly find an infinite supply of sexual opportunities" online (Cooper, cited in Brody, 2000). Although some studies find men who become addicted to online sex to have ample sexual opportunities in the real world, other studies find them to be lonelier than men with those opportunities (Yoder et al., 2005).

Physician Jennifer Schneider (2003, 2004) conducted a survey of 94 family members affected by cybersex addiction and found that it can arise even among people in good relationships and having an abundance of sexual opportunities. "Sex on the 'Net is just so seductive and it's so easy to stumble upon it [that] people who are vulnerable can get hooked before they know it" (cited in Brody, 2000).

Schneider (2005) defends the view that cybersex addiction is a true addiction, characterized by "loss of control, continuation of the behavior despite significant adverse consequences and preoccupation or obsession with obtaining the drug or pursuing the behavior."

As with other addictions, tolerance to cybersex stimulation can develop, prompting the addict to take more and more risks to recapture the initial high. Online viewing that began as a harmless recreation can become all-consuming and even lead to real sexual encounters with people met online. Cybersex compulsives sometimes ignore their partners and children and risk their jobs. Many companies monitor employees' online activities, and visits to sexual sites can cost employees their jobs. Other adverse consequences include broken relationships. Partners often report feeling betrayed, ignored, and unable to compete with the online fantasies.

There are treatments for cybersex addiction that tend to parallel the treatments of drug addiction and for paraphilic disorders. Some of the treatments are medical, and a wide array of medicines have been used with mixed results. Cognitive-behavior therapy (CBT) is the most widely used for of psychotherapy, and there have been some encouraging reports that CBT has reduced the amount of time spent online, masturbation, and the incidence of surfing to meet random and potentially dangerous people. But again: there are many treatment failures (Dhuffar & Griffiths, 2015).

Studies appear to confirm that many paraphilics have higher-than-normal sex drives (Jordan et al., 2011). A German study, for example, found that people with parahilias had shorter refractory periods after orgasm by masturbation than most men and experienced a higher frequency of sexual fantasies and urges (Haake et al., 2003). Kafka (2003) refers to this heightened sex drive as *hypersexual disorder*— the opposite of hypoactive sexual desire disorder (see Chapter 15). The psychiatric community is proposing that the "diagnosis" of **hypersexual disorder** may apply to many individuals with paraphilic disorders and those with problems such as public masturbation, uncontrolled use of pornography, attendance at strip clubs, visiting prostitutes, and engaging in unprotected sex with multiple partners (Levine, 2012). Repetitive unsuccessful efforts to control the behavior are a key feature (Hypersexual disorder, 2012).

But these studies address the strength of the sex drive, not the direction it takes. Some studies have used the electroencephalograph (EEG) to investigate electrical responses in the brain among paraphilics and others who engage in impulsive behavior (e.g., W. Fisher et al., 2011a). One study measured what is termed "evoked electrical potentials" to erotic stimuli in a sample of 62 right-handed men, half of

hypersexual disorder

A new category of sexual disorders characterized by problematic sexual excesses and failed efforts to control them as expressed through paraphilic disorders and other inappropriate sexual activities, such as public masturbation, uncontrolled use of Internet pornography, unprotected sex with multiple partners, finding of sex partners on the Internet, and so forth.

whom were considered to be normal in terms of their sexual fantasies and behaviors (the control subjects), and half of whom had been diagnosed as paraphilic (fetishistic and sexual sadomasochistic) (Waismann et al., 2003). The men were shown three sets of 57 slides each in random order: 57 paraphilic slides that portrayed depicting fetishistic and sexual sadomasochistic themes; 57 "normal" slides that depicted nude women, coitus, and oral sex: and 57 neutral slides of landscapes, street scenes, and the like. An electrical response labeled "P600" was determined to be the best indicator of sexual arousal in the men. It was found that the main site for evoking the P600 response to "normal" sexual stimuli was on the right side of the brain. The main site for paraphilic stimuli was the left, frontal part of the brain. Men diagnosed with paraphilic disorders showed a significantly greater response than the control subjects in the P600 response in the left, frontal part of the brain. Moreover, control subjects were more likely to differentiate between paraphilic and normal stimuli on the right side of the brain.

Another neurological study may offer some insight into sexual masochism disorder. A research team from Massachusetts General Hospital found that the same neural circuits in the brain are often activated either by painful or by pleasurable stimuli (Becerra et al., 2001). The researchers discovered that a painfully hot (115° F) stimulus to the hand-activated areas of the brain believed to involve "reward" circuitry. The researchers had set out to find ways to help chronic pain patients and not to investigate sexual masochism disorder, but their findings certainly have implications for the disorder. Other studies confirm that people who regularly engage in sexual masochistic behavior are less sensitive to pain than other people (Defrin et al., 2015). It is unclear whether their lower sensitivity reflects habituation to painful experiences or a predisposition toward higher tolerance of pain.

As time goes on, we may learn more about potential biological foundations of paraphilic behavior. Better understanding of these atypical patterns of sexual behavior may lead to the development of more effective treatments.

Psychoanalytic Perspectives

LO 14.4 Discuss psychoanalytic perspectives on the paraphilic disorders.

Psychoanalytic theory has attempted explanations of a number of sexual matters. Psychoanalytic theory suggests that paraphilic disorders are psychological defenses, usually against unresolved castration anxiety dating to the Oedipus complex (Friedman & Downey, 2008). Perhaps the sight of a woman's vagina threatens to arouse castration anxiety in the transvestite, reminding him that women do not have penises and that he might suffer the same fate. Sequestering his penis beneath women's clothing symbolically asserts that women do have penises, which provides unconscious reassurance against his own fears of castration. By exposing his genitals, perhaps the exhibitionist unconsciously seeks reassurance that his penis is secure. It is as if he were asserting, "Look! I have a penis!" Shock or surprise on the victim's face confirms that his penis exists, temporarily relieving castration anxiety. Perhaps masturbation with an object such as a shoe allows the fetishist to gratify his sexual desires while keeping a safe distance from the dangers that he unconsciously associates with sexual contact with women. Or the fetishistic object itself—the shoe—may unconsciously symbolize the penis. Are sadists attempting to defend themselves against unconscious feelings of impotence by inflicting pain on others?

One psychoanalyst associates a type of male sexual masochism disorder with a history of suppressed or repressed feelings of sexual guilt and shame (Schrut, 2005). As an adult, the male

Critical Thinking

If people with paraphilic disorders have powerful urges to engage in deviant behavior as a result of biological forces or unconscious fears, can they be expected to control their behavior?

Unintended Consequences?
Psychoanalysts suggest that some cases of early punishment by the mother can lead to the development of aberrant sexual fantasies and atypical variations in sexual behavior.

wants to be punished for feelings of wrongdoing at the same time he experiences sexual arousal. The pain or humiliation makes the experience "okay."

The paraphilic disorders have provided a fertile ground for psychoanalytic theories. However, such evidence as there is consists of case studies and anecdotes, which are open to interpretation.

Cognitive-Behavioral Perspectives

LO 14.5 **Discuss cognitive-behavioral perspectives on the paraphilic disorders.**

Consider the case of Lucy—not the 3-million-year-old ape who may have been a forebear of modern humans, but Lucy the chimp who was raised as a human child in the home of a psychologist a few decades back. "Once she'd blossomed into a young adult, a favorite hobby of Lucy's was masturbating to the nude human male centerfolds from the latest issue of *Playgirl* magazine by carefully spreading out the pages on the floor and then placing her swollen genitals on the image of the man's penis" (Bering, 2013)

Or consider classic research with infant male rats (Fillion & Blass, 1986). The experimenters painted the nipples and vaginal regions of their mothers with a lemon scent. The infants suckled as per usual and were then weaned. When the rats were about 100 days old—young adults—they were presented at random with either of two sexually receptive females. One was a "normal" female and the other female's genitals were treated with the lemon scent. The males presented with the lemon-scent treated females ejaculated rapidly, whereas those paired with the normal females took significantly longer to ejaculate.

Cognitive-behavioral theorists, like psychoanalytic theorists, believe that experience plays a role in the development of sexual preferences. Cognitive-behavioral theorists generally believe that fetishes and other paraphilic disorders are learned through experience. An object may acquire sexually arousing properties through association with sexual arousal or orgasm. Alfred Kinsey and his colleagues (1953) wrote:

> Even some of the most extremely variant types of human sexual behavior may need no more explanation than is provided by our understanding of the processes of learning and conditioning. Behavior which may appear bizarre, perverse, or unthinkably unacceptable to some persons, and even to most persons, may have significance for other individuals because of the way in which they have been conditioned. (pp. 645–646)

For example, a boy who glimpses his mother's stockings hanging on the towel rack while he is masturbating may develop a fetish for stockings. Orgasm in the presence of the object reinforces the erotic connection, especially if it is repeated.

Friedrich and Gerber (1994) studied five adolescent boys with hypoxyphilistic disorder and found extensive early histories of choking in combination with physical or sexual abuse. The combination seems to have encouraged each of the boys to associate choking with sexual arousal.

Cognitive-behavioral explanations of sexual masochism disorder focus on the pairing of sexual excitement with punishment. For example, a child may be punished when discovered masturbating. Or a boy may reflexively experience an erection if his penis accidentally rubs against the parent's body as he is being spanked. With repeated encounters like these, pain and pleasure may become linked.

Many exhibitionists, voyeurs, frotteurs, and other people with paraphilic disorders have few interpersonal skills relating to women and may avoid "normal" social interactions with them for fear of rejection (Griffee et al., 2014; Leue et al., 2004). Their furtive, paraphilic behaviors may provide sexual release without risk of rejection. For some of these individuals, social skills training may be of use to help them foster relationships (Kaplan & Krueger, 2012)

Observational learning may also play a role. Parents, for example, may inadvertently model exhibitionistic behavior to young sons, which can lead the sons to eroticize the act of exposing themselves. Young people may also read books or magazines or view films or TV programs with paraphilic content. Media may give them the idea of trying paraphilic behavior, and they may find it exciting, especially if acts such as self-exposure or voyeurism provide a rush of adrenaline.

Sociological Perspectives

LO 14.6   Discuss sociological perspectives on the paraphilic disorders.

The psychoanalytic and cognitive-behavioral perspectives are psychological; they focus on the behavior and mental processes of the individual. Sociological perspectives tend to focus on the effects of the group and of society in general on individual and group behavior. For example, although most people indulge paraphilic disorders privately, sexual masochists and sadists require a partner. Most sexual sadomasochists learn S&M rituals, make sexual contacts, acquire sexual paraphernalia, and confirm their sexual sadomasochistic self-identities within what is termed an *S&M subculture*—a loosely connected network of S&M clubs, specialty shops, organizations, magazines, and so on. But the S&M subculture exists in the context of the larger society, and its rituals mirror widely based social and gender roles.

Weinberg (1987) proposes a sociological model that focuses on the social context of sexual sadomasochism. S&M rituals generally involve some form of dominance and submission. Weinberg attributes their erotic appeal to the opportunity to reverse the customary power relationships that exist between males and females and between social classes. Within the confines of the carefully scripted S&M encounter, the meek can be powerful and the powerful meek. People from lower social classes or in menial jobs may be drawn to S&M so they can enact a dominant role. Dominance and submission games allow people to accentuate or reverse the gender stereotypes that identify masculinity with dominance and femininity with submissiveness. Interviews with, and observations of, sexual sadomasochists suggest that most often dominance–submission relationships tend to be consistent with traditional masculine and feminine gender roles in society (Damon, 2002; Santtila et al., 2002). Although there are many exceptions, men more often tend to be dominant and women to be submissive in S&M rituals.

An Integrated Perspective: The "Lovemap"

LO 14.7   Discuss the "Lovemap."

Like other sexual patterns, paraphilic disorders may have complex biopsychosocial origins (Downing et al., 2014; Seligman & Hardenburg, 2000). Might our understanding of them thus be best approached from a theoretical framework that incorporates multiple perspectives? John Money (2003), for example, traces the origins of paraphilic disorders to childhood. He believes that childhood experiences etch a pattern in the brain, called a **lovemap**. This lovemap determines the types of stimuli and activities that become sexually arousing to the individual (Goldie, 2014). In the case of paraphilic disorders, lovemaps become distorted or "vandalized" by early traumatic experiences, such as incest, anti-sexual upbringing, and abuse or neglect. For example, "A boy who is sexually abused may develop paraphilic fantasies involving sexual activity with a boy.... Being punished or embarrassed by being cross-dressed as a young boy may lead to some boys eroticizing the experience, which later is expressed as transvestism" (Lehne, 2009, p. 15).

Research suggests that voyeurs and exhibitionists often were the victims of childhood sexual abuse (Barbaree & Blanchard, 2008; Blokland & Lussier, 2015). Not all children exposed to such influences develop paraphilic compulsions, however. For reasons that remain unknown, some children exposed to such influences appear to be more vulnerable to developing distorted lovemaps than are others. A genetic

Lovemap

A representation in the mind and in the brain of the idealized lover and the idealized erotic activity with the lover.

predisposition, hormonal factors, brain abnormalities, or a combination of these and other factors may play a role in determining one's vulnerability to vandalized love-maps (Lehne, 2009).

Treatment of Paraphilic Disorders

The treatment of paraphilic disorders raises a number of issues. First, many people with paraphilic disorders do not want or seek treatment, at least not voluntarily. The Canadian criminologist Ron Langevin (2006), for example, followed nearly 800 sex offenders from the 1960s through the 2000s and found that only about half desired treatment and completed a course of treatment. But many offenders are seen by health-care providers (HCPs) only when they come into conflict with the law or at the urging of their family members or partners.

Second, HCPs may encounter ethical problems when they are asked to contribute to a judicial process by trying to persuade a sex offender that he (virtually all are male) *ought* to change his behavior. HCPs traditionally help clients clarify or meet their own goals; it is not their role to impose societal goals on the individual. Many HCPs believe that the criminal justice system, not they, ought to enforce social standards.

The third issue is a treatment problem. HCPs realize that they are generally less successful with resistant or recalcitrant clients. Unless the motivation to change is present, therapeutic efforts are often wasted.

The fourth problem is the issue of perceived responsibility. Sex offenders typically claim that they cannot control their impulses, and accepting personal responsibility for one's actions is a prelude to change. Thus, if therapy is to be constructive, it is necessary to break through the client's personal mythology that he or she is powerless to control his or her behavior.

Despite these issues, many offenders are referred for treatment by the courts. Some seek therapy themselves because they have come to see how their behavior harms themselves or others (Langevin, 2006). We shall consider psychological and biological approaches to the treatment of people with paraphilic disorders. Most sexual offender treatment programs use a combination of psychoanalytic psychotherapy, cognitive-behavioral treatment, and medication (Marvasti, 2004).

> **Critical Thinking**
> Is it ethical for mental-health professionals to work with clients who do not want treatment?

Psychoanalytic Psychotherapy

LO 14.8 Discuss the psychoanalytic treatment of the paraphilic disorders.

Psychoanalysis focuses on resolving the unconscious conflicts that are believed to originate in childhood and to give rise in adulthood to pathological problems such as paraphilic disorders. The aim of therapy is to help bring unconscious conflicts of childhood into conscious awareness so that they might be worked through in the light of the individual's adult personality (Laws & Marshall, 2003).

Although some favorable case results have been reported, psychoanalytic therapy of the paraphilic disorders is rarely subjected to experimental analysis. Thus, we know little about whether successes are the result of the psychoanalytic treatment itself or to other factors, such as spontaneous improvement or a client's willingness to change.

Cognitive-Behavioral Therapy

LO 14.9 Discuss the cognitive-behavioral treatment of the paraphilic disorders.

Whereas traditional psychoanalysis tends to entail a lengthy process of exploration of the childhood origins of problem behaviors, **cognitive-behavioral therapy** is relatively briefer and focuses directly on changing behavior. Cognitive-behavioral therapy has spawned a number of techniques to help eliminate paraphilic behaviors and strengthen appropriate sexual behaviors: systematic desensitization, relapse prevention training,

cognitive-behavioral therapy
Therapy that attempts to directly change the ways in which people view events and respond to them, relying frequently on principles of learning.

aversion therapy, empathy training, social skills training, anger management, covert sensitization, and orgasmic reconditioning, to name a few (Kaplan & Krueger, 2012; Marshall & Marshall, 2015).

Systematic desensitization attempts to break the link between the sexual stimulus (such as a fetishistic stimulus) and the inappropriate response (sexual arousal). The client is first taught to relax selected muscle groups in the body. Muscle relaxation is then paired repeatedly with each of a series of progressively more arousing paraphilic images or fantasies. Relaxation comes to replace sexual arousal in response to each of these stimuli, even the most provocative. In one case study, a fetishistic transvestite who had become attracted to his mother's lingerie at age 13 was taught to relax when presented with audiotaped scenes representing transvestite or fetishistic themes (Fensterheim & Kantor, 1980). He played such tapes daily while remaining relaxed. He later reported a complete absence of transvestite thoughts or activities.

In **aversion therapy**, the undesirable sexual behavior (for example, masturbation to fetishistic fantasies) is paired repeatedly with an aversive stimulus (such as a harmless but painful electric shock or a nausea-inducing chemical) in the hope that the client will develop a conditioned aversion toward the paraphilic behavior.

Covert sensitization is a variation of aversion therapy in which paraphilic fantasies are paired with an aversive stimulus in imagination. In one study of 38 **pedophiles** and 62 exhibitionists, more than half of whom were court-referred subjects, were treated by pairing imagined aversive odors with fantasies of the problem behavior (Maletzky, 1980). They were instructed to fantasize pedophiliac or exhibitionistic scenes. Then,

> At a point … when sexual pleasure is aroused, aversive images are presented…. Examples might include a pedophiliac fellating a child, but discovering a festering sore on the boy's penis, an exhibitionist exposing to a woman but suddenly being discovered by his wife or the police, or a pedophiliac laying a young boy down in a field, only to lie next to him in a pile of dog feces. (Maletzky, 1980, p. 308)

Maletzky used this treatment weekly for 6 months, then followed it with booster sessions every 3 months over a 3-year period. The procedure resulted in at least a 75% reduction of the deviant activities and fantasies for more than 80% of the study participants at follow-up periods of up to 36 months. At a 25-year follow-up of 7,275 sex offenders who received similar treatment, Maletzky and Steinhauser (2002) found that benefits were maintained for many of the exhibitionists but for fewer of the pedophiles. But fewer than 50% of the original participants could be contacted after this amount of time elapsed. However, the method remains under study (Marshall, 2015).

Social skills training focuses on helping the individual improve his ability to relate to the other gender. The therapist might first model a desired behavior, such as how to ask a woman out on a date or how to handle a rejection. The client might then role-play the behavior, with the therapist playing the part of the woman. Following the role-play enactment, the therapist would provide feedback and additional guidance and modeling to help the client improve his skills. This process would be repeated until the client mastered the skill.

Orgasmic reconditioning aims to increase sexual arousal to socially appropriate sexual stimuli by pairing culturally appropriate imagery with orgasmic pleasure. The person is instructed to become sexually aroused by masturbating to paraphilic images or fantasies. But as he approaches the point of orgasm, he switches to appropriate imagery and focuses on it during orgasm. In a case example, Davison (1977) reports reduction of sadistic fantasies in a 21-year-old college man. The client was instructed to attain an erection in any way he could, even through the use of the sadistic fantasies he wished to eliminate. But once erection was achieved, he was to masturbate while looking at photos of *Playboy* models. Orgasm was thus paired with nonsadistic images. These images and fantasies eventually acquire the capacity to elicit sexual

---

systematic desensitization

A method that uses muscle relaxation to break the connection between a stimulus (such as a fetishistic object) and an inappropriate response (sexual arousal).

aversion therapy

A method for terminating undesirable sexual behavior in which the behavior is repeatedly paired with an aversive stimulus such as electric shock to condition an aversion.

covert sensitization

A form of aversion therapy in which thoughts of engaging in undesirable behavior are paired repeatedly with imagined aversive stimuli.

pedophiles

Persons with a paraphilic disorder involving sexual interest in children.

social skills training

Cognitive-behavioral therapy methods for building social skills that rely on a therapist's coaching and practice.

orgasmic reconditioning

A method for strengthening the connection between sexual arousal and appropriate sexual stimuli (such as fantasies about an adult of the other sex) by repeatedly pairing the desired stimuli with orgasm.

arousal. Orgasmic reconditioning is often combined with other techniques, such as social skills training, so that more desirable social behaviors can be strengthened as well (Marvasti, 2004).

Medical Approaches

LO 14.10   Discuss medical treatment of the paraphilic disorders.

There may be no medical "cure" for paraphilic disorders. No drug or surgical technique eliminates paraphilic ideas while leaving other cognitive functions intact. But some progress has been reported in using selective serotonin reuptake inhibitors (SSRIs), which are mainly used as anti-depressants, in treating exhibitionistic disorder, voyeuristic disorder, and fetishistic disorder (Assumpcao et al., 2014; Thibaut, 2012). Why anti-depressants? In addition to treating depression, SSRIs are often used to treat obsessive-compulsive disorder, a psychological disorder involving recurrent obsessions (intrusive ideas) and/or compulsions (urges to repeat a certain behavior or thought). Paraphilic behavior has an obsessive-compulsive quality. People with paraphilic disorders often experience intrusive, repetitive fantasies and urges.

People who experience such intense urges that they are at risk of committing sexual offenses may be helped by drugs that reduce the level of testosterone in the bloodstream (Kellar & Hignite, 2014; Houts et al., 2011). Testosterone is closely linked to sex drive and interest. *Medroxyprogesterone acetate (MPA)* (trade name Depo-Provera), which is administered in weekly injections, is the anti-androgen that has been used most extensively in the treatment of sex offenders. In men, anti-androgen drugs reduce sexual desire and the frequencies of erections and ejaculations.

Depo-Provera suppresses the sexual appetite in men. It can lower the intensity of sex drive and erotic fantasies and urges so that the man may feel less compelled to act on them (Briken et al., 2011; Houts et al., 2011). Antiandrogens do not, however, eliminate all paraphilic urges or completely change a person's sexual behavior (Thibaut, 2012).

The use of antiandrogens is sometimes incorrectly referred to as *chemical castration*. Surgical castration, the surgical removal of the testes, has sometimes been performed on convicted rapists and violent sex offenders (del Busto & Harlow, 2011). Surgical castration eliminates testicular sources of testosterone. Antiandrogens suppress, but do not eliminate, testicular production of testosterone. Also, unlike surgical castration, the effects of antiandrogens can be reversed when the treatment is terminated.

Although we have amassed a great deal of research on atypical variations in sexual behavior, our understanding of them and our treatment approaches to them remain less than satisfactory.

> **Critical Thinking**
> Which methods of therapy aim to work by reducing the sex drive in general, and which aim to replace sexual response to socially inappropriate stimuli with sexual response to appropriate stimuli?

Chapter Review

LO 14.1 Discuss what is meant by normal versus deviant sexual behavior.

This chapter discusses sexual behaviors that have been labeled abnormal and deviant, and signs of character disorders. Sexual behaviors have been labeled deviant when they are statistically rare, run counter to our values, or—as in the case of the paraphilic disorders—show a persistent preference for nongenital outlets.

LO 14.2 Enumerate and define the paraphilic disorders.

The American Psychiatric Association defines paraphilic disorders as mental disorders that involve sexual arousal in response to unusual stimuli such as children or other nonconsenting people, certain objects, or pain or humiliation. The great majority of paraphilic disorders are found among men. In fetishistic disorder, an inanimate object comes to elicit sexual arousal. In partialism, people are inordinately aroused by a particular body part, such as the feet. Transvestites become sexually excited by wearing articles of clothing of the other sex. An exhibitionist experiences the compulsion to expose himself to strangers. Voyeurs become sexually aroused by watching unsuspecting victims disrobe or engage in sexual activity, and usually do not seek sexual relations with the target. The obscene phone caller becomes sexually aroused by shocking his victim. Such callers typically masturbate during the phone call or shortly afterward. Sexual masochists associate the receipt of pain or humiliation with sexual arousal. Sexual sadism is characterized by persistent, powerful urges and sexual fantasies involving the inflicting of pain and suffering on others to achieve sexual excitement or gratification. Sexual sadists may be dangerous, especially when they seek nonconsenting "partners." Most frotteuristic acts—also known as mashing—take place in crowded places, such as buses, subway cars, or elevators. Zoophiles desire sexual contact with animals. Necrophiles desire sexual contact with dead bodies.

LO 14.3 Discuss biological perspectives on the paraphilic disorders.

Many people with paraphilic disorders have higher-than-normal sex drives. Their brains may also respond differently to deviant and normal sexual stimuli.

LO 14.4 Discuss psychoanalytic perspectives on the paraphilic disorders.

Psychoanalytic theory suggests that paraphilic disorders in males are defenses against castration anxiety.

LO 14.5 Discuss cognitive-behavioral perspectives on the paraphilic disorders.

Some cognitive-behavioral theorists suggest that unusual stimuli may become sexually arousing through being associated with sexual arousal or orgasm at a young age.

LO 14.6 Discuss sociological perspectives on the paraphilic disorders.

According to Weinberg's sociological model, the erotic appeal of S&M rituals may result from the opportunity to reverse the customary power relationships that exist between men and women and between social classes in society.

LO 14.7 Discuss the "Lovemap."

John Money theorized that childhood experiences etch a "lovemap" in the brain that determines the types of stimuli that become sexually arousing. In paraphilic disorders, lovemaps become distorted by early traumatic experiences.

LO 14.8 Discuss the psychoanalytic treatment of the paraphilic disorders.

Psychoanalysis aims to bring unconscious conflicts that prompt paraphilic behavior into awareness so that they can be worked through in adulthood.

LO 14.9 Discuss the cognitive-behavioral treatment of the paraphilic disorders.

Cognitive-behavioral therapy attempts to eliminate paraphilic behaviors through techniques such as systematic desensitization, aversion therapy, social skills training, covert sensitization, and orgasmic reconditioning.

LO 14.10 Discuss medical treatment of the paraphilic disorders.

Selective serotonin reuptake inhibitors (SSRIs), which are usually used as anti-depressants, tend to curb compulsive behavior to some degree, including paraphilic behavior. Both SSRIs and anti-androgen drugs depress sexual response, which lessens sexual desire and helps individuals control sexual urges. Castration has also been used to curb sexual desire and response, although its use is highly controversial.

Test Your Learning

1. People who are excessively aroused by a particular body part, such as the feet, breasts, or buttocks, are said to have _____
   (a) voyeuristic disorder.
   (b) frotteuristic disorder.
   (c) partialism.
   (d) transvestism.

2. When cognitive-behavioral therapists work with people with paraphilic disorders, they may use all of the following methods *except* _____
   (a) covert sensitization.
   (b) orgasmic reconditioning.
   (c) systematic desensitization.
   (d) antidepressant drugs.

3. According to psychoanalytic theory, the _____ is declaring, "Look, I have a penis!"
   (a) exhibitionist
   (b) voyeur
   (c) masher
   (d) sexual sadist

4. A "lovemap" is most likely to become distorted or "vandalized" by _____
   (a) alcohol.
   (b) childhood abuse or neglect.
   (c) unconscious conflicts from the Oedipal period.
   (d) the sexual sadomasochistic subculture.

5. Transvestism is considered to be most closely related to _____
   (a) fetishistic disorder.
   (b) exhibitionistic disorder.
   (c) mashing.
   (d) sexual sadomasochism.

6. Which of the following are most likely to need to risk capture to heighten their sexual arousal?
   (a) sexual sadomasochists
   (b) coprophiliacs
   (c) exhibitionists
   (d) mashers

7. Waismann and colleagues showed men slides and found that the main site for evoking the _____ response to "normal" sexual stimuli was on the right side of the brain.
   (a) P100
   (b) P300
   (c) P400
   (d) P600

8. Paraphilic disorders are characterized by _____
   (a) preference for atypical sexual stimuli.
   (b) statistical rarity of the sexual interest.
   (c) sexual interests that deviate from the core values of a society.
   (d) a high sex drive.

9. The "kink" culture is most closely related to _____
   (a) cybersex addiction.
   (b) frotteurism.
   (c) sadomasochism.
   (d) use of antiandrogen drugs.

10. The text states that it is normal to _____
    (a) expose one's genital organs to shock a stranger.
    (b) grope a nearby person in the subway,
    (c) enjoy exposing one's body to an intimate partner.
    (d) fantasize about sex with corpses.

Answers: 1. c; 2. d; 3. a; 4. b; 5. a; 6. c; 7. d; 8. c; 9. a; 10. c

Chapter 15
Sexual Coercion

 ## Learning Objectives

Rape: The Most Intimate Crime of Violence

LO 15.1 Define rape.

Types of Rape

LO 15.2 Describe the various kinds of rape, focusing on rape in college.

Social Attitudes, Myths, and Cultural Factors That Encourage Rape

LO 15.3 Explain how our culture encourages people to blame the victim of rape and socializes men into becoming sexually aggressive.

Psychological Characteristics of Rapists: Who Are They?

LO 15.4 Discuss the kinds of rapists and their personalities.

Adjustment of Rape Survivors

LO 15.5 Discuss the effects of rape on survivors.

Rape Prevention

LO 15.6 Discuss ways of preventing rape, including college prevention programs and Internet apps.

Childhood Sexual Abuse

LO 15.7 Discuss the origins and effects of sexual child abuse.

Treatment of Rapists and Child Molesters

LO 15.8 Discuss the treatment options for treating rapists and child molesters.

Sexual Harassment

LO 15.9 Discuss the various kinds of sexual harassment.

LO 15.10 Explain things victims of sexual harassment can do to protect themselves.

TRUTH OR FICTION?

Which of the following statements are the truth, and which are fiction? Look for the Truth-or-Fiction items throughout this chapter to find the answers.

1 Women are raped in the United States at a rate of more than one every minute.   **T / F**?

2 Ten times as many women as men are raped in the United States.   **T / F**?

3 The majority of rapes are committed by strangers in deserted neighborhoods or darkened alleyways.   **T / F**?

4 Men who rape other men are gay.   **T / F**?

5 Many women say "no" when they mean "yes."   **T / F**?

6 Most rapists are mentally ill.   **T / F**?

7 Father–daughter incest is the most common type of incest.   **T / F**?

According to a poll conducted by the *Washington Post*–Kaiser Family Foundation (2015), 20% of female respondents aged 17–26 reported they had been sexually assaulted in college. So did 5% of the men. The women told the interviewers things like "We were kind of wrestling around. Things turned more sexual. I told him to stop. He thought I was joking. I froze." "There was no question about consent. I said 'no' and he didn't care."

A quote from a *New York Times* story (Callimachi, 2015) about ISIS, the fundamentalist Islamic group rampaging through Iraq and Syria, and beheading Shiites, Christians, and other "infidels" in videos posted online: "In the moments before he raped the 12-year-old girl, the Islamic State fighter took the time to explain that what he was about to do was not a sin. Because the preteen girl practiced a religion other than Islam, the Quran not only gave him the right to rape her—it condoned and encouraged it, he insisted." ISIS promises sex slaves online as a recruiting tool.

The July 27, 2015 cover of *New York Magazine* showed 35 women aged from young adulthood through late adulthood sitting in chairs (Moyer, 2015). All of them claimed that the comedian and TV personality Bill Cosby had raped them. His modus operandi, they said, was to drug them and then to carry out the sex act while their brains were fogged. There was an empty chair for the next woman who was expected to lodge a complaint.

In the same year, an ex-teacher from Florida was sentenced to 22 years in prison for having sex with three students (Silveretein, 2015). The teacher said she wished it could all be undone. The victims' parents were unforgiving. The teacher was a woman, Jennifer Fichter—one of many attractive young women who have been adjudicated for such crimes in recent years, and the students were underage boys. Although some cynical observers of

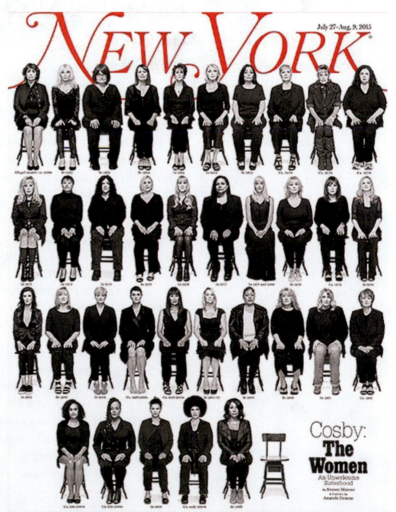

New York Magazine **July 2015 Cover Showed 35 Women Who Have Accused Bill Cosby of Sexual Assault.** The empty chair is for the next woman to come forward.

such proceedings have asked whether the young males inn the cases had truly been victimized or had actually "gotten lucky," bringing the women to court has shown a decline in the double standard that has applied to male and female sex abusers (Finkelhor, 2005a).

Then of course there are the scandals in which male adults have engaged in sexual contact with boys. In 2012, Penn State assistant football coach Jerry Sandusky was sentenced to prison for sexually assaulting boys in the locker room. Louis Freeh, former director of the FBI, released a report on the scandal accusing famed coach Joe Paterno, the university's former president, and other university officials of hiding the facts about Sandusky's sexual abuse, effectively ending their careers. More recently Pope Francis accepted the resignation of an archbishop and other high-ranking Vatican officials who had covered up sexual abuse of minors by pedophile priests (Winfield, 2015). Some observers wondered aloud whether the church's requirement that priests remain celibate had contributed to the problem (Adams, 2003).

This chapter is about the dark underside of human sexuality: sexual coercion in all its forms and faces. Our topics include rape and other forms of sexual pressure, including sexual harassment. As we see in the cases involving minors, sexual coercion also includes *any* sexual activity between an adult and a child. Even when children cooperate, sexual relations with children are coercive because children are younger than the legal age of consent.

Rape: The Most Intimate Crime of Violence

LO 15.1 Define rape.

Critical Thinking

Why do you think rape is a political issue as well as a crime of violence?

Here is an insight into the minds of your authors. We were going to begin this section with a story about date rape and acquaintance rape on campus—believing that we should start where the subject matter hits home. Moreover, this is a book about the science of human sexuality; we should not be sharing opinions. But we can't abide by any of that because some other events in the world today are so outlandish, so outrageous, that they rise to the fore. Following is an excerpt from a *New York Times* column by David Brooks (2015) about ISIS, the Islamic State in Iraq and Syria:

> State-sponsored slavery seemed like a thing of the past, but now ISIS is an unapologetic slave state. [Captured] Yazidi women are carefully catalog[u]ed, warehoused and bid upon.
>
> The rapes are theocratized. The rapists pray devoutly before and after the act. The religious leader's handbook governing the rape program has a handy Frequently Asked Questions section.

For the first few thousand years of history, the only rapes that were punished were those that defiled virgins. These rapes were considered crimes against property (virgins being the property of their fathers)—not crimes against people. In ancient Babylonia, rape laws applied to married women as well. Babylonian law required the assailant *and his victim* to be bound and thrown into a river. As the injured party (after all, *his* property had been damaged), the husband could choose to let his wife drown or save her. Blaming the victim of rape is thus an age-old tradition. The ancient Hebrews stoned to death a married woman who was raped, along with her assailant.

Free Yazidi women in the kurdish part of northern Iraq are receiving military training and resisting the Islamic State in Iraq and Syria (ISIS).

In the ancient Babylonian and Hebrew cultures, the wife was seen as guilty of adultery. Virgins who were raped within the protection of the city gates would also be stoned by the Hebrews. It was thought that they could have maintained their purity by crying out.

The current definition of **rape** varies from state to state. **Forcible rape** is usually defined as sex with a nonconsenting person by the use of force or the threat of force. **Statutory rape** refers to sex with a person who is younger than the age of consent, even if the person cooperates.

Traditionally, a man could not be convicted for raping his wife, even though he might have forced her to submit to sexual activity by physical power or threats. This marital exclusion was derived from the English common law that held that a woman "gives herself over" to her husband when she becomes his wife and cannot retract her consent. Today, however, most states permit the prosecution of husbands who rape their wives.

Rape laws are now also applied to men who rape men and to women who coerce men into sexual activity or assist men in raping other women. Forcible rape is a form of **sexual assault**.

Incidence of Rape

The numbers of women who have been raped are both inconsistent and staggering. First, the inconsistency. The Bureau of Justice Statistics (BJS) of the U.S. Department of Justice reported that 284,350 forcible rapes occurred in 2014 (Langton & Truman, 2015; Truman & Langton, 2015). However, the U.S. Department of Justice tracked only those rapes that were reported to authorities, and the BJS estimates that only one-third (33.6%) of rapes are reported, as compared, say, with three of every five burglaries and five of every six motor vehicle thefts (Truman & Langton, 2015). Let's consider the numbers suggested by the National Intimate Partner and Sexual Violence Survey (NISVS, 2015), administered by the Centers for Disease Control and Prevention (CDC). The NISVS is a continuing telephone survey of a nationally representative sample of some 16,500 adults. (The CDC defined rape as completed forced penetration, forced penetration facilitated by alcohol or other substances, or attempted forced penetration.) According to NISVS (2015) reporting, close to 2 million women are raped each year. If

rape

Sexual activity that takes place without consent. See *forcible rape* and *statutory rape*.

forcible rape

Sexual activity obtained by the use of force or the threat of force.

statutory rape

Sexual activity with a person younger than the age of consent, even when the victim cooperates.

sexual assault

Any sexual activity that involves the use of force or the threat of force.

the NISVS estimate is correct, only 14% of rapes are reported to authorities—that is, one rape in seven. And when respondents are asked about the lifetime incidence of sexual assault, nearly one woman in five reports being raped (NISVS, 2015), which, as we will see, is the same percentage of women who report being raped in college. But there is a lifetime of potential hazards following college.

1 › T / F   Truth or Fiction Revisited   It is true that women in the United States are raped at more than one every minute on the average. As many as 2 *million* American women may be raped each year.

An NISVS report found that about 1 man in 71 had been a rape victim at some time in his life, many earlier than the age of 11. Table 15.1 shows the distribution of types of rape and sexual assault victimizations for the years 2005–2014. Figure 15.1 shows that two out of three female rape victims are between the ages of 11 and 24.

2 › T / F   Truth or Fiction Revisited   Yes—actually more than 10 times as many women are raped as men. The U.S. BJS estimates that 1 man in 71 has been victimized by rape, as compared with one in five women.

How can we explain the discrepancy between the BJS and the NISVS? The fact of the matter is that the vast majority of rapes that occur in the United States go unreported. Why do most rape victims not report the assault to authorities? Many women choose not to report assaults because of concern that they will be humiliated by the criminal justice system. For example, they may be told that they are making something out of nothing by defense attorneys. They may be told that they led the rapist on, that they were wearing suggestive clothing, and, in some cases, that they were already kissing or petting and did not adequately communicate that the rapist must stop. Other women fear reprisal from their families or the rapist. Some simply assume that the offender will not be apprehended or prosecuted. Because Mexican American women live in a

Table 15.1 Distribution of Types of Rape and Sexual Assault Victimizations, 2005–2015

Type of Rape/Sexual Assault	Percentage
Completed rape	30
Attempted rape	23
Sexual assault	24
Unwanted sexual contact without force	6
Verbal threats of rape and sexual assault	18

SOURCE: Table 12, Truman, J. T., & Langton, L. (2015). *Criminal victimization, 2014.* U.S. Department of Justice: Bureau of Justice Statistics. http://www.bjs.gov/content/pub/pdf/cv14.pdf

Figure 15.1 Age at Time of First Completed Rape Victimization.

More than three-quarters of female victims of completed rape (79.6%) were first raped before their 25th birthday with 42.2% experiencing their first completed rape before the age of 18 (29.9% between 11 and 17 years old and 12.3% at or before age 10).

More than one-quarter of male victims of completed rape (27.8%) were first raped when they were 10 years old or younger (data not shown).

SOURCE: Table 12, Truman, J. T., & Langton, L. (2015). *Criminal victimization, 2014.* U.S. Department of Justice: Bureau of Justice Statistics. http://www.bjs.gov/content/pub/pdf/cv14.pdf

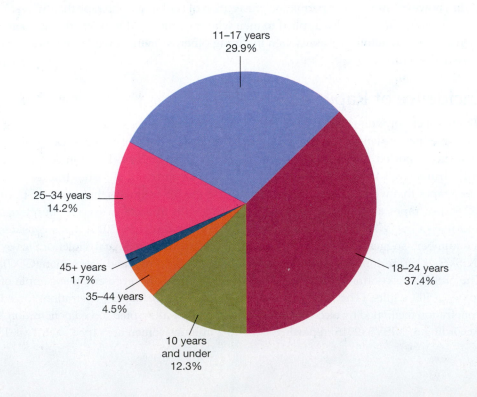

11–17 years 29.9%
25–34 years 14.2%
45+ years 1.7%
35–44 years 4.5%
10 years and under 12.3%
18–24 years 37.4%

culture in which women are often expected to "suffer in silence," they are even more likely to remain quite about rape and sexual abuse than European American women (Chen, 2012; Human Rights Watch, 2012).

There are other reasons that women do not report rape to authorities. Some women mistakenly believe that coercive sex is rape only when the rapist is a stranger. Some other women mistakenly assume that only forced vaginal penetration by the penis is defined as rape. But most states define rape more broadly, also considering nonconsensual anal and oral penetration by the penis or a finger or by a foreign object to be rape. And some count attempted rapes as rape.

The survey also asks respondents about violence by intimate partners. The types of rape include stranger rape, acquaintance rape, partner rape, male rape, and rape by females.

Types of Rape

LO 15.2 **Describe the various kinds of rape, focusing on rape in college.**

Stranger Rape

Stranger rape refers to rape committed by an assailant (or assailants) who is not previously known to the person attacked. The stranger rapist often selects targets that seem vulnerable, such as women who live alone, who are older or mentally retarded, who are walking down deserted streets, or who are asleep or intoxicated. After choosing a target, the rapist may search for a safe time and place to commit the crime—a deserted, run-down part of town, a darkened street, a second-floor apartment without window bars or locks.

stranger rape

Rape that is committed by an assailant previously unknown to the victim.

Acquaintance Rape

Women are more likely to be raped by men they know, such as classmates, fellow office workers, and even their brothers' friends, than by strangers. **Acquaintance rapes** are less likely than stranger rapes to be reported to the police. One reason is that rape survivors may not perceive sexual assaults by acquaintances as rapes. Only about one-quarter of the women in a national college survey who had been sexually assaulted saw themselves as rape victims (Koss & Kilpatrick, 2001; Rozee & Koss, 2001). Let's repeat that: *Only about one-quarter of the women in a national college survey who had been sexually assaulted saw themselves as rape victims!* Despite increased public awareness of acquaintance rape, many still think of rapists as strangers lurking in shadows and that a woman should be able to resist a sexual advance unless the man uses a weapon. Acquaintance rapists tend to rationalize their behavior by believing in myths such as the traditional view that men are expected to assume a sexually aggressive role in dating and the belief that rapists are strangers (Bletzer & Koss, 2006). Even when acquaintance rapes are reported to police, they may be treated as "misunderstandings" or lovers' quarrels rather than violent crimes (Campbell, 2006; Logan et al., 2006).

acquaintance rape

Rape by an acquaintance of the victim.

3 › T / F **Truth or Fiction Revisited** It is *not* true that the majority of rapes are committed by strangers in deserted neighborhoods or darkened alleyways. Most women are raped by men they know—often by men they have come to trust. According to the National Sexual Violence Resource Center (2015), about four in five rapes are committed by acquaintances of the victim.

Date Rape

Date rape is a form of acquaintance rape. Studies of college women show a consistent trend: as many as one college woman in four reports being forced into sexual intercourse by dates (McAnulty, 2012). Date rape is more likely to occur when the couple have too much to drink and then park in the man's car or goes back to his residence (McAnulty, 2012). The man tends to perceive his partner's willingness to return home with him as a signal of sexual interest, even if she resists his advances.

Date rapists may believe that acceptance of a date indicates willingness to have sexual relations. They may think that women should reciprocate with sex if they are taken to dinner. Other men assume that women who frequent places like singles bars are expressing tacit agreement to sex with men who show interest in them. Some date rapists believe that a woman who resists advances is just "protesting too much" so that she will not look "easy." They interpret resistance as coyness—a ploy in the cat-and-mouse game that typifies the so-called battle of the sexes. Date rapists may believe that when a woman says "no," she means "yes," especially when a sexual relationship has already been established (McAnulty, 2012).

According to Roy Baumeister and his colleagues (2001), perpetrators and victims view sexual assaults in different ways. Women see themselves as overpowered and deeply hurt. Men often focus on their own feelings, ignoring those of the victim, and act on their sexual frustration when the woman says it's time to call it quits. The more the man focuses on his own wants and ignores those of the woman, the more likely he is to commit rape (Bushman et al., 2003). In these cases, the motive may be largely sexual, but the man remains a violent criminal who refuses to take no for an answer.

The issue of consent lies at the heart of determining if a sexual act is rape. Unlike cases of stranger rape, date rape occurs within a context in which sexual relations could occur voluntarily. Thus, the issue of consent can become murky. Juries and judges are often faced with a woman plaintiff who alleges that the male defendant, who may appear neatly dressed and looking like the boy next door, forced her into a sexual act against her will. As in the Mike Tyson court appearances, the defendant may admit that sexual intercourse took place but claim that it was consensual. Judges and juries then have to distinguish shadings in meaning regarding "consent."

Cases of date rape often come down to his word against hers. Her word often becomes less persuasive in the eyes of the jury if it was clear that she had consented to acts beforehand, such as sharing dinner, attending the movies together, accompanying him to his home, sharing a drink alone, and perhaps kissing or petting (Maxwell et al., 2003; Osman, 2003). The issue becomes further clouded because some survivors of date rape continue their relationships, and even marry, the perpetrators.

The problem of date rape has been brought within closer public scrutiny in recent years. "Take Back the Night" marches have become a common form of student protest on college campuses against the sexual misconduct of men. Many colleges have mandated date rape seminars and workshops. Let us examine rape on campus in greater depth.

Rape on Campus

"Frank," a fraternity brother, described his technique:

> "We'd be on the lookout for the good-looking girls, especially the freshmen, the really young ones. They were the easiest…. Then we'd get them drinking right away…. They'd be guzzling it, you know, because they were freshmen, kind of nervous."

> "Frank" recounted how he targeted one young woman, plied her with alcohol-spiked punch, and then led her to a bed. "At some point, she started saying things like … 'I don't want to do this right away,' or something like that. I just kept working on her clothes … and she started squirming. But that actually helped, because her blouse came off easier…. She tried to push me off, so I pushed her back down…. I mean, she was so plastered that she probably didn't know what was going on, anyway. I don't know, maybe that's why she started pushing on me. But, you know, I just kept leaning on her, pulling off her clothes."

"Frank" said he kept his arm across her chest, by the base of her neck, to reduce her squirming as he had sex with her. When he was finished, he dressed and returned to the party.

And the woman? "She left."

A *Washington Post*–Kaiser Family Foundation survey (*Washington Post*, 2015), conducted by telephone in 2015, provides a broad view of rape on campus. In contrast with many telephone polls, the interviewees were reached by both land lines and mobile phones. A random nationally representative sample of adults who were in college or had recently been in college was obtained; they were aged 17–26.

Overall, 20% of the women and 5% of the men reported that they had been sexually assaulted (Fig. 15.2). Nine percent of the women said they were overcome by physical force, and 14% said they were assaulted while incapacitated, most often by alcohol, although some women believed they had been slipped a drug. (There was an overlap of 3%, which is why the number who say they were forced and the 14% who say they were incapacitated by alcohol or other drugs "adds up" to 20%. The sample all but universally (96%) agreed that having sex with a person who was incapacitated by alcohol or who had passed out amounted to sexual assault. Only about 20% of women and 30% of men thought that a student would claim that she or he had been sexual assaulted when it was not true.

The news and the literature on sexuality are abuzz with the recent California law stating that college students in the state must provide positive consent for sex to be considered legitimate. We have all heard the expression that "No means no," but the California standard, which has been adopted in about a quarter of states throughout the nation (Shulevitz, 2015), means that "Yes means yes." It seems somewhat similar to couples pausing while engaging in foreplay to apply a condom. Under this ruling, couples are more or less encouraged to pause while making love to ascertain that they are in agreement that they can go farther. Five out of six respondents overall were familiar with the "yes (and only yes!) means yes" standard of consent, and most of them believed that it was a realistic standard. Even so, many students aren't really asking (Keenan, 2015). About half (51%) of the women and a somewhat higher percentage of men (58%) reported that nodding in agreement indicated acceptable consent to proceed with more sexual activity. By contrast, only 15% of women and 30% of men said that kissing or touching provided consent to continue with sexual activity. Only 16% of women and 20% of men believed that *not* saying "no" amounted to permission to continue with sexual activity.

A number of factors were associated with women being victimized by a sexual assault; these included use of alcohol, a history of hooking up in school, and being members of or partying at fraternities and sororities. Although women were aware of the role of alcohol and also did not want to be assaulted, more than one in three (37%) women and two men in five (42%) admitted to drinking more than they should in social situations. In fact, 62% of the women who were assaulted said that they had been drinking before they were assaulted. Overall, 59% of women and 54% of men felt that alcohol and drug use were problems at their school. The likelihood of being assaulted was not connected with the size of the school, whether it was a public or private school, and the student's study habits.

By and large, the attackers were no strangers. One in four or five (22%) female victims of rape or other unwanted sexual contact said they knew the attacker very well, and 25% said they knew him fairly well. Only 28% said they didn't know the attacker at all.*

---

*http://www.washingtonpost.com/graphics/local/sexual assault poll/

Figure 15.2

SOURCE: http://www.washingtonpost.com/sf/local/2015/06/12/1-in-5-women-say-they-were-violated/

Students	Women	Men
who experienced sexual assault	20%	5%
By physical force	9%	1%
While incapacitated (certain it occurred, unable to provide consent)	14%	4%
Experienced both	3%	<1%

Is Aggression on the Playing Field Connected with Aggression off the Field? Are the Lessons Taught in Aggressive College Sports—Such as Taking Out the Competition and Getting It In at All Costs—a Threat to Women?

Nearly three in four (71%) of female survivors told someone about the assault, but only 12% of these reported the incident to the police or college authorities. Why do they avoid telling the authorities? Reporting a sexual assault is embarrassing for many or most victims, and the process of following up with testimony or physical evidence can also be embarrassing, even humiliating. There is also the question as to whether the complaint will go anywhere; only 1 attacker in 10 was ever held responsible or punished for the assault.

A majority of students felt that the following measures might prevent sexual assault at their school: harsher punishments for perpetrators, training students how to defend themselves and to intervene to defend others, and requiring all students, male and female, to attend prevention programs. To be fair, colleges are paying more attention to the problem of sexual assault; 71% of respondents felt that their schools were doing enough to try to prevent sexual assault.

Most students also felt it would help if men paid women more respect, if there were less drinking, and if students avoided casual hookups.

Gang Rape

Exercise of power is a major motive behind gang rapes, although some attackers may also be expressing anger against women. Gang members often believe that once women engage in coitus they are "whores" and therefore (to their minds) deserving of the assault. Thus, each offending gang member may become more aggressive as he takes his turn. The Koss college survey showed that sexual assaults involving a group of assailants tend to be more vicious than individual assaults (Gidycz & Koss, 1990).

Male Rape

Most rapes of men are carried out by other men (Peterson et al., 2010). Many of these rapes occur in prison settings and in military service. Gay and bisexual men appear to be more likely to be victimized than heterosexual men. Males are more often attacked by multiple assailants, held captive longer, and more reluctant to report the assault.

After all, victimization by rape does not fit the male stereotype of toughness. Men are expected to be not only strong but silent. But male rape survivors may suffer traumatic effects similar to those suffered by female survivors (Peterson et al., 2010).

4 › T / F   Truth or Fiction Revisited   It is *not* true that men who rape other men are gay. The statement is too broad to be true. Most male rapists are heterosexual. In addition to any sexual motivation, their motives tend to include domination and control, revenge and retaliation, sadism and degradation, and (when the rape is carried out by a gang member) status and affiliation (Peterson et al., 2010)

Partner Rape

Partner rapes are probably more common than date rapes because a sexual relationship has already been established (Monson et al., 2000; Osman, 2003). A "traditional" man may believe that it is his partner's duty to satisfy his sexual needs even when she is uninterested. However, men who are better educated and less rigid regarding stereotypes about sexual relationships are less likely to rape their partners (Basile, 2002).

Partner rape has been largely unreported and often unrecognized by survivors as actually being rape (Strebeigh, 2009). Women may also fail to report partner rape because of fear that no one will believe them.

Motives for partner rape vary. Sex is a motive, but some people use sex to dominate their partners. Others degrade their partners through sex, especially after arguments. Sexual coercion against one's partner often occurs within a context of a pattern of violence and physical intimidation (Proulx & Beauregard, 2014). In some cases, though, violence is limited to the sexual relationship. Some men see sex as the solution to disputes. They think if they can force their partners into sex, "Everything will be OK."

Survivors of partner rape may be as fearful as survivors of stranger rape of serious injury or death. The long-term effects of partner rape on survivors are also similar to those experienced by survivors of stranger rape, including fear, depression, and sexual dysfunctions (Kaczmarek et al., 2006; Polusny & Arbisi, 2006). Moreover, the woman who is raped by her husband usually continues to live with her assailant and may fear repeated attacks.

Rape by Women

Rape by women is rare. When it does occur, it often involves aiding or abetting men who are attacking another woman. Rape by women may occur in gang rape in which women follow male leaders to gain their approval. In such cases, a woman may be used to lure another woman to a reasonably safe place for the rape. Or the woman may hold the other woman down while she is assaulted.

But some men have been raped by women (Walker et al., 2005; *Washington Post*, 2015). Sarrel and Masters (1982) reported 11 such cases, including a 37-year-old man who was coerced into sexual intercourse by two women at gunpoint. In another

Critical Thinking
Why do you think it was a political struggle to pass laws permitting husbands (and wives) to be prosecuted for marital rape?

case, a 27-year-old man fell asleep in his hotel room with a woman he had just met in a bar and then awakened to find that he was bound to his bed, gagged, and blindfolded. He was then forced into sexual intercourse with four different women, who threatened him with castration if he did not perform satisfactorily. The National Sexual Violence Resource Center (2015) reported that 1 of 71 rape victims was a man.

Social Attitudes, Myths, and Cultural Factors that Encourage Rape

LO 15.3 Explain how our culture encourages people to blame the victim of rape and socializes men into becoming sexually aggressive.

Myths about rape create a social climate that legitimizes rape. Although both men and women are susceptible to rape myths, researchers find that college men show greater acceptance of rape myths than do college women (Stewart, 2014). Men also cling more stubbornly to myths about date rape than do women, even following date rape education classes designed to challenge these views (Maxwell et al., 2003; Maxwell & Scott, 2014). Such myths do not occur in a social vacuum. They are related to other social attitudes, including gender-role stereotyping, perception of sex as adversarial, and acceptance of violence in relationships (Yost & Zurbriggen, 2006).

5 › T / F   Truth or Fiction Revisited   Many people believe a number of myths about rape, such as "women say 'no' when they mean 'yes,'" "all women like a man who is pushy and forceful," "the way women dress, they are just asking to be raped," and "rapists are crazed by sexual desire" (Davies et al., 2012; Hayes et al., 2016). Yet another myth is that deep down inside, women want to be overpowered and forced into sex by men. But none of these myths, including the myth that women say "no" when they mean "yes," is true. Such myths have the effect of blaming the victim and encouraging rape.

Many observers note that our society pushes males into socially and sexually dominant roles (Malamuth et al., 2005). Males are often reinforced from childhood for aggressive and competitive behavior. Gender typing may lead men to reject "feminine" traits such as tenderness and empathy that might restrain aggression (Smith et al., 2015).

Research with college students supports the connection between stereotypical masculine identification and tendencies to rape or condone rape. Studies have compared students who believed strictly in traditional gender roles with student holding less rigid attitudes. The traditionalists express a greater likelihood of committing rape, are more accepting of violence against women, are more likely to blame rape survivors, and are more aroused by depictions of rape (Malamuth et al., 2000; Raichle & Lambert, 2000). College men who identify with the traditional masculine gender role more often report pushing women verbally and by force (R. M. Smith et al., 2015; Steinfeldt & Steinfeldt, 2012).

Do the lessons learned in competitive sports predispose young American males to sexual violence (Steinfeldt & Steinfeldt, 2012)? Boys are often exposed to coaches who emphasize winning at all costs. They are taught to be dominant and to vanquish their

Critical Thinking
Agree or disagree with the following statement, and support your answer: A woman who walks in a dangerous neighborhood or talks to a stranger deserves what she gets.

Are They Capable of Giving Consent to Sex? One survey respondent said that nothing would have happened that night if she hadn't been drinking. But note that an incapacitated person cannot give consent to sex."

Self-Assessment

Ten Cultural Myths That Create a Climate That Supports Rape

Myths about rape create a social climate that legitimizes rape. Although both men and women are susceptible to myths about rape, researchers find that college men show greater acceptance of rape myths than do college women (Davies et al., 2012). These myths tend to blame the victim rather than the rapist. Men also cling more stubbornly to myths about date rape than women do, even following date rape education classes designed to challenges these views. Such myths do not occur in a social vacuum. They are related to other social attitudes, including gender-role stereotyping, perception of sex as adversarial, and acceptance of violence in relationships. Here are some examples of myths about rape that help create a cultural climate that increases the likelihood of rape in the United States. Why not place a checkmark in front of those myths you believe—or did believe—before reading this book.

____ Myth 1: A woman who would go to a man's home or apartment on a first date is implying that she is willing to have sex. *A woman is free to be in a man's residence without expecting that she will be assaulted.*

____ Myth 2: Many women would claim that they have been raped only to call attention to themselves. *Nonsense! One could be just as suspicious anytime anybody complained about anything, such as complaining about a painful toe.*

____ Myth 3: A healthy woman can resist a rapist if she sincerely wants to do so. *The fact is that men are generally stronger than women and can overpower them.*

____ Myth 4: Women who don't use bras or who wear short skirts and other sexually appealing clothing are asking for trouble. *Don't confuse the current style with a sexual invitation.*

____ Myth 5: Most of the victims of rape are promiscuous or have a bad reputation. *It's not true, and even if it were, it wouldn't give men a license to commit rape.*

____ Myth 6: A girl who engages in necking or petting is letting things get out of hand, so you can't blame her partner it he forces sex on her. *Yes, you can. A girl or woman has the right to say "no" at any time.*

____ Myth 7: Women who are hitchhiking get what they deserve. *It may be a sign of poor judgment to hitchhike, but rape is not the appropriate "penalty."*

____ Myth 8: Women who think they're too good to talk to men they pass on the street need to be taught a lesson. *This myth is a perfect example of hatred of women. Women walking on the street should not be victimized by catcalls, leering, and sexual invitations.*

____ Myth 9: Many women have an unconscious desired to be raped. *Nonsense! Even if women, like men, occasionally entertain fantasies about rape, it does not mean they actually want to be raped and certainly doesn't give men an excuse to violently assault them.*

____ Myth 10: Many women who report a rape are angry with them men they accuse and want to punish them, or they find themselves pregnant and don't want to be blamed. *Again, these are just excuses for blaming the victim.*

opponents, even if winning means injuring or taking out the opposition (Stotzer & MacCartney, 2015). Does this philosophy carry over from the playing field into relationships with women?

Sexual behavior and sports in our culture are linked through common idioms. A young man may be taunted by his friends after a date with a woman with such questions as "Did you score?" or more bluntly, "Did you get it in?"

Psychological Characteristics of Rapists: Who Are They?

LO 15.4 **Discuss the kinds of rapists and their personalities.**

Although sexual aggressiveness may be embedded within our social fabric, not all men are equally vulnerable to these cultural influences. Personal factors, then, are also involved. Are rapists mentally disturbed? Intellectually deficient? Driven by insatiable sexual urges?

A CLOSER LOOK

DRUGS USED BY RAPISTS TO INCAPACITATE VICTIMS

"Rophies"; The Date Rape Drug

Rophies, roofies, R2, roofenol, roachies, la rocha, rope, or whatever you call it is dubbed the "date rape drug" because it has been slipped into the drinks of unsuspecting women with the effects of lowering their inhibitions, lessening their ability to resist a sexual assault, and when mixed with alcohol, sometimes causing blackouts that prevent victims from remembering the assault. For this reason, Rohypnol has also been called "the forget pill," "trip-and-fall," and "mind-eraser." The drug has no taste or odor, so the victims don't realize what is happening when an assailant slips it into a drink. About 10 minutes after taking it, the woman may feel dizzy and disoriented, simultaneously too hot and too cold, or nauseated. She may have difficulty speaking and moving and then pass out. She may "black out" for 8 to 24 hours, with little or no memory of what happened.

Rohypnol is not manufactured or sold legally in the United States, but it is prescribed as a treatment for insomnia and as a sedative hypnotic in other countries. It is in the same class of drugs as the tranquilizer Valium, but about 10 times stronger.

Rohypnol is often used with other drugs, such as alcohol, to create a dramatic "high." Rohypnol intoxication is generally associated with impaired judgment, memory, and motor skills and can make a victim unable to resist or recall a sexual attack. Effects begin within 30 minutes, peak within 2 hours, and can persist for 8 hours or more.

Here are some ideas for avoiding problems with Rohypnol:

- Be wary about accepting drinks from anyone you don't know well or long enough to trust.
- Don't put your drink down and leave it unattended, even to go to the restroom.
- If you think that you have been a victim, notify authorities immediately.

Quaaludes: The "Disco Biscuits" of the 1960s and 1970s

Quaaludes—aka Disco Biscuits, Bandits, Ludes, and Quack (not to be confused with "Crack")—are a synthetic barbiturate-like drug that depresses the central nervous system, relaxing people and making them sleepy, distorts perceptions, and sometimes induces feelings of euphoria. It is also highly addictive and overdoses can be deadly. First synthesized in the 1950s, it became a popular recreational drug, but was so dangerous that it is no longer available legally in the United States. Bill Cosby admitted in a 2005–2006 deposition that he had gotten Quaaludes from a Los Angeles physician to give the drugs to women with whom he wanted to have sex (Moghe, 2015).

Most researchers acknowledge that sexual motivation plays a key role in rape (Bushman et al., 2003; Malamuth et al., 2005), but a generation ago some social scientists focused more on emotional and social factors. It was noted that rape can be in part motivated by anger, striving toward power, sadism, or some combination of the three. Anger usually motivates the rapist to use more force than needed to obtain compliance and to force the victim into degrading and humiliating acts. Those who are motivated by power seek to control and dominate the victim (Miller, 2014). Sadistic rapists are most vicious; some torture or murder their victims. It has also been argued that exposure to pornography increases the likelihood that men will sexually assault women. We will see in Chapter 16 that the literature on the issue is mixed, but there is accumulating evidence that even nonviolent pornography can increase attitudes supportive of violence against women—at least among men who are unagreeable (Hald & Malamuth, 2015). The connections between pornography and sexual assault remain of deep concern and are under intense study.

Some of our knowledge of the psychological characteristics of rapists derives from studies of samples of incarcerated rapists. One conclusion that emerges is that there is no single type of rapist. Rapists vary in their psychological characteristics, family backgrounds, mental health, and criminal histories (Lalumière et al., 2005a).

6 › T / F Truth or Fiction Revisited It is *not* true that most rapists are mentally ill, even though their crimes might strike observers as being "sick." Generally speaking, rapists in the general population are no less intelligent or more mentally ill than other people. On the other hand, many rapists have an antisocial personality that enables them to violate their victims without guilt, shame, anxiety, or empathy (Lalumière et al., 2005a; Proulx & Beauregard, 2014b). Some antisocial rapists have long histories of violent behavior (Lalumière et al., 2005a, 2005b). The use of alcohol may also dampen self-restraint and spur sexual aggressiveness.

For some rapists, violence and sexual arousal become enmeshed. Thus, they seek to combine sex and violence to enhance their sexual arousal (Lalumière et al., 2005a). Some rapists are more sexually aroused (as measured by the size of erections) by verbal descriptions, films, or audiotapes that portray themes of rape than are other people (Lalumière et al., 2005a, 2005b, 2005c). Other researchers, however, have failed to find deviant patterns of arousal in rapists (Lalumière et al., 2005a, 2005b, 2005c).

Studies of incarcerated rapists may be criticized on grounds that the samples may not represent the total population of rapists. To offset this methodological concern, researchers have turned to the survey method to study men who anonymously report that they have engaged in sexually coercive behaviors, including rape, but have not been identified by the criminal justice system (Locke & Mahalik, 2005; Yost & Zurbriggen, 2006). Sexually coercive men are more likely than other men to:

- Condone rape and violence against women.
- Hold traditional gender-role attitudes.
- Be sexually experienced.
- Be hostile toward women.
- Engage in sexual activity to express social dominance.
- Be sexually aroused by depictions of rape.
- Be irresponsible and lack a social conscience.
- Have peer groups, such as fraternities, that pressure them into sexual activity.

Adjustment of Rape Survivors

LO 15.5 Discuss the effects of rape on survivors.

Many survivors of stranger rape fear for their lives during the attack (Polusny & Arbisi, 2006). Whether or not weapons or threats are used, the experience of being dominated by an unpredictable and threatening assailant is terrifying. The woman does not know whether she will survive and may feel helpless to do anything about it.

Many survivors are in crisis in the days and weeks following the rape (Bryant-Davis, 2011). They have insomnia and cry frequently. They tend to report eating problems, cystitis, headaches, irritability, mood changes, anxiety and depression, and menstrual irregularity (Kaczmarek et al., 2006; Senn et al., 2015). They may become withdrawn, sullen, and mistrustful. People in the United States tend to believe that women who are raped are at least partly to blame for the assault (Boros et al., 2005); therefore, some survivors experience feelings of guilt and shame. Emotional distress tends to peak in severity by about 3 weeks following the assault and generally remains high before beginning to abate about a month or two later (Duke et al., 2008; Littleton & Henderson, 2009). Many survivors encounter more lasting problems. Victims' feelings of being powerless to affect their own fate can endure and change their personalities (Bryant-Davis, 2011). A study of women in the military who had survived rape and physical abuse revealed health problems a decade afterward (Sadler et al., 2000). Some survivors suffer physical injuries and sexually transmitted infections (STIs).

Survivors may also encounter problems at work, such as problems relating to coworkers or bosses or difficulties in concentrating. Relationships with spouses or partners may suffer. Disturbances in sexual functioning are common and may endure. Survivors often report a lack of sexual desire, fear of sex, and difficulty becoming aroused (Bryant-Davis, 2011).

Most women fail to report sexual assaults to police. Reasons include fears of retaliation, the social stigma attached to the survivors of rape, doubts that others will believe them, feelings that it would be hopeless to try to bring charges against the perpetrator, concerns about negative publicity, and fears about the emotional distress to which they would be subjected if the case were to go to trial (Bryant-Davis, 2011).

Rape and Psychological Disorders

Rape survivors are at higher-than-average risk of developing anxiety disorders and depression, and of abusing alcohol and other substances. The vast majority of female rape victims report experiencing the anxiety disorder known

Many Survivors of Rape Suffer from Posttraumatic Stress Disorder (PTSD).

as–**posttraumatic stress disorder (PTSD)** (NISVS, 2011; Senn et al., 2015). PTSD is brought on by exposure to a traumatic event and is also often seen in soldiers who were in combat. People with PTSD may have flashbacks to the traumatic experience, disturbing dreams, emotional numbing, and nervousness. This disorder may persist for years. The person may also develop fears of situations connected with the traumatic event. For example, a woman who was raped on an elevator may develop a fear of riding elevators by herself. Researchers also report that women who blame themselves for the rape tend to suffer more severe depression and adjustment problems, including sexual problems (Kaczmarek et al., 2006; Vickerman & Margolina, 2009).

posttraumatic stress disorder (PTSD)

A type of stress reaction brought on by a traumatic event and characterized by flashbacks of the experience in the form of disturbing dreams or intrusive recollections, a sense of emotional numbing or restricted range of feelings, and heightened body arousal.

If You Are Raped …

Here are some ideas about what to do if you are raped.

- Don't change anything about your body—don't wash, don't even comb your hair. Leave your clothes as they are. Otherwise you could destroy evidence.

- Strongly consider reporting the incident to police. You may prevent another victim from being assaulted, and you will be taking charge, starting on the path from victim to survivor.

- Ask a relative or friend to take you to a hospital if you can't get an ambulance or a police car. If you call the hospital, tell them why you're requesting an ambulance; the staff may be able to send someone trained to deal with rape cases.

- Seek help in an assertive way. Seek medical help. Injuries you are unaware of may be detected. Insist that a written or photographic record be made to document your condition. If you decide to file charges, the prosecutor may need this evidence to obtain a conviction.

- Question health professionals. Ask about your biological risks. Ask about prophylactic treatment against HIV infection. Ask what treatments are available. Ask for whatever will help make you comfortable. Call the shots. Demand confidentiality if that's what you want. Refuse what you don't want.

If a rape crisis center or rape hotline is available in your area, you may wish to call for advice. A rape crisis volunteer may be available to accompany you to the hospital and help see you through the medical evaluation and police investigation if you report the attack. It is not unusual for rape survivors to try to erase the details of the rape from their minds. However, trying to remember details clearly will permit you to provide an accurate description of the rapist to the police, including his clothing, type of car, and so on. This information may help police apprehend the rapist and assist in the prosecution.

Treatment of Rape Survivors

The treatment of survivors typically involves helping the woman (the vast majority are female) through the crisis following the attack and then helping to foster long-term adjustment (Bryant-Davis, 2011). Crisis intervention typically provides the survivor with support and information to help her express her feelings and develop strategies for coping with the trauma. Psychotherapy, involving group or individual approaches, can help the survivor cope with the emotional consequences of rape, avoid self-blame, improve self-esteem, validate the welter of feelings surrounding the experience, and help her establish or maintain loving relationships. Therapists also recognize the importance of helping the rape survivor mobilize social support. Family, friends, religious leaders, and healthcare specialists are all

A CLOSER LOOK

SLUTWALK

SlutWalk bridges the path between helping rape survivors adjust and rape prevention, which is why we place this feature right here, between the two topics. SlutWalks are marches that protest against the social myth that women who dress in a sexy fashion are asking to be raped, or at worst, really want to be raped.

The idea for SlutWalks originated in Toronto, Canada, in 2011 after a police officer, Michael Sanguinetti, commented that women provoked rape when they dressed like sluts. "I've been told I'm not supposed to say this," said Sanguinetti, "however, women should avoid dressing like sluts in order not to be victimized." Sanguinetti later apologized for his remark, but since that time, women, fed up with insensitive men continuing to blame the victim—and supporters of women's rights—have taken to the streets to protest in places as far flung as Switzerland, the United Kingdom, Canada, and the United States, and across the Pacific, Japan, South Korea, India, and Singapore. In these marches, the women typically dress scantily, some topless, and carry provocative signs asserting that their bodies remain their own regardless of how they choose to dress.

The founders of the SlutWalk movement, Sonya Barnett and Heather Jarvis, reclaimed the negative word *slut* as referring to the empowerment of women. On their Web site they state that "We are tired of being oppressed by slut-shaming; of being judged by our sexuality and feeling unsafe as a result. Being in charge of our sexual lives should not mean that we are opening

Dancers Megan Walsh and Lyz Krieger Pause for a Photo at a Chicago SlutWalk. Their sign addresses the reality that their flirting, their sexy dress, and even their drinking are not causes of rape; rape is caused by rapists.

ourselves to an expectation of violence, regardless if we participate in sex for pleasure or work. No one should equate enjoying sex with attracting sexual assault." College women and even prostitutes have jumped on the bandwagon.

potential sources of help. However, women often find that those from whom they seek support, including family and clergy, blame them for the attack (Bryant-Davis, 2011). In major cities and many towns, concerned men and women have formed rape crisis centers and hotlines, peer counseling groups, and referral agencies geared to assessing and treating survivors' needs after the assault. Some counselors are specially trained to mediate between survivors of rape and their loved ones (husbands, lovers, and so on). These counselors help people to discuss and work through the often complex emotional legacy of rape. Phone numbers for these services can be obtained from feminist groups (for example, your local office of the National Organization for Women [NOW]), the police department, or the telephone directory.

A review of the effectiveness of various kinds of therapy for survivors of rape found that the treatment targets are most often PTSD, depression, and anxiety (Vickerman & Margolina, 2009). The women in the reviewed studies most often experienced chronic (enduring) symptoms. The most effective forms of therapy were cognitive-behavioral (helping the victim view her assault in less self-defeating ways, such as encouraging her not to blame herself for the attack) and helping her approach rather than avoid the "scene of the crime" and other frightful factors so that she learns to cope with them.

Of course, if we work to *prevent* rape, we may not need to help as many survivors adjust.

Rape Prevention

LO 15.6 Discuss ways of preventing rape, including college prevention programs and Internet apps.

The best way to deal with rape is to prevent it—certainly to prevent it from happening to you. Ending rape in society at large will require massive changes in cultural attitudes and socialization processes. Educational intervention on a smaller scale may reduce its incidence, however. Many colleges and universities require that incoming students attend rape-prevention programs, and these programs have apparently reduced the incidence of rape on campus (Gidycz et al., 2011; Vladutiu et al., 2011). These programs aim to develop empathy for the victim by explaining the damage done by rape, exposing traditional cultural myths that endorse rape, and explaining the borders between encouraging a date to have sex and rape.

One program for college men, termed "The Men's Project," addresses the ways in which men are educated about rape and how to prevent it (Stewart, 2014). The program teaches men how gender socialization contributes to rape—how, for example, men are encouraged to be competitive and aggressive, in college sports and in the business world, and how such socialization encourages them to attempt to dominate women. They are also acquainted with the rape myths that increase the likelihood of sexual assault. One myth is that women say "no" but mean "yes." Now these programs debunk this belief by teaching about affirmative consent"—the California ruling adopted on many campuses and in many states which affirms that "'yes' means 'yes,'" and "no," of course, means "no." The concept of affirmative consent applies to same-sex couples as well as male–female couples. They learn that when a woman is silent, confused, and afraid, these responses also mean no. They are also taught that women may dress in a sexy manner and smile at men, even flirt with men, but that these behaviors are not an invitation to sexual assault. Other myths that contribute to rape are shown in the Closer Look feature: "Ten Cultural Myths That Create a Climate That Supports Rape." Men are more likely than women to believe these myths. Prevention programs challenge these myths.

But until the basic cultural attitudes that support rape change, "rape prevention" means that it is up to the woman to be aware of her environment and, if necessary, to take action. A program described by Charlene Senn and her colleagues (2015) includes elements found to be helpful to college women and showed remarkable effectiveness at three universities in Canada. Some 893 first-year students aged 17–24 were enrolled; half were assigned at random to the program, the other half to a control group. The program included lectures, discussion groups, role-playing, and—in the realm of self-defense—practice sessions. One aspect of the program was helping the women develop awareness of the circumstances and behaviors that increase the probability of a sexual assault. They talked about the emotional barriers that make it difficult for many women to resist the advances of men, and they rehearsed resisting verbal coercion. They received 2 hours of training in self-defense based on the Wen-Do method, focusing on defending against attackers who were larger than they. (Women and counselors debate whether women should fight male assailants, but the university setting seems to be a safer environment than the street for trying to fend off a sexual attack.)

One year later, women in the program were almost twice as likely to prevent a sexual assault as women assigned to a control group (5.2% of women from the program were victimized as compared with 9.8% of women in the control group). That amounted to a reduction in risk of 46%. Put another way, one rape was prevented for every 22 women in the program.

Preventing Rape by Strangers

Most of the previous suggestions are focused on preventing rape in or connected with the academic environment. Here are some ides about preventing rape in the larger world:

- Walk with purpose, at a reasonably brisk pace, and as if you're wearing blinders.
- Prearrange signals that you need help with other women in the building or neighborhood.
- List yourself on the mailbox and in the phone directory by first initials only.
- Use dead-bolt locks.
- Keep windows locked.
- Install metal grids on first-floor windows.
- Keep entries well lit.
- Keep keys handy when approaching the car or the door.
- Do not walk alone after dark.
- Avoid deserted areas.
- Do not allow workers into your home without checking their credentials.

SEX IN THE DIGITAL AGE

RAPE PREVENTION? THERE'S AN APP FOR THAT[1] (ACTUALLY THERE ARE SEVERAL)

After one of her colleagues sexually assaulted her, Nancy Schwartzman rode home with him.

She was 24-years-old, living alone in Jerusalem, and she wasn't entirely sure where she was. Living so many miles from her friends and family back in the United States, she didn't have anyone she felt she could rely on to come pick her up. So, after enduring perhaps the most violating, frightening, and confusing experience of her young life, Schwartzman had little choice but to accept a ride from the man who raped her.

Now, Schwartzman, who later made a documentary about her experience called *The Line*, works on technology to ensure that no one ever feels stranded before or after an instance of sexual violence occurs.

Schwartzman is the CEO of Tech 4 Good, the tiny three-person startup behind Circle of 6, an app that makes it easy for users to choose six trusted friends who they can automatically alert in the event of an emergency. Users preprogram their contacts into the app, and with the press of a button, the app will automatically text those contacts. Users can choose a text that asks members of their circle to come get them, to call them, or to give them advice. The app also connects users to national rape support lines.

Circle of 6 is in the process of rolling out custom apps for colleges, which Schwartzman refers to as "petri dishes" for sexual assault. These custom apps come pre-programmed with phone numbers for the school's own support resources and provides those colleges with important information about what's happening on campus. "We know that the first couple of weeks and months of school are really dangerous for young people," Schwartzman says. "The app will enable them to have a safety plan and think about this stuff, without feeling too heavy handed about it."

The app launched in 2012, after winning The White House's Apps Against Abuse Challenge back in 2011 and has since

[1]Adapted from Lapowsky, I. (2014, September 5). This App Is a 21st Century Rape Whistle. *Wired* © Conde Nast

- Keep your car locked.
- Don't live in a risky building. (We recognize this suggestion may be impossible to carry out by poor women who have little choice where they live.)
- Don't stop for hitchhikers (including women hitchhikers).
- Don't talk to strangers on the street.
- Shout "Fire!" not "Rape!" if you are assaulted. People tend to flock to fires but avoid scenes of violence.

Preventing Date Rape

Some ideas about preventing date rape in the larger world:

- Tell your partner how far you would like to go so that he will understand the limits are. If your partner starts fondling you in a way you don't want, say something like "I'd rather you don't touch me there. I prefer not getting so intimate at this point in our relationship."
- Meet new dates in public places.
- When meeting a new date, drive in your own car.
- Firmly refuse unwanted sexual overtures. Make direct eye contact. The firmer you are, the less likely your partner will misinterpret your wishes.

gained 200,000 users across 33 countries. The company's new push onto college campuses comes at a particularly apt time, as awareness of the high rate of sexual violence on campuses has finally turned into national conversation.

In 2014 *The Washington Post* published a study that ranked colleges based on the prevalence of forcible sexual assaults reported on campus and found that the number of reports are on the rise. Although that's perhaps a promising sign that more of these traditionally underreported crimes are actually being reported, the numbers in and of themselves are troubling. Recently, a Columbia University student has drawn national attention, after publicly vowing to carry her dorm room mattress around with her until her rapist is expelled from the school. And earlier this year, the White House even launched its own task force to combat the problem.

Schwartzman is hoping that Circle of 6 can at least be part of the solution to the ongoing rape crisis. The first Circle of 6 app for universities launched this week at Williams College in Massachusetts, and Schwartzman says UCLA will also launch the app in the coming weeks. According to Meg Bossong, the director of sexual assault prevention and response at Williams, the most powerful part of the Circle of 6 app is the fact that it empowers not just potential victims, but also bystanders, to act. "Students are very interested in figuring out how to make campus safer," she says, "but they're not exactly sure how to do that or if they're being asked to do that. This is a great way to let people know when they need help."

Williams is also working with Circle of 6 to collect anonymized data on how people are using the app—whether they're regularly asking friends to come get them or tapping into the app's on campus resources—and using that to inform their on-campus prevention courses.

Of course, Circle of 6 is entering a field that's not without controversy. After a group of students recently invented a nail polish that changes color when it detects date rape drugs, the idea was lambasted in the press for placing the onus of prevention on women. But Bossong says while she agrees with that criticism, she views Circle of 6 differently. "This is about building the culture we want on our campus, a culture in which people feel someone will have their back and a culture in which people feel they owe it to the community to make sure it's safe," she says. "Risk reduction technology, like nail polish, takes for granted that it's going to happen and doesn't push for cultural change."

Still, Schwartzman is the first to admit this tool is just that: a tool, not a solution. Sexual violence is a complex issue, one that Schwartzman says is still all too easy to explain away by blaming the victim or drawing lines around what does or doesn't constitute rape. It's precisely the type of response Schwartzman faced after her assault. Now, she says, the bulk of the work that needs to be done is in truly changing that cultural paradigm. "A mobile tool is a cool, new innovation, and we're glad people are using Circle of 6," she says. "But there's this other stuff that needs to happen too, like consent-based education, justice, and transparency to address the problem in a holistic way."

Cosmopolitan magazine, by the way, has published information about several other apps that will help a woman prevent a sexual assault: On Watch, Safety Siren, Panic Guard, and My Force. Most of them, including Circle of 6, are free. Go to: http://www.cosmopolitan.com/lifestyle/advice/g2170/apps-that-help-prevent-rape/

- Be honest with yourself about your concerns. If you're not sure you should be there—wherever "there" is—leave.

- If you have broken off a relationship with someone you don't really like or feel good about, don't let him into your place.

Confronting A Rapist: Should You Fight, Flee, or Plead?

What if you are accosted by a rapist? Should you try to fight him off, flee, or try to plead with him to stop? Some women have thwarted attacks by pleading or crying. Screaming may help ward off some attacks. Running away sometimes works (Gidycz et al., 2011). No single suggestion is likely to work in all cases.

Self-defense training may help women become better prepared to fend off an assailant (Gidycz et al., 2011; Senn et al., 2015). Yet physical resistance may spur some rapists to become more aggressive. Women who resist increase their chances of preventing the completion of a rape, but resistance also increases the odds of being injured. It may be difficult, if not impossible, for women to think through their options clearly and calmly when they are attacked. Rape experts recommend that women practice various responses to assaults, as did women in the study by Charlene Senn and her colleagues (2015).

Childhood Sexual Abuse

LO 15.7   **Discuss the origins and effects of sexual child abuse.**

Many view sexual assaults on children—such as those committed by Jerry Sandusky—as among the most heinous of crimes. Children who are sexually assaulted often suffer social and emotional problems that impair their development and persist into adulthood, affecting their self-esteem and their ability to form intimate relationships.

No one knows how many children are sexually abused, although researcher David Finkelhor (2012) places the number in the United States at about 200,000 to 300,000 annually. (Finkelhor places the number of children who experience sexual harassment at close to 2 *million*.) Although most sexually abused children are girls, one-quarter to one-third are boys (Edwards et al., 2003). An analysis of 217 studies involving 9.9 million participants estimated that 18% of girls and 7% to 8% of boys had been subjected to childhood sexual abuse (Stoltenborgh et al., 2011). In an anonymous U.S. survey, 232 of 1,521 adult women (15%) reported that they had been sexually abused by an adult other than their father before the age of 18 (Stroebel et al., 2013). The actual percentages might be higher because many people fail to report incidents because of faulty memory, shame, embarrassment, or misinterpretation of events in their histories (Finkelhor, 2015).

Sexual abuse of children ranges from exhibitionism, kissing, fondling, and sexual touching to oral sex and anal intercourse and, with girls, vaginal intercourse. Acts such as touching children's sexual organs while changing or bathing them, sleeping with children, or appearing nude before them are open to interpretation and often innocent. Sexual contact between an adult and a child is abusive, even if the child is willing, since children are legally incapable of consenting. Although the age of consent varies among the states, sexual relations between adults and children below the age of consent are a criminal offense in every state.

Sexual abuse also occurs over the Internet, with pornographic images and invitations to join XXX chat rooms, to interact with women who disrobe online, and to contact prostitutes and women who are (supposedly) seeking clandestine affairs "pop up." In 2010, 9% of children report receiving an unwanted sexual solicitation—a number which actually represents a decrease of about 50% since 2000 (Jones et al., 2012). About one in four children (23%) reported an unwanted exposure to pornography, down from one in three (34%) in 2000. Perhaps the Internet is becoming a safer place for children as parents apply filtering software; and browsers such as Safari and Windows have some filtering mechanisms of their own.

Voluntary sexual activity *between children* of similar ages is not sexual abuse. Children often engage in consensual sex play with peers or siblings, as in "playing doctor" or in mutual masturbation. Although such experiences may be recalled in adulthood with feelings of shame or guilt, they are not typically as harmful as experiences with adults. When the experience involves coercion, or when the other child is significantly older or in a position of power over the younger child, the sexual contact may be considered sexual abuse.

Patterns of Abuse

Children from stable, middle-class families appear to be generally at lower risk of encountering sexual abuse than children from poorer, single parent, or stepfamilies (Amodeo et al., 2006; Turner et al., 2006). In most cases, children who are sexually abused are not accosted by the proverbial stranger lurking in the school yard. Most molesters are close to them: relatives, step-relatives, family friends, and neighbors (Beauregard et al., 2014; LeClerc et al., 2014).

Parents who discover that their child has been abused by a family member are often reluctant to notify authorities (Finkelhor et al., 2012). Some may feel that such problems are "family matters" that are best kept private. Others may be reluctant to notify authorities for fear that it may shame the family or that they may be held accountable for failing to protect the child. The decision to report abuse to the police depends largely on the relationship between the abuser and the person who discovers the abuse (Finkelhor, 2015; Finkelhor et al., 2012). In a Finkelhor survey, none of the parents whose children were abused by family members notified authorities. By contrast, most parents whose children have been abused by strangers did so.

Typically, the child initially trusts the abuser. Physical force is seldom needed to gain compliance, largely because of the child's helplessness, gullibility, and submission to adult authority. Whereas most sexually abused children are abused only once, those who are abused by family members are more likely to suffer repeated abuse.

Genital fondling is the most common type of abuse (Edwards et al., 2003). In one sample of women who had been molested in childhood, most contacts involved genital fondling (38% of cases) or exhibitionism (20% of cases). Intercourse is rare. Repeated abuse by a family member, however, commonly follows a pattern that begins with fondling during preschool, progresses to oral sex or mutual masturbation during the early school years, and then to penetration (vaginal or anal intercourse) in preadolescence or adolescence.

Abused children rarely report the abuse, often because of fear of retaliation from the abuser or because they believe they will be blamed for it. Adults may suspect abuse if a child shows sudden personality changes or develops fears, problems in school, or eating or sleeping problems. A pediatrician may discover physical signs of abuse during a medical examination. The average age at which most children are first sexually abused ranges from 6 to 12 years for girls and 7 to 10 years for boys (Finkelhor et al., 2005b).

Critical Thinking
Why do you think that most cases of child sexual abuse are not reported to the authorities?

Types of Abusers

The overwhelming majority of people who sexually abuse children (both boys and girls) are males (Hamby et al., 2013; Turner et al., 2006). Although most child abusers are adults, some are adolescents. Male adolescent sex offenders are more likely than other adolescents to have been molested themselves as boys. Some adolescent sex offenders may be imitating their own victimization. Adolescent child molesters also tend to feel socially inadequate and to be fearful of social interactions with age-mates of the other gender.

Although the great majority of sexual abusers are male, the number of female sexual abusers may be greater than has been generally believed (Hamby et al., 2013). Many female sexual abusers may go undetected because society accords women a much freer range of physical contact with children than it does men. A woman who fondles a child might be seen as affectionate, or at worst seductive, whereas a man would be more likely to be perceived as a child molester.

What motivates a woman to sexually abuse children, even her own children? Some female abusers have histories of becoming dependent on, or rejected by, abusive males. Some appear to have been manipulated into engaging in sexual abuse by their husbands. Others appear to have unmet emotional needs and low self-esteem and may have been seeking acceptance, closeness, and attention though sexual acts with children (Zernike, 2005). Some, motivated by unresolved feelings of anger, revenge, powerlessness, or jealousy, may view their own and others' children as safe targets for venting these feelings. Some view their crimes as expressions of love.

Sexual interest in children may also be motivated by unusual patterns of sexual arousal. This brings us to pedophilia.

Pedophilia

In 2015, Subway pitchman Jared Fogle pleaded guilty to distributing child pornography—some of the children were as young as 6 years of age—and of buying sex with minor girls (Phillip & Larimer, 2015). Fogle had even offered adult prostitutes bonuses if they would supply him with underage girls. In most states an adult having sex with a minor is rape. It is likely that Fogle can be diagnosed with pedophilia.

Pedophilia is a paraphilia (see Chapter 14) in which an adult finds children to be the preferred and sometimes exclusive objects of sexual desire. The prevalence of pedophilia in the general population is unknown. Some pedophiles are so distressed by their urges that they never act on them. But many molest young children and adolescents, often repeatedly.

Although pedophiles are sometimes called child molesters, not all child molesters are pedophiles. Pedophilia involves persistent or recurrent sexual attraction to children. Some molesters, however, may seek sexual contacts only with children when they are under unusual stress or lack other sexual outlets. Thus, they do not meet the clinical definition of pedophilia.

Pedophiles are almost exclusively male (Hamby et al., 2013), although some female pedophiles have been reported. (See the Closer Look feature: "The Siren Song of Sex with Boys.") Some pedophiles are sexually attracted only to children. Others are sexually attracted to adults as well. Some pedophiles limit their sexual interest in children to incestuous relationships with family members.

pedophilia
A paraphilia that is defined by sexual attraction to children.

Critical Thinking
What political issues are involved in attempting to decide whether or not sex between an adult woman and an adolescent boy be treated differently by the law than sex between an adult man and an adolescent girl?

Former Subway Pitchman Jared Fogle in His "Salad Days"— Launching a Fight-the-Fat Campaign. Fogle pled guilty to distributing child pornography and buying sex with underage girls in 2015. Why do some childhood sexual abusers prefer sex with children to sex with adults?

Others abuse children to whom they are unrelated. Some pedophiles limit their sexual interest in children to looking at them or undressing them. Others fondle them or masturbate in their presence. Some manipulate children into penetration.

Children tend not to be worldly wise. They can often be taken in by pedophiles who tell them that they would like to show them something, teach them something, or do something with them that they would like. Some pedophiles seek to gain the child's affection and discourage the child from disclosing the sexual activity by showering the child with attention and gifts. Others threaten the child or the child's family to prevent disclosure.

Although most pedophiles may not wear trench coats and hang around school yards, there is research evidence that many of them have personality disorders (Madsen et al., 2006). Research finds them to be emotionally unstable, disagreeable, angry, impulsive, and mistrustful.

Some pedophiles that are lacking in social skills may turn to children after failing to establish gratifying relationships with adult women. Yet psychological investigation has found that many pedophiles distort reality in ways that enable them to pursue sexual activity with children (Marziano et al., 2006). Pedophiles often:

- see children as sexual beings who want to have sex with adults.

- believe that sex does not harm children and may be beneficial.

- think of themselves as being so important that they are entitled to sex with whomever they want.

- see others as dangerous and controlling and think they must fight to gain control of their lives.

- believe they cannot control their impulses.

Incest: Breaking Taboos

Incest involves people who are related, usually by blood, or *consanguineous*. Although a few societies have permitted incestuous pairings among royalty, most known cultures have an incest taboo (Argentieri, 2005).

PERSPECTIVES ON THE INCEST TABOO   Speculations about the origin of incest taboos abound. One explanation holds that the incest taboo developed because it was adaptive for ancient humans to prevent the harmful effects of inbreeding that may result when genetic defects or diseases are carried within family bloodlines (Ellis & Bjorklund, 2005). Our ancient ancestors lacked knowledge of genetics, but they may have observed that certain health problems tended to run in families. Evidence suggests that the offspring of close relatives bear an increased rate of genetic diseases, mental retardation, and other physical abnormalities. Inbreeding may also be counterproductive to survival because it reduces genetic variation in the gene pool. Therefore, it can reduce the ability of the population to adapt to changes in the environment.

The incest taboo may also play a part in maintaining stability in the family and establishing kinship ties within the larger group (Argentieri, 2005). The anthropologist Bronislaw Malinowski (1927), for example, argued that the incest taboo reduces sexual competition within the family. If left uncontrolled, competition would create rivalry and hostility such that the family might be unable to function as a unit. Because the family unit fosters survival of a society, the incest taboo may have developed as a means of keeping the family intact.

TYPES OF INCEST   Most of our knowledge of incestuous relationships concerns father–daughter incest. Why? Most identified cases involve fathers who were eventually incarcerated.

incest

Marriage or sexual relations between people who are so closely related that sexual relations are prohibited and punishable by law.

7 › T / F Truth or Fiction Revisited About 1% of a sample of women in five American cities reported a sexual encounter with a father or stepfather (Anderson, 2006), but brother–sister incest, not parent–child incest, is the most common type of incest (Caffaro & Conn-Caffaro, 2005). Brother–sister incest is also believed to be greatly underreported, possibly because it tends to be transient and is apparently less harmful than parent–child incest. Finkelhor (1990) found that 21% of the college men in his sample and 39% of the college women reported incestuous relationships with a sibling of the other sex. Only 4% reported an incestuous relationship with their fathers. Mother–daughter incest is the least common form of incest, but it does occur (Bartolo, 2005; Turton, 2005).

Let us further consider the two most common incest patterns: father–daughter incest and brother–sister incest. Father–daughter incest often begins with affectionate cuddling or embraces and then progresses to teasing sexual play, lengthy caresses, hugs, kisses, and genital contact, even penetration (Crosson-Tower, 2015; Wodarski & Johnson, 2015). In some cases, genital contact occurs more abruptly, usually when the father has been drinking or has been arguing with his wife. Force is not typically used to gain compliance, but daughters are sometimes physically overcome and injured by their fathers.

In sibling incest, the brother usually initiates sexual activity and assumes the dominant role. One study reported that penetration was more frequent in brother–sister incest (71%) than in stepfather–stepdaughter incest (27%) or father–daughter incest (35%) (Cyr et al., 2002). Some younger brothers and sisters may view their sexual activity as natural experimentation or play and not realize it is taboo.

Evidence on the effects of incest between brothers and sisters is mixed. In a study of college undergraduates, those who reported childhood incest with siblings did not reveal greater evidence of sexual adjustment problems than other undergraduates (Greenwald & Leitenberg, 1989). Sibling incest is most likely to be harmful when it is forced or when parental response is harsh (Adams, 2007).

FAMILY FACTORS IN INCEST

> I didn't know what children did with their fathers. Mine told me that his nightly trips to my room for what he called "goodnight loves" were what every girl did with her father. I didn't want his groping touch, his hot breath that reeked of garlic and sometimes booze. I didn't want to keep those things that we did from my mother or brother. No, I didn't want to have my father tell me that I was special because I let him touch me. Let him? I didn't know that I had a choice.

> *Cited in Crosson-Tower, 2015, xvii*

Incest frequently occurs within the context of general family disruption, as in families in which there is spouse abuse, a dysfunctional marriage, or alcoholic or physically abusive parents (Welldon, 2005). Stressful events in the father's life, such as the loss of a job or problems at work, often precede the initiation of incest.

Fathers who abuse older daughters tend to be domineering and authoritarian with their families (Waterman, 1986). Fathers who abuse younger, preschool daughters are more likely to be passive, dependent, and low in self-esteem. As Waterman (1986) notes:

> [The fathers] may need soothing and comforting, and may feel especially safe with preschool children: "I felt safe with her .... I didn't have to perform. She was so little that I knew she wouldn't and couldn't hurt me." p. 215

Marriages in incestuous families tend to be characterized by an uneven power relationship between the spouses. The abusive father is usually dominant. Another thread that frequently runs through incestuous families is a troubled sexual relationship between the spouses. The wife often rejects the husband sexually (Crosson-Tower, 2015; Wodarski & Johnson, 2015).

A number of fathers who commit incest with their daughters are religiously devout, fundamentalist, and moralistic (Crosson-Tower, 2015; Wodarski & Johnson, 2015). Perhaps such men, when sexually frustrated, are less likely to seek extramarital and extrafamilial sexual outlets or to turn to masturbation as a sexual release. He turns to a daughter as a wife surrogate, often when he has been drinking alcohol. The daughter may become, in her father's fantasies, the "woman of the house." This fantasy may become his justification for continuing the incestuous relationship. In some incestuous families, a role reversal occurs. The abused daughter assumes many of the mother's responsibilities for managing the household and caring for the younger children.

Incestuous abuse is often repeated from generation to generation. One study found that in 154 cases of children who were sexually abused within the family, more than one-third of the male offenders and about one-half of the mothers had either been abused themselves or were exposed to abuse as children (Faller, 1989).

Effects of Sexual Abuse on Children

The effects of sexual abuse are variable, and there is no single identifiable syndrome that emerges from sexual abuse (Anderson, 2006; Resick, 2003). Nevertheless, sexual abuse often inflicts great psychological harm on the child, whether perpetrated by a family member, acquaintance, or stranger. Children who are sexually abused may suffer from a litany of short- and long-term psychological complaints, including anger, depression, anxiety, eating disorders, inappropriate sexual behavior, aggressive behavior, self-destructive behavior, sexual promiscuity, drug abuse, suicide attempts, posttraumatic stress disorder, low self-esteem, sexual dysfunction, mistrust of others, and feelings of detachment (Edwards et al., 2003). Sexual abuse may also have physical effects such as genital injuries and cause psychosomatic problems such as stomach aches and headaches.

Abused children commonly "act out." Younger children have tantrums or display aggressive or antisocial behavior. Older children turn to substance abuse (Anderson, 2006; Herrera & McCloskey, 2003). Some abused children become withdrawn and retreat into fantasy or refuse to leave the house. Regressive behaviors, such as thumb sucking, fear of the dark, and fear of strangers, are also common among sexually abused children. On the heels of the assault and in the ensuing years, many survivors of childhood sexual abuse—like many rape survivors—show signs of PTSD. They have flashbacks, nightmares, numbing of emotions, and feelings of estrangement from others (Herrera & McCloskey, 2003).

Sexual development of abused children may also become shaped in dysfunctional ways. The survivor may become prematurely sexually active or promiscuous in adolescence and adulthood (Anderson, 2006). Researchers find that adolescent girls who are sexually abused tend to have consensual sex at earlier ages than nonabused peers (Browning, 2002; Herrera & McCloskey, 2003).

Researchers generally find more similarities than differences between the sexes with respect to the effects of sexual abuse in childhood (Edwards et al., 2003). For example, both boys and girls tend to suffer fears and sleep disturbance. There are some sex differences, however. The most consistent sex difference appears to be that boys more often "externalize" their problems, perhaps by becoming more physically aggressive. Girls more often "internalize" their difficulties, as by becoming depressed (Anderson, 2006).

Late adolescence and early adulthood seem to pose especially difficult periods for survivors of childhood sexual abuse. Studies of women in these age groups

Critical Thinking
Why do you think that boys and girls tend to react differently to childhood sexual abuse?

reveal more psychological and social problems in abused women (Anderson, 2006; Herrera & McCloskey, 2003). Women who blame themselves for the abuse apparently have relatively lower self-esteem and more depression than those who do not (Edwards et al., 2003).

Prevention of Childhood Sexual Abuse

Many of us were taught by our parents never to accept a ride or an offer of candy from a stranger. However, many instances of sexual abuse are perpetrated by familiar adults, often a family member or friend (Zielbauer, 2000). Prevention programs help children understand what sexual abuse is and how they can avoid it. In addition to learning to avoid strangers, children need to recognize the differences between acceptable touching, as in an affectionate embrace or pat on the head, and unacceptable or "bad" touching. Even elementary-school–age children can learn the distinction between "good touching and bad touching." School-based programs can help prepare children to handle an actual encounter with a molester. Children who receive training are more likely to use strategies such as running away, yelling, or saying "no" when they are threatened by an abuser. They are also more likely to report incidents to adults.

How Do We Teach Children the Difference Between Good Touching, as We See Here, and Bad Touching? And how do we teach them what to do about bad touching?

Researchers recognize that children can easily be intimidated or overpowered by adults or older children (Miller, 2005). Children may be unable to say "no" in a sexually abusive situation, even though they want to and know it is the right thing to do. Although children may not always be able to prevent abuse, they can be encouraged to tell someone about it. Most prevention programs emphasize teaching children messages such as "It's not your fault," "Never keep a bad or scary secret," and "Always tell your parents about this, especially if someone says you shouldn't tell them."

Children also need to be alerted to the types of threats they might receive for disclosing the abuse. They are more likely to resist threats if they are reassured that they will be believed if they disclose the abuse, that their parents will continue to love them, and that they and their families will be protected from the molester.

School-based prevention programs focus on protecting the child. In most states, teachers and helping professionals are required to report suspected abuse to authorities. Tighter controls and better screening are needed to monitor the hiring of daycare employees. Administrators and teachers in preschool and daycare facilities also need to be educated to recognize the signs of sexual abuse and to report suspected cases. Treatment programs to help people who are sexually attracted to children *before* they commit abusive acts would also be of use.

Real Students, Real Questions

Q *Does being sexually abused as a child mean someone will sexually abuse their children?*

A It puts a person in a higher-risk category for abusing his or her own children. However, when one is an adult, child abuse is a choice and not a necessity based on one's history. Anyone who feels in danger of harming a child can search "Child Abuse Hotlines" for help and support.

Treatment of Survivors of Sexual Abuse

Because the majority of cases of sexual abuse go unreported during childhood, psychotherapy in adulthood can be the first opportunity for survivors to confront leftover feelings of pain, anger, and misplaced guilt (Finkelhor et al., 2005a). Group or individual therapy can help improve survivors' self-esteem and ability to develop intimate relationships. Social support is an important factor in helping survivors of childhood sexual abuse maintain their self-esteem and minimize the stress they experience (Hyman et al., 2003).

Many therapists recommend a comprehensive approach: individual therapy for the child, mother, and father; group therapy for the adolescent or even preadolescent survivor; art therapy or play therapy for the younger child (e.g., using drawings or puppets to express feelings); marital counseling for the parents; and family therapy for the entire family.

Treatment of Rapists and Child Molesters

LO 15.8 **Discuss the treatment options for treating rapists and child molesters.**

Treating offenders? Just what does *treatment* mean? When a helping professional treats someone, the goal is usually to help that individual. When we speak of treating a sex offender, the goal is as likely, or more likely, to be to help society by eliminating the problem behavior.

Rapists and child molesters are criminals, not patients. Most convicted rapists and child molesters are incarcerated as a form of punishment, not treatment. Some may receive psychological treatment or rehabilitation in prison to help prepare them for release and reentry into society, however. The most common form of treatment is group therapy, which is based on the belief that although offenders may fool counselors, they do not easily fool one another. Yet, most incarcerated sex offenders receive little or no treatment.

The results of prison-based treatment programs are mixed at best. Consider a Canadian study of 54 rapists who participated in a treatment program. Following release from prison, 28% were later convicted of a sexual offense, and 43% were convicted of a violent offense (Rice et al., 1990; Rice & Harris, 2011). Treatment also failed to curb recidivism among a sample of 136 child molesters (Rice & Harris, 2011).

More promising findings may result from programs incorporating cognitive-behavioral techniques such as empathy training and covert sensitization (Ho & Ross, 2012). Empathy training is intended to increase the offender's sensitivity to his victims. One empathy exercise had offenders write about their crimes from the perspective of the victim. Covert sensitization can be used to help offenders resist deviant sex fantasies, which often lead to deviant behavior. The offender would pair, in his imagination, scenes involving rape and molestation with aversive consequences. A child molester might fantasize about sexually approaching a child, only to find himself confronted by police officers. However, "the jury is out" on the effectiveness of cognitive-behavioral—or any other psychological—treatment of sex offenders (Ho & Ross, 2012).

Castration—Surgical and Chemical

Pavel sought surgical castration; most others do not. But in a few places—including the state of Louisiana—it may be required by law for certain sex offenses. The Council of Europe's anti-torture committee has called surgical castration "invasive,

Critical Thinking
Agree or disagree with the following statement, and support your answer: We should punish sex offenders and not worry about "treating" them.

irreversible, and mutilating." Nevertheless, the Czech Republic has allowed some 94 sex offenders to be surgically castrated over the past decade, and is, for now, the only European country that uses the procedure. European countries are now debating use of chemical or surgical castration for some sex offenders (Bilefsky, 2009).

Castration reduces testosterone levels and, consequently, offenders' sex drives. Despite the case of Pavel, experts do not agree on whether castration helps sex offenders control their sexual urges (Rice & Harris, 2011). Many castrated rapists report lowered sex drives, as might be expected from the reductions in testosterone production that result from the removal of the testes. They may retain sexual interest and remain capable of erection, however. And some do repeat their crimes. Other researchers report lower recidivism rates among castrated offenders than among other offenders.

Surgical castration is an extreme measure. It raises ethical concerns because of its invasive character and irreversibility (Phenix & Hoberman, 2016). Anti-androgen drugs such as Depo-Provera chemically reduce testosterone levels (Phenix & Hoberman, 2016). Unlike surgical castration, "chemical castration"—via anti-androgen drugs—is reversible (Phenix & Hoberman, 2016). A typical study showed that anti-androgen drugs decreased pedophilic fantasies and masturbation to pedophilic fantasies in a group of incarcerated offenders (Schober et al., 2005). However, there was no reason to believe that the offenders would voluntarily use such drugs after their release.

Sexual Harassment

LO 15.9 **Discuss the various kinds of sexual harassment.**

Sexual harassment occurs everywhere: in schools and colleges, in the workplace, in the military, and, of course, online., as in cases of bullying and cyberbullying that have led teenage victims to commit suicide. Even so, **sexual harassment** can be difficult to define, although sexual harassment in the workplace is usually defined as deliberate or repeated unwanted comments, gestures, or physical contact (Phenix & Hoberman, 2016). The University Counseling & Testing Center (2016) of the University of Oregon lists the following types of sexual harassment, which make the school, workplace, or other setting a hostile place:

1. Gender Harassment: Sexist remarks and behavior that communicate insulting and degrading attitudes toward women. Also includes offensive graffiti, dirty jokes, and general comments about sex or women.
2. Attempts at Seduction: Unwanted and inappropriate sexual advances, such as repeated sexual invitations, letters, emails, texts, and phone calls.
3. Bribery: Seeking sexual activity in exchange for rewards or the promise of rewards.
4. Sexual Coercion: Forcing sexual behavior through threat of punishment, as in threatening bad job performance evaluations, withholding promotions, or being fired.
5. Physical Sexual Coercion: Forced touching, rubbing, grabbing, or outright sexual assault.

Men or women can both commit, and be subjected to, sexual harassment. However, an astonishing 99% of adult harassers are men (see Table 15.2; University Counseling & Testing Center, 2016). In middle school and high school, larger numbers of sexual harassers and bulliers are female. Moreover, adult males are sexually harassed, and incidents are painful and not to be trivialized (Holland et al., 2015).

Sexual Harassment in the Academic Setting

Sexual harassment starts early, even in middle school (Gruber & Fineran, 2015; Rinehart and Espelage, 2015). Surveys of middle school and high school students—even

sexual harassment

Deliberate or repeated unsolicited verbal comments, gestures, or physical contact of a sexual nature that is considered to be unwelcome by the recipient.

Critical Thinking

What would be the response of a critical thinker to the following argument: Because of all the publicity, people who are intolerant of normal sexual advances, or who want to punish their supervisors, are now crying sexual harassment.

Table 15.2 Sexual Harassment: Myths and Realities.

Myths	Realities
Sexual harassment is rare.	Sexual harassment is extremely widespread. It touches the lives of 40% to 60% of working women, and similar proportions of female students in colleges and universities.
The seriousness of sexual harassment has been exaggerated; most so-called harassment is really trivial and harmless flirtation.	Sexual harassment can be devastating. Studies indicate that most harassment has nothing to do with "flirtation" or sincere sexual or social interest. Rather, it is offensive, often frightening, and insulting to women. Research shows that women are often forced to leave school or jobs to avoid harassment; many experience serious psychological and health-related problems.
Many women make up and report stories of sexual harassment to get back at their employers or others who have angered them.	Research shows that fewer than 1% of complaints are false. Women rarely file false complaints. Women rarely file complaints even when they are justified in doing so.
Women who are sexually harassed generally provoke harassment by the way they look, dress, and behave.	Harassment does not occur because women dress provocatively or initiate sexual activity in the hope of getting promoted and advancing their careers. Studies have found that victims of sexual harassment vary in physical appearance, type of dress, age, and behavior. The only thing they have in common is that more than 99% of them are female.
If you ignore harassment, it will go away.	Harassment does not go away if it is ignored. Research has shown that simply ignoring the behavior is ineffective; harassers generally will not stop on their own. Ignoring such behavior may even be seen as agreement or encouragement.

SOURCE: University Counseling & Testing Center (2016).

elementary school students!—find that many boys and girls had encountered harassment in the form of others grabbing or groping them or subjecting them to sexually explicit putdowns when walking through school hallways (Gådin, 2012; Rahimi & Liston, 2012). Sexual taunts and advances have become part of an unwelcome ritual for many students, especially girls, in trying to make their way through the hallways and stairwells of high schools. Early maturing girls are especially likely to be victimized because late-maturing girls may be jealous, boys of the same age are much less mature, and older boys may see them as socially immature and ripe for picking (Skoog & Ozdemire, 2015).

Many harassers and victims view harassment as "just part of school life" and "no big deal." Many girls who experience sexual harassment at school report that it made them feel that they didn't want to go to school. Some say it makes it more difficult to pay attention in class and lowers their grades.

SEX IN A WORLD OF DIVERSITY

LGBT YOUTH AND SEXUAL HARASSMENT IN THE SCHOOLS

Although early-maturing girls may be special targets for unwanted touching in the schools, LGBT youth are more likely to be targeted for verbal harassment and remarks, and physical violence, according to the National School Climate Surveys (e.g., Kosciw et al., 2014). In the survey reported in 2014:

- Three of four (74%) of LGBT students were verbally harassed—either called names or threatened—in the past year because of their sexual orientation
- Two of three (65%–71%) LGBT students heard homophobic remarks and terms, such as "dyke" and "faggot"
- More than half (55%) of transgendered ("trans") students reported being verbally harassed because of the expression of their gender identity
- More than one in three (36%) were pushed or shoved because of their sexual orientation
- Half (49%) were victims of cyberbullying via Facebook postings or the receipt of text messages
- Three of five (62%) LGBT students who reported an incident to the school said that the school did nothing to help
- Approximately three in five LGBT students reported missing school as a result of the hostile school environment.

A protest against sexual harassment in Egypt.

Estimates of the frequency of sexual harassment of college students vary widely across studies. Overall, 25% to 30% of students report at least one incident of sexual harassment in college, and males are overwhelmingly more likely than females to commit sexual harassment (Wright & Bonita, 2012). The federal law prohibiting sex discrimination in academic institutions permits students to sue their schools for monetary damages for sexual harassment.

Sexual harassment on campus usually involves the less severe forms of harassment, such as sexist comments and sexual remarks, as well as come-ons, suggestive looks, propositions, and light touching (Wright & Bonita, 2012). Relatively few acts involve the use of direct pressure for sexual intercourse. Most students who encounter sexual harassment do not report the incident. If they do, it is usually to a confidant and not a person in authority.

Most forms of harassment involve unequal power relationships between the harasser and the person harassed (Ainsworth & Baumeister, 2012). *Peer harassment* involves cases between people who are equal in power, as in the cases of repeated sexual taunts from fellow employees, students, or colleagues. In some cases, the harasser may even have less formal power than the person harassed. Women professors have been sexually harassed by students, but the traditional social dominance of the male may override the academic position of the woman—at least in the mind of the offender.

One common form of harassment by students, reported by nearly one-third of the female professors polled in one survey, involves sexist remarks (Wright & Bonita, 2012). Other common forms of harassment include obscene phone calls and undue attention.

College women's grades suffer (Huerta et al., 2006) as a result of sexual harassment in the form of unwanted sexual approaches and comments. College women have dropped courses, switched majors, even medical residency programs to avoid sexual harassment (Huerta et al., 2006; Stratton et al., 2005).

African American female college faculty often respond to sexual harassment with silence (Pitt et al., 2015). Jenelle Pitt and her colleagues (2015) note that "Rather than disclose incidents of sexual harassment out of fear of retribution, retaliation, beliefs that the harasser will go unpunished, risk of being ostracized or labeled a troublemaker, or being viewed as a victim, Black women often deal with the issue of sexual harassment in silence, by leaving the organization, or tolerating the behaviors" (p. 217).

Sexual Harassment in the Workplace

Harassers in the workplace can be employers, supervisors, coworkers, or clients of a company. In some cases, clients make unwelcome sexual advances to employees that are ignored or approved of by the boss. If a worker asks a coworker for a date and is refused, it is not sexual harassment. If the coworker persists with unwelcome advances and does not take no for an answer, however, the behavior crosses the line and becomes harassment.

Perhaps the most severe form of sexual harassment, short of an outright assault, involves an employer or supervisor who demands sexual favors as a condition of employment or advancement (Stout, 2011). The definition of sexual harassment in the workplace includes any behavior of a sexual nature that interferes with an individual's work performance or creates a hostile, intimidating, or offensive work environment.

The U.S. Supreme Court has recognized sexual harassment as a form of sex discrimination under Title VII of the Civil Rights Act of 1964. It holds that employers can be held accountable if such behavior was deemed to create a hostile or abusive work environment or to interfere with an employee's work performance. A unanimous 1993 Supreme Court ruling held that a person need not suffer psychological damage to sue an employer on grounds of sexual harassment. Moreover, employers can be held responsible not only for their own actions but also for sexual harassment by their employees when they either knew *or should have known* that harassment was taking place and failed to eliminate it promptly (Resnik, 2011). To protect themselves, many companies and universities have developed programs to educate workers about sexual harassment, established mechanisms for dealing with complaints, and imposed sanctions against harassers.

Under the law, persons subjected to sexual harassment can obtain a court order to have the harassment stopped, have their jobs reinstated (when they have lost them by resisting sexual advances), receive back pay and lost benefits, and obtain monetary awards for the emotional strain imposed by the harassment. However, proving charges of sexual harassment is generally difficult because there are usually no corroborating witnesses or evidence. As a result, relatively few people who encounter sexual harassment in the workplace file formal complaints or seek legal remedies. Like people subjected to other forms of sexual coercion, those experiencing sexual harassment often do not report the offense for fear that they will not be believed or will be subjected to retaliation. Some fear that they will be branded as "troublemakers" or lose their jobs.

Trivialization of Sexual Harassment and Blaming the Victim

Charges of sexual harassment are often ignored or trivialized by school officials, co-workers, and employers. The victim may hear, "Why make a big deal out of it? It's not like you were attacked in the street." Evidence shows, however, that people subjected to sexual harassment do suffer from it. Some become physically ill (Holland & Cortina, 2016). Others report anxiety, irritability, lowered self-esteem, and anger. Some find harassment on the job so unbearable that they resign (Sims et al., 2005).

One reason that sexual harassment is so stressful is that, as with so many other forms of sexual exploitation or coercion, the blame tends to fall on the victim. Some harassers seem to believe that charges of harassment were exaggerated or that the victim "overreacted" or "took me too seriously." In our society, women are expected to be "nice"—to be passive and not "make a scene." The woman who assertively protects her rights may be seen as "strange" and disturbing, or a "troublemaker." "Women are damned if they assert themselves and victimized if they don't" (Chaiyavej & Morash, 2009; Holland & Cortina, 2016; Pitt et al., 2015).

Sexual harassment sometimes has more to do with the abuse of power than sexual desire (Chaiyavej & Morash, 2009). Relatively few cases of sexual harassment involve outright requests for sexual favors. Most involve the expression of power as a tactic to control or frighten someone, usually a woman. The harasser is usually in a dominant position and abuses that position by exploiting the victim's vulnerability. Sexual harassment may be used as a tactic of social control. It may be a means of keeping women "in their place." This is especially so in work settings that are traditional male preserves, such as the firehouse, the police department, the construction site, or the military academy—even in certain areas of medical practice, such as surgery (Stratton et al., 2005). Sexual harassment can be a way of expressing resentment and hostility toward women who venture beyond the boundaries of the traditional feminine role.

Sexual harassment is not confined to the workplace or the university. It may also occur between patients and doctors and between therapists and clients. Therapists may use their power and influence to pressure clients into sexual relations. The harassment may be disguised, expressed in terms of the "therapeutic benefits" of sexual activity.

How to Resist Sexual Harassment

LO 15.10 Explain things victims of sexual harassment can do to protect themselves.

What would you do if you were sexually harassed by an employer or a professor? How would you handle it? Would you try to ignore it and hope that it would stop? Here are some suggestions that may be helpful. Recognize, however, that responsibility for sexual harassment always lies with the perpetrator and the organization that permits sexual harassment to take place, not with the victim.

- *Convey a professional attitude.* Harassment may be stopped cold by responding to the harasser with a businesslike, professional attitude.

- *Discourage harassing behavior, and encourage appropriate behavior.* Harassment may also be stopped cold by shaping the harasser's behavior. Your reactions to the harasser may encourage businesslike behavior and discourage flirtatious or suggestive behavior. If a harassing professor suggests that you come back after school to review your term paper so that the two of you will be undisturbed, set limits assertively. Tell the professor that you'd feel more comfortable discussing the paper during regular office hours. Remain task-oriented. Stick to business. The harasser should quickly get the message that you wish to maintain a strictly professional relationship. If the harasser persists, do not blame yourself. You are responsible only for your own actions. When the harasser persists, a more direct response may be appropriate: "Professor Jones, I'd like to keep our relationship on a purely professional basis, okay?"

- *Avoid being alone with the harasser.* If you are being harassed by your professor but need some advice about preparing your term paper, approach him or her after class when other students are milling about, not privately during office hours. Or bring a friend to wait outside the office while you consult the professor.

- *Maintain a record.* Keep a record of all incidents of harassment as documentation in the event you decide to lodge an official complaint. The record should include the following: (1) where the incident took place; (2) the date and time; (3) what happened, including the exact words that were used, if you can recall them; (4) how you felt; and (5) the names of witnesses. Some people who have been subjected to sexual harassment have carried a hidden tape recorder during contacts with the harasser. Such recordings may not be admissible in a court of law, but they are persuasive in organizational grievance procedures. A hidden tape recorder may be illegal in your state, however. It is thus advisable to check the law.

- *Talk with the harasser.* It may be uncomfortable to address the issue directly with a harasser, but doing so puts the offender on notice that you are aware of the harassment and want it to stop. It may be helpful to frame your approach in terms of a description of the specific offending actions (e.g., "When we were alone in the office, you repeatedly attempted to touch me or brush up against me"); your feelings about the offending behavior ("It made me feel like my privacy was being violated. I'm very upset about this and haven't been sleeping well"); and what you would like the offender to do ("So I'd like you to agree never to attempt to touch me again"). Having a talk with the harasser may stop the harassment. If the harasser denies the accusations, it may be necessary to take further action.

- *Write a letter to the harasser.* Set down on paper a record of the offending behavior, and put the harasser on notice that the harassment must stop. Your letter might (1) describe what happened ("Several times you have made sexist comments about my body"); (2) describe how you feel ("It made me feel like a sexual object when you talked to me that way"); and (3) describe what you would like the harasser to do ("I want you to stop making sexist comments to me").

- *Seek support.* Support from people you trust can help you through the often trying process of resisting sexual harassment. Talking with others allows you to express your feelings and receive emotional support, encouragement, and advice. In addition, it may strengthen your case if you have the opportunity to identify and talk with other people who have been harassed by the offender.

- *File a complaint.* Companies and organizations are required by law to respond reasonably to complaints of sexual harassment. In large organizations, a designated official (sometimes an ombudsman, affirmative action officer, or sexual harassment advisor) is usually charged to handle such complaints. Set up an appointment with this official to discuss your experiences. Ask about the grievance procedures in the organization and your right to confidentiality. Have available a record of the dates of the incidents, what happened, how you felt about it, and so on. The two major government agencies that handle charges of sexual harassment are the Equal Employment Opportunity Commission (look under the government section of your phone book for the telephone number of the nearest office) and your state's Human Rights Commission (listed in your phone book under state or municipal government). These agencies may offer advice on how you can protect your legal rights and proceed with a formal complaint.

- *Seek legal remedies.* Sexual harassment is illegal and actionable. If you are considering legal action, consult an attorney familiar with this area of law. You may be entitled to back pay (if you were fired for reasons arising from the sexual harassment), job reinstatement, and punitive damages.

In closing, we ask not what people who suffer rape, incest, and sexual harassment will do to redress the harm that has been done to them. We ask what all of us will do to reshape our society so that sex is no longer used as an instrument of power, coercion, and violence.

Chapter Review

LO 15.1 Define rape.

The perpetrator of forcible rape coerces a nonconsenting person into sexual activity. Most states do not require actual penetration of the vagina or anus as part of the definition. Statutory rape involves sex with a willing person who is unable to provide consent, as in being too young.

LO 15.2 Describe the various kinds of rape, focusing on rape in college.

Types of rapes include stranger rape, acquaintance rape, partner rape, gang rape, male rape, and rape by females. Women are more likely to be raped by men they know than by strangers. One in five college women reports being raped in college.

LO 15.3 Explain how our culture encourages people to blame the victim of rape and socializes men into becoming sexually aggressive.

Social attitudes such as gender-role stereotyping, seeing sex as adversarial, and acceptance of violence in interpersonal relationships help create a climate that encourages rape. Rape myths also blame the victim for engaging in behaviors such as flirting, dressing provocatively, and drinking alcohol. Social critics also argue that our society breeds rapists by encouraging males to play socially dominant roles.

LO 15.4 Discuss the kinds of rapists and their personalities.

Sexually aggressive men are more likely than other men to condone rape and violence against women, have traditional gender-role attitudes, be hostile toward women, use sex as a way of expressing social dominance, lack empathy, and have peers that pressure them into sexual activity.

LO 15.5 Discuss the effects of rape on survivors.

Rape survivors often experience crisis and stress disorders. Treatment of survivors typically involves supporting them through the crisis and then helping foster long-term adjustment.

LO 15.6 Discuss ways of preventing rape, including college prevention programs and Internet apps.

There are many avenues of rape prevention, including mandatory workshops in colleges, avoiding drinking to excess at get-togethers, taking precautions in one's neighborhood, being specific and assertive when saying "no," using a rape-prevention app, and promoting broad societal change through legal action, education of public officials, and public demonstrations, such as the SlutWalk marches.

LO 15.7 Discuss the origins and effects of sexual child abuse.

Any sexual contact between an adult and a child is abusive because children are legally incapable of providing consent. In most cases, molesters are close to the children they abuse—relatives, step-relatives, family friends, neighbors. Genital fondling is the most common type of abuse. Pedophiles are almost exclusively male. Father–daughter incest is most likely to be reported and prosecuted, but brother–sister incest is most common. Children who are sexually abused often suffer social and emotional problems, affecting their self-esteem and their formation of intimate relationships. Children need to be taught the difference between acceptable touching and "bad" touching.

LO 15.8 Discuss the treatment options for treating rapists and child molesters.

Methods include prison-based rehabilitation programs, often in the form of group therapy, and chemical castration (via anti-androgen drugs) or surgical castration.

LO 15.9 Discuss the various kinds of sexual harassment.

Sexual harassment involves unwanted sexual comments, gestures, or contact. It is often an expression of unequal power relationships. It may be used as a weapon to keep women "in their place," especially in work settings that are traditional male preserves.

LO 15.10 Explain things victims of sexual harassment can do to protect themselves.

Victims of sexual harassment can convey a professional attitude to the harasser, avoid being alone with him, keep a record of instances, write a letter to the harasser that outlines unwanted behaviors, file a complaint, and seek legal remedies.

Test Your Learning

1. All forms of sexual activity between adults and children are coercive because _____
   - **(a)** the children resist.
   - **(b)** the adults need to dominate the children.
   - **(c)** children are hurt by sexual activity.
   - **(d)** children are younger than the age of consent.

2. Which of the following is *not* a reason why the incidence of rape is underreported?
   - **(a)** Some women fear that they will be humiliated by the criminal justice system.
   - **(b)** Some women fear reprisal from their families or the rapist.
   - **(c)** Some women assume that the offender will not be caught or prosecuted.
   - **(d)** Some women are raped by strangers.

3. The most common type of rape is _____
   - **(a)** rape by an acquaintance.
   - **(b)** rape by a stranger.
   - **(c)** marital rape.
   - **(d)** rape by females.

4. Which one of the following is *not* a cultural myth that encourages rape?
   - **(a)** Women say "no" when they mean "yes."
   - **(b)** When women dress provocatively, they are asking to be raped.
   - **(c)** Women do not wish to be forced into sexual activity.
   - **(d)** Women want a truly masculine, sexually aggressive man.

5. Pedophiles often _____
   - **(a)** rape adult victims.
   - **(b)** seek treatment on their own.
   - **(c)** deny that sex is harmful to the child.
   - **(d)** come from liberal backgrounds.

6. Which of the following is the most common form of child sexual abuse?
   - **(a)** Exhibitionism
   - **(b)** Genital fondling
   - **(c)** Oral–genital sex
   - **(d)** Sexual intercourse

7. The *Washington Post* poll found that one woman in _____ had been raped when a college student.
   - **(a)** four
   - **(b)** five,
   - **(c)** ten
   - **(d)** fifty

8. Rohypnol functions as a "date rape" drug because it _____
   - **(a)** can cause forgetfulness.
   - **(b)** is an aphrodisiac.
   - **(c)** multiplies the effects of testosterone.
   - **(d)** encourages women to recall consensual sex as an assault.

9. On-campus rape-prevention programs focus on increasing male students' _____
   - **(a)** academic interests.
   - **(b)** competitiveness.
   - **(c)** interest in sports.
   - **(d)** empathy.

10. Many participants engage in SlutWalk events to show that rape is caused by _____
    - **(a)** flirting.
    - **(b)** provocative dress or partial nudity.
    - **(c)** rapists.
    - **(d)** drinking alcohol.

Chapter 16
Selling Sex

Learning Objectives

Prostitution

LO 16.1 Define prostitution and sex work.

LO 16.2 Summarize what we know about female and male sex workers, including their backgrounds.

LO 16.3 Discuss the relationship between sex work and sexually transmitted infections (STIs).

Pornography

LO 16.4 Define pornography.

LO 16.5 Describe the legal status of pornography.

LO 16.6 Discuss the incidence and use of pornography.

LO 16.7 Discuss gender differences in response to pornography.

LO 16.8 Discuss possible relationships between pornography and violence against women.

Which of the following statements are the truth, and which are fiction? Look for the Truth-or-Fiction items throughout this chapter to find the answers.

1 Prostitution is illegal throughout the United States. **T / F**?

2 The massage and escort services advertised in the Yellow Pages are fronts for prostitution. **T / F**?

3 Most female prostitutes were sexually abused as children. **T / F**?

4 Typical customers of prostitutes have difficulty forming sexual relationships with other women. **T / F**?

5 Only males are sexually aroused by pornography. **T / F**?

6 Pornography causes violence against women. **T / F**?

Millions, perhaps billions, of men (and some women) have paid for sex through the ages. In the caverns of Wall Street, brokers and traders sell stocks and other financial instruments that drive the nation's commercial enterprises. On the floor of Chicago's Board of Trade, brokers trade commodities—soybeans, corn, wheat, and other goods. Prices go up, prices go down, responding to the law of supply and demand. On street corners a few short blocks from these financial institutions another sort of commerce takes place. In New York City and Chicago, as in Hollywood and in the nation's smaller towns and villages, prostitutes—also referred to as *sex workers*—exchange sex for money or for goods such as drugs.

Sex as commerce runs the gamut from adult bookshops to strip clubs, brothels, escort/outcall services, streetwalkers, some "massage parlors," some "tanning salons," cybersex (e.g., sex over the Internet), sex shops, and the use of sex appeal in advertisements for products.

Prostitution and Sex Work

LO 16.1 **Define prostitution and sex work.**

Although **prostitution**, is illegal throughout most of the United States, it is legal in our neighbors, Canada and parts of Mexico, in most countries in Europe, and in many other countries throughout the world.

> **1 › T / F Truth or Fiction Revisited** Prostitution is illegal everywhere in the United States except for some rural counties in Nevada, where it is restricted to state-licensed brothels.

Prostitution is a form of the broader category of **sex work**. Prostitutes sell sexual activity. That is prostitutes engage in body-to-body contact with customers; the contact can be sexual intercourse, oral sex, manual sex (a "hand job"), or even a "foot job." Consumers may also simply wish to fondle prostitutes. All sex work involves the sexual arousal or sexual release of others in exchange for money or other goods of value. But the term sex work also applies to strip tease, to erotic dancing, to "acting" in live sex shows, films, and videos, appearing in pornographic magazines, and sexual surrogates, who may engage in sexual activity with clients as part of sex therapy. Erotic massage can be said to occupy a middle ground in that the sex workers may provide manual release but not undress with clients or allow clients to touch them.

Having made this distinction—or having attempted to make this distinction—let us note that many prostitutes, along with many social commentators and researchers,

prostitution
The sale of sexual activity for money or other goods of value.

sex work
The exchange of various sexual activities for money, such as prostitution, strip tease, erotic dancing, engaging in live sex shows, acting in pornographic magazines and videos, and erotic massage.

have redefined prostitution itself as sex work (Jewkes et al., 2012). Prostitutes have argued that what they do is in fact work and should be accepted as such by society rather than vilified. They would not have their jobs if they were not filling a social need.

In any event, soliciting a prostitute is also illegal in many states, but police rarely crack down on customers, who are often referred to as "johns." Why "johns"? Why not "johns" and janes"? The reason is that most prostitutes are female and virtually all customers are male.

The few customers who are arrested are usually penalized with a small fine (Bennetts, 2011). Melissa Farley, who researches sex work, reports that "for every john arrested for attempting to buy sex, there are up to 50 women in prostitution arrested." On occasion, the names of convicted johns are published in local newspapers to deter men who fear publicity.

Prostitution is often called "the world's oldest profession"—for good reason. (Norma Ramos, 2012, executive director of the Coalition Against Trafficking in Women, who sees sex work as the exploitation of women, comments that sex work "is the world's oldest *oppression*.") Prostitution can be traced at least to ancient Mesopotamia, where temple prostitution flourished. The Greek historian Herodotus noted that all women in the city were expected to put in some time at the temple. They would offer their bodies to passers-by who would make a "religious" donation.

Prostitution flourished in medieval Europe and during the sexually repressive Victorian era. Then, as now, the major motive for the sex workers was Maureen's motive: economic. Many poor women were—and are—drawn to sex work as a means of survival. In Victorian England, it was widely held that women did not enjoy sex. Therefore, it was better for a man to visit a prostitute than "soil" his wife with his carnal passions.

In the nineteenth-century United States, married and single men frequented prostitutes regularly. Use of prostitution cut across all economic and social boundaries. Prostitution most often occurred within two contexts, sexual initiation for males and regular brothel visitation.

Incidence of Prostitution in the United States

LO 16.2 Summarize what we know about female and male sex workers, including their backgrounds.

There are hundreds of thousands of prostitutes in the United States, but no one has an exact number. Prostitutes are found in the streets, in brothels, in adult films, on the Internet, in the phone book, and in classified ads. Geographically speaking, they are found in every state (Dank et al., 2014).

Almost two-thirds of the European American males in Kinsey's sample (Kinsey et al., 1948) reported visiting a prostitute at least once. About 15% to 20% did so regularly. The use of prostitutes varied with educational level. By age 20, about half of Kinsey's non-college-educated single males, but only one-fifth of his college-educated males, had visited a prostitute.

Kinsey's data foreshadowed some falling off of experience with prostitutes that seems linked to the decay of the sexual double standard. Young men in recent generations appear to be less likely to visit prostitutes because they are more likely to become sexually initiated with their girlfriends. Interestingly, concern about sexually transmitted infections (STIs), especially HIV/AIDS, has not markedly reduced the clientele of prostitutes around the world (Hood, 2015; Kawaguchi, 2015). Prostitution continues to flourish.

Female Prostitutes

Female prostitutes—commonly called *hookers, whores, working girls, masseuses* (although state-certified masseuses run legitimate businesses), or *escorts*—are usually classified according to the settings in which they work. The major types of prostitutes today are streetwalkers; brothel or "house" prostitutes, many of whom work in massage parlors; and "escorts" or call girls. Many prostitutes today advertise their wares online, in newspaper ads (where they often say they offer massage), or have their customers "let their fingers do the walking" through the Yellow Pages, where, in some cities, there are multiple pages of escort services and massage parlors.

STREETWALKERS Streetwalkers occupy the bottom rung in the hierarchy of prostitutes. They earn the lowest incomes and are usually considered to be the least desirable or attractive. They also incur the greatest risk of abuse by customers and **pimps**. Streetwalkers tend to come from poverty and to have had unhappy childhoods (Kristof, 2009; Dodge, 2012). Many are survivors of rape, sexual abuse, or incest (Beech et al., 2009; Lloyd, 2012). Many are teenage runaways who turn to drugs and prostitution to survive (Dodge, 2012). Many—in some locales, most—are addicted to drugs (Dank et al., 2014). Some charge as little as $5 for oral sex, although $15 to $25 is a more common figure (Dank et al., 2014). They tend to be U.S. citizens rather than being trafficked in from Europe or Asia.

Streetwalkers operate in the open. They are thus more likely than other prostitutes to draw attention to themselves and risk arrest (Kristof, 2009; McKeganey, 2006). To avoid arrest, streetwalkers may be indirect about their services. They may ask passers-by if they are interested in a "good time" or some "fun" rather than sex per se. In many cities, streetwalkers dress in revealing or provocative fashions. Many cities throughout the United States, Europe, and elsewhere have "red light districts" or "tolerance zones" where prostitutes ply their trade with relatively little interference from police (Miller, 2012).

In most locales, penalties for prostitution involve small fines or short jail terms. Many police departments, besieged by crimes such as drug peddling and violent crimes, consider prostitution a "minor" or "nuisance" crime. Generally, prostitutes

streetwalkers

Sex workers who solicit customers on the streets.

pimps

Men who serve as agents for sex workers and live off their earnings.

Streetwalkers. Male tourists shopping streetwalkers in Pattaya, Thailand.

find the criminal justice system a revolving door. They pay the fine. They spend a night or two in jail. They return to the streets.

A bar prostitute is a variation of the streetwalker. She approaches men in a bar she frequents, rather than on the streets. Payoffs to bar owners or managers secure their cooperation, although the women are sometimes tolerated because they draw customers. Some streetwalkers work in X-rated, or "adult," movie houses and may service their patrons in their seats with manual or oral sex. Payoffs may secure the cooperation of the management.

About 40% to 50% of streetwalkers support a pimp (Dank et al., 2014). A pimp acts as lover-father-companion-master. He provides streetwalkers with protection, bail, and sometimes room and board, in exchange for a high percentage of their earnings. Still, prostitutes are often physically abused by their pimps, who may use threats and beatings as means of control (Nussbaum, 2012). Pimp-controlled prostitutes are more likely than their peers to come from dysfunctional families, to be poorly educated, never to have held legitimate jobs, and to come from racial minority groups (Nussbaum, 2012).

For many streetwalkers, "the life" is a round of sex, violence, disease, and drugs, including cocaine and heroin (Dank et al., 2014). Many street prostitutes feel powerless to control their own fates and are often talked into oral or vaginal sex without protection. Given these realities, streetwalkers do not stay in "the life" very long. Some make the transition to a more traditional life or get married. Others die young from drug abuse, disease, suicide, or physical abuse from pimps or customers (Lloyd, 2012; Love, 2015). Those who survive become less marketable with age. Rachel Lloyd, who as a teenager worked as a prostitute in Germany, where sex work is legal, writes that "Violence is inherent in the sex industry. Numerous studies show that between 70 percent and 90 percent of children and women who end up in commercial sex were sexually abused prior to entry. No other industry is dependent upon a regular supply of victims of trauma and abuse" (Lloyd, 2012).

Researchers also find a high level of psychological disturbance among prostitutes, especially female streetwalkers (Love, 2015; Robitz et al., 2015). Melissa Farley and her colleagues (2005) interviewed 100 prostitutes in Canada. They found that:

- Eighty-two percent had a history of childhood sexual abuse.
- Seventy-two percent had a history of childhood physical abuse.

- Ninety percent had been physically assaulted on the job.

- Seventy-eight percent had been raped on the job.

- Seventy-two percent could be diagnosed with **posttraumatic stress disorder (PTSD)**.

Only 5% of the general population has PTSD, and only 20 to 30% of combat veterans have the disorder. The prostitutes also developed many health problems (other than STIs). From 90 to 95% said that they wanted to get out of "the life" (Farley et al., 2005). However, many who exit the life find themselves back in for financial and social reasons (Ramos, 2012).

Streetwalkers who work in hotels and conventions generally have higher status than those who work on the streets or bars. Clients are typically traveling conventioneers or businessmen. The hotel prostitute must be skilled in conveying subtle messages to potential clients without drawing the attention of hotel management or security. They usually provide sexual services in the client's hotel room. Some hotel managers will tolerate known prostitutes (usually for a payoff under the table), so long as the woman conducts herself discreetly.

BROTHELS   Many brothel prostitutes occupy a middle status in the hierarchy of sex workers, between streetwalkers on one end and call girls on the other. They work in a brothel, or in a massage parlor (Parent & Bruckert, 2005). The ethnic backgrounds of brothel prostitutes tend to vary in different cities. Many in Miami, Dallas, and Washington, D.C. are Latina women; in Denver they are as likely to be Asian as Latina (Dank et al., 2014).

The life of the brothel (or "house") prostitute is usually neither as lucrative as that of the call girl nor as degrading as that of the streetwalker. Some prostitutes in massage parlors or working for escort services may not consider themselves to be "real prostitutes" because they do not walk the streets and because they work for businesses that present a legitimate front. *Cathouse, bordello, cat wagon, parlor house, whorehouse, joy house, sport house, house of ill repute*—these are but a handful of the names given to houses in which prostitutes work. The heyday of the brothel may well be over in the United States. Formal brothels are rare, except in Nevada, where they are legal but regulated. Brothel prostitutes split their fees with management. In addition to their "split," they receive free room and board. They are on duty 3 weeks a month and on call 24 hours a day during that time. When a customer arrives, they step into the living room "lineup." After one has been chosen, they wait again, resting, reading, or watching television.

Barbara Brents, a sociology professor at the University of Nevada, has studied brothel prostitution in Nevada for 15 years. She writes, "In legal brothels, employees report that they feel safe, are free to come and go, and are bound only by their contract. Of the brothel workers we surveyed, 84 percent said that their job felt safe. Workers report that they felt safe largely because the police, employers and co-workers were there to protect them" (Brents, 2012).

Of course some brothel prostitutes lead lives of degradation. Many poor Asian, East European, and African women are kidnapped or lured to the big city or to the West by promises of the good life (Kristof, 2006; Unigwe, 2012).

In *On Black Sisters Street*, Chika Unigwe (2011) describes the experiences of several African women who are trafficked to brothels in Western Europe. Dele, the trafficker, and the women are from Nigeria. Dele tells one of them, "Every month I send gals to Europe. Antwerp. Milan. Madrid. My gals dey there. Every month, four gals. Sometimes five or more," he boasts to Sisi when she first visits his office. "You be fine gal now. Abi, see your backside, kai! Who talk say na dat Jennifer Lopez get the finest *nyansh*? … As for those melons wey you carry for chest, omo, how you no go fin' work?" (Unigwe, 2011).

posttraumatic stress disorder (PTSD)

A stress reaction brought on by flashbacks in the form of disturbing dreams or intrusive recollections, emotional numbing or restricted range of feelings, and heightened vigilance.

Prostitutes Advertising Themselves in Windows in Amsterdam's Red Light District. Prostitutes also advertise themselves in windows in the red light districts in Hamburg, Germany, and in Antwerp, Belgium. Prostitution is tightly regulated in all three places to reduce the risks of sexually transmitted infections and violence against the women. Many prostitutes in these locations have migrated from North Africa and Eastern Europe.

For his services, Dele charges 30,000 euros, which the women are indebted to pay off, and it is money that they really have little hope of repaying. The rent they will owe their madam in Antwerp will further eat at their ability to save money. Elsewhere, Unigwe had some apparently positive words for an Antwerp brothel, but given the frequent indebtedness of the women, for them such places of business are akin to prisons: "Antwerp has apparently one of the best bordellos in Europe, equipped with its own police station and high-tech sensors" (Unigwe, 2012). Thus, the women are unlikely to be physically abused, and strangers will not be sneaking in at night. But leaving the life? For many women, it's only a dream.

ESCORT SERVICES   Conventioneers and businessmen are more likely to turn to the listings for "massage" and "escorts" in the telephone directory, under personal ads in local newspapers, or online than to seek hotel sex workers. Backpage.com, for example, provides ads by masseuses (and massage parlors) and escorts in locations around the world. "Incall" means that the client visits the sex worker. "Outcall" means that the sex worker comes to the client. Some escorts advertise that they will not accept blocked calls. Of course local people as well as travelers avail themselves of escorts in their vicinity.

2 › T / F   Truth or Fiction Revisited   Massage and escort services advertised in the Yellow Pages are typically, but not always, fronts for prostitution. Legitimate masseuses and masseurs often advertise that they are licensed by their states. The acronym CMT stands for "certified massage therapist."

Some escort services are legitimate businesses, providing companions and escorts for men. Indeed, one will find female companionship for corporate functions and for unattached men traveling away from home under "escort services." Many escort services provide only prostitution, however, and clients of any escort service negotiate—or try to negotiate—sexual services after formal escort duties are completed, or in their stead. But it is safe to say that legitimate escort services are a rarity. If the client arranges for the escort through an agency advertised in a telephone

Q   *I worked as a dancer and sometimes had sex for money. Should I tell my present boyfriend (whom I might marry), who does not know my past?*

A   Our advice is that your past is your own and that your future belongs to the two of you, if you decide that you will in fact be a committed couple. Your boyfriend might not be able to live with the details of your past, and if you promise yourself to him, you are promising your future, not your history.

directory, the split between the agency and the prostitute is usually 60–40 or 80–20 in the worker's favor. The agency may tell the caller that they get $60 or $100 and that the rest is between the caller and the prostitute. The prostitute then usually calls the client and gives the client some idea what the tryst will cost.

Escorts advertising on Backpage.com may charge as little as $60 for 15 minutes if the client visits them. Many escorts provided by an agency or advertising online charge $500 an hour or more and more than $1,000 for staying overnight (Dank et al., 2014). As with streetwalkers, ethnicity tends to vary from city to city. In Miami, many are Eastern European women, particularly from Ukraine and Russia. In Denver, they are more likely to be Asian. Dank and her colleagues (2014) describe San Diego escorts provided by agencies as "higher class women."

A CLOSER LOOK

DRIVE-IN SEX

It isn't the drive-in lane at McDonalds or Dunkin Donuts. It's sex boxes.

Prostitution is legal in Switzerland, but that doesn't mean that the average Swiss likes to see women plying their trade on the streets. Consider the Alpine city of Zurich. There are three government-approved zones for sex, including a new group of

The Entrance to the Drive-In Sex Boxes Outside Zurich, Switzerland. Don't try to walk in or to drive in with a truck or motorcycle; only cars allowed.

"sex boxes" just outside the city. Men who solicit streetwalkers outside these zones face fines in the neighborhood of $500.

To handle this problem, do a better job of regulating sex work, fight pimping, and improve security for the women, the city erected nine small wooden sheds that look a lot like shelters for hikers in the woods.

Don't come by without a car. Pedestrians and motorcyclists are not allowed. Some 40 prostitutes line up in the driveway. After the driver talks to a woman and makes a deal, the couple drive up to a vacant shed. Signs in the sheds promote use of condoms. If the woman feels threatened, she can press a button and security will be on its way.

It's about precision, like a Swiss watch.

Other countries in Europe, where prostitution is either legal or tolerated, have also experimented with new venues for sex:

- The German cities of Cologne, Dortmund, and Bonn have also installed various versions of drive-in sex.
- A Love Park for 32 cars was tried at a park near Naples, Italy.
- In Belgium, authorities designed "Eros Centre," complete with 34 rooms and a car park.
- In a twist, in the Dutch city of Utrecht we find "sex house boats."

THE MASSAGE PARLOR   Nature abhors a vacuum. "Massage parlors" have sprung up from coast to coast in the United States to fill the vacuum left by the decline of the brothels (Dank et al., 2014). Many massage parlors are legitimate establishments that provide massage and only massage. Masseuses and masseurs are licensed in many states, and laws prohibit them from offering sexual services. Many localities require that the masseuse keep certain parts of her or his body clothed (some masseuses in suburban Detroit wear a scarf or a garter to comply) and not touch the client's genitals.

Many massage parlors serve as fronts for prostitution, however (Nemoto et al., 2014). They are often found in malls in middle-class suburbs, where there is ample parking. In these establishments, clients typically pay fees for a standard massage and then tip the workers for sexual extras. Masseuses are reviewed by online apps. Clients must subscribe to such services, which means that they identify themselves and are subject to the possibility of identity theft.

Massage parlor sex workers generally offer manual stimulation of the penis, oral sex, or, less frequently, sexual intercourse ("full service"). Typical fees are about $60 to $80 an hour for the house and then whatever additional the client arranges with the masseuse. Manual stimulation of the penis—typically referred to as a "local," a "handjob," or a "happy ending"—will usually cost $40 to $60. Full service is typically between $100 and $200. Some massage parlor prostitutes are better educated than streetwalkers and brothel workers and would not work in those other venues. But many massage parlor workers are Asians who are trafficked from parlor to parlor, from city to city, and then back and forth between the United States and Asia (Dank et al., 2014). According to Dank and her colleagues (2014), masseuses in Miami tend to be primarily Chinese, Thai, and Filipina in Dallas, generally Asian in Washington, D.C., Asian and Latina in Denver, Chinese in Kansas City, and from various places in Asia in San Diego and Seattle. There are exceptions to the rule in every location.

Many masseuses apply a condom to a client. A visitor to a San Francisco parlor reported in a group setting:

> They usually put it (a condom) on you…. You do the shower or bath thing and then you lay down, and then they start rubbing you, and after you do the extra, like kissing on your neck, rubbing your leg, then they do their thing down there. Then, next thing you know the bitch (slang for condom) is on. You know, most of them are pretty smooth by not breaking the moment. (Nemoto et al., 2014)

Men in the group setting also reported that the masseuses will often have oral sex or full service without a condom if the client pays more.

STRIP CLUBS   Many sex workers in strip clubs limit their activity to dancing and doffing their clothes. Others do "lap dances" or "table dances" in which they contact customers as they dance (Rambo & Pruit, 2012). Customers may buy the dance from the club and then also tip the stripper (Frank, 2002, 2003). Some strip clubs have private shows, "VIP rooms," and the like, where strippers may be alone with their customers. What happens in these private shows may be tightly regulated by the club or depend on the size of the tip (Dank et al., 2014; Roach, 2011).

CALL GIRLS   **Call girls** occupy the highest status on the social ladder of female prostitution. Many of them overlap

call girls

Sex workers who arrange for their sexual contacts by telephone. "*Call*" refers both to telephone calls and to being "on call."

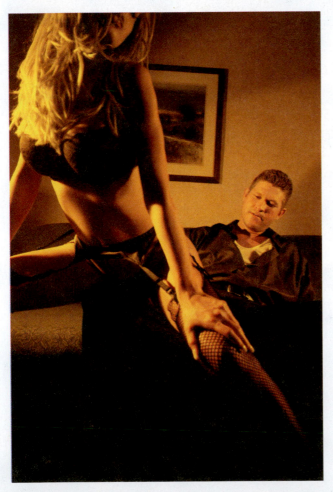

Strippers. Woman giving a lap dance in a "VIP" room at a strip club.

with escorts. Call girls tend to be the most attractive and well-educated prostitutes and tend to charge more for their services. Ashley Dupre met former Governor of New York, Eliot Spitzer, for a reported $5,000 tryst in Washington, D.C. Many call girls come from middle-class backgrounds. Unlike other types of sex workers, call girls usually work on their own. Thus, they need not split their income with a pimp, escort service, or massage parlor. Consequently, they can afford to lead a luxurious lifestyle when business is good, living in expensive neighborhoods and wearing stylish clothes, and to be more selective about the customers they will accept. They do, however, incur expenses for answering services and laundry services, and for payoffs to landlords, doormen, and sometimes to police to maintain their livelihood and avoid arrest.

Often, call girls escort their clients to dinner and social functions and are expected not only to provide sex but also charming and gracious company and conversation. Call girls often give clients the feeling that they are important and attractive (Sanders, 2005). They may effectively simulate pleasure and orgasm and create the illusion that time does not matter. It does, of course. To the call girl, as to other entrepreneurs, time is money.

Call girls may receive clients in their apartments or make outcalls to clients' homes and hotels. Some call girls trade or sell "black books" that list clients and their sexual preferences. To protect themselves from police and abusive clients, call girls may insist on reviewing a client's business card or learning his home telephone number before personal contact is made. They may investigate whether the customer is who he claims to be.

Ashley Dupre. Dupre met former Governor Eliot Spitzer of New York in Washington, D.C., for a reported $5,000 tryst.

GETTING INTO "THE LIFE"   No single factor explains entry into female sex work.

3 ⟩ T / F   Truth or Fiction Revisited   But poverty and sexual or physical abuse figure prominently in the backgrounds of the majority of female sex workers (Carter & Dalla, 2006; Farley et al., 2005; Inciardi et al., 2006). Prostitutes often come from conflict-ridden or single-parent homes in poor urban areas or rural farming communities, or, of course, in the case of Asian and East European sex workers, from overseas.

For young women of impoverished backgrounds and marginal skills, prostitution may seem alluring. It is an alternative to the menial and dismal work that is otherwise available. Poverty accounts for the entry of young women into prostitution in many countries. In some Third World nations, such as Thailand and Cambodia, many rural, impoverished parents actually sell their daughters to recruiters who place them in brothels in cities in their home countries or traffic them overseas (Szablewska & Bradley, 2015). Many of the women send home whatever money they can and also work hard to try to pay off the procurers and break free of their financial bonds.

In the United States and Canada, many initiates into prostitution are teenage runaways. Their family backgrounds vary in socioeconomic status; some come from middle-class or affluent homes, whereas others are reared in poverty. However, family discord and dysfunction frequently set the stage for entry into street life and sex work (Roe-Sepowitz, 2014). Many teenage runaways perceive life on the street to be the only possible escape from family strife and conflict, or from the physical, emotional, or sexual abuse they suffer at home. Despite its dangers, life on the streets appears more attractive than remaining in the troubled family environment.

Some teenagers who have endured sexual abuse or incest learn how to detach themselves emotionally from sex to survive unwanted sexual experiences (Sanders, 2005). The transition to prostitution may represent an extension of this unfortunate learning experience.

"JOHNS": THE CUSTOMERS OF FEMALE PROSTITUTES   Many prostitutes refer to their customers as "johns" or "tricks." Men who use female prostitutes come from all walks of life and represent all socioeconomic and racial groups. Many, perhaps most, are married men of middle-class background (Bennetts, 2011).

Most patrons are *occasional johns.* Examples include traveling salesmen or military personnel who are stopping over in town without their regular sex partners. Men are more interested than women in sexual novelty or variety (Petersen & Hyde, 2011), and variety may provide a major motive because most occasional johns have regular sex partners.

Habitual johns use prostitutes as their major or exclusive sexual outlet. Some habitual johns have never established an intimate sexual relationship. Some wealthy men who wish to avoid intimate relationships habitually patronize call girls.

Compulsive johns feel driven to prostitutes to meet some psychological or sexual need. They may repeatedly resolve to stop using prostitutes but feel unable to control their compulsions. Some compulsive johns engage in acts of fetishism or transvestism with prostitutes but would not inform their wives or girlfriends of their deviant interests. Some compulsive johns have a **whore–Madonna complex**. They see women as either sinners or saints. They can permit themselves to enjoy sex only with prostitutes or would ask only prostitutes to engage in acts such as fellatio. They see marital coitus as a duty or obligation.

MOTIVES FOR USING PROSTITUTES   There appear to be six common motives for using prostitutes:

1. *Sex without negotiation.* A john cited in Bennetts (2011) remarks, "You can have a good time without the servitude." The research on gender differences suggests strongly that men have a stronger sex drive than women do (Petersen & Hyde, 2011). Prostitution evens things up, making women available at the whim of the man. By turning to prostitutes, men need not spend the time, effort, and money to develop a relationship for the sake of sex.

2. *Sex without commitment.* Research on gender differences also shows that men are more willing to enter into sexual activity in the absence of a commitment (Petersen & Hyde, 2011). Prostitutes require no commitment from the customer other than payment for services rendered.

3. *Sex for eroticism and variety.* Many prostitutes offer "something extra" in the way of novel or kinky sex—for example, oral sex, use of costumes (e.g., leather), and S&M rituals (such as B&D). Men may desire such activity but not obtain it with their regular partners. They may even be afraid to mention the idea. Men are also more interested than women in sexual variety (Little et al., 2014; Petersen & Hyde, 2011), and prostitutes provide variety in partners.

4. *Prostitution as sociability.* In the nineteenth and early twentieth centuries, the brothel served not only as a place to obtain sex but also as a kind of "stopping off" place between home and work. Sex was secondary to the companionship and amiable conversation that men would find in brothels, especially in the days of the "bawdy houses" of the pioneer West. (Similarly, women who attend male strip clubs enjoy "bonding" with their friends at the clubs as well as the stripping itself [Montemurro et al., 2003].)

5. *Sex away from home.* The greatest contemporary use of prostitution occurs among male "road warriors"— traveling businessmen. It is also common among sports fans at out-of-town events. In these typical all-male preserves, peer pressure may encourage sexual adventures.

whore–Madonna complex

The rigid stereotyping of women as either sinners or saints.

6. *Problematical sex.* People who have physical disabilities or disfiguring conditions sometimes seek the services of sex workers because of difficulty attracting other partners or because of fears of rejection. (One prostitute at a Nevada brothel said that she was a favorite of the management because she accepted johns with cerebral palsy.) Though some prostitutes are selective about their clients, others will accept anyone who will pay. Men with sexual dysfunctions may also turn to prostitutes who do not "demand" a certain quality of performance. Some men without partners may seek sex workers as substitutes.

Critical Thinking
Agree or disagree with the following statement, and support your answer: Sex work should be legalized throughout the United States.

4 › T / F   Truth or Fiction Revisited   It is *not* true that typical customers of prostitutes have difficulty forming sexual relationships with other women. Many men often turn to prostitutes for sexual variety or because they seek sexual activity when they are away from home.

Male Prostitutes

Males also engage in sex work. Some—especially those who work at strip clubs—have female clients. However, strippers, male and female, typically do not see themselves as prostitutes unless they also have sex with the clientele. Male sex workers who service female clients—*gigolos*—are rare. Gigolos' clients are typically older, wealthy, unattached women. They may serve as escorts or as surrogate sons for the women and may or may not offer sexual services. Many gigolos are struggling actors or models.

Most male prostitutes have male clients (Weitzer, 2012a). The overwhelming majority of male prostitutes service gay men and are called **hustlers**. Their patrons are typically called **scores**. The average hustler is very young—17 to 18 years old—and was initiated into prostitution at age 14 or so. He typically has less than an 11-grade education and few, if any, marketable skills. The majority of hustlers come from working-class and lower-class backgrounds. Many male prostitutes, like many female prostitutes, come from families troubled by conflict, alcoholism, or physical or sexual abuse (Weitzer, 2012a).

hustlers

Males who engage in sex work with male customers.

scores

Customers of hustlers.

Hustlers may be gay, bisexual, or heterosexual. In a large-scale Australian study, half of the male prostitutes surveyed described themselves as gay (Minichiello et al., 2001). About one-third (31%) said they were bisexual, and 5.5% said they were "straight."

A Norwegian study surveyed all adolescents aged 14 to 17 in public and private schools in Oslo, the capital of the country (Pedersen & Hegna, 2003). The response rate was 94%, or 10,828 students. About 1.4% of the sample had sold sexual favors, including three times as many boys as girls. Of these, half had done so more than 10 times. Prostitution was found to be connected with initiation of sexual intercourse at an early age, conduct problems, abuse of alcohol and other drugs, and physical and sexual abuse. The male prostitutes reported that many of their clients were gay or bisexual. The adolescents did not reliably use condoms, which placed them at risk of contracting HIV/AIDS and other STIs.

The major motive for male prostitution, like female prostitution, is money (Weitzer, 2012b). Running away from home typically serves as an entry point. Some males run away because of family problems; others are seeking adventure or independence. Some gay prostitutes are literally thrown out because their families cannot accept their sexual orientation.

Most hustlers are part-timers who continue some form of educational or vocational activity as they support themselves through prostitution. Drug dealing and drug use are also common among hustlers (Weitzer, 2012b).

Male Prostitution. Young male sex worker, Bangkok, Thailand.

Hustlers typically are not attached to a pimp. They generally make contacts with clients in gay bars and social clubs, or by working the streets in areas frequented by gay men. They typically learn to hustle from watching other hustlers ply their trade. Various kinds of male sex workers have been identified:

- Strippers dance and strip. Patrons—female and male—may fondle them or sometimes have sex with them.

- Kept boys have relationships with older, economically secure men who keep them in an affluent lifestyle. The older male, or "sugar daddy," may assume a parental role.

- Call boys, like call girls, may work on their own or through an agency or escort service.

- "Punks" are prison inmates who service other inmates for protection or goods such as cigarettes or drugs.

- Drag prostitutes are transvestites or presurgical male-to-female trans who impersonate females and have sex with men who may be unaware of their gender. Some of them conceal their gender and limit themselves to fellatio. Others take the passive role in anal sex.

- Male brothel prostitutes are rarer than their female counterparts.

- Bar hustlers and street hustlers, like their female counterparts, occupy the lowest status and ply their trade in gay bars or on streets frequented by gay passers-by. Street hustlers are the most common and typically the youngest subtype. They are also the most visible and consequently the ones most likely to draw the attention of the police.

By and large, hustling is an adolescent enterprise. The younger the hustler, the higher the fee he can command and the more tricks he can turn. By the time he reaches his mid-20s, he may be forced to engage in sexual activities he might have rejected when younger or seek clients in sleazier places.

Sexually Transmitted Infections (STIs) and Prostitution

LO 16.3 Discuss the relationship between prostitution and sexually transmitted infections (STIs).

Concerns about the spread of STIs by prostitution is nothing new. In the 1960s, two of three prostitutes surveyed by Gebhard (1969) had contracted gonorrhea or syphilis. Although prostitutes are still exposed to a heightened risk of contracting or spreading these and other STIs, such as chlamydia, the risk of HIV/AIDS poses a deadlier threat. The risk of HIV/AIDS has been linked to both male and female prostitution (Weitzer, 2012a). The risk of HIV/AIDS and other STIs is greater for streetwalkers than brothel

Real Students, Real Questions

Q *Do women use male prostitutes at all? Do they use female prostitutes?*

A The best answer is "sometimes," but certainly not as frequently as men do. When women visit strip clubs and toy with male dancers, they are in effect paying for sex. They may pay for sex (male strippers) at bachelorette parties. And now and then a woman uses a gigolo. As to whether women use female prostitutes, the best evidence we have is that heterosexual women sometimes get talked into using a female prostitute by their male companions—as a couple.

prostitutes (Weitzer, 2012a), and for women working illegally rather than women working legally (Leigh, 2012; Nussbaum, 2012).

Criminologist James Inciardi and his colleagues (2006) interviewed 586 street-walkers in low-income sections of Miami, Florida. Their median age was 38 and they had been in "the life" for a median of 14 years. All women in the sample were heavily involved in alcohol and substance abuse, 42% were homeless, and half (51%) had engaged in unprotected vaginal sex with a customer in the past month. Their blood was tested for various STIs and it was found that:

- 22.4% tested positive for HIV.
- 53.4% tested positive for HBV (the hepatitis B virus).
- 29.7% tested positive for HCV (the hepatitis C virus).

We find another pocket of high infection rates among prostitutes in California, and especially along the border with Mexico, where prostitution is legal. Many Californians visit Tijuana, Mexico, just south of the border, to find prostitutes (Strathdee et al., 2012). Similarly, the incidence of HIV infection is high in Ciudad Juarez, across the border from El Paso, Texas, and in that part of western Texas as well (Strathdee et al., 2010).

An analysis of 102 journal articles on the worldwide incidence of HIV infection among prostitutes confirmed the finding that the burden of disease is "disproportionately high" among prostitutes (Baral et al., 2012). Overall 11.8% of 99,878 female prostitutes were infected with HIV. That infection rate rose to 30.7% in countries with higher overall infection rates.

We have similar findings with men who have sex with male sex workers (Jung et al., 2012). One study looked not only at infection with HIV but also at syphilis, chlamydia, and gonorrhea. High infection levels among the buyers were found among men with lower levels of education who had more sex partners, had anal sex—especially when they had unprotected anal sex—and among men who were more concerned about being infected with an STI. One might think that men who were more anxious about being infected would be more cautious; however, at least in this particular study, it would appear that men who were more anxious had good reason to feel anxious.

Sex with prostitutes is the most important factor in the male–female transmission of HIV in Africa, which is the most affected region by HIV/AIDS, and where HIV is spread mainly by male–female sexual intercourse. Prostitutes incur a greater risk of HIV transmission because they have sexual relations with many partners, often without protection (World Health Organization, 2015c).

Moreover, many prostitutes and their clients and other sex partners inject drugs and share contaminated needles (Strathdee et al., 2010). HIV/AIDS may be spread by unprotected sex from prostitutes to customers, then to the customers' wives or lovers.

Should Prostitution Be Legalized?

As a counterpoint to the transmission of HIV/AIDS and other STIs by many street prostitutes, it can be noted that in the Netherlands and parts of Nevada, where prostitution is legal and carefully regulated by the state, transmission of STIs is extremely low. In Nevada, condoms have been required since 1986, and prostitutes are tested for HIV and other infectious organisms regularly.

Legalization of prostitution has benefits beyond ensuring regular testing for STIs in licensed brothels (Weitzer, 2012a). It also turns prostitutes, other brothel employees, and brothel owners into taxpayers and provides safer venues for prostitution, both for prostitutes and their customers. Safer settings might help sever some of the links between prostitution and drug abuse. Moreover, brothel owners in legal setting are be required to obtain proof of age of prostitutes.

Chika Unigwe, who wrote a novel about African women working in the red-light district of the Belgian city of Antwerp (Unigwe, 2011), supports legal status for prostitutes: "If prostitution is legalized, society gains income tax revenue that would have been otherwise lost. Granted, legalizing the profession might make it attractive for sex traffickers but the benefits outweigh this prospect" (Unigwe, 2012).

Opponents of legalization argue both on moral and practical grounds (Ramos, 2012). Many traditionalists and feminists alike find it morally reprehensible that civilized societies would legalize practices that degrade women and the value of the family. Moreover, given prostitutes' frequent histories of abuse and sexual exploitation, they wonder whether it can be claimed that prostitutes—even as adults—are ever truly making "free" decisions to enter the world's oldest profession.

On the other hand, Martha Nussbaum (2012), a professor of law and ethics at the University of Chicago, writes that "Feminist arguments about prostitution portray financial transactions in the area of female sexuality as demeaning to women. But all of us, with the exception of the independently wealthy and the unemployed, take money for the use of our bodies."

On a more practical level, many writers (e.g., Ramos, 2012) note that globalization and sex trafficking is likely to create a category of sex slaves regardless of whether or not prostitution is legalized or tolerated within a given country. Moreover, social class differences and prejudices are likely to remain such that less attractive prostitutes drawn from minority groups will remain on the streets, and unregulated, rather than finding their ways into the safer brothels.

Economics is to a large degree based on supply and demand. When the sexual experiences desired by individuals are not supplied through personal intimate relationships, sex work of some sort is likely to be in demand. Perhaps we'll give the final word on the matter to Carol Leigh (2012), director of the Bay Area Sex Workers Advocacy Network, which seeks legalization of prostitution in San Francisco: "Prostitution laws in the United States were developed from confused and contradictory impulses, to punish and help sex workers at the same time, reflecting our society's ambivalence and hypocrisy about sex, male desire and women's sexual autonomy."

Pornography

Sexually explicit materials are found nearly everywhere. In addition to the adult magazines and the DVD rentals, millions of people use Google or Yahoo! to search for pornography on the Internet or pay for pornographic films or channels from their cable or satellite dish services.

Pornography is indeed popular, but it is also highly controversial. Many are opposed to pornography on moral grounds. Feminists oppose pornography on the grounds that it portrays women in degrading and dehumanizing roles, as sex objects who are subservient to men's wishes, as sexually insatiable nymphomaniacs, or as sexual masochists who enjoy being raped and violated (DeKeseredy & Corsianos, 2016; Mowlabocus & Wood, 2015). Some feminists hold that depictions of women in sexually subordinate roles may encourage men to treat them as sex objects and increase the potential for rape (DeKeseredy & Corsianos, 2016). On the other hand, many civil libertarians believe that the importance of freedom of speech overrides concerns about pornography.

What Is Pornographic?

LO 16.4 Define pornography.

Webster's Deluxe Unabridged Dictionary defines **pornography** as "writing, pictures, etc., intended to arouse sexual desire." The inclusion of the word *intended* places the determination of what is pornographic in the mind of the person composing

pornography

Sexually explicit material produced for purposes of eliciting or enhancing sexual arousal.

the work. Applying this definition makes it all but impossible to determine what is pornographic. If a filmmaker admits that he or she wanted to arouse the audience sexually, may we judge the work to be pornographic, even if no nudity or explicit sex scenes are shown? On the other hand, explicit representations of people engaged in sexual activity would not be pornographic if the work was intended as an artistic expression, rather than created for its **prurient** value. Many works that were once prohibited in this country because of explicit sexual content—such as the novels *Tropic of Cancer* by Henry Miller, *Lady Chatterley's Lover* by D. H. Lawrence, and *Ulysses* by James Joyce—are now generally considered mainstream literature. Even Mark Twain's *Huckleberry Finn*, John Steinbeck's *The Grapes of Wrath*, and Ernest Hemingway's *For Whom the Bell Tolls* have been banned from place to place because local citizens found them to be offensive, obscene, or morally objectionable.

One alternative definition finds material pornographic when it is judged to be offensive by others. This definition, too, relies on the subjective judgment of the person exposed to the material. In other words, one person's pornography is another person's work of art. On the other hand, most people have no difficulty distinguishing between nudity that is art, nudity that is presented for information (such as illustrations presented in this textbook), and nudity that coincides with pornogrand nudity that coincides with pornography.

Legislative bodies usually write laws about **obscenity** rather than pornography. In the case of *Miller v. California* (1973), Supreme Court Justice William Brennan wrote that obscenity is "incapable of definition with sufficient clarity to withstand attack on vagueness grounds." On the other hand, Justice Potter Stewart quipped that although he could not define obscenity, he knew it when he saw it. But even the Supreme Court has had trouble defining obscenity and determining where, if anywhere, laws against obscenity do not run afoul of the Bill of Rights' guarantee of free speech. Recall that *Huckleberry Finn* was once considered obscene.

Pornography is often classified as either *hard-core* (X-rated) or *soft-core* (R-rated). Hard-core pornography includes graphic and sexually explicit depictions of sex organs and sexual acts. Soft-core porn, as represented by R-rated films, features more stylized nudity and suggested (or simulated) rather than explicit sex acts.

An Erotic Photo from the Late Nineteenth Century. From the erotic wall paintings of Ancient Pompeii to the videos available all over the Internet, we have had pornography as long as we have has drawing and painting, and more recently, photography and film.

prurient

Tending to excite lust; lewd.

obscenity

That which offends people's feelings or goes beyond prevailing standards of decency or modesty.

Pornography, Law, and Politics

LO 16.5 Describe the legal status of pornography.

Laws against obscenity provide the legal framework for outlawing the dissemination of pornography. Because the definition of obscenity relies on offending people or running afoul of community standards, that which is deemed obscene may vary from person to person and from culture to culture. Going topless on a public beach may be deemed obscene in some locales but not along beaches on the French Riviera or Rio de Janeiro, where this style of (un)dress is customary. The word *obscene* extends beyond sexual matters. One could judge TV violence or beer commercials to be obscene because they are personally offensive or are offensive to women, even if such depictions do not meet legal standards of obscenity.

In the United States, legal prohibition of pornography as a form of obscenity dates to the nineteenth century. In 1873, an anti-obscenity bill, the Comstock Act, was passed by Congress. One effect of the bill was to outlaw the dissemination of information about birth control. The Comstock Act and similar laws made it a felony to mail obscene books, pamphlets, photographs, drawings, or letters. But what is obscene?

A landmark case in 1957 helped establish the legal basis of obscenity in the United States. In *Roth v. United States,* the U.S. Supreme Court ruled that portrayal of sexual activity was protected under the First Amendment to the Constitution unless its dominant theme dealt with "sex in a manner appealing to prurient interest" (*Roth v. United States,* 1957, p. 487). In a 1973 case, *Miller v. California,* the U.S. Supreme Court held that obscenity is based on a determination of:

- Whether the average person, applying contemporary community standards, would find that the work, taken as a whole, appeals to the prurient interest ...;

- whether the work depicts or describes, in a patently offensive way, sexual conduct specifically defined by the applicable state law; and

- whether the work, taken as a whole, lacks serious literary, artistic, political, or scientific value. (*Miller v. California,* 1973, p. 24)

Courts have since had to grapple with the *Miller* standard in judging whether material is obscene. *Miller* recognizes that judgments of obscenity may vary with "community standards." As a result, the same material may be considered obscene in one community but not in another. The *Miller* standard raises some questions. For example, who is the "average person" who can speak for a community? Many of us live in ethnically, racially, and religiously diverse communities. Can one viewpoint in *any* community truly represent the community? Even in relatively homogeneous communities, a diversity of opinion may exist on particular issues. Moreover, what is a *community?* Is it one's neighborhood, police precinct, municipality, county, or a larger political unit? What does "patently" offensive mean? Who judges "serious" literary, artistic, political, or scientific value? An attempt to clarify this last question was made in a 1987 case, *Pope v. Illinois,* in which the Supreme Court held that

> The proper inquiry is not whether an ordinary member of any given community would find serious literary, artistic, political, or scientific value in allegedly obscene material, but whether a reasonable person would find such value in the material, taken as a whole. (*Pope v. Illinois,* p. 445)

In this ruling, the court held that sexually explicit material could not be declared obscene if many or most people in a particular community held it to lack serious literary, artistic, political, or scientific value, unless a "reasonable" person were to reach the same judgment. Whether the concept of a "reasonable" person will provide the courts with a clearer standard than that of an "average" or "ordinary" person for adjudicating obscenity cases remains to be seen.

Child pornography and violent, degrading, or dehumanizing pornography complicate matters further. People who do not find explicit depictions of consensual sex between adults to be obscene may regard child pornography or violent pornography as obscene. Child pornography is clearly psychologically harmful to the juvenile actors (McCabe, 2000; Quayle, 2012). Many people also object to sexually explicit material that portrays women as "sex objects," as existing to gratify men's sexual appetites.

Some footnotes: The U.S. Supreme Court ruled (in *Stanley v. Georgia,* 1969) that the possession of obscene material in one's home is not a criminal act. However, most states have criminalized the downloading and possession of child pornography. Police may seize suspects' computers and check them for the presence of child pornography.

Many individuals and communities have sought to ban pornography on the grounds that it discriminates against women (noted in Duggan, 2006a). In other words, pornography damages women's opportunities for equal rights by perpetuating stereotypes of women as subservient to men.

THE REGULATION OF PORNOGRAPHY If the First Amendment has protected people's rights to produce, act in, and possess pornography—with the exception of child pornography—it has not prevented various governing bodies from imposing some regulations on the industry. In sum, actors in adult films must be, in fact, adults, and, in many jurisdictions, they must be certified as free of certain STIs. Actors in southern California, where there are more than 200 adult movie studios, are required to receive monthly tests for HIV, chlamydia, and gonorrhea, and to be tested for other infections on other schedules (AIM Health Care Foundation, 2009). To avoid liability, most studios keep careful records of actors' proof of age and testing.

One might ask why actors are not required to wear condoms, as is common in the Brazilian adult film industry (Clendenning, 2004). The simple answer is that audiences prefer male actors to be "bareback." Very few U.S. studios require actors to use condoms.

FEMINISTS AND ANTI-PORNOGRAPHY CAMPAIGNS The sexual revolution liberated many in society from sexual inhibitions and prompted sexual exploration. As of the late 1960s, pornography became widespread. But many feminists found the proliferation of sexual imagery to be anything but liberating. Instead, it portrayed women as sex objects intended to be subservient to men.

Some feminists joined with conservative Christian groups such as the Moral Majority to try to ban pornography, thereby aligning themselves with what amounted to a moral crusade (Duggan, 2006a). Their efforts ultimately failed, but it did spark conflict within the feminist movement and from some sexual minorities. Some groups claimed that banning pornography not only intrudes on First Amendment rights but also, by legislating what kinds of sexual themes may be portrayed, marginalizes people who derive sexual pleasure from pornography.

Prevalence and Use of Erotica and Pornography

LO 16.6 **Discuss the incidence and use of pornography.**

Nearly all of us have been exposed to sexually explicit materials, whether in the form of a novel, a photo spread in a magazine, an X-rated film, or an adult Web site. DeKeseredy and Corsianos (2016) report that the average age for initial exposure to pornography on the Internet is 11. Adult Web sites have proliferated to the point where many students may be "burning the midnight oil" by surfing sex sites rather than professional journals. A study of 813 students (mean age = 20) from six colleges across the United States found that nearly 9 out of 10 (87%) men and one-third (31%) of women reported making use of pornography (Carroll et al., 2008). Females are more likely to have been exposed to pornography by boyfriends than the reverse. Viewing pornography wasn't associated with much stigma in this sample. Large percentages—two-thirds (67%) of the men and half (49%) of the women—responded that viewing pornography is acceptable.

Pornography is typically used to elicit or enhance sexual arousal, often as a masturbation aid (Kingston et al., 2009; Owens et al., 2012). Couples may use pornographic materials to enliven their sexual appetite and enhance sexual arousal during lovemaking.

Repeated exposure to the same pornographic materials progressively lessens the sexual response to them. People may become aroused by the familiar materials again if some time is allowed to go by. Novel materials are also likely to reactivate a sexual response (Hoffman et al., 2012).

Gender Differences in Response to Pornography

LO 16.7 Discuss gender differences in response to pornography.

Researchers have found that both men and women are physiologically sexually aroused by sexually explicit pictures, movies, or audiotaped passages (Chivers & Timmers, 2012; Diamond & Dickenson, 2012). That is, both men and women respond to pornographic stimuli with vasocongestion of the genitals and myotonia (muscle tension). However, there is a difference between physiological response and subjective feelings of arousal in women (Vilarinho et al., 2014). Despite what is happening within their bodies, women tend to rate romantic scenes as more sexually arousing than cold sexually explicit scenes (Chivers & Timmers, 2012). Women are less accepting than men of sex without emotional involvement (Petersen & Hyde, 2011). It is romance that encourages most women to follow the lead of genital arousal, when they do so. Even in the choice of erotic materials, women are more likely than men to want the element of romance (Petersen & Hyde, 2011).

5 ▶ T / F Truth or Fiction Revisited Both males and females can be physiologically aroused by erotic materials. Yet males and females do not necessarily share the same subjective response to them or the same level of interest in them.

Most erotic visual materials are produced by men for men. Women may read erotic romance novels, but they show relatively less interest in erotic pictures, films, or Web sites (Petersen & Hyde, 2011). Many women find erotica a "turn-off" or disgusting, especially when it portrays women in unflattering roles, as "whorish," and subservient to men.

From the evolutionary perspective, could a basic evolutionary process be at work? Did ancestral men who were more sexually aroused by the sight of a passing female have reproductive advantages over their less arousable peers? Women, however, have fewer mating opportunities than men and must make the most of any reproductive opportunity by selecting the best possible mate and provider. To be sexually aroused by the sight of male genitalia might encourage random couplings, which would undermine their reproductive success.

A Lesbian Sex Scene. This lesbian pornography is one of thousands upon thousands of videos produced in Southern California. They focus on their "art" despite all the camera people and technicians around them. Lesbian pornography is actually produced mainly for men, even though many women respond to it as well.

Pornography and Sexual Coercion

LO 16.8 Discuss possible relationships between pornography and violence against women.

Pornography can be destructive to intimate relationships. Is it also a cause of sexual violence or other antisocial acts? Let us consider several sources of evidence in examining this highly charged question, beginning with history—the findings of a 1970 government commission impaneled to review the evidence that was available at the time.

THE COMMISSION ON OBSCENITY AND PORNOGRAPHY: SCIENTIFIC INVESTIGATION OR POLITICAL AGENDA? In the 1960s, Congress created the Commission on Obscenity and Pornography to study the effects of pornography. After reviewing the research, the commission (Abelson et al., 1970) concluded that there was no evidence that pornography led to crimes of violence or sexual offenses such as exhibitionism, voyeurism, or child molestation. Some people were sexually aroused by pornography and increased the frequency of their usual sexual activity, such as masturbation or sex with regular partners, following exposure. But they did not engage in antisocial behavior. These results have been replicated many times.

Finding pornography basically harmless, the commission recommended that "federal, state, and local legislation should not seek to interfere with the right of adults who wish to read, obtain, or view explicit sexual materials" (Abelson et al., 1970, p. 58). Congress and then-president Richard Nixon rejected the commission's findings and recommendation, however, on moral and political grounds.

THE MEESE COMMISSION REPORT: ANOTHER POLITICAL AGENDA? In 1985, President Ronald Reagan appointed a committee headed by Attorney General Edwin Meese to reexamine the effects of pornography. In 1986, the U.S. Attorney General's Commission on Pornography, known as the Meese Commission, issued a report that reached different conclusions from the 1970 commission. The Meese Commission claimed to find a causal link between sexual violence and exposure to violent pornography (U.S. Department of Justice, 1986). Moreover, the report concluded that exposure to pornography that portrayed women in degrading or subservient roles increased acceptability of rape in the minds of viewers. The commission found no evidence linking exposure to nonviolent, nondegrading pornography (consensual sexual activity between partners in equal roles) and sexual violence but noted that only a small fraction of the pornographic materials on the market was of this type.

Gay Males Are Most Likely to Respond Sexually When Viewing Sex Scenes with Exclusively Male Actors. Many of the actors in these videos are heterosexual and some of them require fluffers to become sexually aroused.

Critics claim that the Meese Commission did not blatantly falsify the data, but it failed to distinguish between the effects of sexually explicit materials per se and the effects of violent materials (Sharp & Joslyn, 2008; Weitzer, 2007). Evidence of links between exposure to sexually explicit materials (without violent content) and sexual aggression is lacking.

PORNOGRAPHY AND SEX OFFENDERS Research comparing the experience of sex offenders and nonoffenders with pornographic materials has been mixed. A review of the research literature found little or no difference in the level of exposure to pornography between incarcerated sex offenders and comparison groups of felons who were incarcerated for nonsexual crimes (Marshall, 1989). Yet, more recent research finds that sexually aggressive individuals are more likely than others to use pornography (Alexy et al., 2009; Quayle, 2012). As many as one in three rapists and child molesters use pornography to become sexually aroused before they commit their crimes (Marshall, 1989). Even so, these studies are correlational and not experimental. It might be that desire to use pornography and commit sexually aggressive acts are both related to other factors, such as a general tendency to seek out sexual images and experiences that humiliate women. Moreover, only 38% of a male college sample reported acting out aggressive sexual fantasies (Williams et al., 2009), but of course 38% is more than enough.

EXPERIMENTS ON THE EFFECTS OF PORNOGRAPHY   According to Catherine Dukes (2015),

> The concepts of pornography and violence can be subjective and emotion-producing terms. Together, the reaction of the word "pornography" to some people can be visceral. A casual conversation linking pornography and violence (as a positive correlation) is not uncommon at cocktail parties and at the water cooler. But what does the research truly reveal? Over 50 million Americans who are porn consumers may not even guess that, contrary to popular belief, the research studies have never shown pornography to cause violence.

Is that possible? Let's look at the research for ourselves, beginning with some classic studies.

In one study (Donnerstein, 1980), 120 college men interacted with a male or female confederate (accomplice) of the experimenter, who treated them in either a neutral or hostile manner. The subjects were then shown neutral, nonviolent pornographic films, or violent pornographic films. In the latter, a man forced himself into a woman's home and raped her. Subjects were then given the opportunity to deliver electric shock to the male or female confederate, presumably to assist the confederate in learning a task. The measure of aggression was the intensity of the shock chosen. No shock was actually delivered, but subjects did not know that the shock apparatus was fake. Unprovoked men who viewed violent pornographic films showed greater aggression toward the women than did unprovoked men who viewed nonviolent films, however. Provoked men who were shown violent pornography selected the highest shock levels of all. The film may have served as a model for retaliation.

In another study, aggression by males against female confederates following exposure to violent pornography (a rape scene) was increased by depictions of the woman being raped as either enjoying the experience or becoming sexually aroused during the rape (Donnerstein & Berkowitz, 1981). These findings suggest that depictions of women enjoying or becoming aroused by their victimization may legitimize violence against women in the viewer's mind, reinforcing the cultural myth that some women need to be dominated and are sexually aroused by an overpowering male.

Some research suggests that it is the violence in violent pornography, and not sexual explicitness, that hardens men's attitudes toward rape survivors. In one study (Donnerstein & Linz, 1987), college men were exposed to films consisting of either violent pornography, nonviolent pornography (a couple having consensual intercourse), or violence that was not sexually explicit. The violent pornographic and nonpornographic films both showed a woman being tied up and slapped at gunpoint, but the nonpornographic version contained no nudity or explicit sexual activity. The men had first been either angered or treated in a neutral manner by a female confederate of the experimenter. The results showed that, in comparison with nonviolent pornography, both violent pornographic films and violent *non-pornographic* films produced greater acceptance of rape myths (see discussion in Chapter 15), increased reported willingness to force a woman into sexual activity, and greater reported likelihood of engaging in rape (if the man also knew that he could get away with it). These effects occurred regardless of whether the man was angered by the woman or not.

Research on the effects of pornography should be interpreted with caution, however (Sharp & Joslyn, 2008). Most of it has employed college students, whose behavior may or may not be typical of people in general or of people with propensities toward sexual violence. Another issue is that most studies in this area are laboratory-based experiments that involve simulated aggression or judgments of sympathy toward hypothetical women who have been portrayed as rape victims. None measured *actual* violence against women outside the lab.

In their comprehensive review of the research literature on pornography and sexual aggression, Neil Malamuth and his colleagues (2000) analyzed data from studies that found no reliable links between pornography and aggression, integrated the findings of multiple summaries of the experimental and naturalistic research literature, and analyzed questionnaire data obtained from a representative sample of 2,972 college men with a mean age of 21. Each method of analysis supported the existence of some reliable connections between the frequent use of pornography and sexually aggressive behavior—particularly in the cases of violent pornography and for men who were likely to engage in sexual aggression.

6 › T / F **Truth or Fiction Revisited** Malamuth and his colleagues conclude not that pornography causes violence, but that relatively aggressive men react differently from nonviolent men to the same pornography. It is not so much that pornography makes men violent; instead, it seems to be more likely that pornography may trigger violence in violent men.

Nonviolent pornography may not contain scenes of sexual violence, but it often portrays women in degrading or dehumanizing roles—as sexually promiscuous, insatiable, and subservient (Itzin et al., 2007). Might such portrayals of women reinforce traditional stereotypes of women as sex objects? Might they lead viewers to condone acts of rape by suggesting that women are essentially promiscuous? Might the depiction of women as readily sexually accessible inspire men to refuse to "take no for an answer"?

In classic research, Zillmann and Bryant (1984) exposed male and female subjects to six sessions of pornography over 6 consecutive weeks. Subjects were exposed to either a massive dose of pornography, consisting of six nonviolent pornographic films during each session; to an intermediate dose consisting of three pornographic and three neutral films each session; or to a no-dose control, consisting of six non-sexual films. When surveyed later, both males and females who received extended exposure to pornography, especially those receiving the massive dose, gave more lenient punishments to a rapist who was depicted in a newspaper article. Moreover, males became more callous in their attitudes toward women.

In a more recent study, 71 men watched one of three films: a film that was sexually explicit and degrading of women, a film that was sexually explicit but *not*

Critical Thinking
Which do you consider to be the greater danger—the danger of widely available pornography or the danger of censorship? Explain your point of view.

degrading of women, and a nonsexual (control) film (Mulac et al., 2002). The men then worked in couples with women to solve problems. Men who watched the sexually explicit films behaved more dominantly toward their problem-solving partners than men who watched the control film. Moreover, men who watched the sexually explicit *and* degrading film showed more dominance than those who watched the sexually explicit but not degrading film.

In a more recent experiment with nonviolent pornography, Gert Hald and Neil Malamuth (2015) used 200 young Danish men and women as their study participants. They looked at the effects of the personality trait of agreeableness, past use of pornography, and exposure to nonviolent pornography on attitudes justifying violence against women. Without even showing the pornography, the researchers found that the more disagreeable the man, and the higher his use of pornography in the past, the more likely he was to think that violence against women could be justified. Experimental exposure to pornography also increased disagreeable men's attitudes supporting violence against women. Perhaps the key takeaway is that men with negative personality traits are more likely to think violence toward women is acceptable when they view—or have viewed—pornography.

Overall, it seems likely that for some men, exposure to pornography renders attitudes toward women more negative and callous (Hald & Malamuth, 2015). Some men who view pornography may come to regard women as sexual playthings who are to be valued for their physical attributes and their role in providing sexual release, and not as individuals.

Another concern is the possible effect of nonviolent pornography on the viewer's attitudes toward committed relationships and family life. Nonviolent pornography typically features impromptu sexual encounters between new acquaintances. Does repeated exposure to nonviolent pornography loosen traditional attitudes? When compared to people who viewed nonsexual films, men and women who were exposed to weekly, hour-long sessions involving scenes of explicit sexual encounters between new acquaintances over a six-week period showed attitudinal changes including greater acceptance of premarital and extramarital sex and of simultaneous sexual relationships with multiple partners (Zillman, 1989). They also reported desiring fewer children and were less likely to say they saw marriage as an "essential institution."

Nonviolent pornography may loosen traditional attitudes about committed relationships and family life by projecting an image of sexual enjoyment without responsibility or obligations (Carroll et al., 2008). Prolonged exposure may also foster dissatisfaction with the physical appearance and sexual performance of one's own intimate partners (Brown, 2003).

In short, we still have a long way to go in figuring out the effects of pornography on viewers' attitudes and behavior. Dukes (2015) may be correct that we cannot conclude that pornography is a direct cause of violence. However, pornography does seem to have a negative effect on what we might call "family values" and men's conceptions of how they should relate to women (Hald & Malamuth, 2015). We can't say that this area of research is in its infancy; rather, we can say that we still have more to learn.

Chapter Review

LO 16.1 Define prostitution.

Prostitution or "sex work" is the sale of sex. Prostitution is illegal everywhere in the United States except rural counties in Nevada. Prostitution is legal or at least tolerated in Canada, much of Mexico, and Europe.

LO 16.2 Summarize what we know about female and male sex workers, including their backgrounds.

The major types of female sex workers are streetwalkers, brothel prostitutes, "masseuses," "escorts," and call girls. Many prostitutes work in adult films and on adult Web sites. Poverty and child abuse figure in the backgrounds of many sex workers. Teenage runaways are vulnerable to being drawn into sex work. Many Asian and East European women are trafficked to work in U.S. brothels and massage parlors.

Most male sex workers service male clients, but some male sex workers—for example, male strippers— have female customers.

LO 16.3 Discuss the relationship between sex work and sexually transmitted infections (STIs).

Sex workers are at greater risk of transmission of HIV and other STIs because they have sexual relations with many partners, often without protection. HIV may be spread by sex workers to customers, then to the customers' regular partners.

LO 16.4 Define pornography.

Pornography is "writing, pictures, etc., intended to arouse sexual desire." What is seen as pornographic or obscene varies from person to person and culture to culture. *Obscenity* refers to statements or materials that offend people or go beyond prevailing standards of decency or modesty.

LO 16.5 Describe the legal status of pornography.

In *Miller v. California,* the U.S. Supreme Court held that obscenity is based on determination of "whether the average person, applying contemporary community standards, would find that the work … appeals to the prurient interest …; whether the work depicts [sexual behavior] in a patently offensive way; [and] whether the work, taken as a whole, lacks serious literary, artistic, political, or scientific value." The downloading or possession of child pornography has been criminalized throughout the United States.

LO 16.6 Discuss the incidence and use of pornography.

The average age of first exposure to Internet pornography is 11. Americans are typically introduced to pornography by their high school years. Pornography is readily available on the Internet, in X-rated magazines, and in books.

LO 16.7 Discuss gender differences in response to pornography.

Although females and males can both be physiologically aroused by pornography, men are relatively more interested. Pornography is frequently used as a masturbation aid.

LO 16.8 Discuss possible relationships between pornography and violence against women.

A 1970 government commission found no harmful effects of pornographic material on normal people. A 1986 government commission reported that exposure to violent pornography is linked with sexual aggression, and exposure to degrading but nonviolent pornography is linked with increased acceptability of rape in the minds of viewers. Scientific experiments suggest that exposure to pornography may stimulate sexually deviant urges in men who are predisposed to commit crimes of sexual violence, and that violent pornography may stimulate college men to act more aggressively toward women.

Test Your Learning

1. _____ occupy the bottom rung in the hierarchy of sex workers.
   (a) Streetwalkers
   (b) Brothel prostitutes
   (c) Massage parlor prostitutes
   (d) Call girls

2. Most patrons of sex workers are "_____ johns."
   (a) habitual
   (b) gay
   (c) occasional
   (d) atypical

3. Men seek sex with sex workers because _____
   (a) they desire sex without commitment,
   (b) they are seeking sexual novelty,
   (c) sex workers do things their regular partners do not do,
   (d) all of the above.

4. _____ are physiologically sexually aroused by pornography.
   (a) Men and women
   (b) Only men
   (c) Only women
   (d) Only gay males and lesbians

5. The Supreme Court decision in *Miller v. California* stated that _____ standards must be considered in defining obscenity.
   (a) biblical
   (b) community
   (c) educational
   (d) universal

6. Research appears to show that _____ pornography is connected with sexual aggression.
   (a) sexually explicit
   (b) gay
   (c) violent
   (d) online

7. U.S. courts have held that the _____ Amendment to the Constitution guarantees freedom to use pornography.
   (a) First
   (b) Second
   (c) Fifth
   (d) Twenty-third

8. A study of 586 streetwalkers in Miami found that about _____ percent tested positive for HIV.
   (a) 22
   (b) 42
   (c) 62
   (d) 82

9. Farley and her colleagues interviewed 100 Canadian prostitutes and found that _____ percent reported a history of childhood sexual abuse.
   (a) 22
   (b) 42
   (c) 62
   (d) 82

10. What is true of the sexual orientation of hustlers?
    (a) They are straight.
    (b) They are gay.
    (c) They are bisexual.
    (d) They may have any sexual orientation.

Answers: 1. a; 2. c; 3. d; 4. a; 5. b; 6. c; 7. a; 8. a; 9. d; 10. d

Appendix

Scoring Keys for Self-Assessments

"Sternberg's Triangular Love Scale" (Chapter 6)

Add your scores for the items on each of the three components—intimacy, passion, and commitment—and divide each total by 15. This procedure will yield an average rating for each subscale. An average rating of 5 points on a particular subscale indicates a moderate level of the component represented by the subscale. A higher rating indicates a greater level. A lower rating indicates a lower level. Examining your ratings on these components will give you an idea of the degree to which you perceive your love relationship to be characterized by these three components of love. For example, you might find that passion is stronger than commitment, a pattern that is common during the early stages of an intense romantic relationship. You might find it interesting to complete the questionnaire a few months or perhaps a year or so from now to see how your feelings about your relationship change over time. You might also ask your partner to complete the scale so that the two of you can compare your respective scores. Comparing your ratings for each component with those of your partner will give you an idea of the degree to which you and your partner see your relationship in a similar way.

Sternberg (1988) reports the results of administering the scale to a sample of 50 men and 51 women (average age, 31 years) from the New Haven, Connecticut, area who were either married or currently involved in a close relationship. Average scores for the three components were 7.39 points for intimacy, 6.51 points for passion, and 7.20 points for commitment. High scores (scores representing approximately the top 15% of scores) were 8.6 points for intimacy, 8.2 points for passion, and 8.7 points for commitment. Low scores, representing the bottom 15% of scores, were 6.2 points, 4.9 points, and 5.7 points for the three components, respectively. Because romantic ardor may be more difficult to maintain over time, the lower average scores for passion may reflect the length of the relationships in which the people in the sample were involved, which averaged 6.3 years. Although you may want to compare your scores with those from this sample, we caution that the Sternberg sample was small and most likely does not accurately represent the general population.

"Pro-Choice or Pro-Life? Where Do You Stand?" (Chapter 10)

First, change the signs of your answers to the following items: 2, 4, 6, 8, 10, 12, 13, 15, 17, and 19. That is, change a plus sign (+) to a minus (–) sign, and a minus sign (–) to a plus (+) sign. For example, if your answer to item 2 was +1, change the answer to –1. If your answer to item 17 was -2, change the answer to +2.

Now add up your scores. Final scores can be positive (+), negative (–), or 0. A positive score indicates agreement with a pro-choice philosophy. A negative score indicates agreement with a pro-life philosophy. The larger the number—ignoring the sign—the more strongly you agree with the position that you endorsed.

Scores may range from –40 to +40 points. Consider scores between –4 and +4 to be in the middle. Scores between 6 and 20 indicate a slight to moderate degree of support for the position you endorse. Scores between 22 and 40 represent a stronger endorsement of your position, with scores between 36 and 40 signifying a "powerful" endorsement of your position.

References

Aarts, H., & van Honk, J. (2009). Testosterone and unconscious positive priming increase human motivation separately. *NeuroReport, 20*(14), 1300–1303.

Abal, Y. N., Marin, J. A. L., & Sánchez, S. R. (2003). A new paraphilia of the XXI century: Chat-scatophilia. *Archivos Hispanoamericanos de Sexologíía, 9*(1), 81–104.

Abelson, H., et al. (1970). Public attitudes toward and experience with erotic materials. In *Technical reports of the commission on obscenity and pornography*. Vol. 6. Washington, DC: U.S. Government Printing Office.

Abma, J. C., et al. (2010). Teenagers in the United States: Sexual activity, contraceptive use, and childbearing. National Survey of Family Growth, 2006–2008. National Center for Health Statistics. *Vital and Health Statistics, 23*(30), http://www.cdc.gov/nchs/data/series/sr_23/sr23_030.pdf

Ackerman, D. (1991). *The moon by whale light*. New York: Random House.

Ackerman, D. (2012, March 24). The brain on love. *The New York Times* (Online). http://opinionator.blogs.nytimes.com/2012/03/24/the-brain-on-love/?_r=0

American College of Obstetricians and Gynecologists (ACOG). (2003, July 31). *Weighing the pros and cons of cesarean delivery*. ACOG news release. www.acog.com/from_home/publications/press_releases/nr07-31-03-3.cfm

Adams, H. E., Wright, L. W., Jr., & Lohr, B. A. (1996). Is homophobia associated with homosexual arousal? *Journal of Abnormal Psychology, 105*, 440–445.

Adams, H., & Phillips, L. (2006). Experiences of two-spirit lesbian and gay Native Americans: An argument for standpoint theory in identity research. *Identity, 6*(3), 273–291.

Adams, K. M. (2003). Clergy sex abuse: A commentary on celibacy. *Sexual Addiction & Compulsivity: The Journal of Treatment and Prevention, 10*(2–3), 91–92.

Adams, N. (2006). Systemic therapy techniques for sexual difficulties. In J. Hiller et al. (Eds.), *Sex, mind, and emotion: Innovation in psychological theory and practice* (pp. 209–227). London, UK: Karnac Books.

Adams, R. A. (2007). College students' attribution of blame in father–daughter incest. *Family and Consumer Sciences Research Journal, 36*(1), 55–62.

Agrawal, A. (1997). Gendered bodies: The case of the "third gender" in India. *Contributions to Indian Sociology, 31*, 273–97.

AIM Health Care Foundation (2009). HIV/STD Testing. http://www.aim-med.org/(Accessed November 6, 2009).

Ainsworth, S. E., & Baumeister, R. F. (2012). Theories of sexology: What have we learned from college students? In R. D. McAnulty (Ed.), *Sex in college: The things they don't write home about* (pp. 45–64). Santa Barbara, CA: ABC-CLIO.

Akolekar, R., et al. (2014). Procedure-related risk of miscarriage following amniocentesis and chorionic villus sampling: A systematic review and meta-analysis. *Ultrasound in Obstetrics & Gynecology*, DOI: 10.1002/uog.14636

Alemozaffar, M., et al. (2011). Prediction of erectile function following treatment for prostate cancer. *Journal of the American Medical Association, 306*(11), 1205–1214.

Alexander, B. (2009, March 26). "Sex surrogates" put personal touch on therapy: Despite dubious legality, some counselors still prescribe practice to patients. http://www.msnbc.msn.com/id/29881206/

Alexander, G. M., Wilcox, T., & Woods, R. (2009). Sex differences in infants' visual interest in toys. *Archives of Sexual Behavior, 38*(3), 427–433.

Alexander, J. (2006). A critical introduction to queer theory. *Sexualities, 9*(1), 115–117.

Alexy, E. M., Burgess, A. W., & Prentky, R. A. (2009). Pornography use as a risk marker for an aggressive pattern of behavior among sexually reactive children and adolescents. *Journal of the American Psychiatric Nurses Association, 14*(6), 442–453.

Ali, M. M., & Dwyer, D. S. (2011). Estimating peer effects in sexual behavior among adolescents. *Journal of Adolescence, 34*(1), 183–190.

Allen, L., & Rasmussen, M. L. (2015). Queer conversation in straight spaces: An interview with Mary Lou Rasmussen about queer theory in higher education. *Higher Education Research & Development, 34*(4), 685–694.

Allen, R. H., Cwiak, C., & Kaunitz, A. M. (2016). Progestin injectable contraceptives. In D. Shoupe & D. R. Mishell (Eds.), *The handbook of contraception* (pp. 125–138). Switzerland: Springer International Publishing.

Allen, S. A. (2015). Sexual stereotypes about ethnic minorities in the United States. In P. Wheelen & A. Bolin (Eds.), *The international encyclopedia of human sexuality* (pp. 1115–1354). Hoboken, NJ: Wiley.

Allison, C. M., & Hyde, J. S. (2011). Early menarche: Confluence of biological and contextual factors. *Sex Roles*. DOI:10.1007/s11199-011-9993-5

Aloi, J. A. (2009). Nursing the disenfranchised: Women who have relinquished an infant for adoption. *Journal of Psychiatric and Mental Health Nursing, 16*(1), 27–31.

Aloni, M., & Bernieri, F. J. (2004). Is love blind? The effects of experience and infatuation on the perception of love. *Journal of Nonverbal Behavior, 28*(4), 287–295.

Althof, S. E. (1994). Paper presented at the annual meeting of the American Urological Association, San Francisco, CA.

Althof, S. E. (2010). What's new in sex therapy? *Journal of Sexual Medicine, 7*, 5–13.

Althof, S. E. (2012). Psychological interventions for delayed ejaculation/orgasm. *International Journal of Impotence Research*. DOI:10.1038/ijir.2012.2

Althof, S. E., & Needle, R. B. (2011). Sex therapy in male sexual dysfunction. *Current Clinical Urology*, Part 5, 731–738.

Althof, S. E., et al. (2014). An update of the International Society of Sexual Medicine's guidelines for the diagnosis and treatment of premature ejaculation (PE). *The Journal of Sexual Medicine, 11*(6), 1392–1422.

Altunkaynak, B. Z., et al. (2012). Effects of diabetes and ovariectomy on a rat hippocampus. *Gynecological Endocrinology, 28*(3), 228–233.

Alvarez, L., et al. (2012). The rate of change in Ca^{2+} concentration controls sperm chemotaxis. *The Journal of Cell Biology, 196*(5), 653–663.

Alvarez, L., Friedrich, B. M., Gompper, G., & Kaupp, U. B. (2014). The computational sperm cell. *Trends in Cell Biology, 24*(3), 198–207.

Alzate, H., & Hoch, Z. (1986). The "G spot" and "female ejaculation": A current appraisal. *Journal of Sex and Marital Therapy, 12*(3), 211–220.

Amato, P. R. (2006). Marital discord, divorce, and children's well-being: Results from a 20-year longitudinal study of two generations. In A. Clarke-Stewart & J. Dunn (Eds.), *Families count: Effects on child and adolescent development* (pp. 179–202). The Jacobs Foundation series on adolescence. New York: Cambridge University Press.

Amato, P. R., & Afifi, T. D. (2006). Feeling caught between parents: Adult children's relations with parents and subjective well-being. *Journal of Marriage and Family, 68*(1), 222–235.

American Academy of Family Physicians. (2006). *Depo-Provera: An injectable contraceptive*. http://familydoctor.org/043.xml?printxml

American Academy of Family Physicians. (2012, June 13). Family planning and contraception. http://www.aafp.org/afp/topicModules/viewTopicModule.htm?topicModuleId=71 (Accessed June 23, 2012).

American Academy of Pediatrics. (2005). Breastfeeding and the use of human milk. *Pediatrics, 115*, 496–506.

American Academy of Pediatrics. (2012, February 27). AAP Reaffirms breastfeeding guidelines. https://www.aap.org/en-us/about-the-aap/aap-press-room/Pages/AAP-Reaffirms-Breastfeeding-Guidelines.aspx (Accessed September 21, 2012).

American Academy of Pediatrics. (2015). Benefits of breastfeeding for mothers. https://www.healthychildren.org/English/ages-stages/baby/breastfeeding/Pages/Benefits-of-Breastfeeding-for-Mom.aspx (Accessed July 13, 2016).

American Academy of Pediatrics Task Force on Circumcision. (2012, August 27). Male circumcision. *Pediatrics*, 2012-1990. DOI:10.1542/peds

American Cancer Society. (2006). *Cancer facts & figures 2006*. www.cancer.org/downloads/STT/CAFF2006f4PWSecured.pdf

American Cancer Society. (2009). *Cancer facts & figures 2009*. http://www.cancer.org/downloads/STT/500809web.pdf

American Cancer Society. (2012a). Breast cancer. http://www.cancer.org/Cancer/BreastCancer/index

American Cancer Society. (2012b). Cervical cancer. http://www.cancer.org/Cancer/CervicalCancer/index

American Cancer Society. (2012c). Endometrial cancer. http://www.cancer.org/Cancer/EndometrialCancer/index

American Cancer Society. (2012d). Ovarian cancer. http://www.cancer.org/Cancer/OvarianCancer/index

American Cancer Society. (2012e). Prostate cancer. http://www.cancer.org/Cancer/ProstateCancer/OverviewGuide/index

American Cancer Society. (2012f). Testicular cancer. http://www.cancer.org/Cancer/TesticularCancer/index

American Cancer Society. (2016a). Cervical cancer. http://www.cancer.org/Cancer/CervicalCancer/index

American Cancer Society. (2016b). Endometrial cancer. http://www.cancer.org/Cancer/EndometrialCancer/index

American Cancer Society. (2016c). Ovarian cancer. http://www.cancer.org/Cancer/OvarianCancer/index

American Cancer Society. (2016d). Breast cancer. http://www.cancer.org/Cancer/BreastCancer/index

American Cancer Society. (2015e). Testicular cancer. http://www.cancer.org/cancer/testicularcancer/index

American Cancer Society. (2015f). Prostate Cancer. http://www.cancer.org/cancer/prostatecancer/index

American Osteopathic College of Dermatology. (2015). Herpes. http://www.aocd.org/?page=Herpes

American Psychiatric Association. (2000). *Diagnostic and statistical manual of mental disorders* (4th ed.). *DSM-IV-TR*. Washington, DC: Author.

American Psychiatric Association. (2012). DSM-5 development. http://www.dsm5.org/Pages/Default.aspx

American Psychiatric Association. (2013). *Diagnostic and statistical manual of mental disorders* (5th ed.). Washington, DC: American Psychiatric Association..

American Psychiatric Association. (2014). Postpartum depression. http://www.psychiatry.org/postpartum-depression

American Sexual Health Association. (2015). Statistics. http://www.ashasexualhealth.org/stdsstis/statistics/

Amnesty International. (2012). Violence against women information. http://www.amnestyusa.org/our-work/issues/women-s-rights/violence-against-women/violence-against-women-information.

Amodeo, M., Griffin, M. K., Fassler, I. R., Clay, C. M., & Ellis, M. A. (2006). Childhood sexual abuse among black women and white women from two-parent families. *Child Maltreatment, 11*(3), 237–246.

Amodio, D. M., & Showers, C. J. (2005). "Similarity breeds liking" revisited: The moderating role of commitment. *Journal of Social and Personal Relationships, 22*(6), 817–836.

Andersen, M. L., Bignotto, M., & Tufik, S. (2003). The effect of apomorphine on genital reflexes in male rats deprived of paradoxical sleep. *Physiology & Behavior, 80*(2–3), 211–215.

Andersen, M. L., & Tufik, S. (2005). Effects of progesterone blockade over cocaine-induced genital reflexes of paradoxical sleep-deprived male rats. *Hormones and Behavior, 47*(4), 477–484.

Andersen, N. E., Dahmani, L., Konishi, K., & Dohbot, V. D. (2012). Eye tracking, strategies, and sex differences in virtual navigation. *Neurobiology of Learning and Memory, 97*(1), 81–89.

Anderson, B. J., & Stein, M. D. (2011). A behavioral decision model testing the association of marijuana use and sexual risk in young adult women. *AIDS and Behavior, 15*(4), 875–884.

Anderson, E. R., Greene, S. M., Hetherington, E. M., & Clingempeel, W. G. (1999). Dynamics of parental remarriage: Adolescent, parent, and sibling influences. In E. M. Hetherington (Ed.), *Coping with divorce, single parenting, and remarriage: A risk and resiliency perspective* (pp. 295–319). Hillsdale, NJ: Erlbaum.

Anderson, G. L., et al. (2012). Conjugated equine oestrogen and breast cancer incidence and mortality in postmenopausal women with hysterectomy: Extended follow-up of the Women's Health Initiative randomised placebo-controlled trial. *Lancet Oncology, 13*(5). http://dx.doi.org/10.1016/S1470-2045(12)70075-X

Anderson, K. M. (2006). Surviving incest: The art of resistance. *Families in Society, 87*(3), 409–416.

Anderson, M., Kunkel, A., & Dennis, M. R. (2011). "Let's (not) talk about that": Bridging the past sexual experiences taboo to build healthy romantic relationships. *Journal of Sex Research, 48*(4), 381–391.

Anderson, S. E., et al. (2003). Relative weight and race influence average age at menarche: Results from two nationally representative surveys of U.S. girls studied 25 years apart. *Pediatrics, 111*, 844–850.

Anderssen, N., Amlie, C., & Ytteroy, E. A. (2002). Outcomes for children with lesbian or gay parents: A review of studies from 1978 to 2000. *Scandinavian Journal of Psychology, 43*(4), 335–351.

Andreano, J. M., & Cahill, L. (2009). Sex influences on the neurobiology of learning and memory. *Learning and Memory, 16*, 248–266.

Andriole, G. L. (2009 March 24). In T. Parker-Pope, Screen or not? What those prostate studies mean. *The New York Times.*

Andriole, G. L., et al. (2009). Mortality results from a randomized prostate-cancer screening trial. *New England Journal of Medicine, 360*, 1310–1319.

Ankee, A. W., & Yazdanifard, R. (2015). The review of the ugly truth and negative aspects of online dating. *Global Journal of Management and Business Research: E marketing, 15*(4), https://globaljournals.org/GJMBR_Volume15/5-The-Review-of-the-Ugly.pdf

Ansari, A., & Klinenberg, E. (2015, June 13). How to make online dating work. *The New York Times,* p. SR6.

Apperloo, M. J. A., et al. (2003). In the mood for sex: The value of androgens. *Journal of Sex & Marital Therapy, 29*(2), 87–102.

Argentieri, S. (2005). Incest yesterday and today: From conflict to ambiguity. In G. Ambrosio (Ed.), *On incest: Psychoanalytic perspectives* (pp. 17–49). London: Karnac Books.

Armstrong, E. A. (2009). Cited in P. L. Brown & C. Pogash. (2009, March 15). The pleasure principle. *The New York Times.* http://www.nytimes.com/2009/03/15/fashion/15commune.html *(Accessed July 13, 2016).*

Arnez, Z. M., et al. (2015). Total phallic reconstruction in female-to-male transsexuals by the pedicle anterolateral (ALT) flap. In C. Trombetta et al. (Eds.), *Management of gender dysphoria* (pp. 241–247). Milan, Italy: Sprinter-Verlag Italia.

Aron, A., et al. (2008). Falling in love. In S. Sprecher, A. Wenzel & J. Harvey (Eds.), *Handbook of relationship initiation* (pp. 315–336). New York: CRC Press.

Arriaga, X. B., & Rusbult, C. E. (1998). Standing in my partner's shoes: Partner perspective taking and reactions to accommodative dilemmas. *Personality & Social Psychology Bulletin, 24*(9), 927–948.

Arthur, B. I., Jr., et al. (1998). Sexual behaviour in *Drosophila* is irreversibly programmed during critical period. *Current Biology, 8*(21), 1187–1190.

Ascher, N. (2006, July 10.) *Fight ignorance before it's too late.* www.classicalvalues.com/archives/003848.html

Ashley–Koch, A., Yang, Q., & Olney, R. S. (2000). Sickle hemoglobin (Hb S) allele and sickle cell disease. *American Journal of Epidemiology, 151*(9), 839–845.

Ask, H., et al. (2012). Non-random mating and convergence over time for alcohol consumption, smoking, and exercise: The Nord-Trøndelag Health Study. *Behavior Genetics, 42*(3), 354–365.

Astley, S. J., & Clarren, S. K. (2001). Measuring the facial phenotype of individuals with prenatal alcohol exposure: Correlations with brain dysfunction. *Alcohol & Alcoholism, 36*(2), 147–159.

Assumpcao, A. A., et al. (2014). Pharmacologic treatment of paraphilias. *Psychiatric Clinics of North America, 37*(2), 173–181.

Aubin, S., Heiman, J. R., Berger, R. E., Murallo, A. V., & Yung-Wen, L. (2009). Comparing sildenafil alone vs. sildenafil plus brief couple sex therapy on erectile dysfunction and couples' sexual and marital quality of life. *Journal of Sex and Marital Therapy, 35*(2), 122–143.

"Australia scientists find flowers dupe lonely bees." (2000, June 16). Reuters News Agency online. http://ww1.utusan.com.my/utusan/info.asp?y=2000&dt=0619&pub=Utusan_Express&sec=OddsEnds&pg=oe_10.htm

Auyeung, B., et al. (2009). Fetal testosterone predicts behavior in girls and in boys. *Psychological Science, 20*(2), 144–148.

Aveline, D. (2006). "Did I have blinders on or what?": Retrospective sense making by parents of gay sons recalling their sons' earlier years. *Journal of Family Issues, 27*(6), 777–802.

Avinum, R., & Knafo-Noam, A. (2015). Socialization, genetics, and their interplay in development. In J. E. Grusec & P. D. Hastings (Eds.). *Handbook of socialization: Theory and Research* (pp. 347–371). New York: Guilford.

Avis, N. E. (2003). Depression during the menopausal transition. *Psychology of Women Quarterly, 27*(2), 91–100.

Ayres, M. M., & Haddock, S. A. (2009). Therapists' approaches in working with heterosexual couples struggling with male partners' online sexual behavior. *Sexual Addiction & Compulsivity, 16*(1), 55–78.

Bach, G., & Deutsch, R. M. (1970). *Pairing: How to achieve genuine intimacy.* New York: Avon Books.

Bäckström T., et al. (2003). The role of hormones and hormonal treatments in premenstrual syndrome. *CNS Drugs, 17*(5), 325–342.

Bacterial Vaginosis. (2015). Centers for Disease Control and Prevention. http://www.cdc.gov/std/bv/default.htm

Bader, M. (2003). *Arousal: The secret logic of sexual fantasies.* New York: Griffin Trade Paperback.

Bagley, C., & D'Augelli, A. R. (2000). Suicidal behaviour in gay, lesbian, and bisexual youth. *British Medical Journal, 320,* 1617–1618.

Bailes, E., et al. (2003). Hybrid origin of SIV in chimpanzees. *Science, 300*(5626), 1713.

Bailey, J. M. (1999). Homosexuality and mental illness. *Archives of General Psychiatry, 56*(10), 883–884.

Bailey, J. M. (2003a). Personal communication.

Bailey, J. M. (2003b). *The man who would be queen: The science of gender-bending and transsexualism.* Washington, DC: Joseph Henry Press.

Bailey, J. M., & Pillard, R. C. (1991). A genetic study of male sexual orientation. *Archives of General Psychiatry, 48,* 1089–1096.

Bailey, J. M., et al. (1999). A family history study of male sexual orientation using three independent samples. *Behavior Genetics, 29*(2), 79–86.

Bakalar, N. (2005, November 22). Premature births increase along with C-sections. *The New York Times,* p. F8.

Bakalar, N. (2014, March 4). Is breast-feeding really better? *The New York Times.* http://well.blogs.nytimes.com/2014/03/04/is-breast-feeding-really-better/?_r=0 (Accessed February 26, 2016).

Baker, J. L., et al. (2008). Breastfeeding reduces postpartum weight retention. *American Journal of Clinical Nutrition, 88,* 1553–1551.

Balon, R. (2015a). Is infidelity biologically determined? *European Psychiatry, 30*(Suppl. 1), 28–31.

Balon, R. (2015b). Paraphilic disorders. In L. W. Roberts & A K. Louie (Eds.). (2015). *Study guide to DSM–5.* (pp. 441–458). Arlington, VA: American Psychiatric Publishing.

Balsam, K. F., et al. (2004). Culture, trauma, and wellness: A comparison of heterosexual and lesbian, gay, bisexual, and two-spirit Native Americans. *Cultural Diversity & Ethnic Minority Psychology, 10*(3), 287–301.

Bamgbose, O. (2002). Teenage prostitution and the future of the female adolescent in Nigeria. *International Journal of Offender Therapy & Comparative Criminology, 46*(5), 569–585.

Bancroft, J. (Ed.). (2003). *Sexual development in childhood.* Bloomington: Indiana University Press.

Bancroft, J., Carnes, L., & Janssen, E. (2005a). Unprotected anal intercourse in HIV-positive and HIV-negative gay men: The relevance of sexual arousability, mood, sensation seeking, and erectile problems. *Archives of Sexual Behavior, 34,* 299–305.

Bancroft, J., Carnes, L., Janssen, E., Goodrich, D., & Long, J. S. (2005b). Erectile and ejaculatory problems in gay and heterosexual men. *Archives of Sexual Behavior, 34*(3), 285–297.

Bancroft, J., et al. (2005c). The relevance of the dual control model to male sexual dysfunction: The Kinsey Institute/BASRT collaborative project. *Sexual & Relationship Therapy, 20,* 13–30.

Bandera, E. V., et al. (2015). Obesity, body fat distribution, and risk of breast cancer subtypes in African American women participating in the AMBER Consortium. *Breast Cancer Research and Treatment, 150*(3), 655–666.

Bangs, R., & Davis, L. E. (2015). America's racial realities. In R. Bangs, & L. E. Davis (Eds.). *Race and social problems: Restructuring inequality* (pp. 3–14). New York: Springer Science+Business Media.

Banszegi, O., et al. (2010). Testosterone treatment of pregnant rabbits affects sexual development of their daughters. *Physiology and Behavior, 101*(4), 422–427.

Barak, A. (2005). Sexual harassment on the Internet. *Social Science Computer Review, 23*(1), 77–92.

Baral, S., et al. (2012). Burden of HIV among female sex workers in low-income and middle-income countries: a systematic review and meta-analysis. *The Lancet Infectious Diseases, 12*(7), 538–549.

Barbaree, H. E., & Blanchard, R. (2008). Sexual deviance over the lifespan. In D. R. Laws and W. T. O'Donohue (Eds.), *Sexual deviance: Theory, assessment, and treatment* (2nd ed., pp. 27–60). New York: Guilford Press.

Barelli, C., Heistermann, M., Boesch, C., & Reichard, U. H. (2008). Mating patterns and sexual swellings in pair-living and multiple groups of wild white-handed gibbons, *Hylobates lar. Animal Behaviour, 75*(3), 991–1001.

Barnard, N. D., Scialli, A. R., Hurlock, D., & Bertron, P. (2000). Diet and sex-hormone binding globulin, dysmenorrhea, and premenstrual symptoms. *Obstetrics & Gynecology, 95,* 245–250.

Barnett, J. E., & Dunning, C. (2003). Clinical perspectives on elderly sexuality. *Archives of Sexual Behavior, 32*(3), 295–296.

Barney, D., & Feenberg, A. (Eds.). (2004). *Community in the digital age: Philosophy and practice.* Lanham, MD: Rowman & Littlefield.

Barrett, S. E., Chin, J. L., Comas–Diaz, L., Espin, O., Greene, B., & McGoldrick, M. (2005). Multicultural feminist therapy: Theory in context. *Women & Therapy, 28*(3–4), 27–61.

Barrionuevo, A. (2009, March 28). Amid abuse of girls in Brazil, abortion debate flares. *The New York Times.* http://www.nytimes.com/2009/03/28/world/americas/28brazil.html (Accessed July 13, 2006).

Barsky, J. L., Friedman, M. A., & Rosen, R. C. (2006). Sexual dysfunction and chronic illness: The role of flexibility in coping. *Journal of Sex & Marital Therapy, 32*(3), 235–253.

Bartels, R. M., & Gannon, T. A. (2011). Understanding the sexual fantasies of sex offenders and their correlates. *Aggression and Violent Behavior, 16*(6), 551–561.

Barth, R. P., et al. (2002). Methodological lessons from the National Survey of Child and Adolescent Well-Being: The first three years of the USA's first national probability study of children and families investigated for abuse and neglect. *Children & Youth Services Review, 24*(6–7), 513–541.

Bartolo, K. C. (2005). Mother–daughter incest: A guide for helping professionals. *Journal of Family Studies, 11*(2), 328–329.

Based on Gallup organization and the Williams Institute at the law school of UCLA, October 18, 2012. Based on telephone interviews June 1–September 30, 2012 of 121, 290 Americans.

Basile, K. C. (2002). Attitudes toward wife rape: Effects of social background and victim status. *Violence & Victims, 17*(3), 341–354.

Basow, S. A., & Rubenfeld, K. (2003). "Troubles talk": Effects of gender and gender-typing. *Sex Roles, 48*(3–4), 183–187.

Basson, B., Davis, S. R., & Rodenberg, C. (2009). Testosterone for low libido. *New England Journal of Medicine, 360*(7), 728–729.

Bastian, L. A., Smith, C. M., & Nanda, K. (2003). Is this woman perimenopausal? *Journal of the American Medical Association, 289,* 895–902.

Bauerle, S. Y., Amirkhan, J. H., & Hupka, R. B. (2002). An attribution theory analysis of romantic jealousy. *Motivation & Emotion, 26*(4), 297–319.

Bauland, C. G., et al. (2012). Similar risk for hemangiomas after amniocentesis and trans-abdominal chorionic villus sampling. *The Journal of Obstetrics and Gynecology Research, 38*(2), 371–375.

Baum, M. J., & Kelliher, K. R. (2009). Complementary roles of the main and accessory olfactory systems in mammalian mate recognition. *Annual Review of Physiology, 71,* 141–160.

Baumeister, R. F. (2000). Gender differences in erotic plasticity: The female sex drive as socially flexible and responsive. *Psychological Bulletin, 126*(3), 347–374.

Baumeister, R. F., Catanese, K. R., & Vohs, K. D. (2001). Is there a gender difference in strength of sex drive? Theoretical views, conceptual distinctions, and a review of relevant evidence. *Personality & Social Psychology Review, 5*(3), 242–273.

Bearak, B. (2006, July 9). The bride price. *The New York Times Magazine.* http://www.nytimes.com/2006/07/09/magazine/09BRI.html (Accessed July 13, 2016).

Beauregard, E., Proulx, J., & LeClerc, B. (2014). Offending pathways: The role of lifestyle and precrime factors in extrafamilial child molesters. In E. Prolux, et al. (Eds.), *Pathways to sexual aggression* (pp. 137–155). New York: Routledge.

Becerra, L., Breiter, H. C., Wise, R., Gonzalez, R. G., & Borsook, D. (2001). Reward circuitry activation by noxious thermal stimuli. *Neuron, 32*(5), 927–946.

Becher, E., & Bechara, A. (2011). Making the diagnosis of erectile dysfunction. *Contemporary Endocrinology,* 69–80.

Becker, J. C., & Swim, J. K. (2012). Reducing endorsement of benevolent and modern sexist beliefs: Differential effects of addressing harm versus pervasiveness of benevolent sexism. *Social Psychology, 43,* 127–137.

Beckman, N., Waern, M., Gustafson, D., & Skoog, I. (2008). Secular trends in self reported sexual activity and satisfaction in Swedish 70 year olds: Cross sectional survey of four populations, 1971–2001. *British Medical Journal, 337,* a279.

Becquet, R., & Dabis, F. (2013). Turning the tide on HIV in women and children: Preventing breast-milk HIV transmission while increasing maternal life expectancy. *Clinical Infectious Diseases, 56*(1), 140–142.

Beech, A., et al. (2009). Evaluating rapists' distorted beliefs and deviant sexual fantasies: A preliminary study. *Journal of Aggression, Conflict, and Peace Research, 1*(1), 25–35.

Beech, A. R., Parrett, N., Ward, T., & Fisher, D. (2009). Assessing female sexual offenders' motivations and cognitions: an exploratory study. *Psychology, Crime & Law, 15*(2–3), 201–216.

Begum, K. S., Khan, N. U., & Akter, F. (2014). Factors affecting the pregnancy outcome in patients with previous one Caesarean section. *Medicine Today, 26*(1), 1–3.

Behrendt, N., Buhl, N., & Seidl, S. (2002). The lethal paraphiliac syndrome: Accidental autoerotic deaths in four women and a review of the literature. *International Journal of Legal Medicine, 116*(3), 148–152.

Belden, M. (2011). *Obstetrics & gynecology: A competency-based companion.* Philadelphia: Saunders.

Belgrave, F. Z., van Oss Marian, B., & Chambers, D. B. (2000). Cultural, contextual, and intrapersonal predictors of risky sexual attitudes among urban African American girls in early adolescence. *Cultural Diversity and Ethnic Minority Psychology, 6*(3), 309–322.

Belkin, L. (2009, April 5). Your old man. *The New York Times Magazine.* http://parenting.blogs.nytimes.com/2009/04/03/your-old-man/comment-page-3/(Accessed July 13, 2016).

Bell, A. P., & Weinberg, M. S. (1978). *Homosexualities: A study of diversity among men and women.* New York: Simon & Schuster.

Bell, A. P., Weinberg, M. S., & Hammersmith, S. K. (1981). *Sexual preference: Its development in men and women.* Bloomington, IN: University of Indiana Press.

Bellavia, G., & Murray, S. (2003). Did I do that? Self esteem-related differences in reactions to romantic partner's mood. *Personal Relationships, 10*(1), 77–95.

Belluck, P. (2006, February 6). Fugitive in gay bar attacks dies after shootout with Arkansas police. *The New York Times.* http://www.nytimes.com/2006/02/06/us/fugitive-in-gay-bar-attacks-dies-after-shootout-with-arkansas-police.html (Accessed July 13, 2016).

Bem, S. L. (1975). Sex role adaptability: One consequence of psychological androgyny. *Journal of Personality and Social Psychology, 31,* 634–643.

Bem, S. L. (1993). *The lenses of gender.* New Haven: Yale University Press.

Bem, S. L., Martyna, W., & Watson, C. (1976). Sex typing and androgyny: Further explorations of the expressive domain. *Journal of Personality and Social Psychology, 34,* 1016–1023.

Bendixen, M., Kennair, L. E. O., & Buss, D. M. (2015). Jealousy: Evidence of strong sex differences using both forced choice and continuous measure paradigms. *Personality and Individual Differences, 86,* 212–216.

Bengoa Vallejo, R. B., et al. (2008). Application of cantharidin and podophyllotoxin for the treatment of plantar warts. *Journal of the American Podiatric Medical Association, 98*(6), 445–450.

Bennetts, L. (2011, July 18). The john next door. *Newsweek* magazine. http://www.newsweek.com/growing-demand-prostitution-68493 (Accessed July 13, 2016).

Benotsch, E. G., & Kalichman, S. C. (2002). Preventing HIV and AIDS. In L. A. Jason & D. S. Glenwick (Eds.), *Innovative strategies for promoting health and mental health across the life span* (pp. 205–226). New York: Springer.

Bentley, T. (2009, June 21). Harem envy. *The New York Times Magazine,* pp. 10–11.

Benvenuto, C., & Weeks, S. C. (2012). Intersexual conflict during mate guarding in an androdioecious crustacean. *Behavioral Ecology, 23*(1), 218–224.

Benvenuto, C., Knott, B., & Weeks, S.C. (2015). Crustaceans of extreme environments. In M. Thiel & L. Watling (Eds.), *Lifestyles and feeding biology* (pp. 379–417). New York: Oxford University Press.

Ben-Zur, H. (2003). Peer risk behavior and denial of HIV/AIDS among adolescents. *Sex Education, 3*(1), 75–85.

Berga, S., & Naftolin, F. (2012). Neuroendocrine control of ovulation. *Gynecological Endocrinology, 28*(S1), 9–13.

Berger, L. (2002, December 10). After long hiatus, new contraceptives emerge. *The New York Times.*

Bergner, D. (2009, January 22). What do women want? *The New York Times.*

Bering, J. (2013). *The sexual deviant in all of us.* New York: Farrar, Straus & Giroux.

Berridge, K. C., & Kringelbach, M. L. (2015). Pleasure systems in the brain. *Neuron, 86*(3), 646–664.

Berke, R. L. (1997, June 15). Suddenly, the new politics of morality. *The New York Times,* p. E3.

Berke, R. L. (1998, August 2). Chasing the polls on gay rights. *The New York Times,* p. WK3.

Berkowitz, D. (2013). Gay men and surrogacy. In A. E Goldberg, & K. R. Allen (Eds.). *LGBT-parent families: Innovations in research and implications for practice* (pp. 71–85). New York: Springer Science+Business Media.

Berman, J. R., & Berman, L. A., et al. (2001). Effect of sildenafil on subjective and physiologic parameters of the female sexual response in women with sexual arousal disorder. *Journal of Sex & Marital Therapy, 27*(5), 411–420.

Bernstein, I. M., et al. (2005). Maternal smoking and its association with birth weight. *Obstetrics & Gynecology, 106,* 986–991.

Bernstein, R. (2009). *The East, the West, and sex: A history of erotic encounters.* New York: Knopf.

Berry, D. A., et al. (2005). Effect of screening and adjuvant therapy on mortality from breast cancer. *The New England Journal of Medicine, 353,* 1784–1792.

Bersamin, M. M., et al. (2014). Risky business: Is there an association between casual sex and mental health among emerging adults? *The Journal of Sex Research, 51*(1), 43–51.

Berscheid, E. (2003). On stepping on land mines. In R. J. Sternberg (Ed.), *Psychologists defying the crowd: Stories of those who battled the establishment and won* (pp. 33–44). Washington, DC: American Psychological Association.

Berscheid, E. (2010). Love in the fourth dimension. *Annual Review of Psychology, 61,* 1–25.

Berscheid, E., & Walster, E. (1978). *Interpersonal attraction.* Reading, MA: Addison-Wesley.

Besiroglu, H., Otunctemur, A., & Ozbek, E. (2015). The relationship between metabolic syndrome, its components, and erectile dysfunction: A systematic review and a meta-analysis of observational studies. *The Journal of Sexual Medicine, 12*(6), 1309–1318.

Beutel, M. E., Stöbel-Richter, Y., & Brähler, E. (2008). Sexual desire and sexual activity of men and women across their lifespans: Results from a representative German community survey. *BJU International, 101*(1), 76–82.

Beyerlein, A., et al. (2011). The relationship between birth weight, smoking during pregnancy, and maternal weight gain. *American Journal of Epidemiology, 113*(5), 590–595.

Bhugra, D. (2004). Literature update: A critical review. *Sexual and Relationship Therapy, 19*(2), 201–208.

Bhugra, D. (2005). Queer theory. *Sexual and Relationship Therapy, 20*(4), 476.

Bhugra, D., Rahman, Q., & Bhintade, R. (2006). Sexual fantasy in gay men in India: A comparison with heterosexual men. *Sexual and Relationship Therapy, 21*(2), 197–207.

Bialy, M., & Sachs, B. D. (2002). Androgen implants in medial amygdala briefly maintain noncontact erection in castrated male rats. *Hormones & Behavior, 42*(3), 345–355.

Bianchi, S. M., & Spain, D. (1997). *Women, work and family in America.* Population Reference Bureau.

Bilefsky, D. (2009, March 11). Europeans debate castration of sex offenders. *The New York Times.* http://www.nytimes.com/2009/03/11/world/europe/11castrate.html *(Accessed July 13, 2016).*

Billy, J. O. G., et al. (1993). The sexual behavior of men in the United States. *Family Planning Perspectives, 25,* 52–60.

Bimbi, D. S. (2007). Male prostitution: Pathology, paradigms and progress in research. *Journal of Homosexuality, 53*(1–2), 7–35.

Binik, Y. M. (2005). Should dyspareunia be retained as a sexual dysfunction in *DSM-V?* A painful classification decision. *Archives of Sexual Behavior, 34*(1), 11–21.

Bird, E. R., Gilmore, A. K., George, W. W., & Lewis, M. (2016). The role of social drinking factors in the relationship between incapacitated sexual assault and drinking before sexual activity. *Addictive Behaviors, 52,* 28–33.

Birnie-Porter, C., & Lydon, J. E. (2012). A prototype approach to understanding sexual intimacy through its relationship to intimacy. *Personal Relationships.* DOI:10.1111/j.1475-6811.2012.01402.x.

Black breast-feeding gatherings battle troubling health gaps. (2015, January 29). http://www.nytimes.com/aponline/2015/01/29/health/ap-us-med-blacks-breast-feeding.html (Accessed February 26, 2015).

Blackwell, D. L., & Lichter, D. T. (2004). Homogamy among dating, cohabiting, and married couples. *Sociological Quarterly, 45*(4), 719–737.

Blake, S. M., et al. (2003). Condom availability programs in Massachusetts high schools: Relationships with condom use and sexual behavior. *American Journal of Public Health, 93,* 955–962.

Blanchard, R. (1988). Nonhomosexual gender dysphoria. *Journal of Sex Research, 24,* 188–193.

Blanchard, R. (1989). The concept of autogynephilia and the typology of male gender dysphoria. *Journal of Nervous & Mental Disease, 177*(10), 616–623.

Blanchard, R. (2010). The DSM criteria for transvestic fetishism. *Archives of Sexual Behavior,* DOI 10.1007/s10508-009-9541-3.

Blanchard, R., Steiner, B. W., & Clemmensen, L. H. (1985). Gender dysphoria, gender reorientation, and the clinical management of transsexualism. *Journal of Consulting and Clinical Psychology, 53,* 295–304.

Blanker, M. H., et al. (2001). Erectile and ejaculatory dysfunction in a community-based sample of men 50 to 78 years old: Prevalence, concern, and relation to sexual activity. *Urology, 57*(4), 763–768.

Bletzer, K. V., & Koss, M. P. (2006). After rape among three populations in the southwest: A time of mourning, a time for recovery. *Violence Against Women, 12*(1), 5–29.

Blickstein, I., Goldman, R. D., & Mazkereth, R. (2000). Risk for one or two very low birth weight twins: A population study. *Obstetrics & Gynecology, 96*(3), 400–402.

Bloch, M., Rotenberg, N., Koren, D., & Ehud, K. (2006). Risk factors for early postpartum depressive symptoms. *General Hospital Psychiatry, 28*(1), 3–8.

Bloemers, J., et al. (2013). Toward personalized sexual medicine (Part 1): Integrating the "dual control model" into differential drug treatments for hypoactive sexual desire disorder and female sexual arousal disorder. *The Journal of Sexual Medicine, 10*(3), 791–809.

Blokland, A., & Lussier, P. (Eds.). (2015). *Sex offenders*. Chichester, UK: Wiley Blackwell.

Blow, A. J., & Hartnett, K. (2005). Infidelity in committed relationships II: A substantive review. *Journal of Family and Marital Therapy, 31*(2), 217–233.

Blow, C. M. (2009, June 27). The prurient trap. *The New York Times.* http://www.nytimes.com/2009/06/27/opinion/27blow.html (Accessed July 13, 2016).

Bockting, W. O., & Fung, L. C. T. (2006). Genital reconstruction and gender identity disorders. In D. B. Sarwer (Ed.), *Psychological aspects of reconstructive and cosmetic plastic surgery: Clinical, empirical, and ethical perspectives* (pp. 207–229). New York: Lippincott Williams & Wilkins.

Bodurtha, J., & Strauss, J. F. (2012). Genomics and perinatal care. *The New England Journal of Medicine, 366*, 64–73.

Bogaert, A. F. (2006). Toward a conceptual understanding of asexuality. *Review of General Psychology, 10*(3), 241–250.

Bogaert, A. F., Visser, B. A., & Pozzebon, J. A. (2015). Gender differences in object of desire self-consciousness sexual fantasies. *Archives of Sexual Behavior, 44*(8), 2299–2310.

Bogin, G. Y. (2006). Out of the darkness: Male adolescents and the experience of sexual victimization. *School Social Work Journal, 30*(2), 1–21.

Bogle, K. (2008). *Hooking up: Sex, dating, and relationships on campus*. New York: New York University Press.

Bolton, J. M., Sareen, J., & Reiss, J. P. (2006). Genital anaesthesia persisting six years after sertraline discontinuation. *Journal of Sex & Marital Therapy, 32*(4), 327–330.

Born, L., Soares, C. N., Phillips, S., Jung, M., & Steiner, M. (2006). Women and reproductive-related trauma. In R. Yehuda (Ed.), *Psychobiology of posttraumatic stress disorders: A decade of progress* (Vol. 1071, pp. 491–494). New York: Blackwell.

Boros, S., Mateuca, A., & Matus, M. (2005). The role of social identity in attributions—Evaluating the guilt in rape assault. *Cognitie Creier Comportament, 9*(1), 35–57.

Bos, H. (2013). Lesbian-mother families formed through donor insemination. In A. E Goldberg, & K. R. Allen (Eds.). *LGBT-parent families: Innovations in research and implications for practice* (pp. 21–37). New York: Springer Science+Business Media.

Bos, H. M. W., Sandfort, T. G. M., de Bruyn, E. H., & Hakvoort, E. M. (2008). Same-sex attraction, social relationships, psychosocial functioning, and school performance in early adolescence. *Developmental Psychology, 44*(1), 59–68.

Boss, S., & Maltz, W. (2001). *Private thoughts: Exploring the power of women's sexual fantasies.* New York: New World Library.

Boston Women's Health Book Collective. (2005). *Our bodies, ourselves: A new edition for a new era.* New York: Touchstone.

Bottorff, J. L., et al. (2014). Tobacco and alcohol use in the context of adolescent pregnancy and postpartum. *Health and Social Care in the Community, 22*(6), 561–574.

Bouchard, K. N., Timmers, A. D., & Chivers, M. L. (2015). Gender-specificity of genital response and self-reported sexual arousal in women endorsing facets of bisexuality. *Journal of Bisexuality, 15*(2), 180–203.

Bower, B. (2009). Infectious voyagers: DNA suggests Columbus took syphilis to Europe. *Science News, 173*(3), 38.

Bowes-Sperry, L., & O'Leary–Kelly, A. M. (2005). To act or not to act: The dilemma faced by sexual harassment observers. *Academy of Management Review, 30*(2), 288–306.

Bowlby, J. (1969). *Attachment and loss* (Vol. 1). New York: Basic Books.

Boxer, S. (2000, July 22). Truth or lies? In sex surveys, you never know. *The New York Times.* http://www.nytimes.com/2000/07/22/arts/truth-or-lies-in-sex-surveys-you-never-know.html?pagewanted=all (Accessed July 13, 2016).

Boynton, P. (2008). A review of "G-strings and sympathy: Strip club regulars and male desire." *Journal of Sex & Marital Therapy, 34*(5), 457–459.

Bozell, B. (2005, December 30). Coming in 2006: Group marriage TV? www.townhall.com/opinion/columns/brentbozell/2005/12/30/180704.html

Bradford, J. M. W. (1998). Treatment of men with paraphilia. *New England Journal of Medicine, 338*, 464–465.

Bradford, J. M. W. (2001). The neurobiology, neuropharmacology, and pharmacological treatment of the paraphilias and compulsive sexual behaviour. *Canadian Journal of Psychiatry, 46*(1), 26–34.

Bradley, S. J., Oliver, G. D., Chernick, A. B., & Zucker, K. J. (1998). Experiment of nurture: Ablatio penis at 2 months, sex reassignment at 7 months, and a psychosexual follow-up in young adulthood. *Pediatrics, 102*(1), e9.

Braithwaite, D. O., Olson, L. N., Golish, T. D., Soukup, C., & Turman, P. (2001). "Becoming a family": Developmental processes represented in blended family discourse. *Journal of Applied Communication Research, 29*(3), 221–247.

Braithwaite, S. R., Coulson, G., Keddington, K., & Fincham, F. D. (2015a). The influence of pornography on sexual scripts and hooking up among emerging adults in college. *Archives of Sexual Behavior, 44*(1), 111–123.

Braithwaite, S. R., et al. (2015b). The influence of religion on the partner selection strategies of emerging adults. *Journal of Family Issues, 36*(2), 212–231.

Bramlett, M. D., & Mosher, W. D. (2002). *Cohabitation, marriage, divorce, and remarriage.* National Center for Health Statistics, *Vital Health Statistics, 23*(22). www.cdc.gov/nchs/data/series/sr_23/sr23_022.pdf

Brassard, A., Dupuy, E., Bergeron, S., & Shaver, P. R. (2015). Attachment insecurities and women's sexual function and satisfaction: The mediating roles of sexual self-esteem, sexual anxiety, and sexual assertiveness. *The Journal of Sex Research, 52*(1), 110–119.

Brauer, M., ter Kuile, M. M., Laan, E., & Trimbos, B. (2009). Cognitive-affective correlates and predictors of superficial dyspareunia. *Journal of Sex & Marital Therapy, 35*(1), 1–24.

Brawley, O. (2009, March 24). In T. Parker-Pope, Screen or not? What those prostate studies mean. *The New York Times.* http://www.nytimes.com/2009/03/24/health/24well.html (Accessed July 13, 2016).

Bray, P. F., et al. (2008). "Undesirable" lipid levels linked to HRT-related coronary events. *Inpharma, 1*, 20.

Breastfeeding. (2010). U.S. Department of Health and Human Services: http://www.womenshealth.gov/breastfeeding (Accessed September 21, 2012).

Brechin, S., & Bigrigg, A. (2006). Male and female sterilization. *Current Obstetrics & Gynaecology, 16*(1), 39–46.

Brents, B. G. (2012, April 19). Nevada's legal brothels make workers feel safer. *The New York Times.* http://www.nytimes.com/roomfordebate/2012/04/19/is-legalized-prostitution-safer/nevadas-legal-brothels-make-workers-feel-safer (Accessed July 13, 2016).

Brewster, K. L., Tillman, K. H., & Jokinen-Gordon, H. (2014). Demographic characteristics of lesbian parents in the United States. *Population Research and Policy Review, 33*, 503–526.

Briken, P., Hill, A., & Berner, W. (2011). Pharmacotherapy of sexual offenders and men who are at risk of sexual offending. In D. P. Boer et al. (Eds.), *International Perspectives on the Assessment and Treatment of Sexual Offenders: Theory, Practice, and Research* (pp. 419–431). Hoboken, NJ: Wiley.

Briken, P., Hill, A., Nika, E., & Berner, W. (2005). Obscene telephone calls—Relations to paraphilias, paraphilia related disorders and stalking. *Psychiatrische Praxis, 32*(6), 304–307.

Brin, D. J. (2004). The use of rituals in grieving for a miscarriage or stillbirth. *Women & Therapy, 27*(3–4), 123–132.

Brisch, K. H., et al. (2005). Effects of previous pregnancy loss on level of maternal anxiety after prenatal ultrasound screening for fetal malformation. *Journal of Loss & Trauma, 10*(2), 131–153.

Brock, G., et al. (2015). Effect of testosterone solution 2% ontestosterone concentration, sex drive and energy in hypogonadal men: Results of a placebo-controlled study. *The Journal of Urology*, DOI: 10.1016/j.juro.2015.10.083

Broder, M. S., Kanouse, D. E., Mittman, B. S., & Bernstein, S. J. (2000). The appropriateness of recommendations for hysterectomy. *Obstetrics & Gynecology, 95*, 199–206.

Brodkin, E. S., et al. (2002). Identification of quantitative trait loci that affect aggressive behavior in mice. *The Journal of Neuroscience, 22*(3), 1165–1170.

Brody, J. E. (1994, March 21). Notions of beauty transcend culture, new study suggests. *The New York Times*, p. A14.

Brody, J. E. (2000, May 16). Cybersex gives birth to a psychological disorder. *The New York Times*, pp. F7, F12.

Brody, J. E. (2012, February 27). Americans get reacquainted with IUDs. *The New York Times*. http://well.blogs.nytimes.com/2012/02/27/americans-get-reacquainted-with-iuds/(*Accessed July 13, 2016*).

Brody, J. E. (2013, October 7). Breakthroughs in prenatal screening. *The New York Times*. http://well.blogs.nytimes.com/2013/10/07/break-throughs-in-prenatal-screening/?mtrref=www.google.com&gwh=60AAB1699BDF363FD26D36156B3EDC7C&gwt=pay (Accessed July 13, 2016).

Brodzinsky, D. M., & Palacios, J. (2005). *Psychological issues in adoption: Research and practice*. Westport, CT: Praeger Publishers/Greenwood Publishing Group.

Bronner, E. (1998, February 1). "Just say maybe. No sexology, please. We're Americans." *The New York Times*, p. WK6.

Brooks, D. (2015, August 28). When ISIS rapists win. *The New York Times*. http://www.nytimes.com/2015/08/28/opinion/david-brooks-when-isis-rapists-win.html (Accessed July 13, 2016).

Bross, D. C. (2005). Invited commentary: Minimizing risks to children when they access the World Wide Web. *Child Abuse & Neglect, 29*(7), 749–752.

Brotto L. A., Bitzer, J., Laan, E., Leiblum, S., & Luria, M. (2010). Women's sexual desire and arousal disorders. *Journal of Sexual Medicine, 7,* 586–614.

Broude, G. J., & Greene, S. J. (1976). Cross-cultural codes on twenty sexual attitudes and practices. *Ethnology, 15,* 409–429.

Brown, D. (2003). Pornography and erotica. In J. Bryant, D. Roskos–Ewoldsen, & J. Cantor (Eds.), *Communication and emotion: Essays in honor of Dolf Zillmann* (pp. 221–253). LEA's communication series. Hillsdale, NJ: Erlbaum.

Brown, G. R., & Haaser, R. C. (2005). Sexual disorders. In J. L. Levenson (Ed.), *The American psychiatric publishing textbook of psychosomatic medicine* (pp. 359–386). Washington, DC: American Psychiatric Publishing.

Brown, J., et al. (2009). Selective serotonin reuptake inhibitors for premenstrual syndrome. *Cochrane Database System Review, 15*(2), CD001396.

Brown, L. M., McNatt, P. S., & Cooper, G. D. (2003). Ingroup romantic preferences among Jewish and non-Jewish white undergraduates. *International Journal of Intercultural Relations, 27*(3), 335–354.

Brown, L. S. (2005). Prostitution, trafficking and traumatic stress. *Journal of Trauma & Dissociation, 6*(3), 143–145.

Brown, P. L., & Pogash, C. (2009, March 15). The pleasure principle. *The New York Times.* http://www.nytimes.com/2009/03/15/fashion/15commune.html (*Accessed July 13, 2016*).

Brown, R., Balousek, S., Mundt, M., & Fleming, M. (2005). Methadone maintenance and male sexual dysfunction. *Journal of Addictive Diseases, 24*(2), 91–106.

Brown, S. L., & Manning, W. D. (2009). Family boundary ambiguity and the measurement of family structure: The significance of cohabitation. *Demography, 46*(1), 85–101.

Brown, T. (2002). A proposed model of bisexual identity development that elaborates on experiential differences of women and men. *Journal of Bisexuality, 2*(4), 67–91.

Browning, C. R. (2002). Trauma or transition: A life-course perspective on the link between childhood sexual experiences and men's adult well-being. *Social Science Research, 31*(4), 473–510.

Browning, D. S., Green, M. C., & Witte Jr., J. (Eds.). (2006). *Sex, marriage, and family in world religions.* New York: Columbia University Press.

Browning, J. R., Hatfield, E., Kessler, D., & Levine, T. (2000). Sexual motives, gender, and sexual behavior. *Archives of Sexual Behavior, 29*(2), 135–153.

Brun, C. C., et al. (2009). Sex differences in brain structure in auditory and cingulate regions. *NeuroReport: For Rapid Communication of Neuroscience Research, 20*(10), 930.

Brunet, P. M., & Schmidt, L. A. (2008). Are shy adults really bolder online? It depends on the context. *CyberPsychology & Behavior, 11*(6), 707–709.

Bruni, F. (2015, August 21). Gay and marked for death. *The New York Times*, p. SR3.

Bryant-Davis, T. (Ed.). (2011). *Surviving sexual violence.* Lanham, MD: Rowman & Littlefield.

Budygin, E. A., et al. (2012). Aversive stimulus differentially triggers subsecond dopamine release in reward regions of the brain. *Neuroscience, 201,* 331–337.

Bugental, D. B., Corpuz, R., & Beaulieu, D. A. (2015). An evolutionary approach to socialization. In J. E. Grusec & P. D. Hastings (Eds.), *Handbook of socialization: Theory and Research* (pp. 325–346). New York. Guilford.

Bullough, V. L. (2002). Masturbation: A historical overview. *Journal of Psychology & Human Sexuality, 14*(2–3), 17–33.

Bunting, L., & McAuley, C. (2004). Teenage pregnancy and motherhood: The contribution of support. *Child & Family Social Work, 9*(2), 207–215.

Burch, B. (2008). Infidelity: Outlaws and in-laws and lesbian relationships. *Journal of Lesbian Studies, 12*(2–3), 145–159.

Burchell, A. N., et al. (2011). Genital transmission of human papillomavirus in recently formed heterosexual couples. *Journal of Infectious Disease, 204*(11), 1723–1729.

Burgess, A. W., & Morgenbesser, L. I. (2005). Sexual violence and seniors. *Brief Treatment and Crisis Intervention, 5*(2), 193–202.

Burke, T. J., & Young, V. J. (2012). Sexual transformations and intimate behaviors in romantic relationships. *Journal of Sex Research, 49*(5), 454–463.

Burri, A., & Rahman, Q. (2015). Common genetic factors among sexual orientation, gender nonconformity, and number of sex partners in female twins: Implications for the evolution of homosexuality. *The Journal of Sexual Medicine, 12*(4), 1004–1011.

Burri, A., Hysi, P., Clop, A., Rahman, Q., & Spector, T. D. (2012). A genome-wide association study of female sexual dysfunction. *PLoS ONE, 7*(4): e35041. DOI:10.1371/journal.pone.0035041

Burt, M. R. (1980). Cultural myths and supports for rape. *Journal of Personality and Social Psychology, 38,* 217–230.

Bushman, B. J., Bonacci, A. M., van Dijk, M., & Baumeister, R. F. (2003). Narcissism, sexual refusal, and aggression: Testing a narcissistic reactance model of sexual coercion. *Journal of Personality and Social Psychology, 84*(5), 1027–1040.

Buss, D. M. (1994). *The evolution of desire: Strategies of human mating.* New York: Basic Books.

Buss, D. M. (2009a). An evolutionary formulation of person–situation interactions. *Journal of Research in Personality, 43*(2), 241–242.

Buss, D. M. (2009b). The great struggles of life: Darwin and the emergence of evolutionary psychology. *American Psychologist, 64*(2), 140–148.

Buss, D. M. (Ed.). (2005). *The handbook of evolutionary psychology.* Hoboken, NJ: Wiley.

Buss, D. M., & Schmitt, D. P. (2011). Evolutionary psychology and feminism. *Sex Roles, 64*(9–10), 768–787.

Bustos, M., Venkataramanan, R., & Caritis, S. (2016). Nausea and vomiting of pregnancy—What's new? *Autonomic Neuroscience,* DOI: 10.1016/j.autneu.2016.05.002

Butler, J. (1993). *Bodies that matter: On the discursive limits of sex.* New York: Routledge.

Butler, J. (2003). *Kritik der ethischen Gewalt.* Adorno lectures, 2002. Frankfurt am Main: Institut fur Sozialforschung an der Johann Wolfgang Goethe-Universitat.

Buvat, J., et al. (2010). Endocrine aspects of male sexual dysfunctions. *Journal of Sexual Medicine, 7,* 1627–1656.

Byerly, M. J., et al. (2006). Sexual dysfunction associated with second-generation antipsychotics in outpatients with schizophrenia or schizoaffective disorder: An empirical evaluation of olanzapine, risperidone, and quetiapine. *Schizophrenia Research, 86*(1–3), 244–250.

Byers, E. S., & Grenier, G. (2003). Premature or rapid ejaculation: Heterosexual couples' perceptions of men's ejaculatory behavior. *Archives of Sexual Behavior, 32*(3), 261–270.

Byrd, J., Hyde, J. S., DeLamater, J. D., & Plant, E. A. (1998). Sexuality during pregnancy and the year postpartum. *Journal of Family Practice, 47*(4), 305–308.

Cacioppo, J. T., Hawkley, L. C., & Berntson, G. G. (2003). The anatomy of loneliness. *Current Directions in Psychological Science, 12*(3), 71–74.

Cacioppo, J. T., Cacioppo, S., Gonzaga, G. C., Ogburn, E. L., & VanderWeele, T. J. (2013). Marital satisfaction and break-ups differ across on-line and off-line meeting venues. *Proceedings of the National Academy of Sciences, 110*(25), 10135–10140.

Cado, S., & Leitenberg, H. (1990). Guilt reactions to sexual fantasies during intercourse. *Archives of Sexual Behavior, 19,* 49–64.

Caffaro, J. V., & Conn-Caffaro, A. (2005). Treating sibling abuse families. *Aggression and Violent Behavior, 10*(5), 604–623.

Cai, R., Alexander, M., & Marson, L. (2008). Activation of somatosensory afferents elicit changes in vaginal blood flow and the urethrogenital reflex via autonomic efferents. *The Journal of Urology, 180*(3), 1167–1172.

Calhoun, K. S., Mouilso, E. R., & Edwards, K. M. (2012). Sexual assault among college students. In R. D. McAnulty (Ed.). *Sex in college: The things they don't write home about* (pp. 263–288). Santa Barbara, CA: ABC-CLIO.

Call, V., Sprecher, S., & Schwartz, P. (1995). The incidence and frequency of marital sex in a national sample. *Journal of Marriage and the Family, 57,* 639–652.

Callahan, R., et al. (2015). Pregnancy and contraceptive use among women participating in the FEM-PrEP Trial. *Journal of Acquired Immune Deficiency Syndrome, 68*(2), 196–203.

Callaway, E. (2012). Fathers bequeath more mutations as they age. *Nature, 488*(412), http://www.nature.com/news/fathers-bequeath-more-mutations-as-they-age-1.11247. (Accessed September 21, 2012).

Callimachi, R. (2015, August 13). ISIS enshrines a theology of rape: Claiming the Quran's support, the Islamic State codifies sex in conquered regions of Iraq and Syria and uses the practice as a recruiting tool. *The New York Times.* http://www.nytimes.com/2015/08/14/world/middleeast/isis-enshrines-a-theology-of-rape.html?mtrref=www.google.com&gwh=8A430E91B4953F98E01E3FE825B5BAC6&gwt=pay (Accessed July 13, 2016).

Calmes, J., & Baker, P. (2012, May 10). Obama says same-sex marriage should be legal. *The New York Times,* p. A1.

Campbell, R. (2006). Rape survivors' experiences with the legal and medical systems: Do rape victim advocates make a difference? *Violence Against Women, 12*(1), 30–45.

Campbell, R., & Wasco, S. M. (2005). Understanding rape and sexual assault: 20 years of progress and future directions. *Journal of Interpersonal Violence, 20*(1), 127–131.

Campbell, W. K., Foster, C. A., & Finkel, E. J. (2002). Does self-love lead to love for others? A story of narcissistic game playing. *Journal of Personality & Social Psychology, 83*(2), 340–354.

Cancer Statistics, 2008. In American Cancer Society. (2009). http://www.cancer.org/downloads/STT/Cancer_Statistics_2008.ppt#405,10,Cancer Sites in Men for Which African American Death Rates Exceed White Death Rates, US, 2000–2004.

Cantor, J. M. (2011). New MRI studies support the Blanchard typology of male-to-female transsexualism. *Archives of Sexual Behavior, 40*(5), 863–864.

Caporaletti, J. (2006, September 20). *Prostitution is a world-wide problem.* www.collegiatetimes.com

Cappelletti, M., & Wallen, K. (2015). Increasing women's sexual desire: The comparative effectiveness of estrogens and androgens. *Hormones and Behavior, 78,* 178–193.

Capron, C., Thérond, C., & Duyme, M. (2007). Brief report: Effect of menarcheal status and family structure on depressive symptoms and emotional/behavioural problems in young adolescent girls. *Journal of Adolescence, 30*(1), 175–179.

Cardwell, M. S. (2012). Pregnancy sickness: A biopsychological perspective. *Obstetrical & Gynecological Survey, 67*(10), 645–652.

Carey, B. (2005, January 11). The secret lives of just about everybody. *The New York Times.* http://www.nytimes.com/2005/01/11/health/psychology/the-secret-lives-of-just-about-everybody.html (Accessed July 13, 2016).

Carlson, N. (2007). *Physiology of behavior* (9th ed.). Boston: Allyn & Bacon.

Carpenter, L. M., Nathanson, C. A., & Kim, Y. J. (2009). Physical women, emotional men: Gender and sexual satisfaction in midlife. *Archives of Sexual Behavior, 38*(1), 87–107.

Carre, J. M., & Olmstead, N. A. (2015). Social neuroendocrinology of human aggression: Examining the role of competition-induced testosterone dynamics. *Neuroscience, 286,* 171–186.

Carroll, J. S., et al. (2008). Generation XXX: Pornography acceptance and use among emerging adults. *Journal of Adolescent Research, 23*(1), 6–30.

Carter, D. J., & Dalla, R. L. (2006). Transactional analysis case report: Street-level prostituted women as mental health care clients. *Sexual Addiction & Compulsivity, 13*(1), 95–119.

Carvalho, J., & Nobre, P. (2010a). Gender issues and sexual desire: The role of emotional and relationship variables. *Journal of Sexual Medicine, 7,* 2469–2478.

Carvalho, J., & Nobre, P. (2010b). Sexual desire in women: An integrative approach regarding psychological, medical, and relationship dimensions. *Journal of Sexual Medicine, 7,* 1807–1813.

Castanho, T. C., et al. (2014). The role of sex and sex-related hormones in cognition, mood and well-being in older men and women. *Biological Psychology, 103,* 158–166.

Castellsague, X., et al. (2002). Male circumcision, penile human papillomavirus infection, and cervical cancer in female partners. *New England Journal of Medicine, 346*(15), 1105–1112.

Castellsague, X., et al. (2011). Intrauterine device use, cervical infection with human papillomavirus, and risk of cervical cancer: A pooled analysis of 26 epidemiological studies. *The Lancet Oncology, 12*(11), 1023–1031.

Caughlin, J. P., Hardesty, J. L., & Middleton, A. V. (2012). Conflict avoidance in families. In P. Noller & G. C. Karantzas (Eds.). *The Wiley-Blackwell handbook of couples and family relationships* (pp. 115–128). Chichester, UK: Wiley.

Cavalot, A. L., & Cossu, D. (2015). Feminization laryngoplasty: Surgical therapy. In C. Trombetta et al. (Eds.). *Management of gender dysphoria* (pp. 135–144). Milan, Italy: Sprinter-Verlag Italia.

Cawley, J., Avery, R., & Eisenberg, M. (2011). The effect of advertising and deceptive advertising on consumption: The case of over-the-counter weight loss products. http://www.iza.org/conference_files/riskonomics2011/cawley_j6697.pdf

Ceci, S. J., Williams, W. M., & Barnett, S. R. (2009). Women's underrepresentation in science. *Psychological Bulletin, 135*(2), 218–261.

Center for Sexual Health Promotion. (2011). *National Survey of Sexual Health and Behavior (NSSHB).* Indiana University, Bloomington: School of Health, Physical Education, and Recreation. http://www.nationalsexstudy.indiana.edu (Accessed August 23, 2012).

Centers for Disease Control and Prevention (CDC). (2001, June). *Genital herpes.* National Center for HIV, STD and TB Prevention. Division of Sexually Transmitted Diseases. www.cdc.gov/nchstp/dstd/Fact_Sheets/facts_.Genital_Herpes.htm

Centers for Disease Control and Prevention (CDC). (2002a). *Oral alternatives to cefixime for the treatment of uncomplicated* Neisseria gonorrhoeae *urogenital infections.* National Center for HIV, STD and TB Prevention. Division of Sexually Transmitted Diseases. www.cdc.gov/STD/treatment/Cefixime.htm

Centers for Disease Control and Prevention (CDC). (2002b). *Laboratory guidelines screening tests to detect Chlamydia trachomatis and Neisseria gonorrhoeae infections.* National Center for HIV, STD and TB Prevention. Division of Sexually Transmitted Diseases. www.cdc.gov/STD/LabGuidelines/default.htm

Centers for Disease Control and Prevention (CDC). (2003). *HIV/AIDS surveillance report: U.S. HIV and AIDS cases reported through December 2002, 14*(2).

Centers for Disease Control and Prevention (CDC). (2005a). *STD surveillance 2005.* www.cdc.gov/std/stats/toc2004.htm

Centers for Disease Control and Prevention (CDC). (2005b). *DES Update: For Consumers.* www.cdc.gov/DES/consumers/index.html.

Centers for Disease Control and Prevention (CDC). (2006). *Sexually transmitted diseases.* Various fact sheets.

Centers for Disease Control and Prevention (CDC). (2008). HIV and AIDS in the United States: A picture of today's epidemic. http://www.cdc.gov/HIV/topics/surveillance/united_states.htm (Accessed December 22, 2008).

Centers for Disease Control and Prevention (CDC). (2009a, February 28). Cases of HIV infection and AIDS in the United States and dependent areas, 2007. http://www.cdc.gov/hiv/topics/surveillance/resources/reports/2007/report/table13.htm.

Centers for Disease Control and Prevention (CDC). (2009b, January 13). Trends in reportable sexually transmitted diseases in the United States, 2007: National surveillance data for chlamydia, gonorrhea, and syphilis. http://www.cdc.gov/std/stats07/trends.htm

Centers for Disease Control and Prevention (CDC). (2013). Sexually transmitted diseases. http://www.cdc.gov/std/pregnancy/stdfact-pregnancy.htm

Cerezales, S. P., Boryshpolets, S., & Eisenbach, M. (2015). Behavioral mechanisms of mammalian sperm guidance. *Asian Journal of Andrology, 17*(4), 628–632.

Chaiyavej, S., & Morash, M. (2009). Reasons for policewomen's assertive and passive reactions to sexual harassment. *Police Quarterly, 12*(1), 63–85.

Champion, D. R. (2006). Sexual harassment: Criminal justice and academia. *Criminal Justice Studies: A Critical Journal of Crime, Law & Society, 19*(2), 101–109.

Chance, S. E., Brown, R. T., Dabbs, J. M., Jr., & Casey, R. (2000). Testosterone, intelligence and behavior disorders in young boys. *Personality & Individual Differences, 28*(3), 437–445.

Chandler, C. H., & Zamudio, K. R. (2008). Reproductive success by large, closely related males facilitated by sperm storage in an aggregate breeding amphibian. *Molecular Ecology, 17*(6), 1564–1576.

Chandra, A., et al. (2008). Does watching sex on television predict teen pregnancy? Findings from a national longitudinal survey of youth. *Pediatrics, 122*(5), 1047–1054.

Chandra, A., et al. (2012). HIV risk-related behaviors in the United States household population aged 15–44 years: Data from the National Survey of Family Growth, 2002 and 2006–2110. *National Health Statistics Reports,* January 19, 2012, No. 46.

Chao, Q., Wang, P., & He, N. (2001). Comparative research on self-concept of middle school students from complete and divorced families. *Chinese Journal of Clinical Psychology, 9*(2), 143.

Charness, M. E., Riley, E. P., & Sowell, E. R. (2016). Drinking during pregnancy and the developing brain: Is any amount safe? *Trends in Cognitive Sciences, 20*(2), 80–82.

Chatham, M. L. (2008). Early predictors of disinhibited attachment behaviors among internationally adopted children. *Dissertation Abstracts International: Section B: The Sciences and Engineering, 69*(3-B), 1985.

Chaturvedi, A. K., et al. (2011). Human papillomavirus and rising oropharyngeal cancer incidence in the United States. *Journal of Clinical Oncology, 29*(32), 4294–4301.

Chavez, M. L., & Spitzer, M. F. (2002). Herbals and other dietary supplements for premenstrual syndrome and menopause. *Psychiatric Annals, 32*(1), 61–71.

Chehab, M., Madala, A., & Trussell, J. C. (2015). On-label and off-label drugs used in treatment of male infertility. *Fertility and Sterility*, DOI: 10.1016/j.fertnstert.2014.12.122

Chen, M. (2012, May 27). Working with your rapist as your supervisor? The widespread sexual abuse of women in farm work. www.alternet.org (Accessed July 16, 2012).

Cheng, H., & Furnham, A. (2002). Personality, peer relations, and self-confidence as predictors of happiness and loneliness. *Journal of Adolescence, 25*(3), 327–339.

Cheryan, S., Plaut, V. C., Handron, C., & Hudson, L. (2013). The stereotypical computer scientist: Gendered media representations as a barrier to inclusion for women. *Sex Roles, 69*(1), 58–71.

Cheryan, S., Master, A., & Meltzoff, A. N. (2015). Cultural stereotypes as gatekeepers: Increasing girls' interest in computer science and engineering by diversifying stereotypes. *Frontiers in Psychology, 6*, 49.

Chesler, P. (2006, February 24). The failure of feminism. *Chronicle of Higher Education, 52*(25).

Cheyne, R. A. (2005). The sanctification of parenting and adoption among special needs adoptive parents. *Dissertation Abstracts International: Section B: The Sciences and Engineering, 66*(1-B), 545.

Chisholm, J., & Greene, B. (2008). Women of color: Perspectives on multiple identities in psychological theory, research, and practice. In F. L. Denmark & M. A. Paludi (Eds.), *Psychology of women* (2nd ed., pp. 40–69). Westport, CT: Greenwood Publishing Group.

Chivers, M., & Bailey, J. M. (2005). A sex difference in features that elicit genital response. *Biological Psychology, 70*(2), 115–120.

Chivers, M. L. (2010). A brief update on the specificity of sexual arousal. *Sexual and Relationship Therapy, 25*(4), 407–414.

Chivers, M. L., & Bailey, J. M. (2007). The sexual physiology of sexual orientation. In E. Janssen (Ed.), *The psychophysiology of sex. The Kinsey Institute series* (pp. 458–474). Bloomington: Indiana University Press.

Chivers, M. L., & Rosen, R. C. (2010). Phosphodiesterase Type 5 inhibitors and female sexual response: Faulty protocols or paradigms? *Journal of Sexual Medicine, 7*(2), 858–872.

Chivers, M. L., & Timmers, A. D. (2012). Effects of gender and relationship context in audio narratives on genital and subjective sexual response in heterosexual men and women. *Archives of Sexual Behavior, 41*(1), 185–197.

Chivers, M. L., Rieger, G., Latty, E., & Bailey, J. M. (2004). A sex difference in the specificity of sexual arousal. *Psychological Science, 15*(11), 736–744.

Chivers, M. L., Seto, M. C., & Blanchard, R. (2007). Gender and sexual orientation differences in sexual response to sexual activities versus gender of actors in sexual films. *Journal of Personality and Social Psychology, 93*(6), 1108–1121.

Chivers, M. L., Seto, M. C., Lalumiere, M. L., Laan, E., & Grimbos, T. (2010). Agreement of self-reported and genital measures of sexual arousal in men and women: A meta-analysis. *Archives of Sexual Behavior, 39*(1), 5–56.

Chlamydia positivity of women by state, 2010. Centers for Disease Control and Prevention. (2011). Sexually Transmitted Diseases (STDs). 2010 Sexually Transmitted Diseases Surveillance. http://www.cdc.gov/std/stats10/figures/11.htm (Accessed October 4, 2012).

Chlamydia statistics, 2012. Centers for Disease Control and Prevention. (2012). Sexually Transmitted Diseases (STDs). Chlamydia statistics. http://www.cdc.gov/std/chlamydia/stats.htm (Accessed October 4, 2012).

Chlamydia—CDC fact sheet, 2012. Centers for Disease Control and Prevention. (2012). Sexually Transmitted Diseases (STDs).

Chlamydia—CDC Fact Sheet. http://www.cdc.gov/std/chlamydia/STDFact-Chlamydia.htm (Accessed October 4, 2012).

Chlamydia—CDC Fact sheet, 2014. Centers for Disease Control and Prevention. http://www.cdc.gov/std/chlamydia/stdfact-chlamydia.htm (Accessed January 1, 2016)

Chlamydis—CDC fact sheet. (2016). http://www.cdc.gov/std/chlamydia/stdfact-chlamydia.htm (Accessed July 8, 2016).

Chlebowski, R, et al. (2003). Influence of estrogen plus progestin on breast cancer and mammography in healthy postmenopausal women: The Women's Health Initiative Randomized Trial. *Journal of the American Medical Association, 289*, 3243–3253.

Chlebowski, R., et al. (2009, May 30). HRT increases risk for death from non-small-cell lung cancer. American Society of Clinical Oncology, 45th Meeting.

Cho, S., Park, E. S., Park, C. I., & Na, S. (2004). Characteristics of psychosexual functioning in adults with cerebral palsy. *Clinical Rehabilitation, 18*(4), 423–429.

CIA (Central Intelligence Agency). (2012). The World Factbook. https://www.cia.gov/library/publications/the-world-factbook/fields/2018.html (Accessed June 23, 2012).

Ciani, A. S. C., et al. (2012). Factors associated with higher fecundity in female maternal relatives of homosexual men. *The Journal of Sexual Medicine, 9*(11), 2878–2887.

Ciccarone, D. (2011). Stimulant abuse: Pharmacology, cocaine, methamphetamine treatment, attempts at pharmacotherapy. *Primary Care: Clinics in Office Practice, 38*(1), 41–58.

Cifu, A. S., & Davis, A. M. (2014). Use of HPV vaccine in males and females. *Journal of the American Medical Association, 312*(18), 1920–1921.

Clark, C., et al. (2013). Relation of neural structure to persistently low academic achievement: A longitudinal study of children with differing birth weights. *Neuropsychology, 27*(3), 364–377.

Claxton, S. E., DeLuca, H. K., & van Dulmen, M. H. M. (2015). The association between alcohol use and engagement in casual sexual relationships and experiences: A meta-analytic review of non-experimental studies. *Archives of Sexual Behavior, 44*(4), 837–856.

Clay, R. A. (2006). Battling the self-blame of infertility. *Monitor on Psychology, 37*(8), 44–45.

Clay, R. A. (2015, October). Sex research at the Kinsey Institute. *Monitor on Psychology, 46*(9), 48–52.

Cleary Bradley, R. P., Friend, D. J., & Gottman, J. M. (2011). Supporting healthy relationships in low-income, violent couples: Reducing conflict and strengthening relationship skills and satisfaction. *Journal of Couple & Relationship Therapy: Innovations in Clinical and Educational Interventions, 10*(2), 97–116.

Cleland, K., Zhu, H., Goldstuck, N., Cheng, L., & Trussell, J. (2012). The efficacy of intrauterine devices for emergency contraception: A systematic review of 35 years of experience. *Human Reproduction, 27*(7), 1994–2000.

Clendenen, T. V., et al. (2009). Postmenopausal levels of endogenous sex hormones and risk of colorectal cancer. *Cancer Epidemiology Biomarkers & Prevention, 18*, 275.

Clendenning, A. (2004, April 29). *Yale global online.* www.yaleglobal.yale.edu

Cnattingius, S. (2004). The epidemiology of smoking during pregnancy: Smoking prevalence, maternal characteristics, and pregnancy outcomes. *Nicotine & Tobacco Research, 6*(Suppl. 2), S125–S140.

Cnattingius, S., Bergstrom, R., Lipworth, L., & Kramer, M. S. (1998). Pre-pregnancy weight and the risk of adverse pregnancy outcomes. *New England Journal of Medicine, 338*, 147–152.

CNN.com. (2015, July 23). Highlights from Bill Cosby's 2005–2006 deposition. http://www.cnn.com/2015/07/23/entertainment/cosby-deposition-quotes/index.html (Accessed July 13, 2016).

Cohen, A. B., & Tannenbaum, I. J. (2001). Lesbian and bisexual women's judgments of the attractiveness of different body types. *Journal of Sex Research, 38*(3), 226–232.

Cohen, D. L., & Belsky, J. (2008). Individual differences in female mate preferences as a function of attachment and hypothetical ecological conditions. *Journal of Evolutionary Psychology, 6*(1), 25–42.

Cohen, L. S., et al. (2006). Relapse of major depression during pregnancy in women who maintain or discontinue antidepressant treatment. *Journal of the American Medical Association, 295*(5), 499–507.

Cohen, M. S. (2000). Preventing sexual transmission of HIV: New ideas from sub-Saharan Africa. *The New England Journal of Medicine, 342*(13), 970–973.

Cohen, S. D., & Goldstein, I. (2016). Diagnosis and management of female orgasmic disorder. In L. I. Lipshultz et al. (Eds.). *Management of sexual dysfunction in men and women* (pp. 261–271). New York: Springer Science+Business Media.

Cohen-Bendahan, C. C. C., van de Beek, C., & Berenbaum, S. A. (2005). Prenatal sex hormone effects on child and adult sex-typed behavior: Methods and findings. *Neuroscience & Biobehavioral Reviews, 29*(2), 353–384.

Cohen-Kettenis, P. Y., & Klink, D. (2015). Adolescents with gender dysphoria. *Best Practice & Research Clinical Endocrinology & Metabolism, 29*(3), 485–495.

Colangelo, J. J., & Keefe-Cooperman, K. (2012). Understanding the impact of childhood sexual abuse on women's sexuality. *Journal of Mental Health Counseling, 34*(1), 14–37.

Colapinto, J. (2000). *As nature made him: The boy who was raised as a girl.* New York. HarperCollins.

Colditz, G. A., & Rosner, B. A. (2000). Cumulative risk for breast cancer to age 70 years according to risk factor status. Data from the Nurses' Health Study. *American Journal of Epidemiology, 152*(10), 950–964.

Colditz, G. A., et al. (2004). Risk factors for breast cancer according to estrogen and progesterone receptor status. *Journal of the National Cancer Institute, 96,* 218–228.

Cole, F. S. (2000). Extremely preterm birth—Defining the limits of hope. *New England Journal of Medicine, 343*(6), 429–430.

Cole, T. B. (2006). Rape at US colleges often fueled by alcohol. *Journal of the American Medical Association, 296*(5), 504–505.

Coleman, E. (2002). Masturbation as a means of achieving sexual health. *Journal of Psychology & Human Sexuality, 14*(2–3), 5–16.

Coleman, M., Ganong, L. H., & Fine, M. (2000). Reinvestigating remarriage: Another decade of progress. *Journal of Marriage & the Family, 62*(4), 1288–1307.

Coles, L. S. (2010). The ethical basis for using human embryonic stem cells in the treatment of aging. *The Future of Aging,Part 1,* 63–86.

Collaer, M. L., & Hill, E. M. (2006). Large sex difference in adolescents on a timed line judgment task: Attentional contributors and task relationship to mathematics. *Perception, 35*(4), 561–572.

Collaer, M. L., & Hines, M. (1995). Human behavioral sex differences: A role for gonadal hormones during early development? *Psychological Bulletin, 118*(1), 55–107.

Collins, C., Harshbarger, C., Sawyer, R., & Hamdallah, M. (2006). The diffusion of effective behavioral interventions project: Development, implementation, and lessons learned. *AIDS Education and Prevention, 18*(Suppl. A), 5–20.

Collins, L. (2004). We are not gay. In K. K. Kumashiro (Ed.), *Restoried selves: Autobiographies of queer Asian/Pacific American activists* (pp. 13–17). New York: Harrington Park Press/The Haworth Press.

Collins, R. L., et al. (2004). Watching sex on television predicts adolescent initiation of sexual behavior. *Pediatrics, 114*(3), e280–e289.

Colson, M.-H., Lemaire, A., Pinton, P., Hamidi, K., & Klein, P. (2006). Sexual behaviors and mental perception, satisfaction and expectations of sex life in men and women in France. *Journal of Sexual Medicine, 3*(1), 121–131.

Comtois, K.A., Schiff, M. A., & Grossman, D. C. (2008). Psychiatric risk factors associated with postpartum suicide attempts in Washington State, 1992–2001. *American Journal of Obstetrics & Gynecology, 199*(2), 120.e1–120.e5.

Conley, S. (2009, March 26). In B. Alexander, "Sex surrogates" put personal touch on therapy: Despite dubious legality, some counselors still prescribe practice to patients. http://www.msnbc.msn.com/id/29881206/

Connaughton, C., & McCabe, M. (2015). Sexuality and aging. In N. A. Pachana (Ed.), *Encyclopedia of geropsychology* (pp. 1–10). Singapore: Springer Science+Business Media.

Conniff, J., & Evensen, A. (2016). Preexposure prophylaxis (PrEP) for HIV prevention: The primary care perspective. *Journal of the American Board of Family Medicine, 29*(1), 143–151.

Connolly, J., Craig, W., Goldberg, A., & Pepler, D. (2004). Mixed-gender groups, dating, and romantic relationships in early adolescence. *Journal of Research on Adolescence, 14*(2), 185–207.

Connor, E. M., et al. (1994). Reduction of maternal–infant transmission of human immunodeficiency virus type 1 with zidovudine treatment. *New England Journal of Medicine, 331,* 1173–1180.

Connor, P. D., Sampson, P. D., Streissguth, A. P., Bookstein, F. L., & Barr, H. M. (2006). Effects of prenatal alcohol exposure on fine motor coordination and balance: A study of two adult samples. *Neuropsychologia, 44*(5), 744–751.

Conroy-Beam, D., Buss, D. M., Pham, M. N., & Shackelford, T. K. (2015). How sexually dimorphic are human mate preferences? *Personality and Social Psychology Bulletin,* DOI: 10.1177/0146167215590987

Cooke, B. M., Breedlove, S. M., & Jordan, C. L. (2003). Both estrogen receptors and androgen receptors contribute to testosterone-induced changes in the morphology of the medial amygdala and sexual arousal in male rats. *Hormones & Behavior, 43*(2), 336–346.

Cooper, A., Delmonico, D. L., & Burg, R. (2000). Cybersex users, abusers, and compulsives: New findings and implications. *Sexual Addiction & Compulsivity, 7*(1–2), 5–29.

Cooper, A., Delmonico, D. L., Griffin-Shelley, E., & Mathy, R. M. (2004). Online sexual activity: An examination of potentially problematic behaviors. *Sexual Addiction & Compulsivity, 11*(3), 129–143.

Cooper, A. J., Galbreath, N., & Becker, M. A. (2004). Sex on the Internet: Furthering our understanding of men with online sexual problems. *Psychology of Addictive Behaviors, 18*(3), 223–230.

Cooper, M. L., O'Hara, R. E., & Martins, J. (2015). Does drinking improve the quality of sexual experience? Sex-specific alcohol expectancies and subjective experience on drinking versus sober sexual occasions. *AIDS and Behavior,* pp. 1–12. DOI: 10.1007/s10461-015-1136-5

Cooper, S. M., Guthrie, B. J., Brown, C., & Metzger, I. (2011). Daily hassles and African American adolescent females' psychological functioning: Direct and interactive associations with gender role orientation. *Sex Roles, 65*(5–6), 397–409.

Corona, G., et al. (2009). The age-related decline of testosterone is associated with different specific symptoms and signs in patients with sexual dysfunction. *International Journal of Andrology,* 10.1111/j.1365-2605.2009.00952.

Corona, L. E., et al. (2015). Use of other treatments before hysterectomy for benign conditions in a statewide hospital collaborative. *American Journal of Obstetrics and Gynecology, 212*(3), 304.e1–304.e7.

Courtenay, W. H. (2000). Engendering health: A social constructionist examination of men's health beliefs and behaviors. *Psychology of Men & Masculinity, 1*(1), 4–15.

Cott, E. (2015, June 11). Sex dolls that talk back. *The New York Times.* http://www.nytimes.com/2015/06/12/technology/robotica-sex-robot-realdoll.html?_r=0 (Accessed July 13, 2016).

Cove, J., & Petrak, J. (2004). Factors associated with sexual problems in HIV-positive gay men. *International Journal of STD & AIDS, 15*(11), 732–736.

Cox, B., Sneyd, M. J., Paul, C., & Skegg, D. C. G. (2006). Risk factors for prostate cancer: A national case-control study. *International Journal of Cancer, 119*(7), 1690–1694.

Cox, D. J. (1988). Incidence and nature of male genital exposure behavior as reported by college women. *Journal of Sex Research, 24,* 227–234.

Cox, L. (2014, January 7). Laverne Cox flawlessly shuts down Katie Couric's invasive questions about transgender people. http://www.salon.com/2014/01/07/laverne_cox_artfully_shuts_down_katie_courics_invasive_questions_about_transgender_people/(Accessed July 13, 2016).

Cox, W. M., & Alm, R. (2005, February 25). Scientists are made, not born. *The New York Times.* http://www.nytimes.com/2005/02/28/opinion/scientists-are-made-not-born.html (Accessed July 13, 2016).

Coyle, J. P. (2006). Treating difficult couples: Helping clients with coexisting mental and relationship disorders. *Family Relations: Interdisciplinary Journal of Applied Family Studies, 55*(1), 146–147.

Craig, R. J. (2005). Harassment. In R. J. Craig (Ed.), *Personality-guided forensic psychology. Personality-guided psychology* (pp. 155–167). Washington, DC: American Psychological Association.

Craighill, P. M., & Somashektar, S. (2015, September 15). Post-ABC poll: Most say Kim Davis should issue marriage licenses to gay couples. *The Washington Post.*

Cramer, D. (2003). Facilitativeness, conflict, demand for approval, self-esteem, and satisfaction with romantic relationships. *Journal of Psychology, 137*(1), 85–98.

Crandall, C. J., et al. (2012). Breast tenderness and breast cancer risk in the estrogen plus progestin and estrogen-alone women's health initiative clinical trials. *Breast Cancer Research and Treatment, 132*(1), 275–285.

Cranney, S. (2015). Internet pornography use and sexual body image in a Dutch sample. *International Journal of Sexual Health, 27*(3), 316–323.

Crawford, T. V., Rawlins, J., McGrowder, D. A., & Adams, R. L. (2011). The Church's response to sexual reproductive health issues. *Journal of Religion and Health, 50*(1), 163–176.

Crepaz, N., Hart, T. A., & Marks, G. (2004). Highly active antiretroviral therapy and sexual risk behavior: A meta-analytic review. *Journal of the American Medical Association, 292*(2), 224–236.

Crespi, B. J. (2015). Oxytocin, testosterone, and human social cognition. *Biological Reviews,* DOI: 10.1111/brv.12175.

Critelli, J. W., & Bivona, J. M. (2008). Women's erotic rape fantasies: An evaluation of theory and research. *Journal of Sex Research, 45*(1), 57–70.

Crofoot, M. C., & Wrangham, R. W. (2010). Intergroup aggression in primates and humans: The case for a unified theory. In P. M. Kappeler & J. B. Silk (Eds.), *Mind the gap: Tracing the origins of human universals* (pp. 171–195). New York: Springer.

Crosby, R., Yarber, W., Sanders, S., & Graham, C. (2005). Condom discomfort and associated problems with their use among university students. *Journal of American College Health* 54(3), 143–147.

Crosson-Tower, C. (2015). *Confronting child and adolescent sexual abuse.* Thousand Oaks, CA: Sage.

Crowley, T., Richardson, D., Goldmeier, D., & BASHH Special Interest Group for Sexual Dysfunction. (2006). Recommendations for the management of vaginismus: BASHH Special Interest Group for Sexual Dysfunction. *International Journal of STD & AIDS, 17*(1), 14–18.

Crozier, I. (2012). Making up Koro: Multiplicity, psychiatry, culture, and penis-shrinking anxieties. *Journal of the History of Medicine and Allied Sciences, 67*(1), 36–70.

Crum, N. F., Furtek, K. J., Olson, P. E., Amling, C. L., & Wallace, M. R. (2005). A review of hypogonadism and erectile dysfunction among HIV-infected men during the pre-and post-HAART eras: Diagnosis, pathogenesis, and management. *AIDS Patient Care and STDs, 19*(10), 869–885.

Csoka, A. B., & Shipko, S. (2006). Persistent sexual side effects after SSRI discontinuation. *Psychotherapy and Psychosomatics, 75*(3), 187–188.

Cuddy, A. J. C., et al. (2015). Men as cultural ideals: Cultural values moderate gender stereotype content. *Journal of Personality and Social Psychology, 109*(4), 622–635.

Cui, Y., Zong, H., Yan, H., & Zhang, Y. (2015). The effect of testosterone replacement therapy in prostate cancer: A systematic review and meta-analysis. *Prostate Cancer and Prostatic Disease, 17*(1), 132–143.

Cullen, K. J. (2011, October 4). In Grady, D., Study cites increase in cancers from HPV. *The New York Times*, p. D5.

Cummings, S. R., et al. (1999). The effect of raloxifene on risk of breast cancer in postmenopausal women: Results from the MORE randomized trial. *Journal of the American Medical Association, 281*, 2189–2197.

Cunningham, A. L., et al. (2006). Prevalence of infection with herpes simplex virus types 1 and 2 in Australia: A nationwide population based survey. *Sexually Transmitted Infections, 82*, 164–168.

Cunningham, M. R., et al. (1995). "Their ideas of beauty are, on the whole, the same as ours": Consistency and variability in the cross-cultural perception of female physical attractiveness. *Journal of Personality and Social Psychology, 68*(2), 261–279.

Curnoe, S., & Langevin, R. (2002). Personality and deviant sexual fantasies: An examination of the MMPIs. *Journal of Clinical Psychology, 58*(7), 803–815.

Cutler, W. B. (1999). Human sex-attractant hormones: Discovery, research, development, and application in sex therapy. *Psychiatric Annals, 29*(1), 54–59.

Cutler, W. B., Friedmann, E., & McCoy, N. L. (1998). Pheromonal influences on sociosexual behavior in men. *Archives of Sexual Behavior, 27*(1), 1–13.

Cuzin, B., et al. (2011). Guidelines for general practitioners for first-line management of erectile dysfunction. *Sexologies, 20*(1), 23–35.

Cyr, M., Wright, J., McDuff, P., & Perron, A. (2002). Intrafamilial sexual abuse: Brother–sister incest does not differ from father–daughter and stepfather–stepdaughter incest. *Child Abuse & Neglect, 26*(9), 957–973.

Czech, D. P., et al. (2012). The human testis-determining factor SRY localizes in midbrain dopamine neurons and regulates multiple components of catecholamine synthesis and metabolism. *Journal of Neurochemistry, 122*(2), 260–271.

D'Angelo, D., et al. (2007). Preconception and interconception health status of women who recently gave birth to a live-born infant—Pregnancy risk assessment monitoring system. *Morbidity and Mortality Weekly Report, 56*(SS10), 1–35.

Dabbs, J. M., Jr., & Morris, R. (1990). Testosterone, social class, and antisocial behavior in a sample of 4,462 men. *Psychological Science, 1*, 1–3.

Dahl, D. W., Sengupta, J., & Vohs, K. D. (2009, January 9). Sex in advertising: Gender differences and the role of relationship commitment, *Journal of Consumer Research 36*(2), 215–231.

Daily Mail. (2007, September 25). "We don't have any gays in Iran," Oranian president tells Ivy League audience. http://www.dailymail.co.uk/news/article-483746/We-dont-gays-Iran-Iranian-president-tells-Ivy-League-audience.html (Accessed July 13, 2016).

Daley, A. (2009). Exercise and premenstrual symptomatology: A comprehensive review. *Journal of Women's Health, 18*(6), 895–899.

Dalla, R. L. (2006). "You can't hustle all your life": An exploratory investigation of the exit process among street-level prostituted women. *Psychology of Women Quarterly, 30*(3), 276–290.

Daly, M., & Wilson, M. (2003). Evolutionary psychology of lethal interpersonal violence. In W. Heitmeyer & J. Hagan (Eds.), *Handbook of research on violence* (pp. 709–734). New York: Westview.

Daly, M., & Wilson, M. (2005). Human behavior as animal behavior. In J. J. Bolhuis & L. A Giraldeau (Eds.), *The behavior of animals. Mechanisms, function, and evolution* (pp. 393–408). Oxford: Blackwell.

Damon, W. (2002). Dominance, sexism, and inadequacy: Testing a compensatory conceptualization in a sample of heterosexual men involved in SM. *Journal of Psychology & Human Sexuality, 14*(4), 25–45.

Dan, A., et al. (2014). Erectile dysfunction in patients with diabetes mellitus: Its magnitude, predictors and their bio-psycho-social interaction: A study from a developing country. *Asian Journal of Psychiatry, 7*, 58–65.

Daneback, K., Ross, M. W., & Månsson, S. (2006). Characteristics and behaviors of sexual compulsives who use the Internet for sexual purposes. *Sexual Addiction & Compulsivity, 13*(1), 53–67.

Dank, M., et al. (2014). *Estimating the size and structure of the underground commercial sex economy in eight major US cities.* Washington, D.C.: The Urban Institute.

Daniels, K., Mosher, W. D., & Jones, J. (2013). Contraceptive methods women have ever used. National Health Statistics Reports, no. 62. Hyattsville, MD: National Center for Health Statistics.

Dantzker, M. L., & Eisenman, R. (2003). Sexual attitudes among Hispanic college students: Differences between males and females. *International Journal of Adolescence & Youth, 11*(1), 79–89.

Darcangelo, S. (2008). Fetishism: Psychopathology and theory. In D. R. Laws & W. T. O'Donohue (Eds.), *Sexual deviance: Theory, assessment, and treatment* (2nd ed., pp. 76–107). New York: Guilford Press.

Darling, C. A., Davidson, J. K., & Jennings, D. A. (1991). The female sexual response revisited: Understanding the multiorgasmic experience in women. *Archives of Sexual Behavior, 20*, 527–540.

Darwin, C. (1871). *The descent of man, and selection in relation to sex.* London: John Murray, pp. 663–664.

Das, A., et al. (2009). Frontiers of retrovirology: Complex retroviruses, retroelements and their hosts. Montpellier, France. 21-23 September 2009. *Retrovirology, 6*(Suppl 2), I24.

Das, V. (2013). South Asia and the states of social theory. In J. G. Carrier & D. B. Gewertz (Eds.). *The handbook of sociocultural anthropology* (pp. 456–470). London: Bloomsbury Academic.

Dauwalder, B. (2011). The roles of *fruitless* and *doublesex* in the control of male courtship. In N. Atkinson (Ed.), *International Review of Neurobiology: Recent advances in the use of Drosophila in neurobiology and neurodegeneration, 99* (pp. 87–107). London: Academic Press.

Davidson, J. K., & Hoffman, L. E. (1986). Sexual fantasies and sexual satisfaction: An empirical analysis of erotic thought. *Journal of Sex Research, 22*(2), 184–205.

Davies, M. (2004). Correlates of negative attitudes toward gay men: Sexism, male role norms, and male sexuality. *Journal of Sex Research, 41*(3), 259–266.

Davis, K. C. (2010). The influence of alcohol expectancies and intoxication on men's aggressive unprotected sexual intentions. *Experimental and Clinical Psychopharmacology, 18*(5), 418–428.

Davis, K. E., Frieze, I. H., & Maiuro, R. D. (Eds.). (2002). *Stalking: Perspectives on victims and perpetrators* (pp. 212–236). New York: Springer.

Davis, R. L. (2010). *More perfect unions: The American search for marital bliss.* Cambridge, MA: Harvard University Press.

Davis, S. (2000). Testosterone and sexual desire in women. *Journal of Sex Education & Therapy, 25*(1), 25–32.

Davis, S. R., & Braunstein, G. D. (2012). Efficacy and safety of testosterone in the management of hypoactive sexual desire disorder in menopausal women. *The Journal of Sexual Medicine, 9*(4), 1134–1148.

Davis, S. R., et al. (2008). Testosterone for low libido in postmenopausal women not taking estrogen. *New England Journal of Medicine, 359*, 2005.

Davison, G. C. (1977). Elimination of a sadistic fantasy by a client-controlled counter-conditioning technique. In J. Fischer & H. Gochios (Eds.), *Handbook of behavior therapy with sexual problems.* New York: Pergamon.

Dawood, K., Bailey, J. M., & Martin, N. G. (2009). Genetic and environmental influences on sexual orientation. In Y-K. Kim (Ed.), *Handbook of behavior genetics* (pp. 269–279). New York: Springer.

Dawson, S. J., Suschinsky, K. D., & Lalumiere, M. L. (2012). Sexual fantasies and viewing times across the menstrual cycle: A diary study. *Archives of Sexual Behavior, 41*(1), 173–183.

De Cuyper, M., de Bolle, M., & de Fruyt, F. (2012). Personality similarity, perceptual accuracy, and relationship satisfaction in dating and married couples. *Personal Relationships, 19*(1), 128–145.

De Graaf, H., & Rademakers, J. (2011). The psychological measurement of childhood sexual development in Western societies: Methodological challenges. *Journal of Sex Research, 48*(2–3), 118–129.

De Graaf, G., Buckley, F., & Skotko, B. G. (2015). Estimates of the live births, natural losses, and elective terminations with Down syndrome in the United States. *American Journal of Medical Genetics Part A., 167*(4), 756–767.

de Souza, A. S., Fernandes, F. S., & do Carmo, M. (2011). Effects of maternal malnutrition and postnatal nutritional rehabilitation on brain fatty acids, learning, and memory. *Nutrition Reviews, 69*(3), 132–144.

De Vries, G. J., et al. (2002). A model system for study of sex chromosome effects on sexually dimorphic neural and behavioral traits. *Journal of Neuroscience, 22*(20), 9005–9014.

Defrin, R., Arad, M., Ben-Sasson, & Ginzburg, K. (2015). Attitudes and emotions towards pain and sensitivity to painful stimuli among people routinely engaging in masochistic behavior. *European Journal of Pain, 19*(9), 1321–1330.

Degenhardt, L., Day, C., Conroy, E., & Gilmour, S. (2006). Examining links between cocaine use and street-based sex work in New South Wales, Australia. *Journal of Sex Research, 43*(2), 107–114.

DeJesus, E., et al. (2012). Co-formulated elvitegravir, cobicistat, emtricitabine, and tenofovir disoproxil fumarate versus ritonavir-boosted atazanavir plus co-formulated emtricitabine and tenofovir disoproxil fumarate for initial treatment of HIV-1 infection: a randomised, double-blind, phase 3, non-inferiority trial. *The Lancet, 379*(9835), 2429–2438.

DeKeseredy, W. S., & Corsianos, M. (2016). *Violence against women in pornography.* New York: Routledge.

Dekker, A., & Schmidt, G. (2002). Patterns of masturbatory behaviour: Changes between the sixties and the nineties. *Journal of Psychology & Human Sexuality, 14*(2–3), 35–48.

DeLamater, J., & Plante, R. F. (2015). The sociological study of sexuality. *Handbook of the sociology of sexualities* (pp. 1–4). Switzerland: Springer International Publishing.

del Busto, E., & Harlow, M. C. (2011). American sex offender castration treatment and legislation. In D. P. Boer et al. (Eds.). *International Perspectives on the Assessment and Treatment of Sexual Offenders: Theory, Practice, and Research* (pp. 543–571). Hoboken, NJ: Wiley.

Del Rio, F. J., Cabello, F., & Fernandez, I. (2015). Influence of substance abuse on the erectile response in sample of drug users. *International Journal of Clinical and Health Psychology, 15,* 37–43.

Del Rosso, J. (2011). The penis as public part: Embodiment and the performance of masculinity in public settings. *Sexualities, 14*(6), 704–724.

Delgado, A. R., & Prieto, G. (2004). Cognitive mediators and sex-related differences in mathematics. *Intelligence, 32*(1), 25–32.

Delgado, J. (1969). *Physical control of the mind.* New York: Harper & Row.

den Tonkelaar, I., & Oddens, B. J. (2000). Determinants of long-term hormone replacement therapy and reasons for early discontinuation. *Obstetrics & Gynecology, 95*(4), 507–512.

Denmark, F., Paludi, M. A., & Lott, B. (2008). *Psychology of women: A handbook of issues and theories.* Santa Barbara, CA: Greenwood Press.

Denmark, F. L., & Williams, D. (2014). Gender bias, overview. In T. Teo (Ed.). *Encyclopedia of critical psychology* (pp. 761–762). New York: Springer Science+Business Media.

Dennerstein, L., & Goldstein, I. (2005). Postmenopausal female sexual dysfunction: At a crossroads. *Journal of Sexual Medicine, 2*(Suppl. 3), 116–117.

Derby, C. A. (2000, October 2). Cited in Study finds exercise reduces the risk of impotence. The Associated Press.

Derlega, V. J., Winstead, B. A., & Greene, K. (2008). Self-disclosure and starting a close relationship. In S. Sprecher, A. Wenzel, & J. Harvey (Eds.), *Handbook of relationship initiation* (pp.153–174). New York: CRC Press.

Devereux, C. (2011). "Last night, I did a striptease for my husband." Erotic dance and the representation of "everyday" femininity. *Feminist media studies,* 10.1080/14680777.2011.615598.

Dew, J., & Wilcox, W. B. (2011, December 8). Give and you shall receive? Generosity, sacrifice, and marital quality. *National Marriage Project Working Paper* No. 11-1.

Dhar, N. B. (2006). Vasectomy men pose pregnancy risk. *British Journal of Urology International, 97,* 773–776.

Dhuffar, M. K., & Griffiths, M. D. (2015). A systematic review of online sex addiction and clinical treatments using CONSORT evaluation. *Current Addiction Reports: Topical Collection on Technology and Addiction, 2*(2), 163–174.

Diamond, L. (2008). *Sexual fluidity: Understanding women's love and desire.* Cambridge, MA: Harvard University Press.

Diamond, L. M. (2000). Sexual identity, attractions, and behavior among young sexual-minority women over a 2-year period. *Developmental Psychology, 36*(2), 241–250.

Diamond, L. M. (2002). "Having a girlfriend without knowing it": Intimate friendships among adolescent sexual-minority women. *Journal of Lesbian Studies, 6*(1) 5–16.

Diamond, L. M. (2003a). Was it a phase? Young women's relinquishment of lesbian/bisexual identities over a 5-year period. *Journal of Personality & Social Psychology, 84*(2), 352–364.

Diamond, L. M. (2003b). What does sexual orientation orient? A biobehavioral model distinguishing romantic love and sexual desire. *Psychological Review, 110*(1), 173–192.

Diamond, L. M. (2008). Female bisexuality from adolescence to adulthood: Results from a 10-year longitudinal study. *Developmental Psychology, 44*(1), 5–14.

Diamond, L. M. (2014). Romantic love. In M. M. Tugade et al. (Eds.). *Handbook of positive emotions* (pp. 311–328). New York: Guilford Press.

Diamond, L. M., & Dickenson, J. A. (2012). The neuroimaging of love and desire: Review and future directions. *Clinical Neuropsychiatry, 9*(1), 39–46.

Diamond, M. (1996). Prenatal predisposition and the clinical management of some pediatric conditions. *Journal of Sex & Marital Therapy, 22*(3), 139–147.

Diamond, M. (2011). Developmental, sexual and reproductive neuroendocrinology: Historical, clinical and ethical considerations. *Frontiers in Neuroendocrinology, 32*(2), 255–263.

DiDonato, M. D., & Berenbaum, S. A. (2011). The benefits and drawbacks of gender typing: How different dimensions are related to psychological adjustment. *Archives of Sexual Behavior, 40*(2), 457–463.

Dijkstra, P., & Buunk, B. P. (2002). Sex differences in the jealousy-evoking effect of rival characteristics. *European Journal of Social Psychology, 32*(6), 829–852.

Dilley, J. W., et al. (2003). Availability of combination therapy for HIV: Effects on sexual risk taking in a sample of high-risk gay and bisexual men. *AIDS Care, 15*(1), 27–37.

Dindia, K., & Allen, M. (1992). Sex differences in self-disclosure: A meta-analysis. *Psychological Bulletin, 112,* 106–124.

Ding, Z., Ingraham, C. M., Rodd, Z. A., & McBride, W. L. (2016). Alcohol drinking increases the dopamine-stimulating effects of ethanol and reduces D_2 auto-receptor and group II metabotropic glutamate receptor function within the posterior ventral tegmental area of alcohol preferring (P) rats. *Neuropharmacology, 109,* 41–48.

Ding, Q. J., & Hesketh, T. (2006). Family size, fertility preferences, and sex ratio in China in the era of the one child family policy: Results from National Family Planning and Reproductive Health Survey. *British Medical Journal, 333*(7564), 371–373.

Dingfelder, S. F. (2011, April). Understanding orgasm. *Monitor on Psychology, 42*(4), 42–45.

Direkvand-Moghadam, A., et al. (2014). Epidemiology of premenstrual syndrome (PMS)—A systematic review and meta-analysis study. *Journal of Clinical and Diagnostic Research, 8*(2), 106–109.

Disney, E. R., Iacono, W., McGue, M., Tully, E., & Legrand, L. (2008). Strengthening the case: Prenatal alcohol exposure is associated with increased risk for conduct disorder. *Pediatrics, 122*(6), e1225–e1230.

Dittert, S., Seidl, O., & Soyka, M. (2005). Zoophilia as a special case of paraphilia. Presentation of three case reports and an Internet survey. *Nervenarzt, 76*(1), 61–67.

Dixson, B. J., Grimshaw, G. M., Linklater, W. L., & Dixson, A. F. (2011). Eye tracking of men's preferences for female breast size and areola pigmentation. *Archives of Sexual Behavior, 40*(1), 51–58.

Dixson, B. J., Duncan, M., & Dixson, A. F. (2015). The role of breast size and areolar pigmentation in perceptions of women's sexual attractiveness, reproductive health, sexual maturity, maternal nurturing abilities, and age. *Archives of Sexual Behavior, 44*(6), 1685–1695.

Do, C., et al. (2009). Statins and erectile dysfunction: Results of a case/non-case study using the French Pharmacovigilance System Database. *Drug Safety, 32*(7), 591–597.

Dodge, B., Schick, V., Herbenick, D., Reece, M., Sanders, S. A., and Fortenberry, J. D. (2014). Frequency, reasons for, and perceptions of lubricant use among a nationally representative sample of self-identified gay and bisexual men in the United States. *Journal of Sexual Medicine, 11*(10), 2396–2405.

Dodge, M. (2012). Female prostitution. In C. D. Bryant (Ed.). *The Routledge handbook of deviant behavior* (pp. 371–377). New York: Routledge.

Doherty, W. (2014). Cited in Miller, C. C. (2014, December 2). The divorce surge is over, but the myth lives on. *The New York Times*, p. A3.

Donald, M., Dower, J., Correa-Velez, I., & Jones, M. (2006). Risk and protective factors for medically serious suicide attempts: A comparison of hospital-based with population-based samples of young adults. *Australian and New Zealand Journal of Psychiatry, 40*(1), 87–96.

Donnerstein, E. (1980). Aggressive erotica and violence against women. *Journal of Personality and Social Psychology, 39*, 269–277.

Donnerstein, E. I., & Linz, D. G. (1987). *The question of pornography.* New York: The Free Press.

Donnerstein, E., & Berkowitz, L. (1981). Victim reactions in aggressive erotic films as a factor in violence against women. *Journal of Personality and Social Psychology, 41*, 710–724.

Downing, L. (2015). Heteronormativity and repronormativity in sexological "perversion theory" and the DSM-5's "paraphilic disorder" categories. *Archives of Sexual Behavior, 44*, 1139–1145.

Downing, L., & Gillett, R. (2011). Viewing critical psychology through the lens of queer. *Psychology and Sexuality, 2*(1), 4–15.

Downing, L., Morland, I., & Sullivan, N. (2014). Fuckology: *Critical essays on John Money's diagnostic concepts.* Chicago: University of Chicago Press.

Downs, M., & Nazario, B. (2003, February 11). *Aphrodisiacs through the ages.* WebMD Features. http://www.webmd.com/sex-relationships/features/aphrodisiacs-through-ages (Accessed July 13, 2016).

Drews, C. D., et al. (1996). The relationship between idiopathic mental retardation and maternal smoking during pregnancy. *Pediatrics, 97*(4), 547–553.

Drigotas, S. M., Rusbult, C. E., & Verette, J. (1999). Level of commitment, mutuality of commitment, and couple well-being. *Personal Relationships, 6*(3) 389–409.

Driver, J., Tabares, A., Shapiro, A., Nahm, E. Y., & Gottman, J. M. (2003). Interactional patterns in marital success and failure: Gottman laboratory studies. In F. Walsh (Ed.), *Normal family processes: Growing diversity and complexity* (3rd ed., pp. 493–513). New York: Guilford.

Drucker, D. J. (2012). A most interesting chapter in the history of science: Intellectual responses to Alfred Kinsey's *Sexual behavior in the human male. History of the Human Sciences, 25*(1), 75–98.

Duby, Z. et al. (2015). Condoms, lubricants and rectal cleansing: Practices associated with heterosexual penile-anal intercourse amongst participants in an HIV prevention trial in South Africa, Uganda, and Zimbabwe. *AIDS and Behavior, 20*(4), 754–762.

Duenwald, M. (2002, July 16). Hormone therapy: One size, clearly, no longer fits all. *The New York Times.* http://www.nytimes.com/2002/07/16/science/hormone-therapy-one-size-clearly-no-longer-fits-all.html?mtrref=www.nytimes.com&gwh=35E29F8F1A4F41B5D31A1C7E883A7A0E&gwt=pay (Accessed July 13, 2016).

Duggan, L. (2006a). Censorship in the name of feminism. In L. Duggan & N. D. Hunter (Eds.), *Sex wars: Sexual dissent and political culture* (10th ed., pp. 29–39). Oxford, UK: Routledge/Taylor & Francis Group.

Duggan, L. (2006b). Feminist historians and antipornography campaigns: An overview. In L. Duggan & N. D. Hunter (Eds.), *Sex wars: Sexual dissent and political culture* (10th ed., pp. 65–69). Oxford, UK: Routledge/Taylor & Francis Group.

Duggan, L., Hunter, N. D., & Vance, C. S. (2006). False promises: Feminist antipornography legislation. In L. Duggan & N. D. Hunter (Eds.), *Sex wars: Sexual dissent and political culture* (10th ed., pp. 43–64). Oxford, UK: Routledge/Taylor & Francis Group.

Duggirala, M. K., et al. (2003). A human papillomavirus type 16 vaccine. *New England Journal of Medicine, 348*, 1402–1405.

Duke, L. A., Allen, D. N., Rozee, P. D., & Bommaritto, M. (2008). The sensitivity and specificity of flashbacks and nightmares to trauma. *Journal of Anxiety Disorders, 22*(2), 319–327.

Dukes, C. (2015). Pornography and violence. *The international encyclopedia of human sexuality.* Hoboken, NJ: Wiley. DOI: 10.1002/9781118896877.wbiehs357

Dunski, S. (2015). Yes, my teenage son is transgender. No, you may not ask about his genitals. *Washington Post.* http://ourqueerstories.com/yes-my-teenage-son-is-transgender-no-you-may-not-ask-about-his-genitals/(Accessed July 13, 2016).

Dural, S., Cetinkaya, H., & Gulbetekin, E. (2015). Hemispheric specialization in the assessment of female physical attractiveness. *Laterality: Asymmetries of Body, Brain and Cognition, 20*(2), 232–248.

Durante, K. M., Li, N. P., & Haselton, M. G. (2008). Changes in women's choice of dress across the ovulatory cycle: Naturalistic and laboratory task-based evidence. *Personality and Social Psychology Bulletin, 34*(11), 1451–1460.

Duru, C., Jha, S., & Lashen, H. (2012). Urodynamic outcomes after hysterectomy for benign conditions: A systematic review and meta-analysis. *Obstetrical and Gynecological Survey, 67*(1), 45–54.

Dvorak, R. D., & Day, A. M. (2014). Marijuana and self-regulation: Examining likelihood and intensity of use and problems. *Addictive Behaviors, 39*(3), 709–712.

Dwyer, P. L. (2011). Skene's gland revisited: Function, dysfunction, and the G-spot. *International Urogynecology Journal, 23*(2), 135–137.

Dye, J. (2013, April 5). U.S. judge widens "morning-after" pill access for young girls. Reuters.

Dzokoto, V. A., & Adams, G. (2005). Understanding genital-shrinking epidemics in West Africa: Koro, juju, or mass psychogenic illness? *Culture, Medicine and Psychiatry, 29*(1), 53–78.

Eadie, M. J., & Vajda, F. J. E. (2016). *Antiepileptic drugs and pregnancy.* Switzerland: Springer International Publishing.

Eardley, I., et al. (2010). Pharmacotherapy for erectile dysfunction. *Journal of Sexual Medicine, 7*, 524–540.

Eason, E., & Feldman, P. (2000). Much ado about a little cut: Is episiotomy worthwhile? *Obstetrics & Gynecology, 95*(4), 616–618.

Eason, E., Labrecque, M., Wells, G., & Feldman, P. (2000). Preventing perineal trauma during childbirth: A systematic review. *Obstetrics & Gynecology, 95*, 464–471.

Eastwick, P. W., & Finkel, E. J. (2008a). Sex differences in mate preferences revisited: Do people know what they initially desire in a romantic partner? *Journal of Personality and Social Psychology, 94*(2), 245–264.

Eastwick, P. W., & Finkel, E. J. (2008b). Speed-dating: A powerful and flexible paradigm for studying romantic relationship initiation. In S. Sprecher, A. Wenzel, & J. Harvey (Eds.), *Handbook of relationship initiation* (pp. 217–234). New York: CRC Press.

Eastwick, P. W., & Hunt, L. L. (2014). Relational mate value: Consensus and uniqueness in romantic evaluations. *Journal of Personality and Social Psychology, 106*(5), 728–751.

Eck, B. A. (2001). Nudity and framing: Classifying art, pornography, information, and ambiguity. *Sociological Forum, 16*(4), 603–632.

Ecuyer-Dab, I., & Robert, M. (2004). Have sex differences in spatial ability evolved from male competition for mating and female concern for survival? *Cognition, 91*(3), 221–257.

Editorial Board. (2015a, August 21). A libido pill and its side effects. *The New York Times*, p. A26.

Editorial Board. (2015b, September 21). Ignoring sexual abuse in Afghanistan. *The New York Times.* http://www.nytimes.com/2015/09/22/opinion/ignoring-sexual-abuse-in-afghanistan.html?_r=0 (Accessed July 13, 2016).

Edser, S. J., & Shea, J. D. (2002). An exploratory investigation of bisexual men in monogamous, heterosexual marriages. *Journal of Bisexuality, 2*(4), 5–29.

Edwards, J., et al. (2011). Developmental coordination disorder in school-aged children born very preterm and/or at very low birth weight: A systematic review. *Journal of Developmental Behavioral Pediatrics, 32*(9), 678–687.

Edwards, T. M. (2000, August 28). Single by choice. *Time Magazine, 156*(9).

Edwards, V. J., Holden, G. W., Felitti, V. J., & Anda, R. F. (2003). Relationship between multiple forms of childhood maltreatment and adult mental health in community respondents: Results from the Adverse Childhood Experiences Study. *American Journal of Psychiatry, 160*(8), 1453–1460.

Egelman, P. C. (2011). *A history of the birth control movement in America.* Santa Barbara, CA: ABC-CLIO.

Eggers, D. (2000, May 7). Intimacies. *The New York Times Magazine*, 76–77.

Eguiguren, M. L., & Ackerman, K. E. (2016). The female athlete triad. In *Contemporary pediatric and adolescent sports medicine* (pp. 57–71). Switzerland: Springer International Publishing.

Eisenberg, M. L., et al. (2010). Socioeconomic, anthropomorphic, and demographic predictors of adult sexual activity in the United States: Data from the National Survey of Family Growth. *Journal of Sexual Medicine, 7*, 50–58.

Eisenberg, M., Shindel, A. W., Smith, J. F., Breyer, B. N., & Lipshultz, L. I. (2010). Socioeconomic, anthropomorphic, and demographic predictors of adult sexual activity in the United States: Data from the national survey of family growth. *Journal of Sexual Medicine, 7*, 50–58.

Eisenberg, N. W., Andreski, S., & Mona, L. R. (2015). Sexuality and physical disability: A disability-affirmative approach to assessment and intervention within health care. *Current Sexual Health Reports, 7*(1), 19–29.

El-Defrawi, M. H., Lotfy, G., Dandash, K. F., Refaat, A. H., & Eyada, M. (2001). Female genital mutilation and its psychosexual impact. *Journal of Sex & Marital Therapy, 27*(5), 465–473.

El-Gibaly, O., Ibrahim, B., Mensch, B. S., & Clark, W. H. (2002). The decline of female circumcision in Egypt: Evidence and interpretation. *Social Science & Medicine, 54*(2), 205–220.

ElleUK. (2015, October). Miley Cyrus is ELLE's October Cover Star. http://www.elleuk.com/now-trending/miley-cyrus-elle-uk-october-2015

Ellingsen, D., et al. (2013). Placebo improves pleasure and pain through opposite modulation of sensory processing. *Proceedings of the National Academy of Sciences, 110*(44), 17993–17998.

Elliot, A. J. (2015). Color and psychological functioning: A review of theoretical and empirical work. *Frontiers in Psychology, 6,* DOI: 10.3389/fpsyg.2015.00368

Elliot, A. J., & Niesta, D. (2008). Romantic red: Red enhances men's attraction to women. *Journal of Personality and Social Psychology, 95*(5), 1150–1164.

Elliot, A. J., & Pazda, A. D. (2012). Dressed for sex: Red as a female sexual signal in humans. *PLoS ONE 7*(4): e34607. DOI:10.1371/journal.pone.0034607

Elliot, A. J., Tracy, J. L., Pazda, A. D., & Beall, A. T. (2013). Red enhances women's attractiveness to men: First evidence suggesting universality. *Journal of Experimental Social Psychology, 49*(1), 165–168.

Elliot, A. J., et al. (2010). Red, rank, and romance in women viewing men. *Journal of Experimental Psychology: General, 139*(3), 399–417.

Ellis, B. J., & Bjorklund, D. F. (Eds.). (2005). *Origins of the social mind: Evolutionary psychology and child development.* New York: Guilford.

Ellis, L., & Ames, M. A. (1987). Neurohormonal functioning and sexual orientation: A theory of homosexuality–heterosexuality. *Psychological Bulletin, 101,* 233–258.

Else-Quest, N. M., & Grabe, S. (2012). The political is personal: Measurement and application of nation-level indicators of gender equity in psychological research. *Psychology of Women Quarterly, 36*(2), 131–144.

Else-Quest, N. M., Hyde, J. S., & Linn, M. C. (2010). Cross-national patterns of gender differences in mathematics: A meta-analysis. *Psychological Bulletin, 136*(1), 103–127.

Else-Quest, N. M., Mineo, C. C., & Higgins, A. (2013). Math and science attitudes at the intersection of gender and ethnicity. *Psychology of Women Quarterly, 37*(3), 293–309.

El-Sheikh, M. & Harger, J. (2001). Appraisals of marital conflict and children's adjustment, health, and physiological reactivity. *Developmental Psychology, 37*(6), 875–885.

Eltahawy, M. (2003, January 9). *Young Africans reject female genital mutilation.* www.feminist.com/news/news141.html.

Emanuel, E. J. (2014, January 18). Sex and the single senior. *The New York Times,* p. SR8.

Emanuele, E., et al. (2006). Raised plasma nerve growth factor levels associated with early-stage romantic love. *Psychoneuroendocrinology, 31*(3), 288–294.

Emetu, R. E., Marshall, A., Sanders, S. A., Yarber, W. L., Milhausen, R. R., Crosby,

R. A., & Graham, C. A. (2014) A novel, self-guided, home-based intervention to improve condom use among young men who have sex with men. *Journal of American College Health, 62,* (2), 118–124.

Emmanuele A., et al. (2011). The controversial role of phosphodiesterase type 5 inhibitors in the treatment of premature ejaculation. *The Journal of Sexual Medicine, 8*(8), 2135–2143.

Emmelot-Vonk, M. H., et al. (2009). Effect of testosterone supplementation on sexual functioning in aging men: A 6-month randomized controlled trial. *International Journal of Impotence Research, 21,* 129–138.

Engelhardt, A., Fischer, J., Neumann, C., Pfeifer, J., & Heistermann, M. (2012). Information content of female copulation calls in wild long-tailed macaques. *Behavioral Ecology and Sociobiology, 66*(1), 121–134.

England, P., & Bearak, J. (2014). The sexual double standard and gender differences in attitudes toward casual sex among U.S. university students. *Demographic Research, 30,* 1327–1338.

Enteen, J. B. (2014). Transitioning online. *Television and News Media, 15*(3), 238–249.

Eriksson, C., Salander, K., & Hamberg, K. (2007). Men's experiences of intense fear related to childbirth investigated in a Swedish qualitative study. *The Journal of Men's Health & Gender, 4*(4), 409–418.

European Commission. Eurostat. (2009). Live births outside marriage. Accessed May 13, 2009.

Evlampidou, I., et al. (2015). Prenatal second-hand smoke exposure measured with urine cotinine may reduce gross motor development at 18 months of age. *The Journal of Pediatrics, 167*(2), 246–252.

Fabre, L. F., et al. (2012). The effect of gepirone-ER in the treatment of sexual dysfunction in depressed men. *Journal of Sexual Medicine, 9*(3), 821–829.

Fabricius, W. V., Sokol, K. R., Diaz, P., & Braver, S. L. (2012). Parenting time, parent conflict, parent–child relationships, and children's physical health. In K. Kuehnle, & L. Drozd. (Eds.). *Parenting plan evaluations: Applied research for the family court* (pp. 188–213). New York: Oxford University Press.

Fagot, B. I., Rodgers, C. S., & Leinbach, M. D. (2000). Theories of gender socialization. In T. Eckes & H. M. Trautner (Eds.), *The developmental social psychology of gender* (pp. 65–89). Mahwah, NJ: Erlbaum.

Faller, K. C. (1989). Why sexual abuse? An exploration of the intergenerational hypothesis. *Child Abuse and Neglect, 13,* 543–548.

Fales, M. R., Frederiack, D. A., Garcia, J. R., Gildersleeve, K. A., Haselton, M. G., & Fisher, H. E. (2016). Mating markets and bargaining hands: Mate preferences for attractiveness and resources in two national U.S. studies. *Personality and Individual Differences, 88,* 78–87.

Fang, A., & Hofmann, S. G. (2010). Relationship between social anxiety disorder and body dysmorphic disorder. *Clinical Psychology Review, 30*(8), 1040–1048.

Farley, M. Citied in Bennets, L. (2011, July 18). The john next door. *Newsweek* magazine.

Farley, M., Lynne, J., & Cotton, A. J. (2005). Prostitution in Vancouver: Violence and the colonization of First Nations Women. *Transcultural Psychiatry, 42*(2), 242–271.

Farr, R. H., & Patterson, C. J. (2013). Lesbian and gay adoptive parents and their children. In A. E. Goldberg, & K. R. Allen (Eds.), *LGBT-parent families: Innovations in research and implications for practice* (pp. 39–55). New York: Springer Science+Business Media.

Fausto-Sterling, A. (May/April 1993). The five sexes: Why male and female are not enough. *The Sciences,* 20–25.

Fausto-Sterling, A. (2012). The dynamic development of gender variability. *Journal of Homosexuality, 59*(3), 398–421.

Fava, N. M., & Bay-Cheng, L. Y. (2012). Young women's adolescent experiences of oral sex: Relation of age of initiation to sexual motivation, sexual coercion, and psychological functioning. *Journal of Adolescence, 35*(5), 1191–1201.

FBI. (2014). Latest Hate Crime Statistics report released. https://www.fbi.gov/news/stories/2014/december/latest-hate-crime-statistics-report-released

Fehr, B., Harasymchuk, C., & Sprecher, S. (2014). Compassionate love in romantic relationships. *Journal of Social and Personal Relationships,* DOI: 10.1177/0265407514533768

Feinberg, D. R., et al. (2006). Menstrual cycle, trait estrogen level, and masculinity preferences in the human voice. *Hormones and Behavior, 49*(2), 215–222.

Feingold, A. (1994). Gender differences in personality: A meta-analysis. *Psychological Bulletin, 116,* 429–456.

Felson, R. B. (2002). *Violence and gender reexamined.* Washington, DC: American Psychological Association.

Fensterheim, H., & Kantor, J. S. (1980). Behavioral approach to sexual disorders. In B. Wolman & J. Money (Eds.), *Handbook of human sexuality.* Englewood Cliffs, NJ: Prentice-Hall.

Fenton, K., et al. (2008). Infectious syphilis in high-income settings in the 21st century. *The Lancet Infectious Diseases, 8*(4), 244–253.

Fergusson, D. M., McLeod, G. F. H., & Horwood, L. J. (2014). Breast feeding, infant growth, and body mass index at 30 and 35 years. *Paediatric and Perinatal Epidemiology, 28*(6), 545–552.

Ferraro, G. (2004). *Cultural anthropology—An applied perspective* (5th ed.). Belmont, CA: Wadsworth.

Ferris, C. F., et al. (2004). Activation of neural pathways associated with sexual arousal in non-human primates. *Journal of Magnetic Resonance Imaging, 19*(2), 168–175.

Festa, E. D., et al. (2004). Sex differences in cocaine-induced behavioral responses, pharmacokinetics, and monoamine levels. *Neuropharmacology, 46*(5), 672–687.

Festini, F., et al. (2006, August 22). The open problems of China's One-Child Family Policy: Men surplus and support of the elders. Available at www.bmj.com.

Fichner-Rathus, L. (2010). *Understanding art* (9th ed.). Belmont, CA: Thomson Learning/Wadsworth.

Fielder, R. L., Walsh, J. L., Carey, K. B., & Carey, M. P. (2013). Predictors of sexual hookups: A theory-based, prospective study of first-year college women. *Archives of Sexual Behavior, 42,* 1425–1441.

Fielder, R. L., Walsh, J. L., Carey, K. B., & Carey, M. P. (2014). Sexual hookups and adverse health outcomes: A longitudinal study of first-year college women. *Journal of Sex Research, 51*(2), 131–144.

Fields, E. L., et al. (2015). "I Always Felt I Had to Prove My Manhood": Homosexuality, Masculinity, Gender Role Strain, and HIV Risk Among Young Black Men Who Have Sex with Men. *American Journal of Public Health, 105*(1), 122–131.

Fillion, T. J., & Blass, E. M. (1986). Infantile experience with suckling odors determines adult sexual behavior in male rats. *Science, 231*(4739), 729–731.

Fine, C. (2014). Neuroscience, genders, and "development to" and "from": The example of toy preferences. In J. Clausen & N Levy (Eds.), *Handbook of neuroethics* (pp. 1737–1755). Dordrecht, Netherlands: Springer Netherlands.

Finer, L. B., & Zolna, M. R. (2011). Unintended pregnancy in the United States: In cadence and disparities. *Contraception, 84*(5), 478–485.

Finkel, E. J., Eastwick, P., Karney, B., Reis, H. T., & Sprecher, S. (2012). Online dating: A critical analysis from the perspective of psychological science. *Psychological Science in the Public Interest*, 1–64. DOI:10.1177/1529100612436522

Finkel, E. J. (2015, February 8). In defense of Tinder. *The New York Times*, p. SR9.

Finkelhor, D. (1990). Early and long-term effects of child sexual abuse: An update. *Professional Psychology: Research and Practice, 21*, 325–330.

Finkelhor, D. (2003). The legacy of the clergy abuse scandal. *Child Abuse & Neglect, 27*(11), 1225–1229.

Finkelhor, D. (2011). Prevalence of child victimization, abuse, crime, and violence exposure. In J. W. White, M. P. Koss, & A. E. Kazdin (Eds.). *Violence against women and children, Vol 1: Mapping the terrain* (pp. 9–29). Washington, DC, US: American Psychological Association.

Finkelhor, D. (2015). Improving surveys on sexual assault. *PsycCRITIQUES, 60*(10), DOI: 10.1037/a0038623

Finkelhor, D., Cross, T. P., & Cantor, E. N. (2005a). The justice system for juvenile victims: A comprehensive model of case flow. *Trauma, Violence, & Abuse, 6*(2), 83–102.

Finkelhor, D., Ormrod, R., Turner, H., & Hamby, S. (2012). *Child and Youth Victimization Known to Police, School, and Medical Authorities. National Survey of Children's Exposure to Violence*. Juvenile Justice Bulletin. Office of Juvenile Justice and Delinquency Prevention.

Finkelhor, D., Ormrod, R., Turner, H., & Hamby, S. L. (2005b). The victimization of children and youth: A comprehensive, national survey. *Child Maltreatment: Journal of the American Professional Society on the Abuse of Children, 10*(1), 5–25.

Finkelman, J. M. (2005). Sexual harassment: The organizational perspective. In A. Barnes (Ed.), *The handbook of women, psychology, and the law* (pp. 64–78). New York: Wiley.

Finkenauer, C., & Hazam, H. (2000). Disclosure and secrecy in marriage: Do both contribute to marital satisfaction? *Journal of Social & Personal Relationships, 17*(2), 245–263.

Firestone, R. W., Firestone, L. A., & Catlett, J. (2006a). *Sex and love in intimate relationships*. Washington, DC: American Psychological Association.

Fisher, A. D., Bandini, E., Casale, H., & Maggi, M. (2011). Paraphilic disorders: Diagnosis and treatment. In M. Maggi (Ed.). *Hormonal therapy for male sexual dysfunction* (pp. 94–110). Hoboken, NJ: Wiley.

Fisher, A. D., Bandini, E., Casale, H., & Maggi, M. (2012). Paraphilic disorders: Diagnosis and treatment. In M. Maggi (Ed.). *Hormonal therapy for male sexual dysfunction* (pp. 94–110). Hoboken, NJ: Wiley.

Fisher, A. D., et al. (2015) Endocrine treatment of transsexual male-to-female persons. In. C. Trombetta et al. (Eds.), *Management of gender dysphoria* (pp. 83–91). Milan, Italy: Sprinter-Verlag Italia.

Fisher, B. S., Daigle, L. E., Cullen, F. T., & Turner, M. G. (2003). Reporting sexual victimization to the police and others: Results from a national-level study of college women. *Criminal Justice & Behavior, 30*(1), 6–38.

Fisher, H. E. (2000). Brains do it: Lust, attraction and attachment. *Cerebrum, 2*, 23–42.

Fisher, T. D., Moore, Z. T., & Pittenger, M. (2012). Sex on the brain? An examination of frequency of sexual cognitions as a function of gender, erotophilia, and social desirability. *Journal of Sex Research, 49*(1), 69–77.

Fisher, W. A., et al. (2005). Improving the sexual quality of life of couples affected by erectile dysfunction: A double-blind, randomized, placebo-controlled trial of vardenafil. *Journal of Sexual Medicine, 2*(5), 699–708.

Fisher, W., Ceballos, N., Matthews, D., & Ficher, L. (2011). Event-related potentials in impulsively aggressive juveniles: A retrospective chart-review study. *Psychiatry Research, 187*(3), 409–413.

Fishman, J. R., & Mamo, L. (2001). What's in a disorder: A cultural analysis of medical and pharmaceutical constructions of male and female sexual dysfunction. *Women & Therapy, 24*(1–2), 179–193.

Flaxman, S. M., & Sherman, P. W. (2000). Morning sickness: A mechanism for protecting mother and embryo. *Quarterly Review of Biology, 75*(2), 113–148.

Fletcher, J. (1966). *Situation ethics*. Philadelphia: Westminster Press.

Fletcher, J. (1967). *Moral responsibility: Situation ethics at work*. Philadelphia: Westminster Press.

Fletcher, J. M., & Sindelar, J. L. (2012). The effects of family stressors on substance abuse initiation in adolescence. *Review of Economics of the Household, 10*(1), 99–114.

Fletcher, S. W., & Colditz, G. A. (2002). Failure of estrogen plus progestin therapy for prevention. *Journal of the American Medical Association, 288*(3), 366–368.

Florence, E., et al. (2004). Prevalence and factors associated with sexual dysfunction among HIV-positive women in Europe. *AIDS Care, 16*(5), 550–557.

Flores, A. R., Herman, J. L., Gates, G. J., & Brown, T. N. T. (2016, June). How many adults identify as transgender in the United States? Los Angeles, CA: The Williams Institute, UCLA School of Law.

Floyd, R. L., O'Connor, M. J., Sokol, R. J., Bertrand, J., & Cordero, F. F. (2005). Recognition and prevention of fetal alcohol syndrome. *Obstetrics & Gynecology, 106*, 1059–1064.

Fod and Drug Administration. (2015). Condoms and sexually transmitted diseases. http://www.fda.gov/ForPatients/Illness/HIVAIDS/ucm126372.htm (Retrieved July 3, 2016).

Forbes, A., While, A., Mathes, L., & Griffiths, P. (2006). Health problems and health-related quality of life in people with multiple sclerosis. *Clinical Rehabilitation, 20*(1), 67–78.

Forbes, G. B., Adams-Curtis, L. E., Pakalka, A. H., & White, K. B. (2006). Dating aggression, sexual coercion, and aggression-supporting attitudes among college men as a function of participation in aggressive high school sports. *Violence Against Women, 12*(5), 441–455.

Ford, C. S., & Beach, F. A. (1951). *Patterns of sexual behavior*. New York: Harper & Row.

Foubert, J. D., & Newberry, J. T. (2006). Effects of two versions of an empathy-based rape prevention program on fraternity men's survivor empathy, attitudes, and behavioral intent to commit rape or sexual assault. *Journal of College Student Development, 47*(2), 133–148.

Fovargue, S., & Bennett, R. (2016). What role should public opinion play in ethico-legal decision making? The example of selecting sex for nonmedical reasons using preimplantation genetic diagnosis. *Medical Law Review, 24*(1), 34–58.

Fox, N. S., et al. (2008). Physical and sexual activity during pregnancy and near delivery. *Journal of Women's Health, 17*, 1431.

Frank, K. (2002). *G-strings and sympathy: Strip club regulars and male desire*. Raleigh, NC: Duke University Press.

Frank, K. (2003). Just trying to relax: Masculinity, masculinizing practices, and strip club regulars. *The Journal of Sex Research, 40*(1), 61–75.

Frank, K. (2007). Thinking critically about strip club research. *Sexualities, 10*(4), 501–517.

Frank, K. (2015). Observational methods in sexuality research. In J. DeLamater, & R. F. Plante (Eds.), *Handbook of the sociology of sexualities* (pp. 123–146). Switzerland: Springer International Publishing.

Franzese, A. T., & Panaggio, N. C. (2016). *Contraception in the United States*, DOI: 10.1002/9781119085621.wbefs407

Frayser, S. (1985). *Varieties of sexual experience: An anthropological perspective on human sexuality*. New Haven, CT: Human Relations Area Files Press.

Frethelm, A., et al. (2013). The impact of an intervention program employing a hands-on technique to reduce the incidence of anal sphincter tears: Interrupted time-series analysis. *British Medical Journal Open*, DOI: 10.1136/bmjopen-2013-003355

Freud, S. (1922/1959). Analysis of a phobia in a 5-year-old boy. In A. J. Strachey (Ed., Trans.), *Collected papers* (Vol. 3). New York: Basic Books. [Original work published 1909].

Freudenmann, R. W., & Schönfeldt–Lecuona, C. (2005). The syndrome of genital retraction from a transcultural psychiatric point of view. Chinese suo yang, Indonesian koro and non-Asian forms (koro-like symptoms). *Nervenarzt, 76*(5), 569–580.

Frey, K. S., & Ruble, D. N. (1992). Gender constancy and the "cost" of sex-typed behavior: A test of the conflict hypothesis. *Developmental Psychology, 28*, 714–721.

Frick, K. D., Pugh, L. C., & Milligan, R. A. (2012). Costs related to promoting breastfeeding among urban low-income women. *Journal of Obstetric, Gynecologic, & Neonatal Nursing, 41*(1), 144–150.

Friday, N. (1973). *My secret garden*. New York: Trident.

Friday, N. (2008). *My secret garden: Women's sexual fantasies*. New York: Simon & Schuster.

Fried, P. A., & Smith, A. M. (2001) A literature review of the consequences of prenatal marihuana exposure: An emerging theme of a deficiency in aspects of executive function. *Neurotoxicology & Teratology, 23*(1), 1–11.

Friedman, R. A. (2015a, August 22). How Changeable Is Gender? *The New York Times.* http://www.nytimes.com/2015/08/23/opinion/sunday/richard-a-friedman-how-changeable-is-gender.html (Accessed July 13, 2016).

Friedman, R. A. (2015b, May 22). Infidelity lurks in your genes. *The New York Times.* http://www.nytimes.com/2015/05/24/opinion/sunday/infidelity-lurks-in-your-genes.html (Accessed July 13, 2016).

Friedman, R. C., & Downey, J. I. (2001). The Oedipus complex and male homosexuality. In P. Hartocollis (Ed.), *Mankind's Oedipal destiny: Libidinal and aggressive aspects of sexuality* (pp. 113–138). Madison, CT: International Universities Press.

Friedman, R. C., & Downey, J. I. (2008). Sexual differentiation of behavior: The foundation of a developmental model of psychosexuality. *Journal of the American Psychoanalytic Association, 56*(1), 147–175.

Friedrich, W., & Gerber, P. N. (1994). Autoerotic asphyxia: The development of a paraphilia. *Journal of the American Academy of Child and Adolescent Psychiatry, 33*(7), 970–974.

Friedrich, W., Fisher, J., Broughton, D., Houston, M., & Shafran, C. R. (1998). Normative sexual behavior in children: A contemporary sample. *Pediatrics, 101*(4), e9.

Frohlich, P. F., & Meston, C. M. (2005). Tactile sensitivity in women with sexual arousal disorder. *Archives of Sexual Behavior, 34*(2), 207–217.

Frohmader, K. S., Bateman, K. L., Lehman, M. N., & Coolen, L. M. (2010). Effects of methamphetamine on sexual performance and compulsive sex behavior in male rats. *Psychopharmacology, 212*(1), 93–104.

Frost, J. J., & Frohwirth, L. A. (2005, July). *Family planning annual report: 2004 Summary.* The Alan Guttmacher Institute.

Frühauf, S., Gerger, H., Schmidt, H. M., Munder, T., & Barth, J. (2013). Efficacy of psychological interventions for sexual dysfunction: a systematic review and meta-analysis. *Archives of Sexual Behavior, 42*, 915–933.

Fuentes-Afflick, E., & Hessol, N. A. (2000). Interpregnancy interval and the risk or premature infants. *Obstetrics & Gynecology, 95*, 383–390.

Fugl-Meyer, K. S., Öberg, K., Lundberg, P. O., Lewin, B., & Fugl-Meyer, A. (2006). On orgasm, sexual techniques, and erotic perceptions in 18- to 74-year-old Swedish women. *Journal of Sexual Medicine, 3*(1), 56–68.

Fulcher, M., Sutfin, E. L., & Patterson, C. J. (2008). Individual differences in gender development: Associations with parental sexual orientation, attitudes, and division of labor. *Sex Roles, 58* (5-6), 330–341.

Furnham, A. (2009). Sex differences in mate selection preferences. *Personality and Individual Differences, 47*(4), 262–267.

Furnham, A., Petrides, K. V., & Constantinides, A. (2005). The effects of body mass index and waist-to-hip ratio on ratings of female attractiveness, fecundity, and health. *Personality and Individual Differences, 38*(8), 1823–1834.

Furstenberg, F. F., & Kiernan, K. E. (2001). Delayed parental divorce: How much do children benefit? *Journal of Marriage & the Family, 63*(2), 446–457.

Gable, S. (2012). Approach and avoidance motivation. In P. Noller & G. C. Karantzas (Eds.). *The Wiley-Blackwell handbook of couples and family relationships* (pp. 193–206). Chichester, UK: Wiley.

Gabriel, T. (1995, June 12). A new generation seems ready to give bisexuality a place in the spectrum. *The New York Times*, p. A12.

Gådin, K. G. (2012). Sexual harassment of girls in elementary school. *Journal of Interpersonal Violence, 27*(9), 1762–1779.

Gagnon, J. H. (1977). *Human sexualities.* Glenview, IL: Scott Foresman.

Galdi, S., Cadinu, M., & Tomasetto, C. (2014). The root of stereotype threat: When automatic associations disrupt girls' math performance. *Child Development, 85*(1), 250–263.

Gallup Poll. (2015). http://www.gallup.com/poll/1576/abortion.aspx

Galperin, A., et al. (2013). Sexual regret: Evidence for evolved sex differences. *Archives of Sexual Behavior, 42*, 1145–1161.

Garcia, J. R., Reiber, C., Massey, S. G., & Merriwether, A. M. (2012). Sexual hookup culture: A review. *Review of General Psychology, 16*(2), 161–176.

Garcia, J. R., Seibold-Simpson, S. M., Massey, S. G., & Merriwether, A. M. (2015). Casual sex: Integrating social, behavioral, and sexual health research. In J. DeLamater, & R. F. Plante (Eds.), *Handbook of the sociology of sexualities* (pp. 203–222). Switzerland: Springer International Publishing.

Garcia-Falgueras, A., & Swaab, D. F. (2010). Sex hormones and the brain: An essential alliance for sexual identity and sexual orientation. In S. Loche et al. (Eds.), *Pediatric neuroendocrinology* (Vol. 17, pp. 22–35). Basel, Switzerland: Karger.

Garwood, S. G., et al. (1980). Beauty is only "name deep": The effect of first name in ratings of physical attraction. *Journal of Applied Social Psychology, 10*, 431–435.

Gass, M. L. S., et al. (2011). Patterns and predictors of sexual activity among women in the Hormone Therapy trials of the Women's Health Initiative. *Menopause, 18*(11), 1160–1171.

Gates, J. (2001). *Survivors of an open marriage.* Anchorage: KiwE Publishing.

Gates, G. J., & Newport, F. (2012, October). Gallup special report: The LGBT vote in the 2012 presidential election. The Williams Institute. http://williamsinstitute.law.ucla.edu/research/census-lgbt-demographics-studies/gallup-special-report-lgbt-vote-18oct-2012/(Accessed October 20, 2012).

Gauthier, K., & Genesee, F. (2011). Language development in internationally adopted children. *Child Development*, DOI: 10.1111/j.1467-8624.2011.01578.x

Gavin, L., et al. (2009, July 17). Sexual and reproductive health of persons aged 10–24 years—United States, 2002–2007. *Morbidity and Mortality Weekly Report, 58*(27), 1–58. Available at http://www.cdc.gov/mmwr/preview/mmwrhtml/ss5806a1.htm

Gavin, N. I., et al. (2005). Perinatal depression: A systematic review of prevalence and incidence. *Obstetrics & Gynecology, 106*, 1071–1083.

Gebhard, P. H. (1969). Misconceptions about female prostitutes. *Medical Aspects of Human Sexuality, 3*, 24–26.

Gebhard, P. H., et al. (1965). *Sex offenders: An analysis of types.* New York: Harper & Row.

Geddes, L. (2008). Ultrasound nails location of the elusive G spot. *The New Scientist, 197*(2644), 6–7.

Genital herpes, 2012. Centers for Disease Control and Prevention. (2012). Sexually Transmitted Diseases (STDs). Genital herpes—CDC fact sheet. http://www.cdc.gov/std/Herpes/STDFact-Herpes.htm (Accessed October 4, 2012).

Genital HPV infection, 2012. Centers for Disease Control and Prevention. (2012). Sexually Transmitted Diseases (STDs). Genital HPV infection—Fact sheet. http://www.cdc.gov/std/HPV/STDFact-HPV.htm (Accessed October 4, 2012).

Genital HPV infection—Fact sheet. (2016). http://www.cdc.gov/std/hpv/stdfact-hpv.htm (Accessed July 8, 2016)

George, D., et al. (2015). Couple similarity on stimulus characteristics and marital satisfaction. *Personality and Individual Differences, 86*, 126–131.

George, W. H., Stoner, S. A., Norris, J., Lopez, P. A., & Lehman, G. L. (2000). Alcohol expectancies and sexuality: A self-fulfilling prophecy analysis of dyadic perceptions and behavior. *Journal of Studies on Alcohol, 61*(1), 168–176.

George, W. H., et al. (2014). Sexual victimization, alcohol intoxication, sexual-emotional responding, and sexual risk in heavy episodic drinking women. *Archives f Sexual Behavior, 43*(4), 645–658.

Gidycz, C. A., & Koss, M. P. (1990). A comparison of group and individual sexual assault victims. *Psychology of Women Quarterly, 14*, 325–342.

Gidycz, C. A., Orchowski, L. M., & Berkowitz, A. D. (2011). Preventing sexual aggression among college men: An evaluation of a social norms and bystander intervention program. *Violence Against Women, 17*(6), 720–742.

Gidycz, C. A., Rich, C. L., Orchowski, L., King, C., & Miller, A. K. (2006). The evaluation of a sexual assault self-defense and risk-reduction program for college women: A prospective study. *Psychology of Women Quarterly, 30*(2), 173–186.

Gietzen, M. S. (2009). Cited in Monica Davey. (2009, June 7). Closed clinic leaves abortion protesters at a loss. *The New York Times.* http://www.nytimes.com/2009/06/08/us/08wichita.html (Accessed July 13, 2016).

Gijs, L., & Gooren, L. (1996). Hormonal and psychopharmacological interventions in the treatment of paraphilias: An update. *Journal of Sex Research, 33*, 273–290.

Gillibrand, R. (2012). Sex, power and consent: Youth culture and the unwritten rules. *Sex Education: Sexuality, Society and Learning, 12*(1), 125–126.

Gillis, J. S., & Avis, W. E. (1980). The maletaller norm in mate selection. *Personality and Social Psychology Bulletin, 6*, 396–401.

Gillison, M. L. (2011, October 4). In Grady, D., Study cites increase in cancers from HPV. *The New York Times*, p. D5.

Gillison, M. L., et al. (2012). Prevalence of Oral HPV Infection in the United States, 2009-2010. *Journal of the American Medical Association. 307*(7), 693–703.

Gilmore, K. (2008). Birth mother, adoptive mother, dying mother, dead mother. In E. L. Jurist et al. (Eds.), *Mind to mind: Infant research, neuroscience, and psychoanalysis* (pp. 373–397). New York: Other Press.

Gil-Rivas, V. (2012). Sexual risk taking among college students: Correlates and consequences. In R. D. McAnulty (Ed.). *Sex in college: The things they don't write home about.* Santa Barbara, CA: ABC-CLIO, LLC.

Ginzburg, E., et al. (2010). Long-term safety of testosterone and growth hormone supplementation: A retrospective study of metabolic, cardiovascular, and other outcomes. *Journal of Clinical Medicine and Research, 2*(4), 159–166.

Giotakos, O., Markianos, M., & Vaidakis, N. (2005). Aggression, impulsivity, and plasma sex hormone levels in a group of rapists, in relation to their history of childhood attention-deficit/hyperactivity disorder symptoms. *Journal of Forensic Psychiatry & Psychology, 16*(2), 423–433.

Giraldi, H. R., et al. (2012). Female sexual arousal disorders. *The Journal of Sexual Medicine,* DOI: 10.1111/j.1743-6109.2012.02820.x

Giussani, D. A. (2011). The vulnerable developing brain. *Proceedings of the National Academy of Sciences, 108*(7), 2641–2642.

Glaesmer, H., et al. (2012). Gender differences in healthcare utilization. *Journal of Applied Social Psychology,* DOI:10.1111/j.1559-1816.2011.00888.x

Glasser, C. L., Robnett, B., & Feliciano, C. (2009). Internet daters' body type preferences: Race–ethnic and gender differences. *Sex Roles, 61*(1–2), 14–33.

Gleason, J. M., et al. (2011). Regular non-steroidal antiinflammatory drug use and erectile dysfunction. *Journal of Urology, 185,* 1388–1393.

Gnagy, S., Ming, E. E., Devesa, S. S., Hartge, P., & Whittemore, A. S. (2000). Declining ovarian cancer rates in U.S. women in relation to parity and oral contraceptive use. *Epidemiology, 11*(2), 102–105.

Goldberg, J., Holtz, D., Hyslop, T., & Tolosa, J. E. (2002). Has the use of routine episiotomy decreased? Examination of episiotomy rates from 1983 to 2000. *Obstetrics & Gynecology, 99*(3), 395–400.

Goldberg, W. A., Kelly, E., Matthews, N. L., Kang, H., & … Sumaroka, M. (2012). The more things change, the more they stay the same: Gender, culture, and college students' views about work and family. *Journal of Social Issues, 68*(4), 814–837.

Goldie, T. (2014). *The man who invented gender.* Vancouver, Canada: UBC Press.

Goldschmidt, L., Day, N. L., & Richardson, G. A. (2000). Effects of prenatal marijuana exposure on child behavior problems at age 10. *Neurotoxicology & Teratology, 22*(3), 325–336.

Goldstein, I. (2012). The hour lecture that changed sexual medicine—The Giles Brindley injection story. *Journal of Sexual Medicine, 9,* 337–342.

Goldstein, I., & Alexander, J. L. (2005). Practical aspects in the management of vaginal atrophy and sexual dysfunction in perimenopausal and postmenopausal women. *Journal of Sexual Medicine, 2*(Suppl. 3), 154–165.

Goldstein, I., et al. (1998). Oral sildenafil in the treatment of erectile dysfunction. *New England Journal of Medicine, 338,* 1397–1404.

Goldstein, I., Meston, C., Davis, S., & Traish, A. (Eds.). (2006). *Female sexual dysfunction.* New York: Parthenon.

Goldstein, J. (2015, September 20). U.S. soldiers told to ignore sexual abuse by Afghan Allies. *The New York Times.* http://www.nytimes.com/2015/09/21/world/asia/us-soldiers-told-to-ignore-afghan-allies-abuse-of-boys.html (Accessed July 13, 2016).

Golish, T. D. (2003). Stepfamily communication strengths: Understanding the ties that bind. *Human Communication Research, 29*(1), 41–80.

Golombok, S., et al. (2008). Developmental trajectories of sex-typed behavior in boys and girls: A longitudinal general population study of children aged 2.5–8 Years. *Child Development, 79*(5), 1583–1593.

Gomes do Espirito, M. E., & Etheredge, G. D. (2003). HIV prevalence and sexual behaviour of male clients of brothels' prostitutes in Dakar, Senegal. *AIDS Care, 15*(1), 53–62.

Gonococcal infections. (2015). Centers for Disease Control and prevention. http://www.cdc.gov/std/tg2015/gonorrhea.htm

Gonorrhea fact sheet, 2012. Centers for Disease Control and Prevention. (2012). Sexually Transmitted Diseases. Gonorrhea—CDC fact sheet. http://www.cdc.gov/std/gonorrhea/STDFact-gonorrhea.htm (Accessed October 4, 2012).

Gonzaga, G. C., Turner, R. A., Keltner, D., Campos, B., & Altemus, M. (2006). Romantic love and sexual desire in close relationships. *Emotion, 6*(2), 63–179.

Goodman, J. J. (2006). Becoming an involved father of an infant. *Journal of Obstetric, Gynecologic, & Neonatal Nursing, 34*(2), 190–200.

Goodson, P., McCormick, D., & Evans, A. (2001). Searching for sexually explicit materials on the Internet: An exploratory study of college students' behavior and attitudes. *Archives of Sexual Behavior, 30*(2), 101–118.

Goodwin, R. D., Canino, G., Ortega, A. N., & Bird, H. R. (2009). Maternal mental health and childhood asthma among Puerto Rican youth: The role of prenatal smoking. *Journal of Asthma, 46*(7), 726–730.

Gooren, L. J. (2011). Ethical and medical considerations of androgen deprivation treatment of sex offenders. *Journal of Clinical endocrinology & Metabolism, 96*(12), 3626–3637.

Gordon, A. E., et al. (2002). Why is smoking a risk factor for sudden infant death syndrome? *Child: Care, Health & Development, 28*(Suppl. 1), 23–25.

Gordon, C. M., & LeBoff, M. S. (Eds.). (2014). *The female athlete triad.* New York: Springer Science+Business Media.

Gordon, K., et al. (2016) A recombinant variant with increased envelope entry efficiency emerged during early infection of an HIV-1 subtype C dual infected rapid progressor. *AIDS Research and Human Retroviruses, 32*(3), 303–310.

Gorelik, G. J., & Shackelford, T. K. (2014). In H. L. Miller (Ed.), *The SAGE encyclopedia of theory in psychology.* Thousand Oaks, CA: Sage.

Gorzalka, B. B., Hill, M. N., & Chang, S. C. H. (2010). Male–female differences in the effects of cannabinoids on sexual behavior and gonadal hormone function. *Hormones and Behavior, 58*(1), 91–99.

Gottman, J. M., & Gottman, J. S. (2008). Gottman method couple therapy. In A. S. Gurman (Ed.), *Clinical handbook of couple therapy* (pp. 138–164). New York: Guilford Press.

Gottman, J. M., & Silver, N. (2015). *The seven principles for making marriage work.* New York: Harmony Books.

Gould, D. C., & Kirby, R. S. (2006). Testosterone replacement therapy for late onset hypogonadism: What is the risk of inducing prostate cancer? *Prostate Cancer and Prostatic Diseases, 9,* 14–18.

Goulet, J. (2006). The "berdache"/"two-spirit": A comparison of anthropological and native constructions of gendered identities among the Northern Athapaskans. *Journal of the Royal Anthropological Institute, 2*(4), 683–701.

Gouveia, V. V., et al. (2009). Versão abreviada da Escala Triangular do Amor: Evidências de validade fatorial e consistência interna. *Estudos de Psicologia, 14*(1), 31–39.

Gow, J. L. (2008). The mating game: Do opposites really attract? *Molecular Ecology, 17*(6), 1399–1400.

Grace, D. M., David, B. J., & Ryan, M. K. (2008). Investigating preschoolers' categorical thinking about gender through imitation, attention, and the use of self-categories. *Child Development, 79*(6), 1928–1941.

Grady, D. (2012, May 14). Taking Truvada to prevent HIV also comes with risks. *The New York Times,* p. D5.

Graham, C. A., Crosby, R. A., Milhausen, R. A., Sanders, S. A, & Yarber, W. L. (2014). Condom-associated erection loss: A study of high-risk young black males residing in the Southern United States. *American Journal of Men's Health,* DOI: 10.1177/1557988314561311

Graham, J. M. (2011). Measuring love in romantic relationships: A meta-analysis. *Journal of Social and Personal Relationships, 28*(6), 748–771.

Granata, A. R., et al. (2012). Hormonal regulation of male sexual desire: The role of testosterone, estrogen, prolactin, oxytocin, vasopressin and others. In M. Maggi (Ed.). Hormonal therapy for male sexual dysfunction (pp. 72–82). Hoboken, NJ: Wiley.

Granata, A. R., Pugni, V., Rochira, V., Zirilli, L., & Carani, C. (2012). Hormonal regulation of male sexual desire: The role of testosterone, estrogen, prolactin, oxytocin, and others. In M. Maggi (Ed.), Hormonal therapy for male sexual dysfunction (pp. 72–82). Hoboken, NJ: Wiley.

Grandoni, D. (2015, July 20). Ashley Madison, a website for straying spouses, is hit by an online attack. *The New York Times,* p. B3.

Gray, R. H., & Wawer, M. J. (2012). Probability of heterosexual HIV-1 transmission per coital act in sub-Saharan Africa. *Journal of Infectious Diseases, 205*(3), 351–352.

Gray, R. H., et al. (2012). The effectiveness of male circumcision for HIV prevention and effects on risk behavior in a post-trial follow-up study. *AIDS, 26*(5), 609–615.

Gray, R., et al. (2009). The role of genital ulcer disease in the efficacy of male circumcision for HIV prevention. Sixteenth Conference on Retroviruses and Opportunistic Diseases. http://www.retroconference.org/2009/PDFs/1063.pdf

Graziano, W. G., & Bruce, J. W. (2008). Attraction and the initiation of relationships. In S. Sprecher, A. Wenzel, & J. Harvey (Eds.), *Handbook of relationship initiation* (pp. 269–296). New York: CRC Press.

Graziottin, A., & Althof, S. E. (2011). What does premature ejaculation mean to the man, the woman, and the couple? *Journal of Sexual Medicine, 8*(Suppl. S4), 304–309.

Green, B. A., Carnes, S., & Carnes, P. J. (2012). Cybersex addiction patterns in a clinical sample of homosexual, heterosexual, and bisexual men and women. *Sexual Addiction and Compulsivity, 19*(1–2), 77–98.

Green, R. (1978). Sexual identity of 37 children raised by homosexual or transsexual parents. *The American Journal of Psychiatry, 135*(6), 692–697.

Green, R., et al. (1986). Lesbian mothers and their children: A comparison with solo parent heterosexual mothers and their children. *Archives of Sexual Behavior, 15*(2), 167–184.

Green, R. (2008). Childhood cross-gender behavior and adult homosexuality: Why the link? *Journal of Gay & Lesbian Mental Health, 12*(1), 17–28.

Greene, B. (2000). African American lesbian and bisexual women. *Journal of Social Issues, 56*(2), 239–249.

Greene, B. (2005). Psychology, diversity and social justice: Beyond heterosexism and across the cultural divide. *Counselling Psychology Quarterly, 18*(4), 295–306.

Greene, B. (2012). Intersections of multiple identities and multiple marginalizations: Clinical and paradigmatic considerations. In R. Nettles, & R. Balter (Eds.), *Multiple minority identities* (pp. 81–94). New York: Springer.

Greene, F. J., Han, L., & Marlow, S. (2013). Like mother, like daughter? Analyzing maternal influences upon women's entrepreneurial propensity. *Entrepreneurship: Theory and Practice, 37*(4), 687–711.

Greenwald, E., & Leitenberg, H. (1989). Long-term effects of sexual experiences with siblings and non-siblings during childhood. *Archives of Sexual Behavior, 18*, 389–399.

Grenz, S. (2006). Review of *The Politics of Prostitution. Women's Movements, Democratic States and the Globalisation of Sex Commerce* and *Not for Sale: Feminists Resisting Prostitution and Pornography. Sexualities, 9*(2), 256–259.

Grey, D. J. R. (2014). Crimes related to sexuality and reproduction. In R. Gartner, & B. McCarthy (Eds.). *The Oxford handbook of gender, sex, and crime* (pp. 225–244). New York: Oxford University Press.

Griffee, K., et al. (2014). Human sexual development is subject to critical period learning: Implications for sexual addiction, sexual therapy, and for child rearing. *Sexual Addiction & Compulsivity, 21*(2), 114–169.

Griffith, L. C. (2014). Neuroscience: What females really want. *Nature, 512*(7513), 138–139.

Griffith, K. H., & Hebl, M. R. (2002). The disclosure dilemma for gay men and lesbians: "Coming out" at work. *Journal of Applied Psychology, 87*(6), 1191–1199.

Griffiths, M D. (2012). Internet sex addiction: A review of empirical research. *Addiction Research & Theory, 20*(2), 111–124.

Grigoriadis, S., & Romans, S. (2006). Postpartum psychiatric disorders: What do we know and where do we go? *Current Psychiatry Reviews, 2*(1), 151–158.

Grodstein, F., Manson, J. E., & Stampfer, M. J. (2006). Hormone therapy and coronary heart disease: The role of time since menopause and age at hormone initiation. *Journal of Women's Health, 15*(1), 35–44.

Grön, G., Wunderlich, A. P., Spitzer, M., Tomczak, R., & Riepe, M. W. (2000). Brain activation during human navigation: Gender-different neural networks as substrate of performance. *Nature Neuroscience, 3*, 404–408.

Gross, J. (2006, April 20). Learning to savor a full life, love life included. *The New York Times*. http://www.nytimes.com/2006/04/20/us/20romance.html (Accessed July 13, 2016).

Grov, C., Bimbi, D. S., Nanin, J. E., & Parsons, J. T. (2006). Race, ethnicity, gender, and generational factors associated with the coming-out process among gay, lesbian, and bisexual individuals. *Journal of Sex Research, 43*(2), 115–121.

Grov, C., Parsons, J. T., & Bimbi, D. S. (2010). The association between penis size and sexual health among men who have sex with men. *Archives of Sexual Behavior, 39*(3), 788–797.

Grubb, A. R., & Harrower, J. (2009). Understanding attribution of blame in cases of rape: An analysis of participant gender, type of rape and perceived similarity to the victim. *Journal of Sexual Aggression, 15*(1), 63–81.

Gruber, J., & Fineran, S. (2015). Sexual harassment, bullying, and school outcomes for high school girls and boys. *Violence Against Women*, DOI: 10.1177/1077801215599079

Grubin, D. (2008). Medical models and interventions in sexual deviance. In D. R. Laws and W. T. O'Donohue (Eds.), *Sexual deviance: Theory, assessment, and treatment* (2nd ed., pp. 594–610). New York: Guilford Press.

Grych, J. H., Fincham, F. D., Jouriles, E. N., & McDonald, R. (2000). Interparental conflict and child adjustment: Testing the mediational role of appraisals in the cognitive–contextual framework. *Child Development, 71*(6), 1648–1661.

Guay, A. T. (2001). Decreased testosterone in regularly menstruating women with decreased libido: A clinical observation. *Journal of Sex & Marital Therapy, 27*(5), 513–519.

Gueguen, N. (2012). Gait and menstrual cycle: Ovulating women use sexier gaits and walking slowly ahead of men. *Gait & Posture, 35*(4), 621–624.

Guerrero, L. K., Hannawa, A. F., & Babin, E. A. (2011). The Communicative Responses to Jealousy Scale: Revision, empirical validation, and associations with relational satisfaction. *Communication Methods and Measures, 5*(3), 223–249.

Guerrero, L. K. (2014). Four on the dark side of communication: Jealousy and relational satisfaction: Actor effects, partner effects, and the mediating role of destructive communicative responses to jealousy. *Western Journal of Communication, 78*(5), 586–611.

Guittar, N. A., & Pals, H. (2014). Intersecting gender with race and religiosity: Do unique social categories explain attitudes toward homosexuality? *Current Sociology, 62*(1), 41–62.

Gustafson, P., & Fransson, U. (2015). Age differences between spouses: Sociodemographic variation and selection. *Marriage & Family Review*, DOI: 10.1080/01494929.2015.1060289

Gutmann, P. (2006). About confusions of the mind due to abnormal conditions of the sexual organs. *History of Psychiatry, 17*(1), 107–111.

Guttmacher Institute. (2009). Various fact sheets. (Accessed November 1, 2009). http://www.guttmacher.org/sections/adolescents.php.

Guttmacher Institute. (2011, August). Facts on induced abortion in the United States. http://www.guttmacher.org/pubs/fb_induced_abortion.html (Accessed June 23, 2012).

Guttmacher Institute. (2012). Facts on American teens' sources of information about sex. http://www.guttmacher.org/pubs/FB-Teen-Sex-Ed.html (Accessed September 23, 2012).

Guttmacher Institute. (2014). Induced abortion in the United States. http://www.guttmacher.org/pubs/fb_induced_abortion.html

Guttmacher Institute. (2015). State policies in brief: Bans on "partial-birth" abortion. http://www.guttmacher.org/statecenter/spibs/spib_BPBA.pdf

Guzick, D. S., & Hoeger, K. (2000). Sex, hormones, and hysterectomies. *The New England Journal of Medicine, 343*, 730–731.

Haake, P., et al. (2003). Acute neuroendocrine response to sexual stimulation in sexual offenders. *Canadian Journal of Psychiatry, 48*(4), 265–271.

Haandrikman, K., Harmsen, C., van Wissen, L. J. G., & Hutter, I. (2008). Geography matters: Patterns of spatial homogamy in the Netherlands. *Population, Space, and Place, 14*, 387–405.

Hackett, G. I. (2008). Disorders of male sexual desire. In D. L. Rowland & L. Incrocci (Eds.), *Handbook of sexual and gender identity disorders*. Hoboken, NJ: Wiley.

Hakim, C. (2015). The male sexual deficit: A social fact of the 21st century. *International Sociology, 30*(3), 314–335.

Hald, G. M., & Malamuth, N. N. (2015). Experimental effects of exposure to pornography: The moderating effect of personality and mediating effect of sexual arousal. *Archives of Sexual Behavior, 44*(1), 99–109.

Halim, M. L., et al. (2014). Pink frilly dresses and the avoidance of all things "girly": Children's appearance rigidity and cognitive theories of gender development. *Developmental Psychology, 50*(4), 1091–1101.

Hall, G., Collins, A., Csemiczky, G., & Landgren, B. (2002). Lipoproteins and BMI: A comparison between women during transition to menopause and regularly menstruating healthy women. *Maturitas, 41*(3), 177–185.

Hall, J. (Ed.). *Female students and culture of violence in cities*. New York: Routledge.

Hallgrímsdóttir, H. K., Phillips, R., Benoit, C., & Walby, K. (2008). Sporting girls, streetwalkers, and inmates of houses of ill repute. *Sociological Perspectives, 51*(1), 119–138.

Halpern, D. (2012). *Sex differences in cognitive abilities* (4th ed.). New York: Psychology Press.

Halpern, D. F. (1997). Sex differences in intelligence: Implications for education. *American Psychologist, 52*, 1091–1102.

Halpern, D. F. (2003). Sex differences in cognitive abilities. *Applied Cognitive Psychology, 17*(3), 375–376.

Halpern, D. F., & LaMay, M. L. (2000). The smarter sex: A critical review of sex differences in intelligence. *Educational Psychology Review, 12*(2), 229–246.

Halpern, D. F., et al. (2007). The science of sex differences in science and mathematics. *Psychological Science in the Public Interest, 8*(1), 1–51.

Halpern-Felsher, B. (2008). Oral sexual behavior: Harm reduction or gateway behavior? *Journal of Adolescent Health, 43*(3), 207–208.

Hamann, S., Herman, R. A., Nolan, C. L., & Wallen, K. (2004). Men and women differ in amygdala response to visual sexual stimuli. *Nature Neuroscience, 7*(4), 411–416.

Hamby, S., Finkelhor, D., & Turner, H. (2013). Perpetrator and victim gender patterns for 21 forms of youth victimization in the National Survey of Children's Exposure to Violence. *Violence and Victims, 28*(6), 915–939.

Hamer, D. H., et al. (1993, July 16). A linkage between DNA markers on the X chromosome and male sexual orientation. *Science, 261,* 321–327.

Hamilton, B. E., & Ventura, S. J. (2012). Birth rates for U.S. teenagers reach historic lows for all age and ethnic groups. NCHS data brief, No. 89. Hyattsville, MD. National Center for Health Statistics.

Hamilton, B. E., Martin, J. A., Osterman, M. J. K., & Curtin, S. C. (2015). Births: Preliminary data for 2014. *National Vital Statistics Reports, 64*(6). Hyattsville, MD.

Hammack, P. L., & Cohler, B. J. (2009). *The story of sexual identity.* New York: Oxford University Press.

Hamplova, D. (2009). Educational homogamy among married and unmarried couples in Europe. *Journal of Family Issues, 30*(1), 28–52.

Harlow, B. L., et al. (2014). Sexual pain prevalence of symptoms consistent with a diagnosis of vulvodyinia: Population-based estimates from 2 geographic reasons. *American Journal of Obstetrics & Gynecology, 210*(1), 40.e1–40.e8.

Harmon-Jones, E., Peterson, C. K., & Harris, C. R. (2009). Jealousy: Novel methods and neural correlates. *Emotion, 9*(1), 113–117.

Harris, A., Battle, J., Pastrana, A., & Daniels, J. (2015). Feelings of belonging: An exploratory analysis of the sociopolitical involvement of black, Latina, and Asian/Pacific Islander sexual minoriy women. *Journal of Homosexuality, 62*(10), 1374–1397.

Harris, G. (2011, October 6). U.S. panel advises against routine use of prostate test. *The New York Times.* http://www.nytimes.com/2011/10/07/health/07prostate.html (Accessed July 13, 2016).

Harris, G. (2015, April 24). Websites in India put a bit of choice into arranged marriages. *The New York Times,* p. A1

Hart, S. D., & Kropp, P. R. (2008). Sexual deviance and the law. In D. R. Laws and W. T. O'Donohue (Eds.), *Sexual deviance: Theory, assessment, and treatment* (2nd ed. pp. 557–570). New York: Guilford Press.

Hart, T. A., et al. (2012). The cumulative effects of medication use, drug use, and smoking on erectile dysfunctions among men who have sex with men. *Journal of Sexual Medicine, 9*(4), 1106–1113.

Hartley, H. (2006). The "pinking" of Viagra culture: Drug industry efforts to create and repackage sex drugs for women. *Sexualities, 9*(3), 363–378.

Hartocollis, A. (2006, June 24). Women have seen it all on subway, unwillingly. *The New York Times.* http://www.nytimes.com/2006/06/24/nyregion/24harass.html *(Accessed July 13, 2016).*

Harvey, J., & Berry, J. (2009). Andropause in the aging male. *Journal for Nurse Practitioners, 5*(3), 207–212.

Haselton, M. G., & Gildersleeve, K. (2011). Can men detect ovulation? *Current Directions in Psychological Science, 20,* 87–92.

Haselton, M. G., & Gildersleeve, K. (2015). Human Ovulation Cues. *Current Opinion in Psychology,* DOI: 10.1016/J.Copsyc.2015.08.020

Haselton, M. G., Mortezaie, M., Pillsworth, E. G., Bleske-Rechek, A., & Frederick, D. A. (2007). Ovulatory shifts in human female ornamentation: Near ovulation, women dress to impress. *Hormones and Behavior, 51*(1), 40–45.

Hassett, J. M., Siebert, E. R., & Wallen, K. (2008). Sex differences in rhesus monkey toy preferences parallel those of children. *Hormones and Behavior, 54*(3), 359–364.

Hatcher, R. A., et al. (2008). *Contraceptive technology,* 19th ed. New York: Ardent Media.

Hatcher, R. A., Trussell, J., Nelson, A. L., Cates, W., Kowal, D., & Policar, M. (Eds.). (2011). *Contraceptive Technology: Twentieth Revised Edition.* New York: Ardent Media.

Hatfield, E., & Rapson, R. L., Passionate love and sexual desire: Cultural and historical perspectives. In A. L. Vangelisti, H. T. Reis, et al. (Eds.), *Stability and change in relationships. Advances in personal relationships* (pp. 306–324). New York: Cambridge University Press.

Hatfield, E., Bensman, L., & Rapson, R. L. (2012). A brief history of social scientists' attempts to measure passionate love. *Journal of Social and Personal Relationships, 29*(2), 143–164.

Hatfield, E., Pillemer, J. T., O'Brien, M. U., & Le, Y-C. L. (2008). The endurance of love: Passionate and companionate love in newlywed and long-term marriages. *Interpersona 2*(1), 35–64.

Hatzichristou, D. G., et al. (2000). Sildenafil versus intracavernous injection therapy: Efficacy and preference in patients on intracaverous injection for more than 1 year. *Journal of Urology, 164,* 1197–1200.

Hatzichristou, D. G., et al. (2005). Vardenafil improves satisfaction rates, depressive symptomatology, and self-confidence in a broad population of men with erectile dysfunction. *Journal of Sexual Medicine, 2*(1), 109–116.

Haugaard, J. J. (2000). The challenge of defining child sexual abuse. *American Psychologist, 55*(9), 1036–1039.

Hawkinson, K., & Zamboni, B. D. (2014). Adult Baby/Diaper Lovers: An exploratory study of an online community sample. *Archives of Sexual Behavior, 43*(5), 863–877.

Hawkley, L. C., Burleson, M. H., Berntson, G. G., & Cacioppo, J. T. (2003). Loneliness in everyday life: Cardiovascular activity, psychosocial context, and health behaviors. *Journal of Personality & Social Psychology, 85*(1), 105–120.

Hawkley, L. C., & Cacioppo, J. T. (2003). Loneliness and pathways to disease. *Brain, Behavior & Immunity, 17*(Suppl. 1), S98–S105.

Hay, D. F. et al. (2011). The emergence of gender differences in physical aggression in the context of conflict between young peers. *British Journal of Developmental Psychology, 29*(2), 158–175.

Hayes, R. M., Abbott, R. L., & Cook, S. (2016). It's her fault: Student acceptance of rape myths on two college campuses. *Violence Against Women,* DOI: 10.1177/1077801216630147

Haynes, A. (2012). Obscenity, sex education, and medical democracy in the antebellum United States. In E. Reis, (Ed.), *American sexual histories* (pp. 165–176). Chichester, UK: Wiley–Blackwell.

Hazan, C., & Selcuk, E. (2015). Normative processes in romantic attachment. In V. Zayas & C. Hazan (Eds.), *Bases of adult attachment* (pp. 3–8). New York: Springer Science+Business Media.

He, C., et al. (2009). Genome-wide association studies identify loci associated with age at menarche and age at natural menopause. *Nature Genetics, 41,* 724–728.

Health risks among sexual minority youth. (2015). Centers for Disease Control and Prevention. http://www.cdc.gov/healthyyouth/disparities/smy.htm

Health24.com. *The girl child.* (2006, February 10). www.health24.com/sex/sexuality_throughout_life.

Heath, R. (1972). Pleasure and brain activity in man. *Journal of Nervous and Mental Disease, 154,* 3–18.

Hegarty, P. (2011). Becoming curious: An invitation to the special issue on queer theory. *Psychology and Sexuality, 2*(1), 1–3.

Heil, P., & Simons, D. (2008). Multiple paraphilias: Prevalence, etiology, assessment, and treatment. In D. R. Laws and W. T. O'Donohue (Eds.), *Sexual deviance: Theory, assessment, and treatment* (2nd ed., pp. 527–556). New York: Guilford Press.

Heiman, J. (2000). The technology of orgasm: "Hysteria," the vibrator, and women's sexual satisfaction. *New England Journal of Medicine, 342*(25), 1925–1926.

Heiman, J. R. (2008). Treating low sexual desire—New findings for testosterone in women. *New England Journal of Medicine, 359*(19), 2047–2049.

Helgeson, V. S. (2015). *Psychology of gender, fourth edition.* London and New York: Routledge.

Hellstrom, W. J. G., Nehra, A., Shabsigh, R., & Sharlip, I. D. (2006). Premature ejaculation: The most common male sexual dysfunction. *Journal of Sexual Medicine, 3*(Suppl. 1), 1–3.

Hemmings, N., & Birkhead, T. R. (2015). Polyspermy in birds: Sperm numbers and embryo survival. *Proceedings B of the Royal Society,* DOI: 10.1098/rspb.2015.1682

Henderson, A. W., Lehavot, K., & Simoni, J. M. (2009). Ecological models of sexual satisfaction among lesbian/bisexual and heterosexual women. *Archives of Sexual Behavior, 38*(1), 50–65.

Hendrick, C., & Hendrick, S. S. (2003). Romantic love: Measuring Cupid's arrow. In S. Lopez & C. R. Snyder (Eds.), *Positive psychological assessment: A handbook of models and measures* (pp. 235–249). Washington, DC: American Psychological Association.

Hendrick, C., Hendrick, S. S., & Reich, D. A. (2006). The Brief Sexual Attitudes Scale. *Journal of Sex Research, 43*(1), 76–86.

Hendrick, S. S., & Hendrick, C. (2002). Love. In C. R. Snyder & S. J. Lopez (Eds.), *Handbook of positive psychology* (pp. 472–484). London: Oxford University Press.

Henshaw, S. K. (2003, May 1). U.S. teenage pregnancy statistics with comparative statistics for women aged 20–24. www.guttmacher.org/pubs/teen_stats.html.

Henslin, J. H. (2007). *Sociology: A down-to-earth approach* (8th ed.). Boston: Allyn & Bacon.

Herbenick, D., & Fortenberry, J. D. (2011). Exercise-induced orgasm and pleasure among women. *Sexual and Relationship Therapy, 26*(4), 373–388.

Herbenick, D., et al. (2009). Prevalence and characteristics of vibrator use by women in the United States: Results from a nationally representative study. *Journal of Sexual Medicine, 6,* 1857–1866.

Herbenick, D., Reece, M., Sanders, S. A., Schick, V., Dodge, B., & Fortenberry, J. D. (2010a). Sexual behavior in the United States: Results from a national probability sample of males and females ages 14 to 94. *Journal of Sexual Medicine, 7*(suppl 5), 255–265.

Herbenick, D., Reece, M., Schick, V., Sanders, S. A., Dodge, B., & Fortenberry, J. D. (2010b). Sexual behaviors, relationships, and perceived health among adult women in the United States: Results from a national probability sample. *Journal of Sexual Medicine, 7*(suppl 5), 277–290.

Herbenick, D., Reece, M., Schick, V., Sanders, S. A., Dodge, B., & Fortenberry, J. D. (2010c). An event-level analysis of the sexual characteristics and composition among adults ages 18 to 59: Results from a national probability sample in the United States. *Journal of Sexual Medicine, 7*(suppl 5), 346–361.

Herbenick, D., et al. (2011). Beliefs about women's vibrator use: Results from a nationally representative probability survey in the United States. *Journal of Sex & Marital Therapy, 37*(5), 329–345.

Herbst, J. H., et al. (2008). Estimating HIV prevalence and risk behaviors of transgender persons in the United States: A systematic review. *AIDS and Behavior, 12*(1), 1–17.

Herdt, G. (1990). Mistaken gender: 5-Alpha reductase hermaphroditism and biological reductionism in sexual identity reconsidered. *American Anthropologist, 92*(2), 433–446.

Herek, G. M., Widaman, K. F., & Capitanio, J. P. (2005). When sex equals AIDS: Symbolic stigma and heterosexual adults' inaccurate beliefs about sexual transmission of AIDS. *Social Problems, 52*(1), 15–37.

Hergenhahn, B. R. (2013). *An introduction to the history of psychology* (7th ed.). Belmont, CA: Cengage.

Hergenhahn, B. R., & Henley, T. (2014). *An introduction to the history of psychology, seventh edition.* Belmont, CA: Wadsworth.

Herpes simplex virus. (2015). 2014 Sexually transmitted diseases surveillance. Centers for Disease Control and Prevention. http://www.cdc.gov/std/stats14/other.htm#herpes

Herrera, V. M., & McCloskey, L. A. (2003). Sexual abuse, family violence, and female delinquency: Findings from a longitudinal study. *Violence & Victims, 18*(3), 319–334.

Herrington, D. M., et al. (2000). Effects of estrogen replacement on the progression of coronary artery atherosclerosis. *New England Journal of Medicine, 343*(8), 522–529.

Herrmann, H. C., Chang, G., Klugherz, B. D., & Mahoney, P. D. (2000). Hemodynamic effects of sildenafil in men with severe coronary artery disease. *New England Journal of Medicine, 342*(22), 1622–1626.

Hertlein, K. M., & Weeks, G. R. (2008). Toward a new paradigm in sex therapy. In K. M. Hertlein, G. R. Weeks, & N. Gambescia (pp. 44–61). *Systemic sex therapy.* New York: CRC Press.

Hertlein, K. M., Weeks, G. R., & Gambescia, N. (Eds.). (2009). *Systemic sex therapy.* New York: Routledge.

Herz, M., & Johansson, T. (2015). The normativity of the concept of heteronormativity. *Journal of Homosexuality, 62*(8), 1009–1020.

Hesketh, T., & Xing, Z. W. (2006). Abnormal sex ratios in human populations: Causes and consequences. *Proceedings of the National Academy of Sciences, 103,* 13271–13275.

Hess, M. J., & Hough, S. (2012). Impact of spinal cord injury on sexuality: Broad-based clinical practice intervention and practical application. *Journal of Spinal Cord Medicine, 35*(4), 211–218.

Hester, J. D. (2005). Eunuchs and the postgender Jesus: Matthew 19:12 and transgressive sexualities. *Journal for the Study of the New Testament, 28*(1), 13–40.

Hetherington, E. M. (2006). The influence of conflict, marital problem solving and parenting on children's adjustment in nondivorced, divorced and remarried families. In A. Clarke-Stewart, & J. Dunn (Eds.). *Families count: Effects on child and adolescent development. The Jacobs Foundation series on adolescence* (pp. 203–237). New York: Cambridge University Press.

Hetherington, E. M., & Kelly, J. (2003). For better or for worse: Divorce reconsidered. *American Journal of Psychiatry, 160*(3), 601–602.

Hicks, T. V., & Leitenberg, H. (2001). Sexual fantasies about one's partner versus someone else: Gender differences in incidence and frequency. *Journal of Sex Research, 38*(1), 43–50.

Hill, B. J., Sanders, S. A., Crosby, R., Ingelhart, K. N., Janssen, E. (2015). Condom-associated erection problems (CAEP): Behavioral responses and attributions in young, heterosexual men. *Sexual Health.* doi: 10.1071/SH14051

Hill, R. A., et al. (2009). Estrogen deficiency results in apoptosis in the frontal cortex of adult female aromatase knockout mice. *Molecular and Cellular Neuroscience, 41*(1), 1–7.

Hill, S. E., & Buss, D. M. (2008). The mere presence of opposite-sex others on judgments of sexual and romantic desirability. *Personality and Social Psychology Bulletin, 34*(5), 635–647.

Hillerer, K. M., Jacobs, V. R., Fischer, T., & Aigner, L. (2014). The maternal brain: An organ with peripartal plasticity. *Neural Plasticity,* http://dx.doi.org/10.1155/2014/574159

Hines, D. A., & Saudino, K. J. (2003). Gender differences in psychological, physical, and sexual aggression among college students using the Revised Conflict Tactics Scales. *Violence & Victims, 18*(2), 197–217.

Hines, M. (2011a). Gender development and the human brain. *Annual Review of Neuroscience, 34,* 69–88.

Hines, M. (2011b). Prenatal endocrine influences on sexual orientation and on sexually differentiated childhood behavior. *Frontiers in Neuroendocrinology, 32*(2), 170–182.

Hines, M., Ahmed, S. F., & Hughes, I. A. (2003). Psychological outcomes and gender-related development in complete androgen insensitivity syndrome. *Archives of Sexual Behavior, 32*(2), 93–101.

Hines, M., Constantinescu, M., & Spencer, D. (2015). Early androgen exposure and human gender development. *Biology of Sex Differences, 6*(3), DOI: 10.1186/s13293-015-0022-1

Hines, T. M. (2001). The G-spot: A modern gynecological myth. *American Journal of Obstetrics and Gynecology, 185*(2), 359–362.

Hird, M. J. (2004). Naturally queer. *Feminist Theory, 5*(1), 85–89.

Hird, M. J. (2006). Sex diversity and evolutionary psychology. *The Psychologist, 19*(1), 30–32.

Hitt, J. (1998, January 18). Who will do abortions here? *The New York Times Magazine,* pp. 20–27, 42, 45–46, 54–55.

HIV in the United States: At a glance. (2015, September 29). Division of HIV/AIDS Prevention, National Center for HIV/AIDS, Viral Hepatitis, Sexual Transmitted Diseases and Tuberculosis Prevention, Centers for Disease Control and Prevention. http://www.cdc.gov/hiv/statistics/overview/ataglance.html

HIV/AIDS surveillance, 2012. Centers for Disease Control and Prevention. (2012). Diagnoses of HIV infection and AIDS in the United States and dependent areas, 2010. *HIV surveillance report, Volume 22.* http://www.cdc.gov/hiv/surveillance/resources/reports/2010report/index.htm (Accessed October 4, 2012).

HIV in the United States: At a glance. (2015). http://www.cdc.gov/hiv/statistics/overview/ataglance.html (Accessed July 8, 2016).

Ho, D. K., & Ross, C. C. (2012). Cognitive behavior therapy for sex offenders. Too good to be true? *Criminal Behaviour and Mental Health, 22*(1), 1–6.

Hofferth, S. L., & Anderson, K. G. (2003). Are all dads equal? Biology versus marriage as a basis for paternal investment. *Journal of Marriage & Family, 65*(1), 213–232.

Hoffmann, H. (2012). Considering the role of conditioning in sexual orientation. *Archives of Sexual Behavior, 41,* 63–71.

Hoffman, H., Peterson, K., & Garner, H. (2012). Field conditioning of sexual arousal in humans. *Socioaffective Neuroscience & Psychology, 2,* 17336 - DOI: 10.3402/snp.v2i0.17336

Hoffman, J. R., et al. (2015). Perceptions and knowledge of voluntary medical male circumcision for HIV prevention in traditionally non-circumcising communities in South Africa. *Global Public Health: An International Journal for Research, Policy and Practice, 10*(5–6), 692–707.

Hogarth, H., & Ingham, R. (2009). Masturbation among young women and associations with sexual health: An exploratory study. *The Journal of Sex Research, 46*(1), 1559–8519.

Holland, K. J., & Cortina, L. M. (2016). Sexual harassment: Undermining the well-being of working women. In M. L. Connerley & J. Wu (Eds.). *Handbook on well-being of working women* (pp. 83–101). Dordrecht, Netherlands: Springer Netherlands.

Holland, K. J., Rabelo, V. C., Gustafson, A. M., Seabrook, R. C., & Cortina, L. M. (2015). Sexual harassment against men: Examining the roles of feminist activism, sexuality, and organizational context. *Psychology of Men & Masculinity,* DOI: 10.1037/a0039151

Hollimon, S. E. (2015). Third gender. *The International Encyclopedia of Human Sexuality.* Hoboken, NJ: Wiley.

Holman, T. B., & Jarvis, M. O. (2003). Hostile, volatile, avoiding, and validating couple-conflict types: An investigation of Gottman's couple-conflict types. *Personal Relationships, 10*(2), 267–282.

Holmes, S. T., & Holmes, R. M. (2002). *Sex crimes.* Thousand Oaks, CA: Sage.

Holmstrom, A. J. (2009). Sex and gender similarities and differences in communication values in same-sex and cross-sex friendships. *Communication Quarterly, 57*(2), 224–238.

Holt-Lunstad, J., Smith, T. B., Baker, M., Harris, T., & Stephenson, D. (2015). Loneliness and social isolation as risk factors for mortality: A meta-analytic review. *Perspectives on Psychological Science, 10*(2), 227–237.

Home tests. (2015, October 16). Division of HIV/AIDS Prevention, National Center for HIV/AIDS, Viral Hepatitis, Sexual Transmitted

Diseases and Tuberculosis Prevention, Centers for Disease Control and Prevention. http://www.cdc.gov/hiv/testing/hometests.html

Homfray, V., et al. (2015). Examining the association between male circumcision and sexual function: evidence from a British probability survey. *AIDS, 29*(11), 1411–1416.

Honeycutt, J. M., & Cantrill, J. G. (2001). *Cognition, communication, and romantic relationships*. Mahwah, NJ: Erlbaum.

Hood, J. (2015). Untangling HIV in China: Social, political, economic, and global–local factors. In M. McLelland & V. Mackie (Eds.). *Routledge handbook of sexuality studies in East Asia* (pp. 356–371). New York: Routledge.

Hoover, K. C. (2010). Smell with inspiration: The evolutionary significance of olfaction. *American Journal of Physical Anthropology, 143*(Suppl 51), 63–74.

Horan, S. M., Guinn, T. D., & Banghart, S. (2015). Understanding relationships among the dark triad personality profile and romantic partners' conflict communication. *Communication Quarterly, 63*(2), 156–170.

Horowitz, H. L. (2002). *Rereading sex: Battles over sexual knowledge and suppression in nineteenth-century America*. New York: Knopf.

Houts, F. W., Taller, I., Tucker, D. E., & Berlin, F. S. (2011). Sexual dysfunction. In R. Balon (Ed.). *Beyond the brain-body connection. Advances in Psychosomatic Medicine, Vol. 31*, 149–163. Basel: Karger.

Hsiao, M., Liu, C., Chen, K., & Hsieh, T. (2002). Characteristics of women seeking treatment for premenstrual syndrome in Taiwan. *Acta Psychiatrica Scandinavica, 106*(2), 150–155.

Hsueh, A. C., Morrison, K. R., & Doss, B. D. (2009). Qualitative reports of problems in cohabiting relationships: Comparisons to married and dating relationships. *Journal of Family Psychology, 23*(2), 236–246. http://caliber.ucpress.net/doi/abs/10.1525/ctx.2007.6.4.28 http://epp.eurostat.ec.europa.eu/portal/page/portal/eurostat/home/.

Hubbard, T. K. (2009). The paradox of "natural" heterosexuality with "unnatural" women. *Classical World, 102*(3), 249–258.

Huberman, J. S., & Chivers, M. L. (2015). Examining gender specificity of sexual response with concurrent thermography and plethysmography. *Psychophysiology, 52*(10), 1382–1395.

Huchard, E., et al. (2009). Studying shape in sexual signals: The case of primate sexual swellings. *Behavioral Ecology and Sociobiology, 63*(8), 1231–1242.

Hucker, S. J. (2008). Sexual masochism: Psychopathology and theory. In D. R. Laws & W. T. O'Donohue (Eds.), *Sexual deviance: Theory, assessment, and treatment* (2nd ed., pp. 250–263). New York: Guilford Press.

Huerta, M., Cortina, L. M., Pang, J. S., Torges, C. M., & Magley, V. J. (2006). Sex and power in the academy: Modeling sexual harassment in the lives of college women. *Personality and Social Psychology Bulletin, 32*(5), 616–628.

Hugh-Jones, S., Gough, B., & Littlewood, A. (2005). Sexual exhibitionism as "sexuality and individuality": A critique of psycho-medical discourse from the perspectives of women who exhibit. *Sexualities, 8*(3), 259–281.

Huizink, A. C. (2013). Prenatal cannabis exposure and infant outcomes: Overview of studies. *Progress in Neuro-Psychopharmacology and Biological Psychiatry*, DOI: 10.1016/j.pnpbp.2013.09.014

Human Rights Watch. (2012, May). Cultivating fear: The vulnerability of immigrant farm workers in the U.S. to sexual violence and sexual harassment. http://www.hrw.org/sites/default/files/reports/us0512ForUpload_1.pdf (Accessed July 16, 2012).

Hummer, T. A., & McClintock, M. K. (2009). Putative human pheromone androstadienone attunes the mind specifically to emotional information. *Hormones and Behavior, 55*(4), 548–559.

Hunt, M. (1974). *Sexual behavior in the 1970's*. New York: Dell Books.

Hunt, S. A., & Kraus, S. W. (2009). Exploring the relationship between erotic disruption during the latency period and the use of sexually explicit material, online sexual behaviors, and sexual dysfunctions in young adulthood. *Sexual Addiction & Compulsivity, 16*(1), 79–100.

Hunter, M. S. (2011). Cortisol, hot flashes, and cardiovascular risk. *Menopause, 18*(3), 251–252.

Hunter, T., & Cattelona, G. (2014). Breastfeeding initiation and duration in first-time mothers: Exploring the impact of father involvement in the early post-partum period. *Health Promotion Perspectives, 4*(2), 132–136.

Hurd, Y. L., Michaelides, M., Miller, M. L., & Jutras-Aswad, D. (2014). Trajectory of cannabis use on addiction vulnerability. *Neuropharmacology, 76*(Part B), 416–424.

Hussain, A. (2002, June 26) It's official. Men really are afraid of commitment.

Hutchings, J. (2004). Color in folklore and tradition—The principles. *Color Research and Application, 29*, 57–66.

Hutton, H. E. (2008, March 11). Gender differences in alcohol use and risky sexual behaviors and STDs among STD clinic patients. Chicago: 2008 National STD Prevention Conference,

Huxley, R. R. (2000). Nausea and vomiting in early pregnancy: Its role in placental development. *Obstetrics & Gynecology, 95*, 779–782.

Hyde, J. S. (Ed.) (2005). *Biological substrates of human sexuality*. Washington, DC: American Psychological Association.

Hyde, J. S. (2014). Gender similarities and differences. *Annual Review of Psychology, 65*, 373–398.

Hyde, J. S., & Mertz, J. E. (2009). Gender, culture, and mathematics performance. *Proceedings of the National Academy of Sciences, 106*, 8801–8807.

Hyde, J. S., Fennema, E., & Lamon, S. J. (1990). Gender differences in mathematics performance: A meta-analysis. *Psychological Bulletin, 107*, 139–155.

Hyde, J. S., Lindberg, S. M., Linn, M. C., Ellis, A. B., & Williams, C. C. (2008). Gender similarities characterize math performance. *Science, 321*, 494–495.

Hyman, S. M., Gold, S. N., & Cott, M. A. (2003). Forms of social support that moderate PTSD in childhood sexual abuse survivors. *Journal of Family Violence, 18*(5), 295–300.

Hypersexual disorder. (2012). Hypersexual disorder. American Psychiatric Association. DSM-5 Development. http://www.dsm5.org/proposedrevision/pages/proposedrevision.aspx?rid=415.

Iemmola, F., & Ciani, A. C. (2009). New evidence of genetic factors influencing sexual orientation in men: Female fecundity increase in the maternal line. *Archives of Sexual Behavior, 38*(3), 393–399.

Illes, J. (October 2000). Beauty secrets of ancient Egypt: Nefertem, Ancient Lord of Perfume. *Tour Egypt Monthly, 5*(1).

Imperato-McGinley, J., et al. (1974). Steroid 5 reductase deficiency in man: An inherited form of male pseudohermaphroditism. *Science, 186*, 1213–1215.

Inciardi, J. A., Surratt, H. L., & Kurtz, S. P. (2006). HIV, HBV, and HCV infections among drug-involved, inner-city, street sex workers in Miami, Florida. *AIDS and Behavior, 10*(2), 139–147.

Intersex Society of North America. Accessed August 22, 2006. www.isna.org.

Irwin, T. W., Morgenstern, J., Parsons, J. T., Wainberg, M., & Labouvie, E. (2006). Alcohol and sexual HIV risk behavior among problem drinking men who have sex with men: An event level analysis of timeline followback data. *AIDS and Behavior, 10*(3), 299–307.

IsHak, W. W., Bokarius, A., Jeffrey, J. K., Davis, M. C., & Bakhta, Y. (2010). Disorders of orgasm in women: A literature review of etiology and current treatments. *Journal of Sexual Medicine, 7*, 3254–3268.

Itzin, C. (2002). Pornography and the construction of misogyny. *Journal of Sexual Aggression, 8*(3), 4–42.

Itzin, C., Taket, A., & Kelly, L. (2007). The evidence of harm to adults relating to exposure to extreme pornographic material: a rapid evidence assessment (REA). Ministry of Justice Research Series 11/07. http://webarchive.nationalarchives.gov.uk/+/http://www.justice.gov.uk/docs/280907.pdf

Jacob, S., & McClintock, M. K. (2000). Psychological state and mood effects of steroidal chemosignals in women and men. *Hormones and Behavior, 37*(1), 57–78.

Jacob, S., Hayreh, D. J. S., & McClintock, M. K. (2001). Context-dependent effects of steroid chemosignals on human physiology and mood. *Physiology & Behavior, 74*(1–2), 15–27.

Jaeger, F., Caflisch, M., & Hohlfeld, P. (2009). Female genital mutilation and its prevention: A challenge for paediatricians. *European Journal of Pediatrics, 168*(1), 27–33.

Jameson, M. (2000, June 12). Childbirth that's not so labor-intensive. *Los Angeles Times*.

Jankowiak, W. R., Volsche, S. L., & Garcia, J. R. (2015). Is the romantic–sexual kiss a near human universal? *American Anthropologist*, DOI: 10.1111/aman.12286

Jannini, E. A., Blanchard, R., Camperio-Ciani, A., & Bancroft, J. (2010a). Male homosexuality: Nature or culture. *Journal of Sexual Medicine, 7*, 3245–3253.

Jannini, E. A., Buison, O., & Rubio-Casillàs, A. (2014). Beyond the G-spot: Clitourethrovaginal complex anatomy in female orgasm. *Nature Reviews: Urology, 11*, 532–538.

Jannini, E. A., McMahon, C., Chen, J., Aversa, A., & Perelman, M. (2011). The controversial role of PDE5 inhibitors in the treatment of premature ejaculation. *Journal of Sexual Medicine, 8*, 2135–2143.

Jannini, E. A., Whipple, B., Kingsberg, S. A., Buisson, O., Foldès, P., & Vardi, Y. (2010b). Who's afraid of the G-spot? *Journal of Sexual Medicine, 7*(1), 25–34.

Jannini, E., et al. (2008). In vivo measurement of the human G-spot. *Sexologies, 17*(S1), S52–S53.

Janssen, E. (Ed.). (2006). *The psychophysiology of sex*. Bloomington, IN: Indiana University Press.

Janssen, E., & Bancroft, J. (2006). The dual-control model: The role of sexual inhibition & excitation in sexual arousal and behavior. In E. Janssen (Ed.), *The psychophysiology of sex*. Bloomington, IN: Indiana University Press.

Janssen, E., Prause, N., & Geer, J. (2006). The sexual response. In J. T. Cacioppo, L. G. Tassinary, & G. G. Berntson (Eds.), *Handbook of psychophysiology* (3rd ed.). New York: Cambridge University Press.

Javed, A., et al. (2015). Hyperandrogenism in female athletes with functional hypothalamic amenorrhea: A distinct phenotype. *International Journal of Women's Health, 7*, 103–111.

Jayaraman, S., & Mann, M. (2012). Male and female sterilization. *Obstetrics, Gynaecology, & Reproductive Medicine, 22*(4), 85–91.

Jayson, S. (2006, May 29). Poll: Boomers go easy on marriage. *USA Today*.

Jayson, S. (2013, April 4). Cohabitation first is the new norm for unmarrieds with kids. *USA Today*.

Jejeebhoy, S. J., Santhya, K. G., Acharya, R., & Prakash, R. (2013). Marriage-related decision-making and young women's marital relations and agency. *Asian Population Studies, 9*(1), 28–49.

Jemmott, J. B., Jemmott, L. S., & Fong, G. T. Efficacy of a theory-based abstinence-only intervention over 24 months. *Archives of Pediatric and Adolescent Medicine, 164*(2), 152–159.

Jena, A. B., Goldman, D. P., & Seabury, S. A. (2015). Incidence of sexually transmitted infections after human papillomavirus vaccination among adolescent females, *JAMA Internal Medicine, 175*(4), 617–613.

Jewkes, R., Morrell, R., Sikweyiya, Y., Dunckle, K., & Penn-Kekana, L. (2012). Transactional relationships and sex with a woman in prostitution: prevalence and patterns in a representative sample of South African men. *BMC Public Health, 12*, 325. http://www.biomedcentral.com/1471-2458/12/325 (Accessed July 18, 2012).

Johannes, C. B., et al. (2000). Incidence of erectile dysfunction in men 40 to 69 years old: Longitudinal results from the Massachusetts male aging study. *Journal of Urology, 163*, 460.

Johanson, R. (2000). Perineal massage for prevention of perineal trauma in childbirth. *Lancet, 355*(9200), 250–251.

Johnson, T. (2015, July 23). Bill Cosby's lawyers claim accuser violated confidential settlement agreement. *Variety*. http://variety.com/2015/biz/news/bill-cosby-andrea-constand-sexual-assault-2-1201547572/

Johnson, W., & Bouchard, T. J. Jr. (2007). Sex differences in mental abilities: *g* masks the dimensions on which they lie. *Intelligence, 35*(1), 23–39.

Johnson, W., & Bouchard, T. J. Jr. (2009). Linking abilities, interests, and sex via latent class analysis. *Journal of Career Assessment, 17*(1), 3–38.

Johnston, L. D., O'Malley, P. M., Bachman, J. G., & Schulenberg, J. E. (2005). *Monitoring the future national results on adolescent drug use: Overview of key findings, 2004*. NIH publication no. 05-5726. Bethesda, MD: National Institute on Drug Abuse.

Johnstone, S. J., et al. (2001). Obstetric risk factors for postnatal depression in urban and rural community samples. *Australian & New Zealand Journal of Psychiatry, 35*(1), 69–74.

Jolie, A. (2013, May 14). My medical choice. *The New York Times*, p. A25.

Jonason, P. K., Li, N. P., & Cason, M. J. (2009a). The "Booty Call" A compromise between men's and women's ideal mating strategies. *Journal of Sex Research, 46*(5), 460–470.

Jonason, P. K., Li, N. P., Webster, G. D., & Schmitt, D. P. (2009b). The dark triad: Facilitating a short-term mating strategy in men. *European Journal of Personality, 23*(1), 5–18.

Jonason, P. K., Hatfield, E., & Boler, V. M. (2015). Who engages in serious and casual sexual relationships? An individual differences perspective. *Personality and Individual Differences, 75*, 205–209.

Jones, B. E., & Hill, M. J. (2002). *Mental health issues in lesbian, gay, bisexual, and transgender communities: Review of Psychiatry* (Vol. 21). Washington, DC: American Psychiatric Publishing.

Jones, K. E., & Hertlein, K. M. (2012). Four key dimensions for distinguishing Internet infidelity from Internet and sex addiction: Concepts and clinical application. *American Journal of Family Therapy, 40*(2), 115–125.

Jones, R. K., & Jerman, J. (2014). Abortion incidence and service availability in the United States, 2011. *Perspectives on Sexual and Reproductive Health, 46*(1), 3–14.

Jones, L. M., Mitchell, K. J., & Finkelhor, D. (2012). Trends in youth Internet victimization: Findings from three youth Internet safety surveys 2000–2010. *Journal of Adolescent Health, 50*(2), 179–186.

Jordan, K., Fromberger, P., Stolpmann, G., & Muller, J. L. (2011). The role of testosterone in sexuality and paraphilia—A neurobiological approach. *Sexual Medicine, 8*(11), 3008–3029.

Jung, M., Lee, J., Kwon, D. D., & Park, B. (2012). Comparison of sexual risky factors of men who have sex with men and sex-buying men as groups vulnerable to sexually transmitted diseases. *Journal of Preventive Medicine & Public Health, 45*(3), 156–163.

Kaczmarek, P., LeVine, E., & Segal, A. F. (2006). Section 6. Civil and criminal trial matters. In P. Kaczmarek, E. LeVine, & A. F. Segal (Eds.), *Law & mental health professionals: New Mexico* (pp. 269–296). Washington, DC: American Psychological Association.

Kaestle, C. E., & Allen, K. R. (2011). The role of masturbation in healthy sexual development: Perceptions of young adults. *Archives of Sexual Behavior, 40*(5), 983–994.

Kafka, M. P. (2003). Sex offending and sexual appetite: The clinical and theoretical relevance of hypersexual desire. *International Journal of Offender Therapy & Comparative Criminology, 47*(4), 439–451.

Kafka, M. P. (2010). The DSM diagnostic criteria for fetishism. *Archives of Sexual Behavior*, DOI: 10.1007/s10508-009-9558-7

Kaiser Family Foundation, Holt, T., Greene, L., & Davis, J. (2003). *National Survey of Adolescents and Young Adults: Sexual health knowledge, attitudes and experiences*. Menlo Park, CA: Henry J. Kaiser Family Foundation.

Kaler, A. (2005). Peer commentaries on Binik (2005): Classifying pain: What's at stake for women with dyspareunia. *Archives of Sexual Behavior, 34*(1), 34–36.

Kaplan, H. S. (1974). *The new sex therapy: Active treatment of sexual dysfunctions*. New York: Brunner/Mazel.

Kaplan, H. S. (1987). *Sexual aversion, sexual phobias, and panic disorder*. New York: Brunner/Mazel.

Kaplan, M. S., & Krueger, R. B. (2012). Cognitive-Behavioral treatment of the paraphilias. *The Israel Journal of Psychiatry and Related Sciences, 49*(4), 291–296.

Karpman, E., Williams, D. H., & Lipshultz, L. I. (2006). Vasectomy reversal: New techniques and role in the era of intracytoplasmic sperm injection. *Canadian Journal of Urology, 13*(Suppl. 1), 22–27.

Kaser-Boyd, N. (2015). Indecent exposure, exhibitionism, and other paraphilias. In C. de Ruiter, & N. Kaser-Boyd (Eds.). *Forensic psychological assessment in practice* (pp. 92–111). New York: Routledge.

Katsiki, N., Wierzbicki, A. S., & Mikhailidis, D. P. (2015). Erectile dysfunctions and coronary heart disease. *Current Opinion in Cardiology, 30*(4), 416–421.

Katz, J., & Tirone, V. (2009). Women's sexual compliance with male dating partners: Associations with investment in ideal womanhood and romantic well-being. *Sex Roles, 60*(5-6), 347–356.

Kawaguchi, K. (2015). Responses to HIV–AIDS in East Asia. In M. McLelland & V. Mackie (Eds.). *Routledge handbook of sexuality studies in East Asia* (pp. 331– 343). New York: Routledge.

Kaylor, L., Jeglic, E. L., & Collins, C. (2016). Examining the impact of technology on exhibitionistic behavior. *Deviant Behavior*, DOI: 10.1080/01639625.2016.1169828

Kayser, D. N., Elliot, A. J., & Feltman, R. (2010). Red and romantic behavior in men viewing women. *European Journal of Social Psychology, 40*(6), 901–908.

Keen, J. D., & Keen, J. E. (2009). What is the point: Will screening mammography save my life? *BMC Medical Informatics and Decision Making, 9*, 18.

Keenan, S. (2015, August 2). Affirmative consent: Are students really asking? *The New York Times*, p. ED10.

Kellar, M. C., & Hignite, L. R. (2014). Chemical castration. *The Encyclopedia of Criminology and Criminal Justice*, 1–4.

Keller, J. J., Liang, Y., & Lin, H. (2012). Association between multiple sclerosis and erectile dysfunction: A nationwide case-control study. *Journal of Sexual Medicine*, DOI: 10.1111/j.1743-6109.2012.02746.x

Kelly, J. B. (2000). Children's adjustment in conflicted marriage and divorce: A decade review of research. *Journal of the American Academy of Child & Adolescent Psychiatry, 39*(8), 963–973.

Kelly, Y., et al. (2013). Light drinking versus abstinence in pregnancy—behavioural and cognitive outcomes in 7-year-old children: A longitudinal cohort study. *British Journal of Gynecology, 120*(11), 1340–1347.

Kendler, K. S., et al. (2000). Childhood sexual abuse and adult psychiatric and substance use disorders in women: An epidemiological and Cotwin control analysis. *Archives of General Psychiatry, 57*(10), 953–959.

Kennair, L. E. O., Grontvedt, T. V., Mehmetoglu, M., Perilloux, C., & Buss, D. M. (2015). Sex and mating strategy impact the 13 basic reasons for having sex. *Evolutionary Psychological Science*, DOI: 10.1007/s40806-015-0024-6

Kennedy, A. (2015). Cited in Supreme Court of the United States. (2015, June 26). *Obergefell et al. v.*

Hodges, Director, Ohio Department of Health, et al. Certiorari to the United States Court of Appeals for the Sixth Circuit. Argued April 28, 2015— Decided June 26, 2015. http://www.supremecourt.gov/opinions/14pdf/14-556_3204.pdf

Kennedy, N., & McDonough, M. (2002). Koro: A case in an eastern European asylum seeker in Ireland. *Irish Journal of Psychological Medicine, 19*(4), 130–131.

Kennedy, R. (2003). *Interracial intimacies: Sex, marriage, identity, and adoption.* New York: Knopf.

Kennedy, S. H., & Rizvi, S. (2009). Sexual dysfunction, depression, and the impact of antidepressants. *Journal of Clinical Psychopharmacology, 29*(2), 157–164.

Kennedy, S., & Bumpass, L. (2011, April 1). Cohabitation and trends in the structure and stability of children's family lives (paper presented at the Annual Meeting of the Population Association of America, Washington, DC, April 1, 2011).

Kenny, M. C., & Wurtele, S. K. (2012). Child sexual behavior inventory: A comparison between Latino and normative samples of preschoolers. *Journal of Sex Research.* DOI:10. 1080/00224499.2011.652265

Kersting, K. (2003). Cognitive sex differences: A "political minefield." *Monitor on Psychology, 34*(5)., 54–55

Kessler, R. C. (2003). Epidemiology of women and depression. *Journal of Affective Disorders, 74*(1), 5–13.

Khoury, M. J., Burke, W., & Thomson, E. J. (Eds.). (2000). *Genetics and public health in the 21st century: Using genetic information to improve health and prevent disease.* New York: Oxford University Press.

Khurana, A., Cooksey, E. C., & Gavazzi, S. M. (2011). Juvenile delinquency and teenage pregnancy. *Psychology of Women Quarterly, 35*(2), 282–289.

Kilchevsky, A., Vardi, Y., Lowenstein, L., & Gruenwald, I. (2012). Is the female G-spot truly a distinct anatomic entity? *Journal of Sexual Medicine, 9*(3), 719–726.

Kim, A. A., Kent, C. K., & Klausner, J. D. (2002). Increased risk of HIV and sexually transmitted disease transmission among gay or bisexual men who use Viagra, San Francisco 2000–2001. *AIDS, 16*(10), 1425–1428.

Kim, H. S. (2011). Consequences of parental divorce for child development. *American Sociological Review, 76*(3), 487–511.

Kim, J., & Hebert, M. F. (2015). Pharmacological treatment of musculoskeletal conditions during pregnancy and lactation. In C. M. Fitzgerald, & N. A. Segal (Eds.). *Musculoskeletal health in pregnancy and postpartum* (pp. 227–242). Switzerland: Springer International Publishing.

Kimble, D. P. (1992). *Biological psychology* (2nd ed.). Fort Worth, TX: Harcourt Brace Jovanovich.

Kimmel, L. G., Miller, J. D., & Eccles, J. S. (2012). Do the paths to the STEMM professions differ by gender? *Peabody Journal of Education, 87*(1). doi:10.1080/0161956X.2012.642276

Kimmel, M., et al. (2015). Family history, not lack of medication use, is associated with the development of postpartum depression in a high-risk sample. *Archives of Women's Mental Health, 18*(1), 113–121.

King, J. A., De Oliveira, W. L., & Patel, N. (2005). Deficits in testosterone facilitate enhanced fear response. *Psychoneuroendocrinology, 30*(4), 333–340.

King, M. (2008). A systematic review of mental disorder, suicide, and deliberate self harm in lesbian, gay and bisexual people. *BMC Psychiatry, 8.* http://www.biomedcentral.com/1471244X/8/70 (Accessed October 15, 2009).

Kingston, D. A., Malamuth, N. M., Fedoroff, P., & Marshall, W. L. (2009). The importance of individual differences in pornography use: Theoretical perspectives and implications for treating sexual offenders. *Journal of Sex Research, 46*(2–3), 216–232.

Kinsey, A. C., Pomeroy, W. B., & Martin, C. E. (1948). *Sexual behavior in the human male.* Philadelphia: W. B. Saunders.

Kinsey, A. C., Pomeroy, W. B., Martin, C. E., & Gebhard, P. H. (1953). *Sexual behavior in the human female.* Philadelphia: W. B. Saunders.

Kippax, S., & Smith, G. (2001). Anal intercourse and power in sex between men. *Sexualities, 4*(4), 413–434.

Kirby, D. (2008). Changes in sexual behaviour leading to the decline in the prevalence of HIV in Uganda: Confirmation from multiple sources of evidence. *Sexually Transmitted Infections, 84*(Suppl 2), ii35–ii41.

Kirby, D. (2011). *Sex education: Access and impact on sexual behavior of young people. United Nations expert group meeting on adolescents, youth and development.* Population Division. Department of Economic and Social Affairs. United Nations Secretariat. New York.

Kirby, D. B., Laris, B. A., & Rolleri, L. A. (2007). Sex and HIV education programs: Their impact on sexual behaviors of young people throughout the world. *Journal of Adolescent Health, 40*(3), 206–217.

Kirchheimer, S., & Smith, M. (2003, May 28). Condoms in schools don't boost teen sex: Key is making condom programs part of overall sex education, says one expert. *WebMD Medical News.* http://www.webmd.com/sex/birth-control/news/20030528/condoms-in-schools-dont-boost-teen-sex (Accessed July 13, 2016).

Kirenskaya-Berus, A. V., & Tkachenko, A. A. (2003). Characteristic features of EEG spectral characteristics in persons with deviant sexual behavior. *Human Physiology, 29*(3), 278–287.

Kirkpatrick, R. C. (2000). The evolution of human homosexual behavior. *Current Anthropology, 41*(3), 385–413.

Kito, M. (2005). Self-disclosure in romantic relationships and friendships among American and Japanese college students. *Journal of Social Psychology, 145*(2), 127–140.

Kjerulff, K. H., et al. (2000). Effectiveness of hysterectomy. *Obstetrics & Gynecology, 95,* 319–326.

Klahr, A. M., McGue, M., Iacono, W. G., & Burt, S. A. (2011). The association between parent-child conflict and adolescent conduct problems over time: Results from a longitudinal adoption study. *Journal of Abnormal Psychology, 120*(1), 46–56.

Klapilová, K. et al. (2015). Sexual satisfaction, sexual compatibility, and relationship adjustment in couples: The role of sexual behaviors, orgasm, and men's discernment of women's intercourse orgasm. *Journal of Sexual Medicine, 12*(3), 667–675.

Klemetti, R., Gissler, M., Sainio, S., & Hemmenki, E. (2014). Associations of maternal age with maternity care use and birth outcomes in primiparous women: a comparison of results in 1991 and 2008 in Finland. *BJOG: An International Journal of Obstetrics & Gynaecology,* DOI: 10.1111/1471-0528.12415

Klusmann, D. (2002). Sexual motivation and the duration of partnership. *Archives of Sexual Behavior, 31,* 275–287.

Klüver, H., & Bucy, P. C. (1939). Preliminary analysis of functions of the temporal lobes in monkeys. *Archives of Neurology and Psychiatry, 42,* 979.

Knaak, S. (2005). Breast-feeding, bottle-feeding and Dr. Spock: The shifting context of choice. *Canadian Review of Sociology and Anthropology, 42*(2), 197–216.

Knafo, D. (2015). Guys and dolls: Relational life in the technological era. *Psychoanalytic Dialogues: The International Journal of Relational Perspectives, 25*(4), DOI: 10.1080/10481885.2015.1055174

Knickmeyer, R., et al. (2005). Gender-typed play and amniotic testosterone. *Developmental Psychology, 41,* 517–528.

Kniffin, K. M., & Wilson, D. S. (2004). The effect of nonphysical traits on the perception of physical attractiveness: Three naturalistic studies. *Evolution and Human Behavior, 25*(2), 88–101.

Knoll, J. L., & Hazelwood, R. R. (2009). Becoming the victim: Beyond sadism in serial sexual murderers. *Aggression and Violent Behavior, 14*(2), 106–114.

Kohler, P. K., Manhart, L. E., & Lafferty, W. E. (2008). Abstinence-only and comprehensive sex education and the initiation of sexual activity and teen pregnancy. *Journal of Adolescent Health, 42*(4), 344–351.

Kosciw, J. G., Greytak, E. A., Palmer, N.A., & Boesen, M. J. (2014). *The 2013 National School Climate Survey: The experiences of lesbian, gay, bisexual, ad transgender youth in our nation's schools.* New York: GLSEN.

Knox, D., Schacht, C., & Zusman, M. E. (1999). Love relationships among college students. *College Student Journal, 33*(1), 149–151.

Knox, D., Gibson, L., Zusman, M., & Gallmeier, C. (1997). Why college students end relationships. *College Student Journal, 31*(4), 449–452.

Knox, D., & Schacht, C. (2002). *Choices in relationships—An introduction to marriage and the family* (7th ed.). Belmont, CA: Wadsworth.

Knudson, G. A., & Kingsberg, S. A. (2010). Hypoactive sexual desire disorder. *Journal of Sexual Medicine, 7*(2), 928–937.

Koblin, B. A., et al. (2006). Risk factors for HIV infection among men who have sex with men. *AIDS, 20*(5), 731–739.

Koehler, N., et al. (2012). Erectile dysfunction after radical prostatectomy: The impact of nerve-sparing status and surgical approach. *International Journal of Impotence Research,* DOI:10.1038/ijir.2012.8

Kohlberg, L. (1966). A cognitive-developmental analysis of children's sex-role concepts and attitudes. In E. E. Maccoby (Ed.), *The development of sex differences.* Stanford, CA: Stanford University Press.

Kohtz, A. S., Paris, J. J., & Frye, C. A. (2010). Low doses of cocaine decrease, and high doses increase, anxiety-like behavior and brain progestogen levels among intact rats. *Hormones and Behavior, 57*(4–5), 474–480.

Kolata, G. (2000a, April 5). Estrogen tied to slight rise in heart attack. *The New York Times*, pp. A1, A20.

Kolata, G. (2000b, April 18). New name for impotence, and new drugs. *The New York Times*, pp. F6, F14.

Kolata, G. (2002, December 22). Chasing youth, many gamble on hormones. *The New York Times*. http://www.nytimes.com/2002/12/22/us/chasing-youth-many-gamble-on-hormones.html?mtrref=www.nytimes.com&gwh=E33E94602F9049A7DB028E53F4290177&gwt=pay (Accessed July 13, 2016).

Kolata, G. (2005, October 27). Screening proves itself in breast cancer fight. *The New York Times*.

Komisaruk, B. R., & Whipple, B. (2005). Brain activity imaging during sexual response in women with spinal cord injury. In J. S. Hyde (Ed.). *Biological substrates of human sexuality* (pp. 109–145). Washington, DC: American Psychological Association.

Komisaruk, B. R., et al. (2011). Women's clitoris, vagina, and cervix mapped on the sensory cortex: fMRI evidence. *Journal of Sexual Medicine, 8*(10), 2822–2830.

Korda, J. B., Goldstein, S. W., & Sommer, F. (2010). The history of female ejaculation. *Journal of Sexual Medicine, 7*, 1965–1975.

Koren, G., Pastuszak, A., & Ito, S. (1998). Drug therapy: Drugs in pregnancy. *New England Journal of Medicine, 338*, 1128–1137.

Kornacki, S. (2008, April 10). Spitzer and Vitter: Equal hypocrisy, unequal punishment.

Korobov, N., & Thorne, A. (2006). Intimacy and distancing: Young men's conversations about romantic relationships. *Journal of Adolescent Research, 21*(1), 27–55.

Koscik, T., O'Leary, D., Moser, D. J., Andreasen, N. C., & Nopoulos, P. (2009). Sex differences in parietal lobe morphology: Relationship to mental rotation performance. *Brain and Cognition, 69*(3), 451–459.

Koss, M. P., & Kilpatrick, D. G. (2001). Rape and sexual assault. In E. Gerrity et al. (Eds.), *The mental health consequences of torture. Plenum series on stress and coping* (pp. 177–193). Dordrecht, the Netherlands: Kluwer Academic Publishers.

Koss, M. P., Bailey, J. A., Yuan, N. P., Herrera, V. M., & Lichter, E. L. (2003). Depression and PTSD in survivors of male violence: Research and training initiatives to facilitate recovery. *Psychology of Women Quarterly, 27*(2), 130–142.

Koss, M. P., Figueredo, A. J., & Prince, R. J. (2002). Cognitive mediation of rape's mental, physical and social health impact: Tests of four models in cross-sectional data. *Journal of Consulting & Clinical Psychology, 70*(4), 926–941.

Kouros-Mehr, H., et al. (2001). Identification of non-functional human VNO receptor genes provides evidence for vestigiality of the human VNO. *Chemical Sciences, 26*(9), 1167–1174.

Kovic, A., Hampson, P., & Gonsiorek, J. C. (2015). Sexual identity and sexual orientation. *The International Encyclopedia of Human Sexuality* (pp. 1115–1354.) Hoboken, NJ: Wiley.

Kraft, J. M., Kulkarni, A., Hsia, J., Jamieson, D. J., & Warner, L. (2012). Sex education and adolescent sexual behavior: Do community characteristics matter? *Contraception, 86*(3), 276–280.

Krahe, B., Waizenhofer, E., & Moller, I. (2003). Women's sexual aggression against men: Prevalence and predictors. *Sex Roles, 49*(5–6), 219–232.

Krajnik, J., et al. (2014). Gender effects and sexual-orientation impact on androstadienone-evoked behavior and neural processing. *Frontiers in Neuroscience, 8*, 195.

Kramer, M. S., et al. (2000). The contribution of mild and moderate preterm birth to infant mortality. *Journal of the American Medical Association, 284*, 843–849.

Kranz, G. S., et al. (2014). White matter microstructure in transsexuals and controls investigated by diffusion tensor imaging. *Journal of Neuroscience, 34*(46), 15466–15475.

Kristof, N. D. (2004, January 24). Going home, with hope. *The New York Times*, p. A15.

Kristof, N. D. (2006, January 22). Slavery in our time. *The New York Times*, Section 4, p. 17.

Kristof, N. D. (2009, May 7). Girls on our streets. *The New York Times*. http://www.nytimes.com/2009/05/07/opinion/07kristof.html?rref=collection%2Fcolumn%2Fnicholas-kristof&action=click&contentCollection=opinion&region=stream&module=stream_unit&version=search&contentPlacement=1&pgtype=collection (Accessed July 13, 2016).

Kristof, N. (2015, May 24). When the rapist doesn't see it as rape. *The New York Times*, p. SR9.

Krouse, A., et al. (2012). Bed-sharing influences, attitudes, and practices: Implications for promoting safe infant sleep. *Journal of Child Health Care*. DOI:10.1177/1367493511432300

Krueger, R. B., & Kaplan, M. S. (2002). Behavioral and psychopharmacological treatment of the paraphilic and hypersexual disorders. *Journal of Psychiatric Practice, 8*(1), 21–32.

Kuehn, B. M. (2009). Sexually transmitted infections. *Journal of the American Medical Association, 301*(8), 817.

Kuhnle, U., Krob, G., & Maier, E. (2003). True hermaphroditism: Presentation, management, outcomes. *Endocrinologist, 13*(3), 214–218.

Kuiper, B., & Cohen-Kettenis, P. (1988). Sex reassignment surgery: A study of 141 Dutch transsexuals. *Archives of Sexual Behavior, 17*, 439–457.

Kuja-Halkola, R., D'Onofrio, B. M., Larsson, H., & Lichtenstein, P. (2014). Maternal smoking during pregnancy and adverse outcomes in offspring. *Behavior Genetics, 44*(5), 456–467.

Kulik, L. (2000). Gender identity, sex typing of occupations, and gender role ideology among adolescents: Are they related? *International Journal for the Advancement of Counselling, 22*(1), 43–56.

Kumashiro, K. K. (Ed.). (2004). *Restoried selves: Autobiographies of Queer Asian/Pacific American activists*. New York: Harrington Park Press/The Haworth Press.

Kurdek, L. A. (2005). What do we know about gay and lesbian couples? *Current Directions in Psychological Science, 14*(5), 251–254.

Kurdek, L. A. (2006). Differences between partners from heterosexual, gay, and lesbian cohabiting couples. *Journal of Marriage and Family, 68*(2), 509–528.

Kurutz, S. (2012, February 22). One is the quirkiest number: The freedom, and perils, of living alone. *The New York Times*, D1.

La Rocque, C. L., & Cloe, J. (2011). An evaluation of the relationship between body image and sexual avoidance. *Journal of Sex Research, 48*(4), 397–408.

Laan, E. (2008). What makes women experience desire? *Feminism & Psychology, 18*(4), 505–514.

Labelle, A., Bourget, D., Bradford, J. M. W., Alda, M., & Tessier, P. (2012). Familial paraphilia: A pilot study with the construction of genograms. *ISRN Psychatry, Volume 2012,* Article ID 692813, 9 pagesDOI:10.5402/2012/692813

Ladas, A. K., Whipple, B., & Perry, J. D. (1982). *The G spot and other recent discoveries about human sexuality.* New York: Holt, Rinehart & Winston.

LaFraniere, S. (2009, April 11). Chinese bias for baby boys creates a gap of 32 million. *The New York Times*. http://www.nytimes.com/2009/04/11/world/asia/11china.html?_r=0&mtrref=www.google.com&gwh=F594F28C63C812302102C59D143B20FF&gwt=pay (Accessed July 13, 2016).

LaGasse, L. L., et al. (2012). Prenatal methamphetamine exposure and childhood behavior problems at 3 and 5 years of age. *Pediatrics, 129*(4), 681–688.

Laier, C., Jaro, P., & Brand, M. (2014). Cybersex addiction in heterosexual female users of Internet pornography can be explained by the gratification hypothesis. *Cyberpsychology, Behavior, and Social Networking, 17*(8), 505–511.

Lalumière, M. L., Harris, G. T., Quinsey, V. L., & Rice, M. E. (2005a). Introduction. In M. L. Lalumière, G. T. Harris, V. L. Quinsey, & M. E. Rice (Eds.), *The causes of rape: Understanding individual differences in male propensity for sexual aggression* (pp. 3–6). Washington, DC: American Psychological Association.

Lalumière, M. L., Harris, G. T., Quinsey, V. L., & Rice, M. E. (2005b). Antisociality and mating effort. In M. L. Lalumière, G. T. Harris, V. L. Quinsey, & M. E. Rice (Eds.). *The causes of rape: Understanding individual differences in male propensity for sexual aggression* (pp. 61–103). Washington, DC: American Psychological Association.

Lalumière, M. L., Harris, G. T., Quinsey, V. L., & Rice, M. E. (2005c). Sexual interest in rape. In M. L. Lalumière, G. T. Harris, V. L. Quinsey, & M. E. Rice (Eds.), *The causes of rape: Understanding individual differences in male propensity for sexual aggression* (pp. 105–128). Washington, DC: American Psychological Association.

Lamanna, M. A., & Riedmann, A. (2005). *Marriages and families* (8th ed.). Belmont, CA: Wadsworth.

Lamar, C. (2012, January 16). An eyewitness account of the most awkward urology lecture ver. *Sexology*, http://io9.com/5876545/an-eyewitness-account-of-the-most-awkward-urology-lecture-ever

Lamaze, F. (1981). *Painless childbirth.* New York: Simon & Schuster.

Lamba, H., Goldmeier, D., Mackie, N. E., & Scullard, G. (2004). Antiretroviral therapy is associated with sexual dysfunction and with increased serum oestradiol levels in men. *International Journal of STD & AIDS, 15*(4), 234–237.

Landovitz, R. J., et al. (2013). Epidemiology, sexual risk behavior, and HIV prevention practices of men who have sex with men using Grindr in Los Angeles, California. *Journal of Urban Health, 90*(4), 729–739.

Lane, R., & Thayer, J. (2008). Sexual dysfunction and coronary artery disease. *American Journal of Medicine, 121*(4), 256–257.

Lane, T., Pettifor, A., Pascoe, S., Fiamma, A., & Rees, H. (2006). Heterosexual anal intercourse increases risk of HIV infection among young South African men. *AIDS, 20*(1), 123–125.

Lang, C., & Kuhnle, U. (2008). Intersexuality and alternative gender categories in non-Western cultures. *Hormone Research in Paediatrics, 69*(4), 240–250.

Langevin, R. (2003). A study of the psychosexual characteristics of sex killers: Can we identify them before it is too late? *International Journal of Offender Therapy & Comparative Criminology, 47*(4), 366–382.

Langevin, R. (2006). Acceptance and completion of treatment among sex offenders. *International Journal of Offender Therapy and Comparative Criminology, 50*(4), 402–417.

Langevin, R., et al. (1979). Experimental studies of the etiology of genital exhibitionism. *Archives of Sexual Behavior, 8*, 307–332.

Langevin, R., et al. (2004). Lifetime sex offender recidivism: A 25-year follow-up study. *Canadian Journal of Criminology and Criminal Justice, 46*(5), 531–552.

Langhinrichsen-Rohling, J., Palarea, R. E., Cohen, J., & Rohlin, M. L. (2002). Breaking up is hard to do: Unwanted pursuit behaviors following the dissolution of a romantic relationship. In K. E. Davis, I. H. Frieze et al. (Eds.). *Stalking: Perspectives on victims and perpetrators* (pp. 212–236). New York: Springer.

Langille, D. B., & Curtis, L. (2002). Factors associated with sexual intercourse before age 15 among female adolescents in Nova Scotia. *Canadian Journal of Human Sexuality, 11*(3), 91–99.

Langlois, J. H., et al. (2000). Maxims or myths of beauty? A meta-analytic and theoretical review. *Psychological Bulletin, 126*(3), 390–423.

Langstrom, N. (2010). The DSM diagnostic criteria for exhibitionism, voyeurism, and frotteurism. *Archives of Sexual Behavior*, DOI 10.1007/s10508-009-9577-4

Långström, N., & Zucker, K. J. (2005). Transvestic fetishism in the general population: Prevalence and correlates. *Journal of Sex & Marital Therapy, 31*(2), 87–95.

Langton, L., & Truman, J. T. (2015). Criminal victimization, 2014. Bureau of Justice Statistics. NCJ 248973. http://www.bjs.gov/index.cfm?ty=pbdetail&iid=5366

Laqueur, T. W. (2003). *Solitary sex: A cultural history of masturbation*. New York: Zone Books.

Larson, V. (2015, July 6). The appeal of time alone for the over 50 crowd. *The New York Times*. http://www.nytimes.com/roomforde-bate/2015/07/06/has-being-single-in-america-changed/the-appeal-of-alone-time-for-the-over-50-crowd (Accessed July 13, 2016).

Larsson, I., & Svedin, C. (2002). Experiences in childhood: Young adults' recollections. *Archives of Sexual Behavior, 31*(3), 263–273.

LaSala, M. C. (2004). Monogamy of the heart: Extradyadic sex and gay male couples. *Journal of Gay & Lesbian Social Services: Issues in Practice, Policy & Research, 17*(3), 1–24.

Laturi, C. A., et al. (2010). Treatment of adolescent gynecomastia. *Journal of Pediatric Surgery, 45*(3), 650–654.

Lau, J. T. F., Siah, P. C., & Tsui, H. Y. (2002). A study of the STD/AIDS related attitudes and behaviors of men who have sex with men in Hong Kong. *Archives of Sexual Behavior, 31*(4), 367–373.

Lau, M., et al. (2009). Dating and sexual attitudes in Asian-American adolescents. *Journal of Adolescent Research, 24*(1), 91–113.

Laumann, E. O., et al. (2006). A cross-national study of subjective sexual well-being among older women and men: Findings from the global study of sexual attitudes and behaviors. *Archives of Sexual Behavior, 35*(2), 145–161.

Laumann, E. O., Gagnon, J. H., Michael, R. T., & Michaels, S. (1994). *The social organization of sexuality: Sexual practices in the United States*. Chicago: University of Chicago Press.

Laumann, E. O., Masi, C. M., & Zuckerman, E. W., et al. (1997, April 2). Circumcision in the United States: Prevalence, prophylactic effects, and sexual practice. *Journal of the American Medical Association, 277*, 1052–1057.

Laumann, E. O., Paik, A., & Rosen, R. C. (1999). Sexual dysfunction in the United States. Prevalence and predictors. *Journal of the American Medical Association, 281*(6), 537–544.

Laurent, S. M., & Simons, A. D. (2009). Sexual dysfunction in depression and anxiety: Conceptualizing sexual dysfunction as part of an internalizing dimension. *Clinical Psychology Review, 29*(7), 573–585.

Lavin, M. (2008). Voyeurism: Psychopathology and theory. In D. R. Laws & W. T. O'Donohue (Eds.), *Sexual deviance: Theory, assessment, and treatment* (2nd ed., pp. 305–319). New York: Guilford Press.

Lawrence, A. A. (2004). Autogynephilia: A paraphilic model of gender identity disorder. *Journal of Gay & Lesbian Psychotherapy, 8*(1–2), 69–87.

Lawrence, A. A. (2005). Sexuality before and after male-to-female sex reassignment surgery. *Archives of Sexual Behavior, 34*(2), 147–166.

Laws, D. R., & Marshall, W. L. (2003). A brief history of behavioral and cognitive behavioral approaches to sexual offenders: Part 1. Early developments. *Sexual Abuse: Journal of Research & Treatment, 15*(2), 75–92.

Laws, D. R., & O'Donohue, W. T. (2008). Introduction. *Sexual deviance: Theory, assessment, and treatment* (2nd ed., pp. 1–20). New York: Guilford Press.

Leaper, C. (2013). Gender development during childhood. In P. D. Zalazo (Ed.), *The Oxford handbook of developmental psychology, Vol. 2: Self and other* (pp. 326–377). New York: Oxford University Press.

Leaper, C., & Bigler, R. S. (2011). In M. K. Underwood & L. H. Rosen (Eds.). *Social development* (pp. 289–315). New York: Guilford.

Leaper, C., & Farkas, T. (2015). The socialization of gender during childhood and adolescence. In J. E. Grusec & P. D. Hastings (Eds.). *Handbook of socialization: Theory and Research* (pp. 541–565). New York: Guilford.

Leaper, C., Farkas, T., & Brown, C. S. (2012). Adolescent girls' experiences and gender-related beliefs in relation to their motivation in math/science and English. *Journal of Youth and Adolescence, 41*(3), 268–282.

Leary, M. R., & Tangney, J. P. (2012). *Handbook of self and identity* (2nd ed.). New York: Guilford.

LeClerc, B., Beauregard, E., Forouzan, E., & Proulx, J. (2014). Offending pathways of intrafamilial child sexual offenders. *aggression* (pp. 156–178). New York: Routledge.

Lederman, M. M., & Valdez, H. (2000). Immune restoration with antiretroviral therapies: Implications for clinical management. *Journal of the American Medical Association, 284*, 223–228.

Lee, F. R. (2006, March 28). "Big love": Real polygamists look at HBO polygamists and find sex. *The New York Times*. http://www.nytimes.com/2006/03/28/arts/television/28poly.html (Accessed July 13, 2016).

Lee, Y. (2006). *Man as the prayer: The origin and nature of humankind*. New York: Trafford.

Legate, N., Ryan, R. M., & Weinstein, N. (2012). Is coming out always a "good thing"? Exploring the relations of autonomy support, outness, and wellness for lesbian, gay, and bisexual individuals. *Social Psychology and Personality Science, 3*(2), 145–152.

Legato, M. J. (2000, May 12). Cited in "Study of children born without penises finds nature determines gender." The Associated Press online.

Lehne, G. K. (2009). Phenomenology of paraphilia: Lovemap theory. In F. M. Saleh et al. (Eds.), *Sex offenders: Identification, risk assessment, treatment, and legal issue* (pp. 12–26). New York: Oxford University Press.

Leiblum, S. R., & Rosen, R. C. (Ed.). (2000). *Principles and practice of sex therapy*. 3rd ed. New York: Guilford Press.

Leigh, C. (2012, April 19). Labor laws, not criminal laws, are the solution. *The New York Times*. http://www.nytimes.com/roomforde-bate/2012/04/19/is-legalized-prostitution-safer/labor-laws-not-criminal-laws-are-the-solution-to-prostitution (Accessed July 13, 2016).

Leinders-Zufall, T., et al. (2000). Ultrasensitive pheromone detection by mammalian vomeronasal neurons. *Nature, 405*, 792–796.

Leitenberg, H., & Henning, K. (1995). Sexual fantasy. *Psychological Bulletin, 117*, 469–496.

Leitenberg, H., Detzer, M. J., & Srebnik, D. (1993). Gender differences in masturbation and the relation of masturbation experience in preadolescence and/or early adolescence to sexual behavior and sexual adjustment in young adulthood. *Archives of Sexual Behavior, 22*, 87–98.

Leland, J. (2000, May 29). The science of women & sex. *Newsweek*, pp. 48–54.

Lesjak, B., Bogadi, M., & Tosic, G. (2004). Zoophilia in comorbidity with other psychiatric disorders. *Socijalna Psihijatrija, 32*(4), 160–164.

Leubsdorf, B., & Nelson, C. M. (2015, June 26). Public's shift on same-sex marriage was swift, broad. *Wall Street Journal*. http://www.wsj.com/articles/publics-shift-on-same-sex-marriage-was-swift-broad-1435359461

Leue, A., Borchard, B., & Hoyer, J. (2004). Mental disorders in a forensic sample of sexual offenders. *European Psychiatry, 19*(3), 123–130.

Leung, E. Y. L. (2015). A report from #BlueJC: Doe the G-spot exist? *BJOG: An International Journal of Obstetrics and Gynaecology, 122*(4), 597.

LeVay, S. (1991). A difference in hypothalamic structure between heterosexual and homosexual men. *Science, 253*, 1034–1037.

Lever, J., Frederick, D. A., & Peplau, L. A. (2006). Does size matter? Men's and women's views on penis size across the lifespan. *Psychology of Men & Masculinity, 7*(3), 129–143.

Levin, R. J. (2003). The G-spot: Reality or illusion? *Sexual and Relationship Therapy, 18*(1), 117–119.

Levin, R. J. (2005a). The mechanisms of human ejaculation—A critical analysis. *Sexual and Relationship Therapy, 20*(1), 123–131.

Levin, R. J. (2005b). The involvement of the human cervix in reproduction and sex. *Sexual and Relationship Therapy, 20*(2), 251–260.

Levin, R. J. (2006). The breast/nipple/areola complex and human sexuality. *Sexual and Relationship Therapy, 21*(2), 237–249.

Levine, D. (2000). Virtual attraction: What rocks your boat. *CyberPsychology & Behavior, 3*(4), 565–573.

Levine, M. P. (2012). Loneliness and eating disorders. *Journal of Psychology: Interdisciplinary and Applied, 146*(1–2), 243–257.

Levine, S. B. (2012). Problematic sexual excesses. *Neuropsychiatry, 2*(1), 69–79.

Levite, A., & Cohen, O. (2012). The tango of loving hate: Dynamics in high-conflict divorce. *Clinical Social Work Journal, 40*(1), 46–55.

Levy, H., & Packman, W. (2004). Sexual abuse prevention for individuals with mental retardation: Considerations for genetic counselors. *Journal of Genetic Counseling, 13*(3), 189–205.

Lewin, T. (1998, January 17). Debate distant for many having abortions. *The New York Times*, pp. A1, A9.

Lewis, A. L., & White, J. (2009). The defense mechanisms of homophobia adolescent males. *Journal of Adolescence, 32*, 435–441.

Lewis, R. W., Fugl-Meyer, K. S., Corona, G., Hayes, R. D., Laumann, E. O., Moreira, E. D., Jr., Rellini, A. H., & Segraves T. (2010). Definitions/Epidemiology/Risk Factors for Sexual Dysfunction. *Journal of Sexual Medicine, 7*, 1598–1607.

Lewin, T. (2014, September 17). Surrogates and couples face a maze of laws, state by state. *The New York Times*. http://www.nytimes.com/2014/09/18/us/surrogates-and-couples-face-a-maze-of-laws-state-by-state.html (Accessed July 13, 2016).

Lewis, J., Maticka-Tyndale, E., Shaver, F., & Schramm, H. (2005). Managing risk and safety on the job: The experiences of Canadian sex workers. *Journal of Psychology & Human Sexuality, 17*(1–2), 147–167.

Lewis, R. W., et al. (2010). Definitions/epidemiology/risk factors for sexual dysfunction. *Journal of Sexual Medicine, 7*, 1598–1607.

Ley, D. J. (2012). *The myth of sex addiction*. Lanham, MD: Rowman & Littlefield Publishers.

Li, N. P., & Kenrick, D. T. (2006). Sex similarities and differences in preferences for short-term mates: What, whether, and why. *Journal of Personality and Social Psychology, 90*(3), 468–489.

Liao, L., Lunn, S., & Baker, M. (2015), Midlife menopause: Male partners talking. *Sexual and Relationship Therapy, 30*(1), 167–180.

Liben, L. S., Bigler, R. S., & Hilliard, L. J. (2014). Gender development: From universality to individuality. In E. T. Gershoff, R. G. Mistry, & D. A. Crosby (Eds.). *Societal contexts of child development: Pathways of influence and implications for practice and policy* (pp. 3–18). New York: Oxford University Press.

Lick, D. J., Tornello, S. L., Riskind, R. G., Schmidt, K. M., & Patterson, C. J. (2012). Social climate for sexual minorities predicts well-being among heterosexual offspring of lesbian and gay parents. *Sexuality Research and Social Policy, 9*(2), 99–112.

Lim, D. (2006, October 22). Mondo multiplex: The snuff film turns respectable. *The New York Times*. http://www.nytimes.com/2006/10/22/movies/22lim.html (Accessed July 13, 2016).

Lindsay, R. (2011). Preventing osteoporosis with a tissue receptive estrogen complex containing bazedoxifene/conjugated estrogens. *Osteoporosis International, 22*(2), 447–451.

Lippa, R. (2001). On deconstructing and reconstructing masculinity–femininity. *Journal of Research in Personality, 35*(2), 168–207.

Lippa, R. (2008). The relation between childhood gender nonconformity and adult masculinity–femininity and anxiety in heterosexual and homosexual men and women. *Sex Roles, 59*, 684–693.

Lippa, R. A. (2012). Effects of sex and sexual orientation on self-reported attraction and viewing times to images of men and women: Testing for category specificity. *Archives of Sexual Behavior, 41*(1), 149–160.

Lippa, R., & Arad, S. (1997). The structure of sexual orientation and its relation to masculinity, femininity, and gender diagnosticity: Different for men and women. *Sex Roles, 37*(3–4), 187–208.

Liptak, A. (2003, January 23). Opponents of circumcision use the legal system and legislatures to combat it. *The New York Times*. http://www.nytimes.com/2003/01/23/us/opponents-of-circumcision-use-the-legal-system-and-legislatures-to-combat-it.html (Accessed July 13, 2016).

Lipworth, L., et al. (2008). Cancer among Scandinavian women with cosmetic breast implants: A pooled long-term follow-up study. *International Journal of Cancer, 124*(2), 490–493.

Lira, L. R., Koss, M. P., & Russo, N. F. (1999). Mexican American women's definitions of rape and sexual abuse. *Hispanic Journal of Behavioral Sciences, 21*(3), 236–265.

Little, A. C., Caldwell, C. A., Jones, B. C., & DeBruine, L. M. (2011). Effects of partner beauty on opposite-sex attractiveness judgments. *Archives of Sexual Behavior, 40*(6), 1119–1127.

Little, A. C., DeBruine, L. M., & Jones, B. C. (2014). Sex differences in attraction to familiar and unfamiliar opposite-sex faces: Men prefer novelty and women prefer familiarity. *Archives of Sexual Behavior, 43*(5), 973–981.

Littleton, H., & Henderson, C. E. (2009). If she is not a victim, does that mean she was not traumatized? Evaluation of predictors of PTSD symptomatology among college rape victims. *Violence Against Women, 15*(2), 148–167.

Liu, G., et al. (2015). Trends and patterns of sexual behaviors among adolescents and adults aged 14 to 59 years: United States. *Sexually Transmitted Diseases, 42*(1), 20–26.

Lloyd, R. (2012, April 19). Legality leads to more trafficking. *The New York Times*. http://www.nytimes.com/roomfordebate/2012/04/19/is-legalized-prostitution-safer/legalizing-prostitution-leads-to-more-trafficking (Accessed July 13, 2016).

Locke, B. D., & Mahalik, J. R. (2005). Examining masculinity norms, problem drinking, and athletic involvement as predictors of sexual aggression in college men. *Journal of Counseling Psychology, 52*(3), 279–283.

Locock, L., & Alexander, J. (2005). "Just a bystander"? Men's place in the process of fetal screening and diagnosis. *Social Science & Medicine, 62*(6), 1349–1359.

Loder, N. (2000). US science shocked by revelations of sexual discrimination. *Nature, 405*, 713–714.

Loe, M. (2012). Pleasure in old age. In L. M. Carpenter, & J. DeLamater (Eds.). *Sex for life* (pp. 278–298). New York: New York University Press.

Logan, C. (2008). Sexual deviance in females. In D. R. Laws & W. T. O'Donohue (Eds.), *Sexual deviance: Theory, assessment, and treatment* (2nd ed., pp. 486–507). New York: Guilford Press.

Logan, T. K., Walker, R., Jordan, C. E., & Leukefeld, C. G. (2006). Justice system options and responses. In T. K. Logan, R. Walker, C. E. Jordan, & C. G. Leukefeld (Eds.), *Women and victimization: Contributing factors, interventions, and implications* (pp. 161–194). Washington, DC: American Psychological Association.

Lohman, D. F., & Lakin, J. M. (2009). Consistencies in sex differences on the Cognitive Abilities Test across countries, grades, test forms, and cohorts. *British Journal of Educational Psychology, 79*(2), 389–407.

Lohmann, R. I. (2004). Sex and sensibility: Margaret Mead's descriptive and rhetorical ethnography. *Reviews in Anthropology, 33*(2), 111–130.

Londoño, D. C., et al. (2012). Population-based study of erectile dysfunction and polypharmacy. *BJUI, 110*(2), 254–259.

Long, C. R., Seburn, M., Averill, J. R., & More, T. A. (2003). Solitude experiences: Varieties, settings, and individual differences. *Personality & Social Psychology Bulletin, 29*(5), 578–583.

Lorant, V., et al. (2005). A European comparative study of marital status and socio-economic inequalities in suicide. *Social Science & Medicine, 60*(11), 2431–2441.

Lorenz, F. O., Wickrama, K. A. S., Conger, R. D., & Elder, G. H., Jr. (2006). The short-term and decade-long effects of divorce on women's midlife health. *Journal of Health and Social Behavior, 47*(2), 111–125.

Lotery, H. E., McClure, N., & Galask, R. P. (2004). Vulvodynia. *Lancet, 363*(9414), 1058–1060.

Loukes, K. (2016). Common LGBT sexual health questions. *Lesbian, Gay, Bisexual, and Transgender Healthcare* (pp. 441–450). Switzerland: Springer International Publishing.

Lovaas, K. E., Elia, J. P., & Yep, G. A. (2007). Shifting ground(s): Surveying the contested terrain of LGBT studies and queer theory. *Journal of Homosexuality, 52*(1-2), 1–18.

Love, R. (2015). Street level prostitution: A systematic literature review. *Issues in Mental Health Nursing, 36*(8), 568–576.

Lu, S., & Chen, C. (2014). Natural history and epidemiology of benign prostatic hyperplasia. *Formosan Journal of Surgery, 47*(6), 207–210.

Lucon, A. M., et al. (2006). Spontaneous recanalization after vasectomy. *TSW Urology, 1*, 71–74.

Luder, M., et al. (2011). Associations between online pornography and sexual behavior among adolescents: Myth or reality? *Archives of Sexual Behavior, 40*(5), 1027–1035.

Lue, T. F. (2000). Drug therapy: Erectile dysfunction. *New England Journal of Medicine, 342*(24), 1802–1813.

Lundström, J. N., & Marilyn Jones-Gotman, M. (2009). Romantic love modulates women's identification of men's body odors. *Hormones and Behavior, 55*(2), 280–284.

Luo, Y., et al. (2015). Sex hormones predict the incidence of erectile dysfunction: From a population-based prospective cohort study (FAMHES). *Journal of Sexual Medicine, 12*(5), 1165–1174.

Lussier, P., & Piché, L. (2008). Frotteurism: Psychopathology and theory. In D. R. Laws & W. T. O'Donohue (Eds.), *Sexual deviance:*

Theory, assessment, and treatment (2nd ed., pp. 131–149). New York: Guilford Press.

Lynn, B. M., McCord, J. L., & Halliwell, J. R. (2007). Effects of menstrual cycle and sex on progesterone hemodynamics. American Journal of Physiology: Regulatory, Integrative, and Comparative Physiology, 292, R1260–R1270.

Lyons, H. A., Manning, W. D., Longmore, M. A., & Giordano, P. C. (2015). Gender and casual sexual activity from adolescence to emerging adulthood: Social and life course correlates. The Journal of Sex Research, 52(5), 543–557.

Maaita, M. J., Bhaumik, J., & Davies, A. E. (2002). Sexual function after using tension-free vaginal tape for the surgical treatment of genuine stress incontinence. British Journal of Urology International, 90(6), 540.

Maartens, L. W. F., Knottnerus, J. A., & Pop, V. J. (2002). Menopausal transition and increased depressive symptomatology: A community based prospective study. Maturitas, 42(3), 195–200.

MacCallum, F., & Keeley, S. (2008). Embryo donation families: A follow-up in middle childhood. Journal of Family Psychology, 22(6), 799–808.

MacCulloch, D. (2011). Christianity: The first three thousand years. New York: Viking.

MacDonald, T. K., MacDonald, G., Zanna, M. P., & Fong, G. T. (2000). Alcohol, sexual arousal, and intentions to use condoms in young men: Applying alcohol myopia theory to risky sexual behavior. Health Psychology, 19, 290–298.

Macedo, S. (2015). Just married: Same-sex couples, monogamy & the future of marriage. Princeton, NJ: Princeton University Press.

Macey, K., Gregory, A., Nunns, D., & das Nair, R. (2015). Women's experiences of using vaginal trainers (dilators) to treat vaginal penetration difficulties diagnosed as vaginismus: A qualitative interview study. BMC Women's Health, 15(49), DOI: 10.1186/s12905-015-0201-6

MacGregor, E. (2009). Estrogen replacement and migraine. Maturitas, 63(1), 51–55.

Mackinnon, C. A. (2007). Women's lives, men's laws. Cambridge, MA: Harvard University Press.

Macy, R. J., Nurius, P. S., & Norris, J. (2006). Responding in their best interests: Contextualizing women's coping with acquaintance sexual aggression. Violence Against Women, 12(5), 478–500.

Madhyastha, T. M., Hamaker, E. L., & Gottman, J. M. (2011). Investigating spousal influence using moment-to-moment affect data from marital conflict. Journal of Family Psychology, 25(2), 292 –300.

Madsen, L., Parsons, S., & Grubin, D. (2006). The relationship between the five-factor model and DSM personality disorder in a sample of child molesters. Personality and Individual Differences, 40(2), 227–236.

Maggi, M. (2012). Hormonal therapy for male sexual dysfunction. Hoboken, NJ: Wiley.

Mahoney, A. R., & Knudson-Martin, C. (2009). Couples, gender, and power. New York: Springer.

Major, B., et al. (2000). Psychological responses of women after first-trimester abortion. Archives of General Psychiatry, 57, 777–784.

Major, B., Kaiser, C. R., & McCoy, S. K. (2003). It's not my fault: When and why attributions to prejudice protect self-esteem. Personality & Social Psychology Bulletin, 29(6), 772–781.

Malamuth, N. M., Addison, T., & Koss, M. (2000). Pornography and sexual aggression:

Are there reliable effects and can we understand them? Annual Review of Sex Research, 11, 26–91.

Malamuth, N. M., Huppin, M., & Paul, B. (2005). Sexual coercion. In D. M. Buss (Ed.), The handbook of evolutionary psychology (pp. 394–418). Hoboken, NJ: Wiley.

Malaspina, D. (2009). Cited in L. Belkin (2009, April 5). Your old man. The New York Times Magazine.

Malec, K. (2003, Summer). The abortion–breast cancer link: How politics trumped science and informed consent. Journal of American Physicians and Surgeons, 8(2). www.abortion-breastcancer.com/jpands.pdf

Maletzky, B. M. (1980). Assisted covert sensitization in the treatment of exhibitionism. Journal of Consulting and Clinical Psychology, 48(1), 306–312.

Maletzky, B. M., & Steinhauser, C. (2002). A 25-year follow-up of cognitive/behavioral therapy with 7,275 sexual offenders. Behavior Modification, 26(2), 123–147.

Malinowski, B. (1927). Sex and repression in savage society. London: Kegan Paul, Trench, Trubner & Co.

Malinowski, B. (1929). The sexual life of savages in north-western Melanesia. New York: Eugenics.

Maner, J. K., Rouby, D. A., & Gonzaga, G. C. (2008). Automatic inattention to attractive alternatives: The evolved psychology of relationship maintenance. Evolution and Human Behavior, 29(5), 343–349.

Maniglio, R. (2011). The role of childhood trauma, psychological problems, and coping in the development of deviant sexual fantasies in sexual offenders. Clinical Psychology Review, 31(5), 748–756.

Mansergh, G., et al. (2008). Alcohol and drug use in the context of anal sex and other factors associated with sexually transmitted infections: Results from a multi-city study of high-risk men who have sex with men in the USA. Sexually Transmitted Infections, 84, 509–511.

Maranda, M. J., Han, C., & Rainone, G. A. (2004). Crack cocaine and sex. Journal of Psychoactive Drugs, 36(3), 315–322.

Marazziti, D. (2005). The neurobiology of love. Current Psychiatry Reviews, 1(3), 331–335.

Marchbanks, P. A., et al. (2002). Oral contraceptives and the risk of breast cancer. New England Journal of Medicine, 346, 2025–2032.

Marcus, D. K., & Miller, R. S. (2003). Sex differences in judgments of physical attractiveness: A social relations analysis. Personality & Social Psychology Bulletin, 29(3), 325–335.

Marquis, C. (2003, March 16). Living in sin. The New York Times, p. WK2.

Marr, S. (2012, April 20). Nevada's legal brothels are coercive too. The New York Times. http://www.nytimes.com/roomfordebate/2012/04/19/is-legalized-prostitution-safer/nevadas-legal-brothels-are-coercive-too (Accessed July 13, 2016).

Marrazzo, J. (2003). Vulvovaginal candidiasis: Over the counter treatment doesn't seem to lead to resistance. British Medical Journal, 326, 993–994.

Marshall, B. L. (2006). The new virility: Viagra, male aging and sexual function. Sexualities, 9(3), 345–362.

Marshall, W. L. (1989). Pornography and sex offenders. In D. Zillmann & J. Bryant (Eds.),

Pornography: Research advances and policy considerations (pp. 185–214). Hillsdale, NJ: Erlbaum.

Marshall, W. L. (2015). Changing deviant sexual interests: Masturbatory reconditioning with a child molester. In D. T. Wilcox, T. Garrett, & L. Harkins (Eds.). Sex offender treatment: A case study approach to issues and interventions (pp. 327–341). Chichester, UK: Wiley Blackwell.

Marshall, W. L., & Marshall, L. E. (2015). Psychological treatment of the paraphilias: A review and appraisal of effectiveness. Current Psychiatry Reports: Topical Collection on Sexual Disorders, 17, 47.

Marsiglio, W. (2004). When stepfathers claim stepchildren: A conceptual analysis. Journal of Marriage & Family, 66(1), 22–39.

Martin, J. A., et al. (2008). Annual summary of vital statistics: 2006. Pediatrics, 121(4), 788–801.

Martin, J. A., Hamilton, B. E., Osterman, M. J. K., Curtin, S. C., & Mathews, T. J. (2015). Births: Final data for 2013. National Vital Statistics Reports, 64(1).

Martin, S. A., et al. (2014). Predictors of sexual dysfunction incidence and remission in men. Journal of Sexual Medicine, 11(5), 1136–1147.

Martinez, G. M., & Abma, J. C. (2015). Sexual activity, contraceptive use, and childbearing of teenagers aged 15–19 in the United States. U.S. Department of Health and Human Services, National Center for Health Statistics. NCHS Data Brief, No. 209.

Martinez, G., Abma, J., & Copen, C. (2010). Educating teenagers about sex in the United States. NCHS data brief, no. 44. Hyattsville, MD: National Center for Health Statistics.

Martinez, G., Copen, C. E., & Abma, J. C. (2011). Teenagers in the United States: Sexual activity, contraceptive use, and childbearing, 2006–1010 National Survey of Family Growth. National Center for Health Statistics. Vital Health Statistics, 23(31).

Martino, S. C., et al. (2006). Exposure to degrading versus nondegrading music lyrics and sexual behavior among youth. Pediatrics, 118, e430–e441.

Martins, Y., Preti, G., Crabtree, C. R., Runyan, T., Vainius, A. A., & Wysocki, C. J. (2005). Preference for human body odors is influenced by gender and sexual orientation. Psychological Science, 16(9), 694.

Marvasti, J. A. (2004). Pharmacotherapy and surgical treatment of paraphiliacs and sexual offenders. In J. A. Marvasti (Ed.), Psychiatric treatment of sexual offenders: Treating the past traumas in traumatizers. A bio-psychosocial perspective. American series in behavioral science and law (pp. 97–115). Springfield, IL: Charles C. Thomas.

Marwick, C. (2000). Consensus panel considers osteoporosis. Journal of the American Medical Association, 283(16), 2093–2095.

Marziano, V., Ward, T., Beech, A. R., & Pattison, P. (2006). Identification of five fundamental implicit theories underlying cognitive distortions in child abusers: A preliminary study. Psychology, Crime & Law, 12(1), 97–105.

Masheb, R. M., Lozano–Blanco, C., Kohorn, E. I., Minkin, M J., & Kerns, R. D. (2004). Assessing sexual function and dyspareunia with the female sexual function index (FSFI) in women with vulvodynia. Journal of Sex & Marital Therapy, 30(5), 315–324.

Master, A., Cheryan, S., & Meltzoff, A. N. (2014). Reducing adolescent girls' concerns about STEM stereotypes: When do female teachers matter? *International Review of Social Psychology, 27*(2), 79–102.

Master, A., Cheryan, S., & Meltzoff, A. N. (2015). Computing whether she belongs: Stereotypes undermine girls' interest and sense of belonging in computer science. *Journal of Educational Psychology,* DOI: 10.1037/edu0000061

Masters, W. H., & Johnson, V. E. (1966). *Human sexual response.* Boston: Little, Brown.

Masters, W. H., & Johnson, V. E. (1970). *Human sexual inadequacy.* Boston: Little, Brown.

Masters, W. H., & Johnson, V. E. (1979). *Homosexuality in perspective.* Boston: Little, Brown.

Mathers, B. M., et al. (2008). Global epidemiology of injecting drug use and HIV among people who inject drugs: A systematic review. *Lancet, 372*(9651), 1733–1745.

Matsui, H.,Sopko, N. A., Hannan, J. L., & Bivalacqua, T. J. (2015). Pathophysiology of erectile dysfunction. *Current Drug Targets, 16*(5), 411–419.

Matthews, A. K., Hughes, T. L., Tartaro, J., Omoto, A. M., & Kurtzman, H. S. (Eds.). (2006). *Sexual orientation and mental health: Examining identity and development in lesbian, gay, and bisexual people. Contemporary perspectives on lesbian, gay, and bisexual psychology.* Washington, DC: American Psychological Association.

Mattson, C. L., Bailey, R. C., Muga, R., Poulussen, R., & Onyango, T. (2005). Acceptability of male circumcision and predictors of circumcision preference among men and women in Nyanza Province, Kenya, *AIDS Care, 17*(2), 182–194.

Mattson, G. (2011). Sin in the suburbs: Nevada's changing brothel industry. *Journal of Sex Research, 48*(6), 599–601.

Maxson, S. C. (1998). Homologous genes, aggression, and animal models. *Developmental Neuropsychology, 14*(1), 143–156.

Maxwell, C. D., Robinson, A. L., & Post, L. A. (2003). The nature and predictors of sexual victimization and offending among adolescents. *Journal of Youth & Adolescence, 32*(6), 465–477.

Maxwell, L. & Scott, G. (2014). A review of the role of radical feminist theories in the understanding of rape myth acceptance. *Journal of Sexual Aggression, 20*(1), 40–54.

Maybach, K. L., & Gold, S. R. (1994). Hyperfemininity and attraction to macho and nonmacho men. *Journal of Sex Research, 31*(2), 91–98.

Mayo Clinic. (2006, October 10). Vulvodynia. www.mayoclinic.com/health/vulvodynia/DS00159.

Mayo Clinic. (2012). Ectopic pregnancy. http://www.mayoclinic.com/health/ectopic-pregnancy/DS00622/DSECTION=risk-factors

Mayo Clinic. (2014). Vulvodyinia. http://www.mayoclinic.org/diseases-conditions/vulvodynia/basics/definition/con-20020326

Mayo Clinic. (2016). Rubella. http://www.mayoclinic.org/diseases-conditions/rubella/basics/definition/con-20020067

Mazur, T. *The infant's developing sexuality.* Accessed February 10, 2006. www2.hu-berlin.de/sexology/GESUND/ARCHIV/SEN/CH07.HTM#b11-CHILDREN%20AND%20SEX.

McAndrew, F. T. (2009). The interacting roles of testosterone and challenges to status in human male aggression. *Aggression and Violent Behavior, 14,* 330–335.

McAnulty, R. (2012). *Sex in college: The things they don't write home about.* Santa Barbara, CA: ABC-CLIO, LLC.

McBride, C. K., Paikoff, R. L., & Holmbeck, G. N. (2003). Individual and familial influences on the onset of sexual intercourse among urban African American adolescents. *Journal of Consulting and Clinical Psychology, 71*(1), 159–167.

McCabe M., et al. (2010). Psychological and interpersonal dimensions of sexual function and dysfunctions. *Journal of Sexual Medicine, 7,* 327–336.

McCabe, K. A. (2000). Child pornography and the Internet. *Social Science Computer Review, 18*(1), 73–76.

McCabe, M. P. (2004). Exacerbation of symptoms among people with multiple sclerosis: Impact on sexuality and relationships over time. *Archives of Sexual Behavior, 33*(6), 593–601.

McCabe, M. P. (2005). The role of performance anxiety in the development and maintenance of sexual dysfunction in men and women. *International Journal of Stress Management, 12*(4), 379–388.

McCabe, S. E., et al. (2005). Selection and socialization effects of fraternities and sororities on US college student substance use: A multicohort national longitudinal study. *Addiction, 100*(4), 512–524.

McCabe, M. P., & Connaughton, C. (2014). Psychosocial factors associated with male sexual difficulties. *The Journal of Sex Research, 51*(1), DOI: 10.1080/00224499.2013.789820

McCarthy, B., Farr, E., & McDonald, D. (2013). Couple sexuality after 60. *Journal of Family Psychotherapy, 24*(1), 38–47.

McCarthy, B., & Pierpaoli, C. (2015). Sexual challenges with aging: Integrating the GES approach in an elderly couple. *Sex & Marital Therapy, 41*(1), 72–82.

McCarthy, B. W., & Fucito, L. M. (2005). Integrating medication, realistic expectations, and therapeutic interventions in the treatment of male sexual dysfunction. *Journal of Sex & Marital Therapy, 31*(4), 319–328.

McCarthy, B. W., Bodnar, L. E., & Handal, M. (2004). Integrating sex therapy and couple therapy. In J. H. Harvey, A. Wenzel, & S. Sprecher (Eds.), *The handbook of sexuality in close relationships* (pp. 573–593). Mahwah, NJ: Erlbaum.

McCarthy, B. W., Ginsberg, R. L., & Fucito, L. M. (2006). Resilient sexual desire in heterosexual couples. *Family Journal: Counseling and Therapy for Couples and Families, 14*(1), 59–64.

McCarthy, J. (2015, May 19). Record-high 60% of Americans support same-sex marriage. Gallup Organization.

McClamrock, H. D., Jones, H. W., & Adashi, E. Y. (2012). Ovarian stimulation and intrauterine insemination at the quarter centennial: Implications for the multiple births epidemic. *Fertility and Sterility, 97*(4), 802–809.

McCormack, S., & Dunn, D. (2015). Pragmatic open-label randomized trial of pre-exposure prophylaxis: The PROUD study. *Conference on Retroviruses and Opportunistic Infections,* Seattle, Washington, February 23–26.

McCoy, N. L., & Pitino, L. (2002). Pheromonal influences on sociosexual behavior in young women. *Physiology & Behavior, 75*(3), 367–375.

McDonough, Y. Z. (1998, January 24). What Barbie really taught me. *The New York Times Magazine,* 70.

McElduff, A., & Beange, H. (2003). Men's health and well-being: Testosterone deficiency. *Journal of Intellectual & Developmental Disability, 28*(2), 211–213.

McEwan, S. I., de Man, A. F., & Simpson-Housley, P. (2005). Acquaintance rape, ego-identity achievement, and locus of control. *Social Behavior and Personality, 33*(6), 587–592.

McGee, R. W. (2016). Do views toward homosexuality differ based on ethnicity? An empirical study of United States opinion. Social Science Research Network, http://papers.ssrn.com/sol3/papers.cfm?abstract_id=2799875.

McGue, M., Elkins, I., Walden, B., & Iacono, W. G. (2005). Perceptions of the parent–adolescent relationship: A longitudinal investigation. *Developmental Psychology, 41*(6), 971–984.

McHugh, M. C., & Hambaugh, J. (2010). She said, he said: Gender, language, and power. *Handbook of Gender Research in Psychology, 5,* 379–410.

McIntyre, S., Formichella, A., Osterhout, M. B., & Gresh, S. (1991). *Tell it like it is: Straight talk about sex.* New York: Avon Books.

McKeganey, N. (2006). Street prostitution in Scotland: The views of working women. *Drugs: Education, Prevention & Policy, 13*(2), 151–166.

McLawsen, J. E., Scalora, M. J., & Darrow, C. (2012). Civilly committed sex offenders: A description and interstate comparison of populations. *Psychology, Public Policy, and Law.* DOI: 10.1037/a0026116

McLeod, J. D., & Knight, S. (2010). The association of socioemotional problems with early sexual initiation. *Perspectives on Sexual and Reproductive Health, 42*(2), 93–101.

McMahon, C. G. (2011). Premature ejaculation. *Journal of Sexual Medicine, 9*(2), 454–465.

McNally, M. R., & Fremouw, W. J. (2014). Examining risk of escalation: A critical review of the exhibitionistic behavior literature. *Aggression and Violent Behavior, 19*(5), 474–485.

McMillen, M. (2011, September 1). Circumcision rates are dropping in the U.S. CDC says circumcision is slightly less common today than a decade ago. WebMD Health News. http://www.webmd.com/parenting/baby/news/20110901/circumcision-rates-are-dropping-in-the-us

McNeil, D. G. (2011, July 13). Two studies show pills can prevent HIV infection. *The New York Times.* http://www.nytimes.com/2011/07/14/health/research/14aids.html?_r=0&mtrref=www.google.com&gwh=9E98D6CA8BA8E47FB17ECB9FBF5B2D95&gwt=pay (*Accessed July 13, 2016).*

McNeil, D. G. (2012, July 3). AIDS: New four-drug pill taken daily tests better than other regimens. *The New York Times,* p. D6.

Mead, M. (1935). *Sex and temperament in three primitive societies.* New York: Dell.

Meadows, S. (2009). Family structure and fathers' well-being: Trajectories of mental health and self-rated health. *Journal of Health and Social Behavior, 50*(2), 115–131.

Medical News Today. (2008, January 17). Circumcision rates highest in Midwest, lowest in West. http://www.medicalnewstoday.com/articles/94200.php.

Medrano, M. A., Hatch, J. P., Zule, W. A., & Desmond, D. P. (2003). Childhood trauma and adult prostitution behavior in a multiethnic heterosexual drug-using population. *American Journal of Drug & Alcohol Abuse, 29*(2), 463–486.

Melo, J., & Creinin, M. D. (2016). Combination oral contraceptive pills. In D. Shoupe, & D. R. Mishell (Eds.). *The handbook of contraception* (pp. 61–77). Switzerland: Springer International Publishing.

Meltzer, A. L., McNulty, J. K., Jackson, G. L., & Karney, B. R. (2014). Men still value attractiveness in a long-term mate more than women. *Journal of Personality and Social Psychology, 106*(3), 435–440.

Meier, B. P., D'Agostino, P. R., Elliot, A. J., Maier, M. A., & Wilkowski, B. M. (2012). Color in context: Psychological context moderates the influence of red on approach- and avoidance-motivated behavior *PLoS ONE, 7*(7): e40333.

Meissner, G. W., et al. (2011). Functional dissection of the neural substrates for sexual behaviors in *Drosophila melanogaster. Genetics, 189*(1), 195–211.

Menard, A. D., et al. (2015). Individual and relationship contributors to optimal sexual experiences in older men and women. *Sexual and Relationship Therapy, 30*(1), 78–93.

Menard, K. S., et al. (2003). Gender differences in sexual harassment and coercion in college students: Developmental, individual, and situational determinants. *Journal of Interpersonal Violence, 18*(10), 1222–1239.

Meston, C. M., & Frohlich, P. F. (2000). The neurobiology of sexual function. *Archives of General Psychiatry, 57*(11), 1012–1030.

Meston, C., & Buss, D. M. (2007). Why humans have sex. *Archives of Sexual Behavior, 36,* 477–507.

Meyer, T. (1998, February 18). *AZT short treatment works.* Associated Press.

Meyer-Bahlburg, H. F. L. (2015). Gender identity and role: clinical-psychological aspects. *The International Encyclopedia of Human Sexuality,* 427–500.

Meyer-Bahlburg, H. F. L., et al. (1995). Prenatal estrogens and the development of homosexual orientation. *Developmental Psychology, 31*(1), 12–21.

Michel, A. & Pedinielli, J.-L. (2005). Vers une conceptualization du transsexualisme. *Annales Medico-Psychologiques, 163*(5), 379–386.

Mikach, S. M., & Bailey, J. M. (1999). What distinguishes women with unusually high numbers of sex partners? *Evolution & Human Behavior, 20*(3) 141–150.

Milhausen, R. R., Buchholz, A. C., Opperman, E. A., & Benson, L. E. (2015). Relationships between body image, body composition, sexual functioning, and sexual satisfaction among heterosexual young adults. *Archives of Sexual Behavior, 44*(6), 1621–1633.

Mill, J. S. (1983). *Utilitarianism.* Indianapolis: Hackett Publishing.

Mills, T. A., & Lavender, T. (2014). Advanced maternal age. *Obstetrics, Gynaecology, & Reproductive Medicine, 24*(3), 85–90.

Miller, D. I., & Halpern, D. F. (2014). The new science of cognitive sex differences. *Trends in Cognitive Sciences, 18*(1), 37–45.

Miller, G., Tybur, J., & Jordan, B. D. (2007). *Evolution and Human Behavior, 28*(6), 375–381.

Miller, J. (2012). In C. D. Bryant (Ed.). *The Routledge handbook of deviant behavior* (pp. 383–389). New York: Routledge.

Miller, L. (2014). Rape: Sex crime, act of violence, or naturalistic adaptation? *Aggression and Violent Behavior, 19*(1), 67–81.

Miller, M. (1998, cited in Bronner, February 1). Just say maybe. No sexology, please. We're Americans. *The New York Times,* p. WK6.

Miller, R. (2005). Overcoming violence against women and girls: The international campaign to eradicate a worldwide problem. *Culture, Health & Sexuality, 7*(5), 519–521.

Miller, S. A., & Byers, E. S. (2004). Actual and desired duration of foreplay and intercourse: Discordance and misperceptions within heterosexual couples. *Journal of Sex Research, 41*(3), 301–309.

Miller, S. L., & Maner, J. K. (2009). Sex differences in response to sexual versus emotional infidelity: The moderating role of individual differences. *Personality and Individual Differences, 46*(3), 287-291.

Millett, G. A., et al. (2008). Circumcision status and risk of HIV and sexually transmitted infections among men who have sex with men: A meta-analysis. *Journal of the American Medical Association, 300*(14), 1674–1684.

Milner, A., McClure, R., & de Leo, D. (2012). Socio-economic determinants of suicide: An ecological analysis of 35 countries. *Social Psychiatry and Psychiatric Epidemiology, 47*(1), 19–27.

Miner, M. M. (2011). Erectile dysfunction and cardiovascular disease: A harbinger for cardiovascular events. *Journal of Sexual Medicine,* Virtual Issue Number 2.

Minichiello, V., et al. (2001). Male sex workers in three Australian cities: Socio-demographic and sex work characteristics. *Journal of Homosexuality, 42*(1), 29–51.

Mirande, A. (2015). Hombres mujeres: An indigenous third gender. *Men and Masculinities,* DOI: 10.1177/1097184X15602746

Missailidis, K., & Gebre–Medhin, M. (2000). Female genital mutilation in eastern Ethiopia. *Lancet, 356,* 137–138.

Mitchell, K. J., Finkelhor, D., & Wolak, J. (2005). Protecting youth online: Family use of filtering and blocking software. *Child Abuse & Neglect, 29*(7), 753–765.

Mock, S. E., & Elbach, R. P. (2012). Stability and change in sexual orientation over a 10-year period in adulthood. *Archives of Sexual Behavior, 41*(3), 641–648.

Mofenson, L. M. (2000). Perinatal exposure to zidovudine—Benefits and risks. *New England Journal of Medicine, 343*(11), 803–805.

Moghe, S. (2015, July 25). Cosby deposition: Quaaludes came from L.A. gynecologist. *CNN.com.* http://www.cnn.com/2015/07/24/us/cosby-deposition-quaaludes/

Mohan, R., & Bhugra, D. (2005). Literature update: A critical review. *Sexual and Relationship Therapy, 20*(1), 115–122.

Money, J. (1994). The concept of gender identity disorder in childhood and adolescence after 39 years. *Journal of Sex and Marital Therapy, 20*(3), 163–177.

Money, J. (2003). History, causality, and sexology. *Journal of Sex Research, 40*(3), 237–239.

Monk, C., Georgieff, M. K., & Osterholm, E. A. (2013). Research review: Maternal prenatal distress and poor nutrition—mutually influencing risk factors affecting infant neurocognitive development. *The Journal of Child Psychology and Psychiatry, 54*(2), 115–130.

Monson, C. M., Langhinrichsen-Rohling, J., & Binderup, T. (2000). Does "no" really mean "no" after you say "yes"? Attributions about date and marital rape. *Journal of Interpersonal Violence, 15*(11), 1156–1174.

Montano, D., Kasprzyk, D., von Haeften, I., & Fishbein, M. (2001). Toward an understanding of condom use behaviours: A theoretical and methodological overview of Project SAFER. *Psychology, Health & Medicine, 6*(2), 139–150.

Montejo, A. L., Montejo, L., & Navarro-Cremades, F. (2015). Sexual side effects of antidepressant and antipsychotic drugs. *Current Opinion in Psychiatry, 28*(6), 418–423.

Montemurro, B., Bloom, C., & Madell, K. (2003). Ladies night out: A typology of women patrons of a male strip club. *Deviant Behavior, 24*(4), 333–352.

Montgomery-Downs, H. E. (2008). Normal sleep development in infants and toddlers. In A. Ivanenko (Ed.), *Sleep and psychiatric disorders in children and adolescents* (pp. 11–21). London: Informa Healthcare.

Montoya, R. M., Horton, R. S., & Kirchner, J. (2008). Is actual similarity necessary for attraction? A meta-analysis of actual and perceived similarity. *Journal of Social and Personal Relationships, 25*(6), 889–922.

Moore, D. R., & Heiman, J. R. (2006). Women's sexuality in context: Relationship factors and female sexual functioning. In I. Goldstein, C. Meston, S. Davis, & A. Traish (Eds.), *Female sexual dysfunction.* New York: Parthenon.

Moore, M. M. (2010). Human nonverbal courtship behavior—A brief historical review. *Journal of Sex Research, 47,* 171–180.

Moore, S., & Leung, C. (2002). Young people's romantic attachment styles and their association with well-being. *Journal of Adolescence, 25*(2), 243–255.

Morley, J. E., & Perry, H. M., III. (2003). Androgens and women at the menopause and beyond. *Journals of Gerontology: Series A: Biological Sciences & Medical Sciences, 58A*(5), 409–416.

Morofushi, M., Shinohara, K., Funabashi, T., & Kimura, F. (2000). Positive relationship between menstrual synchrony and ability to smell 5alpha-androst-16-en-3alpha-ol. *Chemical Senses, 25*(4), 407–411.

Morris, B. J., et al. (2014). Circumcision rates in the United States: Rising or falling? What effect might the new affirmative pediatric policy statement have? *Mayo Clinic Proceedings, 89*(5), 677–686.

Morris, L. B. (2000, June 25). For the partum blues, a question of whether to medicate. *The New York Times.*

Morrison, C. S., & Nanda, K. (2012). Hormonal contraception and HIV: An unanswered question. *The Lancet Infectious Diseases, 12*(1), 2–3.

Morrison, D. R., & Coiro, M. J. (1999). Parental conflict and marital disruption: Do children benefit when high-conflict marriages are dissolved? *Journal of Marriage & the Family, 61*(3), 626–637.

Morrison, E. S., et al. (1980). *Growing up sexual.* New York: Van Nostrand Reinhold.

Morry, M. M. (2005). Allocentrism and friendship satisfaction: The mediating roles of disclosure and closeness. *Canadian Journal of Behavioural Science, 37*(3), 211–222.

Morry, M. M., & Gaines, S. O. (2005). Relationship satisfaction as a predictor of similarity ratings: A test of the attraction–similarity hypothesis. *Journal of Social and Personal Relationships, 22*(4), 561–584.

Morry, M. M., Kito, M., & Ortiz, L. (2011). The attraction–similarity model and dating couples. *Personal Relationships, 18*(1), 125–143.

Mortola, J. F. (1998). Premenstrual syndrome— Pathophysiologic considerations. *New England Journal of Medicine, 338,* 256–257.

Moser, C. (2010). Blanchard's autogynephilia theory: A critique. *Journal of Homosexuality, 57*(6), 790–809.

Moser, S. E., & Alken, L. S. (2011). Cognitive and emotional factors associated with elective breast augmentation among young women. *Psychology and Health, 26*(1), 41–60.

Mosher, W. D., Chandra, A., & Jones, J. (2005). *Sexual behavior and selected health measures: Men and women 15–44 years of age, United States, 2002. Advance data from vital and health statistics.* Centers for Disease Control and Prevention. National Center for Health Statistics, No. 362.

Moshkin, M. P., et al. (2011). Odor as an element of subjectiv assessment of attractiveness of young males and females. *Comparative and Ontogenic Physiology, 47*(1), 69–82.

Mostafa, T., El Khouly, G., & Hassan, A. (2012). Pheromones in sex and reproduction: Do they have a role in humans? *Journal of Advanced Research, 3*(1), 1–9.

Mowlabocus, S., & Wood, R. (2015). Introduction: Audiences and consumers of porn. *Porn Studies, 2*(2–3), 118–122.

Moyer, J. W. (2015, July 27). 35 Bill Cosby accusers on *New York magazine's* cover. http://www. washingtonpost.com/news/morning-mix/wp/2015/07/27/35-bill-cosby-accusers-on-new-york-magazines-cover/

Mukherjee, S., et al. (2009). What is the effect of circumcision on risk of urinary tract infection in boys with posterior urethral valves? *Journal of Pediatric Surgery, 44*(2), 417–421.

Mulac, A., Jansma, L. L., & Linz, D. G. (2002). Men's behavior toward women after viewing sexually-explicit films: Degradation makes a difference. *Communication Monographs, 69*(4), 311–328.

Mulick, P. S., & Wright, L. W., Jr. (2002). Examining the existence of biphobia in the heterosexual and homosexual populations. *Journal of Bisexuality, 2*(4), 45–64.

Mullinax, M., et al. (2016). How condom discontinuation occurs: Interviews with emerging adult women. The Journal of Sex Research, DOI: 10.1080/00224499.2016.1143440

Multidrug-resistant gonorrhea, 2012. Centers for Disease Control and Prevention. (2012). The growing threat of multidrug-resistant gonorrhea. http://www.cdc.gov/about/grand-rounds/archives/2012/May2012.htm (Accessed October 4, 2012).

Munarriz, R., et al. (2002). Androgen replacement therapy with dehydroepiandrosterone for androgen insufficiency and female sexual dysfunction: Androgen and questionnaire results. *Journal of Sex & Marital Therapy, 28*(Suppl. 1), 165–173.

Mundy, L. (2000, July 16). Sex and sensibility. *The Washington Post.* [Online].

Munro, V. E. (2006). Stopping traffic? A comparative study of responses to the trafficking in women for prostitution. *British Journal of Criminology, 46*(2), 318–333.

Murad, M. H., et al. (2010). Hormonal therapy and sex reassignment: A systematic review and meta-analysis of quality of life and psychosocial outcomes. *Clinical Endocrinology, 72*(2), 214–231.

Murphy, S. M., Vallacher, R. R., Shackelford, T. K., Bjorklund, D. F., & Yunger, J. L. (2006). Relationship experience as a predictor of romantic jealousy. *Personality and Individual Differences, 40*(4), 761–769.

Murphy, W. D., & Page, I. J. (2008). Exhibitionism: Psychopathology and theory. In D. R. Laws & W. T. O'Donohue (Eds.), *Sexual deviance: Theory, assessment, and treatment* (2nd ed., pp. 61–75). New York: Guilford Press.

Murphy, W. D., & Page, I. J. (2012). Exhibitionism: Psychopathology and theory. I. D. R. Laws & W. T. O'Donohue (Eds.). *Sexual deviance: Theory, assessment, and treatment* (pp. 61–75). New York: Guilford Press.

Murray, S. H., & Milhausen, R. R. (2012). Sexual desire and relationship duration in young men and women. *Journal of Sex & Marital Therapy, 38*(1), 28–40.

Murray, S. L., & Holmes, J. G. (2000). Seeing the self through a partner's eyes: Why self-doubts turn into relationship insecurities. In A. Tesser, R. B. Felson, et al. (Eds.), *Psychological perspectives on self and identity* (pp. 173–197). Washington, DC: American Psychological Association.

Murray, S. L., Bellavia, G., Feeney, B., Holmes, J. G., & Rose, P. (2001). The contingencies of interpersonal acceptance: When romantic relationships function as a self-affirmational resource. *Motivation & Emotion, 25*(2), 163–189.

Murray, S. O., & Roscoe, W. (1997). *Islamic homosexualities: Culture, history, and literature.* New York: New York University Press.

Myers, J. E., Madathil, J., & Tingle, L. R. (2005). Marriage satisfaction and wellness in India and the United States: A preliminary comparison of arranged marriages and marriages of choice. *Journal of Counseling & Development, 83*(2), 183–190.

Myers, S. M. (2006). Religious homogamy and marital quality: Historical and generational patterns, 1980–1997. *Journal of Marriage and the Family, 68*(2), 292–304.

Myers, S. Myers, J. E., Madathil, J., & Tingle, L. R. (2005). Marriage satisfaction and wellness in India and the United States: A preliminary comparison of arranged marriages and marriages of choice. *Journal of Counseling & Development, 83*(2), 183–190.

Nagourney, A. (2009, April 29). Signs GOP is re-thinking stance on gay marriage. *The New York Times,* p. A15.

Najdowski, C. J., Cleary, H. M. D., & Stevenson, M. C. (2015, September 7). Adolescent sex offender registration policy: Perspectives on general deterrence potential from criminology and developmental psychology. *Psychology, Public Policy, and Law, 22*(1), 114–125.

Najman, J. M., Dunne, M. P., Purdie, D. M., Boyle, F. M., & Coxeter, P. D. (2005). Sexual abuse in childhood and sexual dysfunction in adulthood: An Australian population-based study. *Archives of Sexual Behavior, 34*(5), 517–526.

Nakaya, M. (2002). Fluvoxamine treatment of a Japanese patient with Koro. *Journal of Clinical Psychiatry, 63*(12), 1182–1183.

Nanda, S., & Warms, R. L. (2004). *Cultural anthropology* (8th ed.). Belmont, CA: Wadsworth.

Nappi, R. E., & Albani, F. (2016). Sexual dysfunction in 2015: Recovering sex drive in women—progress and opportunities. *Nature Reviews Urology, 13,* 67-68.

Nappi, R. E., & Nappi, G. (2012). Neuroendocrine aspects of migraine in women. *Gynecological Endocrinology, 28*(1), 37–41.

Nappi, R. E., Wawra, K., & Schmitt, S. (2006). Hypoactive sexual desire disorder in postmenopausal women. *Gynecological Endocrinology, 22*(6), 318–323.

Narchi, H. (2003). Infantile masturbation mimicking paroxysmal disorders. *Journal of Pediatric Neurology, 1*(1), 43–45.

National Campaign to Prevent Teen and Unplanned Pregnancy. (2012). Counting it up: The public costs of teen childbearing: Key data. Washington, DC: The National Campaign to Prevent Teen and Unplanned Pregnancy. Available from http://www.thenationalcampaign.org/costs/pdf/counting-it-up/key-data.pdf (Accessed September 23, 2012).

National Campaign to Prevent Teen Pregnancy. (2003, September 30). *Teens say parents most influence their sexual decisions: New polling data and "Tips for Parents" released.* www.teenpregnancy.org/about/announcements/pr/2003/release9_30_03.asp

National Cancer Institute. (2009). www.nci.nih.gov/

National Cancer Institute. (2012a). Breast cancer. http://www.cancer.gov/cancertopics/types/breast

National Cancer Institute. (2015). Prostate Cancer. Risk Factors. http://www.cancer.gov/cancertopics/wyntk/prostate/page4

National Center for Biotechnology Information (NCBI). (2006, February 1). National Institute of Health. [Online]. www.ncbi.nlm.nih.gov/entrez/query.fcgi?=CMD=Search&db=homologene&term=SRY.

National Institute of Alcohol Abuse and Alcoholism. (2005). Apparent per capita ethanol consumption for the United States, 1850–2002. [Gallons of ethanol, based on population age 15 and older prior to 1970 and on population age 14 and older thereafter]. www.niaaa.nih.gov/databases/consum01.htm.

National Institute of Allergy and Infectious Diseases. (2009, July 14). Herpevac trial for women. (Accessed November 2, 2009). http://www3.niaid.nih.gov/topics/genitalHerpes/research/herpevac/default.htm.

National Institute of Population and Social Security Research. Population statistics of Japan 2008. Accessed May 13, 2009. http://www.ipss.go.jp/indexe.html.

National Science Foundation. (2007). The General Social Survey. Arlington, VA: National Science Foundation. http://www.nsf.gov/pubs/2007/nsf0748/nsf0748.pdf.

National Sexual Violence Resource Center. (2015). Statistics about sexual violence. http://www.nsvrc.org/sites/default/files/publications_nsvrc_factsheet_media-packet_statistics-about-sexual-violence_0.pdf (Accessed July 18,2016)

National Stepfamily Resource Center. (2015). Stepfamily Fact Sheet. http://www.stepfamilies.info/stepfamily-fact-sheet.php (Accessed October 5, 2015)

National Vital Statistics Report, 2016, Vol. 65(3), Table I-5. http://www.cdc.gov/nchs/data/nvsr/nvsr65/nvsr65_03_tables.pdf

Natsuaki, M. N., Leve, L. D., & Mendle, J. (2011). Going through the rites of passage: Timing and transition of menarche, childhood sexual abuse, and anxiety symptoms in girls. *Journal of Youth and Adolescence, 40*(10), 1357–1370.

Nduati, R., et al. (2000). Effect of breastfeeding and formula feeding on transmission of HIV-1. *Journal of the American Medical Association, 283,* 1167–1174.

Neerman-Arbez, M. (2003, June 4). Genes implicated in sexual differentiation. Geneva Foundation for Medical Education and Research. www.gfmer.ch/Endo/Lectures_10/Sexualdi.htm.

Nelson, A. L., & Russo, J. (2016). Barrier contraceptives. *The handbook of contraception* (pp. 181–202). Switzerland: Springer International Publishing.

Nemoto, T., Iwamoto, M., Wong, S., Le, M. N., & Operario, D. (2004). Social factors related to risk for violence and sexually transmitted infections/HIV among Asian massage parlor workers in San Francisco. *AIDS and Behavior, 8*(4), 475–483.

Nemoto, T., et al. (2014). Contexts of HIV-related risk behaviors among male customers at Asian massage parlors in San Francisco. *ISRN Infectious Diseases,* DOI: 10.1155/2014/934839

Newman, G. A. (2006). Woman's place or women's spaces: Intertwining history, herstory, and Christianity. In C. K. Robertson (Ed.), *Religion & sexuality: Passionate debates* (pp. 65–76). New York: Peter Lang Publishing.

Newman, L. (2012). Questions about gender: Children with atypical gender development. *Disorders of Sex Development, 31*–39. DOI:10.1007/978-3-642-22964-0_4

Newman, T. (2009). Cited in Monica Davey. (2009, June 7). Closed clinic leaves abortion protesters at a loss. *The New York Times.*

Nield, J., Magnusson, B., Brooks, C., Chapman, D., & Lapane, K. L. (2015). Sexual discordance and sexual partnering among heterosexual women. *Archives of Sexual Behavior, 44*(4), 885–894.

Nieschlag, E., et al. (2012). *Testosterone, fourth edition.* New York: Cambridge University Press.

Nieto, J. J., Cogswell, D., Jesinger, D., & Hardiman, P. (2000). Lipid effects of hormone replacement therapy with sequential transdermal 17-beta-estradiol and oral dydrogesterone. *Obstetrics & Gynecology, 95,* 111–114.

NISVS. (2011, December 14). Centers for Disease Control and Prevention. The National Intimate Partner and Sexual Violence Survey (NISVS). http://www.cdc.gov/ViolencePrevention/NISVS/index.html (Accessed July 16, 2012).

NISVS (2015). *The National Intimate Partner and Sexual Violence Survey.* Atlanta, GA: Centers for Disease Control and Prevention. Injury Prevention and Control: Division of Violence Prevention. http://www.cdc.gov/violenceprevention/nisvs/

Niu, Z., et al. (2015). Placenta mediates the association between maternal second-hand smoke exposure during pregnancy and small for gestational age. *Placenta,* DOI: 10.1016/j.placenta.2015.05.005

Njus, D. M., & Bane, C. M. H. (2009). Religious identification as a moderator of evolved sexual strategies of men and women. *Journal of Sex Research,* DOI: 10.1080/00224490902867855

Nobre, P. J., & Pinto-Gouveia, J. (2006). Dysfunctional sexual beliefs as vulnerability factors for sexual dysfunction. *Journal of Sex Research, 43*(1), 68–75.

Noller, P. (2012). Conflict in family relationships. In P. Noller & G. C. Karantzas (Eds.). *The Wiley-Blackwell handbook of couples and family relationships* (pp. 129–143). Chichester, UK: Wiley.

North American Menopause Society. (2013). Management of symptomatic vulvovaginal atrophy: 2013 position statement of the North American Menopause Society. *Menopause: The Journal of the North American Menopause Society, 20*(9), 888–902.

Norton-Hawk, M. (2004). A comparison of pimp- and non-pimp-controlled women. *Violence Against Women, 10*(2), 189–194.

Nosek, M. A. (2005). Wellness in the context of disability. In J. E. Myers & T. J. Sweeney, (Eds.), *Counseling for wellness: Theory, research, and practice* (pp. 139–150). Alexandria, VA: American Counseling Association.

Nosek, M. A. (2011). The person with a disability. In D. R. Maki, & V. M. Tarvydas (Eds.). *The professional practice of rehabilitation counseling* (pp. 111–130). New York: Springer.

Nosek, M. A., et al. (2004). The meaning of health for women with physical disabilities: A qualitative analysis. *Family & Community Health, 27*(1), 6–21.

Nour, N. M. (2000). Female circumcision and genital mutilation: A practical and sensitive approach. *Contemporary OB/GYN, 45*(3), 50–55.

Novotny, R., et al. (2011). Puberty, body fat, and breast density in girls of several ethnic groups. *American Journal of Human Biology, 23*(3), 359–365.

Nurnberg, H. G., et al. (2008). Sildenafil treatment of women with antidepressant-associated sexual dysfunction: A randomized controlled trial. *Journal of the American Medical Association, 300*(4), 395–404.

Nussbaum, M. A. (2012, April 19). Ignore the stigma and focus on the need. *The New York Times.* http://www.nytimes.com/roomfordebate/2012/04/19/is-legalized-prostitution-safer/ignore-the-stigma-of-prostitution-and-focus-on-the-need (Accessed July 13, 2016).

Nuttbrock, L., et al. (2011). A further assessment of Blanchard's typology of homosexual versus non-homosexual or autogynephilic gender dysphoria. *Archives of Sexual Behavior, 40*(2), 247–257.

Oakley, S. H., et al. (2013). Innervation and histology of the clitoral–urethral complex: A cross-sectional cadaver study. *The Journal of Sexual Medicine, 10*(9), 2211–2218.

O'Dell, K. M. C., & Kaiser, K. (1997). Sexual behaviour: Secrets and flies. *Current Biology, 7*(6), R345–R347.

O'Doherty, J., et al. (2003a). Beauty in a smile: The role of medial orbitofrontal cortex in facial attractiveness. *Neuropsychologia, 41*(2), 147–155.

O'Donnell, L., et al. (2003b). Long-term influence of sexual norms and attitudes on timing of sexual initiation among urban minority youth. *Journal of School Health, 23*(2), 68–75.

O'Donohue, W., Yeater, E. A., & Fanetti, M. (2003). Rape prevention with college males: The roles of rape myth acceptance, victim empathy, and outcome expectancies. *Journal of Interpersonal Violence, 18*(5), 513–531.

O'Donohue, W. T. (2014). *Case studies in sexual deviance.* New York: Routledge.

Office of Minority Health & Health Disparities. (2010). Eliminate disparities in HIV and AIDS. Retrieved from http://www.cdc.gov/omhd/amh/factsheets/hiv.htm. Accessed February 14, 2016.

O'Hara, M. W., & McCabe, J. E. (2013). Postpartum depression: Current status and future directions. *Annual Review of Clinical Psychology, 9,* 379–407.

O'Keeffe, M. J., et al. (2003). Learning, cognitive, and attentional problems in adolescents born small for gestational age. *Pediatrics, 112*(2), 301–307.

O'Sullivan, L. F. (2003). The development of romantic relationships in adolescence. *Archives of Sexual Behavior, 32*(3), 292–294.

Obald, F. P. (2012). Sigmund Freud and Otto Rank: Debates and confrontations about anxiety and birth. *The International Journal of Psychoanalysis, 93*(3), 449–471.

Ofer, D., & Weitzman, L. (Eds.). (1998). *Women in the Holocaust.* New Haven, CT: Yale University Press.

Oguz, N., & Uygur, N. (2005). A case of diaper fetishism. *Türk Psikiyatri Dergisi, 16*(2), 133–138.

Ohly, N. T., & Westhof, C. L. (2016). Intrauterine contraception: Comparison of the copper T intrauterine device with the Levonorgestrel intrauterine systems. In D. Shoupe, & D. R. Mishell (Eds.). *The handbook of contraception* (pp. 165–180). Switzerland: Springer International Publishing.

Okami, P., Weisner, T., & Olmstead, R. (2002). Outcome correlates of parent–child bedsharing: An eighteen-year longitudinal study. *Journal of Developmental & Behavioral Pediatrics, 23*(4), 244–253.

Olds, J. (1956). Pleasure centers in the brain. *Scientific American, 193,* 105–116.

Olds, J., & Milner, P. (1954). Positive reinforcement produced by electrical stimulation of the septal area and other regions of the rat brain. *Journal of Comparative and Physiological Psychology, 47,* 419–427.

Oleksyk, T. K., et al. (2009, March 19). Extended IL10 haplotypes and their association with HIV progression to AIDS. *Genes and Immunity, 10*(4), 309–322.

Olfson, M., Uttaro, T., Carson, W. H., & Tafesse, E. (2005). Male sexual dysfunction and quality of life in schizophrenia. *Journal of Clinical Psychiatry, 66*(3), 331–338.

Olshen, E., et al. (2006). Use of human immunodeficiency virus postexposure prophylaxis in adolescent sexual assault victims. *Archives of Pediatric Adolescent Medicine, 160,* 674–680.

Ompad, D. C., et al. (2006). Predictors of early initiation of vaginal and oral sex among urban young adults in Baltimore, Maryland. *Archives of Sexual Behavior, 35*(1), 53–65.

Orchowski, L. M., Mastroleo, N. R., & Borsari, B. (2012). Correlates of alcohol-related sex among college students. *Psychology of Addictive Behaviors.* DOI:10.1037/a0027840

Ortega, V., Ojeda, P., Sutil, F., & Sierra, J. C. (2005). Culpabilidad sexual en adolescentes: Estudio de algunos factores relacionados. *Anales de Psicología, 21*(2), 268–275.

Osman, S. L. (2003). Predicting men's rape perceptions based on the belief that "no" really means "yes." *Journal of Applied Social Psychology, 33*(4), 683–692.

Ostrzenski, A. (2011). Cosmetic gynecology in the view of evidence-based medicine and ACOG recommendations: A review. *Archives of Gynecology and Obstetrics, 284*(3), 61–630.

Ostrzenski, A. (2015). Author's comment: A report from #BlueJC: Does the G-spot exist? *BJOG: An International Journal of Obstetrics and Gynaecology, 122*(4), 598.

Osuch, J. R., et al. (2010). Association of age at menarche with adult leg length and trunk height: Speculations in relation to breast cancer risk. *Annals of Human Biology, 37*(1), 76–85.

Oswald, R. F., et al. (2013). LGB families in community context. In A. E Goldberg, & K. R. Allen (Eds.). *LGBT-parent families: Innovations in research and implications for practice* (pp. 193–208). New York: Springer Science+Business Media.

Owens, E. W., Behun, R. J., Manning, J. C., & Reid, R. C. (2012). The impact of Internet pornography on adolescents: Review of the research. *Sexual Addiction & Compulsivity: The Journal of Treatment & Prevention, 19*(2), 99–122.

Owings, M., Uddin, S., & Williams, S. (2013). Trends in circumcision for male newborns in U.S. hospitals: 1979–2010. http://www.cdc.gov/nchs/data/hestat/circumcision_2013/circumcision_2013.htm

Pace, C. S., Cavanna, D., Velotti, P., & Zavattini, G. S. (2014). Attachment representations in late-adopted children. *Adoption & Fostering, 38*(3), 255–270.

Pace, C. S., et al. (2015). Adoptive parenting and attachment: Association of the internal working models between adoptive mothers and their late-adopted children during adolescence. *Frontiers in Psychology,* DOI: 10.3389/fpsyg.2015.01433

Pacik, P. T. (2015). Understanding and treating vaginismus: A multimodal approach. *Obstetrical & Gynecological Survey, 70*(5), 314–316.

Pagliery, J. (2015, August 21). The Ashley Madison hack ruined my life. CNNMoney. http://money.cnn.com/2015/08/21/technology/ashley-madison-ruined-lives/

Paintner, A., Williams, A. D., & Burd, L. (2012). Fetal alcohol spectrum disorders—Implications for child neurology,Part 2: Diagnosis and management. *Journal of Child Neurology, 27*(3), 355–362.

Pakhomou, S. M. (2006). Methodological aspects of telephone scatologia: A case study. *International Journal of Law and Psychiatry, 29*(3), 178–185.

Palace, E. M. (1995). Modification of dysfunctional patterns of sexual arousal through autonomic arousal and false physiological feedback. *Journal of Consulting and Clinical Psychology, 63*, 604–615.

Palefsky, J. M., et al. (2011). HPV vaccine against anal HPV infection and anal intraepithelial neoplasia. *New England Journal of Medicine, 365*, 1576.

Pan, S., Leung, C., Shah, J., & Kilchevsky, A. (2015). Clinical anatomy of the G-spot. *Clinical Anatomy, 28*(3), 363–367.

Parent, C., & Bruckert, C. (2005). Sex work in establishments offering erotic services: A form of marginalised work. *Déviance et Société, 29*(1), 33–53.

Parent, M. C., Moradi, B., Rummell, C. M., & Tokar, D. M. (2011). Evidence of construct distinctiveness for conformity to masculine norms. *Psychology of Men and Masculinity, 12*(4), 354–367.

Parent, M. C., Torrey, C., & Michaels, M. S. (2012). "HIV testing is so gay": The role of masculine gender role conformity in HIV testing. *Journal of Counseling Psychology, 59*(3), 465–470.

Park, C. L., Edmonson, D., & Lee, J. (2012). Development of self-regulation abilities as predictors of psychological adjustment across the first year of college. *Journal of Adult Development, 19*(1), 40–49.

Park, N., Jin, B., & Jin, S. A. (2011). Effects of self-disclosure on relational intimacy in Facebook. *Computers in Human Behavior, 27*(5), 1974–1983.

Parker-Pope, T. (2008a, October 27). Love, sex and the changing landscape of infidelity. *The New York Times.* http://www.nytimes.com/2008/10/28/health/28well.html (Accessed July 13, 2016).

Parker-Pope, T. (2008b, February 5). No answers for men with prostate cancer. *The New York Times.* http://well.blogs.nytimes.com/2008/02/05/no-answers-for-men-with-prostate-cancer/(Accessed July 13, 2016).

Parker-Pope, T. (2009a, March 24). Screen or not? What those prostate studies mean. *The New York Times.* http://www.nytimes.com/2009/03/24/health/24well.html (Accessed July 13, 2016).

Parker-Pope, T. (2009b, May 28). Study urges weight gain be curbed in pregnancy. *The New York Times.* http://www.nytimes.com/2009/05/29/health/research/29pregnant.html (Accessed July 13, 2016).

Parker-Pope, T. (2014, August 6). Prostate cancer screening still not recommended for all. *The New York Times.* http://well.blogs.nytimes.com/2014/08/06/prostate-cancer-screening-still-not-recommended-for-all/(Accessed July 13, 2016).

Parner, E. T., et al. (2012). Parental age and autism spectrum disorders. *Annals of Epidemiology, 22*(3), 143–150.

Parrott, D., Zeichner, A., & Hoover, R. (2006). Sexual prejudice and anger network activation: Mediating role of negative affect. *Aggressive Behavior, 32*(1), 7–16.

Parsons, N. K., Richards, H. C., & Kanter, G. D. (1990). Validation of a scale to measure reasoning about abortion. *Journal of Counseling Psychology, 37*, 107–112.

Passolunghi, M. C., Ferreira, T. I. R., & Tomasetto, C. (2014). Math-gender stereotypes and math-related beliefs in childhood and early adolescence. *Learning and Individual Differences, 34*, 70–76.

Pasupathy, D., & Smith, G. C. (2005). The analysis of factors predicting antepartum stillbirth. *Minerva Ginecology, 57*(4), 397–410.

Path2Parenthood, 2016. www.path2parenthood.org. Accessed various dates in 2016.

Patrick, M. E., & Schulenberg, J. E. (2011). How trajectories of reasons for alcohol use relate to trajectories of binge drinking: National panel data spanning late adolescence to early adulthood. *Developmental Psychology, 47*(2), 311–317.

Patterson, C. J. (2006). Children of lesbian and gay parents. *Current Directions in Psychological Science, 15*(5), 241–244.

Patterson, C. J., & Farr, R. H. (2011). Coparenting among lesbian and gay couples. In J. P. McHale, & K. M. Lindahl (Eds.). *Coparenting: A conceptual and clinical examination of family systems* (pp. 127–146). Washington, DC: American Psychological Association.

Paul, B., & Shim, J. W. (2008). Gender, sexual affect, and motivations for Internet pornography use. *International Journal of Sexual Health, 20*(3), 187–199.

Pauleta, J. R., Pereira, N. M., & Graca, L. M. (2010). Sexuality during pregnancy. *Journal of Sexual Medicine, 7,* 136–142.

Pauls, R. N. (2015). Anatomy of the clitoris and female sexual response. *Clinical Anatomy, 28*(3), 376–384.

Pause, B. M. (2012). Processing of body odor signals by the human brain. *Chemosensory Perception, 5*(1), 55–63.

Paz-Bailey, G., et al. (2013). HIV testing and risk behaviors among gay, bisexual, and other men who have sex with men—United States. *Morbidity and Mortality Weekly Report, 62*(47), 958–962.

Peaceman, A. M., et al. (2009). Previous preterm cesarean delivery and risk of subsequent uterine rupture. *Obstetric Anesthesia Digest, 29*(2), 69–70.

Pear, R. (2012, January 20). U.S. denies exemption sought by Church on coverage for contraceptives. *The New York Times,* p. A17.

Pedersen, W., & Hegna, K. (2003). Children and adolescents who sell sex: A community study. *Social Science & Medicine, 56*(1), 135–147.

Peluso, P. R. (Ed.). (2008). *Infidelity.* Danvers, MA: CRC Press.

Pelvic inflammatory disease, 2011. Centers for Disease Control and Prevention. (2011). Sexually transmitted diseases. Pelvic inflammatory disease (PID)—CDC fact sheet. http://www.cdc.gov/std/PID/STDFact-PID.htm (Accessed October 4, 2012).

Peplau, L. A. (2003). Human sexuality: How do men and women differ? *Current Directions in Psychological Science, 12*(2), 37–40.

Perelman, M. A., & Rowland, D. L. (2008). Retarded and inhibited ejaculation. In D. L. Rowland & L. Incrocci (Eds.), *Handbook of sexual and gender identity disorders* (pp. 100–121). Hoboken, NJ: Wiley.

Peris, A. (2006, February 8). *Fertilitext: At the pharmacy: OTC.* www.fertilitext.org/p3_pharmacy/OTCproducts.html.

Perlman, D., & Sprecher, S. (2012). Sex, intimacy, and dating. In R. D. McAnulty (Ed.). *Sex in college: The things they don't write home about* (pp. 91–118). Santa Barbara, CA: ABC-CLIO, LLC.

Perlroth, N. (2015, August 28). Ashley Madison chief steps down after data breach. *The New York Times,* http://www.nytimes.com/2015/08/29/technology/ashley-madison-ceo-steps-down-after-data-hack.html?hp&action=click&pgtype=Homepage&module=second-column-region&region=top-news&WT.nav=top-news&_r=0 (Accessed July 13, 2016).

Perovic, S. V. (2015). Vaginoplasty in male transsexuals using penile skin and urethral flap. In C. Trombetta et al. (Eds.). *Management of gender dysphoria* (pp. 105–115). Milan, Italy: Sprinter-Verlag Italia.

Perrin, M. C., Brown, A. S., & Malaspina, D. (2007, August 21). Aberrant epigenetic regulation could explain the relationship of paternal age to schizophrenia. *Schizophrenia Bulletin online.* http://schizophreniabulletin.oxfordjournals.org/cgi/content/abstract/sbm093v1.

Perry, J. D., & Whipple, B. (1981). Pelvic muscle strength of female ejaculation: Evidence in support of a new theory of orgasm. *Journal of Sex Research, 17*, 22–39.

Perry, P. J., et al. (2001). Bioavailable testosterone as a correlate of cognition, psychological status, quality of life, and sexual function in aging males: Implications for testosterone replacement therapy. *Annals of Clinical Psychiatry, 13*(2), 75–80.

Petersen, J. L., & Hyde, J. S. (2011). Gender differences in sexual attitudes and behaviors: A review of meta-analytic results and large datasets. *Journal of Sex Research, 48*(2–3), 149–165.

Petersen, J., & Hyde, J. S. (2010). Gender differences in sexuality. *Handbook of Gender Research in Psychology, 6*, 471–491.

Peterson, C. K., & Harmon-Jones, E. (2011). Anger and testosterone: Evidence that situationally-induced anger related to situationally-induced testosterone. *Emotion*, DOI:10.1037/a0025300

Peterson, Z. D., Voller, E. K., Polusny, M. A., & Murdoch, M. (2010). Prevalence and consequences of adult sexual assault of men: Review of empirical findings and state of the literature. *Clinical Psychology Review, 31*, 1–24.

Petrusich, A. (2015, June). Free to be Miley. *Paper magazine.* http://www.papermag.com/2015/06/miley_cyrus_happy_hippie_foundation.php (Accessed July 13, 2016).

Pew Research Center. (2015, July 29). Changing attitudes on gay marriage. http://www.pewforum.org/2015/07/29/graphics-slide-show-changing-attitudes-on-gay-marriage/

Phenix, A., & Hoberman, H. M. (2016). *Sexual offending.* New York: Springer Science+Business.

Philaretou, A. G. (2006). Female exotic dancers: Intrapersonal and interpersonal perspectives. *Sexual Addiction & Compulsivity, 13*(1), 41–52.

Phillip, A., & Larimer, S. (2015). Jared Fogle charged with paying for sex with minors, possessing child porn. *Washington Post,* http://www.washingtonpost.com/news/morning-mix/wp/2015/08/19/jared-fogle-ex-subway-spokesman-faces-child-sex-and-child-pornography-charges/(Accessed July 13, 2016).

Phillips, K. (2009, November 18). Sebelius on mammograms: Don't change what you're doing. *The New York Times* http://prescriptions.blogs.nytimes.com/2009/11/18/health-secretary-on-breast-cancer-screenings-dont-change-what-youre-doing/(Accessed July 13, 2016).

Phipps, A. I., et al. (2011). Long-term use of continuous-combined estrogen-progestin hormone therapy and the risk of endometrial cancer. *Cancer Causes and Control, 22*(2), 1639–1646.

Phoenix, C. H. (2009). Organizing action of prenatally administered testosterone propionate on the tissues mediating mating behavior in the female guinea pig. *Hormones and Behavior, 55*(5), 566.

Pierce, A., Miller, G., Arden, R., & Gottfredson, L. S. (2009). Why is intelligence correlated with semen quality? *Communicative and Integrative Biology, 2*(5), 1–3.

Pike, L. B. (2005, July 1). *Sexuality and your child.* MU Extension, University of Missouri–Columbia.

Pines, H. A., et al. (2015). Individual-level, partnership-level, and sexual event-level predictors of condom use during receptive anal intercourse among HIV-negative men who have sex with men in Los Angeles. *AIDS and Behavior,* 1–15., DOI: 10.1007/s10461-015-1218-4

Pinkerton, S. D., Bogart, L. M., Cecil, H., & Abramson, P. R. (2002). Factors associated with masturbation in collegiate sample. *Journal of Psychology & Human Sexuality, 14*(2–3), 103–121.

Pitt, J. S., Vaughn, M., Shamburger-Rousseau, A., & Harris, L. L. (2015). Black women in academia: The invisible life. In J. L. Martin (Ed.). *Racial battle fatigue: Insights from the front lines of social justice advocacy* (pp. 209–224). Santa Barbara, CA: ABC-CLIO, LLC.

Pitt, A. J. (2015, March 24). Angelina Jolie Pitt: Diary of a surgery. *The New York Times,* p. A23.

Planned Parenthood Federation of America. (2006). www.plannedparenthood.org/pp2/portal.

Plant, E. A., Hyde, J. S., Keltner, D., & Devine, P. G. (2000). The gender stereotyping of emotions. *Psychology of Women Quarterly, 24*(1), 81–92.

Plante, R. F. (2006). The rise of Viagra: How the little blue pill changed sex in America. *Sexualities, 9*(3), 379–380.

Plaut, S. M. (2006). Consent to sexual relations. *Archives of Sexual Behavior, 35*(1), 101–103.

Pliny the Elder, Latin Library, 1 Ad–100 AD, Prose, *Natural history.* Harvard University Press., Loeb Classical Library, p. 549.

Plomin, R., & Asbury, K. (2005). Nature and nurture: Genetic and environmental influences on behavior. *Annals of the American Academy of Political and Social Science, 600,* 86–98.

Polansky, D. C. (2006). The big book of masturbation: From angst to zeal. *Journal of Sex & Marital Therapy, 32*(1), 75–78.

Poll shows decline in sex by high school students. (1998, September 18). *The New York Times,* p. A26.

Pollack, A. (2009, April 14). Promising test for Dendreon's prostate cancer drug. *The New York Times.* http://www.nytimes.com/2009/04/15/business/15cancer.html (Accessed July 13, 2016).

Pollack, H. A. (2001). Sudden infant death syndrome, maternal smoking during pregnancy, and the cost-effectiveness of smoking cessation intervention. *American Journal of Public Health, 91*(3), 432–436.

Polusny, M. A., & Arbisi, P. A. (2006). Assessment of psychological distress and disability after sexual assault in adults. In G. Young et al. (Eds.), *Psychological knowledge in court: PTSD, pain, and TBI* (pp. 97–125). Springer Science + Business Media.

Pomara, C., et al. (2015). Ethical issues for the practitioner work in transgender care. In. C. Trombetta et al. (Eds.). *Management of gender dysphoria* (pp. 325–335). Milan, Italy: Sprinter-Verlag Italia.

Pommier, C. D., et al. (2008). Improved breast cancer survival among hormone replacement therapy users is durable after 5 years of additional follow-up. *American Journal of Surgery, 196,* 505–511.

Poppen, P. J., et al. (2005). Serostatus disclosure, seroconcordance, partner relationship, and unprotected anal intercourse among HIV-positive Latino men who have sex with men. *AIDS Education and Prevention, 17*(3), 227–237.

Porst, H., et al. (2007). The Prematre Ejaculation Prevalence and Attituides (PEPA) survey: Prevalence, comorbidities, and professional help-seeking. *European Urology, 51*(3), 816–824.

Porst, H., et al. (2008). The Premature Ejaculation Prevalence and Attitudes (PEPA) Survey: Prevalence, comorbidities, and professional help-seeking. *European Urology, 51*(3), 816–824.

Potosky, A. L., et al. (2000). Health outcomes after prostatectomy or radiotherapy for prostate cancer: Results from the Prostate Cancer Outcomes Study. *Journal of the National Cancer Institute, 92,* 1582–1592.

Potter, S. J., et al. (2009). Empowering bystanders to prevent campus violence against women. *Violence Against Women, 15*(1), 106–121.

Potts, A., Grace, V. M., Vares, T., & Gavey, N. (2006). "Sex for life?" Men's counter-stories on "erectile dysfunction," male sexuality and ageing. *Sociology of Health & Illness, 28*(3), 306–329.

Potts, M. (2006). China's one child policy. *British Medical Journal, 333,* 361–362.

Powell, E. (1991). *Talking back to sexual pressure.* Minneapolis: CompCare Publishers.

Pradhan, D. S., et al. (2010). Aggressive interactions rapidly increase androgen synthesis in the brain during the non-breeding season. *Hormones and Behavior, 57*(4–5), 381–389.

Pradhan, D. S., Solomon-Lane, T. K., & Grober, M. S. (2015). Contextual modulation of social and endocrine correlates of fitness: Insights from the life history of a sex changing fish. *Frontiers in Neuroscience, 9*(8), DOI: 10.3389/fnins.2015.00008

Prakash, J., et al. (2010). Does androgyny have psychoprotective attributes? A cross-sectional community-based study. *Industrial Psychiatry Journal, 19*(2), 119–124.

Prause, N., Park, J., Leung, S., & Miller, G. (2015) Women's preferences for penis size: A new research method using selection among 3D models. *PLoS ONE 10*(9): e0133079. doi:10.1371/journal.pone.0133079

Premberg, A., & Lundgren, I. (2006). Fathers' experiences of childbirth education. *Journal of Perinatal Education, 15*(2), 21–28.

Prentice, R. L., et al. (2006). Low-fat dietary pattern and risk of invasive breast cancer: The Women's Health Initiative Randomized Controlled Dietary Modification Trial. *Journal of the American Medical Association, 295,* 629–642.

Preterm J., & Valkenburg, P. M. (2011). The use of sexually explicit Internet material and its antecedents: a longitudinal comparison of adolescents and adults. *Archives of Sexual Behavior, 40*(5), 1015–1025.

Preti, G., et al. (1986). Human axillary secretions influence women's menstrual cycles: The role of donor extract of females. *Hormones and Behavior, 20,* 474–482.

Preti, G., Wysocki, C. J., Barnhart, K. T., Sondheimer, S. J., & Leyden, J. J. (2003). Male axillary extracts contain pheromones that affect pulsatile secretion of luteinizing hormone and mood in women recipients. *Biology of Reproduction, 68*(6), 2107–2113.

Price, M., Kafka, M. P., Commons, M. L., Gutheil, T. G., & Simpson, W. (2002). Telephone scatologia: Comorbidity with other paraphilias and paraphilia-related disorders. *International Journal of Law & Psychiatry, 25*(1), 37–49.

Priest, N., et al. (2014). Understanding the complexities of ethnic-racial socialization processes for both minority and majority groups: A 30-year systematic review. *International*

Journal of Intercultural Relations, DOI: 10.1016/j.jijintrel.2014.08.003

Proctor, F., Wagner, N., & Butler, J. (1974). The differentiation of male and female orgasm: An experimental study. In N. Wagner (Ed.), *Perspectives on human sexuality*. New York: Behavioral Publications.

Proulx, J., & Beauregard, E. (2014). Pathways in the offending process of marital rapists. In J. Proulx et al. (Eds.). *Pathways to sexual aggression* (pp. 110–136). New York: Routledge.

Psychology Today. (2006, July 25.) www.psychologytoday.com/images/.PT_MediaKit_Health_2006.pdf.

Public Policy Polling. (2012, February 10). Our polling on the birth control issue. http://www.publicpolicypolling.com/main/2012/02/our-polling-on-the-birth-control-issue.html. (Accessed June 23, 2012).

Puente, S., & Cohen, D. (2003). Jealousy and the meaning (or nonmeaning) of violence. *Personality & Social Psychology Bulletin, 29*(4), 449–460.

Punyanunt-Carter, N. M. (2006). An analysis of college students' self-disclosure behaviors on the Internet. *College Student Journal, 40*(2), 329–331.

Purdie, M. P., et al. (2011). The effects of acute alcohol intoxication, partner risk level, and general intention to have unprotected sex on women's sexual decision making with a new partner. *Experimental and Clinical Psychopharmacology, 19*(5), 378–388.

Puri, S., & Nachtigall, R. D. (2009). The ethics of sex selection: A comparison of the attitudes and experiences of primary care physicians and physician providers of clinical sex selection services. *Fertility and Sterility, 93*(7), 2107–2114.

Puts, D. A., Welling, L. L. M., Burriss, R. P., & Dawood, K. (2011). Men's masculinity and attractiveness predict their female partners' reported orgasm frequency and timing. *Evolution and Human Behavior, 33*(1), 1.

Puts, D. A., Welling, L. L. M., Burriss, R. P., & Dawood, K. (2012). Men's masculinity and attractiveness predict their female partners' reported orgasm frequency and timing. *Evoltuion & Human Behavior, 33*(1), 1–9.

Quartaro, G. K., & Spier, T. E. (2002). We'd like to ask you some questions, but we have to find you first: Internet-based study of lesbian clients in therapy with lesbian feminist therapists. *Journal of Technology in Human Services, 19*(2–3), 109–118.

Quayle, E. (2008). Online sex offending: Psychopathology and theory. In D. R. Laws & W. T. O'Donohue (Eds.), *Sexual deviance: Theory, assessment, and treatment* (2nd ed., pp. 439–458). New York: Guilford Press.

Quayle, E. (2012). Pedophilia, child porn, and cyberpredators. In C. D. Bryant (Ed.). *The Routledge handbook of deviant behavior* (pp. 390–396). New York: Routledge.

Quayle, E., Taylor, M. (2002). Child pornography and the Internet: Perpetuating a cycle of abuse. *Deviant Behavior, 23*(4), 331–362.

Quayle, E., Taylor, M. (2003). Model of problematic Internet use in people with sexual interest in children. *CyberPsychology & Behavior, 6*(1), 93–106.

Quinsey, V. L., Harris, G. T., Rice, M. E., & Cormier, C. A. (2006). Sex offenders. In

V. L. Quinsey, G. T. Harris, M. E. Rice, & C. A. Cormier (Eds.), *Violent offenders: Appraising and managing risk. The law and public policy* (2nd ed. pp. 131–151). Washington, DC: American Psychological Association.

Rabin, R. (2006, January 31). Rethinking hormones, again. *The New York Times*. http://www.nytimes.com/2006/01/31/health/science/rethinking-hormones-again.html (Accessed July 13, 2016).

Rabin, R. C. (2011, December 14). Nearly 1 in 5 women in U.S. survey say they have been sexually assaulted. *The New York Times*, p. A32.

Ragsdale, K., et al. (2012). High-risk drinking among female college drinkers at two reporting intervals: Comparing Spring Break to the 30 days prior. *Sexuality Research and Social Policy, 9*(1), 31–40.

Rahimi, R., & Liston, D. D. (2012). *Pervasive vulnerabilities: Sexual harassment in school.* New York: Peter Lang.

Raichle, K., & Lambert, A. J. (2000). The role of political ideology in mediating judgments of blame in rape victims and their assailants: A test of the just world, personal responsibility, and legitimization hypotheses. *Personality & Social Psychology Bulletin, 26*(7), 853–863.

Rakic, Z., Starcevic, V., Starcevic, V. P., & Marinkovic, J. (1997). Testosterone treatment in men with erectile disorder and low levels of total testosterone in serum. *Archives of Sexual Behavior, 26*(5), 495–504.

Rako, S. (2003). *No more periods? The risks of menstrual suppression and other cutting-edge issues about hormones and women's health.* New York: Crown.

Ralph, D., & McNicholas, T. (2000). UK management guidelines for erectile dysfunction. *British Medical Journal, 321*, 499–503.

Ramasamy, R., Wilken, N., Scovell, J. M., Kovac, J. R., & Lipschultz, L. I. (2014). Hypogonadal symptoms are associated with different serum testosterone thresholds in middle-aged and elderly men. *Urology, 84*, 1378–1382.

Rambo, C., & Pruit, J. (2012). In C. D. Bryant (Ed.). *The Routledge handbook of deviant behavior* (pp. 397–402). New York: Routledge.

Ramos, N. (2012, April 19). Such oppression can never be safe. *The New York Times*.

Randolph, M. E., et al. (2009). Alcohol use and sexual risk behavior among college students. *American Journal of Drug and Alcohol Abuse, 35*(2), 80–84.

Rani, S., & Sharma, V. (2015). Honour killing—Killing humanity. *Journal of Psychiatric Nursing, 4*(1), 27–30.

Raphael, J., & Shapiro, D. L. (2005). Reply to Weitzer. *Violence Against Women, 11*(7), 965–970.

Rasmussen, K. M., et al. (2009, May 27). Institute of Medicine report. In T. Parker-Pope, Study urges weight gain be curbed in pregnancy. *The New York Times*, May 28.

Rasmussen, P. R., & Kilborne, K. J. (2008). Sex in intimate relationships: Variations and challenges. In P. R. Peluso (Ed.), *Infidelity: A practitioner's guide to working with couples in crisis* (pp. 11–30). New York: Routledge.

Rathus, S. A. (2017). *Childhood and Adolescence: Voyages in development.* (6th ed.) Belmont, CA: Cengage.

Rathus, S. A. (2014). *Childhood and adolescence: Voyages in development* (5th ed.). Belmont, CA: Cengage.

Ratnayake, H. (2011, April 29). Co-sleeping with infants can be risky, experts say. *USA Today*.

Rawson, R. A., Washton, A., Domier, C. P., & Reiber, C. (2002). Drugs and sexual effects: Role of drug type and gender. *Journal of Substance Abuse Treatment, 22*(2), 103–108.

Reddy, D. M., et al. (2002). Effect of mandatory parental notification on adolescent girls' use of sexual health care services. *Journal of the American Medical Association, 288*, 710–714.

Reddy, R. C., et al. (2015). Effect of testosterone on neuronal morphology and neuritic growth of fetal lamb hypothalamus-preoptic area and cerebral cortex in primary culture. *PLoS ONE*, DOI: 10.1371/journal.pone.0129521

Reece, M., et al. (2009). Prevalence and characteristics of vibrator use by men in the United States. *Journal of Sexual Medicine, 6*(7), 1867–1874.

Reece, M., et al. (2010a). Background and considerations on the National Survey of Sexual Health and Behavior (NSSHB) from the investigators. *Journal of Sexual Medicine, 7*(suppl 5), 243–245.

Reece, M., et al. (2010b). Sexual behaviors, relationships, and perceived health among adult men in the United States: Results from a national probability sample. *Journal of Sexual Medicine, 7*(suppl 5), 291–304.

Reece, et al. (2010c). Sexual behaviors, relationships, and perceived health among adult men in the United States: Results from a national probability sample. *Journal of Sexual Medicine, 7*(suppl 5), 291–304.

Reece, M., Herbenick, D., Schick, V., Sanders, S. A., & Fortenberry, J. D. (2014). Men's use and perceptions of commercial lubricants: prevalence and characteristics in a nationally representative sample of US adults. *Journal of Sexual Medicine.* DOI:10.1111/jsm.12480. PMID:24612606

Reed, J. B., et al. (2015). Implementation and operational research: Evaluation of loss-to-follow-up and postoperative adverse events in a voluntary male circumcision program in Nyanza Province, Kenya. *Journal of Acquired Immune Deficiency Syndromes, 69*(1), e13–e23.

Reed, M., & Lampe, M. S. (2003). *Margaret Sanger: Her life in her words.* Barricade Books.

Reed, S. C., Levin, F. R., & Evans, S. M. (2008). Changes in mood, cognitive performance and appetite in the late luteal and follicular phases of the menstrual cycle in women with and without PMDD (premenstrual dysphoric disorder). *Hormones and Behavior, 54*(1), 185–193.

Regnerus, M. (2012). How different are the adult children of parents who have same-sex relationships? Findings from the New Family Structures Study. *Social Science Research, 41*(4), 752–770.

Rehor, J. E. (2015). Sensual, erotic, and sexual behaviors of women from the "kink" community. *Archives of Sexual Behavior, 44*(4), 825–836.

Reichenberg, A., et al. (2006). Advancing paternal age and autism. *Archives of General Psychiatry, 63*(9), 1026–1032.

Reiner, W. G. (2000). Cited in Study of children born without penises finds nature determines gender. Associated Press.

Reinisch, J. M. (1990). *The Kinsey Institute new report on sex: What you must know to be sexually literate.* New York: St. Martin's Press.

Reis, H. T., & Aron, A. (2008). Love: What is it, why does it matter, and how does it operate? *Perspectives on Psychological Science, 3*(1), 80–86.

Reis, H. T., Aron, A., Clark, M. S., & Finkel, E. J. (2013). Ellen Berscheid, Elaine Hatfield, and the emergence of relationship science. *Perspectives on Psychological Science, 8*(5), 558–572.

Reis, H. T., Maniaci, M. R., Caprariello, P. A., Eastwick, P. W., & Finkel, E. L. (2011). Familiarity does indeed promote attraction in live interaction. *Journal of Personality and Social Psychology, 101*(3), 557–570.

Reissing, E. D. (2012). Consultation and treatment history and causal attributions in an online sample of women with lifelong and acquired vaginismus. *Journal of Sexual Medicine, 9*(1), 251–258.

Renk, K., Liljequist, L., Simpson, J. E., & Phares, V. (2005). Gender and age differences in the topics of parent–adolescent conflict. *Family Journal: Counseling and Therapy for Couples and Families, 13*(2), 139–149.

Rennie, D. (2014). Grounded theory methodology. In T. Teo (Ed.). *Encyclopedia of critical psychology* (pp. 823–828). New York: Springer Science+Business Media.

Reported STDs in the United States, 2014 national data for chlamydia, gonorrhea, and syphilis. http://www.cdc.gov/std/stats14/std-trends-508.pdf

Rerks-Ngarm, S., et al. (2009). Vaccination with ALVAC and AIDSVAX to prevent HIV-1 infection in Thailand. *New England Journal of Medicine online.* www.nejm.org October 20, 2009 (10.1056/NEJMoa0908492)

Resick, P. A. (2003). Post hoc reasoning in possible cases of child sexual abuse: Just say no. *Clinical Psychology: Science & Practice, 10*(3), 349–351.

Resnik, J. (2011). Cited in Stout, H. (2011, November 6). Less "He Said, She Said" in Sex Harassment Cases. *The New York Times,* p. B10.

Reuters. (2016, June 26). Pope Francis says church should apologize to gays. *The New York Times,* p. A8.

Reynolds, A., & Caron, S. L. (2000). How intimate relationships are impacted when heterosexual men cross dress. *Journal of Psychology & Human Sexuality, 12*(3), 63–77.

Reynolds, C. A., Barlow, T., & Pedersen, N. L. (2006). Alcohol, tobacco and caffeine use: Spouse similarity processes. *Behavior Genetics, 36*(2), 201–215.

Reynolds, G. L., Fisher, D. G., & Rogala, B. (2015). Why women engage in anal intercourse: Results from a qualitative study. *Archives of Sexual Behavior, 44*(4), 983–995.

Reynolds, S. J., et al. (2004). Male circumcision and risk of HIV-1 and other sexually transmitted infections in India. *Lancet, 363*(9414), 1039.

Rhoades, G. K., Stanley, S. M., & Markman, H. J. (2009). Couples' reasons for cohabitation. *Journal of Family Issues, 30*(2), 233–258.

Ricci, E., Parazzini, F, & Pardi, G. (2000). Caesarean section and antiretroviral treatment. *Lancet, 355*(9202), 496–502.

Rice, M. E., & Harris, G. T. (2011). Is androgen deprivation therapy effective in the treatment of sex offenders? *Psychology, Public Policy, and Law, 17*(2), 315–332.

Rice, M. E., Harris, G. T., & Quinsey, V. L. (1990). A follow-up of rapists assessed in a maximum-security psychiatric facility. *Journal of Interpersonal Violence, 5,* 435–448.

Rice, E., Holloway, I., Winetrobe, H., Rhoades, H., Barman-Adhikari, A., et al. (2012) Sex risk among young men who have sex with men who use Grindr, a smartphone geosocial networking application. *Journal of AIDS & Clinical Research,* DOI: 10.4172/2155-6113.S4-005

Rice, M. E., Quinsey, V. L., & Harris, G. T. (1991). Sexual recidivism among child molesters released from a maximum security psychiatric institution. *Journal of Consulting and Clinical Psychology, 59,* 381–386.

Rich, A. J., et al. (2015). Event-level analysis of anal sex roles and sex drug use among gay and bisexual men in Vancouver, British Columbia, Canada. *Archives of Sexual Behavior,* 1–9. DOI: 10.1007/s10508-015-0607-0

Rich, F. (2009, June 28). 40 years later, still second-class Americans. *The New York Times,* p. WK 8.

Richters, J., Hendry, O., & Kippax, S. (2003). When safe sex isn't safe. *Culture, Health & Sexuality, 5*(1), 37–52.

Rickwood, A. M. K., Kenny, S. E., & Donnell, S. C. (2000). Towards evidence based circumcision of English boys: Survey of trends in practice. *British Medical Journal, 321,* 792–793.

Rieger, G., Linsenmeier, J. A. W., Gygax, L., & Bailey, J. M. (2008). Sexual orientation and childhood gender nonconformity: Evidence from home videos. *Developmental Psychology, 44*(1), 46–58.

Rieger, G., & Savin-Williams, R. C. (2012). Gender nonconformity, sexual orientation, and psychological well-being. *Archives of Sexual Behavior, 41*(3), 611–621.

Riggio, H. R., et al. (2015). Internal validation of a self-report measure of perceptions of interpersonal attraction. *Personality and Individual Differences, 74,* 292–296.

Riggio, R. E., & Woll, S. B. (1984). The role of nonverbal cues and physical attractiveness in the selection of dating partners. *Journal of Social and Personal Relationships, 1,* 347–357.

Rimm, E. (May 2000). *Lifestyle may play role in potential for impotence.* Presented at the annual meeting of the American Urological Association, Atlanta, GA.

Rincon, M., & Lam, B. T. (2011). The perspectives of Latina mothers on Latina lesbian families. *Journal of Human Behavior in the Social Environment, 21*(4), 334–349.

Rind, B. (2015). Trends in evolutionary explanations for human male same-sex eroticism. *International Journal of Sexual Health, 27*(3), 199–209.

Rinehart, S. J., & Espelage, D. L. (2015). A multilevel analysis of school climate, homophobic name-calling, and sexual harassment victimization/perpetration among middle school youth. *Psychology of Violence,* DOI: 10/1037.a0039095

Ring-Cassidy, E., & Gentles, I. (2002). *Women's health after abortion: The medical and psychological evidence.* Toronto, Ontario: The deVeber Institute.

Ritner, C., & Roth, J. (1993). *Different voices: Women and the Holocaust.* New York: Paragon House.

Roach, C. M. (2011). *Stripping, sex, and popular culture.* London: Berg Publishers.

Roan, S. (2006, July 22). Newer contraceptives put an end to "the period." *Los Angeles Times.*

Robbers, S. C. C., et al. (2011). Pre-divorce problems in 3-year-olds. *Social Psychiatry and Psychiatric Epidemiology, 46*(4), 311–319.

Robbins, C. L., et al. (2011). Prevalence, frequency, and associations of masturbation with partnered sexual behaviors among U.S. adolescents. *Archives of Pediatrics & Adolescent Medicine, 165*(12), 1087–1093.

Robbins, M. (2015, August 18). Has Tinder replaced dating with hookup culture? http://www.cnn.com/2015/08/18/opinions/robbins-tinder-online-dating/index.html

Robert-McComb, J. J. (2008). The female athletic triad: Disordered eating, amenorrhea, and osteoporosis. In Robert-McComb, J. J., Norman, R., & Zumwalt, M. (Eds.), *The active female: Health issues throughout the lifespan* (pp. 81–92). Totowa, NJ: Humana Press.

Roberts, S. (2006, October 15). It's official: To be married means to be outnumbered. *The New York Times.* http://www.nytimes.com/2006/10/15/us/15census.html?mtrref=www.google.com&gwh=E8830A12C9E57946DBE9D15099C9B939&gwt=pay (Accessed July 13, 2016).

Roberts, S. (2008, March 20). Podcast: Oh, these government affairs. http://cityroom.blogs.nytimes.com/2008/03/20/podcast-oh-these-government-affairs/?scp=5&sq=Spitzer%20Vitter&st=cse

Robinson, J. D., & Parks, C. W. (2003). Lesbian and bisexual women's sexual fantasies, psychological adjustment, and close relationship functioning. *Journal of Psychology & Human Sexuality, 15*(4), 185–203.

Robitz, R., Morrison, L., Ventura, A., Melton, M. C., & Bennett, A. (2015). Sex workers as medical student educators. *Academic Psychiatry, 39,* 329–331.

Roddy, R. E., et al. (1998). A controlled trial of nonoxynol 9 film to reduce male-to-female transmission of sexually transmitted diseases. *New England Journal of Medicine, 339,* 504–510.

Rodriguez, I., Greer, C. A., Mok, M. Y., & Mombaerts, P. (2000). A putative pheromone receptor gene expressed in human olfactory mucosa. *Nature Genetics, 26*(1), 18–19.

Roe-Sepowitz, D. E. (2014) Prostitution. In R. J. R. Levesque (Ed.). *Encyclopedia of Adolescence* (pp. 2195–2200). New York: Springer Science+Business Media.

Rojewski, J. W. (2005). A typical American family? How adoptive families acknowledge and incorporate Chinese cultural heritage in their lives. *Child & Adolescent Social Work Journal, 22*(2), 133–164.

Rolle, L., et al. (2015). Quality of life after sexual reassignment surgery. In C. Trombetta et al. (Eds.). *Management of gender dysphoria* (pp. 193–203). Milan, Italy: Sprinter-Verlag Italia.

Rosario, M., Schrimshaw, E. E., Hunter, J., & Levy-Warren, A. (2009). The coming-out process of young lesbian and bisexual women: Are there butch/femme differences in sexual identity development? *Archives of Sexual Behavior, 38*(1), 34–49.

Roscoe, W. (2000). *Changing ones: Third and fourth genders in native North America.* Palgrave: Macmillan.

Rose, A. M., Hall, C. S., & Martinez-Adler, N. (2014). Aetiology and management of malnutrition in HIV-positive children. *Archives of Disease in Childhood,* DOI:10.1136/archdischild-2012-303348

Rosellii, C. E., Reddy, R. C., & Kaufman, K. R. (2011). The development of male-oriented behavior in rams. *Frontiers in Neuroendocrinology, 32*(2), 164–169.

Rosen, R. C., & Laumann, E. O. (2003). The prevalence of sexual problems in women: How valid are comparisons across studies? Commentary on Bancroft, Loftus, and Long's (2003) "Distress about sex: A national survey of women in heterosexual relationships." *Archives of Sexual Behavior, 32*(3), 209–211.

Rosen, G., & Imperato, P. J. (2015). *A history of public health.* Baltimore: Johns Hopkins University Press.

Rosenblatt, P. C., & Rieks, S. J. (2009). No compromise: Couples dealing with issues for which they do not see a compromise. *The American Journal of Family Therapy, 37*(3), 196–208.

Rosenfeld, M. J., & Thomas, R. J. (2012). Searching for a mate: The rise of the Internet as a social mediary. *American Sociological Review, 77*(4), 523–547.

Rosenthal, A. M., Sylva, D., Safron, A., & Bailey, J. M. (2012). The male bisexuality debate revisited: Some bisexual men have bisexual arousal patterns. *Archives of Sexual Behavior, 41*(1), 135–147.

Rosik, C. H. (2003). Motivational, ethical, and epistemological foundations in the treatment of unwanted homoerotic attraction. *Journal of Marital & Family Therapy, 29*(1), 13–28.

Rosky, C. J. (2009). Like father, like son: Homosexuality, parenthood, and the gender of homophobia. *Yale Journal of Law & Feminism, 20*, 257.

Rösler, A., & Witztum, E. (2000). Pharmacotherapy of paraphilias in the next millennium. *Behavioral Sciences & the Law, 18*(1), 43–56.

Ross, J. L., Roeltgen, D., Feuillan, P., Kushner, H., & Cutler, W. B. (2000). Use of estrogen in young girls with Turner syndrome: Effects on memory. *Neurology, 54*(1), 164–170.

Rothrauff, T., Middlemiss, W., & Jacobson, L. (2004). Comparison of American and Austrian infants' and toddlers' sleep habits: A retrospective, exploratory study. *North American Journal of Psychology, 6*(1), 125–144.

Roughgarden, J. (2004). *Evolution's rainbow: Diversity, gender, and sexuality in nature and people.* Berkeley: University of California Press.

Rowland, D. L., & Incrocci, L. (2008). *Handbook of sexual and gender identity disorders.* Hoboken, NJ: Wiley.

Royce, R. A., Seña, A., Cates, W., Jr., & Cohen, M. S. (1997). Sexual transmission of HIV. *New England Journal of Medicine, 336*, 1072–1078.

Rozee, P. D., & Koss, M. P. (2001). Rape: A century of resistance. *Psychology of Women Quarterly, 25*(4), 295–311.

Rubenson, B., Hanh, L. T., Höjer, B., & Johansson, E. (2005). Young sex-workers in Ho Chi Minh City telling their life stories. *Childhood: A Global Journal of Child Research, 12*(3), 391–411.

Rubin, H., & Campbell, L. (2012). Day-to-day changes in intimacy predict heightened relationship passion, sexual occurrence, and sexual satisfaction: A dyadic diary analysis. *Social Psychological and Personality Science, 3*(2), 224–231.

Rubin, R. (2015). Why the "no brainer" HPV vaccine is being ignored. *Journal of the American Medical Association, 313*(15), 1502–1504.

Rule, N. O., Ambady, N., & Hallett, K. C. (2009). Female sexual orientation is perceived accurately, rapidly, and automatically from the face and its features. *Journal of Experimental Social Psychology, 45*, 1245–1251.

Rule, N. O., Ishii, K., Ambady, N., Rosen, K. S., & Hallett, K. C. (2011). Found in translation: Cross-cultural consensus in the accurate categorization of male sexual orientation. *Personality and Social Psychology Bulletin, 37*, 1499–1507.

Rupp, H. A., & Wallen, K. (2009). Sex-specific content preferences for visual sexual stimuli. *Archives of Sexual Behavior, 38*(3), 417–426.

Rupp, H., et al. (2009). Neural activation in women in response to masculinized male faces: Mediation by hormones and psychosexual factors. *Evolution and Human Behavior, 30*(1), 1–10.

Ruppel, H. (2009, March 26). In B. Alexander, "Sex surrogates" put personal touch on therapy: Despite dubious legality, some counselors still prescribe practice to patients. http://www.msnbc.msn.com/id/29881206/

Rusbult, C. E., & Van Lange, P. A. M. (2003). Interdependence, interaction and relationships. *Annual Review of Psychology, 54*, 351–375.

Rusbult, C. E., Abnew, C. R., & Arriaga, X. B. (2012). The investment model of commitment processes. In P. A. M. Van Lange, et al. (Eds.), *Handbook of theories of social psychology, Vol. 2* (pp. 218–231). Thousand Oaks, CA: Sage.

Rusbult, C. E., Martz, J. M., & Agnew, C. R. (1998). The Investment Model Scale: Measuring commitment level, satisfaction level, quality of alternatives, and investment size. *Personal Relationships, 5*(4), 357–391.

Rush, G., & Schapiro, R. (2009, April 19). Slain masseuse Julissa Brisman once worked for madam Kristin Davis. *Daily News.*

Russell, S. T., van Campen, K. S., & Muraco, J. A. (2012). Sexuality development in adolescence. In L. M. Carpenter, & J. DeLamater (Eds.), *Sex for life* (pp. 70–87). New York: New York University Press.

Russo, N. F., Pirlott, A. G., & Cohen, A. B. (2012). The psychology of women and gender in international perspective: Issues and challenges. *International and Cultural Psychology, 157–178.* DOI:10.1007/978-1-4614-0073-8_8

Rutstein, R. M., Volkman, K. M., Bonda, S., & Shah, S. S. (2015). Ongoing maternal–child transmission of HIV in an urban area, 2003–2012. *Hospital Pediatrics, 5*(2). http://hosppeds.aappublications.org/content/5/2/92.short

Ryan, L. R., Brownlow, S., & Patterson, B. (2015). Women's mental rotation abilities as a function of priming. *Psychology, 6*(3), DOI: 10.4236/psych.2015.63021

Ryan, R. M., & Ryan, W. S. (2012, April 27). Homophobic: Maybe you're gay. *The New York Times,* SR12.

Saad, L. (2009, May 15). More Americans "pro-life" than "pro-choice" for first time. *The New York Times.*

Saad, L. (2012, May 23). Pro-choice Americans at record-low 41%. http://www.gallup.com/poll/154838/pro-choice-americans-record-low.aspx (Accessed June 23, 2012).

Sadalla, E. K., Kenrick, D. T., & Vershure, B. (1987). Dominance and heterosexual attraction. *Journal of Personality and Social Psychology, 52,* 730–738.

Sadker, M., & Sadker, D. (1994). *How America's schools cheat girls.* New York: Scribners.

Sadler, A. G., Booth, B. M., Nielson, D., & Doebbeling, B. N. (2000). Health-related consequences of physical and sexual violence: Women in the military. *Obstetrics & Gynecology, 96*(3), 473–480.

Sagan, C., & Dryan, A. (1990, April 22). The question of abortion: A search for answers. *Parade Magazine,* pp. 4–8.

Sagarin, B. J., Becker, D. V., Guadagno, R. E., Nicastle, L. D., & Millevoi, A. (2003). Sex differences (and similarities) in jealousy. The moderating influence of infidelity experience and sexual orientation of the infidelity. *Evolution & Human Behavior, 24*(1), 17–23.

Sagarin, B. J., et al. (2012). Sex differences in jealousy: A meta-analytic examination. *Evolution and Human Behavior.* Retrieved from http://dx.doi.org/10.1016/j.evolhumbehav.2012.02.006 (Accessed September 15, 2012).

Saigal, S., et al. (2006). Transition of extremely low-birth-weight infants from adolescence to young adulthood. *Journal of the American Medical Association, 295,* 667–675.

Saks, B. R. (2008). Common issues in female sexual dysfunction. *Psychiatric Times, 25*(5), 2.

Saleh, F. M. (2009). Pharmacological treatment of paraphilic sex offenders. In F. M. Saleh et al. (Eds.), *Sex offenders: Identification, risk assessment, treatment, and legal issue* (pp. 189–210). New York: Oxford University Press.

Sales, N. J. (2015, September.) Tinder and the Dawn of the "Dating Apocalypse." *Vanity Fair,* http://www.vanityfair.com/culture/2015/08/tinder-hook-up-culture-end-of-dating

Salgin, B., et al. (2015). Even transient rapid infancy weight gain is associated with higher BMI in young adults and earlier menarche. *International Journal of Obesity, 39,* 939–944.

Sanders, S. A. (2015). Cited in Clay, R. A. (2015). Sex research at the Kinsey Institute, *Monitor on Psychology, 46*(9), 48–52.

Sanders, S.A., Hill, B.J., Crosby, R.A., & Janssen, E. (2014). Correlates of condom associated erection problems (CAEP) in young, heterosexual men: Condom self-efficacy, perceptions, and motivations. *AIDS and Behavior, 18*(1), 128–134.

Sanders, S. A., Yarber, W. L., Kaufman, E. L., Crosby, R. A., Graham, C.A., & Milhausen, R. R. (2012). Condom use errors and problems: A global view. *Sexual Health, 9*(1), 81–95.

Sanders, T. (2005). "It's just acting": Sex workers' strategies for capitalizing on sexuality. *Gender, Work & Organization, 12*(4), 319–342.

Sandin, S., et al. (2012). Advancing maternal age is associated with increasing risk for autism: A review and meta-analysis. *Journal of the American Academy of Child & Adolescent Psychiatry, 51*(5), 477–486.

Sanger, M. (1938). *Margaret Sanger: An autobiography.* New York: Norton.

Sangrador, J. L., & Yela, C. (2000). "What is beautiful is loved": Physical attractiveness in love relationships in a representative sample. *Social Behavior & Personality, 28*(3) 207–218.

Santelli, J. S., et al. (2003). Reproductive health in school-based health centers: Findings from the 1998–99 census of school-based health centers. *Journal of Adolescent Health, 32*(6), 443–451.

Santi, D., et al. (2014). Male sexual dysfunction and HIV—A clinical perspective. *Nature Reviews Urology, 11,* 99–109.

Santtila, P., Sandnabba, N. K., Alison, L., & Nordling, N. (2002). Investigating the underlying structure in sadomasochistically oriented behavior. *Archives of Sexual Behavior, 31*(2), 185–196.

Sarrel, P., & Masters, W. (1982). Sexual molestation of men by women. *Archives of Sexual Behavior, 11*, 117–131.

Sartorius, G. A., & Nieschlag, E. (2009). Paternal age and reproduction. *Human Reproduction Update*, DOI:10.1093/humupd/dmp027

Sasaki, E., et al. (2008). Adverse birth outcomes associated with maternal smoking and polymorphisms in the N-nitrosamine-metabolizing enzyme genes NQ01 and CYP2E1. *American Journal of Epidemiology*, DOI: 10.1093/aje/kwm360

Saul, J. M. (2003). *Feminism: Issues & arguments.* Oxford: Oxford University Press.

Save the Children. (2008). Annual report. www.savethechildren.org

Save the Children. (2008). *State of the world's mothers 2008.* www.savethechildren.org/publications/mothers/2008/SOWM-2008-full-report.pdf

Save the Children. (2011). *State of the World's Mothers 2011.* Westport, CT: Save the Children. www.savethechildren.org

Save the Children. (2013). *State of the world's mothers 2013.* Westport, CT: Save the Children. www.savethechildren.org

Save the Children. (2014). *State of the world's mothers 2014.* Westport, CT: Save the Children. www.savethechildren.org

Save the Children. (2015). *State of the world's mothers 2015.* Fairfield, CT: Save the Children USA.

Savic, I., & Lindström, P. (2008). PET and MRI show differences in cerebral asymmetry and functional connectivity between homo- and heterosexual subjects. Published online on June 16, 2008. *Proceedings of the National Academy of Sciences.* USA, 10.1073/pnas.0801566105.

Savic, I., Berglund, H., & Lindström, P. (2005). Brain response to putative pheromones in homosexual men. *Proceedings of the National Association of Sciences, 102,* 7356–7361.

Savic, I., Garcia-Falgueras, A., & Swaab, D. F. (2010). Sexual differentiation of the human brain in relation to gender identity and sexual orientation. In I. Savic (Ed.), *Sex differences in the human brain, Their underpinnings and implications. Progress in Brain Research, 186* (pp. 41–64). New York: Elsevier.

Savin-Williams, R. C. (2006). Who's gay? Does it matter? *Current Directions in Psychological Science, 15*(1), 40–44.

Savin-Williams, R. C., & Diamond, L. M. (2000). Sexual identity trajectories among sexual-minority youths: Gender comparisons. *Archives of Sexual Behavior, 29*(6), 607–627.

Savin-Williams, R. C., & Vrangalova, Z. (2013). Mostly heterosexual as a distinct sexual orientation group: A systematic review of the empirical evidence. *Developmental Review, 33*(1), 58–88.

Savin-Williams, R., Joyner, K., & Rieger, G. (2012). Prevalence and stability of self-reported sexual orientation identity during young adulthood. *Archives of Sexual Behavior, 41*(1), 103–110.

Savin-Williams, R. C. (2014). An exploratory study of the categorical versus spectrum nature of sexual orientation. *The Journal of Sexual Research, 51*(4), 446–453.

Sax, L. (2002). How common is intersex? A response to Anne Fausto-Sterling. *Journal of Sex Research, 39,* 174–179.

Saywitz, K. J., Mannarino, A. P., Berliner, L., & Cohen, J. A. (2000). Treatment for sexually abused children and adolescents. *American Psychologist, 55*(9), 1040–1049.

Schaller, S., & Træen, B. (2008). Attitudes toward pornography, self-esteem and feelings about sex in a longitudinal sample of Norwegian adolescents. *Sexologies, 17*(Suppl. 1), S148.

Schieve, L. A., et al. (1999). Live-birth rates and multiple-birth risk using in vitro fertilization. *Journal of the American Medical Association, 282,* 1832–1838.

Schlichter, A. (2004). *Contesting "straights," "lesbians," "queer heterosexuals," and the critique of heteronormativity.* Binghamton, NY: Haworth.

Schmidt, H. M., Munder, T., & Gerger, H., Fruhauf, S., & Barth, J. (2014). Combination of psychological intervention and phosphodiesterase-5 inhibitors for erectile dysfunction: A narrative review and meta-analysis. *Journal of Sexual Medicine, 11*(6), 1376–1391.

Schmidt, P. J., et al. (1998). Differential behavioral effects of gonadal steroids in women with and in those without premenstrual syndrome. *New England Journal of Medicine, 338,* 209–216.

Schmidt, S. R., Bonner, B. L., & Chaffin, M. (2012). Understanding and treating adolescents with illegal sexual behavior. In P. Goodyear-Brown (Ed.). *Handbook of child sexual abuse: Identification, assessment, and treatment* (pp. 469–485). Hoboken, NJ: Wiley.

Schmitt, D. P., Realo, A., Voracek, M., & Allik, J. (2008). Whay can't a man be more like a woman? Sex differences in Big Five personality traits across 55 cultures. *Journal of Personality and Social Psychology, 94*(1), 168–182.

Schmitt, D. (2008). An evolutionary perspective on mate choice and relationship initiation. In S. Sprecher, A. Wenzel, & J. Harvey (Eds.), *Handbook of relationship initiation* (pp. 55–74). New York: CRC Press.

Schmitt, D. P. (2003). Universal sex differences in the desire for sexual variety: Tests from 52 nations, 6 continents, and 13 islands. *Journal of Personality and Social Psychology, 85*(1), 85–104.

Schmitt, D. P. (2014). Evaluating evidence of mate preference adaptations: Do we really know what Homo sapiens sapiens really want? In V. A. Weekes-Shackelford, & T. K. Shackelford (Eds.). *Evolutionary perspectives on human sexual psychology and behavior* (pp. 3–39). New York: Springer Science+Business Media.

Schmitt, D. P., & Jonason, P. K. (2014). Attachment and sexual permissiveness. *Cross-Cultural Psychology*, DOI: 10.1177/0022022114551052

Schmitt, D., Jonason, P. K., Byerley, G. J., Flores, S. D., Illbeck, B. E., O'Leary, K. N., & Qudrat, A. (2012). A reexamination of sex differences in sexuality: New studies reveal old truths. *Current Directions in Psychological Science, 21*(2), 135–139.

Schmitt, M. T., Branscombe, N. R., & Postmes, T. (2003). Women's emotional responses to the pervasiveness of gender discrimination. *European Journal of Social Psychology, 33*(3), 297–312.

Schneider, J. P. (2003). The impact of compulsive cybersex behaviours on the family. *Sexual and Relationship Therapy, 18*(3), 329–354.

Schneider, J. P. (2004). Editorial: Sexual addiction & compulsivity: Twenty years of the field, ten years of the journal. *Sexual Addiction & Compulsivity, 11*(1–2), 3–5.

Schneider, J. P. (2005). Addiction is addiction is addiction. *Sexual Addiction & Compulsivity, 12*(2/3), 75–77.

Schneider, J. P., Weiss, R., & Samenow, C. (2012). Really cheating? Understanding the emotional reactions and clinical treatment of spouses and partners affected by cybersex infidelity. *Sexual Addiction and Compulsivity, 19*(1–2), 123–139.

Schneidewind-Skibbe, A., Hayes, R. D., Koochaki, P. E., Meyer, J., & Dennerstein, L. (2007). The frequency of sexual intercourse reported by women: A Review of community-based studies and factors limiting their conclusions. *Journal of Sexual Medicine, 5*(2), 301–335.

Schober, J. M., et al. (2005). Leuprolide acetate suppresses pedophilic urges and arousability. *Archives of Sexual Behavior, 34*(6), 691–705.

Schramm, D. G., Marshall, J. P., Harris, V. W., & Lee, T. R. (2012). Religiosity, homogamy, and marital adjustment. *Journal of Family Issues, 33*(2), 246–268.

Schröder, F. H., et al. (2009). Screening and prostate-cancer mortality in a randomized European study. *New England Journal of Medicine, 360,* 1320–328.

Schroder, J., & Schmiedeberg, C. (2015). Effects of relationship duration, cohabitation, and marriage on the frequency of intercourse in couples: Findings from German panel data. *Social Science Research, 52,* 72–82.

Schroeder–Printzen, I., et al. (2000). Surgical therapy in infertile men with ejaculatory duct obstruction: Technique and outcome of a standardized surgical approach. *Human Reproduction, 15,* 1364–1368.

Schröder, F. H., et al. (2014). Screening and prostate cancer mortality: results of the European Randomised Study of Screening for Prostate Cancer (ERSPC) at 13 years of follow-up. *The Lancet, 384*(9959), 2027–2035.

Schrut, A. (2005). A psychodynamic (nonoedipal) and brain function hypothesis regarding a type of male sexual masochism. *Journal of the American Academy of Psychoanalysis and Dynamic Psychiatry, 33*(2), 333–349.

Schultz, W. W., et al. (2005). Women's sexual pain and its management. *Journal of Sexual Medicine, 2*(3), 301–316.

Schwam-Harris, M. (2008). Achieving permanency in public agency adoptions: Secondary analyses of the national survey of child and adolescent well-being data. *Dissertation Abstracts International Section A: Humanities and Social Sciences, 68*(9-A), 4073.

Schwartz, C. R., & Mare, R. D. (2012). The proximate determinants of educational homogamy. *Demography, 49*(2), 629–650.

Schwartz, H. (2014, September 15). For the first time there are more single American adults than married ones, and here's where they live. *The Washington Post.*

Schwartz, J. (2015, June 26). *Obergefell v. Hodges*: Highlights from the Supreme Court Decision on same-sex marriage. *The New York Times,* http://www.nytimes.com/interactive/2015/

us/2014-term-supreme-court-decision-same-sex-marriage.html?_r=0 (Accessed July 13, 2016).

Schwartz, M. A. (2015). Neurologic disorders. In J. A. Paice (Ed.). *Physical aspects of care* (pp. 103–126). New York: Oxford University Press.

Schwartz, P., & Young, L. (2009). Sexuality Sexual satisfaction in committed relationships. *Research and Social Policy: Journal of NSRC, 6*(1), 1–17.

Sciolino, E., & Mekhennet, S. (2008, June 11). In Europe, debate over Islam and virginity. *The New York Times.* http://www.nytimes.com/2008/06/11/world/europe/11virgin.html (Accessed July 13, 2016).

Scott, B. E., Weiss, H. A., & Viljoen, J. I. (2005). The acceptability of male circumcision as an HIV intervention among a rural Zulu population, KwaZulu-Natal, South Africa. *AIDS Care, 17*(3), 304–313.

Scott-Sheldon, L. A. J., Carey, M. P., & Carey, K. B. (2010). Alcohol and risky sexual behavior among heavy drinking college students. *AIDS and Behavior, 14*(4), 845–853.

Segraves, R. T. (2015). Pharmacotherapy ans psychotherapy for sexual dysfunctions. In P. E. Nathan & J. M. Gorman (Eds.). *Treatments that work* (4th ed., pp. 699–730). New York: Oxford University Press.

Secker-Walker, R. H., & Vacek, P. M. (2003). Relationships between cigarette smoking during pregnancy, gestational age, maternal weight gain, and infant birthweight. *Addictive Behaviors, 28*(1), 55–66.

Segrin, C., Powell, H. L., Givertz, M., & Brackin, A. (2003). Symptoms of depression, relational quality, and loneliness in dating relationships. *Personal Relationships, 10*(1), 25–36.

Seidman, S. M. (2003). The aging male: Androgens, erectile dysfunction, and depression. *Journal of Clinical Psychiatry, 64*(Suppl. 10), 31–37.

Seifert-Klauss V., et al. (2005). Bone metabolism, bone density and estrogen levels in perimenopause: A prospective 2-year study. *Zentralbl Gynakol., 127*(3), 132–139.

Seiffge-Krenke, I., & Kuehnemund, M. (2001). Relationship experiences during adolescence: How important are they for predicting romantic outcomes in young adulthood? *Zeitschrift für Entwicklungspsychologie und Paedagogische Psychologie, 33*(2), 112–123.

Sela, Y., Shackelford, T. K., Pham, M. N., & Zeigler-Hill, V. (2015). Women's mate retention behaviors, personality traits, and fellatio. *Personality and Individual Differences, 85*, 187–191.

Seligman, L., & Hardenburg, S. A. (2000). Assessment and treatment of paraphilias. *Journal of Counseling & Development, 78*(1), 107–113.

Semans, J. (1956). Premature ejaculation: A new approach. *Southern Medical Journal, 49,* 353–358.

Semp, D. (2011). Questioning heteronormativity: Using queer theory to inform research and practice with mental health services. *Psychology and Sexuality, 2*(1), 69–86.

Semple, S. J., Patterson, T. L., & Grant, I. (2003). HIV-positive gay and bisexual men: Predictors of unsafe sex. *AIDS Care, 15*(1), 3–15.

Senbel, A. M. (2011). Interaction between nitric oxide and dopaminergic transmission in the peripheral control of penile erection. *Fundamental and Clinical Pharmacology, 25*(1), 63–71.

Senn, C. Y., et al. (2015). Efficacy of a sexual assault resistance program for university women. *New England Journal of Medicine, 372,* 2326–2335.

Servais, L. (2006). Sexual health care in persons with intellectual disabilities. *Mental Retardation and Developmental Disabilities Research Reviews, 12*(1), 48–56.

Servin, A., Nordenström, A., Larsson, A., & Bohlin, G. (2003). Prenatal androgens and gender-typed behavior: A study of girls with mild and severe forms of congenital adrenal hyperplasia. *Developmental Psychology, 39*(3), 440–450.

Seto, M. C. (2008). Pedophilia: Psychopathology and theory. In D. R. Laws & W. T. O'Donohue (Eds.), *Sexual deviance: Theory, assessment, and treatment* (2nd ed., pp. 164–182). New York: Guilford Press.

Seward, R. R. (2005). Family and community in Ireland. *Journal of Comparative Family Studies, 36*(2), 343–344.

Sex & Tech. (2009). A survey commissioned by The National Campaign to Prevent Teen and Unplanned Pregnancy and *CosmoGirl.com.*

Sexually transmitted disease surveillance, 2014. (2015). Centers for Disease Control and Prevention. Atlanta: U.S. Department of Health and Human Services.

Sexually transmitted disease surveillance. (2015). Atlanta: Centers for Disease Control and Prevention. U.S. Department of Health and Human Services.

Shackelford, T. K., & Goetz, A. T. (2012). *The Oxford handbook of sexual conflict in humans.* New York: Oxford University Press.

Shackelford, T. K., Goetz, A. T., Buss, D. M., Euler, H. A., & Hoier, S. (2005). When we hurt the ones we love: Predicting violence against women from men's mate retention. *Personal Relationships, 12*(4), 447–463.

Shacklett, B. L., & Ferre, A. L. (2011). Mucosal immunity in HIV controllers: The right place at the right time. *Current Opinion in HIV & AIDS, 6*(3), 202–207.

Shafer, L. (2016). Sexual disorders and sexual dysfunction. In T. A. Stern et al. (Eds.). *Massachusetts General Hospital: Comprehensive clinical psychiatry* (pp. 402–412). New York: Elsevier.

Shankar, A., McMunn, A., Banks, J., & Steptoe, A. (2011). Loneliness, social isolation, and behavioral and biological health indicators in older adults. *Health Psychology, 30*(4), 377–385.

Sharp, D. (2002). Telling the truth about sex. *Lancet, 359*(9312), 1084.

Sharp, E. B., & Joslyn, M. (2008). Individual and contextual effects on attributions about pornography. *Journal of Politics, 63,* 501–519.

Shaywitz, B. A., et al. (1995). Sex differences in the functional organization of the brain for language. *Nature, 373,* 607–609.

Sheffield, J. S., & Cunningham, F. G. (2005). Urinary tract infection in women. *Obstetrics & Gynecology, 106,* 1085–1092.

Sherer, R. (2012). The future of HIV care in the USA. *Sexually Transmitted Infections, 88,* 106–111.

Sherwin, B. B. (2012). Estrogen and cognitive functioning in women: Lessons we have learned. *Behavioral Neuroscience, 126*(1), 123–127.

Sherwin, B. B., Gelfand, M. M., & Brender, W. (1985). Androgen enhances sexual motivation in females: A prospective, crossover study of sex steroid administration in the surgical menopause. *Psychosomatic Medicine, 47,* 339–351.

Shevell, T., et al. (2005). Assisted reproductive technology and pregnancy outcome. *Obstetrics & Gynecology, 106,* 1039–1045.

Shick, V., et al. (2011). Prevalence and characteristics of vibrator use among women who have sex with women. *Journal of Sexual Medicine, 8*(12), 3306–3315.

Shields, S. A., & Dicicco, E. C. (2011). The social psychology of sex and gender. *Psychology of Women Quarterly, 35*(3), 491–499.

Shifren, J. L., et al. (2000). Transdermal testosterone treatment in women with impaired sexual function after oophorectomy. *New England Journal of Medicine, 343*(10), 682–688.

Shifren, J. L., et al. (2008). Sexual problems and distress in United States women: Prevalence and correlates. *Obstetrics & Gynecology, 112,* 970–978.

Shiozaki, A., et al. (2014). Multiple pregnancy, short cervix, part-time worker, steroid use, low educational level and male fetus are risk factors for preterm birth in Japan: A multicenter, prospective study. *Journal of Obstetrics and Gynaecology Research, 40*(1), 53–61.

Shipko, S. (2000, February 7). *Antidepressants linked to sexual side effects.* WebMD/Healtheon.

Shlipak, M. G., et al. (2000). Estrogen and progestin, lipoprotein(a), and the risk of recurrent coronary heart disease events after menopause. *Journal of the American Medical Association, 283,* 1845–1852.

Shoag, J., et al. (2015). Efficacy of Prostate-Specific Antigen screening: Use of regression discontinuity in the PLCO cancer screening trial. *JAMA Oncology, 1*(7), 984–986.

Shoveller, J. A., Johnson, J. L., & Savoy, D. M. (2006). Preventing sexually transmitted infections among adolescents: An assessment of ecological approaches and study methods. *Sex Education, 6*(2), 163–183.

Shulevitz, J. (2015, June 28). Regulating sex. *The New York Times*, p. SR1.

Shultz, S. K., Scherman, A., & Marshall, L. J. (2000). Evaluation of a university-based date rape prevention program: Effect on attitudes and behavior related to rape. *Journal of College Student Development, 41*(2), 193–201.

Shuster, S. M., & Sassaman, C. (1997). Genetic interaction between male mating strategy and sex ratio in a marine isopod. *Nature, 388*(6640), 373–377.

Sickle-Cell Disease. (2015). Centers for Disease Control and Prevention. http://www.cdc.gov/ncbddd/sicklecell/data.html

Siegel-Hinson, R. I., & McKeever, W. F. (2002). Hemispheric specialisation, spatial activity experience, and sex differences on tests of mental rotation ability. *Laterality: Asymmetries of Body, Brain and Cognition, 7*(1), 59–74.

Silva, P. (2005). The state of affairs. *Sexual and Relationship Therapy, 20*(2), 261–262.

Silveretein, J. (2015, July 3). Florida ex-teacher gets 22 years for sex with three students. *New York Daily News.* http://www.nydailynews.com/news/national/jennifer-fichter-florida-teacher-sex-article-1.2280215

Simmons, C. (2015). "I had to promise not to ask 'nasty' questions again": African American women and sex and marriage education in the 1940s. *Journal of Women's History, 27*(1), 110–135.

Siminelli, C., Eleuteri, S., Petrucelli, F., & Rossi, R. (2014). Female sexual pain disorders: Dyspareunia and vaginismus. *Current Opinion in Psychiatry, 27*(6), 406–412.

Simon, S. (2011). Report: Breast cancer death rates decline, but more slowly among poor. American Cancer Society. http://www.cancer.org/Cancer/news/News/report-breast-cancer-death-rates-decline-but-more-slowly-among-poor

Simonelli, C., Eleuteri, S., Petruccelli, F., & Rossi, R. (2014). Female sexual pain disorders: Dyspareunia and vaginismus. *Current Opinion in Psychiatry, 27*(6), 406–412.

Simpson, J. L. (2000, June 1). Invasive diagnostic procedures for prenatal genetic diagnosis. *Journal Watch Women's Health.*

Sims, C. S., Drasgow, F., & Fitzgerald, L. F. (2005). The effects of sexual harassment on turnover in the military: Time-dependent modeling. *Journal of Applied Psychology, 90*(6), 1141–1152.

Singer, J., & Singer, I. (1972). Types of female orgasm. *Journal of Sex Research, 8,* 255–267.

Singh, D., Vidaurri, M., Zambrano, R. J., & Dabbs, J. M., Jr. (1999). Lesbian erotic role identification: Behavioral, morphological, and hormonal correlates. *Journal of Personality & Social Psychology, 76*(6), 1035–1039.

Sipski, M. L., Alexander, C. J., & Rosen, R. (2001). Sexual arousal and orgasm in women. *Annals of Neurology, 49*(1), 35–44.

Skoog, T., & Ozdemir, S. B. (2015). Explaining why early-maturing girls are more exposed to sexual harassment in early adolescence, *The Journal of Early Adolescence,* DOI: 10.1177/0272431614568198

Skopek, J., Schulz, F., & Blossfeld, H. (2011). Who contacts whom? Educational homophily in online mate selection. *European Sociological Review, 27*(2), 180–195.

Slackman, M. (2007, September 20). In Egypt, a rising push against genital cutting. *The New York Times.* http://www.nytimes.com/2007/09/20/world/africa/20iht-20girls.7576384.html (Accessed July 13, 2016).

Slovenko, R. (2001). Aphrodisiacs—then and now. *Journal of Psychiatry & Law, 29*(1), 103–116.

Smart, C. (2006). The state of affairs: Explorations in infidelity and commitment. *Sexualities, 9*(2), 259–262.

Smith, C. A., & Konik, J. (2011). Feminism and evolutionary psychology: Allies, adversaries, or both? *Sex Roles, 64*(9–10), 595–602.

Smith, D. K., et al. (2010). Male circumcision in the United States for the prevention of HIV infection and other adverse health outcomes: Report from a CDC consultation. *Public Health Reports, 125*(Suppl 1), 72–82.

Smith, G. D., da Rocha, A. M., & Keller, L. (2014). Microfluidics for sperm selection. In A. Agarwal et al. (Eds.). *Non-invasive sperm selection for in vitro fertilization* (pp. 51–58). New York: Springer Science+Business Media.

Smith, R. M., Parrott, D. J., Swartout, K. M., & Tharp, A. T. (2015). Deconstructing hegemonic masculinity: The roles of antifemininity, subordination to women, and sexual dominance in men's perpetration of sexual aggression. *Psychology of Men & Masculinity, 16*(2), 160–169.

Smith, Y. L. S., Van Goozen, S. H. M., Kuiper, A. J., & Cohen–Kettenis, P. T. (2005). Sex reassignment: Outcomes and predictors of treatment for adolescent and adult transsexuals. *Psychological Medicine, 35*(1), 89–99.

Smock, P. J. (2000, February 15). Cited in E. Nagourney, *Annual Review of Sociology.* Study finds families bypassing marriage. *The New York Times,* p. F8.

Smylie, J., et al. (2014). Socioeconomic position and factors associated with use of a non-supine infant sleep position: Findings from the Canadian Maternity Experiences Survey. *American Journal of Public Health, 104*(3), 539–547.

Snapp, S., Ryu, E., & Kerr, J. (2015). The upside to hooking up: College students' positive hookup experiences. *International Journal of Sexual Health, 27*(1), 43–56.

Sneider, J. T., et al. (2015). Sex differences in spatial navigation and perception in human adolescents and emerging adults. *Behavioural Processes, 111,* 42–50.

Soble, A. (2009). A history of erotic philosophy. *Journal of Sex Research, 46*(2), 104–120.

Sohn, K. (2015). The value of male height in the marriage market. *Economics & Human Biology, 18,* 110–124.

Sommer, F., Goldstein, I., & Korda, J. B. (2010). Bicycle riding and erectile dysfunction: A review. *Journal of Sexual Medicine, 7,* 2346–2358.

Sommerfeld, J. (2000, April 18). *Lifting the curse: Should monthly periods be optional?* MSNBC (Online).

Song, A. V., & Halpern-Felsher, B. L. (2011). Predictive relationship between adolescent oral and vaginal sex: Results from a prospective, longitudinal study. *Archives of Pediatrics & Adolescent Medicine, 165*(3), 243–249.

Spehr, M., et al. (2003). Identification of a testicular odorant receptor mediating human sperm chemotaxis. *Science, 299*(5615).

Spehr, M., Schwane, K., Riffell, J. A., Zimmer, R. K., & Hatt, H. (2006). Odorant receptors and olfactory-like signaling mechanisms in mammalian sperm. *Molecular and Cell Endocrinology, 250*(1-2), 128–136.

Spencer, A. L., & Bonnema, R. (2011). Health issues in oral contraception: Risks, side effects, and health benefits. *Expert Review of Obstetrics & Gynecology, 6*(5), 551–557.

Spencer, N. (2006). Explaining the social gradient in smoking in pregnancy: Early life course accumulation and cross-sectional clustering of social risk exposures in the 1958 British national cohort. *Social Science & Medicine, 62*(5), 1250–1259.

Spencer, T., Biederman, J., & Mick, E. (2006). Attention-deficit/hyperactivity disorder: Diagnosis, lifespan, comorbidities, and neurobiology. *Ambulatory Pediatrics, 7*(1), 73–81.

Spiegel, D. (2001). Breast cancer: Society shapes and epidemic. *New England Journal of Medicine, 334,* 1337–1338.

Spitzer, R. L. (2005). Peer commentaries on Binik: A more radical proposal: Dyspareunia is not a mental disorder. *Archives of Sexual Behavior, 34*(1), 48.

Spitzer, R. L., et al. (1989). *DSM-III-R casebook.* Washington, DC: American Psychiatric Association.

Sprecher, S. (1998). Insiders' perspectives on reasons for attraction to a close other. *Social Psychology Quarterly, 61*(4), 287–300.

Sprecher, S., et al. (2015). Associations between self-expansion and actual and perceived (dis) similarity and their joint effects on attraction in initial interactions. *Self and Identity, 14*(4), 369–389.

Sprecher, S., & Fehr, B. (2011). Dispositional attachment and relationship-specific attachment as predictors of compassionate love for a partner. *Journal of Social and Personal Relationships, 28*(4), 558–574.

Sprecher, S., Barbee, A., & Schwartz, P. (1995). "Was it good for you, too?" Gender differences in first sexual intercourse experiences. *Journal of Sex Research, 32,* 3–15.

Sprecher, S., Sullivan, Q., & Hatfield, E. (1994). Mate selection preferences: Gender differences examined in a national sample. *Journal of Personality and Social Psychology, 66*(6), 1074–1080.

Squeglia, L. M., et al. (2012). Binge drinking differentially affects adolescent male and female brain morphometry. *Psychopharmacology, 220*(3), 529–539.

Squier, S., & Littlefield, M. M. (Eds). (2004). Feminist theory and/of science: Feminist Theory special issue. *Feminist Theory, 5*(2), 123–126.

Stahl, S. M. (2015). Mechanism of action of flibanserin, a multifunctional serotonin agonist (MSAA), in hypoactive sexual desire disorder. *CNS Spectrums, 20*(1), 1–6.

Stake, J. E., & Hoffman, F. L. (2001). Changes in student social attitudes, activism, and personal confidence in higher education: The role of women's studies. *American Educational Research Journal, 38*(2), 411–436.

Stamback, A., & Miriam, D. (2005). Feminist theory and educational policy: How gender has been "involved" in family school choice debates. *Signs, 30*(2), 1633–1658.

Stanyon, R., & Bigoni, F. (2014). Sexual selection and the evolution of behavior, morphology, neuroanatomy and genes in humans and other primates. *Neuroscience & Biobehavioral Reviews, 46*(4), 579–590.

Staras, S., Tobler, A. L., Maldonado-Molina, M., & Cook, R. (2011). Riskier sexual partners contribute to the increased rate of sexually transmitted diseases among youth with substance abuse disorders. *Sexually Transmitted Diseases, 38*(5), 413–418.

Starr, K. E., & Aron, L. (2011). Women on the couch: Genital stimulation and the birth of psychoanalysis. *Psychoanalytic Dialogues: The International Journal of Relational Perspectives, 21*(4), 373–392.

Starratt, V. G., & Alesia, M. N. (2014). Male adaptations to retain a mate. In V. A. Weekes-Shackelford, & T. K. Shackelford (Eds.). *Evolutionary Perspectives on Human Sexual Psychology and Behavior* (pp. 197–205). New York: Springer Science+Business Media.

STDs and Infertility. (2015). Centers for Disease Control and Prevention. http://www.cdc.gov/std/infertility/

Stead, L., et al. (2009). Triple negative breast cancers are increased in Black Women regardless of age or body mass index. *Breast Cancer Research, 11*(2), R18.

Stearns, A. E., Sharp, S. F., & Beutel, A. M. (2015). Women as political bodies in the international speeches of Margaret Sanger. *Feminist Formations, 27*(2), 125–141.

Stearns, V., Beebe, K. L., Iyengar, M., & Dube, E. (2003). Paroxetine controlled release in the treatment of menopausal hot flashes. *Journal of the American Medical Association, 289,* 2827–2834.

Steele, C. M., & Josephs, R. A. (1990). Alcohol myopia: Its prized and dangerous effects. *American Psychologist, 45*, 921–933.

Steensma, T. D., & Cohen-Kettenis, P. Y. (2015). More than two developmental pathways in children with gender dysphoria? *Journal of the American Academy of Child & Adolescent Psychiatry, 54*(2), 147–148.

Stefanick, M. L., et al. (2006). Effects of conjugated equine estrogens on breast cancer and mammography screening in postmenopausal women with hysterectomy. *Journal of the American Medical Association, 295*, 1647–1657.

Stein, C. J., & Colditz, G. A. (2004). Modifiable risk factors for cancer. *Journal of Breast Cancer, 90*(2), 299–303.

Stein, D. J., Black, D. W., Shapira, N. A., & Spitzer, R. L. (2001). Hypersexual disorder and preoccupation with Internet pornography. *American Journal of Psychiatry, 158*(10), 1590–1594.

Stein, Z., & Susser, M. (2000). The risks of having children in later life. *British Medical Journal, 320*(7251), 1681–1682.

Steinemann, S., & Steinemann, M. (2005). Retroelements: Tools for sex chromosome evolution. *Cytogenetic and Genome Research, 110*, 134–143.

Steinfeldt, M., & Steinfeldt, J. A. (2012). Athletic identity and conformity to masculine norms among college football players. *Journal of Applied Sport Psychology, 24*(2), 115–128.

Stengers, J., Van Neck, A., & Hoffmann, K. (2001). *Masturbation: The history of a great terror.* New York: St. Martin's Press.

Stephenson, J. (2000). Widely used spermicide may increase, not decrease, risk of HIV transmission. *Journal of the American Medical Association, 284*(8), 949.

Stephenson, K. R., & Meston, C. M. (2015). The conditional importance of sex: Exploring the association between sexual well-being and life satisfaction. *Journal of Sex & Marital Therapy, 41*(1), 25–38.

Stephenson, K. R., Rellini, A. H., & Meston, C. M. (2012). Relationship satisfaction as a predictor of treatment response during cognitive behavioral sex therapy. *Archives of Sexual Behavior.* DOI:10.1007/s10508-012-9961-3

Stephenson, K. R., Rellini, A. H., & Meston, C. M. (2013). Relationship satisfaction as a predictor of treatment response during cognitive behavioral sex therapy. *Archives of Sexual Behavior, 42*(1), 143–152.

Sternberg, R. J. (1988). *The triangle of love: Intimacy, passion, commitment.* New York: Basic Books.

Sternberg, R. J. (2004). A triangular theory of love. In H. T. Reis & C. E. Rusbult (Eds.), *Close relationships: Key readings* (pp. 213–227). London: Taylor & Francis.

Sternberg, R. J. (2007). Triangulating love. In T. J. Oord (Ed.), *The altruism reader* (pp. 331–374). West Conshohocken, PA: Templeton Press.

Stewart, A. L. (2014). The Men's Project: A sexual assault prevention program targeting college men. *Psychology of Men & Masculinity, 15*(4), 481–485.

Stewart, S. M., Lee, P. W. H., & Tao, R. (2010). Psychiatric disorders in the Chinese. In M. H. Bond (Ed.), *The Oxford handbook of Chinese psychology.* Oxford, UK: Oxford University Press, pp. 367–382.

STI surveillance, 2010. Centers for Disease Control and Prevention. (2010). 2010 Sexually transmitted diseases surveillance. http://www.cdc.gov/std/stats10/tables/trends-snapshot.htm (Accessed October 4, 2012).

STI trends, 2011. Centers for Disease Control and Prevention. (2011). STD Trends in the United States: 2010 National data for gonorrhea, chlamydia, and syphilis. http://www.cdc.gov/std/stats10/trends.htm (Accessed October 4, 2012).

STIs and infertility, 2011. Centers for Disease Control and Prevention. (2011). Sexually transmitted diseases (STDs). STDs and infertility. http://www.cdc.gov/std/infertility (Accessed October 4, 2012).

STIs, 2011. Centers for Disease Control and Prevention. (2011). Sexually Transmitted Diseases (STDs). HIV/AIDS and STDs treatment: Guidelines, research, and updates. http://www.cdc.gov/std/hiv/treatment.htm (Accessed October 4, 2012).

Stobbe, M. (2014, December 2). Circumcision benefits outweigh the risks, CDC says. http://www.today.com/health/circumcision-benefits-outweigh-risks-cdc-says-1D80331010

Stockett, M. K. (2005). On the importance of difference: Re-envisioning sex and gender in ancient Mesoamerica, *World Archaeology, 37*(4), 566–578.

Stoltenborgh, M., et al. (2011). A global perspective on child sexual abuse: Meta-analysis of prevalence around the world. *Child Maltreatment, 16*(2), 79–101.

Stone, B. (2009, May 13). Under pressure, Craigslist to remove "erotic" ads. *The New York Times.* http://www.nytimes.com/2009/05/14/technology/companies/14craigslist.html?mtrref=www.google.com&gwh=9A562AFAA04C396A9E1A1FD48294694D&gwt=pay (Accessed July 13, 2016).

Stopes-Roe, M., & Cochrane, R. (2011). Marriage in two cultures. *British Journal of Social Psychology, 27*(2), 159–169.

Storms, M. D. (1980). Theories of sexual orientation. *Journal of Personality and Social Psychology, 38*, 783–792.

Stotzer, R. L., & MacCartney, D. (2015). The role of institutional factors on on-campus reported rape prevalence. *Journal of Interpersonal Violence,* DOI: 10.1177/0886260515580367

Stout, H. (2011, November 6). Less "he said, she said" in sex harassment cases. *The New York Times,* p. B10.

Stowers, L., & Kuo, T. (2015). Mammalian pheromones: Emerging properties and methods of detection. *Current Opinion in Neurobiology, 34*, 103–109.

Strassberg, D. S., & Holty, S. (2003). An experimental study of women's Internet personal ads. *Archives of Sexual Behavior, 32*(3), 253–260.

Strathdee, S. A., et al. (2010). HIV and risk environment for injecting drug users: The past, present, and future. *The Lancet, 376*(9737), 268–284.

Strathdee, S. A., Magis-Rodriguez, C., Mays, V. M., Jiminez, R., & Patterson, T. L. (2012). The emerging HIV epidemic on the Mexico-U.S. Border: An international case study characterizing the role of epidemiology in surveillance and response. *Annals of Epidemiology, 22*(6), 426–438.

Stratton, T. D., McLaughlin, M. A., Witte, F. M., Fosson, S. E., & Nora, L. M. (2005). Does students' exposure to gender discrimination and sexual harassment in medical school affect specialty choice and residency program selection? *Academic Medicine, 80*(4), 400–408.

Strebeigh, F. (2009). *Equal: Women reshape American law.* New York: Norton.

Stroebel, S. S. et al. (2013). Brother–sister incest: Data from anonymous computer-assisted self interviews. *Journal of Child Sexual Abuse, 22*(3), 255–276.

Strokoff, J., Owen, J., & Fincham, F. D. (2015). Diverse reactions to hooking up among U.S. university students. *Archives of Sexual Behavior, 44*, 935–943.

Studd, J. (2009). Estrogens as first-choice therapy for osteoporosis prevention and treatment in women under 60. *Climacteric, 12*(3), 206–209.

Stulhofer, A. (2006). How (un)important is penis size for women with heterosexual experience? *Archives of Sexual Behavior, 35*(1), 5–6.

Sulak, P. J., et al. (2000). Hormone withdrawal symptoms in oral contraceptive users. *Obstetrics & Gynecology, 95*, 261–266.

Sullum, J. (2007, January 25). 10 million missing Chinese girls reason online. Available at http://www.reason.com/blog/show/118311.html.

Sun, A., & Ren, J. (2012). Estrogen replacement therapy and cardiac function under metabolic syndrome. *Hypertension, 59*, 552–554.

Sun, C. J., et al. (2015, November 2). More than Grindr: A comparison of MSM who use Grindr, other apps, or no apps—Implications for health promotion and disease prevention. Online program presentation 332144. *American Public Health Association,* https://apha.confex.com/apha/143am/webprogram/Paper332144.html

Surratt, H. L., Kurtz, S. P., Weaver, J. C., & Inciardi, J. A. (2005). The connections of mental health problems, violent life experiences, and the social milieu of the "stroll" with the HIV risk behaviors of female street sex workers. *Journal of Psychology & Human Sexuality, 17*(1–2), 23–44.

Sutcliffe, C. G., et al. (2009). Incidence of HIV and sexually transmitted infections and risk factors for acquisition among young methamphetamine users in Northern Thailand. *Sexually Transmitted Diseases, 36*(5), 284–289.

Swirsky, J. M., & Angelone, D. J. (2015). Equality, empowerment, and choice: What does feminism mean to contemporary women? *Journal of Gender Studies,* DOI: 10.1080/09589236.2015.1008429

Symons, D. (1995, Cited in Goleman, D., June 14). Sex fantasy research said to neglect women. *The New York Times,* p. C14.

Syphilis—reported cases, 2011. Centers for Disease Control and Prevention. (2011). 2010 Sexually transmitted diseases surveillance. Figure 34. Syphilis—Reported cases by stage of infection, United States, 1941–2010. http://www.cdc.gov/std/stats10/figures/34.htm (Accessed October 4, 2012).

Syphilis, 2012. Centers for Disease Control and Prevention. (2012). Sexually transmitted diseases (STDs). Syphilis. http://www.cdc.gov/std/syphilis/default.htm (Accessed October 4, 2012).

Syphilis statistics. (2015). Centers for Disease Control and Prevention. http://www.cdc.gov/std/syphilis/stats.htm

Syphilis treatment and care. (2015). Centers for Disease Control and Prevention. http://www.cdc.gov/std/syphilis/treatment.htm

Szablewska, N., & Bradley, C. (2015). Social justice within transitional justice: The case of human trafficking and sex-work in Cambodia and Myanmar. *Current Issues in Transitional Justice, 4,* 261–287.

Szabo, R., & Short, R. V. (2000). How does male circumcision protect against HIV infection? *British Medical Journal, 320,* 1592–1594.

Tabak, J. A., & Zayas, V. (2012). The Roles of featural and configural face processing in snap judgments of sexual orientation. *PLoS ONE, 7*(5), e36671. DOI:10.1371/journal.pone.0036671

Taha, E. T., et al. (2003). Short postexposure prophylaxis in newborn babies to reduce mother-to-child transmission of HIV-1: NVAZ randomised clinical trial. *Lancet, 362*(9391), 1171–1177.

Tamimi, R. M., Hankinson, S. E., Chen, W. Y., Rosner, B., & Colditz, G. A. (2006). Combined estrogen and testosterone use and risk of breast cancer in postmenopausal women. *Archives of Internal Medicine, 166,* 1483–1489.

Tan, H. M., Tong, S. F., & Ho, C. C. K. (2012). Men's health: Sexual dysfunction, physical, and psychological health—Is there a link? *Journal of Sexual Medicine, 9*(3), 663–671.

Tan, R. S. (2002). Managing the andropause in aging men. *Clinical Geriatrics.* www.mmhc.com/cg/articles/CG9907/Tan.html.

Tan, R. S., & Culberson, J. W. (2003). An integrative review on current evidence of testosterone replacement therapy for the andropause. *Maturitas, 45*(1), 15–27.

Tanfer, K., Grady, W. R., Klepinger, D. H., & Billy, J. O. G. (1993). Condom use among U.S. men, 1991. *Family Planning Perspectives, 25,* 61–66.

Tang, C. S., Yeung, D. Y., & Lee, A. M. (2003). Psychosocial correlates of emotional responses to menarche among Chinese adolescent girls. *Journal of Adolescent Health, 33*(3), 193–201.

Tang, M. C., Weiss, N. S., & Malone, K. E. (2000). Induced abortion in relation to breast cancer among parous women: A birth certificate registry study. *Epidemiology, 11*(2), 177–180.

Tavernise, S. (2015, July 5). Colorado's effort against teenage pregnancies is a startling success. *The New York Times.* http://www.nytimes.com/2015/07/06/science/colorados-push-against-teenage-pregnancies-is-a-startling-success.html (Accessed July 13, 2016).

Taylor, K. (2013, July 12). She can play that game, too. *The New York Times,* p. ST1.

Taylor, M. J., Rudkin, L., & Hawton, K. (2005). Strategies for managing antidepressant-induced sexual dysfunction: Systematic review of randomised controlled trials. *Journal of Affective Disorders, 88*(3), 241–254.

Taylor, V., & Rupp, L. J. (2004). Chicks with dicks, men in dresses: What it means to be a drag queen. *Journal of Homosexuality, 46*(3–4), 113–133.

Teen Pregnancy Prevention and United States Students. (2011, July 12). Centers for Disease Control and Prevention. http://www.cdc.gov/healthyyouth/yrbs/pdf/us_pregnancy_combo.pdf (Accessed September 23, 2012).

Telushkin, J. (1991). *Jewish literacy.* New York: HarperCollins.

Temple, J. R., et al. (2012). Teen sexting and its association with sexual behaviors. *Archives of Pediatric & Adolescent Medicine, 166*(9), 828–833.

Templeton, A., & Grimes, D. A. (2011). A request for abortion. *New England Journal of Medicine, 365,* 2198–2204.

Teo, F. H., Oliveira, R. T. D., Mamoni, R. L., Coelho, O. R., & Blotta, M. H. S. L. (2009). I 009 Quantification and Characterization of $CD4^+CD28^{null}$ and $CD4^+CD28^+$ T Cells in Patients with Chronic Coronary Artery Disease and Healthy Subjects. *Atherosclerosis Supplements, 10*(3), 30.

ter Kuile, M. M., Both, S., & van Lankveld, J. J. D. M. (2012). Sexual dysfunctions in women. In P. Sturmey, & M. Hersen (Eds.). *Handbook of evidence-based practice in clinical psychology, adult disorders* (pp. 413–436). Hoboken, NJ: Wiley.

ter Kuile, M. M., et al. (2009). Therapist-aided exposure for women with lifelong vaginismus: A replicated single-case design. *Journal of Consulting and Clinical Psychology, 77,* 149–159.

Terasawa, E., et al. (2012). Body weight impact on puberty: Effects of high-calorie diet on puberty onset in female rhesus monkeys. *Endocrinology, 153*(4), 1696–1705.

Thachil, A., & Bhugra, D. (2006). Literature update: A critical review. *Sexual and Relationship Therapy, 21*(2), 229–235.

Thaler, N. S., et al. (2013). Neuropsychological profiles of six children with anoxic brain injury. *Child Neuropsychology: A Journal on Normal and Abnormal Development in Childhood and Adolescence, 19*(5), 479–494.

Thapar, A., Collishaw, S., Pine, D. S., & Thapar, A. K. (2012). Depression in adolescence. *The Lancet, 379*(9820), 1056–1067.

Thapar, A., Cooper, M., Jefferies, R., & Stergiakoull, E. (2010). What causes attention deficit hyperactivity disorder? *Archives of Disease in Childhood, 97,* 260–265.

The Huffington Post. (2013, May 4). Porn sites get more visitors each month than Netflix, Amazon and Twitter combined. http://www.huffingtonpost.com/2013/05/03/internet-porn-stats_n_3187682.html

The link between HPV and cancer. (2015). Centers for Disease Control and Prevention. http://www.cdc.gov/hpv/parents/cancer.html

The New York Observer. http://www.observer.com/2008/equal-hypocrisy-unequal-punishment.

The New York Times/CBS News Poll, April 22–26, 2009. (2009, April 27). http://graphics8.nytimes.com/packages/images/nytint/docs/new-york-times-cbs-news-poll-obamas-100th-day-in-office/original.pdf.

Thibaut, F. (2011). Pharmacological treatment of sex offenders. *Sexologies, 20*(3),166–168.

Thibaut, F. (2012). Pharmacological treatment of paraphilias. *Israel Journal of Psychiatry and Related Sciences, 49*(4), 297–305.

Thigpen, T. W. (2009). Early sexual behavior in a sample of low-income, African American children. *Journal of Sex Research, 46*(1), 67–79.

Thomas, N. L., & Coughtrie, M. W. H. (2003). Sulfation of apomorphine by human sulfotransferases: Evidence of a major role for the polymorphic phenol sulfotransferase, SULT1A1. *Xenobiotica, 33*(11), 1139–1148.

Thomas, R. M., & Murray, T. R. (2009). *Sex and the American teenager: Seeing through the myths and confronting the issues.* Lanham, MD: L & R Publishers.

Thompson, A. E., O'Sullivan, L. F. (2012). Gender differencs in associaions of sexual and romantic stimuli: Do young men really prefer sex over romance? *Archives of Sexual Behavior, 41*(4), 949–957.

Thompson, B., & Borrello, G. M. (2008). Different views of love: Deductive and inductive lines of inquiry. *Current Directions in Psychological Science, 1*(5), 154–156.

Thompson, E. M., & Morgan, E. M. (2008). "Mostly straight" young women: Variations in sexual behavior and identity. *Developmental Psychology, 44*(1), 15–21.

Thompson, I. M., et al. (2005). Erectile dysfunction and subsequent cardiovascular disease. *Journal of the American Medical Association, 294*(23), 2996–3002.

Thompson, J. K., & Tantleff, S. (1992). Female and male ratings of upper torso: Actual, ideal, and stereotypical conceptions. *Journal of Social Behavior and Personality, 7,* 345–354.

Thorp, J., Palacios, S., Symons, J., Simon, J., & Barour, K. (2014). Improving prospects for treating hypoactive sexual desire disorder (HSDD): Developmental status of flibanserin. *BJOG: An International Journal of Obstetrics and Gynaecology, 121*(11), 1328–1331.

Tobian, A. A. R, et al. (2009). Male circumcision for the prevention of HSV-2 and HPV infections and syphilis. *New England Journal of Medicine, 360,* 1298-1309.

Tobian, A. A. R., & Gray, R. H. (2011). The medical benefits of male circumcision. *Journal of the American Medical Association, 306*(13), 1479–1480.

Tomasetto, C., Alparone, F. R., & Cadinu, M. (2011). Girls' math performances under stereotype threat. *Developmental Psychology, 47*(4), 943–949.

Topper, S. M., Aguilar, S. C., Topper, V. Y., Elbel, E., & Pierce-Shimomura, J. T. (2014). Alcohol disinhibition of behaviors in C. elegans. *PLoS ONE, 9*(3), e92965.

Tornello, S. L., & Patterson, C. J. (2015). Timing of parenthood and experiences of gay fathers: A life course perspective. *Journal of GLBT Family Studies, 11*(1), 35–56.

Totman, R. (2004). *The third sex: Kathoey: Thailand's ladyboys.* London: Souvenir Press.

Touhara, K., & Vosshall, L. B. (2009). Sensing odorants and pheromones with chemosensory receptors. *Annual Review of Physiology, 71,* 307–332.

Townsend, C. L., et al. (2014). Earlier initiation of ART and further decline in mother-to-child HIV transmission rates. *AIDS, 28*(7), 1049–1057.

Townsend, J. M., Wasserman, T. H., & Rosenthal, A. (2015). Gender difference in emotional reactions and sexual coercion in casual sexual relations: An evolutionary perspective. *Personality and Individual Differences, 85,* 41–49.

Traish, A. M., Goldstein, I., Munarriz, R., & Guay, A. (2006). Roles of androgens in women's sexual function & dysfunction: What have we learned in sex decades? *Current Women's Health Reviews, 2*(1), 75–86.

Trichomoniasis. (2015). Centers for Disease Control and Prevention. http://www.cdc.gov/std/tg2015/trichomoniasis.htm

Trichomoniasis—CDC fact sheet. (2016). http://www.cdc.gov/std/trichomonas/stdfact-trichomoniasis.htm (Accessed July 8, 2016)

Trivedi, D., et al. (2012). Can simvastatin improve erectile function and health-related quality of life in men aged ≥40 years with erectile dysfunction? Results of the Erectile Dysfunction and Statins Trial. *BJUI*, DOI: 10.1111/j.1464-410X.2012.11241.x

Troxel, W. M., & Matthews, K. A. (2004). What are the costs of marital conflict and dissolution to children's physical health? *Clinical Child & Family Psychology Review, 7*(1), 29–57.

Trudel, G., Turgeon, L., & Piche, L. (2000). Marital and sexual aspects of old age. *Sexual & Relationship Therapy, 15*(4), 381–406.

Trulsson, O., & Rådestad, I. (2004). The silent child—Mothers' experiences before, during, and after stillbirth. *Birth: Issues in Perinatal Care, 31*(3), 189–195.

Truman, J. T., & Langton, L. (2015). Criminal victimization, 2014. U.S. Department of Justice: Bureau of Justice Statistics. http://www.bjs.gov/content/pub/pdf/cv14.pdf

Tsaliki, L. (2011). Playing with porn: Greek children's explorations in pornography. *Sex Education: Sexuality, Society and Learning, 11*(3), 293–302.

Tucker, J., & Poston, D. L. (Eds.). (2009). *Gender policy and HIV in China: Catalyzing policy change.* Amsterdam: Springer.

Tunariu, A. D., & Reavey, P. (2003). Men in love: Living with sexual boredom. *Sexual & Relationship Therapy, 18*(1), 63–94.

Tuomikoski, P., et al. (2009). Evidence for a role for hot flushes in vascular function in recently postmenopausal women. *Obstetrics and Gynecology, 113*(4), 902–908.

Turkewitz, J. (2015, February 5). Genital cutting cases seen more as immigration rises. *The New York Times*, p. A11.

Turner, H. A., Finkelhor, D., & Ormrod, R. (2006). The effect of lifetime victimization on the mental health of children and adolescents. *Social Science & Medicine, 62*(1), 13–27.

Turton, J. (2005). Perspectives on female sex offending: A culture of denial. *Sexualities, 8*(5), 632–633.

Turton, P., et al. (2006). Psychological impact of stillbirth on fathers in the subsequent pregnancy and puerperium. *British Journal of Psychiatry, 188*(2), 165–172.

Twenge, J. M., Sherman, R. A., & Wells, B. E. (2015). Changes in American adults' sexual behavior and attitudes, 1972–2012. *Archives of Sexual Behavior*, DOI: 10.1007/s10508-015-0540-2

Tyler, M. (2009). No means yes? Perpetuating myths in the sexological construction of women's desire. *Women & Therapy, 32*(1), 40–50.

U.S. Abortion Statistics. (2012, May 24). Facts and figures relating to the frequency of abortion in the United States. http://www.abort73.com/abortion_facts/us_abortion_statistics (Accessed June 23, 2012).

U.S. Bureau of the Census. (2005). *Statistical abstract of the United States* (125th ed.). Washington, DC: U.S. Government Printing Office.

U.S. Bureau of the Census. (2006). U.S. Bureau of the Census, current population reports, estimated median age at first marriage, by sex: 1890–present. www.census.gov/population/socdemo/hh-fam/ms2.pdf.

U.S. Bureau of the Census. (2011). *Families and living arrangements*. Retrieved from http://www.census.gov/population/www/socdemo/hh-fam.html

U. S. Bureau of the Census. (2015). Families and living arrangements main. www.census.gov

U.S. Census Bureau, "America's Families and Living Arrangements" for 2010 (Table UC3). *Current Population Reports*. Available online at www.census.gov/population/www/socdemo/hh-fam/cps2010.html

U.S. Census Bureau. (2011). *America's families and living arrangements for 2010.* (Current Population Reports, Table UC3). Retrieved from www.census.gov/population/www/socdemo/hh-fam/cps2010.html

U.S. Department of Justice. (1986). *Attorney general's commission on pornography: Final report.* Washington, DC: U.S. Government Printing Office.

U.S. Department of Justice. *Criminal victimization in the United States. Statistical tables, 2003.* Office of Justice Programs. Bureau of Justice Statistics. Accessed February 15, 2006. www.ojp.usdoj.gov/bjs/abstract/cvus/rape_sexual_assault.htm.

U.S. Department of Labor, Bureau of Labor Statistics, Economic News Release. (September 2011). Employment situation. Employment status of the civilian population 25 years and over by educational attainment (Table A-4). Available at http://www.bls.gov/news.release/empsit.t04.htm

U.S. National Library of Medicine. (2006). *Androgen insensitivity syndrome.* National Institutes of Health. http://ghr.nlm.nih.gov/condition-androgeninsensitivitysyndrome.

U.S. Preventive Services Task Force. (2009). Screening for breast cancer: U.S. Preventive Services Task Force recommendation statement. *Annals of Internal Medicine, 151*(10), 716–726.

Udry, J. R. (2001). Feminist critics uncover determinism, positivism, and antiquated theory. *American Sociological Review, 66*(4), 611–618.

Ullman, S. E., Filipas, H. H., Townsend, S. M., & Starzynski, L. L. (2006). The role of victim–offender relationship in women's sexual assault experiences. *Journal of Interpersonal Violence, 21*(6), 798–819.

UNAIDS. (2006). *Report on the global AIDS epidemic: Executive summary.* Joint United Nations Programme on HIV/AIDS (UNAIDS). Geneva: UNAIDS.

Unger, J. A. (2014). Mode of delivery and postpartum HIV-1 disease progression and mortality in a Kenyan cohort. *BMC: Pregnancy & Childbirth, 14,* 257ff.

UNICEF. (2012). HIV and Infant Feeding. http://www.unicef.org/programme/breastfeeding/hiv.htm (Accessed September 21, 2012).

Unigwe, C. (2011). *On Black Sisters Street.* New York: Random House.

Unigwe, C. (2012, April 19). Legality brings protection and better care. *The New York Times.* http://www.nytimes.com/roomfordebate/2012/04/19/is-legalized-prostitution-safer/legalizing-prostitution-brings-protection-and-better-care (Accessed July 13, 2016).

United Nations Special Session on AIDS. (2001, June 25–27). *Preventing HIV/AIDS among young people.* New York: United Nations.

University Counseling & Testing Center. (2016). Sexual harassment: Myths and realities. Eugene, Oregon: University of Oregon. https://counseling.uoregon.edu/Topics-Resources/Student-Self-Help/Sexual-Assault-Abuse-Harassment/Sexual-Harassment-Myths (Accessed July 18, 2016).

University of Maryland Medical Center. (2011). Cervical cancer—Prognosis. http://www.umm.edu/patiented/articles/how_serious_cervical_cancer_000046_5.htm

University of Michigan. (2009). *Masturbation.* http://www.med.umich.edu/yourchild/topics/masturb.htm (Accessed September 23, 2012).

Ussher, J. M., Perz, J., & Parton, C. (2015). Sex and the menopausal woman: A critical review and analysis. *Feminism & Psychology*, DOI: 10.1177/0959353515579735

Utian, W. H. (2012). Recent developments in pharmacotherapy for vasomotor symptoms. *Current Obstetrics and Gynecology Reports*, DOI:10.1007/s13669-012-0009-4

Vaculík, M., & Hudecek, T. (2005). Development of close relationships in the Internet environment. *Ceskoslovenská Psychologie, 49*(2), 157–174.

Valkenburg, P. M., Sumter, S. R., & Peter, J. (2011). Gender differences in online and offline self-disclosure in pre-adolescence and adolescence. *British Journal of Developmental Psychology, 29*(2), 253–269.

Valocchi, S. (2005). Not yet queer enough: The lessons of queer theory for the sociology of gender and sexuality. *Gender & Society, 19*(6), 750–770.

van de Beek, C., van Goozen, S. H. M., Buitelaar, J. K., & Cohen-Kettenis, P. T. (2009). Prenatal sex hormones (maternal and amniotic fluid) and gender-related play behavior in 13-month-old infants. *Archives of Sexual Behavior, 38*(1), 6–15.

van den Bree, M. B. M., & Pickworth, W. B. (2005). Risk factors predicting changes in marijuana involvement in teenagers. *Archives of General Psychiatry, 62*(3), 311–319.

van der Made, F., et al. (2008). Childhood sexual abuse, selective attention for sexual cues and the effects of testosterone with or without vardenafil on physiological sexual arousal in women with sexual dysfunction: A pilot study. *Journal of Sexual Medicine, 6*(2), 429–439.

Van Lange, P. A. M., & Rusbult, C. E. (2012). Interdependence theory. In P. A. M. Van Lange et al. (Eds.). *Handbook of theories of social psychology, Vol. 2* (pp. 251–272). Thousand Oaks, CA: Sage.

Van Lange, P. A. M., et al. (1997). Willingness to sacrifice in close relationships. *Journal of Personality & Social Psychology, 72*(6), 1373–1395.

van Lankveld, J. (2008). Problems with sexual interest and desire in women. In D. L. Rowland & L. Incrocci (Eds.), *Handbook of sexual and gender identity disorders.* Hoboken, NJ: Wiley.

van Lankveld, J. (2009). Self-help therapies for sexual dysfunction. *Journal of Sex Research, 46*(2), 143–155.

van Lankveld, J. J. D. M., et al. (2010). Women's sexual pain disorders. *Journal of Sexual Medicine, 7,* 615–631.

van Oort, J. (2012). Augustine and the books of the Manichaeans. In M. Vessey (Ed.). *A companion to Augustine* (pp. 188–199). Chichester, UK: Wiley-Blackwell.

van Straaten, I., Engels, R. C. M. E., Finkenauer, C., & Holland, R. W. (2009). Meeting your match: How attractiveness similarity affects approach behavior in mixed-sex dyads. *Personality and Social Psychology Bulletin, 35*(6), 685–697.

Vasey, P. L., Leca, J., Gunst, N., & VanderLaan, D. P. (2014). Female homosexual behavior and inter-sexual mate competition in Japanese macaques: Possible implications for sexual selection theory. *Neuroscience & Biobehavioral Reviews, 46*(4), 573–578.

Veale, D., et al. (2015a). Environmental and physical risk factors for men to develop body dysmorphic disorder concerning penis size compared to men anxious about their penis size and men with no concerns: A cohort study. *Journal of Obsessive-Compulsive and Related Disorders, 6,* 49–58.

Veale, D., Miles, S., Bramley, S., Muir, G., & Hodsoll, J. (2015b). Am I normal? A systematic review and construction of nomograms for flaccid and erect penis length and circumference in up to 15,521 men. *British Journal of Urology, 115*(6), 978–986.

Vennila, V., et al. (2014). Tetracycline-induced discoloration of deciduous teeth: Case series. *Journal of International Oral Health, 6*(3), 115–119.

Ventura, S. J. (2009, May). Changing patterns of nonmarital childbearing in the United States. NCHS data brief number 18. Hyattsville, MD: National Center for Health Statistics. Accessed May 13, 2009. http://www.cdc.gov/nchs/data/databriefs/db18.htm.

Vickerman, K. A., & Margolina, G. (2009). Rape treatment outcome research: Empirical findings and state of the literature. *Clinical Psychology Review, 29,* 431–448.

Vilarinho, S., et al. (2014). Affective and cognitive determinants of women's sexual response to erotica. *The Journal of Sexual Medicine, 11*(11), 2671–2678.

Villar, F., Villamizar, D. J., & López–Chivrall, S. (2005). Components of loving experience in old age: Older people and long-term relationships. *Revista Espanola de Geriatria y Gerontologia, 40*(3), 166–177.

Vinkhuyzen, A. A. E., et al. (2012). Reconsidering the heritability of intelligence in adulthood: Taking assortative mating and cultural transmission into account. *Behavior Genetics, 42*(2), 187–198.

Vitkova, M., et al. (2014). Health-related quality of life in multiple sclerosis pateints with bladder, bowel and sexual dysfunction. *Disability and Rehabilitation, 36*(12), 987–992.

Vlachopoulos, C. (2015). Definition and assessment of erectile dysfunction. In M. Viigimaa et al. (Eds.). *Erectile dysfunction in hypertension and cardiovascular disease* (pp. 1–8). Switzerland: Springer International Publishing.

Vladutiu, C. J., Martin, S. L., & Macy, R. J. (2011). College- or university-based sexual assault prevention programs: A review of program outcomes, characteristics, and recommendations. *Trauma, Violence, Abuse, 12*(2), 67–86.

Vohs, K. D., & Baumeister, R. F. (2004). Sexual passion, intimacy, and gender. In D. J. Mashek & A. P. Aron (Eds.), *Handbook of closeness and intimacy* (pp. 189–199). Hillsdale, NJ: Erlbaum.

Volk, J. E., et al. (2015). No new HIV infections with increasing use of HIV preexposure prophylaxis in a clinical practice setting. *Clinical Infectious Diseases, 61*(10), 1601–1603.

Vorauer, J. D., Cameron, J. J., Holmes, J. G., & Pearce, D. G. (2003). Invisible overtures: Fears of rejection and the signal amplification bias. *Journal of Personality & Social Psychology, 84*(4), 793–812.

Voyer, D., & Voyer, S. D. (2014). Gender differences in scholastic achievement: A meta-analysis. *Psychological Bulletin, 140*(4), 1174–1204.

Voyeuristic disorder. (2012). U 07 Voyeuristic disorder. American Psychiatric Association. DSM-5 Development. http://www.dsm5.org/proposedrevision/pages/proposedrevision.aspx?rid=190.

Vrangalova, Z., & Savin-Williams, R. (2012). Mostly heterosexual and mostly gay/lesbian: Evidence for new sexual orientation identities. *Archives of Sexual Behavior, 41*(1), 85–101.

Vulvovaginal candidiasis. (2015). Centers for Disease Control and Prevention. http://www.cdc.gov/std/tg2015/candidiasis.htm

Wachtel, M. S., Yang, S., & Morris, B. J. (2015). Countries with high circumcision prevalence have lower prostate cancer mortality. *Asian Journal of Andrology,* http://www.ajandrology.com/preprintarticle.asp?id=159713

Wack, E. R., & Tantleff-Dunn, S. (2008). Cyber sexy: Electronic game play and perceptions of attractiveness among college-aged men. *Body Image, 5*(4), 365–374.

Wagenaar, H. (2006). Democracy and prostitution: Deliberating the legalization of brothels in the Netherlands. *Administration & Society, 38*(2), 98–235.

Wagner, I. V., Sabin, M., & Kiess, W. Influences of childhood obesity on pubertal development. In W. Kiess, et al. (Eds). *Metabolic syndrome and obesity in childhood and adolescence* (pp. 110–125). Basel, Karger.

Waismann, R., Fenwick, P. B. C., Wilson, G. D., Hewett, T. D., & Lumsden, J. (2003). EEG responses to visual erotic stimuli in men with normal and paraphilic interests. *Archives of Sexual Behavior, 32*(2), 135–144.

Wald, A. (2005, November 22). Investigational HPV vaccine shows 100% efficacy. *Journal Watch Women's Health.*

Waldinger, M. D. (2011). The management of premature ejaculation. *Current Clinical Urology,*Part 5, 709–720.

Waldinger, M. D., et al. (2002). The selective serotonin re-uptake inhibitors fluvoxamine and paroxetine differ in sexual inhibitory effects after chronic treatment. *Psychopharmacology, 160*(3), 283–289.

Waldinger, M. D., Zwinderman, A. H., & Olivier, B. (2001). Antidepressants and ejaculation: A double-blind, randomized, placebo-controlled, fixed-dose study with paroxetine, sertraline and nefazodone. *Journal of Clinical Psychopharmacology, 21*(3), 293–297.

Walrave, M., et al. (2015). Whether or not to engage in sexting: Explaining adolescent sexting behaviour by applying the prototype willingness model. *Telematics and Informatics, 32*(4), 796–808.

Walker, A. (2010). Breast milk as the gold standard for protective nutrients. *Journal of Pediatrics, 156*(Suppl. 2), S3–S7.

Walker, J., Archer, J., & Davies, M. (2005). Effects of rape on men: A descriptive analysis. *Archives of Sexual Behavior, 34*(1), 69–80.

Wallen, K., & Hassett, J. M. (2009). Sexual differentiation of behaviour in monkeys: Role of prenatal hormones. *Journal of Neuroendocrinology, 21*(4), 421–426.

Walther, C. S., & Poston, D. L., Jr. (2004). Patterns of gay and lesbian partnering in the larger metropolitan areas of the United States. *Journal of Sex Research, 41*(2), 201–214.

Waltman, M. (2012, April 20). Criminalize only the buying of sex. *The New York Times.* http://www.nytimes.com/roomfordebate/2012/04/19/is-legalized-prostitution-safer/criminalize-buying-not-selling-sex *(Accessed July 13, 2016).*

Walum, H., et al. (2012). Variation in the oxytocin receptor gene is associated with pair-bonding and social behavior. *Biological Psychiatry, 71*(5), 419–426.

Walum, H., Waldman, I. D., & Young, L. J. (2015). Statistical and methodological considerations for the interpretation of intranasal oxytocin studies. *Biological Psychiatry,* DOI: 10.1016/j.biopsych.2015.06.016

Wambach, K. A., et al. (2011). A randomized controlled trial of breastfeeding support and education for adolescent mothers. *Western Journal of Nursing Research, 33*(4), 486–505.

Wandrey, R. L., Mosack, K. E., & Moore, E. M. (2015). Coming out to family and friends as bisexually identified young adult women: A discussion of homophobia, biphobia, and heteronormativity. *Journal of Bisexuality, 15*(2), 204–229.

Wang, W. (2012, February 16). *The Rise of Intermarriage: Rates, Characteristics Vary by Race and Gender.* http://www.pew-socialtrends.org/2012/02/16/the-rise-of-intermarriage/1/(Accessed June 24, 2012).

Wang, X., Dow-Edwards, D., Anderson, V., Minkoff, H., & Hurd, Y. L. (2004). In utero marijuana exposure associated with abnormal amygdala dopamine d-sub-2 gene expression in the human fetus. *Biological Psychiatry, 56*(12), 909–915.

Ward, T., & Gannon, T. A. (2006). Rehabilitation, etiology, and self-regulation: The comprehensive good lives model of treatment for sexual offenders. *Aggression and Violent Behavior, 11*(1), 77–94.

Ward, B. W., Dahlhamer, J. M., Galinsky, A. M., & Joestl, S. S. (2014, July 15). Sexual orientation and health among U.S. adults: National Health Interview Survey, 2013. National Health Statistics Reports (77). Hyattsville, MD: National Center for Health Statistics.

Washington Post. (2015, June 12). One in 5 college women say they were violated. http://www.washingtonpost.com/sf/local/2015/06/12/1-in-5-women-say-they-were-violated/

Washington Post. (2015a, June 12). One in 5 college women say they were violated. http://www.washingtonpost.com/sf/local/2015/06/12/1-in-5-women-say-they-were-violated/

Washington Post-Kaiser Family Foundation. (2015). Washington Post-Kaiser Family Foundation Survey of College Students on Sexual Assault. http://apps.washingtonpost.com/g/page/national/washington-post-kaiser-family-foundation-survey-of-college-students-on-sexual-assault/1726/

Waterman, J. (1986). Overview of treatment issues. In K. MacFarlane et al. (Eds.), *Sexual abuse of young children: Evaluation and treatment* (pp. 197–203). New York: Guilford.

Watts, C., & Zimmerman, C. (2002). Violence against women: Global scope and magnitude. *Lancet, 359*(9313), 1232–1237.

Waylen, A. E. (2010). Romantic and sexual behavior in young adolescents: Repeated surveys in a population-based cohort. *Journal of Early Adolescence, 30*(3), 432–443.

Weaver, L. (2012). A short history of infant feeding and growth. *Early Human Development, 88*(Suppl. 1), S57–S59.

Weeden, J., & Sabini, J. (2005). Physical attractiveness and health in Western societies: A review. *Psychological Bulletin, 131*(5), 635–653.

Weinberg, T. S. (1987). Sadomasochism in the United States: A review of recent sociological literature. *Journal of Sex Research, 23,* 50–69.

Weinrich, J. D., & Klein, F. (2002). Bi-gay, bi-straight, and bi-bi: Three bisexual subgroups identified using cluster analysis of the Klein Sexual Orientation Grid. *Journal of Bisexuality, 2*(4), 109–139.

Weinstein, N., Ryan, W. S., DeHaan, C. R., Przybylski, A. K., Legate, N., & Ryan, R. M. (2012). Parental autonomy support and discrepancies between implicit and explicit sexual identities: Dynamics of self-acceptance and defense. *Journal of Personality and Social Psychology, 102*(4), 815–832.

Weiss, H. A., Wasserheit, J. N., Barnabas, R. V., Hayes, R. J., & Abu-Raddad, L. J. (2008). Persisting with prevention: The importance of adherence for HIV prevention. *Emerging Themes in Epidemiology, 5,* 8.

Weitzer, R. (2007a). Prostitution: Facts and fictions. *Contexts, 6*(4), 28–33.

Weitzer, R. (2012a). *Legalizing prostitution: From illicit vice to lawful business.* New York: New York University Press.

Weitzer, R. (2012b). Male prostitution. In C. D. Bryant (Ed.). *The Routledge handbook of deviant behavior* (pp. 378–382). New York: Routledge.

Weizer, R. (2007b). The social construction of sex trafficking: Ideology and institutionalization of a moral crusade. *Politics & Society, 35*(3), 447–475.

Welldon, E. V. (2005). Incest: A therapeutic challenge. In G. Ambrosio (Ed.), *On incest: Psychoanalytic perspectives* (pp. 81–100). London: Karnac Books.

Welling, L. L. M. (2014). Female orgasm. In V. A. Weekes-Shackelford, & T. K. Shackelford (Eds.). *Evolutionary perspectives on human sexual psychology and behavior* (pp. 223–241). New York: Springer Science+Business Media.

West, S. L., et al. (2008). Prevalence of low sexual desire and hypoactive sexual desire disorder in a nationally representative sample of US women. *Archives of Internal Medicine, 168*(13), 1441–1449.

West, E., & Krychman, M. (2015). Natural aphrodisiacs—A review of selected sexual enhancers. *Sexual Medicine Reviews, 3*(4), 279–288.

Western Resistance. (2006, May 25). *Pakistan: "Hudood" ordinances (Islamic rape/adultery laws) may be repealed.* www.westernresistance.com/blog/archives/002215.html.

Wheeler, J., Newring, K. A. B., & Draper, C. (2008). Transvestic fetishism: Psychopathology and theory. In D. R. Laws & W. T. O'Donohue (Eds.), *Sexual deviance: Theory, assessment, and treatment* (2nd ed., pp. 272–284). New York: Guilford Press.

Whipple, B. (2015). Female ejaculation, G spot, A spot, and should we be looking for spots? *Current Sexual Health Reports, 7*(2), 59–62.

Whipple, B., & Komisaruk, B. R. (1988). Analgesia produced in women by genital self-stimulation. *Journal of Sex Research, 24,* 130–140.

Whisman, M. A., & Snyder, D. K. (2007). Sexual infidelity in a national survey of American women: differences in prevalence and correlates as a function of method of assessment. *The Journal of Family Psychology, 21*(2),147–154.

White, R. G., et al. (2008). Male circumcision for HIV prevention in sub-Saharan Africa: Who, what and when? *AIDS, 22*(14), 1841–1850.

Whitehead, B. D., & Popenoe, D. (2006). The state of our unions: The social health of marriage in America 2006. New Brunswick, NJ: Rutgers University.

Whitley, B. E., Jr. (1983). Sex role orientation and self-esteem: A critical meta-analysis. *Journal of Personality and Social Psychology, 44,* 765–788.

Whitmarsh, L., & Wentworth, D. K. (2012). Gender similarity or gender difference? Contemporary women's and men's career patterns. *The Career Development Quarterly, 60*(1), 47–64.

Wickerham, D. L. et al. (2015). Final updated results of the NRG Oncology/NSABP Protocol P-2: Study of tamoxifen and raloxifene (STAR) in preventing breast cancer. *Journal of Clinical Oncology, 33*(15), 1500ff.

Wierman, M. E., et al. (2010). Endocrine aspects of women's sexual function. *Journal of Sexual Medicine, 7,* 561–585.

Wieselquist, J., Rusbult, C. E., Foster, C. A., & Agnew, C. R. (1999). Commitment, pro-relationship behavior, and trust in close relationships. *Journal of Personality & Social Psychology, 77*(5), 942–966.

Wilcox, A. J., Dunson, D., & Baird, D. D. (2000). The timing of the "fertile window" in the menstrual cycle: Day specific estimates from a prospective study. *British Medical Journal, 321,* 1259–1262.

Wilcox, W. B. (2015, July 26). Marriage remains the gold standard. *The New York Times.* http://www.nytimes.com/roomfordebate/2015/07/06/has-being-single-in-america-changed/marriage-remains-the-gold-standard (Accessed July 13, 2016).

Wilcox, W. B., & Marquardt, E. (Eds.). (2010). *When marriage disappears: The new middle America.* Charlottesville, VA: National Marriage Project/Institute for American Values.

Wilcox, W. B., & Marquardt, E. (Eds.). (2011). *The state of our unions: Marriage in America 2011.* Charlottesville, VA: The National Marriage Project/Institute for American Values.

Willetts, M. C. (2006). Union quality comparisons between long-term heterosexual cohabitation and legal marriage. *Journal of Family Issues, 27*(1), 110–127.

Williams, D. E., & D'Alessandro, J. D. (1994). A comparison of three measures of androgyny and their relationship to psychological adjustment. *Journal of Social Behavior and Personality, 9*(3), 469–480.

Williams, J. E., & Best, D. L. (1994). Cross-cultural views of women and men. In W. J. Lonner & R. Malpass (Eds.), *Psychology and culture.* Boston: Allyn & Bacon.

Williams, K. M., Cooper, B. S., Howell, T. M., Yuille, J. C., & Paulhus, D. L. (2009). Inferring sexually deviant behavior from corresponding fantasies: The role of personality and pornography consumption. *Criminal Justice and Behavior, 36*(2), 198–222.

Williams, M. E. (Ed.). (2001). *Abortion: Opposing viewpoints.* Greenhaven Press.

Williams, S. L. (2011). Gender research then and now: Complexity, intersectionality, and scientific rigor. *Sex Roles, 65*(5–6), 435–437.

Williamson, C., & Cluse–Tolar, T. (2002). Pimp-controlled prostitution: Still an integral part of street life. *Violence Against Women, 8*(9), 1074–1092.

Wilson, J. M. B., Tripp, D. A., & Boland, F. J. (2005). The relative contributions of waist-to-hip ratio and body mass index to judgments of attractiveness. *Sexualities, Evolution & Gender, 7*(3), 245–267.

Wilson, W., et al. (2000). Brain morphological changes and early marijuana use: A magnetic resonance and positron emission tomography study. *Journal of Addictive Diseases, 19*(1), 1–22.

Wilt, T. J., et al. (2008). Systematic review: Comparative effectiveness and harms of treatments for clinically localized prostate cancer. *Annals of Internal Medicine, 148*(6), 435–448.

Winfield, N. (2015, June 15). Pope Francis has started making good on his sex abuse scandal promise. *Business Insider.* http://www.businessinsider.com/pope-francis-has-started-making-good-on-his-sex-abuse-scandal-promise-2015-6

Wing, R. R., et al. (2010). Effects of weight loss intervention on erectile function in older men with type 2 diabetes in the look AHEAD trial. *Journal of Sexual Medicine, 7,* 156–165.

Winter, S. (2003). *Research and discussion paper: Language and identity in transgender: Gender wars and the case of the Thai kathoey.* Paper presented at the Hawaii conference on Social Sciences. Waikiki, HI.

Wismer Fries, A. B., Shirtcliff, E. A., & Pollak, S. D. (2008). Neuroendocrine dysregulation following early social deprivation in children. *Developmental Psychobiology, 50*(6), 588–599.

Wodarski, J. S., & Johnson, S. R. (2015). Contributing factors to child sexual abuse. In J. S. Wodarski, M. J. Holosko, & M. D. Feit (Eds.). *Evidence-informed assessment and practice in child welfare* (pp. 53–65). Switzerland: Springer International Publishing.

Womenshealth.gov. (2009, December). Female genital cutting fact sheet. http://www.womenshealth.gov/publications/our-publications/fact-sheet/female-genital-cutting.cfm

Womenshealth.gov. (2012). Female genital cutting fact sheet. http://womenshealth.gov/publications/our-publications/fact-sheet/female-genital-cutting.html

Wong, C. F., Kipke, M. D., & Weiss, G. (2008). Risk factors for alcohol use, frequent use, and binge drinking among young men who have sex with men. *Addictive Behaviors, 33*(8), 1012–1020.

Wong, D. (2012). Doing gender, doing culture: Division of labour among lesbians in Hong Kong. *Women's Studies International Forum, 35*(4), 266–275.

Wong, W. I., & Hines, M. (2015). Preferences for pick and blue: The development of color preferences as a distinct gender-typed behavior in toddlers. *Archives of Sexual Behavior, 44*(5), 1243–1254.

Wong, W. I., Pasterski, V., Hindmarsh, P. C., Geffner, M. E., & Hines, M. (2012). Are there parental socialization effects on the sex-typed behavior of individuals with congenital adrenal hyperplasia? *Archives of Sexual Behavior.* DOI:10.1007/s10508-012-9997-4

Woo, J. (2013). *Meet Grindr: How one App changed the way we connect*. New York: Jaime Woo.

Woo, J. S. T., Brotto, L. A., & Gorzalka, B. B. (2011). The role of sex guilt in the relationship between culture and women's sexual desire. *Archives of Sexual Behavior, 40*(2), 385–394.

Wood, J. T. (2005). *Gendered lives: Communication, gender, and culture* (6th ed.). Belmont, CA: Wadsworth.

Wood, N. S., et al. (2000). Neurologic and developmental disability after extremely preterm birth. *New England Journal of Medicine, 343*(6), 378–384.

Wooster, R., & Weber, B. L. (2003). Genomic medicine: Breast and ovarian cancer. *New England Journal of Medicine, 348*, 2339–2347.

Wooten, J. M. (2008). Drug-induced sexual problems. *Southern Medical Journal, 101*(11), 1092–1093.

World Health Organization. (2012, February). Female genital mutilation. Fact sheet N 241. http://www.who.int/mediacentre/factsheets/fs241/en/

World Health Organization. (2015a). Female genital mutilation. http://www.who.int/topics/female_genital_mutilation/en/

World Health Organization. (2015b). HIV/AIDS. http://www.who.int/features/qa/71/en/

World Health Organization. (2015c). HIV/AIDS fact sheet number 360. http://www.who.int/mediacentre/factsheets/fs360/en/

Wright, J. L., Lin, D. W., & Stanford, J. L. (2012). Circumcision and the risk of prostate cancer. *Cancer*, DOI: 10.1002/cncr.26653

Wright, L. W., & Bonita, A. G. (2012). A negative campus climate: Sexual harassment and homophobia. In R. D. McAnulty (Ed.). *Sex in college: The things they don't write home about* (pp. 189–210). Santa Barbara, CA: ABC-CLIO.

Wyatt, G. E. (1985). The sexual abuse of Afro-American and white American women in childhood. *Child Abuse and Neglect, 9*, 507–519.

Wyatt, G. E. (1989). Reexamining factors predicting Afro-American and white American women's age at first coitus. *Archives of Sexual Behavior, 18*, 271–298.

Wyatt, G. E., Williams, J. K., & Myers, H. F. (2008). African-American sexuality and HIV/AIDS. *Journal of the National Medical Association, 100*(1), 44–51.

Wyatt, G. E., Williams, J. K., Henderson, T., & Sumner, L. (2009). On the outside looking in: Promoting HIV/AIDS research initiated by African American investigators. *American Journal of Public Health, 99*(S1), S48–S53.

Wyatt, T. (2003). *Pheromones and animal behaviour: Communication by smell and taste.* Cambridge, UK: Cambridge University Press.

Wyatt, T. D. (2009). *Fifty years of pheromones.* Nature, 457, 262–263.

Wyatt, T. D. (2014). *Pheromones and animal behavior* (2nd ed.). Cambridge, UK: Cambridge University Press.

Wyatt, T. D. (2014). *Pheromones and animal behavior, 2nd edition.* United Kingdom: Cambridge University Press.

Xu, J., Burgoyne, P. S., & Arnold, A. P. (2002). Sex differences in sex chromosome gene expression in mouse brain. *Human Molecular Genetics, 11*(12), 1409–1419.

Xu, Y., & Zheng, Y. (2015). The relationship between digit ratio (2D:4D) and sexual orientation in men from China. *Archives of Sexual Behavior*, DOI: 10/1007/s10508-015-0535-z

Yamaguchi, K., et al. (2011). Assessment of possible effects for testosterone replacement therapy in men with symptomatic late-onset hypogonadism. *Andrologia, 43*(1), 52–56.

Yang, M., et al. (2015). Fatty acid patterns and the risk of prostate cancer in the Physicians' Health Study. *The FASEB Journal, 29*(1), Supplement 918.11.

Yarber, W. L., Torabi, M. R., & Veenker, C. H. (1989). Development of a three-component sexually transmitted diseases attitude scale. *Journal of Sex Education & Therapy, 15*, 36–49.

Yates, P. M., Hucker, S. J., & Kingston, D. A. (2008). Sexual sadism: Psychopathology and theory. In D. R. Laws and W. T. O'Donohue (Eds.), *Sexual deviance: Theory, assessment, and treatment* (2nd ed., pp. 213–230). New York: Guilford Press.

Yazzie, A. (2010). Visual-spatial thinking and academic achievement: A concurrent and predictive validity study. *Dissertation Abstracts International: Section A, Humanities and Social Sciences, 70*(8-A), 2897.

Yeap, B. B. (2009). Testosterone and ill-health in aging men. *Nature Clinical Practice Endocrinology & Metabolism, 5*, 113–121.

Yeh, K-Y., Pu, H-F., Wu, C-H., Tai, M-Y., & Tsai, Y-F. (2009). Different subregions of the medial preoptic area are separately involved in the regulation of copulation and sexual incentive motivation in male rats: A behavioral and morphological study. *Behavioural Brain Research, 205*(1), 219–225.

Yehuda, R., Lehrner, A., & Rosenbaum, T. Y. (2015). PTSD and sexual dysfunction and men and women. *Journal of Sexual Medicine, 12*(5), 1107–1119.

Yela, C. (2000). Predictors of and factors related to loving and sexual satisfaction for men and women. *European Review of Applied Psychology, 50*(1), 235–243.

Yela, C. (2006). The evaluation of love: Simplified version of the scales for Yela's tetrangular model based on Sternberg's model. *European Journal of Psychological Assessment, 22*(1), 21–27.

Yeoman, I., & Mars, M. (2012). Robots, men and sex tourism. *Futures, 44*(4), 365–371.

Yoder, V. C., Virden, T. B., III, & Amin, K. (2005). Internet pornography and loneliness: An association? *Sexual Addiction & Compulsivity, 12*(1), 19–44.

Yoshida, M. (2014). Sperm chemotaxis: The first authentication events between conspecific gametes before fertilization. In H. Sawada et al. (Eds.). *Sexual reproduction in animals and plants* (pp. 3–11). Springer Japan.

Yoshimoto, D., et al. (2006). Nonverbal communication coding systems of committed couples. In *The new handbook of methods in nonverbal behavior research* (pp. 369–397). New York: Oxford University Press.

Yost, M. R., & Thomas, G. D. (2011). Gender and binegativity: Men's and women's attitudes toward male and female bisexuals. *Archives of Sexual Behavior.* doi:10.1007/s10508-011-9767-8

Yost, M. R., & Zurbriggen, E. L. (2006). Gender differences in the enactment of sociosexuality: An examination of implicit social motives, sexual fantasies, coercive sexual attitudes, and aggressive sexual behavior. *Journal of Sex Research, 43*(2), 163–173.

YouGov. (2015). A third of young Americans say they aren't 100% heterosexual. https://today.yougov.com/news/2015/08/20/third-young-americans-exclusively-heterosexual/

Young, K. S. (2008). Internet sex addiction: Risk factors, stages of development, and treatment. *American Behavioral Scientist, 52*(1), 21–37.

Yu., G., Wall., M. M., Chiasson, M. A., & Hirshfield, S. (2015). Complex drug use patterns and associated HIV transmission risk behaviors in an Internet sample of U.S. men who have sex with men. *Archives of Sexual Behavior, 44*(2), 421–428.

Zablotska, I. B., et al. (2009). Gay men's current practice of HIV seroconcordant unprotected anal intercourse. *AIDS Care: Psychological and Socio-medical Aspects of AIDS/HIV, 21*(4), 501–510.

Zaidi, A. U., & Shuraydi, M. (2002). Perceptions of arranged marriages by young Pakistani Muslim women living in a Western society. *Journal of Comparative Family Studies, 33*(4), 495–514.

Zalenskaya, I. A., et al. (2011). Increased COX-2 expression in human vaginal epithelial cells exposed to nonoxynol-9, a vaginal contraceptive microbicide that failed to protect women from HIV-1 infection. *American Journal of Reproductive Immunology, 65*(6), 569–577.

Zandbergen, D. L., & Brown, S. G. (2015). Culture and gender differences in romantic jealousy. *Personality and Individual Differences, 72*, 122–127.

Zaviacic, M., & Whipple, B. (1993). Update on the female prostate and the phenomenon of female ejaculation. *Journal of Sex Research, 30*, 148–151.

Zaviacic, M., et al. (1988a). Concentrations of fructose in female ejaculate and urine: A comparative biochemical study. *Journal of Sex Research, 24*, 319–325.

Zaviacic, M., et al. (1988b). Female urethral expulsions evoked by local digital stimulation of the G-spot: Differences in the response patterns. *Journal of Sex Research, 24*, 311–318.

Zeichner, A., Parrott, D. J., & Frey, F. C. (2003). Gender differences in laboratory aggression under response choice conditions. *Aggressive Behavior, 29*(2), 95–106.

Zelenski, J. M., Rusting, C. L., & Larsen, R. J. (2003). Consistency in the time of experimental participation and personality correlates. *Personality & Individual Differences, 34*(4), 547–558.

Zernike, K. (2005, December 11). The siren song of sex with boys. *The New York Times.* http://www.nytimes.com/2005/12/11/weekinreview/the-siren-song-of-sex-with-boys.html (Accessed July 13, 2016).

Zernike, K. (2013, August 19). Christie signs bill outlawing a gay "cure." *The New York Times,* p. A14.

Zerubavel, E. (2006). *The elephant in the room: Silence and denial in everyday life.* New York: Oxford University Press.

Zezima, K. (2006, February 3). Teenager attacks three men at gay bar in Massachusetts. *The New York Times.* http://www.nytimes.com/2006/02/03/us/teenager-attacks-three-men-at-gay-bar-in-massachusetts.html (Accessed July 13, 2016).

Zhang, H., Ho, P. S. Y., & Ylp, P. S. F. (2011). Does similarity breed marital and sexual satisfaction. *Journal of Sex Research*. DOI:10.1080/00224 499.2011.574240

Zhang, J., Pang, X., Zhang, L., Medina, A., & Rozelle, S. (2012, May). Gender inequality in education in China: A meta-regression analysis. Working paper 239. www.reapchina.org/reap.stanford.edu (Accessed June 23, 2012).

Zhou, Q., Zhang, K., Li, Z., Liu, D., & Zhou, X. (2002). Personality of 133 male commercial sex service providers and acceptors. *Chinese Mental Health Journal, 16*(1), 48.

Zhu, B., et al. (2011). Transition from paroxysmal disorder in infancy to the masturbatory orgasm in childhood. *International Journal of Sexual Health, 23*(4), 278–281.

Zielbauer, P. (2000, May 22). Sex offender listings on Web set off debate. *The New York Times*. https://partners.nytimes.com/library/tech/00/05/biztech/articles/22abus.html (Accessed July 13, 2016).

Zieman, M., Hatcher, R., & Allen, A. (2015–2016). *Managing contraception*. Tiger, GA: Bridging the Gap Foundation.

Zietsch, B. P., Westberg, L., Santtila, P., & Jern, P. (2015). Genetic analysis of human extrapair mating: Heretability, between-sex correlation, and receptor genes for vasopressin and oxytocisn. *Evolution & Human Behavior, 36*(2), 130–136.

Zika virus. 2016. https://www.cdc.gov/zika/ (Accessed July 8, 2016).

Zilbergeld, B. (1999). *The new male sexuality* (rev. ed.). New York: Bantam Doubleday Dell.

Zillmann, D. (1989). Effects of prolonged consumption of pornography. In D. Zillmann & J. Bryant (Eds.), *Pornography: Research advances and policy considerations* (pp. 127–157). Hillsdale, to Erlbaum.

Zillmann, D., & Bryant, J. (1984). Effects of massive exposure to pornography. In N. M. Malamuth & E Donnerstein (Eds.), *Pornography and sexual aggression* (pp. 115–138). New York: Academic Press.

Zona, S., et al. (2012). Erectile dysfunction is more common in young to middle-aged HIV-infected men than in HIV-uninfected men. *The Journal of Sexual Medicine*. DOI: 10.1111/j.1743-6109.2012.02750.x

Zosuls, K. M., et al. (2009). The acquisition of gender labels in infancy: Implications for gender-typed play. *Developmental Psychology, 45*(3), 688–701.

Zubeidat, l., Ortega, V., & Sierra, J. C. (2004). Assessment of some determinant factors of sexual desire: Emotional state, sexual attitudes and sexual fantasies. *Análisis y Modificación de Conducta, 30*(129), 105–128.

Zucker, K. J. (2005a). Gender identity disorder in children and adolescents. *Annual Review of Clinical Psychology, 1*(1), 467–492.

Zucker, K. J. (2005b). Gender identity disorder in girls. In D. J. Bell, S. L. Foster, & E. J. Mash (Eds.), *Handbook of behavioral and emotional problems in girls. Issues in clinical child psychology* (pp. 285–319). Kluwer Academic/Plenum Publishers.

Zucker, K. J. (2015). The DSM-5 diagnostic criteria for gender disorder. In C. Trombetta et al. (Eds.). *Management of gender dysphoria* (pp. 33–37). Milan, Italy: Springer-Verlag Italia.

Zuckerman, P. (2012). *Faith no more: Why people reject religion*. New York: Oxford University Press.

Credits

Text Credits

Chapter 1 Page 19: Source: Kennair, L. E. O., et al. (2015). Sex and mating strategy impact the 13 basic reasons for having sex. *Evolutionary Psychological Science*, DOI: 10.1007/s40806-015-0024-6, Figure 1. With permission of Springer.

Chapter 4 Page 115: Dunski, S. (2015). Yes, my teenage son is transgender. No, you may not ask about his genitals. *Washington Post*. Reprinted with permission of the author.; **p. 119:** Hilary Tucker Rosebrock/WIRED; © Conde Nast. 12 Tales of Getting it On in the Digital Age. *Wired*. March 9, 2015.

Chapter 5 Page 146: YouGov. (2015). A third of young Americans say they aren't 100% heterosexual. https://today.yougov.com/news/2015/08/20/third-young-americans-exclusively-heterosexual/. Used with permission.; **p. 147:** Source: You-Gov. (2015). A third of young Americans say they aren't 100% heterosexual. https://today.yougov.com/news/2015/08/20/third-young-americans-exclusively-heterosexual/. Used with permission.

Chapter 6 Page 187: Malone, Clare, "Modern-Day Yentas Have a New Tool." From *The New York Times*, March 15, 2015 © 2015 The New York Times. All rights reserved. Used by permission and protected by the Copyright Laws of the United States. The printing, copying, redistribution, or retransmission of this Content without express written permission is prohibited.

Chapter 7 Page 229: Center for Sexual Health Promotion. (2011) National Survey of Sexual Health and Behavior (NSSHE). Indiana University School of Public Health-Bloomington. http://www.nationalsexstudy.indiana.edu/graph.html (Accessed February 22, 2012). Used with permission.

Chapter 8 Page 246: Republished with permission of Springer Science and Bus Media B V, from Fielder, R. L., Walsh, J. L., Carey, K. B., & Carey, M. p. (2013). Predictors of sexual hookups: A theory-based, prospective study of first-year college women. Archives of Sexual Behavior, 42, 1425–1441, p. 1427; permission conveyed through Copyright Clearance Center, Inc.

Chapter 10 Page 335: Copyright © 2015 Gallup, Inc. All rights reserved. The content is used with permission; however, Gallup retains all rights of republication.; **p. 336:** Copyright © 2015 Gallup, Inc. All rights reserved. The content is used with permission; however, Gallup retains all rights of republication.

Chapter 14 Page 460: Victoria Tang & Lorelei Lee/WIRED; © Conde Nast. 12 Tales of Getting it On in the Digital Age. *Wired*. March 9, 2015.

Chapter 15 Page 478: Brooks, David, "When ISIS Rapists Win," from *The New York Times*. August 28, 2015.; p. **483:** *Washington Post*. (2015, June 12). 1 in 5 college women say they were violated. http://www.washingtonpost.com/sf/local/2015/06/12/1-in-5-women-say-they-were-violated/; **p. 494:** Lapowsky, I. (2014, September 5). This App Is a 21st Century Rape Whistle. *Wired* © Conde Nast.

Photo Credits

Chapter 1 Page 1: Photodisc/Getty Images; **p. 3:** Rubberball/SuperStock; **p. 5:** Maria Teijeiro/Photodisc/Getty Images; **p. 6:** Hola Images/Getty Images; **p. 8:** Patrick Heagney/E+/Getty Images; **p. 9:** BeBa/Iberfoto/The Image Works; **p. 10:** Azoor Photo/Alamy Stock Photo; **p. 11:** Andrew Burton/Getty Images News/Getty Images; **p. 13:** ©David Henley/Pictures From History/The Image Works; **p. 14:** Granger, NYC — All rights reserved.; **p. 18:** Zero Creatives/Cultura/Getty Images; **p. 23 top:** Robert Dodge/Alamy Stock Photo; **p. 23 bottom:** RubberBall/SuperStock; **p. 27:** Wallace Kirkland/The LIFE Picture Collection/Getty Images; **p. 28:** Rubberball/SuperStock; **p. 31:** Rebecca Henry/Mirabel Studios, 2006. Courtesy of Kate Frank; **p. 32:** Behavioral Technology; **p. 33:** Behavioral Technology

Chapter 2 Page 40: Veer; **p. 42 left:** Daniel Sambraus/Science Source; **p. 42 right:** John R. Foster/Science Source; **p. 43:** Rubberball/Alamy Stock Photo; **p. 44:** Nick Savage/Alamy Stock Photo; **p. 52:** Thierry Berrod, Mona Lisa Production /Photo Researchers, Inc.; **p. 56:** Stockbroker/SuperStock; **p. 57 center:** Chris Rout/Alamy; **p. 57 left:** © SIME /eStock Photo – All rights reserved; **p. 57 right:** Chris Rout/Alamy Stock Photo; **p. 59:** MARKA/Alamy Stock Photo; **p. 62:** CHASSENET/BSIP/Age Fotostock; **p. 70 top:** Oote Boe 1/Alamy; **p. 70 bottom:** The North American Menopause Society (NAMS); **p. 76:** Ermolaev Alexandr/Fotolia

Chapter 3 Page 79: plainpicture; **p. 83 left:** John Henderson/Alamy; **p. 83 right:** John Henderson/Alamy Stock Photo; **p. 86:** Evgenii Zadiraka/Alamy Stock Photo; **p. 89:** Michael Abbey/Science Source; **p. 90:** Hogan Imaging/Fotolia; **p. 91:** linejuan moyano/Alamy Stock Photo; **p. 95:** Christopher Malcolm/The Image Bank/Getty Images

Chapter 4 Page 106: Everett Collection Inc/Alamy Stock Photo; **p. 107:** Frazer Harrison/Getty Images; **p. 112:** Dr M.A. Ansary/Science Source; **p. 113:** Courtesy of Kinsey Institute; **p. 114 top:** REUTERS/Str Old; **p. 114 bottom:** WILDLIFE GmbH/Alamy Stock Photo; **p. 116:** epa european pressphoto agency b.v./Alamy Stock Photo; **p. 117:** Stockbroker/SuperStock; **p. 118:** Rubberball/SuperStock; **p. 119:** iPhone/Alamy Stock Photo; **p. 121:** Taxi/Getty Images; **p. 122:** Lonely Planet/Getty Images; **p. 125:** Amble Design /Shutterstock; **p. 130:** Buena Vista Images/The Image Bank; **p. 132:** Rubberball/SuperStock; **p. 133:** Blend Images/Alamy Stock Photo; **p. 135:** J. Howard Miller, artist employed by Westinghouse, poster used by the War Production Co-ordinating Committee

Chapter 5 Page 139: Oredia/Alamy Stock Photo; **p. 140:** Jon Kopaloff/FilmMagic/Getty Images; **p. 143:** Ingram Publishing /SuperStock; **p. 151:** Michael Dwyer/Alamy; **p. 153:** Copyright (2008) National Academy of Sciences, U.S.A.; **p. 158:** Rubberball/Alamy Stock Photo; **p. 159:** Hemis/Alamy Stock Photo; **p. 160:** Jim West/Alamy; **p. 161:** Daniel Acker/Bloomberg/Getty Images; **p. 163:** Hero Images Inc./Alamy Stock Photo; **p. 167 top:** Ryan McVay/Getty Images; **p. 169:** Bloomberg/Getty Images; **p. 170:** Cindy Brown /Alamy Stock Photo

Chapter 6 Page 174: Tetra Images/Alamy Stock Photo; **p. 177:** Journal of Personality & Social Psychology (APA); **p. 177:** Journal of Personality & Social Psychology (APA); **p. 178:** Fancy/Alamy; **p. 180:** Kaspars Grinvalds/Shutterstock; **p. 182:** Steve Stock/Alamy Stock Photo; **p. 183:** Apollofoto/Shutterstock; **p. 185:** StockLite/Shutterstock; **p. 186 bottom:** Artpose Adam Borkowski/Shutterstock; **p. 186 left:** imageBROKER/Alamy Stock Photo; **p. 186 right:** Maria Vazquez/Alamy Stock Photo; **p. 187:** sjscreens /Alamy Stock Photo; **p. 188:** Andor Bujdoso/Alamy Stock Photo; **p. 189 top:** Marmaduke St. John/Alamy Stock Photo; **p. 189 bottom:** Tetra Images/Alamy Stock Photo; **p. 192:** Odua Images/Shutterstock; **p. 197:** Flashon Studio/Shutterstock

Chapter 7 Page 200: Dominique Douieb/PhotoAlto Agency RF Collections/Getty Images; **p. 206:** Yuri Arcurs/Shutterstock; **p. 210:** Michael Ventura/Alamy Stock Photo; **p. 212:** Michael Austen/Alamy; **p. 215:** Golden Pixels LLC /Alamy Stock Photo; **p. 223:** Archives du 7e Art/Annapurna Pictures/Photos 12/Alamy Stock Photo; **p. 224:** ©Mark Antman/The Image Works; **p. 226 top:** Zoran Steiner/age fotostock; **p. 227:** Alloy Photography/VEER; **p. 237 bottom:** Blend Images/Alamy Stock Photo

Chapter 8 Page 241: Blend Images/Alamy Stock Photo; **p. 242:** AF archive /Alamy Stock Photo; **p. 247:** Image Source/Alamy Stock Photo; **p. 248:** Cyberstock/Alamy Stock Photo; **p. 251:** GoGo Images Corporation/Alamy Stock Photo; **p. 253:** Eric Audras/PhotoAlto/Getty Images; **p. 258:** Hill Street Studios/Blend Images/Getty Images; **p. 260:** Dominic Harris/Alamy Stock Photo

Chapter 9 Page 265: Gino's Premium Images/Alamy Stock Photo; **p. 266:** IMAGEMORE Co., Ltd./Alamy Stock Photo; **p. 267:** David Phillips/PRI/Photo Researchers/Getty Images; **p. 269:** Bloomberg/Getty Images; **p. 271:** BURGER/PHANIE/age fotostock; **p. 273:** Cultura Creative (RF)/Alamy Stock Photo; **p. 276:** Kathy deWitt/Alamy Stock Photo; **p. 282:** Stocktrek Images, Inc./Alamy Stock Photo; **p. 288:** imageBROKER/Alamy Stock Photo; **p. 290:** Source Salsa/Alamy Stock Photo; **p. 294:** Illene MacDonald/PhotoEdit; **p. 297:** Herjua/Fotolia; **p. 301:** RooM the Agency/Alamy Stock Photo

Chapter 10 Page 306: Yeko Photo Studio/Fotolia; **p. 308:** AP Photo/File; **p. 311:** Ocean Photography/Veer; **p. 313:** Kristoffer Tripplaar/Alamy Stock Photo; **p. 321:** Comstock/Thinkstock; **p. 323:** CC Studio/Science Source; **p. 325:** Ruth Jenkinson/Dorling Kindersley/Getty Images; **p. 326:** Copyright 2016 Kindara, Inc./ **p. 330 top:** GARO/PHANIE/age fotostock

Chapter 11 Page 343: Image Source Plus/Alamy Stock Photo; **p. 349:** Will Hart/PhotoEdit, Inc; **p. 351:** PhotoAlto/Alamy Stock Photo; **p. 352:** Sean Justice/Riser/Getty Images; **p. 354:** Rubberball/Glow Images; **p. 355:** Peter Mason/Stone/Getty Images; **p. 361:** Corbis Photography/Veer; **p. 365:** Queerstock, Inc./Alamy Stock Photo; **p. 366:** Frank Micelotta/Getty Images; **p. 367:** Blend Images/Shutterstock; **p. 367:** Henrik Sorensen/Iconica/Getty Images; **p. 372:** Mediablitzimages/Alamy Stock Photo; **p. 374:** Tetra Images/Alamy Stock Photo; **p. 375:** George Doyle/Stockbyte/Getty Images; **p. 378:** Rubberball/SuperStock

Chapter 12 Page 383: PhotoAlto Photography/Veer; **p. 384:** Ryan McVay/Digital Vision/Getty Images; **p. 388:** wavebreakmedia/Shutterstock; **p. 392:** Corbis Photography/Veer; **p. 393:** RubberBall/Alamy; **p. 395:** PhotoLink/Photodisc/Getty Images; **p. 397:** BananaStock/Jupiter Images; **p. 398:** MBI/Alamy Stock Photo; **p. 401:** Pearson Education; **p. 403:** Nucleus Medical Art Inc /Alamy Stock Photo; **p. 405:** Alex Segre/Alamy Stock Photo; **p. 409:** BSIP SA/Alamy Stock Photo

Chapter 13 Page 413: Ocean Photography/Veer; **p. 415:** Kevin Jordan/Fancy/age fotostock; **p. 417:** Dr. p. Marazzi/Photo Researchers, Inc; **p. 420:** Sebastian Kaulitzki/Shutterstock; **p. 422:** UIG/Getty Images; **p. 427:** Aubert/Science Source; **p. 431:** Scott Camazine/Photo Researchers, Inc.; **p. 433:** Phanie/Alamy Stock Photo; **p. 434:** Image Source/Stockbyte/Getty Images; **p. 435:** Marc Antoine Saucier/Alamy Stock Photo; **p. 437:** Dr. p. Marazzi/Science Source; **p. 439:** Marazzi/Photo Researchers, Inc.; **p. 441:** E. Gray/Photo Researchers, Inc.; **p. 443:** PBNJ Productions/Blend Images/Getty Images; **p. 444:** 914 collection/Alamy Stock Photo

Chapter 14 Page 449: Sarah Ashun/Dorling Kindersley/Getty Images; **p. 453:** Darrin Klimek/Photonica/Getty Images; **p. 454:** Dimitri Stangl/Alamy Stock Photo; **p. 455:** James Boardman/Alamy Stock Photo; **p. 457:** Taylor Hill/FilmMagic/Getty Images; **p. 458:** PhotoAlto/Alamy Stock Photo; **p. 460:** Jim Lo Scalzo/Aurora Photos; **p. 461:** Blend Images/Veer; **p. 462:** Pictorial Press Ltd/Alamy Stock; **p. 466:** Dariush M/Shutterstock; **p. 468:** PhotoAlto Photography/Veer

Chapter 15 Page 476: Justin Tallis/AFP/GettyImages; **p. 477:** Instagram/Photoshot/Newscom; **p. 479:** Emrah Yorulmaz/Anadolu Agency/Getty Images; **p. 484:** (Doug Kapustin/MCT/Getty Images; **p. 486:** Yuri Arcurs/E+/Getty Images; **p. 488:** MBI/Alamy Stock Photo; **p. 490 bottom:** Martin Dimitrov/E+/Getty Images; **p. 492:** Scott Olson/Getty Images; **p. 494:** Circle of 6; **p. 498:** David Lodge/FilmMagic/Getty Images; **p. 502 top:** PeopleImages/E+/Getty Images; **p. 506:** Ahmed Ismail/Anadolu Agency/Getty Images

Chapter 16 Page 512: Leon Werdinger/Alamy Stock Photo; **p. 514:** EPA/Jim Lo Scalzo/Alamy; **p. 516:** Jonas Gratzer/LightRocket/Getty Images; **p. 518:** Horacio Villalobos/Corbis/Getty Images; **p. 519:** AP Photo/Keystone, Ennio Leanza; **p. 520:** Dazzo/Masterfile; **p. 521:** epa european pressphoto agency b.v./Alamy Stock Photo; **p. 523:** ©Sean Sprague/The Image Works; **p. 524:** Corbis/SuperStock; **p. 527:** Mary Evans Picture Library; **p. 530:** Jim Lo Scalzo/Aurora Photos; **p. 531:** Marin/PhotoAlto/Getty Images

Name Index

Subject Index

Note: Page numbers followed by (*f*) and (*t*) refer to figures and tables, respectively.

Hedonism, 5, 7(*t*)
Height, 176–177
Hepatitis, 440
Hepatitis B virus (HBV), 528
Hepatitis C virus (HCV), 528
Hermaphrodite, 112
Herpes Simplex Virus Type 1 (HSV-1), 418(*t*)
Heteronormativity, 22, 141–142
Heterosexual orientation, 141, 144
Heterosexuality, 22, 148(*f*)
Highly active antiretroviral therapy (HAART), 236
High-risk behaviors, 446
Hijras, 122–123
Hippocrates, 417
HIV-1 nucleic acid tests, 434
Homogamy, 185, 367
Homologous, 44
Homophobia, 164–165
Homophobia, 23
Homosexual orientation, 141, 144
Homosexuality
    activism, 159
    contemporary U.S. attitudes toward, 158–161
    heterosexuality and homosexuality as separate
        dimensions, 148(*f*)
    historical perspectives, 172
    laws, 159
    queer theory, 22
    sexual orientation, 141
    stereotypes and, 160–161
"honeymoon cystitis", 46
Honor killings, 498
Hookup, 243, 245–247, 263
Hopi Native Americans, 17
Hormonal methods of contraception
    contraceptive patch, 314
    injectable contraceptives, 314
    IUC devices, 314–316
    methods of, 310–316, 341
    morning-after pill, 313
    oral contraceptive, 310–313
    under-the-skin implants, 316
Hormone replacement therapy (HRT), 71–73,
    91, 377
Hormones, 64, 110, 125, 129, 215–218, 287
Hourglass figure, 179
HPV test, 51
Human chorionic gonadotropin (HCG), 275–276
Human embryos, 281(*f*)
Human immunodeficiency virus (HIV)
    anal intercourse and, 236
    circumcision and, 85
    diagnosis, 433–434
    effects on immune system, 430–432, 447
    epidemic of, 415–416
    estimated numbers of people in U.S. living
        with, 429(*t*)
    estimates of annual prevalence of new
        infections in U.S., 429(*f*)
    factors affecting risk of sexual transmission
        of, 432–433
    immune system and, 430
    male prostitutes, 523
    non-transmission, 433
    prenatal development, 285–286
    prevalence of, 429–430
    preventing infection with Truvada, 435
    prostitution and, 524
    rape and, 491
    sexual problems, 392–393
    transmission, 432, 447
    treatment of, 434–436, 447
    use of condoms to prevent, 323

Human papilloma virus (HPV), 85, 230–231,
    415, 438–440, 447
Human Potential Movement, 15
Human Sexual Response (Masters & Johnson), 32
Human sexuality
    ancient Greeks, 10
    ancient Hebrews, 9–10
    beginnings of the scientific study of, 14–15
    biological perspective, 16
    Christianity, 11–12
    cross-species perspective, 17
    ethics in research on, 36–37
    evolutionary perspective, 16–17
    Far East, 13–14
    goals of the science of, 25
    historical perspective, 7–16
    Islam, 12
    multiple perspectives on, 23–24
    perspectives on, 7–24
    prehistoric sexuality, 9
    psychological perspectives, 20–21
    recent trends, 16
    research methods in, 24–36
    science of, 4
    sexual revolution, 15–16
    sociological perspectives, 17
    study of, 4
    thinking critically about, 6–7
    value systems and, 5–6, 7
    Victorian period, 14
Hustlers, 523–524
Hyaluronidase, 267
Hymen, 46
Hypogonadism, 216, 392
Hypothalamus, 64, 155
Hypothesis, 24–25
Hypoxyphilistic disorder, 460
Hysterectomy, 55
Hysterosalpingogram, 272
Hysterotomy, 339

Identification, 132
Immune system, 430
In vitro fertilization (IVF), 272–273
Incest
    family factors, 502–503
    perspectives on, 501–502
    types of, 502
Incest taboo, 9
Incidence, 30
Incompatibility, 195(*f*)
Independent variable, 36
Infancy
    ejaculation, 345
    masturbation, 345
    orgasm, 345
    sexual response, 344–345, 381
Infatuation, 190–191
Inferences, 25
Infertility
    female fertility problems, 272
    incidence of, 270
    male fertility problems, 270–271
Infibulation, 45
Infidelity
    attitudes toward, 371
    effects of, 372–373, 381
    evolutionary theory, 370–371
    patterns of, 371
Inflammation, 430
Informed consent, 37
Inguinal canal, 110
Injectable contraceptives, 314

Internal sex organs
    cervix, 51–52
    Cowper's glands, 92
    fallopian tubes, 53
    female, 48–54
    male, 87–92, 104
    ovaries, 53–55
    prostate gland, 90–92
    seminal vesicles, 90, 92
    testes, 64, 87–89
    uterus, 52
    vagina, 48–50
    vas deferens, 89
Internet, 8, 16, 405, 516, 526
Intersexual, 112–113
Interstitial cells, 88
Intimacy, 247–250
Intra-amniotic infusion, 338
Intracytoplasmic Sperm Injection (ICSI), 274
Intrauterine contraceptive (IUC) device,
    314–316, 427
Introitus, 46
Involuntary contractions, 391
Irrational beliefs, 398
Islam, 9, 12

Jaundice, 440
Jealousy
    cognitive perspective on, 252
    communicative responses to, 252–253
    effects on relationship, 263
    evolutionary theory, 251–252
Johns, 522
JSwipe, 187

Kama Sutra, 13
Karma, 13
Khoikhoi tribe, 176
Kink community, 463
Kinsey Confidential, 8
Kinsey Reports, 28
Kinsey sample, 26
Kissing, 226–227, 434
Klinefelter syndrome, 111
Klismaphilistic disorder, 465

Labia majora, 42–43
Labia minora, 41, 43
Laboratory-observation, 32–34
Lack of interest or desire, 387–388
Lactation, 303
"Ladyboys", 123
Lamaze method, 295
Laparoscopy, 272
Lateral-entry position, 234–235
Learning theories, 21, 157
Legalism, 5, 7(*t*)
Lesbians
    adolescence, 359
    coming out, 166–168
    families and, 163
    family building, 273
    hate crimes, 165(*f*)
    homophobia, 164–165
    psychological adjustment of, 162–168
    relationship satisfaction, 256
    sexual orientation, 141
    "treatment" of, 165–166
Leukocytes, 430
Levitra, 210, 239
Leydig's cells, 88
LGBT youth, 507
Limbic system, 214